NEW WEBSTER'S DICTIONARY

edited by
R. F. PATTERSON, M.A., D.Litt.

1988 Edition

New Expanded Webster's Dictionary is not associated with, or published by,
the original publishers of Webster's Dictionary or their successors.

Published by

P.S.I. & Associates, Inc.
10481 S.W. 123rd Street
Miami, Florida 33176

Manufactured in The United States of America
1 2 3 4 5 6 7 8 9 10 — 92 91 90 89 88

New Webster's Dictionary

All entries are arranged in alphabetical order and appear in bold faced type. Following each entry are related words, derivations, and meanings. Each bold entry also includes a special simplified syllabic pronunciation help. Each entry also displays a symbol indicating the specific part of speech.

ABBREVIATIONS USED IN THIS DICTIONARY

a. adjective.
adv adverb.
conj. conjunction.
int. interjection.
n. noun.

n.pl. noun plural.
p.a. participial adjective.
pl. plural.
pp. past participle.
prep. preposition.

pret. preterit.
pron. pronoun.
vi. verb intransitive.
vt. verb transitive.

GUIDE TO PRONUNCIATION

ch, chain; g, go; ng, sing; ŦH, then; th, thin; w, wig; wh, whig; ah, azure; fāte, fär, fat, fall; mē, met, her; pīne, pin; nōte, not, mōve; tūbe, tub, bull; oil, pound.

A

A, the indefinite article, used before a consonant.

Abacus, ab′a-kus, *n.*; pl. **-ci,** or **-cuses.** A square slab forming the crowning of a column.

Abandon, a-ban′dun, *vt.* To forsake entirely; to desert.

Abase, a-bās′, *vt.* (abasing, abased). To bring low; degrade; disgrace.

Abash, a-bash′, *vt.* To put to confusion; to make ashamed.

Abate, a-bāt′, *vt.* (abating, abated). To lessen. *vi.* To become less.

Abbey, ab′i, *n.*; pl. **-eys.** A monastery, or convent.

Abbot, ab′ut, *n.* The male superior of an abbey.

Abbreviate, ab-brē′vi-āt, *vt.* To shorten.

Abbreviation, ab-brē′vi-ā′′shon, *n.* A shortening; contraction.

Abdicate, ab′di-kāt, *vt.* (abdicating, abdicated). To resign voluntarily; to relinquish. *vi.* To resign power.

Abdomen, ab-dō′men, *n.* The lower belly.

Abduct, ab-dukt′, *vt.* To entice or lead away wrongly.

Aberrant, ab-e′rant, *a.* Wandering from; deviating from an established rule.

Aberration, ab-e-rā′shon, *n.* A wandering from; alienation of the mind.

Abet, a-bet′, *vt.* (abetting, abetted). To urge on; to encourage. (Chiefly in a bad sense.)

Abeyance, a-bā′ans, *n.* Temporary extinction. (With *in* before it.)

Abhor, ab-hor′, *vt.* (abhorring, abhorred). To shrink from with horror; to loathe, detest.

Abhorrent, ab-hor′rent, *a.* Hating; inconsistent with. (With *to*).

Abide, a-bīd, *vi.* (abiding, abode or abided). To stay in a place; to dwell.—*vt.* To wait for; to endure.

Ability, a-bil′li-ti, *n.* Power to do anything; talent; skill; in *pl.* the powers of the mind.

Abiogenesis, ab′i-ō-jen′′e-sis, *n.* The doctrine that living matter may be produced by not-living matter.

Abject, ab′jekt, *a.* Mean; despicable.

Abjure, ab-jūr′, *vt.* (abjuring, abjured). To renounce upon oath; to reject.

Ablative, ab′lat-iv, *a.* or *n.* Applied to a case of nouns in Latin and other languages.

Ablaze, a-blāz′, *adv.* On fire; in a blaze.

Able, ā′bl, *a.* Having power sufficient; capable; skilful.

Ablution, ab-lū′shon, *n.* A washing away from; a purification by water.

Ably, ā′bli, *adv.* With ability.

Abnegate, ab′nē-gāt, *vt.* To deny; to renounce.

Abnormal, ab-norm′al, *a.* Deviating from a fixed rule; irregular.

Aboard, a-bōrd′, *adv.* or *prep.* On board; in a ship or vessel.

Abode, a-bōd′, *n.* Residence; habitation.

Abolish, a-bol′ish, *vt.* To destroy; to abrogate.

Abolition, ab-ō-li′shon, *n.* Act of abolishing; state of being abolished.

Abolitionist, ab-ō-li′shon-ist, *n.* One who seeks to abolish anything, especially slavery.

Abominable, a-bom′in-a-bl, *a.* Loathsome.

Abomination, a-bom′in-ā′′shon, *n.* Hatred; object of hatred; loathsomeness.

Aboriginal, ab-ō-rij′in-al, *a.* Primitive.

Aborigines, ab-ō-rij′in-ēz, *n. pl.* The original inhabitants of a country.

Abort, a-bort′, *vi.* To miscarry in giving birth.

Abortion, a-bor′shon, *n.* A miscarriage.

Abound, a-bound′, *vi.* To be, or have, in great plenty.

About, a-bout′, *prep.* Around; near to; relating to; engaged in.—*adv.* Around; round; nearly; here and there.

Above, a-buv′, *prep.* To or in a higher place than; superior to; more than; beyond; before.—*adv.* To or in a higher place; chiefly.

Above-board, a-buv′bōrd, *adv.* Without concealment or deception.

Abrasion, ab-rā′zhon, *n.* A rubbing off; substance worn off by rubbing.

Abreast, a-brest′, *adv.* In a line; side by side.

Abridge, a-brij′, *vt.* To shorten; to condense.

Abroad, a-brad′, *adv.* At large; away from home; in a foreign country.

Abrogate, ab′rō-gāt, *vt.* (abrogating, abrogated). To repeal; to make void.

Abrupt, ab-rupt′, *a.* Broken off; steep; sudden; unceremonious.

Abscess, ab′ses, *n.* A gathering of purulent matter in some part of the body.

Abscind, ab-sind′, *vt.* To cut off.

Abscond, ab-skond′, *vi.* To hide oneself; to fly from justice.

Absence, ab′sens, *n.* State of being absent; inattention to things present.

Absent, ab′sent, *a.* Being away from; not present; wanting in attention.

Absentee, ab-sen-tē′, *n.* One who absents himself.

Absinthe, ab′sinth, *n.* A liqueur consisting of spirit flavored with wormwood.

Absolute, ab′sō-lūt, *a.* Unlimited; unconditional; certain; despotic.

Absolve, ab-solv′, *vt.* To free from, as from guilt or punishment; acquit; pardon.

Absorb, ab-sorb′, *vt.* To drink in; to engross.

Absorbent, ab-sorb′ent, *a.* Imbibing; swallowing.—*n.* That which absorbs.

Absorption, ab-sorp′shon, *n.* Act or process of imbibing or swallowing up.

Abstain, ab-stān′, *vi.* To keep back from; to refrain; to forbear.

Abstinence, ab′sti-nens, *n.* A keeping from the indulgence of the appetites, especially from intoxicating liquors.

Abstract, ab-strakt′, *vt.* To draw from; to separate and consider by itself; to epitomize.

Abstract, ab′strakt, *a.* Existing in the mind only; not concrete; general in language or in reasoning.—*n.* A summary; an abridgment.

Absurd, ab-sėrd′, *a.* Contrary to reason or common sense; ridiculous.

Abundance, a-bun′dans, *n.* Plenteousness; copiousness; wealth.

Abundant, a-bun′dant, *a.* Abounding; plentiful; ample.

Abuse, a-būz′, *vt.* (abusing, abused). To turn from the proper use; to ill-use; to deceive; to vilify; to violate.

Abuse, a-būs′, *n.* Misuse; bad language addressed to a person; insulting words; violation.

Abut, a-but′, *vi.* (abutting, abutted). To border; to meet. (With *upon*.)

Abutment, a-but′ment, *n.* That which abuts; solid support for the extremity of a bridge, arch, etc.

Abyss, a-bis′, *n.* A bottomless gulf; a deep pit or mass of waters; hell.

Acacia, a-kā′shi-a, *n.* A genus of ornamental plants, yielding catechu, gum-arabic, etc.

Academic, Academical, ak-a-dem′ik, ak-a-dem′ik-al, *a.* Belonging to an academy or university.

Academy, a-kad′ē-mi, *n.* A seminary of arts or sciences; a society of persons for the cultivation of arts and sciences.

Acaridan, a-kar′i-dan, *n.* A mite, tick, or allied animal.

Accede, ak-sēd′, *vi.* (acceding, acceded). To assent to; to comply with.

Accelerate, ak-sel′lē-rāt, *vt.* (accelerating, accelerated). To hasten; to quicken the speed of.

Accent, ak′sent, *n.* A tone or modulation of the voice; stress of the voice on a syllable or word; the mark which indicates this stress; manner of speaking.

Accent, ak-sent′, *vt.* To express or note the accent of.

Accept, ak-sept′, *vt.* To receive; to admit; to promise to pay, by attaching one's signature.

Acceptable, ak-sept'a-bl, *a.* That may be accepted; pleasing; gratifying.

Access, ak'ses, *n.* Approach; admission; means of approach; increase.

Accessible, ak-ses'i-bl, *a.* Easy of approach; affable.

Accession, ak-se'shon, *n.* The act of acceding; augmentation; succession to a throne.

Accessory, ak'ses-sō-ri, *a.* Additional, contributing to.—*n.* An accomplice; an adjunct.

Accidence, ak'si-dens, *n.* The changes which inflected parts of speech undergo; a work exhibiting such changes.

Accident, ak'si-dent, *n.* Quality of a being not essential to it; an unfortunate event occurring casually.

Accidental, ak-si-dent'al, *a.* Happening by chance; not necessarily belonging to.—*n.* A property or thing not essential.

Acclaim, ak-klām', *n.* Acclamation.—*vt.* To applaud; to declare by acclamation.

Acclamation, ak-kla-mā'shon, *n.* A shout of applause, assent, or approbation.

Accolade, ak-kō-lād', *n.* A ceremony used in conferring knighthood, usually a blow on the shoulder with the flat of a sword.

Accommodate, ak-kom'mō-dāt, *vt.* (accommodating, accommodated). To make suitable; to adjust; to furnish with.

Accompaniment, ak-kum'pa-ni-ment, *n.* That which accompanies; the subordinate part or parts, in music.

Accompany, ak-kum'pa-ni, *vt.* (accompanying, accompanied). To go with; to associate with; to perform music along with.

Accomplice, ak-kom'plis, *n.* An associate, especially in a crime.

Accomplish, ak-kom'plish, *vt.* To fulfil; to execute fully; to perfect.

Accomplishment, ak-kom'plish-ment, *n.* Fulfilment; acquirement; embellishment.

Accord, ak-kord', *n.* Harmony; agreement; will.—*vt.* To make to agree; to grant, or concede.—*vi.* To agree; to be in correspondence.

Accordance, ak-kord'ans, *n.* Agreement; conformity; harmony.

Accordion, ak-kord'i-on, *n.* A small melodious, keyed wind-instrument.

Accost, ak-kost', *vt.* To speak to first; to address.

Account, ak-kount', *n.* A reckoning; a register of facts relating to money; narration; advantage; end; importance.—*vt.* To reckon; to consider; to deem; to value.—*vi.* To give or render reasons; to explain (with *for*).

Accountant, ak-kount'ant, *n.* One skilled or employed in accounts; one whose profession is to examine accounts.

Accoutre, ak-kö'tér, *vt.* (accoutring, accoutred). To furnish with a military dress and arms.

Accoutrements, ak-kö'tér-ments, *n.pl.* Military dress and arms; dress.

Accredit, ak-kred'it, *vt.* To give credit or authority to; to receive, as an envoy; to bring into vogue, as a word.

Accretion, ak-krē'shon, *n.* A growing to, or increase by natural growth.

Accrue, ak-krö', *vi.* (accruing, accrued). To arise or come; to be added.

Accumulate, ak-kū'mū-lāt, *vt.* (accumulating, accumulated). To heap up; to amass.—*vi.* To increase.

Accumulator, ak-kū'mū-lāt-ér, *n.* A kind of battery which stores electric energy.

Accurate, ak'kū-rāt, *a.* Done with care; exact; without error.

Accursed, ak-kérs'ed, *a.* Lying under a curse; doomed; wicked.

Accusation, ak-kū-zā'shon, *n.* Act of accusing; impeachment; that of which one is accused.

Accusative, ak-kūz'at-iv, *a.* or *n.* A case in grammar, in English the objective.

Accuse, ak-kūz', *vt.* (accusing, accused). To charge with a crime; to impeach; to censure.

Accustom, ak-kus'tum, *vt.* To inure to a custom; to make familiar with by use.

Ace, ās, *n.* A unit; a single point on cards or dice; a distinguished airman, who has destroyed many enemy planes.

Acephalous, a-sef'al-us, *a.* Without a head.

Acerbity, a-sérb'i-ti, *n.* Sourness; bitterness or severity of language.

Acetic, a-set'ik, *a.* Relating to vinegar; sour.

Acetify, a-set'i-fi, *vt.* or *i.* (acetifying, acetified). To turn into acid or vinegar.

Acetylene, a-set'i-lēn, *n.* A gas used for lighting houses, etc.

Ache, āk, *vi.* (aching, ached). To be in pain; to be distressed.—*n.* Continued pain.

Achieve, a-chēv', *vt.* (achieving, achieved). To bring to an end; to accomplish; to obtain by effort.

Aching, āk'ing, *p.a.* Being in continued pain.—*n.* Pain.

Achromatic, ak-rō-mat'ik, *a.* Free from color.

Acid, as'id, *a.* Sharp, or sour to the taste.—*n.* A sour substance; a substance that with certain other substances forms salts.

Acidifier, as-id'i-fi-ér, *n.* A principle whose presence is necessary for acidity.

Acidity, as-id'i-ti, *n.* Sourness.

Acknowledge, ak-nol'lej, *vt.* (acknowledging, acknowledged). To own the knowledge of; to avow; to own or confess.

Acme, ak'mē, *n.* The top or highest point.

Acolyte, ak'ol-īt, *n.* One of the lowest order in the Roman church; an attendant.

Acorn, ā'korn, *n.* The fruit of the oak.

Acotyledon, a-kot'il-ē''don, *n.* A plant whose seeds have no seed-lobes.

Acoustic, a-kous'tik, *a.* Pertaining to the sense of hearing, or to the doctrine of sounds.

Acoustics, a-kous'tiks, *n.* The science of sound.

Acquaint, ak-kwānt', *vt.* To make to know; to make familiar; to inform.

Acquaintance, ak-kwänt'ans, *n.* Familiar knowledge; intimacy; a person well known.

Acquiesce, ak-kwi-es', *vi.* (acquiescing, acquiesced). To rest satisfied; to admit without opposition; to comply.

Acquire, ak-kwīr', *vt.* (acquiring, acquired). To obtain; to procure.

Acquisition, ak-kwi-zi'shon, *n.* Act of acquiring; the thing acquired; gain.

Acquit, ak-kwit', *vt.* (acquitting, acquitted). To set free from a charge or blame; to absolve; to bear or conduct (with refl. pron.).

Acre, ā'kér, *n.* A quantity of land, containing 4840 square yards.

Acreage, ā'kér-āj, *n.* A number of acres in a piece of land.

Acrid, ak'rid, *a.* Sharp; hot or biting to the taste; corroding; harsh.

Acrimony, ak'ri-mo-nt, *n.* Sharpness; harshness; severity.

Acrobat, ak'rō-bat, *n.* A rope-dancer; one who practices vaulting, tumbling, etc.

Acrocephalic, ak'rō-se-fal''ik, *a.* High-skulled.

Acrogen, ak'rō-jen, *n.* A plant increasing by extension of the stem at the top.

Acropolis, a-krop'o-lis, *n.* The citadel of a Greek city, as of Athens.

Across, a-kros', *prep.* or *adv.* From side to side; transversely; crosswise.

Acrostic, a-kros'tik, *n.* A composition in verse, in which the first (or other) letters of the lines form the name of a person, etc.

Act, akt, *vi.* To be in action; to exert power; to conduct oneself.—*vt.* To do; to perform, as an assumed part; to counterfeit.—*n.* A deed; power, or the effect of power, put forth; a state of reality; a part of a play; law, as an act of parliament.

Actinia, ak-tin'i-a, *n.;* pl. **-iae.** A sea-anemone.

Actinism, ak'tin-izm, *n.* The chemical action of the sun's rays.

Action, ak'shon, *n.* A deed; operation; a series of

events; gesture; a suit or process; an engagement, battle.

Active, ak'tiv, *a.* That acts or is in action; busy; quick; denoting action.

Actor, akt'er, *n.* One who acts; an active agent; a stage-player.

Actual, ak'tū-al, *a.* Existing in act; real; certain; positive.

Actuary, ak'tū-a-ri, *n.* A registrar or clerk; a specially able accountant.

Actuate, ak'tū-āt, *vt.* (actuating, actuated). To put into action; to incite.

Aculeate, a-kū'lē-āt, *a.* Having prickles or sharp points.

Acumen, a-kū'men, *n.* Sharpness of perception; sagacity.

Acupressure, ak-ū-pre'shūr, *n.* The stopping of hemorrhage from arteries, in surgical operations, by needles or wires.

Acute, a-kūt', *a.* Sharpened; sharp; ending in a sharp point; penetrating; having nice sensibility; sharp in sound.

Adage, ad'āj, *n.* A proverb; a maxim.

Adagio, a-da''jō, *a.* and *adv.* In *music*, slow; with grace.—*n.* A slow movement.

Adamant, ad'a-mant, *n.* Any substance of impenetrable hardness; the diamond.

Adam's-apple, ad'amz-ap'l, *n.* The prominence on the forepart of the throat.

Adapt, a-dapt', *vt.* To fit; to adjust; to suit.

Add, ad, *vt.* To join to; to annex; to say further.

Addendum, ad-den'dum, *n.*; pl. **-da.** A thing to be added; an appendix.

Adder, ad'er, *n.* A venomous serpent.

Addict, ad-dikt', *vt.* To apply habitually; generally in a bad sense, with refl. pron.

Addicted, ad-dikt'ed, *p.a.* Habitually given to a practice; inclined; prone.

Addition, ad-di'shon, *n.* Act of adding; the thing added; increase.

Additive, ad'it-iv, *a.* That is to be or may be added.

Addle, ad'l, *a.* Rotten; barren.—*vt.* (addling, addled). To make corrupt or barren.

Address, ad-dres', *vt.* To direct, to apply to by words or writing; to speak to; to apply (oneself); to write a name and destination on.—*n.* Verbal or written application; speech or discourse to a person; tact; courtship (generally in *plural*); direction of a letter.

Adduce, ad-dūs', *vt.* (adducing, adduced). To bring forward; to cite.

Adductor, ad-dukt'er, *n.* A muscle which draws one part to another.

Adenoid, ad'en-oid, *a.* Glandular.—*n.pl.* Gland-like morbid growths in the throat behind the soft palate.

Adept, a-dept', *n.* One fully skilled in any art.—*a.* Well skilled; completely versed or acquainted.

Adequate, ad'ē-kwāt, *a.* Equal to; proportionate; fully sufficient.

Adhere, ad-hēr', *vi.* (adhering, adhered). To stick, to cling; to remain firm.

Adhesion, ad-hē'zhon, *n.* Act or state of sticking to; adherence.

Adhibit, ad-hib'it, *vt.* To attach (one's signature).

Adhortatory, ad-hor'ta-tō-ri, *a.* Containing counsel or warning.

Adieu, a-dū', *interj.* Farewell.—*n.*; pl. **-us** or **-ux.** A farewell.

Adipose, ad'i-pōs, *a.* Consisting of or resembling fat; fatty.

Adit, ad'it, *n.* An approach; the horizontal opening into a mine.

Adjacent, ad-jā'sent, *a.* Lying near, adjoining; contiguous; neighboring.

Adjective, ad'jek-tiv, *n.* A word used with a noun, to express some quality or circumstance.

Adjoin, ad-join', *vt.* To join to.—*vi.* To lie or be next; to be contiguous.

Adjourn, ad-jėrn', *vt.* To put off to a future day; to postpone.—*vi.* To leave off for a future meeting.

Adjudge, ad-juj', *vt.* To decree judicially; to decide.

Adjudicate, ad-jū'di-kāt, *vt.* To adjudge; to determine judicially.

Adjunct, ad'jungkt, *n.* A thing (or person) joined to another.—*a.* United with.

Adjure, ad-jūr', *vt.* (adjuring, adjured). To charge on oath; to charge earnestly and solemnly.

Adjust, ad-just', *vt.* To rectify; to make exact; to regulate; to adapt; to settle.

Adjutant, ad'jū-tant, *n.* An officer who assists a commanding officer; a large species of bird allied to the stork.

Admeasure, ad-me'zhūr, *vt.* To ascertain the size or capacity of.

Adminicle, ad-min'i-kl, *n.* Support; aid.

Administer, ad-min'is-tėr, *vt.* To manage; to dispense; to distribute.

Administration, ad-min'is-trā''shon, *n.* Management; executive part of a government.

Admirable, ad'mi-ra-bl, *a.* Worthy of admiration; excellent.

Admiral, ad'mi-ral, *n.* The chief commander of a fleet or navy.

Admiration, ad-mi-rā'shon, *n.* Wonder mingled with delight; esteem.

Admire, ad mīr', *vt.* (admiring, admired). To regard with delight or affection.

Admit, ad-mit', *vt.* (admitting, admitted). To allow to enter; to grant; to concede.

Admittance, ad-mit'ans, *n.* Permission to enter; entrance; allowance.

Admixture, ad-miks'tūr, *n.* That which is mixed with something else; a mixing.

Admonish, ad-mon'ish, *vt.* To warn; to reprove solemnly or quietly; to exhort.

Admonition, ad-mō-ni'shon, *n.* Gentle or solemn reproof; instruction; caution.

Ado, a-dö', *n.* Stir; bustle; difficulty.

Adobe, a-dö'be, *n.* A sun-dried brick.

Adolescent, ad-ō-les'ent, *a.* Advancing to manhood.

Adopt, a-dopt', *vt.* To take and treat as a child, giving a title to the rights of a child; to embrace.

Adorable, a-dōr'a-bl, *a.* Worthy to be adored.

Adoration, a-dōr-ā'shon, *n.* Worship paid to God; profound reverence.

Adore, a-dōr', *vt.* (adoring, adored). To address in prayer; to worship with reverence and awe; to love intensely.

Adorn, a-dorn', *vt.* To deck with ornaments; to embellish; to beautify.

Adrift, a-drift', *adv.* Floating at random; at the mercy of any impulse.

Adroit, a-droit', *a.* Dexterous; skilful; ready.

Adulation, ad-ū-lā'shon, *n.* Servile flattery; excessive praise.

Adult, a-dult', *a.* Grown to maturity.—*n.* A person grown to manhood.

Adultery, a-dul'te-ri, *n.* Unfaithfulness to the marriage-bed.

Adumbrate, ad-um'brāt, *vt.* (adumbrating, adumbrated). To give a faint shadow of; to shadow out; to describe faintly.

Advance, ad-vans', *vt.* (advancing, advanced). To put forward; to promote; (in *commerce*) to pay beforehand; to supply.—*vi.* To go forward; to be promoted.—*n.* A going forward; preferment; first hint or step; rise in value; a giving beforehand.

Advantage, ad-van'tāj, *n.* Favorable state; superiority; gain.—*vt.* (advantaging, advantaged). To benefit; to promote.

Advent, ad'vent, *n.* Arrival; the coming of Christ; the four weeks before Christmas.

Adventitious, ad-ven-ti'shi-us, *a.* Accidental; casual; accessory; foreign.

Adventure, ad-ven'tur, *n.* Hazardous enterprise; a bold undertaking.—*vt.* To risk or hazard.—*vi.* To dare; to venture.

Adventurous, ad-ven'tūr-us, *a.* Prone to incur hazard; daring; full of hazard.

Adverb, ad'verb, *n.* A word which modifies a verb, adjective, or another adverb.

Adversary, ad'ver-sa-ri, *n.* An enemy; an antagonist.

Adversative, ad-vers'at-iv, *a.* Noting or causing opposition.—*n.* A word denoting opposition.

Adverse, ad'vers, *a.* Hostile; unprosperous.

Adversity, ad-vers'i-ti, *n.* Misfortune; affliction; calamity; distress.

Advert, ad-vert', *vi.* To refer or allude to; to regard. (With *to.*)

Advertence, ad-vert'ens, *n.* Regard; attention; heedfulness.

Advertent, ad-vert'ent, *a.* Attentive.

Advertise, ad-ver-tiz', *vt.* (advertising, advertised). To inform; to announce; to publish a notice of.

Advice, ad-vis', *n.* Opinion offered; counsel; information.

Advisable, ad-vis'a-bl, *a.* Fitting or proper to be done; expedient; fit.

Advise, ad-viz', *vt.* (advising, advised). To counsel; to warn; to inform.—*vi.* To deliberate or consider.

Advised, ad-vizd', *p.a.* Cautious; done with advice.

Advocate, ad'vo-kat, *n.* One who pleads for another; an intercessor.—*vt.* (advocating, advocated). To plead in favor of; to vindicate.

Adze, adz, *n.* A kind of axe, with the edge at right angles to the handle.

Aegis, e'jis, *n.* A shield; protection.

Aeolian, e-o'li-an, *a.* Pertaining to Aeolus, the god of the winds; played upon by the wind.

Aerate, a'er-at, *vt.* (aerating, aerated). To put air into; to combine with carbonic acid.

Aerial, a-e'ri-al, *a.* Belonging to the air; high; lofty.—*n.* The overhead structure of a wireless station, used for transmitting and receiving electrical oscillations.

Aerie, e're, *n.* The nest of a bird of prey; a brood of such birds.

Aerolite, a'er-o-lit, *n.* A meteoric stone; a meteorite.

Aerology, a-er-ol'o-ji, *n.* The science of atmospheric phenomena.

Aerometer, a-er-om'et-er, *n.* An instrument for finding the density of air and gases.

Aeronaut, a-er-o-nat, *n.* One who sails or floats in the air.

Aeronautic, a'er-o-nat''ik, *a.* Pertaining to aerial sailing.

Aeronautics, a'er-o-nat''iks, *n.* The science or art of flying in aircraft.

Aerostatics, a'er-o-stat''iks, *n.* The science which treats of air in a state of rest.

Aesculapian, es-ku-la'pi-an, *a.* Pertaining to Aesculapius, the god of medicine.

Afar, a-far', *adv.* At, to, or from a distance.

Affability, af-fa-bil'i-ti, *n.* Courteousness; civility; urbanity.

Affable, af'fa-bl, *a.* Easy to be spoken to; courteous; accessible.

Affair, af-far', *n.* That which is to do, or which is done; business.

Affect, af-fekt', *vt.* To act upon; to move the feelings of; to aim at; to pretend.

Affectation, af-fek-ta'shon, *n.* False pretense; an artificial air put on by a person.

Affectedly, af-fekt'ed-li, *adv.* In an affected manner; feignedly.

Affecting, af-fekt'ing, *p.a.* Pathetic; tender; exciting.

Affection, af-fek'shon, *n.* The state of being affected; fondness; love.

Affectionate, af-fek'shon-at, *a.* Tender; loving; fond.

Afferent, af'fer-ent, *a.* Carrying to or inwards.

Affiance, af-fi'ans, *n.* Faith pledged; marriage contract; reliance.—*vt.* (affiancing, affianced). To pledge one's faith to; to betroth.

Affidavit, af-fi-da'vit, *n.* A written declaration upon oath.

Affiliate, af-fil'li-at, *vt.* (affiliating, affiliated). To adopt; to assign to a father; to unite to a chief society or body.

Affiliation, af-fil'li-a''shon, *n.* Act of affiliating; association.

Affinity, af-fin'i-ti, *n.* Relation by marriage; resemblance; chemical attraction.

Affirm, af-ferm', *vt.* To assert; to declare; to ratify.—*vi.* To declare solemnly.

Affix, af-fiks', *vt.* To fasten to; to subjoin.—*n.* af'fiks. A syllable or letter added to a word.

Afflatus, af-fla'tus, *n.* Inspiration.

Afflict, af-flikt', *vt.* To distress; to grieve; to harass.

Affluent, af'flu-ent, *a.* Flowing to; wealthy; abundant.—*n.* A river that flows into another river.

Afflux, af'fluks, *n.* A flowing to; that which flows to.

Afford, af-ford', *vt.* To yield; to supply; to be able to give, grant, buy, or expend.

Affray, af-fra', *n.* A tumult; brawl.

Affront, af-frunt', *vt.* To insult; to offend.—*n.* Open defiance; insult.

Afield, a-feld', *adv.* To or in the field.

Afloat, a-flot', *adv.* or *a.* Floating; in circulation (as a rumor).

Afoot, a-fut', *adv.* On foot, in action.

Aforementioned, a-for'men-shond, *a.* Mentioned before.

Aforenamed, a-for'namd, *a.* Named before.

Aforesaid, a-for'sad, *a.* Said before.

Afraid, a-frad', *a.* Struck with fear; fearful.

Afresh, a-fresh', *adv.* Anew; again.

African, af'rik-an, *a.* Belonging to Africa.—*n.* A native of Africa.

Afrikander, af'rik-an-der, *n.* A native of South Africa, born of white, especially of Dutch, parents.

After, aft'er, *a.* Later in time; subsequent.—*prep.* Later in time than; behind; according to; in imitation of.—*adv.* Later in time.

Afterbirth, aft'er-berth, *n.* That which is expelled from the uterus after the birth of a child.

Aftermath, aft'er-math, *n.* A second crop of grass in the same season; consequences; results.

Afternoon, aft'er-non, *n.* The part of the day which follows noon.

Afterthought, aft'er-that, *n.* Reflection after an act.

Afterward, Afterwards, aft'er-werd, aft'er-werdz, *adv.* In subsequent time.

Again, a-gen', *adv.* Once more; further.

Against, a-genst', *prep.* In opposition to; in expectation of.

Agape, a-gap', *a.* With the mouth wide open.

Agate, ag'at, *n.* A semi-pellucid mineral.

Age, aj, *n.* A period of time; an epoch; number of years during which a person has lived; decline of life; oldness; legal maturity.—*vi.*and *t.* (aging, aged). To grow or make old; to show signs of advancing age.

Agency, a'jen-si, *n.* Instrumentality; office or business of an agent.

Agenda, a-jen'da, *n.pl.* Memoranda; business to be transacted at a meeting.

Agent, a'jent, *n.* One who acts; a deputy; an active cause or power.

Agglomerate, ag-glom'me-rat, *vt.* To gather into a mass.—*vi.* To grow into a mass.

Agglutinant, ag-glu'tin-ant, *n.* Any viscous or gluey substance.

Agglutinate, ag-glu'tin-at, *vt.* To glue to; to cause to adhere.

Aggrandize, ag'gran-diz, *vt.* To make great; to magnify.

Aggravate, ag'gra-vat, *vt.* (aggravating, aggravated). To intensify; to exasperate.

Aggregate, ag'gre-gat, *vt.* To bring together; to heap up.—*a.* Formed of parts collected.—*n.* A sum, mass, or assemblage of particulars.

Aggression, ag-gre'shon, *n.* The first act of hostility; attack.

Aggressor, ag-gres'or, n. The person who commences hostilities.

Aggrieve, ag-grēv', vt. To pain, oppress, or injure.

Aghast, a-gast', a. or adv. Amazed; stupefied. Also agast.

Agile, aj'il, a. Ready to act; nimble.

Agio, ā'ji-ō, n. The difference in value between paper and metallic money.

Agitate, aj'it-āt, vt. (agitating, agitated). To put in violent motion; to shake briskly; to excite; to consider; to discuss.

Agnomen, ag-nō'men, n. An additional name or epithet conferred on a person.

Agnostic, ag-nos'tik, n. One who disclaims any knowledge of God or of anything but material phenomena.—a. Pertaining to agnostics or their doctrines.

Agnosticism, ag-nos'ti-sizm, n. The doctrines or belief of agnostics.

Ago, a-gō, adv. or a. Past; gone.

Agonize, ag'ō-niz, vi. (agonizing, agonized). To writhe with extreme pain.—vt. To distress with extreme pain; to torture.

Agony, ag'ō-ni, n. Extreme pain of body or mind; anguish; the pangs of death.

Agrarian, a-grā'ri-an, a. Relating to lands.

Agree, a-grē', vi. (agreeing, agreed). To be in concord; to correspond; to suit.

Agreement, a-grē'ment, n. Harmony, conformity; stipulation.

Agriculture, ag'ri-kul-tūr, n. The art or science of cultivating the ground.

Aground, a-ground', adv. Stranded.

Ague, ā'gū, n. An intermittent fever, with cold fits and shivering.

Ahead, a-hed', adv. Before; onward.

Ahoy, a-hoi', exclam. A sea-term used in hailing.

Aid, ād, vt. To help; to relieve.—n. Help; assistance; a helper.

Aide-de-camp, ād-de-konp, n.; pl. **Aides-de-camp.** An officer attendant on a general.

AIDS, ādz, n. Acquired Immune Deficiency Syndrome. A breakdown of the human body's immune system.

Aigret, Aigrette, ā'gret, ā-gret', n. A plume or ornament for the head composed of feathers or precious stones.

Ail, āl, vt. To pain, to affect with uneasiness.—vi. To be in pain or trouble.

Aim, ām, vi. To point with a missive weapon; to intend; to endeavor.—vt. To level or direct as a firearm.—n. That which is aimed at; direction; purpose; drift.

Air, ār, n. The fluid which we breathe; a light breeze; a tune; mien; pl. affected manner.—vt. To expose to the air; to ventilate; to dry.

Air-bladder, ār'blad-dėr, n. The bladder of a fish containing air.

Aircraft, ār-kraft, n. A general name for craft designed for the navigation of the air, such as airplanes, airships or balloons.

Airily, ār'i-li, adj. In an airy manner.

Airiness, ār'i-nes, n. Openness; gaiety.

Airing, ār'ing, n. An exposure to the air or to a fire; an excursion in the open air.

Airplane, ār'o-plān, n. A heavier-than-air power-driven flying-machine having one or two pairs of wings (monoplane or biplane) which support it owing to the reaction of the air.

Airport, ār'pört, n. An area for landing airplanes, usually having customs houses, servicing facilities, etc.

Air-pump, ār'pump, n. A machine for pumping the air out of a vessel.

Air-shaft, ār'shaft, n. A passage for air into a mine.

Air-tight, ār'tīt, a. So tight or compact as not to let air pass.

Airy, ā'ri, a. Open to the free air; high in air; light; thin; vain; gay.

Aisle, il, n. A wing or side of a church; a passage in a church.

Ajar, a-jär', adv. Partly open, as a door.

Akimbo, a-kim'bō, pred.a. or adv. With the elbow outwards and the hand on the hip.

Akin, a-kin', a. Of kin; related to; partaking of the same properties.

Alabaster, al'a-bas-tėr, n. A soft marble-like mineral.—a. Made of alabaster.

Alacrity, a-lak'ri-ti, n. Liveliness; cheerful readiness; promptitude.

Alarm, a-lärm', n. A call to arms; sudden surprise; fright; a notice of danger.—vt. To give notice of danger; to disturb.

Alarm clock, a-lärm' klok, n. A clock which can be set to awaken sleepers at a given time by ringing a small gong.

Alarming, a-lärm'ing, p.a. Terrifying.

Alarmist, a-lärm'ist, n. One prone to excite alarm.—a. Exciting unnecessary alarm.

Alas, a-las', interj. Expressing grief, pity, etc.

Albatross, al'ba-tros, n. An aquatic bird of southern seas, the largest sea-bird known.

Albino, al-bī'nō, n. A person with abnormally white skin and hair, and pink eyes.

Album, al'bum, n. A book for autographs, sketches, etc.

Albumen, al-bū'men, n. The white of an egg; a substance of the same kind found in animals and vegetables.

Alburnum, al-bėr'num, n. Sap-wood of a tree.

Alchemy, al'ke-mi, n. An obsolete science, aiming at changing metals into gold, etc.

Alcohol, al'kō-hol, n. Pure spirit of a highly intoxicating nature.

Alcoholic, al-kō-hol'ik, a. Pertaining to alcohol.

Alcoholism, al'kō-hol-izm, n. The condition of habitual drunkards.

Alcove, al'kov, n. A recess.

Aldehyde, al'dė-hīd, n. A colorless liquid produced by oxidation of alcohol.

Alder, al'dėr, n. A tree generally growing in moist land.

Alderman, al'dėr-man, n.; pl. **-men.** A magistrate of a town.

Ale, āl, n. A fermented malt liquor; beer.

Alee, a-lē', adv. On the lee side of a vessel.

Alembic, a-lem'bik, n. A vessel used in chemical distillation.

Alert, a-lėrt', a. Vigilant; quick; prompt.—n. An air-raid warning.

Alexandrine, al'legz-an''drin, n. A line with six stresses.

Alga, al'ga, n.; pl. **-gae,** A sea-weed.

Algebra, al'je-bra, n. The science of computing by symbols.

Alias, ā'li-as, adv. Otherwise.—n.; pl. **-ses,** An assumed name.

Alibi, al'i-bī, n. The plea of a person who, charged with a crime, alleges that he was elsewhere when the crime was committed.

Alien, āl'yen, a. Foreign; estranged from.—n. A foreigner.

Alienable, āl'yen-a-bl, a. That may be alienated or transferred to another.

Alienate, āl'yen-āt, vt. (alienating, alienated). To transfer to another; to estrange.

Alight, a-līt', vi. To get down; to settle on.

Alike, a-līk', a. Like; similar.—adv. In the same manner, form, or degree.

Aliment, al'i-ment, n. Nourishment; food.

Alimony, al'i-mo-ni, n. Allowance to a woman legally separated from her husband.

Aliped, al'i-ped, n. A wing-footed animal.

Aliquot, al'i-kwot, a. A part of a number which divides the whole without remainder.

Alive, a-līv', a. Living; lively; susceptible.

Alkali, al'ka-li, n.; pl. **-es** or **-is.** A substance, as potash and soda, which neutralizes acids and unites with oil or fat to form soap.

All, al, a. Every part; every one.—n. The whole; everything.—adv. Wholly; entirely.

Allah, al'la, n. The Arabic name of God.

Allay, al-lā', vt. To repress; to assuage.

Allegation, al-lē-gā'shon, n. Affirmation; declaration.

Allege, al-lej', *vt.* (alleging, alleged). To adduce; to assert; to plead in excuse.

Allegiance, al-lē'ji-ans, *n.* Loyalty.

Allegory, al'li-gō-ri, *n.* A speech or discourse which conveys a meaning different from the literal one.

Allegro, al-lā'grō. A word denoting a brisk sprightly movement.

Alleluiah, al-lē-lū'ya, *n.* Praise to Jehovah; a word used to express pious joy.

Allergy, al'er-je, *n.* A state of the body in which the cells are specially sensitive to certain substances, usually proteins.

Alleviate, al-lē'vi-āt, *vt.* (alleviating, alleviated). To make light; to assuage.

Alley, al'i, *n.* A narrow walk or passage.

Alliance, al-lī'ans, *n.* State of being allied; confederacy; league.

Allied, al-lid', *p.a.* United by treaty.

Alligation, al-li-gā'shon, *n.* Act of tying together; a rule of arithmetic.

Alligator, al'li-gā-tor, *n.* The American crocodile.

Alliteration, al-lit-ėr-ā'shon, *n.* The repetition of a letter at the beginning of two or more words in close succession.

Allocate, al'lō-kāt, *vt.* (allocating, allocated). To distribute; to assign to each his share.

Allocution, al-lō-kū'shon, *n.* The act or manner of speaking; a formal address.

Allomorphism, al-lo-mor'fizm, *n.* Difference of form, with sameness of substance.

Allopathy, al-lop'a-thi, *n.* The ordinary mode of curing diseases, by using medicines which produce a condition contrary to that of the disease.

Allot, al-lot', *vt.* (allotting, allotted). To give by lot; to apportion.

Allotrophy, al-lot'ro-pi, *n.* The capability of substances of existing in more than one form.

Allow, al-lou', *vt.* To grant; to admit; to abate; to bestow, as compensation.

Alloy, al-loi', *vt.* To mix with baser metals; to abate by mixture.—*n.* A baser metal mixed with a finer; a metallic compound.

All-spice, al-spis, *n.* Pimento or Jamaica pepper, supposed to combine many different flavors.

Allude, al-lūd', *vi.* (alluding, alluded). To refer to; to hint at.

Allure, al-lūr', *vt.* (alluring, allured). To draw by some lure; to entice; to decoy.

Allusion, al-lū'zhon, *n.* The act of alluding; a hint; a reference.

Alluvial, al-lū'vi-al, *a.* Deposited by water.

Alluvion, al-lū'vi-on, *n.* Land added to a property by soil washed up by the sea or a river.

Ally, al-lī', *vt.* (allying, allied). To unite by friendship, marriage, or treaty; to associate. *n.* One related by marriage or other tie; an associate.

Almanac, al'ma-nak, *n.* A calendar of days, weeks, and months, etc.

Almighty, al-mī'ti, *a.* Omnipotent.—*n.* God.

Almond, a'mund, *n.* The nut of the almond-tree; *pl.* the tonsils of the throat.

Almost, al'most, *adv.* Nearly; well-nigh; for the greatest part.

Alms, ämz, *n.pl.* A charitable gift.

Aloe, al'ō, *n.* A succulent plant; *pl.* a bitter purgative medicine.

Aloft, a-loft', *adv.* In the sky; on high.

Alone, a-lōn', *a.* Solitary.—*adv.* Separately.

Along, a-long', *adv.* Lengthwise; forward.—*prep.* By the side of; lengthwise.

Aloof, a-löf', *adv.* At a distance; apart.

Aloud, a-loud', *adv.* Loudly.

Alp, alp, *n.* A high mountain.

Alpaca, al-pak'a, *n.* A Peruvian animal, with long, soft, and woolly hair; cloth made of its hair, or a similar cloth.

Alpenstock, al'pen-stok, *n.* A long stick shod with iron, used in climbing mountains.

Alpha, al'fa, *n.* The first letter in the Greek alphabet; the first or beginning.

Alphabet, al'fa-bet, *n.* The letters of a language

arranged in the customary order.

Alpine, al'pīn, *a.* Pertaining to high mountains.

Already, al-red'i, *adv.* Before or by this time; even now.

Also, al'sō, *adv.* Likewise; in the same manner, further.

Altar, al'tėr, *n.* An elevated place on which sacrifices were offered; the communion table.

Altar-cloth, al'tėr-kloth, *n.* A cloth to lay upon an altar in churches.

Alter, al'tėr, *vt.* To make some change in; to vary.—*vt.* To vary.

Altercation, al-tėr-kā'shon, *n.* Heated dispute; wrangle.

Alternate, al-tėr'nāt, *a.* Being by turns.—*vt.* (alternating, alternated). To cause to follow by turns; to interchange.—*vi.* To happen or act by turns.

Alternation, al-tėrn-ā'shon, *n.* Reciprocal succession; interchange.

Alternative, al-tėrn'at-iv, *n.* A choice of two things.

Although, al'THŌ', *conj.* Be it so; admit all that.

Altitude, al'ti-tūd, *n.* Height; eminence; elevation.

Alto, al'tō, *a.* High.—*n.* In *music,* contralto.

Altogether, al-tō-geTH'er, *adv.* Wholly; entirely; without exception.

Altruism, al'trö-izm, *n.* Devotion to others or to humanity; the opposite of selfishness.

Alum, al'um, *n.* An astringent salt of great use in medicine and the arts.

Aluminium, al-ū-min'i-um, *n.* A very light metal of a silvery white color.

Alumnus, a-lum'nus, *n.*; pl. **-ni.** A pupil; a graduate of a university.

Alveolar, Alveolate, al-vē'o-lėr, al-vē'o-lāt, *a.* Containing sockets; resembling a honeycomb.

Alvine, al'vin, *a.* Belonging to the lower belly.

Always, al'wāz, *adv.* At all times; continually.

Am, am. The first person singular, present tense, indicative mood, of the verb *to be.*

Amalgam, a-mal'gam, *n.* A compound of quicksilver with another metal; a compound.

Amanuensis, a-man'ū-en''sis, *n.*; pl. **-ses.** One who writes what another dictates.

Amaranth, am'a-ranth, *n.* The unfading flower; a color inclining to purple.

Amaranthine, am-a-ran'thin, *a.* Unfading.

Amass, a-mas', *vt.* To form into a mass; to accumulate; to heap up.

Amateur, am-a-tūr', *n.* A lover of any art or science, not a professor.

Amatory, am'a-tō-ri, *a.* Relating to love; causing love; amorous.

Amaze, a-māz', *vt.* (amazing, amazed). To astonish; to bewilder.

Amazon, am'a-zon, *n.* A warlike or masculine woman; a virago.

Ambassador, am-bas'sa-dor, *n.* A representative of a sovereign or state at a foreign court.

Amber, am'bėr, *n.* A mineralized pale-yellow resin of extinct pine-trees.

Ambergris, am'bėr-grēs, *n.* A fragrant, solid, opaque, ash-colored substance, obtained from the spermaceti whale.

Ambidextrous, am-bi-deks'trus, *a.* Using both hands alike.

Ambient, am'bi-ent, *a.* Encompassing.

Ambiguity, am-bi-gū'i-ti, *n.* Doubtfulness of signification.

Ambiguous, am-big'ū-us, *a.* Of uncertain signification; doubtful.

Ambit, am'bit, *n.* Compass; scope.

Ambition, am-bi'shon, *n.* Desire of preferment or power.

Ambitious, am-bi'shus, *a.* Aspiring.

Amble, am'bl, *vi.* (ambling, ambled). To move, as a horse, by lifting the two legs on each side alternately; to go between a walk and a trot.—*n.* A peculiar motion of a horse; a pace between a walk and a trot.

Ambrosia, am-brō'zhi-a, *n.* The imaginary food of the gods, which conferred immortality.

Ambulance, am'bū-lans, *n.* An itinerant hospital; a wagon for the sick or wounded.

Ambulatory, am'bū-lā-tō-ri, *a.* Movable.—*n.* A part of a building to walk in.

Ambuscade, am-bus-kād', *n.* The act or place of lying in wait in order to surprise; the troops lying in wait; ambush.

Ameliorate, a-mēl'yor-āt, *vt.* To make better.

Amen, ā-men', *adv.* So be it.

Amenable, a-mēn'a-bl, *a.* Accountable; responsible.

Amend, a-mend', *vt.* To correct; to improve.—*vi.* To grow better.

Amendment, a-mend'ment, *n.* A change for the better; correction; reformation.

Amends, a-mendz', *n.pl.* Compensation; satisfaction; recompense.

Amenity, a-men'i-ti, *n.* Pleasantness; agreeableness of situation.

American, a-me'ri-kan, *n.* A native of America.— *a.* Pertaining to America.

Amethyst, am'ē-thist, *n.* A variety of quartz, a precious stone of a violet or purple color.

Amiable, ā'mi-a-bl, *a.* Lovable; sweet-tempered.

Amicable, am'ik-a-bl, *a.* Friendly; kind.

Amidships, a-mid'ships, *adv.* or *pred.a.* In or towards the middle of a ship.

Amiss, a-mis', *a.* In error; improper.—*adv.* In a faulty manner; improperly.

Amity, am'i-ti, *n.* Friendship; harmony.

Ammeter, am'met-ėr, *n.* An instrument for measuring an electric current (in AMPERES).

Ammonia, am-mō'ni-a, *n.* Volatile alkali.

Ammonite, am'mon-īt, *n.* The fossil shell of extinct cuttle-fishes.

Ammunition, am-mu-ni'shon, *n.* Military projectiles; formerly military stores generally.

Amnesty, am'nes-ti, *n.* A general pardon of offenses against a government.

Amnion, am'ni-on, *n.* The innermost membrane surrounding the fetus of mammals, birds, and reptiles.

Amoeba, a-mē'ba, *n.*; pl. **-bae.** A microscopic animal commonly found in fresh water.

Among, Amongst, a-mung', a-mungst', *prep.* Amidst; throughout; of the number.

Amorous, am'or-us, *a.* Inclined to love; enamored; fond; relating to love.

Amorphous, a-mor'fus, *a.* Without shape; of irregular shape.

Amount, a-mount', *vi.* To mount up to; to result in.—*n.* The sum total; effect or result.

Amour, a-mör', *n.* A love intrigue.

Ampere, am-pār', *n.* The unit in measuring the strength of an electric current.

Amphibian, am-fib'i-an, *n.*; pl. **Amphibia,** am-fib'i-a. An animal capable of living both in water and on land; an animal that has both lungs and gills.

Amphibious, am-fib'i-us, *a.* Able to live under water and on land.

Amphibology, am-fi-bol'o-ji, *n.* Speech susceptible of two interpretations.

Amphitheater, am-fi-thē'a-tėr, *n.* An edifice of an oval form, with rows of seats all round, rising higher as they recede from the area.

Ample, am'pl, *a.* Spacious; copious; rich.

Amplification, am'pli-fi-kā''shon, *n.* Act of amplifying; enlargement; discussion.

Amplify, am'plif-ī, *vt.* (amplifying, amplified). To enlarge; to treat copiously.—*vi.* To speak copiously; to be diffuse.

Amplitude, am'pli-tūd, *n.* Ampleness; extent; abundance.

Amply, am'pli, *adv.* Largely; liberally; fully; copiously.

Amputate, am'pū-tāt, *vt.* (amputating, amputated). To cut off, as a limb.

Amuck, a-muk', *n.* or *adv.* Only in phrase *to run amuck,* to rush about frantically, to attack all and sundry.

Amulet, am'ū-let, *n.* A charm against evils or witchcraft.

Amuse, a-mūz', *vt.* (amusing, amused). To entertain; to beguile.

Amyl, am'il, *n.* A hypothetical radical said to exist in many substances.

Amyloid, am'il-oid, *a.* Resembling or of the nature of starch.—*n.* A starchy substance.

An, an, *a.* The indefinite article, used before words beginning with a vowel-sound.

Anabaptist, an-a-bap'tist, *n.* One who maintains that adults only should be baptized.

Anachronism, an-ak'ron-izm, *n.* An error in chronology.

Anaconda, an-a-kon'da, *n.* A large species of serpent tribe.

Anagram, an'a-gram, *n.* A transposition of the letters of a name or sentence, by which a new word or sentence is formed.

Anal, ā'nal, *a.* Pertaining to the anus.

Analogous, an-al'og-us, *a.* Having analogy; corresponding.

Analogy, an-al'o-ji, *n.* Likeness; similarity.

Analyse, an'a-līz, *vt.* (analysing, analysed). To subject to analysis; to resolve into its elements.

Analysis, an-al'i-sis, *n.*; pl. **-ses.** A resolution of a thing into its elements; synopsis.

Anarchist, an'ärk-ist, *n.* An author or promoter of anarchy; one who opposes all existing systems of government.

Anarchy, an'är-ki, *n.* State of being without rule; political confusion.

Anathema, a-nath'e-ma, *n.* An ecclesiastical denunciation; curse.

Anatomy, a-nat'ō-mi, *n.* The art of dissection; doctrine of the structure of the body learned by dissection.

Ancestor, an'ses-tėr, *n.* A progenitor; forefather.

Anchor, ang'kėr, *n.* An iron instrument for holding a ship at rest in water. *vt.* To hold fast by an anchor.—*vi.* To cast anchor.

Anchorage, ang'ker-āj, *n.* A place where a ship can anchor; duty on ships for anchoring.

Anchorite, ang'kō-rīt, *n.* A hermit.

Anchovy, an-chō'vi, *n.* A small fish of the herring kind, furnishing a fine sauce.

Ancient, ān'shent, *a.* That happened in former times; old, antique.

Ancillary, an'sil-la-ri, *a.* Pertaining to a maidservant; subservient or subordinate.

And, and, *conj.* A particle which connects words and sentences together.

Andante, an-dan'te, *a.* In *music,* with slow, graceful movement.

Andiron, and'ī-ėrn, *n.* A metallic support for logs of wood burned on an open hearth.

Anecdote, an'ek-dōt, *n.* A short story.

Anemometer, an-e-mom'et-ėr, *n.* An instrument for measuring the force of the wind.

Anemia, a-nē'mi-a, *n.* Bloodlessness.

Anemone, a-nem'o-nē, *n.* Wind-flower, a genus of plants.

Aneroid, an'ē-roid, *a.* Dispensing with fluid, said of a kind of barometer.

Anesthetic, an-es-thet'ik, *a.* Producing insensibility.—*n.* A substance, as chloroform, which produces insensibility.

Aneurysm, an'ū-rizm, *n.* Dilatation of an artery.

Anew, a-nū', *adv.* On new; fresh.

Angel, ān'jel, *n.* A divine messenger; a spirit; an old English gold coin worth ten shillings.

Anger, ang'gėr, *n.* A violent passion, excited by real or supposed injury; resentment —*vt.* To excite anger; to irritate.

Angina, an-ji'na, *n.* Angina pectoris, a fatal disease characterized by paroxysms of intense pain and a feeling of constriction in the chest.

Angle, ang'gl, *n.* The inclination of two lines which meet in a point but have different directions; a corner.

Angle, ang'gl, *n.* A fishing-hook, or hook with line and rod.—*vi.* (angling, angled). To fish with an angle.

Anglican, ang'glik-an, *a.* Pertaining to England,

or to the English Church.

Anglicize, ang'gli-siz, *vt.* To make English.

Anglomania, ang-glō-mā'ni-a, *n.* Excessive attachment to English people, customs, etc.

Anglophobia, ang-glō-fō'bi-a, *n.* Excessive hatred of English people, customs, etc.

Anglo-Saxon, ang-glō-sak'son, *n.* One of the English race; the English language in its first stage.—*a.* Pertaining to the Anglo-Saxons, or their language.

Angry, ang'gri, *a.* Affected with anger; provoked; wrathful; resentful.

Anguish, ang'gwish, *n.* Extreme pain, either of body or mind; agony; grief.

Angular, ang'gū-lėr, *a.* Having an angle; stiff.

Anile, an'īl, *a.* Aged; imbecile.

Aniline, an'i-lin, *n.* A substance obtained from coal-tar, used in dyeing.

Animadvert, an'i-mad-vert'', *vi.* To criticise; to censure (with *upon*).

Animal, an'i-mal, *n.* A living being having sensation and voluntary motion; a quadruped.—*a.* Belonging to animals; gross.

Animalcule, an-i-mal'kūl, *n.* A minute animal seen by means of a microscope.

Animalism, an'i-mal-izm, *n.* Sensuality.

Animate, an'i-māt, *vt.* (animating, animated). To give natural life to; to enliven.

Animated, an'i-māt-ed, *p.a.* Lively; living.

Animism, an'i-mizm, *n.* The belief that natural phenomena are due to spirits, and that inanimate objects have spirits.

Animosity, an-i-mos'i-ti, *n.* Violent hatred; active enmity; malignity.

Animus, an'i-mus, *n.* Intention; hostile spirit.

Anise, an'is, *n.* An aromatic plant, the seeds of which are used in making cordials.

Ankle, ang'kl, *n.* The joint which connects the foot with the leg.

Annals, an'nalz, *n.pl.* A record of events under the years in which they happened.

Anneal, an'nēl', *vt.* To temper glass or metals by heat; to fix colors laid on glass.

Annelid, an'ne-lid, *n.* An invertebrate animal whose body is formed of numerous small rings, as the worm, leech, etc.

Annex, an-neks', *vt.* To unite at the end; to subjoin; to take possession of.

Annihilate, an-ni'hil-āt, *vt.* (annihilating, annihilated). To reduce to nothing; to destroy the existence of.

Anniversary, an-ni-vėrs'a-ri, *n.* A day on which some event is annually celebrated.

Annotate, an'nō-tāt, *vt.* (annotating, annotated). To write notes upon.

Announce, an-nouns', *vt.* (announcing, announced). To declare; to proclaim.

Announcement, an-nouns'ment, *n.* Declaration.

Annoy, an-noi', *vt.* To hurt; to molest; to vex.

Annual, an'nū al, *a.* Yearly; lasting a year.—*n.* A plant whose root dies yearly; a book published yearly.

Annually, an'nū-al-li, *adv.* Yearly.

Annuitant, an-nū'it-ant, *n.* One who receives an annuity.

Annuity, an-nū'i-ti, *n.* A sum of money payable yearly, etc.

Annul, annul', *vt.* (annulling, annulled). To make void or of no effect; to repeal.

Annular, an'nū-lėr, *a.* Having the form of a ring; pertaining to a ring.

Annulose, an'nū-lōs, *a.* Having a body composed of rings; applied to annelids.

Annunciation, an-nun'si-ā''shon, *n.* The angel's salutation to the Virgin Mary, and its anniversary, the 25th of March.

Anode, an'ōd, *n.* The positive pole of a voltaic current.

Anodyne, an'ō-din, *n.* Any medicine which allays or mitigates pain.—*a.* Assuaging pain.

Anoint, a-noint', *vt.* To rub over with oil; to consecrate by unction.

Anomaly, a-nom'a-li, *n.* Irregularity; deviation

from common rule.

Anonymous, a-non'im-us, *a.* Nameless; without the real name of the author.

Another, an-uTH'ėr, *a.* Not the same; different; any other.

Answer, an'sėr, *vt.* To reply to; to satisfy; to suit.—*vi.* To reply; to be accountable; to succeed.—*n.* A reply; a solution.

Answerably, an'sėr-a-bli, *adv.* In due proportion; suitably.

Ant, ant, *n.* An emmet; a pismire.

Antagonism, an-tag'ō-nizm, *n.* Opposition; contest.

Antagonist, an-tag'ō-nist, *n.* One who struggles with another in combat; an opponent; that which acts in opposition.

Antarctic, ant-ärk'tik, *a.* Relating to the south pole, or to the region near it.

Antecedent, an-tē-sē'dent, *a.* Going before; prior.—*n.* That which goes before; the noun to which a relative refers; *pl.* a man's previous history, etc.

Antechamber, an'tē-chăm-bėr, *n.* An apartment leading into a chief apartment.

Antedate, an'tē-dāt, *n.* Prior date.—*vt.* To date before the true time.

Antediluvian, an'tē-di-lū''vi-an, *a.* Before the flood.—*n.* One who lived before the flood.

Antelope, an'tē-lōp, *n.* An animal resembling the deer, but with hollow, unbranched horns.

Antemeridian, an'tē-mē-rid''i-an, *a.* Before midday; pertaining to the forenoon.

Antemundane, an-tē-mun'dān, *a.* Before the creation of the world.

Antenna, an-ten'na, *n.*; *pl.* **Antennae,** an-ten'nē. The feeler of an insect; an aerial.

Anterior, an-tē'ri-ėr, *a.* Before; prior; in front.

Anteroom, an'tē-röm, *n.* A room in front of a principal apartment.

Anthem, an'them, *n.* A sacred song sung in alternate parts; a piece of Scripture set to music.

Anther, an'thėr, *n.* The summit of the stamen in a flower, containing the pollen.

Anthology, an-thol'o-ji, *n.* A collection of poems.

Anthracite, an'thra-sīt, *n.* A hard, compact coal which burns almost without flame.

Anthropoid, an'thrō-poid, *a.* Resembling man; applied to the higher apes.

Anthropology, an-thrō-pol'o-ji, *n.* The science of man and mankind; the study of the physical and mental constitution of man.

Anthropomorphism, an-thrō'pō-mor''fizm, *n.* The representation of a deity in human form, or with human attributes.

Anthropophagi, an-thrō-pof'a-ji, *n.pl.* Maneaters; cannibals.

Antic, an'tik, *a.* Grotesque; fantastic.—*n.* A buffoon; buffoonery.

Antichrist, an'ti-krīst, *n.* The great adversary of Christ.

Anticipate, an-tis'-i-pāt, *vt.* (anticipating, anticipated). To forestall; to foretaste; to preclude; to expect.

Anti-climax, an-ti-klī'maks, *n.* A sentence in which the ideas become less striking at the close.

Antidote, an'ti-dōt, *n.* A remedy for poison or any evil.

Antimony, an'ti-mo-ni, *n.* A brittle, white-colored metal, used in the arts and in medicine.

Antinomian, an-ti-nō'mi-an, *n.* One who opposes the moral law.

Antipathy, an-tip'a-thi, *n.* Instinctive aversion; dislike; opposition.

Antiphlogistic, an'ti-flo-jis''tik, *a.* Counteracting inflammation.

Antiphrasis, an-tif'ra-sis, *n.* The use of words in a sense opposite to the proper one.

Antipodes, an-tip'o-dēz, *n.pl.* Those who live on opposite sides of the globe; the opposite side of the globe.

Antipyrin, an-ti-pī'rin, *n.* A drug used to reduce fever and relieve pain.

Antiquarianism, an-ti-kwā'ri-an-izm, *n.* Love or knowledge of antiquities.

Antiquary, an'ti-kwa-ri, *n.* One versed in antiquities.

Antiquated, an'ti-kwāt-ed, *a.* Grown old; obsolete.

Antique, an-tēk', *a.* Old; of genuine antiquity.—*n.* Anything very old; an ancient relic.

Antiquity, an-tik'wi-ti, *n.* Ancient times; great age; *pl.* remains of ancient times.

Antiseptic, an-ti-sep'tik, *a.* Counteracting putrefaction.—*n.* A substance which resists or corrects putrefaction.

Antithesis, an-tith'e-sis, *n.*; *pl.* **-theses.** Opposition of thoughts or words; contrast.

Antitype, an'ti-tip, *n.* That which is shadowed out by a type or emblem.

Antler, ant'ler, *n.* A branch of a stag's horn.

Antonym, ant'ō-nim, *n.* A word of directly contrary signification to another: the opposite of a synonym.

Anus, ā'nus, *n.* The opening of the body by which excrement is expelled.

Anvil, an'vil, *n.* An iron block on which smiths hammer and shape their work.

Anxiety, ang-zī'e-ti, *n.* State of being anxious; concern.

Anxious, angk'shus, *a.* Suffering mental distress; solicitous; concerned.

Any, en'i, *a.* One indefinitely; whatever; some.—*adv.* At all; in any degree.

Aorist, ā'or-ist, *n.* An indefinite past tense in the Greek verb.

Aorta, ā-ort'a, *n.* The great artery which rises up from the left ventricle of the heart.

Apart, a-pärt', *adv.* Separately; aside.

Apartment, a-pärt'ment, *n.* A room.

Apathy, ap'a-thi, *n.* Want of feeling; insensibility; indifference.

Ape, āp, *n.* A monkey; an imitator.—*vt.* (aping, aped). To imitate servilely; to mimic.

Aperture, ap'ér-tūr, *n.* An opening; a hole.

Apex, ā'peks, *n.*; *pl.* **-exes** and **-ices.** The summit of anything.

Aphelion, a-fē'li-on, *n.*; *pl.* **-lia.** The point of a planet's orbit farthest from the sun.

Aphorism, af-or-izm, *n.* A precept expressed in few words; a maxim.

Apiary, ā'pi-a-ri, *n.* A place where bees are kept.

Apiece, a-pēs', *adv.* In a separate share; to each; noting the share of each.

Aplomb, a-plong, *n.* Self-possession.

Apocalypse, a-pok'a-lips, *n.* Revelation; the last book of the New Testament.

Apocrypha, a-pok'ri-fa, *n.pl.* Certain books whose authenticity as inspired writings is not generally admitted.

Apogee, ap'ō-jē, *n.* The point in the moon's orbit farthest from the earth.

Apologetic, a-pol'ō-jet''ik, *a.* Containing apology; defending; excusing.

Apologetics, a-pol'ō-jet''iks, *n.pl.* The branch of theology which defends Christianity.

Apologize, a-pol'ō-jīz, *vi.* (apologizing, apologized). To make an apology.

Apology, a-pol'ō-ji, *n.* That which is said in defense; vindication; excuse.

Apophthegm, Apothegm, ap'o-them, *n.* A terse, pointed saying.

Apoplexy, ap'ō-plek'si, *n.* A sudden privation of sense and voluntary motion.

Apostasy, a-pos'ta-si, *n.* Departure from one's faith; desertion of a party.

Apostle, a-pos'l, *n.* One sent to preach the gospel; one of the twelve disciples.

Apostrophe, a-pos'tro-fē, *n.* An addressing of the absent or the dead as if present; a mark (') indicating contraction of a word, or the possessive case.

Apothecary, a-poth'e-ka-ri, *n.* One who prepares and sells drugs or medicines.

Apotheosis, ap-o-thē'ō-sis or -thē-ō'sis, *n.* A deification; a placing among the gods.

Appal, ap-pal', *vt.* (appalling, appalled). To depress with fear; to dismay.

Apparatus, ap-pa-rā'tus, *n.*; *pl.* **-tus,** or **-tuses,** Set of instruments or utensils for performing any operation.

Apparel, ap-pa'rel, *n.* Equipment; clothing. *vt.* (apparelling, apparelled). To dress; to array.

Apparent, ap-pā'rent, *a.* That may be seen; evident; seeming, not real.

Apparition, ap-pa-ri'shon, *n.* An appearance; a specter; a ghost or phantom.

Appeal, ap-pēl', *vi.* To call; to refer to a superior court; to have recourse.—*vt.* To remove to a superior court.—*n.* The removal of a cause to a higher tribunal; a reference to another.

Appear, ap-pēr', *vi.* To be or become visible; to seem.

Appease, ap-pēz', *vt.* (appeasing, appeased). To pacify; to tranquilize.

Appellation, ap-pel-ā'shon, *n.* Name; title.

Appellative, ap-pel'at-iv, *a.* Naming; designating.—*n.* A name; an appellation.

Append, ap-pend', *vt.* To add; to annex.

Appendage, ap-pend'āj, *n.* Something added; a subordinate part.

Appendix, ap-pen'diks, *n.*; *pl.* **-ixes** or **-ices.** An adjunct or appendage; a supplement; a narrow tube with blind end leading out of intestine.

Appertain, ap-pér-tān', *vi.* To belong; to relate.

Appetence, Appetency, ap'pē-tens, ap'pē-ten-si, *n.* Desire; sensual appetite.

Appetite, ap'pē-tīt, *n.* A desire or relish for food or other sensual gratifications.

Applaud, ap-plad', *vt.* To praise by clapping the hands, etc.; to extol.

Apple, ap'l, *n.* The fruit of the apple-tree; the pupil of the eye.

Appliance, ap-plī'ans, *n.* Act of applying; thing applied; article of equipment.

Applicable, ap'pli-ka-bl, *a.* That may be applied; suitable.

Application, ap-pli-kā'shon, *n.* Act of applying; request; close study; assiduity; the thing applied.

Apply, ap-plī', *vt.* (applying, applied). To fasten or attach; to use; to employ with assiduity.—*vi.* To suit; to solicit; to have recourse to.

Appoint, ap-point', *vt.* To fix; to allot; to nominate; to equip.—*vi.* To determine.

Apportion, ap-pōr'shon, *vt.* To portion out; to assign in just proportion.

Apposite, ap'pō-zit, *a.* Suitable; applicable; pat.

Apposition, ap-pō-zi'shon, *n.* In *grammar,* the relation of one noun to another, when it explains its meaning, while agreeing in case.

Appraise, ap-prāz', *vt.* (appraising, appraised) To fix or set a price on; to estimate.

Appreciate, ap-prē'shi-āt, *vt.* (appreciating, appreciated). To value; to estimate justly.

Apprehend, ap-prē-hend', *vt.* To take hold of; to arrest; to conceive; to fear.—*vi.* To think; to imagine.

Apprehensive, ap-prē-hen'siv, *a.* Fearful; suspicious.

Apprentice, ap-pren'tis, *n.* One who is indentured to a master to learn a trade, an art, etc.—*vi.* To bind as an apprentice.

Apprise, ap-prīz', *vt.* (apprising, apprised). To inform; to make known of.

Approach, ap-prōch', *vi.* To come near; to approximate.—*vt.* To come near to; to resemble.—*n.* Act of drawing near; an avenue; access.

Approbation, ap-prō-bā'shon, *n.* Approval; attestation; a liking.

Appropriate, ap-prō'pri-āt, *vt.* (appropriating, appropriated). To take to oneself as one's own; to set apart for.—*a.* Set apart for a particular use or person; suitable; adapted.

Appropriateness, ap-prō'pri-āt-nes, *n.* Peculiar fitness.

Approval, ap-pröv'al, *n.* Approbation.

Approve, ap-pröv', *vt.* (approving, approved) To

deem good; to like; to sanction.—*vi.* To feel or express approbation (with *of*).

Approximate, ap-prok'si-mât, *a.* Near; approaching.—*vt.* (approximating, approximated). To bring near.—*vi.* To come near; to approach.

Appurtenance, ap-pér'ten-ans, *n.* That which pertains to; an appendage.

Apricot, ā'pri-kot, *n.* Stone-fruit, resembling the peach.

April, ā'pril, *n.* The fourth month of the year.

Apron, ā'prun, *n.* A cloth, or piece of leather, worn in front to protect the clothes.

Apropos, ap'rō-pō, *adv.* To the purpose; opportunely.

Apsis, ap'sis, *n.*; pl. **-sides,** -si-dēz. One of the two points in a planet's orbit which mark its greatest and least distance from the body round which it revolves.

Apt, apt, *a.* Suitable; liable; ready.

Apterous, ap'tėr-us, *a.* Destitute of wings.

Apteryx, ap'tė-riks, *n.* A bird of New Zealand, with rudimentary wings, and no tail.

Aptitude, ap'ti-tūd, *n.* Fitness; readiness.

Aptness, apt'nes, *n.* Aptitude.

Aqua, ak'wa, *n.* Water.

Aqua fortis, ak'wa for-tis, *n.* Weak and impure nitric acid.

Aquarium, a-kwā'ri-um, *n.*; pl. **-iums** or **-ia.** A vessel or tank for aquatic plants and animals; a collection of such vessels.

Aquarius, a-kwā'ri-us, *n.* The water-bearer, a sign in the zodiac.

Aquatic, a-kwat'ik, *a.* Living or growing in water.—*n.* A plant which grows in water; pl. sports or exercises in water.

Aqueduct, ak'wē-dukt, *n.* A conduit made for conveying water.

Aqueous, ā'kwē-us, *a.* Watery.

Aquiline, ak'wil-īn, *a.* Belonging to the eagle; hooked like the beak of an eagle.

Arab, a'rab, *n.* A native of Arabia; a street urchin; an Arabian horse.

Arabesque, ar'ab-esk, *n.* A species of ornamentation consisting of fanciful figures and floral forms.

Arabian, a-rā'bi-an, *a.* Pertaining to Arabia.—*n.* A native of Arabia.

Arable, a'ra-bl, *a.* Fit for farming.

Arachnida, a-rak'ni-da, *n.pl.* A class of annulose wingless animals, such as spiders.

Aramaic, Aramean, a-ra-mā'ik, a-ra-mē'an, *a.* Pertaining to the languages, etc., of the Syrians and Chaldeans.

Araucaria, ar-a-kā'ri-a, *n.* A coniferous prickly tree, the monkey-puzzle.

Arbiter, är'bit-ėr, *n.* A person appointed by parties in controversy to decide their differences; an umpire.

Arbitrary, är'bi-tra-ri, *a.* Depending on one's will; despotic.

Arbitrate, är'bi-trāt, *vi.* (arbitrating, arbitrated). To act as an arbiter; to decide.

Arbor, är'bėr, *n.* A bower; a shelter in a garden, formed of trees, etc.

Arboreous, är-bō'rē-us, *a.* Belonging to trees.

Arborescent, är-bor-es'sent, *a.* Growing like a tree; becoming woody.

Arboretum, är-bo-rē'tum, *n.* A place where trees are cultivated for scientific purposes.

Arbutus, är'bū-tus, *n.* An evergreen shrub, with berries like the strawberry.

Arc, ärk, *n.* A part of a circle or curve.

Arcade, är-kād', *n.* A walk arched above; an arched gallery; a covered passage containing shops.

Arcanum, är-kān'um, *n.*; pl. **-na.** Mystery.

Arch, ärch, *a.* Chief; cunning; sly; roguish.

Arch, ärch, *n.* A concave structure supported by its own curve; a vault.—*vt.* To cover with an arch; to form with a curve.

Archeology, är-kē-ol'o-ji, *n.* The science of antiquities; knowledge of ancient art.

Archaic, är-kā'ik, *a.* Antiquated; obsolete.

Archaism, är'kā-izm, *n.* Obsolete word or expression.

Archangel, ärk-ān'jel, *n.* An angel of the highest order.

Archbishop, ärch-bish'up, *n.* A chief bishop; a bishop who superintends other bishops, his suffragans, in his province.

Archdeacon, ärch-dē'kn, *n.* A church dignitary next in rank below a bishop.

Archduke, ärch-dūk', *n.* Formerly a title of princes of the House of Austria.

Archer, ärch'ėr, *n.* A bowman; one who shoots with a bow and arrow.

Archetype, är'kē-tīp, *n.* The original model from which a thing is made.

Archipelago, är-ki-pel'a-gō, *n.* The Aegean Sea; a sea abounding in small islands.

Architect, är'ki-tekt, *n.* One who plans buildings, etc.; a contriver.

Architecture, är'ki-tek-tūr, *n.* The art or science of building; structure.

Architrave, är'ki-trāv, *n.* In *architecture,* the part of an entablature resting on a column.

Archive, är'kīv, *n.* A record; generally *pl.,* records of a kingdom, city, family, etc.

Archly, ärch'li, *adv.* Shrewdly; roguishly.

Archon, är'kon, *n.* One of the chief magistrates of ancient Athens.

Archway, ärch'wā, *n.* A way or passage under an arch.

Arctic, ärk'tik, *a.* Pertaining to the regions about the north pole; frigid; cold.

Ardency, är'den-si, *n.* Ardor; eagerness.

Ardent, är'dent, *a.* Burning; fervent; eager.

Ardor, är'dėr, *n.* Warmth; fervency; eagerness.

Arduous, är'dū-us, *a.* Difficult; laborios.

Are, är. The plural pres. indic. of the verb *to be.*

Area, ā'rē-a, *n.* Any open surface; superficial contents; any inclosed space.

Arena, a-rē'na, *n.* An open space of ground, strewed with sand or saw-dust, for combatants; any place of public contest.

Arenaceous, a-rē-nā'shus, *a.* Sandy.

Areopagus, ar-ē-op'a-gus, *n.* The supreme court of ancient Athens, held on a hill of this name.

Argent, är'jent, *a.* Silvery; like silver.

Argil, är'jil, *n.* White clay; potter's earth.

Argon, är'gon, *n.* A gas existing in the atmosphere in very small quantities; an inert chemical element.

Argonaut, är'go-nat, *n.* One who sailed in the ship *Argo* in quest of the golden fleece.

Argue, är'gū, *vi.* (arguing, argued). To offer reasons; to dispute.—*vt.* To show reasons for; to discuss.

Argument, är'gū-ment, *n.* A reason offered; a plea; subject of a discourse; heads of contents; controversy.

Argus, är'gus, *n.* A fabulous being with a hundred eyes; a watchful person.

Arian, ā'ri-an, *a.* Pertaining to Arius, who denied the divinity of Christ.—*n.* One who adheres to the doctrines of Arius.

Arid, a'rid, *a.* Dry; dried; parched.

Aries, ā'ri-ēz, *n.* The Ram, the first of the twelve signs of the zodiac.

Arise, a-rīz', *vi.* (arising, pret. arose, pp. arisen). To rise up; to proceed from.

Aristocracy, a-ris-tok'ra-si, *n.* Government by the nobility; the nobility.

Aristocrat, a'ris-to-krat, *n.* A noble; one who favors aristocracy.

Aristotelian, a-ris-to-tē'li-an, *a.* Pertaining to Aristotle, or to his philosophy.

Arithmetic, a-rith'met-ik, *n.* The science of numbering; the art of computation.

Ark, ärk, *n.* A chest; a large floating vessel.

Arm, ärm, *n.* The limb from the shoulder to the hand; anything extending from a main body; a weapon; *pl.* war; armor; armorial bearings.—*vt.* To furnish with arms; to fortify.—*vi.* To take up arms.

Armada, är-mä'da, *n*. A fleet of armed ships; a squadron.

Armadillo, är-ma-dil'lō, *n*. A quadruped of the southwestern U.S. with a hard bony shell.

Armament, ärm'a-ment, *n*. A force armed for war; war-munitions of a ship.

Armenian, är-mē'ni-an, *a*. Pertaining to Armenia.—*n*. A native of Armenia; the language of the country.

Arminian, är-min'i-an, *a*. Pertaining to Arminius.—*n*. A Protestant who denies the doctrine of predestination.

Armipotent, är-mip'ō-tent, *a*. Powerful in arms.

Armistice, är'mis-tis, *n*. A cessation of hostilities for a short time; a truce.

Armlet, ärm'let, *n*. A bracelet.

Armorial, är-mō'ri-al, *a*. Belonging to armour, or to the arms of a family.

Armoric, är-mo'rik, *a*. Pertaining to Brittany.—*n*. The language of Brittany.

Armor, ärm'ėr, *n*. Defensive arms.

Armory, ärm'e-ri, *n*. A repository of arms.

Armpit, ärm'pit, *n*. The hollow place under the shoulder.

Army, är'mi, *n*. A body of men armed for war; a great number.

Aroma, a-rō'ma, *n*. Perfume; the fragrant principle in plants, etc.

Aromatic, a-rō-mat'ik, *a*. Fragrant; spicy.—*n*. A fragrant plant or drug.

Around, a-round', *prep*. About; on all sides of; encircling.—*adv*. On every side.

Arouse, a-rouz', *vt*. (arousing, aroused). To rouse; to stir up.

Arrack, a'rak, *n*. A spirituous liquor distilled in the E. Indies from rice, etc.

Arraign, a-rān', *vt*. To indict; to censure.

Arrange, a-rānj', *vt*. (arranging, arranged). To put in order; to classify.

Arrangement, a-rānj'ment, *n*. Orderly disposition; adjustment; classification.

Arrant, a'rant, *a*. Downright; thorough.

Arras, a'ras, *n*. Tapestry.

Array, a-rā', *n*. Order; order of battle; apparel.—*v.t.* To draw up in order; to adorn.

Arrear, a-rēr', *n*. That which remains unpaid. Generally in plural.

Arrest, a-rest', *vt*. To stop; to apprehend.—*n*. A seizure by warrant; stoppage.

Arrive, a-riv', *vi*. (arriving, arrived). To come; to reach; to attain.

Arrogance, a'rō-gans, *n*. Assumption; haughtiness; insolent bearing.

Arrogant, a'rō-gant, *a*. Assuming; haughty.

Arrogate, a'rō-gāt, *vt*. (arrogating, arrogated). To claim unduly; to assume.

Arrow, a'rō, *n*. A straight-pointed weapon, to be discharged from a bow.

Arrowroot, a'rō-röt, *n*. A W. Indian plant; the starch of the plant, a medicinal food.

Arsenal, är'sē-nal, *n*. A public establishment where ammunition and guns are manufactured or stored.

Arsenic, är'sen-ik, *n*. A virulent mineral poison; an oxide of a brittle metal, called also arsenic.

Arson, är'son, *n*. The malicious setting on fire of a house, etc.

Art, ärt, *n*. Practical skill; a system of rules for certain actions; cunning; profession of a painter, etc.

Artery, är'te-ri, *n*. A tube which conveys blood from the heart.

Artesian, är-tē'zi-an, *a*. Designating a well made by boring till water is reached.

Artful, ärt'ful, *a*. Full of art; skilful; crafty.

Arthritis, är-thrī'tis, *n*. Gout.

Artichoke, är'ti-chōk, *n*. An esculent plant somewhat resembling a thistle.

Article, är'ti-kl, *n*. A separate item; stipulation; a particular commodity; a part of speech used before nouns, as *the.*—*vt*. To bind by articles.—*vi*. To stipulate.

Articulate, är-tik'ū-lāt, *a*. Distinct; clear.—*vi*. To utter distinct sounds, syllables, or words.—*vt*. To speak distinctly.

Articulation, är-tik'ū-lā''shon, *n*. Juncture of bones; joint; distinct utterance.

Artifice, ärt'i-fis, *n*. An artful device; fraud; stratagem.

Artificial, ärt-i-fi'shal, *a*. Made by art; not natural.

Artillery, är-til'lė-ri, *n*. Cannon; the troops who manage them; gunnery.

Artisan, ärt'i-zan, *n*. One trained to manual dexterity; a mechanic.

Artist, ärt'ist, *n*. One skilled in some art, especially the fine arts, as painting, etc.

Artiste, är-tēst, *n*. One skilled in some art not one of the fine arts, as singing, dancing.

Artless, ärt'les, *a*. Wanting art; unaffected.

Aryan, är-i-an or ā'ri-an, *a*. Indo-European; belonging to the Hindus, Persians, and most Europeans (except Turks, Hungarians, Finns, etc.), and to their languages.

As, az, *adv*. and *conj*. Like; even; equally; while; since; for example.

Asbestos, as-bes'tos, *n*. A mineral fibrous substance which is incombustible.

Ascend, as-send', *vi*. To rise; to go backward in order of time.—*vt*. To move upward upon; to climb.

Ascendancy, Ascendency, as-send'an-si, as-send'en-si, *n*. Controlling power; sway.

Ascendant, as-send'ant, *a*. Rising; superior; predominant.—*n*. Ascendancy; superiority.

Ascent, as-sent', *n*. Rise; a mounting upward; the means of ascending.

Ascertain, as-ser-tān', *vt*. To make certain; to find out.

Ascetic, as-set'ik, *a*. Unduly rigid in devotion.—*n*. One rigidly austere.

Ascribe, as-krīb', *vt*. (ascribing, ascribed). To attribute; to assign.

Aseptic, a-sep'tik, *a*. Not liable to putrefy.

Ash, ash, *n*. A well-known timber tree.

Ashamed, a-shāmd', *a*. Affected by shame.

Ashes, ash'ez, *n.pl*. The dust produced by combustion; the remains of a dead body.

Ashlar, Ashler, ash'lėr, *n*. A facing of dressed stones on a wall; hewn stone.

Ashore, a-shōr', *adv*. or *pred.a.* On shore.

Ash-Wednesday, ash-wenz'dā, *n*. The first day of Lent, so called from a custom of sprinkling ashes on the head.

Asiatic, ā-shi-at'ik, *a*. Belonging to Asia.—*n*. A native of Asia.

Aside, a-sid', *adv*. On one side; apart; at a small distance.

Asinine, as'i-nīn, *a*. Belonging to or resembling the ass.

Ask, ask, *vt*. To request; to question; to invite.—*vi*. To request or petition; to make inquiry.

Askance, Askant, a-skans', a-skant', *adv*. Awry; obliquely.

Aslant, a-slant', *pred.a.* or *adv*. On slant; obliquely; not perpendicularly.

Asleep, a-slēp', *pred.a.* or *adv*. Sleeping; at rest.

Aslope, a-slōp', *pred.a.* or *adv*. On slope; obliquely.

Asp, asp, *n*. A small venomous serpent of Egypt.

Asparagus, as-pa'ra-gus, *n*. A well-known esculent plant.

Aspect, as'pekt, *n*. Appearance; situation.

Aspen, asp'en, *n*. A species of the poplar.

Asperity, as-pe'ri-ti, *n*. Roughness; harshness.

Asperse, as-pers', *vt*. (aspersing, aspersed). To calumniate; to slander.

Asphalt, as-falt', *n*. A bituminous, hard substance, used for pavement, etc.

Asphodel, as'fō-del, *n*. A kind of lily.

Asphyxia, as-fik'si-a, *n*. Suspended animation from suffocation, etc.

Aspirant, as-pīr'ant, *n*. A candidate.

Aspirate, as'pi-rāt, *vt*. (aspirating, aspirated). To pronounce with an audible breath; to add an *h*-sound to.—*n*. An aspirated letter.

Aspire, as-pīr', *vi.* (aspiring, aspired). To aim at high things; to soar.

Asquint, a-skwint', *adv.* Out of the corner or angle of the eye; obliquely.

Ass, as, *n.* A well-known animal skin to the horse; a dolt.

Assail, as-sāl', *vt.* To attack; to assault.

Assassin, as-sas'sin, *n.* One who kills, or attempts to kill, by surprise or secretly.

Assassinate, as-sas'sin-āt, *vt.* (assassinating, assassinated). To murder by surprise or secretly.

Assault, as-salt', *n.* An attack; a storming.—*vt.* To assail; to storm.

Assay, as-sā', *n.* Proof; trial; determination of the quantity of metal in an ore or alloy.—*vt.* To try; to ascertain the purity or alloy of.—*vi.* To try or endeavor.

Assemblage, as-sem'bläj, *n.* A collection of individuals or things.

Assemble, as-sem'bl, *vt.* (assembling, assembled). To bring together.—*vi.* To come together.

Assembly, as-sem'bli, *n.* An assemblage; a convocation.

Assent, as-sent', *n.* Act of agreeing to anything; consent.—*vi.* To agree; to yield.

Assert, as-sèrt', *vt.* To affirm; to maintain; to vindicate.

Assertive, as-sèrt'iv, *a.* Affirming confidently; peremptory.

Assess, as-ses', *vt.* To fix a charge to be paid upon; to rate.

Assessment, as-ses'ment, *n.* Act of assessing; the sum levied; a tax.

Assets, as'sets, *n.pl.* Goods available to pay debts.

Asseverate, as-sev'ē-rāt, *vt.* (asseverating, asseverated). To declare seriously or solemnly; to protest.

Assiduity, as-si-dū'i-ti, *n.* Close application; diligence.

Assiduous, as-sid'ū-us, *a.* Constantly diligent.

Assign, as-sīn', *vt.* To designate; to allot; to make over to another.—*n.* A person to whom property or any right may be or is transferred.

Assignation, as-sig-nä'shon, *n.* An appointment to meet, as of lovers; a making over by transfer of title.

Assignment, as-sīn'ment, *n.* Act of assigning; thing assigned; a writ of transfer.

Assimilate, as-sim'il-āt, *vt.* (assimilating, assimilated). To make like to; to digest.—*vi.* To become similar or of the same substance.

Assist, as-sist', *vt.* To help.—*vi.* To lend help; to contribute.

Assistance, as-sist'ans, *n.* Help; aid.

Associate, as-sō'shi-āt, *vt.* (associating, associated). To join in company with; to combine.—*vi.* To keep company with.—*n.* A companion; friend.

Association, as-sō'si-ā''shon, *n.* Act of associating; union; confederacy; one of the two principal varieties of football, played by eleven men a side, with a round ball, handling (except by the goalkeeper) being forbidden.

Assoil, as-soil', *vt.* To release; to absolve.

Assonance, as'sō-nans, *n.* Resemblance of sounds.

Assort, as-sort', *vt.* To sort; to arrange.—*vi.* To suit; to agree.

Assortment, as-sort'ment, *n.* Act of assorting; quantity of things assorted; variety.

Assuage, as-swāj', *vt.* (assuaging, assuaged). To allay; to calm.—*vi.* To abate or subside.

Assume, as-sūm', *vt.* (assuming, assumed). To take for granted; to usurp.—*vi.* To claim more than is due; to be arrogant.

Assumption, as-sum'shon, *n.* Act of assuming; the thing assumed; the taking up of any person into heaven.

Assurance, a-shör'ans, *n.* Act of assuring; secure confidence; impudence; positive declaration; insurance.

Assure, a-shör', *vt.* (assuring, assured). To make sure; to confirm; to insure.

Assuredness, a-shör'ed-nes, *n.* State of being assured.

Assyrian, as-sir'i-an, *a.* Pertaining to Assyria or its inhabitants.—*n.* A native of Assyria; the language of the Assyrians.

Astatic, a-stat'ik, *a.* Being without polarity, as a magnetic needle.

Aster, as'tèr, *n.* A genus of composite plants, with flowers somewhat like stars.

Asterisk, as'tė-risk, *n.* The figure of a star, thus *, used in printing.

Astern, a-stern', *adv.* In or at the hinder part of a ship.

Asteroid, as'tér-oid, *n.* A small planet.

Asthma, as'ma or as'thma, *n.* A disorder of respiration, characterized by difficulty of breathing, cough, and expectoration.

Astigmatism, a-stig'mat-izm, *n.* A malformation of the eye, in which rays of light do not properly converge to one point.

Astonish, as-ton'ish, *vt.* To surprise; to astound.

Astound, as-tound', *vt.* To astonish; to stun; to strike dumb with amazement.

Astragal, as'tra-gal, *n.* A moulding surrounding the top or bottom of a column.

Astrakhan, as'tra-kan, *n.* A rough kind of cloth with a curled pile.

Astral, as'tral, *a.* Belonging to the stars.

Astrict, as-trikt', *vt.* To contract; to limit.

Astride, a-strid', *adv.* or *pred.a.* With the legs apart or across a thing.

Astringent, as-trinj'ent, *a.* Contracting tissues of the body; strengthening.—*n.* A medicine which contracts and strengthens.

Astrolabe, as'trō-lāb, *n.* An old instrument for taking the altitude at sea.

Astrology, as-trol'o-ji, *n.* The pretended art of foretelling future events from the stars.

Astronomy, as-tron'o-mi, *n.* The science of the heavenly bodies.

Astute, as-tūt', *a.* Shrewd; crafty.

Asunder, a-sun'dèr, *adv.* or *pred.a.* Apart; into parts; in a divided state.

Asylum, a-si'lum, *n.* A place of refuge; an institution for the care or relief of the unfortunate.

At, at, *prep.* Denoting presence or nearness; in a state of; employed in, on, or with; with direction towards.

Atavism, at'a-vizm, *n.* The resemblance of offspring to a remote ancestor.

Atelier, ä-tl-yā, *n.* A workshop; a studio.

Athanasian, ath-a-nā'si-an, *a.* Pertaining to Athanasius or to his creed.

Atheism, ā'thē-izm, *n.* The disbelief in the existence of a God.

Atheist, ā'thē-ist, *n.* One who disbelieves the existence of a God.

Athenaeum, ath-e-nē'um, *n.* An establishment connected with literature, science, or art.

Athenian, a-thēn'i-an, *a.* Pertaining to Athens.—*n.* A native of Athens.

Athlete, ath-lēt', *n.* One skilled in exercises of agility or strength.

Athletics, ath-let'iks, *n.pl.* Athletic exercises.

Athwart, a-thwart', *prep.* Across; from side to side.—*adv.* Crossly; wrong.

Atlantean, at-lan-tē'an, *a.* Gigantic.

Atlantic, at-lan'tik, *a.* Pertaining to the ocean between Europe, Africa, and America.—*n.* This ocean.

Atlas, at'las, *n.* A collection of maps.

Atmosphere, at'mos-fēr, *n.* The mass of gas around the earth; air; pervading influence.

Atoll, a-tol', *n.* A ring-shaped coral island.

Atom, a'tom, *n.* A minute particle of matter; anything extremely small.

Atomic bomb, a-tom'ik bom, *n.* A bomb in which the splitting of atoms causes vast heating and explosion on a catastrophic scale.

Atomism, at'om-izm, *n.* Atomic philosophy; the doctrine that atoms of themselves formed the universe.

Atone, a-tōn', vi. (atoning, atoned). To make satisfaction.—vt. To expiate.

Atrabilious, at-ra-bil'i-us, a. Melancholic or hypochondriacal. Also *Atrabiliar, Atrabilarious*.

Atrip, a-trip', adv. or pred.a. Just raised from the ground, as an anchor.

Atrocious, a-trō'shus, a. Extremely cruel or wicked; flagitious.

Atrocity, a-tros'i-ti, n. Horrible wickedness.

Atrophy, at'rō-fi, n. A wasting away; emaciation.

Attach, at-tach', vt. To affix; to connect; to arrest; to win.—vi. To adhere.

Attaché, at-ta-shā', n. One attached to the suite of an ambassador. **Attaché case,** n. A small oblong case of leather or fiber, for carrying documents, books, etc.

Attack, at-tak', vt. To assault; to assail.—n. An assault; seizure by a disease.

Attain, at-tān', vi. To come or arrive.—vt. To reach; to gain; to obtain.

Attainder, at-tān'der, n. Extinction of civil rights, in consequence of a capital crime.

Attar, at'tär, n. An essential oil made from roses, forming a valuable perfume.

Attemper, at-tem'per, vt. To temper; to modify; to accommodate.

Attempt, at-temt', vt. To try to do; to make an effort upon.—n. An essay; enterprise.

Attend, at-tend', vt. To wait on; to accompany or be present at.—vi. To pay regard; to hearken; to wait.

Attendant, at-tend'ant, a. Accompanying, as subordinate.—n. One who waits on, is present, or accompanies.

Attention, at-ten'shon, n. Act of attending; heed; courtesy.

Attentive, at-tent'iv, a. Heedful.

Attenuate, at-ten'ū-āt, vt. (attenuating, attenuated). To make slender or thin (as liquids).—vi. To diminish.

Attest, at-test', vt. To bear witness to; to certify; to call to witness.

Attestation, at-test-ā'shon, n. Testimony.

Attic, at'tik, a. Pertaining to Attica or to Athens; pure; elegant in style or language.—n. The dialect of Attica or Athens; the uppermost story of a building; garret.

Attire, at-tir', vt. (attiring, attired). To dress; to array.—n. Dress.

Attitude, at'ti-tūd, n. Posture.

Attorney, at-ter'ni, n. One who acts in place of another; one who practices in law-courts.

Attract, at-trakt', vt. To draw to; to entice.

Attractive, at-trakt'iv, a. Having the power of attracting; enticing.

Attribute, at-trib'ūt, vt. (attributing, attributed). To ascribe; to impute.—n. at'tri-būt. Inherent property; characteristic; an adjectival word or clause.

Attrition, at-tri'shon, n. Act of wearing, or state of being worn, by rubbing.

Attune, at-tūn', vt. (attuning, attuned). To put in tune; to adjust to another sound.

Auburn, a'bern, a. Reddish-brown.

Auction, ak'shon, n. A public sale in which the article falls to the highest bidder.

Audacity, a-das'i-ti, n. Daring; reprehensible boldness; impudence.

Audible, a'di-bl, a. That may be heard.

Audience, a'di-ens, n. Act of hearing; an assembly of hearers; admittance to a hearing; ceremonial interview.

Audit, a'dit, n. An official examination of accounts.—vt. To examine and adjust, as accounts.

Auditory, a'di-tō-ri, a. Pertaining to the sense or organs of hearing.—n. An audience; an auditorium.

Augean, a-jē'an, a. Pertaining to Augeas, King of Elis, in Greece, whose stable for 3000 oxen, uncleaned for thirty years, was cleaned by Hercules in one day.

Auger, a'ger, n. An instrument for boring holes.

Aught, at, n. Anything; any part; a whit.

Augment, ag-ment', vt. To make larger; to add to.—vi. To grow larger.

Augment, ag'ment, n. Increase; a prefix to a word.

Augur, a'ger, n. One who foretold the future by observing the flight of birds; a soothsayer.—vi. To predict; to bode.—vt. To predict or foretell.

August, a-gust', a. Grand; majestic; awful.

August, a'gust, n. The eighth month of the year.

Auk, ak, n. A swimming bird found in the British seas, with very short wings.

Aunt, änt, n. The sister of one's father or mother.

Aureate, a-rē'āt, a. Golden.

Aurelia, a-rē'li-a, n. The chrysalis of an insect.

Aureola, Aureole, a-rē'o-la, a'rē-ōl, n. An illumination represented as surrounding a holy person, as Christ; a halo.

Auricle, a'ri-kl, n. The external ear; either of the two ear-like cavities over the two ventricles of the heart.

Auricula, a-rik'ū-la, n. Species of primrose.

Auriferous, a-rif'er-us, a. Yielding gold.

Aurist, a'rist, n. One skilled in disorders of the ear.

Aurochs, a'roks, n. A species of wild ox, once abundant in Europe.

Aurora, a-rō'ra, n. The dawn; the goddess of the dawn.

Aurora Borealis, a-rō'ra bō-rē-ā'lis, n. The northern lights or streamers.—**Aurora Australis,** a similar phenomenon in the S. hemisphere.

Auscultation, as-kul-tā'shon, n. A method of discovering diseases of the lungs, etc., by listening for the sounds arising there.

Auspice, a'spis, n. Augury from birds; protection; influence.

Auspicious, a-spi'shus, a. Fortunate; propitious.

Austere, a-stēr', a. Rigid; sour; stern; severe.

Austral, as'tral, a. Southern.

Autarky, a'tar-ki, n. Self sufficiency; economic independence.

Authentic, a-then'tik, a. Genuine; authoritative.

Author, a'ther, n. One who creates; an originator; the writer of a book, etc.

Authoritative, a-tho'ri-tā-tiv, a. Having due authority; peremptory.

Authority, a-tho'ri-ti, n. Legal power or right; influence conferred by character or station; person in power; testimony; credibility; precedent.

Autobiography, a'tō-bi-og''ra-fi, n. Memoirs of a person written by himself.

Autocracy, a-tok'ra-si, n. Absolute government by one man.

Auto-de-fe, au'tō-de-fā'', n.; pl. **Autos-de-fe.** The burning of heretics by authority of the Inquisition. **Auto-da-fe,** ou'tō-dä-fā'', is the Portuguese form.

Autograph, a'tō-graf, n. A person's own handwriting; signature.

Automatic, a-tō-mat'ik.—a. Self-acting; moving spontaneously.—n. A pistol which is reloaded by force of the recoil.

Automaton, a-tom'a-ton, n.; pl. **-ta.** A self-moving machine, or one which moves by invisible machinery.

Automobile, a'tō mō bēl'', n. A motor-car or similar vehicle.

Autonomy, a-ton'o-mi, n. The power or right of self-government.

Autopsy, a'top-si, n. Personal observation; post-mortem examination.

Autumn, a'tum, n. The third season of the year, between summer and winter.

Auxiliary, ag-zil'i-a-ri, a. Aiding.—n. One who aids; a verb which helps to form the moods and tenses of other verbs; pl. foreign troops employed in war.

Avail, a-vāl', vt. To profit; to promote.—vi. To be of use; to answer the purpose.—n. Advantage; use.

Avalanche, av'a-lansh, n. A large body of snow

or ice sliding down a mountain.

Avarice, av'a-ris, n. Covetousness.

Avaricious, av-a-ri'shus, a. Covetous; greedy of gain; niggardly.

Avatar, av-a-tär', n. A descent of a Hindu deity; a remarkable appearance of any kind.

Ave, ä've, n. Hail; an abbreviation of the Ave-Maria, or Hail-Mary.

Avenge, a-venj', vt. (avenging, avenged). To vindicate; to take satisfaction for.

Avenue, av'e-nū, n. An approach to; an alley of trees leading to a house, etc.

Aver, a-ver', vt. (averring, averred). To declare positively; to assert.

Average, av'er-āj, n. Medium; mean proportion.—a. Medial; containing a mean proportion.—vt. To find the mean of.—vi. To form a mean.

Averment, a-ver'ment, n. Affirmation; declaration.

Averruncator, av-e-rung'kät-er, n. Shears for pruning trees.

Averse, a-vers', a. Disinclined; not favorable.

Aversion, a-ver'shon, n. Dislike; antipathy.

Avert, a-vert', vt. To turn aside or away from; to keep off or prevent.

Aviary, ä-vi-a-ri, n. A place for keeping birds.

Aviation, ä'vi-ā-shon, n. Aerial navigation by machines heavier than air.

Avidity, a-vid'i-ti, n. Eager desire; greediness; strong appetite.

Avocation, av-ō-kā'shon, n. Business; occupation.

Avoid, a-void', vt. To shun; to evade; to make void.

Avoirdupois, av'er-dū-poiz'', n. or a. A system of weight, in which a pound contains sixteen ounces.

Avow, a-vou', vt. To declare with confidence; to confess frankly.

Await, a-wât', vt. To wait for; to expect; to be in store for.

Awake, a-wäk', vt. (awaking, pret. woke, awaked, pp. awaked). To rouse from sleep or from a state of inaction.—vi. To cease from sleep; to rouse oneself.—a. Not sleeping; vigilant.

Award, a-ward', vt. To adjudge.—vi. To make an award.—n. A judgment; decision of arbitrators.

Aware, a-wär', a. Informed; conscious.

Away, a-wā', adv. Absent; at a distance; in motion from; by degrees; in continuance.—exclam. Begone!

Awe, a, n. Fear; fear mingled with reverence.—vt. (awing, awed). To strike with fear and reverence.

Awful, a'ful, a. Filling with awe; terrible.

Awhile, a-whil', adv. For some time.

Awkward, ak'werd, a. Inexpert; inelegant.

Awkwardly, ak'werd-li, adv. In a bungling manner; inelegantly.

Awl, al, n. A pointed iron instrument for piercing small holes in leather.

Awn, an, n. The beard of corn or grass.

Awning, an'ing, n. A cover of canvas, etc., to shelter from the sun or wind.

Awry, a-rī, pred.a. or adv. Twisted toward one side; distorted; asquint.

Axe, aks, n. An instrument for hewing and chopping.

Axilla, aks-il'la, n. The arm-pit.

Axiom, aks'i-om, n. A self-evident truth; an established principle.

Axis, aks'is, n.; pl. **Axes,** aks'ēz. The straight line, real or imaginary, passing through a body, on which it revolves.

Axle, Axle-tree, aks'l, aks'l-trē, n. The pole on which a wheel turns.

Ay, Aye, ī, adv. Yea; yes.—n. An affirmative vote.

Ayah, ä'yä, n. A native Indian waiting woman.

Azalea, a-zā'lē-a, n. The generic name of certain showy plants of the heath family.

Azimuth, az'i-muth, n. An arc of the horizon between the meridian of a place and a vertical cir-

cle.

Azoic, a-zō'ik, a. Destitute of organic life.

Azote, az'ōt, n. Nitrogen.

Azure, ä'zhūr, a. Sky-colored.—n. The fine blue color of the sky; the sky.

B

Baa, bä, n. The cry of a sheep.—vi. To cry or bleat as sheep.

Babble, bab'bl, vi. (babbling, babbled). To talk idly; to prate.—vt. To utter idly.—n. Idle talk; murmur, as of a stream.

Babel, bä'bel, n. Confusion; disorder.

Baboon, ba-bön', n. A large kind of monkey.

Baby, bä'bi, n. A babe; a young child.—a. Pertaining to a baby.

Babylonian, Babylonish, ba-bi-lōn'i-an, ba-bi-lōn'ish, a. Pertaining to Babylon.

Baccarat, bak-ka-rä, n. A game of cards played by any number and a banker.

Bacchanal, bak'ka-nal, n. A votary of Bacchus; a revel.—a. Characterized by intemperate drinking.

Bachelor, bach'el-er, n. An unmarried man; one who has taken the university degree below that of Master or Doctor.

Bacillus, ba-sil'lus, n.; pl. **-illi.** A microscopic organism which causes disease.

Back, bak, n. The hinder part of the body in man and the upper part in beasts; the hinder part.—vt. To support; to cause to recede; to endorse.—vi. To move back.—adv. To the rear; to a former state; in return.

Backbite, bak'bīt, vt. To speak evil of secretly.

Backbone, bak'bōn, n. The spine; strength.

Backer, bak'er, n. One who backs or supports another in a contest.

Backgammon, bak-gam'mon, n. A game played by two persons on a board, with men and dice.

Background, bak'ground, n. The part of a picture represented as farthest away; a situation little noticed.

Backslide, bak-slīd', vt. To apostatize; to relapse.

Backward, bak'werd, a. Lagging behind; reluctant; late; dull.

Backwoods, bak'wudz, n.pl. Outlying forest districts.

Bacon, bä'kn, n. Swine's flesh cured and dried.

Bacteriology, bak-tē'ri-ol''o-ji, n. The doctrine or study of bacteria.

Bacterium, bak-tē'ri-um, n.; pl. **-ia.** A disease germ.

Bad, bad, a. Not good; wicked; immoral; injurious; incompetent.

Badge, baj, n. A mark or cognizance worn.

Badger, baj'er, n. A burrowing quadruped, nocturnal in habits.—vt. To worry; to pester.

Badinage, bä'di-näzh, n. Raillery; banter.

Badminton, bad'min-ton, n. A game like lawn-tennis played with shuttlecocks.

Baffle, baf'fl, vt. (baffling, baffled). To elude; to frustrate; to defeat.

Bag, bag, n. A sack; what is contained in a bag; a certain quantity of a commodity.—vt. (bagging, bagged). To put into a bag; to distend.—vi. To swell like a full bag.

Bagatelle, bag-a-tel', n. A trifle; a game somewhat like billiards.

Baggage, bag'āj, n. The necessaries of an army; luggage; lumber.

Bagnio, ban'yō, n. A bath; brothel; prison.

Bagpipe, bag'pip, n. A musical wind-instrument.

Bail, bäl, vt. To liberate from custody on security for reappearance; to free (a boat) from water; to bale.—n. Security given for release; the person who gives such security.

Bailiff, bä'lif, n. A subordinate civil officer; a steward.

Bailiwick, bä'li-wik, n. The extent or limit of a bailiff's jurisdiction.

Bait, bāt, n. A substance used to allure fish, etc.; an enticement.—vt. To furnish with a lure; to give food and drink to a beast when traveling; to harass; to annoy.—vi. To take refreshment on a journey.

Baize, bāz, n. A coarse woolen stuff with a long nap.

Bake, bāk, vt. (baking, baked). To heat, dry, and harden by fire or the sun's rays; to cook in an oven.—vi. To do the work of making bread; to be baked.

Bakelite, bāk'l-īt, n. Trade name for a hard, insoluble, infusible substance derived by heat treatment from phenol and formaldehyde.

Balance, bal'ans, n. A pair of scales; equilibrium; surplus; difference of two sums; the sum due on an account.—vt. (balancing, balanced). To bring to an equilibrium; to weigh, as reasons; to settle, as an account.—vi. To be in equilibrium; to be equal when added up; to hesitate.

Balcony, bal'ko-ni, n. A platform projecting from a window.

Bald, bald, a. Wanting hair; unadorned; bare; paltry.

Bale, bāl, n. A bundle or package of goods.—vt. (baling, baled). To make up in a bale; to free from water; to bail. **Bale out**, vi. To leave aircraft by parachute.

Baleful, bāl'ful, a. Calamitous; deadly.

Balk, bak, n. A ridge of land left unploughed; a great beam; a barrier; a disappointment.—vt. To baffle; to disappoint.

Ball, bal, n. A round body; a globe; a bullet; an entertainment of dancing.—vi. To form, as snow, into balls, as on horses' hoofs.

Ballad, bal'lad, n. A short narrative poem; a popular song.

Ballast, bal'last, n. Heavy matter carried in a ship to keep it steady; that which confers steadiness.—vt. To load with ballast; to make or keep steady.

Ballet, bal'lā, n. A theatrical dance.

Ballistic, bal-lis'tik, a. Pertaining to projectiles.—n.pl. The science of projectiles in motion.

Balloon, bal-lön', n. A spherical hollow body; a large bag filled with a gas which makes it rise and float in the air.

Ballot, bal'lot, n. A ball, paper, etc., used for voting in private; the system of voting by such means.—vi. To vote by ballot.

Balm, bäm, n. Balsam; that which heals or soothes; the name of several aromatic plants. vt. To anoint with balm; to soothe.

Balsam, bal'sam, n. An oily, aromatic substance got from trees; a soothing ointment.

Baluster, bal'us-tèr, n. A small column or pillar, used for balustrades.

Bamboo, bam-bö', n. A tropical plant of the reed kind.

Bamboozle, bam-bö'zl, vt. (bamboozling, bamboozled). To hoax; to humbug; to perplex.

Ban, ban, n. A public proclamation; curse; excommunication; pl. proclamation of marriage.—vt. (banning, banned). To curse.

Banal, ban'al, or ba-nal', a. Hackneyed; vulgar.

Banana, ba-nä'na, n. A plant allied to the plantain, with soft luscious fruit.

Band, band, n. That which binds; a bond; a fillet; a company; a body of musicians.—vt. To bind together; to unite in a troop or confederacy.—vi. To unite in a band.

Bandage, band'āj, n. A band; a cloth for a wound, etc.—vt. (bandaging, bandaged). To bind with a bandage.

Bandbox, band'boks, n. A slight box for caps, bonnets, etc.

Bandit, ban'dit, n.; pl. -itti, -its. An outlaw; a robber; a highwayman.

Bandolier, ban-dō-lēr', n. A shoulder-belt for carrying cartridges.

Bandy, ban'di, n. A bent club for striking a ball; a play at ball with such a club.—vt. (bandying, bandied). To strike to and fro; to exchange (compliments, etc.).

Bandy-legged, ban'di-legd, a. Having crooked legs.

Bane, bān, n. That which causes hurt or death; ruin; poison; mischief.

Bang, bang, vt. To thump; to treat with violence.—n. A heavy blow.

Bangle, bang'gl, n. An ornamental ring worn upon the arms and ankles.

Banish, ban'ish, vt. To drive away; to exile.

Banister, ban'is-tèr, n. A baluster.

Banjo, ban'jō, n. A six-stringed musical instrument.

Bank, bangk, n. Ground rising from the side of a river, lake, etc.; any heap piled up; a bench of rowers; place where money is deposited; a banking company.—vt. To fortify with a bank; to deposit in a bank.

Bankrupt, bangk'rupt, n. One who cannot pay his debts.—a. Unable to pay debts.

Banner, ban'nèr, n. A flag bearing a device or national emblem; a standard.

Banquet, bang'kwet, n. A feast; a sumptuous entertainment.—vt. To treat with a feast.—vi. To feast.

Banshee, ban'shē, n. An Irish fairy believed to attach herself to a house or family.

Bantam, ban'tam, n. A small breed of domestic fowl with feathered shanks.

Banter, ban'tèr, vt. To attack with jocularity; to rally.—n. Raillery; pleasantry.

Banyan, ban'yan, n. An Indian tree of the fig genus.

Baptism, bap'tizm, n. An immersing in or sprinkling with water, as a religious ceremony.

Baptist, bap'tist, n. One of those Protestants who believe in adult baptism by immersion.

Bar, bär, n. A bolt; obstacle, a long piece of wood or metal; inclosure in an inn or court; a tribunal; body of barristers; obstruction at the mouth of a river; a counter where liquors are served.—vt. (barring, barred). To secure; to hinder; to prohibit; to except.

Barb, bärb, n. The points which stand backward in an arrow, hook, etc.; a Barbary horse.—vt. To furnish with barbs or points.

Barbarian, bär-bā'ri-an, a. Belonging to savages; uncivilized.—n. A savage.

Barbarous, bär'bär-us, a. In a state of barbarism; cruel; inhuman.

Barbecue, bär-be-kū, n. A hog, etc., roasted whole; a feast in the open air.—vt To dress and roast whole.

Barber, bär'bèr, n. One who shaves beards and dresses hair.

Barberry, bär'be-ri, n. A thorny shrub bearing red berries.

Barcarolle, bär'ka-rōl, n. A melody sung by Venetian gondoliers.

Bard, bärd, n. A Celtic minstrel; a poet.

Bare, bār, a. Uncovered; empty; scanty; worn.—vt. (baring, bared). To make naked.

Barebacked, bär'bakt, a. Unsaddled.

Barefaced, bär'fāst, a. Shameless; glaring.

Bargain, bär'gin, n. A contract; a gainful transaction; a thing bought or sold.—vi. To make a bargain.—vt. To sell.

Barge, bärj, n. A boat of pleasure or state; a flat-bottomed boat of burden.

Baritone, ba'ri-tōn, a. Having a voice ranging between tenor and bass.—n. A male voice between tenor and bass.

Bark, bärk, n. The outer rind of a tree; a barque; the noise made by a dog, wolf, etc.—vt. To strip bark off; to treat with bark; to make the cry of dogs, etc.

Barley, bär'li, n. A species of grain used especially for making malt.

Barmaid, bär'mād, n. A woman who tends a bar where liquors are sold.

Barn, bärn, n. A building for grain, hay, etc.

Barnacle, bär'na-kl, n. A shell-fish, often found on ships' bottoms; a species of goose.

Barograph, ba'rō-graf, *n.* An instrument for recording changes in the atmosphere.

Barometer, ba-rom'et-èr, *n.* An instrument for measuring the weight of the atmosphere.

Barque, bärk, *n.* A sailing vessel; a three-masted ship, the mizzen-mast without yards.

Barrack, ba'rak, *n.* A building for soldiers, especially in garrison (generally in *pl.*).

Barrage, bar'aj, *n.* The discharge of artillery in such a manner as to keep a selected zone under continuous fire.

Barrel, ba'rel, *n.* A round wooden cask; the quantity which a barrel holds; a hollow cylinder.—*vt.* (barreling, barreled). To pack in a barrel.

Barren, ba'ren, *a.* Sterile; unfruitful; unsuggestive.

Barricade, ba-ri-kād', *n.* A temporary fortification to obstruct an enemy; a barrier.—*vt.* To obstruct; to bar.

Barrier, ba'ri-èr, *n.* Fence; obstruction.

Barrister, ba'ris-tèr, *n.* A counselor at law; a lawyer whose profession is to speak in court on behalf of clients.

Barrow, ba'rō, *n.* A small hand or wheel carriage; a sepulchral mound.

Barter, bär'tèr, *vi.* To traffic by exchange.—*vt.* To exchange in commerce.—*n.* Traffic by exchange.

Basalt, ba-zalt', *n.* A dark volcanic rock, often found in columnar form.

Bascule, bas'kūl, *n.* An arrangement in bridges by which one part balances another.

Base, bās, *a.* Low in value or station; worthless; despicable.—*n.* Foundation; lower side; support; chief ingredient of a compound; the gravest part in music.—*vt.* (basing, based). To place on a basis; to found.

Base-ball, bās'bal, *n.* The national game of the U.S.A. played with bat and ball by two sides of nine men each.

Base-born, bās'born, *a.* Illegitimate.

Basement, bās'ment, *n.* The ground floor of a building.

Bash, bash, *vt.* To beat violently.

Bashful, bash'ful, *a.* Modest; wanting confidence.

Basil, baz'il, *n.* An aromatic pot-herb.

Basilica, ba-sil'i-ka, *n.* An ancient Roman public hall; a church in imitation thereof.

Basilisk, baz'il-isk, *n.* A fabulous serpent, lizard, or cockatrice; a genus of crested lizards; an old kind of cannon.

Basin, bā'sn, *n.* A broad circular dish; a reservoir; a dock; tract of country drained by a river.

Basis, bās'is, *n.*; pl. **-ses.** A base; foundation; groundwork.

Bask, bask, *vt.* To lie in warmth, or in the sun; to enjoy ease and prosperity.—*vt.* To warm by exposure to heat.

Basket, bas'ket, *n.* A domestic vessel made of twigs, etc.; the contents of a basket.—*vt.* To put in a basket.

Bass, bās, *n.* The American linden; a mat made of bast; a fish allied to the perch.

Bass, bās, *n.* The lowest part in musical harmony; the lowest male voice.

Basset, bas'set, *n.* The outcrop of a stratum.

Bassinet, bas'si-net, *n.* A wicker cradle; a type of perambulator.

Bassoon, bas-sön', *n.* A musical wind-instrument which serves for a bass.

Bass-relief, bäs'rē-lēf, *n.* Bas-relief.

Bast, bast, *n.* The inner bark of the lime tree.

Bastard, bas'tèrd, *n.* An illegitimate child.—*a.* Illegitimate; not genuine.

Baste, bāst, *vt.* (basting, basted). To beat with a stick; to drip fat or butter on meat while roasting; to sew with temporary stitches.

Bastion, bas'ti-on, *n.* A large mass of earth or masonry standing out from a rampart.

Bat, bat, *n.* A flying mammal, like a mouse; a heavy stick; a club used to strike the ball in cricket, etc.—*vi.* (batting, batted). To play with a bat.

Batch, bach, *n.* Quantity of bread baked at one time; a quantity.

Bath, bäth, *n.* Place to bathe in; immersion in water, etc.; a Jewish measure.

Bathe, bäTH, *vt.* (bathing, bathed). To immerse in water, etc.—*vi.* To take a bath.

Bathometer, ba-thom'et-èr, *n.* An apparatus for taking soundings.

Bathos, bā'thos, *n.* A ludicrous sinking in writing or speech; anti-climax.

Batist, Batiste, ba-tēst', *n.* A kind of cambric.

Baton, ba'ton, *n.* A staff; a truncheon; a badge of office carried by field-marshals.

Battalion, bat-ta'li-on, *n.* A body of infantry, consisting of from 300 to 1000 men.

Batter, bat'tèr, *vt.* To beat with violence; to wear by hard usage.—*n.* A mixture beaten together with some liquid.

Battle, bat'l, *n.* Encounter of two armies; a combat.—*vi.* (battling, battled). To contend in fight.

Battledore, bat'l-dör, *n.* An instrument to strike a ball or shuttlecock.

Bauble, ba'bl, *n.* A trifling piece of finery; a gewgaw.

Bawdy, ba'di, *a.* Obscene; unchaste.

Bawl, bal, *vi.* To shout; to clamor.

Bay, bā, *a.* Reddish-brown.—*n.* An arm of the sea; the laurel tree; a laurel-crown, fame (generally in *pl.*); a deep-toned bark of a dog.—*vi.* To bark.—*vt.* To bark at; to follow with barking. **At bay,** so pressed by enemies as to be compelled to face them.

Bayonet, bā'on-et, *n.* A dagger-like weapon fixed to a rifle.—*vt.* (bayoneting, bayoneted). To stab with a bayonet.

Bay-rum, bā'rum, *n.* A spirituous liquor containing the oil of the bayberry of Jamaica.

Bay-window, bā'win-dō, *n.* A projecting window which forms a recess within.

Bazaar, ba-zär', *n.* A place of sale; a sale of articles for a charitable purpose.

Bdellium, del'li-um, *n.* An aromatic gum-resin.

Be, bē, *vi. substantive* (being, been; pres. am, art, is, are; pret. was, wast or wert, were). To exist; to become; to remain.

Beach, bēch, *n.* The shore of the sea.—*vt.* To run (a vessel) on a beach.

Beacon, bē'kn, *n.* A light to direct seamen; a signal of danger.—*vt.* To afford light, as a beacon; to light up.

Bead, bēd, *n.* A little ball strung on a thread, any small globular body; a small molding.

Beagle, bē'gl, *n.* A small hunting dog.

Beak, bēk, *n.* The bill of a bird; anything like a bird's beak.

Beaker, bēk'èr, *n.* A large drinking-cup.

Beam, bēm, *n.* A main timber in a building; part of a balance which sustains the scales; pole of a carriage; a ray of light.—*vt.* To send forth, as beams; to emit.—*vi.* To shine.

Bean, bēn, *n.* A name of several kinds of pulse.

Bear, bār, *vt.* (bearing, pret. bore, pp. borne). To carry; to suffer; to produce; to have; to permit; to behave (oneself).—*vi.* To suffer; to be patient; to produce; to take effect; to be situated as to the point of the compass; to refer (with *upon*).

Bear, bār, *n.* A large carnivorous plantigrade quadruped; one of two constellations, the Greater and Lesser; an uncouth person; one who tries to bring down the price of stock.

Beard, bērd, *n.* The hair on the chin, etc.; the awn of corn.—*vt.* To defy to the face.

Beast, bēst, *n.* Any four-footed animal; a brutal man.

Beat, bēt, *vt.* (beating, pret. beat, pp. beat, beaten). To strike repeatedly; to overcome; to crush; to harass.—*vi.* To throb, as a pulse; to sail against the wind.—*n.* A stroke; a pulsation; a course frequently trodden.

Beatify, bē-at'i-fī, *vt.* (beatifying, beatified). To make happy; to declare a person blessed.

Beating, bēt'ing, *n.* Act of striking; chastisement by blows; a conquering; defeat.

Beatitude, bē·at'i·tūd, *n.* Blessedness; bliss; one of the declarations of blessedness to particular virtues made by Christ.

Beauty, bū'ti, *n.* Loveliness; elegance; grace; a beautiful woman.

Beaver, bē'vėr, *n.* A rodent quadruped; beaver-fur, or a hat made of it; the face-guard of a helmet; a visor.—*a.* Made of beaver, or of its fur.

Because, bē·kaz'. By cause; on this account that.

Beccafico, bek·a·fē'kō, *n.* A bird resembling the nightingale; the garden-warbler.

Bechamel, besh'a·mel, *n.* A fine white sauce thickened with cream.

Beckon, bek'n, *vi.* To make a sign by nodding, etc.—*vt.* To make a sign to.

Become, bē·kum', *vi.* (becoming, pp. become, pret. became). To come to be; to change to.—*vt.* To suit; to add grace to; to be worthy of.

Bed, bed, *n.* Something to sleep or rest on; the channel of a river; place where anything is deposited; a layer; a stratum.—*vt.* (bedding, bedded). To lay in a bed; to sow; to stratify.—*vi.* To go to bed.

Bedchamber, bed'chām·bėr, *n.* An apartment for a bed.

Bedizen, bē·dī'zn, *vt.* To adorn gaudily.

Bedouin, bed'ö·in, *n.* A nomadic Arab living in tents in Arabia, Syria, Egypt, etc.

Bedraggle, bē·drag'l, *vt.* To soil by drawing along on mud.

Bedrid, Bedridden, bed'rid, bed'rid·n, *a.* Confined to bed by age or infirmity.

Bedroom, bed'röm, *n.* A sleeping apartment.

Bedstead, bed'sted, *n.* A frame for supporting a bed.

Bee, bē, *n.* The insect that makes honey.

Beech, bēch, *n.* A large smooth-barked tree yielding a hard timber and nuts.

Beef, bēf, *n.* The flesh of an ox, bull, or cow.—*a.* Consisting of such flesh.

Beef-wood, bēf'wud, *n.* The wood of some Australian trees.

Bee-line, bē'lin, *n.* The direct line between two places.

Beer, bēr, *n.* A fermented alcoholic liquor made from barley and hops.

Bees'-wax, bēz'waks, *n.* The wax collected by bees, of which their cells are made.

Beet, bēt, *n.* A vegetable with thick, fleshy roots, yielding sugar.

Beetle, bē'tl, *n.* A coleopterous insect; a heavy wooden mallet.—*vi.* (beetling, beetled). To jut; to hang over.

Beetling, bē'tl·ing, *a.* Jutting; overhanging.

Befall, bē·fal', *vt.* To happen to.—*vi.* To happen.

Befit, bē·fit', *vt.* To suit; to become.

Before, bē·fōr', *prep.* In front of; in presence of; earlier than; in preference to.—*adv.* In time preceding; further; onward; in front.

Beforehand, bē·fōr'hand, *a.* In good pecuniary circumstances.—*adv.* In advance.

Beg, beg, *vt.* (begging, begged). To ask in charity; to ask earnestly; to take for granted.—*vi.* To ask or live upon alms.

Beget, bē·get', *vt.* (begetting, pp. begot, begotten, pret. begot). To procreate; to produce.

Beggar, beg'gėr, *n.* One who begs.—*vt.* To impoverish.

Begin, bē·gin', *vi.* (pp. begun, pret. began). To take rise; to do the first act; to commence.—*vt.* To enter on; to originate.

Beginning, bē·gin'ing, *n.* The first cause, act, or state; origin; commencement.

Begonia, bō·gō'ni·a, *n.* A showy tropical plant much cultivated in hothouses.

Begrudge, bē·gruj', *vt.* To envy the possession of.

Beguile, bē·gil', *vt.* (beguiling, beguilded). To practice guile on; to dupe; to while away.

Behalf, bē·haf', *n.* Interest; support.

Behave, bē·hāv', *vt.* (behaving, behaved). To conduct (oneself).—*vi.* To act; to conduct oneself.

Behavior, bē·hāv'i·ėr, *n.* Conduct; deportment.

Behemoth, bē·hē'moth, *n.* A huge beast mentioned in the Book of Job and supposed to be an elephant or hippopotamus.

Behest, bē·hest', *n.* Command; precept.

Behind. bē·hind', *prep.* In the rear of; remaining after; inferior to.—*adv.* In the rear; backwards; remaining.

Behold, bē·hōld', *vt.* (beholding, beheld). To look upon; to regard with attention.—*vi.* To look; to fix the mind.

Behove, bē·hōv', *vt.* (behoving, behoved). To be meet or necessary for (used impersonally).

Beige, bāzh, *n.* A fabric made of unbleached or undyed wool, a greyish-brown color.

Being, bē'ing, *n.* Existence; a creature.

Belabor, bē·lā'bėr, *vt.* To beat soundly; to thump.

Belated, bē·lāt'ed, *p.a.* Made late; benighted.

Belch, belch, *vt.* To eject, as wind from the stomach; to cast forth violently.—*vi.* To eject wind from the stomach; to issue out, as by eructation.—*n.* Eructation.

Beleaguer, bē·lē'gėr, *vt.* To surround with an army; to blockade; to besiege.

Belemnite, bel'em·nit, *n.* A dart-shaped fossil common in the chalk formation.

Belfry, bel'fri, *n.* A bell-tower; place where a bell is hung.

Belial, bē'li·al, *n.* An evil spirit; Satan.

Belie, bē·li', *vt.* (belying, belied). To represent falsely; to be in contradiction to; to fail to equal.

Belief, bē·lēf', *n.* Assent of the mind; persuasion; creed; opinion.

Believe, bē·lēv', *vt.* (believing, believed). To give belief to; to credit; to expect with confidence.—*vi.* To have a firm persuasion.

Belittle, bē·lit'l, *vt.* To make smaller; to speak disparagingly of.

Bell, bel, *n.* A metallic vessel used for giving sounds by being struck; anything in form of a bell.—*vi.* To flower.—*vt.* To put a bell on.

Belladonna, bel·la·don'na, *n.* A European plant yielding a powerful medicine.

Belle, bel, *n.* A lady of great beauty.

Belles-lettres, bel·let'tr, *n.pl.* Polite literature, including poetry, rhetoric, history, etc.

Bellicose, bel'li·kōs, *a.* Warlike; pugnacious.

Belligerent, bel·lij'ėr·ent, *a.* Waging war. *n.* A nation or state waging war.

Bellow, bel'ō, *vi.* To make a hollow loud noise, as a bull; to roar.—*n.* A roar.

Bellows, bel'ōz, *n.sing.* and *pl.* An instrument for blowing fires, supplying wind to organ-pipes, etc.

Bell-wether, bel'weṯh-ėr, *n.* A sheep which leads the flock with a bell on his neck.

Belly, bel'li, *n.* That part of the body which contains the bowels.—*vt.* and *i.* (bellying, bellied). To swell; bulge.

Belong, bē·long', *vi.* To be the property; to appertain; to be connected; to have original residence.

Below, bē·lō', *prep.* Under in place; beneath; unworthy of.—*adv.* In a lower place; beneath; on earth; in hell.

Belt, belt, *n.* A girdle; a band.—*vt.* To encircle.

Bemoan, bē·mōn', *vt.* To lament; bewail.

Bemused, bē·mūzd', *a.* Muddled; stupefied.

Bench, bensh, *n.* A long seat; seat of justice; body of judges.—*vt.* To furnish with benches.

Bend, bend, *vt.* (pp. and pret. bent and bended). To curve; to direct to a certain point; to subdue.—*vi.* To become crooked; to lean or turn; to yield.—*n.* A curve.

Beneath, bē·nēth', *prep.* Under; lower in place, rank, dignity, etc., unworthy of.—*adv.* In a lower place; below.

Benediction, ben·ē·dik'shon, *n.* Act of blessing; invocation of happiness.

Benefaction, ben·ē·fak'shon, *n.* The doing of a benefit; a benefit conferred.

Benefactor, ben·ē·fak'tėr, *n.* He who confers a benefit.

Benefice, ben´ē-fĭs, *n.* An ecclesiastical living.
Beneficent, bē-nef´ĭ-sent, *a.* Kind; bountiful.
Beneficial, ben-ē-fĭ´shal, *a.* Conferring benefit.
Beneficiary, ben-ē-fĭ´shĭ-a-ri, *n.* A person who is benefited or assisted.
Benefit, ben´ē-fit, *n.* An act of kindness; a favor; advantage.—*vt.* To do a service to.—*vi.* To gain advantage.
Benevolent, bē-nev´ō-lent, *a.* Kind; charitable.
Benight, bē-nīt´, *vt.* To involve in night; to overwhelm in moral darkness or ignorance.
Benign, bē-nīn´, *a.* Gracious; kind; mild.
Benignant, bē-nig´nant, *a.* Gracious; favorable.
Benison, ben´ĭ-zn, *n.* A blessing, benediction.
Bent, bent, pret. and pp. of *bend.*—*n.* Bias of mind; inclination; a wiry grass; a wild piece of land.
Benumb, bē-num´, *vt.* To deprive of sensation; to make torpid; to stupefy.
Benzene, ben´zēn, *n.* A liquid used to remove grease spots, etc.
Benzoin, Benzoine, ben-zō´in or ben´zoin, *n.* A fragrant resinous juice.
Bequeath, bē-kwēTH´, *vt.* To leave by will; to hand down.
Bequest, bē-kwest´, *n.* A legacy.
Bereave, bē-rēv´, *vt.* (bereaving, pp. and pret. bereaved and bereft). To deprive of.
Beret, be´ri, *n.* A close-fitting round woolen cap.
Bergamot, bėrg´a-mot, *n.* A species of pear; perfume from the fruit of the lime; a coarse tapestry.
Beri-beri, ber´ĭ-ber´ĭ, *n.* A dangerous disease endemic in parts of India and Ceylon, characterized by paralysis, difficult breathing, and other symptoms.
Berlin, bėr´lin or bėr-lin´, *n.* A four-wheeled vehicle; a wool for fancy work.
Berry, be´ri, *n.* A pulpy fruit containing many seeds.
Berth, bėrth, *n.* A station in which a ship lies; a place for sleeping in a ship, etc.—*vt.* To allot a berth to.
Beryl, be´ril, *n.* A hard greenish mineral.
Beseech, bē-sēch´, *vt.* (beseeching, besought). To entreat; to solicit.
Beseem, bē-sēm´, *vt.* To become; to be fit.
Beset, bē-set´, *vt.* (besetting, beset). To surround; to press on all sides.
Beside, Besides, bē-sīd´, bē-sīdz´, *prep.* By the side of; near; over and above; distinct from.—*adv.* Moreover; in addition.
Besiege, bē-sēj´, *vt.* (besieging, besieged). To lay siege to; to beset.
Besom, bē´zum, *n.* A brush of twigs; a broom.
Besot, bē-sot´, *vt.* (besotting, besotted). To make sottish.
Bespangle, bē-spang´gl, *vt.* To adorn with spangles.
Bespatter, bē-spat´tėr, *vt.* To spatter over.
Bespeak, bē-spēk´, *vt.* (pp. bespoke, bespoken, pret. bespoke). To speak for beforehand; to indicate.
Bessemer-steel, bes´e-mėr-stēl, *n.* Steel made directly from molten cast-iron by driving through it air to carry off impurities.
Best, best, *a.superl.* Most good; having good qualities in the highest degree; exceeding all.—*n.* The utmost; highest endeavor.—*adv.* In the highest degree; beyond all others.
Bestial, bes´ti-al, *a.* Belonging to a beast; brutish; vile.
Bestiary, bes´ti-a-ri, *n.* A book of the middle ages treating fancifully of beasts.
Bestir, bē-stėr´, *vt.* To stir up; to put into brisk action. (Usually with *refl.* pron.)
Bestow, bē-stō´, *vt.* To lay up; to give; to confer; to dispose of; to apply.
Bestride, bē-strīd´, *vt.* (pp. bestrid, bestridden, pret. bestrid, bestrode). To stride over; to place a leg on each side of.
Bet, bet, *n.* A wager; that which is pledged in a contest.—*vt.* (betting, betted). To wager.
Betray, bē-trā´, *vt.* To disclose treacherously; to entrap.

Betroth, bē-trōтн´, *vt.* To affiance; to pledge to marriage.
Better, bet´tėr, *a.comp.* More good; improved.—*adv.* More excellently; in a higher degree.—*vt.* To make better; to advance.—*n.* A superior (generally in *pl.*).
Between, bē-twēn´, *prep.* In the middle; from one to another of; belonging to two.
Bevel, be´vel, *n.* An instrument for taking angles; an angle not a right angle.—*a.* Slant; oblique.—*vt.* (beveling, beveled). To cut to a bevel angle.
Beverage, bev´ér-āj, *n.* Drink; liquor.
Bevy, be´vi, *n.* A flock of birds; a company of females.
Bewail, bē-wāl´, *vt.* To lament.—*vi.* To utter deep grief.
Beware, bē-wār´, *vi.* To take care (with *of*).
Bewilder, bē-wil´dėr, *vt.* To confuse; to perplex.
Bewitch, bē-wich´, *vt.* To enchant; to fascinate; to overpower by charms.
Beyond, bē-yond´, *prep.* On the further side of; farther onward than; out of the reach of; above.—*adv.* At a distance.
Bezel, bez´el, *n.* The part of a ring which holds the stone.
Bezique, be-zēk´, *n.* A game at cards.
Bhang, bang, *n.* A narcotic drug prepared from an Indian hemp.
Biangular, bī-ang´gū-lėr, *a.* Having two angles.
Bias, bī´as, *n.*; pl. **-ses.** Weight on one side; a leaning of the mind; bent.—*vt.* To incline to one side; to prejudice.
Bib, bib, *n.* A cloth worn by children over the breast.
Bible, bī´bl, *n.* The Holy Scriptures.
Bibliography, bib-li-og´ra-fi, *n.* A history of books and their editions; list of books by one author or on one subject.
Bibliomania, bib´li-ō-mā´´ni-a, *n.* A rage for possessing rare books.
Bibliophile, bib´li-ō-fīl, *n.* A lover of books.
Bibulous, bib´ū-lus, *a.* Spongy; addicted to intoxicants.
Bicarbonate, bī-kär´bon-āt, *n.* A carbonate containing two equivalents of carbonic acid to one of a base.
Bicentenary, bī-sen´te-na-ri, *n.* Two hundred years.
Biceps, bī´seps, *n.* A muscle of the arm and of the thigh.
Bicker, bik´ér, *vt.* To skirmish; to quarrel.
Bicycle, bī´si-kl, *n.* A two-wheeled vehicle propelled by the rider.
Bid, bid, *vt.* (bidding, pp. bid, bidden, pret. bid, bade). To ask; to order; to offer.—*n.* An offer, as at an auction.
Bidding, bid´ing, *n.* Invitation; order; offer.
Bide, bid, *vi.* (biding, bode). To dwell; to remain.—*vt.* To endure; to abide.
Biennial, bī-en´ni-al, *a.* Continuing for two years; taking place once in two years.—*n.* A plant which lives two years.
Bier, bēr, *n.* A carriage or frame for conveying a corpse to the grave.
Bifid, bī´fid, *a.* Cleft into two parts; forked.
Bifurcate, bī-fėr´kät, *a.* Forked.
Big, big, *a.* Great; large; pregnant; arrogant.
Bigamy, big´a-mi, *n.* The crime of having two wives or husbands at once.
Bight, bit, *n.* A small bay; a loop.
Bigot, big´ot, *n.* A person obstinately wedded to a particular creed.
Bigotry, big´ot-ri, *n.* Blind zeal in favor of a creed, party, sect, or opinion.
Bilateral, bī-lat´ér-al, *a.* Two-sided.
Bilberry, bil´be-ri, *n.* The whortleberry or blaeberry.
Bile, bīl, *n.* A yellowish bitter liquid secreted in the liver; spleen; anger.
Bilge, bilj, *n.* The protuberant part of a cask; the breadth of a ship's bottom.—*vi.* (bilging, bilged). To leak in the bilge.

Bilingual, bī-lin'gwal, *a.* In two languages.

Biliteral, bī-lit'ẽr-al, *a.* Consisting of two letters.

Bilk, bilk, *vt.* To defraud; to elude.

Bill, bil, *n.* The beak of a bird; anything resembling a bird's beak; an instrument for pruning, etc.; a military weapon now obsolete; an account of money due; draught of a proposed new law; a placard.—*vi.* To join bills, as doves; to fondle.—*vt.* To announce by bill; to stick bills on.

Billet, bil'et, *n.* A small note in writing; a ticket directing soldiers where to lodge; a situation; a stick of wood.—*vt.* To quarter, as soldiers.—*vi.* To be quartered.

Billet-doux, bil-e-dö', *n.* A love-letter.

Billiards, bil'yẽrdz, *n.pl.* A game played on a table with balls and cues.

Billion, bil'yon, *n.* A million of millions.

Billow, bil'lō, *n.* A great wave of the sea.—*vi.* To roll in large waves.

Bimensal, bī-men'sal, *a.* Occurring every two months.

Bimetallism, bī-met'al-izm, *n.* A system of currency which recognizes silver and gold as legal tender to any amount.

Bimonthly, bī-munth'li, *a.* Occurring every two months.

Bin, bin, *n.* A receptacle for corn, etc.; a partition in a wine-cellar.

Binary, bī'na-ri, *a.* Twofold.

Bind, bīnd, *vt.* (binding, bound). To tie; to confine; to oblige; to cover (a book); to render costive; to make firm.—*vi.* To grow hard; to be obligatory.

Binnacle, bin'a-kl, *n.* A case in which a ship's compass is kept.

Binocular, bī-nok'ū-lẽr, *a.* Adapted for both eyes.—*n.* A small telescope for using with both eyes at once.

Binomial, bī-nō'mi-al, *a.* or *n.* An algebraic expression consisting of two terms.

Biochemistry, bī-ō-kem'ist-ri, *n.* The study of the chemistry of living things.

Biogenesis, bī-ō-jen'e-sis, *n.* The doctrine that living organisms can spring only from living parents.

Biographer, bī-og'ra-fẽr, *n.* A writer of biography.

Biography, bī-og'ra-fi, *n.* An account of one's life and character.

Biology, bī-ol'o-ji, *n.* The science of life.

Bioplasm, bī'ō-plazm, *n.* The germinal matter in plants and animals.

Bipartite, bī-pärt'īt, *a.* Having two parts.

Biped, bī'ped, *n.* An animal with two feet.

Birch, bẽrch, *n.* A tree having small leaves, white bark, and a fragrant odor.

Bird, bẽrd, *n.* One of the feathered race.

Biretta, Beretta, bi-ret'ta, be-ret'ta, *n.* A square cap worn by ecclesiastics.

Birth, bẽrth, *n.* Act of bearing or coming into life; extraction.

Birthright, bẽrth'rīt, *n.* Any right to which a person is entitled by birth.

Biscuit, bis'ket, *n.* Hard bread made into cakes; unglazed porcelain.

Bisect, bī-sekt', *vt.* To cut into two equal parts.

Bishop, bish'up, *n.* Head of a diocese; a piece in chess which moves diagonally.

Bismuth, bis'muth, *n.* A brittle yellowish or reddish-white metal.

Bison, bī'zon, *n.* A quadruped of the ox family; the American buffalo.

Bisque, bisk, *n.* Unglazed white porcelain; odds given at tennis, etc.

Bit, bit, *n.* A morsel; fragment; the metal part of a bridle inserted in a horse's mouth; a boring tool.—*vt.* (bitting, bitted) To put the bit in the mouth.

Bitch, bich, *n.* A female dog; a name of reproach for a woman.

Bite, bīt, *vt.* (biting, pp. bit, bitten, pret. bit). To crush or sever with the teeth; to cause to smart; to wound by reproach, etc.; to corrode.—*n.* Act of biting; wound made by biting; a mouthful.

Biting, bīt'ing, *p.a.* Sharp; severe; sarcastic.

Bitter, bit'ẽr, *a.* Sharp to the taste; severe; painful; calamitous; distressing.

Bittern, bit'ẽrn, *n.* A bird of the heron kind.

Bitters, bit'ẽrz, *n.pl.* A liquor in which bitter herbs or roots are steeped.

Bitumen, bi-tū'men, *n.* A mineral, pitchy, inflammable substance.

Bivalve, Bivalvular, bī'valv, bī-valv'ū-lẽr, *a.* Having two shells which open and shut, as the oyster.

Bivouac, bi'vö-ak, *n.* Encampment of soldiers for the night in the open air.—*vi.* (bivouacking, bivouacked). To encamp during the night without covering.

Biweekly, bī-wēk'li, *a.* Occurring every two weeks.

Bizarre, bi-zär', *a.* Odd; fantastical.

Blab, blab, *vt.* (blabbing, blabbed). To tell indiscreetly.—*vi.* To talk indiscreetly.

Black, blak, *a.* Destitute of light; dark; gloomy; sullen; astrocious; wicked.—*n.* The darkest color; a negro.—*vt.* To make black.

Black-ball, blak'bal, *n.* A composition for blacking shoes; a ball used as a negative in voting.—*vt.* To reject by private voting.

Blackberry, blak'be-ri, *n.* A plant of the bramble kind, and its fruit.

Blackbird, blak'bẽrd, *n.* A species of thrush.

Blackboard, blak'bōrd, *n.* A board for writing on with chalk for instruction.

Blacken, blak'n, *vt.* To make black; to defame.—*vi.* To grow black or dark.

Blackguard, blak'gärd or bla'gärd, *n.* A scoundrel.—*vt.* To revile in scurrilous language.

Blacking, blak'ing, *n.* A substance used for blacking shoes.

Black-lead, blak'led, *n.* A dark mineral substance used for pencils; plumbago.

Black-mail, blak'māl, *n.* Money paid for protection; extortion by intimidation.

Black-market, blak-mär'ket, *n.* Illegal dealing in goods or currencies which are scarce or controlled.

Black-out, blak'out, *n.* In war-time, the period between dusk and dawn during which no light must be visible through windows and doors.

Black-sheep, blak'shēp, *n.* One whose conduct is discreditable.

Blacksmith, blak'smith, *n.* A smith who works in iron.

Blackthorn, blak'thorn, *n.* The sloe.

Bladder, blad'ẽr, *n.* A thin sac in animals containing the urine, bile, etc.; a blister; anything like the animal bladder.

Blade, blād, *n.* A leaf; cutting part of a sword, knife, etc.; flat part of an oar.

Blame, blām, *vt.* (blaming, blamed). To censure; to reprimand.—*n.* Censure; fault.

Blanch, blansh, *vt.* To make white.—*vi.* To grow white; to bleach.

Blanc-mange, bla-mängzh', *n.* A dish of arrow-root or maize-flour boiled with milk.

Bland, bland, *a.* Mild; soothing; gentle.

Blandishment, bland'ish-ment, *n.* Soft words; artful caresses; flattery.

Blank, blangk, *a.* White; pale; void; void of writing; without rhyme.—*n.* A white unwritten paper; a void space; the white mark which a shot is to hit.

Blanket, blang'ket, *n.* A woolen covering for a bed, horses, etc.

Blank-verse, blangk'vẽrs, *n.* Ten-syllabled line without rhyme.

Blare, blār, *vi.* (blaring, blared). To give forth a loud sound.—*vt.* To sound loudly; to proclaim noisily.—*n.* Sound like that of a trumpet; roar.

Blarney, blär'ni, *n.* Excessively complimentary language; gammon.—*vt.* To flatter.

Blasé, blä-zä, *a.* Satiated; used up; bored.

Blaspheme, blas-fēm', *vt.* (blaspheming, blasphemed). To speak irreverently of, as of God; to speak evil of.—*vi.* To utter blasphemy.

Blast, blast, *n.* A gust of wind; sound of a wind-instrument; violent explosion of gunpowder; pernicious influence, as of wind; blight.—*vt.* To blight; to strike with some sudden plague, etc.; to destroy; to blow up by gunpowder.—*vi.* To wither; to be blighted.

Blatant, blā'tant, *a.* Bellowing; noisy.

Blaze, blāz, *n.* A flame; brilliance; a bursting out; a white spot.—*vi.* (blazing, blazed). To flame; to send forth a bright light.—*vt.* To noise abroad; to proclaim.

Blazer, blāz'ėr, *n.* A bright-colored coat suited for sports.

Bleach, blēch, *vt.* To make white or whiter.—*vi.* To grow white.

Bleak, blēk, *a.* Exposed; chill; dreary.

Blear, blēr, *a.* Sore; dimmed, as the eyes.—*vt.* To dim or impair.

Bleat, blēt, *vi.* To cry as a sheep.—*n.* The cry of a sheep.

Bleed, blēd, *vi.* (bleeding, bled). To emit blood; to die by slaughter; to feel agony, as from bleeding; to drop, as blood.—*vt.* To take blood from; to extort money from.

Blemish, blem'ish, *vt.* To mar; to tarnish.—*n.* A mark of imperfection; dishonor.

Blend, blend, *vt.* To mix together.—*vi.* To be mixed.—*n.* A mixture.

Blenheim, blen'em, *n.* A spaniel.

Bless, bles, *vt.* (blessing, blessed or blest). To make happy; to wish happiness to; to consecrate.

Blessing, bles'ing, *n.* A prayer imploring happiness upon; piece of good fortune.

Blight, blīt, *n.* That which withers up; mildew.—*vt.* To wither up; to corrupt with mildew; to frustrate.

Blind, blīnd, *a.* Destitute of sight; wanting discernment; having no outlet.—*n.* A screen; something to mislead; a pretext.—*vt.* To make blind; to obstruct the view.

Blindfold, blīnd'fōld, *a.* Having the eyes covered.—*vt.* To cover the eyes of.

Blindness, blīnd'nes, *n.* Want of sight or discernment; ignorance.

Blink, blingk, *vi.* To wink; to twinkle.—*vt.* To shut the eyes upon; to avoid.—*n.* A twinkle; a glimpse or glance.

Blinker, bling'kėr, *n.* A flap to prevent a horse from seeing sideways.

Bliss, blis, *n.* Blessedness; perfect happiness.

Blister, blis'tėr, *n.* A thin bladder on the skin; a pustule; something to raise a blister.—*vi.* To rise in blisters.—*vt.* To raise a blister or blisters on; to apply a blister to.

Blithe, blīтн, *a.* Joyful; gay; mirthful.

Blitz, blitz, *n.* A concentrated attack by air.

Blizzard, bliz'ėrd, *n.* A violent snow-storm, with high wind and intense cold.

Bloat, blōt, *vt.* To make turgid; to cure by salting and smoking.—*vi.* To grow turgid.

Blob, blob, *n.* A small globe of liquid.

Block, blok, *n.* A heavy piece of wood or stone; a lump of solid matter; piece of wood in which a pulley is placed; a mass of buildings; an obstacle; a stupid person.—*vt.* To shut up; to obstruct; to form into blocks.

Blockade, blok-ād', *n.* A close siege by troops or ships.—*vt.* (blockading, blockaded). To besiege closely.

Blockhead, blok'hed, *n.* A stupid fellow.

Blond, Blonde, blond, *a.* Of a fair complexion.—*n.* A person of fair complexion.

Blood, blud, *n.* The fluid which circulates in animals; kindred; high birth; the juice of fruits.—*a.* Pertaining to blood; of a superior breed.—*vt.* To bleed; to stain with blood; to inure to blood.

Blood-heat, blud'hēt, *n.* The heat of the human blood, about 98° Fah.

Blood-horse, blud'hors, *n.* A horse of the purest breed.

Blood-hound, blud'hound, *n.* A hound of remarkably acute smell.

Blood-money, blud'mu-ni, *n.* Money earned by the shedding of blood or murder.

Blood-shot, blud'shot, *a.* Inflamed.

Blood-stone, blud'stōn, *n.* A greenish stone with red spots.

Blood-sucker, blud'suk-ėr, *n.* Any animal that sucks blood; an extortioner.

Bloodthirsty, blud'thėrs-ti, *a.* Eager to shed blood.

Blood-vessel, blud'ves-sel, *n.* An artery or a vein.

Bloom, blöm, *n.* A blossom; a flower; state of youth; native flush on the cheek; the powdery coating on plums, etc.; a lump of puddled iron.—*vi.* To blossom; to flourish; to show the freshness of youth.

Blossom, blos'om, *n.* The flower of a plant.—*vi.* To bloom; to flower; to flourish.

Blot, blot, *vt.* (blotted, blotting). To spot; to stain; to cancel (with *out*); to dry.—*n.* A spot or stain; an obliteration.

Blotch, bloch, *n.* Pustule upon the skin; an eruption; a confused patch of color.

Blotter, blot'ėr, *n.* One who blots; a piece of blotting-paper.

Blouse, blouz, *n.* A light loose upper garment.

Blow, blō, *vi.* (blowing, pp. blown, pret. blew). To make a current of air; to emit air or breath; to pant; to sound by being blown; to bloom; to flourish.—*vt.* To impel by wind; to inflate; to sound by the breath; to infect with the eggs of flies.—*n.* A blast; a blossoming; bloom; a stroke; a calamitous event.

Blowzy, blouz'i, *a.* Fat and ruddy.

Blubber, blub'bėr, *n.* The fat of whales and other large sea-animals; the sea-nettle.—*vi.* To weep in a noisy manner.

Blucher, bluch'ėr or blö'kėr, *n.* A strong half-boot.

Bludgeon, blud'jon, *n.* A short club with one end loaded.

Blue, blü, *n.* The color which the sky exhibits; (*pl.*) depression, the dumps.—*a.* Of a blue color; sky-colored.—*vt.* (bluing, blued). To dye of a blue color.

Bluebell, blü'bel, *n.* The wild hyacinth (in England), the harebell (in Scotland).

Blue-print, blü'print, *n.* A print obtained by the action of light on prepared paper over which a transparent drawing is laid. The exposed part of the paper becomes covered with Prussian blue, and the drawing is shown in white.

Blue-stocking, blü'stok-ing, *n.* A learned and pedantic lady.

Blue-stone, blü'stōn, *n.* Sulphate of copper.

Bluff, bluf, *a.* Steep; blustering; burly; hearty.—*n.* A steep projecting bank.—*vt.* and *i.* To impose on by a show of boldness or strength.

Blunder, blun'dėr, *vi.* To err stupidly; to stumble.—*vt.* To confound.—*n.* A gross mistake; error.

Blunt, blunt, *a.* Dull on the edge or point; not sharp; dull in understanding; unceremonious.—*vt.* To make blunt or dull.

Blur, blėr, *n.* A stain; a blot.—*vt.* (blurring, blurred). To stain; to obscure; to render indistinct.

Blurb, blėrb, *n.* A brief epitome or eulogy of a book, often printed on its jacket.

Blurt, blėrt, *vt.* To utter suddenly or unadvisedly.

Blush, blush, *vi.* To redden in the face; to bear a blooming red color.—*n.* A red color caused by shame, confusion, etc.; sudden appearance or glance.

Bluster, blus'tėr, *vi.* To roar like wind; to swagger.—*n.* A violent gust of wind; swagger.

Boa, bō'a, *n.* A genus of large serpents without fangs and venom; a long piece of fur, etc., worn round the neck.

Boar, bōr, *n.* The male of swine.

Board, bōrd, *n.* A piece of timber broad and thin; a table; food; persons seated round a table; council; the deck of a ship; a thick stiff paper.—*vt.* To cover with boards; to supply with food; to place as a boarder; to enter a ship by force.—*vi.* To live in a house at a certain rate.

Boarder, bōrd'ėr, *n.* One who receives food and lodging at a stated charge; one who boards a ship in action.

Boarding-school, bōrd'ing-skōl, *n.* A school which supplies board as well as tuition.

Boast, bōst, *vi.* To brag; to talk ostentatiously.— *vt.* To brag of; to magnify.—*n.* A vaunting; the cause of boasting.

Boat, bōt, *n.* A small open vessel, usually impelled by oars; a small ship.—*vt.* To transport in a boat.—*vi.* To go in a boat.

Boatswain, bō'sn, *n.* A ship's officer who has charge of boats, sails, etc.

Bob, bob, *n.* A pendant; something that plays loosely; a short jerking motion; a docked tail; (slang) a shilling.—*vt.* (bobbing, bobbed). To move with a short jerking motion.—*vi.* To play backward and forward, or loosely.

Bobbin, bob'in, *n.* A small pin of wood to wind the thread on in weaving lace, etc.

Boche, bosh, *n.* A German.

Bode, bōd, *vt.* (boding, boded). To portend; to be the omen of.—*vi.* To presage.

Bodice, bod'is, *n.* Something worn round the waist; a corset.

Bodily, bo'di-li, *a.* Relating to the body; actual.— *adv.* Corporeally; entirely.

Bodkin, bod'kin, *n.* An instrument for piercing holes; a kind of large needle.

Body, bo'di, *n.* The trunk of an animal; main part; matter; a person; a system; strength; reality; any solid figure.—*vt.* (bodying, bodied). To give a body to; to embody with *forth*).

Bog, bog, *n.* A quagmire; a morass.—*vt.* (bogging, bogged). To whelm, as in mud.

Boggle, bog'l, ī (boggling, boggled). To stop; to hesitate; to waver.

Boggy, bog'i, *a.* Containing bogs.

Bogus, bō'gus, *a.* Counterfeit; sham.

Bohemian, bō-hē'mi-an, *n.* A native of Bohemia; a gypsy; an artist who leads an unconventional life.

Boil, boil, *vi.* To bubble from the action of heat; to seethe; to be cooked by boiling; to be in a state of agitation.—*vt.* To heat to a boiling state; to prepare by boiling.—*n.* A sore swelling or tumor.

Boisterous, bois'tėr-us, *a.* Stormy; noisy.

Bold, bōld, *a.* Daring; courageous; impudent; steep and abrupt.

Bole, bōl, *n.* The body or stem of a tree; a kind of fine clay.

Bolero, bo-lar'o, *n.* A Spanish dance.

Bolshevik, bol'shev-ik, *n.* The Russian name for the majority party in the 1903 split of the Social Democrats; revolutionists; extreme Socialists.

Bolster, bōl'stėr, *n.* A long pillow; a pad.—*vt.* To support with a bolster; to hold up; to maintain.

Bolt, bōlt, *n.* An arrow; a thunderbolt; a bar of a door; anything which fastens or secures.—*vi.* To leave suddenly.—*vt.* To fasten; to swallow hurriedly; to sift.

Bomb, bom, *n.* An iron shell filled with explosive material.

Bombard, bom-bärd', *vt.* To attack with shot and shell—*n.* An old short cannon.

Bombast, bom'bast, *n.* High-sounding words.

Bombastic, bom-bast'ik, *a.* Inflated; turgid.

Bona fide, bō'na fī'dē, *adv.* and *a.* With good faith.

Bon-bon, bong-bong, *n.* A sweetmeat.

Bond, bond, *n.* That which binds; obligation; state of being bonded; a writing by which a person binds himself; in *pl.* chains, imprisonment.—*a.* In a servile state.—*vt.* To grant a bond in security for money; to store till duty is paid.

Bondage, bond'āj, *n.* Slavery; thraldom.

Bonded, bond'ed, *a.* Secured by bond; under a bond to pay duty; containing goods liable to duties.

Bone, bōn, *n.* A hard substance, forming the

framework of an animal; something made of bone.—*vt.* (boning, boned). To take out bones from.

Bonfire, bon'fir, *n.* A large fire in the open air expressive of joy.

Bon-mot, bong-mō, *n.* A witticism.

Bonnet, bon'net, *n.* A dress for the head.

Bonny, bon'ni, *a.* Beautiful; blithe.

Bonus, bō'nus, *n.* A premium; extra dividend to shareholders.

Bony, bōn'i, *a.* Pertaining to or consisting of bones; full of bones; stout; strong.

Book, buk, *n.* A printed or written literary work; a volume; division of a literary work.—*vt.* To enter in a book.

Book-keeper, buk'kēp-ėr, *n.* One who keeps the accounts of a business house.

Book-maker, buk'māk-ėr, *n.* One who compiles books; one who bets systematically.

Bookworm, buk'wėrm, *n.* A worm that eats holes in books; a close student of books.

Boom, bōm, *n.* A long pole to extend the bottom of a sail; a chain or bar across a river or mouth of a harbor; a hollow roar; briskness in commerce.—*vi.* To make a humming sound; to roar, as waves or cannon.

Boomerang, bōm'e-rang, *n.* An Australian missile of hard wood, which can return to hit an object behind the thrower.

Boon, bōn, *n.* Answer to a prayer; a favor, gift, or grant.—*a.* Merry; pleasant.

Boor, bör, *n.* A rustic; an ill-mannered or illiterate fellow.

Boot, bōt, *vt.* To benefit; to put on boots.—*n.* Profit; a covering for the foot and leg; *pl.* a male servant in a hotel.

Booth, bōᴛн, *n.* A temporary shed.

Boot-jack, bōt'jak, *n.* An instrument for drawing off boots.

Booty, bō'ti, *n.* Spoil; plunder.

Borax, bō'raks, *n.* A salt found crude, or prepared from boracic acid and soda.

Border, bor'dėr, *n.* The outer edge of anything; boundary; margin.—*vi.* To approach near; to touch at the confines; to be contiguous.—*vt.* To surround with a border.

Bore, bōr, *vt.* (boring, bored). To make a hole in; to weary.—*vi.* To pierce.—*n.* The hole made by boring; the diameter of a round hole; a person or thing that wearies; a sudden rise of the tide in certain estuaries.

Boreal, bo're-al, *a.* Northern.

Born, born, *pp.* of *bear,* to bring forth.

Borne, born, *pp.* of *bear,* to carry.

Borough, bu'ro, *n.* A town with a municipal government.

Borrow, bo'rō, *vt.* To ask or receive as a loan; to appropriate.

Bort, bort, *n.* Fragments of diamonds.

Boscage, Boskage, bos'kāj, *n.* A mass of growing trees, groves, or thickets.

Bosky, bosk'i, *a.* Woody or bushy.

Bosom, bö'zum, *n.* The breast; the seat of the affections.—*vt.* To conceal.—*a.* Much beloved; confidential.

Boss, bos, *n.* A knob; an ornamental projection; a master.

Botany, bot'a-ni, *n.* The science which treats of plants.

Botch, boch, *n.* A swelling on the skin; a clumsy patch; bungled work.—*vt.* To mend or perform clumsily.

Both, bōth, *a.* and *pron.* The two, taken by themselves; the pair.—*conj.* As well; on the one side.

Bother, boᴛн'ėr, *vt.* To annoy.—*vi.* To trouble oneself.—*n.* A trouble, vexation.

Bothersome, boᴛн'er-sum, *a.* Causing trouble.

Bott, Bot, bot, *n.* A maggot found in the intestines of horses, etc.; generally in *pl.*

Bottle, bot'l, *n.* A narrow-mouthed vessel of glass, leather, etc., for liquor; the contents of a bottle.—*vt.* (bottling, bottled). To put into a bottle or bottles.

Bottle-nose, bot'l-nōz, n. A kind of whale.
Bottom, bot'tom, n. The lowest part; the ground under water; foundation; a valley; native strength; a ship; dregs.—vt. To found or build upon.
Boudoir, bö-dwar', n. A lady's private room.
Bough, bou, n. A branch of a tree.
Boulder, bōl'dér, n. A large roundish stone.
Boulevard, bōl-vär, n. A wide street planted with trees.
Bounce, bouns, vi. (bouncing, bounced). To spring or rush out suddenly; to thump; to boast or bully.—n. A strong sudden thump; a rebound; a boast.
Bound, bound, n. A boundary; a leap.—vt. To limit; to restrain.—vi. To leap; to rebound.—p.a. Obliged; sure.—a. Ready; destined.
Boundary, bound'a-ri, n. A mark designating a limit; border.
Bountiful, boun'ti-ful, a. Munificent; generous.
Bounty, boun'ti, n. Liberality; generosity; a gratuity; premium to encourage trade.
Bouquet, bŏ-kā', n. A bunch of flowers; a nosegay; an agreeable aromatic odor.
Bourgeois, börzh-wa, n. A citizen; a man of middle rank.
Bourgeoisie, börzh-wa-zē, n. The middle classes, especially those dependent on trade.
Bout, bout, n. As much of an action as is performed at one time; turn; debauch.
Bovine, bō'vīn, a. Pertaining to oxen.
Bow, bou, vt. To bend; to bend the head or body in token of respect; to depress.—vi. To bend; to make a reverence; to yield.—n. A bending of the head or body, in token of respect; the rounding part of a ship's side forward.
Bow, bō, n. An instrument to shoot arrows; the rainbow; a curve; a fiddlestick; an ornamental knot.
Bowel, bou'el, n. One of the intestines; pl. the intestines; the seat of pity; compassion.
Bower, bou'ér, n. An anchor carried at the bow; a shady recess; an arbor.
Bowie-knife, bō'i-nīf, n. A knife from 10 to 15 inches long and about 2 inches broad.
Bowl, bōl, n. A large roundish cup; a ball, of wood, etc.; used for rolling on a level plat of ground; pl. the game played with such bowls.—vi. To play with bowls; to deliver a ball at cricket; to move rapidly.—vt. To roll as a bowl; to deliver (a ball) at cricket, etc.
Bowler, bōl'ér, n. One who bowls; a round-shaped felt hat.
Bowling, bōl'ing, n. Act or art of playing with bowls; art or style of a bowler.
Bowman, bō'man, n. An archer.
Bowsprit, bō'sprit, n. A large spar which projects over the bow of a ship.
Box, boks, n. A case of wood, metal, etc.; quantity that a case contains; a seat in a playhouse, etc.; driver's seat on a coach; a sportsman's house; a blow on the ear; a tree or shrub, yielding a hard wood.—vt. To put in a box; to strike with the hand.—vi. To fight with the fists.
Boxwood, boks'wud, n. The hard-grained wood of the box-tree; the plant itself.
Boy, boi, n. A male child; a lad.
Boycott, boi'kot, vt. To combine in refusing to have dealings with.
Boy Scout, boi skout, n. A member of an organization founded in England in 1908 by Lord Baden-Powell with the object of promoting good citizenship.
Brace, brās, n. That which holds; a bandage; a couple.—vt. (bracing, braced). To tighten; to strain up; to strengthen.
Bracelet, brās'let, n. An ornament for the wrist.
Brachial, brā'ki-al, a. Belonging to the arm.
Bracing, brās'ing, a. Invigorating.
Bracken, brak'en, n. A kind of large fern.
Bracket, brak'et, n. A support for something fixed to a wall; a mark in printing to enclose words, etc.—vt. To place within or connect by brackets.

Brackish, brak'ish, a. Salt; saltish.
Bract, brakt, n. An irregularly developed leaf at the base of a flower.
Brad, brad, n. A small nail with no head.
Brag, brag, vi. (bragging, bragged). To bluster; to talk big.—n. A boast.
Braggadocio, brag-a-dō'shi-ō, n. A boasting fellow; boastful words.
Brahman, Brahmin, brä'man, brä'min, n. A Hindu of the sacerdotal caste.
Braid, brād, vt. To weave, knit, or wreathe; to intertwine.—n. A narrow woven band of silk, cotton, etc.; something braided.
Braille, brāl, n. A system of reading with raised letters for the blind.
Brain, brān, The nervous matter within the skull; seat of sensation and of the intellect; the understanding.—vt. To dash out the brains of.
Braise, Braize, brāz, vt. (braising, braised). To cook with herbs, etc., in a close pan.
Brake, brāk, n. A place overgrown with brushwood, etc.; a thicket; the bracken; an instrument to break flax; a harrow for breaking clods; a contrivance for retarding the motion of wheels; a large wagonette.
Bramble, bram'bl, n. A prickly shrub of the rose family; its berry.
Bran, bran, n. The husks of ground corn.
Branch, bransh, n. The shoot of a tree or plant; the offshoot of anything, as of a river, family, etc.; a limb.—vi. To spread in branches.—vt. To divide or form into branches.
Brand, brand, n. A burning piece of wood; a sword; a mark made with a hot iron; a note of infamy; a trade-mark; a kind or quality.—vt. To mark with a hot iron; to stigmatize as infamous.
Brandish, brand'ish, vt. To shake, wave, or flourish.—n. A waving; a flourish.
Brandy, bran'di, n. An ardent spirit distilled from wine.
Brash, brash, n. A confused heap of fragments; small fragments of crushed ice.
Brasier, brā'zhér, n. One who works in brass; a pan for holding coals.
Brass, bras, n. A yellow alloy of copper and zinc; a utensil, etc., made of brass; impudence.
Brat, brat, n. A child, so called in contempt.
Bravado, bra-vä'dō, n. A boast or brag; would-be boldness.
Brave, brāv, a. Daring; bold; valiant; noble.—n. A daring person; a savage warrior.—vt. (braving, braved). To challenge; to defy; to encounter with courage.
Brawl, bral, vi. To quarrel noisily.—n. A noisy quarrel; uproar.
Brawn, bran, n. The flesh of a boar; the muscular part of the body; muscle.
Bray, brā, vt. To beat or grind small.—vi. To make a loud harsh sound, as an ass.—n. The cry of an ass.
Braze, brāz, vt. (brazing, brazed). To cover with brass; to solder with brass.
Brazen, brāz'n, a. Made of brass; impudent.—vt. To behave with insolence (with it).
Breach, brēch, n. The act of breaking, or state of being broken; infringement; quarrel.—vt. To make a breach or opening in.
Bread, bred, n. Food made of flour or meal baked; food; sustenance.
Breadfruit-tree, bred'frōt-trē, n. A tree of the Pacific Islands, producing a fruit which forms a substitute for bread.
Breadth, bredth, n. The measure across any plane surface; width; liberality.
Break, brāk, vt. (breaking, pret. broke, pp. broke, broken). To sever by fracture; to rend; to open; to tame; to make bankrupt; to discard; to interrupt; to dissolve any union; to tell with discretion.—vi. To come to pieces; to burst; to burst forth; to dawn; to become bankrupt; to decline in vigor; to change in tone.—n. An open-

ing; breach; pause; the dawn; a brake for vehicles; a large wagonette.

Breaker, brāk'ẽr, n. One who or that which breaks; a rock; a wave broken by rocks.

Breakfast, brek'fast, n. The first meal in the day.—vi. To eat the first meal in the day.—vt. To furnish with breakfast.

Breakwater, brāk'wa-tẽr, n. A mole to break the force of the waves.

Bream, brēm, n. A fish.—vt. To clean a ship's bottom by means of fire.

Breast, brest, n. The fore part of the body, between the neck and the belly; the heart; the conscience; the affections.—vt. To bear the breast against; to meet in front.

Breath, breth, n. The air drawn into and expelled from the lungs; life; a single respiration; pause; a gentle breeze.

Breathe, brēTH, vi. (breathing, breathed). To draw into the eject air from the lungs; to live; to take breath; to rest.—vt. To inspire and exhale; to infuse; to utter softly or in private; to suffer to take breath.

Breech, brēch, n. The lower part of the body behind; the hinder part of a gun, etc.—vt. To put into breeches.

Breeches, brēch'ez, n.pl. A garment worn by men on the legs.

Breed, brēd, vt. (breeding, bred). To bring up; to educate; to engender; to bring forth; to occasion; to rear, as live stock.—vi. To produce offspring; to be with young; to be produced.—n. Offspring; kind; a brood.

Breeze, brēz, n. A light wind.

Breton, bret'on, a. Relating to Brittany.—n. The native language of Brittany.

Breve, brēv, n. A written mandate; a note of time equal to four minims.

Brevet, brev'et, n. A commission entitling an officer to rank above his actual rank or pay.—a. Taking rank by brevet.

Breviary, brē'vi-a-ri, n. A book containing the daily service of the R. Catholic Church.

Brevity, bre'vi-ti, n. Shortness; conciseness.

Brew, brö, vt. To prepare, as ale or beer, from malt, etc.; to concoct; to plot.—vi. To make beer; to be forming.—n. The mixture formed by brewing.

Briar, brī'ar, n. The root of the white heath, used extensively in the manufacture of tobacco-pipes.

Bribe, brīb, n. A gift to corrupt the conduct or judgment. vt. (bribing, bribed). To gain over by bribes.

Bric-à-brac, brik-a-brak, n. Articles of interest or value from rarity, antiquity, etc.

Brick, brik, n. A rectangular mass of burned clay, used in building, etc.; a loaf shaped like a brick.—a. Made of brick.—vt. To lay with bricks.

Bridal, brid'al, n. A wedding-feast; a wedding.— a. Belonging to a bride or to a wedding.

Bride, brīd, n. A woman about to be or newly married.

Bridegroom, brīd'gröm, n. A man about to be or newly married.

Bride's-maid, brīdz'mād, n. A woman who attends on a bride at her wedding.

Bridge, brij, n. A structure across a river, etc., to furnish a passage; the upper part of the nose.— vt. (bridging, bridged). To build a bridge over.

Bridge, brij, n. A game of cards resembling whist.

Bridgehead, brij'hed, n. Defensive work protecting approach to a bridge on side nearest to the enemy.

Bridle, brī'dl, n. The part of harness with which a horse is governed; a curb; a check.—vt. (bridling, bridled). To put a bridle on; to restrain — vi. To hold up the head and draw in the chin.

Brief, brēf, a. Short; concise.—n. A short writing; a writ or precept; an abridgment of a client's case.

Brier, brī'ẽr, n. A prickly shrub, species of the rose.

Brig, brig, n. A vessel with two masts, square-rigged.

Brigand, bri'gand, n. A freebooter.

Brigantine, brig'an-tin, n. A light swift vessel, two-masted and square-rigged.

Bright, brīt, a. Clear; shining; glittering; acute; witty; lively; cheerful.

Brilliant, bril'yant, a. Shining; sparkling; spendid; of great talents.—n. A diamond of the finest cut; a small printing type.

Brim, brim, n. The rim of anything; the upper edge of the mouth of a vessel.—vi. (brimming, brimmed). To be full to the brim.

Brimstone, brim'stōn, n. Sulphur.

Brindled, brind'ld, a. Marked with brown streaks.

Brine, brin, n. Salt water; the sea.

Bring, bring, vt. (bringing, brought). To lead or cause to come; to fetch; to produce; to attract; to prevail upon.

Brink, bringk, n. The edge of a steep place.

Briquette, bri-ket', n. A lump of fuel, in the form of a brick, made from coal-dust.

Brisk, brisk, a. Lively; bright; effervescing.

Brisket, brisk'et, n. The breast of an animal, or that part next to the ribs.

Bristle, bris'l, n. A stiff hair of swine; stiff hair of any kind. vt. (bristling, bristled). To erect in bristles.— vi. To stand erect, as bristles; to show anger, etc.

British, brit'ish, a. Pertaining to Britain or its inhabitants.

Brittle, brit'l, a. Apt to break; not tough or tenacious.—vt. To cut up a deer.

Broach, brōch, n. A spit; a brooch.—vt. To pierce, as with a spit; to tap; to open up; to publish first.

Broad, brad, a. Having extent from side to side; wide; unrestricted; indelicate.

Broaden, brad'n, vi. To grow broad.—vt. To make broad.

Broadside, brad'sid, n. A discharge of all the guns on one side of a ship; a sheet of paper printed on one side.

Brocade, brō-kād', n. A silk or satin stuff variegated with gold and silver.

Broccoli, brok'o-li, n. A kind of cauliflower.

Brochure, brō-shör', n. A pamphlet.

Brogue, brōg, n. A shoe or raw hide; the pronunciation of English peculiar to the Irish.

Broil, broil, n. A brawl; a noisy quarrel.—vt. To cook over a fire, to subject to strong heat.—vi. To be subjected to heat; to be greatly heated.

Broker, brō'kẽr, n. An agent who buys and sells for others; a pawn-broker.

Bromide, brō'mid, n. A compound of bromine with another element.

Bromine, brō'min or brō'min, n. A simple non-metallic element with a rank odor.

Bronchial, brong'ki-al, a. Belonging to the tubes branching from the windpipe through the lungs.

Bronchitis, brong-ki'tis, n. Inflammation of the bronchial tubes.

Bronze, bronz, n. An alloy of copper and tin; a color to imitate bronze; a figure made of bronze.—vt. (bronzing, bronzed). To make appear on the surface like bronze.

Brooch, brōch, n. An ornamental pin or buckle used to fasten dress.

Brood, bröd, vi. To sit on eggs; to ponder anxiously (with over or on).—n. That which is bred; birds of one hatching; offspring.

Brook, bruk, n. A natural stream smaller than a river.—vt. To bear; to endure.

Broom, bröm, n. A shrub with yellow flowers and angular branches; a brush.

Broth, broth, n. Liquor in which flesh, or some other substance, has been boiled.

Brothel, broth'el, n. A house of ill-fame.

Brother, bruTH'ẽr, n.; pl. **Brothers**, **Brethren**, bruTH'ẽrz, breTH'ren. A male born of the same parents; an associate; a fellow-creature.

Brougham, bröm or brö'am, *n.* A one-horse close carriage.

Brow, brou, *n.* The ridge over the eye; the forehead; the edge of a steep place.

Browbeat, brou'bēt, *vt.* To bear down with stern looks or arrogant speech.

Brown, broun, *a.* Of a dusky color, inclining to red.—*n.* A color resulting from the mixture of red, black, and yellow.—*vt.* To make brown.

Brownie, brou'ni, *n.* A domestic spirit of benevolent character; a junior Girl Guide, between the ages of 8 and 11.

Browse, brouz, *vt.* (browsing, browsed). To pasture or feed upon.—*vi.* To crop and eat food.

Bruin, brö'in, *n.* A familiar name of a bear.

Bruise, bröz, *vt.* (bruising, bruised). To crush; to make a contusion on.—*n.* A contusion; a hurt from a blow.

Bruit, bröt, *n.* Report; rumor.—*vt.* To noise abroad.

Brumal, brö'mal, *a.* Belonging to winter.

Brunette, brö-net', *n.* A woman with a brownish or dark complexion.

Brunt, brunt, *n.* The heat of battle; onset; shock.

Brush, brush, *n.* An instrument to clean by rubbing or sweeping; a painter's large pencil; a skirmish; a thicket; the tail of a fox.—*vt.* To sweep, rub, or paint with a brush; to touch lightly in passing.—*vi.* To move nimbly or in haste; to skim.

Brusque, brusk, *a.* Abrupt in manner; rude.

Brussels-sprouts, brus'elz-sprouts, *n.pl.* A variety of cabbage.

Brutal, bröt'al, *a.* Cruel; ferocious.

Brute, bröt, *a.* Senseless; bestial; uncivilized.—*n.* A beast; a brutal person.

Bubble, bub'bl, *n.* A small vesicle of fluid inflated with air; a vain project; a swindle.—*vi.* (bubbling, bubbled). To rise in bubbles.—*vt.* To cheat; to swindle.

Bubo, bū'bō, *n.*; pl. **-oes.** A swelling or abscess in a glandular part of the body.

Bubonic, bū-bon'ik, *a.* Pertaining to bubo.

Buccaneer, buk-a-nēr', *n.* A pirate.

Buck, buk, *n.* The male of deer, goats, etc.; a gay young fellow; a lye for steeping clothes in.—*vt.* To steep in lye.—*vi.* To leap, as a horse, so as to dismount the rider.

Bucket, buk'et, *n.* A vessel in which water is drawn or carried.

Buckle, buk'l, *n.* An instrument to fasten straps, etc.—*vt.* (buckling, buckled). To fasten with a buckle; to bend or warp.—*vi.* To apply with vigor (with *to*).

Buck-shot, buk'shot, *n.* A large kind of shot used for killing large game.

Buckwheat, buk'whēt, *n.* A plant bearing small seeds which are ground into meal.

Bucolic, bū-kol'ik, *a.* Pastoral.—*n.* A pastoral poem.

Bud, bud, *n.* The first shoot of a leaf, etc.; a germ.—*vi.* (budding, budded). To put forth buds or germs; to begin to grow.—*vt.* To graft by inserting a bud.

Buddhism, bud'izm, *n.* The religion founded in India by Buddha.

Budding, bud'ing, *n.* A mode of grafting buds.

Budge, buj, *vt.* (budging, budged). To move; to stir.

Budgerigar, bud'jer-ē-gär'', *n.* The grass or zebra parakeet; the Australian love-bird.

Budget, buj'et, *n.* A little sack with its contents; a stock; the annual statement respecting the British finances.

Buff, buf, *n.* Leather prepared from the skin of the buffalo, elk, etc.; a dull light yellow.—*a.* Light yellow; made of buff.

Buffalo, buf'fa-lō, *n.* A species of ox, larger than the common ox; the American bison.

Buffer, buf'er, *n.* An apparatus for deadening concussion.

Buffet, buf'et, *n.* A cupboard for wine, glasses, etc.; a place for refreshments (pron. bu-fe).

Buffet, buf'et, *n.* A blow; a slap.—*vt.* To beat; to box; to contend against.

Buffoon, buf-fön', *n.* One who makes sport by low jests and antic gestures; a droll.

Bug, bug, *n.* A name for various insects, particularly one infesting houses and inflicting severe bites.

Bugbear, bug'bār, *n.* Something real or imaginary that causes terror.

Buggy, bug'i, *n.* A light one-horse carriage.

Bugle, bū'gl, *n.* A hunting-horn; a military instrument of music; a long glass bead, commonly black.

Buhl, böl, *n.* Unburnished gold or brass used for inlaying; articles so ornamented.

Build, bild, *vt.* (building, built). To construct; to raise on a foundation; to establish.—*vi.* To form a structure.—*n.* Construction; make; form.

Bulb, bulb, *n.* A round root; a round protuberance.

Bulbul, bul'bul, *n.* The Persian nightingale.

Bulge, bulj, *n.* A swelling; bilge.—*vi.* (bulging, bulged). To swell out; to be protuberant.

Bulk, bulk, *n.* Magnitude; the majority; extent.

Bull, bul, *n.* The male of cattle; a sign of the zodiac; one who raises the price of stock; a letter or edict of the pope; a ludicrous contradiction in language.

Bull-dog, bul'dog, *n.* A species of dog.

Bulldozer, bul'dōz-er, *n.* A machine provided with a blade for spreading and levelling material.

Bullet, bul'et, *n.* A small ball; a conical projectile generally of lead intended to be discharged from small-arms.

Bulletin, bul'e-tin, *n.* An official report.

Bull-fight, bul'fīt, *n.* A combat between armed men and bulls in a closed arena.

Bullfinch, bul'finsh, *n.* A British song-bird.

Bull-frog, bul'frog, *n.* A large species of frog in N. America, with a loud bass voice.

Bullion, bul'yon, *n.* Uncoined gold or silver.

Bull's-eye, bulz'ī, *n.* A circular opening for light or air; the centre of a target.

Bully, bul'i, *n.* An overbearing quarrelsome fellow.—*vt.* (bullying, bullied). To insult and overbear.—*vi.* To bluster or domineer.

Bulrush, bul'rush, *n.* A large, strong kind of rush.

Bulwark, bul'werk, *n.* A bastion; a fortification; a means of defense or safety.

Bumble-bee, bum'bl-bē, *n.* A large bee.

Bump, bump, *n.* A heavy blow, or the noise of it; a lump produced by a blow.—*vi.* To make a loud, heavy, or hollow noise.—*vt.* To strike heavily against.

Bumpkin, bump'kin, *n.* An awkward rustic; a lout.

Bun, bun, *n.* A kind of cake or sweet bread.

Bunch, bunsh, *n.* A knob or lump; a cluster.—*vi.* To swell out in a protuberance; to cluster.

Bundle, bun'dl, *n.* A number of things bound together; a package.—*vt.* (bundling, bundled). To tie in a bundle; to dispose of hurriedly.—*vi.* To depart hurriedly (with *off*).

Bung, bung, *n.* The stopper of a cask.—*vt.* To stop with a bung; to close up.

Bungalow, bung'ga-lō, *n.* A single-storied house.

Bungle, bung'gl, *vi.* (bungling, bungled). To perform in a clumsy manner.—*vt.* To make or mend clumsily; to manage awkwardly.—*n.* A clumsy performance.

Bunk, bungk, *n.* A wooden box serving as a seat and bed; a sleeping berth.

Bunker, bung'ker, *n.* A large bin or receptacle; a sandy hollow on a golf course.

Bunkum, Buncombe, bung'kum, *n.* Talking for talking's sake; mere words.

Bunting, bunt'ing, *n.* A bird allied to finches and sparrows; stuff of which flags are made; flags.

Bunyon, Bunion, bun'yon, *n.* An excrescence on some of the joints of the feet.

Buoy, boi, *n.* A floating mark to point out shoals,

etc.; something to keep a person or thing up in the water.—*vt.* To keep afloat; to bear up.—*vi.* To float.

Buoyant, boi'ant, *a.* Floating; light; elastic.

Burden, Burthen, bér'dn, bér'THn, *n.* That which is borne; load; freight; that which is oppressive; chorus of a song; that which is often repeated.—*vt.* To load; to oppress.

Burdock, bér'dok, *n.* A plant with a rough prickly head.

Bureau, bū-rō', *n.*; pl. -**eaux,** -rōz, or -**eaus.** A writing table with drawers; an office or court; a government office.

Bureaucracy, bū-rō'kra-si, *n.* Centralized administration of a country, through regularly graded officials; such officials collectively.

Burglar, bérg'lér, *n.* One who robs a house by night.

Burgundy, bér'gun-di, *n.* A kind of wine, so called from Burgundy in France.

Burin, bū'rin, *n.* A tool for engraving.

Burlesque, bér-lesk', *a.* Tending to excite laughter.—*n.* A composition tending to excite laughter; caricature.—*vt.* (burlesquing, burlesqued). To turn into ridicule; to make ludicrous.

Burly, bér'li, *a.* Great in size; boisterous.

Burn, bérn, *vt.* (burning, burnt or burned). To consume with fire; to scorch; to inflame; to harden by fire.—*vi.* To be on fire; to be inflamed with desire; to rage fiercely.—*n.* A hurt caused by fire; a rivulet.

Burnish, bér'nish, *vt.* To polish.—*vi.* To grow bright or glossy.—*n.* Gloss; luster.

Burr, bér, *n.* A guttural sounding of the letter *r*; a rough or projecting ridge; bur.

Burrow, bu'rō, *n.* A hole in the earth made by rabbits, etc.—*vi.* To excavate a hole underground; to hide.

Burst, bérst, *vi.* (bursting, burst). To fly or break open; to rush forth; to come with violence.—*vt.* To break by force; to open suddenly.—*n.* A violent disruption; a rupture.

Bury, be'ri, *vt.* (burying, buried). To put into a grave; to overwhelm; to hide.

Bush, bush, *n.* A shrub with branches; a thicket; the backwoods of Australia; a lining of hard metal in the nave of a wheel, etc.—*vi.* To grow bushy.

Bushel, bush'el, *n.* A dry measure containing eight gallons or four pecks.

Business, biz'nes, *n.* Occupation; concern; trade.—*a.* Pertaining to traffic, trade, etc.

Buss, bus, *n.* A kiss.—*vt.* To kiss.

Bust, bust, *n.* The chest and thorax; a sculptured figure of the head and shoulders.

Bustle, bus'l, *vi.* (bustling, bustled). To hurry and be busy.—*n.* Hurry; tumult; a pad formerly worn by ladies at the back below the waist.

Busy, bi'zi, *a.* Occupied; actively engaged; officious.—*vt.* (busying, busied). To make or keep busy.

But, but, *conj. prep. adv.* Except; unless; only; however; nevertheless.

Butcher, buch'ér, *n.* One who kills animals for market; one who sells meat; one who delights in bloody deeds.—*vt.* To kill animals for food; to slaughter cruelly.

Butler, but'lér, *n.* A male servant who has the care of wines, etc.

Butt, but, *n.* The end of a thing; a mark to be shot at; the person at whom ridicule, etc., is directed; a cask holding 126 gallons of wine.—*vi.* To thrust the head forward.—*vt.* To strike with the head or horns.

Butter, but'tér, *n.* An oily substance obtained from cream by churning; any substance resembling butter.—*vt.* To spread with butter; to flatter grossly.

Butterfly, but'tér-flī, *n.* The name of a group of winged insects.

Buttermilk, but'ér-milk, *n.* The milk that remains after the butter is separated.

Buttock, but'tok, *n.* The protuberant part of the body behind; the rump.

Button, but'n, *n.* A knob to fasten the parts of dress; a knob or stud; pl. a page-boy.—*vt.* To fasten with buttons.

Buttress, but'tres, *n.* A projecting support for a wall; a prop.—*vt.* To support by a buttress; to prop.

Buxom, buks'um, *a.* Gay; brisk; wanton.

Buy, bī, *vt.* (buying, bought). To acquire by payment; to purchase; to bribe.—*vi.* To negotiate or treat about a purchase.

Buzz, buz, *vi.* To hum, as bees; to whisper.—*vt.* To whisper.—*n.* The noise of bees; a confused humming noise.

Buzzard, buz'érd, *n.* A species of hawk; a blockhead.

By, bī, *prep.* Used to denote the instrument, agent, or manner; at; near; beside; through or with; in; for; according to; at the rate of; not later than.—*adv.* Near; passing. In *composition,* secondary, side.

Bye, bī, *n.* A term in certain games; e.g. in cricket an odd or side run; the odd man in a game where the players pair off in couples.

By-law, bī'la, *n.* A local law of a city, society, etc.; an accessory law.

By-play, bī'plā, *n.* Action carried on aside, and commonly in dumb-show.

By-stander, bī'stand-ér, *n.* One who stands near; a spectator; a mere looker-on.

By-word, bī'wérd, *n.* A common saying; a proverb.

Byzantine, biz-an'tin or biz', *a.* Pertaining to Byzantium or Constantinople and the Greek Empire of which it was the capital.

C

Cabal, ka-bal', *n.* An intrigue; persons united in some intrigue.—*vi.* (caballing, caballed). To combine in plotting.

Cabaret, kab'a-ret, ka-ba-rā, *n.* A tavern; a restaurant in which singing and dancing performances are given.

Cabbage, kab'āj, *n.* A culinary vegetable.—*vt.* (cabbaging, cabbaged). To purloin, especially pieces of cloth.

Cabin, kab'in, *n.* A hut; an apartment in a ship.—*vt.* To confine, as in a cabin.

Cabinet, kab'in-et, *n.* A closet; a small room; a set of drawers for curiosities; the ministers of state.

Cable, kā'bl, *n.* The strong rope or chain to hold a ship at anchor; a large rope or chain; a submarine telegraph wire.—*vt.* (cabling, cabled). To furnish with a cable; to send by ocean telegraph.

Cablegram, kā'bl-gram, *n.* A message sent by an oceanic telegraph cable.

Cacao, ka-kā'ō, *n.* The chocolate-tree.

Cackle, kak'l, *vi.* (cackling, cackled). To make the noise of a goose or hen; to chatter.—*n.* The noise of a hen, etc.; idle talk.

Cacophony, ka-kof'ō-ni, *n.* Unpleasant vocal sound; a discord.

Cactus, kak'tus, *n.*; pl. -**tuses** or -**ti.** A spiny shrub of numerous species.

Cad, kad, *n.* A mean, vulgar fellow.

Cadaverous, ka-dav'ér-us, *a.* Resembling a dead human body; pale; ghastly.

Caddie, kad'i, *n.* A golfer's attendant.

Caddy, kad'i, *n.* A small box for tea.

Cadence, kā'dens, *n.* A fall of the voice at the end of a sentence; rhythm; the close of a musical passage or phrase.

Cadet, ka-det', *n.* A younger brother; a young man in a military school.

Cadge, kaj, *vt.* and *i.* (cadging, cadged). To carry about for sale; to go about begging.

Cadmium, kad'mi-um, *n.* A whitish metal.

Caduceus, ka-dū'sē-us, *n.* Mercury's rod.

Café, kaf-ā, *n.* A coffee-house; a restaurant.

Cafeteria, kaf-e-tēr'i-a, *n.* A restaurant in which customers serve themselves.

Caffeine, ka-fē'in, *n.* A slightly bitter alkaloid found in coffee, tea, etc.

Cage, kāj, *n.* An inclosure of wire, etc., for birds and beasts.—*vt.* (caging, caged). To confine in a cage.

Cairn, kārn, *n.* A rounded heap of stones.

Caisson, kās'son, *n.* An ammunition chest; a structure to raise sunken vessels; a structure used in laying foundations in deep water.

Cajole, ka-jōl', *vt.* (cajoling, cajoled). To coax; to court; to deceive by flattery.

Cake, kāk, *n.* A composition of flour, butter, sugar, etc., baked; a mass of matter concreted.—*vt.* (caking, caked). To form into a cake or mass.—*vi.* To form into a hard mass.

Calabash, kal'a-bash, *n.* A gourd shell dried.

Calamitous, ka-lam'it-us, *a.* Miserable; afflictive.

Calamity, ka-lam'i-ti, *n.* Misfortune; disaster.

Calcine, kal-sīn', *vt.* (calcining, calcined). To reduce to a powder by fire.—*vi.* To be converted by heat into a powder.

Calculate, kal'ku-lāt, *vt.* (calculating, calculated). To compute; to adjust; to make suitable.—*vi.* To make a computation.

Calculus, kal'ku-lus, *n.*; pl. **-li.** The stone in the bladder, kidneys, etc.; a method of calculation in mathematics.

Caldron, kal'dron, *n.* A large kettle or boiler.

Caledonian, kal-i-dō'ni-an, *a.* Pertaining to Scotland.—*n.* A Scot.

Calends, ka'lendz, *n.pl.* Among the Romans, the first day of each month.

Calf, käf, *n.*; pl. **Calves,** kävz. The young of the cow; a kind of leather; the fleshy part of the leg below the knee.

Caliber, ka'li-bėr, *n.* Diameter of the bore of a gun; extent of mental qualities; a sort or kind.

Calico, ka'li-kō, *n.* Cotton cloth.

Calk, kak, *vt.* See Caulk.

Calkin, Calker, kak'in, kak'ėr, *n.* The part of a horse-shoe bent downwards and pointed.

Call, kal, *vt.* To name; to style; to summon; to ask, or command to come; to appoint; to appeal to; to utter aloud; to awaken.—*vi.* To utter a loud sound; to make a short visit.—*n.* A vocal utterance; summons; demand; divine vocation; a short visit.

Calligraphy, kal-lig'ra-fi, *n.* The art of beautiful writing; penmanship.

Calling, kal'ing, *n.* Vocation; profession.

Callipers, kal'i-pėrz, *n.pl.* Compasses for measuring caliber.

Callisthenics, kal-is-then'iks, *n.* Exercise for health, strength, or grace of movement.

Callosity, ka-los'i-ti, *n.* Hardness of skin; horny hardness.

Callous, kal'us, *a.* Hardened; unfeeling; obdurate.

Calm, käm, *a.* Still; free from wind; peaceable; composed.—*n.* Absence of wind; tranquillity.—*vt.* To make calm; to still; to assuage.—*vi.* To become calm.

Caloric, ka-lo'rik, *n.* The principle or simple element of heat; heat.

Calumet, kal'ū-met, *n.* The North American Indians' pipe of peace.

Calumniate, ka-lum'ni-āt, *vt.* (calumniating, calumniated). To defame maliciously; to slander.—*vi.* To utter calumnies.

Calumny, kal'lum-ni, *n.* False and malicious defamation; backbiting.

Calvary, kal'va-ri, *n.* A place of skulls, particularly the place where Christ was crucified.

Calvinism, kal'vin-izm, *n.* The theological tenets of Calvin.

Calyx, kā-liks, *n.*; pl. **-yces** or **-yxes.** The outer covering of a flower; the flower-cup.

Cam, kam, *n.* A projection on a wheel to give alternating motion to another wheel, etc.

Camber, kam'bėr, *n.* A convexity upon an upper surface, as a ship's deck, a bridge, a road, a beam.

Cambrian, kam'bri-an, *a.* Pertaining to Wales.—*n.* A Welshman.

Cambric, kām'brik, *n.* A fine white linen.

Camel, kam'el, *n.* A large ruminant hoofed quadruped used in Asia and Africa for carrying burdens.

Camellia, ka-mel'i-a or ka-mēl'ya, *n.* A genus of beautiful shrubs of the tea family.

Cameo, kam'ē-ō, *n.* A stone or shell of different colored layers cut in relief.

Camera, kam'e-ra, *n.* An arched roof; a council chamber; an apparatus for taking photographs.

Camomile, kam'ō-mīl, *n.* A bitter medicinal plant.

Camouflage, kam-ö-fläzh, *n.* The art of disguising; especially the art of disguising material in warfare.

Camp, kamp, *n.* The ground on which an army pitch their tents; an encampment.—*vi.* To pitch a camp; to encamp.

Campaign, kam-pān', *n.* The time an army keeps the field every year, during a war; its operations.—*vi.* To serve in a campaign.

Campanile, kam-pa-nē'lā or kam'pa-nil, *n.*; pl. **-ili** or **-iles.** A bell-tower.

Camphor, kam'fėr, *n.* A whitish, bitter, strong-smelling substance used in medicine.

Campion, kam'pi-on, *n.* A popular name of certain plants of the Pink family.

Can, kan, *n.* A cup or vessel for liquors.

Can, kan, *vi.* (pret. could). To be able; to have sufficient moral or physical power.

Canal, ka-nal', *n.* A channel; an artificial watercourse for boats; a duct of the body.

Canard, ka-när or ka-närd', *n.* An absurd story; a false rumor.

Canary, ka-nā'ri, *n.* Wine made in the Canary Isles; a finch from the Canary Isles.

Cancel, kan'sel, *vt.* (cancelling, cancelled). To obliterate; to revoke; to set aside.—*n.* Act of cancelling.

Cancer, kan'sėr, *n.* One of the signs of the zodiac; a malignant growth in the body.

Candelabrum, kan-de-lā'brum, *n.*; pl. **-ra.** A branched ornamental candlestick.

Candid, kan'did, *a.* Sincere; ingenuous.

Candidate, kan'di-dāt, *n.* One who proposes himself, or is proposed, for some office; one who aspires after preferment.

Candied, kan'did, *a.* Preserved with sugar, or incrusted with it.

Candle, kan'dl, *n.* A cylindrical body of tallow, wax, etc., surrounding a wick, and used for giving light.

Candlestick, kan'dl-stik, *n.* An instrument to hold a candle.

Candor, kan'dėr, *n.* Frankness; sincerity.

Candy, kan'di, *vt.* (candying, candied). To conserve with sugar; to form into crystals.—*vi.* To take on the form of candied sugar.—*n.* Crystallized sugar; a sweetmeat.

Cane, kān, *n.* A reed; a walking-stick.—*vt.* (caning, caned). To beat with a cane.

Canine, ka'nin, *a.* Pertaining to dogs.

Canister, kan'is-tėr, *n.* A small box for tea, coffee, etc.; a case containing shot which bursts on being discharged.

Canker, kang'kėr, *n.* A malignant ulcer; a disease of trees; a disease in horses' feet; something that gnaws or corrodes.—*vt.* and *i.* To corrode or corrupt.

Cannibal, kan'ni-bal, *n.* A savage who eats human flesh.—*a.* Relating to cannibalism.

Cannon, kan'un, *n.* A great gun; the striking of a ball on two other balls successively.—*vi.* To strike with rebounding collision; to make a cannon at billiards.

Canny, Cannie, kan'i, *a.* Cautious; wary.

Canoe, ka-nö', *n.* A boat made of the trunk of a

tree, or of bark or skins; a light boat propelled by paddles.

Canon, kan'on, n. A rule of doctrine or discipline; a law in general; the genuine books of the Holy Scriptures; a member of the cathedral chapter; a catalogue of saints canonized; a formula; a large kind of printing type.

Canon, Canyon, kan'yun, n. A long and narrow mountain gorge.

Canonize, kan'on-iz, vt. (canonizing, canonized). To enroll in the canon as a saint.

Canopy, kan'ō-pi, n. A covering over a throne, bed, or person's head, etc.—vt. (canopying, canopied). To cover with a canopy.

Cant, kant, vi. To speak in a whining tone; to sham piety.—vt. To tilt up; to bevel.—n. A whining hypocritical manner of speech; jargon; slang; inclination from a perpendicular or horizontal line; a toss or jerk.—a. Of the nature of cant or slang.

Cantankerous, kan-tang'kėr-us, a. Ill-natured; cross; contentious.

Cantata, kan-tä'ta, n. A short musical composition in the form of an oratorio.

Canteen, kan-tēn', n. A vessel used by soldiers for carrying liquor; a place in barracks where provisions, etc., are sold.

Canter, kan'tėr, n. A moderate gallop.—vi. To move in a moderate gallop.

Cantharides, kan-tha'ri-dēz, n.pl. Spanish flies, used to raise a blister.

Canticle, kan'ti-kl, n. A song; a passage of Scripture for chanting; in pl. the Song of Solomon.

Cantilever, kan'ti-lēv-ėr, n. A bracket to carry moldings, eaves, balconies, etc.; one of two long arms projecting toward each other from opposite banks or piers, used in bridgemaking.

Cantle, kan'tl, n. A corner; a piece; the hind part of a saddle.

Canto, kan'tō, n. A division of a poem; the treble part of a musical composition.

Canton, kan'ton, n. A division of territory or its inhabitants.—vt. To divide into cantons; to allot separate quarters to different parts of an army. (In milit. lan. pron. kan-tön'.)

Canvas, kan'vas, n. A coarse cloth; sailcloth; sails of ships; cloth for painting on; a painting.

Canvass, kan'vas, vt. To scrutinize; to solicit the votes of—vi. To solicit votes or interest; to use efforts to obtain.—n. Scrutiny; solicitation of votes.

Cap, kap, n. A covering for the head; something used as a cover; a top piece.—vt. (capping, capped). To put a cap on; to complete; to crown; to excel.

Capable, kā'pa-bl, a. Having sufficient skill or power; competent; susceptible.

Capacious, ka-pā'shus, a. Wide; large; comprehensive.

Capacitate, ka-pas'i-tāt, vt. To make able; to qualify.

Capacity, ka-pas'i-ti, n. Power of holding; extent of space; ability; state.

Caparison, ka-pa'ri-son, n. A covering laid over the saddle of a horse; clothing.—vt. To cover with a cloth; to dress richly.

Cape, kāp, n. The point of a neck of land extending into the sea; a loose cloak hung from the shoulders.

Caper, kā'pėr, vi. To prance; to spring.—n. A skip, spring, jump; the flower-bud of the caper-bush, much used for pickling.

Capillary, ka-pil'la-ri, or kap'il la ri, a. Resembling a hair; having a bore of very small diameter.—n. A tube with a very small bore; a fine vessel or canal in an animal body.

Capital, kap'it-al, a. First in importance; metropolitan; affecting the head; punishable with death.—n. The uppermost part of a column; the chief city; the stock of a bank, tradesman, etc.; a large letter or type.

Capitalist, kap'it-al-ist, n. A man who has a capital or wealth.

Capitation, kap-it-ā'shon, n. Numeration by heads or individuals.

Capitol, kap'it-ol, n. The temple of Jupiter in Rome; a citadel; a state-house.

Capitulate, ka-pit'ū-lāt, vi. (capitulating, capitulated). To surrender on conditions.

Capon, kā'pon, n. A young castrated cock.

Caprice, ka-prēs', n. A freak; a sudden or unreasonable change of opinion or humor.

Capricorn, ka'pri-korn, n. The he-goat, one of the signs of the zodiac; the southern tropic.

Capsicum, kap'si-kum, n. The generic name of some tropical plants yielding chilies and cayenne pepper.

Capsize, kap-siz', vt. (capsizing, capsized). To upset or overturn.

Capstan, kap'stan, n. An apparatus in ships to raise great weights, weigh anchors, etc.

Capsule, kap'sūl, n. A dry, many-seeded seed-vessel; an envelope for drugs.

Captain, kap'tin, n. A head officer; the commander of a ship, troop of horse, or company of infantry; a leader.

Caption, kap'shon, n. Seizure; arrest; heading or short title of a division of a book, or of a scene in a cinematograph film.

Captious, kap'shus, a. Ready to find fault; carping.

Captive, kap'tiv, n. One taken in war; one ensnared by love, beauty, etc.—a. Make prisoner; kept in bondage.

Capture, kap'tūr, n. Act of taking; the thing taken.—vt. (capturing, captured). To take by force or stratagem.

Capuchin, ka-pū-shēn', n. A Franciscan monk; a cloak with a hood.

Car, kär, n. A chariot; a vehicle in pageants; a railway or tramway carriage.

Carafe, ka'raf, n. A glass water-bottle.

Caramel, ka'ra-mel, n. Burnt sugar, used to color spirits.

Carat, ka'rat, n. A weight of four grains, for weighing diamonds, etc.; a word employed to denote the fineness of gold, pure gold being of twenty-four carats.

Caravan, ka'ra-van, n. A company of travelers associated together for safety; a large close carriage.

Caraway, ka'ra-wā, n. A biennial, aromatic plant whose seeds are used in baking, etc.

Carbide, kär'bid, n. A compound of carbon with a metal.

Carbine, kär'bin, n. A short-barreled rifle used by cavalry, police, etc.

Carbolic, kär-bol'ik, a. An antiseptic and disinfecting acid obtained from coal-tar.

Carbon, kär'bon, n. Pure charcoal; an element, a tary substance, bright and brittle.

Carbonate, kär'bon-āt, n. A salt formed by the union of carbonic acid with a base.

Carbuncle, kär'bung-kl, n. A fiery red precious stone; an inflammatory tumor.

Carburetor, kär'bū-ret-ėr, n. A device for vaporizing the light oil fuel used in the engines of motor-cars, airplanes, etc.

Carcass, kär'kas, a. A dead body; anything decayed; a framework; a kind of bomb.

Card, kärd, n. A piece of pasteboard with figures, used in games; a piece of pasteboard containing a person's name, etc.; a printed invitation; a note; the dial of a compass; a large comb for wool or flax.—vt. To comb wool, flax, hemp, etc.

Cardamom, kär'da-mum, n. The aromatic capsule of various plants of the ginger family.

Cardboard, kärd'bōrd, n. A stiff kind of paper or pasteboard for making cards, etc.

Cardiac, kär'di-ak, a. Pertaining to the heart; stimulating.—n. A cordial.

Cardigan, kär'di-gan, n. A knitted waistcoat.

Cardinal, kär'din-al, a. Chief; fundamental.—n. A dignitary in the Roman Catholic Church next to the pope; a lady's short cloak.

Care, kär, n. Solicitude; attention; object of watchful regard.—vi. (caring, cared). To be solicitous; to be inclined; to have regard.

Careen, ka-rēn', vt. To lay (a ship) on one side, for the purpose of repairing.—vi. To incline to one side.

Career, ka-rēr', n. A race; course of action.—vi. To move or run rapidly.

Careful, kär'ful, a. Solicitous; cautious.

Caress, ka-res', vt. To fondle; to embrace affectionately.—n. An act of endearment.

Caret, kā'ret, n. In writing, this mark, ʌ, noting insertion.

Care-taker, kär'tā-kėr, n. A person put in charge of a house, farm, or the like.

Cargo, kär'gō, n. The freight of a ship.

Cariboo, Caribou, ka'ri-bō, n. An American variety of the reindeer.

Caricature, ka-ri-ka-tūr', n. A portrait or description so exaggerated as to excite ridicule.—vt. (caricaturing, caricatured). To represent by caricature.

Caries, kā'ri-ēz, n. Ulceration of a bone.

Carillon, ka'ril-lon, n. A chime of bells; simple air adapted to a set of bells.

Carious, kā'ri-us, a. Ulcerated; decayed.

Carminative, kär'min-āt-iv, n. A medicine for flatulence, etc.

Carmine, kär'min, n. A bright crimson color.

Carnage, kär'nāj, n. Great slaughter in war; massacre; butchery.

Carnal, kär'nal, a. Fleshly; sensual.

Carnation, kär-nā'shon, n. Flesh-color; a sweet-scented plant with pink flowers.

Carnelian, kär-nē'li-an, n. A red or flesh-colored stone, a variety of chalcedony.

Carnival, kär'ni-val, n. A festival during the week before Lent; a revel.

Carnivora, kär-niv'ō-ra, n.pl. Animals that feed on flesh.

Carob, ka'rob, n. A tree with sweet nutritious pods called locust-beans.

Carol, ka'rol, n. A song of joy or devotion; a warble.—vt. (caroling, caroled). To sing; to warble.—vt. To celebrate in song.

Carotid, ka-rot'id, a. Pertaining to the two great arteries in the neck conveying the blood to the head.

Carouse, ka-rouz', vi. (carousing, caroused). To drink freely with noisy jollity.—n. A drinking bout.

Carp, kärp, vi. To cavil; to find fault.—n. A voracious fish, found in rivers and ponds.

Carpenter, kär'pen-tėr, n. One who works in timber.

Carpet, kär'pet, n. A woven fabric for covering floors, etc.—vt. To cover with a carpet.

Carpet-bagger, kär'pet-bag-ėr, n. An outsider who takes part in political affairs.

Carriage, ka'rij, n. Act of carrying; that which carries; a vehicle; conveyance; price of carrying; behavior; demeanor.

Carrion, ka'ri-on, n. Dead and putrefying flesh.—a. Relating to putrefying carcasses; feeding on carrion.

Carrot, ka'rot, n. A yellowish or reddish esculent root of a tapering form.

Carry, ka'ri, vt. (carrying, carried). To bear, convey, or transport; to gain; to capture; to import; to behave.—vi. To convey; to propel.—n. Onward motion.

Cart, kärt, n. A carriage of burden with two wheels.—vt. To carry or place on a cart.

Carte-blanche, kärt-blänsh, n. A blank paper; unconditional terms.

Cartel, kär'tel, n. A challenge; an agreement for the exchange of prisoners.

Cartilage, kär'ti-läj, n. Gristle; an elastic substance from which bone is formed.

Cartography, kär-tog'ra-fi, n. The art or practice of drawing up charts.

Cartoon, kär-tön', n. A drawing for a fresco or tapestry; a pictorial sketch relating to a prevalent topic.

Cartouch, kär-tösh', n. A cartridge or cartridge-box; a sculptured ornament.

Cartridge, kär'trij, n. A case containing the charge of a gun or any firearm.

Carve, kärv, vt. (carving, carved). To cut; to engrave; to shape by cutting.—vi. To cut up meat; to sculpture.

Caryatid, ka'ri-at-id, n.; pl. **-ids** or **-ides.** A figure of a woman serving as a column.

Cascade, kas'kād, n. A waterfall.

Case, kās, n. That which contains; a box; a receptacle; covering; an event; condition; a suit in court; a form in the inflection of nouns, etc.—vt. (casing, cased). To cover with a case; to put in a case.

Casein, Caseine, kā'sē-in, n. That ingredient in milk which forms curd and cheese.

Casement, käz'ment, n. A case for a window.

Caseous, kā'sē-us, a. Pertaining to cheese.

Cash, kash, n. Money; ready money; coin.—vt. To turn into money.

Cashier, kash-ēr', n. One who has charge of money.—vt. To deprive of office; to dismiss; to break.

Cashmere, kash'mēr, n. A rich kind of shawl; a fine woolen stuff.

Casino, ka-sē'nō, n. A public dancing, singing, or gaming saloon.

Cask, kask, n. A vessel for containing liquors.

Cassava, kas-sä'va or sä'va, n. A tropical shrub yielding a nutritious starch formed into tapioca, etc.

Casserole, kas'e-rōl, n. A sauce-pan; a kind of stew.

Cassia, kash'i-a, n. A sweet spice; wild cinnamon; a plant which yields senna.

Cassock, kas'ok, n. A close garment worn by clergymen under the surplice.

Cassowary, kas'sō-wa-ri, n. A running bird allied to the ostrich.

Cast, kast, vt. (casting, cast). To throw; to impel; to throw off; to let fall; to condemn; to compute; to model; to found; to scatter (seed); to bring forth immaturely.—vi. To revolve in the mind; to contrive (with about); to warp.—n. A throw; the thing thrown; manner of throwing; distance passed by a thing thrown; a squint; form; a tinge; manner; that which is formed from a mould; the actors to whom the parts of a play are assigned.

Castanet, kas'ta-net, n. Small pieces of wood or ivory struck together in dancing.

Castaway, kast'a-wä, n. A person abandoned; a reprobate.

Caste, kast, n. A distinct hereditary order among the Hindus; a class of society.

Castigate, kas'ti-gāt, vt. (castigating, castigated). To chastise; to punish by stripes.

Cast-iron, kast'i-ern, n. Iron which has been cast into pigs or molds.

Castle, kas'l, n. A fortified building; a large and imposing mansion; a piece in chess.

Castor, kas'tėr, n. A small cruet; a small wheel on the leg of a table, etc.

Castor-oil, kas'tėr-oil, n. A medicinal oil obtained from a tropical plant.

Castrate, kas'trāt, vt. (castrating, castrated). To geld; to emasculate; to expurgate.

Cast-steel, kast'stēl, n. Steel melted and cast into ingots and rolled into bars.

Casual, ka'zhū-al, a. Happening by chance; occasional; contingent.

Casualty, ka'zhū-al-ti, n. Accident, especially one resulting in death or injury; death or injury caused by enemy action.

Casuistry, ka'zū-is-tri, n. The science of determining cases of conscience; sophistry.

Cat, kat, n. A domestic animal of the feline tribe; a strong tackle; a double tripod; an instrument for flogging.

Cataclysm, kat'a-klizm, n. A deluge; a sudden overwhelming catastrophe.

Catacomb, ka'ta-kōm, n. A subterranean place for the burial of the dead.

Catafalque, kat'a-falk, n. A temporary structure representing a tomb.

Catalectic, kat-a-lek'tik, a. Incomplete.

Catalepsy, ka'ta-leps-i, n. A nervous affection suspending motion and sensation.

Catalogue, ka'ta-log, n. A list; a register.—vt. (cataloguing, catalogued). To make a list of.

Catamaran, kat'a-ma-ran'', n. A kind of raft; a cross-grained woman.

Catapult, kat'a-pult, n. An apparatus for throwing stones, etc.

Cataract, kat'a-rakt, n. A great waterfall; a disease of the eye.

Catarrh, ka-tär', n. A flow of mucus from the nose, etc.; a cold.

Catastrophe, ka-tas'trō-fē, n. Calamity or disaster; final event.

Catch, kach, vt. (catching, caught). To lay hold on; to stop the falling of; to grasp; to entangle; to receive by contagion; to be seized with; to get.—vi. To lay hold; to be contagious.—n. Act of seizing; anything that takes hold; a sudden advantage taken; something desirable; a capture; a song.

Catechism, ka'tē-kizm, n. A manual of instruction by questions and answers, especially in religion.

Catechumen, ka-tē-kū'men, n. One who is being instructed in the first rudiments of Christianity.

Category, kat'ē-go-ri, n. One of the highest classes to which objects of thought can be referred; class; a general head.

Catena, ka-tē'na, n. A chain; series of extracts, arguments, etc.

Cater, kā'tér, vi. To buy or procure provisions, food, entertainment, etc.

Caterpillar, kat'ér-pil-ér, n. The hairy worm-like grub of butterflies and moths; a traction device consisting of an endless chain encircling the wheels of the tractor.

Caterwaul, kat'ér-wal, vi. To cry as cats.

Catgut, kat'gut, n. The intestines of a cat; intestines made into strings for musical instruments, etc.; a kind of linen or canvas.

Cathartic, ka-thär'tik, a. Purging.—n. A medicine that purges.

Cathedral, ka-thē'dral, n. The principal church in a diocese.

Catheter, kath'e-tér, n. A tubular instrument, to be introduced into the bladder.

Cathode, kath'ōd, n. The negative pole of an electric current.

Catholic, ka'thol-ik, a. Universal; liberal; pertaining to the universal Church; pertaining to the Roman Catholic Church.—n. A member of the universal Christian Church; an adherent of the Roman Catholic Church.

Catkin, kat'kin, n. The blossom of the willow, birch, etc., resembling a cat's tail.

Catmint, Catnip, kat'mint, kat'nip, n. A strong-scented labiate plant.

Catoptrics, kat-op'triks, n. The part of optics treating of vision by reflected light.

Cat's-eye, kats'ī, n. A variety of chalcedony.

Cat's-paw, kats'pa, n. A light breeze; a dupe; a tool.

Cattle, kat'tl, n.pl. Domestic quadrupeds serving for tillage or food; bovine animals.

Caucus, ka'kus, n. A private committee to manage election matters.

Caudal, ka'dal, a. Pertaining to a tail.

Caul, kal, n. A net for the hair; a membrane investing some part of the intestines.

Cauliflower, ka'li-flou-ér, n. A variety of cabbage.

Caulk, kak, vt. To drive oakum into the seams of (a ship) to prevent leaking.

Causative, kaz'a-tiv, a. That expresses a cause or reason that effects.

Cause, kaz, n. That which produces an effect; reason; origin; sake; purpose; a suit in court;

that which a person or party espouses.—vt. (causing, caused). To effect; to bring about.

Causeway, Causey, kaz'wā, kaz'i, n. A raised road; a paved way.

Caustic, kas'tik, a. Burning; corroding; cutting.—n. A substance which burns the flesh.

Cauterization, ka'tér-iz-ā''shon, n. Act of cauterizing.

Cauterize, ka'tér-iz, vt. To burn with caustics, or hot iron, as morbid flesh.

Caution, ka'shon, n. Care; wariness; warning; pledge.—vt. To warn.

Cavalcade, ka'val-kād, n. A procession of persons on horseback.

Cavalier, ka-va-lér', n. A horseman; a gay military man; a beau.—a. Gay; brave; haughty; supercilious.

Cavalry, ka'val-ri, n. A body of troops mounted.

Cave, kāv, n. A hollow place in the earth; a den.

Caveat, ka've-at, n. A warning; a process to stop proceedings in a court.

Cavern, ka'vérn, n. A large cave.

Caviare, Caviar, ka-vi-är', n. The roe of the sturgeon salted and prepared for food.

Cavil, ka'vil, vi. (caviling, caviled). To carp; to find fault with insufficient reason.—n. A captious objection.

Cavity, ka'vi-ti, n. A hollow place.

Cayenne, kā-en', n. A pepper made from capsicum seeds.

Cease, sēs, vi. (ceasing, ceased). To leave off; to fail; to stop; to become extinct.—vt. To put a stop to.

Cedar, sē'dér, n. A large coniferous tree.—a. Made of cedar; belonging to cedar.

Cede, sēd, vt. (ceding, ceded). To give up; to surrender.—vi. To yeild; to lapse.

Cedilla, sē-dil'la, n. A mark under c (thus ç), to show that it is to be sounded like s.

Ceiling, sēl'ing, n. The upper inside surface of a room.

Celebrate, sel'ē-brāt, vt. (celebrating, celebrated). To honor by solemn rites; to praise; to commemorate.

Celebrated, se'lē-brāt-ed, a. Famous.

Celerity, sē-le'ri-ti, n. Speed; quickness.

Celery, se'le-ri, n. An umbelliferous plant cultivated for the table.

Celestial, sē-les'ti-al, a. Heavenly; pertaining to heaven.—n. An inhabitant of heaven.

Celibacy, se'li-ba-si, n. The unmarried state; a single life.

Celibate, se'li-bāt, n. One who intentionally remains unmarried.—a. Unmarried.

Cell, sel, n. A small room; a cave; a small mass of protoplasm forming the structural unit in animal tissues.

Cellar sel'lér, n. An apartment underground used for storage.

Cellophane, sel'ō-fān, n. Trade name for a thin, waterproof solidification of viscose, much used for wrapping.

Celluloid, sel'lū-loid, n. An artificial substitute for ivory, bone, coral, etc.

Cellulose, sel'lū-lōs, n. The substance of which the permanent cell membranes of plants are always composed, in many respects allied to starch.

Celt, selt, n. One of a race of Western Europe; a prehistoric cutting instrument.

Cement, sē-ment', n. An adhesive substance which unites bodies; mortar; bond of union.—vt. To unite closely.—vi. To unite and cohere.

Cemetery, se'mē-te-ri, n. A burial-place.

Cenotaph, sen'ō-taf, n. A monument to one who is buried elsewhere.

Censer, sens'ér, n. A vase or pan in which incense is burned.

Censor, sen'sér, n. One who examines manuscripts, etc., before they are published; one who censures; in war-time, an official who controls the public press, etc., and who also supervises private correspondence.

Censorious, sen-sō'ri-us, a. Addicted to censure.

Censure, sen'shūr, n. Severe judgment; reproof. —vt. (censuring, censured). To judge unfavorably of; to blame.

Census, sen'sus, n. An enumeration of the inhabitants of a country.

Cent, sent, n. A hundred; a copper coin in America, etc.; the hundredth part of a dollar. Per cent, a certain rate by the hundred.

Centaur, sen'tar, n. A fabulous being, half man and half horse.

Centenarian, sen-ten-ā'ri-an, n. A person a hundred years old.

Centennial, sen-ten'ni-al, a. Consisting of a hundred years; happening every hundred years.

Centesimal, sen-tes'i-mal, a. The hundredth.—n. The hundredth part.

Centigrade, sen'ti-grād, a. Divided into a hundred degrees.

Centimeter, sen'ti-mē-tèr, n. The hundredth part of a meter, about two-fifths of an inch.

Centipede, sen'ti-pēd, n. An insect having a great number of feet.

Central, sen'tral, a. Placed in the center; relating to the center.

Center, sen'tèr, n. The middle point; a nucleus.— vt. (centering, centered). To fix on a center; to collect to a point.—vi. To be collected to a point; to have as a center.

Centrifugal, sen-trif'ū-gal, a. Tending to fly from a center.

Centripetal, sen-trip'et-al, a. Tending toward the center.

Centuple, sen'tū-pl, a. Hundredfold.

Centurion, sen-tū'ri-on, n. Among the Romans the captain of a hundred men.

Century, sen'tū-ri, n. A hundred; the period of a hundred years.

Cephalic, se-fal'ik, a. Pertaining to the head.

Ceramic, se-ram'ik, a. Pertaining to the manufacture of porcelain and earthenware.

Cerate, sē'rāt, n. A thick ointment, composed of wax and oil.

Cere, sēr, n. The wax-like skin that covers the base of the bill in some birds.—vt. (cering, cered). To wax or cover with wax.

Cereal, sē'rē-al, a. Pertaining to corn.—n. A grain plant.

Cerebral, se'rē-bral, a. Pertaining to the brain.

Ceremony, se'rē-mō-ni, n. Outward rite; form; observance; formality.

Cerise, se-rēz', n. Cherry-color.

Certain, sèr'tān, a. Sure; undeniable; decided; particular; some; one.

Certificate, sèr-tif'i-kāt, n. A written testimony; a credential.

Certify, sèr'ti-fī, vt. (certifying, certified). To give certain information; to testify to in writing.

Cerulean, sē-rū'lē-an, a. Sky-colored.

Cerumen, sē-rū'mēn, n. The wax or yellow matter secreted by the ear.

Cervine, sèr'vin, a. Pertaining to deer.

Cess, ses, n. A rate or tax.—vt. To rate, or impose a tax on.

Cessation, ses-ā'shon, n. Stoppage.

Cession, se'shon, n. Surrender; a yielding up.

Cesspool, ses'pöl, n. A receptacle for sewage.

Cetaceous, sē-tā'shus, a. Pertaining to animals of the whale kind.

Chafe, chāf, vt. (chafing, chafed). To make warm by rubbing; to fret by rubbing; to enrage.—vi. To be fretted by friction; to rage.—n. A heat; a fretting.

Chafer, chāf'èr, n. A beetle that eats roots, leaves, and young shoots.

Chaff, chaf, n. The husk of corn and grasses; banter.—vt. To banter.

Chagrin, sha-grēn', n. Ill-humor; vexation.—vt. To vex; to mortify.

Chain, chān, n. A series of links; a line of things connected; that which binds; a line formed of links, 66 feet long; (pl.) bondage; slavery.—vt. To bind with a chain; to confine.

Chair, chār, n. A movable seat; an official seat; professorship.—vt. To place or carry in a chair.

Chairman, chār'man, n. The presiding officer of an assembly; a president.

Chalcedony, kal-sed'ō-ni, n. A variety of quartz, having a whitish color.

Chaldaic, Chaldean, Chaldee, kal-dā'ik, kal-dē'an, kal'dē, a. Pertaining to Chaldea.—n. The language of the Chaldeans.

Chalice, cha'lis, n. A drinking-cup.

Chalk, chak, n. A white calcareous earth or carbonate of lime.—vt. To mark with chalk.

Challenge, chal'lenj, n. A summons to fight; a calling in question; an exception taken.—vt. (challenging, challenged). To summon to a fight; to defy; to call in question; to object to.

Chalybeate, ka-lib'ē-āt, a. Impregnated with particles of iron.—n. A liquid into which iron or steel enters.

Chamber, chām'bèr, n. An apartment; an office; a hall of justice or legislation; a legislative body.

Chameleon, ka-mē'lē-on, n. A species of lizard, whose color changes.

Chamfer, cham'fèr, n. A small furrow in wood, etc.; a bevel.—vt. To cut a chamfer in; to bevel.

Chamois, sham'i or sham'wa, n. A species of antelope; a soft leather.

Champ, champ, vt. To devour with violent action of the teeth; to bite the bit, as a horse.—vi. To keep biting.

Champagne, sham-pān', n. A kind of brisk sparkling wine.

Champion, cham'pi-on, n. A combatant for another, or for a cause; a hero; one victorious in contest.—vt. To fight for.

Chance, chans, n. That which happens; accident; possibility of an occurrence; opportunity.—vi. (chancing, chanced). To happen.—a. Happening by chance; casual.

Chancel, chan'sel, n. That part of a church where the altar is placed.

Chancellor, chan'sel-lèr, n. A high judicial officer who presides over a court of chancery, etc.; a presiding official.

Chancery, chan'se-ri, n. A court of public affairs; in England, a division of the High Court of Justice.

Chancre, shang'kèr, n. An ulcer which arises from the venereal virus.

Chandelier, shan-dē-lēr', n. A frame with branches for candles or lamps.

Change, chānj, vt. (changing, changed). To cause to turn from one state to another; to substitute; to give one kind of money for another.—vt. To be altered.—n. Variation; small money.

Changeling, chānj'ling, n. A child substituted for another; a fool; one apt to change.

Channel, chan'nel, n. A water-course; a narrow sea; means of passing or transmitting.—vt. (channelling, channelled). To form into a channel; to groove.

Chant, chant, vt. and i. To sing; to sing after the manner of a chant.—n. Song; a kind of sacred music; a part of church srvice.

Chanticleer, chan'ti-klēr, n. A cock.

Chantry, chant'ri, n. A chapel where priests sing or say mass for the souls of others.

Chaos, kā'os, n. Confused mass; disorder.

Chap, chap, vt. (chapping, chapped). To cause to crack.—vt. To open in slits.—n. A crack in the skin; the jaw; a young fellow.

Chapel, chap'el, n. A place of worship; a church; a sanctuary.

Chaperon, sha'pe-rōn, n. A married lady who attends a young lady to public places.—vt. To act as chaperon to.

Chaplain, chap'lān, n. A clergyman of the army, navy, court, etc.

Chapter, chap'tèr, n. Division of a book; a society of clergymen belonging to a cathedral or collegiate church; an organized branch of some fratrnity.

Char, chär, *vt.* (charring, charred). To reduce to a carbon by burning; to burn slightly.—*n.* A charred body; a lake fish or the salmon kind.

Character, ka'rak-tér, *n.* A mark engraved; a letter or figure; manner of writing; distinctive qualities of a person or thing; certificate of qualifications; a person in fiction or drama; a peculiar person.

Charade, sha-räd', *n.* A species of riddle upon the syllables of a word.

Charcoal, chär'kōl, *n.* Coal made by charring wood; the residue of animal, vegetable, and many mineral substances, when heated to redness in close vessls.

Charge, chärj, *vt.* (charging, charged). To load; to put a price on; to entrust; to impute, as a debt or crime; to command; to confide; to attack.—*vi.* To make a charge or onset.—*n.* That which is laid on; that which loads a rifle, etc.; an assault or onset; order; instruction; person or thing committed to another's care; accusation; cost.

Chargé d'affaires, shär-zhä dä-fär, *n.* One who transacts diplomatic business in place of an ambassador.

Chariot, cha'ri-ot, *n.* A stately carriage with four wheels.

Charioteer, cha'ri-ot-ēr'', *n.* The person who drives or conducts a chariot.

Charitable, cha'rit-a-bl, *a.* Liberal to the poor; pertaining to charity; indulgent.

Charitably, cha'rit-a-bli, *adv.* In a charitable manner; kindly; liberally.

Charity, cha'ri-ti, *n.* A disposition to relieve the wants of others; benevolence; alms; a charitable institution.

Charlatan, shär'la-tan, *n.* A quack.

Charm, chärm, *n.* A spell; fascination; a locket, etc.—*vt.* To enthrall; to delight.

Chart, chärt, *n.* A map; delineation of coasts, etc.; tabulated facts.

Charter, chär'tér, *n.* A writing given as evidence of a grant, contract, etc.—*vt.* To establish by charter; to hire or to let (a ship).

Chary, chā'ri, *a.* Careful; wary; frugal.

Chase, chās, *vt.* (chasing, chased). To pursue; to hunt; to enchase; to cut into the form of a screw. —*n.* Pursuit; hunt; that which is pursued; a printer's frame.

Chasm, kazm, *n.* A wide opening; an abyss.

Chaste, chāst, *a.* Free from impure desires; undefiled; pure in taste and style.

Chasten, chās'n, *vt.* To afflict in order to reclaim; to chastise; to correct.

Chastise, chas-tīz', *vt.* (chastising, chastised). To correct by punishment.

Chastity, chas'ti-ti, *n.* Purity of the body, mind, language, and style.

Chasuble, chas'ū-bl, *n.* A priest's uppermost vestment when celebrating the eucharist.

Chat, chat, *vi.* (chatting, chatter). To talk familiarly.—*n.* Familiar talk; a small song-bird.

Château, shä'tō, *n.* A castle; a country seat.

Chattel, chat'el, *n.* Any article of movable goods; in law, all goods except such as have the nature of freehold.

Chatter, chat'ér, *vi.* To make a noise by repeated clashing of the teeth; to jabber.—*n.* Sounds like those of a magpie or monkey; idle talk.

Chauffeur, shō'fér, *n.* A person regularly employed to drive a private motor-car.

Chauvinism, shō'vin-izm, *n.* Absurdly exaggerated patriotism or military enthusiasm.

Cheap, chēp, *a.* Of a low price; common; not respected.

Cheat, chēt, *vt.* To defraud; to deceive.—*n.* A deceitful act; a swindler.

Check, chek, *vt.* To stop; to curb; to chide; to compare with corresponding evidence.—*vi.* To stop, to clash or interfere.—*n.* An attack made on the king in chess; a stop; control; a counterfoil; a token; a cheque; cloth with a square pattern.

Checkmate, chek'māt, *n.* A move in chess which ends the game; defeat.—*vt.* To give checkmate

to; to frustrate; to defeat.

Cheddar, ched'ér, *n.* A rich English cheese.

Cheek, chēk, *n.* The side of the face below the eyes on each side; impudence.

Cheep, chēp, *vi.* and *t.* To pule; to chirp.—*n.* A chirp.

Cheer, chēr, *n.* Expression of countenance; gaiety; viands; a shout of joy.—*vt.* To brighten the countenance of; to gladden; to applaud.—*vi.* To grow cheerful

Cheese, chēz, *n.* Coagulated milk pressed into a firm mass, and used as food; anything in the form of cheese.

Chef, shef, *n.* A head cook.

Chemise, she-mēz', *n.* An under garment worn by women.

Chemistry, kem'ist-ri, *n.* The science which treats of the properties and nature of elementary substances.

Cherish, che'rish, *vt.* To treat with tenderness; to encourage.

Cheroot, she-röt', *n.* A kind of cigar with both ends cut square off.

Cherry, che'ri, *n.* A tree and its fruit, of the plum family.—*a.* Like a cherry in color.

Cherub, che'rub, *n.*; pl. **-ubs** and **-ubim.** An angel of the second order; a beautiful child.

Chess, ches, *n.* A game played by two, with 16 pieces each on a board of 64 squares.

Chest, chest, *n.* A large close box; the part of the body containing the heart, lungs, etc.—*vt.* To reposit in a chest.

Chestnut, ches'nut, *n.* A kind of tree; its fruit or nut; a stale joke or anecdote.—*a.* Of the color of a chestnut; reddish-brown.

Chew, chō, *vt.* To grind with the teeth; to masticate.

Chic, shēk, *n.* Easy elegance; smartness.

Chicane, Chicanery, shi-kān', shi-kān'é-ri, *n.* Trickery; artifice.—*Chicane, vt.* (chicaning, chicaned). To use chicane or artifices.

Chick, Chicken, chik, chik'en, *n.* The young of various birds; a child.

Chicken-pox, chik'en-poks, *n.* An eruptive disease, generally appearing in children.

Chicory, chik'o-ri, *n.* A common English plant, often used to mix with coffee.

Chide, chīd, *vt.* and *i.* (chiding, pret. chid, pp. chid, chidden). To reprove; to scold.

Chief, chēf, *a.* Being at the head; first; leading.— *n.* A principal person; a leader.

Chilblain, chil'blān, *n.* A blain or sore produced on the hands and feet by cold.

Child, chīld, *n.*; pl. **Children.** An infant; one very young; a son or daughter; offspring.

Childbirth, chīld'bérth, *n.* The act of bringing forth a child; travail; labor.

Chill, chil, *n.* A shivering with cold; a cold fit; that which checks or disheartens.—*a.* Cold; tending to cause shivering; dispiriting.—*vt.* To make cold; to discourage.

Chime, chīm, *n.* A set of bells tuned to each other; their sound; harmony; the brim of a cask. —*vi.* (chiming, chimed). To sound in consonance; to agree.—*vt.* To cause to sound in harmony; to cause to sound.

Chimera, ki-mē'ra, *n.* A fire-breathing monster of fable; a vain or idle fancy.

Chimere, shi-mēr', *n.* A bishop's upper robe, to which the lawn sleeves are attached.

Chimerical, ki-me'rik-al, *a.* Wildly or vainly conceived.

Chimney, chim'nē, *n.* The funnel through which the smoke is conveyed; a flue; a glass funnel for a lamp, etc.

Chimpanzee, chim'pan-zē, *n.* A large W. African ape.

Chin, chin, *n.* The lower part of the face; the point of the under jaw.

China, chi'na, *n.* A species of fine porcelain.

Chinchilla, chin-chil'la, *n.* A genus of S. American rodent animals; their fur.

Chinese, chī-nēz', *n. sing.* and *pl.* A native of

China; the language of China.

Chink, chingk, *n.* A narrow opening; a cleft; a sharp metallic sound; money.—*vi.* To crack; to make a sound as by the collision of coins.—*vt.* To jingle, as coins.

Chintz, chints, *n.* Cotton cloth printed with colored designs.

Chip, chip, *n.* A fragment; a small piece.—*vt.* (chipping, chipped). To cut into chips; to cut off chips.—*vi.* To fly off in small pieces.

Chirography, kī-rog'ra-fi, *n.* Handwriting; fortune-telling by examination of the hand.

Chiropodist, kir-op'od-ist, *n.* One who extracts corns, removes bunions, etc.

Chirp, chėrp, *vi.* To make the lively noise of small birds.—*n.* A short, shrill note of birds.

Chisel, chiz'el, *n.* A cutting tool, used in woodwork, masonry, sculpture, etc.—*vt.* (chiselling, chiselled). To cut, gouge, or engrave with a chisel.

Chit, chit, *n.* A note; an order or pass.

Chivalry, shi'val-ri, *n.* Knighthood; customs pertaining to the orders of knighthood; heroic defense of life and honor.

Chloral, klō'ral, *n.* An oily liquid produced from chlorine and alcohol; a narcotic.

Chloride, klō'rid, *n.* A compound of chlorine and some other substance.

Chlorine, klō'rīn, *n.* A gaseous substance obtained from common salt, used in bleaching and disinfecting.

Chlorodyne, klō'rō-dīn, *n.* An anodyne, containing morphia, chloroform, and prussic acid.

Chloroform, klō'rō-form, *n.* A volatile thin liquid, used as an anesthetic.

Chlorophyll, klō'rō-fil, *n.* The green coloring matter of plants.

Chocolate, cho'kō-lāt, *n.* A preparation from the kernels of the cacao-nut.—*a.* Dark, glossy brown.

Choice, chois, *n.* Act of choosing; option; the thing chosen; best part of anything; the object of choice.—*a.* Select; precious.

Choir, kwīr, *n.* A body of singers in a church; part of a church set apart for the singers.

Choke, chōk, *vt.* (choking, choked). To strangle by compressing the throat of; to block up; to stiffle.—*vi.* To be suffocated; to be blocked up.

Choler, ko'lėr, *n.* Anger; wrath.

Cholera, ko'lė-ra, *n.* A disease accompanied by purging and vomiting.

Choose, chöz, *vt.* (choosing, pret. chose, pp. chosen). To take by preference.—*vi.* To make choice; to prefer.

Chop, chop, *vt.* (chopping, chopped). To cut into small pieces; to barter or exchange.—*vi.* To change; to turn suddenly.—*n.* A piece chopped off; a small piece of meat; a crack or cleft; a turn or change; the jaw; the mouth.

Chopsticks, chop'stiks, *n.* Two sticks of wood, ivory, etc., used by the Chinese in eating.

Chord, kord, *n.* String of a musical instrument; the simultaneous combination of different sounds; a straight line joining the ends of the arc of a circle or curve.

Chorus, kō'rus, *n.* A company of singers; a piece performed by a company in concert; verses of a song in which the company join the singer; any union of voices in general.

Chosen, chōz'n, *a.* Select; eminent.

Chrism, krizm, *n.* Consecrated oil.

CHRIST, krīst, *n.* THE ANOINTED; the Messiah; the Saviour.

Christen, kris'n, *vt.* To baptize; to name.

Christendom, kris'n-dum, *n.* The countries inhabited by Christians; the whole body of Christians.

Christian, kris'ti-an, *n.* A professed follower of Christ.—*a.* Pertaining to Christ or Christianity.

Christmas, kris'mas, *n.* The festival of Christ's nativity, observed annually on 25th December.—*a.* Belonging to Christmas time.

Chromatic, kō-mat'ik, *a.* Relating to color; proceeding by semitones.

Chrome, Chromium, krōm, krō'mi-um, *n.* A steel-gray, hard metal, from which colored preparations are made.

Chronic, kron'ik, *a.* Continuing a long time; lingering; continuous.

Chronicle, kron'i-kl, *n.* An historical account of events in order of time.—*vt.* (chronicling, chronicled). To record.

Chronology, kro-nol'o-ji, *n.* Arrangement of events according to their dates.

Chronometer, kro-nom'et-ėr, *n.* An instrument that measures time.

Chrysalis, kris'a-lis, *n.*; pl. **-ides** or **-ises**. The form of certain insects before they arrive at their winged state.

Chrysanthemum, kri-san'thē-mum, *n.* The name of numerous composite plants.

Chub, chub, *n.* A small river fish of the carp family.

Chubby, chub'i, *a.* Round or full-cheeked; plump; having a large fat face.

Chuck, chuk, *vi.* To make the noise of a hen.—*vt.* To call, as a hen her chickens; to tap under the chin; to throw with quick motion; to pitch.—*n.* The call of a hen; a slight blow under the chin; a short throw.

Chuckle, chuk'l, *vi.* (chuckling, chuckled). To laugh in the throat; to feel inward triumph or exultation.—*n.* A short and suppressed laugh in the throat.

Chunk, chungk, *n.* A short, thick piece.

Church, chėrch, *n.* A house consecrated to the worship of God among Christians; the collective body of Christians; a particular body of Christians; the body of clergy; ecclesiastical authority.—*vt.* To give or receive a service in church, as after childbirth.

Churl, chėrl, *n.* A rude, ill-bred man; a rustic laborer; a miser.

Churn, chėrn, *n.* a vessel in which butter is made.—*vt.* To agitate cream for making butter; to shake with violence.

Chyle, kil, *n.* A milky fluid separated from aliments in the intestines and entering the blood.

Chyme, kim, *n.* The pulp of partially digested food before the chyle is extracted.

Cicatrix, Cicatrice, si-kā'triks, sik'a-tris, *n.* A scar; a mark of a wound or ulcer.

Cider, sī'dėr, *n.* A fermented drink prepared from the juice of apples.

Cigar, si-gär', *n.* A roll of tobacco for smoking.

Cigarette, sig-a-ret', *n.* A little cut tobacco rolled up in rice paper, used for smoking.

Cilia, sil'i-a, *n.pl.* Minute hairs on plants or animals.

Ciliary, sil'i-a-ri, *a.* Belonging to or of the nature of eyelashes.

Cimmerian, sim-mē'ri-an, *a.* Pertaining to the fabulous Cimmerians, who dwelt in perpetual darkness; extremely dark.

Cinchona, sin-kō'na, *n.* A genus of S. American trees whose bark yields quinine; Peruvian bark.

Cincture, singk'tūr, *n.* A girdle.

Cinder, sin'dėr, *n.* A burned coal; an ember; a piece of dross or slag.

Cinema, sin'e-ma, *n.* A picture-house or theater for the exhibition of moving pictures.

Cinerary, si'ne-ra-ri, *a.* Pertaining to ashes.

Cingalese, sing'ga-lēz, *a.* Pertaining to Ceylon.

Cinnabar, sin'na-bär, *n.* Red sulphide of mercury; vermilion.

Cinnamon, sin'na-mon, *n.* The inner bark of a tree, a native of Ceylon; a spice.

Cipher, sī'fėr, *n.* The figure 0 or nothing; any numeral; a person or thing of no importance; a device; a secret writing.—*vi.* To use figures.—*vt.* To write in secret characters.

Circle, sėr'kl, *n.* A plane figure contained by a curved line, every point of which is equally distant from a point within the figure, called the center; the curved line itself; a ring; enclosure;

a class; a coterie.—vt. (circling, circled). To move round; to enclose.—vi. To move circularly.

Circuit, sêr'kit, n. Act of going round; space measured by travelling round; the journey of judges to hold courts; the district visited by judges; path of an electric current.

Circular, sêr'kū-lêr, a. Round; addressed to a number of persons.—n. A paper addressed to a number of persons.

Circulate, sêr'kū-lāt, vi. (circulating, circulated). To move in a circle; to have currency.—vt. To spread; to give currency to.

Circumcise, sêr'kum-sīz, vt. (circumcising, circumcised). To cut off the foreskin, according to Jewish and Mohammedan law.

Circumference, sêr-kum'fē-rens, n. The bounding line of a circle.

Circumflex, sêr'kum-fleks, n. An accent on long vowels, generally marked thus (̂).

Circumfuse, sêr-kum-fūz', vt. To pour round; to spread round.

Circumlocution, sêr-kum'lō-kū''shon, n. A roundabout mode of speaking.

Circumnavigate, sêr-kum-na'vi-gāt, vt. To sail round.

Circumscribe, sêr'kum-skrīb, vt. To draw a line round; to limit; to restrict.

Circumspect, sêr'kum-spekt, a. Watchful on all sides; wary; thoughtful.

Circumstance, sêr'kum-stans, n. Something attending, or relative to a main fact or case; event; (pl.) state of affairs; condition.

Circumvent, sêr-kum-vent', vt. To encompass; to outwit.

Circus, sêr'kus, n.; pl. -ses. Among the Romans, a place for horse-races; a place for feats of horsemanship and acrobatic displays.

Cirrus, sir'rus, n.; pl. **Cirri.** A tendril; a light fleecy cloud at a high elevation.

Cistern, sis'têrn, n. An artificial receptacle for water, etc.; a natural reservoir.

Citadel, sit'ta-del, n. A fortress in or near a city.

Citation, sī-tā'shon, n. Quotation; a summons.

Cite, sīt, vt. (citing, cited). To summon to appear in a court; to quote; to adduce.

Citizen, si'ti-zen, n. An inhabitant of a city; one who has full municipal and political privileges.—a. Having the qualities of a citizen.

Citric, sit'rik, a. Belonging to citrons, or to lemons or limes.

Citrine, sit'rin, n. A yellow pellucid variety of quartz.

Citron, sit'ron, n. The fruit of the citron tree, a large species of lemon; the tree itself.

City, si'ti, n. A large town; a borough or town corporate; the inhabitants of a city.

Civic, si'vik, a. Pertaining to a city or citizen; relating to civil affairs.

Civil, si'vil, a. Relating to the government of a city or state; polite; political; lay; legislative, not military; intestine, not foreign.

Civilian, si-vil'i-an, n. One skilled in the civil law; one engaged in civil, not military or clerical pursuits.

Civility, si-vil'i-ti, n. Quality of being civil; good breeding; (pl.) acts of politeness.

Civilize, si'vil-īz, vt. (civilizing, civilized). To reclaim from a savage state.

Claim, klām, vt. To ask; to demand as due.—n. A demand as of right; a title to something in the possession of another; a pretension.

Clairvoyance, klār-voi'ans, n. A power attributed to a mesmerised person, by which he discerns objects concealed from sight, etc.

Clam, klam, vt. (clamming, clammed). To smear with viscous matter.—n. A clamp; a bivalve shell-fish.

Clamant, klam'ant, a. Crying aloud; urgent.

Clamber, klam'bêr, vi. To climb with difficulty, or with hands and feet.

Clammy, klam'i, a. Sticky; adhesive.

Clamor, klam'êr, n. Loud and continued noise, uproar.—vi. To call aloud; to make importunate demands.

Clamp, klamp, n. A piece of timber or iron, used to strengthen or fasten; a heavy footstep.—vt. To fasten or strengthen with clamps; to tread heavily.

Clan, klan, n. A family; a tribe; a sect.

Clandestine, klan-des'tin, a. Secret; underhand.

Clang, klang, vt. or i. To make a sharp sound, as by striking metallic substances.—n. A loud sound made by striking together metallic bodies.

Clank, klangk, n. The loud sound made by the collison of metallic bodies.—vi. or t. To sound or cause to sound with a clank.

Clap, klap, vt. (clapping, clapped or clapt). To strike together so as to make a noise; to strike with something broad; to shut hastily; to pat.—vi. To move together suddenly with noise; to strike the hands together in applause.—n. A noise made by sudden collision; a sudden explosive sound; a striking of hands in applause.

Claret, kla'ret, n. A French red wine.—a. Of the color of claret wine.

Clarification, kla'ri-fi-kā''shon, n. The clearing of liquids by chemical means.

Clarify, kla'ri-fī, vt. (clarifying, clarified). To purify; to make clear.—vi. To become clear, pure, or fine.

Clarion, kla'ri-on, n. A kind of trumpet with a shrill tone.

Clarionet, Clarinet, kla'ri-on-et, kla'rin-et, n. A musical wind instrument of wood.

Clash, klash, vi. To make a noise by collision; to meet in opposition; to interfere.—vt. To strike noisily together.—n. Noisy collision; opposition.

Clasp, klasp, n. An embrace; a hook for fastening; a catch; a bar added to a military medal to commemorate a particular battle or campaign.—vt. To fasten together with a clasp; to inclose in the hand; to embrace closely.

Clasp-knife, klasp'nīf, n. A knife the blade of which folds into the handle.

Class, klas, n. A rank of persons or things; an order; a group.—vt. To arrange in classes.

Classic, klas'ik, a. Of the first rank; standard in literary quality; pertaining to Greek and Roman antiquity; pure in style.—n. An author of the first rank; a Greek or Roman author of this character; a work of the first rank.

Classification, klas'i-fi-kā''shon, n. Act of forming into a class or classes.

Classify, klas'i-fī, vt. (classifying, classified). To distribute into classes.

Clatter, klat'têr, vi. To make repeated rattling noises; to talk fast and idly.—vt. To cause to rattle.—n. A rattling, confused noise.

Clause, klaz, n. A member of a sentence; a distinct part of a contract, will, etc.

Claustrophobia, klas'trō-fo''bē-a, n. Morbid fear of confined spaces.

Clavicle, klav'i-kl, n. The collar-bone.

Claw, kla, n. The sharp hooked nail of an animal; that which resembles a claw.—vt. To scrape, scratch, or tear.

Clay, klā, n. A tenacious kind of earth; earth in general; the body.—vt. To cover with clay; to purify and whiten with clay, as sugar.

Clean, klēn, a. Free from dirt; pure.—adv. Quite; fully.—vt. To purify; to cleanse.

Cleanse, klenz, vt. (cleansing, cleansed). To make clean or pure; to free from guilt.

Clear, klēr, a. Bright; shining; open; fair; plain; shrill; cheerful; acute; free from debt; free from guilt; exempt.—adv. Manifestly; quite; indicating entire separation.—vt. To make clear; to free from obstructions or obscurity; to cleanse; to justify; to make gain as profit; to prepare, as waste land, for tillage or pasture; to leap over; to pay customs on a cargo.—vi. To become clear; to become fair; to exchange checks.

Clear-story, Clere-story, klēr'stō-ri, n. The upper story of a cathedral or church.

Cleat, klēt, n. A piece of wood or iron in a ship to

fasten ropes upon; a wedge.

Cleave, klēv, *vi.* (pret. clave, cleaved, pp. cleaved). To stick; to adhere.

Cleave, klēv, *vt.* (pret. clove, cleaved, cleft, pp. cloven, cleaved, cleft). To split; to sever.—*vi.* To part asunder.

Cleek, klēk, *n.* A large hook; an iron-headed club used in golf.

Clef, klef, *n.* A character prefixed to a staff in music to determine the pitch.

Cleft, kleft, *n.* A crevice; a fissure.

Clematis, klem'a-tis, *n.* The generic name of woody climbing plants.

Clement, kle'ment, *a.* Mild; humane.

Clench, klensh, *vt.* To secure; to confirm; to grasp.

Clergy, klėr'ji, *n.pl.* The body or order of men set apart to the service of God, in the Christian church.

Clericalism, kle'rik-al-izm, *n.* Clerical power to influence; sacerdotalism.

Clerk, klärk, *n.* A clergyman; one who reads the responses in church; one who is employed under another as a writer.

Clever, kle'vėr, *a.* Adroit; talented; excuted with ability.

Cliché, klē'shā, *n.* A hackneyed phrase.

Click, klik, *vi.* To make a small sharp noise, or a succession of such sounds.—*n.* A small sharp sound.

Client, klī'ent, *n.* A person under patronage; one who employs a lawyer.

Clientele, klī'en-tēl, *n.* One's clients collectively.

Cliff, klif, *n.* A precipice; a steep rock.

Climacteric, kli-mak-te'rik, *n.* A critical period in human life.

Climate, klī'māt, *n.* The condition of a country in respect of temperature, dryness, wind, etc.

Climax, klī'maks, *n.* A figure of rhetoric, in which the language gradually rises in strength and dignity; culmination; acme.

Climb, klīm, *vi.* To creep up step by step; to ascend.—*vt.* To ascent.

Clime, klīm, *n.* A region of the earth.

Clinch, klinsh, *vt.* To rivet; to clench; to make conclusive.—*n.* A catch; a pun.

Clincher, klinsh'ėr, *n.* A kind of nail; a conclusive argument.

Cling, kling, *vi.* (clinging, clung). To hang by twining round; to adhere closely.

Clinic, Clinical, klin'ik, klin'ik-al, *a.* Pertaining to a sick-bed.—*n.* One confined to bed.

Clink, klingk, *vt.* To cause to ring or jingle.—*vi.* To ring.—*n.* A sound made by the collision of small sonorous bodies.

Clinker, klingk'ėr, *n.* A partially vitrified brick; a mass of incombustible slag.

Clinometer, klīn-om'et-ėr, *n.* An instrument for measuring the dip of rock strata.

Clip, klip, *vt.* (clipping, clipped). To shear; to trim with scissors; to cut short.—*n.* Act or product of sheep-shearing.

Clique, klēk, *n.* A party; a coterie; a set.

Cloak, klōk, *n.* A loose outer garment; a disguise; a pretext.—*vt.* To cover with a cloak; to hide; to veil.

Clock, klok, *n.* An instrument which measures time.

Clod, klod, *n.* A lump of earth; a stupid fellow.—*vt.* (clodding, clodded). To pelt with clods.

Clog, klog, *vt.* (clogging, clogged). To hinder; to impede; to trammel.—*vi.* To be loaded.—*n.* Hindrance; a shoe with a wooden sole.

Cloister, klois'tėr, *n.* A monastery or nunnery; an arcade round an open court.—*vt.* To shut up in a cloister; to immure.

Close, klōz, *vt.* (closing, closed). To shut; to finish.—*vi.* To come close together; to end; to grapple; to come to an agreement.—*n.* End.

Close, klōs, *a.* Shut fast; tight; dense; near; stingy; trusty; intense; without ventilation; disposed to keep secrets.—*adv.* Tightly; in contact, or very near.—*n.* An inclosed place; precinct of a cathedral.

Clot, klot, *n.* A mass of soft or fluid matter concreted.—*vi.* (clotting, clotted). To become thick; to coagulate.

Cloth, kloth, *n.* A woven material or fabric; the covering of a table; the clerical profession.

Clothe, klōᴛʜ, *vt.* (clothing, clothed or clad). To put clothes on; to cover or spread over.

Cloud, kloud, *n.* A collection of visible vapor, suspended in the air; something similar to this; what obscures, threatens, etc.; a great multitude, a mass.—*vt.* To obscure; to darken; to sully; to make to appear sullen.—*vi.* To grow cloudy.

Clout, klout, *n.* A patch of cloth, leather, etc.; a rag; a blow.—*vt.* To patch; to join clumsily.

Clove, klōv, *n.* The dried spicy bud of an East Indian tree; the tree itself; a small bulb in a compound bulb, as in garlic.

Cloven-footed, Cloven-hoofed, klōv'n-fut-ed, klōv'n-höft, *a.* Having the foot or hoof divided into two parts, as the ox.

Clover, klō'vėr, *n.* A leguminous plant with three-lobed leaves.

Clown, kloun, *n.* An awkward country fellow; a lout; a professional jester.

Cloy, kloi, *vt.* To glut; to fill to loathing.

Club, klub, *n.* A cudgel; a card of the suit marked with trefoils; a staff with a heavy head for driving the ball in golf, etc.; an association for some common object; the meeting-place of such an association.—*vt.* To beat with a club.—*vi.* To join for some common object.

Club-footed, klub'fut-ed, *a.* Having short, crooked, or deformed feet.

Cluck, kluk, *vi.* To make the noise of the hen when calling chickens.—*n.* Such a sound.

Clue, klö, *n.* A ball of thread; a thread serving to guide; something helping to unravel a mystery.

Clump, klump, *n.* A lump; a cluster of trees or shrubs.

Clumsy, klum'zi, *a.* Unwieldy; ungainly; rude in make.

Cluster, klus'tėr, *n.* A bunch, as of grapes; a knot; a small crowd.—*vi.* To be or to keep close together; to grow in bunches; to collect in masses.—*vt.* To collect into a body.

Clutch, kluch, *vt.* To seize hold of; to grasp.—*n.* A grasp; talon; a merciless hand; something that holds fast.

Clutter, klut'tėr, *n.* A confused noise; a bustle.—*vt.* To crowd together in disorder.—*vi.* To make a bustle.

Coach, kōch, *n.* A large four-wheeled close vehicle; a tutor.—*vi.* To ride in a coach; to tutor.

Coagulate, kō-ag'ū-lāt, *vt.* (coagulating, coagulated). To change from a fluid into a fixed state.—*vi.* To curdle; to congeal.

Coal, kōl, *n.* Any combustible substance in a state of ignition; charcoal; a solid, black, fossil substance used as fuel.—*vt.* or *i.* To supply with coals; to take in coals.

Coalesce, kō-al-es', *vi.* (coalescing, coalesced). To grow together; to unite.

Coalition, kō-al-i'shon, *n.* Act of coalescing; union of persons, parties, etc., into one body; alliance; confederation.

Coarse, kōrs, *a.* Rude; not refined; crude; inelegant; gross.

Coast, kōst, *n.* The sea-shore; the country near the sea.—*vi.* To sail along a shore; to sail from port to port.

Coat, kōt, *n.* An upper garment; vesture, as indicating office; hair or fur covering of animals; a layer; a covering; that on which ensigns armorial are portrayed.—*vt.* To cover; to spread over.

Coax, kōks, *vt.* To wheedle; to persuade by fondling and flattering.

Cob, kob, *n.* A round knob; the head of clover or wheat; a smallish thick-set horse; a male swan.

Cobalt, kō'balt, *n.* A mineral of grayish color, and a metal obtained from it yielding a permanent blue; the blue itself.

Cobble, kob´l, *vt.* (cobbling, cobbled). To mend coarsely, as shoes; to botch.—*n.* A roundish stone.

Coble, kō´bl, *n.* A flattish-bottomed boat.

Cobra, Cobra-de-capello, kob´ra, kob´ra-de-ka-pel´lō, *n.* A hooded venomous snake.

Cobweb, kob´web, *n.* A spider's net; something flimsy.

Coca, kō´ka, *n.* The dried leaf of a S. American plant which gives power of enduring fatigue.

Cocaine, kō´ka-in, *n.* The active principle of coca, used as a local anesthetic.

Cochineal, ko´chi-nēl, *n.* An insect which forms a scarlet dye; a dye-stuff consisting of the bodies of these insects.

Cock kok, *n.* The male of the domestic fowl; the male of other birds; a vane; a person or thing having resemblance to a cock; a chief man; a tap for drawing off liquids; the hammer of a gun; a small pile of hay.—*vt.* To set erect; to set on the head with an air of pertness; to draw back the cock of a gun.

Cockatoo, kok-a-tō´, *n.* A crested bird of the parrot family.

Cockle, kok´l, *n.* A weed that chokes corn; a small shell-fish.—*vi.* or *t.* To wrinkle; to shrink.

Cockney, kok´nē, *n.* An effeminate citizen; a native of London.—*a.* Pertaining to a cockney.

Cockroach, kok´rōch, *n.* The black beetle.

Cock's-comb, koks´kōm, *n.* The comb of a cock; a plant. *See* Coxcomb.

Cocktail, kok´tāl, *n.* A species of beetle; a half-bred horse; a short drink or appetizer, usually consisting of gin, bitters, and some flavoring, and often iced.

Coco, Cocoa, kō´kō, *n.* A tropical palm-tree.

Cocoa, kō´kō, *n.* The seed of the cacao prepared for a beverage; the beverage itself.

Coco-nut, Cocoa-nut, kō´kō nut, *n.* The fruit of the coco palm.

Cocoon, kō´kōn´, *n.* The silky case in which the silkworm involves itself when still a larva; the envelope of other larvae.

Cod, kod, *n.* A species of sea fish allied to the haddock; a husk; a pod.

Coddle, kod´l, *vt.* (coddling, coddled). To fondle.

Code, kōd, *n.* A digest of laws; a collection of rules; a system of signals, etc.

Codicil, ko´di-sil, *n.* A writing by way of supplement to a will.

Codify, kōd´i-fī, *vt.* (codifying, codified). To reduce to a code.

Codling, kod´ling, *n.* A young codfish.

Cod-liver oil, kod´li-vėr oil, *n.* A medicinal oil obtained from the livers of the cod.

Coefficient, kō-ef-fi´shent, *a.* Jointly efficient; co-operating.—*n.* That which co-operates; a number or quantity that multiplies or measures another.

Coerce, kō-ėrs´, *vt.* (coercing, coerced). To restrain by force; to compel.

Coeval, kō-ē´val, *a.* Of the same age; contemporary.—*n.* One of the same age.

Coexist, kō-egz-ist´, *vi.* To live at the same time with another.

Coffee, kof´i, *n.* A tree and its fruit or berries; a beverage made from the seeds.

Coffee-house, kof´i-hous, *n.* A house where coffee and refreshments are supplied.

Coffer, kof´ėr, *n.* A chest for holding gold, jewels, etc.

Coffer-dam, kof´ėr-dam, *n.* A case of piling, water-tight, serving to exclude water in laying the foundations of piers, bridges, etc.

Coffin, kof´fin, *n.* The chest in which a dead human body is buried.—*vt.* To inclose in a coffin.

Cog, kog, *n.* The tooth of a wheel.—*vt.* (cogging, cogged). To furnish with cogs; to trick, deceive; to manipulate dice unfairly.—*vi.* To cheat; to lie.

Cogent, kō´jent, *a.* Forcible; convincing.

Cogitate, ko´jit-āt, *vi.* (cogitating, cogitated). To ponder; to meditate.

Cognac, kō´nyak, *n.* A kind of brandy.

Cognate, kog´nāt, *a.* Born of the same stock; akin; of the same nature.

Cognition, kog-ni´shon, *n.* Knowledge from personal view or experience.

Cognizable, kog´niz-a-bl, *a.* That may be known; that may be tried and determined.

Cognizance, kog´niz ans, *n.* Knowledge; judicial notice; trial, or right to try; a badge.

Cognomen, kog-nō´men, *n.* A name added to a family name; a surname.

Cohabit, kō hab´it, *vi.* To dwell together; to live as husband and wife, though not married.

Cohere, kō-hēr´, *vi.* (cohering, cohered). To stick together; to be consistent.

Coherent, kō-hēr´ent, *a.* Sticking together; consistent.

Cohesion, kō-hē´zhon, *n.* Act of sticking together; the attraction by which bodies are kept together; coherence.

Coiffure, koif´ūr, *n.* Mode of dressing the hair in women.

Coil, koil, *vt.* To wind into a ring.—*n.* A ring or rings into which a rope, etc., is wound.

Coin, koin, *n.* A piece of metal stamped, as money; that which serves for payment.—*vt.* To stamp and convert metal into money; to mint; to invent; to fabricate.

Coincide, kō-in-sid´, *vi.* (coinciding, coincided). To agree in position; to happen at the same time; to concur.

Coition, kō-i´shon, *n.* Sexual intercourse.

Coke kōk, *n.* Coal charred and deprived of gas.—*vt.* (coking, coked). To turn into coke.

Cola, kō´la, *n.* An African tree with nuts containing much caffeine and yielding an invigorating beverage.

Colander, ko´lan-dėr, *n.* A strainer; sieve.

Cold, kōld, *a.* Not hot; chill; indifferent; reserved; stoical; unaffecting.—*n.* Absence of heat; sensation produced by the escape of heat; an ailment occasioned by cold.

Colic, kol´ik, *n.* A painful affection of the intestines.

Colitis, kō-lī´tis, *n.* Inflammation of the large intestine, especially of its mucous membrane.

Collaborator, kol-la´bo-rāt-ėr, *n.* An associate in literary or scientific labor.

Collapse, kol-laps´, *n.* A wasting of the body; a sudden and complete failure.—*vi.* (collapsing, collapsed). To fall together, as the sides of a vessel; to break down.

Collar, kol´ėr, *n.* A part of dress that surrounds the neck; something worn round the neck.—*vt.* To seize by the collar; to put a collar on; to roll up and bind with a cord.

Collar-bone, kol´ėr-bōn, *n.* Each of the two bones of the neck.

Collate, kol-lāt´, *vt.* (collating, collated). To lay together and compare, as books, etc.; to place in a benefice; to gather and place in order.—*vi.* To place in a benefice.

Collateral, kol-lat´er-al, *a.* Placed side by side; running parallel; descending from the same stock, but not one from the other; connected.—*n.* A kinsman.

Collator, kol-lāt´ėr, *n.* One who collates.

Colleague, kol´lēg, *n.* An associate in office.

Collect, kol´ekt, *n.* A short comprehensive prayer; a short prayer adapted to a particular occasion.

Collected, kol-lekt´ed, *p.a.* Cool; self-possessed.

Collectivism, kol-lek´tiv-izm, *n.* The doctrine that the state should own or control the land and all means of production.

College, kol´lej, *n.* A society of men, invested with certain powers, engaged in some common pursuit; a seminary of the higher learning; the building occupied for such purposes.

Collide, kol-lid´, *vi.* (colliding, collided). To strike against each other; to meet in opposition.

Collie, kol´i, *n.* A dog common in Scotland, much used for sheep.

Collier, kol´yėr, *n.* A ship that carries coals.

Collimate, kol'li-māt, *vt.* To adjust to the proper line of sight.

Collision, kol-li'zhon, *n.* Act of striking together; state of contrariety; conflict.

Collocate, kol'lō-kāt, *vt.* To place; to set; to station.

-lō-kā'shon, *n.* Act of collocating; disposition.

Collodion, kol-lō'di-on, *n.* A solution of gun-cotton in ether, forming a thin film.

Colloid, kol'loid, *a.* Like glue or jelly; *chem.* applied to uncrystallizable liquids.

Colloquial, kol-lō'kwi-al, *a.* Pertaining to common conversation or discourse.

Colloquy, kol'lō-kwi, *n.* A speaking together; mutual discourse; dialogue.

Collude, 'kol-lūd', *vi.* (colluding, colluded). To conspire in a fraud; to connive.

Colon, kō'lon, *n.* A mark of punctuation, thus (:); the largest of the intestines.

Colonel, kér'nel, *n.* The chief commander of a regiment of troops.

Colonial, ko-lō'ni-al, *a.* Pertaining to a colony.—*n.* A person belonging to a colony.

Colonize, ko'lon-iz, *vt.* (colonizing, colonized). To establish a colony in; to migrate to and settle in as inhabitants.

Colonnade, ko-lon-ād', *n.* A range of columns placed at regular intervals.

Colony, ko'lō-ni, *n.* A body of people transplanted from their mother country to inhabit some distant place; the country colonized.

Colophon, ko'lo-fon, *n.* An inscription or device formerly on the last page of a book, now usually in its preliminary pages.

Color, kul'ér, *n.* That which gives bodies different appearances independently of form; a pigment; complexion; appearance to the mind; pretense; (*pl.*) a flag.—*vt.* To give some kind of color to; to give a specious appearance to; to exaggerate in representation.—*vi.* To show color; to blush.

Color-blindness, kul'ér-blind-nes, *n.* Inability to distinguish colors.

Coloring, kul'ér-ing, *n.* Act of giving a color; color applied; a specious appearance; fair artificial representation.

Colossal, kō-los'al, *a.* Huge; gigantic.

Colossus, kō-los'us, *n.*; *pl.* **-lossi.** A statue of gigantic size.

Colporteur, kol'pōr-tér, *n.* One who travels for the sale or distribution of moral books, etc.

Colt, kōlt, *n.* A young male of the horse kind; a young foolish fellow.

Columbine, ko'lum-bin, *n.* A plant of the buttercup family; the female companion of Harlequin in pantomimes.

Columbium, kō-lum'bi-um, *n.* A rare metal.

Column, ko'lum, *n.* A pillar; a formation of troops, narrow in front, and deep from front to rear; a perpendicular section of a page; a perpendicular line of figures.

Colure, kō-lūr', *n.* Either of two great circles of the heavens, passing through the solstitial and the equinoctial points of the ecliptic.

Coma, kō'ma, *n.* Deep sleep; stupor; the hair-like envelope round the nucleus of a comet.

Comb, kōm, *n.* An instrument for separating hair, wool, etc.; the crest of a cock; honeycomb.—*vt.* To separate and adjust with a comb.

Combat, kom'bat, *vi.* To fight; to act in opposition.—*vt.* To oppose; to resist.—*n.* A fighting; an engagement; a duel.

Combine, kom-bin', *vt.* (combining, combined). To cause to unite; to join.—*vi.* To come into union; to coalesce; to league together.—kom'bin, *n.* A union.

Combustible, kom-bust'i-bl, *a.* Capable of catching fire; inflammable.—*n.* A substance easily set on fire.

Combustion, kom-bust'shon, *n.* A burning; chemical combination, attended with heat and light.

Come, kum, *vi.* (coming, pret. came, pp. come). To move hitherward; to draw nigh; to arrive; to happen; to appear; to rise; to result.

Comedian, ko-mē'di-an, *n.* An actor in or writer of comedies.

Comedy, ko'mē-di, *n.* A drama of the lighter kind.

Comely, kum'li, *a.* Good-looking; handsome; becoming.

Comestible, kom'es-ti-bl, *n.* An eatable.

Comet, kom'et, *n.* A heavenly body having a luminous tail or train.

Comfit, kum'fit, *n.* A sweetmeat.

Comfort, kum'fért, *vt.* To console; to gladden.—*n.* Consolation; relief; moderate enjoyment.

Comforter, kum'fért-ér, *n.* One who comforts; the Holy Spirit; a woollen scarf.

Comic, kom'ik, *a.* Relating to comedy; comical.

Coming, kum'ing, *p.a.* Future.—*n.* Approach.

Comity, ko'mi-ti, *n.* Courtesy; civility.

Comma, kom'ma, *n.* A mark of punctuation, thus (,); an interval in music.

Command, kom-mand', *vt.* To order; to govern; to have at one's disposal.—*vi.* To have chief power.—*n.* Order; control; power of overlooking; power of defending.

Commandment, kom-mand'ment, *n.* A command; a precept of the moral law.

Commando, kom-man'dō, *n.* A member of a body of troops specially trained and selected for hazardous enterprises.

Commemorate, kom-mem'o-rāt, *vt.* To call to remembrance by a solemn act; to celebrate with honor and solemnity.

Commence, kom-mens', *vi.* (commencing; commenced). To take the first step; to begin to be.—*vt.* To begin; to originate.

Commend, kom-mend', *vt.* To commit to the care of; to recommend; to praise.

Commensal, kom-men'sal, *n.* One that eats at the same table; one living with another.

Commensurate, kom-men'sūr-āt, *a.* Proportional; having equal measure.

Comment, kom-ment', *vi.* To make remarks or criticisms.—*vt.* To annotate.—*n.* kom'-ment. An explanatory note; criticism.

Commentary, kom'ment-a-ri, *n.* Book of comments; an historical narrative.

Commerce, kom'mérs, *n.* Exchange of goods by barter or purchase; trade; intercourse.

Commercial, kom-mér'shal, *a.* Pertaining to commerce; trading; mercantile.

Comminatory, kom-mi'na-to-ri, *a.* Threatening.

Commingle, kom-ming'gl, *vt.* To blend.—*vi.* To unite together.

Comminute, kom'mi-nūt, *vt.* To make small or fine; to pulverize.

Commiserate, kom-miz'é-rāt, *vt.* (commiserating, commiserated). To pity; to condole with.

Commissary, kom'mis-sa-ri, *n.* A delegate; an officer of a bishop; an officer who has the charge of furnishing provisions, clothing, etc., for an army.

Commission, kom-mi'shon, *n.* Trust; warrant; a written document, investing one with an office; allowance made to an agent, etc., for transacting business; a body of men joined in an office or trust, or their appointment; perpetration.—*vt.* To appoint; to depute.

Commissure, kom'mis-sūr, *n.* A joint or seam; juncture.

Commit, kom-mit', *vt.* (committing, committed). To intrust; to consign; to send to prison; to perpetrate; to endanger or compromise (oneself).

Committee, kom-mit'tē, *n.* A body of persons appointed to manage any matter.

Commix, kom-miks', *vt.* To blend; to mix.

Commode, kom-mōd', *n.* A kind of small sideboard; a lady's head-dress; a night-stool.

Commodious, kom-mō'di-us, *a.* Convenient; spacious and suitable.

Commodity, kom-mo'di-ti, *n.* Something useful; any article of commerce; (*pl.*) goods;; merchandise.

Commodore, kom'mo-dōr, *n.* A captain in the navy who is discharging duties rather more important than those usually assigned to a captain.

Common, kom'mon, *a.* Having no separate owner; general; usual; of no rank; of little value,—*n.* An open public ground; *pl.* the untitled people; the lower House of Parliament; food at a common table; food in general.

Commonplace, kom'mon-plās, *n.* A usual topic; a trite saying.—*a.* Ordinary; trite.

Common sense, kom'mon sens, *n.* Sound practical judgment.

Commonwealth, kom'mon-welth, *n.* The public good; the state; body politic; a form of government; a republic.

Commotion, kom-mō'shon, *n.* Violent agitation; tumultuous disorder.

Commune, kom'mūn, *n.* A small administrative district in France; a socialist body which ruled over Paris in 1871.

Communicable, kom-mū'ni-ka-bl, *a.* Capable of being imparted to another.

Communicant, kom-mū'ni-kant, *n.* One who communicates; a partaker of the Lord's supper.

Communicate, kom-mū'ni-kāt, *vt.* (communicating, communicated). To cause to be common to others; to impart, as news, disease, etc.; to bestow; to reveal.—*vi.* To share with others; to partake of the Lord's supper; to have intercourse; to correspond.

Communion, kom-mūn'yon, *n.* A mutual participation in anything; mutual intercourse; concord; celebration of the Lord's supper.

Communism, kom'mūn-izm, *n.* The doctrine of a community of property by which the state owns and controls all means of production.

Communist, kom'mūn-ist, *n.* One who holds the doctrines of communism; member of the communist party.

Community, kom-mū'ni-ti, *n.* Mutual participation; the public; a society of persons under the same laws.

Commutable, kom-mūt'a-bl, *a.* That may be exchanged; convertible into money.

Commute, kom-mūt', *vt.* (commuting, commuted). To exchange; to put one thing for another.

Compact, kom-pakt', *a.* Closely united; solid; dense; brief.—*vt.* To consolidate; to unite firmly.—*n.* kom'pakt. An agreement; a contract.

Companion, kom-pan'yon, *n.* A comrade; an associate; one of the third rank in an order of knighthood; a raised cover to the cabin stair of a merchant vessel.

Company, kum'pa-ni, *n.* Companionship; an assembly of persons; partners in a firm; a division of a battalion, consisting of four platoons, and commanded by a major or mounted captain, with a captain as second-in-command; the crew of a ship.—*vi.* To associate with.

Comparative, kom-pa'ra-tiv, *a.* Estimated by comparison; not positive or absolute.

Compare, kom-pār', *vt.* (comparing, compared). To bring together and examine the relations between; to estimate one by another; to inflect in the degrees of comparison.—*vi.* To hold comparison.

Comparison, kom-pa'ri-son, *n.* Act of comparing; state of being compared; relation; the formation of an adjective in its degrees of signification; a simile.

Compartment, kom-pärt'ment, *n.* A division or part of a general design.

Compass, kum'pas, *n.* A round; a circuit; limit; extent; range; an instrument for directing the course of ships; an instrument for describing circles (often in *pl.*).—*vt.* To pass round; to inclose; to obtain; to contrive.

Compassable, kum'pas-a-bl, *a.* Capable of being accomplished.

Compassion, kom-pa'shon, *n.* Fellow-suffering; pity; sympathy.

Compatible, kom-pat'i-bl, *a.* Consistent; suitable; not incongruous.

Compatriot, kom-pā'tri-ot, *n.* One of the same country.

Compeer, kom-pēr', *n.* An equal; an associate.

Compel, kom-pel', *vt.* (compelling, compelled). To drive; to urge; to necessitate.

Compellation, kom-pel-lā'shon, *n.* An addressing; a ceremonious appellation.

Compendium, kom-pen'di-um, *n.* An abridgment; a summary; an epitome.

Compensate, kom-pens'āt, *vi.* (compensating, compensated). To give equal value to; to make amends for; to requite.—*vt.* To make amends; to supply an equivalent.

Compete, kom-pēt', *vi.* (competing, competed). To strive for the same thing as another; to contend.

Competent, kom'pē-tent, *a.* Suitable, sufficient; qualified; having adequate right.

Competition, kom-pē-ti'shon, *n.* Contest for the same object; rivalry.

Compile, kom-pīl', *vt.* (compiling, compiled). To gather from various sources; to draw up by collecting parts from different authors.

Complacence, Complacency, kom-plā'sens, kom-plā'sen-si, *n.* A feeling of quiet satisfaction; complaisance.

Complain, kom-plān', *vi.* to express grief or distress; to lament; to express dissatisfaction; to make a formal accusation.

Complaisance, kom-plā-zans, *n.* A pleasing deportment; courtesy; urbanity.

Complement, kom'plē-ment, *n.* That which fills up; full quantity or number.

Complete, kom-plēt', *a.* Having no deficiency; finished; total; absolute.—*vt.* (completing, completed). To make complete; to finish; to fulfil.

Complex, kom'pleks, *a.* Of various parts; involved; composite.—*n.* A series of emotionally accentuated ideas in a repressed state.

Complexion, kom-plek'shon, *n.* The color of the face; general appearance.

Compliance, kom-plī'ans, *n.* Submission; consent.

Complicate, kom'pli-kāt, *vt.* (complicating, complicated). To make complex or intricate; to entangle.

Complicity, kom-plis'i-ti, *n.* State or condition of being an accomplice.

Compliment, kom'pli-ment, *n.* Act or expression of civility or regard; delicate flattery; a favor bestowed.—*vt.* To pay a compliment to; to congratulate; to praise.

Complot, kom'plot, *n.* A joint plot.—*vt.* and *i.* To plot together.

Comply, kom-plī', *vi.* (complying, complied). To yield; to assent; to acquiesce.

Component, kom-pōn'ent, *a.* Composing; forming an element of a compound.—*n.* A constituent part; ingredient.

Comport, kom-pōrt', *vi.* To agree; to suit.—*vt.* To bear or carry (oneself); to behave.

Compose, kom-pōz', *vt.* (composing, composed). To form by uniting; to constitute; to write, to calm; to set types in printing.

Composer, kom-pōz'ér, *n.* An author, especially a musical author.

Composite, kom'po-zit or -zit, *a.* Compound; noting a rich order of architecture; noting plants whose flowers are arranged in dense heads.

Compost, kom'pōst, *n.* A mixture for manure.

Composure, kom-pō'zhūr, *n.* A settled frame of mind; calmness; tranquillity.

Compound, kom-pound', *vt.* and *i.* To put together; to mix; to adjust; to discharge a debt by paying a part.—*a.* kom'pound. Composed of two or more ingredients, words, or parts.—*n.* A mass composed of two or more elements; inclosure in which houses stand.

Comprehend, kom-prē-hend', *vt.* To embrace within limits; to understand.

Comprehensive, kom-prē-hens'iv, *a.* Comprising much; capacious; able to understand.

Compress, kom-pres', *vt.* To press together; to

squeeze; to condense.—n. kom'pres. A soft mass or bandage used in surgery.

Compressible, kom-pres'i-bl, a. Capable of being compressed.

Comprise, kom-prīz, vt. (comprising, comprised). To embrace; to contain; to inclose.

Compromise, kom'prō-mīz, n. An amicable agreement to settle differences; mutual concession.—vi. To settle by mutual concessions; to involve; to endanger the interests of.

Comptroller, kon-trōl'ẽr, n. A controller; an officer who examines the accounts of collectors of public money.

Compulsion, kom-pul'shon, n. Act of compelling; state of being compelled; force.

Compulsory, kom-pul'so-ri, a. Constraining; co-ercive; obligatory.

Compunction, kom-pungk'shon, n. Remorse; contrition.

Compurgation, kom-pẽr-gā'shon, n. Act of justi-fying a man by the oath of others.

Compute, kom-pūt', vt. (computing, computed). To count; to estimate.

Comrade, kom'rād, n. A mate; a companion; an associate.

Con, kon, vt. (conning, conned). To learn; to fix in the mind; to peruse carefully; to direct the steering of (a ship).

Concatenate, kon-ka'tē-nāt, vt. To link together; to unite in a series.

Concave, kon'kāv, a. Hollow, as the inner surface of a sphere; opposed to convex.—n. A hollow; an arch or vault.

Conceal, kon-sēl', vt. To hide; to secrete; to dis-guise.

Concede, kon-sēd', vt. (conceding, conceded). To yield; to grant.—vi. To make concession.

Conceit, kon-sēt', n. Conception; fancy; self-flattering opinion; vanity.

Conceive, kon-sēv', vt. (conceiving, conceived). To form in the womb; to take into the mind; to comprehend.—vi. To become pregnant; to have or form an idea.

Concentrate, kon'sen-trāt, vt. (concentrating, concentrated). To bring together; to direct to one object; to condense.

Concentric, kon-sen'trik, a. Having a common center.

Concept, kon'sept, n. An object conceived by the mind; a general notion of a class of objects.

Conception, kon-sep'shon, n. Act of conceiving; state of being conceived; thing conceived; image in the mind; mental faculty which origi-nates ideas.

Conceptualist, kon-sep'tū-al-ist, n. One who holds that the mind can give independent exis-tence to general conceptions.

Concern, kon-sẽrn', vt. To belong to; to affect the interest of; to make anxious.—n. That which re-lates to one; affair; care; anxiety; a commercial establishment.

Concert, kon-sẽrt', vt. To plan together; to contrive.—n. kon'sẽrt. Agreement in a design; harmony; performance of a company of play-ers, singers, etc.

Concertina, kon-sẽrt-ē'na, n. A musical instru-ment of the accordion species.

Concerto, kon-chär'tō, n. A musical composition for one principal instrument, with accompani-ments for a full orchestra.

Concession, kon-se'shon, n. Act of conceding; the thing yielded; a grant.

Conch, kongk, n. A marine shell.

Conciliate, kon-si'li-āt, vt. (conciliating, concili-ated). To bring to friendliness; to win the favor or consent; to reconcile; to propitiate.

Concise, kon-sīs', a. Brief; abridged; comprehen-sive.

Conclave, kon'klāv, n. A private apartment; the assembly of cardinals for the election of a pope; a close assembly.

Conclude, kon-klūd', vt. (concluding, concluded). To end; to decide; to deduce.—vi. To end; to form

a final judgment.

Concoct, kon-kokt', vt. To devise; to plot.

Concomitance, Concomitancy, kon-kom'i-tans, kon-kom'i-tan-si, n. A being together or in con-nection with another thing.

Concord, kong'kord, n. Union in feelings, opin-ions, etc.; harmony; agreement of words in con-struction.

Concordance, kon-kord'ans, n. Agreement; index of the principal words of a book.

Concourse, kong'kōrs, n. Confluence; an assem-bly; crowd.

Concrete, kon'krēt, a. Composed of particles united in one mass; congealed; existing in a subject; not abstract.—n. A mass formed by concretion; a hard mass formed of lime, sand, etc.—vi. kon-krēt' (concreting, concreted). To unite in a mass; to become solid.

Concubine, kong'kū-bīn, n. A woman who co-habits with a man; a mistress.

Concupiscence, kon-kū'pis-ens, n. Lust.

Concur, kon-kẽr', vi. (concurring, concurred). To unite; to agree; to assent.

Concussion, kon-ku'shon, n. A violent shock.

Concussive, kon-kus'iv, a. Having the power or quality of shaking; agitating.

Condemn, kon-dem', vt. To pronounce to be wrong; to censure; to sentence.

Condense, kon-dens', vt. (condensing, con-densed). To reduce in compass; to reduce from a gaseous to a liquid or solid state.—vi. To be-come dense; to grow thick.

Condenser, kon-dens'ẽr, n. One who or that which condenses; a vessel in which vapors are re-duced to liquid by coldness; a chamber in which steam in condensed; an instrument for storing an electric charge.

Condescend, kon-dē-send', vi. To descend from the privileges of superior rank; to deign.

Condign, kon-dīn', a. Deserved; suitable.

Condiment, kon'di-ment, n. Seasoning; relish.

Condition, kon-di'shon, n. State; case; external circumstances; temper; stipulation.

Conditionally, kon-di'shon-al-li, adv. With cer-tain limitatons.

Condole, kon-dōl', vi. (condoling, condoled). To grieve with another; to sympathize.

Condone, kon-dōn', vt. (condoning, condoned). To pardon; to imply forgiveness of.

Condor, kon'dor, n. A S. American vulture.

Conduce, kon-dūs', vi. (conducing, conduced). To lead; to tend; to contribute.

Conduct, kon'dukt, n. Personal behavior; man-agement; escort.—vt. kon-dukt'. To lead or guide; to escort; to manage; to behave (oneself); to transmit, as heat, etc.

Conduction, kon-duk'shon, n. Property by which bodies transmit heat or electricity.

Conductor, kon-dukt'ẽr, n. A leader; a director; a body that transmits heat, electricity, etc.

Conduit, kon'dit or kun'dit, n. A channel or pipe to convey water, etc., or to drain off filth; a chan-nel or passage.

Cone, kōn, n. A solid body having a circle for its base, and tapering to a point; the fruit of firs, pine-trees, etc.

Confabulate, kon-fab'ū-lāt, vi. (confabulating, confabulated). To talk familiarly.

Confection, kon-fek'shon, n. A mixture; a sweet-meat.

Confectioner, kon-fek'shon-ẽr, n. One who makes or sells sweetmeats.

Confederacy, kon-fe'de-ra-si, n. A confederation; the parties united by a league.

Confederate, kon-fe'de-rāt, a. Allied by treaty.—n. One united with others in a league.—vt. and i. (confederating, confederated). To unite in a league.

Confederation, kon-fe'de-rā''shon, n. A league; alliance, particularly of states, etc.

Confer, kon-fẽr', vi. (conferring, conferred). To consult together.—vt. To give or bestow.

Conference, kon'fẽr-ens, n. A meeting for consultation, or for the adjustment of differences; bestowal.

Confess, kon-fes', vt. To own, as a crime, debt, etc.; to admit; publicly to declare adherence to; to hear a confession, as a priest.—vi. To make confession.

Confession, kon-fe'shon, n. Act of confessing; that which is confessed; a formulary of articles of faith; a creed.

Confessional, kon-fe'shon-al, n. The place where a priest sits to hear confessions.

Confetti, kon-fet'i, n. Small pieces of colored paper thrown at each other by revellers at carnivals, or at the bride and groom by wedding guests.

Confidant, kon'fi-dant, n.m.; **Confidante,** kon-fi-dant', n.f. A confidential friend.

Confide, kon-fid', vi. (confiding, confided). To trust wholly; to have firm faith (with in).—vt. To intrust; to commit to the charge of.

Confidence, kon'fi-dens, n. Firm belief or trust; self-reliance; boldness; assurance; a secret.

Confidential, kon-fi-den'shal, a. Enjoying confidence; trusty; private; secret.

Configuration, kon-fig'ūr-ā''shon, n. External form; contour.

Confine, kon'fin, n. Boundary; territory near the end; border (generally in pl.).—vt. kon-fin' (confining, confined). To restrain; to limit; to shut up; to imprison.—**To be confined,** to be in childbed.

Confirm, kon-ferm', vt. To make firm or more firm; to establish; to make certain; to administer the rite of confirmation to.

Confirmation, kon-ferm-ā'shon, n. Act of confirming; additional evidence; ratification; the laying on of a bishop's hands in the rite of admission to the privileges of a Christian.

Confiscate, kon'fis-kāt, vt. (confiscating, confiscated). To seize as forfeited to the public treasury.

Conflagration, kon-fla-grā'shon, n. A great fire.

Conflict, kon'flikt, n. a struggle; clashing of views or statements.—vi. kon-flikt'. To meet in opposition; to be antagonistic.

Confluence, kon'flū-ens, n. A flowing together; meeting, or place of meeting, of rivers; a concourse; a crowd.

Conform, kon-form', vt. To cause to be of the same form; to adapt.—vi. To comply.

Conformation, kon-for-mā'shon, n. The act of conforming; structure; configuration.

Conformist, kon-for'mist, n. One who conforms; one who complies with the worship of the established church.

Confound, kon-found', vt. To confuse; to astound; to overthrow; to mistake.

Confounded, kon-foun'ded, a. Excessive; odious; detestable; reprehensible.

Confraternity, kon-fra-ter'ni-ti, n. A brotherhood; a society or body of men.

Confrère, kong-frār, n. A colleague.

Confront, kon-frunt', vt. To face; to oppose; to bring into the presence of; to set together for comparison.

Confucian, kon-fū'shi-an, a. and n. Pertaining to, or a follower of, Confucius, the famous Chinese philosopher.

Confuse, kon-fūz', vt. (confusing, confused). To mix without order; to derange; to confound; to disconcert.

Confute, kon-fūt', vt. (confuting, confuted). To prove to be false; to refute.

Congé, kon'jē, n. Leave to depart; leavetaking; a bow. Also the form **Congee** (kon'jē), and sometimes as a verb: to take leave; to make a bow (congeeing, congeed).

Congeal, kon-jēl', vt. To freeze; to coagulate.—vi. To pass from a fluid to a solid state.

Congener, kon'je-ner, n. One of the same origin or kind.

Congenial, kon-jē'ni-al, a. Of like taste or disposition; kindly; adapted.

Congeniality, kon-jē'ni-al''i-ti, n. Natural affinity; suitableness.

Congenital, kon-jen'it-al, a. Pertaining to an individual from his birth.

Conger, kong'ger, n. The sea-eel.

Congeries, kon-jē'ri-ēz, n. A heap or pile; a collection of several bodies in one mass.

Congest, kon-jest', vt. and i. To accumulate to excess, as blood, population, etc.

Congestion, kon-jest'shon, n. Excessive accumulation; undue fullness of blood-vessels in an organ.

Conglobation, kon-glōb-ā'shon, n. Act of forming into a ball; a round body.

Conglomerate, kon-glom'er-āt, a. Gathered into a ball; composed of fragments of rock cemented together.—n. A rock composed of pebbles cemented together.—vt. To gather into a ball or round mass.

Congratulate, kon-grat'ū-lāt, vt. (congratulating, congratulated). To express sympathy to in good fortune; to felicitate.

Congregate, kong'grē-gāt, vt. (congregating, congregated). To collect together.—vi. To come together; to assemble.

Congregation, kong-grē-gā'shon, n. Act of congregating; an assembly; an assembly met for divine worhip.

Congregationalist, kong-grē-gā'shon-al-ist, n. One who adheres to the system in which each separate congregation or church forms an independent body.

Congress, kong'gres, n. An assembly; a meeting of ambassaors, etc., for the settlement of affairs between different nations; the legislature of the United States.

Congruence, **Congruency,** kong'gru-ens, kong'gru-en-si, n. Accordance; consistency.

Congruity, kon-gru'i-ti, n. Suitableness; accordance; consistency.

Conic, Conical, kon'ik, kon'ik-al, a. Having the form of a cone; pertaining to a cone.

Conics, kon'iks, n. That part of geometry which treats of the cone.

Coniferous, kon-if'er-us, a. Bearing cones, as the pine, fir, etc.

Conjecture, kon-jek'tūr, n. Supposition; opinion without proof; surmise.—vt. (conjecturing, conjectured). To judge by guess; to surmise.—vi. To form conjectures.

Conjoin, kon-join', vt. To join together; to unite; to associate.

Conjugal, kon'jū-gal, a. Pertaining to marriage; connubial.

Conjugate, kon'jū gāt, vt. (conjugating, conjugated). To join together; to inflect (a verb) through its several forms.—a. Joined in pairs; kindred in origin and meaning.

Conjunction, kon-jungk'shon, n. Act of joining; state of being joined; connection; a connecting word.

Conjuncture, kon-jungk'tūr, n. A combination of important events; a crisis.

Conjure, kon-jūr', vt. (conjuring, conjured). To call upon solemnly; to beseech.

Conjure, kon'jer, vt. (conjuring, conjured). To summon up by enchantments.—vi. To practice the arts of a conjurer.

Connate, kon'nāt, a. Born with another; being of the same birth; united in origin.

Connatural, kon-na'tūr-al, a. Connected by nature; innate; congenital.

Connect, kon-nekt', vt. To conjoin; to combine; to associate.—vi. To unite or cohere together; to have a close relation.

Connection, kon-nek'shon, n. Act of connecting; state of being connected; a relation by blood or marriage; relationship.

Connective, kon-nekt'iv, a. Having the power of connecting; tending to connect.—n. A word that connects other words and sentences; a conjunction.

Connivance, kon-niv'ans, n. Voluntary blindness

to an act; pretended ignorance.

Connive, kon-niv', *vi.* (conniving, connived). To wink; to pretend ignorance or blindness; to forbear to see (with *at*).

Connoisseur, kon'i-sūr, *n.* A judge of any art, particularly painting and sculpture.

Connotation, kon-ŏ-tā'shon, *n.* That which constitutes the meaning of a word.

Connote, kon-nōt', *vt.* (connoting, connoted). To include in the meaning; to imply.

Connubial, kon-nū'bi-al, *a.* Pertaining to marriage; conjugal; matrimonial.

Conoild, kŏn'oid, *n.* A body resembling a cone.— *a.* Resembling a cone. Also *conoidal.*

Conquer, kong'kér, *vt.* To gain by force; to vanquish; to subjugate; to surmount,—*vi.* To overcome; to gain the victory.

Conquest, kong'kwest, *n.* Act of conquering; that which is conquered; a gaining by struggle.

Conscience, kon'shens, *n.* Internal knowledge or judgment of right and wrong; the moral sense; morality.

Conscionable, kon'shon-a-bl, *a.* Reasonable.

Conscious, kon'shus, *a.* Knowing in one's own mind; knowing by sensation or perception; aware; sensible; self-conscious.

Consciousness, kon'shus-nes, *n.* State of being conscious; perception of what passes in one's own mind; sense of guilt or innocence.

Conscript, kon'skript, *a.* Registered; enrolled.— *n.* One compulsorily enrolled to serve in the army or navy.

Consecrate, kon'sē-kr āt, *vt.* (consecrating, consecrated). To appropriate to sacred uses; to dedicate to God.—*a.* Sacred; consecrated.

Consecutive, kon-sek'ū-tiv, *a.* Following in regular order; following logically.

Consent, kon-sent', *n.* Agreement to what is proposed; concurrence; compliance.—*vi.* To be of the same mind; to assent; to comply.

Consentient, kon-sen'shi-ent, *a.* Consenting; agreeing; accordant.

Consequence, kon'sē-kwens, *n.* That which follows as a result; inference; importance.

Consequent, kon'sē-kwent, *a.* Following, as the natural effect, or by inference.—*n.* Effect; result; inference.

Consequential, kon-sē-kwen'shal, *a.* Following as the effect; pompous.

Conservation, kon-sérv-ā'shon, *n.* Preservation; the keeping of a thing entire.

Conservative, kon-sérv'at-iv, *a.* Preservative; adhering to existing institutions.—*n.* One opposed to political changes of a radical nature; a Tory.

Conservatoire, kong-sér-vä-twär, *n.* A public establishment for the study of music.

Conservator, kon-sérv-āt-ér, *n.* A preserver; a custodian; a guardian.

Conservatory, kon-sérv'a-to-ri, *n.* A greenhouse for exotics.

Conserve, kon-sérv', *vt.* (conserving, conserved). To keep in a sound state; to candy or pickle.—*n.* kon'sérv. That which is conserved, particularly fruits.

Consider, kon-si'dér, *vt.* To fix the mind on; to ponder; to have respect to; to regard to be.—*vi.* To think seriously; to ponder.

Considerable, kon-si'dér-a-bl, *a.* Worthy of consideration; moderately large.

Considerate, kon-si'dér-āt, *a.* Given to consideration; mindful of others; deliberate.

Considerately, kon-si'dér-āt-li, *adv.* In a considerate manner.

Consideration, kon-si'dér-ā''shon, *n.* Mental view; serious deliberation; importance; motive of action; an equivalent.

Considering, kon-si'dér-ing, *prep.* Taking into account; making allowance for.

Consign, kon-sin', *vt.* To deliver over to another by agreement; to intrust; to commit; to deposit.

Consist, kon-sist', *vi.* To be in a fixed state; to be comprised; to be made up; to be compatible; to agree.

Consistence, Consistency, kon-sis'tens, kon-sis'ten-si, *n.* A degree of density; firmness or coherence, harmony; agreement.

Consistent, kon-sis'tent, *a.* Fixed; firm; not contradictory; compatible.

Consistory, kon'sis-to-ri, *n.* A spiritual court; the court of a diocesan bishop; college of cardinals.

Consociation, kon-sō'shi-ā''shon, *n.* Association; alliance; fellowship.

Consolation, kon-sōl-ā'shon, *n.* A solace; alleviation of misery; what helps to cheer; what gives comfort.

Console, kon-sōl', *vt.* (consoling, consoled). To comfort; to soothe; to cheer.

Console, kon'sōl, *n.* A bracket to support a cornice, vase, etc.

Consolidate, kon-sol'id-āt, *vt.* (consolidating, consolidated). To make solid or firm; to unite into one; to compact.—*vi.* To grow firm and solid.

Consonance, kon'sō-nans, *n.* Concord; agreement; consistency.

Consonant, kon'sō-nant, *a.* Having agreement; accordant; consistent.—*n.* A letter always sounded with a vowel.

Consort, kon'sort, *n.* A partner; a wife or husband; a companion.—*vi.* kon-sort'. To associate; to accord.

Conspectus, kon-spek'tus, *n.* A comprehensive view of a subject; abstract or sketch.

Conspicuous, kon-spik'ū-us, *a.* Standing clearly in view; manifest; distinguished.

Conspiracy, kon-spi'ra-si, *n.* A plot; a treasonable combination.

Conspire, kon-spīr', *vi.* (conspiring, conspired). To plot; to combine for some evil purpose; to tend to one end.

Constable, kun'sta-bl, *n.* An officer of the peace; policeman.

Constant, kon'stant, *a.* Steadfast; perpetual; assiduous; resolute.—*n.* That which remains unchanged; a fixed quantity.

Constellation, kon-stel-lā'shon, *n.* A group of fixed stars; an assemblage of splendors or excellences.

Consternation, kon-stér-nā'shon, *n.* Prostration of the mind by terror, dismay, etc.

Constipate, kon'sti-pāt, *vt.* (constipating, constipated). To make costive.

Constituent, kon-stit'ū-ent, *a.* Forming; existing as an essential part.—*n.* An elector; an essential part.

Constitute, kon'sti-tūt, *vt.* (constituting, constituted). To set up or establish; to compose; to appoint; to make and empower.

Constitution, kon-sti-tū'shon, *n.* The particular frame or character of the body or mind; established form of government; a system of fundamental laws; a particular law.

Constitutional, kon-sti-tū'shon-al, *a.* Adherent in the human constitution; consistent with the civil constitution; legal.—*n.* A walk for the sake of health.

Constrain, kon-strān', *vt.* To urge by force; to necessitate; to restrain.

Constraint, kon-strānt', *n.* Necessity; reserve; restraint.

Constrict, kon-strikt', *vt.* To draw together; to contract.

Constriction, kon-strik'shon, *n.* Contraction.

Constrictor, kon-strik'tér, *n.* That which constricts; a muscle that closes an orifice; a serpent which crushes its prey.

Construct, kon-strukt', *vt.* To build; to frame with contrivance; to devise.

Construction, kon-struk'shon, *n.* Structure; arrangement of words in a sentence; sense; interpretation.

Constructive, kon-strukt'iv, *a.* Having ability to construct; created or deduced by construction; inferred.

Construe, kon'strū, *vt.* (construing, construed). To arrange words so as to discover the sense of a sentence; to interpret.

Consubstantiality, kon-sub-stan'shi-al''i-ti, *n.* Participation of the same nature.

Consubstantiation, kon-sub-stan'shi-ā''shon, *n.* The doctrine of the presence of the body and blood of Christ in the sacramental elements.

Consuetude, kon'swē-tūd, *n.* Custom.

Consul, kon'sul, *n.* One of the two chief magistrates of ancient Rome; a person appointed by government to reside in a foreign country, and protect the commercial interests of his own country.

Consult, kon-sult', *vi.* To seek the opinion of another; to deliberate in common; to consider.—*vt.* To ask advice of, to refer to for information; to have regard to.

Consume, kon-sūm', *vt.* (consuming, consumed). To reduce to nothing; to burn up; to squander.—*vi.* To waste away slowly; to be exhausted.

Consummate, kon'sum-āt, *vt.* To finish; to perfect.—*a.* kon-sum'āt. Complete; perfect.

Consumption, kon-sum'shon, *n.* Act of consuming; quantity consumed; a gradual wasting away of the body; phthisis.

Contact, kon'takt, *n.* A touching together; close union or juncture of bodies.

Contagion, kon-tā'jon, *n.* Communication of a disease by contact; poisonous emanation; infection.

Contain, kon-tān', *vt.* To hold; to be able to hold; to comprise; to restrain.

Contaminate, kon-tam'in-āt, *vt.* To corrupt; to taint; to vitiate.

Contamination, kon-tam'in-ā''shon, *n.* Pollution; defilement; taint.

Contemn, kon-tem', *vt.* To despise; to scorn.

Contemplate, kon'tem-plāt, *vt.* To view with continued attention; to meditate on; to design; to purpose.—*vi.* To study; to meditate.

Contemporaneous, kon-tem'pō-rā''nē-us, *a.* Living or being at the same time.

Contemporary, kon-tem'pō-ra-ri, *a.* Living or occurring at the same time. *n.* One who lives at the same time with another.

Contempt, kon-temt', *n.* Act of contemning; scorn; disregard; disobedience to the rules; etc., of a court.

Contemptible, kon-tem'ti-bl, *a.* Worthy of contempt; despicable; vile; mean.

Contemptuous, kon-tem'tū-us, *a.* Manifesting contempt; scornful; insolent.

Contend, kon-tend', *vi.* To strive; to vie; to dispute; to wrangle.

Content, kon-tent', *a.* Easy in mind; satisfied.—*vt.* To satisfy the mind of; to please or gratify.—*n.* State of being contented; contentment. Kon'tent' or kon'tent, things contained in a vessel, book, etc.: in these senses *pl.*; capacity; space occupied: in these senses *sing.*

Contented, kon-tent'ed, *a.* Satisfied; easy in mind.

Contention, kon-ten'shon, *n.* Struggle; quarrel; debate; emulation.

Contentment, kon-tent'ment, *n.* State of being contended; satisfaction; content.

Conterminous, conterminal, kon-tėr'min-us, kon-tėr'min-al, *a.* Having the same bounds; contiguous.

Contest, kon-test', *vt.* To call in question; to strive for.—*vi.* To strive; to contend; to emulate.—*n.* kon'test. Struggle for victory; encounter; debate; competition.

Context, kon'tekst, *n.* The parts which precede or follow a passage quoted.

Contexture, kon-teks'tūr, *n.* The interweaving of several parts into one body; disposition of parts; texture.

Contiguous, kon-tig'ū-us, *a.* Touching one another; in contact; adjacent.

Continence, Continency, kon'ti-nens, kona-ti-nen-si, *n.* Restraint of the desires and passions; chastity; temperance.

Continent, kon'ti-nent, *a.* Chaste; moderate.—*n.*

A connected tract of land of great extent; the mainland of Europe.

Contingence, Contingency, kon-tin'jens, kon-tin'jen-si, *n.* Quality of being contingent; an event which may occur; chance; juncture.

Contingent, kon-tin'jent, *a.* Happening by chance; incidental; dependent upon an uncertainty.—*n.* A contingency; a quota; a quota of troops or a joint enterprise.

Continual, kon-tin'ū-al, *a.* Not intermitting; uninterrupted; often repeated.

Continuance, kon-tin'ū-ans, *n.* Permanence in one state; duration.

Continuation, kon-tin'ū-ā''shon, *n.* Succession; extension; prolongation.

Continue, kon-tin'ū, *vi.* (continuing, continued). To remain in a state or place; to be durable; to persevere; to be steadfast.—*vt.* To prolong; to extend; to persevere in.

Continuity, kon-ti-nū'i-ti, *n.* Close union of parts; unbroken texture; cohesion.

Continuous, kon-tin'ū-us, *a.* Joined together closely; conjoined; continued.

Contort, kon-tort', *vt.* To twist; to writhe; to draw or pull awry.

Contortionist, kon-tor'shon-ist, *n.* An acrobat who practices contortions of the body.

Contour, kontör', *n.* The line that bounds a body; outline.

Contour-map, kon-tör' map, *n.* A map showing elevations about sea-level by curves (*contour lines*) drawn through places of equal elevation.

Contraband, kon'tra-band, *n.* Illegal traffic; smuggling.—*a.* Prohibited.

Contract, kon-trakt', *vt.* To draw together; to cause to shrink; to reduce; to betroth; to bring on; to incur.—*vi.* To shrink up; to make a mutual agreement.—*n.* kon'trakt. Agreement; bond; the writing which contains stipulations; betrothment.

Contracted, kon-trakt'ed, *a.* Limited; narrow; mean.

Contractile, kon-trakt'īl, *a.* Having the power of contracting, as living fibers.

Contraction, kon-trak'shon, *n.* Shrinking; shortening; abbreviation.

Contractor, kon-trakt'ėr, *n.* One who contracts to perform any work or service, or to furnish supplies, at a certain price or rate.

Contradict, kon-tra-dikt', *vt.* To assert to be the contrary; to deny; to oppose.

Contradiction, kon-tra-dik'shon, *n.* A contrary assertion; inconsistency with itself.

Contradictory, kon-tra-dik'to-ri, *a.* Implying contradiction; inconsistent.

Contradistinction, kon'tra-dis-tingk''shon, *n.* Distinction by opposites.

Contradistinguish, kon'tra-dis-tin''gwish, *vt.* To distinguish by opposite qualities.

Contralto, kon-tral'tō, *n.* The lowest voice of a woman or boy.

Contraposition, kon'tra-pō-zi'shon, *n.* A placing over against; opposite position.

Contrapuntist, kon-tra-punt'ist, *n.* One skilled in counterpoint.

Contrariety, kon-tra-rī'e-ti, *n.* Opposition; repugnance; inconsistency.

Contrary, kon'tra-ri, *a.* Opposite; repugnant; inconsistent.—*adv.* In an opposite manner; in opposition.—*n.* A thing that is contrary.

Contrast, kon-trast', *vt.* To set in opposition; to show the difference or heighten the effect.—*vi.* To stand in contrast to.—*n.* kon'trast. Opposition or comparison of things; a person or thing strikingly different.

Contravene, kon-tra-vēn', *vt.* (contravening, contravened). To oppose; to trangress.

Contretemps, kong-tr-tong, *n.* An unexpected and untoward accident.

Contribute, kon-trib'ūt, *vt.* (contributing, contributed). To give in common with others.—*vi.* To give a part; to conduce.

Contribution, kon-tri-bū'shon, *n.* Act of contributing; that which is contributed; an article sent to a periodical, etc.

Contrite, kon'trīt, a. Broken-hearted for sin; penitent.

Contrition, kon-tri'shon, n. Grief of heart for sin.

Contrivance, kon-triv'ans, n. Scheme; invention; artifice.

Contrive, kon-trīv', vt. (contriving, contrived). To invent; to devise.—vi. To form or design.

Control, kon-trōl', n. Restraint; superintendence; authority.—vt. (controlling, controlled). To restrain; to regulate.

Controller, kon-trōl'er, n. An officer who checks the accounts of collectors of public moneys.

Controversy, kon'trō-vėr-si, n. A disputation, particularly in writing; litigation.

Controvert, kon'trō-vert, vt. To dispute by reasoning; to attempt to disprove or confute.

Contumacious, kon-tū-mā'shus, a. Opposing rightful authority; obstinate.

Contumacy, kon'tū-mā-si, n. Resistance to authority; perverseness.

Contumelious, kon-tū-mē'li-us, a. Contemptuous; insolent; proudly rude.

Contumely, kon'tū-me-li, n. Haughty insolence; contemptuous language.

Contuse, kon-tūz', vt. (contusing, contused). To bruise; to injure without breaking the skin or substance.

Contusion, kon-tū'zhon, n. A severe bruise; injury without breaking of the skin.

Conundrum, kō-nun'drum, n. A sort of riddle turning on some odd resemblance between things quite unlike.

Convalesce, kon-va-les', vi. (convalescing, convalesced). To recover health.

Convalescence, kon-va-les'ens, n. The state of one convalescent; gradual recovery after illness.

Convene, kon-vēn', vi. (convening, convened). To assemble.—vt. To cause to assemble; to convoke.

Convenience, Conveniency, kon-vē'ni-ens, kon-vē'ni-en-si, n. Ease; comfort; suitable opportunity; an appliance or utensil.

Convenient, kon-vē'ni-ent, a. Suitable; adapted; opportune.

Convent, kon'vent, n. A body of monks or nuns; a monastery; a nunnery.

Conventicle, kon-ven'ti-kl, n. A secret meeting; a meeting of religious dissenters; their meeting-place.

Convention, kon-ven'shon, n. An assembly; an agreement; recognized social custom.

Conventional, kon-ven'shon-al, a. Formed by agreement; tacitly understood; resting on mere usage.

Conventionalism, kon-ven'shon-al-izm, n. Arbitrary custom; a conventional phrase, ceremony, etc.

Conventual, kon-ven'tū-al, a. Belonging to a convent.—n. A monk or nun.

Converge, kon-vėrj', vi. (converging, converged). To tend to the same point; to approach in position or character.

Convergence, Convergency, kon-vėrj'ens, kon-vėrj'en-si, n. Tendency to one point.

Convergent, kon-vėrj'ent, a. Tending to one point or object; approaching.

Conversant, kon'vėrs-ant, a. Having intercourse or familiarity; versed in; proficient; occupied or concerned.

Conversation, kon-vėr-sā'shon, n. Familiar intercourse; easy talk.

Converse, kon-vėrs', vi. (conversing, conversed). To hold intercourse; to talk familiarly; to commune.—n. kon'vėrs. Conversation; familiarity; something forming a counterpart.—a. Put the opposite or reverse way.

Conversion, kon-vėr'shon, n. Change from one state, religion, or party to another; interchange of terms in logic.

Convert, kon-vėrt', vt. and i. To change from one

state, use, religion, or party to another; to turn from a bad life to a good; to interchange conversely.—n. kon'vėrt. One who has changed his opinion, practice, or religion.

Convertible, kon-vėrt'i-bl, a. Transformable; interchangeable.

Convex, kon'veks, a. Rising on the exterior surface into a round form; opposed to concave.

Convey, kon-vā, vt. To transport; to deliver; to impart.

Conveyance, kon-vā'ans, n. Act or means of conveying; a carriage; transference; a deed which transfers property.

Conveyancer, kon-va'ans-ėr, n. One who draws deeds by which property is transferred.

Convict, kon-vikt', vt. To prove or decide to be guilty—n. kon'vikt. A person found guilty; one undergoing penal servitude.

Conviction, kon-vik'shon, n. Act of finding a person guilty; strong belief; state of being sensible of wrong-doing.

Convince, kon-vins', vt. (convincing, convinced). To persuade by argument; to satisfy by evidence or proof.

Convivial, kon-vi'vi-al, a. Festive; festal; jovial; social.

Convocation, kon-vō-kā'shon, n. Act of convoking; an assembly, particularly of clergy or heads of a university.

Convoke, kon-vōk', vt. (convoking, convoked). To call together; to summon to meet.

Convolution, kon-vō-lū'shon, n. Act of rolling together or on itself; a winding; a spiral.

Convolve, kon-volv', vt. To roll together or on itself; to coil up.

Convolvulus, kon-volv'ū-lus, n. Bind-weed; a genus of slender twining plants.

Convoy, kon-voi', vt. To accompany for defense; to escort.—n. kon'voi. A protecting force; escort.

Convulse, kon-vuls', vt. (convulsing, convulsed). To contract violently, as the muscles; to affect by irregular spasms; to disturb.

Convulsion, kon-vul'shon, n. A violent involuntary contraction of the muscles; a violent irregular motion; disturbance.

Cony, Coney, kō'ni, n. A rabbit; simpleton.

Coo, kö, vi. (cooing, cooed). To make a low sound, as doves; to act in a loving manner.

Cook, kuk, vt. To prepare food by fire or heat; to concoct; to tamper with.—n. One who prepares victuals for the table.

Cool, köl, a. Moderately cold; dispassionate; self-possessed; impudent.—n. A moderate degree or state of cold.—vt. To make cool; to moderate; to calm; to render indifferent.—vi. To lose heat, ardor, affection, etc.

Cool-headed, köl'hed-ed, a. Having a temper not easily excited.

Coolie, kö'li, n. An Oriental porter.

Coolness, köl'nes, n. Moderate degree of cold; indifference; calm assurance.

Coop, köp, n. A barrel or cask; a box for poultry, etc.—vt. To confine in a coop; to shut up in a narrow compass.

Cooper, kö'pėr, n. One who makes barrels.—vt. and i. To do the work of a cooper.

Co-operate, kō-op'ėr-āt, vi. To act with another; to concur in producing the same effect.

Co-operative, kō-op'ėr-āt-iv, a. Operating jointly to the same end.

Co-ordinate, kō-or'din-āt, a. Holding the same rank or degree.—vt. To arrange in due order.

Coot, köt, n. A black wading bird.

Copal, kō-pal', n. The juice of certain trees, used as a varnish.

Coparcener, kō-pär'sen-ėr, n. One who has an equal portion of an inheritance.

Copartner, kö-pärt'nėr, n. An associate.

Cope, köp, n. A sacerdotal cloak; the arch of the sky; the roof of a house; the arch over a door, etc.—vt. (coping, coped). To cover, as with a cope; to strive, or contend; to oppose with success (with *with*).

Copernican, kō-pėr'ni-kan, *a.* Pertaining to Copernicus, or to his astronomical system.

Copestone, kōp'stōn, *n.* Head or top stone; hence, what finishes off.

Copier, Copyist, ko'pi-ėr, ko'pi-ist, *n.* One who copies; a transcriber; an imitator.

Coping, kōp'ing, *n.* The covering course of a wall, parapet, etc.

Copious, kō'pi-us, *a.* Abundant; exuberant; diffuse.

Copper, kop'ėr, *n.* A reddish colored ductile and malleable metal; a large boiler; a copper coin.—*a.* Consisting of or resembling copper.—*vt.* To cover with sheets of copper.

Copperas, kop'ėr-as, *n.* Green vitriol or sulphate or iron.

Copperplate, kop'ėr-plāt, *n.* A plate of polished copper, on which designs are engraved; a print from a copperplate.

Coppersmith, kop'ėr-smith, *n.* One who works in copper.

Coppice, Copse, kop'is, kops, *n.* A wood of small growth; a thicket.

Coprolite, kop'ro-līt, *n.* The petrified dung of extinct animals.

Coptic, kop'tik, *a.* Pertaining to the descendants of the ancient Egyptians, called *Copts.*—*n.* The language of the Copts.

Copula, kop'ū-la, *n.* The word which unites the subject and predicate of a proposition, part of *to be*; a bond; a link.

Copulate, kop'ū-lāt, *vi.* (copulating, copulated). To come together, as different sexes.

Copulation, kop-ū-lā'shon, *n.* Coition.

Copulative, kop'ū-lāt-iv, *a.* That unites.—*n.* A conjunction.

Copy, ko'pi, *n.* An imitation; a transcript; a pattern; a single example of a book, etc.; matter to be set up in type.—*vt.* (copying copied). To imitate; to transcribe.

Copyright, kop'i-rīt, *n.* The exclusive right to print or produce, given for a limited number of years to an author, artist, etc., or his assignee.—*a.* Relating to, or protected by copyright.—*vt.* To secure by copyright.

Coquet, .kō-ket', *vi.* (coquetting, coquetted). To trifle in love; to endeavor to excite admiration from vanity.

Coquetry, kō'ket-ri, *n.* The arts of a coquette; trifling in love.

Coquette, kō-ket', *n.* A vain, trifling woman; a flirt.

Coracle, kor'a-kl, *n.* A boat made of wickerwork covered with leather or oil-cloth.

Coral, ko'ral, *n.* A hard calcareous substance found in the ocean; a piece of coral.—*a.* Made of coral; resembling coral.

Coralline, ko'ral-in, *a.* Consisting of, like, or containing coral.—*n.* A sea-weed; an orange-red color; a coral zoophyte.

Corbel, kor'bel, *n.* A piece projecting from a wall as a support.—*vt.* (corbelling, corbelled). To support on corbels; to provide with corbels.

Cord, kord, *n.* A small rope; a band; a sinew; a pile of wood, 8 feet long, 4 high, and 4 broad.—*vi.* To bind with a cord.

Cordate, kor'dāt, *a.* Heart-shaped.

Cordelier, kord'el-ėr, *n.* A Franciscan friar.

Cordial, kor'di-al, *a.* Hearty; heartfelt; invigorating.—*n.* A medicine or beverage which increases strength; anything that gladdens or exhilarates.

Cordite, kor'dīt, *n.* A smokeless explosive introduced in 1889.

Cordon, kor'don, *n.* A line of military posts; a ribbon worn across the breast by knights.

Cordovan, kor'dō-van, *n.* Spanish leather.

Corduroy, kor-dė-roi', *n.* A thick cotton stuff corded or ribbed.

Core, kōr, *n.* The heart or inner part; the central part of fruit.

Co-respondent, kō-rē-spond'ent, *n.* A joint re-

spondent; a man charged with adultery in a divorce case.

Corgi, kor'ji, *n.* A small Welsh breed of dog.

Coriander, ko-ri-an'dėr, *n.* A plant which produces aromatic seeds.

Corinthian, ko-rin'thi-an, *a.* Pertaining to Corinth; denoting an order in architecture, distinguished by fluted columns and ornamental capitals.—*n.* A gay fellow.

Cork, kork, *n.* The bark of a species of oak; the tree itself; a stopple made of cork.—*vt.* To stop with a cork.

Cormorant, kor'mō-rant, *n.* A large voracious sea-bird; a glutton.

Corn, korn, *n.* Grain; the seeds of plants which grow in ears, and are made into bread; a horny excrescence on a toe or foot.—*vt.* To preserve with salt in grains; to granulate.

Cornea, kor'nē-a, *n.* The horny transparent membrane in the fore part of the eye.

Corned, kornd, *a.* Cured by salting.

Corneous, kor'nē-us, *a.* Horny; hard.

Corner, kor'nėr, *n.* A projecting extremity; angle; a secret or retired place; a nook.—*vt.* To buy up the whole stock of a commodity.

Corner-stone, kor'nėr-stōn, *n.* The stone which lies at the corner of two walls, and unites them; the principal stone.

Cornet, kor'net, *n.* A sort of trumpet; formerly a cavalry officer, of the lowest commissioned rank, who bore the standard.

Cornice, kor'nis, *n.* A molded projection crowning a part; uppermost molding of a pediment, room, etc.

Cornish, korn'ish, *a.* Pertaining to Cornwall.—*n.* The language of Cornwall.

Cornucopia, kor-nū-kō'pi-a, *n.* The representation of a horn filled with fruit, flowers, and grain, a symbol of plenty and peace.

Cornuted, kor-nūt'ed, *a.* Horned.

Corolla, ko-rol'la, *n.* The inner covering of a flower.

Corollary, ko'rol-la-ri, ko-rol'a-ri, *n.* Something added to a proposition demonstrated; an inference, deduction.

Coronal, ko'rō-nal, *a.* Belonging to the crown of the head.—*n.* A crown, garland.

Coronation, ko-rō-nā'shon, *n.* Act or solemnity of crowning a sovereign.

Coroner, ko'rō-nėr, *n.* An officer who holds a court of inquiry in a case of sudden death.

Coronet, ko'rō-net, *n.* A small crown worn by peers and peeresses; an ornamental head-dress; something that surmounts.

Corporal, kor'po-ral, *n.* A non-commissioned officer ranking below a sergeant.—*a.* Belonging or relating to the body; material.

Corporate, kor'po-rāt, *a.* Formed into a legal body, and empowered to act in legal processes as an individual.

Corporation, kor-po-rā'shon, *n.* A body corporate, empowered to act as an individual; the human body or frame.

Corporeal, kor-pō'rē-al, *a.* Having a body; material; opposed to spiritual.

Corps, kōr, *n.*; pl. **Corps,** kōrz. A body of troops. *Army Corps.* Two or more divisions.

Corpse, korps, *n.* The dead body of a human being; a carcass; remains.

Corpulence, Corpulency, kor'pū-lens, kor'-pū-len-si, *n.* The state of being corpulent; excessive fatness.

Corpuscle, kor'pus-l, *n.* A minute particle or physical atom; a minute animal cell.

Corral, kor-räl', *n.* A pen for cattle; an inclosure formed by wagons; a stockade for capturing elephants.

Correct, ko-rekt', *a.* Right; accurate; exact.—*vt.* To make right; to chastise; to counteract.

Correction, ko-rek'shon, *n.* Act of correcting, state of being corrected; discipline; chastisement; counteraction.

Correctness, ko-rekt'nes, *n.* Freedom from faults

or errors; accuracy; exactness.

Correlate, kor'ē-lāt, *n.* A correlative.—*vi.* (correlating, correlated). To be reciprocally related.—*vt.* To place in reciprocal relation; to determine the relations between.

Correlative, ko-rel'at-iv, *a.* Having a mutual relation, as father and son.—*n.* One who or that which stands in reciprocal relation.

Correspond, ko-rē-spond', *vi.* To answer one to another; to be congruous; to fit; to hold intercourse by letters.

Correspondence, ko-rē-spond'ens, *n.* Act or state of corresponding; fitness; congruity; intercourse by letters; the letters interchanged.

Correspondent, ko-rē-spond'ent, *a.* Corresponding; suitable; congruous.—*n.* One who has intercourse by letters.

Corridor, ko'ri-dör, *n.* A passage in a building, or round a court.

Corrigenda, ko-ri-jen'da, *n.pl.* Things to be corrected.

Corrigible, ko'ri-ji-bl, *a.* That may be corrected or reformed; punishable.

Corrival, ko-ri'val, *n.* A competitor.

Corroborant, ko-rob'ō-rant, *a.* Strengthening.

Corroborate, ko-rob'ō-rāt, *vt.* (corroborating, corroborated). To strengthen; to confirm.

Corrode, ko-rōd', *vt.* (corroding, corroded). To eat or wear away by degrees; to prey upon; to poison, blight, canker.

Corrosion, ko-rō'zhon, *n.* Action of corroding; state of being corroded.

Corrosive, ko-rōs'iv, *a.* Having the power of corroding; vexing; blighting.—*n.* That which has the quality of corroding.

Corrugate, ko'rū-gāt, *vt.* To wrinkle; to contract into folds or furrows.

Corrugation, ko-rū-gā'shon, *n.* A wrinkling; contraction into wrinkles.

Corrupt, ko-rupt', *vt.* To make putrid; to deprave; to taint; to bribe; to infect with errors.—*vi.* To become putrid or vitiated.—*a.* Tainted; depraved; infected with errors.

Corruptible, ko-rupt'i-bl, *a.* That may be corrupted; subject to decay, destruction, etc.

Corruption, ko-rup'shon, *n.* Act or process of corrupting; depravity; pollution; taint of blood; bribe-taking; bribery.

Corset, kor'set, *n.* An article of dress laced closely round the body; stays.

Cortège, kor'tāzh, *n.* A train of attendants.

Cortex, kor'teks, *n.* The bark of a tree; a membrane enveloping part of the body.

Cortical, kor'tik-al, *a.* Belonging to, consisting of, or resembling bark; belonging to the external covering.

Coruscate, ko-rus'kāt, *vi.* (coruscating, coruscated). To flash intermittently; to glitter.

Coruscation, ko-rus-kā'shon, *n.* A glittering or flashing; a quick vibration of light; intellectual brilliancy.

Corvine, kor'vin, *a.* Pertaining to the crow.

Corymb, kō'rimb, *n.* A form of inflorescence in which the blossoms form a mass with a convex or level top.

Coryphaeus, ko-ri-fē'us, *n.*; p. **-aei.** The leader of the chorus; the chief of a company.

Cosh, kosh, *n.* A bludgeon; a flexible tube filled with some heavy substance for use as a weapon.

Cosmetic, koz-met'ik, *a.* Improving beauty.—*n.* An application to improve the complexion.

Cosmic, Cosmical, koz'mik, koz'mik-al, *a.* Relating to the whole frame of the universe.

Cosmic rays, koz-mik rāz', *n.pl.* Penetrating radiation of shorter wavelength than X-rays, believed to reach the earth from outer space.

Cosmogony, koz-mog'on-i, *n.* The origin, or doctrine of the origin, of the universe.

Cosmography, koz-mog'ra-fi, *n.* A description of the world; the science of the construction of the universe.

Cosmology, koz-mol'o-ji, *n.* The science of the world or universe; cosmogony.

Cosmopolitan, Cosmopolite, koz-mō-pol'i-tan, koz-mop'o-līt, *n.* One who is at home in every place.—*a.* Free from local prejudices; common to all the world.

Cosmos, koz'mos, *n.* The universe; the system of order and harmony in creation.

Cost, kost, *vt.* (costing, cost). To be bought for; to require to be laid out or borne.—*n.* That which is paid for anything; expenditure; loss; (*pl.*) expenses of a lawsuit.

Costal, kos'tal, *a.* Pertaining to the ribs.

Costive, kos'tiv, *a.* Having the bowels bound; constipated.

Costly, kost'li, *a.* Of a high price; valuable, precious; dear; sumptuous.

Costmary, kost'ma-ri, *n.* A perennial fragrant plant a native of S. Europe.

Costume, kos'tūm, *n.* An established mode of dress; garb; attire.

Costumier, kos-tū'mi-ėr, *n.* One who prepares costumes; one who deals in costumes.

Co-surety, kō-shür'ti, *n.* A joint surety; one who is surety with another.

Cosy, kō'zi, *a.* Snug; comfortable.—*n.* Padded covering put over a teapot to keep in the heat after the tea has been infused.

Cot, kot, *n.* A small house; a hut; a small bed.

Cote, kōt, *n.* A shelter for animals (as a dove-*cote*); a sheepfold; a cottage or hut.

Coterie, kō'te-rē, *n.* A circle of familiar friends who meet for social or literary intercourse; an exclusive society; a clique.

Cotillion, ko-til'yon, *n.* A brisk dance; a kind of quadrille.

Cottage, kot'tāj, *n.* A cot; a small country or suburban house.

Cotton, kot'tn, *n.* A soft, downy substance in the pods of several plants; cloth made of cotton.—*a.* Pertaining to, or consisting of cotton.—*vi.* To agree; to become friendly.

Cotton-wood, kot'tn-wud, *n.* A large tree of the poplar kind.

Cotton-wool, kot'tn-wul, *n.* Cotton in the raw state.

Cotyledon, kot-i-lē'don, *n.* The seed-leaf, or first leaf or leaves, of the embryo plant.

Couch, kouch, *vi.* To lie down; to bend down; to lie close and concealed.—*vt.* To lay down; to place upon a bed; to comprise; to express; to fix a spear in rest; to depress a cataract in the eye.—*n.* A bed; a place for rest and ease.

Cougar, kö'gär, *n.* A large carnivorous quadruped of the cat kind; the puma.

Cough, kof, *n.* A violent convulsive effort of the lungs to throw off offending matter.—*vi.* To make a violent effort, with noise, to expel the airs from the lungs, and throw off any offensive matter.—*vt.* To expel from the lungs by a violent effort with noise; to expectorate.

Could, kud, *pret.* of *can.* Was able.

Coulter, kōl'tėr, *n.* The blade of a plow that cuts the earth in advance of the share.

Council, koun'sil, *n.* An assembly for consultation; a body of men designated to advise a sovereign or chief magistrate; a convocation.

Counsel, koun'sel, *n.* Deliberation; consultation; advice; design; a barrister.—*vt.* (counselling, counselled). To advise; to warn.

Count, kount, *vt.* To enumerate; to compute; to consider; to judge.—*vi.* To reckon; to rely; to be reckoned.—*n.* Reckoning; a particular charge in an indictment; a continental title of nobility, equivalent to the English earl.

Countenance, koun'ten-ans, *n.* The human face; air; aspect; favor; encouragement.—*vt.* To favor; to encourage; to vindicate.

Counter, kount'ėr, *n.* One who or that which counts; anything used to reckon, as in games; a shop table.—*adv.* Contrary; in an opposite direction.—*a.* Adverse; opposing.

Counteract, koun-tėr-akt', *vt.* To act in opposition to; to render ineffectual.

Counterbalance, koun-ter-bal´ans, vt. To weigh against with an equal weight; to act against with equal power.—n. Equal weight, power, or agency, acting in opposition.

Countercheck, koun-ter-chek´, vt. To oppose by some obstacle; to check.—n. Check; check that controls another check.

Counterfeit, koun´ter-fit, vt. and i. To forge; to copy; to feign.—a. Made in imitation; fraudulent.—n. An imposter; a forgery.

Counter-irritant, koun´ter-i-rit-ant, n. An irritant employed to relieve another irritation or inflammation.

Countermand, koun´ter-mand´, vt. To annul or revoke a former command.—n. A contrary order; revocation of a former order.

Counterpane, koun´ter-pān, n. A bed-cover.

Counterpart, koun´ter-pärt, n. A corresponding part; a duplicate; a supplement.

Counterplot, koun´ter-plot´, vi. To oppose one plot by another.—vt. To plot against in order to defeat another plot; to baffle by an opposite plot.—n. A plot to frustrate another.

Counterpoint, koun´ter-point, n. The art, in music, of adding to a given melody one or more melodies.

Counterpoise, koun´ter-poiz, vt. To counterbalance.—n. A weight which balances another; equivalence of power or force; equilibrium.

Countersign, koun-ter-sīn´, vt. To sign with an additional signature.—n. A military watchword.

Countervail, koun-ter-vāl´, vt. To act against with equal power or effect.

Countess, kount´es, n. The wife or widow of an earl or count.

Country, kun´tri, n. A large tract of land; a region; a kingdom or state; the inhabitants of a region; the public; rural parts.—a. Pertaining to the country; rural.

Countryman, kun´tri-man, n. One born in the same country with another; one who dwells in the country; a rustic.

County, koun´ti, n. A particular portion of a state or kingdom; a shire.—a. Pertaining to a county.

Couple, ku´pl, n. A band or leash; a pair; a brace; a man and his wife.—vt. and i. (coupling, coupled). To join together; to unite.

Couplet, kup´let, n. Two lines that rhyme.

Coupling, kup´ling, n. The act of one who couples; that which couples; a hook, chain, or other contrivance forming a connection.

Coupon, kö´pon, n. An interest certificate attached to a bond; one of a series of tickets which guarantee the holder to obtain a certain value or service for each at different periods.

Courage, ku´rij, n. Intrepidity; dauntlessness; hardihood.

Courageous, ku-rā´je-us. a. Bold; brave; heroic; fearless.

Courier, kö´rē-ėr, n. A messenger sent express with dispatches; a travelling attendant.

Course, kōrs, n. A running, passage; route; career; ground run over; line of conduct; order of succession; series of lectures, etc.; range of subjects taught; a layer of stones in masonry; part of a meal served at one time.—vt. (coursing, coursed). To hunt; to run through or over.—vi. To move with speed.

Courser, kōrs´ėr, n. A swift horse.

Court, kōrt, n. An inclosed area; residence of a sovereign; the family and retinue of a sovereign; judges assembled for deciding causes; the place where judges assemble; a judicial body; attention directed to gain favor; flattery.—vt. To endeavor to please by civilities, to woo, to seek.

Courteous, kort´e-us, a. Polite; complaisant; affable; respectful.

Courtesan, Courtezan, kör´te-zan, n. A loose woman, a prostitute.

Courtesy, kört´e-si, n. Urbanity; complaisance; act of kindness or civility.

Courthouse, kört´hous, n. A house in which established courts are held.

Courtier, kört´i-ėr, n. A man who attends courts; a person of courtly manners; one who solicits favors.

Court-martial, kört´mär´shal, n.; pl. **Courts-martial.** A court consisting of military or naval officers for the trial of offenses of a military or naval character.

Courtship, kört´ship, n. Act of courting a woman in view of marriage; wooing.

Courtyard, kört´yärd, n. A court or inclosure round or near a house.

Cousin, kuz´n, n. The son or daughter of an uncle or aunt; a kinsman.

Cove, kōv, n. A small inlet or bay; a sheltered recess in the sea-shore; a concave molding; a man, fellow.—vt. To arch over.

Covenant, kuv´en-ant, n. A contract; compact; a writing containing the terms of an agreement.—vi. To enter into a formal agreement; to stipulate.—vt. To grant by covenant.

Cover, kuv´er, vt. To overspread; to cloak; to secrete; to defend; to wrap up; to brood on; to be sufficient for; to include.—n. Anything spread over another thing; disguise; shelter; articles laid at table for one person.

Coverlet, kuv´er-let, n. The cover of a bed.

Covert, kuv´ert, a. Kept secret; private; insidious.—n. A shelter; a thicket.

Coverture, kuv´er-tür, n. Shelter; defense; the legal state of a married woman.

Covet, kuv´et, vt. To long for (in a good sense); to desire unlawfully; to hanker after.—vi. To have inordinate desire.

Covey, kuv´i, n. A hatch of birds; a small flock of birds (especially partridges) together; a company.

Cow, kou, n. The female of the bull, or of bovine animals generally.—vt. To sink the spirits or courage of; to dishearten.

Coward, kou´erd, n. A person who wants courage to meet danger; a craven; a dastard.—a. Destitute of courage; dastardly.

Cowardice, kou´erd-is, n. Want of courage to face danger.

Cow-catcher, kou´kach-ėr, n. A frame in front of locomotives to remove obstructions.

Cower, kou´ėr, vi. To crouch; to sink by bending the knees; to shrink through fear.

Cowhide, kou´hid, n. The hide of a cow; a leather whip.—vt. To flog with a leather whip.

Cowl, koul, n. A monk's hood; a chimney cover which turns with the wind; a vessel carried on a pole by two persons.

Coxcomb, koks´kōm, n. The comb worn by fools in their caps; the cap itself; a fop, a vain, showy fellow.

Coxswain, kok´sn, n. The man who steers a boat, or who has the care of a boat and its crew.

Coy, koi, a. Shy; reserved; bashful.

Cozen, kuz´n, vt. To cheat, to defraud; to beguile.—vi. To act deceitfully.

Crab, krab, n. A crustaceous fish with strong claws; a portable windlass, etc.; Cancer, a sign of the zodiac; a wild sour apple; a morose person.

Crabbed, krab´ed, a. Perverse; peevish; perplexing.

Crack, krak, n. A chink or fissure; a sudden or sharp sound; a sounding blow; a chat.—vt. and i. To break with a sharp, abrupt sound; to break partially; to snap; to boast of; to utter with smartness; to chat.

Cracked, krakt, a. Having fissures but not in pieces; impaired; crazy.

Cracker, krak´er, n. One who or that which cracks; a small firework; a hard biscuit.

Crackle, krak´l, vi. (crackling, crackled). To make small abrupt noises rapidly repeated.

Crackling, krak´ling, n. The act or noise of the verb to crackle; the brown skin of roasted pork.

Cradle, krā´dl, n. A small bed in which infants are rocked; a frame to support or hold together.—*vt.* (cradling, cradled). To lay or rock in a cradle.

Craft, kraft, *n.* Ability; skill; artifice; guile; manual art; trade; a vessel or ship.

Craftsman, krafts'man, *n.* An artificer.

Crag, krag, *n.* A steep rugged rock; a cliff; gravel or sand mixed with shells.

Cram, kram, *vt.* (cramming, crammed). To thrust in by force; to stuff; to coach for an examination.—*vi.* To stuff; to eat beyond satiety; to prepare for an examination.

Cramp, kramp, *n.* A spasmodic contraction of a limb or muscle; restraint; piece of iron bent at the ends, to hold together pieces of timber, stones, etc.—*vt.* To affect with spasms; to restrain, hinder.

Cranberry, kran'be-ri, *n.* A wild sour berry.

Crane, krān, *n.* A migratory bird with long legs and neck; a machine for raising great weights; a crooked pipe for drawing liquor out of a cask.—*vi.* To stretch out one's neck.

Craniology, krā-ni-ol'o-ji, *n.* The knowledge of the cranium or skull.

Cranium, krā'ni-um, *n.* The skull; the bones which inclose the brain.

Crank, krangk, *n.* A contrivance for producing a horizontal or perpendicular motion by means of a rotary motion, or the contrary; a bend or turn.—*a.* Liable to be overset; loose.

Cranny, kran'ni, *n.* A narrow opening; chink.

Crash, krash, *vi.* To make the loud, clattering sound of many things falling and breaking at once.—*n.* The sound of things falling and breaking; a commercial collapse.

Crasis, krā'sis, *n.* The mixture of bodily constituents; temperament; constitution; the contraction of vowels into one long vowel.

Crass, kras, *a.* Gross; coarse; dense.

Crate, krāt, *n.* A basket of wicker-work, for crockery, etc.

Crater, krā'tėr, *n.* A bowl; the circular cavity or mouth of a volcano; hole in the ground caused by the explosion of a shell, bomb, or mine.

Cravat, kra-vat', *n.* A neck-cloth.

Crave, krāv, *vt.* (craving, craved). To ask earnestly or submissively; to desire strongly.—*n.* Strong desire.

Craven, krā'vn, *n.* A coward; a weak-hearted, spiritless fellow.—*a.* Cowardly.

Craw, kra, *n.* The crop or first stomach of fowls.

Crawl, kral, *vi.* To creep; to advance slowly, slyly, or weakly.

Crayfish, Crawfish, krā'fish, kra'fish, *n.* A crustacean found in streams; also the spiny lobster, a sea crustacean.

Crayon, krā'on, *n.* A pencil of colored clay, chalk, or charcoal, used in drawing; a drawing made with crayons.—*vt.* To sketch.

Craze, krāz, *vt.* (crazing, crazed). To shatter; to impair the intellect of.—*vi.* To become crazy.—*n.* An inordinate desire.

Crazy, krāz'i, *a.* Decrepit; deranged; weakened or disordered in intellect.

Creak, krēk, *vi.* To make a grating sound.—*n.* A sharp, harsh, grating sound.

Cream, krēm, *n.* That part of a liquor which collects on the surface; the richer part of milk; best part of a thing.—*vt.* To take off cream from.—*vi.* To gather cream; to mantle.

Creamery, krē'mėr-i, *n.* A place where milk is made into butter and cheese.

Crease, krēs, *n.* A mark made by folding; a hollow streak like a groove; lines near the wickets in cricket.—*vt.* (creasing, creased). To make a mark in by compressing or folding.

Create, krē-āt', *vt.* (creating, created). To bring into being from nothing; to cause to be; to shape; to beget; to bring about; to invest with a new character; to constitute or appoint.

Creation, krē-ā'shon, *n.* Act of creating; the aggregate of created things; the universe; conferring of a title or dignity.

Creature, krē'tūr, *n.* Something created; a human being; something imagined; a person who owes his rise to another; a mere tool.

Credential, krē-den'shi-al, *n.* That which gives a title to credit; (*pl.*) documents showing that one is entitled to credit, or is invested with authority.

Credit, kred'it, *n.* Reliance on testimony; faith; reputed integrity; transfer of goods, etc., in confidence of future payment; reputation for pecuniary worth; time given for payment of goods sold on trust; side of an account in which payment is entered; money possessed or due.—*vt.* To trust; to believe; to sell or lend to, in confidence of future payment; to procure credit or honor to; to enter on the credit side of an account; to attribute.

Credulity, kred-dū'li-ti, *n.* A disposition to believe on slight evidence.

Creed, krēd, *n.* A system of principles believed or professed; a brief summary of the articles of Christian faith.

Creek, krēk, *n.* A small bay; a small harbor; a brook.

Creep, krēp, *vi.* (creeping, crept). To move as a reptile; to crawl; to grow along the ground, or on another body; to move secretly, feebly, or timorously; to be servile; to shiver.

Cremate, krē-māt', *vt.* To burn; to dispose of (a human body) by burning.

Crenate, Crenated, krē'nāt, krē'nāt-ed, *a.* Notched; indented.

Creole, krē'ōl, *n.* A native of the W. Indies or Spanish America, but not of indigenous blood.

Creosote, krē'ō-sōt, *n.* An antiseptic liquid obtained from wood-tar.

Crepitate, krep'i-tāt, *vi.* To crackle.

Crepuscular, krē-pus'kūl-ėr, *a.* Pertaining to twilight.

Crescent, kres'ent, *n.* The moon in her state of increase; anything resembling the shape of the new moon; the Turkish standard; buildings in the form of a crescent.

Cress, kres, *n.* The name of various plants, mostly cruciferous, used as a salad.

Crest, krest, *n.* A tuft on the head of certain birds; the plume of feathers or tuft on a helmet; the helmet itself; the top; a lofty mien; a sort of heraldic badge.—*vt.* To furnish with a crest.

Crestfallen, krest'fal-en, *a.* Dejected.

Cretaceous, krē-tā'shus, *a.* Chalky.

Cretinism, krē'tin-izm, *n.* A disease resembling rickets, but accompanied with idiocy.

Crevice, kre'vis, *n.* A crack; cleft; cranny.

Crew, krö, *n.* A company; a gang; the company of sailors belonging to a vessel.

Crewel, krö'el, *n.* A kind of fine worsted.

Crib, krib, *n.* A child's bed; a small habitation; a rack; a stall for oxen; a framework; a literal translation.—*vt.* (cribbing, cribbed). To shut up in a narrow habitation; to pilfer.

Cribbage, krib'āj, *n.* A game at cards.

Crick, krik, *n.* A local spasm or cramp; a stiffness of the neck.

Cricket, krik'et, *n.* An insect which makes a creaking or chirping sound; an open-air game played with bats, ball, and wickets.

Crime, krīm, *n.* A breach of law, divine or human; any great wickedness.

Criminal, krim'in-al, *a.* Guilty; wicked; relating to crime.—*n.* A malefactor; a convict.

Criminate, krim'in-āt, *vt.* To charge with or involve in a crime.

Crimp, krimp, *a.* Easily crumbled; friable; brittle.—*vt.* To curl or crisp; to seize; to pinch; to decoy for the army or navy.

Crimson, krim'zn, *n.* A deep-red color; a red tinged with blue.—*a.* Of a beautiful deep-red.—*vt.* To dye of a deep-red color.—*vi.* To become of a deep-red color; to blush.

Cringe, krinj, *vi.* (cringing, cringed). To bend; to bend with servility; to fawn.—*n.* A bow; servile civility.

Crinkle, kring'kl, *vi.* (crinkling, crinkled). To

bend in little turns; to wrinkle.—*vt.* To form with short turns or wrinkles.—*n.* A winding or turn; a wrinkle.

Crinoline, krin′o-lin, *n.* A fabric of horsehair and linen thread; a hooped petticoat.

Cripple, krip′l, *n.* A lame person.—*vt.* (crippling, crippled). To lame; to disable.

Crisis, krī′sis, *n.;* pl. **-ses.** Turning-point of a disease; a decisive stage; time when anything is at its height; conjuncture.

Crisp, krisp, *a.* Brittle; easily broken or crumbled; fresh; brisk.—*vt.* To curl; to make wavy.—*vi.* To form little curls.

Cristate, kris′tāt, *a.* Crested; tufted.

Criterion, krī-tē′ri-un, *n.;* pl. **-ia.** Standard of judging; a measure; test.

Critic, kri′tik, *n.* One skilled in judging literary or artistic work; a reviewer; a severe judge.—*a.* Relating to criticism.

Critical, kri′tik-al, *a.* Relating to or containing criticism; nicely judicious; inclined to find fault; relating to a crisis; momentous.

Criticism, kri′ti-sizm, *n.* Act or art of criticizing; exhibition of the merits of literary or artistic work; a critical essay; censure.

Criticize, kri′ti-sīz, *vi.* and *t.* (criticizing, criticized). To examine or judge critically; to pick out faults; to animadvert upon.

Critique, kri-tēk′, *n.* A written estimate of the merits of a literary or artistic work.

Croak, krōk, *vi.* To make a low hoarse noise in the throat, as a frog or crow; to forebode evil without much cause; to murmur.—*n.* The low harsh sound of a frog, raven, etc.

Crochet, krō′shā, *n.* A species of knitting performed by means of a small hook.

Crockery, krok′e-ri, *n.* Earthenware; vessels formed of clay, glazed and baked.

Crocodile, kro′kō-dīl, *n.* A large aquatic reptile of the lizard kind.—*a.* Pertaining to or like a crocodile; affected (tears).

Crocus, krō′kus, *n.* A bulbous plant of the iris family; saffron.

Crone, krōn, *n.* An old woman.

Crony, krō′ni, *n.* A familiar friend.

Crook, krōk, *n.* A bend; a curving instrument; a shepherd's staff; a pastoral staff; a criminal, swindler.—*vt.* and *i.* To bend; to make a hook on.

Crop, krop, *n.* The first stomach of birds; the craw; harvest; corn, etc., while growing; act of cutting, as hair, a short whip without a lash.—*vt.* (cropping, cropped). To cut off the ends of; to cut close; to browse; to gather before it falls; to cultivate.

Crop-eared, krop′ērd, *a.* Having the ears cut short.

Croquet, krō′kā, *n.* An open-air game played with mallets, balls, hoops, and pegs.

Cross, kros, *n.* An instrument of death, consisting of two pieces of timber placed transversely; the symbol of the Christian religion; the religion itself; a monument or sign in the form of a cross; anything that thwarts; a hybrid.—*a.* Athwart; adverse; fretful.—*vt.* To draw a line or lay a body across; to mark with a cross; to cancel; to pass from side to side of; to thwart; to perplex; to interbreed.—*vi.* To be athwart; to move across.

Cross-bones, kros′bōnz, *n.pl.* A symbol of death; two human thigh-bones places crosswise, generally in conjunction with a skull.

Crossbow, kros′bō, *n.* A weapon for shooting, formed by fixing a bow crosswise on a stock.

Cross-breed, kros′brēd, *n.* A breed from a male and female of different breeds.

Cross-examine, kros′egz-am-in, *vt.* To examine a witness of the opposite party.

Cross-grained, kros′grānd, *a.* Having the fiber across or irregular; perverse.

Cross-purpose, kros′pėr-pus, *n.* A contrary purpose; a misunderstanding.

Crossword puzzle, kros′wėrd puz′l, *n.* A diagram of squares, each of which, except certain

blanks, is to be filled with a letter so that the words formed, when read down and across, correspond to definitions given.

Crotch, kroch, *n.* A fork or forking.

Crotchet, kroch′et, *n.* A note in music, half the length of a minim; a whim; a perverse conceit; a bracket in printing.

Croton, krō′ton, *n.* An E. Indian shrub whose seeds yield a violently purgative oil.

Crouch, krouch, *vi.* To bend low; to lie close to the ground; to cringe.

Croup, krōp, *n.* A disease of the windpipe in children; the rump of certain animals; the place behind the saddle.

Croupier, krō′pē-ėr, *n.* One who at a public dinner sits at the lower end of the table; person in charge of the money at a gaming table.

Crow, krō, *n.* A black bird of the genus Corvus, including the raven, rook, jackdaw, etc.; a crowbar; the sound which a cock utters.—*vi.* (crowing, *pret.* crew, crowed, *pp.* crowed). To cry as a cock; to exult; to boast.

Crowbar, krō′bär, *n.* A bar of iron with a bent or forked end, used as a lever.

Crowd, kroud, *n.* A number of persons or things; a throng; the populace.—*vt.* To fill by pressing together; to fill to excess.—*vi.* To press in numbers; to throng.

Crowded, kroud′ed, *a.* Filled by a promiscuous multitude.

Crown, kroun, *n.* An ornament for the head in the form of a wreath; a diadem; a badge of royalty; perfection; completion; the top of anything, especially the head; a coin.—*vt.* To invest with a crown; to cover; to adorn; to finish; to perfect.

Crow's-feet, krōz′fēt, *n.pl.* The wrinkles at corners of the eyes, the effects of age.

Crucial, krō′shi-al, *a.* Relating to a cross; severe; searching; decisive.

Crucible, krō′si-bl, *n.* A melting pot, used by chemists and others.

Crucifix, krō′si-fiks, *n.* A cross with the figure of Christ crucified on it.

Crucifixion, krō-si-fik′shon, *n.* The act of crucifying; the death of Christ.

Crucify, krō′si-fī, *vt.* (crucifying, crucified). To put to death by nailing the hands and feet of to a cross, to mortify; to torment.

Crude, krōd, *a.* Raw; unripe; in its natural state; not brought to perfection.

Cruel, krō′el, *a.* Unmerciful; hard-hearted; ferocious; brutal; severe.

Cruet, krō′et, *n.* A vial or small glass bottle for holding vinegar, oil, etc.

Cruise, krōz, *vi.* (cruising, cruised). To sail hither and thither.—*n.* A sailing to and fro in search of an enemy's ships, or for pleasure.

Cruiser, krōz′ėr, *n.* A person or a ship that cruises; a swift armed vessel to protect or destroy shipping.

Crumb, krum, *n.* A fragment; a small piece of bread broken off; the soft part of bread.—*vt.* To break into small pieces with the fingers; to cover with bread-crumbs.

Crumble, krum′bl, *vt.* (crumbling, crumbled). To break into small fragments; to pulverize.—*vi.* To part into small fragments; to decay.

Crumpet, krum′pet, *n.* A sort of muffin.

Crumple, krum′pl, *vt.* (crumpling, crumpled). To press into wrinkles; to rumple.—*vi.* To shrink; to shrivel.

Crunch, krunch, *vt.* To crush between the teeth.

Crupper, krup′ėr, *n.* A strap of leather to prevent a saddle from shifting forward; the buttocks.

Crural, krōr′al, *a.* Belonging to the leg; shaped like a leg or root.

Crusade, krō-sād′, *n.* A military expedition against the infidels of the Holy Land; a romantic or enthusiastic enterprise.

Crush, krush, *vt.* To squeeze; to bruise; to pound; to overpower; to oppress.—*vi.* To be pressed; to force one's way amid a crowd.—*n.* A violent pressing or squeezing; a crowding.

Crust, krust, *n.* The hard outer coat of anything; the outside of a loaf; a piece of hard bread; a deposit from wine.—*vt.* and *i.* To cover with a crust or hard coat.

Crustacea, krus-tā'shē-a, *n.pl.* A division of animals, comprising crabs, shrimps, etc., having an external skeleton or shell.

Crustacean, krus-tā'shē-an, *n.* and *a.* One of, or pertaining to, the crustaceans.

Crusty, krust'i, *a.* Pertaining to, having, or like a crust; snappish; surly.

Crutch, kruch, *n.* a staff with a cross-piece used by cripples; a support.

Cry, krī, *vi.* (crying, cried). To utter the loud shrill sounds of weeping, joy, fear, surprise, etc.; to clamor; to weep.—*vt.* To shout; to proclaim.—*n.* The loud voice of man or beast; a shriek or scream; acclamation; weeping; importunate call; a political catchword.

Crypt, kript, *n.* A subterranean cell for burying purposes; a subterranean chapel.

Cryptic, Cryptical, krip'tik, krip'tik-al, *a.* Hidden; secret; occult.

Cryptogam, krip'tō-gam, *n.* One of those plants which do not bear true flowers, such as lichens, mosses, ferns, etc.

Cryptogram, Cryptograph, krip'tō-gram, krip'tō-graf, *n.* Something written in secret characters.

Crystal, kris'tal, *n.* Pure transparent quartz; a superior kind of glass; articles, collectively, made of this material; a regular solid mineral body with smooth surfaces.—*a.* Consisting of or like crystal; clear; pellucid.

Ctenoid, ten'oid, *a.* Comb-shaped; having the posterior edge with teeth: said of the scales of fishes; having scales of this kind.

Cub, kub, *n.* The young of certain quadrupeds, as the bear and fox.—*vi.* (cubbing, cubbed). To bring forth cubs.

Cube, kūb, *n.* A regular solid body, with six equal square sides, the third power, or the product from multiplying a number twice by itself.—*vt.* To raise to the third power.

Cubicle, kū'bi-kl, *n.* A sleeping-place; a compartment for one bed in a dormitory.

Cubit, kū'bit, *n.* The forearm; the length from the elbow to the extremity of the middle finger, usually taken as 18 inches.

Cuckold, kuk'old, *n.* A man whose wife is false to his bed.—*vt.* To make a cuckold of.

Cuckoo, ku'kō, *n.* A migratory bird, so named from the sound of its note.

Cucumber, kū'kum-bėr, *n.* An annual plant of the gourd family.

Cud, kud, *n.* The food which ruminating animals bring up from the first stomach to chew.

Cuddle, kud'dl, *vi.* (cuddling, cuddled). To lie close and snug.—*vt.* To hug; to embrace; to fondle.

Cudgel, kuj'el, *n.* A short thick stick; a club.—*vt.* (cudgelling, cudgelled). To beat with a cudgel; to beat in general.

Cue, kū, *n.* The last words of an actor's speech; catch-word; hint; the part which any man is to play in his turn; humor; the straight rod used in billiards.

Cuff, kuf, *n.* A blow; slap; part of a sleeve near the hand.—*vt.* To beat; to strike with talons or wings, or with fists.

Cuisine, kwē-zēn', *n.* Style of cooking.

Cul-de-sac, köl'de-sak, *n.* A blind alley.

Culinary, kū'lin-a-ri, *a.* Relating to the kitchen, or cookery; used in kitchens.

Cull, kul, *vt.* To pick out, to gather.

Culminate, kul'min-āt, *vi.* To come or be in the meridian; to reach the highest point, as of rank, power, size, etc.

Culmination, kul-min-ā'shon, *n.* The transit of a heavenly body over the meridian; highest point; consummation.

Culpable, kulp'a-bl, *a.* Blameworthy; guilty; criminal; immoral; sinful.

Culprit, kul'prit, *n.* A person arraigned in court for a crime, or convicted of a crime; a criminal; an offender.

Cult, kult, *n.* A system of belief and worship; a subject of devoted study.

Cultivate, kul'ti-vāt, *vt.* To till; to refine; to foster; to improve.

Culture, kul'tūr, *n.* Cultivation; the rearing of certain animals, as oysters; the application of labor, or other means of improvement; the result of such efforts; refinement.—*vt.* To cultivate.

Culvert, kul'vėrt, *n.* An arched drain under a road, railway, etc., for the passage of water.

Cumber, kum'bėr, *vt.* To embarrass; to entangle; to obstruct; to distract.

Cumbersome, kum'bėr-sum, *a.* Troublesome; unwieldy; unmanageable.

Cumin, Cummin, kum'in, *n.* An annual umbelliferous plant, whose seeds have stimulating and carminative properties.

Cummer-bund, kum'ėr-bund, *n.* A girdle or waistband.

Cumulate, kū-mū-lāt, *vt.* (cumulating, cumulated). To form a heap; to heap together.

Cumulation, kū-mū-lā'shon, *n.* A heaping up; a heap; accumulation.

Cumulus, kū'mū-lus, *n.*; pl. **-li.** A cloud in the form of dense convex or conical heaps.

Cuneiform, kū-nē'i-form, *a.* Wedge-shaped; applied to the arrow-headed characters on old Babylonian and Persian inscriptions.

Cunning, kun'ing, *a.* Astute; artful.—*n.* Faculty or act of using stratagem; craftiness; artifice.

Cup, kup, *n.* A small vessel to drink out of; anything hollow, like a cup; a glass vessel for drawing blood; liquor in a cup.—*vt.* (cupping, cupped). To apply a cupping-glass.

Cupboard, kup'bōrd, *n.* A case or inclosure for cups, plates, dishes, etc.

Cupel, kū'pel, *n.* A small cup or vessel used in refining precious metals.

Cupellation, kū-pel-lā'shon, *n.* The process of refining gold or silver in a cupel.

Cupid, kū'pid, *n.* The god of love.

Cupidity, kū-pid'i-ti, *n.* A longing to possess; inordinate or unlawful desire; covetousness.

Cupola, kū-pō-la, *n.* A spherical vault on the top of a building; a dome.

Cur, kėr, *n.* A mongrel dog; a contemptible man.

Curaçoa, Curaçao, kö-ra-sö'a, kö-ra-sä'o, *n.* A liqueur flavored with orange-peel, etc.

Curate, kū'rāt, *n.* One to whom the cure of souls is committed; a clergyman employed to assist in the duties of a rector or vicar.

Curative, kū'rāt-iv, *a.* Relating to the cure of diseases; tending to cure.

Curator, kū-rāt'ėr, *n.* A superintendent; custodian; guardian.

Curb, kėrb, *vt.* To control; to check; to restrain with a curb, as a horse; to strengthen by a curb-stone.—*n.* Check; restraint; part of a bridle; a curb-stone.

Curd, kėrd, *n.* Coagulated milk.—*vt.* and *i.* To curdle; to congeal.

Curdle, kėrd'l, *vt.* and *i.* (curdling, curdled). To change into curds; to coagulate.

Cure, kūr, *n.* Act of healing; a remedy; the care of souls; spiritual charge.—*vt.* (curing, cured). To heal; to remedy; to pickle.—*vi.* To effect a cure.

Curé, kū-rā, *n.* A curate; a parson.

Curfew, kėr'fū, *n.* An evening bell; an old utensil for covering a fire.

Curia, kū'ri-a, *n.* The Roman see in its temporal aspect.

Curio, kū'ri-ō, *n.*; pl. **-os,** A curiosity; an interesting and curious article.

Curiosity, kū-ri-os'i-ti, *n.* Inquisitiveness; a thing unusual; a rarity.

Curl, kėrl, *vt.* To form into ringlets,—*vi.* To take a twisted or coiled form; to play at the game of curling.—*n.* A ringlet of hair, or anything of a like form; a waving; flexure.

Curling, kėrl'ing, *n.* A winter game in which large smooth stones are propelled on the ice.

Curmudgeon, ker-muj'on, *n.* An avaricious churlish fellow; a miser; a churl.

Currant, ku'rant, *n.* A small dried grape; the name of several shrubs and of their fruit.

Currency, ku'ren-si, *n.* Circulation; circulating medium; the aggregate of coin, notes, etc., in circulation; general esteem; vogue.

Current, ku'rent, *a.* Running; circulating; general; present in its course.—*n.* A running; a stream; progressive motion of water; successive course; the passage of electricity from one pole of an apparatus to the other; often used for strength, amount, or intensity of current.

Curriculum, ku-rik'ū-lum, *n.* A course of study in a university, school, etc.

Currier, ku'ri-ėr, *n.* A man who dresses leather after it is tanned.

Curry, ku'ri, *n.* A highly spiced sauce or mixture; a dish cooked with curry.—*vt.* (currying, curried). To flavor with curry; to dress leather; to rub and clean (a horse) with a comb; to seek (favor).

Curse, kėrs, *vt.* (cursing, cursed). To utter a wish of evil against; a blight; to torment with calamities.—*vi.* To utter imprecations; to blaspheme.—*n.* Imprecation of evil; execration; torment.

Cursive, kėr'siv, *a.* Running, flowing.

Cursory, kėr'so-ri, *a.* Hasty; superficial.

Curt, kėrt, *a.* Short; concise; somewhat rude.

Curtail, kėr-tāl', *vt.* To cut short; to abridge.

Curtain, kėr'tan, *n.* A hanging cloth for a window, bed, etc.; a screen in a theater—*vt.* To inclose or furnish with curtains.

Curtly, kėrt'li, *adv.* Shortly; briefly.

Curtsy, Curtsey, kėrt'si, *n.* A gesture of respect by a female.—*vi.* (curtsying or curtseying, curtsied or curtseyed). To drop or make a crutsy.

Curve, kėrv, *a.* Bending; inflected.—*n.* A bending without angles; a bent line.—*vt.* (curving, curved). To bend.

Curvilinear, Curvilineal, kėrv-i-lin'ē-ėr, kėrv-i-lin'ē-al, *a.* Consisting of curved lines; bounded by curved lines.

Curvirostral, kėrv-i-ros'tral, *a.* Having a crooked beak.

Cushion, kush'on, *n.* A pillow for a seat; something resembling a pillow.—*vt.* To seat on a cushion; to furnish with cushions.

Cusp, kusp, *n.* The point of the moon, or other luminary; a point formed by the meeting of two curves.

Custard, kus'tėrd, *n.* A composition of milk and egg, sweetened, and baked or boiled.

Custodian, kus-tō'di-an, *n.* One who has care of a library, public building, etc.

Custody, kus'tō-di, *n.* A keeping; guardianship; imprisonment; security.

Custom, kus'tum, *n.* Habit; established practice; fashion; a buying of goods; business support; a tax on goods; *pl.* duties on merchandise imported or exported.

Customer, kus'tum-ėr, *n.* An accustomed buyer at a shop, etc., one who buys goods.

Custom-house, kus'tum-hous, *n.* The office where customs are paid.

Cut, kut, *vt.* (cutting, cut). To divide into pieces; to fell or mow; to clip; to carve; to affect deeply; to intersect; to castrate; to divide, as cards; to refuse to recognize.—*vi.* To make an incision; to be severed by a cutting instrument; to pass straight and rapidly.—*a.* Gashed; carved; intersected; deeply affected.—*n.* The action of an edged instrument, a wound, a stroke with a whip; a severe remark; a channel; any small piece; a lot; a near passage; a carving or engraving; act of dividing a pack of cards; form; fashion; refusal to recognize a person.

Cutaneous, kū-tā'nē-us, *a.* Pertaining to the skin.

Cuticle, ku'ti-kl, *n.* The thin exterior coat of the skin; a vesicular membrane in plants.

Cutlass, kut'las, *n.* A broad, curving sword.

Cutlery, kut'le-ri, *n.* Knives and edged instruments collectively.

Cutlet, kut'let, *n.* A small piece of meat for cooking, generally off the ribs.

Cutting, kut'ing, *p.a.* Serving to cut; wounding the feelings; severe.—*n.* A piece cut off; an incision; an excavation; a twig or scion.

Cuttle, Cuttle-fish, kut'tl, kut'tl-fish, *n.* A mollusc which ejects a black fluid to conceal itself..

Cyanean, si-ā'nē-an, *a.* Of a dark-blue color.

Cyanide, si'an-id, *n.* A combination of cyanogen with a metallic base.

Cyanogen, si-an'ō-jen, *n.* A poisonous gas of a strong and peculiar odor.

Cycle, si'kl, *n.* An orbit in the heavens; a circle of years; a bicycle or tricycle.—*vi.* To recur in a cycle; to ride a bicycle.

Cycloid, si'kloid, *n.* A geometrical curve.

Cyclone, si'klōn, *n.* A circular storm; a rotatory system of winds revolving round a calm center, and advancing.

Cyclops, si'klops, *n.sing.* and *pl.*; pl. also **Cyclopes,** si-klō'pēz. A one-eyed race of giants in Greek fable.

Cygnet, sig'net, *n.* A young swan.

Cylinder, si'lin-dėr, *n.* An elongated round body of uniform diameter.

Cymbal, sim'bal, *n.* A basin-shaped musical instrument of brass, used in pairs.

Cynic, sin'ik, *n.* One of a sect of Greek philosophers who professed contempt of riches, arts, etc.; a morose man.

Cynic, Cynical, sin'ik, sin'i-kal, *a.* Belonging to the Cynics; surly; sneering; captious.

Cynicism, sin'i-sizm, *n.* A morose contempt of the pleasures and arts of life.

Cynosure, si'nō-zhōr, *n.* The constellation of the Little Bear; a center of attraction.

Cypress, si'pres, *n.* An evergreen tree; the emblem of mourning.

Cyst, sist, *n.* A bag in animal bodies containing matter.

Czar, tsär or zär, *n.* Formerly, the title of the Emperor of Russia.

Czech, chek, *n.* One of the Slavonic inhabitants of Bohemia; the language of the Czechs.

D

Dab, dab, *vt.* (dabbing, dabbed). To hit lightly with something soft or moist.—*n.* A gentle blow; a small mass of anything soft or moist; a small flat fish; an adept or expert.

Dabble, dab'bl, *vt.* (dabbling, dabbled). To wet; to sprinkle.—*vi.* To play in water; to do anything in a superficial manner; to meddle.

Dachshund, däks'hunt, *n.* A long-bodied, short-legged dog, with short hair.

Dactyl, dak'til, *n.* A poetical foot of one long or accented syllable followed by two short.

Dad, Daddy, dad, dad'di, *n.* A childish or pet name for father.

Dado, dā'dō, *n.* That part of a pedestal between the base and the cornice; the finishing of the lower part of the walls in rooms.

Daffodil, daf'fō-dil, *n.* A plant of the amaryllis family with yellow flowers.

Dagger, dag'ėr, *n.* A short sharp-pointed sword.

Dahlia, da'li-a, *n.* A genus of composite plants, consisting of tuberous-rooted herbs.

Daily, dā'li, *a.* Happening or being every day; diurnal.—*adv.* Day by day.

Dainty, dān'ti, *a.* Toothsome, nice, delicate, elegant.—*n.* Something nice; a delicacy.

Dairy, dā'ri, *n.* The place where milk is converted into butter or cheese; a shop where milk, butter, etc., are sold.—*a.* Pertaining to the keeping of cows, managing of milk, etc.

Dais, dā'is, *n.* The high table at the upper end of the dining-hall; the raised floor on which the table stood; a canopy.

Daisy, dā'zi, n. The day's eye; a well-known plant, bearing a white flower with a tinge of red, and a yellow center.

Dale, dāl, n. A valley; a place between hills.

Dally, dal'li, vi. (dallying, dallied). To trifle; to wanton; to linger.

Dam, dam, n. A female parent; a bank to confine or raise water.—vt. (damming, dammed). To obstruct or confine by a dam.

Damage, dam'āj, n. Hurt; injury; money compensation (generally in pl.).—vt. (damaging, damaged). To injure; to impair.

Damask, dam'ask, n. A fabric, of various materials, with figures of flowers, etc.; a pink color.—a. Pink or rosy.—vt. To form or imprint flowers or figures on.

Damn, dam, vt. To send to hell; to condemn.

Damnation, dam-nā'shon, n. Condemnation; sentence to punishment in the future state.

Damned, damd, a. Hateful; detestable.

Damning, dam'ing or dam'ning, a. That condemns or exposes to damnation.

Damp, damp, a. Moist; humid.—n. Moist air; fog; noxious exhalation from the earth; depression of spirits; discouragement.—vt. To moisten; to dispirit; to restrain.

Damper, dam'per, n. One who or that which damps; a plate across a flue or a furnace, etc., to regulate the draught of air.

Damsel, dam'zel, n. A young unmarried woman; a girl.

Damson, dam'zn, n. A small dark plum.

Dance, dans, vi. (dancing, danced). To move with measured steps, regulated by a tune; to leap and risk.—vt. To make to dance; to dandle.—n. A leaping or stepping to the measure of a tune; the tune itself.

Dandelion, dan'di-li-un, n. A composite plant bearing a bright yellow flower.

Dandle, dan'dl, vt. (dandling, dandled). To shake on the knee; as an infant; to fondle; to trifle with.

Dandruff, dan'druff, n. A scurf on the head.

Danger, dān'jer, n. Exposure to injury; jeopardy; risk.

Dangerous, dān'jer-us, a. Perilous; causing risk of harm; unsafe; insecure.

Dangle, dang'gl, vi. (dangling, dangled). To hang loose; to follow officiously.—vt. To carry suspended loosely; to swing.

Dank, dangk, a. Damp; moist; humid.

Danseuse, däng-sez, n. A female stage-dancer.

Dapper, dap'er, a. Little and active; neat.

Dapple, dap'l, n. A spot.—a. Marked with spots.—vt. (dappling, dappled). to variegate with spots.

Dare, dār, vi. (daring, pret. dared pp. dared). To have courage; to be bold enough; to venture.—vt. To challenge; to defy; to venture on.

Daring, dār'ing, a. Bold; intrepid; fearless.—n. Courage; audacity.

Dark, därk, a. Destitute of light; clouded; black or blackish; disheartening; involved in mystery; keeping designs in concealment.—n. Darkness; obscurity; secrecy; a state of ignorance.

Darkness, därk'nes, n. Absence of light; blackness; gloom; ignorance; privacy.

Darling, där'ling, a. Dearly beloved.—n. One much beloved; a favorite.

Darn, därn, vt. To mend by imitating the texture of the stuff with thread and needle; to sew together.—n. A place so mended.

Dart, därt, n. A pointed missile thrown by the hand; a sudden rush or bound.—vt. To throw with a sudden thrust; to shoot.—vi. To fly or shoot, as a dart; to start and run.

Darwinism, där'win-izm, n. The doctrine as to the origin and modifications of species taught by Darwin; evolution.

Dash, dash, vt. To cause to strike suddenly or violently; to throw or cast; to sprinkle; to mix slightly; to sketch out hastily; to obliterate; to frustrate; to abash.—vi. To rush with violence to strike or be hurled.—n. A violent striking of two bodies; admixture; a rushing or onset vigor in attack; bluster; a mark in writing or printing (—).

Dashing, dash'ing, a. Spirited; showy.

Dastard, das'terd, n. A coward.—a. cowardly.

Date, dāt, n. The time when any event happened era; age; a soft fleshy drupe, the fruit of the date-palm.—vt. (dating, dated). To note the time of.—vi. To reckon time; to have origin.

Date-palm, Date-tree, dāt'päm, dāt'trē, n. The kind of palm which bear dates.

Dative, dāt'iv, a. or n. A grammatical case, followowing verbs that express giving, etc.

Datum, dā'tum, n.; pl. **-ta.** A fact, proposition etc., granted or known, from which other facts etc., are to be deduced.

Daub, dab, vt. To smear; to cover with mud or other soft substance; to paint coarsely; to flat ter grossly.—n. Coarse painting; a smear.

Dauby, dab'i, a. Viscous; glutinous.

Daughter, da'ter, n. A female child or descendant.

Daughter-in-law, da'ter-in-la, n. A son's wife.

Daunt, dant, vt. To subdue the courage of; to intimidate; to discourage.

Dauntless, dant'les, a. Fearless; intrepid.

Dawdle, da'dl, vi. (dawdling, dawdled). To waste time; to trifle; to saunter.

Dawn, dan, vi. To begin to grow light in the morning; to glimmer obscurely; to begin to open or appear.—n. The break of day; beginning; first appearance.

Day, dā, n. The time between the rising and setting of the sun; the time of one revolution of the earth; or 24 hours; light; time specified; age time; anniversary.

Daybreak, dā'brāk, n. The dawn; first appearance of light in the morning.

Day-dream, dā'drēm, n. A vision to the waking senses; a reverie.

Daylight, dā'līt, n. The light of the day.

Daze, dāz, vt. (dazing, dazed). To stupefy; to stun

Dazzle, daz'zl, vt. (dazzling, dazzled). To over power with light or splendor.—vi. To be in tensely bright; to be overpowered by light.—n. A dazzling light; glitter.

Deacon, dē'kon, n. A person in the lowest degree of holy orders; a church officer; the president of an incorporated trade.

Dead, ded, a. Without life; deceased; perfectly still; dull; cold; tasteless; spiritless; utter; unerring.

Deaden, ded'n, vt. To abate in vigor, force, or sen sation; to darken, dull, or dim.

Dead-heat, ded'hēt, n. A race in which the com petitors finish at the same time.

Dead-letter, ded'let-ter, n. A letter which cannot be delivered, and is returned to the sender; a law, treaty, etc., which has ceased to be acted on.

Dead-lock, ded'lok, n. Complete stand-still.

Deadly, ded'li, a. That may cause death; mortal implacable.—adv. In a deadly manner.

Dead-weight, ded'wāt, n. A heavy or oppressive burden.

Deaf, def, a. Wanting the sense of hearing; not listening or regarding.

Deaf-mute, def'mūt, n. A deaf and dumb person

Deal, dēl, n. A part; an indefinite quantity, de gree, or extent; the distribution of playing cards; a board or plank; fir or pine timber.—vt (dealing, dealt). To distribute.—vi. To traffic; to behave; to distribute cards.

Dean, dēn, n. A dignitary in cathedral and colle giate churches who presides over the chapter an officer in a university or college.

Dear, dēr, a. Bearing a high price; valuable; ex pensive; a high estimation; beloved.—n. A darling.—adv. Dearly.

Dearth, derth, n. Scarcity; want; famine.

Death, deth, *n.* Extinction of life; decease; cause of decease; damnation.

Deathly, deth 'li, *a.* Deadly; fatal.

Death's-head, deths 'hed, *n.* A figure of a human skull; a kind of moth.

Debacle, dē-bak 'l, *n.* A sudden breaking up of ice; a confused rout; a crash in the social or political world.

Debar, dē-bär', *vt.* (debarring, debarred). To hinder from approach, entry, or enjoyment.

Debase, de-bas', *vt.* (debasing, debased). To lower; to degrade; to vitiate.

Debasement, dē-bās 'ment, *n.* Act of debasing; state of being debased.

Debate, dē-bāt', *n.* Contention in words or arguments; discussion; controversy.—*vt.* (debating, debated). To dispute; to argue; to discuss.—*vi.* To examine different arguments in the mind; to deliberate.

Debauch, dē-bach', *vt.* To corrupt; to pervert.—*vi.* To riot; to revel.—*n.* Excess in eating or drinking; lewdness.

Debaucher, dē-bach 'ėr, *n.* One who debauches or corrupts others.

Debauchery, dē-bach 'e-ri, *n.* Gluttony; intemperance; habitual lewdness.

Debenture, dē-ben 'tūr, *n.* A deed charging property with the repayment of money lent, and with interest; a certificate of drawback.

Debilitate, dē-bil 'i-tāt, *vt.* (debilitating, debilitated). To enfeeble; to enervate.

Debility, dē-bil 'i-ti, *n.* Weakness; feebleness.

Debit, deb 'it, *n.* A recorded item of debt; the lefthand page or debtor side of a ledger or account.—*vt.* To charge with debt.

Debonair, de-bō-nār', *a.* Gracious; courteous.

Debouch, dē-bösh', *vi.* To issue or march out of a narrow place.

Debris, dē-brē', *n.sing.* or *pl.* Fragments; rubbish.

Debt, det, *n.* That which is due from one person to another; obligation; guilt.

Début, dā-bu', *n.* First appearance in public.

Débutant, dā-bu-täng, *fem.* **Débutante,** dā-butängt, *n.* One who makes a début.

Decade, de 'kād, *n.* The number of ten; a period of ten years.

Decadence, Decadency, dē-kā 'dens, dē-kā '-densi or dek 'a-, *n.* A falling off; decay.

Decagon, dē 'ka-gon, *n.* A figure having ten sides.

Decahedron, de-ka-hē 'dron, *n.* A solid figure or body having ten sides.

Decalogue, de 'ka-log, *n.* The ten commandments given by God to Moses.

Decamp, dē-kamp', *vi.* To depart from a camp; to march off; to take oneself off.

Decant, dē-kant', *vt.* To pour from one vessel into another.

Decanter, dē-kant 'ėr, *n.* A glass bottle used for holding wine or other liquors.

Decapitate, dē-kap 'it-āt, *vt.* (decapitating, decapitated). To behead.

Decapod, dek 'a-pod, *n.* A crustacean having ten feet, as a crab; also a cuttle-fish with ten prehensile arms.

Decay, dē-kā', *vi.* To pass from a sound or prosperous state; to waste; to wither; to fail.—*n.* Gradual loss of strength, excellence, etc.; corruption; putrefaction.

Decease, dē-sēs', *n.* Departure from this life; death.—*vi.* (deceasing, deceased). To die.

Deceit, dē-sēt', *n.* Fraud; guile; cunning.

Deceitful, dē-sēt 'ful, *d.* Fraudulent; delusive; false; hollow.

Deceive, dē-sēv', *vt.* (deceiving, deceived). To mislead the mind of; to impose on; to delude; to frustrate (hopes, etc.).

December, dē-sem 'bėr, *n.* The twelfth and last month of the year.

Decency, dē 'sen-si, *n.* The state or quality of being decent; decorum; modesty.

Decennial, dē-sen 'ni-al, *a.* Consisting of ten years, happening every ten years.

Decent, dē 'sent, *a.* Becoming; seemly; respectable; modest; moderate.

Decentralize, dē-sen 'tral-īz, *vt.* To remove from direct dependence on a central authority.

Deception, dē-sep 'shon, *n.* Act of deceiving; state of being deceived; artifice practiced; fraud; double-dealing.

Decide, dē-sīd', *vt.* (deciding, decided). To determine; to settle; to resolve.—*vi.* To determine; to pronounce a judgment.

Deciduous, dē-sid 'ū-us, *a.* Not permanent; having leaves that fall in autumn.

Decimal, de 'si-mal, *a.* Tenth; reckoned by ten.—*n.* A tenth.

Decimate, de 'si-māt, *vt.* (decimating, decimated). To kill every tenth man of; to tithe; to destroy a large number of.

Decimation, de-si-mā 'shon, *n.* Act of decimating; a tithing.

Decipher, dē-sī 'fėr, *vt.* To explain what is written in ciphers; to read what is not clear; to interpret.

Decision, dē-si 'zhon, *n.* Determination of a difference, doubt, or event; final judgment; firmness of purpose or character.

Deck, dek, *vt.* To clothe; to adorn; to furnish with a deck, as a vessel.—*n.* The platform or floor of a ship.

Declaim, dē-klām', *vi.* To make a formal speech; to harangue; to inveigh.

Declamation, dē-kla-mā 'shon, *n.* The art or act of declaiming; a harangue.

Declaration, de-kla-rā 'shon, *n.* Act of declaring; that which is declared; an explicit statement; a solemn affirmation.

Declarative, dē-klär 'at-iv, *a.* Explanatory; making proclamation.

Declare, dē-klār', *vt.* (declaring, declared). To show clearly; to tell explicitly; to testify; to reveal.—*vt.* To make a declaration.

Declension, dē-klen 'shon, *n.* The act or state of declining; refusal; the change of the terminations of nouns, adjectives, and pronouns to form the oblique cases.

Declination, dē-klin-ā 'shon, *n.* A bending downwards; decay; deviation from rectitude; angular distance of a heavenly body north or south from the equator; variation of the magnetic needle from the true meridian of a place.

Decline, dē-klin', *vi.* (declining, declined). To bend downwards; to serve; to fail; not to comply.—*vt.* To bend downward; to refuse; to change the termination of a noun, etc.—*n.* A falling off; decay; deterioration; consumption.

Declinometer, dek-li-nom 'et-ėr, *n.* An instrument for measuring the declination of the magnetic needle.

Declivity, dē-kli 'vi-ti, *n.* Inclining downward; a downward slope.

Decoct, dē-kokt', *vt.* To prepare by boiling; to digest by heat.

Decollate, dē-kol 'āt, *vt.* To behead.

Decompose, dē-kom-pōz, *vt.* To resolve into original elements.—*vi.* To become resolved into elementary particles; to decay.

Decorate, dek 'ō-rāt, *vt.* (decorating, decorated). To adorn; to embellish.

Decoration, dek 'ō-rā 'shon, *n.* Act of decorating; that which adorns; a badge or medal.

Decorum, dē-kō 'rum, *n.* Propriety of speech or behavior; seemliness.

Decoy, dē-koi', *n.* An enclosure for catching ducks or wild fowls; a lure.—*vt.* To lure into a snare; to entice.

Decrease, dē-krēs', *vi.* (decreasing, decreased). To grow less.—*vt.* To cause to become less.—*n.* Gradual diminution; decay; the wane of the moon.

Decree, dē-krē', *n.* An edict; an order or law; predetermined purpose; judicial decision.—*vt.* (decreeing, decreed). To enact; to award; to determine judicially.—*vi.* To make an edict; to appoint by edict.

Decrement, de 'krē-ment, *n.* Decrease; quantity

D

lost by diminution or waste.

Decrepit, dē-krep'it, *a.* Broken down with age; being in the last stage of decay.

Decrepitate, dē-krep'it-āt, *vt.* To calcine in a strong heat, with a continual crackling of the substance.—*vi.* To crackle when roasting.

Decretal, dē-krēt'al, *a.* Containing a decree.—*n.* A decree of the pope; a collection of papal decrees.

Decretive, dē-krēt'iv, *a.* Having the force of a decree; making a decree.

Decretory, de'krē-to-ri, *a.* Established by a decree; judicial; definitive.

Decry, dē-krī', *vt.* To cry down; to rail against; to censure; to depreciate.

Decumbent, dē-kum'bent, *a.* Lying down; recumbent; prostrate.

Decuple, dē-kū-pl, *a.* Tenfold.—*n.* A number ten times repeated.

Decussate, dē-kus'āt, *vt.* and *i.* To intersect; to cross.—*a.* Crossing; intersected.

Dedicate, ded'i-kāt, *vt.* (dedicating, dedicated). To consecrate to a sacred purpose; to devote (often refl.); to inscribe to a friend.

Dedication, ded-i-kā'shon, *n.* Act of devoting to some person, use, or thing; inscription or address.

Deduce, dē-dūs', *vt.* (deducing, deduced). To draw or bring; to gather from premises; to infer; to derive.

Deduct, dē-dukt', *vt.* To subtract.

Deduction, dē-duk'shon, *n.* Inference; abatement; discount.

Deed, dēd, *n.* That which is done; an act; feat; reality; a written agreement; an instrument conveying real estate.

Deem, dēm, *vt.* To judge; to think.—*vi.* To judge; to be of opinion; to estimate.

Deep, dēp, *a.* Being far below the surface; descending far downward; low in situation; not obvious; sagacious; designing; grave in sound; very still or solemn; thick; strongly colored; mysterious; heartfelt; absorbed.—*n.* The sea; the abyss of waters; any abyss.

Deer, dēr, *n. sing.* and *pl.* A quadruped of several species, as the stag, the fallow-deer, the roebuck, the reindeer, etc.

Deface, dē-fās', *vt.* To destroy or mar the surface of a thing; to disfigure; to erase.

Defalcate, dē-fal'kāt, *vt.* To take away or deduct.

Defalcation, dē-fal-kā'shon, *n.* A deficit; a fraudulent abstraction of money.

Defamation, de-fa-mā'shon, *n.* Act of defaming; slander; calumny.

Defame, dē-fām', *vt.* (defaming, defamed). To accuse falsely and maliciously; to slander.

Default, dē-falt', *n.* An omission; neglect to do what duty or law requires; failure to appear in court.—*vi.* To fail in fulfilling an engagement, contract, etc.

Defeat, dē-fēt', *n.* Frustration; overthrow; loss of battle.—*vt.* To frustrate; to foil, to overthrow; to conquer.

Defecate, de'fē-kāt, *vt.* To clear from lees; to purify.—*vi.* To void excrement.

Defect, dē-fekt', *n.* Want; a blemish; fault; flaw.

Defective, dē-fekt'iv, *a.* Having a defect; deficient; faulty.

Defend, dē-fend', *vt.* To guard; to support; to resist; to vindicate; to act as defendant.—*vi.* To make defense or opposition.

Defendant, dē-fen'dant, *n.* A defender; in *law,* the person that opposes a charge, etc.

Defense, dē-fens', *n.* A guarding against danger; protection; fortification; vindication; apology; plea; method adopted by one against whom legal proceedings are taken; skill in fencing.

Defensive, dē-fens'iv, *a.* Proper for defense; carried on in resisting attack; in a state or posture to defend.—*n.* That which defends; state or posture of defense.

Defer, dē-fer', *vt.* (deferring, deferred). To put off to a future time; to postpone.—*vi.* To yield to an-

other's opinion; to submit courteously or from respect.

Deference, de'fer-ens, *n.* A yielding in opinion; regard; respect; submission.

Deferment, dē-fer-ment, *n.* Postponement.

Defiance, dē-fi'ans, *n.* Act of defying; a challenge to fight; contempt of opposition or danger.

Deficient, de-fi'shent, *a.* Defective; imperfect; not adequate.

Deficit, de'fi-sit, *n.* Deficiency of revenue.

Defile, dē-fil', *vt.* (defiling, defiled). To make foul to pollute; to violate the chastity of; to march off in a line, or file by file.—*n.* A narrow way in which troops may march only in a line, or with a narrow front; a long narrow pass.

Define, dē-fin', *vt.* (defining, defined). To limit; to explain exactly.

Definite, de'fin-it, *a.* Having fixed limits; precise exact; clear.

Definition, de-fi-ni'shon, *n.* The act of defining; a brief description of a thing by its properties; an explanation in words.

Definitive, dē-fin'it-iv, *a.* Limiting; positive; determining; final.—*n.* A word used to limit the signification of a noun.

Deflagrate, de'flā-grāt, *vi.* To burn with a sudden and violent combustion.—*vt.* To set fire to.

Deflect, dē-flekt', *vi.* To deviate; to swerve.—*vt.* To cause to turn aside.

Defloration, dē-flor-ā'shon, *n.* Act of deflowering rape.

Deflower, Deflour, dē-flou'er, dē-flour', *vt.* To strip of flowers, or of bloom and beauty; to deprive of virginity.

Defluxion, dē-fluk'shon, *n.* A discharge of fluid from a mucous membrane.

Defoliation, dē-fō'li-ā''shon, *n.* The fall of the leaf, or shedding of leaves.

Deform, dē-form', *vt.* To mar in form; to disfigure

Defraud, dē-frad', *vt.* To deprive of or withhold from wrongfully.

Defray, dē-frā', *vt.* To discharge or pay, as the expenses of anything.

Deft, deft, *a.* Apt; clever.

Defunct, dē-fungkt', *a.* Dead; deceased.—*n.* A dead person; one deceased.

Defy, dē-fi', *vt.* (defying, defied). To provoke to combat; to dare; to challenge; to set at nought

Degeneracy, dē-jen'e-ra-si, *n.* A growing worse or inferior; decline in good qualities; departure from the virtue of ancestors.

Degenerate, dē-jen'e-rat, *vi.* To become worse than one's kind; to decay in good qualities. —*a* Fallen from primitive or natural excellence mean; corrupt.

Deglutition, dē-glū-ti'shon, *n.* Act or power of swallowing.

Degrade, dē-grād', *vt.* (degrading, degraded). To reduce to a lower rank; to strip of honors, to debase; to depose; to dishonor.

Degree, dē-grē', *n.* A step; step in relationship rank quality, etc.; measure; extent; the 360th part of the circumference of a circle; a mark of distinction conferred by universities; divisions marked on scientific instruments.

Dehydration, dē-hī-drā'shon, *n.* Process of free ing a compound from water.

Deify, dē'i-fi, *vt.* (deifying, deified). To exalt to the rank of a deity; to extol as an object of supreme regard.

Deign, dān, *vi.* To vouchsafe; to condescend.—*vt* To condescend to give.

Deist, dē'ist, *n.* One who acknowledges the exis tence of a God, but denies revealed religion; a freethinker.

Deity, dē'i-ti, *n.* Godhead; the Supreme Being; a fabulous god or goddess; a divinity.

Deject, dē-jekt', *vt.* To dispirit; to depress.

Dejection, dē-jek'shon, *n.* Depression; melan choly; lowness of spirits.

Déjeuner, dā-zhö-nä, *n.* Breakfast; luncheon.

Delay, dē-lā', *vt.* To defer; to retard; to stop; to protract.—*vi.* To linger; to stop for a time.—*n.* A lingering; stay; hindrance.

Delectable, dē-lekt´a-bl, *a.* Delightful.

Delectation, dē-lek-tā´shon, *n.* A giving of pleasure or delight.

Delegate, de´lē-gāt, *vt.* (delegating, delegated). To send as a representative; to depute; to commit to another's care.—*n.* A representative; a deputy.

Delete, dē-lēt´, *vt.* (deleting, deleted). To blot out; to erase; to efface.

Deleterious, de-lē-te´ri-us, *a.* Hurtful; poisonous; pernicious.

Delf, delf, *n.* Earthenware, covered with enamel or white glazing in imitation of chinaware or porcelain.

Deliberate, dē-lib´e-rāt, *vi.* To weigh well in one's mind; to consider; to consult; to debate.—*vt.* To balance well in the mind; to consider.—*a.* Cautious; discreet; well advised.

Deliberation, dē-lib´e-rā´´shon, *n.* Thoughtful consideration; prudence; discussion of reasons for and against a measure.

Delicacy, de´li-ka-si, *n.* The quality of being delicate; fineness of texture; tenderness; minute accuracy; refined taste; a dainty.

Delicate, de´li-kāt, *a.* Pleasing to the taste or senses; choice; fine; soft; smooth; nice in forms; minute; easily hurt or affected; tender; not robust

Delicious, dē-li´shus, *a.* Highly pleasing to the taste; delightful.

Delight, dē-līt´, *n.* That which yields great pleasure; a high degree of pleasure; joy.—*vt.* To affect with great pleasure; to give high satisfaction to.—*vi.* To take great pleasure; to be rejoiced.

Delimit, dē-lim´it, *vt.* To mark or settle distinctly the limits of.

Delineate, dē-lin´ē-āt, *vt.* To draw the lines showing the form of; to sketch; to describe.

Delinquent, dē-lin´kwent, *a.* Neglecting duty.—*n.* One who fails to perform his duty; one who commits a fault or crime.

Delirium, dē-li´ri-um, *n.* Temporary disorder of the mind; violent excitement.

Delitescence. Delitescency, del-i-tes´ens, del-i-tes´en-si, *n.* The state of being concealed, or not active or manifest.

Deliver, dē-liv´ėr, *vt.* To free, as from danger or bondage; to disburden a woman of a child; to surrender; to commit, to give forth in words or in action.

Deliverance, de-liv´ėr-ans, *n.* Release; rescue; an authoritative judgment.

Delivery, dē-liv´e-ri, *n.* Act of delivering; childbirth; rescue; surrender; distribution (of letters); manner of speaking.

Dell, del, *n.* A small valley; a glen.

Delta, del´ta, *n.* The space between diverging mouths of a river, as the Nile.

Deltoid, del´toid, *a.* Triangular.

Delude, dē-lūd´, *vt.* (deluding, deluded). To impose on; to deceive; to circumvent.

Deluge, del´ūj, *n.* A flood; an inundation; the flood in the days of Noah; a sweeping or overwhelming calamity.—*vt.* (deluging, deluged). To inundate; to drown; to overwhelm.

Delusion, dē-lū´zhon, *n.* Act of deluding; a false belief; illusion; fallacy.

Delusive, dē-lū´siv, *a.* Apt to deceive.

Delve, delv, *vt.* and *i.* (delving, delved). To dig.

Demagnetize, dē´mag´not-īz, *vt.* To deprive of magnetic polarity.

Demagogue, dem´a-gog, *n.* A leader of the people; a factious orator.

Demand, dē-mand´, *vt.* To ceek as due by right; to require; to interrogate.—*n.* A claim by virtue of a right; an asking with authority; debt; the calling for in order to purchase; desire to purchase or possess.

Demarcation, dē-mär-kā´shon, *n.* Act of setting a limit; a limit fixed.

Demean, dē-mēn´, *vt.* To conduct; to behave; to debase (oneself).

Demeanor, dē-mēn´ėr, *n.* Manner of conducting oneself; behavior.

Demented, dē-ment´ed, *a.* Insane; infatuated.

Demerit, dē-me´rit, *n.* Fault; vice.

Demi-god, de´mi-god, *n.* Half a god; one partaking of the divine nature.

Demi-monde, demi´mongd, *n.* The class of fashionable courtesans.

Demise, dē-mīz´, *n.* Death; conveyance of an estate by lease or will.—*vt.* (demising, demised). To transfer; to lease; to bequeath.

Demit, dē-mit´, *vt.* (demitting, demitted). To lay down formally, as an office.

Demiurge, Demiurgus, dē´mi-ėrj, dē-mi-ėr-gus, *n.* A maker; the Creator.

Demobilize, dē-mō´bil-īz, *vt.* To disband.

Democracy, dē-mok´ra-si, *n.* A form of government in which the supreme power is vested in the people.

Demolish, dē-mol´ish, *vt.* To pull down; to destroy.

Demon, dē´mon, *n.* A spirit, holding a place below the celestial deities of the pagans; an evil spirit; a devil; a fiend-like man.

Demonetize, dē-mon´e-tīz, *vt.* To deprive of standard value, as money; to withdraw from circulation.

Demoniac, dē-mō´ni-ak, *n.* A human being possessed by a demon.

Demonism, dē´mon-izm, *n.* Belief in demons.

Demonize, dē´mon-īz, *vt.* To fill with the spirit of a demon.

Demonstrate, de-mon´strāt, *vt.* (demonstrating, demonstrated). To prove beyond doubt; to make evident; to exhibit.

Demonstration, de-mon-strā´shon, *n.* Act or process of demonstrating; proof; massing of troops to deceive the enemy; a gathering to exhibit sympathy with a person or cause.

Demoralize, dē-mo´ral-īz, *vt.* To corrupt the morals of; to deprave.

Demoralizing, dē-mo´ral-īz-ing, *p.a.* Tending to destroy morals or moral principles.

Demos, dē´mos, *n.* The people at large.

Demotic, dē-mot´ik, *a.* Pertaining to the common people; applied to the popular alphabet of the ancient Egyptians, as distinguished from the *hieratic.*

Demulcent, dē-mul´sent, *a.* Softening; mollifying.—*n.* A medicine to soothe irritation.

Demur, dē-mėr, *vi.* (demurring, demurred). To hesitate; to object.—*n.* Pause; suspense of proceeding or decision; objection stated.

Demure, dē-mūr´, *a.* Consciously grave; affectedly modest.

Den, den, *n.* A cave; a dell; a haunt.

Denary, dē-na-ri, *a.* Containing ten; proceeding by tens.—*n.* The number ten.

Dendriform, den´dri-form, *a.* Having the form or appearance of a tree.

Dendritic, Dendritical, den-drit´ik, den-drit´i-kal, *a.* Resembling a tree; marked by figures resembling shrubs, moss, etc.

Denial, dē-nī´al, *n.* Act of denying; contradiction; refusal to grant or acknowledge.

Denigrate, den´i-grāt, *vt.* To blacken; to sully.

Denim, den´im, *n.* A coarse cotton drill used for making aprons, overalls, etc.

Denizen, de´ni-zn, *n.* A stranger admitted to residence in a foreign country

Denominate, dē-nom´in-āt, *vt.* (denominating, denominated). To name; to designate.

Denomination, dē-nom´in-ā´´shon, *n.* Act of naming; title; class; religious sect.

Denominationalism, dē-nom´in-ā´´shon al izm, *n.* A class spirit; system of religious sects having each their own schools.

Denominative, dē-nom´in-at-iv, *a.* That confers a distinct appellation.

Denominator, dē-nom´in-āt-ėr, *n.* One who or that which denominates; that number placed below the line in vulgar fractions.

D

Denote, dē-nōt´, vt. To indicate; to imply.

Dénouement, dā-nö´mäng, n. The winding up of a plot in a novel or drama; solution of a mystery; issue; the event.

Denounce, dē-nouns´, vt. (denouncing, denounced). To threaten; to accuse publicly; to stigmatize.

Dense, dens, a. Thick; close; compact.

Dent, dent, n. A mark made by a blow on a solid body.—vt. To make a dent on.

Dental, den´tal, a. Pertaining to the teeth; pronounced by the teeth and the tip of the tongue.—n. A dental letter or sound, as d, t, th.

Dentifrice, den´ti-fris, n. A powder or other substance for cleansing the teeth.

Dentine, den´tin, n. The ivory tissue forming the body of the tooth.

Dentist, den´tist, n. One whose occupation is to extract, repair, or replace teeth.

Dentition, den-ti´shon, n. The cutting of teeth in infancy; the system of teeth peculiar to an animal.

Denture, den´tūr, n. A set of false teeth.

Denude, dē-nūd´, vt. (denuding, denuded). To make bare; to divest; to uncover.

Denunciation, dē-nun´si-ā´´shon, n. Act of denouncing; public menace; arraignment.

Deny, dē-ni´, vt. (denying, denied). To declare not to be true; to disavow; to refuse to grant or acknowledge; not to afford or yield.

Deodorize, dē-ō´dėr-iz, vt. (deodorizing, deodorized). To deprive of fetid odor.

Deoxidate, Deoxidize, dē-ok´sid-āt, dē-ok´sid-īz, vt. To reduce from the state of an oxide.

Depart, dē-pärt´, vi. To go away; to desist; to abandon; to deviate; to die.

Department, dē-pärt´ment, n. A separate part; a division of territory; a distinct branch, as of science, etc.

Depend, dē-pend´, vi. To hang from; to be contingent or conditioned; to rest or rely solely; to trust.

Dependant, Dependent, dē-pend´ant, dē-pend´ent, n. One who depends on another; a retainer. (The spelling with -ant is more common in the noun, with -ent in the adj.).

Dependent, Dependant, dē-pend´ent, dē-pend´ant, a. Hanging down; subordinate; relying solely on another; contingent.

Depict, dē-pikt´, vt. To paint; to delineate; to represent in words.

Depilate, dep´i-lāt, vt. To strip of hair.

Depilatory, dē-pil´ä-to-ri, n. An application to remove hair from the skin.

Deplete, dē-plēt´, vt. (depleting, depleted). To empty, reduce, or exhaust.

Deplorable, dē-plōr´a-bl, a. To be deplored; lamentable; grievous; pitiable.

Deplore, dē-plōr´, vt. (deploring, deplored). To feel or express deep grief for; to bewail.

Deploy, dē-ploi´, vt. To open out; to extend from column to line as a body of troops.—vi. To form a more extended front or line.

Deplume, dē-plūm´, vt. To strip of feathers.

Depolarize, dē-pō´lär-īz, vt. To deprive of polarity.

Depone, dē-pōn´, vi. (deponing, deponed). To give testimony; to depose.

Deponent, dē-pōn´ent, a. Laying down; that has a passive form but an active signification.—n. One who gives testimony under oath; a deponent verb.

Depopulate, dē-po´pū-lāt, vt. To deprive of inhabitants; to dispeople.

Deport, dē-pōrt´, vt. To transport; to demean; to conduct (oneself).

Deportation, dē-pōrt-ā´shon, n. Removal from one country to another; exile.

Deportment, dē-pōrt´ment, n. Carriage; demeanor; manner of acting.

Depose, dē-pōz´, vt. (deposing, deposed). To dethrone; to divest of office; to degrade.—vi. To bear witness; to give testimony in writing.

Deposit, dē-poz´it, vt. To lay down; to lodge in a place; to lay in a place for preservation; to intrust; to commit as a pledge.—n. Any matter laid down or lodged; anything intrusted to another; a thing given as security.

Depositary, dē-poz´it-a-ri, n. One to whom a thing is lodged in trust; a guardian.

Deposition, dē-pō-zi´shon, n. Act of depositing and of deposing; attested written testimony; declaration; act of dethroning a king, or degrading an official.

Depot, dep´ō, n. A place of deposit; headquarters of a regiment; a railway-station.

Deprave, dē-prāv´, vt. (depraving, depraved). To make bad or worse; to impair the good qualities of; to corrupt; to vitiate.

Depravity, dē-prav´i-ti, n. Corruption of moral principles; wickedness; profligacy.

Deprecate, de´prē-kāt, vt. (deprecating, deprecated). To pray for deliverance from; to plead against; to express regret or disapproval.

Deprecatory, Deprecative, de´prē-kā-to-ri, de´prē-kāt-iv, a. That serves to deprecate; containing protest or entreaty.

Depreciate, dēprē´shi-āt, vt. (depreciating, depreciated). To bring down the price or value of; to undervalue; to disparage; to traduce.—vi. To fall in value.

Depredate, de´prē-dāt, vt. To plunder; to waste.

Depress, dē-pres´, vt. To press down; to lower; to humble; to deject.

Depression, dē-pre´shon, n. Act of depressing; state of being depressed; a low state; a sinking of a surface; a hollow; abasement; dejection; a state of dulness.

Deprivation, de-pri-vā´shon, n. Act of depriving; state of being deprived; want; bereavement; deposition of a clergyman.

Deprive, dē-prīv´, vt. (depriving, deprived). To take from; to dispossess; to hinder from possessing or enjoying.

Depth, depth, n. Deepness; a deep place; the darkest or stillest part, as of the night; the inner part; abstruseness; unsearchableness; intensity; extent of penetration.

Deputy, de´pū-ti, n. A person appointed to act for another; a substitute; a delegate; an agent.

Deracinate, dē-ras´in-āt, vt. To pluck up by the roots; to extirpate.

Derange, dē-rānj´, vt. (deranging, deranged). To disturb the regular order of; to displace; to disconcert; to disorder the mind of.

Derangement, dē-rānj´ment, n. A putting out of order; disorder; insanity.

Derelict, de´re-likt, a. Abandoned.—n. Anything forsaken or left, especially a ship.

Dereliction, de-re-lik´shon, n. Act of forsaking; state of being forsaken; neglect.

Deride, dē-rid´, vt. (deriding, derided). To laugh at in contempt; to ridicule; to jeer.

Derision, dē-ri´zhon, n. Act of deriding; scorn; ridicule; mockery.

Derivation, de-ri-vā´shon, a. Act of deriving; the tracing of a word from its root; deduction.

Derivative, de-riv´āt-iv, a. Derived; secondary.—n. That which is derived; a word which takes its origin in another word.

Derive, de-rīv´, vt. (deriving, derived). To draw or receive, as from a source or origin; to trace the etymology of.—vi. To come from.

Derma, Dermis, Derm, dėr´ma, dėr´mis, dėrm, n. The true skin, or under layer of the skin.

Dermatology, dėr-ma-tol´o-ji, n. The science which treats of skin and its diseases.

Dermo-skelton, dėr´mo-skel´´e-ton, n. The covering of scales, plates, shells, etc., of many animals, as crabs, crocodiles, etc.

Derogate, de´rō-gāt, vt. (derogating, derogated). To detract from; to disparage.—vi. To detract.

Derogatory, dē-rog´ā-to-ri, a. Tending to lessen in repute, effect, etc.; disparaging.

Derrick, de´rik, n. A kind of crane for hoisting heavy weights.

Descant, des´kant, n. A discourse; discussion; a

song or tune with various modulations.—*vi.* des-kant'. To discourse or animadvert freely; to add a part to a melody.

Descend, dĕ-send', *vi.* To pass or move down; to invade; to be derived; to pass to an heir.—*vt.* To pass or move down, on, or along.

Descendant, dĕ-send'ant, *n.* Offspring from an ancestor; issue.

Descent, dĕ-sent', *n.* Act of descending; declivity; invasion; a passing from an ancestor to an heir; lineage; distance drom the common ancestor; descendants; a rank in the scale of subordination.

Describe, dĕ-skrīb', *vt.* (describing, described). To mark or trace out; to represent on paper, etc.; to portray; to relate.

Description, dĕ-skrip'shon, *n.* Act of describing; account; relation; class, species, kind.

Descry, dĕ-skri', *vt.* (descrying, descried). To espy; to discover from a distance.

Desecrate, de'sĕ-krāt, *vt.* (desecrating, desecrated). To divert from a sacred purpose; to profane.

Desert, de'zĕrt, *a.* Waste; uncultivated.—*n.* An uninhabited tract; a vast sandy plain.

Desert, dĕ-zĕrt', *vt.* To leave, as service; to abandon; to quit.—*vi.* To run away; to quit a service without permission.—*n.* That which is deserved; merit or demerit; reward.

Deserter, dĕ-zĕrt'ĕr, *n.* One who deserts; a soldier or seaman who quits the service without permission.

Deserve, dĕ-zĕrv', *vt.* (deserving, deserved). To merit by qualities or services; to be worthy of.— *vi.* To merit; to be worthy of.

Deshabille, dez-a-bēl', *n.* The state of being in undress, or not fully dressed.

Desiccant, Desiccative, des'i-kant, or dĕ-sik'ant, dĕ-ski'a-tiv, *a.* Drying.—*n.* An application that dries a sore.

Desiccate, dĕ-sik'āt, *vt.* To exhaust of moisture; to dry.

Desiderate, dĕ-sid'ĕr-āt, *vt.* To desire; to want; to miss.

Desideratum, dĕ-sid'ĕr-ā''tum, *n.*; pl. **-ata** That which is not possessed, but is desirable; something much wanted.

Design, dĕ-sīn', *vt.* To delineate by drawing the outline of; to form in idea; to plan; to propose; to mean.—*vi.* To intend.—*n.* A representation of a thing by an outline; first idea represented by lines; a plan drawn out in the mind; purpose; aim; project.

Designate, de'sig-nāt, *vt.* (designating, designated). To point out; to name; to characterize; to appoint; to allot.

Designer, de-sin'ĕr, *n.* One who designs; a contriver; a plotter.

Desirable, dĕ-zīr'a-bl, *a.* Worthy of desire; pleasing; agreeable.

Desire, dĕ-zīr', *n.* Eagerness to obtain or enjoy; aspiration; longing; a request to obtain; the object of desire; love; lust.—*vt.* (desiring, desired). To wish for the possession or enjoyment of; to covet; to ask; to petition.

Desist, dĕ-sist', *vi.* To cease to act or proceed; to forbear; to leave off. (With *from.*)

Desk, desk, *n.* An inclining table to write or read upon; a portable case for the same purpose; a lectern; a pulpit.

Desolate, de'sō-lāt, *a.* Destitute of inhabitants; waste; laid waste; afflicted; forlorn.—*vt.* (desolating, desolated). To deprive of inhabitants; to make desert; to ravage.

Despair, dĕ-spār', *n.* A hopeless state; despondency; that which causes despair; loss of hope.—*vi.* To give up all hope; to despond.

Desperado, des-pē-rä'dō, *n.* A desperate fellow; a reckless ruffian.

Desperate, des'pē-rāt, *a.* Without care of safety; reckless; frantic; beyond hope; past cure.

Desperation, des-pē-rä'shon, *n.* A giving up of hope; fury; disregard of danger; despair.

Despicable, des'pik-a-bl, *a.* Contemptible; vile; base; mean.

Despise, dĕ-spiz', *vt.* (despising, despised). To hold in contempt; to scorn; to disdain.

Despite, dĕ-spīt', *n.* Extreme malice; defiance with contempt; an act of malice.—*vt.* To despise; to spite.—*prep.* In spite of; notwithstanding.

Despoil, dĕ-spoil', *vt.* To take from by force; to rob; to bereave; to rifle.

Despond, dĕ-spond', *vi.* To be cast down or dejected; to lose heart, hope, or resolution.

Despondence, Despondency, dĕ-spond'ens, dĕ-spond'en-si, *n.* Hopelessness; dejection.

Despot, des'pot, *n.* An absolute ruler (generally in a bad sense); a tyrant.

Desquamate, dĕ-skwā'māt, *vt.* or *i.* to come off in scales; to peel off.

Dessert, dĕ-zĕrt', *n.* That which is served at the close of a dinner, as fruits, etc.

Destination, des-tin-ā'shon, *n.* Act of destining; ultimate design; predetermined end.

Destine, des'tin, *vt.* (destining, destined). To set or appoint to a purpose; to design; to doom; to ordain.

Destiny, des'ti-ni, *n.* State appointed or predetermined; fate; invincible necessity.

Destitute, des'ti-tūt, *a.* Wanting; needy; comfortless; forlorn.

Destitution, des-ti-tū'shon, *n.* Want; poverty; indigence.

Destroy, dĕ-stroi', *vt.* To pull down; to overthrow; to devastate; to annihilate.

Destroyer, dĕ-stroi'ĕr, *n.* One who or that which destroys; a swift class of vessel intended for the destruction of torpedo-craft, and itself armed with guns and torpedoes.

Destruction, dĕ-struk'shon, *n.* A pulling down; demolition; overthrow; death; slaughter; cause of destruction.

Desultory, de'sul-to-ri, *a.* Passing from one subject to another, without order; unconnected; rambling.

Detach, dĕ-tach', *vt.* To separate; to disengage.

Detachment, dĕ-tach'ment, *n.* Act of detaching; a body of troops, or number of ships, sent from the main army or fleet.

Detail, dĕ-tāl, *vt.* To relate in particulars; to specify; in military affairs, to appoint to a particular service.—*n.* dĕ-tāl' or dē'tāl. An individual fact, circumstance, or portion; an item; a report of particulars.

Detain, dĕ-tān', *vt.* To keep back or from; to withhold; to arrest; to check; to retard.

Detect, dĕ-tekt', *vt.* To discover; to bring to light.

Detection, dĕ-tek'shon, *n.* Act of detecting; discovery of a person or thing.

Detective, dĕ-tek'tiv, *a.* Skilled or employed in detecting.—*n.* A police officer whose duty is to detect criminals; one who investigates cases for hire.

Detent, dĕ-tent', *n.* A pin, stud, or lever forming a check in a clock, watch, etc.

Deter, dĕ-tĕr', *vt.* (deterring, deterred). To prevent by prohibition or danger; to discourage.

Detergent, dĕ-tĕrj'ent, *a.* Cleansing; purging.—*n.* That which cleanses.

Deteriorate, dĕ-tē'ri-ō-rāt, *vi.* (deteriorating, deteriorated). To grow worse; to degenerate.—*vt.* To reduce in quality.

Determent, dĕ-tĕr'ment, *n.* Act of deterring; that which deters.

Determination, dĕ-tĕr'min-ā''shon, *n.* Act of determining; firm resolution; judgment; strong direction to a given point; end.

Determine, dĕ-tĕr'min, *vt.* (determining, determined). To bound; to fix permanently; to decide; to establish; to give a direction to; to resolve on; to bring to an end.—*vi.* To resolve; to conclude.

Detest, dĕ-test', *vt.* To abhor; to loathe.

Detestable, dĕ-test'a-bl, *a.* Extremely hateful; abominable; odious.

Detestation, dĕ-test-ā'shon, *n.* Extreme hatred; abhorrence; loathing.

D

Dethrone, dē-thrōn´, vt. (dethroning, dethroned). To divest of royal authority and dignity; to depose.

Detonate, de´tō-nāt, vt. (detonating, detonated). To cause to explode; to cause to burn with a sudden repot.—vi. To explode.

Detract, dē-trakt´, vt. To draw away; to disparage.—vi. To take away from (especially reputation).

Detriment, de´tri-ment, n. Loss; damage; injury; prejudice; mischief; harm.

Detritus, dē-trīt´us, n. A mass of matter worn off from solid bodies by attrition; disintegrated materials of rocks.

Detruncate, dē-trung´kāt, vt. To cut off; to lop; to shorten by cutting.

Deuce, dūs, n. A card or die with two spots; the devil; perdition.

Deuteronomy, dū-tėr-on´o-mi, n. The second law, or second giving of the law by Moses; the fifth book of the Pentateuch.

Devastate, de´vas-tāt, vt. (devastating, devastated). To lay waste; to ravage.

Develop, dē-vel´up, vt. To unfold; to lay open to view; to make to grow.—vi. To be unfolded; to become manifest; to grow or expand; to be evolved.

Deviate, dē´vi-āt, vi. (deviating, deviated). To stray; to wander; to swerve; to err.

Device, dē-vīs´, n. That which is devised; contrivance; scheme; an emblem.

Devil, de´vil, n. An evil spirit; Satan; a very wicked person; a machine for cutting, tearing, etc.—vt. (devilling, devilled). To pepper excessively and broil; to tease or cut up.

Devil-may-care, de´vil-mā-kār, a. Rollicking; reckless.

Devious, dē´vi-us, a. Out of the common way or track; erring; rambling.

Devise, dē-vīz´, vt. (devising, devised). To form in the mind; to contrive; to invent; to give or bequeath by will.—n. Act of bequeathing by will; a will; a share of estate bequeathed.

Devoid, dē-void´, a. Destitute; not possessing; free from.

Devoir, de-vwär´, n. Service or duty; act of civility or respect.

Devote, dē-vōt´, vt. (devoting, devoted). To set apart by vow; to consecrate; to addict (oneself); to apply closely to; to consign.

Devotee, dev-o-tē´, n. One wholly devoted, particularly to religion; a votary.

Devotion, dē-vō´shon, n. Act of devoting or state of being devoted; prayer; devoutness; ardent love or affection; attachment; earnestness.

Devour, dē-vour´, vt. To eat ravenously; to swallow up; to waste; to look on with keen delight.

Devout, dē-vout´, a. Pious; expressing devotion; earnest; solemn.

Dew, dū, n. Moisture from the atmosphere condensed into drops on the surface of cold bodies, as grass, etc.; damp.—vt. To wet with dew; to moisten; to damp.

Dew-lap, dū´lap, n. The fold of skin that hangs from the throat of oxen, etc.

Dew-point, dū´point, n. The temperature at which dew begins to form.

Dexterity, deks-te´ri-ti, n. Right-handedness; adroitness; expertness; skill.

Dexterous, deks´tėr-us, a. Expert in manual acts; adroit; done with dexterity.

Dextrine, deks´trin, n. A gummy matter prepared from starch.

Dextrose, deks´tros, n. Grape-sugar.

Diabetes, dī-a-bē´tēz, n. Disease characterized by a morbid discharge of urine.

Diabolic, Diabolical, dī-a-bol´ik, dī-a-bol´ik-al, a. Devilish; atrocious.

Diaconate, dī-ak´on-āt, n. Office of a deacon; body of deacons.

Diacoustics, dī-a-kous´tiks, n. The science of refracted sound.

Diacritical, dī-a-krit´ik-al, a. Separating; distinc-

tive; applied to a mark used to distinguish letters similar in form.

Diadem, dī´a-dem, n. A badge of royalty worn on the head; a crown; a coronet.

Diaeresis, dī-ē´re-sis, n. Separation of one syllable into two; a mark signifying such a division, as in *aërial*.

Diagnose, dī-ag-nōs´, vt. To ascertain from symptoms the true nature of.

Diagnosis, dī-ag-nō´sis, n. The ascertaining from symptoms the true nature of diseases.

Diagonal, dī-ag´on-al, a. Extending from one angle to another of a quadrilateral figure; lying in an oblique direction.—n. A straight line drawn between opposite angles of a quadrilateral figure.

Diagram, dī´a-gram, n. A drawing to demonstrate the properties of any figure; an illustrative figure in outline.

Dial, dī´al, n. An instrument for showing the hour by the sun's shadow; face of a clock, etc.

Dialect, dī´a-lekt, n. The idiom of a language peculiar to a province; language; manner of speaking.

Dialectics, dī-a-lek´tiks, n.sing. The art of reasoning; that branch of logic which teaches the rules and modes of reasoning; word-fence. Also **Dialectic** in same sense.

Dialling, dī´al-ing, n. The science which explains the principles of measuring time by dials; the art of constructing dials.

Dialogue, dī´a-log, n. A conversation between two or more persons.

Dial-plate, dī´al-plāt, n. The plate or face of a dial, clock, or watch.

Diamagnetic, dī-a-mag-net´´ik, a. Applied to substances which, when under the influence of magnetism, point east and west.

Diameter, dī-am´et-ėr, n. A straight line passing through the center of a circle, and terminated by the circumference; the distance through the center of any object.

Diamond, dī´a-mond, n. A valuable gem, remarkable for its hardness and transparency; a rhombus; a card of the suit marked with such figures in red; a very small printing type.—a. Resembling a diamond; set with diamonds.

Diapason, dī-a-pā´zon, n. The entire compass of a voice or instrument; an organ stop.

Diaper, dī´a-pėr, n. A figured linen or cotton cloth.—vt. To variegate or diversify with figures.—vi. To draw flowers or figures on.

Diaphanous, dī-af´an-us, a. Having power to transmit rays of light; transparent.

Diaphragm, dī´a-fram, n. The midriff, a muscular partition separating the thorax from the abdomen.

Diarrhea, dī-a-rē´a, n. A morbidly frequent evacuation of the intestines.

Diary, dī´a-ri, n. A register of daily events or transactions; a journal.

Diastole, dī-as´to-lē, n. Dilatation of the heart in beating.

Diathermal, Diathermous, dī-a-thėr´mal, dī-a-thėr´mus, a. Freely permeable by heat.

Diathesis, dī-ath´e-sis, n. Predisposition.

Diatomic, dī-a-tom´ik, a. Consisting of two atoms.

Diatonic, dī-a-ton´ik, a. In *music*, applied to the major or minor scales.

Diatribe, dī´a-trīb, n. A continued disputation; a lengthy invective.

Dibble, dib´bl, n. A pointed instrument to make holes for planting seeds, etc.—vt. (dibbling, dibbled). To make holes for planting seeds, etc.

Dice, dīs, n.; pl. of **Die**, for gaming.—vi. (dicing, diced). To play with dice.

Dichotomous, dī-kot´o-mus, a. In *botany*, regularly divided by pairs from top to bottom.

Dickey, Dicky, dik´i, n. A false shirt-front; the driver's seat in a carriage.

Dicotyledon, dī´kot-i-lē´´don, n. A plant whose seeds contain a pair of cotyledons.

Dictaphone, dik´ta-fōn, n. Trade name for an instrument into which correspondence is dictated, to be transcribed afterwards.

Dictate, dik'tāt, *vt.* (dictating, dictated). To deliver, as an order or direction; to prescribe; to tell what to say or write; to instigate.—*n.* An order delivered; an authoritative precept or maxim; an impulse.

Dictator, dik-tāt'er, *n.* One invested with absolute authority.

Diction, dik'shon, *n.* Choice of words; mode of expression; style.

Dictionary, dik'shon-a-ri, *n.* A book containing the words of a language arranged alphabetically, with their meanings, etc.; a work explaining the terms, etc., of any subject under heads alphabetically arranged.

Dictum, dik'tum, *n.*; pl. **Dicta.** An authoritative saying or assertion.

Did, did, *pret of do.*

Didactic, Didactical, di-dak'tik, di-dak'tik-al, *a.* Adapted to teach; instructive.

Die, dī, *vi.* (dying, died). To cease to live; to expire; to sink gradually; to vanish.

Die, dī, *n.*; pl. **Dice,** dis, in first sense, in the others **Dies,** diz. A small cube with numbered faces; any cubic body; the dado of a pedestal; a stamp used in coining money; an implement for turning out things of a regular shape.

Dielectric, dī-ē-lek'trik, *n.* Any medium through or across which electric induction takes place between two conductors.

Diesel, dēs'el, *n.* An oil-burning internal-combustion engine.

Diet, dī'et, *n.* A person's regular food; food prescribed medically; a meeting of dignitaries or delegates for legislative or other purposes.—*vt.* To furnish provisions for.—*vi.* To eat according to rules prescribed.

Dietetics, dī-et-et'iks, *n.* Principles for regulating the diet.

Differ, dif'er, *vi.* To be unlike or distinct; to disagree; to be at variance.

Difference, dif'er-ens, *n.* State of being different; dissimilarity; that which distinguishes; dispute; point in dispute; remainder after a sum is subtracted.

Differential, dif-er-en'shi-al, *a.* Creating a difference; discriminating.—*n.* An infinitesimal difference between two states of a variable quantity; a differential gear.

Differentiate, dif-er-en'shi-āt, *vt.* To mark or distinguish by a difference.—*vi.* To acquire a distinct character.

Difficult, dif'fi-kult, *a.* Not easy to be done, etc.; perplexed; hard to please; unyielding.

Diffidence, dif'fi-dens, *n.* Want of confidence; modest reserve; bashfulness.

Diffract, dif-frakt', *vt.* To bend from a straight line; to deflect.

Diffraction, dif-frak'shon, *n.* The modifications which light undergoes when it passes by the edge of an opaque body; deflection.

Diffuse, dif-fūz', *vt.* (diffusing, diffused). To pour out and spread; to circulate; to proclaim.—*a.* dif-fūs'. Widely spread; prolix; verbose.

Diffusion, dif-fū'zhon, *n.* A spreading or scattering; dispersion; circulation.

Dig, dig, *vt.* (digging, digged or dug). To open and turn up with a spade; to excavate.—*vi.* To work with a spade.

Digest, di-jest', *vt.* To arrange under proper heads; to think out; to dissolve in the stomach; to soften by a heated liquid; to bear with patience.—*vi.* To undergo digestion, as food.—*n.* dī'jest. A collection of laws, systematic sum mary.

Digestion, di-jest'yon, *n.* Act of digesting; process of dissolving aliment in the stomach; operation of heating with some solvent.

Digit, di'jit, *n.* A finger; three-fourths of an inch; the twelfth part of the diameter of the sun or moon; any integer under 10.

Dignify, dig'ni-fī, *vt.* (dignifying, dignified). To in-

vest with dignity; to exalt in rank or office; to make illustrious.

Dignity, dig'ni-ti, *n.* Nobleness or elevation of mind; honorable place; degree of excellence; grandeur of mien; an elevated office; one who holds high rank.

Digress, di-gres' or dī'gres, *vi.* To depart from the main subject; to deviate.

Digression, di-gre'shon or dī-, *n.* Act of digressing; departure from the main subject; the part of a discourse which digresses.

Dike, Dyke, dīk, *n.* A ditch; an embankment; a wall; a vein of igneous rock.—*vt.* (diking, diked). To surround with a dike; to secure by a bank; to drain by ditches.

Dilacerate, dī-la'se-rāt, *vt.* To rend asunder; to separate by force.

Dilapidate, di-la'pi-dāt, *vt.* To make ruinous; to squander.—*vi.* To go to ruin; to fall by decay.

Dilapidation, di-la'pi-dā''shon, *n.* Decay; ruin; destruction; ruining or suffering to decay of a church building.

Dilatation, Dilation, dil-at-ā'shon, dī-lā'shon, *n.* Act of dilating; expansion; state of being expanded or distended.

Dilate, dī-lāt', *vt.* (dilating, dilated). To expand; to distend.—*vi.* To swell or extend in all directions; to speak copiously; to dwell on in narration (with *on* or *upon*).

Dilatory, di'la-tō-ri, *a.* Tardy; given to procrastination; making delay; sluggish.

Dilemma, di-lem'ma, *n.* An argument with two alternatives, each conclusive against an opponent; a difficult or doubtful choice.

Dilettante, dil-e-tan'tā, *n.*; pl. **Dilettanti,** dil-e-tan'tē. An amateur or trifler in art.

Diligence, di'li-jens, *n.* Steady application; assiduity; a four-wheeled stage-coach.

Diligent, di'li-jent, *a.* Steady in application; industrious; persevering; prosecuted with care and constant effort.

Dilute, di-lūt', *vt.* (diluting, diluted). To render liquid or more liquid; to weaken by admixture of water.—*vi.* To become attenuated or diluted.—*a.* Thin; reduced in strength.

Diluvium, di-lū'vi-um, *n.* A deluge or inundation; a deposit of sand, gravel, etc., caused by a flood.

Dim, dim, *a.* Not seeing clearly; not clearly seen; mysterious; tarnished.—*vt.* (dimming, dimmed). To dull; to obscure; to sully.

Dime, dīm, *n.* A silver coin the tenth of a dollar.

Dimension, di-men'shon, *n.* Extension in a single direction; measure of a thing, its size, extent, capacity, (usually in *pl.*).

Diminish, di-min'ish, *vt.* To reduce; to abate; to degrade.—*vi.* To become less.

Diminutive, di-min'ūt-iv, *a.* Small; little.—*n.* A word formed from another word to express a little thing of the kind.

Dimissory, di-mis'so-ri, *a.* Dismissing to another jurisdiction; granting leave to depart.

Dimity, di'mi-ti, *n.* A stout cotton fabric woven with raised stripes or figures.

Dimly, dim'li, *adv.* Obscurely.

Dimple, dim'pl, *n.* A small natural depression in the cheek or chin.—*vi.* (dimpling, dimpled). To form dimples.

Din, din, *n.* A loud sound long continued.—*vt.* (dinning, dinned). To stun with noise; to harass with clamor.

Dine, dīn, *vi.* (dining, dined). To eat a dinner.—*vt.* To give a dinner to.

Dinghy, ding'gi, *n.* A small boat used by a ship.

Dingy, din'ji, *a.* Of a dusky color; soiled.

Dinner, din'ner, *n.* The principal meal of the day.

Diocese, dī'ō-sēs, *n.* An ecclesiastical division of a state, subject to a bishop.

Dioptrics, dī-op-triks, *n.* The science of the refractions of light passing through mediums, as air, water, or lenses.

Diorama, dī-ō-rä'ma, *n.* A contrivance for giving a high degree of optical illusion to painted scenes.

Dip, dip, vt. (dipping, dipped). To plunge in a liquid; to baptize by immersion.—vi. To dive into a liquid and emerge; to engage in a desultory way; to look cursorily; to choose by chance; to incline.—n. Act of dipping; a bath; candle; downward slope.

Diphtheria, dif-thē'ri-a, n. An epidemic inflammatory disease of the throat.

Diphthong, dif'thong, n. A union of two vowels pronounced in one syllable.

Diploma, di-plō-ma, n. A document conferring some power, privilege, or honor

Diplomacy, di-plō'ma-si, n. The art or practice of conducting international negotiations; skill in securing advantages.

Diplomatic, Diplomatical, dip-lō-mat'ik, dip-lō-mat'ik-al, a. Pertaining to diplomacy; skilful in gaining one's ends by tact; relating to diplomatics.

Diplomatics, dip-lō-mat'iks, n. The science of deciphering ancient writings, and of ascertaining their authenticity, date, etc.

Dipper, dip'ér, n. He or that which dips; a ladle; a bird, the water-ousel.

Dipsomania, dip-sō-mā'ni-a, n. An uncontrollable craving for stimulants.

Dire, dīr, a. Dreadful; dismal; terrible.

Direct, di-rekt', a. Straight; right; in the line of father and son; not ambiguous; express.—vt. To point or aim at; to show the right course to; to conduct; to order; to instruct.

Directory, di-rek'to-ri, n. A rule to direct; a book containing directions for public worship; a book containing a list of the inhabitants of a place, with their addresses; a board of directors.

Dirge, dérj, n. A song or tune intended to express grief, sorrow, and mourning.

Dirk, dérk, n. A kind of dagger or poniard.

Dirt, dért, n. Any foul or filthy substance.—vt. To make foul; to defile.

Dirty, dért'i, a. Soiled with dirt; mean; despicable; rainy; squally, etc.—vt. (dirtying, dirtied). To soil; to sully.

Disable, dis-ā'bl, vt. (disabling, disabled). To deprive of power; to disqualify; to incapacitate.

Disabuse, dis-a-būz', vt. To undeceive.

Disadvantage, dis-ad-van'tāj, n. Want of advantage; unfavorable state; detriment.

Disaffect, dis-af-fekt', vt. To make less faithful or friendly; to make discontented.

Disaffirm, dis-af-fèrm', vt. To deny; to annul.

Disagree, dis-a-grē', vi. To be of a different opinion; to dissent; to be unfriendly; to be unsuitable.

Disagreement, dis-a-grē'ment, n. Difference; unsuitableness; discrepancy; discord.

Disallow, dis-al-lou', vt. To refuse to allow; to disapprove of; to reject.

Disannul, dis-an-nul', vt. To annul.

Disappear, dis-ap-pēr', vi. To vanish from sight; to cease, or seem to cease, to be.

Disappoint, dis-ap-point', vt. To defeat of expectation or intention; to frustrate.

Disappointment, dis-ap-point'ment, n. Failure of expectation or intention.

Disapprobation, dis-ap'prō-bā''shon, n. Disapproval; censure, expressed or unexpressed.

Disapprove, dis-ap-pröv', vt. To censure as wrong; to regard with dislike; to reject.

Disarm, dis-ärm', vt. To take the arms or weapons from; to render harmless.—vi. To lay down arms; to disband.

Disarrange, dis-a-rānj', vt. To put out of arrangement or order; to derange.

Disarray, dis-a-rā', vt. To undress; to throw into disorder.—n. Disorder; undress.

Disaster, diz-as'tér, n. An unfortunate event; mishap; catastrophe; reverse.

Disavow, dis-a-vou', vt. To deny to be true; to reject; to dissent from.

Disband, dis-band', vt. To dismiss from military service; to disperse.—vi. To retire from military service; to dissolve connection.

Disbar, dis-bär', vt. To expel from being a member of the bar.

Disbelief, dis-bē-lēf', n. Refusal of credit or faith; distrust.

Disburden, dis-bér'dn, vt. To remove a burden from; to relieve.

Disburse, dis-bérs', vt. (disbursing, disbursed). To pay out, as money; to expend.

Disbursement, dis-bérs'ment, n. Act of disbursing; the sum paid out.

Disc, Disk, disk, n. A flat circular plate; the face of the sun, or a planet; the central part of a composite flower.

Discard, dis-kärd', vt. To throw away; to cast off; to dismiss; to discharge.

Discern, dis-sérn' or di-zérn', vt. To distinguish; to discriminate; to descry.—vi. To see or understand difference; to have clearness of mental sight.

Discernment, dis-sérn'ment, n. Act or power of discerning; judgment; sagacity.

Discharge, dis-chärj', vt. To unload; to let fly or go, as a missile; to fire off; to give vent to; to clear off by payment; to perform; to acquit; to dismiss; to release.—vi. To get rid of or let out a charge or contents.—n. Act of discharging; unloading; a firing off; emission; dismissal; release from obligation, debt, or penalty; absolution from a crime; ransom; performance; release; payment, as of a debt.

Disciple, dis-sī'pl, n. A learner; a pupil; an adherent to the doctrines of another.

Disciplinarian, dis'si-plin-ā''ri-an, a. Pertaining to discipline.—n. One who enforces discipline; a martinet.

Discipline, dis'si-plin, n. Training; method of government; order; subjection to laws; punishment; correction; execution of ecclesiastical laws.—vt. (disciplining, disciplined). To subject to discipline; to train up well; to chastise.

Disclaim, dis-klām', vt. To deny all claim to; to reject; to disown.

Disclose, dis-klōz', vt. To open; to uncover; to reveal; to divulge.

Disclosure, dis-klō'zhūr, n. Act of disclosing; utterance of what was secret; that which is disclosed.

Discolor, dis-kul'ér, vt. To alter the color of; to stain; to tinge.

Discomfit, dis-kom'fit, vt. To rout; to defeat.—n. Rout; overthrow.

Discomfort, dis-kum'fért, n. Want of comfort; uneasiness; inquietude.—vt. To deprive of comfort; to grieve.

Discommend, dis-kom-mend', vt. To blame; to censure; to mention with disapprobation.

Discompose, dis-kom-pōz', vt. To disturb.

Discomposure, dis-kom-pō'zhūr, n. Disorder; agitation; disturbance; perturbation.

Disconcert, dis-kon-sért', vt. To disturb; to unsettle; to confuse; to ruffle.

Disconnect, dis-kon-nekt', vt. To separate; to disunite.

Disconsolate, dis-kon'sō-lāt, a. Comfortless; hopeless; gloomy; cheerless.

Discontent, dis-kon-tent', n. Want of content; uneasiness of mind; dissatisfaction.

Discontinuance, dis-kon-tin'ū-ans, n. A breaking off; cessation.

Discontinue, dis-kon-tin'ū, vt. To leave off; to cause to cease; to cease to take or receive.—vi. To cease.

Discord, dis'kord, n. Want of concord; disagreement; disagreement of sounds.

Discordance, Discordancy, dis-kord'ans, dis-kord'an-si, n. Want of concord; disagreement; inconsistency; discord.

Discount, dis'kount, n. A sum deducted for prompt or advanced payment.—vt. dis-kount'. To advance the amount of, as of a bill, deducting a certain rate per cent; to make an allowance for supposed exaggeration; to disregard.

Discountenance, dis-koun'ten-ans, vt. To restrain by censure, cold treatment, etc.

Discourage, dis-ku'rāj, vt. (discouraging, discouraged). To dishearten; to dissuade.

Discouragement, dis-ku'rāj-ment, n. Act of discouraging; that which discourages.

Discourse, dis-kōrs', n. A speech; treatise; sermon; conversation.—vi. (discoursing, discoursed). To talk; to converse; to treat of formally; to expatiate.—vt. To utter.

Discourtesy, dis-kōr'te-si, n. Incivility; rudeness; act of disrespect.

Discover, dis-kuv'er, vt. To lay open to view; to reveal; to have the first sight of; to find out; to detect.

Discovery, dis-kuv'e-ri, n. Act of discovering; disclosure; that which is discovered.

Discredit, dis-kred'it, n. Want of credit; disrepute; disbelief; distrust.—vt. To give no credit to; to deprive of credit; to make less reputable; to bring into disesteem.

Discreet, dis-krēt, a. Prudent; wary; judicious.

Discrepance, Discrepancy, dis-krep'ans, dis-krep'an-si, n. Discordance; disagreement.

Discrete, dis'krēt, a. Separate; distinct.

Discriminate, dis-krim'in-āt, vt. (discriminating, discriminated). To distinguish; to select from.—vt. To make a distinction.—a. Having the difference marked; distinct.

Discrimination, dis-krim'in-ā''shon, n. Discernment; judgment; distinction.

Discursive, dis-kers'iv, a. Passing from one subject to another, desultory; rambling.

Discus, dis'kus, n. A round, flat piece of iron, etc., thrown in play; a quoit.

Discuss, dis-kus', vt. To drive away or dissolve (a tumor, etc.); to debate; to examine by disputation, to make a trial of, as food; to consume.

Discussion, dis-ku'shon, n. Dispersion; debate; examination.

Disdain, dis-dān', vt. To think unworthy; to deem worthless; to scorn; to contemn.—n. Contempt; scorn; haughtiness; pride.

Disease, diz-ēz', n. Any state of a living body in which the natural functions are disturbed; illness; disorder.—vt. (diseasing, diseased). To afflict with disease; to infect; to derange.

Disembark, dis-em-bärk', vt. To remove from a vessel to the land.—vi. To go ashore.

Disembarrass, dis-em-ba'ras, vt. To free from perplexity; to clear; to extricate.

Disembody, dis-em-bo'di, vt. To divest of body; to free from connection with the human body; to disband (troops).

Disembowel, dis-em-bou'el, vt. (disembowelling, disembowelled). To take out the bowels of.

Disembroil, dis-em-broil', vt. To disentangle; to free from perplexity.

Disenchant, dis-en-chant', vt. To free from enchantment.

Disencumber, dis-en-kum'ber, vt. To free from encumbrance or obstruction.

Disendow, dis-en-dou', vt. To deprive of endowment, as a church.

Disengage, dis-en-gāj', vt. To free from engagement; to detach; to release; to extricate.

Disengagement, dis-en-gāj'ment, n. Release from engagement; separation; extrication; leisure.

Disentail, dis-en-tāl', vt. To free from being entailed.—n. The act of breaking the entail of an estate.

Disentangle, dis-en-tang'gl, vt. To free from entanglement; to clear.

Disenthrall, dis-en-thral', vt. To give freedom to.

Disentitle, dis-en-tī'tl, vt. To deprive of title.

Disestablish, dis-es-tab'lish, vt. To cause to cease to be established; to withdraw (a church) from connection with the state.

Disesteem, dis-es-tēm', n. Want of esteem.—vt. To dislike moderately; to slight.

Disfavor, dis-fā'ver, n. Want of favor; unfavorable

regard.—vt. To withhold favor from; to discountenance.

Disfigure, dis-fi'gūr, vt. (disfiguring, disfigured). To mar the figure of; to impair the beauty, symmetry, or excellence of.

Disfranchise, dis-fran'chiz, vt. To deprive of the rights of a free citizen.

Disgorge, dis-gorj', vt. To vomit; to discharge violently; to surrender.

Disgrace, dis-grās', n. State of being deprived of grace or favor; cause of shame; dishonor.—vt. (disgracing, disgraced). To bring to shame; to degrade; to dishonor.

Disguise, dis-gīz', vt. (disguising, disguised). To conceal by an unusual habit or mask; to dissemble; to give an unusual appearance to.—n. A dress intended to conceal; an assumed appearance, intended to deceive.

Disgust, dis-gust', n. Distaste; loathing; repugnance.—vt. To cause distaste in; to offend the mind or moral taste of.

Dish, dish, n. A broad open vessel for serving up meat at table; the meat served; any particular kind of food.—vt. To put in a dish; to make (a wheel) hollow or concave.

Dishearten, dis-härt'n, vt. To discourage; to depress.

Dishevel, di-she'vel, vt. (dishevelling, dishevelled). To put out of order, or spread loosely, as the hair.

Dishonest, dis-on'est, a. Void of honesty; fraudulent; knavish; perfidious.

Dishonor, dis-on'er, n. Want of honor; disgrace; ignominy.—vt. To deprive of honor; to treat with indignity; to violate the chastity of; to decline to accept or pay, as a draft.

Disillusionize, dis-il-lū'zhon-īz, vt. To free from illusion.

Disinclination, dis-in'klin-ā''shon, n. Want of propensity, desire, or affection.

Disincline, dis-in-klin', vt. To take away inclination from; to make disaffected.

Disinfect, dis-in-fekt', vt. To cleanse from infection.

Disingenuous, dis-in-jen'ū-us, a. Not open, frank, and candid; crafty; cunning.

Disinherit, dis-in-he'rit, vt. To cut off from hereditary right.

Disintegrate, dis-in'tē-grāt, vt. To separate, as the integral parts of a body.

Disinter, dis-in-tėr', vt. To take out of a grave; to bring into view.

Disinterested, dis-in'tėr-est-ed, a. Not interested; free from self-interest; not dictated by private advantage; impartial.

Disinterment, dis-in-tėr'ment, n. Act of disinterring or taking out of the earth.

Disjoin, dis-join', vt. To part asunder; to sever.—vi. To part.

Disjoint, dis-joint', vt. To separate, as parts united by joints; to put out of joint; to make incoherent.

Disjunction, dis-jungk'shon, n. Act of disjoining; disunion.

Disjunctive, dis-jungk'tiv, a. Separating; uniting words or sentences in construction, but disjoining the sense.—n. A word that disjoins, as or, nor.

Dislike, dis-līk', n. A feeling the opposite of liking; a moderate degree of hatred; aversion; antipathy.—vt. To regard with some aversion or displeasure.

Dislocate, dis'lō-kāt, vt. To displace, to put out of joint.

Dislodge, dis-loj', vt. To remove or drive from a place of rest or a station.—vi. To go from a place of rest.

Disloyal, dis-loi'al, a. Void of loyalty; false to a sovereign; faithless.

Dismal, diz'mal, a. Dark; gloomy; doleful; calamitous; sorrowful.

Dismantle, dis-man'tl, vt. To strip; to divest; to unrig; to deprive or strip, as of military equipment or defenses; to break down.

Dismask, dis-mask', vt. To strip off a mask from; to uncover.

Dismay, dis-mā', vt. To produce terror in; to appal; to dishearten.—n. Loss of courage; consternation; fright.

Dismember, dis-mem'bėr, vt. To sever limb from limb; to separate; to mutilate.

Dismiss, dis-mis', vt. To send away; to permit to depart; to discharge.

Dismount, dis-mount', vi. To descend from a horse, etc.—vt. To unhorse; to throw cannon from their carriages or fixed positions.

Disobedience, dis-ō-bē'di-ens, n. Neglect or refusal to obey.

Disobey, dis-ō-bā', vt. To neglect or refuse to obey; to violate an order.

Disoblige, dis-ō-blīj', vt. To fail to oblige; to be unaccommodating to.

Disorder, dis-or'dėr, n. Want of order; confusion; disease.—vt. To put out of order; to disturb; to produce indisposition; to craze.

Disorganize, dis-or'gan-īz, vt. To destroy organic structure or connected system in; to throw into confusion.

Disown, dis-ōn', vt. To refuse to acknowledge; to renounce; to repudiate.

Disparage, dis-pa'rāj, vt. (disparaging, disparaged). To dishonor by comparison with something inferior; to derogate from; to decry.

Disparagement, dis-pa'rāj-ment, n. Injury by union or comparison with something inferior; indignity; detraction.

Disparity, dis-pa'ri-ti, n. Inequality; difference in degree, age, rank, etc.

Dispart, dis-pärt', vt. and i. To separate.

Dispassionately, dis-pa'shon-āt-li, adv. Without passion; calmly; coolly.

Dispatch, dis-pach', vt. To send away in haste; to put to death; to perform quickly; to conclude.— n. Act of dispatching; communication on public business; speedy performance; due diligence.

Dispel, dis-pel', vt. (dispelling, dispelled). To scatter; to banish.—vi. To fly different ways; to disappear.

Dispensary, dis-pens'a-ri, n. A place where medicines are dispensed to the poor, and medical advice is given gratis; a place where medicines are compounded.

Dispensation, dis-pens-ā'shon, n. Act of dispensing; distribution; good or evil dealt out by providence; exemption.

Dispense, dis-pens', vt. (dispensing, dispensed). To deal out in portions; to administer; to apply; to exempt; to grant dispensation for.—vi. To do without (with with).

Disperse, dis-pėrs', vt. To scatter; to dispel; to diffuse; to distribute.—vi. To be scattered; to vanish.

Dispersion, dis-pėr'shon, n. Act of dispersing; diffusion; dissipation.

Dispirit, dis-pi'rit, vt. To deprive of spirit; to discourage; to daunt.

Displace, dis-plās', vt. To remove from its place; to derange; to dismiss.

Displacement, dis-plās'ment, n. Act of displacing; quantity of water displaced by a floating body.

Displant, dis-plant', vt. To pluck up from the spot where planted; to remove from the usual place of residence; to depopulate.

Display, dis-plā', vt. To unfold; to spread before the eyes or mind; to show; to parade.—vi. To make a show; to talk without restraint.—n. An opening or unfolding; exhibition; parade.

Displease, dis-plēz', vt. To offend; to dissatisfy; to provoke.—vi. To disgust.

Displeasure, dis-ple'zhŭr, n. Dissatisfaction; resentment.

Dispose, dis-pōz', vt. (disposing, disposed). To arrange; to apply to a particular purpose; to incline.—vi. To regulate; (with of) to part with, to employ.

Disposed, dis-pōzd', p.a. Inclined.

Disposition, dis-pō-zi'shon, n. Act of disposing; state of being disposed; arrangement; natural fitness; frame of mind; inclination.

Dispossess, dis-poz-zes', vt. To deprive of possession.

Dispraise, dis-prāz, n. The opposite of praise; blame; censure.—vt. To blame; to mention with disapprobation.

Disproportion, dis-prō-pōr'shon, n. Want of proportion or symmetry.—vt. To violate proportion; to join unfitly.

Disproportionate, dis-prō-pōr'shon-āt, a. Not proportioned; unsymmetrical; inadequate.

Disprove, dis-pröv', vt. To prove to be false; to confute.

Disputant, dis-pūt-ant, n. One who argues in opposition to another.

Disputation, dis-pūt-ā'shon, n. Act of disputing; controversy in words; debate.

Dispute, dis-pūt', vi. (disputing, disputed). To contend in argument; to debate; to strive with.—vt. To attempt to prove to be false; to impugn; to contest; to strive to maintain.—n. Controversy in words; strife.

Disqualify, dis-kwo'li-fī, vt. To divest of qualifications; to incapacitate.

Disquiet, dis-kwī'et, n. Uneasiness; anxiety.—vt. To make uneasy or restless.

Disquietude, dis-kwī'et-ūd, n. Uneasiness; anxiety.

Disquisition, dis-kwi-zi'shon, n. A systematic inquiry into any subject, by arguments; a treatise or dissertation.

Disregard, dis-rē-gärd', n. Neglect; slight.—vt. To omit to take notice of; to slight.

Disrelish, dis-rel'ish, n. Distaste; dislike.—vt. To dislike the taste of; to feel some disgust at.

Disrepair, dis-rē-pār', n. A state of being not in repair.

Disreputable, dis-re'pūt-a-bl, a. Discreditable; low; mean.

Disrepute, dis-rē-pūt', n. Loss or want of reputation; disesteem; disgrace.

Disrespect, dis-rē-spekt', n. Want of respect; incivility.—vt. To show disrespect to.

Disrobe, dis-rōb, vt. To undress; to uncover; to divest of any surrounding appendage.

Disroot, dis-röt', vt. To tear up the roots.

Disruption, dis-rup'shon, n. Act of rending asunder; breach; rent; rupture.

Dissatisfaction, dis-sa'tis-fak''shon, n. Want of satisfaction; discontent.

Dissatisfy, dis-sa'tis-fī, vt. To fail to satisfy; to render discontented.

Dissect, dis-sekt', vt. To cut up; to anatomize; to divide and examine minutely.

Dissection, dis-sek'shon, n. Act of cutting up an atomically; act of separating into parts for the purpose of critical examination.

Dissemble, dis-sem'bl, vt. and i. (dissembling, dissembled). To hide under a false appearance; to conceal under some pretense.

Disseminate, dis-se'min-āt, vt. (disseminating, disseminated). To scatter; to spread.

Dissension, dis-sen'shon, n. Disagreement in opinion; discord; strife.

Dissent, dis-sent', vi. To disagree in opinion; to separate from an established church, in doctrines, rites, or government.—n. Disagreement; separation from an established church.

Dissentient, dis-sen'shi-ent, a. Declaring dissent; disagreeing.—a. One who declares his dissent.

Dissertation, dis-sėr-tā'shon, n. A formal discourse; treatise; disquisition.

Disservice, dis-sėr'vis, n. An ill-service; injury; harm; mischief.

Dissever, dis-sev'ėr, vt. To part in two; to disunite.

Dissident, dis'si-dent, a. Dissenting.—n. A dissenter.

Dissilient, dis-si'li-ent, a. Starting asunder; opening with an elastic force.

Dissimilitude, dis-si-mil'i-tūd, n. Unlikeness;

want of resemblance.

Dissimulate, dis-sim'ū-lāt, *vt.* and *i.* To dissemble.

Dissipate, dis'si-pāt, *vt.* (dissipating, dissipated). To scatter; to spend; to squander.—*vi.* To scatter; to disperse; to vanish.

Dissipation, dis-si-pā'shon, *n.* Dispersion; waste; dissolute conduct; diversion.

Dissociate, dis-sō'shi-āt, *vt.* (dissociating, dissociated). To separate, as from society; to disunite; to part.

Dissoluble, dis'so-lū-bl, *a.* Capable of being dissolved.

Dissolution, dis-sō-lū'shon, *n.* Act of dissolving; a melting or liquefaction; separation of parts; decomposition; death; destruction; the breaking up of an assembly.

Dissolve, diz-zolv', *vt.* To melt; to break up; to put an end to; to cause to vanish.—*vi.* To be melted; to become soft or languid; to waste away; to perish; to break up.

Dissolvent, diz-zolv'ent, *a.* Having power to dissolve.—*n.* That which has the power of melting; a solvent.

Dissonance, dis'so-nans, *n.* Disagreement in sound; discord.

Dissuade, dis-swād', *vt.* (dissuading, dissuaded). To exhort against; to turn from a purpose by argument.

Dissyllable, dis'sil-la-bl, *n.* A word of two syllables only.

Distaff, dis'taf, *n.* The staff to which a bunch of flax or tow is tied, and from which the thread is drawn in spinning.

Distance, dis'tans, *n.* Remoteness in place or time; extent of interval between two things; the remoteness which respect requires; reserve; coldness.—*vt.* (distancing, distanced). To leave behind in a race; to outdo or excel.

Distaste, dis-tāst', *n.* Aversion of the taste or mind; dislike.—*vt.* To dislike.

Distemper, dis-tem'pér, *n.* Any morbid state of the body; disorder; a disease of young dogs; bad constitution of the mind; a kind of painting in which the pigments are mixed with size; a pigment so mixed.—*vt.* To disease; to derange; to ruffle.

Distemperature, dis-tem'pér-ā-tūr, *n.* Tumult; perturbation of mind.

Distend, dis-tend', *vt.* To stretch by force from within; to swell.—*vi.* To swell; to dilate.

Distich, dis'tik, *n.* A couple of poetic lines.

Distil, dis'til', *vi.* (distilling, distilled). To fall in drops; to practice distillation.—*vt.* To let fall in drops; to extract spirit from, by evaporation and condensation.

Distillery, dis-til'é-ri, *n.* The building where distilling is carried on.

Distinct, dis-tingkt', *a.* Separated by some mark; not the same in number or kind; separate in place; clear; definite.

Distinction, dis-tingk'shon, *n.* Act of distinguishing; that which distinguishes; difference, elevation of rank in society; eminence; a title or honor.

Distinguish, dis-ting'gwish, *vt.* To mark out by some peculiarity; to perceive; to make eminent; to signalize.—*vi.* To make a distinction; to find or show the difference.

Distort, dis-tort', *vt.* To twist; to pervert.

Distortion, dis-tor'shon, *n.* Act of distorting; a writhing motion; deformity; perversion of the true meaning of words.

Distract, dis-trakt', *vt.* To draw towards different objects; to perplex; to disorder the reason of; to render furious.

Distraction, dis-trak'shon, *n.* Derangement; frenzy; diversion.

Distrain, dis-trān', *vt.* To seize, as goods, for debt.—*vi.* To make seizure of goods.

Distraught, dis-trat', *a.* Distracted.

Distress, dis-tres', *n.* Anguish of body or mind; affliction; state of danger or destitution; act of

distraining.—*vt.* To afflict with pain or anguish; to perplex.

Distribute, dis-tri'būt, *vt.* (distributing, distributed). To divide among two or more; to apportion; to administer, as justice; to classify.

Distributive, dis-tri'būt-iv, *a.* That distributes; expressing separation or division.—*n.* A word that divides or distributes, as *each, every, either*.

District, dis'trikt, *n.* A limited extent of country; a circuit; a region.

Distrust, dis-trust', *vt.* To have no trust in, to doubt; to suspect.—*n.* Want of trust; doubt; suspicion; discredit.

Disturb, dis-tèrb', *vt.* To throw into disorder; to agitate; to hinder; to move.

Disturbance, dis-tèrb'ans, *n.* State of being disturbed; commotion; excitement; interruption of a right.

Ditch, dich, *n.* A trench in the earth for drainage or defense.—*vi.* To dig a ditch.—*vt.* To dig a ditch in; to drain by a ditch; to surround with a ditch.

Ditto, dit'tō, *n.* A word used in lists, etc., meaning same as above; often written *Do*.

Ditty, dit'ti, *n.* A song; a poem to be sung.

Diuretic, dī-ū-rēt'ik, *a.* Tending to produce discharges of urine.—*n.* A medicine that has this effect.

Diurnal, dī-èrn'al, *a.* Relating to day; daily.—*n.* In the Roman Catholic Church, a book containing the office of each day.

Divagation, dī-va-gā'shon, *n.* Deviation.

Divan, di-van', *n.* Among the Turks, a court of justice; a council or council-chamber; a cushioned seat standing against the wall of a room.

Divaricate, dī-va'ri-kāt, *vi.* To branch off; to fork.

Dive, dīv, *vi.* (diving, dived). To plunge into water head-foremost; to go under water to execute some work; to go deep.

Diverge, di-vèrj', *vi.* (diverging, diverged). To proceed from a point in different directions; to deviate; to vary.

Divergence, Divergency, di-vèrj'ens, di-vèr'jen-si, *n.* Act of diverging; a receding from each other.

Divers, dī'vèrz, *a.* Different; various; sundry; more than one, but not many.

Diverse, di-vèrs', *a.* Different; unlike; various.

Diversification, di-vèrs'i-fi-kā''shon, *n.* Act of diversifying; variation; variegation.

Diversify, di-vèrs'i-fī, *vt.* (diversifying, diversified). To make diverse in form or qualities; to variegate; to give diversity to.

Diversion, di-vèr'shon, *n.* Act of diverting; that which diverts; amusement; a feigned attack.

Diversity, di-vèrs'i-ti, *n.* State of being diverse; contrariety; variety.

Divert, di-vèrt', *vt.* To turn aside; to amuse.

Divest, di-vest', *vt.* To strip of clothes; to deprive.

Divide, di-vid', *vt.* (dividing, divided). To part asunder; to separate; to keep apart; to distribute, allot; to set at variance.—*vi.* To part; to be of different opinions; to vote by the division of a legislative house into parties.

Dividend, di'vi-dend, *n.* A number which is to be divided; share of profit; share divided to creditors.

Divination, di-vin-ā'shon, *n.* Act of divining; a foretelling future events, or discovering things secret, by magical means.

Divine, di-vīn', *a.* Of or belonging to God; excellent in the highest degree.—*n.* One versed in divinity; a clergyman.—*vt.* (divining, divined). To foretell; to presage; to guess.—*vi.* To practice divination; to have or utter presages; to guess.

Diving-bell, dīv'ing-bel, *n.* An apparatus by means of which persons may descend below water to execute various operations.

Divining-rod, di-vīn'ing-rod, *n.* A hazel rod, which is said to point downwards over a spot where water or treasure is to be found.

Divinity, di-vin'i-ti, *n.* The state of being divine; God; a deity; the science of divine things; theology.

Division, di·vi'zhon, *n.* Act of dividing; state of being divided; separation; partition; portion; a separate body of men; a process or rule in arithmetic; part of an army, comprising all arms and services in due proportion.

Divisive, di·vīz'iv, *a.* Creating division or discord.

Divisor, di·vīz'or, *n.* In *arithmetic,* the number by which the dividend is divided.

Divorce, di·vōrs', *n.* A legal dissolution of marriage; disunion of things closely united.—*vt.* (divorcing, divorced). To dissolve the marriage contract between; to separate.

Divot, div'ot, *n.* A piece of turf cut out by a golfer when striking the ball.

Divulge, di·vulj', *vt.* (divulging, divulged). To make public; to disclose.

Divulsion, di·vul'shon, *n.* A pulling, tearing, or rending asunder, or separating.

Dizziness, diz'zi·nes, *n.* Giddiness; vertigo.

Dizzy, diz'zi, *a.* Having a sensation of whirling in the head; giddy; causing giddiness.—*vt.* (dizzying, dizzied). To make giddy.

Do, dö, *vt.* or *auxiliary* (doing, pret. did, pp. done). To perform; to bring about; to pay (as honor, etc.); to transact; to finish; to prepare; to cook.—*vi.* To act or behave; to fare in health; to succeed; to suffice; to avail.

Docile, dō'sīl, *a.* Easily taught; ready to learn; tractable; pliant.

Dock, dok, *n.* A troublesome weed; the tail of a beast cut short; the stump of a tail; an inclosed area on the side of a harbor or bank of a river for ships; the place where the accused stands in court.—*vt.* To cut off; to curtail; to deduct from; to put a ship in dock.

Docket, dok'et, *n.* A summary; a bill tied to goods; a list of cases in a court.—*vt.* To make an abstract of; to mark the contents of papers on the back; to attach a docket to.

Dockyard, dok'yärd, *n.* A yard near a dock for naval stores.

Doctor, dok'ter, *n.* A person who has received the highest degree in a university faculty; one licensed to practice medicine; a physician.—*vt.* To treat medically; to adulterate.

Doctorate, dok'ter·āt, *n.* The degree of a doctor.

Doctrinaire, dok·tri·när', *n.* A political theorist.

Doctrine, dok'trin, *n.* Instruction; whatever is taught; a principle in any science; dogma; a truth of the gospel.

Document, do'kū·ment, *n.* Written evidence or proof; any authoritative paper containing instructions or proof.—*vt.* To furnish with documents.

Dodecagon, dō·de'ka·gon, *n.* A figure with twelve sides.

Dodge, doj, *vt.* (dodging, dodged). To start aside; to quibble.—*vt.* To evade by a sudden shift of place.—*n.* An artifice; an evasion.

Dodo, dō'dō, *n.* An extinct bird of Mauritius, having a massive, clumsy body, short strong legs, and wings useless for flight.

Doe, dō, *n.* A female deer.

Does, duz. The third sing. present of *do.*

Doeskin, dō'skin, *n.* The skin of a doe; a compact twilled woollen cloth.

Doff, dof, *vt.* To put off.

Dog, dog, *n.* A domestic quadruped of many varieties; a mean fellow; a gay young man.—*vt.* (dogging, dogged). To follow insidiously; to worry with importunity.

Dog-day, dog'dā, *n.* One of the days when Sirius, the Dog-star, rises and sets with the sun.

Doge, dōj, *n.* The chief magistrate in republican Venice.

Dog-eared, dog'ērd, *a.* Having the corners of the leaves turned down (said of a book).

Dog-fish, dog'fish, *n.* A species of shark.

Dogged, dog'ed, *a.* Determined; pertinacious.

Doggerel, dog'e·rel, *n.* A loose irregular kind of versification; wretched verse.

Dogma, dog'ma, *n.* A settled opinion or belief; tenet; a doctrinal point.

Dogmatics, dog·mat'iks, *n.* Doctrinal theology; essential doctrines of Christianity.

Dogmatism, dog'mat·izm, *n.* Positiveness in assertion; arrogance in opinion.

Dogmatize, dog'mat·īz, *vi.* (dogmatizing, dogmatized). To assert with undue confidence; to advance principles with arrogance.

Dog-star, dog'stär, *n.* Sirius, a star of the first magnitude.

Doily, doi'li, *n.* A small ornamental mat for glasses, etc.

Doldrums, dol'drumz, *n.pl.* The dumps.

Dole, dōl, *n.* That which is dealt out; share; gratuity; grief; sorrow.—*vt.* (doling, doled). To deal out; to distribute.

Doleful, dōl'ful, *a.* Full of pain, grief, etc.; expressing or causing grief; gloomy.

Dolichocephalic, Dolichocephalous, dol'i·kō·se·fal''ik, dol'i·kō·sef''a·lus, *a.* Long-skulled; used to denote skulls in which the diameter from side to side is small in proportion to the diameter from front to back.

Doll, dol, *n.* A child's puppet in human form.

Dollar, dol'ler, *n.* A coin of the United States and Canada (= 100 cents).

Dolmen, dol'men, *n.* An ancient structure consisting of one large unhewn stone resting on others; a cromlech.

Dolomite, dol'o·mīt, *n.* A granular crystalline or schistose rock compounded of carbonate of magnesia and carbonate of lime.

Dolorous, dō'ler·us, *a.* Sorrowful; doleful.

Dolor, dō'ler, *n.* Sorrow; lamentation.

Dolphin, dol'fin, *n.* A small species of whale remarkable for gambolling in the water; a fish celebrated for its changes of color when dying.

Dolt, dōlt, *n.* A blockhead.

Domain, dō·mān', *n.* Territory governed; estate; a demesne.

Dome, dōm, *n.* A hemispherical roof of a building; a large cupola.

Domestic, dō·mes'tik, *a.* Belonging to the house or home; tame; not foreign.—*n.* A household servant.

Domesticate, dō·mes'tik·āt, *vt.* To accustom to remain much at home; to tame.

Domicile, do'mi·sīl, *n.* A habitation; family residence.—*vt.* (domiciling, domiciled). To establish in a residence.

Dominant, dom'in·ant, *a.* Governing; predominant; ascendant.

Dominate, dom'in·āt, *vt.* (dominating, dominated). To rule; to predominate over.

Domination, dom·in·ā'shon, *n.* Rule; tyranny.

Domineer, dom·in·ēr', *vi.* To rule tyrannically or with insolence (with *over*).

Dominical, dō·min'ik·al, *a.* Noting Sunday; relating to God.

Dominican, dō·min'ik·an, *n.* A Black-friar.

Dominion, dō·min'i·on, *n.* Sovereign authority; district governed; region.

Domino, do'mi·nō, *n.* A masquerade dress; a half-mask; a person wearing a domino; *pl.* **(Dominoes),** a game played with pieces of ivory or bone dotted like dice.

Don, don, *n.* A Spanish title, corresponding to Eng. Mr.; an important personage; a resident Fellow of a college at Oxford or Cambridge.—*vt.* (donning, donned). To put on; to invest with.

Donate, dō'nāt, *vt.* To bestow.

Donation, dō·nā'shon, *n.* Act of giving; that which is given; a gift; a present.

Donkey, dong'ki, *n.* An ass.

Donna, don'na, *n.* A lady; as, *prima donna,* the first female singer in an opera, etc.

Donor, dō'ner, *n.* One who gives.

Doom, döm, *n.* Judicial sentence; fate; ruin.—*vt.* To condemn to punishment; to destine.

Doomsday, dömz'dā, *n.* The day of judgment.

Door, dōr, *n.* The entrance of a house or room; the frame of boards that shuts such an entrance; avenue; means of approach.

Doric, dor'ik, *a.* Pertaining to Doris in Greece; denoting the earliest and plainest of the Grecian orders of architecture.

Dormant, dor'mant, *a.* Sleeping; not used; inactive.

Dormer, Dormer-window, dor'mėr, dor'mėr-win-dō, *n.* A window in a sloping roof, the frame being placed vertically.

Dormitory, dor'mi-to-ri, *n.* A place to sleep in; a room in which a number sleep.

Dormouse, dor'mous, *n.;* pl. **Dormice,** dor'mīs. A small rodent which passes the winter in a lethargic or torpid state.

Dormy, dor'mi, *a.* In golf, applied to a player leading by as many holes as still remain to be played.

Dorsal, dor'sal, *a.* Pertaining to the back.

Dory, dō'ri, *n.* A European yellow fish, with a protrusible mouth; a small boat.

Dose, dōs, *n.* The quantity of medicine given at one time; something given to be swallowed.—*vt.* (dosing, dosed). To give in doses; to give medicine to.

Dossier, dos'ē-ā, *n.* A collection of documents of information about a person or incident.

Dot, dot, *n.* A small point, as made with a pen, etc.; a speck.—*vt.* (dotting, dotted). To mark with a dot; to diversify with small objects.—*vi.* To make dots.

Dotage, dōt'āj, *n.* Feebleness of mind, particularly in old age; excessive fondness.

Dotal, dōt'al, *a.* Pertaining to dower.

Dotard, dōt'ėrd, *n.* One whose mind is impaired by age; one foolishly fond.

Dote, dōt, *vi.* (doting, doted). To have the intellect impaired by age; to be foolishly fond.

Double, du'bl, *a.* Twofold; forming a pair; of extra size, quality, etc.; doceitful.—*vt.* (doubling, doubled). To make twofold; to fold; to increase by adding an equal amount to; to sail round (a cape, etc.).—*vi.* To increase twofold; to turn or wind in running; to use sleights.—*n.* Twice as much; a turn in running; a shift; a duplicate; a wraith.

Double-bass, du'bl-bās, *n.* The lowest-toned instrument of the violin class.

Double-dealing, du'bl-dēl-ing, *n.* Deceitful practice; duplicity.

Double-entry, du'bl-en-tri, *n.* A mode of book-keeping in which every transaction is entered on the debit side of one account and the credit side of another.

Doublet, du'blet, *n.* A close-fitting body garment; one of a pair; one of two words really the same but different in form.

Doubling, du'bl-ing, *n.* Act of making double; a fold; a lining.

Doubloon, dub-lōn', *n.* A Spanish gold coin.

Doubt, dout, *vi.* To waver in opinion or judgment; to question; to suspect.—*vt.* To deem uncertain; to distrust.—*n.* A wavering in opinion; uncertainty; suspicion.

Douceur, dö-sér', *n.* A gift; bribe; gratuity.

Douche, dösh, *n.* A jet of water directed upon some part of the body.

Dough, dō, *n.* Flour or meal moistened and kneaded, but not baked; paste of bread.

Doughty, dou'ti, *a.* Noble; brave; valiant.

Doughy, dō'i, *a.* Like dough; soft; pale.

Douse, Dowse, dous, *vt.* and *i.* To plunge into water; to drench.

Dove, duv, *n.* A pigeon; a word of endearment.

Dove-cot, Dove-cote, duv'kot, duv'kōt, *n.* A place for pigeons.

Dovetail, duv'tāl, *n.* A mode of joining boards by letting one piece into another in the form of a dove's tail spread, or wedge reversed.—*vt.* and *i.* To unite by the above method, to fit exactly.

Dowager, dou'ā-jėr, *n.* A title given to the widow of a person of title, provided that she is mother, grandmother, or stepmother of the successor.

Dowdy, dou'di, *n.* An awkward, ill-dressed woman.—*a.* Ill-dressed; vulgar-looking.

Dowel, dou'el, *n.* A pin of wood or iron to join boards, etc.—*vt.* (dowelling, dowelled). To fasten by dowels.

Dower, dou'ėr, *n.* That portion of the property of a man which his widow enjoys during her life; the property which a woman brings to her husband in marriage; dowry.

Down, doun, *n.* The fine soft feathers of birds; fine hair; the pubescence of plants; a hill; a dune; a tract of naked, hilly land.—*adv.* In a descending direction; on the ground; into less bulk; paid in ready money.—*prep.* Along in descent; toward the mouth of.—*a.* Downcast; dejected.

Downcast, doun'kast, *a.* Cast downward; dejected.

Downfall, foun'fal, *n.* A falling down; loss of wealth or high position; ruin.

Downpour, doun'pōr, *n.* A pouring down; especially, a heavy or continuous shower.

Downright, doun'rit, *adv.* Right down; in plain terms; utterly.—*a.* Directly to the point; plain; blunt; utter.

Downtrodden, doun'trod-n, *a.* Trodden down; oppressed.

Downy, doun'i, *a.* Covered with, or pertaining to, down, soft; soothing.

Dowry, dou'ri, *n.* The property which a woman brings to her husband in marriage; a dower; gift.

Doxology, doks-ol'o-ji, *n.* A hymn or form of giving glory to God.

Doze, dōz, *vi.* (dozing, dozed). To sleep lightly; to be half asleep.—*vt.* To pass or spend in drowsiness.—*n.* A slight sleep; a slumber.

Dozen, du'zn, *n.* Twelve things regarded collectively.

Drab, drab, *n.* A sluttish woman; a strumpet; a thick woollen cloth of a dun color; a dull brownish color.—*a.* Of a dull brown color.

Draconic, Draconian, drā-kon'ik, drā-kō'ni-an, *a.* Relating to Draco, the Athenian lawgiver; extremely severe.

Draft, dräft, *n.* A detachment of men or things; an order for money; the first sketch of any writing; a sketch.—*vt.* To make a draft of; to sketch; to select.

Drag, drag, *vt.* (dragging, dragged). To draw along the ground by main force; to haul; to explore with a drag.—*vi.* To hang so as to trail on the ground; to move slowly.—*n.* A net drawn along the bottom of the water; an instrument to catch hold of things under water; a machine for dredging; a low cart; a long coach; a contrivance to stop a wheel of a carriage; whatever serves to retard.

Drag-net, drag'net, *n.* A net to be drawn along the bottom of a river or pond.

Dragon, dra'gon, *n.* A fabulous winged monster; a fierce person; a kind of small lizard.

Dragon-fly, dra'gon-fli, *n.* A fly that preys upon other insects.

Dragoon, dra-gön', *n.* A heavy cavalry soldier.—*vt.* To harass; to compel by force.

Drain, drān, *vt.* To draw off; to filter; to make dry; to exhaust.—*vi.* To flow off gradually.—*n.* A channel for liquid; a sewer; gradual or continuous withdrawal.

Drake, drāk, *n.* The male of ducks.

Dram, dram, *n.* The eighth part of an ounce, or sixty grains apothecaries' measure; the sixteenth part of an ounce avoirdupois; as much spirituous liquor as is drunk at once.

Drama, drä'ma, *n.* A representation on a stage; a play; dramatic literature.

Dramatist, drä'mat-ist, *n.* The author of a dramatic composition.

Dramatize, drä'mat-iz, *vt.* To compose in the form of the drama.

Dramaturgy, dräm'a-tėr-ji, *n.* The science of dramatic composition and representation.

Drape, drāp, *vt.* (draping, draped). To cover with cloth or drapery.

Drapery, drāp'ė-ri, *n.* The occupation of a dra-per; fabrics of wool or linen; clothes or hangings.

Drastic, dras'tik, a. Acting with strength or violence.—n. A strong purgative.

Draught, dräft, n. The act of drawing; quantity drunk at once; a sketch or outline; the depth a ship sinks in water; a current of air; pl. a game played on a checkered board.—vt. To draw out; to draft.—a. Used for drawing; drawn from the barrel, etc.

Draughtsman, dräfts'man, n. One who draws plans or designs; one of the pieces in the game of draughts.

Draughty, dräf'ti, a. Of or pertaining to draughts of air; exposed to draughts.

Draw, dra, vt. (drawing, pret. drew, pp. drawn). To pull along or towards; to cause to come; to unsheathe; to suck; to attract; to inhale; to stretch; to lead, as a motive; to represent by lines drawn on a surface; to describe; to infer; to derive; to draft; to require a certain depth of water; to bend (a bow); to end indecisively.—vi. To pull; to shrink; to advance; to practice drawing; to make a written demand for money.—n. Act of drawing; the lot or chance drawn; a drawn game.

Drawback, dra'bak, n. What detracts from profit or pleasure; duties on goods paid back when exported.

Drawbridge, dra'brij, n. A bridge which may be raised or drawn aside.

Drawer, dra'ér, n. One who or that which draws; he who draws a bill; a sliding box in a case, etc.; pl. an under-garment for the lower limbs.

Drawing, dra'ing, n. Act of one who draws; representation of objects by lines and shades; delineation.

Drawl, dral, vi. To speak with slow, prolonged utterance.—vt. To utter in a slow tone.—n. A lengthened utterance.

Dread, dred, n. Fear, united with respect; terror; the person or the thing dreaded.—a. Exciting great fear; terrible; venerable.—vt. and i. To fear in a great degree.

Dreadnought, dred'nat, n. A person that fears nothing; a thick cloth with a long pile; a garment made of such cloth; a general term for a battleship.

Dream, drēm, n. The thought of a person in sleep; a vain fancy.—vi. To have images in the mind, in sleep; to imagine; to think idly.—vt. To see in a dream; to spend idly.

Dreamer, drēm'ér, n. One who dreams; a fanciful man; a visionary.

Dreary, drē'ri, a. Dismal; gloomy; oppressively monotonous.

Dredge, drej, n. An oyster net; a dredging-machine.—vt. (dredging, dredged). To take with a dredge; to deepen with a dredging-machine; to powder; to sprinkle flour on meat while roasting.

Dregs, dregz, n.pl. Lees; grounds; the most vile and despicable part.

Drench, drensh, vi. To wet thoroughly; to soak; to purge violently.—n. A draught; a large dose of liquid medicine for an animal.

Dress, dres, vt. To make straight; to put in good order; to cleanse and cover a wound; to prepare; to curry, rub, and comb; to clothe; to array; to trim.—vi. To arrange in a line; to put on clothes; to pay regard to dress.—n. Apparel; attire; a lady's gown.

Dribble, drib'l, vi. (dribbling, dribbled). To fall in a quick succession of drops; to trickle; to take a football up the field by means of a series of short kicks, keeping the ball near to the foot and under control.—vt. To throw down in drops.

Drift, drift, n. That which is driven by wind or water; impulse; tendency; aim; velocity of a current; the distance a vessel is driven by a current; rocks conveyed by glaciers and deposited over a country while submerged; in S. Africa, a ford.—vi. To move along like anything

driven; to accumulate in heaps; to float or be driven by a current.—vt. To drive into heaps.—a. Drifted by wind or currents.

Drill, dril, vt. To pierce with a drill; to teach soldiers their proper movements, etc.; to teach by repeated exercise; to sow in rows; to furrow.—vi. To sow in drills; to muster for exercise.—n. A pointed instrument for boring holes; act of training soldiers; a row of seeds; a furrow.

Drill, dril, n. A kind of coarse linen or cotton cloth.

Drink, dringk, vi. (drinking, pret. drank, pp. drunk or drunken). To swallow liquor; to take spirituous liquors to excess.—vt. To swallow, as liquids; to absorb.—n. Liquor to be swallowed; any beverage; potion.

Drip, drip, vi. (dripping, dripped). To fall in drops.—vt. To let fall in drops.—n. A falling in drops; the eaves; a projecting moulding.

Dripping, drip'ing, n. A falling in drops; the fat which falls from meat in roasting.

Drive, drīv, vt. (driving, pret. drove, pp. driven). To impel; to hurry on; to impel and guide; to convey in a carriage; to carry on.—vi. To be impelled along; to aim at; to strike with force.—n. A journey in a vehicle; a road for driving on; a sweeping blow.

Drivel, dri'vel, vi. (drivelling, drivelled). To slaver; to dote; to talk rubbish.—n. Slaver; senseless twaddle.

Driver, drīv'ér, n. One who or that which drives; a large quadrilateral sail; a main wheel; a golf club for long strokes.

Drizzle, driz'l, vi. (drizzling, drizzled). To rain in small drops.—vt. To shed in small drops or particles.—n. A small or fine rain.

Drollery, drōl'é-ri, n. Buffoonery; comical stories.

Dromedary, drom'é-da-ri, n. A swift camel, usually the Arabian, with one hump, in distinction from the Bactrian, which has two.

Drone, drōn, n. The male or non-working bee; an idler; a low humming sound; a large tube of the bagpipe.—vi. (droning, droned). To give a low dull sound; to hum.

Droop, dröp, vi. To hang down; to languish; to fail; to be dispirited.—vt. To let sink or hang down.—n. A drooping position or state.

Drop, drop, n. A globule of any liquid; an earring; a small quantity; part of a gallows; a distance to fall.—vt. (dropping, dropped). To pour or let fall in drops; to let fall; to let down; to quit; to utter casually.—vi. To fall in drops; to fall; to cease; to come unexpectedly.

Drop-scene, drop'sēn, n. A scenic picture, which descends in front of the stage.

Dropsy, drop'si, n. An unnatural collection of water in any part of the body.

Dross, dros, n. The scum of metals; waste matter; refuse.

Drought, drout, n. Dry weather; want of rain; aridness; thirst; lack.

Drove, drōv, n. A collection of cattle driven; a crowd of people in motion.

Drown, droun, vt. To deprive of life by immersion in water, etc.; to inundate; to overwhelm.—vi. To be suffocated in water, etc.

Drowse, drouz, vi. (drowsing, drowsed). To nod in slumber; to doze; to look heavy.—vt. To make heavy with sleep, or stupid.

Drub, drub, vt. (drubbing, drubbed). To cudgel; to thrash.—n. A blow; a thump.

Drudge, druj, vi. (drudging, drudged). To labor at mean work.—n. One who labors hard in servile employments; a slave.

Drudgery, druj'é-ri, n. Hard labor; toilsome work; ignoble toil.

Drug, drug, n. Any substance used in medicine; an article of slow sale.—vt. (drugging, drugged). To mix with drugs; to introduce a narcotic into; to dose to excess with drugs.

Druid, drü'id, n. A priest and judge among the ancient Celtic nations.

Drum, drum, n. A hollow cylindrical instrument

of music beaten with sticks; something in the form of a drum; the tympanum of the ear.—*vi.* (drumming, drummed). To beat a drum; to beat with the fingers, as with drumsticks; to beat rapidly.—*vt.* To expel or summon by beat of drum.

Drumhead, drum'hed, *n.* The head of a drum; the top part of a capstan.

Drunk, drungk, *a.* Overcome with alcoholic liquor; intoxicated.

Drunkard, drungk'erd, *n.* A person who is habitually or frequently drunk.

Drupe, dröp, *n.* A stone fruit, as the plum.

Dry, drī, *a.* Destitute of moisture; arid; free from juice; thirsty; uninteresting; sarcastic; harsh; cold.—*vt.* (drying, dried). To free from moisture; to deprive of natural juice; to drain.—*vi.* To lose moisture; to evaporate wholly.

Dryad, drī'ad, *n.* A nymph of the woods.

Dryer, Drier, drī'er, *n.* One who or that which dries; that which exhausts moisture.

Dry-rot, drī'rot, *n.* A decay of timber, occasioned by various species of fungi.

Dual, dū'al, *a.* Expressing the number two; existing as two; twofold.

Dub, dub, *vt.* (dubbing, dubbed). To tap with a sword and make a knight, to speak of as; to smooth; to trim.

Dubious, dū'bi-us, *a.* Wavering in opinion; doubtful; uncertain.

Duchess, duch'es, *n.* The wife of a duke; a lady who has the sovereignty of a duchy.

Duchy, duch'i, *n.* The dominion of a duke.

Duck, duk, *vt.* and *i.* To plunge in water; to bow, stoop, or nod.—*n.* A water-fowl; a term of endearment; an inclination of the head; a canvas or coarse cloth.

Duct, dukt, *n.* A canal or tube, especially in animal bodies and plants.

Ductility, duk-til'i-ti, *n.* The property of metals which renders them capable of being drawn out without breaking; obsequiousness; ready compliance.

Dud, dud, *n.* A shell which fails to explode; hence an incompetent person or a defective thing.

Dudgeon, du'jon, *n.* A small dagger, or the handle of a dagger; ill-will; sullenness.

Due, dū, *a.* Owed; owing; suitable; proper; attributable; that ought to have arrived by the time specified.—*adv.* Directly.—*n.* That which law, office, rank, etc., require to be paid or done; fee; right; just title.

Duel, dū'el, *n.* A premeditated combat between two persons; single combat; contest.

Duet, dū'et, *n.* A piece of music for two performers, vocal or instrumental.

Dug-out, dug-out, *n.* A rudely hollowed-out canoe from trunk of tree; an underground shelter from shells; an elderly officer recalled to duty from retirement.

Duke, dūk, *n.* One of the highest order of nobility; a sovereign prince.

Dulcet, dul'set, *a.* Sweet; harmonious.

Dulcimer, dul'si-mèr, *n.* A stringed instrument of music, played on by two sticks.

Dull, dul, *a.* Stupid; slow; blunt; drowsy; cheerless; not bright or clear; tarnished; uninteresting.—*vt.* To make dull; to stupefy; to blunt; to make sad; to sully.—*vi.* To become dull, blunt, or stupid.

Dulness, Dullness, dul'nes, *n.* Stupidity; heaviness; slowness; dimness.

Duly, dū'li, *adv.* Properly; fitly.

Dumb, dum, *a.* Incapable of speech; mute; silent; not accompanied with speech.

Dumb-bell, dum'bel, *n.* One of a pair of weights used for exercise.

Dumbly, dum'li, *adv.* Mutely.

Dumdum, dum-dum, *n.* A soft-nosed bullet which expands and lacerates on striking.

Dumfound, Dumbfound, dum-found', *vt.* To strike dumb; to confuse. Also *Dumfounder.*

Dummy, dum'i, *n.* One who is dumb; the exposed hand when three persons play at whist; a sham article.

Dump, dump, *n.* A heap of refuse, a place where refuse is deposited; a large concentration of military stores, especially of ammunition.

Dumpling, dump'ling, *n.* A pudding of boiled suet paste, with or without fruit.

Dumpy, dump'i, *a.* Short and thick.

Dun, dun, *a.* Of a dark dull color; swarthy.—*vt.* (dunning, dunned). To demand a debt from; to urge importunately.—*n.* An importunate creditor; urgent demand for payment.

Dunce, duns, *n.* One slow at learning; a dullard; a dolt.

Dune, dūn, *n.* A sand-hill on the sea-coast.

Dung, dung, *n.* The excrement of animals.—*vt.* To manure; to immerse (calico) in cow-dung and water.—*vi.* To void excrement.

Dungeon, dun'jon, *n.* A strong tower in the middle of a castle; a deep, dark place of confinement.

Duodecimal, dū-ō-de'si-mal, *a.* Proceeding in computation by twelves; twelfth.

Duodenum, dū-ō-dē'num, *n.* The first portion of the small intestines.

Dupe, dūp, *n.* One who is cheated; one easily deceived.—*vt.* (duping, duped). To impose on.

Duplex, dū'pleks, *a.* Double; twofold.

Duplicate, dū'pli-kāt, *a.* Double; twofold.—*n.* A copy; a transcript.—*vt.* To double.

Duplicity, dū-pli'si-ti, *n.* Doubleness of heart or speech; guile; deception.

Durable, dūr'a-bl, *a.* Having the quality of lasting long; permanent; firm.

Dura-mater, dū'ra-mā-tèr, *n.* The outer membrane of the brain.

Durance, dūr'ans, *n.* Imprisonment; custody.

Duration, dūr-ā'shon, *n.* Continuance in time; power of continuance; permanency.

Duress, dūr'es, *n.* Constraint; imprisonment.

During, dūr'ing, *prep.* For the time of the continuance of.

Dusk, dusk, *a.* Tending to darkness; moderately black.—*n.* A middle degree between light and darkness; twilight.

Dust, dust, *n.* Fine dry particles of earth, etc.; powder; earth as symbolic of mortality; a low condition.—*vt.* To free from dust; to sprinkle, as with dust.

Dutch, duch, *a.* Pertaining to Holland, or to its inhabitants.—*n.pl.* The people of Holland; *sing* their language.

Duty, dū'ti, *n.* That which a person is bound to perform; obligation; act of reverence or respect; business, service, or office; tax, impost or customs.

Dwarf, dwarf, *n.* A person or plant much below the ordinary size.—*vt.* To stunt; to make or keep small; to cause to appear small by comparison.—*a.* Below the common size; stunted.

Dwell, dwel, *vi.* (pret. and pp. dwelled). To live in a place; to reside; to hang on with fondness; to continue.

Dwindle, dwin'dl, *vi.* (dwindling, dwindled). To diminish gradually; to shrink; to sink.

Dye, dī, *vt.* (dyeing, dyed). To stain; to give a new and permanent color to.—*n.* A coloring liquid or matter; tinge.

Dying, dī'ing, *a.* Mortal; destined to death; uttered, given, etc., just before death; pertaining to death; fading away.

Dynamics, dī-nam'iks, *n.* The science which investigates the action of force.

Dynamite, din'a-mit, *n.* An explosive substance consisting of some powdery matter impregnated with nitro-glycerine.

Dynamo, dī'na-mō, *n.* A machine for producing an electric current by mechanical power.

Dynasty, dī'nas-ti, *n.* A race of kings of the same family.

Dyne, dīn, *n.* A unit of force, being that force which, acting on a gram for one second, generates a velocity of a centimeter per second.

Dysentery, dis'en-te-ri, *n.* A disorder of the intestines; a flux in which the stools consist chiefly of blood and mucus.

Dyspepsia, Dyspepsy, dis-pep'si-a, dis-pep'si, *n.* Indigestion; difficulty of digestion.

E

Each, ēch, *a.* and *pron.* Every one of any number considered individually.

Eager, ē'gėr, *a.* Sharp; ardent; keenly desirous; impetuous; earnest; intense.

Eagerness, ē'gėr-nes, *n.* Ardent desire; vehemence; fervor; avidity.

Eagle, ē'gl, *n.* A large bird of prey, of great powers of flight and vision; a military standard.

Ear, ēr, *n.* The organ of hearing; power of distinguishing musical sounds; heed; regard; anything resembling an ear or ears; a spike, as of corn.—*vi.* To form ears, as corn.—*vt.* To plow or till.

Ear-ache, ēr'āk, *n.* Pain in the ear.

Ear-drum, ēr'drum, *n.* The tympanum or middle ear.

Earl, ėrl, *n.* A British title of nobility, below a marquis and above a viscount.

Earless, ēr'les, *a.* Without ears.

Earn, ėrn, *vt.* To gain by labor; to deserve.

Earnest, ėrn'est, *a.* Ardent in the pursuit of an object; eager; zealous; serious.—*n.* Seriousness; a reality; first-fruits; a part given beforehand as a pledge for the whole; indication; token.

Earnest-money, ėrn'est-mun-i, *n.* Money paid as earnest, to bind a bargain, etc.

Earnings, ėrn'ingz, *n.pl.* That which is gained or merited by labor or performance; wages; reward.

Ear-ring, ēr'ring, *n.* A jewel or ornament worn in the ear; a pendant.

Ear-shot, ēr'shot, *n.* The distance at which words may be heard.

Earth, ėrth, *n.* The globe we inhabit; the world; the fine mold on the surface of the globe; dry land; the ground; the hiding hole of a fox, etc.—*vt.* To cover with earth.—*vi.* To retire underground; to burrow.

Earthenware, ėrth'en-wår, *n.* Ware made of clay; crockery; pottery.

Earthquake, ėrth'kwāk, *n.* A shaking, trembling, or concussion of the earth.

Earth-worm, ėrth'wėrm, *n.* The common worm; a mean, sordid wretch.

Earthy, ėrth'i, *a.* Consisting of or resembling earth; gross; not refined.

Ease, ēz, *n.* Freedom from toil, pain, anxiety, etc.; freedom from difficulty; freedom from stiffness or formality; unaffectedness.—*vt.* (easing, eased). To give ease to; to relieve; to calm; to alleviate; to shift a little.

Easel, ēz'el, *n.* The frame on which pictures are placed while being painted.

Easement, ēz'ment, *n.* That which gives ease; accommodation; privilege.

East, ēst, *n.* That part of the heavens where the sun rises; the countries east of Europe.—*a.* In or toward the east; easterly.—*adv.* Eastwards.

Easter, ēs'tėr, *n.* A festival of the Christian church in March or April, in commemoration of Christ's resurrection.

Eastertide, ēst'ėr-tīd, *n.* The time at which Easter is celebrated.

Easy, ēz'i, *a.* Being at ease; free from pain or anxiety; not difficult; gentle; complying; affluent; not stiff or formal.

Easy-chair, ēz'i-chår, *n.* A large, padded armchair.

Eat, ēt, *vt.* (pret. ate, pp. eaten or eat). to chew and swallow, as food; to wear away; to gnaw; to consume.—*vi.* To take food; to taste or relish; to corrode.

Eating, ēt'ing, *n.* The act of chewing and swallowing food; what is eaten.

Eau de Cologne, ō dė ko-lōn, *n.* A perfumed spirit.—**Eau de vie,** ō dė vē, *n.* Brandy.

Eaves, ēvz, *n.pl.* That part of the roof of a building which overhangs the walls.

Eavesdrop, ēvz'drop, *n.* The water which drops from the eaves.—*vi.* To listen to what is said within doors; to watch for opportunities of hearing private conversation.

Ebb, eb, *n.* The flowing back of the tide; decline; decay.—*vi.* To flow back; to decay; to decline.

Ebony, eb'on-i, *n.* A hard, heavy, dark wood admitting of a fine polish.

Ebullient, ē-bul'yent, *a.* Boiling over, as a liquor; over enthusiastic.

Ebullition, ē-bul-li'shon, *n.* The operation of boiling; a sudden burst, as of passion; an overflowing; outbreak.

Eburnean, Eburnine, ē-bėr'nē-an, ē-bėr'nin, *a.* Relating to or made of ivory.

Eccentric, ek,sen'trik, *a.* Not having its axis in the center; not having the same center; deviating from usual practice, etc.; anomalous; whimsical.—*n.* An eccentric person; mechanical contrivance for converting circular into reciprocating rectilinear motion.

Ecclesiastes, ek-klē'zi-as''tēz, *n.* A canonical book of the Old Testament.

Ecclesiastical, ek-klē'zi-as''tik-al, *a.* Pertaining to the church; not civil or secular.

Echelon, esh'e-lon, *n.* The position of troops or ships in parallel lines, each line being a little to the right or left of the preceding one.

Echo, e'kō, *n.* A sound repeated or reverberated.—*vi.* To give out an echo.—*vt.* To reverberate or send back, as sound; to repeat with assent.

Eclat, e-klä', *n.* A burst of applause; renown; splendor.

Eclectic, ek-lek'tik, *a.* Proceeding by the method of selection; applied to certain philosophers who selected from the principles of various schools what they thought sound.—*n.* One who follows an eclectic method in philosophy, etc.

Eclipse, ē-klips', *n.* An interception of the light of the sun, moon, etc., by some other body; darkness; obscuration.—*vt.* (eclipsing, eclipsed). To cause an eclipse of; to excel.

Ecliptic, ē-klip'tik, *n.* The apparent path of the sun round the earth.—*a.* Pertaining to the ecliptic or an eclipse; suffering an eclipse.

Economic, Economical, ē-kon-om'ik, ē-kon-om'ik-al, *a.* Pertaining to economy or economics; frugal; careful.

Economics, ē-kon-om'iks, *n.* The science of the application of wealth; political economy.

Economize, ē-kon'om-īz, *vt.* and *i.* (economizing, economized). To manage with prudence or frugality.

Economy, ē-kon'o-mi, *n.* Frugal use of money; the regular operations of nature; due order of things; judicious management.

Ecstasy, ek'sta-si, *n.* A trance; excessive joy; rapture; enthusiasm.

Ecumenic, Ecumenical, ek-ū-men'ik, ek-ū-men'i-kal, *a.* General; universal: applied to church councils.

Eczema, ek'ze-ma, *n.* A skin disease.

Edacious, ē-dā'shus, *a.* Voracious.

Eddy, ed'i, *n.* A circular current of water or air.—*a.* Whirling.—*vi.* (eddying, eddied). To move circularly, or as an eddy.

Edelweiss, ā'dl-vīs, *n.* An Alpine plant.

Eden, ē'den, *n.* The garden of Adam and Eve; a delightful region or residence.

Edentata, ē-den-tā'ta, *n.pl.* An order of mammals with no, or rudimentary, teeth.

Edge, ej, *n.* The cutting side of an instrument; an abrupt border or margin; sharpness; keenness.—*vt.* (edging, edged). To bring to an edge; to sharpen; to fringe; to exasperate; to move by little and little.—*vi.* To move sideways or gradually.

Edging, ej'ing, *n.* A border; fringe.

Edible, ĕd'i-bl, *a.* Eatable.

Edict, ē'dikt, *n.* An order issued by a prince; a decree; manifesto.

Edification, ed'i-fi-kā''shon, *n.* A building up; improvement in knowledge, morals, etc.; instruction.

Edifice, ed'i-fis, *n.* A structure; a fabric; a large or splendid building.

Edify, ed'i-fī, *vt.* (edifying, edified). To build up, in a moral sense; to instruct or improve generally.

Edit, ed'it, *vt.* To prepare for publication; to conduct, as regards literary contents.

Edition, ē-di'shon, *n.* A published book as characterized by form or editorial labors; the whole number of copies of a work published at once.

Editorial, ed-i-tō'ri-al, *a.* Pertaining to or written by an editor.—*n.* A leading article in a newspaper.

Educate, ed'ū-kāt, *vt.* (educating, educated). To teach; to cultivate and train; to enlighten.

Education, ed-ū-kā'shon, *n.* Act of educating; instruction and discipline; schooling.

Educe, ē-dūs', *vt.* (educing, educed). To draw out; to elicit; to extract.

Eel, ēl, *n.* A slimy serpent-like fish.

Eerie, ē'ri, *a.* Inspiring superstitious fear; weird.

Efface, ef-fās', *vt.* To remove from the face or surface of anything; to render illegible; to blot out; to wear away.

Effect, ef-fekt', *n.* That which is produced; result; purpose; validity; striking appearance; impression produced by a work of art, etc.; *pl.* goods; movables; personal estate.—*vt.* To produce; to cause; to fulfil; to execute.

Effectuate, ef-fek'tū-āt, *vt.* To carry into effect; to bring to pass; to fulfil.

Effeminacy, ef-fem'in-a-si, *n.* State or character of being effeminate.

Effeminate, ef-fem'in-āt, *a.* Womanish; unmanly; weak; voluptuous.—*vt.* To unman; to weaken.—*vi.* To grow womanish or weak.

Effervesce, ef-fėr-ves', *vi.* To bubble or sparkle, as any fluid when part escapes in gas; to exhibit signs of excitement.

Effervescence, ef-fėr-ves'ens, *n.* Act of effervescing; strong excitement.

Effete, ef-fēt', *a.* Worn out; exhausted; barren.

Efficacy, ef'fi-ka-si, *n.* Power to produce effects; production of the effect intended; virtue; force; energy.

Efficiency, ef-fi'shen-si, *n.* The state or character of being efficient; effectual agency.

Efficient, ef-fi'shent, *a.* Effecting; capable; qualified for duty.

Effigy, ef'fi-ji, *n.* The image or likeness of a person; portrait; figure.

Effluence, ef'flu-ens, *n.* A flowing out; that which issues from any body or substance.

Effluent, ef'flu-ent, *a.* Flowing out.—*n.* A stream that flows out of another, or out of a lake.

Effluvium, ef-flū'vi-um, *n.*; *pl.* **-via.** Something flowing out invisibly; a disagreeable odor; a noxious exhalation.

Efflux, ef'fluks, *n.* Act or state of flowing out in a stream; flow; emanation.

Effort, ef'fort, *n.* An exertion of strength; strenuous endeavor; struggle.

Effrontery, ef-frun'te-ri, *n.* Audacious impudence; shameless boldness.

Effulgence, ef-fulj'ens, *n.* A flood of light; great luster; splendor.

Effuse, ef-fūz', *vt.* (effusing, effused). To pour out; to shed.—*vi.* To emanate.

Effusion, ef-fū'zhon, *n.* Act of pouring out; that which is poured out; in *pathology*, the escape of fluid out of its proper vessel into another part; cordiality of manner; a literary production.

Egg, eg, *n.* A roundish body produced by many female animals besides birds, from which their young is produced; something resembling an egg.—*vt.* To urge on; to instigate.

Egotism, eg'ot-izm or ē', *n.* The practice of too frequently using the word *I*; an exaggerated love of self; self-exaltation.

Egotist, eg'ot-ist or ē', *n.* One always talking of himself; one who magnifies his own achievements.

Egregious, e-grē'jus, *a.* Remarkable; extraordinary; enormous.

Egress, ē'gres, *n.* Act of going out; power of departing from any confined place; exit.—*vi.* To go out.

Egret, eg'ret or ē'gret, *n.* A species of heron; an aigret.

Egyptian, ē-jip'shun, *a.* Pertaining to Egypt.—*n.* A native of Egypt; a gipsy.

Eider, Eider-duck, ī'dėr, ī'dėr-duk, *n.* A species of sea-duck, producing down of the finest and softest kind.

Eight, āt, *a.* One more than seven and less than nine.—*n.* This number; the symbol representing this number; an eight-oared racing boat or its crew.

Eighteenth, āt'ēnth, *a.* and *n.* Next in order after the seventeenth; one of eighteen parts.

Eighth, ātth, *a.* and *n.* Next after the seventh; one of eight parts; an octave.

Either, ē'THėr or ī'THėr, *a.* or *pron.* One or the other; one of two; each;.—*conj.* or *adv.* Used disjunctively as correlative to *or.*

Ejaculate, ē-jak'ū-lāt, *vt.* To exclaim; to utter suddenly and briefly.

Eject, ē'jekt, *vt.* To throw out; to dismiss; to dispossess of land or estate; to expel.

Ejection, ē-jek'shon, *n.* Act of casting out; expulsion; dismission.

Eke, ēk, *vt.* (eking, eked). To add to; to lengthen; to prolong.—*n.* An addition.—*adv.* Also; in addition.

Elaborate, ē-lab'o-rāt, *vt.* (elaborating, elaborated). To produce with labor; to refine by successive operations.—*a.* Wrought with labor; studied; high-wrought.

Elaboration, ē-lab'o-rā''shon, *n.* Refinement by successive operations; the process in animal and vegetable organs by which something is produced.

Elapse, ē-laps', *vi.* (elapsing, elapsed). To slip or glide away.

Elastic, ē-las'tik, *a.* Having the power of returning to the form from which it is bent or distorted; rebounding.—*n.* Cord or ribbon made of cotton or silk, etc., with strands of rubber.

Elate, ē-lāt', *a.* Elevated in mind; flushed, as with success.—*vt.* (elating, elated). To exalt; to puff up; to make proud.

Elbow, el'bo, *n.* The bend or joint of the arm; an angle.—*vt.* To push with the elbow; to push, as through a crowd.—*vi.* To project; to push one's way.

Elder, eld'ėr, *a.* Older; having lived a longer time; senior.—*n.* One who is older; an office-bearer in the Presbyterian Church; a small tree with a spongy pith and dark purple or red berries.

Elect, ē-lekt', *vt.* To pick or choose; to select for an office.—*a.* Chosen; chosen to an office, but not yet in office.—*n. sing.* or *pl.* One or several chosen; those favored by God.

Election, ē-lek'shon, *n.* Act of choosing; choice; voluntary preference; divine choice; predestination.

Elective, ē-lekt'iv, *a.* Pertaining to or consisting in choice; exerting the power of choice.

Electric, Electrical, ē-lek'trik, ē-lek'tri-kal, *a.* Containing, conveying, or produced by electricity; full of fire or spirit, and capable of communicating it.

Electricity, ē-lek-tris'i-ti, *n.* The force that manifests itself in lightning and in many other phenomena; the science which deals with these phenomena.

Electrify, ē-lek'tri-fī, *vt.* (electrifying, electrified). To communicate electricity to; to thrill.—*vi.* To become electric.

Electro-biology, ē-lec'trō-bī-ol''o-ji, *n.* The science of electric currents in living organisms; mesmerism or animal magnetism.

Electrocute, ē-lek'trō-kŭt, *vt.* To execute a criminal by means of electricity.

Electrode, ē-lek'trōd, *n.* One of the terminals or poles of the voltaic circle.

Electro-dynamics, ē-lek'trō-di-nam''iks, *n.* The science of mechanical actions exerted on one another by electric currents.

Electrolysis, ē-lek-trol'i-sis, *n.* Decomposition by means of electricity.

Electrolyte, ē-lek'trō-līt, *n.* A compound decomposable by electricity.

Electron, ē-lek'tron, *n.* One of the extremely small particles of negative electricity, which form essential constituents of atoms, and by which, according to the electron theory, heat and electricity are conducted.

Electroplate, ē-lek'trō-plāt, *vt.* To give a coating of silver or other metal by means of electricity.—*n.* Articles so coated.

Electrotype, ē-lek'trō-tīp, *n.* The art of producing copies of types, wood-cuts, etc., by the electric deposition of copper on a cast from the original; a copy thus produced.

Electuary, ē-lek'tū-a-ri, *n.* A medicine incoporated with some conserve or syrup.

Eleemosynary, el-ē-mos'i-na-ri, *a.* Given in or relating to charity; founded to dispense some gratuity.—*n.* One who subsists on charity.

Elegance, Elegancy, el'ē-gans, el'ē-gan-si, *n.* Quality of being elegant; beauty resulting from propriety; refinement.

Elegiac, el'ē-ji'ak, *a.* Belonging to elegy; plaintive.—*n.* Elegiac verse.

Elegy, el'ē-ji, *n.* A poem or a song expressive of sorrow and lamentation.

Element, el'ē-ment, *n.* A fundamental part or principle; an ingredient; proper sphere; suitable state of things; *pl.* first principles of an art or science; data employed in a calculation; the bread and wine used in the Lord's supper.

Elementary, el-ē-ment'ar-i, *a.* Primary; uncompounded; teaching first principles or rudiments.

Elephant, el'ē-fant, *n.* A huge quadruped, having a long trunk and tusks.

Elevate, el'ē-vāt, *vt.* (elevating, elevated). To raise; to refine or dignify; to elate; to cheer.

Elevation, el-ē-vā'shon, *n.* Act of elevating; state of being elevated; an elevated station; a hill; representation of a building in vertical section.

Elevator, el'ē-vāt-er, *n.* One who or that which elevates; a hoist.

Eleven, ē-lev'n, *a.* Ten and one added.—*n.* The sum of ten and one; the symbol representing this number; a side of players in association football, cricket, etc.

Elf, elf, *n.; pl.* **Elves,** elvz. A fairy; a goblin; a mischievous person.

Elfin, elf'in, *a.* Relating to elves.—*n.* An elf; a little urchin.

Elicit, ē-lis'it, *vt.* To draw out by reasoning, discussion, etc.; to educe.

Elide, ē-līd', *vt.* (eliding, elided). To strike out; to cut off or suppress (a syllable).

Eligibility, el'i-ji-bil''i-ti, *n.* Worthiness or fitness to be chosen.

Eligible, el'i-ji-bl, *a.* Fit to be chosen; suitable; legally qualified.

Eliminate, ē-lim'in-āt, *vt.* (eliminating, eliminated). To throw off; to cancel; to leave out of consideration.

Elision, ē-li'zhon, *n.* Act of eliding; suppression of a vowel or syllable.

Elite, ā-lēt', *n.pl.* A select body; the best.

Elixir, ē-lik'ser, *n.* A liquor sought by the alchemists to transmute metals into gold or to prolong life; quintessence; a cordial.

Elizabethan, ē-liz'a-bēth''an, *a.* Pertaining to Queen Elizabeth or her times.

Elk, elk, *n.* The largest species of deer.

Ellipse, el-lips', *n.* An oval figure.

Ellipsis, el-lips'is, *n.; pl.* -**ses.** A figure of syntax by which words are omitted; suppression of letters or words in printing.

Elm, elm, *n.* A tree valuable for its timber.

Elocution, e-lō-kū'shon, *n.* Management of the voice and gesture in speaking; pronunciation; delivery.

Elongate, ē-long'gāt, *vt.* (elongating, elongated). To lengthen.—*vi.* To recede apparently from the sun.—*a.* Long and slender.

Elongation, ē-long-gā'shon, *n.* Act of lengthening; state of being extended; continuation; apparent distance of a planet from the sun.

Elope, ē-lōp', *vi.* (eloping, eloped). To escape privately; to run away with a lover.

Eloquence, e'lō-kwens, *n.* The quality or faculty of being eloquent; oratory.

Eloquent, e'lō-kwent, *a.* Having the power of fluent, elegant, or forcible speech; characterized by eloquence.

Else, els, *a.* or *adv.* Other; besides; in addition.—*conj.* Otherwise; in the other case.

Elsewhere, els'whār, *adv.* In any other place; in some other place.

Elucidate, ē-lū'sid-āt, *vt.* To make clear; to free from obscurity; to explain.

Elude, ē-lūd', *vt.* (eluding, eluded). To avoid by artifice or dexterity; to baffle; to evade.

Elysium, ē-li'zhi-um, *n.* The place of future happiness; any delightful place.

Elytron, Elytrum, el'i-tron, el'i-trum, *n.; pl.* **Elytra,** el'i-tra. The wing-sheath which covers the true wing in beetles.

Emaciate, ē-mā'shi-āt, *vi.* and *t.* (emaciating, emaciated). To become or make lean.

Emaciation, ē-mā'shi-ā''shon, *n.* Act of emaciating; leanness.

Emanate, em'a-nāt, *vi.* (emanating, emanated). To flow out; to issue; to spring.

Emancipate, ē-man'si-pāt, *vt.* (emancipating, emancipated). To set free from slavery; to liberate.

Emancipation, ē-man'si-pā''shon, *n.* Liberation; freedom; enfranchisement.

Emasculate, ē-mas'kū-lāt, *vt.* To castrate; to render effeminate; to expurgate.

Embalm, em-bäm', *vt.* To preserve a dead body by aromatics; to cherish the memory of.

Embank, em-bangk', *vt.* To inclose or defend with a bank, mounds, or dikes.

Embankment, em-bangk'ment, *n.* Act of embanking; a bank raised for protecting against inundation, or for a railway, etc.

Embargo, em-bär'gō, *n.* Prohibition on ships from sailing; restraint or hindrance.—*vt.* To put an embargo on.

Embark, em-bärk', *vt.* To put on board a ship; to engage in.—*vi.* To go on board of a ship; to engage in; to take a share.

Embarrass, em-ba'ras, *vt.* To involve in difficulties; to entangle; to disconcert.

Embarrassment, em-ba'ras-ment, *n.* Entanglement; trouble; abashment.

Embassy, em'bas-si, *n.* The mission, charge or residence of an ambassador; an important message.

Embattle, em-bat'l, *vt.* To arrange in order of battle; to furnish with battlements.—*vi.* To be ranged in order of battle.

Embellish, em-bel'lish, *vt.* To make beautiful; to adorn.

Embellishment, em-bel'lish-ment, *n.* Act of embellishing; that which embellishes.

Ember, em'bér, *n.* A glowing cinder; chiefly in *pl.*

Ember-days, em'bér-dāz, *n.pl.* Days appointed for fasting, being a Wednesday, Friday, and Saturday in each of the four seasons.

Embezzle, em-bez'l, *vt.* (embezzling, embezzled). To appropriate by breach of trust.

Embezzlement, em-bez'l-ment, *n.* Act of fraudently appropriating money, etc., intrusted to one's care.

Embitter, em-bit'ẽr, vt. To make bitter or more bitter; to exasperate.

Emblem, em'blem, n. A picture representing one thing and suggesting another; a symbol; type; device.

Embody, em-bo'di, vt. (embodying, embodied). To invest with a body; to form into a body (as troops), or into a system; to collect.

Embolden, em-bōld'en, vt. To give boldness to; to encourage.

Embolism, em'bol-izm, n. Obstruction of a blood-vessel by a clot of blood.

Emboss, em-bos', vt. To form bosses on; to fashion in relievo or raised work.

Embouchure, em'bö-shör, n. A mouth or aperture, as of a river, cannon, etc.

Embowel, em-bou'el, vt. To take out the bowels of; to eviscerate; to imbed.

Embower, em-bou'ẽr, vt. To inclose in or cover with a bower; to shade.

Embrace, em-brās', vt. (embracing, embraced). To take within the arms; to press to the bosom; to seize ardently; to include; to accept.—vi. To join in an embrace.—n. Clasp with the arms; a hug; conjugal endearment.

Embrasure, em-brā'zhŭr, n. An opening in a wall or parapet through which cannon are fired.

Embrocate, em'brö-kāt, vt. To moisten and rub, as a diseased part of the body.

Embroider, em-broi'dẽr, vt. To adorn with ornamental needlework or figures.

Embroidery, em-broi'de-ri, n. Embroidered work; variegated needlework.

Embroil, em-broil', vt. To confuse; to disorder; to involve in troubles; to disturb.

Embryo, em'bri-ō, n. The first rudiments of an animal in the womb or of a plant in the seed; the first state of anything.—a. Pertaining to anything in its first rudiments.

Embryology, em-bri-ol'o-ji, n. The doctrine of the development of embryos.

Emend, ē-mend', vt. To remove faults from; to improve the text or reading of.

Emerald, e'me-rald, n. A precious stone, akin to the beryl, usually green; a small printing type.—a. Of a bright-green color.

Emerge, ē-mérj', vi. (emerging, emerged). To rise out of a fluid or other substance; to issue; to rise into view; to reappear.

Emergency, ē-mérj'en-si, n. Act of emerging; unforeseen occurrence; pressing necessity.

Emeritus, e-mer'i-tus, a. Discharged from duty with honor on account of infirmity, age, or long service.

Emersion, ē-mér'shon, n. Act of rising out of a fluid or other substance; reappearance of a heavenly body after eclipse, etc.

Emery, e'me-ri, n. A hard mineral used in cutting gems and for polishing.

Emetic, ē-met'ik, a. Causing vomiting.—n. A medicine that provokes vomiting.

Emigrant, em'i-grant, a. Emigrating; pertaining to emigration or emigrants.—n. One who emigrates.

Emigrate, em'i-grāt, vi. (emigrating, emigrated). To remove from one country or state to another for the purpose of residence.

Eminence, om'in-ons, n. A rising ground, elevation; top; distinction; fame; a title of honor given to cardinals, etc.

Eminent, em'in-ent, a. Exalted; high in office; distinguished; illustrious.

Emissary, em'is-sa-ri, n. One sent on private business; a secret agent; a spy.

Emit, ē-mit', vt. (emitting, emitted). To send out; to discharge; to vent.

Emollient, ē-mol'li-ent, a. Softening; making supple.—n. A substance which softens or allays irritation.

Emolument, ē-mol'ū-ment, n. Profit arising from office or employment; salary; gain.

Emotion, ē-mō'shon, n. Any agitation of mind; feeling.

Empale, em-pāl', vt. (empaling, empaled). To put to death by fixing on a stake.

Emperor, em'pér-ér, n. The sovereign of an empire.

Emphasis, em'fa-sis, n. A stress laid on a word or clause to enforce a meaning; impressiveness; weight.

Emphasize, em'fa-sīz, vt. (emphasizing, emphasized). To place emphasis on.

Empire, em'pīr, n. Supreme power in governing; sway; dominion of an emperor; region over which dominion is extended.

Empiric, em-pi'rik, n. One whose knowledge is founded exclusively on experience; a quack; a charlatan.

Empiricism, em-pi'ri-sizm, n. The methods or practice of an empiric; quackery; the doctrine that knowledge comes solely from experience.

Employ, em-ploi', vt. To occupy; to engage in one's service; to keep at work; to make use of.—n. Business; occupation; engagement.

Employee, em-ploi'ē, n. One who works for an employer.

Employer, em-ploi'ér, n. One who employs; one who keeps men in service.

Emporium, em-pō'ri-um, n.; pl. -ia or -iums. A commercial center; a warehouse or shop.

Empower, em-pou'ér, vt. To give legal or moral power to; to authorize.

Empress, em'pres, n. The consort of an emperor; a female invested with imperial power.

Empty, em'ti, a. Containing nothing, or nothing but air; void; unsatisfactory; unburdened; hungry; vacant of head.—vt. (emptying, emptied). To make empty.—vi. To become empty.—n. An empty packingcase, etc.

Empyrean, em-pi-rē'an, em-pi'rē-an, a. The highest heaven.

Emu, Emeu, ē-mū', n. A large Australian bird, allied to the ostrich and cassowary.

Emulate, em'ū-lāt, vt. (emulating, emulated). To strive to equal or excel; to vie with.

Emulsion, ē-mul'shon, n. A soft liquid remedy resembling milk; any milk-like mixture.

Enable, en-ā'bl, vt. (enabling, enabled). To make able; to empower; to authorize.

Enact, en-akt', vt. To establish by law; to decree; to perform; to act.

Enactment, en-akt'ment, n. The passing of a bill into a law; a decree; an act.

Enamel, en-am'el, n. A substance of the nature of glass, used as a coating; that which is enamelled; a smooth glossy surface of various colors; the smooth substance on a tooth.—vt. (enamelling, enamelled). To lay enamel on; to paint in enamel; to form a surface like enamel; to adorn with different colors.—vi. To practice the art of enamelling.

Enamor, en-am'ér, vt. To inspire with love; to charm; to fill with delight.

Encamp, en-kamp', vi. To take up position in a camp; to make a camp.—vt. To form into or place in a camp.

Enceinte, ang-sangt', n. The rampart which surrounds a fortress; the area thus surrounded.—a. Pregnant; with child.

Encephalon, en-sef'a-lon, n. The contents of the skull; the brain.

Enchain, en-chān', vt. To fasten with a chain; to hold in bondage; to confine.

Enchant, en-chant', vt. To practice sorcery on; to charm; to enrapture; to fascinate.

Enchanter, en-chant'ér, n. A sorcerer; one who charms or delights.

Enchantment, en-chant'ment, n. Act of enchanting; incantation; magic; overpowering influence of delight; fascination.

Enchase, en-chās', vt. To inclose in a border; to surround with an ornamental setting; to adorn by embossed work.

Encircle, en-sér'kl, vt. To inclose with a circle; to encompass; to embrace.

Enclave, en-klăv or ang-klav, *n.* A place surrounded entirely by the territories of another power.

Enclitic, Enclitical, en-klit´ik, en-klit´ik-al, *a.* Said of a particle or word so united to the preceding word as to seem a part of it; throwing back the accent on the foregoing syllable.—*n.* An enclitic word.

Encomiast, en-kō´mi-ast, *n.* One who praises another; a panegyrist.

Encomium, en-kō´mi-um, *n.*; pl. **-iums.** Panegyric; eulogy; praise.

Encompass, en-kum´pas, *vt.* To encircle; to hem in; to go or sail round.

Encore, ang-kōr´. Again; once more; a call for a repetition of a performance.—*vt.* (encoring, encored). To call for a repetition of.

Encounter, en-koun´tėr, *n.* A meeting in contest; a conflict; a meeting; controversy; debate.—*vt.* To meet face to face; to meet suddenly; to strive against.—*vi.* To meet unexpectedly; to conflict.

Encourage, en-ku´rāj, *vt.* (encouraging, encouraged). To give courage to; to stimulate; to embolden; to countenance.

Encroach, en-krōch´, *vi.* To trespass on the rights and possessions of another; to intrude; to infringe; with *on* or *upon.*

Encroachment, en-krōch-ment, *n.* Act of encroaching; invasion; inroad; that which is taken by encroaching.

Encumber, en-kum´bėr, *vt.* To impede the motion of with a load; to embarrass; to load with debts or legal claims.

Encumbrance, en-kum´brans, *n.* That which encumbers; burden; hindrance; legal claims or liabilities; mortgage.

Encyclic, Encyclical, en-sī´klik, en-sī´kli-kal, *a.* Sent to many persons or places; circular.—*n.* A letter on some important occasion sent by the pope to the bishops.

Encyclopedia, Encyclopaedia, en-sī´klō-pē´´di-a, *n.* A collection, usually alphabetical, of articles on one or more branches of knowledge.

End, end, *n.* The extreme point; the last part; final state; completion; close of life; death; issue; result; aim; drift.—*vt.* To bring to an end; to conclude; to destroy.—*vi.* To come to an end; to close; to cease.

Endanger, en-dān´jėr, *vt.* To bring into danger; to expose to loss or injury.

Endear, en-dēr´, *vt.* To make dear; to make more beloved.

Endeavor, en-dev´ėr, *n.* Effort; attempt; exertion; essay; aim.—*vi.* To try; to strive; to aim.—*vt.* To try to effect; to strive after.

Endemic, Endemical, en-dem´ik, en-dem´ik-al, *a.* Peculiar to a people or region, as a disease.—*n.* A disease of endemic nature.

Ending, end´ing, *n.* Termination.

Endive, en´div, *n.* A plant allied to chicory; garden succory.

Endless, end´les, *a.* Without end; everlasting; infinite; incessant.

Endogen, en´dō-jen, *n.* A plant whose stem grows by additions developed from the inside, as palms and grasses.

Endogenous, en-doj´e-nus, *a.* Pertaining to endogens; developing from within.

Endorse, en-dors´, *vt.* (endorsing, endorsed). To write on the back of, as one's name on a bill; to assign by endorsement; to ratify.

Endorsement, en-dors´ment, *n.* The act of endorsing; a docket; signature of one who endorses; sanction or approval.

Endoskeleton, en´dō-skel-e-ton, *n.* The internal bony structure of animals.

Endow, en-dou´, *vt.* To settle a dower on; to enrich or furnish, as with any gift, quality, or faculty; to indue; to invest.

Endowment, en-dou´ment, *n.* Act of endowing; revenue permanently appropriated to any object; natural capacity.

Endurance, en-dūr´ans, *n.* State of enduring;

continuance; patience; fortitude.

Endure, en-dūr´, *vi.* (enduring, endured). To continue in the same state; to last; to abide; to submit.—*vt.* To sustain; to bear; to undergo; to tolerate.

Enema, en´e-ma, *n.* A liquid or gaseous medicine injected into the rectum; a clyster.

Enemy, en´e-mi, *n.* One who is unfriendly; an antagonist; a hostile army.

Energetic, Energetical, en-ėr-jet´ik, en-ėr-jet´ik-al, *a.* Acting with energy; forcible; potent; active; vigorous.

Energy, en´ėr-ji, *n.* Inherent power to operate or act; power exerted; force; vigor; strength of expression; emphasis; in physics, power to do work; it may be mechanical, electrical, thermal, chemical, etc.

Enervate, en´ėr-vāt or ē-nėrv´āt, *vt.* (enervating, enervated). To deprive of strength or force; to unnerve; to debilitate.

Enfeeble, en-fē´bl, *vt.* (enfeebling, enfeebled). To make feeble; to weaken.

Enfilade, en-fi-lād, *vt.* (enfilading, enfiladed). To rake with shot through the whole length of a line or work; to fire in the flank of.—*n.* A firing in such a manner; the line of fire.

Enforce, en-fōrs´, *vt.* To urge with energy; to impress on the mind; to compel; to put in execution.

Enforcement, en-fōrs´ment, *n.* Act of enforcing; compulsion; a giving of force or effect to; a putting in execution, as law.

Enfranchise, en-fran´chiz, *vt.* (enfranchising, enfranchised). To set free; to admit to the privileges of a citizen; to endow with the franchise.

Engage, en-gāj´, *vt.* (engaging, engaged). To bind by pledge or contract; to attach; to attract; to attack.—*vi.* To bind oneself; to embark on any business; to begin to fight.

Engagement, en-gāj´ment, *n.* Act of engaging; obligation; betrothal; avocation; business; conflict; battle.

Engaging, en-gāj´ing, *p.a.* Winning; attractive; pleasing.

Engender, en-jen´dėr, *vt.* To breed; to beget; to occasion.—*vi.* To be caused or produced.

Engine, en´jin, *n.* Any instrument in some degree complicated; a machine to drive machinery, to propel vessels, railway trains, etc.—*vt.* (engining, engined). To furnish with an engine or engines.

Engineer, en-ji-nēr´, *n.* One who constructs or manages engines; one who plans works for offense or defense; one who constructs roads, railways, etc.—*vt.* To direct the making of in the capacity of engineer.

English, ing´glish, *a.* Belonging to England, or to its inhabitants.—*n.* The people or language of England.—*vt.* To translate into English.

Engrail, en-grāl´, *vt.* To notch; to indent; to jag at the edges.

Engrain, en-grān´, *vt.* To dye with grain; to dye deep; to paint in imitation of wood.

Engrave, en-grāv´, *vt.* (engraving, engraved). To cut figures on with a burin; to represent by incisions; to imprint; to impress deeply.

Engraving, en-grāv´ing, *n.* Act or art of engraving; an engraved plate; an impression from an engraved plate.

Engross, en-grōs´, *vt.* To take up the whole of; to occupy, engage; to write a correct copy in legible characters; to take in undue quantities or degrees.—*vi.* To be employed in making fair copies of writings.

Engulf, en-gulf´, *vt.* To ingulf; to swallow up.

Enhance, en-hans´, *vt.* (enhancing, enhanced). To raise to a higher point; to increase; to aggravate.—*vi.* To grow larger.

Enigma, ē-nig´ma, *n.* An obscure statement or question; riddle; anything inexplicable.

Enjoin, en-join´, *vt.* To order with urgency; to admonish; to prescribe.

Enjoy, en-joi´, *vt.* To feel gladness in; to have, use, or perceive with pleasure.

Enjoyment, en-joi'ment, *n.* State of enjoying; pleasure; satisfaction; fruition.

Enlarge, en-lärj', *vt.* (enlarging, enlarged). To make large or larger; to set free.—*vi.* To grow large or larger; to expatiate.

Enlargement, en lärj'ment, *n.* Act of enlarging; state of being enlarged; expansion; release; addition.

Enlighten, en-lit'en, *vt.* To make clear; to enable to see more clearly; to instruct.

Enlist, en-list', *vt.* To enter on a list; to engage in public service, especially military; to engage the services of.—*vi.* To engage voluntarily in public service; to enter heartily into a cause.

Enliven, en-liv'en, *vt.* To give life or vivacity to; to gladden; to invigorate.

Enmity, en'mi-ti, *n.* Quality of being an enemy; hostility; ill-will; opposition.

Ennoble, en-nō'bl, *vt.* (ennobling, ennobled). To make noble; to exalt; to dignify.

Ennui, än-nwē, *n.* Dullness of spirit; weariness; listlessness; tedium.

Enormity, ē-nor'mi-ti, *n.* State or quality of being enormous; depravity; atrocity.

Enormous, ē-nor'mus, *a.* Great beyond the common measure; huge; outrageous.

Enough, ē-nuf', *a.* That satisfies desire; that may answer the purpose.—*n.* A sufficiency; that which is equal to the powers or abilities.—*adv.* Sufficiently; tolerably.

Enrage, en-rāj', *vt.* To excite rage in; to incense.

Enrapture, en-rap'tūr, *vt.* To transport with rapture; to delight beyond measure.

Enrich, en-rich', *vt.* To make rich; to fertilize; to supply with an abundance of anything desirable; to adorn.

Enroll, Enrol, en-rōl', *vt.* To write in a roll or register; to record.

Ensanguine, en-sang'gwin, *vt.* To stain or cover with blood; to smear with gore.

Ensconce, en-skons', *vt.* To cover, as with a sconce; to protect; to hide.

Ensemble, ong-säm-bl, *n.* All parts of a thing considered together; general effect.

Enshrine, en-shrin', *vt.* To inclose in a shrine or chest; to cherish.

Enshroud, en-shroud', *vt.* To cover with a shroud; to envelope.

Ensign, en'sīn, *n.* A mark of distinction; the flag of a company of soldiers or a vessel; formerly the lowest rank of commissioned officer in the infantry.

Ensilage, en'sil-āj, *n.* A mode of storing green fodder, vegetables, etc., by burying in pits or silos.

Enslave, en-slāv', *vt.* (enslaving, enslaved). To reduce to slavery; to overpower.

Ensnare, en-snâr, *vt.* To entrap; to insnare.

Ensue, en-sū', *vi.* (ensuing, ensued). To follow as a consequence; to succeed.

Ensure, en-shōr', *vt.* To make sure.

Entail, en-tal', *vt.* To cut off an estate from the heirs general; to settle, as the descent of lands by gift to a man and to certain heirs; to devolve as a consequence or of necessity.—*n.* The act of entailing; an estate entailed; rule of descent settled for an estate.

Entangle, en-tang'gl, *vt.* To knit or interweave confusedly; to involve; to hamper.

Enter, en'tér, *vt.* To go or come into; to begin; to set down in writing; to register; to take possession of.—*vi.* To go or come in; begin; engage in; be an ingredient in.

Enteric, en-ter'ik, *a.* Belonging to the intestines.—*Enteric fever,* same as *Typhoid fever.*

Enterprise, en'ter-priz, *n.* That which is undertaken; a bold or hazardous attempt; adventurous spirit; hardihood.—*vt.* To undertake.

Entertain, en-tér-tān', *vt.* To receive as a guest; to cherish; to treat with conversation; to please; to admit, with a view to consider—*vi.* To give entertainments.

Entertainment, en-tér-tān'ment, *n.* Act of entertaining; hospitable treatment; a festival; amusement.

Enthrall, Enthral, en-thral', *vt.* To reduce to the condition of a thrall; to enslave.

Enthrone, en-thrōn, *vt.* (enthroning, enthroned). To place on a throne.

Enthusiasm, en-thū'zi-azm, *n.* An ecstasy of mind, as if from divine or spiritual influence; ardent zeal; elevation of fancy.

Entice, en-tis', *vt.* (enticing, enticed). To draw on, by exciting hope or desire; to allure.

Enticement, en-tis'ment, *n.* Act or means of enticing; blandishment; wile.

Entire, en-tīr', *a.* Whole; unshared; complete; sincere; hearty; in full strength.

Entirely, entīr'li, *adv.* Wholly; fully.

Entitle, en-ti'tl, *vt.* (entitling, entitled). To give a title to; to style; to characterize; to give a claim to; to qualify.

Entity, en'ti-ti, *n.* Being; essence; existence.

Entomb, en-töm', *vt.* To deposit in a tomb; to bury; to inter.

Entomologist, en-to-mol'o-jist, *n.* One versed in the science of insects.

Entomology, en-to-mol'o-ji, *n.* That branch of zoology which treats of the structure, habits, and classification of insects.

Entozoon, en-to zō'on, *n.,* pl. **-zoa.** An intestinal worm; an animal living in some part of another animal.

Entrail, en'trāl, *n.* One of the intestines; generally in *pl.;* the bowels.

Entrain, en-trān', *vt.* To put on board a railway train.—*vi.* To take places in a train.

Entrance, en'trans, *n.* Act or power of entering into a place; the door or avenue by which a place may be entered; beginning; act of taking possession.

Entrance, en-trans', *vt.* To put in a trance or ecstasy; to enrapture; to transport.

Entrap, en-trap', *vt.* To catch in a trap; to inveigle; to decoy.

Entreat, en-trēt', *vt.* To beg earnestly; to beseech; to supplicate.—*vi.* To make an earnest request; to pray.

Entrée, äng-trā, *n.* Freedom of access; a dish served at table.

Entry, en'tri, *n.* Act of entering; entrance; the passage by which persons enter a house; act of taking possession of lands, etc.; act of committing to writing.

Entwine, en-twin', *vt.* To twine; to twist round; to intwine.

Enumerate, ē-nū'me-rāt, *vt.* (enumerating, enumerated). To count number by number; to reckon or mention a number of things, each separately.

Enunciate, ē-nun'si-āt, *vt.* (enunciating, enunciated). To utter; to pronounce; to proclaim.

Enunciation, ē-nun'si-ā'shon, *n.* Act or manner of enunciating; expression; declaration; public attestation.

Envelop, en-vel'op, *vt.* To cover by wrapping or folding; to lie around and conceal.

Envelope, en'vel-ōp, *n.* That which infolds; a wrapper; a covering for a letter, etc.; an investing integument.

Environ, en-vī'ron, *vt.* To encompass; to encircle; to besiege; to invest.

Environment, en-vī'ron-ment, *n.* Act of environing; state of being environed; that which environs; conditions under which one lives.

Envisage, en-viz'āj, *vt.* To look in the face of; to apprehend directly or by intuition.

Envoy, en'voi, *n.* One sent on a mission; a person next in rank to an ambassador, deputed to transact business with a foreign power.

Envy, en'vi, *n.* Pain or discontent excited by another's superiority or success; malice; object of envy.—*vt.* (envying, envied). To feel envy towards or on account of; to begrudge.—*vi.* To be affected with envy.

Eocene, ē'ō-sēn, *a.* and *n.* A term applied to the series of strata at the base of the tertiary formations.

Eozoic, ē-ō-zō'ik, *a.* Pertaining to the oldest fossiliferous rocks.

Epact, ē'pakt, *n.* Days forming the excess of the solar over the lunar year; the moon's age at the end of the year.

Epaulet, Epaulette, e'pal-et, *n.* A shoulder knot; a badge worn on the shoulder by military men or naval officers.

Epergne, e-pärn', *n.* An ornamental stand for the center of a table.

Ephemeral, e-fē'me-ral, *a.* Continuing one day only; short-lived; fleeting.

Ephemeris, e-fem'e-ris, *n.*; pl. **Ephemerides,** e-feme'ri-dēz. A diary; an astronomical almanac; periodical literature.

Ephod, e'fod, *n.* A vestment worn by the Jewish high-priest.

Epic, ep'ik, *a.* Composed in a lofty narrative style; heroic.—*n.* A poem of elevated character, describing the exploits of heroes.

Epicure, ep'i-kūr, *n.* One devoted to sensual enjoyments; a voluptuary.

Epicurean, ep'i-kū-rē''an, *a.* Luxurious; given to luxury.—*n.* A follower of Epicurus; a luxurious eater; an epicure.

Epicycle, ep'i-sī-kl, *n.* A little circle whose center moves round in the circumference of a greater circle.

Epideictic, Epideictical, ep-i-dīk'tik, ep-i-dīk'tikal, *a.* Serving to display; having a rhetorical character; demonstrative.

Epidemic, Epidemical, ep-i-dem'ik, ep-i-dem'ik-al, *a.* Affecting a whole community, as a disease; prevalent.—**Epidemic,** ep-i-dem'ik, *n.* A disease which attacks many people at the same period.

Epidermis, ep-i-der'mis, *n.* The cuticle or scarf-skin of the body; the exterior coating of the leaf or stem of a plant.

Epiglottis, ep-i-glot'is, *n.* The cartilage at the root of the tongue that covers the glottis during the act of swallowing.

Epigram, ep'i-gram, *n.* A short poem, usually keenly satirical; a pointed or antithetical saying.

Epigraph, ep'i-graf, *n.* An inscription; quotation; motto.

Epilepsy, ep'i-lep-si, *n.* The falling-sickness; a disease characterized by spasms and loss of sense.

Epilogue, ep'i-log, *n.* A speech or short poem spoken by an actor at the end of a play.

Epiphany, ē-pif'a-ni, *n.* A church festival on January 6th, celebrating the manifestation of Christ to the wise men of the East.

Epiphyte, ep'i-fit, *n.* A plant growing upon another plant, but not nourished by it.

Episcopalian, ē-pis'kō-pā''li-an, *a.* Pertaining to bishops, or government by bishops.—*n.* One who belongs to an episcopal church.

Episcopate, ē-pis'kō-pāt, *n.* A bishopric; the collective body of bishops.

Episode, ep'i-sōd, *n.* A separate story introduced to give greater variety to the events related in a poem, etc.; an incident.

Epistle, ē-pis'l, *n.* A writing communicating intelligence to a distant person; a letter.

Epitaph, ep'i-taf, *n.* That which is written on a tomb; an inscription, or a composition, in honor of the dead.

Epithalamium, ep'i-tha-lā'mi-um, *n.*; pl. **-iums** or **-ia.** A nuptial song or poem.

Epithet, ep'i-thet, *n.* Any word implying a quality attached to a person or thing.

Epitome, e-pit'o-mi, *n.* A brief summary; abridgment; compendium.

Epitomize, e-pit'om-īz, *vt.* To make an epitome of; to abstract; to condense.

Epoch, ē'pok, *n.* A fixed point of time, from which years are numbered; period; era; date.

Eponym, ep'o-nim, *n.* A name of a place or people derived from that of a person.

Epopee, e-po-pē', *n.* An epic poem; the subject of an epic poem.

Epsom-salt, ep'sum-salt, *n.* The sulphate of magnesia, a cathartic.

Equable, ē-kwa-bl, *a.* Uniform; even; steady.

Equal, ē'kwal, *a.* The same in extent, number, degree, rank, etc.; same in qualities; uniform; proportionate; adequate; just.—*n.* One not inferior or superior to another.—*vt.* (equalling, equalled). To make equal to; to become or be equal to.

Equanimity, ē-kwa-nim'i-ti or ek-, *n.* Evenness of mind; steadiness of temper.

Equate, ē-kwāt, *vt.* (equating, equated). To make equal; to reduce to an equation; to reduce to mean time or motion.

Equation, ē-kwā'shon, *n.* The act of equating; an expression asserting the equality of two quantities; a quantity to be taken into account in order to give a true result.

Equator, ē-kwā'tėr, *n.* The great circle of our globe which divides it into the northern and southern hemispheres; a circle in the heavens coinciding with the plane of the earth's equator.

Equestrian, ē-kwes'tri-an, *a.* Pertaining to horses or horsemanship; on horseback; skilled in horsemanship.—*n.* A horseman.

Equidistant, ē-kwi-dis'tant or ek-, *a.* Being at an equal distance from.

Equilateral, ē-kwi-lat'ėr-al or ek-, *a.* Having all the sides equal.

Equilibrist, ē-kwil'i-brist or ek-, *n.* One who keeps his balance in unnatural positions.

Equilibrium, ē-kwi-li'bri-um or ek-, *n.* State of rest produced by the counteraction of forces; balance.

Equine, ē-kwīn,', *a.* Pertaining to a horse; denoting the horse kind.

Equinoctial, ē-kwi-nok'shal, or ek-, *a.* Pertaining to the equinoxes.—*n.* The celestial equator: when the sun is on it, the days and nights are of equal length.

Equinox, ē'kwi-noks or ek', *n.* The time when the day and night are of equal length, about March 21st and September 23rd.

Equip, ē-kwip', *vt.* (equipping, equipped). To fit out or furnish, as for war; to dress; to array.

Equipage, ek'wi-pāj, *n.* An equipment; retinue; carriage of state and attendants; accoutrements.

Equipment, ē-kwip'ment, *n.* Act of equipping; habiliments; warlike apparatus; necessary adjuncts.

Equipose, ē'kwi-poiz or ek', *n.* Equality of weight or force; equilibrium.

Equiponderance, ē-kwi-pon'dėr-ans or ek-, *n.* Equality of weight; equipoise.

Equitable, ek'wit-a-bl, *a.* Distributing equal justice; just; upright; impartial.

Equity, ek'wi-ti, *n.* The giving to each man his due; impartiality; uprightness; a system of supplementary law founded upon precedents and established principles.

Equivalent, ē-kwiv'a-lent or ek-, *a.* Equal in excellence, worth, or weight; of the same import or meaning.—*n.* That which is equal in value, etc.; compensation.

Equivocate, ē-kwiv'ō-kāt, *vi.* To use ambiguous expressions to mislead; to quibble.

Equivocation, ē-kwiv'ō-kā''shon, *n.* Act of equivocating; ambiguity.

Era, ē'ra, *n.* A fixed point of time, from which years are counted; epoch; age.

Eradicate, ē-rad'i-kāt, *vt.* To root out; to destroy; to exterminate.

Erase, ē-rās', *vt.* (erasing, erased). To scrape out; to efface; to expunge.

Eraser, ē-rās'ėr, *n.* One who erases; an appliance to erase writing, etc.

Erastian, ē-ras'ti-an, *n.* A follower of Thomas Erastus, a 16th-century German, who maintained that the church is dependent on the state for its government and discipline.—*a.* Relating to the Erastians or their principles.

Erect, ē-rekt′, *a.* Upright; bold; undismayed.—*vt.* To raise and set upright; to build; to found; to cheer.

Ergot, ėr′got, *n.* A disease of rye and other grasses; this diseases growth, used in medicine.

Ermine, ėr′mĭn, *n.* An animal of the weasel kind, a native of N. Europe and America, valued for its white fur; the fur of the ermine.

Erode, ē-rōd′, *vt.* (eroding, eroded). To gnaw off or away; to corrode.

Erotic, ē-rot′ik, *a.* Pertaining to or prompted by love; treating of love.

Err, er, *vi.* To wander; to stray; to depart from rectitude; to blunder.

Errand, e′rand, *n.* A message; mandate; business to be transacted by a messenger.

Erratic, e-rat′ik, *a.* Wandering; irregular; eccentric.

Erratum, e-rā′tum, *n.*; pl. **-ata.** An error or mistake in writing or printing.

Error, e′rėr, *n.* A deviation from truth or what is right; a mistake; a blunder; fault; offense.

Eructation, ē-ruk-tā′shon, *n.* Act of belching; a belch; a violent bursting forth or ejection of matter from the earth.

Erudition, e-rū-di′shon, *n.* Learning; knowledge gained by study; scholarship.

Erupt, ē-rupt′, *vt.* To throw out by volcanic action.

Eruption, ē-rup′shon, *n.* A breaking forth; a violent emission; a sudden hostile excursion; a breaking out of pimples, pustules, etc.

Erysipelas, e-ri-si′pe-las, *n.* A disease accompanied by fever and an eruption of a fiery acrid humor, chiefly on the face.

Escalator, es′ka-lā-tėr, *n.* A mechanism consisting of a series of steps which are carried up and down by means of a continuous chain; a moving stairway.

Escapade, es-ka-pād′, *n.* A runaway adventure; a freak; a mad prank.

Escape, es-kāp′, *vt.* (escaping, escaped). To get out of the way of; to pass without harm; to pass unobserved; to avoid.—*vi.* To be free; to avoid; to regain one's liberty.—*n.* Flight; to shun danger; an evasion of legal retraint or custody

Escarpment, es-kärp′ment, *n.* A steep declivity; ground cut away nearly vertically.

Eschatology, es-ka-tol′o-ji, *n.* The doctrine of the last or final things, as death.

Eschew, es-chō′, *vt.* To shun; to avoid.

Escort, es′kort, *n.* A guard attending an officer or baggage, etc.; persons attending as a mark of honor.—*vt.* es-kort′. To attend and guard.

Escritoire, es-kri-twär′, *n.* A chest of drawers with appliances for writing; a writing-desk.

Esophagus, ē-sof′a-gus, *n.* The gullet; the canal through which food and drink pass to the stomach.

Esoteric, es-ō-te′rik, *a.* Taught to a select few; private; select.

Espalier, es-pa′li-ėr, *n.* A trellis-work or lattice-work on which to train fruit-trees and shrubs; a tree or row of trees so trained.

Espionage, es′pi-on-āj, *n.* Practice or employment of spies; practice of watching others without being suspected

Esplanade, es-pla-nād′, *n.* An open space between the glacis of a citadel and the houses of the town; any level space near a town for walks or drives; a terrace by the sea-side.

Espousal, es-pouz′al, *n.* Betrothal; nuptials: in this sense generally in *pl*; the adopting of a cause.

Espouse, es-pouz′, *vt.* (espousing, espoused). To give or take in marriage; to betroth; to wed; to embrace or adopt; to uphold.

Esprit, es-prē, *n.* Soul; spirit; mind; wit.

Esquire, es-kwīr′, *n.* A shield-bearer; a title of dig-

nity next to a knight; a title of courtesy.

Essay, es-sā′, *vt.* To try; to make experiment of.—*n.* es′sā. An endeavor or experiment; a literary composition to prove or illustrate a particular subject; a short treatise.

Essence, es′sens, *n.* The nature, substance, or being of anything; predominant qualities of a plant or drug; an extract; perfume; fundamental doctrines, facts, etc., of a statement, etc.—*vt.* To perfume; to scent.

Essential, es-sen′shal, *a.* Relating to or containing the essence; necessary to the existence of; indispensable; highly rectified; volatile; diffusible (oils).—*n.* Something necessary; the chief point; constituent principle.

Establish, es-tab′lish, *vt.* To make stable; to found permanently; to institute; to enact; to sanction; to confirm; to make good.

Establishment, es-tab′lish-ment, *n.* Act of establishing; state of being established; confirmation; sanction; that which is established; a civil or military force or organization; form of doctrine and church government established under state control; place of residence or business; the number of men in a regiment, etc.

Estate, es-tāt′, *n.* State; condition; rank; landed property; possessions; an order or class of men in the body politic.

Esteem, es tēm′, *vt.* To set a value on; to regard with respect; to prize.—*n.* Judgment of merit or demerit; estimation; great regard.

Estimate, es′tim-āt, *vt.* (estimating, estimated). To form an opinion regarding; to calculate; to appraise; to esteem.—*n.* Valuation; calculation of probable cost.

Estrange, es-trānj′, *vt.* (estranging, estranged). To alienate, as the affections.

Estuary, es′tū-a-ri, *n.* The mouth of a river where the tide meets the current; a firth.

Etch, ech, *vt.* To produce designs on a copper or other plate by lines drawn through a thin coating, and then eaten into the plate by a strong acid; to draw finely in ink.—*vi.* To practice etching.

Etching, ech′ing, *n.* The act or art of the etcher; a mode of engraving; the impression taken from an etched plate.

Eternal, ē-tėrn′al, *a.* Everlasting; without beginning or end of existence; unchangeable.—*n.* An appellation of God.

Eternity, ē-tėrn′i-ti, *n.* Continuance without beginning or ond; duration without end; the state or time after death.

Ether, ē′thėr, *n.* The clear upper air; refined air; a hypothetical medium of extreme tenuity universally diffused, and the medium of the transmission of light, heat, etc.; a very light, volatile, and inflammable fluid obtained from alcohol, used as a stimulant and anesthetic.

Ethereal, ē-thē′rē-al, *a.* Formed of ether; heavenly; aerial; intangible.

Ethic, Ethical, eth′ik, eth′ik-al, *a.* Relating to morals; treating of morality; delivering precepts of morality.

Ethics, eth′iks, *n.* The doctrine of morals; moral philosophy; a system of moral principles.

Ethnic, Ethnical, eth′nik, eth′nik-al, *a.* Pertaining to the gentiles; pagan; ethnological.

Ethnography, eth-nog′ra-fi, *n.* That branch of science which treats of the manners, customs, etc., peculiar to different nations.

Ethnology, eth-nol′o-ji, *n.* That branch of science which treats of the different races of men.

Ethology, eth-ol′o-ji, *n.* The science of ethics; the doctrine of the formation of character.

Etiolate, ē′ti-ō-lāt, *vi.* To be whitened by exclusion of sunlight.—*vt.* To whiten.

Etiquet, et-i-ket′, *n.* Forms of ceremony or decorum; social observance.

Etruscan, ē-trus′kan, *a.* Relating to Etruria, an ancient country in Italy.—*n.* A native of ancient Etruria.

Etymology, et-i-mol′o-ji, *n.* that part of philology

E

which traces the origin of words; the derivation or history of any word.

Eucalyptus, ū-ka-lip'tus, *n.*; pl. **-tuses** or **-ti.** The generic name of some Australian trees of the myrtle order, usually called gum-trees.

Eucharist, ū'ka-rist, *n.* The sacrament of the Lord's Supper.

Eugenics, ū-jen'iks, *n.* The theory dealing with the production or treatment of a fine, healthy race.

Eulogistic, ū-lo-jis'tik, *a.* Commendatory; full of praise.

Eulogize, ū'lo-jiz, *vt.* (eulogizing, eulogized). To praise; to extol.

Eulogy, ū'lo-ji, *n.* A speech or writing in commendation; praise; panegyric.

Eunuch, ū'nuk, *n.* A castrated man.

Eupepsia, Eupepsy, ū-pep'si-a, ū-pep'si, *n.* Good digestion.

Euphemism, ū'fem-izm, *n.* A mode of speaking by which a delicate word or expression is substituted for one which is offensive; a word or expression so substituted.

Euphony, ū'fo-ni, *n.* An easy, smooth enunciation of sounds; harmony of sound.

Eurasian, ū-rā'shi-an, *n.* One born in India of a native mother and European father.

European, ū-rō-pē'an, *a.* Pertaining to Europe.—*n.* A native of Europe.

Euthanasia, ū-tha-nā'zi-a, *n.* An easy death; a putting to death by painless means.

Evacuate, ē-vak'ū-āt, *vt.* (evacuating, evacuated). To make empty; to quit; to withdraw from; to discharge.

Evade, ē-vād', *vt.* (evading, evaded). To avoid by dexterity; to slip away from; to elude; to baffle.—*vi.* To practice evasion.

Evaluate, ē-val'ū-āt, *vt.* To value carefully; to ascertain the amount of.

Evanesce, ev-a-nes', *vi.* To vanish.

Evanescence, ev-an-es'ens, *n.* A vanishing away; state of being liable to vanish.

Evangel, ē-van'jel, *n.* The gospel.

Evangelist, ē-van'jel-ist, *n.* One of the four writers of the history of Jesus Christ; a preacher of the gospel; a missionary.

Evangelize, ē-van'jel-īz, *vt.* and *i.* (evangelizing, evangelized). To preach the gospel to and convert.

Evaporable, ē-va'pėr-a-bl, *a.* That may evaporate or be evaporated.

Evaporate, ē-va'pėr-āt, *vi.* (evaporating, evaporated). To pass off in vapor; to exhale; to be wasted.—*vt.* To convert into vapor; to disperse in vapors.

Evasion, ē-vā'zhon, *n.* Act of evading; artifice to elude; shift; equivocation.

Even, ē'vn, *a.* Level; smooth; equable; on an equality; just; settled; balanced; capable of being divided by 2 without a remainder.—*vt.* To make even or level; to equalize; to balance.—*adv.* Just; exactly; likewise; moreover.—*n.* The evening.

Evening, ē'vn-ing, *n.* The close of the day; the decline of anything.—*a.* Being at the close of day.

Event, ē'vent', *n.* That which happens; an incident; the consequence of anything; issue; result; conclusion.

Eventful, ē-vent'ful, *a.* Full of incidents; producing numerous or great changes.

Eventual, ē-vent'ū-al, *a.* Pertaining to a final issue; happening as a consequence; final; ultimate.

Eventuality, ē-vent'ū-al''i-ti, *n.* That which happens; a contingent result.

Ever, ev'ėr, *adv.* At all times; at any time; continually; in any degree.

Evergreen, ev'ėr-grēn, *n.* A plant that always retains its greenness.—*a.* Always green.

Everlasting, ev-ėr-last'ing, *a.* Enduring forever; eternal.—*n.* Eternity; the Eternal Being; a plant whose flowers endure for many months after being plucked.

Eversion, ē-vėr'shon, *n.* An overthrowing; destruction; subversion.

Every, ev'ri, *a.* Each one; all taken separately.

Evict, ē-vikt', *vt.* To dispossess by judicial process; to expel from lands, etc., by law.

Evidence, ev'i-dens, *n.* That which demonstrates that a fact is so; testimony; proof; witness.—*vt.* To make evident; to prove.

Evil, ē'vil, *a.* Not good; bad; wrong; unhappy; calamitious.—*n.* That which is not good; anything which produces pain, calamity, etc.; wrong; malady.—*adv.* Not well; ill.

Evince, ē-vins', *vt.* (evincing, evinced). To show in a clear manner; to manifest.

Eviscerate, ē-vis'sē-rāt, *vt.* To take out the entrails of; to disembowel.

Evocation, ev-ō-kā'shon, *n.* A calling forth.

Evoke, ē-vōk', *vt.* (evoking, evoked). To call forth or out; to summon forth.

Evolution, ev-o-lū'shon, *n.* An unfolding; development; extraction of roots in arithmetic and algebra; systematic movement of troops or ships in changing their position; that theory which sees in the history of all things a gradual advance from a rudimentary condition to one more complex and of higher character.

Evolve, ē-volv', *vt.* (evolving, evolved). To unfold; to develop; to open and expand.—*vi.* To open or disclose itself.

Ewe, ū, *n.* A female sheep.

Ewer, ū'ėr, *n.* A kind of pitcher or vessel for holding water.

Exacerbate, eks-as'ėr-bāt, *vt.* To exasperate; to increase the violence of.

Exacerbation, eks-as'ėr-bā''shon, *n.* Increase of malignity; periodical increase of violence in a disease.

Exact, egz-akt', *a.* Strictly accurate; methodical; precise; true.—*vt.* To extort by means of authority; to demand of right; to compel.—*vi.* To practice extortion.

Exaction, egz-ak'shon, *n.* Act of exacting; extortion; that which is exacted.

Exaggerate, egz-aj'ē-rāt, *vt.* (exaggerating, exaggerated). To increase beyond due limits; to depict extravagantly.

Exalt, egz-alt', *vt.* To raise high; to raise to power or dignity; to extol.

Examination, egz-am'in-ā''shon, *n.* Act of examining; inquiry into facts, etc., by interrogation; scrutiny by study.

Examine, egz-am'in, *vt.* (examining, examined). To inspect carefully; to inquire into; to interrogate, as a witness, a student, etc.; to discuss.

Example, egz-am'pl, *n.* A sample; pattern; model; precedent; instance.

Exasperate, egz-as'pė-rāt, *vt.* (exasperating, exasperated). To irritate; to enrage; to make worse; to aggravate.

Excavate, eks'ka-vāt, *vt.* (excavating, excavated). To hollow out.

Exceed, ek-sēd', *vt.* To go beyond, as any limit; to surpass; to outdo.—*vi.* To go too far; to bear the greater proportion.

Excel, ek-sel', *vt.* (excelling, excelled). To surpass; to transcend; to outdo.—*vi.* To be eminent or distinguished.

Excellence, Excellency, ek'sel-lens, ek'sel-len-si, *n.* Superiority; pre-eminence; any valuable quality; an official title of honor.

Except, ek-sept', *vt.* To take or leave out of any number specified; to exclude.—*vi.* to object; to make objection.—*prep.* Exclusively of; without.—*conj.* Unless.

Exception, ek-sep'shon, *n.* Act of excepting; state of being excepted; that which is excepted; an objection; offense.

Excerpt, ek-sėrpt', *n.* An extract; a passage selected from an author.—*vt.* To pick out from a book, etc.; to cite.

Excess, ek-ses', *n.* That which exceeds; superabundance; intemperate conduct; that by which one thing exceeds another.

Exchange, eks-chānj′, *vt.* To change one thing for another; to commute; to bargain.—*n.* Act of exchanging; interchange; barter; the thing interchanged; place where merchants, etc., of a city meet to transact business; a method of finding the equivalent to a given sum in the money of another country.

Excise, ek-sīz′, *n.* A tax on certain commodities of home production and consumption, as beer, etc.; also for licenses to deal in certain commodities.—*vt.* (excising, excised). To impose a duty on articles produced and consumed at home; to cut out.

Excision, ek-si′zhon, *n.* A cutting out or off; amputation; extirpation.

Excitability, ek-sīt′a-bil′′i-ti, *n.* The state or quality of being excitable.

Excite, ek-sīt′, *vt.* (exciting, excited). To call into action; to rouse; to stimulate.

Excitement, ek-sīt′ment, *n.* Act of exciting; stimulation; agitation.

Exclaim, eks-klām′, *vi.* To call out; to shout.—*vt.* To declare with loud vociferation.

Exclamation, eks-klam-ā′shon, *n.* A loud outcry; a passionate sentence; a note by which emphatical utterance is marked, thus, !; an interjection.

Exclude, eks-klūd′, *vt.* (excluding, excluded). To shut out; to thrust out; to debar; to prohibit; to except.

Exclusive, eks-klū′siv, *a.* Excluding; not including; debarring from fellowship; illiberal.

Excogitate, eks-ko′jit-āt, *vt.* To invent or devise by thinking; to think out.

Excommunicate, eks-kom-mū′ni-kāt, *vt.* To eject from the communion of the church; to expel from fellowship.

Excoriate, eks-kō′ri-āt, *vt.* To break or wear off the cuticle of.

Excorticate, eks-kor′ti-kāt, *vt.* To strip of the bark or rind.

Excrement, eks′kre-ment, *n.* That which is separated from the nutriment by digestion, and discharged from the body; ordure; dung.

Excrescence, eks-kres′ens, *n.* Anything which grows out of something else and is useless or disfiguring; a troublesome superfluity.

Excrete, eks-krēt′, *vt.* (excreting, excreted). To separate and discharge from the body by vital action.

Excruciate, eks-krö′shi-āt, *vt.* To torture; to rack.

Exculpate, eks-kul′pāt, *vt.* To clear from a charge of fault or guilt; to absolve

Excursion, eks-ker′shon, *n.* A journey for pleasure or health; a ramble; a trip.

Excursive, eks-ker′siv, *a.* Rambling; wandering; deviating.

Excursus, eks-ker′sus, *n.*; pl. **-suses.** A dissertation appended to a book; digression.

Excusable, eks-kuz′a-bl, *a.* Admitting of excuse or justification; pardonable.

Excuse, eks-kūz′, *vt.* (excusing, excused). To acquit of guilt; to pardon; to free from a duty.—*n.* eks-kūs′. A plea in extenuation of a fault; apology; that which excuses.

Execrable, eks′sē-kra-bl, *a.* Deserving to be execrated or cursed; hateful; detestable.

Execrate, ek′sē krāt, *vt.* (execrating, execrated). To curse; to abominate.

Executant, eks-ek′ū-tant, *n.* A performer.

Execute, ek′sē-kūt, *vt.* (executing, executed). To effect; to achieve; to inflict capital punishment on; to make valid, as by signing and sealing; to perform.—*vi.* To perform.

Execution, ek-sē-kū′shon, *n.* Act of executing; act of signing and sealing a legal instrument; capital punishment; mode of performing a work of art; facility of voice or finger in music.

Executioner, ek-sē-kū′shon-er, *n.* One who puts to death by law.

Executive, egz-ek′ūt-iv, *a.* That executes; carrying laws into effect, or superintending their enforcement.—*n.* The person or persons who administer the government.

Executor, egz-ek′ūt-er, *n.* One who executes or performs; the person appointed by a testator to execute his will.

Exegesis, eks-ē-jē′sis, *n.* An exposition; the science or art of literary interpretation, particularly of the Bible.

Exegetics, eks-ē-jet′iks, *n.pl.* A branch of theology dealing with scriptural interpretation.

Exemplar, egz-em′plér, *n.* A pattern; copy.

Exemplary, egz′em-pla-ri, *a.* Serving as a pattern; worthy of imitation; explanatory.

Exemplify, egz-em′pli-fi, *vt.* (exemplifying, exemplified). To show by example; to serve as an instance of.

Exempt, egz-emt′, *vt.* To free from; to privilege; to grant immunity from.—*a.* Free by privilege; not liable.

Exemption, egz-em′shon, *n.* Act of exempting; state of being exempt; immunity.

Exercise, eks′ér-sīz, *n.* Practice; use; drill; act of divine worship; application; a lesson or example for practice.—*vt.* (exercising, exercise). To employ; to practice; to train; to give anxiety to; to afflict.—*vi.* To take exercise.

Exert, egz-ért, *vt.* To put forth, as strength; to put in action. (*refl.*) to use efforts; to strive.

Exfoliate, eks-fō′li-āt, *vt.* and *i.* To scale off.

Exhale, egz-hāl′, *vt.* (exhaling, exhaled). To breathe out; to cause to be emitted in vapor or minute particles; to evaporate.—*vi.* To fly off as vapor.

Exhaust, egz-ast′, *vt.* To drain off contents; to expend entirely; to treat thoroughly; to tire.

Exhibit, egz-ib′it, *vt.* To show; to display; to administer by way of remedy.—*n.* Anything exhibited.

Exhibition, eks-i-bi′shon, *n.* Act of exhibiting; display; any public show, a benefaction for students in English universities.

Exhilarate, egz-il′a-rāt, *vt.* (exhilarating, exhilarated). To make cheerful; to inspirit.

Exhilaration, egz-il′a-rā′′shon, *n.* Act of exhilarating; cheerfulness; gaiety.

Exhort, egz-hort′, *vt.* To urge to a good deed; to encourage; to warn.

Exhume, eks′hūm, *vt.* (exhuming, exhumed). To unbury; to disinter.

Exigence, Exigency, eks′i-jens, eks′i-jen-si, *n.* Pressing necessity; urgency.

Exile, eks′īl or egz′il, *n.* State of being expelled from one's native country; banishment; the person banished.—*vt.* (exiling, exiled). To banish from one's country.

Exist, egz-ist′, *vi.* To be; to live; to endure.

Existence, egz-ist′ens, *n.* State of being; life; continuation; anything that exists.

Exit, eks′it, *n.* A going out; the departure of a player from the stage; death; a way out.

Exodus, eks′o-dus, *n.* Way out; departure; the second book of the Old Testament.

Exogen, eks′o-ien, *n.* A plant whose stem grows by additions to the outside of the wood.

Exonerate, egz-on′ē-rāt, *vt.* To exculpate; to acquit; to justify.

Exorable, eks′ōr-a-bl, *a.* That can be persuaded; placable.

Exorbitant, ogz or′bit ant, *a.* Excessive; extravagant.

Exorcise, eks′or-sīz, *vi.* (exorcising, exorcised). To purify from evil spirits by adjurations.

Exoskeleton, ek′sō-skel-e-ton, *n.* The external skeleton, as the shell of a crustacean; the dermoskeleton.

Exosmose, ek′sos-mōs, *n.* The passage of gases or liquids through membrane or porous media, from within outward.

Exoteric, Exoterical, eks-ō-te′rik, eks-ō-te′rik-al, *a.* Suitable to be imparted to the public; public; opposed to *esoteric* or secret.

Exotic, egz-ot′ik, *a.* Introduced from a foreign country; not native.—*n. a.* Anything introduced from a foreign country.

Expand, ek-spand′, vt. and i. To spread out; to enlarge; to distend; to dilate.

Expanse, ek-spans′, n. A surface widely extended; a wide extent of space or body.

Expansion, ek-span′shon, n. Act of expanding; state of being expanded; dilatation; distension; enlargement.

Ex-parte, eks-pär′te, a. One-sided; partial.

Expatiate, ek-spā′shi-āt, vi. (expatiating, expatiated). To move at large; to enlarge in discourse or writing.

Expatriate, eks-pā′tri-āt, vt. (expatriating, expatriated). To exile.

Expatriation, eks-pā′tri-ā′′shon, n. Exile; the forsaking of one's own country.

Expect, ek-spekt′, vt. To wait for; to look for to happen; to anticipate.

Expectance, **Expectancy**, ek-spek′tans, ek-spek′tan-si, n. Act or state of expecting; expectation; hope.

Expectation, ek-spek-tā′shon, n. Act or state of expecting; prospect of good to come; prospect of reaching a certain age.

Expectorate, eks-pek′tō-rāt, vt. (expectorating, expectorated). To expel, as phlegm, by coughing; to spit out.

Expectoration, eks-pek′tō-rā′′shon, n. Act of expectorating; matter expectorated.

Expedient, eks-pē′di-ent, a. Tending to promote the object proposed; proper under the circumstances; advantageous.—n. Means to an end; shift; plan.

Expedite, eks′pē-dīt, vt. (expediting, expedited). To free from hindrance; to accelerate; to hasten by making easier.

Expedition, eks-pē-di′shon, n. State of being unimpeded; dispatch; a march or voyage for hostile purposes; journey by a body of men for some valuable end; such body of men.

Expeditious, eks-pē-di′shus, a. Speedy; prompt; nimble; active.

Expel, eks-pel′, vt. (expelling, expelled). To drive out; to eject; to banish.

Expend, ek-spend′, vt. To spend; to use or consume; to waste.

Expenditure, ek-spend′i-tūr, n. Act of expending; a laying out, as of money; money expended; expense.

Expense, ek-spens′, n. That which is expended; cost; charge; price.

Experience, eks-pē′ri-ens, n. Personal trial; continued observation; knowledge gained by trial or observation; trial and knowledge from suffering or enjoyment; suffering itself.—vt. (experiencing, experienced). To try; to know by trial; to have happen; to undergo.

Experiment, eks-pe′ri-ment, n. A trial; an operation designed to discover something unknown, or to establish it when discovered.—vi. To make trial or experiment.

Expert, eks-pert′, a. Skillful; dexterous; adroit.—n. eks′pert. An expert person; a scientific witness.

Expiate, eks′pi-āt, vt. (expiating, expiated). To atone for; to make reparation for.

Expiation, eks-pi-ā′shon, n. Act of expiating; atonement; reparation.

Expiration, eks-pir-ā′shon, n. Act of breathing out; death; end; expiry.

Expire, eks-pīr′, vt. (expiring, expired). To breathe out; to exhale.—vi. To emit the last breath; to die; to terminate.

Explain, eks-plān′, vt. To make plain or intelligible; to expound; to elucidate.—vi. To give explanations.

Explanation, eks-pla-nā′shon, n. Act of explaining; interpretation; clearing up of matters between parties at variance.

Expletive, eks′plēt-iv, a. Serving to fill out; superfluous.—n. A word or syllable inserted to fill a vacancy or for ornament; an oath or interjection.

Explicate, eks′pli-kāt, vt. To unfold the meaning of; to explain.

Explicit, eks-plis′it, a. Plain in language; express, not merely implied; open.

Explode, eks-plōd′, vt. (exploding, exploded). To drive out of use or belief; to cause to burst with violence and noise.—vi. To burst with noise; to burst into activity or passion.

Exploit, eks-ploit′, n. A deed; a heroic act; a deed of renown.—vt. To make use of; to work.

Exploitation, eks-ploi-tā′shon, n. Successful application of industry on any object, as land, mines, etc.

Exploration, eks-plō-rā′shon, n. Act of exploring; strict or careful examination.

Explore, eks-plōr′, vt. (exploring, explored). To travel with the view of making discovery; to search; to examine closely.

Explosion, eks-plō′zhon, n. Act of exploding; a bursting with noise; a violent outburst of feeling.

Explosive, eks-plō′siv, a. Causing explosion; readily exploding.—n. Anything liable to explode, as gunpowder; a mute or non-continuous consonant, as k, t, b.

Exponent, eks-pō′nent, n. One who explains or illustrates; that which indicates; the index of a power in algebra.

Export, eks-pōrt′, vt. To convey, in traffic, to another country.—n. eks′pōrt. Act of exporting; quantity of goods exported; a commodity exported.

Exportation, eks-pōr-tā′shon, n. Act of conveying goods to another country.

Expose, eks-pōz′, vt. (exposing, exposed). To put or set out; to disclose; to lay open to attack, censure, &c; to make liable; to exhibit.

Exposé, eks-po-zā, n. Exposure; statement.

Exposition, eks-pō-zi′shon, n. Act of exposing; explanation; exhibition.

Expositor, eks-poz′it-er, n. One who expounds; an interpreter.

Ex-post-facto, eks-pōst-fak′tō, a. After the deed is done; retrospective.

Expostulate, eks-pos′tū-lāt, vi. To remonstrate; to reason earnestly with a person on some impropriety.

Expostulation, eks-pos′tū-lā′′shon, n. Act of expostulating; remonstrance.

Exposure, eks-pō-zhūr, n. Act of exposing; state of being exposed; situation.

Expound, eks-pound′, vt. To explain; to interpret; to unfold.

Express, eks-pres′, vt. To press out; to set forth in words; to declare; to make known by any means; (refl.) to say what one has got to say.—a. Clearly exhibited; given in direct terms; intended or sent for a particular purpose; traveling with special speed.—n. A messenger or vehicle sent on a particular occasion; a message specially sent; a specially fast railway train.—adv. For a particular purpose; with special haste.

Expression, eks-pre′shon, n. Act of expressing; a phrase or mode of speech; manner of utterance; a natural and lively representation in painting and sculpture; musical tone, grace, or modulation; play of features; representation of a quantity in algebra.

Expropriate, eks-prō′pri-āt, vt. To take for public use; to dispossess.

Expulsion, eks-pul′shon, n. A driving away by violence; state of being driven away.

Expunge, ek spunj′, vt. (expunging, expunged). To blot out, as with a pen; to erase; to obliterate.

Expurgate, eks-per′gāt or eks′per-gāt, vt. (expurgating, expurgated). To render pure; to strike offensive passages out of (a book).

Expurgation, eks-per-gā′shon, n. Act of purging or cleansing; purification.

Exquisite, eks′kwi-zit, a. Select; highly finished; excellent; extreme; matchless; as pain or pleasure keenly felt.—n. A fop; a dandy.

Extant, eks′tant, a. Still existing; in being.

Extemporary, eks-tem´pō-ra-ri, *a.* Arising out of the time or occasion; extemporaneous.

Extemporize, eks-tem´pō-riz, *vi.* To speak without preparation.—*vt.* To make without forethought; to prepare in haste.

Extend, eks-tend´, *vt.* To stretch out; to spread; to prolong; to bestow on.—*vi.* To stretch; to reach; to become larger.

Extension, eks-ten´shon, *n.* Act of extending; state of being extended; that property of a body by which it occupies a portion of space; enlargement; in *logic,* the objects to which a term may be applied.

Extensive, eks-ten´siv, *a.* Having great extent; large; comprehensive.

Extensor, eks-ten´sėr, *n.* A muscle which serves to extend or straighten.

Extent, eks-tent´, *n.* Space or degree to which a thing is extended; compass; size.

Extenuate, eks-ten´ū-āt, *vt.* To lessen; to weaken the force of; to palliate.

Exterior, eks-tē´ri-ėr, *a.* External; on the outside; foreign.—*n.* The outward surface; that which is external.

Exterminate, eks-tėr´min-āt, *vt.* To destroy utterly; to extirpate; to root out.

External, eks-tėr´nal, *a.* On the outside; exterior; not being within, as causes or effects visible; foreign.

Exterritorial, eks-ter´i-tō´´ri-al, *a.* Beyond the jurisdiction of the country in which one resides.

Extinct, ek-stingkt´, *a.* Extinguished; abolished; having died out.

Extinction, ek-stingk´shon, *n.* Act of extinguishing; state of being extinguished; destruction; extermination.

Extinguish, ek-sting´gwish, *vt.* To put out; to quench; to destroy; to eclipse.

Extirpate, eks-tėrp´āt or eks´tėrp-āt, *vt.* To root out; to eradicate; to destroy totally.

Extirpation, eks-tėrp-ā´shon, *n.* Act of rooting out; eradication; total destruction.

Extol, eks-tol´, *vt.* (extolling; extolled). To exalt in eulogy; to magnify; to glorify.

Extort, eks-tort´, *vt.* To exact by force; to wrest or wring.

Extortion, eks-tor´shon, *n.* Act of extorting; illegal or oppressive exaction.

Extra, eks´tra, *a.* and *adv.* Additional; beyond what is usual, due, etc.—*n.* Something in addition.

Extract, eks-trakt´, *vt.* To draw out or forth; to select; to draw or copy out; to find the root of a number.—*n.* eks´trakt. That which is extracted; a quotation; an essence, tincture, etc.

Extraction, eks-trak´shon, *n.* Act of extracting; lineage; operation of drawing essences; tinctures; etc.; operation of finding the roots of numbers.

Extradite, eks´tra-dīt, *vt.* To deliver up (a criminal) to the authorities of the country from which he has come.

Extradition, eks-traa-di´shon, *n.* The delivery, under a treaty, of a fugitive from justice by one government to another.

Extramundane, eks-tra-mun´dān, *a.* Beyond the limit of the material world.

Extraneous, eks-trā´nē-us, *a.* That is without; foreign; not intrinsic; irrelevant.

Extraordinary, eks-tra-or´din-a-ri, *a.* Beyond that which is ordinary; unusual; remarkable; special.

Extravagance, Extravagancy, eks-trav´-a-gans, eks-trav´a-gan-si, *n.* A going beyond due bounds; excess; wastefulness.

Extravaganza, eks-trav´a-gan´´za, *n.* A wild literary or musical composition.

Extreme, eks-trēm´, *a.* Outermost; furthest; most violent; last; worst or best; most pressing.—*n.* The utmost point or verge of a thing; end; furthest or highest degree; (*pl.*) points at the greatest distance from each other.

Extremist, eks-trēm´ist, *n.* A supporter of extreme doctrines or practice.

Extremity, eks-trem´i-ti, *n.* That which is extreme; utmost point, part, or degree; utmost distress or violence.

Extricate, eks´tri-kāt, *vt.* (extricating, extricated). To disentangle; to set free.

Extrinsic, Extrinsical, eks-trin´sik, eks-trin´-sik-al, *a.* Being on the outside; extraneous; accessory.

Extrude, eks-tröd´, *vt.* (extruding, extruded). To thrust out; to expel.

Extrusion, eks-trö´zhon, *n.* Act of extruding; a driving out; expulsion.

Exuberant, eks-ū-bē-rant, *a.* Superabundant; ovrflowing; luxuriant.

Exude, eks-ūd, *vt.* (exuding, exuded). To discharge through the pores; to let ooze out.—*vi.* To flow through pores; to ooze out like sweat.

Exult, egz-ult´, *vi.* To rejoice exceedingly; to triumph.

Exultation, egz-ult-ā´shon, *n.* Lively joy; triumph; rapture; ecstasy.

Eye, ī, *n.* The organ of vision; sight or view; power of perception; something resembling an eye in form; a small hole; a loop or ring for fastening.—*vt.* (eyeing, eyed). To fix the eye on; to observe or watch narrowly.

Eyebrow, ī´brou, *n.* The brow or hairy arch about the eye.

Eyelash, ī´lash, *n.* The line of hair that edges the eyelid.

Eyeless, ī´les, *a.* Wanting eyes; blind.

Eyelet, Eyelet-hole, ī´let, ī´let-hōl, *n.* A small eye or hole to receive a lace.

Eyelid, ī´lid, *n.* The cover of the eye; the movable skin with which an animal covers or uncovers the eyeball.

Eye-service, ī´sėr-vis, *n.* Service performed only under the eye of an employer.

Eyeshot, ī´shot, *n.* Range of vision; view.

Eyesight, ī´sīt, *n.* The sight of the eye; view; observation; the sense of seeing.

Eyesore, ī´sōr, *n.* Something ugly to look at.

Eye-tooth, ī´töth, *n.* A tooth under the eye; a canine tooth; a fang.

Eye-witness, ī´wit-nes, *n.* One who sees a thing done.

Eyrie, Eyry, ī´ri, *n.* An aerie; nest of a bird of prey.

F

Fable, fā´bl, *n.* A fictitious narrative to instruct or amuse, often to enforce a precept; falsehood; an idle story; the plot in a poem or drama.—*vi.* (fabling, fabled). To tell fables or falsehoods.—*vt.* To feign; to invent.

Fabric, fab´rik, *n.* Frame or structure of anything; a building; texture; cloth.

Fabricate, fab´ri-kāt, *vt.* (fabricating, fabricated). To make or fashion; to form by art or labor; to devise falsely.

Fabulous, fa´bū-lus, *a.* Containing or abounding in fable; feigned; mythical; incredible.

Façade, Facade, fa-säd´, fa-sād´, *n.* Front view or elevation of an edifice.

Face, fās, *n.* The front part of an animal's head, particularly of the human head; the visage; front; effrontery; assurance; dial of a watch, etc.—*vt.* (facing; faced). To meet in front; to stand opposite to; to oppose with firmness; to finish or protect with a thin external covering; to dress the face of (a stone, etc.).—*vi.* To turn the face; to look.

Facetious, fa-sē´shus, *a.* Witty; humorous, jocose; sprightly.

Facial, fā´shi-al, *a.* Pertaining to the face.

Facile, fa´sil, *a.* Easy; easily persuaded; yielding; dexterous.

Facilitate, fa-sil´it-āt, *vt.* To make easy; to lessen the labor of.

Facility, fa-sil´i-ti, *n.* Easiness to be performed;

Facing, fās'ing, n. A covering in front for ornament or defense; a mode of adulterating tea; the movement of soldiers in turning round to the left, right, etc.; pl. trimmings on regimental garments.

Facsimile, fak-sim'i-lē, n. An exact copy or likeness.

Fact, fakt, n. Anything done; a deed; event; circumstance; reality; truth.

Faction, fak'shon, n. A party in political society in opposition to the ruling power; a party unscrupulously promoting its private ends; discord; dissension.

Factious, fak'shus, a. Given to faction; prone to clamor against public measures or men; pertaining to faction.

Factitive, fak'ti-tiv, a. Causative: applied to verbs expressing an action that produces a new condition in the object.

Factor, fak'ter, n. An agent, particularly a mercantile agent; in Scotland, one appointed to manage an estate; one of two or more numbers or quantities, which, when multiplied together, form a product; one of several elements which contribute to a result.

Factory, fak'to-ri, n. An establishment where factors in foreign countries reside to transact business for their employers; buildings appropriated to the manufacture of goods; a manufactory.

Factotum, fak-tō'tum, n. A person employed to do all kinds of work; confidential agent.

Facula, fak'ū-lē, n.pl. Spots sometimes seen on the sun's disc, which appear brighter than the rest of the surface.

Faculty, fak'ul-ti, n. Any mental or bodily power; capacity; special power or authority; the body of individuals constituing one of the learned professions; a department of a university, or its professors.

Fad, fad, n. A favorite theory; crotchet; hobby.

Fade, fād, vi. (fading, faded). To lose color, strength, or freshness; to wither; to perish; to become indistinct.—vt. To cause to wither.

Faggot, Fagot, fag'ot, n. A bundle of sticks or twigs; a bundle of pieces of iron or steel for remanufacture; one hired to take the place of another at the muster of a military company; a shriveled old woman.—vt. To tie up; to collect promiscuously.

Fahrenheit, fä'ren-hīt, a. The name of the thermometer in which the freezing point is 32° and the boiling 212°.

Fail, fāl, vi. To become deficient; to decline; to become extinct; not to produce the effect; to be unsuccessful; to be guilty of omission or neglect; to become bankrupt.—vt. To cease or omit to afford aid, supply, or strength to; to forsake.—n. Omission; failure; want.

Failing, fāl'ing, n. A natural weakness; foible; fault in character or disposition.

Failure, fāl'ūr, n. A failing; cessation of supply or total defect; non-performance; want of success; a becoming bankrupt.

Fain, fān, a. Glad; pleased; inclined; content to accept.—adv. Gladly.

Faint, fānt, vi. To become feeble; to become senseless and motionless; to swoon; to lose spirit; to vanish.—a. Enfeebled so as to be inclined to swoon; weak; indistinct; depressed.—n. A fainting fit; a swoon.

Faint-hearted, fānt'härt-ed, a. Cowardly; timorous; dejected.

Fair, fār, a. Pleasing to the eye; beautiful; white or light in respect of complexion; not stormy or wet; favorable; reasonable; impartial; honorable; plain; unspotted; moderately good; middling.—adv. Openly; frankly; honestly; on good terms.—n. A fair woman; the fair, the female sex; a stated market.

Fairy, fā'ri, n. An imaginary being of human form, supposed to play a variety of pranks.—a. Belonging to fairies; given by fairies.

Faith, fāth, n. Belief; trust; confidence; conviction in regard to religion; system of religious beliefs; strict adherence to duty and promises; word or honor pledged.

Falcon, fa'kn, or fal'kon, n. The name of various small or medium-sized raptorial birds; a hawk of any kind trained to sport.

Falconry, fa'kn-ri, n. The art of training hawks; hawking.

Fall, fal, vi. (pret. fell, pp. fallen). To sink to a lower position; to drop down; to empty or disembogue; to sink into sin, weakness, or disgrace; to come to an end suddenly; to decrease; to assume an expression of dejection, etc.; to happen; to pass or be transferred; to belong or appertain; to be uttered carelessly.—n. Descent; tumble; death; ruin; cadence; a cascade or cataract; extent of descent; declivity; autumn; that which falls; a kind of ladies' veil; lapse or declension from innocence or goodness; naut. the part of a tackle to which the power is applied in hoisting.

Fallacious, fal-lā'shus, a. Deceitful; misleading; sophistical; delusive.

Fallacy, fal'la-si, n. Deception; deceitfulness; a misleading or mistaken argument.

Fallible, fal'i-bl, a. Liable to mistake or be deceived.

Fallow, fal'ō, a. Pale red or pale yellow; ploughed, but not sowed; uncultivated.—n. Land left unsown after being ploughed.—vt. To plough and harrow land without seeding it.

False, fals, a. Not true; forged; feigned; fraudulent; treacherous; inconstant; constructed for show or a subsidiary purpose.

Falsehood, fals'hod, n. Quality of being false; untruth; fiction; a lie.

Falsetto, fal-set'tō, n. A false or artifical voice; the tones above the natural compass of the voice.

Falsification, fals'i-fi-kā''shon, n. Act of falsifying; willful misrepresentation.

Falsify, fals'i-fi, vt. (falsifying, falsified). To make false; to garble; to prove to be false; to break by falsehood.—vi. To violate the truth.

Falsity, fals'i-ti, n. The quality of being false; that which is false; a falsehood.

Falter, fal'ter, vi. To hestiate in speech; to fail in exertion; to fail in the regular exercise of the understanding.

Fame, fām, n. A public report or rumor; favorable report; celebrity; reputation.

Familiar, fa-mil'i-er, a. Well acquainted; intimate; affable; well known; free; unconstrained.—n. An intimate; one long acquainted; a demon supposed to attend at call.

Family, fam'i-li, n. Household; the parents and children alone; the children as distinguished from the parents; kindred; line of ancestors; honorable descent; a group or class of animals or plants.

Famine, fam'in, n. Scarcity of food; dearth.

Famish, fam'ish, vt. To kill or exhaust with hunger; to starve; to kill by denial of anything necessary.—vi. To die of hunger; to suffer extreme hunger or thirst.

Famous, fām'us, a. Much talked of and praised; renowned; distinguished; admirable.

Fan, fan, n. An instrument for winnowing grain; an instrument to agitate the air and cool the face; something by which the air is moved; a wing.—vt. (fanning, fanned). To cool and refresh by moving the air with a fan; to winnow, to stimulate.

Fanatic, Fanatical, fa-nat'ik, fa-nat'ik-al, a. Wild in opinions, particularly in religious opinions; excessively enthusiastic.—**Fanatic,** fa-nat'ik, n. A person affected by excessive enthusiasm, particularly on religious subjects; an enthusiast; a visionary.

Fancier, fan'si-er, n. One who fancies; one who

has a hobby for certain things.

Fancy, fan'si, *n.* A phase of the intellect of a lighter cast than the imagination; thought due to this faculty; embodiment of such in words; opinion or notion; liking; caprice; false notion.— *vi.* (fancying, fancied). To imagine; to suppose without proof.—*vt.* To imagine; to like; to be pleased with.—*a.* Fine; ornamental; adapted to please the fancy; beyond intrinsic value.

Fandango, fan-dang'gō, *n.* A lively Spanish dance by two persons, male and female.

Fanfare, fan'fär, *n.* A flourish of trumpets; an ostentatious boast; a bravado.

Fang, fang, *n.* A long, pointed tooth; the tusk of an animal; the hollow poison tooth of a serpent; a prong; a claw or talon.

Fan-light, fan'lit, *n.* A window over a door and forming part of the door-opening.

Fantasia, fan-tä'zē-a, *n.* A species of music ranging amidst various airs and movements.

Fantasy, fan'ta-si, *n.* Fancy; a vagary of the imagination; a fanciful artistic production.—*vt.* To picture in fancy.

Far, fär, *a.* Remote; distant, *adv.* To a great extent or distance in space or in time; in great part; very much; to a certain point.

Farad, far'ad, *n.* The unit of quantity in the measurement of electricity.

Farce, färs, *n.* A play full of extravagant drollery; absurdity; mere show.—*vt.* To stuff with forcemeat or mingled ingredients.

Fare, fär, *vi.* (faring, fared). To go; to travel; to be in any state, good or bad; to be entertained with food; to happen well or ill.—*n.* Sum charged for conveying a person; person conveyed; food; provisions of the table.

Farewell, fär'wel, *interj.* May you fare or prosper well.—*n.* Good-bye; departure; final attention.— *a.* Leave-taking; valedictory.

Far-fetched, fèr'fect, *a.* Brought from afar; not naturally introduced; forced.

Farina, fa-ri'na, *n.* Meal; flour.

Farm, färm, *n.* A portion of land under cultivation; ground let to a tenant for tillage, pasture, etc.—*vt.* To let out or take on lease, as lands; to cultivate; to lease, as taxes, imposts, etc.—*vi.* To cultivate the soil.

Farmer, färm'ėr, *n.* One who cultivates a farm; one who collects taxes, etc., for a certain rate per cent.

Farrago, fa-rä'gō, *n.* A mass composed of various materials; a medley.

Farrier, fa'ri-ėr, *n.* A smith who shoes horses; one who combines horse-shoeing with veterinary surgery.

Farrow, fa'rō. *n.* A pig; a litter of pigs.—*vt.* or *i.* To bring forth pigs.

Farther, fär'THėr-mėr, *a. comp.* More remote.— *adv.* At or to a greater distance; beyond; moreover; in addition.

Fascinate, fas'si-nāt, *vt.* (fascinating, fascinated). To bewitch; to charm; to captivate.

Fascination, fas-si-nā'shon, *n.* Act of bewitching; enchantment; charm; spell.

Fascist, fash'ist, *n.* A member of an Italian organization formed to oppose Bolshevism, Communism, and Socialism in all their forms.

Fashion, fa'shon, *n.* The make or form of anything; external appearance; form of a garment; prevailing mode; custom; genteel life—*vt.* To give shape to; to mold; to adapt.

Fast, fäst, *a.* Firmly fixed; closely adhering; steadfast; durable; swift; dissipated.—*adv.* Firmly; rapidly; durably; near; with dissipation.—*vi.* To abstain from eating and drinking, or from particular kinds of food.—*n.* Abstinence from food; a religious mortification by abstinence; the time of fasting.

Fasten, fäs'n, *vt.* To fix firmly, closely, or tightly; to hold together; to affix.—*vi.* To become fixed; to seize and hold on.

Fastidious, fas-tid'i-us, *a.* Squeamish; delicate to a fault; difficult to please.

Fat, fat, *a.* Fleshy; plump; unctuous; heavy; stupid; rich; fertile.—*n.* A solid oily substance found in parts of animal bodies; the best or richest part of a thing.—*vt.* (fatting, fatted). To make fat.

Fatal, fāt'al, *a.* Proceeding from fate; causing death; deadly; calamitous.

Fatalism, fāt'al-izm, *n.* The doctrine that all things take place by inevitable necessity.

Fatality, fa-tal'i-ti, *n.* State of being fatal; invincible necessity; fatalism; fatal occurence; calamitous accident.

Fate, fat, *n.* Destiny; inevitable necessity; death; doom; lot; *pl.* the three goddesses supposed to preside over the birth and life of men.

Father, fä'THėr, *n.* A male parent; the first ancestor; the oldest member of a society or profession; the first to practice any art; a creator; a name given to God; a dignitary of the church; one of the early expounders of Christianity.—*vt.* To become a father to; to adopt; to profess to be the author of; to ascribe to one as his offspring or production.

Father-in-law, fä'THėr-in-la, *n.* The father of one's husband or wife.

Fatherland, fä'THėr-land, *n.* One's native country.

Fathom, faTH'um, *n.* A measure of length containing six feet.—*vt.* To try the depth of; to sound; to master; to comprehend.

Fatigue, fa-tēg', *vt.* (fatiguing, fatigued). To employ to weariness; to tire; to harass with toil or labor.—*n.* Weariness from bodily or mental exertion; exhaustion; toil; labors of soldiers distinct from the use of arms.

Fatten, fat'n, *vt.* To make fat; to feed for slaughter; to make fertile.—*vi.* To grow fat.

Fatuity, fa-tū'i-ti, *n.* State or quality of being fatuous; foolishness; imbecility.

Fauces, fa'sēz, *n.pl.* The back part of the mouth.

Faucet, fa'set, *n.* A pipe to be inserted in a cask, for drawing liquor.

Fault, falt, *n.* A slight offence; a defect; a flaw; a break or dislocation of strata.

Faulty, falt'i, *a.* Marked by faults; defective; imperfect; blamable; bad.

Fauna, fa'na, *n.* A collective term for the animals peculiar to a region or epoch.

Faux-pas, fō-pä, *n.* A false step; a breach of manners or moral conduct.

Favor, fä'vėr, *n.* Good-will; kindness; a kind act; leave; a yielding to another; a token of good-will; a knot of ribbons; advantage; prejudice — *vt.* To regard with good-will or kindness; to befriend; to show partiality to; to facilitate; to resemble in features.

Favorite, fä'vėr-it, *n.* A person or thing regarded with peculiar favor; a darling; a minion; one unduly favored.—*a.* Regarded with particular favor.

Favoritism, fä'vėr-it-izm, *n.* Disposition to favor one or more persons or classes, to the neglect of others having equal claims; exercise of power by favorites.

Fawn, fan, *n.* A young deer; a buck or doe of the first year; a light-brown color; a servile cringe or bow; mean flattery.—*vi.* To bring forth a fawn; to show a servile attachment; to cringe to gain favor.—*a.* Light brown.

Fawningly, fan'ing-li, *adv.* In a cringing servile way; with mean flattery.

Fealty, fē'al-ti, *n.* Fidelity to a superior; loyalty.

Fear, fär, *n.* Painful emotion excited by apprehension of impending danger; dread; the object of fear; filial regard mingled with awe; reverence.—*vt.* To feel fear; to apprehend; to dread; to reverence.—*vi.* To be in apprehension of evil; to be afraid.

Feasibility, fēz-i-bil'i-ti, *n.* Quality of being feasible; practicability.

Feasible, fēz-i-bl, *a.* That may be done; practicable.

Feast, fēst, *n.* A festal day; a sumptuous enterainment; a banquet; a festival; that which delights and entertains.—*vi*. To partake of a feast; to eat sumptuously; to be highly gratified.—*vt*. To entertain sumptuously.

Feat, fēt, *n*. An exploit, an extraordinary act of strength, skill, or cunning.

Feather, feᴛʜ'ėr, *n*. One of the growths which form the covering of birds; a plume; projection on a board to fit into another board; kind of nature; birds collectively; a trifle.—*vt*. To cover or fit with feathers; to turn (an oar) horizonatally over the water.

Feature, fē'tūr, *n*. The make or cast of any part of the face; any single lineament; a prominent part or characteristic.

Febrile, fē'bril, *a*. Pertaining to fever; indicating fever, or derived from it.

February, feb'rū-a-ri, *n*. The second month in the year.

Feces, fē'sēz, *n.pl*. Grounds; dregs; excrement.

Feculent, fe'kū-lent, *a*. Abounding with sediment; foul or filthy; impure.

Fecund, fē'kund, *a*. Fruitful in progeny; prolific; fertile; productive.

Fecundate, fē'kund-āt, *vt*. To make fruitful or prolific; to impregnate.

Fecundity, fē-kund'i-ti, *n*. State or quality of being fecund; fertility; richness of invention.

Federal, fed'ér-al, *a*. Pertaining to a league or contract; confederated; founded on alliance between states which unite for national purposes.—*n*. One who upholds federal government.

Federalism, fed'ér-al-izm, *n*. The principles of federal government.

Federation, fed-ér-ā'shon, *n*. Act of uniting in a league; confederacy.

Fee, fē, *n*. A reward for services; recompense for professional services; a fief; a freehold estate held by one who is absolute owner.—*vt*. (feeing, feed). To pay a fee to; to engage in one's service by advancing a fee to.

Feeble, fē'bl, *a*. Weak; impotent; deficient in vigor, as mental powers, sound, light, etc.

Feed, fēd, *vt*. (feeding, fed). To give food to; to furnish with anything of which there is constant consumption; to fatten.—*vi*. To take food; to eat; to prey; to graze; to grow fat.—*n*. That which is eaten; fodder; portion of provender given to a horse, cow, etc.

Feel, fēl, *vt*. (feeling, felt). To perceive by the touch; to have the sense of; to be affected by; to examine by touching.—*vi*. To have perception by the touch; to have the sensibility moved; to have perception mentally.—*n*. Act of feeling; perception caused by the touch.

Feign, fān, *vt*. To pretend; to counterfeit; to simulate.—*vi*. To represent falsely; to pretend.

Feint, fānt, *n*. A pretense; an appearance of aiming at one part when another is intended to be struck.—*vi*. To make a feigned blow or thrust.

Felicitate, fe-lis'it-āt, *vt*. To congratulate.

Felicity, fē-lis'i-ti, *n*. State of being in extreme enjoyment; bliss; the joys of heaven; skillfulness; appropriateness.

Feline, fē'līn, *a*. Pertaining to cats; like a cat.

Fellow, fel'ō, *n*. A partner; a companion; one of the same kind; an appellation of contempt; a member of a college or incorporated society.

Fellowship, fel'ō-ship, *n*. Companionship; joint interest; an association; an establishment in colleges for maintaining a fellow.

Felon, fe'lon, *n*. One who has committed felony; a culprit; a whitlow.—*a*. Fierce; malignant; malicious.

Felony, fe'lon-i, *n*. Any crime which incurs the forfeiture of lands or goods; a heinous crime.

Felspar, fel'spär, *n*. A mineral consisting of silica and alumina, with potash, soda, or lime, a principal constituent in granite, porphyry, etc. Called also *Feldspar, Felspath*.

Felt, felt, *n*. A fabric made of wool, or wool and fur, wrought into a compact substance by rolling, beating, etc.; an article made of felt.—*vt*. To make into felt; to cover with felt.

Female, fē'māl, *n*. One of that sex which conceives and brings forth young.—*a*. Belonging to the sex which produces young; feminine; weak.

Feminine, fem'in-in, *a*. Pertaining to females; womanly; effeminate; denoting the gender of words which signify females.

Femoral, fem'o-ral, *a*. Belonging to the thigh.

Femur, fē'mėr, *n*. The thigh-bone.

Fen, fen, *n*. A marsh; bog; swamp where water stagnates.

Fence, fens, *n*. That which defends or guards; a wall, railing, etc., forming a boundary, etc.; defense; fencing; skill in fencing or argument; a purchaser or receiver of stolen goods.—*vt*. (fencing, fenced). To defend; to secure by an enclosure; to ward off by argument or reasoning.—*vi*. To practice the swordsman's art; to parry arguments; to prevaricate.

Fencing, fens'ing, *n*. The art of using a sword or foil in attack or defense; material used in making fences; that which fences.

Fend, fend, *vt*. To keep or ward off.—*vi*. To act on the defensive; to provide a livelihood.

Fenestration, fen-es-trā'shon, *n*. The arrangement of windows in a building.

Fennel, fen'el, *n*. A plant cutivated for the aromatic flavor of its seeds and for its leaves.

Feral, fē'ral, *a*. Having become wild after a state of domestication or cultivation.

Ferment, fėr'ment, *n*. That which causes fermentation, as yeast, etc.; intestine motion; agitation.—*vt*. fėr-ment'. To produce fermentation in; to set in agitation.—*vi*. To undergo fermentation; to be in agitation.

Fermentation, fėr-ment-ā'shon, *n*. Decomposition or conversion of an organic substance into new compounds by a ferment, indicated by the development of heat, bubbles, etc.; process by which grape juice is converted into wine; agitaion; excitement.

Fern, fėrn, *n*. The name of many cryptogams producing leaves called fronds.

Ferocious, fē-rō'shus, *a*. Fierce; savage; cruel.

Ferocity, fē-ros'i-ti, *n*. Savage wildness; fury; fierceness.

Ferreous, fe'rē-us, *a*. Partaking of or pertaining to iron.

Ferret, fe'ret, *n*. An animal allied to the weasel, employed in unearthing rabbits; a narrow tape made of woolen thread, cotton, or silk.—*vt*. To hunt with ferrets; to search out cunningly.

Ferruginous, fe-rū'jin-us, *a*. Of the color of the rust or oxide of iron; partaking of or containing iron.

Ferrule, fe'rūl, *n*. A ring of metal round the end of a stick to strengthen it.

Ferry, fe'ri, *vt*. (ferrying, ferried). To carry over a river or other water in a boat.—*n*. Place where boats pass over to convey passengers; regular conveyance provided at such a place; a boat that plies at a ferry.

Fertile, fér'til, *a*. Fruitful; prolific; inventive; able to produce abundantly.

Fertility, fér-til'i-ti, *n*. Fruitfulness; rickness; fertile invention.

Fertilize, fér'til-īz, *vt*. To make fertile or fruitful; to enrich; to impregnate.

Fervent, fér'vent, *a*. Burning; vehement; ardent; earnest.

Fervor, fér'vér, *n*. Heat or warmth; ardor; intensity of feeling; zeal.

Fester, fes'tér, *vi*. To suppurate; to rankle; to putrefy; to grow virulent.—*n*. A small inflammatory tumor.

Festival, fes'tiv-al, *a*. Festive; joyous.—*n*. The time of feasting; a feast; an anniversary day of joy, civil or religious.

Festivity, fes-tiv'i-ti, *n*. Festive gaiety; social joy or mirth at an entertainment.

Festoon, fes-tön', *n*. A string of flowers, foliage, etc., suspended in a curve or curves; carved work in the form of a wreath of flowers, etc. —*vt*.

To form in festoons; to adorn with festoons.

Fetch, fech, *vt*. To bring or draw; to make; to heave, as a sigh; to obtain as its price.—*vi*. To move or turn; to bring things.—*n*. A stratagem or trick; a wraith.

Fête, fāt, *n*. A feast or festival; a holiday.—*vt*. To honor with a feast.

Fetlock, fet'lok. *n*. The tuft of hair that grows behind on a horse's feet; the joint on which this hair grows; an instrument fixed to a horse's leg to prevent him from running off.

Fetter, fet'ér, *n*. A chain for the feet; anything that confines or restrains from motion; generally in *pl*.—*vt*. To put fetters upon; to restrain.

Fetus, fē'tus. *n*.; **pl. -uses.** The young or an animal in the womb, or in the egg, after being perfectly formed.

Feud, fūd, *n*. Hostility; a hereditary quarrel; a fief.

Fever, Fē'vér, *n*. A disease characterized by an accelerated pulse, heat, thirst, and diminished strength; agitation; excitement.—*vt*. To put in a fever.—*vt*. To be seized with fever.

Few, fū, *a*. Not many; small in number.

Fey, fā, *a*. On the verge of a sudden or violent death; fated soon to die and often showing this by unnatural gaiety.

Fez, fez, *n*. A close-fitting red cap with a tassel, worn in Turkey, Egypt, etc.

Fiancé, Fiancée, fē-äng-sā', *n*., *masc*. and *fem*. An affianced or betrothed person.

Fiasco, fē-as'kō, *n*. An ignominious failure.

Fiat, fī'at, *n*. A decree; a command.

Fib, fib, *n*. A falsehood (a softer expression than *lie*).—*vi*. (fibbing, fibbed). To tell fibs.

Fiber, fibér, *n*. A thread; a fine, slender body which constitutes a part of animals, plants, or minderals.

Fickle, fik'l, *a*. Of a changeable mind; vacillating; capricious.

Fiction, fik'shon, *n*. A feigned story; literature in the form of novels, tales, etc., a falsehood; fabrication.

Fiddle, fid'l, *n*. A stringed instrument of music; a violin; the wooden framework fixed on tables on board ship in rough weather, to keep the crockery from sliding off.—*vt*. (fiddling, fiddled). To play on a fiddle; to trifle; to trifle with the hands.—*vt*. To play on a fiddle.

Fidelity, fi-del'i-ti, *n*. Faithfulness; trustiness; loyalty; integrity.

Fidget, fij'et, *vi*. To move uneasily or in fits and starts.—*n*. An uneasy restless motion.

Fiduciary, fi-dū'shi-a-ri, *a*. Held in trust; having the nature of a trust.—*n*. One who holds a thing in trust; a trustee.

Field, fēld, *n*. A piece of land suitable for tillage or pasture; piece of enclosed land; place of battle; battle; open space for action; sphere; blank space on which figures are drawn; those taking part in a hunt or race.—*vi. and t*. To watch and catch the ball, as in cricket.

Fiend, fēnd, *n*. A demon; the devil; a wicked or cruel person.

Fierce, fērs, *a*. Wild; savage; outrageous; violent.

Fiery, fī'e-ri, *a*. Consisting of fire; like fire; impetuous; irritable; fierce.

Fife, fif, *n*. A small wind-instrument used chiefly in martial music. *vi*. (fifing, fifed). To play on a fife.

Fifteen, fif'tēn, *a. and n*. Five and ten; a Rugby football team.

Fifth, fifth, *a*. The ordinal of five.—*n*. A fifth part.

Fifty, fif'ti, *a. and n*. Five tens; five times ten.

Fig, fig, *n*. The fruit of a tree of the mulberry family; the tree itself; a mere trifle; dress.

Fight, fit, *vi*. (fighting, fought). To strive for victory; to contend in arms.—*vt*. To war against; to contend with in battle; to win by struggle.—*n*. A struggle for victory; a battle; an encounter.

Fighter, fit'ér, *n*. One who fights; a combatant; a warrior; an aeroplane designed for aerial combat.

Figment, fig'ment, *n*. A fiction; fabrication.

Figurant, fig'ūr-ant, *n*. A character on the stage who has nothing to say.

Figuration, fig-ūr-ā'shon, *n*. Act of giving figure; configuration; form.

Figurative, fig'ūr-āt-iv, *a*. Containing a figure or figures; representing by resemblance; typical metaphoric; abounding in figures of speech.

Figure, fig'ūr, *n*. The form of anything as expressed by the outline; appearance; representation; a statue; a character denoting a number; a diagram; type; mode of expression in which words are turned from their ordinary signification; price.—*vt*. (figuring, figured). To make a likeness of; to represent by drawing, etc.; to cover or mark with figures; to image in the mind.—*vi*. To make a figure; to be distinguished.

Figure-head, fig'ūr-hed, *n*. The ornamental figure on a ship under the bowsprit.

Filament, fil'a-ment, *n*. A slender thread; a fine fiber.

Filatory, fil'a-to-ri, *n*. A machine which spins threads.

Filbert, fil'bért, *n*. The fruit of the cultivated hazel.

Filch, filsh or filch, *vt*. To pilfer; to steal.

File, fil, *n*. A line or wire on which papers are strung; the papers so strung; a row of soldiers one behind another; a steel instrument for cutting and smoothing iron, wood, etc.—*vt*. (filing, filed). To arrange or place on or in a file; to bring before a court by presenting the proper papers; to rub or cut with a file; to polish.—*vi*. To march in a line one after the other.

Filial, fil'i-al, *a*. Pertaining to or becoming a son or daughter.

Filigree, fil'i-gre, *n*. Ornamental open work in fine gold or silver wire.

Filings, fil'ingz, *n.pl*. Fragments or particles rubbed off by the act of filing.

Fill, fil, *vt*. To make full; to occupy; to pervade; to satisfy; to surfeit; to supply with an occupant; to hold; to possess and perform the duties of.—*vi*. To grow or become full.—*n*. As much as fills or supplies want.

Fillet, fil'et, *n*. A little band to tie about the hair; the fleshy part of the thigh in veal; meat rolled together and tied round; something resembling a fillet or band.—*vt*. (filleting, filleted). To bind with a little band.

Film, film, *n*. A thin skin; a pellicle; *(pl.)* a cinema-show; the pictures.—*vt*. To cover with a thin skin.

Filter, fil'tér, *n*. A strainer; any substance through which liquors are passed.—*vt*. To purify by passing through a filter.—*vi*. To percolate; to pass through a filter.

Filth, filth, *n*. That which defiles; dirt; pollution.

Filtrate, fil'trāt, *vt*. To filter.

Filtration, fil-trā'shon, *n*. Act or process of filtering.

Fin, fin, *n*. One of the organs which enable fishes to balance themselves and regulate their movements; anything resembling a fin.

Final, fin'al, *a*. Pertaining to the end; last; ultimate; conclusive; decisive.

Finale, fē-nä'lā, *n*. The last part of a piece of music, the last piece or scene in a performance.

Finality, fi-nal'i-ti, *n*. Final state; state of being final; the doctrine that nothing exists except for a determinate end.

Finance, fi-nans', *n*. The science of public revenue and expenditure; management of money matters; *pl*. public funds or resources of money; private income.—*vi*. (financing, financed). To conduct financial operations.—*vt*. To manage the financial affairs of.

Finch, finsh, *n*. A small singing bird.

Find, find, *vt*. (finding, found). To come upon; to discover; to recover; to get; to perceive; to supply; to declare by verdict.—*n*. A discovery; the thing found.

Finding, find'ing, *n*. Discovery; act of discovering; that which is found; a verdict.

Fine, fīn, *a.* Slender; minute; keen; delicate; refined; elegant; amiable; noble; splendid.—*n.* Payment of money imposed as a punishment; conclusion *(in fine).*—*vt.* (fining, fined). To make fine; to purify; to impose a pecuniary penalty on.

Finery, fīn'é-ri, *n.* Fine things; showy articles of dress; a furnace where cast-iron is converted into malleable iron.

Finesse, fi-nes', *n.* Artifice; stratagem.—*vi.* To use finesse or artifice.

Finger, fing'gėr, *n.* One of the five members of the hand; something resembling a finger; skill in playing on a keyed instrument.—*vt.* To handle with the fingers; to touch lightly; to pilfer.—*vi.* To dispose the fingers aptly in playing on an instrument.

Fingering, fing'gėr-ing, *n.* Act of touching lightly; manner of touching an instrument of music; a loose worsted for stockings, etc.

Finis, fī'nis, *n.* An end; conclusion.

Finish, fin'ish, *vt.* To bring to an end; to perfect; to polish to a high degree.—*vi.* To come to an end; to expire.—*n.* Completion; the last touch to a work; polish.

Finite, fī'nīt, *a.* Limited; bounded; circumscribed; not infinite.

Finn, fin, *n.* A native of Finland.

Fiord, Fjord, fyord, *n.* An inlet of the sea, such as are common in Norway.

Fir, fėr, *n.* A resinous coniferous tree.

Fire, fīr, *n.* Heat and light emanating from a body; fuel burning; a conflagration; discharge of firearms; splendor; violence of passion; vigor of fancy; animation; ardent affection; affliction.—*vt.* (firing, fired). To set on fire; to irritate; to animate; to bake; to cause to explode; to discharge (firearms).—*vi.* To take fire; to be inflamed with passion; to discharge firearms.

Firearm, fīr'ärm, *n.* A weapon which expels its projectile by the combustion of powder.

Fire-brand, fīr'brand, *n.* A piece of wood kindled; an incendiary; one who inflames factions.

Fire-engine, fīr'en-jin, *n.* An engine for throwing water to extinguish fire.

Fire-escape, fīr'es-kāp, *n.* A machine to facilitate escape from a building on fire.

Fire-fly, fīr'flī, *n.* A winged insect which emits a brilliant light at night.

Fire-irons, fīr'ī-ėrnz, *n.pl,* A shovel, tongs, poker, etc.

Fireman, fīr'man, *n.* A man who extinguishes fires, or tends the fires of an engine.

Fire-proof, fīr'pröf, *a.* Incombustible.

Fire-side, fīr'sīd, *n.* A place near the fire or hearth; home; domestic life.

Firework, fīr'wėrk, *n.* Preparation of gunpowder, sulphur, etc., used for making a show, a signal, etc.

Firm, fėrm, *a.* Steady; stable; strong; dense; hard; not fluid; fixed; resolute.—*n.* A partnership or commercial house.—*vt.* To make firm or solid.—*vi.* To become firm.

Firmament, fėrm'a-ment, *n.* The sky or heavens; region of the air; an expanse.

First, fėrst, *a.* Foremost in time, place, rank, value, etc.; chief; highest; the ordinal of *one.*—*adv.* Before all others in time, place, etc.

First-born, fėrst'born, *a.* Eldest.

First-fruit, fėrst'fröt, *n.* The fruit or produce first collected; first profits; first or earliest effect, in good or bad sense.

First-hand, fėrst'hand, *a.* Obtained direct from the first source, producer, maker, etc.

Firstling, fėrst'ling, *n.* The first produce or offspring, as of sheep or cattle.

First-rate, fėrst'rāt, *a.* Of highest excellence; preeminent; of largest size.

Fiscal, fis'kal, *a.* Pertaining to the public treasury.—*n.* A treasurer; a public prosecutor, as in Scotland.

Fish, fish, *n.* An animal that lives in water; the

flesh of such animals used as food.—*vi.* To attempt to catch fish; to attempt to obtain by artifice.—*vt.* To catch or try to catch fish in; to draw out or up when in water.

Fisherman, fish'ėr-man, *n.* One whose occupation is to catch fish.

Fission, fi'shon, *n.* The act of splitting into parts; reproduction in animals of a low type through the body dividing into parts.

Fissure, fi'shūr, *n.* A cleft; a longitudinal opening.—*vt.* To cleave; to crack.

Fist, fist, *n.* The hand clenched; the hand with the fingers doubled into the palm.—*vt.* To strike with the fist.

Fistula, fis'tū-la, *n.* A shepherd's pipe; a deep, narrow, sinuous ulcer.

Fistular, fis'tū-lėr, *a.* Hollow like a pipe.

Fit, fit, *n.* A sudden activity followed by a relaxation; paroxysm; convulsion; due adjustment of dress to the body.—*a.* Conformable to a standard of right, duty, taste, etc.; suitable; proper; congruous; qualified; adequate.—*vt.* (fitting, fitted). To make fit or suitable; to furnish with anything; to adapt; to qualify for.—*vi.* To be proper or becoming; to suit; to be adapted.

Five, fiv, *a.* and *n.* Four and one added; the half of ten.

Fix, fiks, *vt.* To make fast or firm; to settle; to define; to appoint; to deprive of volatility.—*vi.* To settle or remain permanently; to cease to be fluid; to congeal.—*n.* A condition of difficulty; dilemma.

Fixation, fiks-ā'shon, *n.* Act of fixing; state in which a body resists evaporation.

Fixative, fiks'a-tiv, *a.* Tending or causing to fix.—*n.* A substance that causes something to be stable or not fleeting.

Fixture, fiks'tūr, *n.* That which is fixed; that which is permanently attached; an appendage.

Fizz, Fizzle, fiz, fiz'l, *vi.* To make a hissing sound. Also used as a noun.

Flabbergast, flab'ėr-gast, *vt.* To strike with astonishment or dismay.

Flabby, flab'i, *a.* Soft; yielding to the touch; languid; feeble.

Flaccid, flak'sid, *a.* Flabby; soft and weak; drooping; limber.

Flag, flag, *n.* A cloth, usually attached to a pole, and bearing devices expressive of nationality, etc.; a banner; a flat stone for paving; an aquatic plant with sword-shaped leaves.—*vt.* (flagging, flagged). To hang loose; to droop; to languish; to slacken.—*vt.* To lay with broad flat stones.

Flagellant, fla'jel-lant, *n.* One who whips himself in religious discipline.

Flagellate, fla'jel-lāt, *vt.* To whip.

Flageolet, fla'jel-et, *n.* A small wind-instrument like a flute with a mouth-piece.

Flagging, flag'ing, *n.* Flag-stones; a pavement or side-walk of flag-stones.

Flagrant, flā'grant, *a.* Flaming in notice; glaring; notorious; enormous.

Flail, flāl, *n.* A wooden instrument for thrashing or beating grain, etc.

Flake, flāk, *n.* A loose, filmy mass of anything; a scale; a fleecy or feathery particle, as of snow; a flock, as of wool.—*vt.* (flaking, flaked). To form into flakes.—*vi.* To break in layers; to peel off.

Flamboyant, flam-boi'ant, *a.* Noting that style of gothic architecture characterized by wavy tracery in the windows; florid.

Flame, flām, *n.* Light emitted from fire; a blaze; fire; heat of passion; ardor of temper or imagination; ardent love; rage; one beloved.—*vi.* (flaming, flamed). To blaze; to glow; to rage.

Flamingo, fla-ming'gō, *n.* A web-footed, long-necked bird about 5 to 6 feet high.

Flange, flanj, *n.* A projecting rim or edge on any substance; a raised edge on a wheel, etc.—*vt.* (flanging, flanged). To furnish with a flange.

Flank, flangk, *n.* The part of the side of an animal, between the ribs and the hip; the side of an

rmy; the extreme right or left; the side of any
building.—*vt.* To be situated at the side of; to
place troops so as to command or attack the
flank; to pass round the side of.

annel, flan'el, *n.* A soft, nappy, woollen cloth of
loose texture; garment made of flannel.

ap, flap, *n.* Something broad and flexible that
hangs loose; the motion or sound of anything
broad and loose, or a stroke with it; tail of a
coat, etc.—*vt.* (flapping, flapped). To beat with a
flap; to move; as something broad.—*vi.* To
move, as wings; to wave loosely.

ap-jack, flap'jak, *n.* A sort of broad pancake;
an apple-puff; a flat powder-compact.

are, flār, *vi.* (flaring, flared). To burn with an unsteady light; to glitter with transient luster; to
give out a dazzling light.—*n.* An unsteady
strong light.

ash, flash, *n.* A sudden burst of flame and light;
gleam.—*a.* Vulgarly showy; counterfeit.—*vi.*
to burst or break forth with a flash; to dart.—*vt.*
to throw out like a burst of light.

ash-point, Flashing-point, flash'point,
flash'ing-point, *n.* The temperature at which
the vapor of oils will ignite and flash.

ask, flask, *n.* A kind of bottle; a bottle for the
pocket; a vessel for powder.

at, flat, *a.* Having an even surface; level; fallen;
tasteless; vapid; depressed; dull; absolute; below the true pitch, as a sound.—*n.* A level; a
shallow; the broad side of something; a mark in
music ♭ indicating lowering of pitch; a story or
floor of a house; a simpleton.

atten, flat'n, *vt.* To make flat; to level; to render
less acute or sharp, as a sound.—*vi.* To grow or
become flat.

atter, flat'er, *vt.* To gratify by praise; to compliment; to praise falsely.

attery, flat'e-ri, *n.* False praise; sycophancy; ca-
jolery.

atulent, flat'ū-lent, *a.* Affected with gases in
the stomach and intestines; generating wind in
the stomach; empty; puffy.

aunt, flant, *vi.* and *t.* To display ostentatiously.—*n.* Bold or impudent parade.

avor, flā'ver, *n.* The quality of a substance
which affects the smell or taste; relish; zest.—
t. To give a flavor to.

aw, fla, *n.* A crack; a defect; a speck; a gust of
wind.—*vt.* To make a flaw in.

awless, fla'les, *a.* Without defect; perfect.

ax, flaks, *n.* A plant, the fibers of which are
formed into linen threads; the fibers prepared
or manufacture.

ay, flā, *vt.* To strip the skin off an animal.

ea, flē, *n.* An insect that leaps with great agil-
ty, and whose bite causes itch

eck, flek, *n.* A spot; streak; dapple.—*vt.* To spot;
to streak or stripe; to dapple.

ection, flek'shon, *n.* Act of bending; state of being bent.

edge, flej, *vt.* (fledging, fledged). To supply with
the feathers necessary for flight.

ee, flē, *vi.* (fleeing, fled). To run away; to hasten
from.—*vt.* To shun.

eece, flēs, *n.* The coat of wool that covers a
sheep, or is shorn at one time.—*vt.* (fleecing,
fleeced). To strip of the fleece; to rob or cheat
heartlessly; to cover as with a fleece.

eet, flēt, *n.* A squadron or body of ships; navy.—
. Swift of pace; nimble.—*vi.* To fly swiftly; to be
n a transient state.

eeting, flēt'ing, *a.* Not durable; transient; momentary.

emish, flem'ish, *a.* Pertaining to Flanders.—*n.*
The language of the Flemings.

esh, flesh, *n.* The muscular part of an animal;
animal food; beasts and birds used as food; the
body, as distinguished from the soul; mankind;
corporeal appetites; kindred; family.—*vt.* To
feed with flesh; to initiate to the taste of flesh.

eshly, flesh'li, *a.* Carnal; worldly; lascivious;
human; not spiritual.

Flesh-wound, flesh'wönd, *n.* A wound which affects the flesh only.

Fleshy, flesh'i, *a.* Muscular; fat; corpulent;
plump; pulpy.

Flex, fleks, *vt.* To bend.

Flexibility, fleks-i-bil'i-ti, *n.* Quality of being flexible; pliancy, readiness to comply.

Flexible, fleks'i-bl, *a.* That may be bent; pliant;
supple; tractable; plastic.

Flexion, flek'shon, *n.* Act of bending; a bend; part
bent.

Flexor, fleks'er, *n.* A muscle which produces flexion.

Flick, flik, *n.* A sharp sudden stroke, as with a
whip; a flip.—*vt.* To strike with a flick; to flip.

Flicker, flik'er, *vi.* To flutter; to waver, as an unsteady flame.—*n.* A wavering gleam.

Flight, flīt, *n.* Act of fleeing or flying; power or
manner of flying; a flock of birds; a volley, as of
arrows; pace passed by flying; a soaring; lofty
elevation, as of fancy; extravagant sally; a series of steps or stairs.

Flimsy, flim'zi, *a.* Thin; slight; weak; without
force; shallow.

Flinch, flinsh, *vi* to shrink; to withdraw; to wince;
to fail.

Fling, fling, *vt.* (flinging, flung). To cause to fly
from the hand; to hurl; to scatter; to throw to
the ground.—*vi.* To fly into violent and irregular
motions; to flounce; to rush away angrily.—*n.* A
throw; a gibe; a lively Scottish dance.

Flint, flint, *n.* A very hard siliceous stone, which
strikes fire with steel; anything proverbially
hard.

Flinty, flint'i, *a.* Consisting of or like flint; very
hard; cruel; inexorable.

Flippant, flip'ant, *a.* Speaking confidently, without knowledge; heedlessly pert; shallow.

Flipper, flip'er, *n.* The paddle of a sea-turtle; the
broad fin of a fish; the arm of a seal.

Flirt, flert, *vt.* To throw with a jerk; to make co-
quettish motions with (a fan).—*vi.* To run and
dart about; to coquette; to play at courtship.—
n. A sudden jerk; one who plays at courtship; a
coquette.

Float, flōt, *n.* That which is borne on water or any
fluid; a raft.—*vi.* To be borne on the surface of a
fluid; to be buoyed up; to move with a light, irregular course.—*vt.* To cause to be conveyed on
water; to flood; to get (a company, scheme, etc.)
started.

Flock, flok, *n.* A lock of wool or hair; stuffing for
mattresses, etc.; a company, as of sheep, birds,
etc.; a Christian congregation in relation to
their pastor.—*vi.* To gather in companies; to
crowd; to move in crowds.

Floe, flō, *n.* A mass of ice floating in the ocean.

Flog, flog, *vt.* (flogging, flogged). To whip; to chastise with repeated blows.

Flood, flud, *n.* A great flow of water; a deluge; a
river; the flowing of the tide; a great quantity;
abundance.—*vt.* To overflow; to deluge; to overwhelm.

Floor, flōr, *n.* That part of a building on which we
walk; bottom of a room; story in a building; a
flat, hard surface of loam, lime, etc., used in
some kinds of business, as in malting.—*vt.* To
lay a floor upon; to strike down.

Flop, flop, *vt.* and *i* (flopping, flopped). To clap or
flap; to let down suddenly; to plump down.—*n.*
A sudden sinking to the ground.

Flora, flō'ra, *n.* The plants of a particular district
or period; a work describing them.

Florescence, flō-res'ens, *n.* A flowering; season'
when plants expand their flowers.

Floret, flō'ret, *n.* A flowcret; the separate little
flower of an aggregate flower; a fencing foil; silk
yarn or floss.

Florid, flo'rid, *a.* Flowery; bright in color; flushed
with red; embellished with flowers of rhetoric;
highly decorated.

Florist, flo'rist, *n.* A cultivator of flowers; one who
writes a flora.

Floss, floss, *n.* A downy or silky substance in plants; fine untwisted silk used in embroidery.

Flotation, flōt-ā'shon, *n.* Act of floating; the doctrine of floating bodies.

Flotilla, flō-til'la, *n.* A little fleet, or fleet of small vessels.

Flotsam, flot'sam, *n.* Portion of a wreck that continues floating.

Flounce, flouns, *vi.* (flouncing, flounced). To spring or turn with sudden effort; to start away in anger.—*vt.* To deck with a flounce or flounces.—*n.* A strip of cloth sewed around a gown with the lower border loose and spreading.

Flounder, floun'dėr, *n.* A flat fish found in the sea near the mouths of rivers.—*vi.* To struggle, as in mire; to roll, toss, and tumble.

Flour, flour, *n.* Finely ground meal of wheat or other grain; fine powder of any substance.—*vt.* To convert into flour; to sprinkle with flour.

Flourish, flu'rish, *vi.* To grow luxuriantly; to thrive; to live; to use florid language; to make ornamental strokes in writing, etc.; to move in bold and irregular figures.—*vt.* To adorn with flowers or figures; to ornament with anything showy; to brandish.—*n.* Showy splendor; parade of words and figures; fanciful stroke of the pen; decorative notes in music; brandishing.

Flout, flout, *vt.* To mock or insult; to jeer at.—*n.* A mock; an insult.

Flow, flō, *vi.* To move, as water; to issue; to abound; to glide smoothly; to hang loose and waving; to rise, as the tide; to circulate, as blood.—*vt.* To flow over; to flood.—*n.* A moving along, as of water; stream; current; rise of water; fullness; free expression; feeling.

Flower, flou'ėr, *n.* The delicate and gaily-colored leaves or petals on a plant; a bloom or blossom; youth; the prime; the best part; one most distinguished; an ornamental expression; *pl.* a powdery substance.—*vi.* To blossom; to bloom.—*vt.* To embellish with figures of flowers.

Flowing, flō'ing, *p.a.* Moving as a steam; abounding; fluent; undulating.

Fluctuate, fluk'tū-āt, *vi.* To move as a wave; to waver; to hesitate; to experience vicissitudes.

Fluctuation, fluk-tū-ā'shon, *n.* A rising and falling; change; vicissitude.

Flue, flō, *n.* A passage for smoke or heated air; a pipe for conveying heat; light downy matter; fluff.

Fluent, flu'ent, *a.* Flowing; ready in the use of words; voluble; smooth.

Fluff, fluf, *n.* Light down or nap such as rises from beds, cotton, etc.

Fluid, flu'id, *a.* Capable of flowing; liquid or gaseous.—*n.* Any substance whose parts easily move and change their relative position without separation; a liquid.

Fluke, flōk, *n.* That part of an anchor which fastens in the ground; an accidental success; a flat-fish; a parasitic worm.

Flume, flōm, *n.* A channel for the water that drives a mill-wheel; an artifical channel for gold-washing.

Flummery, flum'mė-ri, *n.* A sort of jelly made of flour or meal; flattery; nonsense.

Flunkey, flung'ki, *n.* A male servant in livery; a cringing flatterer; a toady.

Fluor-spar, flō'or-spär, *n.* A mineral exhibiting yellow, green, blue, and red tints.

Flurry, flu'ri, *n.* Bustle; hurry; a gust of wind; light things carried by the wind.—*vt.* (flurrying, flurried). To agitate or alarm.

Flush, flush, *vi.* To become suddenly red, to blush.—*vt.* To cause to redden suddenly; to elate; to excite; to wash out by copious supplies of water; to cause to start up.—*n.* A sudden flow of blood to the face; sudden thrill; vigor; flow of water; run of cards of the same suit.—*a.* Fresh; full of vigor; affluent; even with the adjacent surface.

Fluster, flus'tėr, *vt.* To agitate; to make hot with

drink.—*n.* Agitation; confusion; heat.

Flute, flōt, *n.* A small wind-instrument with hole and keys; a channel cut along the shaft of column; a similar channel.—*vi.* (fluting, fluted) To play on a flute.—*vt.* To play or sing in note like those of a flute; to form flutes or channel in.

Flutist, flōt'ist, *n.* A performer on the flute.

Flutter, flut'ėr, *vi.* To move or flap the wings rap idly; to be in agitation; to fluctuate.—*vt.* To ag tate; to throw into confusion.—*n.* Quicl confused motion; agitation; disorder.

Fluvial, flō'vi-al, *a.* Belonging to rivers.

Flux, fluks, *n.* Act of flowing, any flow of matte dysentery; flow of the tide; anything used t promote fusion; fusion; liquid state from the o eration of heat.—*vt.* To melt; to fuse.

Fluxion, fluk'shon, *n.* Act of flowing; flux; a flo of blood or other fluid; an infintely small qua tity; *pl.* the analysis of infintely small variabl quantities.

Fly, flī, *vi.* (flying, pret. flew, pp. flown). To mov through air by wings; to move in air by th force of wind, etc.; to rise in air; to move rapidl to pass away; to depart suddenly; to spring; t flutter.—*vt.* To flee from; to cause to float in th air.—*n.* A winged insect; a revolving mech nism to regulate the motion of machinery; light carriage; a cab.

Fly-fishing, flī'fish-ing, *n.* Angling for fish wit flies, natural or artifical.

Flying-fish, flī'ing-fish, *n.* A fish which can su tain itself in the air for a time by means of i long pectoral fins.

Fly-leaf, flī'lēf, *n.* A leaf of blank paper at the b ginning and end of a book.

Fly-paper, flī'pā-pėr, *n.* A paper for destroyin flies.

Fly-wheel, flī'whēl, *n.* A wheel to equalize th motive power of a machine.

Foal, fōl, *n.* The young of a mare, she-ass, etc.; colt or filly.—*vt.* To bring forth, as a colt or filly.— *vi.* To bring forth a foal.

Foam, fōm, *n.* Froth; spume.—*vi.* To froth; to sho froth at the mouth; to rage.—*vt.* To cause to giv out foam; to throw out with rage or violence.

Fob, fob, *n.* A little pocket for a watch in the wais band of the breeches.

Focus, fō'kus, *n.*; *pl.* **-cuses** or **-ci.** A point i which rays of light meet after being reflected c refracted; point of concentration.—*vt.* To brin to a focus.

Fodder, fod'ėr, *n.* Food for cattle, etc.—*vt.* To fu nish with fodder.

Foe, fō, *n.* An enemy; an opposing army; one wh opposes anything.

Fog, fog, *n.* A dense vapor near the surface of th land or water; mental confusion; dimness; se ond growth of grass; long grass that remains i pastures till winter.

Fogey, Fogy, fō'gi, *n.*; *pl.* **-eys, -ies.** A stupid fe low; an old-fashioned person.

Foible, foi'bl, *n.* A weak point in character; a fai ing; the weak part of a sword.

Foil, foil, *vt.* To frustrate; to baffle; to balk.—*n.* D feat; frustration; a sword used in fencing; a thi leaf of metal; anything which serves to set off thing to advantage; something resembling leaf; a curve in the tracery of Gothic window etc.

Foist, foist, *vt.* To introduce or insert surrept tiously or without warrant; to palm off.

Fold, fōld, *n.* The doubling or doubled part of an flexible substance; a plait; an enclosure fo sheep; a flock of sheep; the Church.—*vt.* To dov ble; to lay in plaits; to embrace; to confine, a sheep in a fold.—*vi.* To close together; to b come folded.

Foliage, fō'li-āj, *n.* Leaves collectively; orname tal representation of leaves.

Foliation, fō-li-ā'shon, *n.* The leafing of plant operation of spreading foil over a surface; pro erty in certain rocks of dividing into lamina tracery of Gothic windows.

olio, fō'li-ō, n. A book of the largest size, formed by sheets of paper once doubled; a page; number appended to each page; a written page of a certain number of words.

olk, fōk, n. People in general; certain people discriminated from others, as old *folks*.

olk-lore, fōk'lōr, n. Rural superstitions, tales, traditions, or legends.

ollicle, fol'li-kl, n. A little bag or vesicle in animals or plants.

ollow, fol'ō, vt. To go or come after; to chase; to accompany; to succeed; to result from; to understand; to copy, to practice, to be occupied with; to be guided by.—vi. To come after another; to ensure; to result.

olly, fol'i, n. Foolishness; imbecility; a weak or foolish act; criminal weakness.

oment, fō-ment', vt. To apply warm lotions to; to abet; to stir up (in a bad sense).

ond, fond, a. Foolish; foolishly tender and loving; doting; loving; relishing.

ondle, fon'dl, vt. (fondling, fondled). To treat with fondness; to caress.

ont, font, n. A large basin in which water is contained for baptizing; a complete assortment of printing types of one size.

ood, fōd, n. Whatever supplies nourishment to animals or plants; nutriment; provisions, whatever feeds or augments.

ool, fōl, n. One destitute of reason; a simpleton; a silly person; a buffoon.—vi. To play the fool; to trifle.—vt. To make a fool of; to deceive.

oolhardy, fōl'här-di, a. Daring without judgment; foolishly bold; venturesome.

oolish, fōl'ish, a. Void of understanding; acting without judgment or discretion, silly, ridiculous; unwise.

oot, fut, n.; pl. **feet**, fēt. The lower extremity of the leg; that on which a thing stands; the base; infantry; a measure of twelve inches; a measure of syllables in a verse.—vi. To dance; to tread to measure or music; to skip; to walk.—vt. To tread; to dance; to trip; to add a foot to, as to a stocking.

ootball, fut'bal, n. An inflated leather ball to be driven by the foot; a game played with such a ball.

ootfall, fut'fal, n. A footstep; a stumble.

oothold, fut'hōld, n. That on which one may tread or rest securely; firm standing.

ooting, fut'ing, n. Ground for the foot; established place; basis; tread.

oot-lights, fut'līts, n.pl. A row of lights in a theater on the front of the stage.

ootpath, fut'path, n. A narrow path for foot passengers only.

oot-sore, fut'sōr, a. Having the feet sore or tender, as by much walking.

ootstep, fut'step, n. A track; the mark of the foot; vestige; pl. example; course.

or, for, prep. In the place of; because of; in favor of; toward; during; in quest of; according to; as far as; notwithstanding; in proportion to.—conj. Because.

orage, fo'rāj, n. Food for horses and cattle; act of providing forage.—vi. (foraging, foraged). To collect forage; to rove in search of food.—vt. To strip of provisions for horses, etc.; to supply with forage. **Forage cap**, n. Undress cap worn by soldiers of all branches of the army.

orament, fō-rā'men, n.; pl. **Foramina**, fō-ram'in-a. A small natural opening in animals or plants.

oraminifera, fō-ram'i-nif''ér-a, n.pl. An order of minute animals furnished with a shell perforated by pores.

oray, fo'rā, vt. To ravage; to pillage.—n. A predatory excursion; a raid.

orbear, for-bār', vi. To keep away; to cease; to delay; to refrain.—vt. To abstain from; to avoid doing.

orbid, for-bid', vt. To prohibit; to oppose; to

obstruct.—vi. To utter a prohibition.

Force, fōrs, n. Strength; active power; might; violence; coercion; cogency; efficacy; power for war; troops; a waterfall.—vt. (forcing, forced). To compel; to impel; to take by violence; to ravish; to twist or overstrain; to ripen by artificial means; to stuff; to farce.—vi. To use force or violence.

Forcemeat, fōrs'mēt, n. Meat chopped and seasoned, served up alone or as stuffing.

Forceps, for'seps, n. A surgical instrument on the principle of pincers for holding anything difficult to be held by the hand.

Forcible, fōrs'i-bl, a. Efficacious, potent; cogent; done by force; suffered by force.

Forcing, fōrs'ing, n. Art of raising plants or fruits, at an earlier season than the natural one, by artifical heat.

Ford, fōrd, n. A shallow place in a river or other water, where it may be passed on foot.—vt. To cross by walking; to wade through.

Fore, fōr, a. In front of; anterior; coming first in time; prior.—adv. In the part that precedes or goes first.

Fore-arm, fōr'ärm, n., vt. The part of the arm between the elbow and the wrist.

Forearm, fōr'ärm', vt. To arm for attack or resistance before the time of need.

Forebode, fōr-bōd', vt. To foretell, to prognosticate; to be prescient of.

Forecast, fōr-kast', vt. To foresee; to scheme beforehand.—vi. To foresee.—n. fōr'kast. Contrivance beforehand; foresight; estimate of what will happen.

Foreclose, fōr-klōz', vt. To preclude; to stop.

Forefather, fōr'fä-THér, n. A progenitor; an ancestor.

Forefinger, fōr'fing-gér, n. The finger next to the thumb.

Fore-foot, fōr'fut, n. One of the anterior feet of a quadruped.

Forefront, fōr'frunt, n. The foremost part.

Forego, fōr-gō', vt. To go before; to precede. See FORGO.

Foregone, fōr-gon', or fōr'gon, p.a. Past; preceding; predetermined.

Foreground, fōr'ground, n. The part of a scene or picture represented as nearest the observer.

Forehead, fōr'hed or fo'red, n. The part of the face above the eyes; the brow.

Foreign, fo'rin, a. Belonging to another nation or country; alien; not to the purpose; irrelevant.

Forejudge, fōr-juj', vt. To judge beforehand, or before hearing the facts and proof.

Foreknow, fōr-nō', vt. To know beforehand; to foresee.

Forolog, fōr'log, n. One of the anterior logs of an animal, chair, etc.

Forelock, fōr'lok, n. The lock of hair that grows from the fore part of the head.

Foreman, fōr'man, n. The first or chief man; chief man of a jury; chief workman.

Foremost, fōr'mōst, a. First in place, time, rank, or dignity; most advanced.

Forenoon, fōr'nōn, n. The part of the day before noon, or from morning to noon.

Forensic, fō-ren'sik, a. Belonging to courts of justice, or to public debate; used in courts or legal proceedings.

Forepart, fōr'pärt, n. The anterior part; part first in time; part most advanced in place; beginning.

Forerunner, fōr'run-ér, n. One who runs before; harbinger; precursor; prognostic.

Foresee, fōr-sē', vt. To see beforehand; to foreknow.

Foreshadow, fōr-sha'dō, vt. To shadow or typify beforehand.

Foreshorten, fōr-short'n, vt. To shorten, in drawing and painting, the parts of figures that stand forward.

Foresight, fōr'sit, n. Foreknowledge; provident care; forethought; sight on muzzle of gun or rifle.

Forest, fo'rest, n. An extensive wood; a district devoted to the purposes of the chase; a tract once a royal forest.—a. Relating to a forest; sylvan; rustic.—vt. To convert into a forest.

Forestall, fōr-stal', vt. To anticipate; to hinder by preoccupation.

Foretaste, fōr'tāst, n. A taste beforehand; anticipation.—vt. to taste before possession; to anticipate.

Foretell, fōr-tel', vt. To tell beforehand; to predict.—vi. To utter prophecy.

Forethought, fōr'that, n. A thinking beforehand; foresight; provident care.

Forever, for-ev'èr, adv. At all times; through endless ages; eternally.

Forewarn, fōr-warn', vt. To warn beforehand, to give previous notice to.

Foreword, fōr'wèrd, n. A preface.

Forfeit, for'fit, vt. To lose by a misdeed.—n. That which is forfeited; fine; penalty.

Forfeiture, for'fit-ūr, n. Act of forfeiting; loss of some right, estate, honor, etc., by a crime or fault; fine; penalty.

Forge, fōrj, n. A furnace in which iron is heated and wrought; a smithy.—vt. (forging, forged). To frame or fabricate; to form by heating and hammering; to counterfeit.—vi. To commit forgery; to move on slowly and laboriously; to work one's way.

Forgery, fōrj'é-ri, n. The crime of counterfeiting; that which is forged or counterfeited.

Forget, for-get', vt. (forgetting, pret. forgot, pp. forgot, forgotten). To lose the remembrance of; to slight; to neglect.

Forgetfulness, for-get'ful-nes, n. Oblivion; obliviousness; inattention.

Forgive, for-giv', vt. (forgiving, pret. forgave, pp. forgiven). To pardon; to remit; to overlook.

Forgiveness, for-giv'nes, n. Act of forgiving; pardon; disposition to pardon; remission.

Forgo, for-gō', vt. To forbear to enjoy or possess; to renounce; to resign.

Fork, fork, n. An instrument with two or more prongs, used for lifting or pitching anything; a branch or division; a prong.—vi. To shoot into branches; to divide into two.—vt. To raise or pitch with a fork, as hay, etc.

Forlorn, for-lorn', a. Deserted; abandoned; miserable.—**Forlorn hope,** a body of men appointed to perform some specially perilous service.

Form, form, n. Shape; manner; pattern; order; empty show; prescribed mode; ceremony; schedule; a long seat; a bench; a class; the seat or bed of a hare.—vt. To shape or mold; to arrange; to invent; to make up.—vi. To take a form.

Formal, form'al, a. Relating to outward form; according to form; precise; ceremonious; having mere appearance.

Formality, form-al'i-ti, n. Quality of being formal; ceremony; a mere form.

Format, for'mä, n. Size of a book as regards length and breadth; get-up.

Formation, form-ā'shon, n. Act of forming; production; manner in which a thing is formed; any assemblage of rocks or strata, referred to a common origin; arrangement.

Formative, form'at-iv, a. Giving form; plastic; derivative.—n. That which serves to give form to a word, and is no part of the root.

Former, form'èr, n. He who forms.—a. comp. deg. Before in time; long past; mentioned before another.

Formicary, for'mi-ka-ri, n. A colony of ants; an ant-hill.

Formidable, for'mid-a-bl, a. Exciting fear or apprehension; difficult to deal with or undertake.

Formula, for'mū-la, n.; pl. **-lae.** A prescribed form; a confession of faith; expression for resolving certain problems in mathematics; expression of chemical composition.

Formulate, for'mū-lāt, vt. To express in a formula; to put into a precise and comprehensive statement.

Fornicate, for'ni-kāt, vi. To have unlawful sexual intercourse.

Fornication, for-ni-kā'shon, n. Incontinence of unmarried persons.

Forsake, for-sāk', vt. (forsaking, pret. forsook, pp. forsaken). To abandon; to renounce; to withdraw from.

Forswear, for-swär', vt. To renounce upon oath; to abjure; to swear falsely; to perjure oneself.—vi. To swear falsely.

Fort, fōrt, n. A fortified place; a fortress.

Forte, fōr'tä, adv. A direction to sing or play with force.

Forte, fōrt, n. The strong portion of a swordblade; peculiar talent; strong point; chief excellence.

Forthcoming, fōrth-kum'ing, a. Coming forth; making appearance; ready to appear.

Fortification, for'ti-fi-kā'shon, n. The art or science of fortifying places; the works erected in defense; a fortified place; additional strength.

Fortify, for'ti-fi, vt. (fortifying, fortified). To make strong; to strengthen by forts, batteries, etc.; to invigorate; to increase the strength of.

Fortissimo, for-tis'sē-mō, adv. Direction to sing or play with the utmost loudness.

Fortitude, for'ti-tūd, n. Firmness of mind to encounter danger or to bear pain or adversity; resolute endurance.

Fortnight, fort'nit, n. The space of fourteen days; two weeks.

Fortress, fort'res, n. A fortified place; stronghold; place of security.

Fortuitous, for-tū'it-us, a. Happening by chance; accidental; incidental.

Fortunate, for'tū-nāt, a. Having good fortune; successful; coming by good luck.

Fortune, for'tūn, n. Chance; luck; the good or ill that befalls man; means of living; estate; great wealth; destiny; the power regarded as determining the lots of life.

Forty, for'ti, a. and n. Four times ten.

Forum, fō'rum, n. A public place in ancient Rome, where causes were tried; a tribunal; jurisdiction.

Forward, for'wèrd, adv. Toward a place in front; onward.—a. Near or towards the forepart; in advance of something; ready; bold; pert; advanced beyond the usual degree; too ready.—vt. To help onward; to hasten; to send forward; to transmit.—n. In football, hockey, etc., one of the players in the front line.

Forwardness, for'wèrd-nes, n. Promptness; eagerness; want of due reserve or modesty; pertness; earliness.

Fossil, fos'sil, a. Dug out of the earth; petrified and preserved in rocks.—n. Petrified remains of plants and animals found in the strata composing the surface of our globe.

Fossilize, fos'sil-iz, vt. To convert into a fossil state.—vi. To be changed into a fossil state; to become antiquated.

Foster, fos'tèr, vt. To nourish; to bring up; to encourage; to promote.

Foster-child, fos'tèr-child, n. A child nursed by a woman not the mother; or bred by a man not the father. (Also foster-brother, -mother, -parent, etc.).

Foul, foul, a. Covered with or containing extraneous matter which is offensive; turbid; obscene; rainy or tempestuous; unfair; loathsome; entangled or in collision.—vt. To defile; to dirty.—vi. To become dirty; to come into collision; to become clogged.—n. A colliding, or impeding due motion; an unfair piece of play.

Found, found, vt. To lay the base of; to establish; to institute; to form by melting metal and pouring it into a mold; to cast.—vi. To rest or rely (with on or upon). Pret. and pp. of find.

Foundation, found-ā'shon, n. Act of founding; base of an edifice; base; endowment; endowed institution.

Founder, found´er, *n*. One who lays a foundation; an originator; an endower; one who casts metal.—*vi*. To fill with water and sink; to miscarry; to go lame, as a horse.

Foundry, found´ri, *n*. An establishment for casting metals.

Fountain, fount´än, *n*. A spring or source of water; an artificial jet or shower; head of a river; original; source.

Fountainhead, fount´än-hed, *n*. The head of a stream; primary source; origin.

Four, för, *a*. and *n*. Twice two; three and one.

Fourscore, för´skör, *a*. and *n*. Eighty.

Foursquare, för-skwär, *a*. Having four sides and four angles equal; quadrangular.

Fourteen, för´tën, *a*. and *n*. Four and ten.

Fowl, foul, *n*. A bird; a domestic or barndoor bird.—*vt*. To catch wild fowls for game or food.

Fox, foks, *n*. A carnivorous animal, remarkable for cunning; a sly cunning fellow.—*vt*. and *i*. To turn sour; to become marked with brown spots, as paper.

Foxglove, foks´gluv, *n*. A British plant yielding a powerful medicine, both sedative and diuretic; digitalis.

Fox-hound, foks´hound, *n*. A hound for chasing foxes.

Fracas, fra-käs´, *n*. An uproar; a brawl.

Fraction, frak´shon, *n*. A fragment; a very small part; one or more of the equal parts into which a unit or number is divided.

Fractious, frak´shus, *a*. Snappish; peevish; cross.

Fracture, frak´tür, *n*. A breach or break; breaking of a bone; manner in which a mineral breaks.—*vt*. (fracturing, fractured). To break.

Fragility, fra-jil´i-ti, *n*. Quality of being fragile; delicacy of substance.

Fragment, frag´ment, *n*. A part broken off; an imperfect thing.

Fragrance, Fragrancy, frä´grans, frä´gran-si, *n*. Quality of being fragrant; sweetness of smell; perfume.

Fragrant, frä´grant, *a*. Sweet-smelling; spicy; balmy; aromatic.

Frail, fräl, *a*. Easily broken; weak; liable to fail and decay.—*n*. A kind of basket.

Frailty, frāl´ti, *n*. State or quality of being frail; infirmity; liableness to be deceived or seduced; failing; foible.

Frame, främ, *vt*. (framing, framed). To make; to construct; to devise; to adjust; to shape; to place in a frame.—*n*. Anything composed of parts fitted together; structure; bodily structure; framework; particular state, as of the mind; mood or disposition.

Framework, främ´werk, *n*. A structure or fabric for supporting anything; a frame.

Framing, främ´ing, *n*. Act of constructing a frame; frame thus constructed; rough timberwork of a house.

Franchise, fran´chīz, *n*. Right granted by a sovereign or government; right of voting for a member of parliament.

Franciscan, fran-sis´kan, *n*. A mendicant friar of the order of St. Francis; a Gray Friar.

Frangible, fran´ji-bl, *a*. That may be broken; brittle; fragile.

Frank, frangk, *a*. Free in uttering real sentiments; candid; outspoken.—*n*. Signature of a privileged person formerly securing free transmission of a letter.—*vt*. To exempt from postage.

Frankincense, frangk´in-sens, *n*. An odoriferous gum-resin used as a perfume.

Frantic, fran´tik, *a*. Mad; raving; furious; outrageous; distracted.

Fraternal, fra-ter´nal, *a*. Brotherly; pertaining to brethren; becoming brothers.

Fraternity, fra-ter´ni-ti, *n*. State or relationship of a brother; brotherhood; society, class, or profession.

Fraternize, frat´er-niz, *vi*. (fraternizing, frater-

nized). To associate as brothers, or as men of like occupation or disposition.

Fratricide, fra´tri-sīd, *n*. Murder of a brother; one who murders a brother.

Fraud, frad, *n*. Artifice by which the right or interest of another is injured; deception.

Fray, frä, *n*. An affray; a broil; a night; a frayed place in cloth.—*vt*. To rub; to fret, as cloth, by wearing.—*vi*. Top become worn by rubbing.

Freak, frēk, *n*. A sudden causeless turn of the mind; a caprice; a sport.—*vt*. To variegate.

Freckle, frek´l, *n*. A yellowish spot in the skin; any small spot or discoloration.—*vt*. or *i*. (freckling, freckled). To give or acquire freckles.

Free, frē, *a*. Being at liberty; instituted by a free people; not arbitrary or despotic; open; clear; disjoined; licentious; candid; generous; gratuitous; guiltless.—*vt*. (freeing, freed). To set free; to liberate; to disentangle; to exempt; to absolve from some charge.

Freedman, frēd´man, *n*. A man who has been a slave and is set free.

Freedom, frē´dum, *n*. State of being free; liberty; particular privilege; facility of doing anything; frankness; undue familiarity.

Freehand, frē´hand, *a*. Applied to drawing in which the hand is not assisted by any guiding or measuring instruments.

Freeman, frē´man, *n*. One who is free; one who enjoys or is entitled to a franchise.

Freemason, frē´mä-sn, *n*. A member of a secret friendly society or organization.

Freestone, frē´ston, *n*. Any stone composed of sand or grit, easily cut.

Free-thinker, frē´thingk-er, *n*. One who is free from the common modes of thinking in religious matters; a deist; a sceptic.

Free-trade, frē´träd, *n*. Commerce free from customs on foreign commodities.

Free-will, frē´wil, *n*. The power of directing our own actions, without restraint by necessity or fate.—*a*. Spontaneous.

Freeze, frēz, *vi*. (freezing, pret. froze, pp. frozen or froze). To be congealed by cold; to be hardened into ice; to be of that degree of cold at which water congeals; to stagnate; to shiver or stiffen with cold.—*vt*. To congeal; to chill; to make credits, etc., temporarily unrealizable.

Freight, frat, *n*. The cargo of a ship; lading; hire of a ship; charge for the transportation of goods.—*vt*. To load with goods; to hire for carrying goods.

Freighter, frät´er, *n*. One who charters and loads a ship.

French, frensh, *a*. Pertaining to France or its inhabitants.—*n*. The language spoken by the people of France; the people of France.

Frenetic, Frenetical, fre-net´ik, fre-net´ik-al, *a*. Frenzied; frantic.

Frenzy, fren´zi, *n*. Madness; distraction; violent agitation of the mind.

Frequent, frē´kwent, *a*. That takes place repeatedly; often seen or done; doing a thing often.—*vt*. frē-kwent´. To visit often; to resort to habitually.

Fresco, fres´kō, *n*. A method of painting with mineral and earthy pigments on walls of which the plaster is not quite dry.

Fresh, fresh, *a*. Full of health and strength; vigorous; brisk; bright; not faded; in good condition; not stale; cool and agreeable; clearly remembered; new; not salt; unpracticed; unused.

Freshen, fresh´n, *vt*. To make fresh; to revive.—*vi*. To grow fresh.

Freshet, fresh´et, *n*. A small stream of fresh water; flood of a river.

Fret, fret, *vt*. (fretting, fretted). To eat into; to corrode; to wear away; to chafe; to vex; to ornament or furnish with frets; to variegate.—*vi*. To be vexed; to utter peevish expressions; to rankle.—*n*. Irritation; peevishness; an ornament of bands or fillets; a piece of perforated work; one of the crossbars on the finger-board

F

of some stringed instruments.

Fretwork, fret'werk, *n.* Ornamental work consisting of a series or combination of frets.

Friable, fri'a-bl, *a.* Easily rubbed down, crumbled, or pulverized.

Friar, fri'er, *n.* A monk; a male member of a monastery.

Fricassee, fri-kas-se', *n.* A dish made by cutting chickens or rabbits, etc., into pieces, and dressing them in a frying-pan, etc., with strong sauces.

Friction, frik'shon, *n.* A rubbing; effect of rubbing; resistance which a moving body meets with from the surface on which it moves.

Friday, fri'dā, *n.* The sixth day of the week.— **Good Friday,** the Friday preceding Easter, sacred as the day of Christ's crucifixion.

Friend, frend, *n.* One attached to another by affection; a favorer; one who is propitious; a favorite; a Quaker.

Friendliness, frend'li-nes, *n.* Friendly disposition.

Friendship, frend'ship, *n.* Intimacy resting on mutual esteem; kindness; aid.

Frieze, frēz, *n.* A coarse woolen cloth with a nap on one side; that part of the entablature of a column between the architrave and the cornice; upper part of the wall of a room and its decoration.—*vt.* (friezing, friezed). To form a nap on cloth; to frizzle; to curl.

Fright, frit, *n.* Sudden and violent fear; terror; consternation; an ugly or ill-dressed person.— *vt.* To frighten.

Frighten, frit'n, *vt.* To strike with fright or fear; to terrify; to scare; to alarm.

Frigid, fri'jid, *a.* Cold; wanting spirit or zeal; stiff; formal; lifeless.

Frigidity, fri-jid'i-ti, *n.* Coldness; coldness of affection; dullness.

Frill, fril, *n.* A crisp or plaited edging on an article of dress; a ruffle.—*vt.* To decorate with frills.

Fringe, frinj, *n.* An ornamental appendage to furniture or dress, consisting of loose threads; margin; extremity.—*vt.* (fringing, fringed). To border with fringe or a loose edging.

Frisk, frisk, *vi.* To dance, skip, and gambol in frolic and gaiety.—*n.* A frolic; a fit of wanton gaiety.

Frit, frit, *n.* The matter of which glass is made after it has been calcined.

Fritter, frit'er, *n.* A kind of small cake fried; a small piece of meat fried; a small piece.—*vt.* To cut into small pieces to be fried; to break into small pieces; to waste by degrees (with *away*).

Frivolity, fri-vol'i-ti, *n.* Acts or habit of trifling; unbecoming levity.

Frivolous, fri'vol-us, *a.* Trivial; trifling; petty.

Frizz, friz, *vt.* To curl; to crisp; to form the nap of cloth into little burs.

Frock, frok, *n.* An ecclesiastical garment; a lady's gown; a child's dress; a blouse for men.

Frog, frog, *n.* An amphibious animal, remarkable for its activity in swimming and leaping; a kind of button or tassel on a coat or vestment; a loop used to support a sword or bayonet; horny growth on sole of horse's hoof.

Frolic, fro'lik, *a.* Joyous; merry; frisky; *poetic.—n.* A merry prank; merry-making.—*vi.* To play merry pranks; to gambol.

From, from, *prep.* Out of the neighborhood or presence of; by reason of; denoting source, distance, absence, departure, etc.

Frond, frond, *n.* The leaf of a fern or other cryptogamic plant.

Front, frunt, *n.* The forehead; the whole face; the fore part; boldness; impudence; the area of military operations.—*a.* Relating to the front or face.—*vt.* To stand with the front opposed to; to oppose; to face; to supply with a front.—*vi.* To face; to look.

Frontage, frunt'āj, *n.* The front part of an edifice, quay, etc.

Frontal, frunt'al, *a.* Belonging to the forehead.— *n.* An ornament for the forehead; a frontlet; a small pediment.

Frontier, fron'tēr, *n.* That part of a country which fronts another country; extreme part of a country.—*a.* Bordering; conterminous.

Frontispiece, fron'tis-pēs, *n.* The principal face of a building; an illustration facing the title-page of a book.

Frost, frost, *n.* That temperature of the air which causes freezing; frozen dew; rime; coldness or severity of manner.—*vt.* To injure by frost; to ornament with anything resembling hoar-frost; to frunish with frost-nails.

Frost-bite, frost'bit, *n.* Insensibility or deadness in any part of the body caused by exposure to frost.—*vt.* To affect with frost-bite.

Frosting, frost'ing, *n.* The composition, resembling hoar-frost, used to cover cake, etc.

Froth, froth, *n.* Bubbles caused by fermentation or agitation; spume; empty talk; light unsubstantial matter.—*vt.* To cause to foam.—*vi.* To foam; to throw up spume.

Frouzy, Frowzy, frou'zi, *a.* Fetid; musty; dingy; in disorder; slatternly.

Froward, frō'werd, *a.* Perverse; ungovernable; disobedient; peevish.

Frown, froun, *vi.* To express displeasure by contracting the brow; to look stern; to scowl.—*n.* A wrinkling of the brow; a sour or stern look; any expression of displeasure.

Fructification, fruk'ti-fi-kā''shon, *n.* Act of fructifying; the bearing of fruit; arrangement of the organs of reproduction in plants.

Fructify, fruk'ti-fi, *vt.* (fructifying, fructified). To make fruitful; to fertilize.—*vi.* To bear fruit.

Frugality, frō-gal'i-ti, *n.* Prudent economy; thrift.

Frugivorous, frō-jiv-er-us, *a.* Feeding on fruits, seeds, or corn, as birds.

Fruit, frōt, *n.* Whatever of a vegetable nature is of use to man or animals; the reproductive produce of a plant; such products collectively; the seed or matured ovary; that which is produced; offspring; effect; outcome.—*vi.* To produce fruit.

Fruitful, frōt'ful, *a.* Very productive; fertile; plenteous; prolific.

Fruition, frō-i'shon, *n.* A using or enjoying; enjoyment; gratification; pleasure derived from use or possession.

Frumentaceous, frō-men-tā'shus, *a.* Having the character of or resembling wheat or other cereal.

Frustrate, frus'trāt, *vt.* (frustrating, frustrated). To balk; to foil; to bring to nothing; to render of no effect.

Frustration, frus-trā'shon, *n.* Disappointment; defeat.

Fry, fri, *vt.* (frying, fried). To cook by roasting over a fire.—*vi.* To be cooked as above; to simmer; to be in agitation.—*n.* A dish of anything fried; state of mental ferment; young fishes at an early stage; swarm of small fishes, etc.; insignificant objects.

Fuchsia, fū'shi-a, *n.* A beautiful flowering shrub.

Fuddle, fud'l, *vt.* (fuddling, fuddled). To make stupid by drink; to spend in drinking.—*vi.* To drink to excess.

Fuel, fū'el, *n.* That which serves to feed fire, or to increase excitement. etc.—*vt.* To feed or furnish with fuel.

Fugitive, fū-jit-iv, *a.* Apt to flee away; volatile; fleeting; vagabond; temporary.—*n.* One who flees from duty or danger; refugee.

Fugue, fūg, *n.* A musical composition in which the parts seem to chase each other.

Fulcrum, ful'krum, *n.*; pl. **-ra** or **-rums.** A support; that by which a lever is sustained, or the point about which it moves.

Fulfill, ful-fil', *vt.* To carry into effect, as a prophecy, promise, etc.; to answer in execution or event; to perform; to complete.

Fulfillment, ful-fil'ment, *n.* Accomplishment; execution; performance.

Fulgency, ful'jen-si, *n.* Splendor; glitter.

Full, ful, *a.* Having all it can contain; abounding

crowded; entire; strong; loud; clear; mature; perfect; ample.—*n.* Complete measure; the highest state or degree (usually with *the*).—*adv.* Quite; altogether; exactly; directly.—*vt.* To scour and thicken, as woolen cloth, in a mill.

Full-blown, ful'blōn, *a.* Fully expanded, as a blossom.

Fulminate, ful'min-āt, *vi.* (fulminating, fulminated). To lighten and thunder; to detonate; to issue threats, denunciations, etc.—*vt.* To utter or send out, as a denunciation or censure; to cause to explode.—*n.* A compound substance which explodes by percussion, friction, or heat.

Fulsome, ful'sum, *a.* Offensive from excess of praise; gross; nauseous.

Fumble, fum'bli, *vi.* (fumbling, fumbled). To grope about awkwardly; to attempt or handle something bunglingly.

Fume, fūm, *n.* Smoke; vapor; exhalation from the stomach, as of liquor; heat of passion.—*vi.* (fuming, fumed). To yield vapor or visible exhalations; to be hot with anger.—*vt.* To smoke; to perfume; to disperse in vapors.

Fumigate, fūm'i-gāt, *vt.* (fumigating, fumigated). To smoke; to purify from infection, etc.

Fun, fun, *n.* Sportive acts or words; merriment

Function, fungk'shon, *n.* Performance; office; duty; proper office of any organ in animals or vegetables; a ceremonial; a mathematical quantity connected with and varying with another.

Fund, fund, *n.* A stock or capital; money set apart for any object more or less permanent; store; supply.—*vt.* To provide and appropriate a fund for paying the interest of, as a debt; to place in a fund, as money.

Fundamental, fun-da-ment'al, *a.* Pertaining to the foundation; essential; primary.—*n.* A leading principle which serves as the groundwork of a system; an essential.

Fundamentalist, fun-da-ment'al-ist, *n.* One who believes in the literal interpretation and the infallibility of the Bible.

Funeral, fū'né-ral, *n.* Burial; ceremony of burying a dead body.—*a.* Used at the interment of the dead.

Funereal, fū-nē'rē-al, *a.* Suiting a funeral; dark; dismal; mournful.

Fungus, fung'gus, *n.*; pl. **Fungi** or **Funguses,** fun'jī, fung'gus-es A mushroom; a toadstool; spongy excrescence in animal bodies; as proud flesh formed in wounds.

Funicle, fū'ni kl, *n.* A small cord or ligament

Funnel, fun'el, *n.* A utensil for conveying liquids into close vessels; the shaft of a chimney through which smoke ascends.

Funny, fun'i, *a.* Making fun; droll; comical.

Fur, fér, *n.* The short, fine, soft hair of certain animals, growing thick on the skin; furred animals collectively; something resembling fur.—*a.* Pertaining to or made of fur.—*vt.* (furring, furred). To line or cover with fur.

Furbelow, fér'bē-lō, *n.* A kind of flounce; plaited border of a petticoat or gown.

Furbish, fér'bish, *vt.* To rub or scour to brightness; to burnish.

Furcate, Furcated, fér'kāt, fér'kāt-ed, *a.* Forked; branching like the prongs of a fork.

Furious, fū'ri-us, *a.* Full of rage; violent; impetuous; frantic.

Furl, férl, *vt.* To wrap a sail close to a yard, etc., and fasten by a cord.

Furlong, fér'long, *n.* The eighth of a mile.

Furlough, fér'lō, *n.* Leave of absence to a soldier for a limited time.—*vt.* To grant leave of absence from military service.

Furnace, fér'nås, *n.* A structure in which a vehement fire may be maintained for melting ores, heating water, etc.; place or occasion of torture or trial.

Furnish, fér'nish, *vt.* To supply; to equip; to yield; to provide.

Furniture, fér'ni-tūr, *n.* That with which anything is furnished; equipment; outfit; movable wooden articles in a house.

Furor, fū'ror, *n.* Fury; rage.

Furrow, fu'rō, *n.* A trench made by a plough; a groove; a wrinkle.—*vt.* To make furrows in; to groove; to wrinkle.

Further, fér'ᴛʜér, *adv.* More in advance; besides; farther.—*a.* More distant; farther.—*vt.* To help forward; to advance.

Furthest, fér'ᴛʜest, *a.* and *adv.* Most advanced; farthest.

Furtive, fér'tiv, *a.* Stolen; sly; stealthy.

Fury, fū'ri, *n.* Rage; a violent rushing; frenzy; a goddess of vengeance, in mythology; a violent woman.

Fuse, fūz, *n.* A length of easily melted metal inserted in an electrical circuit as a safety device.—*vt.* (fusing, fused). To liquefy by heat; to dissolve; to blend or unite.—*vi.* To be melted; to become blended.

Fuse, Fuze, fūz, *n.* A tube or case filled with combustible matter, used in blasting or in discharging a shell, etc.

Fuselage, fū'sel-āj, *n.* The long, narrow, somewhat spindle-shaped body of an airplane.

Fusel-oil, fū'zel-oil, *n.* A colorless oily spirit separated in the rectification of ordinary distilled spirits.

Fusion, fū'zhon, *n.* Act or operation of fusing; state of being melted or blended; complete union.

Fuss, fus, *n.* Bustle; much ado about trifles.—*vi.* To make a fuss or bustle.

Fusty, fus'ti, *n.* Tasting or smelling of a foul or moldy cask; moldy; ill-smelling.

Futile, fū'til *a.* Serving no useful end; trivial; worthless.

Futility, fū-til'i-ti, *n.* Quality of being futile; worthlessness; unimportance.

Future, fū'tūr, *a.* That is to be; pertaining to time to come.—*n.* The time to come; all that is to happen; the future tense.

Fuzz, fuz, *vi.* To fly off in minute particles.—*n.* Fine particles; loose, volatile matter.

G

Gab, gab, *vi.* (gabbling, gabbed). To talk much; to chatter.—*n.* Idle talk.

Gabble, gab'l, *vi.* (gabbling, gabbled). To talk fast, or without meaning.—*n.* Rapid talk without meaning; inarticulate sounds rapidly uttered

Gable, gā'bl, *n.* The pointed end of a house; the triangular part of the end of a house.

Gad, gad, *n.* A spike; a wedge or ingot of steel or iron.—*vi.* (gadding, gadded). To rove or ramble idly.

Gadget, gad'jet, *n.* A tool, appliance, or contrivance.

Gaelic, gāl'ik, *a.* Pertaining to the Celtic inhabitants of Scotland.—*n.* Their language.

Gaff, gaf, *n.* A hook used by anglers in landing large fish; a spar to extend the upper edge of some fore-and-aft sails.—*vt.* To strike or secure (a salmon) by means of a gaff.

Gag, gag, *vt.* (gagging, gagged). To prevent from speaking by fixing something in the mouth; to silence by authority or force.—*n.* Something thrust into the mouth to hinder speaking; interpolations in an actor's part.

Gage, gāj, *n.* A pledge; a security; a kind of plum.—*vt.* (gaging, gaged). To pledge; to bind by pledge or security; to engage. *See* GAUGE.

Gaiety, gā'e-ti, *n.* State or quality of being gay; mirth; entertainment; showiness.

Gain, gān, *vt.* To obtain; to get, as profit or advantage; to receive, as honor; to win to one's side; to conciliate; to reach, arrive at.—*vi.* To reap advantage or profit; to make progress.—*n.* Something obtained as an advantage; profit;

benefit.

Gainsay, găn'sā, vt. To contradict; to oppose in words; to dispute.

Gait, găt, n. Walk; manner of walking or stepping; carriage.

Gala, gal'a, n. An occasion of public festivity.

Galantine, gal-an-tēn', n. A dish of veal or chicken, without bones, served cold.

Galaxy, ga'lak-si, n. The Milky Way; that long, luminous track in the heavens, formed by a multitude of stars; an assemblage of splendid persons or things.

Gale, gāl, n. A strong wind; a storm; a small shrub found in bogs.

Galena, ga-lē'na, n. The principal ore of lead.

Gall, gal, n. A bitter fluid secreted in the liver; bile; rancor; malignity; an excrescence produced by the egg of an insect on a plant, especially the oak; a sore place in the skin from rubbing.—vt. To make a sore in the skin of by rubbing; to fret; to vex; to harass.

Gallant, gal'ant, a. Gay in attire; handsome; brave; showing politeness and attention to ladies (in this sense also pron. ga-lant').—n. A gay sprightly man; a daring spirit; (pron. also ga-lant') a man attentive to ladies; suitor; paramour.—vt. ga-lant'. To act the gallant towards; to be very attentive to (a lady).

Gallantry, gal'ant-ri, n. Show; bravery; intrepidity; polite attentions to ladies; vicious love or pretentions to love.

Gallery, gal'ė-ri, n. A long apartment serving as a passage of communication, or for the receptio of pictures, etc.; upper floor of a church, theatre, etc.; a covered passage; frame like a balcony projected from a ship.

Galley, gal'i, n. A low, flat-built vessel navigated with sails and oars; the cook-room of a large ship; a frame used in printing.

Gallic, gal'ik, a. Pertaining to Gaul, or France.

Galling, gal'ing, p.a. Adapted to gall or chagrin; keenly annoying.

Gallon, gal'lun, n. A liquid measure of four quarts or eight pints.

Gallop, gal'up, vi. To move or run with leaps; to ride at this pace; to move very fast.—n. The pace of a horse, by springs or leaps.

Gallows, gal'ōz, n. sing. or pl.; also **Gallowses,** gal'ōz-ez, in pl. A structure for the hanging of criminals; one of a pair of braces for the trousers.

Galoche, Galosh, ga-losh', n. A shoe worn over another shoe to keep the foot dry.

Galore, ga-lōr', n. Abundance; plenty.

Galvanism, gal'van-izm, n. A species of electricity developed by the action of various metals and chemicals upon each other.

Galvanize, gal'van-īz, vt. (galvanizing, galvanized). To affect with falvanism; to electroplate; to coat with tin or zinc; to restore to consciousness; to give spurious life to.

Galvanometer, gal-van-om'et-ėr, n. An instrument for detecting the existence and determining the strength and direction of an electric current.

Gambit, gam'bit, n. An opening in chess incurring the sacrifice of a pawn.

Gamble, gam'bl, vi. (gambling, gambled). To play for money.

Gambling, gam'bl-ing, n. The act or practice of gaming for money or anything valuable.

Gambol, gam'bol, vi. (gamboling, gamboled). To skip about in sport; to frisk; to frolic.—n. A skipping about in frolic; a prank.

Game, gām, n. Sport of any kind; exercise for amusement, testing skill, etc.; scheme pursued; field-sports; animals hunted.—vi. (gaming, gamed). To play at any sport; to play for a stake or prize; to practice gaming. **To die game,** to maintain a bold spirit to the last.

Gamester, gām'stėr, n. A person addicted to gaming; a gambler.

Gamin, gam'in, n. A street arab; a neglected street-boy.

Gaming, gām'ing, n. The act or practice of gambling.

Gamut, gam'ut, n. A scale on which notes in mu sic are written, consisting of lines and spaces range or compass.

Gander, gan'dėr, n. The male of the goose.

Gang, gang, n. A crew or band; a squad; a vein ir mining; a gangue.

Ganglion, gang'gli-on, n.; pl. **-ia** or **-ions.** An en largement in the course of a nerve; a mass o nervous matter giving origin to nervefibers; ε tumor on a tendon.

Gangrene, gang'grēn, n. An eating away of the flesh; first stage of mortification.—vt. (gangren ing, gangrened). To mortify.—vi. To become mortified.

Gangster, gang'stėr, n. A member of a crimina organization.

Gap, gap, n. An opening; breach; hiatus; chasm

Gape, gāp, vi. (gaping, gaped). To open the mouth wide; to yawn; to open in fissures; tε stand open.—n. A gaping; the width of the mouth when opened, as of a bird, fish, etc.

Garage, gar'aj, n. A place for housing or repair ing motor-cars.

Garb, gärb, n. Dress; clothes; mode of dress.—vt To dress.

Garbage, gärb'āj, n. Waste matter; offal; vegeta ble refuse.

Garble, gär'bl, vt. (garbling, garbled). To pick ou such parts as may serve a purpose; to falsify by leaving out parts; to corrupt.

Garden, gär'dn, n. A piece of ground appropri ated to the cultivation of plants; a rich, well cultivated tract; a delightful spot.—a. Pertain ing to or produced in a garden.—vi. To lay ou and to cultivate a garden.

Gargle, gär'gl, vt. (gargling, gargled). To wash as the throat.—n. Any liquid preparation fo washing the throat.

Gargoyle, gär'goil, n. A projecting waterspou on a building, often grotesque.

Garish, gär'ish, a. Gaudy; showy; dazzling.

Garland, gär'land, n. A wreath or chaplet o flowers, leaves, etc.; a collection of pieces o prose or verse.—vt. To deck with a garland.

Garlic, gär'lik, n. A plant allied to the onion, with a pungent taste and strong odor.

Garment, gär'ment, n. An article of clothing, as ε coat, a gown, etc.

Garner, gär'nėr, n. A granary; a store.—vt. Tc store in a granary; to store up.

Garnet, gär'net, n. A precious stone, generally o a red color.

Garnish, gär'nish, vt. To adorn; to embellish (ε dish) with something laid round.—n. Orna ment; an embellishment round a dish.

Garret, ga'ret, n. A room in a house on the upper most floor, immediately under the roof.

Garrison, ga'ri-sn, n. A body of troops stationed in a fort or town.—vt. To place a garrison in.

Garrotte, ga-rot', vt. To rob by seizing a persor and compressing his windpipe till he become helpless.

Garrulity, ga-rū'li-ti, n. Loquacity; practice oı habit to talking much.

Garter, gär'tėr, n. A band to hold up a stocking the badge of the highest order or knighthood ir Great Britain; the order itself.—vt. To bind with a garter.

Gas, gas, n. An elastic aeriform fluid; coalgas used for giving light; any similar substance.

Gasconade, gas-kon-ād', n. A boast or boasting a bravado.—vi. To boast; to brag.

Gash, gash, vt. To make a long deep incision in to cut; to slash.—n. A deep and long cut, partic ularly in flesh.

Gasify, gas'i-fī, vt. To convert into gas by heat.

Gasket, gas'ket, n. A cord on the yard of a ship tc tie the sail to it; material used for packing joints, etc.

Gas-mask, gas-mask, n. A covering for the face

used to give protection against poisonous gases in warfare.

Gasp, gasp, *vi.* To open the mouth wide to catch breath; to labor for breath; to pant.—*vt.* To emit with a gasp.—*n.* Short painful catching of the breath.

Gasteropod, Gastropod, gas'tėr-o-pod, gas'trō-pod, *n.* A mollusc such as snails, having a broad muscular foot attached to the ventral surface.

Gastric, gas'trik, *a.* Belonging to the stomach.

Gastronomy, gas-tron'o-mi, *n.* The art or science of good eating; epicurism.

Gate, gāt, *n.* A large door or entrance; a frame of timber, iron, etc., closing an entrance, etc.; a way or passage; the frame which stops the passage of water through a dam, lock, etc.

Gate-crasher, gāt-krash'ėr, *n.* An uninvited guest; one who obtains admission to a public entertainment without a ticket.

Gateway, gāt'wā, *n.* A way through the gate of some enclosure; the gate itself.

Gather, gaᴛн'ėr, *vt.* To bring together; to collect; to acquire; to pucker; to deduce by inference.—*vi.* To assemble; to increase.—*n.* A fold in cloth, made by drawing; a pucker.

Gathering, gaᴛн'ėr-ing, *n.* The act of collecting or assembling; an assembly; a collection of pus; an abscess.

Gaucherie, gōsh'rē, *n.* Awkwardness.

Gaucho, gou'chó, *n.* A native of the S. American Pampas, of Spanish descent.

Gaudy, gad'i, *a.* Showy; ostentatiously fine; tastelessly or glaringly adorned.

Gauge, gāj, *vt.* (gauging, gauged). To ascertain the contents of; to measure.—*n.* A measuring-rod; a measure; distance between the rails of a railway, caliber; size or dimensions.

Gaunt, gant, *a.* Emaciated; lean; thin; famished.

Gauntlet, gant'let, *n.* A large iron glove formerly worn as armor; a long glove covering the hand and wrist.

Gauze, gaz, *n.* A very thin, slight, transparent stuff.

Gay, gā, *a.* Merry; frolicsome; showy; dressed out; dissipated.

Gaze, gāz, *vi.* (gazing, gazed). To fix the eyes and look earnestly; to stare.—*n.* A fixed look; a look of eagerness, wonder or admiration.

Gazelle, ga-zel', *n.* A small elegant species of antelope, with soft, lustrous eyes.

Gazette, ga-zet', *n.* A newspaper, especially an official newspaper. *vt.* (gazetting, gazetted). To insert in a gazette; to announce or public officially.

Gazetteer, ga-zet-tēr', *n.* A writer or publisher of news; a dictionary of geographical information.

Gear, gēr, *n.* Dress; ornaments; apparatus; harness; tackle; a train of toothed wheels.—*vt.* To put gear on; to harness.

Gelatine, jel'a-tin, *n.* A concrete transparent substance obtained by boiling from certain parts of animals; the principle of jelly; glue.

Geld, geld, *vt.* To castrate; to emasculate.

Gelding, geld'ing, *n.* Act of castrating; a castrated animal, but chiefly a horse.

Gelid, je'lid, *a.* Icy cold; frosty or icy.

Gem, jem, *n.* A precious stone of any kind; a jewel; anything remarkable for beauty or rarity.—*vt.* (gemming, gemmed). To adorn, as with gems; to bespangle; to embellish.

Gemini, jem'i-nī, *n.pl.* The Twins, a sign of the zodiac, containing the two stars Castor and Pollux.

Gemma, jem'a, *n.*; pl. -ae. A bud; a leafbud.

Gendarme, zhäng-därm, *n.* A private in the armed police of France.

Gender, jen'dėr, *n.* Sex, male or female; difference in words to express distinction of sex.—*vt.* To beget.—*vi.* To copulate; to breed.

Genealogy, jen-ê-al'o-ji, *n.* An account of the descent of a person or family from an ancestor; pedigree; lineage.

General, jen'ė-ral, *a.* Of or belonging to a genus; not special; public; common; extensive, though not universal; usual; taken as a whole.—*n.* The whole; a comprehensive notion; a military officer of the highest rank.

Generality, jen-ė-ral'i-ti, *n.* State of being general; the bulk; the greatest part.

Generalize, jen'ė-ral-īz, *vt.* To make general; to bring under a general law or statement.—*vi.* To classify under general heads; to reason by induction.

Generate, jen'ė-rāt, *vt.* (generating, generated). To beget; to produce; to cause to be.

Generation, jen-ė-rā'shon, *n.* Act of generating; single succession in natural descent; people living at the same time; race.

Generosity, jen-ė-ros'i-ti, *n.* Nobleness of soul; liberality; munificence.

Generous, jen'ė-rus, *a.* Noble; bountiful; liberal; full of spirit, as wine; courageous, as a steed.

Genesis, jen'e-sis, *n.* Act of producing; origin; first book of the Old Testament.

Genetic, Genetical, jen-net'ik, je-net'ik-al, *a.* Relating to origin or production.

Genial, jē'ni-al, *a.* Cordial kindly; contributing to life and cheerfulness.

Geniality, jē-ni-al'i-ti, *n.* Sympathetic cheerfulness or cordiality.

Genitals, jen'it-alz, *n.pl.* the parts of generation; sexual organs.

Genitive, jen'it-iv, *a.* and *n.* Applied to a case of nouns, pronouns, etc., in English called the possessive.

Genius, jē'ni-us, *n.*; pl. **Geniuses,** jē'ni-us-ez; in first sense **Genii,** jē'ni-ī. A tutelary deity; aptitude of mind for a particular study or course of life; uncommon powers of intellect; a man with uncommon intellectual faculties; nature; peculiar character.

Genre, zhäng-r, *n.* A term applied to the department of painting which depicts scenes of ordinary life.

Genteel, jen-tēl, *a.* Having the manners of well-bred people; refined; elegant.

Gentian, jen'shan, *n.* A bitter herbaceous plant, valued medicinally as a tonic.

Gentile, jen'tīl, *a.* Pertaining to a family, race, or nation; pertaining to pagans.—*n.* Any person not a Jew or a Christian; a heathen.

Gentility, jen-til'i-ti, *n.* Politeness of manners; fashionable style or circumstances.

Gentle, jen'tl, *a.* Well-born; refined in manners; mild; placid; not rough, violent, or wild; soothing.—*n.* A person of good birth.

Gentleman, jen'tl-man, *n.* A man of good social position; technically any man above the rank of yeoman, comprehending noblemen; a man of good breeding or of high honor; a polite equivalent for 'man.'

Genuflection, jen-ū-flek'shon, *n.* The act of bending the knee, particularly in worship.

Genuine, jen'ū-in, *a.* Belonging to the original stock; real; pure; true.

Genus, jē'nus, *n.*; pl. **Genera** jen'ė-ra. A kind, class, or sort; an assemblage of species having distinctive characteristics in common.

Geocentric, Geocentrical, jē-o-sen'trik, jē-o-sen'trik-al, *a.* Having reference to the earth as a center, applied to the position of a celestial object.

Geodesy, jē-od'e-si, *n.* The geometry of the earth.

Geognosy, jē-of'no-si, *n.* The science of the structure of the earth.

Geographer, jē-og'ra-fėr, *n.* One versed in geography or who writes on it.

Geography, jē-og'ra-fi, *n.* The science of the external features of the world; a book describing the earth or part of it.

Geologist, jē-ol'o-jist, *n.* One versed in the science of geology.

Geology, jē-ol'o-ji, *n.* The science of the structure of the earth as to its rocks, strata, soil, minerals, organic remains, and changes.

Geometry, jĕ-om'e-tri, *n.* The science of magnitude; that branch of mathematics which treats of the properties and relations of lines, angles, surfaces, and solids.

Geothermic, jĕ-o-thĕr'mik, *a.* Pertaining to the internal heat of the earth.

Geranium, je-rā'ni-um, *n.* A plant cultivated for its beautiful flowers; the crane's-bill genus of plants.

Germ, jĕrm, *n.* The earliest form of any animal or plant; origin; microbe; bacillus.

German, jĕr'man, *a.* Belonging to Germany.—*n.* A native of Germany; the German language.

Germane, jĕr'mān, *a.* Closely allied; relevant; pertinent.

Germinate, jĕrm'in-āt, *vi.* (germinating, germinated). To sprout; to bud; to begin to vegetate or grow, as seeds.

Gerrymander, ge'ri-man-dėr, *vt.* To arrange so as to get an unfair result from the distribution of voters in political elections.

Gerund, je'rund, *n.* A kind of verbal noun in Latin; a verbal noun, such as 'teaching' in 'fit for teaching boys.'

Gestation, jest-ā'shon, *n.* The carrying of young in the womb from conception to delivery; pregnancy.

Gesticulate, jes-tik'ū-lāt, *vi.* To make gestures or motions, as in speaking.—*vt.* To represent by gesture; to act.

Gesture, jes'tūr, *n.* A posture or motion of the body of limbs; action intended to express an idea or feeling; or to enforce an argument.

Get, get, *vt.* (getting, pret, got, pp. got, gotten). To obtain; to gain; to reach; to beget; to learn; to induce.—*vi.* To arrive at any place or state by degrees; to become; to make gain.

Geyser, gi'zėr, *n.* A hot-water spring, the water rising in a column.

Ghastly, gast'li, *a.* Deathlike in looks; hideous; frightful, as wounds.

Gherkin, gėr'kin, *n.* A small-fruited variety of cucumber used for pickling.

Ghetto, get'to, *n.* Jewish pen or quarter, a Jewry; the quarters closed and locked at night, in Italian and Rhine-valley towns, in which Jews lived.

Ghost, gōst, *n.* The soul of man; a disembodied spirit; apparition; shadow.

Ghoul, gōl, *n.* An imaginary evil being which preys upon human bodies.

Giant, jī'ant, *n.* A man of extraordinary stature; a person of extraordinary powers, bodily or intellectual.—*a.* Like a giant; extraordinary in size.

Gibberish, gib'bėr-ish, *n.* Rapid and inarticulate talk; unmeaning words.

Gibbet, jib'bet, *n.* A gallows; the projecting beam of a crane, on which the pulley is fixed.—*vt.* To hang on a gibbet; to expose to scorn, infamy, etc.

Gibbosity, gib-os'i-ti, *n.* A round or swelling prominence; convexity.

Gibe, jīb, *vi.* (gibing, gibed). To utter taunting, sarcastic words; to flout; to sneer.—*vt.* To scoff at; to mock.—*n.* A scoff; taunt; reproach.

Giblet, jib'let, *n.* One of those parts of poultry usually excluded in roasting, as the head, gizzard, liver, etc.; usually in *pl.*

Giddy, gid'i, *a.* Having in the head a sensation of whirling or swimming; dizzy; fickle; heedless; rendered wild by excitement.

Gift, gift, *n.* Anything given; act of giving; power of giving; talent or faculty.—*vt.* To endow with any power or faculty.

Giggle, gig'l, *n.* A kind of laugh, with short catches of the voice or breath.—*vi.*(giggling, giggled). To laugh with short catches of the breath; to titter.

Gigot, jig'ot, *n.* A leg of mutton.

Gild, gild, *vt.* (pret. and pp. gilded or gilt). To overlay with gold in leaf or powder; to illuminate; to give a fair and agreeable appearance to.

Gill, gil, *n.* The organ of respiration in fishes; th flap below the beak of a fowl; the flesh on th lower part of the cheeks.

Gilt, gilt, pp. of *gild.* Overlaid with gold; brightl adorned.—*n.* Gold laid on the surface of a thing gilding.

Gimbals, jim'balz, *n.pl.* A contrivance of tw movable hoops, used to keep the mariner' compass, etc., always horizontal.

Gimlet, gim'let, *n.* A small borer with a pointe screw at the end.

Gin, jin, *n.* A distilled spirit flavored with junipe berries; a machine for driving piles, raisin great weights, etc.; a machine for separatin the seeds from cotton; a trap, snare.—*vt.* (gir ning, ginned). To clear of seeds by a cotton-gir to catch in a trap.

Ginger, jin'jėr, *n.* A tropical plant, the root c which has a hot, spicy quality.

Gingerly, jin'jėr-li, *adv.* Cautiously; timidly; del cately; gently.

Gingham, ging'am, *n.* A kind of striped cotto cloth.

Ginseng, jin'seng, *n.* The name of two plants, th roots of which are a favorite Chinese medicine

Gipsy, jip'si, *n.* One of an oriental vagabond rac scattered over Europe, etc., believed to hav come originally from India; the language of th Gipsies; a name of slight reproach to a woma implying roguishness.—*a.* Pertaining to or re sembling the Gipsies.

Giraffe, ji-raf', *n.* The camelopard, the tallest c animals.

Gird, gėrd, *vt.* (pp. girded or girt). To bind; t make fast by binding; to invest; t encompass.—*vi.* To gibe; to sneer.—*n.* A strok with a whip; a twitch; a sneer.

Girder, gėrd'ėr, *n.* One who girds; a main bea supporting a superstructure.

Girdle, gėr'dl, *n.* That which girds; a band c belt; something drawn round the waist and tie or buckled.—*vt.* (girdling, girdled). To bind wit a girdle; belt, or sash; to gird.

Girl, gėrl, *n.* A female child; young woman.

Girth, gėrth, *n.* That which girds; band fastenir a saddle on a horse's back; measure round person's body or anything cylindrical.

Gist, jist, *n.* The main point of a question; su stance or pith of a matter.

Give, giv, *vt.* (giving, pret, gave, pp. given). To b stow; to deliver; to impart; to yield; to afford; utter; to show; to send forth; to devote (onesel to pledge; to allow; to ascribe.—*vi.* To ma gifts; to yield to pressure; to recede.

Gizzard, giz'ėrd, *n.* The muscular stomach of bird.

Glacier, glā'shi-ėr, *n.* An immense mass of i formed in valleys above the snow-line, and ha ing a slow movement downwards.

Glad, glad, *a.* Affected with pleasure; please cheerful; imparting pleasure.—*vt.* (gladdin gladded). To make glad; to gladden.

Glade, glād, *n.* A green clear space or opening a wood.

Gladiator, glad'i-ā-tėr, *n.* Among the Roman one who fought with swords, etc., for the ente tainment of the people; a prize-fighter.

Gladiolus, gla-di-ō'lus, *n.*; pl. **-li.** A beauitful g nus of bulbous-rooted plants, abundant in Africa; sword-lily.

Glamor, glam'ėr, *n.* Magic influence causing person to see objects differently from what th really are; witchery.

Glance, gläns, *n.* A sudden shoot of light or sple dor; a glimpse or sudden look.—*vi.* (glancin glanced). To shine; to gleam; to dart aside; look with a sudden rapid cast of the eye; move quickly; to hint.—*vt.* To shoot or dart su denly or obliquely; to cast for a moment.

Gland, gland, *n.* An acorn; any acorn-shap fruit; a roundish organ in many parts of t body secreting some fluid; a secreting organ plants.

Glare, glär, *n.* A bright dazzling light; a fierce piercing look.—*vi.* (glaring, glared). To shine with excessive luster; to look with fierce piercing eyes.

Glass, gläs, *n.* A hard transparent substance; a small drinking vessel of glass; a mirror; quantity of liquor that a glass vessel contains; a lens, a telescope; a barometer; *pl.* spectacles.—*a.* Made of glass; vitreous.

Glass-blower, gläs´blō-er, *n.* One who blows and fashions glass vessels.

Glaucoma, Glaucosis, gla-kō´ma, gla-kō´sis, *n.* An opacity of the vitreous humor of the eye, giving it a bluish-green tint.

Glaucous, gla´kus, *a.* Of a sea-green color; covered with a fine bluish or greenish bloom or powder.

Glaze, gläz, *vt.* (glazing, glazed). To furnish with glass; to incrust with a vitreous substance; to make smooth and glossy.—*n.* A vitreous or transparent coating.

Glazier, glā´zher, *n.* One whose business is to set window-glass.

Gleam, glēm, *n.* A small stream of light; brightness.—*vi.* To shoot or dart, as rays of light; to shine; to flash.

Glean, glēn, *vt.* and *i.* To gather stalks and ears of grain left behind by reapers; to pick up here and there; to gather slowly and assiduously.

Glee, glē, *n.* Joy; mirth; a composition for voices in three or more parts.

Glen, glen, *n.* A narrow valley; a dale; a depression or space between hills.

Glib, glib, *a.* Smooth; slippery; having plausible words always ready.

Glide, glid, *vi.* (gliding, glided). To flow gently; to move or slip along with ease.—*n.* Act of moving smoothly.

Glider, glid´er, *n.* A modification of the airplane, which can travel through the air for a certain time without engine power.

Glimmer, glim´er, *vi.* To shine faintly, and with frequent intermissions; to flicker.—*n.* A faint light; a twinkle.

Glimpse, glimps, *n.* A gleam or flash of light; short transitory view; faint resemblance; slight tinge.—*vi.* To appear by glimpses.

Glint, glint, *vi.* To glance; to give a flash of light.—*n.* A glance, flash, gleam.

Glisten, glis´n, *vi.* To glitter; to sparkle.

Glitter, glit´er, *vi.* To sparkle with light; to be showy, specious, or striking.—*n.* Brightness; luster.

Gloaming, glōm´ing, *n.* Fall of the evening; the twilight; decline.

Gloat, glōt, *vi.* To gave earnestly; to feast the eyes; to contemplate with evil satisfaction.

Globe, glōb, *n.* A round solid body; a sphere; the earth; an artificial sphere on whose surface is drawn a map of the earth or heavens.—*vt.* To gather into a round mass.

Globule, glob´ūl, *n.* A little globe; a small spherical particle; one of the red particles of the blood.

Globulin, glob´ū-lin, *n.* The main ingredient of blood globules and resembling albumen.

Gloom, glōm, *n.* Obscurity; thick shade; sadness, aspect of sorrow; darkness of prospect or aspect.—*vi.* To shine obscurely; to be cloudy or dark; to be sullen or sad.

Glorify, glō´ri-fī, *vt.* (glorifying, glorified). to make glorious; to ascribe glory or honor to; to extol.

Glorious, glō´ri-us, *a.* Full of glory; renowned; celebrated; grand; brilliant.

Glory, glō´ri, *n.* Praise, honor, admiration, or distinction; renown; magnificence; celestial bliss; the divine presence; the divine perfections; that of which one may be proud.—*vi.* (glorying, gloried). To boast; to rejoice; to be proud with regard to something.

Gloss, glos, *n.* Brightness from a smooth surface; sheen; specious appearance; an interpretation; comment.—*vt.* To give superficial luster to; to give a specious appearance to; to render plausible; to comment; to annotate.

Glossary, glos´a-ri, *n.* A vocabulary explaining antiquated or difficult words or phrases.

Glossology, Glottology, glos-ol´o-ji, glot-ol´o-ji, *n.* The science of language; comparative philology.

Glossy, glos´i, *a.* Smooth and shining; highly polished.

Glottis, glot´is, *n.* The narrow opening at the upper part of the windpipe.

Glove, gluv, *n.* A cover for the hand.—*vt.* (gloving, gloved). To cover with a glove.

Glow, glō, *vi.* To burn with intense heat, especialy without flame; to feel great heat of body; to be flushed; to be ardent; to rage.—*n.* White heat; brightness of color; animation.

Glowworm, glō´werm, *n.* A wingless female beetle which emits a greenish light.

Glucose, glō´kōs, *n.* Grape-sugar, a sugar produced from grapes, starch, etc.

Glue, glö, *n.* A tenacious, viscid matter which serves as a cement.—*vt.* (gluing, glued). To join with glue; to unite.

Glum, glum, *a.* Sullen; moody; dejected.

Glut, glut, *vt.* (glutting, glutted). To swallow greedily; to cloy; to satiate; to furnish beyond sufficiency.—*n.* Plenty, even to loathing; supply of an article beyond the demand.

Gluten, glö´ten, *n.* A tough, elastic, nitrogenous substance in the flour of wheat, etc.

Glutinate, glö´tin-āt, *vt.* To unite with glue.

Glutinous, glö´tin-us, *a.* Gluey; viscous; viscid; tenacious; resembling glue.

Glutton, glut´n, *n.* One who eats to excess; one eager of anything to excess; a carnivorous quadruped.

Glycerine, glis´er-in, *n.* A transparent, colorless, sweet liquid obtained from fats.

Glyphic, glif´ik, *a.* Of or pertaining to carving or sculpture.

Glyptic, glip´tik, *a.* Pertaining to the art of engraving on precious stones.

Gnarl, närl, *n.* A protuberance on the outside of a tree; a knot.

Gnash, nash, *vt.* To strike together, as the teeth.—*vi.* To strike or dash the teeth together, as in rage or pain.

Gnat, nat, *n.* A small two-winged fly, the female of which bites.

Gnaw, nä, *vt.* To bite by little and little; to bite in agony or rage; to fret; to corrode.—*vi.* To use the teeth in biting; to cause steady annoying pain.

Gneiss, nis, *n.* A species of rock composed of quartz, feldspar, and mica, and having a slaty structure.

Gnome, nōm, *n.* A sprite supposed to inhabit the inner parts of the earth; a dwarf; a maxim, aphorism.

Gnomic, Gnomical, nō´mik, nō´mik-al, *a.* Containing or dealing in maxims.

Gnomon, nō´mon, *n.* The style or pin of a dial; a geometrical figure.

Gnostic, nos´tik, *n.* One of an early religious sect whose doctrines were based partly on Christianity and partly on Greek and Oriental philosophy.

Gnu, nū, *n.* A large south African antelope.

Go, gō, *vi.* (going, pret, went, pp. gone). To move; to proceed; to depart; to be about to do; to circulate; to tend; to be guided; to be alienated or sold; to reach; to avail; to conduce; to die; to fare; to become.

Goad, gōd, *n.* A pointed instrument to make a beast move faster; anything that stirs into action. *vt.* To drive with a goad; to instigate.

Goal, gol, *n.* The point set to bound a race; a mark that players in some outdoor sport must attain; a success scored by reaching this; final purpose; end.

Goat, gōt, *n.* A ruminant quadruped with long hair and horns.

Gobble, gob´l, *vt.* (gobbling, gobbled). To swallow.

in large pieces or hastily.—*vi.* To make a noise in the throat, as a turkey.

Gobbler, gob'lėr, *n.* One who gobbles; a greedy eater; a gormandizer; a turkey-cock.

Go-between, gō'bē-twēn, *n.* Intermediary.

Goblet, gob'let, *n.* A kind of cup or drinking vessel without a handle.

Goblin, gob'lin, *n.* A mischievous sprite; an elf.

God, god, *n.* The Supreme Being; a divinity; a deity.

Goddess, god'es, *n.* A female deity; a woman of superior charms.

Godfather, god'fä-THėr, *n.* A man who becomes sponsor for a child at baptism. (Also *godmother, -son, -daughter,* and *-child.*).

Godhead, god'hed, *n.* Godship; divinity; divine nature or essence.

Godlike, god'līk, *a.* Resembling God; divine; resembling a deity; of superior excellence.

Godliness, god'li-nes, *n.* Quality of being godly; piety; reverence for God.

Godsend, god'send, *n.* An unexpected acquisition or good fortune.

God-speed, god'spēd, *n.* Success; prosperity.

Goggle, gog'l, *vi.* (goggling, goggled). To roll or strain the eyes.—*a.* Prominent, rolling, or staring (eyes).—*n.* A strained or affected rolling of the eye; *pl.* a kind of spectacles to protect the eyes or cure squinting.

Going, gō'ing, *n.* Act of one who goes; departure; way; state of roads.—**Goings-on,** actions; behavior.

Goiter, goi'tėr, *n.* A morbid enlargment of the thyroid gland, forming a masss on the front of the neck.

Gold, gōld, *n.* A precious metal of a bright yellow color; money; something pleasing or valuable; a bright yellow color.—*a.* Made or consisting of gold.

Golden, gōld'n, *a.* Made of gold; like gold; splendid; most valuable; auspicious.

Goldfinch, gōld'finsh, *n.* A beautiful singing bird.

Gold-fish, gōld'fish, *n.* A fresh-water fish of the carp family, of a bright orange color.

Gold-leaf, gōld'lēf, *n.* Gold beaten into a thin leaf.

Goldsmith, gōld'smith, *n.* One who manufacturers articles of gold and silver.

Golf, golf, *n.* A game played over links with a small ball driven by clubs.—*vi.* To play golf.

Gondola, gon'dō-la, *n.* A long narrow pleasure-boat, used in Venice.

Gong, gong, *n.* A kind of metallic drum; a similar article used instead of a bell.

Good, gud, *a.* The opposite of bad; wholesome; useful; fit; virtuous; valuable; benevolent; clever; adequate; valid; able to fulfil engagements; considerable; full or complete; immaculate.—*n.* What is good or desirable; advantage; welfare; virtue; *pl.* commodities, chattels, movables.—**For good,** to close the whole business; finally.—*interj.* Well; right.

Good-for-nothing, gud'for-nu-thing, *n.* An idle; worthless person.—*a.* Worthless.

Good-humor, gud-hū'mėr, *n.* A cheerful temper or state of mind.

Good-nature, gud-nā'tūr, *n.* Natural mildness and kindness of disposition.

Goodness, gud'nes, *n.* State or quality of being good; excellence, virtue, etc.; a euphemism for God.

Good-will, gud-wil', *n.* Benevolence; business connecton of some established business.

Goose, gös, *n.; pl.* **Geese,** gēs. A swimming bird larger than the duck; a tailor's smoothing-iron; a silly person.

Gooseberry, gös'be-ri, *n.* The fruit of a prickly shrub, and the shrub itself.

Gopher, gō'fėr, *n.* The name given in America to several burrowing animals.

Gordian knot, gor'di-an not. An inextricable difficulty; *to cut the Gordian knot,* to remove a difficulty by bold measures.

Gore, gōr, *n.* Blood that is shed; thick or clotted blood; a wedge-shaped piece of land or cloth; a gusset.—*vt.* (goring, gored). To cut in a triangular form; to pierce with a pointed instrument, or an animal's horns.

Gorge, gorj, *n.* The throat; the gullet; a narrow passage between hills or mountains; entrance into a bastion.—*vt.* and *i.* (gorging, gorged). To swallow with greediness; to glut; to satiate.

Gorgeous, gor'jus, *a.* Showy; splendid; magnificent.

Gorgon, gor'gon, *n.* A monster of Greek mythology, one of three sisters.—*a.* Like a gorgon; very ugly or terrific.

Gorgonzola, gor-gon-zō'la, *n.* A kind of Italian ewe-milk cheese.

Gorilla, gor-il'la, *n.* The largest animal of the ape kind.

Gormand, gor'mand, *n.* A glutton.

Gormandize, gor'mand-īz, *vi.* To eat greedily or to excess.

Gory, gō'ri, *a.* Covered with gore; bloody; murderous.

Gosling, goz'ling, *n.* A young goose.

Gospel, gos'pel, *n.* The history of Jesus Christ; any of the four records of Christ's life by his apostles; scheme of salvation as taught by Christ; any general doctrine.—*a.* Relating to the gospel; accordant with the gospel.

Gossamer, gos'a-mėr, *n.* A fine, filmy substance, like cobwebs, floating in the air in calm, sunny weather; a thin fabric.

Gossip, gos'ip, *n.* An idle tattler; idle talk. *vi.* To prate; to run about and tattle.

Gothic, goth'ik, *a.* Pertaining to the Goths; rude; barbarous; denoting the style of architecture characterized by the pointed arch.—*n.* The language of the Goths; the Gothic order of architecture.

Gouda, gou'da, *n.* A kind of cheese from *Gouda,* A town in Holland.

Gouge, gouj, gōj, *n.* A chisel with a hollow or grooved blade.—*vt.* (gouging, gouged). To scoop out with, or as with, a gouge.

Gourd, gōrd, *n.* The popular name of the family of plants represented by the melon, cucumber, etc.; a cup made from the rind of a gourd.

Gourmet, gor-mā or gor'met, *n.* A connoisseur in wines and meats; a nice feeder.

Gout, gout, *n.* A painful disease, affecting generally the small joints; a drop; a clot or coagulation.

Govern, gu'vėrn, *vt.* To direct and control; to regulate; to steer; to affect so as to determine the case, etc., in grammar.—*vi.* To exercise authority; to administer the laws.

Governess, gu'vėrn-es, *n.* A female who governs or instructs.

Government, gu'vėrn-ment, *n.* Rule; control; administration of public affairs; system of polity in a state; territory ruled by a governor; executive power; the influence of a word in grammar in regard to construction.

Governor, gu'vėrn-ėr, *n.* One who governs; one invested with supreme authority; a tutor; a contrivance in machinery for maintaining a uniform velocity.

Gown, goun, *n.* A woman's outer garment; a long, loose garment worn by professional men, as divines.—*vt.* To put on a gown.

Grab, grab, *vt.* (grabbing, grabbed). To seize; to snatch.—*n.* A sudden grasp; implement for clutching objects.

Grace, grās, *n.* Favor; kindness; love and favor of God; state of reconciliation to God; pardon; license or privilege; expression of thanks before or after meals; title of a duke or archbishop; elegance with appropriate dignity; an embellishment; one of three ancient goddesses in whose gift were grace and beauty; in *music,* a trill, shake, etc.—*vt.* (gracing, graced). To lend grace to; to adorn; to favor.

Gracious, grā'shus, *a.* Full of grace; favorable;

Gradation, gra-dā'shon, n. Arrangement by grades; regular advance step by step; rank; series; regular process by degrees.

Grade, grād, n. A step; degree; rank; gradient.— vt. (grading, graded). To arrange in order of rank, etc.; to reduce to a suitable slope.

Gradient, grā'di-ent, a. Moving by steps; rising or descending by regular degrees.—n. The degree of ascent or descent in a road, etc.; part of a road which slopes.

Graduate, grad'ū-āt, vt. (graduating, graduated). To divide into regular intervals or degrees; to mark with such; to arrange by grades; to confer a university degree on; to reduce to a certain consistency by evaporation.—vi. To receive a university degree; to change gradually.—n. One who has received a degree of a university, etc.

Graft, graft, n. A small scion of a tree inserted in another tree which is to support and nourish the scion; corrupt gains or practices in politics.—vt. To insert a graft on; to propagate by a graft; to join on as if organically; a part.

Grail, Graal, grāl, n. The holy vessel containing the last drops of Christ's blood, brought to England by Joseph of Arimathea, and being afterwards lost, eagerly sought for by King Arthur's knights.

Grain, grān, n. A single seed of a plant; corn in general; a minute particle; a small weight; fibers of wood with regard to their arrangement; substance of a thing with respect to the size, form, or direction of the constituent particles; texture; dye.—vt. To paint in imitation of fibers; to granulate.

Gram, gram, n. The French unit of weight, equal to 15.43 grains troy.

Grammar, gram'ėr, n. A system of principles and rules for speaking or writing a language; propriety of speech; an outline of any subject.

Grammatical, Grammatic, gram-mat'ik-al, gram-mat'ik, a. Belonging to grammar; according to the rules of grammar.

Granary, gra'na-ri, n. A storehouse for grain after it is thrashed.

Grand, grand, a. Great, figuratively; majestic; magnificent; noble.

Grandchild, grand'chīld, n. A son's or daughter's child.

Grand-daughter, grand'da-tėr, n. The daughter of a son or daughter.

Grandeur, grand'yūr, n. Greatness; sublimity; splendor; magnificence.

Grandfather, grand'fä-тнėr, n. A father's or mother's father.

Grandiloquence, grand-il'ō-kwens, n. Lofty speaking; pompous language.

Grandiose, gran'di-ōs, a. Impressive from grandeur; bombastic; turgid.

Grandmother, grand'mūтн-ėr, n. The mother of one's father or mother.

Grandson, grand'sun, n. The son of a son or daughter.

Grand-stand, grand'stand, n. An erection of a race-course, etc., affording a good view.

Grange, grānj, n. A farm, with the buildings, stables, etc.

Granitic, gran-it'ik, a. Like granite; pertaining to or consisting of granite.

Granivorous, grān-iv'ō-rus, a. Feeding on grain or seeds.

Grant, grant, vt. To bestow; to confer on; to admit as true; to convey by deed or writing; to cede.— n. A bestowing; a gift, a conveyance in writing; the thing conveyed.

Granulate, gran'ū-lāt, vt. and i (granulating, granulated). To form into grains; to make or become rough on the surface.

Granulation, gran-ū-lā'shon, n. Act of forming into grains; a process by which minute fleshy bodies are formed on wounds during healing; the fleshy grains themselves.

Grape, grāp, n. A single berry of the vine; grapeshot.

Grapefruit, grāp'frōt, n. A pale-yellow fruit akin to the orange, but larger and sourer.

Graph, graf, n. A diagram representing the relation between two varying magnitudes by means of a curve or series of lines.

Graphic, Graphical, graf'ik, graf'ik-al, a. Pertaining to the art of writing or delineating; pictorial; vivid.

Graphite, graf'īt, n. A form of carbon, made into pencils; plumbago; black lead.

Grapnel, grap'nel, n. A small anchor with four or five claws.

Grapple, grap'l, vt. (grappling, grappled). To lay fast hold on, with hands or hooks.—vi. To contend in close fight, as wrestlers.—n. A seizing; close hug in contest; grappling-iron.

Grappling-iron, grap'ling-i-ėrn, n. An instrument of four or more iron claws for grappling and holding fast; a grapnel.

Grasp, grāsp, vt. To seize and hold by the fingers or arms; to take possession of; to comprehend.—vi. To make a clutch or catch.— n. Gripe of the hand; reach of the arms; power of seizing or comprehending.

Grass, gräs, n. Herbage; any plant of the family to which belong the grain-yielding and pasture plants.—vt. To cover with grass; to bleach on the grass.

Grasshopper, gräs'hop-ėr, n. An insect that hops among grass, allied to the locusts.

Grate, grāt, n. A frame composed of parallel or cross-bars; grating; iron frame for holding coals used as fuel.—vt. (grating, grated). To furnish or make fast with cross-bars; to wear away in small particles by rubbing; to offend, as by a discordant sound.—vi. To rub roughly on; to have an annoying effect; to sound harshly.

Grateful, grāt'ful, a. Pleasing; gratifying; feeling or expressing gratitude.

Garter, grät'ėr, n. An instrument for rubbing off small particles of a body.

Gratification, grat'i-fi-kā''shon, n. Act of gratifying; that which affords pleasure; satisfaction; recompense.

Gratify, grat'i-fi, vt. (gratifying, gratified). To please; to indulge, delight, humor.

Gratifying, grat'i-fi-ing, p.a. Giving pleasure; affording satisfaction.

Grating, grāt'ing, n. A frame or partition of bars or lattice-work.

Gratis, grā'tis, adv. Without recompense; freely.—a. Given or done for nothing.

Gratitude, grat'i-tūd, n. Quality of being grateful; an emotion of the heart, excited by a favor received; thankfulness.

Gratuitous, gra-tū'it-us, a. That is done out of favor; free; voluntary; asserted or taken without proof.

Gratuity, gra-tū'i-ti, n. A free gift; donation; something given in return for a favor.

Gravamen, gra-vā'men, n. Ground or burden of complaint.

Grave, grāv, vt. (graving, pret. graved, pp. graven, graved). To make incisions on; to engrave; to impress deeply; as on the mind; to clean, as a ship's bottom, and cover with pitch.—n. A pit for the dead; a tomb.—a. Weighty; serious; staid; thoughtful; not gay; not tawdry; in music, low.

Gravel, gra'vel, n. Small pebbles; a disease produced by small concretions in the kidneys and bladder.—vt. (gravelling, gravelled). To cover with gravel; to cause to stick in the sand or gravel; to puzzle.

Gravely, grāv'li, adv. In a grave, solemn manner; soberly; seriously.

Gravid, grav'id, a. Being with young; pregnant.

Gravitate, grav'i-tāt, vt. To be affected by gravitation; to tend towards the center.

Gravitation, grav-i-tā'shon, n. The force by which

bodies are drawn towards the center of the earth; tendency of all matter toward all other matter.

Gravity, grav'i-ti, *n.* The tendency of matter toward some attracting body, particularly toward the center of the earth; state or character of being grave; weight; enormity.

Gravy, grā'vi, *n.* The juice that comes from flesh in cooking.

Gray, grā, *a.* Of the color of hair whitened by age; white with a mixture of black; having gray hairs.—*n.* A gray color; a gray animal, as a horse; early morning twilight.

Graze, grāz, *vt.* (grazing, grazed). To rub or touch lightly in passing; to feed with growing grass, as cattle; to feed on.—*vi.* to pass so as to rub lightly; to eat grass; to supply grass.—*n.* A slight rub or brush.

Grease, grēs, *n.* Animal fat in a soft state; oily matter.—*vt.* (greasing, greased). To smear with grease.

Great, grāt, *a.* Large in bulk or number; long-continued; of vast power and excellence; eminent; majestic; pregnant; distant by one more generation, as *great*-grandfather, etc.

Grecian, grē'shan, *a.* Pertaining to Greece.—*n.* A Greek; one well versed in the Greek language.

Greed, grēd, *n.* Eager desire; avarice.

Greek, grēk, *a.* Pertaining to Greece.—*n.* A native of Greece; the language of Greece.

Green, grēn, *a.* Having the color of growing plants; verdant; fresh; containing its natural juices; unripe; young; easily imposed upon.—*n.* A green color; a grassy plain or plot; *pl.* leaves and stems of young plants used in cookery.—*vt.* and *i.* To make or grow green.

Greenhorn, grēn'horn, *n.* One easily imposed upon; a raw inexperienced person.

Greenhouse, grēn'hous, *n.* A building in which tender plants are cultivated.

Green-room, grēn'rōm, *n.* A retiring-room for actors in a theater.

Greet, grēt, *vt.* To salute; to meet and address with kindness.—*vi.* To meet and salute.

Gregarious, grē-gā'ri-us, *a.* Assembling or living in a flock; not habitually solitary.

Grenade, gre-nād', *n.* A small bomb, thrown by hand or fired from a rifle.

Greyhound, grā'hound, *n.* A tall, slender, fleet dog kept for the chase.

Griddle, grid'l, *n.* A circular plate of iron, or a shallow pan, for baking cakes.

Grief, grēf, *n.* Pain of mind produced by loss, misfortune, etc.; sorrow; cause of sorrow; trouble.

Grievance, grēv'ans, *n.* A wrong suffered; cause of complaint; trouble.

Grieve, grēv, *vt.* (grieving, grieved). To cause grief to; to deplore.—*vi.* To feel grief; to sorrow; to lament.

Griffin, Griffon, grif'in, grif'on, *n.* A fabled monster, in the fore part an eagle, in the hinder a lion.

Grill, gril, *vt.* To broil on a gridiron; to torment, as if by broiling.—*vi.* To suffer, as if from grilling.—*n.* A grated utensil for broiling meat, etc.

Grim, grim, *a.* of a forbidding or fear-inspiring aspect; stern; sullen; surly; ugly.

Grimace, gri-mās', *n.* A distortion of the countenance; air of affectation.—*vi.* To make grimaces.

Grime, grīm, *n.* Foul matter.—*vt.* (griming, grimed). To sully or soil deeply.

Grin, grin, *vi.* (grinning, grinned). To show the teeth, as in laughter, scorn, or anguish—*n.* Act of showing the teeth; a forced smile or restrained laugh.

Grind, grind, *vt.* (grinding, ground). To reduce to fine particles; to sharpen or polish by friction; to rub together; to oppress; to crush in pieces.—*vi.* To turn a mill; to be moved or rubbed together; to be puverized by friction; to study hard.—*n.* Act of one who grinds; a laborious spell of work.

Grindstone, grind'stōn, *n.* A circular stone, made to revolve, to sharpen tools.

Grip, grip, *n.* The act of grasping; grasp; a fast hold; a hilt or handle.—*vt.* and *i* (gripping, gripped). To grasp by the hand; to clutch; to hold fast.

Gripe, grip, *vt.* and *i* (griping, griped). To grasp by the hand; to hold fast; to pinch; to give pain to the bowels.—*n.* Grasp; grip; something which grasps; *pl.* pinching pain in the bowels.

Grisly, griz'li, *a.* Dreadful; fearful; ghastly.

Grist, grist, *n.* Corn ground, or for grinding.

Gristle, gris'l, *n.* Cartilage.

Grit, grit, *n.* Sand or gravel; hard sandstone, texture of a stone; firmness of mind; coarse part of meal.

Groan, grōn, *vi.* To utter a mournful voice, as in pain or sorrow; to moan.—*n.* A deep, mournful sound, uttered in pain, sorrow, or disapprobation; any low rumbling sound.

Groats, grōts, *n.pl.* Oats or wheat with the husks taken off.

Grocer, grō'sèr, *n.* A merchant who deals in tea, sugar, spices, etc.

Grocery, grō'sè-ri, *n.* A grocer's shop; the commodities sold by grocers.

Grog, grog, *n.* A mixture of spirit and water not sweetened.

Groggy, grog'i, *a.* Overcome with grog; tipsy; moving in an uneasy, hobbling manner.

Groin, groin, *n.* The part of the human body between the belly and thigh in front; the angular projecting curve made by the intersection of simple vaults at any angle.

Groom, grōm, *n.* A man or boy who has the charge of horses; a bridegroom.—*vt.* To feed and take care of, as a groom does horses.

Groomsman, grōmz'man, *n.* One who acts as attendant on a bridegroom at his marriage.

Groove, grōv, *n.* A channel or long hollow cut by a tool; fixed routine of life.—*vt.* (grooving, grooved). To cut a groove in; to furrow.

Grope, grōp, *vi.* (groping, groped). To search in the dark by feeling; to feel one's way.—*vt.* To search out by feeling in the dark.

Gross, grōs, *a.* Thick; coarse; obscene; palpable; dense; shameful; dull; whole.—*n.* Main body; bulk; the number of twelve dozen.

Grotesque, grō-tesk', *a.* Wildly formed; extravagant; fantastic.—*n.* Whimsical figures or scenery.

Grotto, grot'tō, *n.* A natural cave; an artificial ornamented cave.

Ground, ground, *n.* Surface of the earth; soil; land; basis; reason; foil or background; predominating color; *pl.* dregs, sediment; ornamental land about a mansion—*vt.* To set on the ground; to found; to fix firmly; to instruct in first principles.—*vi.* To strike the bottom and remain fixed, as a ship.

Groundless, ground'les, *a.* Wanting foundation or reason; baseless; false.

Ground-swell, ground'swel, *n.* Heaving of the sea caused by a distant storm.

Groundwork, ground'werk, *n.* Basis; fundamentals.

Group, grōp, *n.* A cluster; an assemblage; an artistic combination of figures; a class.—*vt.* To form into a group or groups.

Grouping, grōp'ing, *n.* The art of arranging or mode of arrangement in a picture or work of art.

Grout, grout, *n.* Coarse meal; a thin mortar; dregs.—*vt.* To fill up with grout or mortar.

Grove, grōv, *n.* A shady cluster of trees; a small wood.

Grovel, gro'vel, *vi.* (grovelling, grovelled). To lie prone, or creep on the earth; to be low or mean.

Grow, grō, *vi.* (pret. grew, pp. grown). To be augmented by natural process; to increase; to make progress; to become; to accrue; to swell.—*vt.* To raise from the soil; to produce.

Growl, groul, *vi.* To murmur or snarl, as a dog; to

utter an angry, grumbling sound.—*vt.* to express by growling.—*n.* Angry sound of a dog; grumbling murmur.

Grown, grōn, *p.a.* Increased in growth; having arrived at full size or stature.

Growth, grōth, *n.* Act or process of growing; product; increase; advancement.

Grub, grub, *vi.*(grubbing, grubbed). To dig; to be employed meanly.—*vt.* To dig; to root out by digging.—*n.* The larva of an insect; caterpillar; maggot.

Grudge, gruj, *vi.* (grudging, grudged). To cherish ill-will; to be envious.—*vt.* To permit or grant with reluctance; to envy.—*n.* Reluctance in giving; secret enmity.

Gruel, grü´el, *n.* A light food made by boiling meal in water.

Gruesome, grö´sum, *a.* Causing one to shudder; frightful; horrible; repulsive.

Gruff, gruf, *a.* Of a rough or stern manner or voice; surly; harsh.

Grumble, grum´bl, *vi.* (grumbling, grumbled). To murmur with discontent.

Grunt, grunt, *vi.* To make a noise like a hog; to utter a deep guttural sound.—*n.* A deep guttural sound, as of a hog.

Gruyère, grü-yår´, *n.* Cheese made from a mixture of goats' and ewes' milk.

Guano, gwä´nō, *n.* A rich manure composed chiefly of the excrements of sea-fowls, and brought from S. America and the Pacific.

Guarantee, ga-ran-tē´, *n.* An undertaking by a third person that a covenant shall be observed by the contracting parties or by one of them; one who binds himself to see the stipulations of another performed.—*vt.* (guaranteeing, guaranteed). To warrant; to pledge oneself for.

Guard, gärd, *vt.* To keep watch over; to secure against injury, loss, or attack.—*vi.* To watch, by way of caution or defense; to be in a state of caution or defense.—*n.* Defense; protector; sentinel; escort; attention; caution; posture of defense.

Guard-house, Guard-room, gärd´hous, gärd´rōm, *n.* A house or room for the accommodation of a guard of soldiers, and where military defaulters are confined.

Guardian, gärd´i-an, *n.* One who guards; one appointed to take charge of an orphan or ward.—*a.* Protecting.

Guava, gwä´va, *n.* A small tropical tree of the myrtle family

Guerrilla, Guerilla, ge-ril´la, *n.* An irregular petty war, one engaged in such.

Guess, ges, *vt.* To conjecture; to form an opinion without certain means of knowledge; to surmise.—*vi.* To conjecture; to judge at random.—*n.* Conjecture; surmise.

Guest, gest, *n.* A visitor or friend entertained in the house or at the table of another.

Guffaw, guf-fa´, *n.* A loud burst of laughter.—*vi.* To burst into a loud laugh.

Guidance, gid´ans, *n.* The act of guiding; direction; government; a leading.

Guide, gid, *vt.* (guiding, guided). To lead; to direct; to influence; to regulate.—*n.* A person who guides; a director; a regulator; a guide-book.

Guild, Gild, gild, *n.* A corporation of craftsmen, etc., for mutual aid and protection.

Guildhall, gild-hal´, *n.* Hall where a guild assembles; a town or corporation hall.

Guile, gil, *n.* Wile; fraud; duplicity.

Guillotine, gil-ō-tēn´, *n.* A machine for beheading persons; a machine for cutting paper.—*vt.* To behead by the guillotine.

Guilt, gilt, *n.* Criminality; sin; wickedness.

Guilty, gilt´i, *a.* Justly chargeable with guilt; criminal; pertaining to or indicating guilt.

Guinea-fowl, gin´ē-foul, *n.* A fowl allied to the peacocks and pheasants.

Guinea-pig, gin´ē-pig, *n.* A tailless rodent about 7 inches in length.

Guise, giz, *n.* External appearance; dress; mien; cast of behavior.

Guitar, gi-tär´, *n.* A musical instrument having six strings.

Gulch, gulch, *n.* A gully; dry bed of a torrent.

Gulf, gulf, *n.* An arm of the sea extending into the land; bay; chasm; whirlpool; anything insatiable; a wide interval.

Gull, gul, *vt.* To cheat.—*n.* One easily cheated; a simpleton; a marine swimming bird.

Gullet, gul´et, *n.* The passage in the neck of an animal by which food and liquor are taken into the stomach.

Gully, gul´i, *n.* A channel worn by water; a ravine.—*vt.* To wear into a gully.

Gulp, gulp, *vt.* To swallow eagerly.—*n.* Act of taking a large swallow.

Gum, gum, *n.* The fleshy substance of the jaws round the teeth; a juice which exudes from trees, etc., and thickens; a viscous substance.—*vt.* (gumming, gummed). To smear with or unite by a viscous substance.

Gumption, gum´shon, *n.* Understanding; capacity; shrewdness: *colloq.*

Gun, gun, *n.* Any species of firearm.

Gunman, gun´man, *n.* An armed bandit.

Gunner, gun´er, *n.* One who has the charge of ordnance.

Gunnery, gun´é-ri, *n.* The art of firing cannon; the science of artillery.

Gunpowder, gun´pou-der, *n.* An explosive mixture of saltpeter, sulphur, and charcoal.

Gunshot, gun´shot, *n.* Range of a cannon-shot; firing of a gun.—*a.* Made by the shot of a gun.

Gunwale, Gunnel, gun´wäl, gun´el, *n.* The upper edge of a ship's side.

Gurgle, gėr´gl, *vi.* (gurgling, gurgled). To run or flow in a broken noisy current.—*n.* Sound produced by a liquid flowing from or through a narrow opening.

Gush, gush, *vi.* To issue with violence and rapidity, as a fluid; to be effusively sentimental.—*n.* A sudden and violent issue of a fluid; the fluid thus emitted; effusive display of sentiment.

Gusset, gus´et, *n.* A piece of cloth inserted in a garment.

Gust, gust, *n.* Taste; relish; a sudden blast of wind; a violent burst of passion.

Gusto, gust´ō, *n.* Relish; zest; taste.

Gusty, gust´i, *a.* Subject to sudden blasts of wind; stormy.

Gut, gut, *n.* The intestinal canal of an animal; *pl.* the entrails; a preparation of the intestines for various purposes; a channel.—*vt.* (gutting, gutted). To take out the entrails of; to plunder of contents; to destroy the interior of.

Gutter, gut´er, *n.* A channel at the side of a road, etc., for water.—*vt.* To cut or form gutters in.—*vi.* To become channelled.

Guttural, gut´tèr-al, *a.* Pertaining to the throat; formed in the throat.—*n.* A letter pronounced in the throat; any guttural sound.

Guy, gi, *n.* A rope to steady anything; a person of queer looks or dress.—*vt.* To steady or direct by means of a guy.

Guzzle, guz´l, *v.* and *t.* (guzzling, guzzled). To swallow greedily or frequently.—*n.* A debauch.

Gymnasium, jim-nä´zi-um, *n.*; pl. **ia** or **-iums.** A place for athletic exercises; a school for the higher branches of education.

Gymnast, jim´nast, *n.* One who teaches or practices gymnastic exercises.

Gynecology, jin- or jin-ē-kol´o-ji, *n.* The medical science of the functions and diseases peculiar to women.

Gypsum, jip´sum, *n.* A mineral found as alabaster or as plaster of Paris.

Gyrate, ji´rāt, *vi.* (gyrating, gyrated). To move in a circle or spirally.—*a.* Moving in a circle.

Gyration, ji-rā´shon, *n.* A turning or whirling round.

Gyre, jir, *n.* A circular motion, or a circle described by a moving body; a turn.

Gyroscope, Gyrostat, ji´rō-skōp, ji´rō-stat, *n.* An apparatus for illustrating peculiarities of rotation.

H

Haberdasher, ha'bér-dash-ér, n. A dealer in drapery goods, as woollens, silks, ribbons, etc.

Habilitate, ha-bil'i-tät, vi. To qualify.

Habit, ha'bit, n. State of body, natural or acquired; mode of growth of a plant; aptitude acquired by practice; custom; manner; dress; outer dress worn by ladies on horseback.—vt. To dress; to clothe; to array.

Habitat, ha'bit-at, n. The natural abode or locality of a plant or animal.

Habitation, ha-bit-ä'shon, n. Occupancy; abode; residence.

Habitual, ha-bit'ū-al, a. Formed or acquired by habit; customary; usual.

Habituate, ha-bit'ū-āt, vt. (habituating, habituated). To train to a habit; to make familiar by frequent use; to inure.

Habitué, a-bé-tu-ā, n. A habitual frequenter of any place.

Hack, hak, n. A notch; cut; kick at football; a horse kept for hire; a worn-out horse; a literary drudge; frame for drying fish, etc.; rack for cattle.—vt. To cut irregularly; to notch; to mangle; to let out for hire.—a. Hired; much used or worn.

, n. A rude two-wheeled cart of India drawn by oxen.

Hacking, hak'ing, p.a. Short and interrupted; as, a *hacking* cough.

Hackle, hak'l, n. A comb for dressing flax; raw silk; any flimsy substance unspun; a long pointed feather; a fly for angling.—vt. (hackling, hackled). To comb (flax or hemp).

Hackneyed, hak'nid, p.a. Much used; trite.

Hades, hä'dēz, n. The abode of the dead; state of departed souls.

Haft, haft, n. A handle; that part of an instrument which is taken into the hand.—vt. To set in a haft.

Hag, hag, n. An ugly old woman; a witch; an eel-shaped fish that eats into other fishes.

Haggard, hag'ärd, a. Wild; intractable; having the face worn and pale; gaunt.—n. An untrained or refractory hawk.

Haggle, hag'l, vt. (haggling, haggled). To cut into small pieces; to mangle.—vi. To be difficult in bargaining; to stick at small matters; to chaffer.

Hail, hāl, n. Frozen drops of rain; a wish of health; a call.—vi. To pour down hail; to have as one's residence, or belong to (with *from*).—vt. To pour down in the manner of hail; to salute; to call to; to designate as.—interj. A salutation expressive of well-wishing.

Hailstone, hāl'stōn, n. A single pellet of hail falling from a cloud.

Hair, här, n. A small filament issuing from the skin of an animal; the mass of filaments growing from the skin of an animal; anything similar; a very small distance.

Hair-breadth, Hair's-breadth, här'bredth, härz'bredth, n. The diameter of a hair; a very small distance.—a. Of the breadth of a hair; very narrow.

Hair-splitting, här'split-ing, n. The making minute distinctions in reasoning.

Hairy, här'i, a. Overgrown with hair; consisting of hair; resembling hair.

Halcyon, hal'si-on, n. The kingfisher, fabled to have the power of producing calm weather during the period of incubation.—a. Calm; peaceful.

Hale, hāl, a. Sound; healthy; robust.—n. A violent pull.—vt. (haling, haled). To take, pull, or drag by force.

Half, häf, n.; pl. **Halves,** hävz. One part of a thing divided into two equal parts.—a. Consisting of a half.—adv. In part, or in an equal part or degree.

Half-back, häf-bak, n. Player in football or hockey who plays between the forwards and the backs.

Half-brother, häf'bruTH-ér, n. A brother by one parent, but not by both.

Half-hearted, häf-härt'ed, a. Far from enthusiastic; lukewarm.

Half-sister, häf'sis-tér, n. A sister by one parent, but not by both.

Half-witted, häf-wit'ed, a. Weak in intellect.

Hall, hal, n. A large room, especially a large public room; a large room at the entrance of a house; a manor-house; the name of certain colleges at Oxford and Cambridge.

Halleluiah, Hallelujah, hal-lē-lu'ya, n. and *interj.* A word used in sacred songs of praise, signifying *praise ye Jehovah.*

Hall-mark, hal'märk, n. The official stamp affixed to articles of gold and silver, as a mark of their legal quality.

Halloo, ha-lö', interj. and n. An exclamation to invite attention; hunting cry to a dog.—vi. (hallooing, hallooed). To cry out.—vt. To encourage with shouts; to call or shout to.

Hallow, hal'ō, vt. To make holy; to set apart for religious use; to treat as sacred.

Hallow-e'en, Hallow-even, hal'ō-ēn, hal'ō-ē-vn, n. The eve or vigil of All-Hallows' or All-Saints' Day.

Hallucination, hal-lū'si-nā''shon, n. A mistaken notion; mere dream or fancy; morbid condition in which objects are believed to be seen and sensations experienced; object or sensation thus erroneously perceived.

Halo, hä'lō, n. A luminous ring round the sun or moon; any circle of light, as the glory round the head of saints; an ideal glory investing an object.—vi. To form itself into a halo.—vt. To surround with a halo.

Halt, halt, vi. To limp; to be lame; to hesitate; to cease marching.—vt. To stop; to cause to cease marching.—a. Lame; limping.—n. A limp; a stopping; stoppage on march.

Halter, hal'tér, n. A rope or strap and headstall for leading or confining a horse; a rope for hanging.—vt. To put a halter on.

Halve, häv, vt. (halving, halved). To divide into two equal parts.

Ham, ham, n. The hind part of the knee; the back of the thigh; the thigh of an animal, particularly of a hog, salted and dried in smoke.

Hamlet, ham'let, n. A small village.

Hammer, ham'ér, n. An instrument for driving nails, beating metals, and the like.—vt. To beat or forge with a hammer; to contrive by intellectual labor.—vi. To work with a hammer; to labor in contrivance.

Hammock, ham'ok, n. A kind of hanging bed.

Hamper, ham'pér, n. A large basket for conveying things to market, etc.; something that encumbers; a clog.—vt. To put into a hamper; to hinder or impede; to embarrass.

Hamstring, ham'string, n. One of the tendons of the ham.—vt. (pp. hamstrung or hamstringed). To cut the tendons of the ham, and thus to lame or disable.

Hand, hand, n. The extremity of the arm, consisting of the palm and fingers; a measure of four inches; side or direction; skill; manner of acting; power; cards held at a game; a game; an index; a male or female in relation to an employer; a person with some special faculty; style of penmanship.—vt. To give with the hand; to lead with the hand; to conduct; to handle.—a. Belonging to, or used by the hand.

Handcuff, hand'kuf, n. A fetter for the hands or wrists.—vt. To manacle with handcuffs.

Handful, hand'ful, n. As much as the hand will grasp or hold; a small quantity or number.

Handicap, hand'i-kap, n. In racing, games, etc., an allowance to bring superior competitors to an equality with the others; a race or contest so arranged.—*vt.* To put a handicap on; to equalize by a handicap.

Handicraft, hand'i-kraft, *n.* Work performed by the hand; manual occupation.

Handiwork, hand'i-werk, *n.* Product of manual labor; work or deed of any person.

Handkerchief, hand'ker-chif, *n.* A cloth carried about the person for wiping the mouth, nose, etc.; a cloth worn about the neck.

Handle, hand'dl, *vt.* (handling, handled). To feel, use, or hold with the hand; to discuss; to deal with; to treat or use well or ill.—*n.* That part of an instrument, etc., held in the hand; instrument for effecting a purpose.

Handrail, hand'rāl, *n.* A rail for the hand, supported by balusters, etc., as in staircases.

Handsome, hand'sum, *a.* Well formed; having a certain share of beauty along with dignity; ample; generous.

Handwriting, hand-rīt'ing, *n.* The writing peculiar to each person; any writing.

Hang, hang, *vt.* (pret. and pp. hung and hanged). To suspend; to furnish with anything suspended; to cause to droop; to fit so as to allow of free motion; to put to death by suspending by the neck.—*vi.* To be suspended; to dangle; to adhere; to linger, to lean, to have a steep declivity; to be executed.

Hangar, hang'ar, *n.* A shed for housing airplanes.

Hanging, hang'ing, *n.* Act of suspending; death by the halter; *pl.* linings for rooms, of tapestry, paper, etc.

Hank, hangk, *n.* A skein of silk, yarn, etc.; a coil.—*vt.* To form into hanks.

Hanker, hang'ker, *vi.* To desire eagerly; to think of something longingly (with *after*).

Haphazard, hap-ha'zerd, *n.* Chance; accident.

Hapless, hap'les, *a.* Unlucky; unhappy.

Happen, hap'n, *vi.* To come by chance; to occur.

Happiness, hap'i-nes, *n.* State of being happy; enjoyment of pleasure; good luck.

Happy, hap'i, *a.* Being in the enjoyment of agreeable sensations from the possession of good; fortunate; propitious; well suited; apt.

Harangue, ha-rang', *n.* A noisy or pompous address; a declamatory public address; a tirade.—*vi.* (haranguing, harangued). To make a harangue.—*vt.* To address by a harangue.

Harass, ha'ras, *vt.* To vex; to tire with labor; to fatigue with importunity.

Harbinger, här'bin-jer, *n.* A forerunner; that which precedes and gives notice of something else.—*vt.* To precede as harbinger.

Harbor, här'ber, *n.* A shelter; a haven for ships; an asylum.—*vt.* To shelter; to entertain in the mind.—*vi.* To take shelter; to lodge or abide for a time.

Hard, härd, *a.* Not easily penetrated or separated; firm; difficult to understand; arduous; unfeeling; severe; unjust; harsh; stiff; grasping; applied to certain sounds, as sibilants contrasted with gutturals: applied to water not suitable for washing, from holding minerals.—*adv.* Close; diligently; with difficulty; fast; copiously; with force.

Harden, härd'n, *vt.* To make hard or more hard; to confirm in effrontery, obstinacy, wickedness, etc.; to make unfeeling; to inure; to render less liable to injury by exposure or use.—*vi.* To become hard or more hard; to become unfeeling; to become inured.

Hardihood, härd'i-hud, *n.* Quality of being hardy; boldness; intrepidity; audacity; effrontery.

Hardness, härd'nes, *n.* State or quality of being hard in all its senses; firmness; difficulty; obduracy; rigor; niggardliness, etc.

Hardship, härd'ship, *n.* Privation; affliction; oppression; injustice; grievance.

Hardware, härd'wār, *n.* Wares made of iron or other metal, as pots, knives, etc.

Hardy, härd'i, *a.* Bold; intrepid; full of assurance;

inured to fatigue; capable of bearing exposure.

Harelip, här'lip, *n.* A perpendicular division of one or both lips, but commonly the upper one, like that of a hare.

Harem, hā'rem, *n.* The apartments of the female members of a Mohammedan family; the occupants.

Haricot, ha'ri-kō, *n.* A ragout of meat and roots; the kidney-bean or French bean.

Hark, härk, *vi.* To listen; to lend the ear.

Harlequin, här'le-kwin, *n.* A performer in a pantomime, masked, dressed in tight spangled clothes, and armed with a magic wand; a buffoon in general.

Harlot, här'lot, *n.* A prostitute.

Harm, härm, *n.* Injury; hurt; evil.—*vt.* To hurt; to damage; to impair.

Harmless, härm'les, *a.* Free from harm; not causing harm; inoffensive; uninjured.

Harmonic, Harmonical, här-mon'ik, här-mon'ik-al, *a.* Pertaining to harmony; concordant; musical.—**Harmonic,** här-mon'ik, *n.* A less distinct tone accompanying a principal tone.

Harmonica, här-mon'i-ka, *n.* A musical toy played by striking rods or plates of glass or metal with small hammers.

Harmonics, här-mon'iks, *n.* The doctrine of harmony or of musical sounds.

Harmonious, här-mō'ni-us, *a.* Having harmony; having the parts adapted to each other; concordant; friendly.

Harmonize, här'mon-iz, *vi.* To be in harmony; to agree in sound or sense; to be in friendship.—*vt.* To bring into harmony; to set accompanying parts to.

Harmony, här'mo-ni, *n.* The just adaptation of parts to each other; musical concord; agreement; peace and friendship.

Harness, här'nes, *n.* Armor; furniture of a carriage or draft horse.—*vt.* To dress in armor; to put harness on.

Harp, härp, *n.* A stringed musical instrument of triangular form played with the fingers.—*vi.* To play on the harp; to dwell on tediously.

Harpoon, här-pön', *n.* A spear or javelin, used to strike whales, etc.—*vt.* To strike, catch, or kill with a harpoon.

Harpy, här'pi, *n.* A fabulous winged monster with the face of a woman; any rapacious animal; an extortioner.

Harridan, ha'ri-dan, *n.* A hag; an odious old woman; a vixenish woman; a trollop.

Harrow, ha'rō, *n.* A frame set with spikes, to prepare plowed land for seed or to cover the seed.—*vt.* To draw a harrow over; to lacerate; to torment.

Harrowing, ha'rō-ing, *p.a.* Causing acute distress to the mind.

Harry, ha'ri, *vt.* (harrying, harried). To pillage; to plunder; to ravage.

Harsh, härsh, *a.* Grating to the touch, taste, or ear; jarring; rough; severe.

Hart, härt, *n.* A stag or male of the red-deer.

Harum-scarum, hā'rum-skā'rum, *a.* Harebrained; unsettled; giddy; rash.

Harvest, här'vest, *n.* The season of gathering a crop, especially corn; the crop gathered; the product of labor; fruit or fruits; effects; consequences.—*vt.* To reap or gather.

Hash, hash, *vt.* To hack; to chop; to mince and mix.—*n.* That which is chopped; cooked meat chopped up and served again; a repetition; bungle.

Hashish, hash'ēsh, *n.* Bhang.

Hasp, hasp, *n.* A clasp that passes over a staple to be fastened by a padlock.—*vt.* To fasten with a hasp.

Hassock, has'ok, *n.* A thick mat or cushion used for kneeling on, etc.

Haste, hāst, *n.* Speed; hurry; sudden excitement of passion; precipitance.—*vt.* (hasting, hasted). To drive or urge forward; to hurry.—*vi.* To move with celerity; to be speedy.

Hasten, hås'n, *vt.* and *i.* To haste.

Hat, hat, *n.* A covering for the head.

Hatch, hach, *vt.* To produce from eggs; to contrive; to shade by crossing lines in drawing, etc.—*vi.* To produce young; to bring the young to maturity.—*n.* A brood; act of exclusion from the egg; frame of cross-bars over the opening in a ship's deck; the opening itself; hatchway; trap-door.

Hatchet, hach'et, *n.* A small axe with a short handle, used with one hand.

Hatchway, hach'wā, *n.* An opening in a ship's deck for communication with the interior.

Hate, hāt, *vt.* (hating, hated). To detest; to loathe; to abhor.—*n.* Great dislike; hatred.

Hateful, hāt'ful, *a.* Exciting hate; odious; loathsome; malignant.

Hatred, hāt'red, *n.* Great dislike or aversion; ill-will; rancor; abhorrence.

Haughty, hat'i, *a.* Proud and disdainful; lofty and arrogant.

Haul, hal, *vt.* To pull or draw with force; to drag; to compel to go.—*n.* A violent pull; draught of fish in a net; that which is taken or gained at once.

Haunch, hansh, *n.* The hip; the thigh; part of an arch between the springing and the crown; the flank.

Haunt, hant, *vt.* To frequent; to resort to often; to appear in or about, as a specter.—*vi.* To be much about; to visit often.—*n.* A place much frequented; a favorite resort.

Hauteur, ō-tér', *n.* Haughty manner or spirit; pride.

Have, hav, *vt.* (having, had). To possess; to accept; to enjoy; to hold in opinion; to be under necessity, or impelled by duty; to procure; to bring forth.

Haven, hā'vn, *n.* A harbor; port; shelter.

Haversack, hav'ér-sak, *n.* A soldier's bag for provisions on the march.

Having, hav'ing, *n.* What one has; possession; goods.

Havoc, hav'ok, *n.* Devastation; wide and general destruction; slaughter.

Hawk, hak, *n.* A rapacious bird of the falcon family.—*vi.* To catch birds by means of hawks; to practice falconry; to take prey on the wing; to force up phlegm with noise.—*vt.* To carry about for sale from place to place.

Hawser, ha'sér, *n.* A small cable.

Hawthorn, ha'thorn, *n.* The hedge-thorn; the white-thorn, much used for hedges.

Hay, hā, *n.* Grass cut and dried for fodder.—*vt.* To make into hay.

Hazard, ha'zérd, *n.* A game at dice, etc.; risk; venture; chance; fortuitous event.—*vt.* To risk; to put in danger of loss or injury.

Haze, hāz, *n.* Vapor which renders the air thick, though not so damp as in foggy weather; dimness; mental fog.

Hazel, hā'zl, *n.* A small tree of the oak family that bears edible nuts.—*a.* Pertaining to the hazel; of a light-brown color.

Hazy, hāz'i, *a.* Thick with haze; mentally obscure or confused.

He, hē, *pron.* of the third person, nominative. A substitute for the third person masculine, representing the man or male named before; prefixed to names of animals to specify the male.

Head, hed, *n.* The anterior part of animals; uppermost part of the human body; seat of the brain; etc.; intellect; an individual; a chief; first place; top; chief part; principal source; crisis; height; promontory; division of discourse; headway.—*vt.* To form a head to; to behead; to lead; to go in front of in order to stop; to oppose.—*vi.* To form a head; to be directed, as a ship.

Headache, hed'āk, *n.* Pain in the head.

Heading, hed'ing, *n.* That which stands at the head; title of a section; passage excavated in the line of an intended tunnel.

Headland, hed'land, *n.* A cape; a promontory; a ridge or strip of unplowed land at the end of furrows.

Headlong, hed'long, *adv.* With the head foremost; precipitately.—*a.* Steep; precipitous; precipitate.

Headmost, hed'mōst, *a.* Most advanced.

Headquarters, hed-kwar'térz, *n.pl.* The quarters of a commander; place where one chiefly resides or carries on business.

Head-stone, hed'stön, *n.* The chief or corner stone; stone at the head of a grave.

Headstrong, hed'strong, *a.* Resolute; obstinate; violent.

Headway, hed'wā, *n.* Progress made by a ship in motion; progress or success.

Head-wind, hed'wind, *n.* A wind that blows right against a ship, etc.

Heady, hed'i, *a.* Rash; hasty; headstrong; intoxicating.

Heal, hēl, *vi.* To make hale or sound; to cure; to reconcile.—*vt.* To grow whole or sound; to recover.

Health, helth, *n.* A sound state of body or mind; freedom from disease; bodily conditions; wish of health and happiness (used in drinking).

Healthy, helth'i, *a.* Being in health; sound; hale; salubrious; wholesome.

Heap, hēp, *n.* A mass; large quantity; pile.—*vt.* To raise in a heap; to amass; to pile.

Hear, hēr, *vt.* (hearing, heard). To perceive by the ear; to give audience to; to listen; to obey; to regard; to attend favorably; to try in a court of law; to learn; to approve.—*vi.* To enjoy the faculty of perceiving sound; to listen; to be told; to receive by report.

Hearing, hēr'ing, *n.* The faculty or sense by which sound is perceived; audience; opportunity to be heard; judicial trial; reach of the ear.

Hearsay, hēr'sā, *n.* Report; rumor.—*a.* Given at second hand.

Hearse, hérs, *n.* A carriage for conveying the dead to the grave; bier.

Heart, härt, *n.* The primary organ of the blood's motion; the inner, vital, or most essential part; seat of the affections, will, etc.; disposition of mind; conscience; courage; spirit; what represents a heart; one of a suit of playing cards marked with such a figure.

Heartache, härt'āk, *n.* Sorrow; anguish.

Heartburn, härt'bérn, *n.* A burning sensation in the stomach from indigestion.

bern-ing, *n.* Discontent; ssecret enmity.

Hearten, härt'n, *vt.* To give heart or courage to; to encourage; to animate.

Heartfelt, härt'felt, *a.* Deeply felt; deeply affecting, either as joy or sorrow.

Hearth, härth, *n.* The part of a floor on which a fire is made; the house and its inmates; the fireside.

Heartless, härt'les, *a.* Without heart; spiritless; without feeling or affection.

Heart-rending, härt'rend-ing, *a.* Overpowering with anguish; deeply afflictive.

Hearty, härt'i, *a.* Warm; cordial; healthy; having a keen appetite; large to satisfaction.

Heat, hēt, *n.* The sensation produced by bodies that are hot; hot air; hot weather; high temperature; degree of temperature; a single effort; a course at a race; animal excitement; rage; ardor; animation in thought or discourse; fermentation.—*vt.* To make hot; to warm with passion or desire; to rouse into action.—*vi.* To grow warm or hot.

Heath, hēth, *n.* A small flowering shrub growing on waste or wild places; a place overgrown with heath; waste tract.

Heathen, hē'THen, *n.* A pagan; one who worships idols; a barbarous person.—*a.* Gentile; pagan.

Heathenism, hē'THen-izm, *n.* Paganism; idolatry.

Heather, heTH'ér, *n.* Common heath, a low shrub with clusters of rose-colored flowers.

Heave, hēv, *vt.* (heaving, pret. and pp. heaved,

hove). To lift; to move upward; to cause to swell; to raise or force from the breast, as a groan; to throw; to turn in some direction.—*vi.* To rise; to swell, as the sea; to pant; to retch; *to heave in sight,* to appear, as a ship.—*n.* A rising or swell; an effort upward; a throw; a swelling, as of the breast.

Heaven, hev'n, *n.* The blue expanse surrounding the earth; the sky; the abode of God and of his angels; God or Providence; supreme felicity; bliss.

Heavenly, hev'n-li, *a.* Pertaining to heaven; divine; inhabiting heaven; enchanting.—*adv.* In a heavenly manner.

Heavy, he'vi, *a.* That is heaved or lifted with difficulty; weighty; sad; grievous; burdensome; drowsy; wearisome; not easily digested; soft and miry; difficult; large in amount; dense; abundant; forcible.

Hebraic, Hebraical, hē-brā'ik, hē-brā'ik-al, *a.* Pertaining to the Hebrews or their language; Jewish.

Hebrew, hē'brō, *n.* An Israelite; a Jew; the Hebrew language.—*a.* Pertaining to the Hebrews.

Heckle, hek'l, *n.* A sort of comb for flax or hemp; a hackle or hatchel.—*vt.* (heckling, heckled). To dress with a heckle; to question or catechize severely.

Hector, hek'tėr, *n.* A bully.—*vt.* To bully; to treat with insolence.—*vi.* To play the bully.

Hedge, hej, *n.* A fence consisting of thorns or shrubs.—*vt.* (hedging, hedged). To enclose with a hedge; to surround or restrain.—*vi.* To hide oneself; to bet on both sides; to skulk; to dodge or trim.—*a.* Pertaining to a hedge; mean; rustic.

Hedonism, hē'don-izm, *n.* The doctrine that the chief good of man lies in pursuit of pleasure.

Hedonist, hē'don-ist, *n.* One who professes hedonism.

Heed, hēd, *vt.* To look to or after; to regard with care; to notice.—*vi.* To mind; to consider.—*n.* Care; attention; regard.

Heedless, hēd'les, *a.* Inattentive; careless; remiss; negligent.

Heel, hēl, *n.* The hind part of the foot; a cant.—*vt.* To add a heel to; to furnish with heels, as shoes.—*vi.* To cant over from a vertical position.

Heft, heft, *n.* The act of heaving; effort; weight; gist.

Hegelian, he-gē'li-an, *a.* Pertaining to Hegel (hā'gl) or his system of philosophy.—*n.* A follower of Hegel.

Hegemony, hē-jem'o-ni (or with g hard), *n.* Leadership; preponderance of one state among others.

Hegira, hej'i-ra, *n.* The flight of Mohammed from Mecca (July 16th, 622); the beginning of the Mohammedan era.

Heifer, hef'ėr, *n.* A young cow.

Height, hit, *n.* The condition of being high; distance of anything above its base or above the earth; eminence; any elevated ground; extent, degree; utmost degree.

Heighten, hit'n, *vt.* To raise higher; to improve; to increase.

Heinous, hān'us, *a.* Hateful; characterized by great wickedness; flagrant.

Heir, ār, *n.* One who succeeds or is to succeed another in the possession of property.

Heirloom, ār'lōm, *n.* Any personal chattel which, by law, descends to the heir or has belonged to a family for a long time.

Heliacal, hē-li'ak-al, *a.* Coincident with the rising or setting of the sun.

Helicopter, hel-i-kop'tėr, hel'i-kop-tėr, *n.* A type of aircraft supported in flight by a propeller rotating about a vertical axis. It can rise and descend vertically.

Heliocentric, hē'li-o-sen''trik, *a.* Relating to the sun as a center; appearing as if seen from the sun's center.

Heliograph, Heliostat, hē'li-o-graf, hē'li-o-stat, *n.* A sun telegraph; apparatus for reflecting the sun's light to a distance.

Helium, hē'li-um, *n.* An inert gas present in the air in small quantities, the lightest element next to hydrogen.

Helix, hē'liks, *n.*; pl. **Helices,** hel'i-sēz. A spiral line, as of wire in a coil; something that is spiral.

Hell, hel, *n.* The place or state of punishment for the wicked after death; the abode of the devil and his angels; the infernal powers; a gambling-house.

Hellenic, hel-len'ik or hel-lēn'ik, *a.* Pertaining to the inhabitants of Greece; Greek.

Hellenism, hel'len-izm, *n.* A Greek idiom; type of character peculiar to the Greeks.

Helm, helm, *n.* A helmet; instrument by which a ship is steered; the rudder, tiller, etc.; place or post of management.—*vt.* To cover or furnish with a helmet.

Helmet, hel'met, *n.* A covering for the head in war; head armor; a head-piece.

Help, help, *vt.* To lend strength or means towards effecting a purpose; to aid; to relieve; to remedy; to prevent; to avoid.—*vi.* To lend aid.—*n.* Aid; remedy; an assistant.

Helpful, help'ful, *a.* That gives help, aid, or assistance; useful.

Helpless, help'les, *a.* Without help in oneself; needing help; affording no help; beyond help.

Helpmate, help'māt, *n.* A companion who helps; an assistant; a wife.

Helter-skelter, hel'tėr-skel'tėr, *adv.* A word suggestive of hurry and confusion.

Helvetian, Helvetic, hel-vē'shan, hel-vet'ik, *a.* Of or pertaining to Switzerland.

Hem, hem, *n.* The border of a garment, doubled and sewed to strengthen it; edge; border.—*interj.* and *n.* A sort of half cough, suggested by some feeling.—*vt.* (hemming, hemmed). To form a hem or border on; to enclose and confine; to make the sound expressed by the word *hem.*

Hematite, he'ma-tit, *n.* A name of two ores of iron, red hematite and brown hematite.

Hemisphere, he'mi-sfėr, *n.* One half of a sphere; half the celestial or terrestrial sphere.

Hemlock, hem'lok, *n.* An umbelliferous plant whose leaves and root are poisonous.

Hemorrhage, he'mor-āj, *n.* A bursting forth of blood; any discharge of blood from the blood-vessels.

Hemorrhoids, he'mor-oidz, *n.pl.* Piles.

Hemp, hemp, *n.* An annual herbaceous plant of the nettle family, the fiber of which, also called hemp, is made into sail-cloth, ropes, etc.

Hen, hen, *n.* The female of the domestic fowl; any female bird.

Henpeck, hen'pek, *vt.* To rule: said of a wife who has the upper hand of her husband.

Hepatic, hē-pat'ik, *a.* Pertaining to the liver.

Heptagon, hep'ta-gon, *n.* A plane figure having seven angles and seven sides.

Heptateuch, hep'ta-tūk, *n.* The first seven books of the Old Testament.

Her, hėr, *pron.* The possessive and objective case of *she:* when the possessive is used without a noun it becomes *hers:*

Herald, he'rald, *n.* An officer whose business was to proclaim war or peace, bear messages, etc.; a forerunner; an officer who regulates matters relating to public ceremonies; one who records and blazons arms, etc.—*vt.* To introduce, as by a herald; to proclaim.

Herb, hėrb, *n.* Any plant with a succulent stem which dies to the root every year.

Herbalist, hėrb'al ist, *n.* One skilled in herbs, or who makes collections of them.

Herbarium, hėr-bā'ri-um, *n.*; pl. **-iums** and **-ia.** A collection of herbs or plants dried and preserved.

Herbivorous, hėrb-iv'or-us, *a.* Eating herbs; subsisting on herbaceous plants.

Herculean, hėr-kū'lē-an, *a.* Belonging to or resembling Hercules; of extraordinary strength;

H

very great or difficult.

Herd, herd, *n*. A number of animals feeding or driven together; flock; crowd; rabble; a keeper of cattle or sheep.—*vi*. and *t*. To unite into a herd, as beasts; to congregate.

Herdsman, herdz'man, *n*. One employed in tending herds of cattle.

Here, hēr, *adv*. In this place; at this point; hither.

Hereafter, hēr-af'tér, *adv*. After this time; in a future state.—*n*. The time after this; a future state.

Hereditary, he-red'it-a-ri, *a*. Relating to an inheritance; descending to an heir; that is or may be transmitted from a parent to a child.

Heredity, he-red'i-ti, *n*. Hereditary transmission of qualities; the doctrine that the offspring inherits parental characteristics.

Heresy, he're-si, *n*. A fundamental error in religion; error in doctrine; heterodoxy.

Heretic, he're-tik, *n*. One guilty of heresy.

Heritage, he'rit-āj, *n*. Inheritance; lot or portion by birth.

Hermaphrodite, her-maf'rod-it, *n*. An animal in which the characteristics of both sexes are really or apparently combined; a flower that contains both the stamen and the pistil.—*a*. Including or being of both sexes.

Hermeneutics, her-mē-nū'tiks, *n*. The science of interpretation, particularly of interpreting the Scriptures.

Hermetic, Hermetical, her-met'ik, her-met'ik-al, *a*. Pertaining to alchemy or to occult science; effected by fusing together the edges of the aperture, as of a bottle; perfectly close and airtight.

Hermit, her'mit, *n*. One who lives in solitude; a recluse.

Hernia, her'ni-a, *n*. A protrusion of some organ of the abdomen through an interstice; a rupture.

Hero, hē'rō, *n*.; pl. **Heroes,** hē'rōz. A man of distinguished valor; the person who has the principal share in some exploit, or in a play, novel, etc.

Heroic, he-rō'ik, *a*. Pertaining to a hero or heroes; intrepid and noble; reciting achievements of heroes; epic.

Heroin, her'o-in, *n*. A narcotic drug derived from morphia.

Heroine, he'rō-in, *n*. A female hero.

Heroism, he'rō-izm, *n*. The qualities of a hero; intrepidity; magnanimity.

Heron, her'un, *n*. A wading bird with a long bill, long slender legs and neck.

Herpes, her'pez, *n*. A skin disease characterized by eruption or inflamed vesicles.

Herpetology, her-pe-tol'o-ji, *n*. The natural history of reptiles.

Herring, he'ring, *n*. One of those small food fishes which go in shoals in northern seas.

Herring-bone, he'ring-bōn, *a*. Applied to masonry, sewing, etc., which bears resemblance to the backbone of a herring.

Hesitate, he'zi-tāt, *vi*. (hesitating, hesitated). To pause respecting decision or action; to stop in speaking; to stammer.

Hesitation, he-zi-tā'shon, *n*. Act of hesitating; doubt; a stopping in speech.

Heteroclite, he'te-rō-klīt, *n*. A word irregular in declension or conjugation; something abnormal or anomalous.

Heterodox, he'te-rō-doks, *a*. Holding opinions different from those established or prevalent; not orthodox; heretical.

Heterogeneous, he'te-rō-jē''nē-us, *a*. Of a different kind or nature; composed of dissimilar parts.

Hew, hū, *vt*. (pret. hewed, pp. hewed or hewn). To cut with an axe, etc.; to cut; to hack; to make smooth, as stone; to shape.

Hexagon, heks'a-gon, *n*. A plane figure of six angles and six sides.

Hexahedron, heks-a-hē'dron, *n*. A regular solid body of six sides; a cube.

Hexameter, heks-am'et-ér, *n*. A verse of six metrical feet.—*a*. Having six metrical feet.

Heyday, hā'dā, *interj*. An exclamation of cheerfulness.—*n*. The bloom or height; the wildness or frolicsome period of youth.

Hiatus, hī-ā'tus, *n*.; pl. **Hiatuses.** A gap; break; lacuna; meeting of vowel sounds.

Hibernal, hī-bér'nal, *a*. Belonging to winter; wintry.

Hibernate, hī-bér'nāt, *vt*. To pass the winter in sleep or seclusion; to winter.

Hibernian, hī-bér'ni-an, *a*. Pertaining to Ireland; Irish.—*n*. A native of Ireland.

Hiccup, Hiccough, hik'up, *n*. A spasmodic affection of the diaphragm and glottis; a convulsive catch of the respiratory muscles.—*vt*. and *i*. To have a hiccup; to utter with hiccups.

Hickory, hik'ō-ri, *n*. An American tree of the walnut family, valuable for timber.

Hide, hīd, *vt*. (hiding, pret. hid, pp. hid, hidden). To withhold or withdraw from sight or knowledge; to screen; to secrete.—*vi*. To be or to lie concealed; to keep oneself out of view.—*n*. The skin of an animal, either raw or dressed; the human skin; an old measure of land of about 80 acres.

Hide-bound, hīd'bound, *a*. Having the hide abnormally tight; having the bark so close or firm as to hinder growth.

Hideous, hid'ē-us, *a*. Frightful; shocking to the eye or ear.

Hiding, hīd'ing, *n*. Concealment; state of being hidden.

Hiemation, hī-e-mā''shon, *n*. The spending or passing of winter.

Hierarch, hī-ér-ärk, *n*. One who has authority in sacred things.

Hierarchy, hī'ér-är-ki, *n*. Authority in sacred things; clergy in whom is confided the direction of sacred things; ecclesiastical or clerical rule.

Hieroglyph, Hieroglyphic, hī'ér-o-glif, hī'ér-o-glif''ik, *n*. A figure of an animal, plant, etc., implying a word, idea, or sound, such as those in use among the ancient Egyptians; a character difficult to decipher.

Hierology, hī'ér-ol'o-ji, *n*. Sacred lore; knowledge of hieroglyphics or sacred writing.

High, hī, *a*. Having a great extent from base to summit; elevated; lofty; far above the earth; elevated in rank or office; dignified; proud; violent; solemn; strong; vivid; dear; remote; sharp; far advanced; committed against the sovereign or state; tending towards putrefaction; strong-scented.—*adv*. In a high manner; to a great altitude or degree; eminently; greatly.

Highbrow, hī'brou, *n*. A person who pretends to be of a superior culture to the majority.

High-handed, hī'hand-ed, *a*. Violent; overbearing; oppressive.

Highland, hī'land, *n*. A mountainous region: often in pl.—*a*. Pertaining to mountainous regions, or to the Highlands of Scotland.

High-minded, hī'mind-ed, *a*. Proud; arrogant; having honorable pride.

High-pressure, hī'prē-shúr, *a*. Having or involving a pressure exceeding that of the atmosphere, or having a pressure greater than 50 lbs. to the square inch.

Highway, hī'wā, *n*. A public road; direct course; train of action.

Hike, hīk, *vi*. To tramp; to go on a long or fairly long walking expedition.

Hilarity, hi-la'ri-ti, *n*. Cheerfulness; merriment; good humor; jollity.

Hill, hil, *n*. A natural elevation of less size than a mountain; an eminence.

Hilt, hilt, *n*. A handle, particularly of a sword.

Himself, him-self', *pron*. The emphatic and reflexive form of *he* and *him*.

Hind, hīnd, *n*. The female of the red-deer or stag; a farm servant; a rustic.—*a*. Backward; back; pertaining to the backward part.

Hinder, hīnd'ér, *a*. Posterior; in the rear; latter;

after.

Hinder, hin'dèr, vt. To prevent from moving or acting; to obstruct; to thwart; to check.—vi. To interpose obstacles or impediments.

Hindrance, hin'drans, n. Act of hindering; impediment; obstruction.

Hinge, hinj, n. The hook or joint on which a door, etc., hangs and turns; that on which anything depends or turns.—vt. (hinging, hinged). To furnish with hinges.—vi. To stand or turn, as on a hinge.

Hinny, hin'i, n. A mule; the produce of a stallion and a she-ass.

Hint, hint, vt. To suggest indirectly; to insinuate.—vi. To make an indirect allusion. n. A distant allusion; a suggestion.

Hip, hip, n. The fleshy projecting part of the thigh; the haunch; the joint of the thigh; the fruit of the dog-rose or wild brier.—interj. Exclamation expressive of a call to anyone. Hip, hip, hurrah! the signal to cheer.

Hippodrome, hip'ō-drōm, n. A racecourse for horses and chariots; a circus.

Hippopotamus, hip-ō-pot'a-mus, n.; pl. -amuses or -ami. A large, hoofed pachydermatous animal, inhabiting the Nile and other rivers in Africa.

Hip-shot, hip'shot, a. Having the hip dislocated.

Hircine, hèr'sīn, a. Pertaining to or resembling a goat.

Hire, hīr, vt. (hiring, hired). To procure for temporary use, at a certain price; to engage in service for a stipulated reward; to let; to lease (with out).—n. Price paid for temporary use of anything; recompense for personal service; wages; pay.

Hirsute, hèr-sūt', a. Hairy; shaggy.

Hiss, his, vi. To make a sound like that of the letter s, in contempt or disapprobation; to emit a similar sound; to whizz.—vt. To condemn by hissing.—n. The sound expressed by the verb.

Histology, his-tol'o-ji, n. The doctrine of animal or vegetable tissues.

Historian, his-tō'ri-an, n. A writer or compiler of history.

Historic, Historical, his-to'rik, his-to'rik-al, a. Pertaining to, connected with, contained in, or deduced from history.

History, his'to-ri, n. An account of facts, particularly respecting nations or states; that branch of knowledge which deals with past events; narration; a story; an account of existing things, as animals or plants.

Histrionics, his-tri-on'iks, n. The art of theatrical representation.

Hit, hit, vt. (hitting, hit). To strike or touch with some force; to give a blow to; not to miss; to reach; to light upon; to suit.—vi. To strike; to come in contact; to reach the intended point; to succeed.—n. A stroke; a blow; a lucky chance; happy thought or expression.

Hitch, hich, vi. To move by jerks; to be entangled, hooked, or yoked.—vt. To fasten; to hook; to raise by jerks.—n. A catch; act of catching, as on a hook, etc.; knot or noose in a rope; a jerk; a temporary obstruction.

Hither, hiᴛʜ'èr, adv. To this place.—a. Nearer; toward the person speaking.

Hive, hīv, n. A box or receptacle for honey-bees; the bees inhabiting a hive; a place swarming with busy occupants.—vt. (hiving, hived). To collect into a hive; to lay up in store.—vi. To take shelter together; to reside in a collective body.

Hoar, hōr, a. White or whitish; hoary.—vi. To become moldy or musty.

Hoard, hōrd, n. A store, stock, or large quantity of anything; a hidden stock.—vt. To collect; to store secretly.—vi. To form a hoard; to lay up in store.

Hoar-frost, hōr'frost, n. The white particles of frozen dew; rime.

Hoarse, hōrs, a. Having a grating voice, as when affected with a cold; discordant; rough; grating.

Hoary, hōr'i, a. White or whitish; white or gray with age.

Hoax, hōks, n. Something done for deception or mockery; a practical joke.—vt. To deceive; to play a trick upon without malice.

Hobble, hob'l, vi. (hobbling, hobbled). To walk lamely or awkwardly; to limp; to halt.—vt. To hopple.—n. An unequal, halting gait; perplexity.

Hobby, hob'i, n. A small but strong British falcon; an active, ambling nag; a hobby-horse; any favorite object or pursuit.

Hobgoblin, hob-gob'lin, n. A goblin; an imp; something that causes terror.

Hobnail, hob'nāl, n. A nail with a thick, strong head.

Hobnob, hob'nob, vi. (hobnobbing, hobnobbed). To drink familiarly; to be boon companions.

Hock, Hough, hok, n. The joint between the knee and fetlock; in man, the posterior part of the knee-joint.—vt. To hamstring.

Hockey, hok'i, n. A game at ball played with a club curved at the lower end.

Hocus-pocus, hō'kus-pō'kus, n. A juggler's trick; trickery used by conjurers.

Hod, hod, n. A kind of trough for carrying mortar and brick on the shoulder.

Hodge-podge, hoj'poj, n. A mixed mass; a medley of ingredients; a hotch-potch.

Hoe, hō, n. An instrument to cut up weeds and loosen the earth.—vt. (hoeing, hoed). To dig or clean with a hoe.—vi. To use a hoe.

Hog, hog, n. A swine; a castrated boar; a sheep of a year old; a brutal or mean fellow.—vi. To bend, as a ship's bottom.

Hogshead, hogz'hed, n. A large cask; an old measure of capacity, containing about 52½ imperial gallons.

Hoist, hoist, vt. To heave up; to lift upward by means of tackle.—n. Act of raising; apparatus for raising goods, etc.; an elevator.

Hold, hōld, vt. (pret. held, pp. held,). To have in the grasp; to keep fast; to confine; to maintain; to consider; to contain; to possess; to withhold; to continue; to celebrate.—vi. To take or keep a thing in one's grasp; to stand as a fact or truth; not to give way or part; to refrain; to adhere; to derive title (with of).—n. A grasp; something which may be seized for support; power of keeping, seizing, or directing; influence; place of confinement; stronghold; interior cavity of a ship.

Hole, hōl, n. A hollow place in any solid body, a perforation, crevice, etc.; a den; a subterfuge.—vt. (holing, holed). To make a hole or holes in; to drive into a hole.

Holiday, ho'li-dā, n. A holy or sacred day; a festival; day of exemption from labor.—a. Pertaining to a festival.

Holiness, hō'li-nes, n. State or quality of being holy; moral goodness; sanctity.—**His Holiness,** a title of the pope.

Holism, hol'izm, n. A philosophical theory according to which a fundamental feature of nature is the existence of 'wholes,' which are more than assemblages of parts, and which are always tending to become more highly developed and comprehensive.

Hollow, hol'lō, a. Containing an empty space; not solid; deep; false; deceitful.—n. A depression or excavation; a cavity.—vt. To make a hole in; to excavate.

Holly, hol'i, n. An evergreen tree or shrub, with thorny leaves and scarlet berries.

Hollyhock, hol'i-hok, n. a tall biennial plant of the mallow family.

Holocaust, hol'o-kast, n. A burnt-sacrifice, of which the whole was consumed by fire; a great slaughter.

Holograph, hol'o-graf, n. A deed or document written wholly by the person from whom it proceeds.

Holometabolic, hol'o-met-a-bol''ik, a. Applied to

insects which undergo a complete metamorphosis.

Holster, hōl'stér, n. A leathern case for a pistol.

Holy, hō'li, a. Free from sin; immaculate; consecrated; sacred.

Homage, hom'āj, n. An act of fealty on the part of a vassal to his lord; obeisance; reverential worship.

Home, hōm, n. One's own abode; the abode of one's family; residence; one' own country; an establishment affording the comforts of a home.—a. Domestic; close; severe; poignant.—adv. To one's own habitation or country; to the point; effectively.

Homely, hōm'li, a. Belonging to home; of plain features; plain; coarse.

Homeopathy, hō-mē-op'a-thi, n. A system of curing diseases by drugs (usually in very small doses) which produce in healthy persons symptoms like those of the disease.

Homeric, hō-me'rik, a. Pertaining to or like Homer or his poetry.

Home-sickness, hōm'sik-nes, n. Depression of spirits occasioned by absence from one's home or country; nostalgia.

Homespun, hōm'spun, a. Spun or wrought at home; plain; coarse; homely.

Homestead, hōm'sted, n. A house with the grounds and buildings contiguous; a home; native seat.

Homeward, hōm'wérd, adv. Toward one's habitation or country.—a. Being in the direction of home.

Homicide, ho'mi-sīd, n. Manslaughter; a person who kills another.

Homiletics, ho-mi-let'iks, n. The art of preaching.

Homily, ho'mi-li, n. A sermon; a familiar religious discourse; a serious discourse or admonition.

Homing, hōm'ing, a. Coming home: applied to birds such as the carrier-pigeons.

Hominy, hom'i-ni, n. Maize hulled or coarsely ground, prepared for food by being boiled.

Homogeneous, ho-mō-jē'nē-us, a. Of the same kind or nature; consisting of similar parts or elements.

Homogenesis, ho-mō-jen'e-sis, n. Sameness of origin; reproduction of offspring similar to their parents.

Homologate, hō-mol'o-gāt, vt. To approve; to ratify.

Homologous, hō-mol'o-gus, a. Having the same relative position, proportion, or structure; corresponding.

Homonym, ho'mō-nim, n. A word which agrees with another in sound, and perhaps in spelling, but differs in signification.

Hone, hōn, n. A stone of a fine grit, used for sharpening instruments.—vt. (honing, honed). To sharpen on a hone.

Honest, on'est, a. Free from fraud; upright; just; sincere; candid; virtuous.

Honey, hun'i, n. A sweet viscous juice collected by bees from flowers; sweetness; a word of tenderness.—vt. To sweeten.

Honey-comb, hun'i-kōm, n. The waxy structure formed by bees for honey; anything having cells like a honey-comb.

Honeymoon, hun'i-mön, n. The first month after marriage; interval spent by a newly-married pair before settling down at home.

Honeysuckle, hun'i-suk-l, n. A beautiful flowering and climbing shrub; woodbine.

Honorarium, on-ér-ā'ri-um, n. A fee for professional services.

Honorary, on'ér-a-ri, a. Relating to honor; conferring honor; possessing a title or place without performing services or without receiving a reward.

Honor, on'ér, n. Respect; esteem; testimony of esteem; dignity; good name; a nice sense of what is right; scorn of meanness; a title of respect or distinction; one of the highest trump cards; pl.

civilities paid; public marks of respect; academic and university distinction.—vt. To regard or treat with honor; to bestow honor upon; to exalt; to accept and pay when due, as a bill.

Honorable, on'ér-a-bl, a. Worthy of honor; actuated by principles of honor; conferring honor; consistent with honor; performed with marks of honor; not base; honest; fair; a title of distinction.

Hood, hud, n. A soft covering for the head; a cowl; a garment worn as part of academic dress, which indicates by its colors, material and shape the degree and University of its wearer; anything resembling a hood.—vt. To dress in a hood; to cover; to blind.

Hoodwink, hud'wingk, vt. To blind by covering the eyes of; to impose on.

Hoof, höf, n.; pl. **Hoofs,** rarely **Hooves.** The horny substance that covers the feet of certain animals, as the horse.

Hook, hök, n. A bent piece of iron or other metal for catching; that which catches; a sickle.—vt. To catch with a hook; to ensnare.—vi. To bend; to be curving.

Hookah, hö'kä, n. A tobacco-pipe with a large bowl and long pliable tube, so constructed that the smoke passes through water.

Hoop, höp, n. A band of wood or metal confining the staves of casks, tubs, etc.; a crinoline; a ring; a loud shout.—vt. To bind with hoops; to encircle.—vi. To shout; to whoop.

Hooping-cough, höp'ing-kof, n. A contagious ailment common in childhood, characterized by a convulsive cough.

Hoot, höt, vi. To shout in contempt; to cry as an owl.—vt. To utter contemptuous cries at.—n. A cry or shout in contempt.

Hop, hop, n. A leap on one leg; a spring; a bitter plant of the hemp family used to flavor malt liquors.—vi. To leap or spring on one leg; to skip; to limp; to pick hops.—vt. To impregnante with hops.

Hope, höp, n. A desire of some good, accompanied with a belief that it is attainable; trust; one in whom trust or confidence is placed; the object of hope.—vi. (hoping, hoped). To entertain hope; to trust.—vt. To desire with some expectation of attainment.

Hopeful, höp'ful, a. Full of hope; having qualities which excite hope; promising.

Hopeless, höp'les, a. Destitute of hope; desponding; promising nothing desirable.

Hopper, hop'ér, n. One who hops; a wooden trough through which grain passes into a mill; a boat to convey dredged matter.

Horal, hör'al, a. Relating to an hour.

Horary, hör'a-ri, a. Hourly; noting the hours; continuing an hour.

Horatian, ho-rä'shan, a. Relating to or resembling Horace or his poetry.

Horde, hörd, n. A tribe or race of nomads; a gang; migratory crew; rabble.—vi. (hording, horded). To live together like migratory tribes.

Horizon, ho-rī'zon, n. The circle which bounds tht part of the earth's surface visible from given point; the apparent junction of the earth and sky.

Hormones, hor'mōnz, n.pl. Products of the ductless glands, affecting other organs by way of the blood stream.

Horn, horn, n. A hard projection on the heads of certain animals; the material of such horns; wind-instrument of music; extremity of the moon; drinking-cup; powder-horn; something resembling a horn; the feeler of a snail, etc.

Hornet, horn'et, n. A large stinging species of wasp.

Horny, horn'i, a. Consisting of horn; resembling horns; hardened by labor; callous.

Horologe, ho'ro-lōj, n. A time-piece of any kind.

Horology, ho-rol'o-ji, n. The science of measuring time; art of constructing machines for measuring time, as clocks, dials.

Horoscope, hor'os-kōp, *n.* In *astrology,* a figure or scheme of the heavens from which to cast nativities and foretell events.

Horrible, hor'ri-bl, *a.* Exciting horror; dreadful; frightful; awful; hideous.

Horrid, hor'rid, *a.* That does or may excite horror; horrible; shocking.

Horrify, hor'ri-fi, *vt.* (horrifying, horrified). To strike or impress with horror.

Horror, hor'rer, *n.* A powerful feeling of fear and abhorrence; that which may excite terror; something frightful or shocking.

Horse, hors, *n.* A well-known quadruped, used for draft and carriage in war; the male animal; cavalry; a name of various things resembling or analogous to a horse.—*vt.* (horsing, horsed). To supply with a horse; to carry on the back; to bestride.

Horse-chestnut, hors'ches-nut, *n.* A flowering tree, the nuts of which have been used as food for animals.

Horseman, hors'man, *n.* A rider on horseback; a man skilled in riding; a soldier who serves on horseback.

Horse-play, hors'plā, *n.* Rough or rude practical jokes or the like; rude pranks.

Horse-power, hors'pou-ėr, *n.* The power of a horse, or its equivalent, estimated as a power which will raise 32,000 lbs. avoirdupois one foot per minute: the standard for estimating the power of a steam-engine or motor, etc.

Horseradish, hors'rad-ish, *n.* A perennial plant, having a root of a pungent taste.

Horseshoe, hors'shō, *n.* A shoe for horses, commonly of iron shaped like the letter U; anything shaped like a horse-shoe.—*a.* Having the form of a horse-shoe.

Hortatory, hort'a-to-ri, *a.* Giving exhortation or advice; encouraging.

Horticulture, hor'ti-kul-tūr, *n.* The art of cultivating gardens.

Hosanna, hō-zan'na, *n.* An exclamation of praise to God, or an invocation of blessings.

Hose, hōz, *n. sing.* or *pl.* A covering for the thighs, legs, or feet; close-fitting breeches; stockings; in these senses plural; a flexible pipe used for conveying water.

Hospice, hos'pis, *n.* A place of refuge and entertainment for travellers, as among the Alps.

Hospitable, hos'pit-a-bl, *a.* Kind to strangers and guests.

Hospital, hos'pit-al, *n.* A building for the sick, wounded, etc., or for any class of persons requiring public help.

Hospitaller, hos'pit-al-ėr, *n.* One of a religious community, whose office it was to relieve the poor, the stranger, and the sick; one of the Knights of Malta.

Host, hōst, *n.* One who entertains a stranger or guest; an innkeeper; an army; any great number or multitude; the consecrated bread in the R. Catholic sacrament of the mass.

Hostage, host'āj, *n.* A person delivered to an enemy, as a pledge to secure the performance of conditions.

Hostel, Hostelry, hos'tel, hos'tel-ri, *n.* An inn; a lodging-house.

Hostile, hos'til, *a.* Belonging to an enemy; unfriendly; antagonistic; adverse.

Hostility, hos-til'i-ti, *n.* State or quality of being hostile; state of war between nations or states; the actions of an open enemy (in *pl.*); animosity; enmity; opposition.

Hot, hot, *a.* Having sensible heat; burning; glowing, easily exasperated; vehement; eager; lustful; biting; pungent in taste.

Hot-bed, hot'bed, *n.* A bed of earth heated by fermenting substances, and covered with glass, used for early or exotic plants; a place which favors rapid growth.

Hot-blast, hot'blast, *n.* A current of heated air injected into a smelting furnace by means of a blowing-engine.

Hot-blooded, hot'blud-ed, *a.* High-spirited; irritable.

Hotel, hō-tel', *n.* A superior house for strangers or travellers; an inn; in France, a large mansion in a town.

Hot-headed, hot'hed-ed, *a.* Of ardent passions; vehement; violent; rash.

Hot-house, hot'hous, *n.* A house kept warm to shelter tender plants; a conservatory.

Hot-tempered, hot'tem-pėrd, *a.* Of a fiery wrathful temper.

Hound, hound, *n.* A dog; a dog used in the chase; a dog-fish.—*vt.* To set on in chase; to hunt; to urge on.

Hour, our, *n.* The twenty-fourth part of a day, consisting of sixty minutes; the particular time of the day; an appointed time; *pl.* certain prayers in the R. Catholic Church.

Hour-glass, our'glas, *n.* A glass for measuring time by the running of sand from one compartment to the other.

House, hous, *n.; pl.* **Houses,** hou'zez. A building or erection for the habitation or use of man; any building or edifice; a dwelling; a household; a family; a legislative body of men; audience or attendance; a commercial establishment.—*vt.* (housing, housed). To put or receive into a house; to shelter.—*vi.* To take shelter; to take up abode.

Household, hous'hōld, *n.* Those who dwell under the same roof and compose a family.—*a.* Domestic.

Housekeeper, hous'kēp-ėr, *n.* A householder; a female servant who has the chief care of the house or family.

Housel, hou'zel, *n.* The eucharist.

House-warming, hous'warm-ing, *n.* A feast on a family's entrance into a new house.

Housewife, hous'wif, *n.* The mistress of a family; a female manager of domestic affairs; a hussif (pronounced huz'if).

Housing, houz'ing, *n.* A horse-cloth; *pl.* the trappings of a horse.—*p.n.* Placing in houses; sheltering.

Hovel, ho'vel, *n.* A mean house; an open shed for cattle, etc.—*vt.* To put in a hovel.

Hover, ho'vėr, *vi.* To hang fluttering in the air; to be in doubt; to linger near.

How, hou, *adv.* In what manner; to what extent; for what reason; by what means; in what state.

However, hou-ev'ėr, *adv.* In whatever manner or degree; in whatever state.—*conj.* Nevertheless; yet; still; though.

Howl, houl, *vi.* To cry as a dog or wolf; to utter a loud mournful sound; to roar, as the wind.—*vt.* To utter or speak with outcry.—*n.* A loud protracted wail; cry of a wolf, etc.

Hub, hub, *n.* The central cylindrical part of a wheel in which the spokes are set.

Hubbub, hub'bub, *n.* A great noise of many confused voices; tumult; uproar.

Huckster, huk'ster, *n.* A retailer of small articles; a hawker.—*vi.* To deal in small articles; to higgle.—*vt.* To hawk.

Huddle, hud'l, *vi.* (huddling, huddled). To crowd or press together promiscuously.—*vt.* To throw or crowd together in confusion; to put on in haste and disorder.—*n.* A confused mass; confusion.

Hue, hū, *n.* Color; tint; dye; a shouting; outcry; alarm.

Huff, huf, *n.* A fit of peevishness or petulance; anger.—*vt.* To treat with insolence; to bully; to make angry.—*vi.* To swell up; to bluster; to take offense.

Hug, hug, *vt.* (hugging, hugged). To press close in an embrace; to hold fast; to cherish; to keep close to.—*n.* A close embrace; a particular grip in wrestling.

Huge, hūj, *a.* Of immense bulk; enormous; prodigious.

Huguenot, hū'ge-not, *n.* A French Protestant of the period of the religious wars in France in the

16th century.

Hulk, hulk, *n.* the body of an old vessel; anything bulky or unwieldy.

Hull, hul, *n.* The outer covering of anything, particularly of a nut or of grain; husk; frame or body of a ship.—*vt.* To strip off the hull or hulls; to pierce the hull of a ship with a cannon-ball.

Hum, hum, *vi.* (humming, hummed). To utter the sound of bees; to make an inarticulate, buzzing sound.—*vt.* To sing in a low voice; to sing or utter inarticulately.—*n.* The noise of bees or insects; a low, confused noise; a low, inarticulate sound.—*interj.* A sound with a pause, implying doubt and deliberation.

Human, hū'man, *a.* Belonging to man or mankind; having the qualities of a man.

Humane, hū-mān', *a.* Having the feelings and dispositions proper to man; compassionate; merciful; tending to refine.

Humanitarian, hū-man'i-tā''ri-an, *n.* A philanthropist; one who believes Christ to have been but a mere man; one who maintains the perfectibility of human nature without the aid of grace.

Humanity, hū-man'i-ti, *n.* The quality of being human or humane; mankind collectively; kindness; benevolence; classical and polite literature: generally plural, *'the humanities.'*

Humble, hum'bl, *a.* Of a low, mean, or unpretending character; lowly; modest; meek.—*vt.* (humbling, humbled). To make humble; to abase; to lower.

Humbles, hum'blz, *n.pl.* The heart, liver, kidneys, etc., of a deer.

Humbling, hum'bl-ing, *a.* Adapted to abase pride and self-dependence.

Humbug, hum'bug, *n.* A hoax; a cheat; a trickish fellow.—*vt.* (humbugging, humbugged). To impose on.

Humdrum, hum'drum, *a.* Commonplace; dull.—*n.* A droning tone; dull monotony.

Humid, hū'mid, *a.* Moist; damp.

Humidity, hū-mid'i-ti, *n.* State of being humid; moisture.

Humiliate, hū-mil'i-āt, *vt.* To humble; to depress; to mortify.

Humility, hū-mil'i-ti, *n.* Humbleness of mind; modesty; sense of insignificance.

Humming-bird, hum'ing-bėrd, *n.* A family of minute but richly-colored birds that make a humming sound with their wings.

Hummock, hum'ok, *n.* A rounded knoll.

Humorist, hū'mėr-ist or ū', *n.* One that makes use of a humorous style in speaking or writing; a wag.

Humor, hū'mėr or ū'mėr, *n.* Moisture or moist mater; fluid matter in an animal body, not blood; disposition; mood; a caprice; jocularity; a quality akin to wit, but depending for its effect less on point or brilliancy of expression.—*vt.* To comply with the inclination of; to soothe by compliance; to indulge.

Hump, hump, *n.* A protuberance, especially that formed by a crooked back; a hunch.

Humpback, hump'bak, *n.* A back with a hump; a humpbacked person; a kind of whale.

Humus, hū'mus, *n.* Vegetable mold.

Hunch, hunsh, *n.* A hump; a protuberance; a thick piece; a push or jerk with the fist or elbow.—*vt.* To bend so as to form a hump; to push with the elbow.

Hundred, hun'dred, *a.* Ten times ten.—*n.* The sum of ten times ten; the number 100; a division or part of a county in England.

Hundredweight, hun'dred-wāt, *n.* A weight of a hundred and twelve pounds avoirdupois, twenty of which make a ton.

Hunger, hung'gėr, *n.* An uneasy sensation occasioned by the want of food; a craving of food; a strong or eager desire.—*vi.* To feel the uneasiness occasioned by want of food; to desire with great eagerness.

Hungry, hung'gri, *a.* Feeling uneasiness from want of food; having an eager desire; lean; barren.

Hunt, hunt, *vt.* To chase or search for, for the purpose of catching or killing; to follow closely; to use or manage, as hounds; to pursue animals over.—*vi.* To follow the chase; to search.—*n.* The chase of wild animals for catching them; pursuit; an association of huntsmen; a pack of hounds.

Hunter, hunt'ėr, *n.* One who hunts; a horse used in the chase; a kind of watch with a hinged case which protects the glass.

Hurdle, hėr'dl, *n.* A movable frame made of twigs or sticks, or of bars or rods.—*vt.* (hurdling, hurdled). To make up, cover, or close with hurdles.

Hurl, hėrl, *vt.* To send whirling through the air; to throw with violence; to utter with vehemence.—*n.* Act of throwing with violence.

Hurricane, hu'ri-kän, *n.* A violent storm of wind traveling over 75 miles per hour.

Hurry, hu'ri, *vt.* (hurrying, hurried). To drive or press forward with more rapidity; to urge to act with more celerity; to quicken.—*vi.* To move or act with haste; to hasten.—*n.* Act of hurrying; urgency; bustle.

Hurt, hėrt, *n.* A wound; bruise; injury; harm.—*vt.* (pret. and pp. hurt). To cause physical pain to; to bruise; to harm; to impair; to injure; to wound the feelings of.

Hurtle, hėr'tl, *vi.* (hurtling, hurtled). To meet in shock; to clash; to fly with threatening noise; to resound.

Husband, huz'band, *n.* A married man; the correlative of wife; a good manager; a steward.—*vt.* To manage with frugality; to use with economy.

Hush, hush, *a.* Silent; still; quiet.—*n.* Stillness; quiet.—*vt.* To make quiet; to repress, as noise.—*vi.* To be still; to be silent.

Husk, husk, *n.* The covering of certain fruits or seeds.—*vt.* To strip the husk from.

Husky, husk'i, *a.* Abounding with husks; consisting of husks; resembling husks; rough, as sound; harsh; hoarse.

Hussy, huz'i, *n.* A worthless woman; a jade; a pert, frolicsome wench; a quean.

Hustle, hus'l, *vt.* and *i.* (hustling, hustled). To shake or shuffle together; to push or crowd; to jostle.

Hut, hut, *n.* A small house, hovel, or cabin; a temporary building to lodge soldiers.—*vt.* (hutting, hutted). To place in huts, as troops.—*vi.* To take lodgings in huts.

Hutch, huch, *n.* A chest or box; a corn bin; a box for rabbits; a low wagon used in coal-pits; a measure of 2 bushels.

Hyacinth, hī'a-sinth, *n.* A flowering, bulbous plant, of many varieties; a red variety of zircon, tinged with yellow or brown: also applied to varieties of garnet, sapphire, and topaz.

Hyaline, hī'al-in, *a.* Glassy; transparent.

Hyalography, hī-al-og'ra-fi, *n.* The art of engraving on glass.

Hybrid, hib'rid, *n.* A mongrel; an animal or plant produced from the mixture of two species.—*a.* Mongrel.

Hydra, hī'dra, *n.* A many-headed monster of Greek mythology.

Hydrangea, hī-dran'jē-a, *n.* An Asiatic shrub with beautiful flowers, cultivated in gardens.

Hydrant, hī'drant, *n.* A pipe with valves, etc., by which water is drawn from a main pipe.

Hydrate, hī'drāt, *n.* A chemical compound in which water or hydrogen is a characteristic ingredient.

Hydraulic, hī-dral'ik, *a.* Pertaining to fluids in motion, or the action of water utilized for mechanical purposes.

Hydrocarbon, hī-drō-kär'bon, *n.* A chemical compound of hydrogen and carbon.

Hydrocephalus, hī-drō-sef'a-lus, *n.* Water in the head.

Hydrogen, hī′drō-jen, *n.* The gaseous elementary substance which combines with oxygen to form water.

Hydrography, hī-drog′ra-fi, *n.* The science of the measurements and representation by charts of seas, rivers, etc.

Hydrology, hī-drol′o-ji, *n.* The science of water, its properties and laws.

Hydrometer, hī-drom′et-ėr, *n.* An instrument for measuring the specific gravities of liquids, and the strength of spirituous liquors.

Hydrophobia, hī-drō-fō′bi-a, *n.* A morbid dread of water; a disease produced by the bite of a mad animal, especially a dog.

Hydroponics, hī drō-pon′iks, *n.* The cultivation of plants in chemical solutions without soil.

Hydrostatic, hī-drō-stat′ik, *a.* Relating to hydrostatics.

Hydrostatics, hī-drō-stat′iks, *n.* The science which treats of the weight, pressure, and equilibrium of fluids, particularly water, when in a state of rest.

Hyena, hī-ē′na, *n.* A carnivorous quadruped of Asia and Africa, feeding chiefly on carrion.

Hygiene, hī′ji-ēn, *n.* A system of principles designed for the promotion of health; sanitary science.

Hygrometer, hī-grom′et-ėr, *n.* An instrument for measuring the moisture of the atmosphere.

Hygroscope, hī′grō-skōp, *n.* An instrument for indicating the presence of moisture in the atmosphere.

Hymen, hī′men, *n.* The god of marriage.

Hymn, him, *n.* A song of praise; a song or ode in honor of God.—*vt.* To praise or celebrate in song.—*vi.* To sing in praise.

Hymnal, him′nal, *n.* A collection of hymns, generally for use in public worship.

Hyoid, hī′oid, *a.* Applied to a movable U-shaped bone between the root of the tongue and the larynx.

Hyperbola, hī-pėr′bō-la, *n.* A conic section, a curve formed by a section of a cone, when the cutting plane makes a greater angle with the base than the side of the cone makes.

Hyperbole, hī-pėr′bō-lē, *n.* Exaggeration; a figure of speech exceeding the truth.

Hyperborean, hī-pėr-bō′rē-an, *a.* Being in the extreme north; arctic; frigid.—*n.* An inhabitant of the most northern regions.

Hypercritic, hī pėr krit′ik, *n.* One critical beyond measure; a captious censor.

Hyphen, hī′fen, *n.* A character, thus (-), implying that two words or syllables are to be connected.

Hypnotism, hip′no-tizm, *n.* A sleep-like condition caused by artificial means.

Hypochondria, hī-po-kon′dri-a, *n.* An ailment characterized by exaggerated anxiety, mainly as to the health; low spirits.

Hypocrisy, hi-pok′ri-si, *n.* A feigning to be what one is not; insincerity; a counterfeiting of religion.

Hypocrite, hi′pō-krit, *n.* One who feigns to be what he is not; a dissembler.

Hypodermal, Hypodermic, hi-pō-dėr′mal, hi-pō-dėr′mik, *a.* Pertaining to parts under the skin, or to the introduction of medicines under the skin.

Hypotenuse, hī-pot′ē-nūs, *n.* The side of a right-angled triangle opposite the right angle.

Hypothesis, hī-poth′e-sis, *n.*; pl. -ses, -sēz. A supposition; something assumed for the purpose of argument; a theory assumed to account for what is not understood.

Hypothetic, Hypothetical, hī-pō-thet′ik, hī-pō-thet′ik al, *a.* Relating to or characterized by hypothesis; conjectural.

Hypsometer, hip-som′et-ėr, *n.* An apparatus for measuring altitudes.

Hyssop, his′sop, *n.* An aromatic plant possessing stimulating, stomachic, and carminative properties.

Hysteria, Hysterics, his-tē′ri-a, his-ter′iks, *n.* A nervous affection chiefly attacking women, characterized by laughing and crying, convulsive struggling, sense of suffocation, etc.

I

I, ī, *pron.* The pronoun of the first person in the nominative case; the word by which a speaker or writer denotes himself.

Iambus, ī-am′bus, *n.*; pl. -buses or -bi. A poetic foot of two syllables, the first short and the last long, as in *delight*.

Iberian, ī-be′ri-an, *a.* Spanish.—*n.* One of the primitive inhabitants of Spain, or their language.

Ibex, ī′beks, *n.* An animal of the goat family.

Ice, īs, *n.* Water or other fluid congealed; ice-cream.—*vt.* (icing, iced). To cover with ice; to convert into ice; to cover with concreted sugar; to freeze.

Iceberg, īs′bėrg, *n.* A vast body of ice floating in the ocean.

Ice-cream, īs′krēm, *n.* A confection of cream, sugar, etc., frozen.

Icheumon, ik-nū′mon, *n.* A carnivorous Egyptian animal resembling a weasel, which hunts out crocodiles' eggs.

Ichor, ī′kor, *n.* In *mythology*, the ethereal juice that flowed in the veins of the gods; in *medicine*, a watery, acrid humor or discharge.

Ichthyology, ik-thi-ol′o ji, *n.* That part of zoology which treats of fishes.

Ichthyosaurus, ik′thi-ō-sa′′rus, *n.* A fishlike lizard; an immense fossil marine reptile.

Icicle, īs′i-kl, *n.* A pendent, conical mass of ice.

Iconoclast, ī-kon′o-klast, *n.* A breaker of images; one who attacks cherished beliefs.

Iconography, ī-ko-nog′ra-fi, *n.* The knowledge of ancient statues, paintings, gems, etc.

Icy, īs′i, *a.* Abounding with ice; made of ice; resembling ice; chilling; frigid; destitute of affection or passion.

Idea, ī-dē′a, *n.* That which is seen by the mind's eye; an image in the mind; object of thought; notion; conception; abstract principle; ideal view.

Ideal, ī-dē′al, *a.* Existing in idea or fancy; visionary; imaginary; perfect.—*n.* An imaginary model of perfection.

Idealism, ī′dē′al-izm, *n.* The system that makes everything to consist in ideas, and denies the existence of material bodies, or which denies any ground for believing in the reality of anything but percipient minds and ideas.

Idealize, ī-dē′al-iz, *vt.* To make ideal; to embody in an ideal form.

Identical, ī-den′tik-al, *a.* The same.

Identify, ī-den′ti-fi, *vt.* To make to be the same; to consider as the same in effect; to ascertain or prove to be the same.

Identity, ī den′ti-ti, *n.* Sameness, as distinguished from similitude and diversity; sameness in every possible circumstance.

Ideograph, Ideogram, id′ē-ō-graf, id′ē-ō-gram, *n.* A character, symbol, or figure which suggests the idea of an object; a hieroglyphic.

Ideology, ī-dē-ol′o-ji, *n.* The doctrine of ideas, or operations of the understanding.

Ides, īdz, *n.pl.* In the ancient Roman calendar the 15th day of March, May, July, and October, and the 13th day of the other months.

Idiograph, id′i-ō-graf, *n.* A private or trade mark.

Idiom, id′i-om, *n.* A mode of expression peculiar to a language; the genius or peculiar cast of a language; dialect.

Idiomatic, id′i-om-at′′ik, *a.* Pertaining to the particular genius or modes of expression of a language.

Idiopathy, id-i-op′a-thi, *n.* A morbid state not produced by any preceding disease.

Idiosyncrasy, id′i-o-sin′′kra-si, *n.* Peculiarity of temperament or constitution; mental or moral

I

characteristic distinguishing an individual.

Idiot, i'di-ot, *n.* One void of understanding; one hopelessly insane.

Idle, I'dl, *a.* Not engaged in any occupation; inactive; lazy; futile; affording leisure; trifling; trivial.—*vi.* (idling, idled). To be idle; to lose or spend time in inaction.—*vt.* To spend in idleness.

Idleness, i'dl-nes, *n.* Inaction; sloth; triviality; uselessness.

Idol, i'dol, *n.* An image or symbol of a deity consecrated as an object of worship; a person honored to adoration; anything on which we set our affections inordinately.

Idolater, i-dol'at-er, *n.* A worshipper of idols; a pagan; a great admirer.

Idolatry, i-dol'at-ri, *n.* The worship of idols; excessive attachment to or veneration for any person or thing.

Idolize, i'dol-iz, *vt.* To worship as an idol; to love or reverence to adoration.

Idyl, id'il or i'dil, *n.* A short highly wrought descriptive poem; a short pastoral poem.

If, if, *conj.* Granting or supposing that; on condition that; whether; although.

Igneous, ig'ne-us, *a.* Pertaining to or consisting of fire; resembling fire; proceeding from the action of fire.

Ignite, ig-nit', *vt.* (igniting, ignited). To set on fire.—*vi.* To take fire.

Ignoble, ig-no'bl, *a.* Not noble; of low birth or family; base; dishonorable.

Ignominy, ig'no-mi-ni, *n.* Public disgrace; loss of character or reputation; infamy; shame; contempt.

Ignorance, ig-no-rans, *n.* State of being illiterate, uninformed, or uneducated; want of knowledge.

Ignore, ig-nor', *vt.* (ignoring, ignored). To pass over or overlook as if ignorant of; to disregard.

Iguana, ig-wä'na, *n.* An American reptile of the lizard family.

Iliac, il'i-ak, *a.* Pertaining to the lower bowels.

Ill, il, *a.* Bad or evil; producing evil, unfortunate; cross; crabbed; sick or indisposed; impaired; ugly; unfavorable; rude.—*n.* Evil; misfortune; calamity; disease; pain.—*adv.* Not well; badly; with pain or difficulty.

Illegal, il-le'gal, *a.* Not legal; contrary to law; prohibited; illicit.

Illegible, il-le'ji-bl, *a.* Not legible; that cannot be read.

Illegitimate, il-le-jit'i-mat, *a.* Not legitimate; born out of wedlock; illogical; not authorized.—*vt.* To render illegitimate.

Illicit, il-lis'it, *a.* Not permitted; unlawful; lawless.

Illiterate, il-lit'er-at, *a.* Unlettered; ignorant of letters or books; not educated.

Ill-mannered, il-man'erd, *a.* Having bad manners; rude; boorish; impolite.

Illness, il'nes, *n.* State or quality of being ill; ailment; malady; sickness.

Illogical, il-lo'jik-al, *a.* Not logical; contrary to logic or sound reasoning.

Ill-timed, il'timd, *a.* Done or said at an unsuitable time.

Illuminate, il-lüm'in-āt, *vt.* (illuminating, illuminated). To light up; to adorn with festal lamps or bonfires; to enlighten intellectually; to adorn with colored pictures, etc., as manuscripts.

Illuminati, il-lü'mi-nä''ti, *n.pl.* A term applied to persons who affect to possess extraordinary knowledge.

Illumination, il-lüm'in-ä''shon, *n.* Act of illuminating; festive display of lights, etc.; splendor; infusion of intellectual or spiritual light; the adorning of manuscripts and books by hand with ornamental designs; such ornaments themselves.

Illusion, il-lü'zhon, *n.* Deception; deceptive appearance; hallucination.

Illusory, il-lü'so-ri, *a.* Deceiving by false appear-

ances; fallacious.

Illustrate, il-lus'trāt or il'lus-trāt, *vt.* (illustrating illustrated). To make clear or obvious; to ex plain; to explain and adorn by means of pic tures; drawings, etc.

Illustration, il-lus-trä'shon, Act of illustrating that which illustrates; an example; design to il lustrate the text of a book.

Illustrious, il-lus'tri-us, *a.* Renowned; celebrated noble; conferring honor or renown; glorious.

Image, im'āj, *n.* A representative of any person or thing; a statue; an idol; embodiment; a pic ture drawn by fancy; the appearance of any ob ject formed by the reflection or refraction of the rays of light.—*vt.* (imaging, imaged). To repre sent by an image; to mirror; to form a likeness of in the mind.

Imagery, im'āj-e-ri, *n.* Images in general; forms of the fancy; rhetorical figures.

Imaginary, im-aj'in-a-ri, *a.* Existing only in imag ination; ideal; visionary.

Imagination, im-aj'in-ä''shon, *n.* The act o imagining; the faculty by which we form a men tal image, or new combinations of ideas; menta image; a mere fancy; notion.

Imagine, im-aj'in, *vt.* (imagining, imagined). To picture to oneself; to fancy; to contrive; to think; to deem.—*vi.* To conceive; to have a no tion or idea.

Imago, im-ā'go, *n.* The last or perfect state of an insect.

Imbecile, im'be-sil, *a.* Destitute of strength; men tally feeble; fatuous; extremely foolish.—*n.* A poor, fatuous, or weak-minded creature.

Imbibe, im-bib', *vt.* (imbibing, imbibed). To drink in; to absorb; to admit into the mind.

Imbricate, Imbricated, im'bri-kāt, im'bri-kāt-ed *a.* Bent and hollowed, like a roof tile; lapping over each other, like tiles.

Imbroglio, im-brō'lyō, *n.* An intricate and per plexing state of affairs; a misunderstanding o a complicated nature.

Imbue, im-bü', *vt.* (imbuing, imbued). To tinge deeply; to dye; to inspire or impregnate (the mind).

Imitate, im'i-tāt, *vt.* (imitating, imitated). To follow as a model or example; to copy; to mimic; to counterfeit.

Imitation, im-i-tä'shon, *n.* Act of imitating; tha which is made or produced as a copy; resem blance; a counterfeit.

Immaculate, im-ma'kū-lāt, *a.* Without spot; un defiled; pure.

Immanate, im'ma-nāt, *vi.* To flow or issue in: said of something intangible.

Immanent, im'ma-nent, *a.* Remaining in o within; inherent and indwelling.

Immaterial, im-ma-tē'ri-al, *a.* Not consisting o matter; unimportant.

Immature, im-ma-tūr', *a.* Not mature; not perfec or completed; premature.

Immeasurable, im-me'zhŭr-a-bl, *a.* That canno be measured; immense.

Immediate, im-mē'di-āt, *a.* Without anything in tervening; acting without a medium; direct; no acting by secondary causes; present; withou intervention of time.

Immemorial, im-me-mō'ri-al, *a.* Beyond memory extending beyond the reach of record or tradi tion.

Immense, im-mens', *a.* Immeasurable; huge; pro digious; enormous.

Immerge, im-merj', *vt.* (immerging, immerged) To dip or plunge; to immerse.—*vi.* To disappea by entering into any medium.

Immerse, im-mers', *vt.* (immersing, immersed). to plunge into water or other fluid; to overwhelm to engage deeply.

Immesh, im-mesh', *vt.* To entangle in the meshe of a net, etc.

Immigrant, im'mi-grant, *n.* A person who immi grates into a country.

Immigrate, im'mi-grāt, *vi.* To come into a coun

try for permanent residence.

Imminent, im'mi·nent, *a.* Hanging over; impending; threatening; near at hand.

Immobile, im-mōb'il, *a.* Not mobile; immovable; fixed; stable.

Immoderate, im-mo'dèr-āt, *a.* Exceeding just or usual bounds; excessive; intemperate.

Immodest, im-mo'dest, *a.* Not modest; indelicate; indecent; lewd.

Immolate, im'mō-lāt, *vt.* (immolating, immolated). To sacrifice; to kill, as a victim offered in sacrifice; to offer in sacrifice.

Immoral, im-mo'ral, *a.* Not moral; wicked; depraved; licentious.

Immorality, im-mō-ral'i-ti, *n.* Quality of being immoral; any immoral act or practice; vice; licentiousness; depravity.

Immortal, im-mor'tal, *a.* Not mortal; everlasting; imperishable; not liable to fall into oblivion.—*n.* One who is exempt from death.

Immortality, im-mor-tal'i-ti, *n.* Condition or quality of being immortal; life destined to endure without end.

Immortalize, im-mor'tal-īz, *vt.* To render immortal; to make famous for ever.

Immovable, im-möv'a·bl, *a.* That cannot be moved from its place; not to be moved from a purpose; fixed; unchangeable; unfeeling.

Immunity, im-mū'ni-ti, *n.* Freedom from service or obligation; particular privilege or prerogative; state of not being liable.

Immure, im-mūr', *vt.* (immuring, immured). to inclose within walls; to imprison.

Immutable, im-mū'ta-bl, *a.* Unchangeable; unalterable; invariable.

Imp, imp, *n.* A young or little devil; a mischievous child.—*vt.* (imping, imped). To graft; to mend a deficient wing by the insertion of a feather; to strengthen.

Impact, im'pakt, *n.* A forcible touch; a blow; the shock of a moving body that strikes against another.

Impair, im-pār', *vt.* To make worse; to lessen in quantity, value, excellence, or strength.

Impale, im-pāl', *vt.* (impaling, impaled). To put to death by fixing on a stake; to join, as two coats of arms on one shield, with an upright line between.

Impalpable, im-pal'pa-bl, *a.* Not to be felt; so fine as not to be perceived by the touch; not easily or readily apprehended by the mind.

Imparity, im-pa'ri-ti, *n.* Inequality.

Impart, im-pärt', *vt.* To give, grant, or communicate; to bestow on another; to confer, to reveal; to disclose.

Impartial, im-pär'shal, *a.* Not partial; not biassed; equitable; just.

Impartiality, im-pär'shi-al''-ti, *n.* State or quality of being impartial; freedom from bias; equity.

Impassible, im-pas'i-bl, *a.* Incapable of passion or suffering; not to be moved to passion or sympathy; unmoved.

Impassion, im-pa'shon, *vt.* To move or affect strongly with passion.

Impassioned, im-pa'shond, *p.a.* Actuated by passion; having the feelings warmed, as a speaker; expressive of passion, as a harangue.

Impassive, im-pas'iv, *a.* Not susceptible of pain or suffering; impassible; unmoved.

Impatient, im-pā'shent, *a.* Not patient; uneasy under given conditions and eager for change; not suffering quietly, not enduring delay.

Impeach, im-pēch', *vt.* To charge with a crime; to bring charges of maladministration against a minister of state, etc.; to call in question; to disparage.

Impeccable, im-pek'a-bl, *a.* Not peccable, or liable to sin.

Impecunious, im-pē-kū'ni-us, *a.* Not having money; without funds.

Impede, im-pēd', *vt.* (impeding, impeded). To entangle or hamper; to obstruct.

Impediment, im-ped'i-ment, *n.* That by which one is impeded; obstruction.

Impel, im-pel', *vt.* (impelling, impelled). To drive or urge forward; to press on; to instigate; to incite; to actuate.

Impend, im-pend', *vi.* To hang over; to threaten; to be imminent.

Impenetrability, im-pe'ne-tra-bil''i-ti, *n.* Quality of being impenetrable; that quality of matter by which it excludes all other matter from the space it occupies.

Impenetrable, im-pe'ne-tra-bl, *a.* That cannot be penetrated; not admitting the entrance or passage of other bodies; impervious; obtuse or unsympathetic.

Impenitence, im-pe'ni-tens, *n.* Obduracy; hardness of heart.

Imperative, im-pe'rat-iv, *a.* Expressive of command; obligatory; designating a mood of the verb which expresses command, etc.

Imperceptible, im-pèr-sep'ti-bl, *a.* Not perceptible; not easily apprehended by the senses; fine or minute.

Imperfect, im-pèr'fekt, *a.* Not perfect; not complete; not perfect in a moral view; faulty; *imperfect tense,* a tense expressing an uncompleted action or state, especially in time past.

Imperforate, im-pèr'fo-rāt, *a.* Not perforated or pierced; having no opening or pores.

Imperial, im-pē'ri-al, *a.* Pertaining to an empire or emperor; suitable for an emperor; of superior excellence.—*n.* A tuft of hair beneath a man's lower lip; a size of paper measuring 30 by 22 inches.

Imperil, im-pe'ril, *vt.* (imperilling, imperilled). To bring into peril; to endanger.

Imperious, im-pē'ri-us, *a.* Commanding; haughty; domineering; arrogant; urgent; authoritative.

Imperishable, im-pe'rish-a-bl, *a.* Not perishable; indestructible; everlasting.

Impermeable, im-pèr'mē-a-bl, *a.* Not permeable; not permitting fluids to pass through; impervious.

Impersonal, im-pèr'son-al, *a.* Not having personal existence; not endued with personality; not referring to any particular person; *impersonal verb,* a verb (such as *it rains*) used only with an impersonal nominative.—*n.* That which wants personality; an impersonal verb.

Impersonate, im-pèr'son-āt, *vt.* To invest with personality; to assume the character of; to represent in character; as on the stage.

Impertinent, im-pèr'ti-nent, *a.* Not pertinent; irrelevant; petulant and rude; pert; intrusive.

Imperturbable, im-pèr-tèrb'a-bl, *a.* That cannot be agitated; unmoved; calm.

Impervious, im-pèr'vi-us, *a.* Not pervious; impassable; impenetrable.

Impetuous, im-pe'tū-us, *a.* Rushing with great force; forcible; precipitate; vehement of mind; hasty; passionate.

Impetus, im'pe-tus, *n.* The force with which any body is driven or impelled; momentum.

Impiety, im-pī'e-ti, *n.* Want of piety; irreverence toward the Supreme Being; ungodliness; an act of wickedness.

Impinge, im-pinj', *vi.* (impinging, impinged). To dash against; to clash.

Impious, im'pi-us, *a.* Destitute of piety; irreverent toward the Supreme Being; profane; tending to dishonor God or his laws.

Implacable, im-plā'ka-bl, *a.* Not to be appeased; inexorable; unrelenting.

Implant, im-plant', *vt.* To set, fix, or plant; to insert; to instil; to infuse.

Implement, im'plē-ment, *n.* A tool, utensil, or instrument.—*vt.* To fulfil the conditions of; to perform.

Implicate, im'pli-kāt, *vt.* (implicating, implicated). To involve or bring into connection with; to prove to be connected or concerned, as in an offense.

Implication, im-pli-kā'shon, *n.* Act of implicating;

state of being implicated; entanglement; a tacit inference; something to be understood though not expressed.

Implicit, im-pli'sit, *a*. Implied; fairly to be understood, though not expressed in words; trusting to another; unquestioning.

Implore, im-plōr', *vt*. and *i*. (imploring, implored). To call upon or for, in supplication; to beseech, entreat.

Imply, im-plī', *vt*. (implying, implied). To involve or contain in substance or by fair inference; to signify indirectly; to presuppose.

Impolite, im-pō-līt', *a*. Not polite; not of polished manners; uncivil.

Impolitic, im-po'lit-ik, *a*. Not politic; wanting policy or prudence; inexpedient.

Imponderable, im-pon'dėr-a-bl, *a*. Not having weight that can be measured.

Import, im-pōrt', *vt*. To bring into a place from abroad; to bear or convey, as the meaning; to signify; to imply; to be of moment or consequence to; to concern.—*n*. im'pōrt. That which is brought into a country from abroad; signification; purport; drift; importance.

Importance, im-pōrt'ans, *n*. Quality of being important; weight; moment; rank or standing; weight in self-estimation.

Important, im-pōrt'ant, *a*. Full of import; momentous; influential; grave; consequential.

Importune, im-por-tūn', *vt*. (importuning, importuned). To press with solicitation; to urge with frequent application.—*vi*. To solicit earnestly and repeatedly.

Impose, im-pōz', *vt*. (imposing, imposed). To place, set, or lay on; to lay on, as a tax, penalty, duty, etc.; to lay on, as hands; to obtrude fallaciously; to palm or pass off.—*vi*. Used in phrase *to impose on* or *upon*, to deceive; to victimize.

Imposing, im-pōz'ing, *p.a*. Impressive in appearance; commanding; stately; majestic.

Impossible, im-pos'i-bl, *a*. Not possible; that cannot be or be done.

Imposter, im-pos'tėr, *n*. One who imposes on others; a deceiver under a false character.

Imposture, im-pos'tūr, *n*. Imposition; fraud; deception.

Impotence, Impotency, im'pō-tens, im'pō-ten-si, *n*. State or quality of being impotent; want of ability or power; want of the power of procreation.

Impotent, im'pō-tent, *a*. Entirely wanting vigor of body or mind; feeble; destitute of the power of begetting children.

Impound, im-pound', *vt*. To confine in a pound or close pen; to confine; to take possession of for use when necessary.

Impoverish, im-po'vėr-ish, *vt*. To make poor; to reduce to indigence; to exhaust the strength or fertility of, as of soil.

Impracticable, im-prak'ti-ka-bl, *a*. Not practicable; unmanageable; stubborn; incapable of being passed.

Imprecate, im'prē-kāt, *vt*. (imprecating, imprecated). To invoke, as a curse or some evil.

Impregnable, im-preg'na-bl, *a*. That cannot be taken by force; able to resist attack; invincible, as affection.

Impregnate, im-preg'nāt, *vt*. To make pregnant; to imbue; to saturate.

Impress, im-pres', *vt*. To press into; to imprint; to stamp on the mind; to inculcate; to compel to enter into public service, as seamen; to take for public use.—*n*. im'press. That which is impressed; mark made by pressure; impression; character; act of compelling to enter into public service.

Impression, im-pre'shon, *n*. Act of impressing; that which is impressed; mark; effect produced on the mind; an indistinct notion; idea; copy taken by pressure from type, etc.; edition; copies forming one issue of a book.

Impressionist, im-pre'shon-ist, *n*. One who lays stress on impressions; an artist who depicts

scenes by their most striking characteristics as they first impress the spectator.

Impressive, im-pres'iv, *a*. Making an impression; solemn; awe-inspiring.

Imprimatur, im-pri-mā'tėr, *n*. A license to print a book, etc.; mark of approval in general.

Imprint, im-print', *vt*. To impress; to stamp; to fix on the mind or memory.—*n*. im'print. The name of the printer or publisher of a book, etc., with place and time of publication.

Imprison, im-pri'zn, *vt*. To put into a prison; to confine; to deprive of liberty.

Improbable, im-pro'ba-bl, *a*. Not probable; not likely to be true; unlikely.

Improbity, im-prō-bi-ti, *n*. Dishonesty.

Impromptu, im-promp'tū, *n*. A saying, poem, etc., made off-hand; an extemporaneous composition.—*a*. Off-hand; extempore.—*adv*. Off-hand. ·

Improper, im-pro'pėr, *a*. Not proper; unfit; not decent; erroneous; wrong.

Impropriety, im-prō-pri'e-ti, *n*. Quality of being improper; that which is improper; an unsuitable act, expression, etc.

Improvable, im-pröv'a-bl, *a*. That may be improved; susceptible of improvement.

Improve, im-pröv', *vt*. (improving, improved). To better; to ameliorate; to mend; to rectify; to use to good purpose; to apply to practical purposes.—*vi*. To grow better.

Improvement, im-pröv'ment, *n*. Act of improving; state of being improved; a change for the better; that which improves; a beneficial or valuable addition or alteration.

Improvident, im-pro'vi-dent, *a*. Not provident; wanting foresight or forethought; careless.

Improvise, im-pro-viz', To form on the spur of the moment; to compose and recite, etc., without previous preparation.

Imprudence, im-prö'dens, *n*. Want of prudence; indiscretion; a rash act.

Impudent, im'pū-dent, *a*. Offensively forward in behavior; bold-faced; impertinent.

Impugn, im-pūn', *vt*. To attack by words or arguments; to contradict; to call in question.

Impulse, im'puls, *n*. Force communicated instantaneously; effect of a sudden communication of motion; influence acting on the mind; motive; sudden determination.

Impulsive, im-puls'iv, *a*. Having the power of impelling; actuated or governed by impulse.

Impunity, im-pū'ni-ti, *n*. Freedom from punishment or injury, loss, etc.

Impure, im-pūr', *a*. Not pure; mixed with extraneous substance; obscene; unchaste; lewd; defiled by sin or guilt; unholy.

Imputation, im-pū-tā'shon, *n*. The act of imputing; attribution; censure; reproach.

Impute, im-pūt', *vt*. (imputing, imputed). To set to the account of; to ascribe.

In, in, *prep*. Within; inside of; surrounded by; indicating presence or situation within limits, whether of place, time, circumstances, etc.—*adv*. In or within some place, state, circumstances, etc.; not out.

Inability, in-a-bil'i-ti, *n*. Want of ability; want of adequate means.

Inaccessible, in-ak-ses'i-bl, *a*. Not accessible; not to be obtained; forbidden access.

Inaccurate, in-ak'kū-rāt, *a*. Not accurate; not exact or correct; erroneous.

Inaction, in-ak'shon, *n*. Want of action; forbearance of labor; idleness; rest.

Inadequate, in-ad'ē-kwāt, *a*. Not equal to the purpose; disproportionate; defective.

Inadmissible, in-ad-mis'i-bl, *a*. Not admissible; not proper to be admitted, allowed, or received.

Inadvertence, Inadvertency, in-ad-vėrt'ens, in-ad-vėrt'en-si, *n*. Quality of being inadvertent; any oversight or fault which proceeds from negligence or want of attention.

Inadvertent, in-ad-vėrt'ent, *a*. Not paying strict attention; heedless; unwary; negligent.

Inalienable, in-āl′yen-a-bl, *a.* Incapable of being alienated or transferred to another.

Inamorata, in-ä′mō-rä′′tä, *n.* A female in love; a mistress.

Inamorato, in-ä′mō-rä′′tō, *n.* A male lover.

Inane, in-ān′, *a.* Empty; void; void of sense or intelligence.—*n.* Infinite void space.

Inanimate, in-an′i-māt, *a.* Not animate; destitute of animation or life; inactive; dull; spiritless.

Inanity, in-an′i-ti, *n.* The quality of being inane; vacuity; mental vacuity; silliness.

Inapplicable, in-ap′pli-ka-bl, *a.* Not applicable; not suitable; inappropriate.

Inappreciable, in-ap-prē′shi-a-bl, *a.* Not appreciable; so small as hardly to be noticed.

Inapproachable, in-ap-prōch′a-bl, *a.* Not approachable; unapproachable.

Inappropriate, in-ap-prō′pri-āt, *a.* Not appropriate; unsuited; not proper.

Inaptitude, in-apt′ti-tūd, *n.* Want of aptitude; unsuitableness.

Inarticulate, in-är-tik′ū-lāt, *a.* Not articulate; not jointed or articulated; not uttered distinctly.

Inasmuch, in-az-much′, *adv.* Seeing; seeing that; this being the fact.

Inattention, in-at-ten′shon, *n.* Want of attention; heedlessness; neglect.

Inaudible, in-a′di-bl, *a.* Not audible; that cannot be heard.

Inaugurate, in-a′gū-rāt, *vt.* To induct into an office with suitable ceremonies; to perform initiatory ceremonies in connection with.

Inauguration, in-a′gū-rā′′shon, *n.* Act of inaugurating; ceremonies connected with such an act.

Inauspicious, in-a-spi′shus, *a.* Not auspicious; ill-omened; unfavorable.

Inboard, in′bōrd, *a.* Within a ship or other vessel.—*adv.* On board of a vessel.

Inborn, in′born, *a.* Born in; innate; implanted by nature; natural; inherent.

Inbreathe, in-brēTH′, *vt.* To breathe in, or infuse by breathing.

Inbred, in′bred, *a.* Bred within; innate.

Inca, in′ka, *n.* A king or prince of Peru before its conquest by the Spaniards.

Incalculable, in-kal′kū-la-bl, *a.* Not calculable; very great.

Incandescent, in-kan-des′ent, *a.* White or glowing with heat.—**Incandescent light,** a form of gas light; a form of electric light given forth from a filament of carbon inclosed in an airless glass globe.

Incantation, in-kan-tā′shon, *n.* The act of using certain words and ceremonies to raise spirits, etc.; the form of words so used; a magical charm or ceremony.

Incapable, in-kā′pa-bl, *a.* Not capable; possessing inadequate power or capacity; not susceptible; incompetent; unqualified or disqualified.—*n.* One physically or mentally weak.

Incapacitate, in-ka-pa′si-tāt, *vt.* To render incapable; to deprive of competent power or ability; to disqualify.

Incapacity, in-ka-pa′si-ti, *n.* Want of capacity; incompetency; disqualification.

Incarcerate, in-kär′se-rāt, *vt.* To imprison; to shut up or inclose.

Incarnate, in-kär′nāt, *vt.* To clothe with flesh; to embody in flesh.—*a.* Invested with flesh; embodied in flesh.

Incarnation, in-kär-nā′shon, *n.* Act of taking on a human body and the nature of man; the state of being incarnated; a vivid exemplification in person or act.

Incautious, in-ka′shus, *a.* Not cautious; unwary; heedless; imprudent.

Incendiary, in-sen′di-a ri, *n.* A person who maliciously sets fire to property; one guilty of arson; one who inflames factions; a firebrand; small bomb dropped from an airplane and intended to cause a fire;—*a.* Relating to arson; tending to excite sedition or quarrels.

Incense, in′sens, *n.* Aromatic substance burned in religious rites; odors of spices and gums, burned in religious rites; flattery or agreeable homage.—*vt.* (incensing, incensed). To perfume with incense.

Incense, in-sens′, *vt.* (incensing, incensed). To inflame to violent anger; to exasperate.

Incentive, in-sen′tiv, *a.* Inciting; encouraging.—*n.* That which incites; that which prompts to good or ill; motive; spur.

Inception, in-sep′shon, *n.* The act of beginning; first or initial stage.

Inceptive, in-sep′tiv, *a.* Pertaining to inception; beginning; applied to a verb which expresses the beginning of an action.—*n.* An inceptive verb.

Incessant, in-ses′ant, *a.* Unceasing; unintermitted; continual; constant.

Incest, in′sest, *n.* Sexual commerce between near blood relations.

Inch, insh, *n.* The twelfth part of a foot in length; a small quantity or degree.—*vt.* To drive or force by inches.

Inchoate, in′kō-āt, *a.* Recently begun; incipient; rudimentary.

Incident, in′si-dent, *a.* Falling or striking; happening; liable to happen; appertaining to or following another thing.—*n.* That which happens; event; an appertaining fact.

Incidental, in-si-dent′al, *a.* Casual; occasional; appertaining and subsidiary.

Incinerate, in-sin′e-rāt, *vt.* To burn to ashes.

Incipient, in-si′pi-ent, *a.* Beginning.

Incise, in-sīz′, *vt.* (incising, incised). To cut in or into; to carve; to engrave.

Incision, in-si′zhon, *n.* Act of cutting into; cut; gash; sharpness; trenchancy.

Incisive, in-sī′siv, *a.* Having the quality of cutting into anything; sharply and clearly expressive; trenchant.

Incisor, in-sīz′er, *n.* A front tooth which cuts or separates.

Incite, in-sīt′, *vt.* (inciting, incited). To move to action by impulse or influence; to instigate, to encourage.

Inclement, in-kle′ment, *a.* Not clement; harsh; stormy; rigorously cold.

Inclination, in-klin-a′shon, *n.* The act of inclining; deviation from a normal direction; a leaning of the mind or will; tendency; bent; bias; predilection; liking.

Incline, in-klin′, *vi.* (inclining, inclined). To deviate from a direction regarded as normal; to slope; to be disposed; to have some wish or desire.—*vt.* To cause to lean or bend towards or away from; to give a leaning to; to dispose.—*n.* An ascent or descent; a slope.

Inclose, in-klōz′, *vt.* (inclosing, inclosed). To shut up or confine on all sides; to environ; to cover with a wrapper or envelope.

Inclosure, in-klō′zhūr, *n.* Act of inclosing; what is inclosed; a space inclosed or fenced; something inclosed with a letter, etc.

Include, in-klōd′, *vt.* (including, included). To hold or contain; to comprise; to comprehend.

Inclusive, in-klō′siv, *a.* Inclosing; comprehended in the number or sum; comprehending the stated limit.

Incognito, in-kog′ni-tō, *pred.a.* or *adv.* In disguise.—*n.* (fem. being **Incognita**). One passing under an assumed name; assumption of a feigned character.

Incognizance, in-kog′ni-zans or in-kon′i-zans, *n.* Failure to recognize or apprehend.

Incoherent, in-kō-hēr′ent, *a.* Not coherent; wanting rational connection, as ideas, language, etc.; rambling and unintelligible.

Incombustible, in-kom-hust′i-bl, *a.* Not combustible; that cannot be burned.

Income, in′kum, *n.* Receipts or emoluments regularly coming in from property or employment; annual receipts; revenue.

Income-tax, in′kum-taks, *n.* A tax levied on incomes according to their amount.

Incommensurable, in-kom-men'sūr-a-bl, a. Not commensurable; having no common measure.

Incommensurate, in-kom-men'sūr-āt, a. Not commensurate; incommensurable; inadequate; insufficient.

Incommode, in-kom-mōd', vt. (incommoding, incommoded). To give trouble to; to inconvenience; to embarrass.

Incommunicative, in-kom-mū'ni-kāt-ive, a. Not communicative; not inclined to impart information.

Incomparable, in-kom'pa-ra-bl, a. Not comparable; that admits of no comparison with others; matchless.

Incompatibility, in-kom-pat'i-bil''i-ti, n. State or quality of being incompatible; inconsistency; disposition or temper entirely out of harmony.

Incompatible, in-kom-pat'i-bl, a. Not compatible; inconsistent; irreconcilably different; that cannot be made to accord.

Incompetence, Incompetency, in-kom'pē-tens, in-kom'pē-ten-si, n. State or quality of being incompetent; want of suitable faculties, adequate means, or proper qualifications.

Incompetent, in-kom'pē-tent, a. Not competent; incapable; wanting legal qualifications; not admissible.

Incomplete, in-kom-plēt', a. Not complete; imperfect; defective.

Incomprehensible, in-kom'prē-hens''i-bl, a. Not comprehensible; beyond the reach of the human intellect.

Incompressible, in-kom-pres'i-bl, a. Not compressible; resisting compression.

Inconceivable, in-kon-sēv'a-bl, a. Incapable of being conceived or thought of.

Inconclusive, in-kon-klōs'iv, a. Not conclusive; not settling a point in debate.

Incondensable, in-kon-dens'a-bl, a. Not condensable; incapable of being condensed.

Incondite, in-kon'dīt, a. Rude; unpolished; said of literary compositions.

Incongruity, in-kong-gru'i-ti, n. Want of congruity; inconsistency; absurdity.

Incongruous, in-kong'gru-us, a. Not congruous; not such as to mingle well or unite in harmony; inconsistent.

Inconsequent, in-kon'sē-kwent, a. Not consequent; not having due relevance; not following from the logical premises.

Inconsiderable, in-kon-sid'ėr-a-bl, a. Not considerable; unimportant; insignificant.

Inconsiderate, in-kon-sid'ėr-āt, a. Not considerate; hasty; thoughtless; injudicious.

Inconsistence, Inconsistency, in-kon-sist'ens, in-kon-sist'en-si, n. The condition or quality of being inconsistent; opposition or disagreement of particulars; self-contradiction; incongruity; discrepancy.

Inconsolable, in-kon-sōl'a-bl, a. Not to be consoled; grieved beyond consolation.

Inconspicuous, in-kon-spik'ū-us, a. Not conspicuous; unobtrusive.

Inconstant, in-kon'stant, a. Not constant; subject to change of opinion or purpose; not firm in resolution; fickle.

Incontestable, in-kon-test'a-bl, a. Not contestable; not to be disputed; unquestionable.

Incontinent, in-kon'ti-nent, a. Not continent; not restraining the passions or appetites; unchaste; unable to restrain discharges.

Incontrovertible, in-kon'trō-vėrt''i-bl, a. Not controvertible; too clear to admit of dispute.

Inconvenience, in-kon-vē'ni-ens, n. The quality of being inconvenient; annoyance; molestation; trouble; disadvantage.—vt. To put to inconvenience; to trouble.

Inconvertible, in-kon-vėrt'i-bl, a. Not convertible; that cannot be changed into or exchanged for something else.

Incorporate, in-kor'pō-rāt, vt. To form into one body; to unite; to blend; to associate with another whole, as with a government; to form into a legal body or corporation.—vi. To unite; to grow into or coalesce.—a. Incorporated; united in one body.

Incorporeal, in-kor-pō'rē-al, a. Not corporeal; not consisting of matter; spiritual.

Incorrect, in-ko-rekt', a. Not correct; inaccurate; erroneous; faulty; untrue.

Incorrigible, in-ko'ri-ji-bl, a. That cannot be corrected; bad beyond correction or reform.

Incorrupt, in-ko-rupt', a. Not corrupt; not marred by corruption or decay; pure; untainted; above the power of bribes.

Incorruptible, in-ko-rupt'i-bl, a. Not corruptible; that cannot corrupt or decay; inflexibly just and upright.

Increase, in-krēs', vi. (increasing, increased). To become greater; to augment; to advance in any quality, good or bad; to multiply by the production of young.—vt. To make greater or larger; to add to.—n. in'krēs. A growing larger in size, quantity, etc.; augmentation; addition; increment; profit; interest; offspring.

Incredible, in-kred'i-bl, a. Not credible; too improbable to admit of belief.

Incredulous, in-kred'ū-lus, a. Not credulous; refusing or withholding belief.

Increment, in'krē-ment, n. Act or process of increasing; increase; increase in the value of real property from adventitious causes.

Incriminate, in-krim'in-āt, vt. To bring an accusation against; to charge with a crime or fault.

Incrust, in-krust', vt. To cover with a crust or hard coat; to form a crust on.

Incrustation, in-krust-ā'shon, n. Act of incrusting; a crust or hard coat on the surface of a body; a covering or inlaying of marble or mosaic, etc.

Incubate, in'kū-bāt, vi. To brood or sit on eggs for hatching.

Incubation, in-kū-bā'shon, n. The act of incubating; the maturation of a contagious poison in the animal system.

Incubator, in'kū-bāt-ėr, n. One who or that which incubates; an apparatus for hatching eggs by artificial heat.

Incubus, in'kū-bus, n.; pl. -buses or -bi. A name of nightmare; something that weighs heavily on a person; burden or incumbrance; dead weight.

Inculcate, in-kul'kāt, vt. To press or urge forcibly and repeatedly; to teach.

Inculpate, in-kul'pāt, vt. To show to be in fault; to impute guilt to; to incriminate.

Incumbent, in-kum'bent, a. Lying on; resting on a person, as duty or obligation.—n. One in possession of an ecclesiastical benefice or other office.

Incunable, Incunabulum, in-kū'na-bl, in-kū-nab'ū-lum, n.; pl. -ula. A book printed before the year 1500.

Incur, in-kėr', vt. (incurring, incurred). To expose oneself to; to become liable to; to bring on or contract, as expense.

Incurable, in-kūr'a-bl, a. That cannot be cured; not admitting remedy; irremediable.—n. A person diseased beyond cure.

Incursion, in-kėr'shon, n. An entering into a territory with hostile intention; inroad.

Incurvate, in-kėrv'āt, a. Curved inward or upward.

Incuse, in-kūz', vt. To impress by stamping.—a. Impressed by stamping.

Indebted, in-det'ed, a. Being in debt; obliged by something received.

Indecency, in-dē'sen-si, n. The quality of being indecent; what is indecent in language, actions, etc.; indecorum; immodesty.

Indecipherable, in-dē-sī'fėr-a-bl, a. Incapable of being deciphered.

Indecision, in-dē-si'zhon, n. Want of decision; irresolution; hesitation.

Indeclinable, in-dē-klin'a-bl, a. Not declinable; not varied by terminations of case, etc.

ndecorous, in-dē-kō´rus or in-de´kō-rus, *a*. Not decorous; unseemly; indecent; unbecoming.

ndeed, in-dēd´, *adv*. In reality; in fact; really; truly.

ndefatigable, in-dē-fat´ig-a-bl, *a*. That cannot be wearied; untiring; unremitting.

ndefensible, in-dē-fens´i-bl, *a*. Not defensible; untenable.

ndefinable, in-dē-fīn´a-bl, *a*. Incapable of being defined; not to be clearly explained.

ndefinite, in-def´i-nit, *a*. Not definite; not limited; not precise; uncertain; vague.

ndelible, in-de´li-bl, *a*. Not to be deleted or blotted out; that cannot be obliterated.

ndelicate, in-de´li-kāt, *a*. Wanting delicacy; offensive to modesty or nice sense of propriety; somewhat immodest.

ndemnify, in-dem´ni-fī, *vt*. To make safe from loss or harm; to reimburse or compensate.

ndemnity, in-dem´ni-ti, *n*. Security given against loss, damage, or punishment; compensation for loss or injury sustained.

ndent, in-dent´, *vt*. To notch; to cut into points or inequalities; to bind by indenture.—*n*. A cut or notch; an indentation.

ndenture, in-den´tūr, *n*. That which is indented; a deed under seal between two or more parties, each having a duplicate.—*vt*. To indent; to bind by indenture.

ndependence, in-dē-pend´ens, *n*. State of being independent; complete exemption from control; self-reliance; political freedom.

ndependent, in-dē-pend´ent, *a*. Not dependent; not subject to control; moderately wealthy; not subject to bias or influence; free; bold; separate from; irrespective.—*n*. One who is independent; (with *cap*.) one who maintains that every congregation is an independent church.

ndestructible, in-dē-strukt´i-bl, *a*. That cannot be destroyed; imperishable.

ndeterminate, in-dē-tėr´min-āt, *a*. Not determinate; not settled or fixed; uncertain.

ndex, in´deks, *n*.; pl. **Indexes** or **Indices,** in´dek-sez, in´di-sez. Something that points out; the hand *or* used by printers, etc.; a table of contents; list of books disapproved of by R. Catholic authorities; the forefinger; the figure denoting to what power any mathematical quantity is involved.—*vt*. To provide with an index; to place in an index.

ndian, in´di-an, *a*. Pertaining to India, or to the Indies, East or West; pertaining to the aborigines of America.

ndicate, in´di-kāt, *vt*. To point out; to show; to intimate; to suggest.

ndication, in-di-ka´shon, *n*. Act of indicating; what points out; mark; token; sign.

ndicative, in-dik´a-tiv, *a*. That serves to point out; serving as an indication; designating a mood of the verb that declares directly or asks questions.—*n*. The indicative mood.

ndict, in-dīt´, *vt*. To charge with a crime or misdemeanor in due form of law.

ndictment, in-dīt´ment, *n*. The act of indicting; a formal charge; a written accusation of a crime or a misdemeanor.

ndifferent, in-dif´ėr-ent, *a*. Impartial; unconcerned; apathetic; immaterial or of little moment; middling; tolerable.

ndigenous, in-di´jen-us, *a*. Native, as persons; not foreign or exotic, as plants.

ndigent, in´di-jent, *a*. Destitute of means of comfortable subsistence; needy.

ndigested, in-di-jest´ed, *a*. Not digested; not reduced to due form; crude.

ndigestion, in-di-jest´yon, *n*. Incapability of or difficulty in digesting; dyspepsia.

ndignation, in-dig-nā´shon, *n*. A feeling of displeasure at what is unworthy or base; anger, mingled with contempt, disgust, or abhorrence; violent displeasure.

ndignity, in-dig´ni-ti, *n*. An insult; an affront; an outrage.

Indigo, in´di-go, *n*. A blue vegetable dye, from India and other places; the leguminous plant that produces the dye.

Indirect, in-di-rekt´, *a*. Not direct; circuitous; not tending directly to a purpose or end; not straightforward; not resulting directly.

Indiscreet, in-dis-krēt´, *a*. Not discreet; injudicious; inconsiderate.

Indiscretion, in-dis-kre´shon, *n*. The condition or quality of being indiscreet; imprudence; an indiscreet act.

Indiscriminate, in-dis-krim´in-āt, *a*. Without discrimination; confused.

Indispensable, in-dis-pens´a-bl, *a*. Not to be dispensed with; necessary or requisite.

Indispose, in-dis-pōz´, *vt*. To disincline; to disquality; to affect with indisposition.

Indisputable, in-dis´pūt-a-bl, *a*. Not to be disputed; unquestionable; certain.

Indissoluble, in-dis´sō-lū-bl, *a*. Not capable of being dissolved; perpetually binding or obligatory; not to be broken.

Indistinct, in-dis-tingkt´, *a*. Not distinct; faint; confused; imperfect or dim.

Indistinguishable, in-dis-ting´gwish-a-bl, *a*. Incapable of being distinguished.

Indite, in-dīt´, *vt*. and *i*. (inditing, indited). To compose or write; to direct or dictate.

Individual, in-di-vid´ū-al, *a*. Subsisting as one indivisible entity; pertaining to one only; peculiar to a single person or thing.—*n*. A being or thing forming one of its kind; a person.

Individuality, in-di-vid´ū-al´´i-ti, *n*. Quality or condition of being individual; separate existence; the sum of the traits peculiar to an individual.

Individualize, in-di-vid´ū-al-īz, *vt*. To single out; to distinguish by distinctive characters.

Indivisibility, in-di-viz´i-bil´´i-ti, *n*. State or quality of being indivisible.

Indivisible, in-di-viz´i-bl, *a*. Not divisible; not separable into parts.—*n*. An elementary part or particle.

Indocile, in-dō´sīl or in-dos´il, *a*. Not docile or teachable; intractable.

Indoctrinate, in-dok´trin-āt, *vt*. To imbue with any doctrine; to teach; to instruct.

Indolence, in´dō-lons, *n*. Habitual love of ease; laziness; idleness.

Indomitable, in-dom´it-a-bl, *a*. Not to be tamed or subdued; irrepressible.

Indoor, in´dōr, *a*. Being within doors; being within the house.—**Indoors,** in´dōrz, *adv*. Within doors; inside a house.

Indubitable, in-dū´bit-a-bl, *a*. Not to be doubted; too plain to admit of doubt; evident.

Induce, in-dūs´, *vt*. (inducing, induced). To lead by persuasion or argument; to prevail on; to actuate; to produce or cause.

Induct, in-dukt´, *vt*. To lead or bring into; to put in possession of an ecclesiastical living or office, with customary ceremonies.

Induction, in-duk´shon, *n*. The act of inducting; introduction of a clergyman into a benefice, etc.; a prologue or prelude; method of reasoning from particulars to generals; the conclusion thus arrived at; process by which one body, having electrical or magnetic properties, causes like properties in another body without direct contact.

Indue, in-dū´, *vt*. (induing, indued). To put on; to invest; to supply with.

Indulge, in-dulj´, *vt*. (indulging, indulged). To give free course to; to gratify by compliance; to humor to excess.—*vi*. To indulge oneself; to practice indulgence.

Indulgence, in-dulj´ens, *n*. The act or practice of indulging; a favor; intemperance; gratification of desire; tolerance; remission of the penance attached to certain sins.

Indurate, in-dū-rāt, *vi*. To grow hard.—*vt*. To make hard; to deprive of sensibility.

Industrious, in-dus´tri-us, *a*. Given to or charac-

I

terized by industry; diligent; active.

Industry, in'dus-tri, *n.* Habitual diligence; steady attention to business; the industrial arts generally, or any one of them; manufacture; trade.

Inebriate, in-ē'bri-āt, *vt.* To make drunk; to intoxicate.—*n.* An habitual drunkard.

Ineffective, in-ef-fekt'iv, *a.* Not effective; inefficient; useless; impotent.

Ineffectual, in-ef-fek'tū-al, *a.* Not effectual; inefficient; impotent; fruitless.

Inefficacious, in-ef'fi-kā''shus, *a.* Not producing the effect desired.

Inefficiency, in-ef-fi'shen-si, *n.* Condition or quality of being inefficient; inefficacy.

Inelegant, in-el'ē-gant, *a.* Not elegant; wanting elegance, beauty, polish, or refinement.

Ineligible, in-el'i-ji-bl, *a.* Not capable of being elected; not worthy to be chosen.

Inept, in-ept', *a.* Unsuitable; improper; foolish; silly; nonsensical.

Ineptitude, in-ept'i-tūd, *n.* Condition or quality of being inept; unfitness; silliness.

Inequality, in-ē-kwol'i-ti, *n.* Condition of being unequal; want of equality; an elevation or depression in a surface; diversity.

Inert, in-ėrt', *a.* Destitute of the power of moving itself, or of active resistance to motion impressed; lifeless; sluggish; inactive.

Inertia, in-ėr'shi-a, *n.* Passiveness; inactivity; the property of matter by which it tends to retain its state of rest or of uniform rectilinear motion.

Inestimable, in-es'tim-a-bl, *a.* That cannot be estimated; invaluable; priceless.

Inevitable, in-ev'it-a-bl, *a.* Not to be avoided; unavoidable; certain to befall.

Inexact, in-egz-akt', *a.* Not exact; not precisely correct or true.

Inexcusable, in-eks-kūz'a-bl, *a.* Not to be excused; unjustifiable; indefensible.

Inexhaustible, in-egz-ast'i-bl, *a.* Incapable of being exhausted; unfailing.

Inexorable, in-eks'ōr-a-bl, *a.* Not to be persuaded by entreaty or prayer; unbending; unrelenting; implacable.

Inexpedient, in-eks-pē'di-ent, *a.* Not expedient; not advisable or judicious.

Inexperience, in-eks-pē'ri-ens, *n.* Want of experience.

Inexplicable, in-eks'pli-ka-bl, *a.* That cannot be explained or interpreted; unaccountable; mysterious.

Inexplicit, in-eks-plis'it, *a.* Not explicit; not clear in statement.

Inexpressible, in-eks-pres'i-bl, *a.* Not to be expressed; unspeakable; indescribable.

Inexpressive, in-eks-pres'iv, *a.* Not expressive; wanting in expression; inexpressible.

Inextinguishable, in-eks-ting'gwish-a-bl, *a.* That cannot be extinguished.

Inextricable, in-eks'tri-ka-bl, *a.* Not to be extricated or disentangled.

Infallibility, in-fal'i-bil''i-ti, *n.* Quality of being infallible; exemption from liability to error.

Infallible, in-fal'i-bl, *a.* Not fallible; not liable to fail; certain.

Infamous, in'fa-mus, *a.* Notoriously vile; detestable; branded with infamy.

Infamy, in'fa-mi, *n.* Total loss of reputation; public disgrace; qualities detested and despised; extreme vileness.

Infancy, in'fan-si, *n.* State of being an infant; early childhood; period from birth to the age of twenty-one; first age of anything.

Infant, in'fant, *n.* A very young child; one under twenty-one years of age.—*a.* Pertaining to infants.

Infanticide, in-fant'i-sīd, *n.* Child murder; a slayer of infants.

Infantry, in'fant-ri, *n.* The soldiers or troops that serve on foot.

Infatuate, in-fa'tū-āt, *vt.* To make foolish; to inspire with an extravagant passion.

Infatuation, in-fa'tū-ā''shon, *n.* Act of infatuat-

ing; state of being infatuated; foolish passion.

Infect, in-fekt', *vt.* To taint with disease; to communicate bad qualities to; to corrupt.

Infection, in-fek'shon, *n.* Act or process of infecting; communication of disease; contagion; the thing which infects.

Infelicity, in-fē-lis'i-ti, *n.* Unhappiness.

Infelt, in'felt, *a.* Felt within or deeply.

Infer, in-fėr', *vt.* (inferring, inferred). To gather by induction or deduction; to deduce.

Inference, in'fėr-ens, *n.* The act of inferring; that which is inferred; deduction.

Inferior, in-fē'ri-ėr, *a.* Lower in place, station, age, value, etc.; subordinate.—*n.* A person lower in rank, importance, etc.

Infernal, in-fėr'nal, *a.* Pertaining to the lower regions or hell; very wicked and detestable; diabolical.—**Infernal machine,** an explosive apparatus contrived for assassination or other mischief.

Infertile, in-fėr'til, *a.* Not fertile; barren.

Infertility, in-fėr-til'i-ti, *n.* Barrenness.

Infest, in-fest', *vt.* To attack; to molest; to annoy continually.

Infidel, in'fi-del, *n.* A disbeliever; a sceptic; one who does not believe in God or in Christianity.—*a.* Unbelieving; sceptical.

Infidelity, in-fi-del'i-ti, *n.* Want of faith or belief; scepticism; unfaithfulness in married persons; dishonesty; treachery.

Infiltrate, in-fil'trāt, *vi.* To enter by the pores or interstices; to percolate.

Infinite, in'fi-nit, *a.* Not finite; without limits; not circumscribed in any way; vast.—*n.* The Infinite Being; infinite space.

Infinitesimal, in'fi-ni-tes''i-mal, *a.* Infinitely or indefinitely small.—*n.* An infinitely small quantity.

Infinitive, in-fin'it-iv, *a.* Designating a mood of the verb which expresses action without limitation of person or number, as, *to love.*—*n.* The infinitive mood.

Infinity, in-fin'i-ti, *n.* State or quality of being infinite; unlimited extent of time, space, quantity, etc.; immensity.

Infirmary, in-fėrm'a-ri, *n.* A place where the sick and injured are nursed; a hospital.

Infirmity, in-fėrm'i-ti, *n.* State of being infirm; unsound state of the body; weakness of mind or resolution; failing; malady.

Infix, in-fiks', *vt.* To fix or fasten in; to implant, as principles, etc.

Inflame, in-flām', *vt.* To set on fire; to kindle; to excite or increase; to incense; to make morbidly red and swollen.—*vi.* To grow hot, angry, and painful; to take fire.

Inflammation, in-flam-ā'shon, *n.* Act of inflaming; state of being inflamed; a redness and swelling attended with heat, pain, and feverish symptoms.

Inflate, in-flāt', *vt.* (inflating, inflated). To disten by injecting air; to puff up; to elate; to raise above the real or normal value.

Inflation, in-flā'shon, *n.* Act of inflating; state of being distended with air; state of being puffed up, as with vanity; over-issue of currency, tending to cause a general rise in prices.

Inflatus, in-flā'tus, *n.* A blowing or breathing in; inspiration.

Inflect, in-flekt', *vt.* To bend; to decline or conjugate; to modulate, as the voice.

Inflection, in-flek'shon, *n.* Act of inflecting; state of being inflected; grammatical variation of nouns, verbs, etc.; modulation of the voice; deflection or diffraction.

Inflexed, in-flekst', *a.* Curved; bent inward.

Inflexibility, in-fleks'i-bil''i-ti, *n.* Firmness of purpose; unbending pertinacity or obstinacy.

Inflexible, in-fleks'i-bl, *a.* That cannot be bent; firm in purpose; pertinacious; inexorable.

Inflict, in-flikt', *vt.* To cause to bear or suffer from; to impose, as pain, punishment, etc.

Inflow, in'flō, *n.* The act of flowing in or into; that which flows in; influx.

nfluence, in'flu-ens, n. Agency or power serving to affect, modify, etc.; sway; effect; acknowledged ascendency with people in power.—vt. To exercise influence on; to bias; to sway.

nfluential, in-flu-en'shal, a. Exerting influence, physical or other; possessing power.

nfluenza, in-flu-en'za, n. An epidemic catarrh or cold of an aggravated kind.

nflux, in'fluks, n. Act of flowing in; a coming in; importation in abundance; point at which one stream runs into another or into the sea.

nfold, in-fold', vi. To fold in; to involve; to wrap up; to inclose; to embrace.

nform, in-form', vt. To give form to; to give life to; to communicate knowledge to; to instruct, etc.—vi. To give information.

nformal, in-form'al, a. Not in the usual form or mode; not with the official or customary forms; without ceremony.

nformation, in-form-ā'shon, n. The act of informing; intelligence communicated or gathered; a charge or accusation before a magistrate; instructive.

nformatory, Informative, in-form'a-to-ri, in-form'a-tiv, a. Affording knowledge or information; instructive.

nformer, in-form'ėr, n. One who informs; one who makes a practice of informing against others for the sake of gain.

nfraction, in-frak'shon, n. Act of infringing; breach; violation; infringement.

nfrangible, in-fran'ji-bl, a. Not to be broken; not to be violated.

nfra-red, in'fra-red, a. Of the part of the spectrum beyond the red end of the visible spectrum.

nfrequent, in-frē'kwent, a. Not frequent; seldom happening, rare.

nfringe, in-frinj', vt. (infringing, infringed). To break, as laws, agreements, etc.; to violate; to contravene.—vi. To encroach (with on or upon).

nfuriate, in-fū'ri-āt, vt. To madden; to enrage.—a. Enraged; mad; raging.

nfuse, in-fūz', vt. (infusing, infused). To pour in, as a liquid; to instil, as principles; to steep in liquor without boiling, in order to extract solutions, etc.

nfusion, in-fū'zhon, n. Act or process of infusing; that which is infused; liquor obtained by infusing or steeping.

ngenious, in-jē'ni-us, a. Possessed of cleverness or ability; apt in contriving; contrived with ingenuity; witty or well conceived.

ngenuity, in-jen-ū'i-ti, n. Quality of being ingenious; ready invention; skill in contrivance.

ngenuous, in-jen'ū-us, a. Open, frank, or candid; free from reserve or dissimulation.

ngest, in-jest', vt. To throw into the stomach.

nglorious, in-glō'ri-us, a. Not glorious; not bringing honor or glory; disgraceful.

ngot, in'got, n. A mass of gold or silver cast in a mold; a mass of unwrought metal.

ngratiate, in-grā'shi-āt, vt. To get into another's good-will or confidence; to recommend; to insinuate; always refl.

ngratitude, in-grat'i-tūd, n. Want of gratitude; unthankfulness.

ngredient, in-grē'di-ent, n. That which is a component part of any mixture; an element, component, or constituent.

ngress, in'gres, n. Entrance; power of entrance; means of entering.

nguinal, in'gwin-al, a. Pertaining to the groin.

ngulf, in-gulf', vt. To swallow up; to absorb; to overwhelm by swallowing.

nhabit, in-ha'bit, vt. To live or dwell in; to occupy as a place of settled resident.—vi. To dwell; to live; to abide.

nhalation, in-ha-lā'shon, n. Act of inhaling; that which is inhaled.

nhale, in-hāl', vt. (inhaling, inhaled). To draw into the lungs; to suck in.

nharmonious, in här mō'ni-us, a. Not harmoni-

ous; unmusical; discordant.

Inherent, in-hēr'ent, a. Naturally pertaining; innate.

Inherit, in-he'rit, vt. To come into possession of as an heir; to receive by nature from a progenitor; to hold as belonging to one's lot.—vi. To take or have possession of property.

Inheritance, in-he'rit-ans, n. Act of inheriting; that which is or may be inherited; what falls to one's lot; possession.

Inhibit, in-hib'it, vt. To hold in or back; to restrain; to forbid; to interdict.

Inhospitable, in-hos'pit-a-bl, a. Not hospitable; wanting in hospitality; affording no entertainment to strangers.

Inhuman, in-hū'man, a. Destitute of the kindness and tenderness that belong to a human being; cruel; merciless.

Inhume, in-hūm', vt. (inhuming, inhumed). To bury; to inter (a dead body).

Inimical, in-im'ik-al, a. Unfriendly; hostile; adverse; hurtful; prejudicial.

Inimitable, in-im'it-a-bl, a. That cannot be imitated or copied; surpassing imitation.

Iniquity, in-ik'wi-ti, n. Want of equity; injustice; a sin or crime; wickedness.

Initial, in-i'shal, a. Placed at the beginning, pertaining to the beginning; beginning.—n. The first letter of a word; pl. the first letter in order of the words composing a name.—vt. (initialing, initialled). To put one's initials to; to mark by initials.

Initiate, in-i'shi-āt, vt. To begin; to be the first to practice or bring in; to instruct in rudiments; to introduce into any society or set; to let into secrets; to indoctrinate.

Initiative, in-i'shi-āt-iv, a. Serving to initiate.—n. An introductory step; first active procedure in any enterprise; power of taking the lead.

Inject, in-jekt', vt. To throw, cast, or put in or into; to dart in; to cast or throw in.

Injection, in-jek'shon, n. Act of injecting; the throwing of a liquid medicine into the body by a syringe or pipe; that which is injected.

Injudicious, in-jū'di'shus, a. Not judicious; acting without judgment; indiscreet.

Injunction, in-jungk'shon, n. Act of enjoining; a command; a precept; urgent advice; admonition.

Injure, in'jėr, vt. (injuring, injured). To do harm to; to hurt; to damage.

Injurious, in-jū'ri-us, a. Causing injury; tending to injure; hurtful; harmful.

Injury, in'jū-ri, n. The doing of harm; harm or damage; mischief; detriment.

Injustice, in-just'is, n. Want of justice or equity; iniquity; wrong.

Ink, ingk, n. A colored liquid, usually black, for writing, printing, etc.—vt. To black or daub with ink.

Inkling, ingk'ling, n. A hint or whisper; a slight notion or idea.

Inland, in'land, a. Interior; remote from the sea; domestic, not foreign; confined to a country.—adv. In or towards the interior of a country.—n. The interior part of a country.

Inlay, in-lā', vt. (inlaying, inlaid). To lay in; to ornament by laying in thin slices of fine wood, ivory, etc., on some other surface.

Inlet, in'let, n. A passage for entrance; place of ingress; a narrow recess in a shore.

Inmate, in'māt, n. One who dwells in the same house with another; one of the occupants of hospitals, asylums, prisons, etc.

Inmost, in'mōst, a. Furthest within; remotest from the surface or external parts.

Inn, in, n. A house for the lodging and entertainment of travellers.

Innate, in-nāt', a. Inborn; natural; native; inherent.

Inner, in'ėr, a. Interior; further inward than something else; internal.—n. A shot which strikes the target between the bull's-eye and the innermost ring.

Innermost, in'ēr-mōst, a. Furthest inward; most remote from the outward part.

Innervate, in-nėr'vāt, vt. To supply with nervous strength or stimulus.

Inning, in'ing, n. The ingathering of grain; pl. turn for using the bat in baseball, cricket, etc.

Innkeeper, in'kēp-ėr, n. One who keeps an inn or tavern.

Innocent, in'nō-sent, a. Not noxious or hurtful; free from guilt; simple-hearted; guileless.—n. One free from guilt or harm; a natural or simpleton.

Innocuous, in-nok'ū-us, a. Harmless; not injurious; producing no ill effect.

Innovate, in'nō-vāt, vi. To introduce novelties or changes.

Innovation, in-nō-vā'shon, n. The act of innovating; change made in anything established.—**Innovator,** in'nō-vāt-ėr, n. One who innovates.

Innoxious, in-nok'shus, a. Free from mischievous qualities; innocent; harmless.

Innuendo, in-nū-en'dō, n.; pl. **Innuendos** or **-does,** dōz. An oblique hint; insinuation.

Innumerable, in-nū'mėr-a-bl, a. Incapable of being numbered for multitude; extremely numerous; countless.

Inobservant, in-ob-zėrv'ant, a. Not observant; not keen in observation; heedless.

Inoculate, in-ok'ū-lāt, vt. To graft by inserting a bud; to communicate a disease to by morbid matter introduced into the blood; to infect; to contaminate.

Inoffensive, in-of-fens'iv, a. Giving no offense or annoyance; harmless.

Inofficial, in-of-fi'shal, a. not official; not clothed with the usual forms of authority.

Inoperative, in-o'pe-rāt-iv, a. Not operative; not active; producing no effect.

Inopportune, in-op'por-tūn, a. Not opportune; inconvenient; unseasonable.

Inordinate, in-or'din-āt, a. Excessive; immoderate.

Inorganic, in-or-gan'ik, a. Not organic; devoid of the structure of a living being; pertaining to substances without carbon.

In-patient, in'pā'shent, n. A patient who is lodged as well as treated in a hospital.

Inquest, in'kwest, n. Inquiry; a judicial inquiry before a jury; the jury itself.

Inquietude, in-kwī'et-ūd, n. Want of quiet; uneasiness, either of body or mind.

Inquire, in-kwīr', vi. (inquiring, inquired). Often **enquire.** To ask a question; to seek for truth by discussion or investigation.—vt. To ask about; to seek by asking.

Inquiry, in-kwī'ri, n. Often **enquiry.** The act of inquiring; a question; research; investigation; examination.

Inquisition, in-kwi-zi'shon, n. The act of inquiring; inquiry; inquest; a R. Catholic court for the examination and punishment of heretics.

Inquisitive, in-kwiz'i-tiv, a. Addicted to inquiry; given to pry; troublesomely curious.

Inquisitor, in-kwiz'i-tėr, n. One whose duty it is to inquire and examine; a member of the Inquisition.

Inroad, in'rōd, n. A hostile incursion; an invasion; attack; encroachment.

Insalubrious, in-sa-lū'bri-us, a. Not salubrious; unfavorable to health.

Insalutary, in-sal'ū-ta-ri, a. Not salutary; unhealthy; productive of evil.

Insane, in-sān', a. Not sane; deranged in mind or intellect; intended for insane persons; senseless.

Insanity, in-san'i-ti, n. The state of being insane; derangement of intellect; lunacy.

Insatiable, in-sā'shi-a-bl, a. Not satiable; incapable of being satisfied or appeased.

Insatiate, in-sā'shi-āt, a. Not satisfied; insatiable.

Inscribe, in-skrīb', vt. (inscribing, inscribed). To write down; to imprint on, as on the memory; to

address or dedicate; to mark with letters o words; to draw a figure within another.

Inscription, in-skrip'shon, n. The act of inscribing; words engraved; address of a book, etc., to a person.

Inscrutable, in-skrö'ta-bl, a. Unsearchable; tha cannot be penetrated or understood by human reason.

Insect, in'sekt, n. One of those small animal that have three divisions of the body—head thorax, and abdomen—and usually three pair of legs and two pairs of wings, as flies, etc.; puny, contemptible person.—a. Pertaining to in sects; like an insect; mean.

Insecticide, in-sek'ti-sīd, n. One who or tha which kills insects; the killing of insects.

Insectivore, in-sek'ti-vōr, n. An animal that eat insects.

Insecure, in-sē-kūr', a. Not secure; not confiden of safety; unsafe.

Insecurity, in-sē-kū'ri-ti, n. The state of being ir secure; want of security.

Insensate, in-sens'āt, a. Destitute of sense or ser sation; stupid; irrational.

Insensibility, in-sens'i-bil''i-ti, n. State or qualit of being insensible; want of sensation; callous ness; apathy.

Insensible, in-sens'i-bl, a. Not perceived or pe ceptible by the senses; void of feeling; unfee ing; callous; indifferent.

Inseparable, in-sep'a-ra-bl, a. Not separable; nc to be parted; always together.

Insert, in-sėrt', vt. To put, bring, or set in; t thrust in; to set in or among.

Insertion, in-sėr'shon, n. Act of inserting; thin inserted; place or mode of attachment of a par or organ to its support.

Inset, in-set', vt. To set in; to implant.—n. in'se That which is set in; insertion.

Inside, in'sīd, n. The interior side or part of thing.—a. Interior; internal.—prep. In the inte rior of; within.

Insidious, in-sid'i-us, a. Treacherous; guilefu working evil secretly.

Insight, in'sit, n. Sight into; thorough knowledge discernment; penetration.

Insignia, in-sig'ni-a, n.pl. Badges or distinguisl ing marks of office or honor.

Insignificant, in-sig-ni'fi-kant, a. Not significan void of signification; trivial or trifling; mea contemptible.

Insincere, in-sin-sēr', a. Not sincere; wanting sin cerity; hypocritical; deceitful.

Insinuate, in-sin'ū-āt, vt. To introduce by win ings or gently; to work gradually into favor; t introduce by gentle or artful means; to hint.—vi. To creep or wind; to make an insinuation; t wheedle.

Insipid, in-sip'id, a. Destitute of taste; vapid; fla dull; heavy; spiritless.

Insist, in-sist', vi. To rest or dilate on; to be urgen or peremptory.

Insnare, in-snār', vt. To catch in a snare; to e trap; to entangle; to involve.

Insobriety, in-sō-brī'e-ti, n. Want of sobriety; i temperance; drunkenness.

Insolate, in'so-lāt, vt. To dry or prepare in th sun's rays.

Insolent, in'sō-lent, a. Showing haughty disr gard of others; impudent; insulting.

Insoluble, in-sol'ū-bl, a. Incapable of being di solved; not to be solved or explained.

Insolvable, in-sol'va-bl, a. Not solvable; not to b solved or explained.

Insolvent, in-sol'vent, a. Not solvent; not havin money, etc., sufficient to pay debts.—n. One u able to pay his debts.

Insomnia, in-som'ni-a, n. Want of sleep; morbi or unnatural sleeplessness.

Inspect, in-spekt', vt. To view or examine to a certain the quality or condition, etc.

Inspiration, in-spi-rā'shon, n. The act of inspi ing; the drawing in of breath; the divine infl ence by which the sacred writers were instructed; influence emanating from any object; the state of being inspired; something conveyed to the mind when under extraordinary influence.

Inspire, in-spīr', vt. (inspiring, inspired). To breathe in; to breathe into; to communicate divine instructions to; to infuse ideas or poetic spirit into; to animate in general.—vi. To draw in breath; to inhale air into the lungs.

Instability, in-sta-bil'i-ti, n. Want of stability; inconstancy; fickleness.

Install, in-stal', vt. To place in a seat; to invest with any office with due ceremony.

Installment, in-stal'ment, n. Act of installing; a part of a whole produced or paid at various times; part payment of a debt.

Instance, in'stans, n. Act or state of being instant or urgent; urgency; an example; an occurrence.—vt. To mention as an instance, example, or case.

Instant, in'stant, a. Pressing or urgent; immediate; making no delay; present or current.—n. A moment.

Instantaneous, in-stant-ā'nē-us, a. Done or occurring in an instant.

Instate, in-stāt', vt. (instating, instated). To set or place; to install.

Instead, in-sted', adv. In the place or room of; in place of that.

Instep, in'step, n. The fore part of the upper side of the foot, near its junction with the leg.

Instigate, in'sti-gāt, vt. To spur on; to urge; to incite; to impel.

Instil, in-stil', vt. (instilling, instilled). To pour in, as by drops; to infuse by degrees; to insinuate imperceptibly.

Instinct, in'stingkt, n. Spontaneous or natural impulse; the knowledge and skill which animals have without experience; intuitive feeling.—a. in-stingkt'. Animated or stimulated from within; inspired.

Institute, in'sti-tūt, vt. To set up or establish; to found; to begin; to appoint to an office; to invest with a benefice.—n. That which is instituted; established law; principle; a literary or scientific body; an institution; pl. a book of elements or principles.

Instruct, in-strukt', vt. To impart knowledge to; to teach; to advise or give notice to.

Instruction, in-struk'shon, n. Act of instructing; information; education; authoritative direction; command.

Instructive, in-struk'tiv, a. Conveying instruction or a useful lesson.

Instrument, in'stru-ment, n. A tool; implement; one subservient to the execution of a plan; means used; any contrivance from which music is produced; a writing instructing one in regard to something agreed upon.

Instrumentalist, in-stru-ment'al-ist, n. One who plays on a musical instrument.

Instrumentation, in'stru-men-tā''shon, n. The use of instruments; music for a number of instruments; art of arranging such music.

Insubordinate, in-sub-or'din-āt, a. Not submitting to authority; riotous.

Insuetude, in'swē-tūd, n. State or quality of not being in use.

Insufferable, in-suf'er-a-bl, a. Not to be suffered; intolerable.

Insufficient, in-suf-fi'shent, a. Not sufficient; deficient; inadequate.

Insular, in'sū-lėr, a. Pertaining to an island; forming an island, narrow minded.

Insulate, in'sū-lat, vt. To make into an island; to detach; to separate, as an electrified body, by interposition of non-conductors.

Insulator, in'sū-lāt-ėr, n. One who or that which insulates; a body that interrupts the communication of electricity; non-conductor.

Insulin, ins'ū-lin, n. A substance extracted from the pancreas of animals, and found beneficial in diabetes.

Insult, in'sult, n. Any gross affront or indignity; act or speech of insolence or contempt.—vt. insult'. To treat with insult and insolence.—vi. To behave with insolent triumph.

Insuperable, in-sū'pėr-a-bl, a. That cannot be overcome; insurmountable.

Insupportable, in-sup-pōrt'a-bl, a. That cannot be supported or borne; intolerable.

Insuppressible, in-sup-pres'i-bl, a. Not to be suppressed.

Insurance, in-shōr'ans, n. Act of insuring against loss, etc.; a system of securing, by making certain payments, a certain sum of money at death, etc.

Insure, in-shōr', vt. (insuring, insured). To make sure; to contract for the receipt of a certain sum in the event of loss, death, etc.

Insurgent, in-sėr'jent, a. Rising in opposition to lawful authority; rebellious.—n. One who rises in opposition to authority.

Insurrection, in-sėr-rek'shon, n. A rising against authority; rebellion.

Insusceptible, in-sus-sept'i-bl, a. Not susceptible; not capable of being affected.

Intact, in-takt', a. Untouched; unimpaired.

Intaglio, in-tal'yō, n. Any figure engraved or cut into a substance; a gem with a figure or device sunk below the surface.

Intangible, in-tan'ji-bl, a. That cannot be touched; not perceptible to the touch.

Integer, in'ti-jer, n. A whole; whole number, in contradistinction to a fraction.

Integral, in'ti-gral, a. Whole; forming a necessary part of a whole; not fractional.—n. A whole; an entire thing.

Integrate, in'ti-grāt, vt. To make or form into one whole; to give the sum or total of.

Integrity, in-teg'ri-ti, n. State of being entire; an unimpaired state; honesty; probity.

Intellect, in'tel-lekt, n. That mental faculty which receives ideas; the understanding; mental power; mind.

Intellectual, in-tel-lek'tū-al, a. Relating or appealing to the intellect; having intellect.

Intelligence, in-tel'i-jens, n. The capacity to know; knowledge imparted or acquired; notice; an intelligent or spiritual being.

Intelligent, in-tel'i-jent, a. Endowed with the faculty of understanding or reason; endowed with a good intellect, well informed.

Intelligible, in-tel'i-ji-bl, a. Capable of being understood; comprehensible; clear.

Intemperate, in-tem'pėr-ēt, a. Not temperate; addicted to an excessive use of alcoholic liquors; excessive or immoderate.—n. One not temperate.

Intend, in-tend', vt. To design; to purpose; to mean.

Intended, in-tend'ed, p.a. Purposed; betrothed.—n. An affianced lover.

Intense, in-tens', a. Closely strained; strict; extreme in degree; violent; severe.

Intensify, in-ten'si-fi, vt. To render intense or more intense; to aggravate.—vi. To become intense.

Intensive, in-ten'siv, a. Serving to give emphasis.—n. Something giving emphasis.

Intent, in-tent', a. Having the mind bent on an object; sedulously applied.—n. Design or purpose; meaning; drift.

Intention, in-ten'shon, n. Act of intending; purpose; design; intension; method of treatment in surgery; a general concept.

Inter, in-tėr', vt. (interring, interred). To bury; to inhume.

Interact, in'tėr-akt, n. Interval between two acts of a drama; any intermediate employment of time.—vt. To act reciprocally.

Intercede, in-tėr-sēd', vi. (interceding, interceded). To mediate; to plead in favor of one; to make intercession.

Intercept, in-tėr-sept', vt. To take or seize on by

the way; to stop on its passage; to obstruct the progress of; to cut or shut off.

Intercession, in-tér-se'shon, *n.* Act of interceding; mediation; prayer or solicitation to one party in favor of another.

Interchange, in-tér-chānj', *vt.* To change, as one with the other; to exchange; to reciprocate.—*n.* in'tér-chānj. Mutual change; exchange; alternate succession.

Intercourse, in'tér-kōrs, *n.* Reciprocal dealings between persons or nations; fellowship; familiarity; sexual connection.

Interdict, in-tér-dikt', *vt.* To forbid; to place under an interdict or prohibition.—*n.* in'tér-dikt. A prohibition; a papal prohibition of the administration of religious rites.

Interest, in'tér-est, *vt.* To concern; to engage the attention of.—*n.* Concern or regard; advantage; profit; profit per cent from money lent or invested; influence with a person.

Interfere, in-ter-fēr', *vi.* (interfering, interfered). To clash; to interpose; to take a part in the concerns of others.

Interim, in'tér-im, *n.* The meantime; time intervening.—*a.* Belonging to an intervening time; temporary.

Interior, in-tē'ri-ér, *a.* Internal; being within; inland.—*n.* The inner part of a thing; the inside; the inland part of a country, etc.

Interject, in-tér-jekt', *vt.* To throw in between; to insert.

Interjection, in-tér-jek'shon, *n.* Act of throwing between; a word thrown in between words to express some emotion; an exclamation.

Interlace, in-tér-lās', *vt.* To weave together.—*vi.* To have parts intercrossing.

Interleave, in-tér-lēv', *vt.* To insert, as blank leaves in a book between other leaves.

Interline, in-tér-līn', *vt.* To put a line or lines between; to write or print in alternate lines or between lines.

Interlock, in-tér-lok', *vi.* and *t.* To unite or lock together by a series of connections.

Interlocution, in'tér-lō-kū''shon, *n.* Dialogue; interchange of speech; an intermediate act or decree before final decision.

Interlocutory, in-tér-lo'kū-to-ri, *a.* Consisting of dialogue; not final or definitive.

Interlope, in-tér-lōp', *vi.* To traffic without proper license; to intrude.

Interlude, in'tér-lūd, *n.* A short entertainment between the acts of a play, or between the play and the afterpiece; a piece of music between certain more important passages.

Interlunar, in-tér-lū'nér, *a.* Belonging to the time when the moon is invisible.

Intermarry, in-tér-ma'ri, *vi.* To become connected by marriage, as families.

Intermediary, in-tér-mē'di-a-ri, *a.* Intermediate.—*n.* An intermediate agent.

Intermediate, in-tér-mē'di-āt, *a.* Being between two extremes; intervening.

Interment, in-tér'ment, *n.* Burial.

Intermezzo, in-tér-met'zō, *n.* A short musical composition, generally of a light sparkling character; an interlude.

Interminable, in-tér'min-a-bl, *a.* Admitting no limit; boundless; endless.

Interminate, in-tér'min-āt, *a.* Unbounded; unlimited; endless.

Intermingle, in-tér-ming'gl, *vt.* To mingle together.—*vi.*•To be mixed or incorporated..

Intermission, in-tér-mi'shon, *n.* Act or state of intermitting; pause; rest.

Intermit, in-tér-mit', *vt.* (intermitting, intermitted). To cause to cease for a time; to suspend.—*vi.* To cease for a time.

Intermittent, in-tér-mit'ent, *a.* Ceasing at intervals; ceasing and then returning, as certain fevers.—*n.* A fever which intermits.

Intermix, in-tér-miks', *vt.* To mix together.—*vi.* To be mixed together.

Intern, in-tern', *vt.* To send to and cause to remain in the interior of a country; to disarm and quarter in some place, as defeated troops.

Internal, in-tern'al, *a.* Inward; not external; domestic; not foreign.

International, in-ter-na'shon-al, *a.* Relating to or mutually affecting nations; regularing the mutual intercourse between nations.

Internecine, in-tér-nē'sin, *a.* Marked by destructive hostilities; causing great slaughter.

Interpolate, in-tér'pō-lāt, *vt.* To foist in; to add a spurious word or passage to.

Interpose, in-tér-pōz', *vt.* (interposing, interposed). to place between.—*vi.* To mediate; to put in or make a remark.

Interpret, in-tér'pret, *vt.* To explain the meaning of; to expound; to construe; to represent artistically (as an actor).

Interpretation, in-tér'pret-ā''shon, *n.* Act of interpreting; explanation; representation of a character on the stage.

Interregnum, in-tér-reg'num, *n.* The time between reigns; intermission or break in succession.

Interrelation, in'tér-rē-lā''shon, *n.* Mutual or corresponding relation; correlation.

Interrogate, in-te'rō-gāt, *vt.* To question; to examine by asking questions.

Interrogation, in-te'rō-gā''shon, *n.* Act of interrogating; question put; a sign that marks a question, thus (?).

Interrupt, in-tér-rupt', *vt.* To break in upon the progress of; to cause to stop in speaking.

Interruption, in-tér-rup'shon, *n.* Act of interrupting; a break or breach; obstruction or hindrance; cause of stoppage.

Intersect, in-tér-sekt', *vt.* To cut in between; to divide; to cut or cross mutually.—*vi.* To meet and cut or cross each other.

Intersection, in-tér-sek'shon, *n.* Act or state of intersecting; the point or line in which two lines or two planes cut each other.

Intersperse, in-tér-spérs', *vt.* To scatter or set here and there among other things.

Interstellar, Interstellary, in-tér-stel'lér, in-tér-stel'la-ri, *a.* Intervening between the stars; situated beyond the solar system.

Interstice, in-térs'tis, *n.* A narrow space between things closely set; a chink.

Intertwine, in-tér-twīn', *vt.* To unite by twining or twisting.—*vi.* To be interwoven.

Interval, in'tér-val, *n.* A space between things; amount of separation between ranks, degrees, etc.; difference in gravity or acuteness between sounds.

Intervene, in-tér-vēn', *vi.* (intervening, intervened). To come or be between; to interpose or interfere.

Interview, in'tér-vū, *n.* A meeting between persons; a conference.—*vt.* To have an interview with to get information for publication.

Interweave, in-tér-wēv', *vt.* To weave together; to unite intimately; to interlace.

Intestate, in-test'āt, *a.* Dying without having made a will; not disposed of by will.—*n.* A person who dies without making a will.

Intestine, in-tes'tin, *a.* Internal; domestic; not foreign. *n.* The canal extending from the stomach to the anus; *pl.* entrails or viscera in general.

Intimate, in'ti-māt, *a.* Inward or internal; close in friendship; familiar; close.—*n.* An intimate or familiar friend.—*vt.* (intimating, intimated). To hint or indicate; to announce.

Intimation, in-ti-mā'shon, *n.* Act of intimating; a hint; announcement.

Intimidate, in-tim'id-āt, *vt.* To put in fear or dread; to cow; to deter with threats.

Into, in'tö, *prep.* In and to: expressing motion or direction towards the inside of, or a change of condition.

Intolerable, in-tol'ér-a-bl, *a.* That cannot be borne; unendurable; insufferable.

Intolerant, in-tol'ér-ant, *a.* That cannot bear; not enduring difference of opinion or worship;

refusing to tolerate others.

Intonate, in'tōn-āt, *vi.* To sound the notes of the musical scale; to modulate the voice.—*vt.* To pronounce with a certain modulation.

Intone, in-tōn', *vi.* To use a musical monotone in pronouncing.—*vt.* To pronounce with a muscial tone; to chant.

Intoxicate, in-toks'i-kāt, *vt.* To make drunk; to elate to enthusiasm or madness.—*vi.* To cause intoxication.

Intoxication, in-toks'i-kā''shon, *n.* Act of intoxicating; state of being drunk; delirious excitement; frenzy.

Intractable, in-trakt'a-bl, *a.* Not tractable; not to be governed or managed; refractory.

Intramural, in-tra-mū'ral, *a.* Being within the walls, as of a town or university.

Intransigent, in-tran'si-jent, *a.* Irreconcilable.—*n.* An irreconcilable person.

Intransitive, in-trans'it-iv, *a.* Designating a verb which expresses an action or state limited to the subject.

Intrench, in-trensh', *vt.* To dig a trench around, as in fortification; to fortify with a ditch and parapet; to lodge within an intrenchment.—*vi.* To invade; to encroach.

Intrepid, in-tre'pid, *a.* Undaunted; fearless; bold; daring; courageous.

Intricate, in'tri-kāt, *a.* Involved; complicated.

Intrigue, in-trēg', *n.* An underhand plot or scheme; plot of a play, etc.; an illicit intimacy between a man and woman.—*vi.* (intriguing, intrigued). To engage in an intrigue; to carry on forbidden love.

Intrinsic, Intrinsical, in-trin'sik, intrin'sik-al, *a.* Being within; inherent; essential.

Introduce, in-trō-dūs', *vt.* To lead or bring in; to insert; to bring to be acquainted; to present; to make known; to import; to bring before the public.

Introduction, in-trō-duk'shon, *n.* Act of introducing; act of making persons known to each other; act of bringing something into notice; a preliminary discourse.

Introspect, in-trō-spekt', *vt.* To look into or within.

Introspection, in-trō-spek'shon, *n.* The act of looking inwardly; examination of one's own thoughts or feelings.

Introvert, in-trō-vert', *vt.* To turn inward.

Intrude, in-trōd', *vi.* (intruding, intruded). to thrust oneself in; to force an entry or way in without permission, right, or invitation; to encroach.—*vt.* To thrust in.

Intuition, in-tū-i'shon, *n.* A looking on; direct apprehension of a truth without reasoning.

Intuitive, in-tū'it-iv, *a.* Perceived by the mind immediately without reasoning; based on intuition; self-evident.

Inundate, in-un'dāt or in'-, *vt.* To spread or flow over; to flood; to overwhelm.

Inuro, in ūr', *vt.* (inuring, inured). To accustom, to harden by use.—*vi.* To be applied.

Invade, in-vād', *vt.* (invading, invaded). To enter wiht hostile intentions; to make an inroad on; to encroach on; to violate.

Invalid, in-va'lid, *a.* Not valid; having no force or effect; void; null.

Invalid, in'va-lēd, *n.* One weak or infirm; a person disabled for active service.—*a.* In ill health; infirm; disabled.—*vt.* To render an invalid; to enrol on the list of invalids.

Invalidate, in-va'li-dāt, *vt.* To render of no force or effect.

Invaluable, in-va'lū-a-bl, *a.* Precious above estimation; inestimable; priceless.

Invariable, in-vā'ri-a-bl, *a.* Not variable; unchangeable; always uniform.

Invasion, in-vā'zhon, *n.* Act of invading; hostile entrance; infringement; violation.

Invective, in-vek'tiv, *n.* Violent utterance of censure; railing language; vituperation.—*a.* Containing invectives; abusive.

Inveigh, in-vā', *vi.* To attack with invectives; to rail against; to reproach; to upbraid.

Inveigle, in-vē'gl, *vt.* To persuade to something evil; to entice; to seduce.

Invent, in-vent', *vt.* To devise or produce, as something new; to fabricate; to concoct.

Invention, in-ven'shon, *n.* Act of inventing; contrivance of that which did not before exist; device; power of inventing; ingenuity; faculty by which an author produces plots, etc.

Inventory, in'ven-to-ri, *n.* An account of or catalogue of the goods and chattels of a deceased person; a catalogue of particular things.—*vt.* to make an inventory of.

Inverse, in'vers or in vers', *a.* Opposite in order or relation; inverted.

Inversion, in-ver'shon, *n.* Act of inverting; state of being inverted; change of order so that the last becomes first, and the first last; a turning backward.

Invert, in-vert', *vt.* To turn upside down; to place in a contrary position; to reverse.

Invertebrate, in-ver'tē-brāt, *a.* Destitute of a backbone or vertebral column.—*n.* An animal (one of the invertebrata) in which there is no backbone.

Inverted, in-vert'ed, *p.a.* Turned upside down; changed in order.

Invest, in-vest', *vt.* To clothe; to array; to clothe with office or authority; to endow; to besiege; to lay out as money in some species of property.—*vi.* To make an investment.

Investigate, in-ves'ti-gāt, *vt.* To search into; to make careful examination of.

Investiture, in-ves'ti-tūr, *n.* Act of investing or giving possession of any manor, office, or benefice; clothing; covering.

Investment, in-vest'ment, *n.* Act of investing; act of besieging; money laid out for profit; that in which money is invested.

Inveterate, in-vet'ėr-āt, *a.* Long established; deep-rooted; obstinate; confirmed.

Invidious, in-vid'i-us, *a.* Envious; malignant; likely to incur hatred or to provoke envy.

Invigorate, in-vi'gor-āt, *vt.* To give vigor to; to give life and energy to.

Invincible, in-vin'si-bl, *a.* Not to be conquered or overcome; insurmountable.—*n.* One who is invincible.

Inviolable, in-vī'ō-la-bl, *a.* Not to be violated; that ought not to be injured or treated irreverently; not susceptible or hurt.

Inviolate, in-vī'ō-lāt, *a.* Not violated; uninjured; unprofaned, unbroken.

Invisible, in-vi'zi-bl, *a.* Not visible; that cannot be seen; imperceptible.

Invitation, in-vi-tā'shon, *n.* Act of inviting; bidding to an entertainment, etc.

Invite, in-vīt', *vt.* (inviting, invited). To ask to do something; to ask to an entertainment, etc.; to allure or attract.—*vi.* To give invitation; to allure.

Invocation, in-vō-kā'shon, *n.* Act of invoking; the form or act of calling for the assistance of any being, particularly a divinity.

Invoice, in'vois, *n.* A written account of the merchandise sent to a person, with the prices annexed.—*vt.* (invoicing, invoiced). To make an invoice of; to enter in an invoice.

Invoke, in-vōk', *vt.* (invoking, invoked). To call upon; to address in prayer; to call on for assistance and protection.

Involuntary, in-vo'lun-ta-ri, *a.* Not voluntary; independent of will or choice.

Involute, in'vō-lūt, *n.* A curve traced by any point of a tense string when it is unwound from a given curve.—*a.* Involved; rolled inward from the edges.

Involve, in-volv', *vt.* (involving, involved). To roll up; to envelop to imply; to include; to implicate; to complicate; in algebra, etc., to raise a quantity to any assigned power.

Invulnerable, in-vul'nėr-a-bl, *a.* That cannot be

wounded; incapable of receiving injury.

Inward, in'wĕrd, *a.* Internal; being within; intimate; in the mind, soul, or feelings.—*adv.* Toward the inside; into the mind.—*n.pl.* The inner parts of an animal; the viscera.

Iodide, ī'ō-dīd, *n.* A compound of iodine and metal.

Iodine, ī'ō-dīn, ī'ō-dĕn, *n.* A non-metallic element chiefly extracted from the ashes of sea-weeds, and much used in medicine.

Iodoform, ī-od'ō-form, *n.* A compound of carbon, hydrogen, and iodine, an antiseptic.

Ion, ī'on, *n.* An electrified particle formed by the transfer of electrons when molecules of gas are broken up.

Ionic, ī-on'ik, *a.* Relating to Ionia, or the Ionian Greeks; denoting an order of architecture distinguished by the volutes of its capital.

Iota, ī-ō'ta, *n.* The name of Greek letter *i*; an insignificant amount.

I O U, ī'ō ū, *n.* A signed paper having on it these letters and a sum of money borrowed, serving an an acknowledgment of a debt.

Irascible, ī-ras'i-bl, *a.* Readily made angry; easily provoked; irritable.

Irate, ī-rāt', *a.* Angry; enraged; incensed.

Ire, īr, *n.* Anger; wrath; rage.

Iridescent, ī-rid-es'ent, *a.* Exhibiting colors like the rainbow; shimmering wth rainbow colors.

Iris, ī'ris, *n.*; pl. **Irises,** ī'ris-ez. The rainbow; an appearance resembling the rainbow; the colored circle round the pupil of the eye; the flag-flower.

Irish, ī'rish, *a.* Pertaining to Ireland or its inhabitants.—*n.* Natives of Ireland; the Celtic language of the natives of Ireland.

Irk, ĕrk, *vt.* To weary; to annoy; to vex. (Used impersonally.)

Irksome, ĕrk'sum, *a.* Wearisome; vexatious.

Iron, ī'ĕrn, *n.* The most common and useful metal; an instrument made of iron; a utensil for smoothing cloth; *pl.* fetters; chains; handcuffs.—*a.* Made of iron; consisting of or like iron; harsh; severe; binding fast; vigorous; inflexible.—*vt.* To smooth with an iron; to fetter; to furnish or arm with iron.

Ironware, ī'ĕrn-wār, *n.* Iron worked up into utensils, tools, etc.

Irony, ī'ron-i, *n.* A mode of speech which expresses a sense contrary to that conveyed by the words; a subtle kind of sarcasm.

Irradiate, ī-rā'di-āt, *vt.* To send forth rays of light upon; to enlighten.—*vi.* To emit rays.

Irradiation, ir-rā'di-ā''shon, *n.* Act of irradiating; illumination; apparent enlargement of an object strongly illuminated.

Irrational, ir-ra'shon-al, *a.* Not rational; void of reason or understanding; foolish; in *mathematics,* surd.

Irreconcilable, ir-re'kon-sil''a-bl, *a.* Not reconcilable; inconsistent; incompatible.—*n.* One who is not to be reconciled; one who will not work in harmony with associates.

Irredeemable, ir-rē-dēm'-a-bl, *a.* Not redeemable; not subject to be paid at its nominal value.

Irreducible, ir-rē-dūs'i-bl, *a.* Not reducible; that cannot be reduced.

Irrefutable, ir-rē-fūt'a-bl or ir-ref'ūt-a-bl, *a.* That cannot be refuted; unanswerable.

Irregular, ir-re'gū-lĕr, *a.* Not regular; not according to rule or custom; anomalous; vicious; crooked; variable; deviating from the common rules in its inflections.—*n.* A soldier not in regular service.

Irrelevant, ir-rē'lĕ-vant, *a.* Not relevant; not applicable; not to the purpose.

Irreligtious, ir-rēli'jus, *a.* Not religious; contrary to religion; impious; ungodly; profane.

Irremediable, ir-rē-mē'di-a-bl, *a.* Not to be remedied; incurable; irreparable.

Irremissible, ir-rē-mis'i-bl, *a.* Not to be remitted or pardoned; unpardonable.

Irremovable, ir-rē-möv'a-bl, *a.* Not removable;

firmly fixed.

Irreparable, ir-rē'pa-ra-bl, *a.* Not reparable; irretrievable; irremediable.

Irrepressible, ir-rē-pres'i-bl, *a.* Not repressible; incapable of being repressed.

Irreproachable, ir-rē-prŏch'a-bl, *a.* Incapable of being reproached; upright; faultless.

Irreprovable, ir-rē-prŏv'a-bl, *a.* Not reprovable; blameless; upright; unblamable.

Irresistible, ir-rē-zist'i-bl, *a.* Not resistible; that cannot be resisted; resistless.

Irresolute, ir-re'zō-lūt, *a.* Not resolute; not firm in purpose; undecided; wavering.

Irrespective, ir-rē-spekt'iv, *a.* Having no respect to particular circumstances (with *of*).

Irresponsible, ir-rēspons'iv, *a.* Not responsive.

Irretrievable, ir-rē-trēv'a-bl, *a.* That cannot be retrieved; irreparable.

Irreverence, ir-rev'er-ens, *n.* Want of reverence; want of veneration for the deity or for things sacred; want of due regard to a superior; irreverent conduct or action.

Irreversible, ir-rē-vĕr'si-bl, *a.* Not reversible; not to be annulled.

Irrevocable, ir-re'vŏk-a-bl, *a.* Not to be recalled, revoked, or annulled; irreversible.

Irrigate, ir'ri-gāt, *vt.* To bedew or sprinkle; to water by means of channels or streams.

Irritant, ir'rit-ant, *a.* Irritating; producing inflammation.—*n.* That which irritates; a medical application that causes pain or heat.

Irritate, ir'rit-āt, *vt.* To rouse to anger; to provoke; to inflame.

Irritation, ir-rit-ā'shon, *n.* Act of irritating; exasperation; annoyance; vital action in muscles or organs caused by some stimulus.

Irruption, ir-rup'shon, *n.* A bursting in; a sudden invasion or incursion.

Is, iz. The third pers, sing. of the verb *to be.*

Islam, is'lam, *n.* The religion of Mohammed; the whole body of those who profess it.

Island, ī'land, *n.* A piece of land surrounded by water; anything resembling an island.—*vt.* To cause to become or appear like an island; to dot, as with islands.

Isobar, ī'sō-bär, *n.* A line on a map connecting places at which the mean height of the barometer at sea-level is the same.

Isochronal, Isochronous, ī-sok'ron-al, ī-sok'ron-us, *n.* Uniform in time; of equal time; performed in equal times.

Isolate, ī'sō-lāt, *vt.* To place in or as in an island; to place by itself; to insulate.

Isolationist, is-ō-lā'shon-ist, *n.* One who favors keeping aloof from other countries politically.

Isometric, Isometrical, ī-sō-met'rik, ī-sō-met'rik-al, *a.* Pertaining to or characterized by equality of measure.

Isosceles, ī-sos'e-lēz, *a.* Having two legs or sides only that are equal (an *isosceles* triangle).

Israelite, iz'ra-el-īt, *n.* A descendant of *Israel* or Jacob; a Jew.

Issuable, ish'ū-a-bl, *a.* That may be issued.

Issue, ish'ū, *n.* The act of passing or flowing out; delivery; quantity issued at one time; event; consequence; progeny; offspring; an artifical ulcer to promote a secretion of pus; matter depending in a lawsuit.—*vi.* (issuing, issued). To pass or flow out; to proceed; to spring; to grow or accrue; to come to an issue in law; to terminate.—*vt.* To send out; to put into circulation; to deliver for use.

Isthmus, ist'mus or is'mus, *n.* A neck of land connecting two much larger portions.

It, it, *pron.* A pronoun of the neuter gender, third person, nominative or objective case.

Italian, i-ta'i-an, *a.* Pertaining to Italy.—*n.* A native of Italy; the language of Italy.

Italic, i-ta'lik, *a.* Pertaining to Italy; the name of a printing type sloping towards the right.—*n.* An italic letter or type.

Itch, ich, *n.* A sensation in the skin causing a desire to scratch; a constant teasing desire—*vi.* To feel an itch; to have a teasing sensation impelling to something.

Item, ī'tem, *adv.* Also.—*n.* A separate particular; a scrap of news.—*vt.* To make a note of.

Iterate, it'ėr-āt, *vt.* To repeat; to utter or do a second time.

Itinerant, i- or ī-tin'ėr-ant, *a.* Passing or travelling from place to place; not settled.—*n.* One who travels from place to place.

Itinerary, i- or ī-tin'ėr-a-ri, *n.* A work containing notices of places of a particular line of road; a travel route; plan of a tour.—*a.* Travelling; pertaining to a journey.

Its, its, *pron.* The possessive case singular of *it.*

Itself, it-self', *pron.* The neuter reflexive pronoun corresponding to *himself.*

Ivory, ī'vo-ri, *n.* The substance composing the tusks of the elephants, etc. something made of ivory.—*a.* Consisting or made of ivory.

Ivy, ī'vi, *n.* A plant which creeps along the ground, or climbs walls, trees, etc.

J

Jabber, jab'ėr, *vi.* To gabble; to talk rapidly or indistinctly; to chatter.—*vt.* To utter rapidly with confused sounds.—*n.* Rapid and indistinct talk.

Jack, jak, *n.* A name of various implements; a boot-jack; a contrivance for raising great weights by the action of screws; a contrivance for turning a spit; a coat serving as mail; a pitcher of waxed leather; a ball used for a mark in bowls; a flag on a bowsprit; the union flag; the male of certain animals; a young pike; the knave in a pack of cards.

Jackal, jak'äl, An animal resembling a fox, and closely akin to the dog.

Jackass, jak'as, *n.* The male of the ass; a dolt; a blockhead.

Jackdaw, jak'da, *n.* A small species of crow.

Jacket, jak'et, *n.* A short outer garment; a casing of cloth, felt, wood, etc.

Jade, jād, *n.* A mean or poor horse; a low woman; a huzzy; a hard tenacious green stone of a resinous aspect when polished.—*vt.* (jading, jaded). To ride or drive severely; to weary or fatigue.—*vi.* To become weary; to sink.

Jag, jag, *vt.* (jagging, jagged). To cut into notches or teeth; to notch.—*n.* A notch; a ragged protuberance.

Jaguar, ja-gwär', *n.* The American tiger, a spotted carnivorous animal, the most formidable feline quadruped of the New World.

Jail, jāl, *n.* A prison; place of confinement.

Jailer, Jailor, jāl'ėr, *n.* The keeper of a jail.

Jam, jam, *n.* A conserve of fruits boiled with sugar and water.—*vt.* (jamming, jammed). To crowd; to squeeze tight; to wedge in.

Jamb, jam, *n.* The side-post or vertical sidepiece of a door, window, etc.

Jangle, jang'gl, *vi.* (jangling, jangled). To sound harshly; to wrangle; to bicker.—*vt.* To cause to sound discordantly.—*n.* Prate; discordant sound.

Janitor, ja'ni-tor, *n.* A doorkeeper; one who looks after a public building.

January, ja'nū-a-ri, *n.* The first month of the year.

Jar, jär, *vi.* (jarring, jarred). To strike together discordantly; to clash; to interfere; to be inconsistent.—*vt.* To shake; to cause a short tremulous motion in.—*n.* A rattling vibration of sound; a harsh sound; contention; clash of interests or opinions; a vessel of earthenware or glass.

Jardinière, zhär-dēn yār, *n.* An ornamental stand for plants and flowers.

Jargon, jär'gon, *n.* Confused, unintelligible talk; gibberish; phraseology peculiar to a sect, profession, etc.; a variety of zircon.

Jasmine, jas'min, *n.* A fragrant shrub, bearing white or yellow flowers.

Jasper, jas'pėr, *n.* A variety of quartz, of red, yellow, and some dull colors.

Jaundice, jan'dis, *n.* A disease characterized by yellowness of the eyes and skin, loss of appetite, and general lassitude.—*vt.* To affect with jaundice, or with prejudice, envy, etc.

Jaunt, jänt, *vi.* To ramble here and there; to make an excursion.—*n.* A trip; a tour; an excursion; a ramble.

Jaunty, jän'ti, *a.* Gay and easy in manner or actions; airy; sprightly; showy.

Javelin, jav'lin, *n.* A light spear thrown from the hand.

Jaw, ja, *n.* The bones of the mouth in which the teeth are fixed.

Jazz, jaz, *n.* Syncopated or rag-time music, originally of negro origin.

Jealous, je'lus, *a.* Uneasy through fear of, or on account of, preference given to another; suspicious in love; apprehensive of rivalry; anxiously fearful or careful.

Jean, jän, *n.* A twilled cotton cloth.

Jeep, jēp, *n.* Small 4-wheel drive military car for carrying army personnel.

Jeer, jēr, *vi.* To flout; to mock; to utter severe, sarcastic reflections.—*vt.* To treat with scoffs or derision.—*n.* A scoff; biting jest; jibe.

Jehovah, jē-hō'va, *n.* An old Hebrew name of the Supreme Being.

Jelly, je'li, *n.* Matter in a glutinous state; the thickened juice of fruit boiled with sugar; transparent matter obtained from animal substances by boiling.—*vi.* To become a jelly.

Jelly-fish, jel'i-fish, *n.* A gelatinous marine animal.

Jeopardy, je'pėrd-i, *n.* Hazard; risk; exposure to death, loss, or injury.

Jerk, jėrk, *vt.* To give a sudden pull, thrust, or push to; to throw with a quick motion.—*vi.* to make a sudden motion.—*n.* A sudden thrust, push, or twitch; a sudden spring; a spasmodic movement.

Jerked, jėrkt, *p.a.* Cut into thin slices, and dried, as beef.

Jersey, jėr'zi, *n.* A kind of close-fitting knitted woollen shirt.

Jest, jest, *n.* A joke; plesantry; object of laughter; a laughing-stock.—*vi.* To make merriment; to joke.

Jesuit, je'zū-it, *n.* One of the Society of Jesus, so called, founded by Ignatius Loyola, in 1534; a crafty person, an intriguer.

Jesus, jē'zus, *n.* The Savior of men; Christ.

Jet, jot, *n.* A shooting forth or spouting; what issues from an orifice, as water, gas, etc.; a compact and very black species of coal, used for ornaments.—*vt.* (jetting, jetted). To emit in a jet.—*vi.* To issue in a jet.

Jet-propulsion, jet-prō-pul'shon, *n.* Propulsion by the reaction to a jet of gas expelled from an engine.

Jetsam, Jetson, jet'sam, jet'sun, *n.* The throwing of goods overboard to lighten a ship in distress; goods so thrown away.

Jettison, jet'i-son, *n.* Jetsam.—*vt.* To throw overboard.

Jew, jū, *n.* A Hebrew or Israelite.

Jewel, jū'el, *n.* A personal ornament of precious stones; a precious stone.—*vt.* (jewelling, jewelled). To adorn with jewels.

Jew's-harp, jūz'härp, *n.* A small musical instrument held between the teeth, sounding by the vibration of a steel tongue.

Jib, Jibe, jib, jīb, *vt.* and *i.* (jibbed, jibed, jibd, jībd; jibbing, jibing, jib'ing, jib'ing). To shift (as a fore-and-aft sail) from one side to the other; to pull against the bit, as a horse; to move restively.

Jiffy, jif'i, *n.* A moment, an instant. (Colloq.)

Jig, jig, *n.* A quick tune; a light lively dance; a mechanical contrivance of various kinds.—*vi.* (jigging, jigged). to dance a jig; to jolt.—*vt.* To jerk; to jolt.

Jilt, jilt, *n.* A woman who gives her lover hopes and capriciously disappoints him.—*vt.* To deceive in love.—*vi.* To play the jilt.

Jingle, jing'gl, *vi.* and *t.* (jingling, jingled). To sound with a tinkling metallic sound; to clink.—*n.* A rattling or clinking sound.

Job, job, *n.* A piece of work undertaken; a public transaction done for private profit.—*vt.* (jobbing, jobbed). To let out in separate portions or jobs; to let out for hire, as horses; to engage for hire; to peck or stab with something sharp.—*vi* To work at chance jobs; to buy and sell as a broker; to let or hire horses.

Jockey, jok'i, *n.* A man who rides horses in a race; a dealer in horses; one who takes undue advantage in trade.—*vt.* To play the jockey to; to ride in a race; to jostle by riding against; to cheat.

Jocose, jōk-ōs', *a.* Given to jokes and jesting; facetious; merry; waggish.

Jocular, jok'ū-lėr, *a.* Given to jesting; jocose; humorous; sportive.

Jocund, jok' or jok'und, *a.* Blithe; merry.

Jog, jog, *vt.* (jogging, jogged). To push with the elbow or hand; to excite attention by a slight push.—*vi.* To move at a slow trot; to walk or travel idly or slowly.—*n.* A push; a shake or push to awaken attention.

Join, join, *vt.* To bind, unite, or connect; to unite in league or marriage; to associate; to add; to couple.—*vi.* To unite; to be close, or in contact; to unite with in marriage, league, etc.—*n.* Place, act, etc., of joining.

Joiner, join'ėr, *n.* A mechanic who does the woodwork of houses; a carpenter.

Joint, joint, *n.* A joining; joining of two or more bones; articulation; a fissure in strata; part of an animal cut off by a butcher.—*a.* Joined; united; shared; acting in concert.—*vt.* To form with joints; to fit together; to divide into joints or pieces.—*vi.* To coalesce as by joints, or as parts fitted to each other.

Joist, joist, *n.* One of the pieces of timber to which the boards of a floor or the laths of a ceiling are nailed.—*vt.* To fit with joists.

Joke, jōk, *n.* A jest; something said to excite a laugh; raillery; what is not in earnest.—*vi.* (joking, joked). To jest; to sport.—*vt.* To cast jokes at; to rally.

Joker, jōk'ėr, *n.* One who jokes; a merry fellow; odd card in pack, used in some games as highest trump.

Jolly, jol'i, *a.* Merry; gay; mirthful; jovial; festive; plump and agreeable in appearance.

Jolt, jōlt, *vi.* and *t.* To shake with sudden jerks.—*n.* A shake by a sudden jerk.

Jonquil, jon'kwil, *a.* A species of narcissus or daffodil.

Jostle, jos'l, *vt.* (jostling, jostled). To push or knock against.—*vi.* To hustle.

Jot, jot, *n.* An iota; a tittle.—*vt.* (jotting, jotted). To set down in writing.

Journal, jėr'nal, *n.* A diary; an account of daily transactions, or the book containing such; a daily or periodical paper; a narrative of the transactions of a society, etc.; that part of an axle which moves in the bearings.

Journalist, jėr'nal-ist, *n.* The writer of a journal; a newspaper editor or contributor.

Journey, jėr'ni, *n.* A travelling from one place to another; tour; excursion; distance travelled.—*vi.* To travel from place to place.

Journeyman, jėr'ni-man, *n.* A workman who has fully learned his trade.

Jovial, jō'vi-al, *a.* Gay; merry; jolly.

Jowl, jōl, *n.* The cheek.—**Cheek by jowl,** with heads close together; side by side.

Joy, joi, *n.* Pleasure caused by the acquisition or expectation of good; delight; exultation; cause of joy or happiness.—*vi.* To rejoice; to be glad.—*vt.* To gladden.

Jubilation, jū-bi-lā'shon, *n.* A rejoicing; exultation; feeling of triumph.

Judaism, jū'dā-izm, *n.* The religious doctrines and rites of the Jews; conformity to the Jewish rites and ceremonies.

Judaize, jū'dā-īz, *vi.* and *t.* To conform to the religious doctrines and rites of the Jews.

Judas, jū'das, *n.* A treacherous person.

Judge, juj, *n.* A civil officer who hears and determines causes in courts; one who has skill to decide on anything; a critic; a connoisseur.—*vi.* (judging, judged). To act as an judge; to pass sentence; to form an opinion; to estimate.—*vt.* To hear and determine; to examine into and decide; to try; to esteem.

Judgment, juj'ment, *n.* Act of judging; good sense; discernment; opinion or estimate; mental faculty by which man ascertains the relations between ideas; sentence pronounced; a calamity regarded as a punishment of sin; final trial of the human race.

Judicatory, jū'di-kā-to-ri, *a.* Pertaining to the passing of judgment; dispensing justice.—*n.* A court of justice; administration of justice.

Judicial, jū-di'shal, *a.* Pertaining to courts of justice; inflicted as a penalty or in judgment; enacted by law or statute.

Judiciary, jū-di'shi-a-ri, *a.* Relating to courts of justice.—*n.* The system of courts of justice in a government; the judges taken collectively.

Judicious, jū-di'shus, *a.* Prudent; sagacious.

Jug, jug, *n.* A vessel for liquors, generally with a handle; a mug; a pitcher.—*vt.* (jugging, jugged). To put in a jug; to cook by putting into a jug, and this into boiling water (*jugged* hare).

Juggernaut, jug'ėr-nat, *n.* Any idea, custom, etc., to which one devotes himself or is ruthlessly sacrificed.

Juggle, jug'l, *vi.* (juggling; juggled). To play tricks by sleight of hand; to practice imposture.—*vt.* To deceive by artifice.—*n.* A trick by legerdemain; an imposture.

Jugular, ju'gū-lėr, *a.* Pertaining to the throat or neck.

Juice, jūs, *n.* Sap of vegetables, especially fruit; fluid part of animal substances.

Jujitsu, jö-jit'sö, *n.* A style of Japanese wrestling based on a knowledge of muscular action.

Jujube, jū'jūb, *n.* The fruit of a piny shrub or small tree; the tree itself; a confection made with gum-arabic or gelatine.

Julep, jū'lep, *n.* A sweet drink.

July, jū-lī', *n.* The seventh month of the year.

Jumble, jum'bl, *vt.* (jumbling, jumbled). To mix in a confused mass.—*vi.* To meet, mix, or unite in a confused manner.—*n.* Confused mass; disorder; confusion.

Jump, jump, *vi.* To leap; to skip; to spring; to agree, tally, coincide.—*vt.* To pass over by a leap; to pass over hastily.—*n.* Act of jumping; leap; spring; bound.

Junction, jungk'shon, *n.* Act or operation of joining; state of being joined; point of union; place where railways meet.

Juncture, jungk'tūr, *n.* A joining or uniting; line or point of joining; point of time; point rendered critical by circumstances.

June, jūn, *n.* The sixth month of the year.

Jungle, jung'gl, *n.* Land covered with trees, brushwood, etc., or coarse, reedy vegetation.

Junior, jū'ni-ėr, *a.* Younger; later or lower in office or rank.—*n.* A person younger than another or lower in standing.

Juniper, jū'ni-pėr, *n.* A coniferous shrub, the berries of which are used to flavor gin.

Junket, jung'ket, *n.* Curds mixed with cream, sweetened and flavored; a sweetmeat; a feast.—*vi.* and *t.* To feast.

Junta, jun'ta, *n.* A meeting; a junto; a grand Spanish council of state.

Junto, jun'tō, *n.* A select council which deliberates in secret on any affair or government; a faction; a cabal.

Jupiter, jū'pi-tėr, *n.* The chief deity of the Romans; the largest and brightest planet.

Jurassic, jū-ras'ik, *a.* Of or belonging to the formation of the *Jura* Mountains; Oolitic.

Juridical, jū-rid'ik-al, *a*. Relating to the administration of justice or to a judge.

Jurisdiction, jū-ris-dik'shon, *n*. Judicial power; right of exercising authority; district within which power may be exercised.

Jurisprudence, jū-ris-prö'dens, *n*. The science of law; the knowledge of the laws, customs, and rights of men necessary for the due administration of justice.

Jurist, jū'rist, *n*. A man who professes the science of law; one versed in the law, or more particularly, in the civil law.

Jury, jū'ri, *n*. A number of men selected according to law and sworn to declare the truth on the evidence; a body who jointly decides as to prizes.—*a*. In *ships*, applied to a temporary substitute, as a *jury*-mast.

Just, just, *a*. Right; acting rightly; upright, impartial; fair; due; merited; exact.—*adv*. Exactly; precisely; near or nearly; almost; merely; barely.

Justice, jus'tis, *n*. Quality of being just; rectitude; propriety; impartiality; fairness; just treatment; merited reward or punishment; a judge holding a special office.

Justification, just'i-fi-kā''shon, *n*. Act of justifying; state of being justified; vindication; defense; remission of sin.

Justify, just'i-fī, *vt*. (justifying, justified). To prove or show to be just; to defend or maintain; to excuse; to judge rightly of; to adjust.

Justly, just'li, *adv*. Rightly; fairly; properly.

Justness, just'nes, *n*. Quality of being just; uprightness; equity.

Jut, jut, *vi*. (jutting, jutted). To project beyond the main body.—*n*. A projection.

Juvenile, jū've-nil, *a*. Young; youthful; pertaining to youth.—*n*. A young person.

Juxtapose, juks-ta-pōz', *vt*. To place near or next. Also **Juxtaposit**, jux-ta-poz'it.

Juxtaposition, juks'ta-pō-si''shon, *n*. A placeing or being placed near.

K

Kail, Kale, kāl, *n*. A kind of cabbage; colewort; cabbage or greens in general.

Kaleidoscope, ka-lī'dos-kōp, *n*. An optical instrument which exhibits an endless variety of colored figures.

Kangaroo, kang'ga-rö, *n*. An Australian marsupial quadruped that moves forward by leaps.

Keel, kēl, *n*. The principal timber in a ship, extending from stem to stern at the bottom; the corresponding part in iron vessels; the whole ship; something resembling a keel; a coal-barge.—*vi*. To capsize.

Keen, kēn, *a*. Acute of mind; shrewd; sharp; eager; piercing; severe; bitter.

Keep, kēp, *vt*. (keeping, kept). To hold; to preserve; to guard; to detain; to attend to; to continue any state, course, or action; to obey; to perform; to observe or solemnize; to confine to one's own knowledge; not to betray; to have in pay.—*vt*. To endure; not to perish or be impaired.—*n*. Care; guard; sustenance; a donjon or strong tower.

Keepsake, kēp'sāk, *a*. Anything kept or given to be kept for the sake of the giver.

Keg, keg, *n*. A small cask or barrel.

Kelp, kelp, *n*. Large sea-weeds; alkaline substance yielded by sea-weeds when burned.

Kennel, ken'el, *n*. A house or cot for dogs; a pack of hounds; hole of a fox, etc.; a haunt; a gutter.—*vi* and *t*. (kenneling, kenneled) To lodge in a kennel.

Kerchief, kėr'chif, *n*. A cloth to cover the head; any loose cloth used in dress.

Kernel, kėr'nel, *n*. The edible substance contained in the shell of a nut; the core; the gist.—

vi. (kernelling, kernelled). To harden or ripen into kernels, as the seeds of plants.

Kerosene, ke'ro-sēn, *n*. A lamp-oil from petroleum, extensively used in America.

Kettle, ket'l, *n*. A vessel of iron or other metal, used for heating and boiling water, etc.

Key, kē, *n*. An instrument for shutting or opening a lock; a little lever by which certain musical instruments are played on by the fingers; fundamental tone in a piece of music; that which serves to explain a cipher, etc.—*vt*. To furnish or fasten with a key.

Key-board, kē'bōrd, *n*. The series of levers in a keyed musical instrument upon which the fingers press.

Keystone, kē'stōn, *n*. The top stone of an arch, which, being the last put in, enters like a wedge, and fastens the work together.

Khaki, kä'ki, *a*. Of a brownish-yellow earth color.—*n*. A brownish-yellow earthy color; cloth of this color worn by soldiers.

Kick, kik, *vt*. To strike with the foot; to strike in recoiling, as a gun.—*vi*. To strike with the foot or feet; to manifest opposition to restraint; to recoil.—*n*. A blow with the foot or feet; recoil of a firearm.

Kid, kid, *n*. A young goat; leather made from its skin; a small wooden tub.—*vt*. (kidding, kidded). To bring forth a kid.

Kidnap, kid'nap, *vt*. (kidnapping, kidnapped). To steal or forcibly abduct a human being.

Kidney, kid'ni, *n*. Either of the two glands which secret the urine; sort or character.

Kill, kil, *vt*. To deprive of life; to slay; to slaughter for food; to deaden.(pain); to overpower.

Kiln, kil, *n*. A fabric of brick or stone, which may be heated to harden or dry anything.

Kilogram, kil'ō-gram, *n*. A French measure of weight, being 1000 grams or 2.2 lbs. avoir.

Kiloliter, kil'ō-lē-tr, *n*. A French measure, 1000 liters or 220.09 gallons.

Kilometer, kil'ō-mä-tr, *n*. A French measure; 1000 meters, about $5/8$ of a mile or 1093.633 yards.

Kilt, kilt, *n*. A kind of short petticoat worn by the Highlanders of Scotland in lieu of trousers.—*vt*. To tuck up or plait like a kilt.

Kimono, kim-ō'nō, *n*. A loose robe with short wide sleeves, worn by both sexes in Japan; a type of dressing-gown.

Kin, kin, *n*. Race; family; consanguinity or affinity; kindred.—*a*. Kindred; congenial.

Kind, kind, *n*. Race; genus; variety; nature; character.—**In kind**, to pay with produce or commodities. *a*. Humane; having tenderness or goodness of nature; benevolent, friendly.

Kindergarten, kin'der-gär-tn, *n*. An infants' school in which amusements are systematically combined with instruction.

Kindle, kin'dl, *vt*. (kindling, kindled). To set on fire; to light; to rouse; to excite to action.—*vi*. To take fire; to be roused or exasperated.

Kindly, kīnd'li, *a*. Of a kind disposition, congenial; benevolent; mild.—*adv*. In a kind manner; favorably.

Kindred, kin'dred, *n*. Relationship by birth; affinity; relatives by blood.—*a*. Related; of like nature; cognate.

Kinematics, ki-nē-mat'iks, *n*. That branch of mechanics which treats of motion without reference to the forces producing it.

Kinetic, ki-net'ik, *a*. Causing motion; applied to force actually exerted.

King, king, *n*. The sovereign of a nation; monarch; a playing card having the picture of a king; chief piece in the game of chess; in draughts, a piece which has reached the opponent's base, and which can move backwards as well as forwards.

Kingdom, king'dum, *n*. The dominion of a king; realm; a primary division of natural objects (*e.g.* the mineral kingdom); place where anything prevails and holds sway.

Kink, kingk, *n*. A twist in a rope or thread; a

K

crotchet.—*vi*. To twist or run into knots.

Kinsfolk, kinz'fölk, *n*. People of the same kin; kindred; relations.

Kinsman, kinz'man, *n*. A man of the same kin; a relative.

Kipper, kip'ėr, *n*. A salmon at the spawning season; a fish split open, salted, and dried or smoked.—*vt*. To cure (fish) by splitting open, salting, and drying.

Kismet, kis'met, *n*. Fate or destiny.

Kiss, kis, *vi*. To touch with the lips; to caress by joining lips; to touch gently.—*vi*. To join lips; to come in slight contact.—*n*. A salute given with the lips.

Kitchen, ki'chen, *n*. The room of a house appropriated to cooking.

Kitchen-garden, ki'chen-gär-dn, *n*. A garden for raising vegetables for the table.

Kite, kit, *n*. A bird of the falcon family; a light frame of wood and paper constructed for flying in the air.

Kith, kith, *n*. Relatives or friends collectively.

Kitten, kit'n, *n*. A young cat.—*vi*. To bring forth young, as a cat.

Kleptomania, klep-tō-mä'ni-a, *n*. An irresistible mania for pilfering.

Knack, nak, *n*. Facility of performance; dexterity.

Knap, nap, *vt*. (knapping, knapped). To break short (as flints); to snap; to bite off.—*n*. A short sharp noise; a snap.

Knapsack, nap'sak, *n*. A bag for necessaries borne on the back by soldiers, etc.

Knave, näv, *n*. A petty rascal; a dishonest man; a card with a soldier or servant on it.

Knead, nēd, *vt*. To work into a mass or suitable consistency for bread, etc.

Knee, nē, *n*. The joint connecting the two principal parts of the leg; a similar joint; piece of bent timber or iron used in a ship, etc.

Knee-cap, nē'kap, *n*. The movable bone covering the knee-joint in front.

Kneel, nēl, *vi*. (pret. and pp. kneeled and knelt). To bend the knee; to rest on the bended knees.

Knell, nel, *n*. The sound of a bell rung at a funeral; a death signal.—*vi*. To sound, as a funeral bell; to toll; to sound as a bad omen.

Knick-knack, nik'nak, *n*. A trinket.

Knife, nīf, *n*.; pl. **Knives**, nīvz. A cutting instrument consisting of a blade attached to a handle; cutting part of a machine.

Knight, nit, *n*. Formerly one admitted to a certain military rank; now one who holds a dignity entitling him to have *Sir* prefixed to his name, but not hereditary; a champion; a piece in chess.—*vt*. To dub or create a knight.

Knit, nit, *vt*. (knitting, knitted or knit). To tie in a knot; to form in a fabric by looping a continuous thread; to unite closely; to draw together; to contract.—*vi*. To interweave a continuous thread; to grow together.

Knitting, nit'ing, *n*. Formation of a fabric by knitting-needles; fabric thus formed.

Knob, nob, *a*. A hard protuberance; a boss; a round ball at the end of anything.

Knock, nok, *vt*. To strike with something thick or heavy; to strike against; to clash.—*vi*. To strike.—*n*. A stroke; a blow; a rap.

Knocker, nok'ėr, *n*. One who knocks; something on a door for knocking.

Knoll, nōl, *n*. A little round hill; ringing of a bell; knell.—*vt*. and *i*. To sound, as a bell.

Knot, not, *n*. A complication of threads or cords; a tie; ornamental bunch of ribbon, etc.; hard protuberant joint of a plant; a knob; bunch; group; a difficult question; a natutical mile (= 1.151 ordinary mile).—*vt*. (knotting, knotted). To tie in a knot; to unite closely.—*vi*. To become knotted; to knit knots.

Know, nō, *vt*. (pret. knew, pp. known). To perceive with certainty; to understand; to be aware of; to distinguish; to be acquainted with; to have experience of.—*vi*. To have knowledge; not to be doubtful.

Knowledge, nol'ej, *n*. The result or condition of knowing; clear perception; learning; information; skill; acquaintance.

Knuckle, nuk'l, *n*. The joint of a finger, particularly at its base; knee-joint of a calf or pig.—*vt* (knuckling, knuckled). To strike with the knuckles.—**To knuckle down**, or **under**, to yield

Koran, kô'ran, *n*. The book regulating the faith and practice of Mohammedans, written by Mohammed

Kudos, kū'dos, *n*. Glory; fame; renown.

Kyanize, kī'an-īz, *vt*. To preserve (timber) from dry-rot by steeping in a solution of corrosive sublimate.

L

Label, lā'bel, *n*. A slip of paper, etc., affixed to something and stating name, contents, etc.; a slip affixed to deeds to hold the seal.—*vt*. (labelling, labelled). To affix a label to.

Labial, lā'bi-al, *a*. Pertaining to the lips.—*n*. A vowel or consonant formed chiefly by the lips as *b*, *m*, *p*, *o*.

Labium, lā'bi-um, *n*. A lip, especially the lower lip of insects.

Laboratory, lab-or'a-to-ri, *n*. A building or room for experiment in chemistry, physics, etc.; a chemist's work-room.

Labor, lā'bėr, *n*. Exertion, physical or mental; toil work done or to be done; laborers in the aggregate; the pangs and efforts of childbirth.—*vi*. To engage in labor; to work; to proceed with difficulty; to be burdened.—*vt*. To cultivate; to prosecute with effort.

Laborer, lā'bėr-ėr, *n*. One who labors; a man who does work that requires little skill, as distinguished from an artisan.

Labrum, lā'brum, *n*. An upper or outer lip.

Labyrinth, lab'i-rinth, *n*. A place full of intricacies; a maze; an inexplicable difficulty; a part of the internal ear.

Lace, lās, *n*. A cord used for fastening boots, etc. ornamental cord or braid; a delicate fabric of interlacing threads.—*vt*. (lacing, laced). To fasten with a lace; to adorn with lace; to interlace to mingle in small quantity.

Lacerate, la'sėr-āt, *vt*. To tear; to rend; to torture to harrow.

Lachrymal, lak'rim-al, *a*. Generating or secreting tears; pertaining to tears.

Lachrymose, lak'rim-ōs, *a*. Full of tears; tearful in a sentimental way; lugubrious.

Lacing, lās'ing, *n*. A fastening with a lace o cord; a cord used in fastening.

Lack, lak, *vt*. To want; to be without; to need; to require.—*vi*. To be in want.—*n*. Want; deficiency; need; failure.

Lackadaisical, lak-a-dā'zik-al, *a*. Affectedly pensive; weakly sentimental.

Lack-luster, lak'lus-tėr, *a*. Wanting luster.

Laconic, Laconical, la-kon'ik, la-kon'ik-al, *a*. Expressing much in a few words; brief; sententious; pithy.

Lacquer, lak'ėr, *n*. A varnish containing lac, etc ware coated with lacquer.—*vt*. To varnish or coat with lacquer.

Lacros, la-kros', *n*. A game at ball, played with a large battledore or *crosse*.

Lactation, lak-tā'shon, *n*. Act or time of giving suck; function of secreting milk.

Lacteal, lak'tē-al, *a*. Pertaining to milk; conveying chyle.—*n*. A vessel in animal bodies for conveying the chyle from the alimentary canal.

Lactine, Lactose, lak'tin, lak'tōs, *n*. Sugar of milk.

Lacuna, la-kū'na, *n*.; pl. **-nae**. A small depression; a blank space; gap; hiatus.

Lad, lad, *n*. A stripling; a young man.

Ladder, lad'ėr, *n*. An article of wood, rope, etc consisting of two long side-pieces connected b cross-pieces forming steps; means of rising to mience; vertical flaw in stocking, etc.

Laden, lād'n, *p.a.* Loaded; burdened.

Lading, lād'ing, *n.* That which constitutes a load or cargo; freight; burden.

Ladle, lā'dl, *n.* A utensil with a long handle for serving out liquor from a vessel.—*vt.* (lading, ladled). To serve with a ladle.

Lady, lā'di, *n.* A woman of rank or distinction, or of good breeding; a title given to a woman whose husband is not of lower rank than a knight; or whose father was not lower than an earl; the mistress of an estate.

Lag, lag, *a.* Coming behind; sluggish; tardy.—*n.* Quantity of retardation of some movement.—*vt.* (lagging, lagged). To loiter, tarry.

Lager-beer, lā'gėr-bėr, *n.* A German beer stored for some months before use.

Laggard, lag'ärd, *a.* Slow; sluggish; backward.—*n.* One who lags; a loiterer.

Lagoon, Lagune, la-gön', *n.* A shallow lake connected with the sea or a river.

Lair, lār, *n.* A place to lie or rest; the resting-place of a wild beast, etc.

Laisser-faire, lā-sā-fār', *n.* A letting alone, non-interference.

Laity, lā'i-ti, *n.* The people, as distinguished from the clergy; non-professional people.

Lake, lāk, *n.* A body of water wholly surrounded by land; a pigment of earthy substance with red (or other) coloring matter.

Lamb, lam, *n.* The young of the sheep; one as gentle or innocent as a lamb.—*vi.* To bring forth young, as sheep.

Lame, lām, *a.* Crippled in a limb or limbs; disabled; limping; defective; not satisfactory; not smooth.—*vt.* (laming, lamed). To make lame; to render imperfect and unsound.

Lamella, la-mel'la, *n.*; pl. **Lamellae.** A thin plate or scale.

Lament, la-ment', *vi.* To express sorrow; to weep; to grieve.—*vt.* To bewail; to deplore.—*n.* A lamentation; an elegy or mournful ballad.

Lamentation, la-ment-ā'shon, *n.* Act of lamenting; expression of sorrow; complaint.

Lamina, la'mi-na, *n.*; pl. **-nae.** A thin plate or scale; a layer lying over another; the blade of a leaf.

Lamp, lamp, *n.* A vessel for containing oil to be burned by means of a wick; any contrivance for supply artificial light.

Lampoon, lam-pön', *n.* A scurrilous or personal satire in writing; a satiric attack.—*vt.* To write a lampoon against.

Lamprey, lam'prā, *n.* The name of eel-like, scaleless fishes with suctorial mouths, inhabiting fresh and salt waters.

Lance, lans, *n.* A weapon consisting of a long shaft with a sharp-pointed head; a long spear.—*vt.* (lancing, lanced). To pierce with a lance; to open with a lancet.

Land, land, *n.* The solid matter which constitutes the fixed part of the surface of the globe; soil; estate; country; people of a country or region.—*vt.* and *i.* To set or go on the land; to disembark.

Landing, land'ing, *n.* Act of or place for going or setting on shore; level part of a staircase between the flights.

Landlocked, land'lokt, *a.* Inclosed by land, or nearly so, as a part of the sea.

Landlord, land'lord, *n.* The lord of land; owner of land or houses who has tenants under him; master of an inn, etc.

Landlubber, land'lub-ėr, *n.* A seaman's term of contempt for one not a sailor.

Landmark, land'mark, *n.* A mark to designate the boundary of land; an object on land that serves as a guide to seamen.

Landscape, land'skāp, *n.* A portion of land which the eye can comprehend in a single view; a country scene; picture representing a piece of country.

Landslip, Landslide, land'slip, land'slīd, *n.* A portion of a hill which slips down; the sliding down of a piece of land.

Land-surveying, land'sėr-vā-ing, *n.* Act of surveying land; art of determining the boundaries and extent of land.

Lane, lān, *n.* A narrow way or street; a passage between lines of men.

Language, lang'gwāj, *n.* Human speech; speech peculiar to a nation; words especially used in any branch of knowledge; general style of expression; expresson of thought or feeling in any way.

Languid, lang'gwid, *a.* Wanting energy; listless; dull or heavy; sluggish.

Languish, lang'gwish, *vi.* To be or become faint, feeble or spiritless; to fade; to sink under sorrow or any continued passion; to look with tenderness.

Languor, lang'gėr, lang'gwėr, *n.* Languidness; lassitude; a listless or dreamy state.

Lank, langk, *a.* Loose or lax; not plump; gaunt.

Lanoline, lan'ō-lin, *n.* A greasy substance obtained from unwashed wool, used as an ointment.

Lantern, lan'tėrn, *n.* A case in which a light is carried; part of a lighthouse in which is the light; erection on the top of a dome, etc., to give light; a tower with the interior open to view.—*vt.* To provide with a lantern.

Lanyard, lan'yärd, *n.* A short piece of rope or line, used in ships.

Lap, lap, *n.* The loose lower part of a garment; the clothes on the knees of a person when sitting; the knees in this position; part of a thing that covers another; single round of a course in races; a lick, as with the tongue; sound as of water rippling on the beach.—*vt.* (lapping, lapped). To lap; to infold; to lick up; to wash gently against.—*vi.* To lie or be turned over; to lick up food; to ripple gently.

Lapel, la-pel', *n.* That part of the coat which laps over the facing, etc.

Lapidary, lap'i-da-ri, *n.* One who cuts and engraves precious stones.—*a.* Pertaining to the art of cutting stones.

Lapse, laps, *n.* A slipping or gradual falling; unnoticed passing; a slip; a failing in duty; deviation from rectitude.—*vi.* (lapsing, lapsed). To pass slowly; to glide; to slip in moral conduct; to fail in duty; to pass from one to another by some omission.

Larceny, lär'se-ni, *n.* Theft of goods or personal property.

Lard, lard, *n.* The fat of swine, after being melted and separated from the flesh.—*vt.* To apply lard to; to fatten; to stuff with bacon; to interlard.

Large, lärj, *a.* Great in size, number, etc.; not small; copious; big; bulky; wide.—**At large,** without restraint; with all details.

Largely, lärj'li, *adv.* Widely; copiously; amply.

Largess, lärj-es', *n.* A present; a bounty bestowed.

Lariat, lā'ri-at, *n.* The lasso; a long cord or thong of leather with a noose used in catching wild horses, etc.

Lark, lärk, *n.* A small song-bird; a frolic.

Larva, lär'va, *n.*; pl. **Larvae.** An insect in the caterpillar or grub state.

Larynx, la'ringks, *n.*; pl. **Larynxes, Larynges,** la'ringks-ez, la-rin'jēz. The upper part of the windpipe, a cartilaginous cavity serving to modulate the sound of the voice.

Lascivious, las-si'vi-us, *a.* Wanton; lewd; lustful.

Lash, lash, *n.* The thong of a whip; a whip; a stroke with a whip; a stroke of satire; a cutting remark.—*vt.* To strike with a lash; to satirize; to dash against, as waves; to tie with a rope or cord.—*vi.* To ply the whip; to strike at.

Lass, las, *n.* A young woman; a girl.

Lassitude, las'i-tūd, *n.* Faintness; languor of body or mind.

Lasso, las'sō, *n.* A rope with a running noose, used for catching wild horses, etc.—*vt.* To catch with a lasso.

Last, läst, *a.* That comes after all the others; latest; final; next before the present; utmost.—*adv.* The last time; in conclusion.—*vi.* To continue in time; to endure; not to decay or perish.—*vt.* To form on or by a last.—*n.* A mold of the foot on which boots are formed; a weight of 4000 lbs.

Latch, lach, *n.* A catch for fastening a door.—*vt.* To fasten with a latch.

Late, lāt, *a.* Coming after the usual time; slow; not early; existing not long ago, but not now; deceased; recent; modern; last or recently in any place, office, etc.—*adv.* At a late time or period; recently.

Latent, lā'tent, *a.* Not apparent; under the surface.

Lateral, lat'ėr-al, *a.* Pertaining to or on the side; proceeding from the side.

Lath, läth, *n.* A long piece of wood nailed to the rafters to support tiles or plaster.—*vt.* To cover or line with laths.

Lathe, lāTH, *n.* A machine by which articles of wood, etc., are turned and cut into a smooth round form.

Lather, laTH'ėr, *n.* Foam or froth made by soap and water; foam or froth from profuse sweat, as of a horse.—*vt.* To spread over with the foam of soap.—*vi.* To become frothy.

Latin, laïtin, *a.* Pertaining to the Latins, a people of Latium, in Italy; Roman.—*n.* The language of the ancient Romans.

Latitude, la'ti-tūd, *n.* Breadth; width; extent from side to side; scope; laxity; distance north or south of the equator, measured on a meridian; distance of a star north or south of the ecliptic.

Latrine, la-trēn', *n.* A privy, especially one in an institution or camp.

Latter, lat'ėr, *a.* Later; opposed to former; mentioned the last of two; modern; lately done or past.

Lattice, lat'is, *n.* A structure of crossed laths or bars forming small openings like network; a window made of laths crossing like network.—*a.* Furnished with a lattice.—*vt.* To form with cross bars and open work.

Laud, lad, *n.* Praise; a hymn of praise; *pl.* a service of the church comprising psalms of praise.—*vt.* To praise; to celebrate.

Laudanum, la'da·num, *n.* Opium prepared in spirit of wine; tincture of opium.

Laugh, läf, *vi.* To make the involuntary noise which sudden merriment excites; to treat with some contempt; to appear gay, bright, or brilliant.—*vt.* To express by laughing; to affect or effect by laughter.—*n.* The act of laughing; short fit of laughing.

Laughter, läf'tėr, *n.* Act or sound of laughing, expression of mirth peculiar to man.

Launch, länsh or lansh, *vt.* To throw; to cause to slide into the water; to put out into another sphere of duty, etc.—*vi.* To glide, as a ship into the water; to enter on a new field of activity; to expatiate in language.—*n.* Act of launching; the largest boat carried by a man-of-war.

Laundry, län'dri or lan'dri, *n.* Place where clothes are washed and dressed.

Laurel, la'rel, *n.* The bay-tree, a fragrant tree or shrub used in ancient times in making wreaths for victors, etc.; *pl.* a crown of laurel; honor; distinction.

Lava, la'va, *n.* Rock-matter that flows in a molten state from volcanoes.

Lave, lāv, *vt.* (laving, laved). To wash; to bathe; to throw out, as water; to bale.—*vi.* To bathe; to wash oneself; to wash, as the sea on the beach.

Lavender, lav'en-dėr, *n.* An aromatic plant of the mint family, which yields an essential oil and a perfume; a pale blue color with a slight mixture of gray.

Lavish, lav'ish, *a.* Profuse; liberal to a fault; extravagant; superabundant.—*vt.* To expend with profusion; to squander.

Law, la, *n.* A rule prescribed by authority; a stat-

ute; a precept; such rules or statues collectively; legal procedure; litigation; a principle deduced from practice or observation; a formal statement of facts observed in natural phenomena.

Lawless, la'les, *a.* Not subject to law; contrary to law; illegal; capricious.

Lawn, lan, *n.* An open space between woods; a space of smooth level ground covered with grass; a fine linen or cambric.

Lawsuit, la'sūt, *n.* A suit in law for the recovery of a supposed right.

Lawyer, la'yėr, *n.* One versed in the laws, or a practitioner of law.

Lax, laks, *a.* Loose; flabby; soft; slack; vague equivocal; not strict; remiss; having too frequent discharges from the bowels.

Laxative, laks'at-iv, *a.* Having the power of relieving from constipation.—*n.* A gentle purgative.

Laxity, laks'i-ti, *n.* State or quality of being lax want of strictness; looseness.

Lay, lā, *vt.* (pret. and pp. laid). To place in a lying position; to set or place in general; to impose; to bring into a certain state; to settle; to allay; to place at hazard; to wager; to contrive.—*vi.* To bring forth eggs; wager.—*n.* A stratum; a layer one rank in a series reckoned upward; a song; a narrative poem.—*a.* Not clerical; not professional.

Layer, lā'ėr, *n.* One who or that which lays; a stratum; a coat, as of paint; a row of masonry, etc. a shoot of a plant, not detached from the stalk partly laid underground for growth.—*vt.* To propagate by bending a shoot into the soil.

Layman, lā'man, *n.* One not a clergyman.

Lazy, lā'zi, *a.* Disinclined to exertion; slothful; indolent; slow.

Lead, led, *n.* A soft and heavy metal; a plummet a thin plate of type-metal, used to separate lines in printing; plumbago in pencils; *pl.* the leaden covering of a roof.—*a.* Made of lead; produced by lead.—*vt.* To cover with lead; to fit with lead.

Lead, lēd, *vt.* (pret. and pp. led). To guide or conduct; to direct and govern; to precede; to entice to influence; to spend; to begin.—*vi.* To go before and show the way; to be chief or commander; to draw; to have a tendency.—*n.* Guidance; precedence.

Leaden, led'n, *a.* Made of lead; like lead; heavy inert; dull.

Leader, lēd'ėr, *n.* One who leads; a guide; captain; head of a party; editorial article in a news paper.

Leaf, lēf, *n.*; pl. **Leaves,** lēvz. One of the thin, expanded, deciduous growths of a plant; a part of a book containing two pages; a very thin plate the movable side of a table; one side of a double door.—*vi.* To shoot out leaves; to produce leaves

League, lēg, *n.* A combination between states for their mutual aid; an alliance; a compact; a measure of three miles or knots.—*vi.* (leaguing leagued). To form a league; to confederate.

Leak, lēk, *n.* A fissure in a vessel that admits water, or permits it to escape; the passing of fluid through an aperture.—*vi.* To let water in or out of a vessel through a crevice.

Lean, lēn, *vi.* (pret. and pp. leaned). To slope or slant; to incline; to tend; to bend so as to rest on something; to depend.—*vt.* To cause to lean; to support or rest.

Lean, lēn, *a.* Wanting flesh or fat on the body meager; not fat; barren.—*n.* That part of flesh which consists of muscle without fat.

Leap, lēp, *vi.* (pret. and pp. leaped). To spring from the ground; to jump; to rush with violence to bound.—*vt.* To pass over by leaping.—*n.* A jump; a spring; space passed by leaping; a sudden transition.

Leap-frog, lēp'frog, *n.* A game in which one stoops down and others leap over him.

Leap-year, lēp'yėr, *n.* A year containing 366 days

every fourth year.

Learn, lėrn, *vt.* (pret. and pp. learned). To gain knowledge of or skill in; to acquire by study.—*vi.* To gain knowledge; to receive instruction.

Learned, lėrn'ed, *a.* Having much knowledge; erudite; scholarly.

Lease, lēs, *n.* A letting of lands, etc., for a rent, written contract for such letting; any tenure by grant or permission.—*vt.* (leasing, leased). To let; to grant by lease.

Leash, lēsh, *n.* A thong or line by which a dog or hawk is held; three creatures of any kind.—*vt.* To bind by a leash.

Least, lēst, *a.* Smallest.—*adv.* In the smallest or lowest degree.—**At least, at the least,** to say no more; at the lowest degree.

Leather, leṮH'ėr, *n.* The skin of an animal prepared for use; tanned hides in general.—*a.* Leathern.

Leave, lēv, *n.* Permission; liberty granted; a formal parting of friends.—*vt.* (leaving, left). To let remain; to have remaining at death; to bequeath; to quit; to abandon; to refer.—*vi.* To depart; to desist.

Leaven, lev'n, *n.* A substance that produces fermentation, as in dough; yeast; barm.—*vt.* To mix with leaven; to excite fermentation in; to imbue.

Lecher, lech'ėr, *n.* A man given to lewdness.—*vi.* To practice lewdness; to indulge lust.

Lectern, lek'tėrn, *n.* A reading-desk in a church.

Lecture, lek'tūr, *n.* A discourse on any subject; a reprimand; a formal reproof.—*vi.* (lecturing, lectured). To deliver a lecture or lectures.—*vt.* To reprimand; to reprove.

Ledge, lej, *n.* A narrow shelf; a ridge or shelf of rocks.

Ledger, lej'ėr, *n.* The principal book of accounts among merchants and others.

Lee, lē, *n.* The quarter toward which the wind blows; shelter caused by an object keeping off the wind.—*a.* Pertaining to the side towards which the wind blows.

Leech, lēch, *n.* A blood-sucking wormlike animal.—*vt.* To treat or heal; to bleed by the use of leeches.

Leek, lēk, *n.* A culinary vegetable allied to the onion.

Leer, lēr, *n.* A side glance; an arch or affected glance.—*vi.* To give a leer; to look meaningly.—*vt.* To turn with a leer; to affect with a leer.

Leeway, lē'wa, *n.* The drifting of a ship to the leeward.—**To make up leeway,** to overtake work in arrear.

Left, left, *a.* Denoting the part opposed to the right of the body.—*n.* The side opposite to the right.

Left-handed, left'hand-ed, *a.* Using the left hand and arm with more dexterity than the right; sinister; insincere; awkward.

Leg, leg, *n.* The limb of an animal; a lower or posterior limb; the long or slender support of anything.

Legacy, leg'a-si, *n.* A bequest; a particular thing given by last will.

Legal, lē'gal, *a.* According to, pertaining to, or permitted by law; lawful; judicial.

Legalize, lē'gal-iz, *vt.* To make legal or lawful; to authorize; to sanction.

Legate, le'gāt, *n.* An ambassador; the pope's ambassador to a foreign state.

Legation, lē-gā'shon, *n.* An embassy; a diplomatic minister and his suite.

Legend, le'jend or lē'jend, *n.* A marvellous story handed down from early times; a nonhistorical narrative; an inscription.

Legerdemain, lej'er-de-mān'', *n.* Sleight of hand; an adroit trick.

Legible, le'ji-bl, *a.* That may be read.

Legion, lē'jon, *n.* A Roman body of infantry soldiers, in number from 3000 to above 6000; a military force; a great number.

Legislate, le'jis-lāt, *vi.* To make or enact a law or laws.

Legislation, le-jis-lā'shon, *n.* Act of making a law or laws; laws or statutes enacted.

Legislator, le'jis-lāt-ėr, *n.* A lawgiver; one who makes laws.

Legislature, le'jis-lāt-ūr, *n.* The body of men invested with power to make laws.

Legitimate, lē-jit'i-māt, *a.* Accordant with law; born in wedlock; genuine; following by logical or natural sequence; allowable; valid.—*vi.* To make legitimate.

Legume, leg'ūm, le-gūm', *n.* A seed-vessel of two valves; a pod; *pl.* pulse, pease, beans, etc.

Leisure, lē'zhùr or lezh'ùr, *n.* Freedom from occupation; vacant time.—*a.* Not spent in labor; vacant.

Lemma, lem'ma, *n.* A subsidiary proposition in mathematics.

Lemming, lem'ing, *n.* A small rodent mammal.

Lemon, le'mon, *n.* An acid fruit of the orange kind; the tree that produces this fruit.

Lemonade, le-mon-ād', *n.* A beverage, usually aerated, consisting of lemon-juice mixed with water and sweetened.

Lemur, lē'mėr, *n.* A quadrumanous mammal, allied to monkeys and rodents.

Lend, lend, *vt.* (lending, lent). To furnish on condition of the thing being returned; to afford or grant; *refl.* to accommodate.

Length, length, *n.* State or quality of being long; extent from end to end; extenstion; long duration; extent or degree.—**At length,** at full extent; at last.

Lengthen, length'n, *vt.* To make long or longer; to extend.—*vi.* To grow longer.

Lengthwise, length'wiz, *adv.* In the direction of the length; longitudinally.

Lenient, lē'ni-ent, *a.* Acting without rigor; gentle; clement.

Lens, lenz, *n.*; pl. **Lenses,** len'zes. A transparent substance, usually of glass, by which objects appear magnified or diminished; one of the glasses of a telescope, etc.

Lent, lent, *n.* A fast of forty days, from Ash Wednesday till Easter.

Lentil, len'til, *n.* A pea-like plant, having seeds forming a very nutritious diet.

Leo, lē'ō, *n.* The Lion, the fifth sign of the zodiac.

Leonine, lē'ō-nin, *a.* Belonging to a lion; resembling a lion; applied to a rhyming Latin measure of hexameter and pentameter verses.

Leopard, lep'ard, *n.* A large carnivorous animal of the cat genus, with a spotted skin.

Leper, lep'ėr, *n.* One affected with leprosy.

Lepidopterous, lep-i-dop'tėr-us, *a.* Belonging to the order of insects called Lepidoptera, comprising butterflies and moths.

Leprosy, lep'rō-si, *n.* A foul cutaneous disease, characterized by dusky red or livid tubercles on the face or extremities.

Lesion, lē'zhon, *n.* Injury; wound; derangement.

Less, les, *a.* Smaller; not so large or great.—*adv.* In a smaller or lower degree.—*n.* A smaller quantity.

Lessen, les'n, *vt.* To make less; to lower; to depreciate.—*vi.* To become less; to abate.

Lesson, les'n, *n.* Portion which a pupil learns at one time; portion of Scripture read in divine service; something to be learned; severe lecture; truth taught by experience.

Let, let, *vt.* (letting, let). To permit; to allow; to lease.—*vi.* To be leased or let.

Let, let, *vt.* To hinder; to impede.—*n.* A hindrance; impediment.

Lethal, lēth'al, *a.* Deadly; mortal; fatal.

Lethargy, le'thär-ji, *n.* Morbid drowsiness; profound sleep; dulness.

Letter, let'ėr, *n.* A mark used as the representative of a sound; a written message; an epistle; the literal meaning; in *printing,* a single type; *pl.* learning; erudition.—*vt.* To impress or form letters on.

Lettuce, let'is, *n.* An annual composite plant,

L

used in salads.

Leucoma, lū-kō'ma, n. A white opacity of the cornea of the eye.

Leucopathy, lū-kop'a-thi, n. The condition of an albino.

Levant, le-vant', n. The eastern coasts of the Mediterranean.—vi. To run away without paying debts.

Levee, lev'ā or lev'ē, n. A morning reception of visitors held by a prince; in America, a river embankment.

Level, le'vel, n. An instrument for detecting variation from a horizontal surface; an instrument by which to find a horizontal line; a horizontal line or plane; a surface without inequalities; usual elevation; equal elevation with something else; horizontal gallery in a mine.—a. Horizontal; even; flat; having no degree of superiority.—vt. (leveling, leveled). To make level; to lay flat on the ground; to reduce to equality; to point, in taking aim.—vi. To point a gun, etc.; to aim.

Lever, lē'vér, n. A bar used for raising weights, etc.; a kind of watch.

Leverage, lē'vér-āj, n. Action or power of a lever; mechanical advantage gained by using a lever.

Leviathan, lē-vī'a-than, n. An immense seamonster.

Levite, lē'vīt, n. One of the tribe of Levi; a priest; a cleric.

Levity, le'vi-ti, n. Lightness; inconstancy; giddiness; want of seriousness.

Levy, le'vi, vt. (levying, levied). To raise (troops); to collect (taxes); to being (war).—n. Act of raising troops or taxes; the troops or taxes raised.

Lewd, lūd, a. Lustful; sensual; vile.

Lexicographer, leks-i-kog'ra-fér, n. The author or compiler of a dictionary.

Lexicography, leks-i-kog'ra-fi, n. The act or art of compiling a dictionary.

Lexicon, leks'i-kon, n. A word-book; a dictionary; a vocabulary containing an alphabetical arrangement of the words in a language, with the definition of each.

Liable, lī'a-bl, a. Answerable for consequences; responsible; subject; exposed: with to.

Liaison, lē-ā-zōng, n. A bond of union; an illicit intimacy between a man and woman.

Liar, lī'ér, n. One who utters falsehood.

Libation, lī-bā'shon, n. Act of pouring a liquor, usually wine, on the ground or on a victim in sacrifice, in honor of some deity; the wine or other liquor so poured.

Libel, lī'bel, n. A defamatory writing; a malicious publication; the written statement of a plaintiff's ground of complaint against a defendant.—vt. (libelling, libelled). To frame a libel against; to lampoon; to exhibit a charge against in court.

Liberal, lī'bér-al, a. Generous ample; profuse; favorable to reform or progress; not too literal or strict; free.—n. One who advocates great political freedom.

Liberality, li-bér-al'i-ti, n. Largeness of mind; width of sympathy; generosity.

Liberate, lī'bér-āt, vt. To free; to deliver; to set at liberty; to disengage.

Libertine, lī'bér-tin, n. A freedman; one who indulges his lust without restraint; a debauchee.—a. Licentious; dissolute.

Liberty, lī'bér-ti, n. State or condition of one who is free; privilege; immunity; license; district within which certain exclusive privileges may be exercised; freedom of action or speech beyond civility or decorum; state of being disengaged.

Libidinous, li-bid'i-nus, a. Characterized by lust; lascivious; lewd.

Libra, lī'bra, n. The Balance, the seventh sign in the zodiac.

Librarian, li-brā'ri-an, n. The keeper of a library or collection of books.

Library, lī'bra-ri, n. A collection of books; edifice or apartment for holding books.

Librate, lī'brāt, vt. To poise; to balance.—vi. To move, as a balance; to be poised.

Libretto, lī-bret'ō, n. The book of words of an opera, etc.

License, lī'sens, n. Authority or liberty given to do any act; a certificate giving permission; excess of liberty; deviation from an artistic standard.—**License,** vt. (licensing, licensed). To grant a license to; to authorize to act in a particular character.

Licentious, lī-sen'shus, a. Characterized by license; profligate; libidinous.

Lichen, lī'ken or lich'en, n. A plant without stem and leaves, growing on the bark of trees, on rocks, etc.; an eruption of small red or white pimples.

Lick, lik, vt. To draw the tongue over the surface of; to lap; to take in by the tongue; to beat.—n. A drawing of the tongue over anything; a slight smear or coat; a blow.

Licorice, lik'or-is, n. Liquorice.

Lid, lid, n. A movable cover of a vessel or box; eyelid.

Lie, lī, vi. (lying, lied). To utter falsehood with deceitful intention.—n. A falsehood; an intentional violation of truth.

Lie, lī, vi. (lying, pret. lay, pp. lain). To occupy a horizontal position; to rest on anything lengthwise; to be situated; to remain; to be incumbent; to exist; to depend; to be sustainable in law.—**To lie in,** to be in childbed.—**To lie to,** to stop and remain stationary.—n. Relative position of objects; general bearing or direction.

Lien, lī'en, n. A legal claim; a right over the property of another until some claim or due is satisfied.

Lieu, lū, n. Place; stead: preceded by in.

Lieutenant, lū-ten'ant, n. An officer who supplies the place of a superior in his absence; a commissioned army officer next in rank below a captain; commissioned naval officer below a lieutenant-commander.

Life, līf, n.; pl. **Lives,** līvz. State of animals and plants in which the natural functions are performed; vitality; present state of existence; time from birth to death; manner of living; animal being; spirit; vivacity; the living form; exact resemblance; rank in society; human affairs; a person; narrative of a life; eternal felicity.

Life-blood, līf'blud, n. The blood necessary to life; vital blood.

Life-boat, līf'bōt, n. A boat for saving men in cases of shipwreck.

Lifeless, līf'les, a. Deprived of life; dead; inanimate; dull; heavy; inactive.

Lifelike, līf'līk, a. Like a living person; true to the life.

Lifetime, līf'tīm, n. The time that life continues; duration of life.

Lift, lift, vt. To raise to a higher position; to hoist; to elevate; to raise in spirit; to collect when due.—vi. To raise; to rise.—n. Act of lifting; assistance; that which is to be raised; an elevator or hoist.

Ligament, li'ga-ment, n. That which unites one thing to another; a band; a substance serving to bind one bone to another.

Ligature, li'ga-tūr, n. Anything that binds; a band or bandage.

Light, līt, n. That by which objects are rendered visible; day; that which gives or admits light; illumination of mind; knowledge; open view; explanation; point of view; situation; spiritual illumination.—a. Bright; clear; not deep, as color; not heavy; not difficult; easy to be digested; active; not laden; slight; moderate; unsteady; gay; trifling; wanton; sandy; having a sensation of giddiness; employed in light work.—adv. Lightly; cheaply.—vt. (pret. and pp. lighted or lit). To give light to; to enlighten; to ignite.—vi. To brighten; to descend, as from a horse, etc.; to alight; to come by chance.

Lighten, lit'n, vi. To become brighter; to shine; to flash, as lightning.—vt. To illuminate; to enlighten; to flash forth; to make less heavy; to alleviate; to cheer; to gladden.

Light-footed, lit'fut-ed, a. Nimble; active.

Light-hearted, lit'härt-ed, a. Free from grief or anxiety; gay; cheerful; merry.

Lighthouse, lit'hous, n. A tower with a light on the top to direct seamen at night.

Lightning, lit'ning, n. The sudden and vivid flash that precedes thunder, produced by a discharge of atmospheric electricity.

Lights, lits, n.pl. The lungs of animals.

Lignite, lig'nit, n. Fossil wood or brown-coal.

Like, lik, a. Equal; similar; resembling; likely; feeling disposed.—adv. or prep. In the same manner; similarly; likely.—vt. (liking, liked). To be pleased with; to approve.—vi. To be pleased; to choose.—n. Some person or thing resembling another; a counterpart; a liking; a fancy.

Likelihood, lik'li-hud, n. Probability; appearance of truth or reality.

Liken, lik'en, vt. To compare; to represent as resembling or similar.

Likeness, lik'nes, n. Quality or state of being like; resemblance; similarity; one who resembles another; a portrait.

Lilac, li'lak, n. A shrub with flowers generally bluish or white.

Lilliputian, lil-i-pū'shan, n. A person of very small size.—a. Very small.

Lilt, lilt, vt. and i. To sing cheerfully; to give musical utterance.—n. A song; a tune.

Lily, lil'i, n. A bulbous plant with showy and fragrant flowers.

Limb, lim, n. The arm or leg, especially the latter; a branch of a tree; graduated edge of a quadrant, etc.; border of the disc of the sun, moon, etc.—vt. To supply with limbs; to tear off the limbs of.

Limber, lim'ber, a. Flexible; pliant.—n. A carriage with ammunition boxes attached to the gun-carriage.—vt. and i. To attach the limber to the gun-carriage.

Limbo, lim'bo, n. A supposed region beyond this world for souls of innocent persons ignorant of Christianity; any similar region; a prison of confinement.

Lime, lim, n. Any viscous substance; calcareous earth used in cement; mortar made with lime; the linden-tree; a tree producing an inferior sort of lemon.—vt. (liming, limed). To smear or manure with lime; to ensnare; to cement.

Limerick, lim'er-ik, n. A nonsense verse form of five lines, popularized by Edward Lear (1812-88) in his *Book of Nonsense* (1840).

Limestone, lim'ston, n. A kind of stone consisting of varieties of carbonate of lime.

Limit, lim'it, n. Boundary; border; utmost extent; restraint; restriction. vt. To bound; to circumscribe; to restrain; to restrict.

Limited, lim'it-ed, a. Narrow; circumscribed; confined; restricted.

Limp, limp, vi. To halt; to walk lamely.—n. A halt; act of limping.—a. Easily bent; pliant; flaccid.

Limpid, lim'pid, a. Clear; crystal; pellucid.

Line, lin, n. A small rope or cord; a threadlike marking; a stroke or score; a row of soldiers, ships, words, etc.; a verse; an outline; a short written communication; course of procedure, etc.; connected series, as of descendants; series of public conveyances, as steamers; the twelfth part of an inch; the equator; the regular infantry of an army; pl. works covering extended positions and presenting a front in only one direction to the enemy.—vt. (lining, lined). To draw lines upon; to set with men or things in lines; to cover on the inside; to put in the inside of.

Lineament, lin'ē-a-ment, n. One of the lines which mark the features; feature; form.

Linen, lin'en, n. Cloth made of flax; under clothing.—a. Made of flax; resembling linen cloth.

Linger, ling'ger, vi. To delay; to loiter; to hesitate; to remain long.—vt. To spend wearily.

Lingo, ling'go, n. Language; speech; contemptuous term for a peculiar language.

Lingual, ling'gwal, a. Pertaining to the tongue.—n. A sound pronounced with the tongue, as l.

Linguist, ling'gwist, n. A person skilled in languages.

Liniment, lin'i-ment, n. A species of soft ointment; an embrocation.

Lining, lin'ing, n. The covering of the inner surface of anything.

Link, lingk, n. A single ring of a chain; anything closed like a link; anything connecting; a measure of 7.92 inches; a torch.—vi. To be connected.—vt. To join or connect, as by links; to unite.

Linseed, lin'sed, n. Flax-seed.

Lintel, lin'tel, n. The horizontal part of the door or window frame.

Lion, li'on, n. A carnivorous animal of the cat family; a sign in the zodiac, Leo; an object of interest and curiosity.

Lion-hearted, li'on-härt-ed, a. Having a lion's courage; brave and magnanimous.

Lionize, li'on-iz, vt. To treat as an object of curiosity and interest.

Lip, lip, n. One of the two fleshy parts covering the front teeth in man, etc.; edge or border.—vt. (lipping, lipped). To touch as with the lip.

Lipstick, lip-stik, n. A cosmetic used by women for heightening the color of the lips.

Liquefaction, lik-wē-fak'shon, n. Act or operation of melting; state of being melted.

Liquefy, lik'wē-fi, vt. To melt; to dissolve by heat.—vi. To become liquid.

Liqueur, li-kūr' or li-kör', n. An alcoholic beverage sweetened and containing some infusion of fruits or aromatic substances.

Liquid, lik'wid, a. Fluid; not solid; soft; smooth; devoid of harshness.—n. A fluid; a letter with a smooth flowing sound, as l and r.

Liquidate, lik'wid-āt, vt. To clear from obscurity; to adjust; to settle, adjust, and apportion, as a bankrupt's affairs.

Liquor, lik'er, n. A liquid; spirituous fluids; drink.

Lisp, lisp, vi. To pronounce the sibilant letters imperfectly, as in pronouncing th for s; to speak imperfectly, as a child.—vt. To pronounce with a lisp, or imperfectly.—n. The habit or act of lisping.

Lissom, lis'um, a. Supple; flexible; lithe; nimble; active.

List, list, n. The selvedge of cloth; a limit or border; a roll or catalogue; inclination to one side; pl. a field inclosed for a combat.—vt. To enroll; to enlist.—vi. To enlist, as in the army; to desire; to be disposed; to hearken.

Listen, lis'n, vi. To hearken; to give heed. vi. To hear; to attend.

Listless, list'les, a. Having no wish; indifferent; uninterested; languid; weary.

Litany, li'ta-ni, n. A solemn supplication; a collection of short supplications uttered by the priest and people alternately.

Liter, lē'tr, n. The French standard measure of capacity, equal to 61.028 cubic inches; the English imperial gallon being fully 4½ liters.

Literal, li'ter-al, a. According to the exact meaning; not figurative; expressed by letters.

Literary, li'ter-a-ri, a. Pertaining to letters or literature; versed in letters.

Literate, li'ter-āt, a. Learned; literary.

Literature, li'ter-a-tūr, n. Learning; literary knowledge; collective writings of a country or period; belles-lettres; the literary profession.

Lithe, liᵺH, a. Pliant; flexible; limber.

Lithium, lith'i-um, n. The lightest of all known solids.

Lithology, li-thol'o-ji, n. The knowledge of rocks; study of the mineral structure of rocks.

Litigant, li'ti-gant, a. Disposed to litigate; en-

L

gaged in a lawsuit.—*n*. One engaged in a lawsuit.

Litigate, li'ti-gāt, *vt*. To contest in law.—*vi*. To carry on a suit by judicial process.

Litigious, li-tij'us, *a*. Apt to go to law; disputable; contentious.

Litmus, lit'mus, *n*. A coloring matter procured from certain lichens, used as a chemical test.

Litter, lit'ér, *n*. A frame supporting a bed in which a person may be borne; straw used as a bed for animals; the young produced at a birth by a quadruped; scattered rubbish; a condition of disorder.—*vt*. To furnish with bedding; to scatter in a slovenly manner; to bring forth.—*vi*. To lie in litter; to give birth to a litter.

Little, lit'l, *a*. Small in size or extent, short in duration; slight; mean.—*n*. A small quantity, space, etc.—**A little,** somewhat.—*adv*. In a small degree or quantity.

Liturgy, li'tér-ji, *n*. A ritual or established formulas for public worship.

Live, liv, *vi*. (living, lived). To exist; to be alive; to dwell; to conduct oneself in life; to feed or subsist; to acquire a livelihood; to be exempt from spiritual death.—*vt*. To lead, pass, or spend.

Live, līv, *a*. Having life; alive; not dead, ignited; vivid, as color.

Livelihood, līv'li-hud, *n*. Means of living; maintenance; sustenance.

Lively, līv'li, *a*. Vivacious; active; gay; vivid.—*adv*. Briskly; vigorously.

Liver, liv'ér, *n*. One who lives; the organ in animals which secretes the bile.

Livid, liv'id, *a*. Black and blue; of a lead color; discolored, as flesh by contusion.

Living, liv'ing, *p.a*. Having life; existing; in action or use.—*n*. Means of subsistence; manner of life; the benefice of a clergyman.

Lizard, li'zérd, *n*. A four-footed, tailed reptile.

Llama, lä'mä or lyä'mä, *n*. A S. American ruminating animal allied to the camel, but smaller and without a hump.

Lloyd's, loidz, *n*. A society in London for the collection and diffusion of maritime intelligence, the insurance, classification, and certification of vessels, etc.

Load, lōd, *vt*. To charge with a load; to burden; to encumber; to bestow in great abundance; to charge, as a gun.—*n*. A burden; cargo; a grievous weight; something that oppresses.

Loadstar, Lodestar, lōd'stär, *n*. A star that serves to guide; the pole-star.

Loadstone, Lodestone, lōd'stōn, *n*. An ore of iron; the magnetic oxide of iron, which can attract iron; a magnet.

Loaf, lōf, *n*.; pl. **Loaves,** lōvz. A mass of bread formed by the baker; a conical lump of sugar.—*vi*. To lounge.—*vt*. To spend idly.

Loam, lōm, *n*. A rich species of earth or mold.—*vt*. To cover with loam.

Loan, lōn, *n*. Lending; that which is lent; a sum of money lent at interest.—*vt*. and *i*. To lend.

Loath, Loth, lōth, *a*. Disliking; unwilling; averse; not inclined; reluctant.

Loathe, lōтн, *vt*. (loathing, loathed). To feel disgust at; to abhor; to abominate.—*vi*. To feel nausea or abhorrence.

Loathing, lōтн'ing, *n*. Extreme disgust or aversion; abhorrence; detestation.

Loathness, lōтн'sum, *a*. Exciting disgust; disgusting; detestable; abhorrent.

Lob, lob, *n*. A dolt; a lout.—*vt*. (lobbing, lobbed). To throw or toss slowly.

Lobby, lob'i, *n*. An apartment giving admission to others; an entrance-hall.

Lobe, lōb, *n*. A round projecting part of something; such a part of the liver, lungs, brain, etc.; the lower soft part of the ear.

Lobster, lob'stér, *n*. A ten-footed crustacean with large claws, allied to the crab.

Local, lō'kal, *a*. Pertaining to a particular place; confined to a spot or definite district.—*n*. A local item of news; a local railway train.

Locality, lō-kal'i-ti, *n*. State of being local; position; situation; place.

Localize, lō'kal-īz, *vt*. To make local; to discover or detect the place of.

Locate, lō'kāt, *vt*. (locating, located). To place; to settle.—*vi*. To reside.

Lock, lok, *n*. An appliance for fastening doors, etc.; mechanism by which a firearm is discharged; a fastening together; inclosure in a canal, with gates at either end; a tuft or ringlet of hair.—*vt*. To fasten with a lock and key; to shut up or confine; to join firmly; to embrace closely.—*vi*. To become fast; to unite closely by mutual insertion.

Locket, lok'et, *n*. A little case worn as an ornament, often containing a lock of hair.

Locksmith, lok'smith, *n*. An artificer who makes or mends locks.

Locomotion, lō-kō-mō'shon, *n*. Act or power of moving from place to place.

Locomotive, lō-kō-mō'tiv, *a*. Moving from place to place.—*n*. A steam-engine placed on wheels, and employed in moving a train of carriages on a railway.

Locust, lō'kust, *n*. A large insect allied to the grasshopper; the locust-tree.

Lode, lōd, *n*. An open ditch; a metallic vein, or any regular mineral vein.

Lodge, loj, *n*. A small country house; a temporary abode; place where members of a society, as freemasons, meet; the society itself.—*vt*. (lodging, lodged). To furnish with temporary accommodation; to set or deposit for keeping; to beat down (growing crops).—*vi*. To have a temporary abode; to settle; to reside.

Loft, loft, *n*. The space below and between the rafters; a gallery raised within a larger apartment or in a church.

Lofty, loft'i, *a*. Elevated in place; rising to a great height; proud; haughty; sublime; stately.

Log, log, *n*. A bulky piece of timber unhewed; a floating contrivance for measuring the rate of a ship's velocity; a log-book.

Logan-berry, lō'gan-be''ri, *n*. A cross between a blackberry and a raspberry.

Logarithm, log'a-rithm, *n*. In *mathematics*, the exponent of the power to which a given invariable number must be raised in order to produce another given number.

Log-book, log'buk, *n*. Register of a ship's way, and of the incidents of the voyage.

Loggerhead, log'ér-hed, *n*. A blockhead; a dunce.—**At loggerheads,** quarrelling.

Logic, lo'jik, *n*. The science or art of reasoning; mode of arguing.

Logistic, lō-jis'tik, *a*. Pertaining to judging, estimating, or calculating.

Log-rolling, log'rōl-ing, *n*. The joining of a number of persons to collect logs; union for mutual assistance or praise.

Loin, loin, *n*. The part of an animal on either side between the ribs and the haunch-bone.

Loiter, loi'tér, *vi*. To be slow in moving; to spend time idly; to hang about.—*vi*. To waste carelessly; with *away*.

Loll, lol, *vi*. (lolling, lolled). To lean idly; to lie at ease; to hang out, as the tongue of a dog.—*vt*. To suffer to hang out.

Lone, lōn, *a*. Solitary; unfrequented; single.

Lonely, lōn'li, *a*. Unfrequented by men; retired; solitary.

Long, long, *a*. Drawn out in a line; drawn out in time; tedious; protracted; late; containing much verbal matter.—*n*. Something that is long.—*adv*. To a great extent in space or in time; at a point of duration far distant.—*vi*. To desire eagerly; with *for*.

Longevity, lon-jev'i-ti, *n*. Great length of life.

Longhand, long'hand, *n*. Ordinary written characters, as distinguished from shorthand, etc.

Longitude, lon'ji-tūd, *n*. Length; distance on the surface of the globe east or west, measured by meridians.

Long-suffering, long'suf-ér-ing, *a.* Patient; not easily provoked.—*n.* Patience of offense.

Long-winded, long'wind-ed, *a.* Not easily exhausted of breath; tedious.

Loofah, lö'fa, *n.* The dried fibrous interior of a kind of gourd, used as a flesh-brush.

Look, luk, *vi.* To direct the eye so as to see; to gaze; to consider; to expect; to heed; to face; to appear.—*vt.* To see; to express by a look.—*n.* Act of looking; sight; gaze; glance; mien; aspect.

Look-out, luk-out', *n.* A careful watching for any object; place from which such observation is made; person watching.

Loom, löm, *n.* A frame or machine by which thread is worked into cloth; that part of an oar within the boat in rowing.—*vi.* To appear larger than the real dimensions, and indistinctly; to appear to the mind faintly.

Loop, löp, *n.* A noose; a doubling of a string, etc.; a small narrow opening.—*vt.* To form into or fasten with a loop.

Loophole, löp'höl, *n.* A small opening in a fortification through which small-arms are discharged; a hole that affords means of escape; underhand method of evasion.

Loose, lös, *a.* Not attached; untied; not dense or compact; vague; careless; having lax bowels; unchaste.—*vt.* (loosing, loosed). To untie or unbind; to detach; to set free; to relax; to loosen.

Loot, löt, *n.* Booty; plunder, especially such as is taken in a sacked city.—*vt.* To plunder.

Lop, lop, *vt.* (lopping, lopped). To cut off; to trim by cutting.—*n.* That which is cut from trees.

Lop-sided, lop'sid-ed, *a.* Heavier at one side than the other; inclining to one side.

Loquacious, lo-kwä'shus, *a.* Talkative; garrulous; babbling.

Loquacity, lo-kwas'i-ti, *n.* Quality of being loquacious; garrulity.

Lord, lord, *n.* A master; a ruler; proprietor of a manor; a nobleman; a British title applied to peers, sons of dukes and marquises, and the eldest sons of earls; honorary title of certain high officials; (with *cap.*) the Supreme Being.—*vi.* To act as a lord; to rule with arbitrary or despotic sway.

Lore, lôr, *n.* Learning; erudition; space between the bill and the eye of a bird.

Lorgnette, lor-nyet', *n.* An opera-glass.

Lose, löz, *vt.* (losing, lost). To cease to possess, as through accident; to fail to keep, to forfeit, not to gain or win; to miss; to cease or fail to see or hear; to misuse.—*vt.* To suffer loss; not to win.

Loss, los, *n.* Act of losing; failure to gain; that which is lost; failure to utilize.

Lost, lost, *p.a.* Gone from our hold, view, etc.; not to be found; ruined; wasted; forfeited; perplexed; alienated.

Lot, lot, *n.* A person's part or share; fate which falls to one; part in life allotted to a person; a distinct portion; a considerable quantity or number; something used to decide what is yet undecided.—*vt.* (lotting, lotted). To assign by lot; to sort; to sort.

Lothario, lö-thä'ri-ö, *n.* A gay libertine.

Lotion, lö'shon, *n.* A wash for the complexion; a fluid applied externally in ailments.

Lottery, lot'e-ri, *n.* A scheme for the distribution of prizes by lot or chance.

Lotus, lö'tus, *n.* A tree, the fruit of which was fabled to cause forgetfulness of the past; also the Egyptian water lily and other plants.

Loud, loud, *a.* Having a great sound; noisy; showy.—*adv.* Loudly.

Loudspeaker, loud-spē'kėr, *n.* A device for converting electrical energy into sounds capable of being heard at a distance.

Lounge, lounj, *vi.* (lounging, lounged). To loiter; to loll.—*n.* An idle gait or stroll; act of reclining at ease; a place for lounging.

Louse, lous, *n.;* pl. **Lice,** lis. A wingless insect, parasitic on man and other animals.

Lout, lout, *n.* A mean, awkward fellow.—*vt.* To bend or stoop down.

Lovable, luv'a-bl, *a.* Worthy of love; amiable.

Love, luv, *vt.* (loving, loved). To regard with affection; to like; to delight in.—*vi.* To love; to be tenderly attached.—*n.* Warm affection; fond attachment; the passion between the sexes; the object beloved; a word of endearment; Cupid, the god of love; the score of nothing at tennis, etc.

Lovely, luv'li, *a.* That may excite love; beautiful; charming; delightful.

Lover, luv'ėr, *n.* One who loves; a suitor; a wooer; one who likes strongly.

Loving-kindness, luv-ing-kïnd'nes, *n.* Tender regard; mercy; favor.

Low, lö, *a.* Depressed below any given surface or place; not high; deep; below the usual rate; not loud; wanting strength; mean; dishonorable; not sublime; plain.—*adv.* Not aloft; under the usual price; near the ground; not loudly.

Low, lö, *vi.* To bellow, as an ox or cow.

Lower, lö'ėr, *vt.* To make lower; to let down; to abase; to reduce.

Lowering, lou'ėr-ing, *p.a.* Threatening a storm; cloudy; overcast.

Lowing, lö'ing, *n.* The bellow of cattle.

Loyal, loi'al, *a.* Faithful to a government, plighted love, duty, etc.; constant to friends or associates.

Loyalty, loi'al-ti, *n.* State or quality of being loyal; fidelity; constancy.

Lozenge, lo'zenj, *n.* A figure with four equal sides, having two acute and two obtuse angles; a small cake of sugar, etc.; a small diamond-shaped pane of glass.

Lubricant, lü'brik-ant, *n.* A substance for oiling or greasing.

Lubricate, lü-brik-āt, *vt.* To make smooth; to smear with oil, to diminish friction.

Lubricity, lü-bris'i-ti, *n.* Smoothness of surface; slipperiness; lasciviousness.

Lucent, lü'sent, *a.* Shining; resplendent.

Lucid, lü'sid, *a.* Full of light; shining; bright; clear; not darkened or confused by delirium; easily understood.

Lucifer, lü'si-fėr, *n.* The morning-star; Satan; a match ignitible by friction.

Luck, luk, *n.* That which happens to a person, chance; hap; fortune; success.

Lucky, luk'i, *a.* Meeting with good luck or success; fortunate; auspicious.

Lucrative, lü'krat-iv, *a.* Pertaining to gain; gainful; profitable.

Ludicrous, lü'di-krus, *a.* That serves for sport; laughable; droll; ridiculous.

Luggage, lug'āj, *n.* Anything cumbersome and heavy; a traveller's baggage.

Lugubrious, lü-gü'bri-us, *a.* Mournful; indicating sorrow; doleful.

Lukewarm, lük'warm, *a.* Moderately warm; tepid; not zealous; indifferent.

Lull, lul, *vt.* To sing to, as to a child; to soothe.—*vi.* To subside; to become calm. *n.* A season of quiet or cessation.

Lullaby, lul'a-bï, *n.* A song to lull or quiet babes; that which quiets.

Lumbago, lum-bā'gô, *n.* A rheumatic affection of the muscles about the loins.

Lumbar, lum'bar, *n.* Pertaining to or near the loins.

Lumber, lum'bėr, *n.* Anything useless and cumbersome; in America, timber sawed or split for use.—*vt.* To fill with lumber; to heap together in disorder.—*vi.* To move heavily, as a vehicle; in America, to cut and prepare timber.

Luminary, lü'min-a-ri, *n.* Any body that gives light.

Luminosity, lü-min-os'i-ti, *n.* The quality of being luminous; brightness; clearness.

Luminous, lü'min-us, *a.* Shining; bright; giving light; clear; lucid.

Lump, lump, *n.* A small mass of matter; a mass of things.—*vt.* To throw into a mass; to take in the gross.

Lunacy, lū'na-si, n. Mental derangement; madness; insanity; craziness; mania.

Lunar, lū'nar, a. Pertaining to the moon; measured by the revolutions of the moon.

Lunch, Luncheon, lunsh, lunsh'on, n. A slight repast between breakfast and dinner.—vi. To take a lunch.

Lune, lūn, n. Anything in the shape of a half-moon or a crescent.

Lung, lung, n. Either of the two organs of respiration in air-breathing animals.

Lunge, lunj, n. A sudden thrust or pass, as with a sword.—vi. (lunging, lunged). To make a thrust.

Lunular, lū'nū-lėr, a. Having the form of a small crescent.

Lupine, lū'pin, n. A leguminous flowering plant.—a. lū'pin. LIke a wolf; wolfish.

Lupus, lū'pus, n. A disease which eats away the flesh of the face.

Lurch, lėrch, vi. To lurk; to roll or sway to one side.—n. A sudden roll or stagger; a difficult or helpless position.

Lure, lūr, n. Something held out to call a trained hawk; a bait; any enticement.—vt. (luring, lured). To attract by a lure or bait; to entice.

Lurid, lū'rid, a. Pale yellow, as flame; ghastly pale; wan; gloomy; dismal.

Lurk, lėrk, vi. To lie hid; to lie in wait.

Luscious, lu'shus, a. Very sweet; delicious; sweet to excess.

Lush, lush, a. Fresh, succulent.

Lust, lust, n. Longing desire; carnal appetite; depraved affections.—vi. To desire eagerly; to have carnal desire.

Luster, lus'ter, n. Brightness; brilliancy; renown; a branched chandelier ornamented with cut glass; a glossy fabric for dress.

Lustily, lust'i-li, adv. In a lusty manner; with vigor of body; stoutly.

Lustral, lus'tral, a. Used in purification; pertaining to purification.

Lustrate, lus'trāt, vt. To purify as by water.

Lustrous, lus'trus, a. Full of luster; bright; shining; luminous.

Lusty, lust'i, a. Vigorous; robust; healthful; bulky; large; lustful.

Lute, lūt, n. A stringed instrument of the guitar kind; a composition of clay, etc.—vt. (luting, luted). To play on the lute; to close or coat with lute.

Lutheran, lū'thėr-an, a. Pertaining to Martin Luther, the reformer.—n. A follower of Luther.

Luxate, luks'āt, vt. To put out of joint, as a limb; to dislocate.

Luxuriant, luks-ū'ri-ant, a. Exuberant in growth; abundant.

Luxuriate, luks-ū'ri-āt, vi. To grow exuberantly; to feed or live luxuriously; to indulge without restraint.

Luxurious, luks-ū'ri-us, a. Given to luxury; voluptuous; furnished with luxuries.

Luxury, luks'ū-ri, n. Extravagant indulgence; that which gratifies a fastidious appetite; anything delightful to the senses.

Lycanthropy, lī-kan'thro-pi, n. A kind of insanity in which the patient supposes himself to be a wolf.

Lyceum, lī-sē'um, n. A literary institute; a higher school.

Lye, lī, n. Water impregnated with alkaline salt imbibed from the ashes of wood; solution of an alkali.

Lymph, limf, n. Water; a watery fluid; a colorless fluid in animal bodies.

Lymphatic, lim-fat'ik, a. Pertaining to lymph; phlegmatic; sluggish.—n. A vessel in animal bodies which contains or conveys lymph.

Lynch, linsh, vt. To inflict punishment upon, without the forms of law, as by a mob.

Lynx, lingks, n. A carnivorous animal resembling the cat, noted for its keen sight.

Lyre, līr, n. A stringed instrument of the harp kind much used by the ancients.

Lyric, Lyrical, li'rik, li'rik-al, a. Pertaining to a lyre; designating that species of poetry which has reference to the individual emotions of the poet, such as songs.—**Lyric,** li'rik, n. A lyric poem; an author of lyric poems.

M

Macabre, mak-a'br, a. Gruesome; terrible.

Macaroni, ma-ka-rō'ni, n. A paste of fine wheat flour made into small tubes; a kind of dandy in fashion in London about 1760.

Macaroon, ma-ka-rön', n. A small sweet-cake, containing almonds.

Macaw, ma-ka', n. A bird of the parrot tribe with long tail-feathers.

Mace, mās, n. A staff with a heavy metal head; an ensign of authority borne before magistrates; a spice, the dried covering of the seed of the nutmeg.

Macerate, ma'se-rāt, vt. To steep almost to solution; to make lean or cause to waste away.

Machiavelian, ma'ki-a-vēl'i-an, a. Pertaining to *Machiavelli*, or denoting his principles; cunning in political management.

Machinate, mak'i-nāt, vt. and i. To plot or plan; to form, as a plot or scheme.

Machine, ma-shēn', n. Any contrivance which serves to regulate the effect of a given force or to produce or change motion; an organized system; a person who acts as the tool of another.—vt. To apply machinery to; to produce by machinery.

Machinery, ma-shēn'e-ri, n. The component parts of a complex machine; machines in general.

Mackerel, mak'ėr-el, n. An edible sea fish.

Macrocosm, mak'ro-kozm, n. The great world; the universe, analogous to the *microcosm*.

Macula, ma'kū-la, n.; pl. **-lae.** A spot, as on the skin.

Maculate, ma'kū-lāt, vt. To spot; to stain.—a. Marked with spots; impure.

Mad, mad, a. Disordered in intellect; insane; crazy; frantic; furious; infatuated.—vt. (madding, madded). To make mad.

Madden, mad'n, vt. To make mad.—vi. To become mad; to act as if mad.

Madeira, ma-dē'ra, n. A rich wine made on the isle of Madeira.

Madness, mad'nes, n. Lunacy; frenzy; extreme folly.

Madonna, ma-don'na, n. The Virgin Mary; a picture representing the Virgin.

Madrigal, mad'ri-gal, n. A pastoral song; vocal composition in five or six parts.

Maestro, mä-es'trō, n. A master of any art; a musical composer.

Magazine, mag'a-zēn, n. A storehouse; a repository for ammunition or provisions; a serial publication.

Magenta, ma-jen'ta, n. A brilliant blue-red color derived from coal-tar.

Maggot, ma'got, n. The larva of a fly or other insect; a grub; an odd fancy.

Magi, mä'jī, n.pl. The caste of priests among the ancient Medes and Persians; holy men or sages of the East.

Magic, ma'jik, n. The art of producing effects by superhuman means; sorcery; enchantment; power similar to that of enchantment.—a. Pertaining to magic; working or worked by or as if by magic.

Magician, ma-ji'shan, n. One skilled in magic; an enchanter.

Magisterial, ma-jis-tē'ri-al, a. Pertaining to a master or magistrate; imperious; haughty; authoritative.

Magistrate, ma'jis-trāt, n. A public civil officer, with executive or judicial authority.

agnanimity, mag-na-nim´i-ti, *n.* Quality of being magnanimous; greatness of soul or mind.

agnate, mag´nāt, *n.* A great man; a person of rank or wealth.

agnesia, mag-nē´si-a, *n.* Oxide of magnesium, a white slightly alkaline powder.

agnet, mag´net, *n.* The loadstone, which has the property of attracting iron; a bar of iron or steel to which the properties of the loadstone have been imparted.

agnetic, mag-net´ik, *a.* Pertaining to the magnet; possessing the properties of the magnet; attractive.

agnetism, mag´net-izm, *n.* A property of certain bodies whereby they naturally attract or repel one another; that branch of science which treats of magnetic phenomena; power of attraction.

agneto, mag-nēt´ō, *n.* The igniting apparatus of a petrol engine.

agnificence, mag-nif´i-sens, *n.* Grandeur of appearance; splendor; pomp.

agnify, mag´ni-fi, *vt.* To make great or greater; to increase the apparent dimensions of; to extol; to exaggerate.—*vi.* To possess the quality of causing objects to appear larger.

agnitude, mag´ni-tūd, *n.* Greatness; size; bulk; importance; consequence.

agnum, mag´num, *n.* A bottle holding two English quarts.

agpie, mag´pī, *n.* A chattering bird of the crow tribe with black and white plumage; a shot on the target between an inner and an outer.

ahogany, ma-hog´a-ni, *n.* A tree of tropical America; its wood, reddish in color, used for cabinet work.

aid, mād, *n.* A young unmarried woman; a girl; a virgin; a female servant.

aiden, mād´n, *n.* A maid or virgin; an old Scottish instrument of capital punishment resembling the guillotine.—*a.* Pertaining to maidens; unpolluted; unused; first.

aidenhair, mād´n-hār, *n.* An elegant fern found growing on rocks and walls.

aidenhead, mād´n-hed, *n.* Virginity; the hymen.

ail, māl, *n.* A bag for conveying letters, etc.; letters conveyed; person or conveyance carrying the mail; armor of chain-work, etc.—*vt.* (mailing, mailed). To send by mail; to post; to arm with mail.

aim, mām, *vt.* To mutilate; to disable.—*n.* An injury by which a person is maimed.

ain, mān, *a.* Chief, or most important, mighty, vast; directly applied; used with all one's might —*n.* Strength; great effort; chief or main portion; the ocean; a principal gas or water pipe in a street; a hand at dice; a match at cockfighting.

ainland, mān´land, *n.* The principal land, as opposed to an isle; the continent.

ain-spring, mān´spring, *n.* The principal spring of any piece of mechanism; the main cause of any action.

aintain, mān-tān´, *vt.* To hold or keep in any particular state; to sustain; to continue; to uphold; to vindicate; to assert.—*vi.* To affirm a position; to assert.

aintenance, mān´ten-ans, *n.* Act of maintaining; means of support or livelihood; continuance.

aize, māz, *n.* Indian corn.

ajestic, ma-jes´tik, *a.* Having majesty; august; sublime; lofty; stately.

ajesty, ma´jes-ti, *n.* Grandeur or dignity; a title of emperors, kings, and queens.

ajolica, ma-jol´i-ka, *n.* A kind of pottery richly colored and enameled.

ajor, mā´jėr, *a.* The greater in number, quantity, or extent; the more important.—*n.* A military officer next above a captain; a person aged twenty-one years complete.

ajority, ma-jo´ri-ti, *n.* The greater number; excess of one number over another; full age; rank or commission of a major.

Make, māk, *vt.* (making, made). To produce or effect; to cause to be; to compose; to constitute; to perform; to cause to have any quality; to force; to gain; to complete; to arrive at; to have within sight.—*vi.* To act or do; to tend; to contribute; to flow toward land.—*n.* Form; structure; texture.

Make-believe, māk´bē-lēv, *n.* Pretense; sham.—*a.* Unreal; sham.

Maker, māk´ėr, *n.* One who makes; the Creator.

Make-shift, māk´shift, *n.* An expedient to serve a present purpose.

Make-up, māk´up, *n.* The manner in which one is dressed for a part in a play.

Making, māk´ing, *n.* Workmanship; what is made at one time; material; means of bringing successs in life; state of being made.

Maladjustment, mal-ad-just´ment, *n.* A bad or wrong adjustment.

Maladroit, mal-a-droit´, *a.* Awkward.

Malady, mal´a-di, *n.* Any disease of the human body; moral or mental disorder.

Malar, mā´lėr, *a.* Pertaining to the cheek or cheek-bone.

Malaria, ma-lā´ri-a, *n.* Noxious exhalations causing fever; fever produced by this cause.

Malcontent, mal´kon-tent, *n.* A discontented person.—*a.* Discontented with the rule under which one lives.

Male, māl, *a.* Pertaining to the sex that begets young; masculine.—*n.* One of the sex that begets young; a plant which has stamens only.

Malefactor, mal-e-fak´tėr, *n.* A criminal; a culprit; a felon.

Malevolence, ma-lev´ō-lens, *n.* Ill-will; personal hatred.

Malformation, mal-form-ā´shon, *n.* Ill or wrong formation; deformity.

Malice, mal´is, *n.* A disposition to injure others; spite; ill-will; rancor.

Malign, ma-lin´, *a.* Of an evil nature or disposition; malicious; pernicious.—*vt.* To defame; to villify.

Malignance, Malignancy, ma-lig´nans, ma-lig´nan-si, *n.* Extreme malevolence; virulence.

Malignant, ma-lig´nant, *a.* Having extreme malevolence; unpropitious; virulent; dangerous to life; extremely heinous.—*n.* A man of extreme enmity.

Malinger, ma-ling´gėr, *vi.* To feign illness in order to avoid military duty.

Mall, mal, *n.* A heavy wooden beetle or hammer; a public walk; a level shaded walk.

Mallard, mal´ard, *n.* The common wild duck.

Malleable, mal´lē-a-bl, *a.* Capable of being beaten out with a hammer; easily persuaded.

Mallet, mal´et, *n.* A wooden hammer; a long-handled mallet is used in polo, croquet, etc.

Malnutrition, mal-nū-tri´shon, *n.* Faulty feeding.

Malpractice, mal-prak´tis, *n.* Evil practice.

Malt, malt, *n.* Barley or other grain steeped in water till it germinates, then dried in a kiln and used in brewing.—*vt.* To make into malt.—*vi.* To become malt.

Malt-liquor, malt´lik-ėr, *n.* A liquor prepared from malt by fermentation, as beer.

Maltreat, mal-trēt, *vt.* To treat ill or roughly; to abuse.

Malversation, mal-vėr-sā´shon, *n.* Fraudulent tricks; corruption in office.

Mama, Mamma, ma mä´, *n.* Mother.

Mamma, mam´ma, *n.* pl. **mae.** The breast; the organ that secretes the milk.

Mammalia, mam-mā´li-a, *n.pl.* The highest class in the animal kingdom, whose distinctive characteristic is that the female suckles the young.

Mammilla, mam-mil´la, *n.* A nipple, or something of this form.

Mammon, mam´on, *n.* A Syrian god of riches; riches; wealth.

Mammoth, mam´oth, *n.* An extinct species of elephant.—*a.* Very large; gigantic.

M

Man, man, *n.*; pl. **Men,** men. A human being; a male adult of the human race; mankind; the male sex; a male servant; a piece in a game, as chess, etc.—*vt.* (manning, manned). To furnish with men; to guard with men; *refl.* to infuse courage into.

Manacle, man′a-kl, *n.* An instrument of iron for fastening the hands; a handcuff; used chiefly in the *plural.—vt.* (manacling, manacled). To put manacles on; to fetter.

Manage, man′āj, *vt.* (managing, managed). To wield; to direct in riding; to conduct or administer; to have under command; to treat with judgment.—*vi.* To conduct affairs.

Management, man′āj-ment, *n.* Act of managing; administration; manner of treating, body directing a business, etc.

Manatee, man-a-tē′, *n.* The sea-cow, an aquatic herbivorous mammal.

Mandamus, man-dā′mus, *n.* A writ requiring a person, corporation, or inferior court to do some specified act.

Mandarin, man-da-rēn′, *n.* A Chinese public official; the court-language of China.

Mandate, man′dāt′, *n.* A command; written authority to act for a person.

Mandatory, man′da-to-ri, *a.* Containing a command; preceptive; directory.

Mandible, man′di-bl, *n.* An animal's jaw.

Mandoline, Mandolin, man′dō-lin, *n.* A musical instrument of the guitar kind.

Mandrill, man′dril, *n.* The great blue-faced or rib-nosed baboon.

Mane, mān, *n.* The long hair on the neck of a horse, lion, etc.

Manful, man′ful, *a.* Having the spirit of a man; bold; honorable; energetic.

Manganese, man-gan-ēz′, *n.* A metal resembling iron.

Manganite, man′gan-īt, *n.* An ore of manganese, used in the manufacture of glass.

Mange, mānj, *n.* A skin disease of horses, cattle, dogs, etc.

Manger, mān′jer, *n.* A trough in which food is placed for cattle and horses.

Mangle, mang′gl, *vt.* (mangling, mangled). To mutilate; to lacerate; to smooth, as linen.—*n.* A rolling press, or small calender, for smoothing cotton or linen.

Mango, mang′gō, *n.* The fruit of the mango-tree, a native of Asia.

Mangrove, man′grōv, *n.* A tropical tree growing on shores.

Manhole, man′hōl, *n.* A hole for admitting a man into a drain, steam-boiler, etc.

Manhood, man′hud, *a.* State of one who is a man; humanity; virility; manliness.

Mania, mā′ni-a, *n.* Insanity; madness; eager desire for anything; morbid craving.

Maniac, mā′ni-ak, *a.* Affected with mania; mad.—*n.* A madman.

Manicure, man′i-kūr, *n.* One whose occupation is to trim the nails, etc., of the hand.

Manifest, man′i-fest, *a.* Clearly visible; evident; obvious.—*vt.* To make manifest; to display or exhibit.—*n.* A document stating a ship's cargo, destination, etc.

Manifesto, man-i-fest′ō, *n.* A public declaration; a proclamation.

Manifold, man′i-fōld, *a.* Numerous and various; of divers kinds.—*vt.* To multiply impressions of, as by a copying apparatus.

Manipulate, ma-nip′ū-lāt, *vt.* To treat with the hands; to handle; to operate upon so as to disguise.

Mankind, man-kind′, *n.* The species of human beings; the males of the human race.

Manliness, man′li-nes, *n.* The best qualities of a man; manhood; bravery.

Manna, man′na, *n.* A substance furnished as food for the Israelites in the wilderness; the sweet juice of a species of ash.

Mannequin, man′ē-kin, *n.* Person employed by dressmakers, etc., to wear and display co tumes.

Manner, man′er, *n.* The mode in which anythin is done; method; bearing or conduct; *pl.* ca riage or behavior; civility in society; sort (kind.

Mannerism, man′er-izm, *n.* Adherence to th same manner; tasteless uniformity of style; p culiarity of personal manner.

Mannish, man′ish, *a.* Characteristic of or reser bling a man; bold or masculin.

Maneuver, ma-nū′ver or ma-nö′ver, *n.* A reg lated movement, particularly of troops or ship management with address; strategem.—\ (maneuvering, maneuvered). To perform mi tary or naval maneuvers; to employ stratager to manage with address.-*vt.* To cause to pe form maneuvers.

Manometer, ma-nom′et-er, *n.* An instrument measure the elastic force of gases.

Mansion, man′shon, *n.* A large dwelling-hous abode; house of the lord of a manor.

Manslaughter, man′sla-ter, *n.* Murder; the u lawful killing of a man without malice.

Mantel, Mantel-piece, man′tel, man′tel-pēs, The ornamental work above a fireplace; a na row shelf or slab there.

Mantilla, man-til′la, *n.* A mantle or hood; Spanish lady's veil.

Mantle, man′tl, *n.* A kind of cloak worn ov other garments; something that covers ar conceals; incandescent hood for gas jet.—\ (mantling, mantled). To cloak; to cover as with mantle.—*vi.* To become covered with a coatin to cream; to display superficial changes of hu

Manual, man′ū-al, *a.* Performed by the han used or made by the hand.—*n.* A small book; compendium; the service-book of the R. Cath lic Church; keyboard of an organ.

Manufacture, man-ū-fak′tūr, *n.* The process making anything by hand or machinery; som thing made from raw materials.—*vt.* (manufa turing, manufactured). To fabricate from ra materials; to fabricate without real grounds. *vi.* To be occupied in manufactures.

Manumit, man-ū-mit′, *vt.* (manumitting, man mitted). To release from slavery.

Manure, man-ūr′, *vt.* (manuring, manured). fertilize with nutritive substances.—*n.* Any su stance added to soil to accelerate or increas the production of the crops.

Manuscript, man′ū-skript, *n.* A paper writte with the hand; often contracted to *MS.*, *MSS.—a.* Written with the hand.

Many, me′ni, *a.* Forming or comprising a nur ber; numerous.—**The many,** the great majori of people; the crowd.—**So many,** the same nur ber of; a certain number indefinitely.

Maori, mä′o-ri, *n.* One of the native inhabitan of New Zealand.

Map, map, *n.* A representation of the surface the earth or of any part of it.—*vt.* (mappin mapped). To draw in a map; to plan.

Maple, mā′pl, *n.* A tree of the sycamore kind.

Mar, mär, *vt.* (marring, marred). To injure in ar manner; to hurt, impair, disfigure, etc.

Marabou, ma′ra-bö, *n.* A large stork yieldir valuable white feathers.

Maraud, ma-rad′, *vi.* To rove in quest of plunde to make an excursion for booty.

Marble, mär′bl, *n.* A calcareous stone of cor pact texture; a little hard ball used by boys play; an inscribed or sculptured marb stone.—*a.* Made of or like marble.—*vt.* (ma bling, marbled). To stain like marble.

March, märch, *vi.* To move by steps and in ord as soldiers; to walk in a stately manner; progress; to be situated next.—*vt.* To cause march.—*n.* The measured walk of a body men; a stately walk; distance passed over; musical composition to regulate the march troops, etc.; a frontier or boundary (usually *pl.*); the third month of the year.

Mare, mār, n. The female of the horse.

Margarine, mär´ga-rin, n. An imitation of butter, made from animal fat.

Margin, mär´jin, n. An edge, border, brink; edge of a page left blank; difference between the cost and selling price.—vt. To furnish with a margin; to enter in the margin.

Marginal, mär´jin-al, a. Pertaining to a margin; written or printed in the margin.

Marigold, ma´ri-gōld, n. A composite plant bearing golden-yellow flowers.

Marine, ma-rēn´, a. Pertaining to the sea; found in the sea; used at sea; naval; maritime.—n. A soldier who serves on board of a man-of-war; collective shipping of a country; whole economy of naval affairs.

Marionette, ma´ri-o-net´´, n. A puppet moved by strings.

Maritime, ma´ri-tim, a. Relating to the sea; naval; bordering on the sea; having a navy and commerce by sea.

Marjoram, mär´jō-ram, n. A plant of the mint family.

Mark, märk, n. A visible sign or impression on something; a distinguishing sign; indication or evidence; pre-eminence or importance; a characteristic; heed or regard; object aimed at; proper standard; extreme estimate; a German coin.—vt. To make a mark or marks on; to denote (often with out); to regard, observe, heed.—vi. To note; to observe critically; to remark.

Marked, märkt, p.a. Pre-eminent; outstanding; prominent; remarkable.

Market, mär´ket, n. An occasion on which goods are publicly exposed for sale; place in which goods are exposed for sale; rate of purchase and sale; demand for commodities; privilege of keeping a public market.—vi. To deal in a market.—vt. To offer for sale in a market.

Market-garden, mär´ket-gär-dn, n. A garden growing vegetables, etc., for market.

Marksman, märks´man, n. One who is skilful to hit a mark; one who shoots well.

Marl, märl, n. A rich calcareous earth much used for manure.—vt. To manure with marl.

Marmalade, mär´ma-lād, n. A preserve made from various fruits, especially acid fruits, such as the orange.

Marmoreal, mär-mō´rē-al, a. Pertaining to marble; made of marble.

Marmot, mär´mot, n. A hibernating rodent animal of northern latitudes.

Maroon, ma-rön, n. A fugitive slave in the W. Indies; a brownish crimson or claret color.—vt. To land and leave on a desolate island.

Marquetry, mär´ket-ri, n. Inlaid work.

Marriage, mar´rij, n. The act or ceremony of marrying; matrimony; wedlock.

Marrow, ma´rō, n. A soft substance in the cavities of bones; the best part; a kind of gourd, also called vegetable marrow.

Marry, ma´ri, vt. (marrying, married). To unite in wedlock; to dispose of in wedlock; to take for husband or wife.—vi. To take a husband or a wife—interj. Indeed; forsooth.

Mars, märz, n. The god of war; a planet.

Marsh, märsh, n. A swamp; a tract of low wet land.—a. Pertaining to boggy places.

Marshal, mär´shal, n. One who regulates rank and order at a feast, procession, etc.; a military officer of the highest rank, generally called field-marshal.—vt. (marshalling, marshalled). To dispose in order; to array.

Marsupial, mär-sū´pi-al, n. and a. One of a large group of mammalians whose young are born in an imperfect condition and nourished in an external abdominal pouch.

Marten, mär´ten, n. A fierce kind of weasel, valued for its fur.

Martial, mär´shal, a. Pertaining to war; warlike.

Martin, mär´tin, n. A species of swallow.

Martinet, mär´ti-net, n. A precise, punctilious, or strict disciplinarian.

Martingale, mär´tin-gāl, n. A strap to prevent a horse from rearing; a short spar under the bowsprit.

Martyr, mär´tėr, n. One who suffers death or persecution on account of his belief; one greatly afflicted.—vt. To put to death for adhering to one's belief.

Marvel, mär´vel, n. A wonder; something very astonishing.—vi. (marvelling, marvelled). To feel admiration or astonishment.

Marvellous, mär´vel-us, a. Exciting wonder or surprise; wonderful; astonishing.

Mascot, mas´kot, n. A thing supposed to bring good luck to its owner.

Masculine, mas´kū-lin, a. Male, manly; robust; bold or unwomanly; designating nouns which are the names of male animals, etc.

Mash, mash, n. A mixture of ingredients beaten or blended together; a mixture of ground malt and warm water yielding wort.—vt. To mix; to beat into a confused mass.

Mask, mask, n. A cover for the face; a masquerade; a sort of play common in the 16th and 17th centuries; pretense.—vt. To cover with a mask; to disguise; to hide.

Masochism, mas´ō-kism, n. Pathological sexual condition in which pleasure is derived from cruel treatment by the associate.

Mason, mä´sn, n. One who prepares stone, and constructs buildings; a freemason.

Masonic, ma-son´ik, a. Pertaining to the craft or mysteries of freemasons.

Masonry, mä´sn-ri, n. The art or occupation of a mason; stonework; the doctrines and practices of freemasons.

Masquerade, mas-kėr-ād´, n. An assembly of persons wearing masks; a disguise.—vi. To assemble in masks; to go in disguise.

Mass, mas, n. A body of matter; a lump; magnitude; an assemblage; collection; the generality; the communion service in the R. Catholic Church.—The Masses, the populace.—vt. and i. To form into a mass; to assemble in crowds.

Massacre, mas´sa-kėr, n. Ruthless, unnecessary, or indiscriminate slaughter.—vt. (massacring, massacred). To kill with indiscriminate violence; to slaughter.

Massage, ma-säzh´ or mas´āj, n. A process of kneading, rubbing, pressing, etc., parts of a person's body to effect a cure.—vt. (massaging, massaged). To treat by this process.

Masseur, mas-ör, n. One who practices massage.

Masseter, mas-sé´tėr, n. Either of the pair of muscles which raise the under jaw.

Massive, mas´iv, a. Bulky and heavy; ponderous; pertaining to a mass; not local or special.

Mast, mast, n. A long upright timber in a vessel, supporting the yards, sails, and rigging; the fruit of the oak, beech, etc. (no pl.).—vt. To supply with a mast or masts.

Master, mäs´tėr, n. One who rules or directs; an employer; owner; captain of a merchant ship; teacher in a school; a man eminently skilled in some art; a word of address for men (written Mr. and pron. mis´tèr) and boys (written in full); a vessel having masts.—vt. To bring under control; to make oneself master of.—a. Belonging to a master; chief.

Master-key, mäs´tėr-kē, n. The key that opens many locks.

Masterpiece, mäs´tėr-pēs, n. Chief performance; anything done with superior skill.

Master-stroke, mäs´tėr-strōk, n. A masterly act or achievement.

Masticate, mas´ti-kāt, vt. To chew and prepare for swallowing.

Mastiff, mas´tif, n. A large heavy dog with deep and pendulous lips.

Mastodon, mas´to-don, n. An extinct quadruped like the elephant, but larger.

Mat, mat, n. An article of interwoven rushes, twine, etc., used for cleaning or protecting; anything growing thickly or closely interwoven.—

M

vt. (matting, matted'). To cover with mats; to entangle.—*vi.* To grow thickly together.

Matador, ma·ta·dōr', *n.* The man appointed to kill the bull in bull-fights; a card in ombre and quadrille.

Match, mach, *n.* A person or thing equal to another; union by marriage; one to be married; a contest; a small body that catches fire readily or ignites by friction.—*vt.* To equal; to show an equal to; to set against as equal in contest; to suit; to marry.—*vi.* To be united in marriage; to suit; to tally.

Mate, māt, *n.* A companion; a match; a husband or wife; second officer in a ship.—*vt.* (mating, mated). To equal; to match; to marry; to checkmate.

Material, ma·tē'ri·al, *a.* Consisting of matter; not spiritual; important; essential; substantial.—*n.* Anything composed of matter; substance of which anything is made.

Materialize, ma·tē'ri·al·īz, *vt.* To reduce to a state of matter; to regard as matter.

Maternal, ma·tér'nal, *a.* Motherly; pertaining to a mother; becoming a mother.

Maternity, ma·tér'ni·ti, *n.* The state, character, or relation of a mother.

Mathematics, ma·thē·ma'tiks, *n.* The science of magnitude and number, comprising arithmetic, geometry, algebra, etc.

Matinée, mat'i·nā, *n.* An entertainment or reception held early in the day.

Matricide, mat'ri·sīd, *n.* The killing of a mother; the murderer of his or her mother.

Matriculate, ma·trik'ū·lāt, *vt.* To enroll; to admit to membership, particularly in a university.—*vi.* To be entered as a member.

Matrimony, mat'ri·mō·ni, *n.* Marriage; wedlock; the married or nuptial state.

Matrix, mā'triks, *n.*; pl. **Matrices** (mā'tri·sēz). The womb; a mold; substance in which a mineral, etc., is embedded.

Matron, mā'tron, *n.* An elderly married woman, or an elderly lady; head nurse or superintendent of a hospital, etc.

Matted, mat'ed, *p.a.* Laid with mats; entangled.

Matter, mat'ér, *n.* Not mind; body; that of which anything is made; substance as distinct from form; subject; business; circumstance; import; moment; pus.—*vi.* To be of importance; to signify; to form pus.

Matter-of-fact, mat'ér-ov-fakt, *a.* Treating of facts; precise; prosaic.

Mattock, mat'ok, *n.* A pick-axe with one or both of its ends broad.

Mattress, mat'res, *n.* A bed stuffed with hair, or other soft material, and quilted.

Maturative, ma·tū'ra·tiv, *a.* Ripening; conducing to suppuration.

Mature, ma·tūr', *a.* Ripe; perfect; completed; ready; having become payable.—*vt.* (maturing, matured). To make mature; to advance toward perfection.—*vi.* To become ripe or perfect; to become payable.

Maudlin, mad'lin, *a.* Over-emotional; sickly sentimental; approaching to intoxication.

Maul, mal, *n.* A large hammer or mallet.—*vt.* To beat with a maul; to maltreat severely.

Maunder, man'dér, *vi.* To speak with a beggar's whine; to drivel.

Mausoleum, ma·sō·lē'um, *n.* A magnificent tomb or sepulchral monument.

Mauve, mōv, *n.* A purple dye obtained from aniline.

Maw, ma, *n.* The stomach, especially of animals; paunch; crop of fowls.

Mawkish, mak'ish, *a.* Apt to cause satiety or loathing; insipid; sickly.

Maxilla, mak·sil'la, *n.*; pl. **ae.** A jaw-bone; a jaw.

Maxim, mak'sim, *n.* An established principle; axiom; aphorism; a light machine-gun.

Maximum, mak'sim·um, *n.* The greatest degree or quantity.—*a.* Greatest.

May, mā, *n.* The fifth month of the year; haw-thorn blossom.—*vi.* To celebrate the festivitie of May-day.—*v. aux.* (pret. might, mit). Used imply possibility, opportunity, permission, d sire, etc.

Mayonnaise, mā·on·āz, *n.* A sauce of yolks eggs, oil, etc.

Mayor, mā'ér, *n.* The chief magistrate of a city borough.

May-pole, mā'pōl, *n.* A pole to dance round May-day.

Mazarine, maz·a·rēn', *n.* A deep blue color.

Maze, māz, *vt.* (mazing, mazed). To bewilder; amaze.—*n.* Perplexed state of things; bewilde ment; a labyrinth; a confusing network of patl or passages.

Me, mē, *pron. pers.* The objective of *I.*

Mead, mēd, *n.* A fermented liquor made fro honey and water; a meadow: *poet.*

Meadow, me'dō, *n.* A low level tract of land und grass.—*a.* Belonging to a meadow.

Meager, mē'gér, *a.* Thin; lean; poor; scanty.

Meal, mēl, *n.* Portion of food taken at one time; repast; ground grain; flour.

Mealy-mouthed, mēl'i·mouᴛʜd, *a.* Unwilling tell the truth in plain language; soft-spoken; i clined to hypocrisy.

Mean, mēn, *a.* Low in rank or birth; humbl base; comtemptible; occupying a middle pos tion; middle; intermediate.—*n.* What is interm diate; average rate or degree; medium; ɟ measure or measures adopted; agency (gene ally used as *sing.*); income or resources.—*ı* (pret. and pp. *meant*). To have in the mind; intend; to signify; to import.—*vi.* To ha thought or ideas, or to have meaning.

Meander, mē·an'dér, *n.* A winding course; a ben in a course; a labyrinth.—*vi.* To wind about; be intricate.

Meaning, mēn'ing, *p.a.* Significant.—*n.* Desig signification; purport; force.

Meanly, mēn'li, *adv.* In a mean manner; poorl basely; shabbily.

Meantime, mēn'tim, *adv.* During the interval; the intervening time.—*n.* The interval betwee one period and another.

Measles, mē'zlz, *n.* A contagious disease in ma characterized by a crimson rash.

Measure, me'zhūr, *n.* The extent or magnitude a thing; a standard of size; a measuring rod line; that which is allotted; moderation; just d gree; course of action; legislative proposal; m sical time; meter; a grave solemn dance; ɟ beds or strata.—*vt.* (measuring, measured). ascertain the extent or capacity of; to estimat to value; to pass through or over; to proportio to allot.—*vi.* To have a certain extent.

Measurement, me'zhūr·ment, *n.* Act of measu ing; amount ascertained.

Meat, mēt, *n.* Food in general; the flesh of ar mals used as food; the edible portion of som thing (the *meat* of an egg).

Mechanic, me·kan'ik, *a.* Mechanical.—*n.* An ar san; an artisan employed in making and r pairing machinery.

Mechanical, me·kan'ik·al, *a.* Pertaining to mec anism or machinery; resembling a machin done by the mere force of habit; pertaining material forces; physical.

Mechanics, me·kan'iks, *n.* The science whic treats of motion and force.

Mechanism, mek'an·izm, *n.* A mechanical co trivance; structure of a machine.

Medal, med'al, *n.* A piece of metal in the form a coin, stamped with some figure or device, a memento or reward.

Medallion, me·dal'yon, *n.* A large antiqu medal; a circular or oval tablet.

Meddle, med'l, *vi.* (meddling, meddled). To inte fere; to intervene officiously.

Meddlesome, med'l·sum, *a.* Given to interferin meddling; officiously intrusive.

Medial, mē'di·al, *a.* Middle; mean; pertaining a mean or average.

Median, mē'di-an, *a.* Situated in the middle; passing through or along the middle.

Mediate, mē'di-āt, *a.* Middle; intervening; acting as a means; not direct.—*vi.* (mediating, mediated). To negotiate between contending parties, with a view to reconciliation; to intercede.

Mediation, mē-di-ā'shon, *n.* Act of mediating; intercession; entreaty for another.

Mediative, mē'di-āt-iv, *a.* Of or belonging to a mediator.

Medical, med'i-kal, *a.* Pertaining to the art of curing diseases; tending to cure.

Medicate, med'i-kāt, *vt.* (medicating, medicated). To treat with medicine; to impregnate with anything medicinal.

Medicinal, me-dis'in-al, *a.* Pertaining to medicine; containing healing ingredients.

Medicine, med'sin, *n.* Any substance used as a remedy for disease; a drug; the science and art of curing diseases.

Medieval, mē-di-ēv'al, *a.* Pertaining to the middle ages.

Mediocre, mē'di-ō-kèr, *a.* Of moderate degree; middling.

Mediocrity, mē-di-ok'ri-ti, *n.* State of being mediocre; a moderate degree or rate; a person of mediocre talents or abilities.

Meditate, med'i-tāt, *vi.* (meditating, meditated). To dwell on anything in thought; to cogitate.—*vt.* To think on; to scheme; to intend.

Mediterranean, med'i-te-rā'nē-an, *a.* Surrounded by land: now applied exclusively to the *Mediterranean* Sea.

Medium, mē'di-um, *n.*; pl. **-ia, -iums.** Something holding a middle position; a mean; means of motion or action; agency of transmission; instrumentality.—*a.* Middle; middling.

Medley, med'li, *n.* A mingled mass of ingredients; a miscellany; a jumble.

Medulla, me-dul'la, *n.* Marrow.

Medullary, Medullar, me-dul'la-ri, me-dul'lèr, *a.* Pertaining to, consisting of, or resembling marrow.

Medusa, me-dū'sa, *n.*; pl. **-ae.** A general name for the jelly-fishes or sea-nettles.

Meek, mēk, *a.* Soft, gentle, or mild of temper; forbearing; humble; submissive.

Meerschaum, mēr'shum, *n.* A silicate of magnesium, used for tobacco-pipes; a tobacco-pipe made of this.

Meet, mēt, *vt.* (meeting, met). To come face to face with; to come in contact with; to encounter; to light on; to receive; to satisfy.—*vi.* To come together; to encounter; to assemble.—*n.* A meeting, as of huntsmen.—*a.* Fit; suitable; proper.

Meeting, mēt'ing, *n.* A coming together; an interview; an assembly; encounter.

Megalithic, meg-a-lith'ik, *a.* Consisting of large stones.

Megaphone, meg'a-fōn, *n.* A cone-shaped speaking-trumpet.

Megrim, mē'grim, *n.* A neuralgic pain in the side of the head; *pl.* low spirits; whims or fancies.

Melancholy, mel'an-ko-li, *n.* Mental alienation characterized by gloom and depression; hypochondria; dejection; sadness.—*a.* Gloomy; dejected; calamitous; somber.

Melanochroic, mel'an-ō-krō''ik, *a.* A term applied to the dark-skinned white races of man.

Mêlée, mā-lā', *n.* A confused fight; an affray.

Meliorate, mē'lyor-āt, *vt.* To make better; to improve.—*vi.* To grow better.

Mellifluence, mel-if'lu-ens, *n.* A flow of honey or sweetness; a sweet smooth flow.

Mellow, mel'ō, *a.* Soft with ripeness; soft to the ear, eye, or taste; toned down by time; half-tipsy.—*vt.* To make mellow; to soften.—*vi.* To become mellow.

Melodic, me-lod'ik, *a.* Of the nature of melody; relating to melody.

Melodrama, me-lō-dra'ma, *n.* Properly a musical drama; a serious play, with startling incidents, exaggerated sentiment, and splendid decora-

tion.

Melody, me'lō-di, *n.* An agreeable succession of sounds; sweetness of sound; the particular air or tune of a musical piece.

Melon, me'lon, *n.* A kind of cucumber and its large, fleshy fruit.

Melt, melt, *vt.* To reduce from a solid to a liquid state by heat; to soften; to overcome with tender emotion.—*vi.* To become liquid; to dissolve; to be softened to love, pity, etc.; to pass by imperceptible degrees.

Member, mem'bèr, *n.* An organ or limb of an animal body; part of an aggregate; one of the persons composing a society, etc.; a representative in a legislative body.

Membrane, mem'brān, *n.* A thin flexible texture in animal bodies; a similar texture in plants.

Memento, mē-men'tō, *n.* That which reminds; a souvenir; a keepsake.

Memoir, mem'oir, mem'wär, *n.* A written account of events or transactions; a biographical notice; recollections of one's life (usually in the *pl.*).

Memorabilia, mem'or-a-bil''i-a, *n.pl.* Things worthy of remembrance or record.

Memorable, mem'or-a-bl, *a.* Worthy to be remembered; signal; remarkable; famous.

Memorandum, mem-or-an'dum, *n.*, pl. **-dums** or **-da.** A note to help the memory; brief entry in a diary; formal statement.

Memorial, mē-mō'ri-al, *a.* Pertaining to memory or remembrance; serving to commemorate.—*n.* That which preserves the memory of something; a monument; memorandum; a written representation of facts, made as the ground of a petition.

Memorize, mem'or-īz, *vt.* To cause to be remembered; to record.

Memory, mem'ō-ri, *n.* The faculty of the mind by which it retains knowledge or ideas; remembrance; recollection; the time within which a person may remember what is past; something remembered.

Menace, men'ās, *n.* A threat; indication of probable evil.—*vt.* (menacing, menaced). To threaten.

Menage, men-äzh', *n.* A household; housekeeping; household management.

Menagerie, me-naj'èr-i, *n.* A collection of wild animals kept for exhibition.

Mend, mend, *vt.* To repair; to restore to a sound state; to amend.—*vi.* To advance to a better state; to improve.

Mendacious, men-dā'shus, *a.* Lying; false; given to telling untruths.

Mendicant, men'di-kant, *a.* Begging.—*n.* A beggar; one who makes it his business to beg alms; a begging friar.

Menial, mē'ni-al, *a.* Belonging to household servants; low with regard to employment.—*n.* A domestic servant (used mostly disparagingly).

Meningitis, men-in-ji'tis, *n.* Inflammation of the membranes of the brain or spinal cord.

Menses, men'sēz, *n.pl.* The monthly discharge of a woman.

Menstrual, men'stru-al, *a.* Monthly; pertaining to the menses of females.

Mensuration, men-sūr-ā'shon, *n.* The act, process, or art of measuring.

Mental, men'tal, *a.* Pertaining to the mind, performed by the mind; intellectual.

Menthol, men'thol, *n.* A white crystalline substance obtained from oil of peppermint.

Mention, men'shon, *n.* A brief notice or remark about something.—*vt.* To make mention of; to name.

Mentor, men'tor, *n.* A friend or sage adviser.

Menu, mēn'ō, *n.* A list of dishes to be served at a dinner, etc.; a bill of fare.

Mephitis, me-fī'tis, *n.* Noxious exhalations.

Mercantile, mèr'kan-til, *a.* Pertaining to merchandise; trading; commercial.

Mercenary, mèr'se-na-ri, *a.* Hired; venal; that may be hired; greedy of gain; sordid. *n.* One who is hired; a soldier hired into foreign service.

Merchandise, mėr'chand-īz, n. The goods of a merchant; objects of commerce; trade.

Merchant, mėr'chant, n. One who carries on trade on a large scale; a man who exports and imports goods.—a. Relating to trade; commercial.

Merciful, mėr'si-ful, a. Full of mercy; compassionate; tender; clement; mild.

Merciless, mėr'si-les, a. Destitute of mercy; pitiless; cruel; hard-hearted.

Mercurial, mėr-kū'ri-al, a. Like the god Mercury; flighty; fickle; pertaining to or containing quicksilver.

Mercury, mėr'kū-ri, n. Quicksilver, a heavy metal, liquid at all ordinary temperatures; the planet nearest the sun.

Mercy, mėr'si, n. Willingness to spare or forgive; clemency; pity; a blessing; benevolence; unrestrained exercise of authority.

Mere, mėr, a. This or that and nothing else; simple, absolute, entire, utter.—n. A pool or small lake; a boundary.

Meretricious, me-rē-tri'shus, a. Pertaining to prostitutes; alluring by false show; gaudy.

Merge, mėrj, vt. (merging, merged). To cause to be swallowed up or incorporated.—vi. To be sunk, swallowed, or lost.

Meridian, mē-rid'i-an, n. Pertaining to midday or noon; pertaining to the acme or culmination.—n. Mid-day; point of greatest splendor; any imaginary circle passing through both poles, used in marking longitude; a similar imaginary line in the heavens passing through the zenith of any place.

Meringue, mer-ang', n. A mixture of white of egg and pounded sugar; a light cake of this material with whipped cream in the center.

Merino, me-rē'no, a. Belonging to a Spanish variety of sheep with long and fine wool; made of the wool of the merino sheep.—n. A merino sheep; a woollen stuff twilled on both sides.

Merit, me'rit, n. What one deserves; desert; value; good quality.—vt. To deserve; to have a just title to; to incur.

Meritorious, me-rit-ō'ri-us, a. Having merit; praiseworthy.

Mermaid, mėr'mād, n. A fabled marine creature, having the upper part like a woman and the lower like a fish.

Merriment, me'ri-ment, n. Mirth; noisy gaiety; hilarity.

Merry, me'ri, a. Joyous; jovial; hilarious; gay and noisy; mirthful; sportive.

Mesentery, me'sen-te-ri, a. A membrane retaining the intestines in a proper position.

Mesh, mesh, n. The space between the threads of a net; something that entangles; implement for making nets.—vt. To catch in a net.

Mesmerism, mez'mėr-izm, n. The doctrine that some persons can exercise influence over the will and nervous system of others; animal magnetism; hypnotism.

Mesmerize, mez'mėr-īz, vt. To bring into a state of mesmeric or hypnotic sleep.

Mesocephalic, Mesocephalous, mes'o-se-fal''ik, mes-o-sef'a-lus, a. Applied to the human skull when of medium breadth.

Mesozoic, mes-o-zō'ik, a. In *geology*, pertaining to the secondary age, between the palaeozoic and cainozoic.

Mess, mes, n. A dish of food; food for a person at one meal; a number of persons who eat together, especially in the army or navy; a disorderly mixture; muddle.—vi. To take meals in common with others.

Message, mes'āj, n. A communication, written or verbal; an official written communication.

Messenger, mes'en-jėr, n. One who bears a message; a harbinger.

Messiah, mes-sī'a, n. The Anointed One; Christ, the Anointed.

Metabolism, me-tab'ol-izm, n. Change or metamorphosis; chemical change of nutriment taken into the body.

Metal, me'tal, n. An elementary substance, such as gold, iron, etc., having a peculiar luster and generally fusible by heat; the broken stone for covering roads.

Metallurgy, me'tal-ėr-ji, n. Art of working metals; art or operation of separating metals from their ores by smelting.

Metamorphose, me-ta-mor'fōs, vt. To change into a different form; to transform.

Metamorphosis, me-ta-mor'fos-is, n.; pl. **-ses.** Change of form or shape; transformation.

Metaphor, me'ta-for, n. A figure of speech founded on resemblance, as 'that man is a fox.'

Metaphrase, me'ta-frāz, n. A verbal translation from one language into another.

Metaphysics, me-ta-fi'ziks, n. The science of the principles and causes of all things existing; the philosophy of mind as distinguished from that of matter.

Metathesis, me-ta'the-sis, n. Transposition, as of the letters or syllables of a word.

Mete, mēt, vt. (meting, meted). To measure; to measure out; to dole.

Meteor, mē'tē-ėr, n. An atmospheric phenomenon; a transient luminous body; something that transiently dazzles.

Meteoric, mē-tē-or'ik, a. Pertaining to or consisting of meteors; proceeding from a meteor; transiently or irregularly brilliant.

Meteorology, mē'tē-ėr-ol''o-ji, n. the science of atmospheric phenomena.

Meter, mē'tėr, n. One who or that which measures.

Method, me'thod, n. Mode or manner of procedure; system; classification.

Methodic, Methodical, me-thod'ik, me-thod'ik-al, a. Systematic; orderly.

Methodism, me'thod-izm, n. Observance of method or system; (with *cap.*) the doctrines and worship of the Methodists.

Methodist, me'thod-ist, n. One who observes method; (with *cap.*) one of a sect of Christians founded by John Wesley.

Metonymy, me-ton'i-mi, n. A figure of speech in which one word is put for another, as when we say, 'We read *Virgil*', meaning his *poetry*.

Meter, mē'tėr, n. Rhythmical arrangement of syllables into verses, etc.; rhythm; verse.

Metric, met'rik, a. Pertaining to the decimal system.

Metric, Metrical, met'rik, met'rik-al, a. Pertaining to rhythm; consisting of verse.

Mettle, met'l, n. Moral or physical constitution; spirit; courage; fire.

Mew, mū, n. A sea-mew; a gūll; moulting of a hawk; a coop for fowls; a place of confinement; the cry of a cat.—vt. To moult; to shut up, as in a cage.—vi. To moult; to cry as a cat.

Mezzo soprano, a treble voice between soprano and contralto.

Miasma, mī-az'ma, n.; pl. **Miasmata**, mī-az'ma-ta. The effluvia of any putrefying bodies; noxious emanation; malaria.

Mica, mī'ka, n. A mineral cleavable into thin shining elastic plates.

Microbe, mī'krōb, n. A microscopic organism such as a bacillus or bacterium.

Microcosm, mī'krō-kozm, n. The little world; used for man, according to an old view an epitome of the *macrocosm*.

Micrometer, mī-krom'et-ėr, n. An instrument for measuring small objects, spaces, or angles.

Microphone, mī'krō-fōn, n. An instrument to augment small sounds by means of electricity.

Microphyte, mī'krō-fīt, n. A microscopicplant, especially one that is parasitic.

Microscope, mī'krō-skōp, n. An optical instrument for magnifying.

Micturate, mik'tūr-āt, vi. To pass urine.

Mid-air, mid'ār, n. The middle of the sky; a lofty position in the air.

Mid-day, mid'dā, n. The middle of the day; noon.—a. Pertaining to noon.

Middle, mid'l, a.; no compar.; superl. middlemost. Equally distant from the extremes; intermediate; intervening.—**Middle ages,** the period from the fall of the Roman Empire to about 1450.—n. Point or part equally distant from the extremities; something intermediate.

Middle-aged, mid'l-ājd, a. Being about the middle of the ordinary age of man.

Middle-class, mid'l-klås, n. The class of people holding a social position between the working-classes and the aristocracy.—a. Of or relating to the middle-classes.

Middleman, mid'l-man, n. An intermediary between two parties; an agent between producers and consumers.

Midnight, mid'nīt, n. The middle of the night; twelve o'clock at night.—a. Pertaining to midnight; dark as midnight.

Midriff, mid'rif, n. The diaphragm.

Midsummer, mid'sum-ėr, n. The middle of summer; the summer solstice, about June 21.

Midway, mid'wā, n. The middle of the way or distance.—a. and adv. In the middle of the way; half-way.

Midwife, mid'wīf, n. A woman that assists other women in childbirth.

Mien, mēn, n. Look; bearing; carriage.

Might, mit, n. Great power or ability to act; strength; force.—v. aux. Pret. of may.

Mighty, mit'i, a. Having might; strong; powerful; potent; very great; vast.

Migrate, mi'grāt, vi. (migrating, migrated). To remove to a distant place or country.

Migration, mi'grā-shon, n. Act of migrating; removal from one place to another.

Milch, milsh, a. Giving milk, as cows.

Mild, mild, a. Gentle in temper or disposition; merciful; soft; bland; mellow.

Mildew, mil'dū, n. A minute parastic fungus that causes decay in vegetable matter; condition so caused.—vt. and i. To taint with mildew.

Mile, mil, n. A measure of length or distance equal to 1760 yards.

Militant, mil'i-tant, a. Serving as a soldier; fighting; combative.

Militarism, mil'i-ta-rizm, n. The system that leads a nation to pay excessive attention to military affairs.

Military, mil'i-ta-ri, a. Pertaining to soldiers or war; martial; soldierly; belligerent.—n. The whole body of soldiers; the army.

Militate, mil'i-tat, vi. (militating, militated). To stand arrayed; to have weight or influence.

Militia, mi-li'sha, n. A body of soldiers not permanently organized in time of peace.

Milk, milk, n. A whitish fluid secreted in female animals, serving as nourishment for their young; what resembles milk; white juice of plants.—vt. To draw milk from.

Mill, mil, n. A machine for making meal or flour; a machine for grinding, etc.; building that contains the machinery for grinding, etc.—vt. To pass through a mill; to stamp in a coining press; to throw, as silk; to full, as cloth.

Milled, mild, p.a. Passed through a mill; having the edge transversely grooved, as a coin.

Millenary, mil'le-na-ri, a. Pertaining to a thousand.—n. Period of a thousand years; commemoration of an event that happened a thousand years ago.

Millennial, mil-len'i-al, a. Pertaining to the millennium, or to a thousand years.

Millennium, mil-lon'i-um, n. An aggregate of a thousand years; the thousand years of Christ's reign on earth.

Milleped, Milliped, mil'le-ped, mil'li-ped, n. A worm-like animal with many feet; a woodlouse.

Miller, mil'ėr, n. One who keeps or attends a mill for grinding grain.

Millet, mil'et, n. A kind of small grain of various species used for food.

Milliard, mil-yärd', n. A thousand millions.

Milligram, mil'i-gram, n. The thousandth part of a gram.

Millimeter, mil-i-mā'tr, n. The thousandth part of a meter.

Milliner, mil'in-ėr, n. One who makes head-dresses, hats, etc., for females.

Milling, mil'ing, n. The process of grinding or passing through a mill; the transverse grooves on the edge of a coin.

Million, mil'yon, n. A thousand thousands; a very great number, indefinitely.

Millionaire, mil'yon-ār, n. One worth a million dollars, etc.; a very rich person.

Mill-pond, mil'pond, n. A pond furnishing water for driving a mill-wheel.

Mill-race, mil'rās, n. The stream of water driving a mill-wheel; channel in which it runs.

Millstone, mil'stön, n. One of the stones used in a mill for grinding grain.

Mill-wheel, mil'whēl, n. A wheel used to drive a mill; a water-wheel.

Mimic, mim'ik, a. Imitative; consisting of imitation.—n. One who imitates or mimics.—vt. (mimicking, mimicked). To imitate, especially for sport; to ridicule by imitation.

Minaret, min'a-ret, n. A slender lofty turret on Mohammedan mosques, with one or more balconies; a small spire.

Minatory, min'a-to-ri, a. Threatening; menacing.

Mince, mins, vt. (mincing, minced). To cut or chop into very small pieces; to extenuate or palliate; to utter with affected softness; to clip, as words.—vi. To walk with short steps; to speak with affected nicety.—n. Mince-meat.

Mince-meat, mins'mēt, n. A mixture of raisins and currants with chopped candied peel, suet, apples, etc.

Mincing, mins'ing, p.a. Speaking or walking affectedly; affectedly elegant.

Mind, mind, n. The intellectual power in man; understanding; cast of thought and feeling; inclination; opinion; memory.—vt. To attend to; to observe; to regard.

Mindful, mind'ful, a. Bearing in mind; attentive; regarding with care; heedful.

Mine, min, adj. pron. My, belonging to me.—n. A pit from which coal, ores, etc., are taken; an underground passage in which explosives may be lodged for destructive purposes; a contrivance floating on or near the surface of the sea, to destroy ships by explosion; a rich source or store of wealth.—vi. (mining, mined). To dig a mine; to dig for ores, etc.; to burrow.—vt. To undermine; to sap.

Mineral, mi'ne-ral, n. An inorganic body existing on or in the earth.—a. Pertaining to or consisting of minerals; impregnated with mineral matter.

Mineralogist, mi-ne-ral'o-jist, n. One who is versed in the science of minerals.

Mineralogy, mi-ne-ral'o-ji, n. The science of the properties of mineral substances.

Mingle, ming'gl, vt. (mingling, mingled). To mix up together; to blend; to debase by mixture.—vi. To be mixed; to join.

Miniature, min'i-a-tūr, n. A painting of very small dimensions, usually in water-colors, on ivory, vellum, etc.; anything represented on a greatly reduced scale; a small scale.—a. On a small scale; diminutive.

Minimize, min'i-miz, vt. (minimizing, minimized). To reduce to a minimum; to represent as of little moment; to depreciate.

Minimum, min'i-mum, n. The least quantity assignable; the smallest amount or degree.

Mining, min'ing, a. Pertaining to mines.—n. The act or employment of digging mines.

Minion, min'yon, n. An unworthy favorite; a servile dependant; a minx; a small kind of printing type.

Minister, min'is-tėr, n. A servant; attendant;

M

agent; a member of a government; a political representative or ambassador; the pastor of a church.—*vt*. To give; to supply.—*vi*. To perform service; to afford supplies; to contribute.

Ministerial, min-is-tē'ri-al, *a.* Pertaining to ministry, ministers of state, or ministers of the gospel.

Ministration, min-is-trā'shon, *n.* Act of ministering; service; ecclesiastical function.

Ministry, min'is-tri, *n.* The act of ministering; service; instrumentality; state of being a minister; profession of a minister of the gospel; the clergy; the administration.

Minium, min'i-um, *n.* Red oxide of lead; red-lead.

Mink, mingk, *n.* A quadruped allied to the polecat and weasel.

Minnow, min'ō, *n.* A very small British fish inhabiting fresh-water streams.

Minor, mi'nor, *a.* Lesser; smaller; of little importance; petty; in *music,* less by a lesser semitone.—*n.* A person not yet 21 years of age.

Minority, mi-no'ri-ti, *n.* State of being a minor; period from birth until 21 years of age; the smaller number or a number less than half; the party that has the fewest vores.

Minstrel, min'strel, *n.* A musician; a bard; a singer.

Mint, mint, *n.* The place where money is coined; a source of abundant supply; a herbaceous aromatic plant.—*vt*. To coin; to invent; to forge; to fabricate.

Minuend, mi'nū-end, *n.* The number from which another is to be subtracted.

Minuet, mi'nū-et, *n.* A slow graceful dance; the tune or air for it.

Minus, mi'nus, *a.* Less; less by so much; wanting; the sign (-).

Minute, mi-nūt', *a.* Very small; precise; particular; exact.

Minute, mi'nit, *a.* The sixtieth part of an hour or degree; short sketch of an agreement, etc., in writing; a note to preserve the memory of anything.—*vt*. (minuting, minuted). To write down a concise state or note of.

Minutiae, mi-nū'shi-ē, *n.pl.* Small or minute things; minor or unimportant details.

Miracle, mi'ra-kl, *n.* A marvel; a supernatural event; a miracle-play.

Miracle-play, mi'ra-kl-plā, *n.* Formerly a dramatic representation exhibiting the lives of the saints, or other sacred subjects.

Miraculous, mi-ra'kū-lus, *a.* Performed supernaturally; wonderful; extraordinary.

Mirage, mi-räzh', *n.* An optical illusion, causing remote objects to be seen double, or to appear as if suspended in the air.

Mire, mir, *n.* Wet, muddy soil; mud.—*vt*. and *i.* (miring, mired). To sink in mire; to soil with mud.

Mirror, mi'rer, *n.* A looking-glass; any polished substance that reflects images; an exemplar.—*vt*. To reflect, as in a mirror.

Mirth, merth, *n.* The feeling of being merry; merriment; glee; hilarity.

Misadventure, mis-ad-ven'tūr, *n.* An unlucky accident; misfortune; ill-luck.

Misalliance, mis-al-li'ans, *n.* Improper association; an unequal marriage.

Misanthrope, Misanthropist, mis'an-thrōp, mis-an'thrōp-ist, *n.* A hater of mankind.

Misanthropy, mis-an'thrō-pi, *n.* Hatred or dislike to mankind.

Misapply, mis-ap-plī', *vt*. To apply amiss; to apply to a wrong purpose.

Misapprehend, mis-ap'prē-hend'', *vt*. To misunderstand; to take in a wrong sense.

Misappropriate, mis-ap-prō'pri-āt, *vt*. To appropriate wrongly.

Misbecome, mis-bē-kum', *vt*. Not to become; to suit ill.

Misbegotten, mis-bē-got'n, *p.a.* Unlawfully or irregularly begotten.

Misbehave, mis-bē-hāv', *vi*. To behave ill; to conduct oneself improperly.

Misbelief, mis-bē-lēf', *n.* Erroneous belief; false religion.

Miscalculate, mis-kal'kū-lāt, *vt*. To calculate erroneously.

Miscarry, mis-ka'ri,*vi.* To fail to reach its destination; to fail of the intended effect; to bring forth young before the proper time.

Miscellaneous, mis-sel-lā'nē-us, *a.* Consisting of several kinds; promiscuous; producing written compositions of various sorts.

Miscellany, mis'sel-la-ni, *n.* A mixture of various kinds; a collection of various literary productions.

Misconception, mis-kon-sep'shon, *n.* An erroneous conception;; misapprehension.

Misconduct, mis-kon'dukt, *n.* Misbehavior; mismanagement.—*vt*. mis-kon-dukt'. To conduct amiss; *refl.* to misbehave.

Misconstruction, mis-kon-struk'shon, *n.* Wrong construction or interpretation.

Misconstrue, mis-kon'strö, *vt*. To construe or interpret erroneously.

Miscreant, mis'krē-ant, *n.* A vile wretch; an unprincipled scoundrel.

Misdate, mis-dāt', *vt*. To date erroneously.—*n.* A wrong date.

Misdeed, mis-dēd', *n.* An evil action; transgression.

Misdemeanor, mis-dē-mēn'ėr, *n.* Ill behavior; an offense inferior to felony.

Misdirect, mis-di-rekt', *vt*. To direct to a wrong person or place.

Misdoubt, mis-dout', *n.* Suspicion of crime or danger.—*vt*. To suspect of deceit or danger.

Misemploy, mis-em-ploi', *vt*. To employ amiss or to no purpose; to misuse.

Miser, mi'zėr, *n.* A niggard; one who in wealth acts as if suffering from poverty.

Miserable, miz'ėr-a-bl, *a.* Very unhappy; wretched; worthless; despicable.

Miserly, mi'zėr-li, *a.* Like a miser in habits; penurious; sordid; niggardly.

Misery, miz'ėr-i, *n.* Great unhappiness; extreme distress; wretchedness.

Misfeasance, mis-fē'zans, *n.* In *law,* a wrong done; wrong-doing in office.

Misfit, mis-fit', *n.* A bad fit.—*vt*. To make (a garment, etc.) of a wrong size; to supply with something not suitable.

Misfortune, mis-for'tūn, *n.* Ill fortune; calamity; mishap.

Misgiving, mis-giv'ing, *n.* A failing of confidence; doubt; distrust.

Misguide, mis-gīd', *vt*. To guide into error; to direct to a wrong purpose or end.

Mishap, mis-hap', *n.* A mischance; an unfortunate accident.

Misinform, mis-in-form', *vt*. To give erroneous information to.

Misinterpret, mis-in-tėr'pret, *vt*. To interpret erroneously.

Misjudge, mis-juj', *vt*. To judge erroneously.—*vi*. To err in judgment.

Mislay, mis-lā', *vt*. To lay in a wrong place; to lay in a place not recollected.

Mislead, mis-lēd', *vt*. To lead astray; to cause to mistake; to deceive.

Mismanage, mis-man'āj, *vt*. To manage ill; to administer improperly.

Misnomer, mis-nō'mer, *n.* A mistaken or inapplicable name or designation.

Misogamist, mi-sog'am-ist, *n.* A hater of marriage.

Misogynist, mi-soj'in-ist, *n.* A woman-hater.

Misplace, mis-plās, *vt*. To put in a wrong place; to set on an improper object.

Misprint, mis-print', *vt*. To print wrongly.—*n.* A mistake in printing.

Mispronounce, mis-prō-nouns', *vt*. or *i.* To pronounce erroneously.

Misquote, mis-kwōt, *vt*. To quote erroneously; to cite incorrectly.

Misreport, mis-rē-pōrt', *vt*. To give an incorrect account of.—*n*. An erroneous report.

Misrepresent, mis-rep'rē-zent'', *vt*. To represent falsely.

Misrule, mis-röl', *n*. Bad rule; misgovernment.—*vt*. To govern badly or oppressively.

Miss, mis, *vt*. To fail in hitting, obtaining, finding, etc.; to feel the loss of; to omit; to let slip.—*vi*. To fail to strike what is aimed at; to miscarry.—*n*. A failure to hit, obtain, etc.; loss; want; an unmarried woman.

Missal, mis'al, *n*. The R. Catholic mass-book.

Misshapen, mis-shāp'n, *a*. Ill-formed; ugly.

Missile, mis'il, *a*. Capable of being thrown.—*n*. A weapon or projectile thrown with hostile intention, as an arrow, a bullet.

Mission, mi'shon, *n*. A sending or delegating; duty on which one is sent; destined end or function; persons sent on some political business or to propagate religion; a station of missionaries.

Missionary, mi'shon-a-ri, *n*. One sent to propagate religion.—*a*. Pertaining to missions.

Missive, mis'iv, *a*. Such as is sent; proceeding from some authoritative source.—*n*. A message; a letter or writing sent.

Misspell, mis-spel', *vt*. To spell wrongly.

Misspent, mis-spent', *p.a*. Ill-spent; wasted.

Misstatement, mis-stāt'ment, *n*. A wrong statement.

Mist, mist, *n*. Visible watery vapor; aqueous vapor falling in numerous but almost imperceptible drops; something which dims or darkens.

Mistake, mis-tāk', *vt*. To misunderstand or misapprehend; to regard as one when really another.—*vi*. To err in opinion or judgment.—*n*. An error in opinion or judgment; blunder; fault.

Mistletoe, mis'l-tō or miz'l-tō, *n*. A plant that grows parasitically on various trees, and was held in veneration by the Druids.

Mistranslate, mis-trans-lāt', *vt*. To translate erroneously.

Mistress, mis'tres, *n*. The female appellation corresponding to *master*; a woman who has authority, ownership, etc.; a female teacher; a concubine; a title of address applied to married women (written *Mrs*. and pronounced mis'iz).

Mistrust, mis-trust', *n*. Want of confidence or trust; suspicion.—*vt*. To distrust; to suspect; to doubt.

Misunderstand, mis-un'der-stand'', *vt*. To understand wrongly; to mistake.

Misuse, mis-ūz', *vt*. To use to a bad purpose; to abuse.—*n*. mis-ūs'. Improper use, misapplication.

Mite, mīt, *n*. A minute animal of the class Arachnida (cheese-*mite*, etc.); a very small coin formerly current; a very little creature.

Mitigant, mi'ti-gant, *a*. Softening; soothing.

Mitigate, mi'ti-gāt, *vt*. To make soft or mild; to assuage, lessen, abate, moderate.

Miter, mī'tèr, *n*. A high pointed cap worn by bishops.—*vt*. (mitering, mitered). To adorn with a miter.

Mitten, mit'n, *n*. A covering for the hand without fingers, or without a separate cover for each finger.

Mix, miks, *vt*. (mixing, mixed). To unite or blend promiscuously; to mingle; to associate.—*vi*. To become united or blended; to join; to associate.

Mixed, mikst, *p.a*. Promiscuous; indiscriminate; miscellaneous.

Mixture, miks'tūr, *n*. Act of mixing; state of being mixed; a compound; a liquid medicine of different ingredients.

Mnemonics, nē mon'iks, *n*. The art of memory; rules for assisting the memory.

Moan, mōn, *vi*. To utter a low dull sound through grief or pain.—*vt*. To bewail or deplore.—*n*. A low dull sound due to grief or pain; a sound resembling this.

Moat, mōt, *n*. A deep trench round a castle or other fortified place.—*vt*. To surround with a ditch for defense.

Mob, mob, *n*. A crowd; disorderly assembly; rabble.—*vt*. (mobbing, mobbed). To attack in a disorderly crowd; to crowd round and annoy.

Mobile, mō'bil, *a*. Capable of being easily moved; changeable; fickle.

Moccasin, mok'a-sin, *n*. A shoe of deer-skin or soft leather, worn by N. American Indians; a venomous serpent of the United States.

Mock, mok, *vt*. To mimic in contempt or derision; to flout; to ridicule; to set at naught; to defy.—*vi*. To use ridicule; to gibe or jeer.—*n*. A derisive word or gesture; ridicule; derision.—*a*. Counterfeit; assumed.

Mockery, mok'ė-ri, *n*. Derision; sportive insult; counterfeit appearance; vain effort.

Mode, mōd, *n*. Manner; method; fashion; custom.

Model, mo'del, *n*. A pattern; an image, copy, facsimile; standard, plan, or type; a person from whom an artist studies his proportions, postures, etc.—*vt*. (modelling, modelled). To plan after some model; to form in order to serve as a model; to mold.—*vi*. To make a model.

Moderate, mo'de-rāt, *vt*. To restrain from excess; to temper, lessen, allay.—*vi*. To become less violent or intense; to preside as a moderator.—*a*. Not going to extremes; temperate; medium; mediocre.—*n*. One not extreme in opinions.

Moderator, mo'de-rāt'ér, *n*. One who or that which moderates; a president, especially of courts in Presbyterian churches.

Modern, mod'érn, *a*. Pertaining to the present time; of recent origin; late; recent.—*n*. A person of modern times.

Modernize, mod'érn-īz, *vt*. To adapt to modern ideas, style, or language.

Modest, mod'est, *a*. Restrained by a sense of propriety; bashful; diffident; chaste; moderate; not excessive.

Modicum, mod'i-kum, *n*. A little; a small quantity; small allowance or share.

Modify, mod'i-fī, *vt*. (modifying, modified). To qualify; to change or alter; to vary.

Modish, mōd'ish, *a*. According to the mode or fashion; affectedly fashionable.

Modulate, mod'ū-lāt, *vt*. To proportion; to adjust; to vary (the voice) in tone; to transfer from one key to another.—*vi*. To pass from one key into another.

Modulation, mod-ū-lā'shon, *n*. Act of modulating; act of inflecting the voice; melodious sound; change from one scale to another.

Module, mod'ūl, *n*. In *architecture*, a measure to regulate the proportions of a building.

Modulus, mod'ū-lus, *n*. In *mathematics*, etc., a constant quantity used in connection with some variable quantity.

Modus, mō'dus, *n*. A way, manner, or mode.

Mohair, mō'hār, *n*. The hair of the Angora goat; cloth made of this hair; an imitation wool and cotton cloth.

Mohammedan, mō-ham'med-an, *a*. Pertaining to Mohammed, or the religion founded by him.—*n*. A follower of Mohammed.

Moire, mwär, *n*. A watered appearance on metals or cloths; watered silk.

Moisture, mois'tūr, *n*. A moderate degree of wetness; humidity.

Molar, mō'lér, *a*. Serving to grind the food in eating.—*n*. A grinding or double tooth.

Molasses, mō-las'ez, *n.sing*. A syrup from sugar in the process of making; treacle.

Mold, mōld, *n*. Fine soft earth; mustiness or mildew; dust from incipient decay; form in which a thing is cast; model; shape; character.—*vt*. To cause to contract mold; to cover with mold or soil; to model; to shape; to fashion.—*vi*. To become moldy.

Molding, mōld'ing, *n*. Anything cast in a mold; ornamental contour or form in wood or stone along an edge or a surface.

Mole, mōl, *n*. A small discolored protuberance on the human body; a mound or break-water to protect a harbor from the waves; a small bur-

M

rowing insectivorous animal.

Molecule, mo'le-kūl, *n.* A very minute particle of matter.

Mole-hill, mōl'hil, *n.* A little hillock of earth thrown up by moles; a very small hill.

Molest, mō-lest', *vt.* To annoy; to disturb; to harass; to vex.

Mollify, mol'i-fī, *vt.* (mollifying, mollified). To soften; to assuage; to appease; to reduce in harshness; to tone down.

Mollusc, Mollusk, mol'usk, *n.* An animal whose body is soft, as mussels, snails, cuttle-fish, etc.; one of the *Mollusca.*

Molten, mōlt'n, old pp. of *melt.* Melted; made of melted metal.

Moment, mō'ment, *n.* A minute portion of time; a second; momentum; importance; gravity.

Momentary, mō-ment-a-ri, *a.* Done in a moment; continuing only a moment.

Momentous, mō-ment'us, *a.* Of moment; important; weighty.

Momentum, mō-ment'um, *n.*; pl. **-ta.** The force possessed by a body in motion; impetus.

Monachism, mon'ak-izm, *n.* The monastic life or system.

Monad, mon'ad, *n.* An ultimate atom.

Monadic, mon-ad'ik, *a.* Having the nature or character of a monad.

Monarch, mon'ärk, *n.* A supreme governor of a state; a sovereign; one who or that which is chief of its kind.—*a.* Supreme; ruling.

Monarchy, mon'är-ki, *n.* Government in which the supreme power is lodged in a single person, actually or nominally; a kingdom.

Monastery, mon'as-te-ri, *n.* A house for monks, sometimes for nuns; abbey; priory; convent.

Monatomic, mon-a-tom'ik, *a.* Said of an element one atom of which will combine with only one atom of another element.

Monday, mun'dā, *n.* The second day of the week.

Monetary, mo'ne-ta-ri, *a.* Relating to money; consisting in money.

Money, mun'i, *n.* Coin; pieces of gold, silver, or other metal, stamped by public authority and used as the medium of exchange; a circulating medium; wealth; affluence.

Mongol, Mongolian, mon'gol, mon-gō'li-an, *n.* A native of Mongolia.—*a.* Belonging to Mongolia.

Mongoose, mong' or mung'gōs, *n.* A common ichneumon of India.

Mongrel, mung'grel, *a.* Of a mixed breed; hybrid.—*n.* An animal of a mixed breed.

Monitor, mo'ni-tėr, *n.* One who admonishes; one who warns of faults or informs of duty; a senior pupil in a school appointed to instruct and look after juniors; a lizard.

Monk, mungk, *n.* A male inhabitant of a monastery, bound to celibacy.

Monkey, mung'ki, *n.* A long-tailed quadrumanous animal; a playful or mischievous youngster.

Monochrome, mon'ō-krōm, *n.* A painting in one color, but with light and shade.

Monogamy, mon-og'a-mi, *n.* The practice or principle of marrying only once; the marrying of only one at a time.

Monogram, mon'ō-gram, *n.* A cipher composed of several letters interwoven.

Monograph, mon'ō-graf, *n.* An account of a single person, thing, or class of things.

Monolith, mon'ō-lith, *n.* A pillar, column, etc., consisting of a single stone.

Monologue, mon'ō-log, *n.* A speech uttered by one person alone; a soliloquy.

Monomania, mon-ō-mā'ni-a, *n.* Insanity in regard to a single subject or class of subjects; a craze.

Monopoly, mo-nop'o-li, *n.* An exclusive trading privilege; assumption of anything to the exclusion of others.

Monosyllabic, mon'ō-sil-lab''ik, *a.* Consisting of one syllable, or of words of one syllable.

Monotheism, mon'ō-thē-izm, *n.* The doctrine of the existence of one God only.

Monotone, mon'ō-tōn, *n.* A single tone; unvaried pitch of the voice.

Monotony, mon-ot'o-ni, *n.* Uniformity of sound; a dull uniformity; an irksome sameness or want of variety.

Monsoon, mon-sön', *n.* The trade-wind of the Indian seas, blowing from N.E. from November to March, and S.W. from April to October.

Monster, mon'stėr, *n.* An animal of unnatural form or of great size; one unnaturally wicked or evil.—*a.* Of inordinate size.

Monstrous, mon'strus, *a.* Unnatural in form; enormous; huge; horrible.—*adv.* Exceedingly.

Month, munth, *n.* The period measured by the moon's revolution (the lunar month, about $29^1/_2$ days); one of the twelve parts of the year (the calendar month, 30 or 31 days).

Monthly, munth'li, *a.* Done or happening once a month, or every month.—*n.* A publication appearing once a month.—*adv.* Once a month; in every month.

Monument, mon'ū-ment, *n.* Anything by which the memory of a person or of an event is preserved; a memorial; a singular or notable instance.

Mood, möd, *n.* Temper of mind; disposition; a fit of sullenness; a form of verbs expressive of certainty, contingency, etc.; a form of syllogism.

Moon, mön, *n.* The changing luminary of the night; the heavenly body next to the earth, revolving round it in about $29^1/_2$ days; a satellite of any planet; a month.

Moonlight, mön'līt, *n.* The light afforded by the moon.—*a.* Illuminated by the moon; occurring during moonlight.—**Moon-lit,** mön'lit, *a.* Illuminated by the moon.

Moonshine, mön'shīn, *n.* The light of the moon; show without substance; pretense; illegally distilled corn whiskey.

Moonstone, mön'stōn, *n.* A translucent variety of felspar used in trinkets, etc.

Moonstruck, mön'struk, *a.* Affected by the influence of the moon; lunatic.

Moor, mör, *n.* A tract of waste land, or of hilly ground on which game is preserved; a native of the northern coast of Africa.—*vt.* To secure a ship in a particular station, as by cables and anchors.—*vi.* To be confined by cables.

Mooring, mör'ing, *n.* Act of one who moors; pl. the anchor, etc., by which a ship is moored; the place where a ship is moored.

Moose, mös, *n.* The American variety of the elk.

Moot, möt, *vt.* To debate; to discuss.—*a.* Debatable; subject to discussion.

Moot-point, möt'point, *n.* A point debated or liable to be debated.

Mop, mop, *n.* A cloth or collection of yarns fastened to a handle, and used for cleaning; a grimace.—*vt.* (mopping, mopped). To rub with a mop; to wipe.—*vi.* To grimace.

Mope, mōp, *vi.* (moping, moped). To show a downcast air; to be spiritless or gloomy.—*n.* One who mopes.

Moraine, mō-rān', *n.* An accumulation of debris on glaciers or in the valleys at their foot.

Moral, mo'ral, *a.* Relating to morality or morals; ethical; virtuous; supported by reason and probability.—*n.* The practical lesson inculcated by any story; pl. general conduct as right or wrong; mode of life; ethics.

Morale, mō-räl', *n.* Mental condition of soldiers, etc., as regards courage, zeal, hope.

Moralist, mo'ral-ist, *n.* One who teaches morals; a writer or lecturer on ethics; one who inculcates or practices moral duties.

Morality, mō-ral'i-ti, *n.* The doctrine of moral duties; ethics; moral character or quality; quality of an action in regard to right and wrong; an old form of drama in which the personages were allegorical representations of virtues, vices, etc.

Moralize, mo'ral-īz, *vt.* To apply to a moral purpose; to draw a moral from.—vi. To make moral reflections; to draw practical lessons from the facts of life.

Morass, mō-ras', n. A tract of low, soft, wet ground; a marsh; a swamp; a fen.

Morbid, mor'bid, a. Diseased; sickly; not sound and healthful.

Mordacious, mor-dā'shus, a. Biting; pungent; sarcastic.

Mordant, mor'dant, n. A substance, such as alum, which fixes colors; matter by which gold-leaf is made to adhere.—a. Biting; severe.

More, mōr, a. comp. of much and many. Greater in amount, extent, degree, etc.; greater in number.—adv. In a greater degree, extent, or quantity; in addition.—n. A greater quantity or number; something further.

Moreover, mōr'ō'vėr, adv. Further; besides; likewise!

Moribund, mo'ri-bund, a. in a dying state.

Mormon, mor'mon, n. A member of a sect founded in the United States in 1830, who practice polygamy; a Latter-day Saint. Also **Mormonite, Mormonist.**

Morning, morn'ing, n. The first part of the day; the time between dawn and the middle of the forenoon; the first or early part. Often used as an adj.

Morning-star, n. The planet Venus when it rises before the sun.

Morocco, mŏrok'ō, n. A find kind of leather prepared from goat skin.

Moron, mo'ron, n. A feeble-minded or degenerate person.

Morose, mō-rōs', a. Of a sour or sullen temper; gloomy; churlish; surly.

Morphia, Morphine, mor'fi-a, mor'fin, n. The narcotic principle of opium, a powerful anodyne.

Morphology, mor-fol'o-ji, n. The science which treats of the form and arrangement of the structures of plants and animals.

Morsel, mor'sel, n. A bite; a mouthful; a fragment; a little piece in general.

Mortal, mor'tal, a. Subject to death; deadly; fatal; human.—n. A being subject to death; a human being.

Mortality, mor-tal'i-ti, n. State of being mortal; actual death of great numbers of men or beasts; death-rate.

Mortar, mor'tär, n. A vessel, in which substances are pounded with a pestle; a short piece of ordnance, thick and wide, for throwing shells, etc.; a mixture of lime and sand with water, used as a cement for building.

Mortgage, mor'gäj, n. A conveyance of land or house property as security for a debt; the deed effecting this conveyance.—vt. (mortgaging, mortgaged). To grant or assign on mortgage; to pledge.

Mortification, mor'ti-fi-kā''shon, n. Act of mortifying; condition of being mortified; death of a part of an animal body while the rest is alive; the subduing of the passions by penance, abstinence, etc.; chagrin.

Mortify, mor'ti-fi, vt. (mortifying, mortified). To affect with gangrene or mortification; to subdue by abstinence or rigorous severities, to humiliate; to chagrin.—vi. To lose vitality while yet a portion of a living body.

Mortise, mor'tis, n. A hole cut in one piece of material to receive the tenon of another piece.—vt. To cut a mortise in; to join by a tenon and mortise.

Mortuary, mor'tū-a-ri, n. A place for the temporary reception of the dead.—a. Pertaining to the burial of the dead.

Mosaic, mō-zā'ik, n. Inlaid work of marble, precious stones, etc., disposed on a ground of cement so as to form designs.—a. Pertaining to or composed of mosaic.

Moslem, moz'lem, n. An orthodox Mohammedan.

Mosque, mosk, n. A Mohammedan place of worship.

Mosquito, mos-kē'tō, n. A sting gnat or fly.

Moss, mos, n. A small plant with simple branching stems and numerous small leaves; a bog; a place where peat is found,—vt. To cover with moss by natural growth.

Most, mōst, a. superl. of more. Greatest in any way.—adv. In the greatest degree, quantity, or extent; mostly; chiefly.—n. The greatest number; the majority; greatest amount; utmost extent, degree, etc.

Mote, mōt, n. A small particle; anything proverbially small.

Moth, moth, n. The name of numerous nocturnal insects allied to the butterflies.

Mother, muᴛʜ'er, n. A female parent; a woman who has borne a child; source or origin; an abbess or other female at the head of a religious institution; a slimy substance that gathers in vinegar, etc.—a. Native; natural; inborn; vernacular.

Mother-country, muᴛʜ'er-kun-tri, n. A country which has sent out colonies; a country as the producer of anything.

Mother-in-law, muᴛʜ'er-in-la, n. The mother of one's husband or wife.

Mother-of-pearl, muᴛʜ'er-ov-perl, n. The hard silvery brilliant internal layer of several kinds of shells.

Motile, mō'til, a. Having inherent power of motion.

Motion, mō'shon, n. Act or process of moving; power of moving; movement; internal impulse; proposal made; evacuation of the intestines.—vi. To make a significant gesture with the hand.

Motive, mō'tiv, n. That which incites to action; cause, inducement; purpose; theme in a piece of music; prevailing idea of an artist.—a. Causing motion.—vt. To supply a motive to or for; to prompt.

Motley, mot'li, a. Variegated in color; particolored; heterogeneous; diversified—n. A dress of various colors.

Motor, mō'tor, n. A moving power; force or agency that sets machinery in motion; a motorcar.—a. Imparting motion.

Mottle, mot'l, n. A blotched or spotted character of surface.—vt. (mottling, mottled). To mark with spots or blothes as if mottled.

Motto, mot'tō, n.; pl. -oes, or -os. A short sentence or phrase, or a single word, adopted as expressive of one's guiding idea.

Moult, mōlt, vi. and t. To shed or cast the hair, feathers, skin, horns, etc., as birds and other animals.—n. Act or process of changing the feathers, etc.; time of moulting.

Mound, mound, n. An artificial elevation of earth; a bulwark, a rampart; the globe which forms part of the regalia.

Mount, mount, n. A hill; a mountain; that with which something is fitted; a setting, frame, etc.; opportunity or means of riding on horseback; a horse.—vi. To rise; to get on horseback or upon any animal; to amount.—vt. To raise aloft; to climb; to place oneself upon, as on horseback; to furnish with horses; to set in or cover with something; to set off to advantage.

Mountain, moun'tin, n. An elevated mass larger than a hill; anything very large.—a. Pertaining to a mountain; found on mountains.

Mountaineer, moun-tin-ēr', n. An inhabitant of a mountainous district; a climber of mountains.—vi. To practice the climbing of mountains.

Mountebank, moun'ti-bangk, n. One who mounts a bench or stage in a public place, and vends medicines or nostrums; a quack; any boastful and false pretender.

Mounting, mount'ing, n. Act of one who mounts; that with which an article is mounted or set off; trimming, setting, etc.

Mourn, mōrn, vi. To sorrow; to lament; to wear the customary habit of sorrow.—vt. To grieve

M

for; to deplore.

Mourning, mörn'ing, n. Lamentation; dress worn by mourners.—a.. Employed to express grief.

Mouse, mous, n.; pl. **Mice,** mīs. A small rodent quadruped that infests houses, fields, etc.—vi. mouz (mousing, moused). To hunt for or catch mice.

Moustache, mus-tash', n. The long hair on the upper lip.

Mouth, mouth, n.; pl. **Mouths,** mouᴛʜz. The opening in the head of an animal into which food is received, and from which voice is uttered; opening of anything hollow, as of a pitcher, or of a cave, pit, etc.; the part of a river, etc., by which it joins with the ocean.—vt. mouᴛʜ. To take into the mouth; to utter with a voice affectedly big.—vi. To speak with a loud, affected voice; to vociferate.

Mouth-organ, mouth-or'gan, n. A small popular wind-instrument, flat in shape, with openings for the various notes, which are produced by inhalation and exhalation.

Mouth-piece, mouth'pēs, n. The part of a wind-instrument to which the mouth is applied; a tube by which a cigar, etc., is held in the mouth; one who believes the opinions of others.

Move, möv, vt. (moving, moved). To cause to change place, posture, or position; to set in motion; to affect; to rouse; to prevail on; to propose, as a resolution.—vi. To change place or posture; to stir; to begin to act; to shake; to change residence; to make a proposal to a meeting.—n. The act of moving; a movement; proceeding; action taken.

Movement, möv'ment, n. Act of moving; motion; change of position; manner of moving; gesture; an agitation to bring about some result desired; wheel-work of a clock.

Mow, mō, vt. (pret. mowed, pp. mowed or mown). To cut down, as grass, etc.; to cut the grass from; to cut down in great numbers.—vi. To cut grass; to use the scythe.

Much, much, a.; comp. more, superl. most. Great in quantity or amount; abundant.—adv. In a great degree; by far; greatly.—n. A great quantity; something strange or serious.

Mucilage, mū'si-lāj, n. A solution in water of gummy matter; a gummy substance found in certain plants.

Muck muk, n. Dung in a moist state; something mean, vile, or filthy.—vt. To manure with muck; to remove muck from.

Mucous, Mucose, mū'kus, a. Pertaining to mucus, or resembling it; slimy.—**Mucous membrane,** a membrane that lines all the cavities of the body which open externally, and secretes mucus.

Mucus, mū'kus, n. A viscid fluid secreted by the mucous membrane.

Mud, mud, n. Moist and soft earth; sediment from turbid waters; mire.—vt. (mudding, mudded). To soil with mud; to make turbid.

Muddle, mud'l, vt. (muddling, muddled). To make muddy; to intoxicate partially; to confuse; to make a mess of.—vi. To become muddy; to act in a confused manner.—n. A mess; confusion; bewilderment.

Muffin, muf'in, n. A light spongy cake.

Muffle, muf'l, vt. (muffling, muffled). To cover close, particularly the neck and face; to conceal; to deaden the sound of by wrapping cloth, etc., round.—n. The tumid and naked portion of the upper lip and nose of ruminants and rodents.

Muffler, muf'lėr, n. A cover for the face or neck; a stuffed glove for lunatics.

Mug, mug, n. A small vessel of earthenware or metal for containing liquor; a jug.

Muggy, Muggish, mug'i, mug'ish, a. Damp and close; moist; moldy.

Mulatto, mū-lat'tō, n. A person who is the offspring of a white and a negro.

Mulch, mulsh, n. Dungy material protecting the roots of newly-planted shrubs, etc.

Mulct, mulkt, n. A fine.—vt. To fine; to deprive.

Mule, mūl, n. The offspring of an ass and mare, or a horse and she-ass; a hybrid animal.

Mull, mul, vt. To heat, sweeten, and flavor with spices, as ale or wine.

Mullion, mul'yon, n. An upright division between the lights of windows, screens, etc., in Gothic architecture.

Multifarious, mul-ti-fā'ri-us, a. Having great diversity or variety.

Multiform, mul'ti-form, a. Having many forms, shapes, or appearances.

Multilateral, mul-ti-lat'ėr-al, a. Having many sides; many-sided.

Multipartite, mul'ti-pär-tīt, a Divided into several or many parts.

Multiple, mul'ti-pl, a. Manifold; having many parts or divisions.—n. A number which contains another an exact number of times.

Multiplex, mul'ti-pleks, a. Manifold; complex.

Multiplicand, mul'ti-pli-kand'', n. A number to be multiplied by another.

Multiplication, mul'ti-pli-kā''shon, n. Act or process of multiplying; state of being multiplied; reproduction of animals.

Multiplicity, mul-ti-plis'i-ti, n. State of being multiplex or manifold; great number.

Multiplier, mul-ti-pli-ėr, n. One who or that which multiplies; the number by which another is multiplied.

Multiply, mul'ti-plī, vt. (multiplying, multiplied). To increase in number; to add to itself any given number of times.—vi. To increase in number, or to become more numerous by reproductive; to extend.

Multitude, mul'ti-tūd, n. State of being many; a great number, collectively or indefinitely; a crowd.—**The multitude,** the populace.

Mumble, mum'bl, vi. (mumbling, mumbled). To mutter; to speak with mouth partly closed; to eat with the lips close.—vt. To utter with a low, inarticulate voice.

Mummy, mum'i, n. A dead human body embalmed after the manner of the ancient Egyptians, with wax, balsams, etc.

Mumps, mumps, n. Silent displeasure; sullenness; a disease consisting in an inflammation of the salivary glands.

Munch, munsh, vt. and i. To chew audibly.

Mundane, mun'dān, a. Belonging to this world; worldly; earthly.

Municpal, mū-ni'si-pal, a. Belonging to a corporation or city.

Municipality, mū-ni'si-pal''i-ti, n. A town possessed of local self-government; community under municipal jurisdiction.

Munificence, mū-ni'fi-sens, n. A bestowing liberally; liberality; generosity.

Munition, mū-ni'shon, n. Military stores; ammunition; material for any enterprise.

Murder, mér'dėr, n. Act of killing a human being with premeditated malice.—vt. To kill (a human being) with premeditated malice; to mar by bad execution.

Muriatic, mū-ri-at'ik, a. Pertaining to or obtained from brine or sea-salt; hydrochloric.

Murky, mėr'ki, a. Dark; obscure; gloomy.

Murmur, mėr'mėr, n. A low continued or repeated sound; a hum; a grumble or mutter.—vi. To utter a murmur or hum; to grumble.—vt. To utter indistinctly; to mutter.

Murrain, mu'rän, n. A deadly and infectious disease among cattle, etc.

Muscadel, Muscatel, Muscadine, mus'ka-del, mus'ka-tel, mus'ka-din, a. and n. A sweet and strong Italian or French wine; the grapes which produce this wine; a delicious pear.

Muscle, mus'l n. A definite portion of an animal body consisting of fibers susceptible of contraction and relaxation, and thus effecting motion; a mussel.

Muscular, mus'kū-lėr, a. Pertaining to or consisting of muscle; performed by a muscle; strong; brawny; vigorous.

Muse, mūz, *n.* One of the nine sister goddesses of the Greeks and Romans presiding over the arts; poetic inspiration; a fit of abstraction.—*vi.* (musing, mused). To ponder; to meditate in silence; to be absent in mind.—*vt.* To meditate on.

Museum, mū-zē'um, *n.* A repository of interesting objects connected with literature, art, or science.

Mushroom, mush'röm, *n.* An edible fungus; an upstart,—*a.* Pertaining to mushrooms; resembling mushrooms in rapidity of growth.

Music, mū'zik, *n.* Melody of harmony; the science of harmonious sounds; the written or printed score of a composition.

Musical, mū'zik·al, *a.* Belonging to music; producing music; melodious; harmonious; fond of or skilled in music.

Musing, mūz'ing, *n.* Meditation.

Musk, musk, *n.* A strong-scented substance obtained from the musk-deer; the animal itself; a musky smell; a plant giving out such a smell.—*vt.* To perfume with musk.

Musk-deer, musk'dēr, *n.* A deer of Central Asia, the male of which yields the perfume musk.

Musky, musk'i, *a.* Having the odor of musk; fragrant.

Muslin, muz'lin, *n.* A fine thin cotton cloth.—*a.* Made of muslin.

Mussel, mus'el, *n.* The common name of a genus of bivalve shell-fish.

Must, must, *vi.* without inflection, and present or past. A defective or auxiliary verb expressing obligation or necessity.—*n.* New wine unfermented.

Mustard, mus'terd, *n.* An annual plant cultivated for its pungent seeds; the condiment obtained from its seeds.

Muster, mus'ter, *vt.* To collect, as troops; to assemble or bring together—*vi.* To assemble; to meet in one place.—*n.* An assembling of troops; register of troops mustered; an array.

Musty, mus'ti, *a.* Moldy; sour; stale.

Mutable, mūta·bl, *a.* Changeable; inconstant; unstable; variable; fickle.

Mutation, mū-tā'shon, *n.* Act or process of changing; change; alteration, either in form or qualities; modification.

Mute, mūt, *a.* Silent; incapable of speaking; dumb; not pronounced, or having its sound chocked by a contact of the vocal organs, as certain consonants (*t, p, k, etc.*).—*n.* A dumb person; a hired attendant at a funeral; a mute consonant.—*vi.* (muting, muted). To eject the contents of the bowels as birds.

Mutilate, mū'ti-lāt, *vt.* To injure or disfigure by cutting a piece from; to maim; to render imperfect.

Mutinous, mū-ti-nus, *a.* Exciting or engaging in mutiny; seditious.

Mutiny, muti-ni, *n.* An insurrection of soldiers or seamen; revolt against constituted authority.—*vi.* (mutinying, mutinied). To rise against lawful authority.

Mutter, mut'er, *vi.* To utter words with compressed liips; to mumble; to murmur.—*vt.* To utter with a low, murmuring voice.—*n.* Murmur; obscure utterance.

Mutton, mut'n, *n.* The flesh of sheep, raw or dressed for food.

Mutual, mū'tū-al, *a.* Reciprocal; interchanged; given and received on both sides.

Muzzle, muz'l, *n.* The projecting mouth and nose of an animal; the open end of a gun or pistol, etc.; a cover for the mouth which hinders an animal from biting.—*vt.* (muzzling, muzzled). To cover the mouth of to prevent biting or eating; to gag.

My, mi, *pron.* The possessive case sing. of I*yopy; belonging to me.

Mycology, mī-kol'o-ji, *n.* That department of botany which investigates fungi.

Myology, mī-ol'o-ji, *n.* The science and description of the muscles.

Myopia, Myopy, mī-ō'pi-a, mī'o-pi, *n.* Shortsightedness; near-sightedness.

Myriad, mi'ri-ad, *n.* A countless number; the number of ten thousand collectively.—*a.* innumerable.

Myrmidon, mer'mi-don, *n.* A soldier of a rough character; a ruffian under an unscrupulous leader.

Myrrh, mer, *n.* An aromatic gum resin exuded by a spiny Arabian shrub.

Myrtle, mer'tl, *n.* An evergreen shrub.

Myself, mi-self', *compd. pron.*; pl. **Ourselves,** ourselvz'. As a nominative it is used, generally after I, to express emphasis—I, and not another; in the objective often used reflexively and without any emphasis.

Mysterious, mis-tē'ri-us, *a.* Containing mystery; beyond human comprehension; untelligible; enigmatical.

Mystery, mis'ter-i, *n.* Something above human intelligence; a secret; an old form of drama in which the characters and events were drawn from sacred history; a trade craft, or calling.

Mystic, Mystical, mis'tik, mis'tik-al, *a.* Obscure to human comprehension; involving some secret meaning or import; mysterious; pertaining to mysticism.

Mysticism, mis'ti-sizm, *n.* Views in religion based on communication between man and God through spiritual perception; obscurity of doctrine.

Mystify, mis'ti-fi, *vt.* (mystifying, mystified). To perplex intentionally; to bewilder; to befog.

Myth, mith, *n.* A tradition or fable embodying the notions of a people as to their gods, origin early history etc.; an invented story.

Mythological, Mythologic, mith-o-loj'ik-al, mith-o-loj'ik, *a.* Relating to or proceeding from mythology; fabulous.

Mythology, mith-ol'o-ji, *n.* The science or doctrine of myths; the myths of a people collectively.

N

Nab, nab, *vt.* (nabbing, nabbed). To catch or seize suddenly or unexpectedly.

Nacre, nā'ker, *n.* Mother-of-pearl.

Nadir, nā'der, *n.* That point of the lower hemisphere of the heavens directly opposite to the zenith; the lowest point.

Nag, nag, *n.* A small horse; a horse in general.—*t.* and *i.* (nagging, nagged). To find fault constantly.

Naif, nä-ēf, *a.* Ingenuous; having a natural luster without being cut, as jewels.

Nail, nāl, *n.* The horny substance at the end of the human finger and toes; a claw, a small pointed piece of metal, to be driven into timber, etc.; a stud or boss; a measure of 2¼ inches.—*vt.* To fasten or stud with nails; to hold fast or make secure.

Naïve, nä-ēv', *a.* Ingenuous; simple; artless.

Naïveté, nä-ēv'tā, *n.* Native simplicity; unaffected ingenuousness.

Naked, nā'ked, *a.* Not having clothes on; bare; nude; open to view; mere, bare, simple; destitute; unassisted.

Name, nām, *n.* That by which a person or thing is designated; appellation; title; reputation; eminence; sound only; not reality; authority; behalf; a family.—*vt.* (naming, named). To give a name to; to designate; to style; to nominate; to speak of or mention as.

Namely, nām'li, *adv.* By name; particularly; that is to say.

Nap, nap, *n.* The woolly substance on the surface of cloth, etc.; the downy substance on plants; a short sleep.—*vi.* (napping, napped). To have a short sleep; to drowse.

Nape, nāp, *n.* The prominent joint of the neck behind; the back part of the neck.

Naphtha, naf'tha or nap', *n.* A volatile, limpid, bituminous liquid, of a strong peculiar odor and very inflammable.

Napkin, nap'kin, *n.* A sort of towel used at table; a handkerchief.

Narcissus, när-sis'us, *n.* An extensive genus of bulbous flowering plants.

Narcotic, när-kot'ik, *n.* A substance which relieves pain and produces sleep.—*a.* Having the properties of a narcotic.

Nard, närd, *n.* An aromatic plant, usually called spikenard; an unguent prepared from the plant.

Narrate, na-rāt' or nar', *vt.* (narrating, narrated). To tell or relate, orally or in writing.

Narrative, nar'a-tiv, *a.* Pertaining to narration.— *n.* That which is narrated or related; a relation orally or in writing.

Narrow, na'rō, *a.* Of little breadth; not wide or broad; very limited; straitened; not liberal; bigoted; near; close; scrutinizing.—*n.* A narrow channel; a strait: usually in *pl.*—*vt.* To make narrow.—*vi.* To become narrow; to contract in breadth.

Nasal, nā'zal, *a.* Pertaining to the nose; formed or affected by the nose, as speech.—*n.* An elementary sound uttered partly through the nose.

Nascent, nas'ent, *a.* Arising; coming into being; springing up.

Nasturtium, nas-tėr'shi-um, *n.* A genus of herbs, including the common water-cress.

Nasty, nas'ti, *a.* Filthy; dirty; indecent; disagreeable in taste or smell; troublesome.

Natal, nā'tal, *a.* Pertaining to birth; dating from one's birth; pertaining to the buttocks.

Natant, nā'tant, *a.* Floating; swimming.

Nation, nā'shon, *n.* A body of people inhabiting the same country, or united under the same government; great number.

National, na'shon-al, *a.* Pertaining to a nation; public; attached to one's own country.

Nationality, na-shon-al'i-ti, *n.* Quality of being national; national character; strong attachment to one's own nation; a nation.

Native, nā'tiv, *a.* Pertaining to the place or circumstances of one's birth; indigenous; inborn; occurring in nature pure or unmixed.—*n.* One born in a place or country; an indigenous animal or plant; an oyster raised in an artificial bed.

Nativity, na-tiv'i-ti, *n.* Birth; time, place, and manner of birth.

Natty, nat'i, *a.* Neat; tidy; spruce.

Natural, na'tūr-al, *a.* Pertaining to nature; produced or effected by nature; consistent with nature; not artificial; according to the life; not revealed; bastard; unregenerated.—*n.* An idiot; a fool.

Naturalization, na'tūr-al-izā''shon, *n.* Act of investing an alien with the privileges of a native citizen.

Nature, nā'tūr, *n.* The universe; the total of all agencies and forces in the creation; the inherent or essential qualities of anything; individual constitution; sort; natural human instincts; reality as distinct from that which is artificial.

Naughty, na'ti, *a.* Bad; mischievous.

Nausea, nā'shē-a, *n.* Sickness.

Nauseate, na'she-āt, *vi.* To feel nausea.—*vt.* To loathe; to affect with disgust.

Nautical, na'tik-al, *a.* Pertaining to ships, seamen, or navigation; naval; marine.

Nautilus, na'ti-lus, *n.* A mollusc with a many-chambered shell in the form of a flat spiral.

Naval, nā'val, *a.* Pertaining to ships; pertaining to a navy; nautical; maritime.

Nave, nāv, *n.* The central block or hub of a wheel; middle part, lengthwise, of a church.

Navel, nā'vl, *n.* A depression in the center of the abdomen, the end of the umbilical cord.

Navigate, na'vi-gāt, *vi.* To conduct or guide a ship; to sail.—*vt.* To manage in sailing, as a vessel; to sail or guide a ship over.

Navigator, na'vi-gāt-ėr, *n.* One who directs the course of a ship.

Navy, nā'vi, *n.* All the ships of a certain class belonging to a country; the whole of the ships of war belonging to a nation.

Nazarean, Nazarene, naz'a-rē-an, naz-a-rēn', *n.* An inhabitant of Nazareth; a name given in contempt of Christ and the early Christians.

Nazarite, naz'a-rit, *n.* A Jew who bound himself to extraordinary purity of life.

Near, nėr, *a.* Not distant in place, time, or degree; intimate; affecting one's interest or feelings; parsimonious; narrow; on the left of a horse; not circuitous.—*prep.* Close to; nigh.—*adv.* Almost; within a little; close to the wind.—*vt.* and *i.* To approach; to come near.

Neat, nēt, *n.* Cattle of the bovine genus.—*a.* Pure; clean; trim; tidy; clever; smart; without water added.

Nebula, neb'ū-la, *n. pl.* **-ae.** Celestial objects like white clouds, generally clusters of stars.

Nebulous, neb'ū-lus, *a.* Cloudy; hazy.

Necessary, ne'ses-sa-ri, *a.* Such as must be; inevitable; essential; acting from necessity.—*n.* Anything indispensably requisite.

Necessitate, nē-ses'si-tāt, *vt.* To make necessary; to render unavoidable; to compel.

Necessity, nē-ses'si-ti, *n.* Condition of being necessary; need; irresistible compulsion; what is absolutely requisite; extreme indigence.

Neck, nek, *n.* The part of an animal's body between the head and the trunk; a narrow tract of land; the slender part of a vessel, as a bottle.

Necklace, nek'kås, *n.* A string of beads, precious stones, etc., worn round the neck.

Necrolatry, nek-rol'a-tri, *n.* Excessive veneration for or worship of the dead.

Necrology, nek-rol'o-ji, *n.* A register of deaths; a collection of obituary notices.

Necromancy, nek'rō-man-si, *n.* The revealing of future events through pretended communication with the dead; sorcery.

Necropolis, nek-rō'po-lis, *n.* A city of the dead, a cemetery.

Necrosis, nek-rō'sis, *n.* Death or mortificatioon of a bone; a disease of plants.

Nectar, nek'tar, *n.* The fabled drink of the gods; any very sweet and pleasant drink; the honey of a flower.

Nectarine, nek'ta-rin, *a.* Sweet as nectar.—*n.* A variety of the common peach.

Nectary, nek'ta-ri, *n.* The part of a flower that contains or secretes the nectar.

Née, nā, *pp.* Born: a term indicating a married woman's maiden name.

Need, nēd, *n.* A state that requires supply or relief; urgent want; necessity; poverty; destitution.—*vt.* To have necessity or need for; to lack, require.—*vi.* To be necessary: used impersonally.

Needle, nē'dl, *n.* An instrument for interweaving thread; a small steel instrument for sewing; a magnetized piece of steel in a compass attracted to the pole; anything in the form of a needle.

Needless, nēd'les, *a.* No needed or wanted; unnecessary; not requisite; useless.

Needle-work, nē'dl-wėrk, *n.* Work done with a needle; business of a seamstress.

Needy, nēd'i, *a.* Being in need; necessitous; indigent; very poor.

Nefarious, nē-fā'ri-us, *a.* Wicked in the extreme; infamous; atrocious.

Negation, nē-gā'shon, *n.* A denial; contradiction or contradictory condition.

Negative, neg'at-iv, *a.* That denies; implying denial or negation; implying absence; the opposite of positive.—*n.* A word which denies, as *not, no*; a proposition by which something is denied;

a veto; a photographic picture on glass or celluloid, in which the lights and shades are the opposite of those in nature.—vt. To prove the contrary of; to reject by vote.

Neglect, neg-lekt′, vt. To treat with no regard; to slight; to set at naught; to overlook.—n. Omission; slight; negligence.

Negligé, neg′lé-zhã, n. Easy or unceremonious dress; a loose gown—a. Carelessly arrayed; careless. Also *negligée.*

Negligence, neg′li-jens, n. Quality of being negligent; neglect; carelessness.

Negotiable, nē-gō′shi-a-bl, a. That may be negotiated; that may be transferred by assignment or indorsement.

Negotiate, nē-gō′shi-āt, vi. To treat with another respecting purchase and sale; to hold diplomatic intercourse; to conduct communications in general.—vt. To procure or bring about by negotiation; to pass into circulation (as a bill of exchange).

Negotiation, nē-gō-shi-ã′′shon, n. A negotiating; the treating with another regarding sale or purchase; diplomatic bargaining.

Negro, nē′grō, n. A black man; a male of the African race.

Neigh, nã, vi. To utter the cry of a horse; to whinny.—n. The voice of a horse.

Neighbor, nã′ber, n. One who lives or dwells near, or on friendly terms with another; a fellow-being.—vt. To be near to; to adjoin.

Neighborhood, nã′ber-hud, n. Condition of being neighbors; neighbors collectively; vicinity; locality.

Neither, nē′THer or nī′THer, pron. and pron. adj. Not either; not the one or the other.—conj. Not either; nor.

Nematoid, nem′a-toid, n. A round-worm; one of an order of entozoa or intestinal worms.—a. Pertaining to or resembling the nematoids.

Nemesis, nem′e-sis, n. A female Greek divinity personifying retributive justice; just retribution or punishment.

Neo-Latin, nē′ō-lat-in, a. and n. Applied to the Romance languages.

Neolithic, ne′ō-lith′ik, a. Belonging to a period in which implements of polished stone were used, the more recent of the two stone periods.

Neologism, nē-ol′ō-jizm, n. A new word or phrase, or new use of a word.

Neology, nē-ol′ō-ji, n. The introduction of a new word or of new words; novel doctrines; rationalistic views in theology.

Neon, nē′on, n. An inert gas present in small amount of air.

Neophyte, nē′ō-fīt, n. One newly implanted in the church; proselyte; novice; tyro.—a. Newly entered on some state.

Neoteric, nē-ō-te′rik, a. New; recent; modern.

Nephew, ne′vū, n. The son of a brother or sister.

Nephritic, ne-frit′ik, a. Pertaining to the kidneys.

Nephritis, nē-frī′tis, n. Inflammation of the kidneys.

Nepotism, nē′pot-izm, n. Undue patronage of relations; favoritism shown to nephews and other relatives.

Neptune, nep′tūn, n. The god of the sea; a planet, the remotest from the sun except Pluto.

Nerve, nerv, n. One of the fibrous threads in animal bodies whose function is to convey sensation and originate motion; fortitude; courage; energy; something resembling a nerve.—vt. (nerving, nerved). To give strength or vigor to; to steel.

Nervous, nerv′us, a. Pertaining to the nerves; affecting the nerves; having the nerves easily affected; easily agitated; having nerve or bodily strength; vigorous; sinewy.

Nescience, nē′shi-ens, n. Want of knowledge; ignorance.

Nest, nest, n. The place or bed formed by a bird for laying and hatching her eggs; a number of persons frequenting the same haunt; a snug

abode.—vi. To build a nest; to nestle.

Nestle, nes′l, vi. (nestling, nestled). To make or occupy a nest; to lie close and snug.—vt. To shelter, as in a nest; to cherish.

Net, net, n. A texture of twine, etc., with meshes, commonly used to catch fish, birds, etc.; a snare.—vt. (netting, netted). To make into a net; to take in a net; to capture by wile.

Net, Nett, net, a. Being clear of all deductions; estimated apart from all expenses.—vt. (netting, netted). To gain as clear profit.

Nether, ne′THer, a. Lowest.

Nettle, net′l, n. A weed with stinging hairs.—vt. (nettling, nettled). To irritate or annoy somewhat; to pique.

Neural, nū′ral, a. Pertaining to the nerves or nervous system.

Neuralgia, nū-ral′ji-a, n. Pain in a nerve.

Neurology, nū-rol′ō-ji, n. That branch of science which treats of the nerves.

Neurotic, nū-rot′ik, a. Relating to the nerves; liable to nervous diseases; hysterical.

Neuter, nū′ter, a. Neutral; neither masculine nor feminine; neither active nor passive, as a verb.—n. An animal or neither sex; a plant with neither stamens nor pistils; a noun of the neuter gender.

Neutral, nū′tral, a. Not siding with any party in a dispute; indifferent; neither acid nor alkaline.—n. A person or nation that takes no part in a contest between others.

Neutralize, nū′tral-īz, vt. To render neutral or inoperative; to counteract.

Neutron, nū′tron, n. An uncharged particle of the same mass as a proton.

Never, nev′er, adv. Not ever; at no time; in no degree; not at all.

Nevertheless, nev′er-THe-les′′, adv. Not the less; notwithstanding; yet; however.

New, nū, a. Recent in origin; novel; not before known; different; unaccustomed; fresh after any event; not second-hand.—adv. Newly; recently.

Newel, nū′el, n. The upright structure in a winding staircase supporting the steps.

Newfoundland, nū-found′land or nū′found-land, n. A large dog, remarkable for sagacity and swimming powers.

News, nūz, n. Recent intelligence or information; tidings; a newspaper.

Newspaper, nūz′pã-per, n. A sheet of paper printed periodically for circulating news.

Newt, nūt, n. A small amphibian of lizard-like appearance.

Next, nekst, a. superl. of *nigh.* Nearest in place, time, rank, or degree.—adv. At the time or turn nearest.

Nexus, nek′sus, n. Tie; connection.

Nib, nib, n. The bill or beak of a bird; the point of anything, particularly of a pen.—vt. (nibbing, nibbed). To furnish with a nib; to mend the nib of, as a pen.

Nibble, nib′l, vt. and i. (nibbling, nibbled). To bite by little at a time; to bite at; to carp at.—n. A little bite.

Niblick, nib′lik, n. A golf-club with a small heavy iron head.

Nice, nis, a. Fastidious; punctilious; accurate; pleasant; delicate; dainty.

Niche, nich, n. A recess in a wall for a statue, a vase, etc.

Nick, nik, n. The exact point of time, the critical time; a notch; a score.—vt. To hit upon exactly; to make a nick in; to mark with nicks.

Nickel, nik′el, n. A valuable metal of a white color and great hardness, magnetic, and when pure malleable and ductile.

Nickel-silver, nik′el-sil-vor, n. An alloy composed of copper, zinc, and nickel.

Nickname, nik′nãm, n. A name given in contempt or jest.—vt. To give a nickname to.

Nicotine, nik′ō-tin, n. A volatile alkaloid from tobacco, highly poisonous.

Nictate, Nictitate, nik'tāt, nik'ti-tāt, *vi.* To wink.

Nidificate, Nidify, nid'i-fi-kāt, nid'i-fi, *vi.* To make a nest and bring out young.

Nidor, ni'dor, *n.* Scent; smell of cooked food.

Nidus, ni'dus, *n.* Any part of a living organism where a parasite finds nourishment; bodily seat of a zymotic disease.

Niece, nēs, *n.* The daughter of one's brother or sister.

Niggard, nig'ėrd, *n.* A miser; a stingy person; a sordid, parsimonious wretch.—*a.* Miserly; stingy; sordidly parsimonious.

Night, nit, *n.* The daily period of darkness; the time from sunset to sunrise; a state or time of darkness, depression, etc.; ignorance; obscurity; death.

Nightfall, nit'fal, *n.* The close of the day; evening.

Nightingale, nit'in-gāl, *n.* A small insectivorous migratory bird that sings at night.

Nightmare, nit'mār, *n.* A feeling of suffocation during sleep, accompanied by intense anxiety or horror; some oppressive or stupefying influence.

Nightshade, nit'shād, *n.* A plant of the potato genus, etc., which possesses narcotic or poisonous properties.

Nigrescent, ni-gres'ent, *a.* Approaching to blackness.

Nihilism, ni'hil-izm, *n.* Nothingness; the doctrine that nothing can be known; principles of a Russian secret society of communists.

Nil, nil, *n.* Nothing.

Nimble, nim'bl, *a.* Quick in motion; moving with ease and celerity; agile; prompt.

Nimbus, nim'bus, *n.* A rain-cloud; a halo surrounding the head in representations of divine or sacred personages.

Nine, nīn, *a.* and *n.* One more than eight.

Nineteen, nīn'tēn *a.* and *n.* Nine and ten.

Ninety, nīn'ti, *a.* and *n.* Nine times ten.

Ninth, ninth, *a.* The ordinal of nine.—*n.* A ninth part.

Nip, nip, *vt.* (nipping, nipped). To catch and compress sharply; to pinch; to snip or bite off; to blast, as by frost; to benumb.—*n.* A pinch as with the fingers; a blast by frost; a small drink.

Nippers, nip'ėrz, *n.pl.* Small pincers.

Nipple, nip'l, *n.* A teat; pap; something like a nipple; nozzle.

Nit, nit, *n.* The egg of a louse, etc.

Niter, ni'tėr, *n.* Nitrate of potassium or saltpeter, used for making gunpowder, in dyeing, medicine, etc.

Nitrate, ni'trāt, *n.* A salt of nitric acid.

Nitric, ni'trik, *a.* Pertaining to neter; containing nitrogent and oxygen.

Nitrogen, ni'tro-jen, *n.* The elementary unflammable gas constituting about four-fifths of the atmospheric air.

Nitro-glycerine, ni-trō-glis'ėr-in, *n.* A powerful explosive produced by the action of nitric and sulphuric acids on glycerine.

Nitrous, ni'trus, *a.* Pertaining to niter; applied to compounds containing less oxygen than those called *nitric.*

Nival, ni'val, *a.* Snowy; growing among snow, or flowering during winter.

No, nō, *adv.* A word of denial or refusal; not in any degree; not.—*n.* A denial; a negative vote.—*a.* Not any; none.

Noble, nō'bl, *a.* Of lofty lineage; belonging to the peerage; illustrious; lofty in character; magnanimous; magnificent; stately.—*n.* A person of rank; a peer; an old English gold coin.

Nobody, nō'bo-di, *n.* No person; no one; a person of no standing or position.

Noctambulist, nok-tam'bū-list, *n.* A nightwalker or somnambulist.

Nocturn, nok'tėrn, *n.* A religious service formerly used in the R. Catholic Church at midnight, now a part of matins.

Nocturne, nok'tėrn, *n.* A painting or piece of music expressing some of the characteristic effects of night.

Nod, nod, *vi.* (nodding, nodded). To make a slight bow; to let the head sink from sleep; to incline the head, as in assent or salutation, etc.—*vt.* To incline; to signify by a nod.—*n.* A quick inclination of the head.

Node, nōd, *n.* A knot; a protuberance; a sort of knot on a stem where leaves arise; one of the two points in which two great circles of the celestial sphere intersect.

Nodule, nod'ūl, *n.* A little know or lump.

Noetic, nō-et'ik, *a.* Relating to the mind.

Noise, noiz, *n.* A sound of any kind; a din; clamor; frequent talk.—*vt.* (noising, noised). To spread by rumor or report.

Noisome, noi'sum *a.* Noxious to health; offensive; disgusting; fetid.

Noisy, noiz'i, *a.* Making a loud noise; turbulent; obstreperous.

Nomad, nō'mad, *n.* One who leads a wandering of pastoral life.

Nomenclature, no'men-kla-tür, *n.* A system of names; vocabulary of terms appropriated to any branch of science

Nominal, no'mi-nal, *a.* Pertaining to a name; titular; not real; merely so called.

Nominate, no'mi-nāt, *vt.* To name; to designate or propose for an office.

Nomination, no-mi-nā'shon *n.* Act of nominating; power of appointing to office; state of being nominated.

Nominative, no'mi-nāt-iv, *a.* A term applied to the case of a noun or pronoun when subject of a sentence.—*n.* The nominative case; a nominative word.

Nominee, no-mi-nē', *n.* A person nominated; one proposed to fill a place or office.

Nonagenarian, non'a-je-nā''ri-an, *n.* One between ninety and a hundred years old.

Nonagon, non'a-gon, *n.* A plane figure having nine sides and nine angles.

Nonchalance, non'sha-lans, *n.* Indifference.

Non-conductor, non-kon-dukt'ér, *n.* A substance which does not conduct, or transmits with difficulty, heat, electricity, etc.

Nonconformist, non-kon-form'ist, *n.* One who does not conform to the established church.

Nonconformity, non-kon-form'i-ti, *n.* Neglect or failure of conformity; refusal to unite with an established church.

Nondescript, non'dė-skript, *a.* That has not been described; abnormal; odd; indescribable.—*n.* A person or thing not easily described or classed.

None, nun, *n.* or *pron.* Not one; not any; not a part; not the least portion.

Nonentity, non-en'ti-ti, *n.* Non-existence; a thing not existing; a person utterly without consequence or importance.

Nonesuch, non'such, *n.* A person or thing that has not its equal or parallel.

Nonpareil, non-pa-rel', *n.* A person or thing having no equal; a nonesuch; a sort of apple; a very small printing type.

Nonplus, non'plus, *n.* A state in which one can say or do no more,—*vt.* (nonplussing, nonplussed). To bring to a stand; to puzzle.

Nonsense, non'sens, *n.* Words without meaning; absurdity; things of no importance.

Nonsuit, non'sūt, *n.* Stoppage of a suit at law by the plaintiff failing to make out a cause of action.—*vt.* To subject to a nonsuit.

Nook, nök, *n.* A corner; A secluded retreat.

Noology, nō-ol'o-ji, *n.* The science of intellectual facts or phenomena.

Noon, nön, *n.* The middle of the day; twelve o'clock; the prime.

Noonday, nön'dā, *n.* Mid-day; noon.—*a.* Pertaining to mid-day; meridional.

Noose, nös or nöz, *n.* A running knot, which binds the closer the more it is drawn.—*vt.* (noosing, noosed). To tie or catch in a noose; to entrap.

Nor, nor, *conj.* A word used to render negative a

subsequent member of a clause or sentence; correlative to *neither* or other negative; also equivalent to *and not*.

Nordic, nor'dik, *a.* Of or belonging to those peoples of Northern Europe who are long-headed, tall, blue-eyed and fair-haired.

Norm, norm, *n.* A rule; a pattern; a type.

Normal, nor'mal, *a.* According to a rule; conforming with a certain type or standard; regular; perpendicular.—**Normal school,** a training-college for teachers.—*n.* A perpendicular.

Norse, nors, *n.* The language of Norway and Iceland.—*a.* Belonging to ancient Scandinavia.

North, north, *n.* One of the cardinal points, the opposite of *south*; a region opposite to the south.—*a.* Being in the north.

North-east, north-ēst', *n.* The point midway between the north and east.—*a.* Northeastern.—*adv.* North-eastward.

Northerly, norTH'ér-li, *a.* Pertaining to the north; northern; proceeding from the north.—*adv.* Toward the north.

Northern, norTH'érn, *a.* Being in the north; toward the north; proceeding from the north.—*n.* An inhabitant of the north.

Northernmost, norTH'érn-mōst, *a.* Situated at the point farthest north.

North-west, north-west', *n.* The point midway between the north and west.—*a.* North-western,—*adv.* North-westward.

Norwegian, nor-wē-jan, *a.* Belonging to Norway.—*n.* A native of Norway.

Nose, nōz, *n.* The organ of smell, employed also in respiration and speech; the power of smelling; scent; sagacity; a nozzle.—*vt.* and *i.* (nosing, nosed). To smell; to wange through the nose; to pry officiously.

Nosology, no-sol'o-ji, *n.* Arrangement or classification of diseases.

Nostalgia, nos-tal'ji-a, *n.* Vehement desire to revisit one's native country; home-sickness.

Nostril, nos'tril, *n.* One of the two apertures of the nose.

Nostrum, nos'trum, *n.* A quack medicine, the ingredients of which are kept secret.

Not, not, *adv.* A word that expresses negation, denial, or refusal.

Notability, nōt-a-bil'i-ti, *n.* Notableness; a notable person or thing; a person of note.

Notable, nōt'a-bl, *a.* Worthy of note; remarkable; conspicuous.—*n.* A person or thing of note or distinction

Notary, nōt'a-ri, *n.* An officer authorized to attest documents, to protest bills of exchange, etc.: called also *Notary Public.*

Notation, nōt-ā'shon, *n.* Act of recording anything by marks, or the marks employed, as in algebra, music, etc.

Notch, noch, *n.* An incision; nick; indentation.—*vt.* To cut a notch in; to indent.

Note, nōt, *n.* A mark, sign, or token; an explanatory or critical comment; a memorandum; a bill, account; a paper promising payment; a communication in writing; notice; reputation; distinction; a character representing a musical sound, or the sound itself.—*vt.* (noting, noted). To observe carefully; to mark; to set down in writing.

Noted, nōt'ed, *p.a.* Celebrated; famous.

Noteworthy, nōt'wér-THi, *a.* Deserving notice; worthy of observation or notice.

Nothing, nu'thing, *n.* Not anything; non-existence; a trifle; a cipher.—*adv.* In no degree.

Notice, nōt'is, *n.* Act of noting; regard; information; order; intimation; civility; a brief critical review.—*vt.* (noticing, noticed). To take note of; to perceive; to make observations on; to treat with attention.

Noticeable, nōt'is-a-bl, *a.* That may be noticed; worthy of observation.

Notify, nōt'i-fi, *vt.* To make known; to declare; to give notice to; to inform.

Notion, nō'shon, *n.* A mental conception; idea; opinion; slight feeling or inclination.

Notoriety, nō-tō-rī'e-ti, *n.* State of being notorious; discreditable publicity; one who is notorious.

Notorious, nō-tō'ri-us, *a.* Publicly known and spoken of; known to disadvantage.

Notwithstanding, not-wiTH-stand'ing, *prep.* and *conj.* In spite of; nevertheless.

Noumenon, nou'men-on, *n.* An object conceived by the understanding, as opposed to *phenomenon*.

Noun, noun, *n.* A word that denotes any object of which we speak.

Nourish, nu'rish, *vt.* To feed; to supply with nutriment; to encourage; to foster.

Nourishment, nu'rish-ment, *n.* Act of nourishing; nutrition; food; nutriment.

Nous, nous, *n.* Intellect; mind; talent.

Novel, no'vel, *a.* Of recent origin or introduction; new and striking; unusual.—*n.* A fictitious prose narrative picturing real life.

Novelist, no'vel-ist, *n.* A writer of novels.

Novelty, no'vel-ti, *n.* Quality of being novel; a new or strange thing.

November, nō-vem'ber, *n.* The eleventh month of the year.

Novice, no'vis, *n.* One who is new in any business; a beginner; a tyro; a probationer.

Now, nou, *adv.* and *conj.* At the present time; at that time; after this; things being so.—*n.* The present time.

Nowhere, nō'whār, *adv.* Not in any place or state.

Noxious, nok'shus, *a.* Hurtful; pernicious; unwholesome; corrupting to morals.

Nozzle, noz'l, *n.* The projecting spout of something; terminal part of a pipe.

Nuance, nu-ängs, *n.* A gradation of color; delicate degree in transitions.

Nubile, nū'bil, *a.* Marriageable (used only of a woman).

Nuciferous, nū-sif'ér-us, *a.* Bearing or producing nuts.

Nucleus, nū'klē-us, *n.*; pl. **-lei.** A kernel or something similar; a mass about which matter is collected; body of a comet.

Nude, nūd, *a.* Naked; bare; undraped.

Nudge, nuj, *n.* A jog with the elbow.—*vt.* (nudging, nudged). To give a jog with the elbow.

Nugget, nug'et, *n.* A lump, as of gold.

Nuisance, nū'sans, *n.* That which annoys or is offensive; a plague or pest; a bore.

Null, nul, *a.* Of no force or validity; of no importance or account.—*n.* A cipher.

Nullify, nul'i-fi, *vt.* (nullifying, nullified). To render null; to deprive of force.

Numb, num, *a.* Benumbed; without sensation and motion; torpid.—*vt.* To make numb or torpid; to deaden.

Number, num'bér, *n.* An aggregate of units, or a single unit; a numeral; many; one of a numbered series of things; part of a periodical; metrical arrangement of syllables; difference of form in a word to express unity or plurality.—*vt.* To reckon; to enumerate; to put a number on; to reach the number of.

Numeral, nū'mér-al, *a.* Pertaining to number; consisting of or representing number.—*n.* A figure used to express a number.

Numerate, nū'mér-āt, *vt.* (numerating, numerated). To count; to enumerate.

Numerator, nū'mér-āt-ér, *n.* One who numbers; the number (above the line) in vulgar fractions which shows how many parts of a unit are taken.

Numerical, nū-me'rik-al, *a.* Belonging to number; consisting in numbers.

Numerous, nū'mér-us, *a.* Consisting of a great number of individuals; many.

Numismatic, nū-mis-mat'ik, *a.* Pertaining to coins or medals.

Numismatist, nū-mis'mat-ist, *n.* One versed in

numismatics.

Numskull, num'skul, n. A blockhead; a dunce; a dolt; a stupid fellow.

Nun, nun, n. A woman devoted to religion who lives in a convent; a female monk.

Nuncio, nun'shi-o, n. An ambassador of the pope at the court of a sovereign.

Nuncupative, Nuncupatory, nun-kū'pat-iv, nun-kū'pa-to-ri, a. Orally pronounced; not written, as a will.

Nunnery, nun'é-ri, n. A house in which nuns reside.

Nuptial, nup'shal, a. Pertaining to marriage.

Nurse, nėrs, n. One who suckles or nourishes a child; one who tends the young, sick, or infirm; an attendant in a hospital; one who or that which nurtures or protects.—vt. (nursing, nursed). To act as nurse to; to suckle; to rear; to tend in sickness or infirmity; to foment; to foster.

Nursery, nėr'se-ri, n. The place in which children are nursed and taken care of; a place where trees, plants, etc., are propagated.

Nurture, nėr'tūr, n. Upbringing; education; nourishment.—vt. (nurturing, nurtured). To nourish; to educate; to bring or train up.

Nut, nut, n. A fruit containing a seed or kernel within a hard covering; a small block of metal or wood with a grooved hole, to be screwed on the end of a bolt.—vi. (nutting, nutted). To gather nuts.

Nutation, nū-tā'shon, n. A nodding, a slight gyratory movement of the earth's axis.

Nutmeg, nut'meg, n. The aromatic kernel of the fruit of a tree of the Malay Archipelago.

Nutrient, nū'tri-ent, a. Nutritious.—n. Any substance which nourishes.

Nutrition, nū-tri'shon, n. Act or process of nourishing; that which nourishes; nutriment.

Nutritious, nū-tri'shus, a. Serving to nourish; containing or supplying nutriment.

Nut-shell, nut'shel, n. The hard shell inclosing the kernel of a nut.

Nuzzle, nuz'l, vi. and t. (nuzzling, nuzzled). To rub or work with the nose; to put a ring into the nose of; to lie snug; to nestle.

Nylon, ni'lon, n. A strong, synthetic textile material, used as a substitute for silk, etc.

Nymph, nimf, n. A goddess of the mountains, forests, meadow, or waters; a young and attractive woman; a maiden; the chrysalis of an insect.

Nymphomania, nim-fō-mā'ni-a, n. Morbid or unnatural sexual desire in women.

O

O, ō. An exclamation used in earnest or solemn address; often distinguished from *Oh*, which is more strictly expressive of emotion.

Oaf, ōf, n. A fairy changeling; a dolt.

Oak, ōk, n. A valuable tree of many species.

Oar, ōr, n. A long piece of timber used to propel a boat.—vt. To impel by rowing.

Oarsman, ōrz'man, n. One who rows at the oar.

Oasis, ō-ā'sis, n.; pl. **-ses.** A fertile spot where there is water in a desert.

Oat, ōt, n. A cereal plant valuable for its grain.

Oath, ōth, n. An appeal to God for the truth of what is affirmed; an imprecation.

Oat-meal, ōt'mēl, n. Meal of oats produced by grinding or pounding.

Obdurate, ob'dū-rāt, a. Hardened in heart; hardened against good; stubborn; inflexible.

Obedience, ō-bē'di-ens, n. Act of obeying; quality of being obedient; submission to authority.

Obeisance, ō-bā'sans, n. A bow or curtsy; act of reverence, deference, or respect.

Obelisk, o'be-lisk, n. A tall four-sided pillar, tapering as it rises, and terminating in a small pyramid; a mark (†) used in printing.

Obesity, ō-bēs'i-ti, n. State or quality of being

obese; excessive corpulency.

Obey, ō-bā', vt. To comply with, as commands or requirements; to be ruled by; to yield to.—vi. To submit to authority.

Obfuscate, ob-fus'kāt, vt. To darken; to confuse.

Obituary, ō-bit'ū-a-ri, n. An account of a person or persons deceased; list of the dead.—a. Relating to the decease of a person.

Object, ob'jekt, n. That about which any faculty of the mind is employed; end; purpose; a concrete reality; the word, clause, etc., governed by a transitive verb or by a preposition.—vt. objekt'. To oppose; to offer as an objection.—vi. To oppose in words or arguments.

Objective, ob-jek'tiv, a. Pertaining to an object; relating to whatever is exterior to the mind (also pron. ob'jek-tiv); belonging to the case which follows a transitive verb or preposition.—n. The objective case; object, place, etc., aimed at.

Objuration, ob-jū-rā'shon, n. Act of binding by oath.

Objurgate, ob-jėr'gāt, vt. and i. To chide, reprove, or reprehend.

Oblate, ob-lāt', a. Flattened or depressed at the poles, as a sphere or globe.

Oblation, ob-lā'shon, n. Anything offered in sacred worship; a sacrifice.

Obligation, ob-li-gā'shon, n. That which morally obliges; binding power of a promise, contract, or law; a favor bestowed and binding to gratitude; a bond with a condition annexed, and a penalty for non-fulfilment.

Oblige, ō-blīj', vt. (obliging, obliged). To constrain; to bind by any restraint; to lay under obligation of gratitude; to render service or kindness to.

Oblique, ob-lēk', a. Neither perpendicular nor parallel; slanting; indirect; sinister.

Obliterate, ob-lit'e-rāt, vt. To blot out; to efface; to cause to be forgotten.

Oblivion, ob-li'vi-on, n. State of being forgotten; forgetfulness; act of forgetting.

Oblivious, ob-li'vi-us, a. That easily forgets; forgetful; causing forgetfulness.

Oblong, ob'long, a. Rectangular, and longer than broad.—n. An oblong figure.

Obloquy, ob'lō-kwi, n. Censorious speech; contumely; odium; infamy.

Obnoxious, ob-nok'shus, a. Odious; offensive; hateful; unpopular.

Oboe, ō'bō, n. A musical wind-instrument made of wood; a hautboy.

Obscene, ob-sēn', a. Indecent; offensive to chastity and delicacy; inauspicious.

Obscure, ob-skūr', a. Darkened; dim; not easily understood; abstruse; unknown to fame; indistinct.—vt. (obscuring, obscured). To darken; to make less visible, legible, or intelligible; to tarnish.

Obsequies, ob'se-kwiz, n.pl. Funeral rites and solemnities.

Obsequious, ob-sē'kwi-us, a. Promptly obedient or submissive; compliant; fawning.

Observance, ob-zėrv'ans, n. Act of observing; respect; performance of rites, etc.; rule of practice; thing to be observed.

Observation, ob-zėr-vā'shon, n. The act, power, or habit of observing; information or notion gained by observing; a remark; due performance.

Observatory, ob-zėr'va-to-ri, n. A place for astronomical observations; place of outlook.

Observe, ob-zėrv', vt. (observing, observed). To take notice of; to behold with attention; to remark; to keep religiously; to celebrate; to comply with; to practice.—vi. To remark; to be attentive.

Obsession, ob-sesh'on, n. Act of besieging; persistent attack; state of being beset.

Obsolescent, ob-sō-les'ent, a. Becoming obsolete; passing into desuetude.

Obsolete, ob'sō-lēt, a. Antiquated; out of date; rudimentary.

Obstacle, ob'sta-kl, *n.* A stoppage; hindrance; obstruction; impediment.

Obstetric, Obstetrical, ob-stet'rik, ob-stet'rik-al, *a.* Pertaining to midwifery.

Obstetrician, ob-stet-rish'an, *n.* One skilled in obstetrics; an accoucheur.

Obstinate, ob'sti-nāt, *a.* Inflexible; stubborn; fixed firmly in opinion or resolution.

Obstreperous, ob-strep'ėr-us, *a.* Making a tumultuous noise; loud; noisy; clamorous.

Obstruct, ob-strukt', *vt.* To block up, as a way or passage; to impede; to hinder in passing; to retard; to interrupt.

Obstruction, ob-struk'shon, *n.* Act of obstructing; that which impedes progress; obstacle; impediment; check.

Obstruent, ob'stru-ent, *a.* Obstructing.—*n.* Anything that obstructs the natural passages in the body.

Obtain, ob-tān', *vt.* To get possession of; to acquire; to earn.—*vi.* To be received in common use; to prevail; to hold good.

Obtest, ob-test', *vt.* To call upon earnestly; to implore; to supplicate.

Obtrude, ob-trōd', *vt.* (obtruding, obtruded). To thrust prominently forward; to offer with unreasonable importunity.—*vi.* To enter when not desired.

Obtrusive, ob-trö'siv, *a.* Disposed to obtrude; forward.

Obturate, ob'tū-rāt, *vt.* To block or plug up, as a passage.

Obtuse, ob-tūs', *a.* Not pointed or acute; greater than a right angle; dull; stupid.

Obverse, ob'vėrs, *n.* and *a.* That side of a coin or medal which has the face or head or principal device on it.

Obviate, ob'vi-āt, *vt.* (obviating, obviated). To meet, as difficulties or objections; to get over; to remove.

Obvious, ob'vi-us, *a.* Easily discovered, seen, or understood; evident; manifest.

Obvolute, ob'vo-lūt, *a.* Rolled or turned in.

Occasion, ok kā'zhon, *n.* Occurrence; incident; opportunity; cause; need; juncture.—*vt.* To cause; to produce.

Occasional, ok kā'zhon-al, *a.* Occurring at times; made as opportunity admits; incidental.

Occident, ok'si-dent, *n.* The west.

Occiput, ok'si-put, *n.* That part of the skull which forms the hind part of the head.

Occult, ok-kult', *a.* Hidden; invisible and mysterious.—*vt.* To conceal by way of eclipse.

Occupancy, ok'kū-pan-si, *n.* Act of occupying; a holding in possession; term during which one is occupant.

Occupation, ok-kū-pā'shon, *n.* Act of occupying; act of taking possession; tenure; business; employment; vocation.

Occupy, ok'ku-pi, *vt.* (occupying, occupied). To take possession of; to hold and use; to cover or fill; to employ; to engage: often *refl.*—*vi.* To be an occupant.

Occur, ok-kėr', *vi.* (occurring, occurred). To come to the mind; to happen; to be met with; to be found here and there.

Occurrence, ok-ku'rens, *n.* The act of occurring or taking place; any incident or accidental event; an observed instance.

Ocean, ō'shan, *n.* The vast body of water which covers more than three-fifths of the globe; the sea; one of the great areas into which the sea is divided; any immense expanse.—*a.* Pertaining to the great sea.

Ocellus, ō-sel'lus, *n.*; pl. **-li.** One of the minute simple eyes of insects, spiders, etc.

Ochlocracy, ok-lok'ra-si, *n.* The rule of the mob or multitude.

Ochre, ō'kėr, *n.* A clay used as a pigment, of a pale-yellow or brownish-red color.

Octagon, ok'ta-gon, *n.* A plane figure having eight angles and sides.

Octahedron, ok-ta-hed'ron, *n.* A solid figure having eight faces or sides.

Octave, ok'tāv, *a.* Eighth; denoting eight.—*n.* An eighth; the eighth day or the eight days after a church festival; a stanza of eight lines; in *music,* an interval of seven degrees or twelve semitones.

October, ok-tō'bėr, *n.* The tenth month of the year.

Octogenarian, ok'tō-je-nā''ri-an, *n.* One between eighty and ninety years of age.

Octopus, ok'tō-pus, *n.*; pl. **-puses.** A two-gilled cuttle-fish, having eight arms furnished with suckers.

Ocular, ok'ū-lėr, *a.* Pertaining to or depending on the eye; received by actual sight.

Oculist, ok'ū-list, *n.* One skilled in diseases of the eyes.

Odd, od, *a.* Not even; not exactly divisible by 2; not included with others; incidental; casual; belonging to a broken set; queer.

Oddity, od'i-ti, *n.* Singularity; a singular person or thing.

Odds, odz, *n. sing.* or *pl.* Inequality; excess; difference in favor of one; advantage; amount by which one bet exceeds another.

Ode, ōd, *n.* A song; a short poem; a lyric poem of a lofty cast.

Odious, ō'di-us, *a.* Hateful; offensive; disgusting.

Odium, ō'di-um, *n.* Hatred; dislike; the quality that provokes hatred, blame, etc.

Odontoid, ō-don'toid, *a.* Tooth-like.

Odontology, ō-don-tol'o-ji, *n.* The science which treats of the teeth.

Odoriferous, ō-dor-if'ėr-us, *a.* Diffusing smell; perfumed; fragrant.

Odor, ō'dor, *n.* Any scent or smell; fragrance; reputation.

Odorless, ō'dor-les, *a.* Free from odor.

Of, ov, *prep.* Denoting source, cause, motive, possession, quality, condition, material; concerning, relating to, about.

Off, of, *adv.* Away; distant; not on; from; not toward.—**Well off, ill off,** in good or bad circumstances. *a.* Distant; farther away; as applied to horses; right hand.—*prep.* Not on; away from; to seaward from.—*interj.* Begone!

Offal, of'al, *n.* The parts of an animal butchered which are unfit for use; refuse.

Offense, of-fens', *n.* Injury; an affront, insult, or wrong; displeasure; transgression of law; misdemeanor.

Offend, of-fend', *vt.* To displease; to shock; to cause to sin or neglect duty.—*vi.* To sin; to commit a fault; to cause dislike or anger.

Offensive, of-fens'iv, *a.* Causing offense; causing displeasure or annoyance; disgusting; impertinent; used in attack; aggressive.—*n.* Act or posture of attack.

Offer, of'ėr, *vt.* To present for acceptance or rejection; to tender; to bid, as a price or wages.—*vi.* To present itself; to declare a willingness; to make an attempt.—*n.* Act of offering; act of bidding a price; the sum bid.

Offertory, of'ėr-to-ri, *n.* Sentences read or repeated in church while the alms or gifts are collecting; the alms collected.

Off-hand, of'hand, *a.* Done without thinking or hesitation; unpremeditated.—*adv.* On the spur of the moment; promptly.

Office, of'is, *n.* Special duty or business; high employment or position under government; function; service; a formulary of devotion; a place where official or professional business is done; persons intrusted with certain duties; persons who transact business in an office; pl. kitchens, outhouses, etc., of a mansion or farm.

Officer, of'is-ėr, *n.* A person invested with an office; one who holds a commission in the army or navy.—*vt.* To furnish with officers.

Official, of-fi'shal, *a.* Pertaining to an office or public duty; made by virtue of authority.—*n.* One invested with an office of a public nature.

Officiate, of-fi'shi-āt, *vi.* To perform official duties; to act in an official capacity.

Officious, of-fi'shus, *a.* Troublesome in trying to serve; intermeddling.

Offset, of'set, *n.* A shoot or scion; a sum or amount set off against another as an equivalent; a contrast or foil.—*vt.* To set off, as one account against another.

Offshoot, of'shŏt, *n.* A shoot of a plant; anything growing out of another.

Offspring, of'spring, *n. sing.* or *pl.* That which springs from a stock or parent; a child or children; progeny; issue.

Often, of'n, *adv.* Frequently; many times.

Ogle, ō'gl, *vt.* (ogling, ogled). To view with side glances.—*n.* A side glance or look.

Ogre, ō'gėr, *n.* A monster in fairy tales, who lived on human flesh; one like an ogre.

Oh, ō, *exclam.* (*See* O.) Denoting surprise, pain, sorrow, or anxiety.

Ohm, ōm, *n.* The unit of electric resistance.

Oil, oil, *n.* An unctuous inflammable liquid drawn from various animal and vegetable substances; a similar substance of mineral origin; an oil-color.—*vi.* To smear or rub over with oil.

Oil-color, oil'kul-ėr, *n.* A pigment made by grinding a coloring substance in oil.

Oil-painting, oil'pänt-ing, *n.* Art of painting with oil-colors; picture painted in oil-colors.

Ointment, oint'ment, *n.* Any soft, unctuous substance used for smearing the body or a diseased part; an unguent.

Old, ōld, *a.* Grown up to maturity and strength; aged; of some particular age; long made or used; not new or fresh; ancient; antiquated.—**Of old,** long ago; in ancient times.

Oleaginous, ō-lē-a'jin-us, *a.* Oily; unctuous.

Oleander, ō-lē-an'dėr, *n.* An evergreen flowering shrub.

Olfactory, ol-fak'to-ri, *a.* Pertaining to smelling; having the sense of smelling.—*n.* An organ of smelling.

Oligarchy, o'li-gär-ki, *n.* Government in which the supreme power is in a few hands; those who form such a class or body.

Olive, o'liv, *n.* An evergreen tree; its fruit, from which a valuable oil is expressed; the color of the olive; the emblem of peace.—*a.* Relating to, or of the color of the olive.

Olympiad, ō-lim'pi-ad, *n.* A period of four years reckoned from one celebration of the Olympic games to another, the first Olympiad beginning 776 B.C.

Omega, ō'me-ga or ō-me'ga, *n.* The last letter of the Greek alphabet, long o; the last, or the ending.

Omelet, o'me-let, *n.* A kind of pancake or fritter made with eggs, etc.

Omen, ō'men, *n.* An event thought to portend good or evil; an augury; presage.—*vi.* To augur; to betoken.—*vt.* To predict.

Ominous, o'min-us, *a.* Containing an omen, and especially an ill omen; inauspicious.

Omission, ō-mi'shon, *n.* Act of omitting; neglect or failure to do something required; failure to insert or mention; something omitted.

Omit, ō-mit', *vt.* (omitting, omitted). To pass over or neglect; not to insert or mention.

Omnibus, om'ni-bus, *n.* A large vehicle for conveying passengers; a book which contains a variety of items.

Omnifarious, om-ni-fā'ri-us, *a.* Of all varieties, forms, or kinds.

Omnipotence, om-nip'ō-tens, *n.* Almighty or unlimited power; an attribute of God.

Omnipresence, om-ni-prez'ens, *n.* Presence in every place at the same time.

Omniscience, Omnisciency, om-ni'shi-ens, om-ni'shi-en-si, *n.* The faculty of knowing all things; universal knowledge.

Omnivorous, om-niv'or-us, *a.* All-devouring; eating food of every kind.

Omphalic, om-fal'ik, *a.* Pertaining to the navel.

On, on, *prep.* Above and touching; by contact with the surface or upper part; in addition to; at or near; immediately after and as a result; in reference or relation to; toward or so as to affect; at the peril of; among the staff of; pointing to a state, occupation, etc.—*adv.* Onward; in continuance; adhering; not off.

Once, wuns, *adv.* One time; formerly; immediately after; as soon as.—**At once,** all together; suddenly; forthwith.

Oncoming, on'kum-ing, *a.* Approaching; nearing.—*n.* Approach.

One, wun, *a.* Being but a single thing or a unit; closely united; forming a whole; single.—*n.* The first of the simple units; the symbol representing this (=1).—**At one,** in union or concord.—*pron.* Any single person; any man; any person; a thing; particular thing.

Oneness, wun'nes, *n.* State or quality of being one; singleness; individuality; unity.

Onerous, on'e-rus, *a.* Burdensome; heavy.

Oneself, wun-self', *pron.* Oneself; one's own person.

One-sided, wun-sid'ed, *a.* Having one side only; limited to one side; partial; unfair.

Onion, un'yun, *n.* A plant with a bulbous root, used as an article of food.

Onlooker, on'luk-ėr, *n.* A spectator.

Only, ōn'li, *a.* Single; sole; alone.—*adv.* For one purpose alone; simply; merely; solely.—*conj.* But; excepting that.

Onomatopeia, on'o-ma-tō-pē''a, *n.* The formation of words by imitation of sounds.

Onrush, on'rush, *n.* A rapid onset.

Onset, on'set, *n.* A violent attack; assault.

Onslaught, on'slat, *n.* An attack; onset.

Ontology, on-tol'o-ji, *n.* The doctrine of being; that part of metaphysics which treats of things or existences.

Onus, ō'nus, *n.* A burden.

Onward, *a.* Advanced or advancing; progressive; improved.

Onyx, o'niks, *n.* A semi-pellucid gem with variously-colored veins, a variety of quartz; an agate with layers of chalcedony.

Oology, ō-ol'o-ji, *n.* The study of birds' eggs.

Ooze, öz, *n.* A soft flow, as of water; soft mud or slime; liquor of a tan-vat.—*vi.* (oozing, oozed). To flow or issue forth gently; to percolate.—*vt.* To emit in the shape of moisture.

Opal, ō-pal, *n.* A precious stone, which exhibits changeable reflections of green, blue, yellow, and red.

Opalescent, ō-pal-es'ent, *a.* Resembling opal; having the iridescent tints of opal.

Opaque, ō-pāk', *a.* Not transparent.

Open, ō'pn, *a.* Not shut, covered, or blocked; not restricted; accessible; public; spread out; free, liberal, bounteous; candid; clear; exposed; fully prepared; attentive; amenable; not settled; enunciated with a full utterance.—*n.* An open or clear space.—*vt.* To make open; to unclose; to cut into; to spread out; to begin; to make public; to declare open; to reveal.—*vi.* To unclose itself; to be parted; to begin.

Opening, ō'pn-ing, *a.* First in order; beginning.—*n.* Act of one who or that which opens; an open place; aperture; beginning; vacancy; opportunity of commencing a business, etc.

Opera, o'pe-ra, *n.* A dramatic composition set to music and sung and acted on the stage; a theater where operas are performed.

Operate, o'pe-rāt, *vi.* (operating, operated). To work; to act; to produce effect; to exert moral power or influence.—*vt.* To act; to effect; to drive, as a machine.

Operation, o-pe-rā'shon, *n.* Act or process of operating; agency; action; process; surgical proceeding to which the human body is subjected; movements of troops or war-ships.

Operative, o'pe-rāt-iv, *a.* That operates; producing the effect; having to do with manual or other operations.—*n.* One who works or labors; an artisan.

Operculum, ō-pėr'kū-lum, *n.* A little lid or cover, especially applied in zoology and botany.

Operetta, op-e-ret'ta, *n.* A short musical drama of a light character.

Ophiology, of-i-ol'o-ji, *n.* That branch of zoology which treats of serpents.

Ophthalmia, of-thal'mi-a, *n.* Inflammation of the eye or its appendages.

Ophthalmist, of-thal'mist, *n.* An oculist.

Opiate, ō'pi-āt, *n.* Any medicine that contains opium; a narcotic.

Opinion, ō-pin'yon, *n.* A judgment or belief; notion; persuasion; estimation.

Opium, ō'pi-um, *n.* The inspissated juice of a kind of poppy, one of the most energetic of narcotics.

Opossum, ō-pos'um, *n.* The name of several marsupial mammals of America.

Opponent, op-pō'nent, *a.* Opposing; antagonistic; opposite.—*n.* One who opposes; an adversary; an antagonist.

Opportune, op-or-tūn', *a.* Seasonable; timely; well-timed; convenient.

Opportunist, op-or-tūn'ist, *n.* One who waits upon favorable opportunities; a politician more influenced by place and power than principle.

Opportunity, op-or-tūn'i-ti, *n.* A fit or convenient time; favorable conjuncture.

Oppose, op-pōz', *vt.* (opposing, opposed). To place over against; to place as an obstacle; to act against; to resist; to check.—*vi.* To make objections; to act obstructively.

Opposite, op'pō-zit, *a.* Facing; adverse; contrary; inconsistent.—*n.* An adversary.

Opposition, op-pō-zi'shon, *n.* Act of opposing; attempt to check or defeat; contradiction; inconsistency; the collective body of opponents of a ministry.

Oppress, op-pres', *vt.* To press or weigh down unduly; to harass; to overpower; to overburden.

Oppressive, op-pres'iv, *a.* Burdensome; unjustly severe; tyrannical.

Opprobrium, op-prō'bri-um, *n.* Scurrilous language; disgrace; scurrility; infamy.

Oppugn, op-pūn', *vt.* To attack by arguments or the like; to oppose or resist.

Optative, op'ta-tiv, *a.* Expressing a desire; designating that mood of the verb in which desire is expressed.—*n.* The optative mood of a verb.

Optic, op'tik, *a.* Pertaining to sight; relating to the science of optics.—*n.* An organ of sight; an eye.

Optician, op ti'chan, *n.* A person skilled in optics; one who makes or sells optical instruments.

Optics, op'tiks, *n.* The science which treats of the nature and properties of light and vision, optical instruments, etc.

Optimism, op'tim-izm, *n.* The opinion or doctrine that everything is for the best; tendency to take the most hopeful view.

Option, op'shon, *n.* Choice; free choice; power of choosing.

Opulence, op'ū-lens, *n.* Wealth; riches.

Or, or, *conj.* A particle that marks an alternative, and frequently corresponds with *either* and *whether.*—*adv.* Ere; before.—*n.* Heraldic name for gold.

Oracle, o'ra-kl, *n.* Among the Greeks and Romans, the answer of a god to an inquiry respecting some future event; place where the answers were given; the sanctuary of the ancient Jews; any person reputed uncommonly wise; a wise or authoritative utterance.

Oral, ō'ral, *a.* Pertaining to the mouth; spoken, not written.

Orange, o'ranj, *n.* An evergreen fruit-tree, and also its fruit; the color of this fruit, a reddish yellow.—*a.* Belonging to an orange; colored as an orange.

Orange-peel, o'ranj-pēl, *n.* The rind of an orange separated from the fruit; the peel of the bitter orange dried and candied.

Orate, ō'rāt, *vi.* (orating, orated). To make an oration; to talk loftily; to harangue.

Oration, ō-rā'shon, *n.* A formal public speech; an eloquent speech or address.

Orator, o'ra-tėr, *n.* A public speaker; a skilled or eloquent speaker.

Oratorio, o-ra-tō'ri-ō, *n.* A sacred musical composition.

Orb, orb, *n.* A sphere; a heavenly body; a circular disc; a hollow globe.—*vt.* To encircle.

Orbit, or'bit, *n.* The path of a planet or comet; cavity in which the eye is situated.

Orchard, or'chėrd, *n.* An inclosure devoted to the culture of fruit-trees.

Orchestra, or'kes-tra, *n.* That part of the Greek theater allotted to the chorus; that part of a theater, etc., appropriated to the musicians; a body of musicians.

Orchestration, or-kes-trā'shon, *n.* Arrangement of music for an orchestra; instrumentation.

Orchid, Orchis, or'kid, or'kis, *n.* A perennial plant with tuberous fleshy root and beautiful flowers.

Ordain, or-dān', *vt.* To establish authoritatively; to decree; to invest with ministerial or sacerdotal functions.

Ordeal, or'dē-al, *n.* A trial by fire and water; severe trial or strict test.

Order, or'dėr, *n.* Regular disposition; proper state; established method; public tranquillity; command; instruction to supply goods or to pay money; rank, class, division, or dignity; a religious fraternity; division of natural objects; *pl.* clerical character, specially called holy orders.—**In order,** for the purpose.—*vt.* To place in order; to direct; to command; to give an order or commission for.—*vi.* To give command.

Ordinal, or'din-al, *a.* Expressing order or succession.—*n.* A number denoting order (as *first*); a book containing an ordination service.

Ordinance, or'din-ans, *n.* That which is ordained; law, statute, edict, decree.

Ordinary, or'din-a-ri, *a.* Conformable to order; regular; customary; common; of little merit.—*n.* An ecclesiastical judge; a judge who takes cognizance of causes in his own right; an eating-house where the prices are settled.—**In ordinary,** in actual and constant service; statedly attending; as a physician; but a ship *in ordinary* is one laid up.

Ordinate, or'din-āt, *a.* Regular; methodical.—*n.* In *geometry,* a line of reference determining the position of a point.

Ordination, or-din-ā'shon, *n.* Act of ordaining; act of conferring sacerdotal power; act of setting a Presbyterian clergyman in a charge.

Ordnance, ord'nans, *n.* Cannon or great guns collectively; artillery.—**Ordnance survey,** the detailed survey of Britain.

Ordure, or'dūr, *n.* Dung; excrement.

Ore, ōr, *n.* A mineral substance from which metals are obtained by smelting; metal.

Organ, or'gan, *n.* An instrument or means; a part of an animal or vegetable by which some function is carried on; a medium of conveying certain opinions; a newspaper; the largest wind-instrument of music.

Organic, or-gan'ik, *a.* Pertaining to or acting as an organ; pertaining to the animal and vegetable worlds; organized; systematized.

Organism, or'gan-izm, *n.* Organic structure; a body exhibiting organic life.

Organization, or'gan-i-zā'shon, *n.* Act or process of organizing; suitable disposition of parts for performance of vital functions.

Organize, or'gan-iz, *vt.* To give an organic structure to; to establish and systematize; to arrange so as to be ready for service.

Orgasm, or'gazm, *n.* Immoderate excitement or action.

Orgy, or'ji, *n.* A wild or frantic revel; a drunken party.

Orient, ō'ri-ent, *a.* Rising, as the sun;; eastern;

oriental; bright.—*n.* The East; luster as that of a pearl.—*vt.* To define the position of; to cause to lie from east to west.

Oriental, ō·ri·ent´al, *a.* Eastern; from the east.— *n.* A native of some eastern country.

Orientation, ōr´i·en·tā´´shon, *n.* A turning towards the east; position east and west.

Orifice, or´ri·fis, *n.* The mouth or aperture of a tube, pipe, etc.; an opening; a vent.

Origin, o´ri·jin, *n.* Source; beginning; derivation; cause; root; foundation.

Original, ō·ri´jin·al, *a.* Pertaining to origin; primitive; first in order; having the power to originate; not copied.—*n.* Origin; source; first copy; model; that from which anything is translated or copied; a person of marked individuality.

Originate, ō·ri´jin·āt, *vt.* (originating, originated). To give origin to; to produce.—*vi.* To have origin; to be begun.

Oriole, ō´ri·ōl, *n.* A bird with golden plumage.

Orion, ō·rī´on, *n.* A constellation near the equator.

Ormolu, or´mō·lū, *n.* A fine kind of brass made to imitate gold; gilt bronze.

Ornament, or´na·ment, *n.* That which adorns or embellishes; decoration.—*vt.* To decorate; to adorn.

Ornate, or´nāt, *a.* Richly ornamented; adorned; of a florid character.

Ornithology, or·ni·thol´o·ji, *n.* The science which treats of birds.

Orography, ō·rog´ra·fi, *n.* The scientific treatment of mountains; orology.

Orotund, ō´rō·tund, *a.* Characterized by fulness and clearness; rich and musical.

Orphan, or´fan, *n.* A child bereaved of father or mother, or of both.—*a.* Bereaved of parents.—*vt.* To reduce to being an orphan.

Orphean, or·fē´an, *a.* Pertaining to Orpheus; melodious.

Orris, o´ris, *n.* A sort of gold or silver lace; a kind of iris.

Orthodox, or´thō·doks, *a.* Sound in opinion or doctrine; sound in religious doctrines; in accordance with sound doctrine.

Orthoepy, or´thō·e·pi or or·thō´e·pi, *n.* Correct pronunciation of words.

Orthography, or·thog´ra·fi, *n.* The art of writing words with the proper letters; spelling.

Orthopter, Orthopteran, or·thop´ter, or·thop´ter·an, *n.* One of an order of insects including cockroaches, grasshoppers, and locusts.

Oscillate, os´sil·lāt, *vi.* To swing; to vibrate; to vary or fluctuate.

Osculate, os´kū·lāt, *vt.* and *i.* To kiss; to touch, as curves.

Osmose, os´mōs, *n.* The tendency of fluids to pass through porous partitions and mix.

Osprey, os´prā, *n.* A kind of hawk or eagle which feeds on fish; one of its feathers.

Osseous, os´ē·us, *a.* Bony; like bone.

Ossicle, os´i·kl, *n.* A small bone.

Ossification, os´i·fi·kā´´shon, *n.* The process of changing into a bony substance.

Ossify, os´i·fī, *vt.* and *i.* To change into bone, or into a substance of the hardness of bone.

Ostensible, os·ten´si·bl, *a.* Put forth as having a certain character; apparent and not real; pretended; professed.

Ostentation, os·ten·tā´shon, *n.* Ambitious display; vain show; parade; pomp.

Osteology, os·tē·ol´o·ji, *n.* The science which treats of the bones and bone-tissue.

Osteopathy, os·tē·op´a·thi, *n.* A system of medical treatment, based on the view that the proper adjustment of the vital mechanism is a more important factor than chemical intake in the maintenance of health.

Ostracize, os´tra·sīz, *vt.* To banish by ostracism; to expel; to banish from society.

Ostrich, os´trich, *n.* A large running bird of Africa, Arabia, and S. America, the largest of existing birds.

Other, uᴛʜ´er, *a.* and *pron.* Not the same; second of two; not this; opposite; often used reciprocally with *each.*

Otherwise, uᴛʜ´er·wīz, *adv.* In a different manner; not so; by other causes; in other respects.— *conj.* Else; but for this.

Otology, ō·tol´o·ji, *n.* Knowledge of the ear and its diseases.

Otter, ot´er, *n.* An aquatic carnivorous animal resembling the weasel, but larger.

Ottoman, ot´tō·man, *a.* Pertaining to or derived from the Turks.—*n.* A Turk; a kind of couch introduced from Turkey.

Oubliette, ö´blē·et, *n.* A dungeon with an opening only at the top.

Ought, at, *n.* Aught.—*v.* To be held or bound in duty or moral obligation.

Ounce, ouns, *n.* The twelfth part of a pound troy, and the sixteenth of a pound avoirdupois; an Asiatic animal like a small leopard.

Our, our, *a.* or *pron.* Pertaining or belonging to us. **Ours** is used when no noun follows.

Oust, oust, *vt.* To eject; to turn out.

Out, out, *adv.* On or towards the outside; not in or within; forth; beyond usual limits; not in proper place; public; exhausted; deficient; not in employment; loudly; in error; at a loss; having taken her place as a woman in society.—*n.* One who is out; a nook or corner.—*vt.* To put out.— *interj.* Away! begone!

Outbreak, out´brāk, *n.* A breaking forth; eruption; sudden manifestation as of anger, disease, etc.

Outburst, out´berst, *n.* A bursting or breaking out; an outbreak.

Outcast, out´kāst, *p.a.* Cast out; rejected.—*n.* An exile; one driven from home or country.

Outcome, out´kum, *n.* The issue; result; consequence.

Outcrop, out´krop, *n.* Exposure of strata at the surface of the ground.

Outcry, out´krī, *n.* A loud cry; exclamation; clamor; noisy opposition.

Outdistance, out·dis´tans, *vt.* To excel or leave behind in any competition.

Outdo, out·dö´, *vt.* To excel; to surpass.

Outdoor, out´dōr, *a.* In the open air; being without the house.

Outer, out´er, *a.* Being on the outside; external.— *n.* That part of a target beyond the circles surrounding the bull's-eye; a shot which hits this part.

Outermost, out´er·mōst, *a.* Being farthest out; being on the extreme external part.

Outfit, out´fit, *n.* A fitting out, as for a voyage; equipment of one going abroad.

Outflank, out·flangk´, *vt.* To maneuver so as to attack in the flank; to get the better of.

Outgo, out·gō´, *vt.* To go beyond; to excel.—*n.* out´gō. Expenditure.

Outgrow, out·grō´, *vt.* To surpass in growth; to grow too great or old for anything.

Outing, out´ing, *n.* A short excursion; an airing; short time spent out-of-doors.

Outlandish, out·land´ish, *a.* Foreign; strange; uncouth; bizarre.

Outlaw, out´la, *n.* A person excluded from the benefit of the law.—*vt.* To deprive of the benefit and protection of law; to proscribe.

Outlay, out´lā, *n.* Expenditure.

Outlet, out´let, *n.* Place by which anything is discharged; exit; a vent.

Outline, out´lin, *n.* The line by which a figure is defined; contour; general scheme.—*vt.* To draw the exterior line of; to sketch.

Outlive, out·liv´, *vt.* To survive.

Outlook, out´luk, *n.* A looking out; vigilant watch; place of watch; prospect.

Outlying, out´lī·ing, *a.* Lying at a distance from the main body; being on the frontier.

Outmaneuver, out·ma·nö´ver, or ·nü´ver, *vt.* To surpass in maneuvering.

Out-of-the-way, out·ov·the·wā, *a.* Secluded; unusual; uncommon.

Out-patient, out'pā-shent, n. A patient not residing in a hospital, but who receives medical advice, etc., from the institution.

Outpost, out'pōst, n. A station at a distance from the main body of an army; troops placed at such a station.

Output, out'put, n. Quantity of material produced within a specified time.

Outrage, out'rāj, vt. (outraging, outraged). To do extreme violence or injury to; to abuse; to commit a rape upon.—n. Excessive abuse; injurious violence.

Outre, ö-trā, a. Extravagant; bizarre.

Outreach, out-rēch', vt. To go or extend beyond.

Outright, out'rīt, adv. Completely; utterly.

Outrun, out-run', vt. To exceed in running; to leave behind; to go beyond.

Outset, out'set, n. Beginning.

Outshine, out-shīn', vi. To shine out or forth.—vt. To excel in luster.

Outside, out'sīd, n. The external surface or superficies; exterior; the utmost; extreme estimate.—a. Exterior; superficial.—prep. On the outside of.

Outskirt, out'skėrt, n. Parts near the edge of an area; border; purlieu; generally in pl.

Outspoken, out'spō-kn, a. Free or bold of speech; candid; frank.

Outspread, out-spred', vt. To spread out; to diffuse.—a. Extended; expanded.

Outstanding, out-stand'ing, a. Projecting outward; prominent; unpaid; undelivered.

Outstrip, out-strip', vt. To outgo; to outrun; to advance beyond; to exceed.

Outwalk, out-wak', vt. To walk farther, or faster than; to leave behind in walking.

Outward, out'wėrd, a. External; exterior; visible; adventitious.—adv. Tending toward the exterior; from a port or country.

Outweigh, out-wā', vt. To exceed in weight, value, etc.; to overbalance.

Outwit, out-wit', vt. (outwitting, outwitted). To overreach; to defeat by superior ingenuity.

Oval, ō'val, a. Shaped like an egg; elliptical.—n. A figure shaped like an egg or ellipse.

Ovariotomy, ō-vā'ri-ot''o-mi, n. The operation of removing a tumor in the ovary.

Ovary, ō'va-ri, n. The female organ in which ova are formed.

Ovate, ō'vāt, a. Egg-shaped; oval.

Ovation, ō-vā'shon, n. A lesser triumph among the ancient Romans; triumphal reception; public marks of respect.

Oven, uv'n, n. A place built in closely for baking, heating, or drying.

Over, ō'vėr, prep. Above; denoting motive, occasion, or superiority; across; throughout; upwards of.—adv. From side to side; in width; on all the surface; above the top or edge; in excess; completely; too.—a. Upper; covering.—n. (cricket) The number of balls (six or eight) which the bowler delivers in succession from one end of the pitch, before a change is made to the other side.

Overact, ō-vėr-akt', vt. To perform to excess.

Overalls, ō'vėr-alz, n.pl. Loose trousers worn over others to protect them.

Overbalance, ō-vėr-bal'ans, vt. To weigh down; to exceed in importance; to destroy the equilibrium of.—n. Excess.

Overbear, ō-vėr-bār', vt. To bear down; to overpower; to domineer over.

Overboard, ō'vėr-bōrd, a. Over the side of a ship; out of a ship.

Overburden, ō-vėr-ber'dn, vt. To load with too great weight; to overload.

Overcast, ō-vėr-kāst', vt. To cloud; to darken; to sew coarsely over a rough edge.

Overcharge, ō-vėr-chärj', vt. To charge or burden to excess; to fill too numerously.—n. ō'vėr-chärj. An excessive charge.

Overcoat, ō'vėr-kōt, n. An upper coat; top-coat.

Overcome, ō-vėr-kum', vt. To be victorious over; to master; to get the better of.—vi. To gain the superiority.

Overcrowd, ō-vėr-kroud', vt. To crowd to excess, especially with human beings.

Overdo, ō-vėr-dö', vt. To do to excess; to fatigue; to boil, bake, or roast too much.

Overdose, ō'vėr-dōs, n. Too great a dose.—vt. ō-vėr-dōs'. To dose excessively.

Overdue, ō'vėr-dū, a. Past the time of payment or arrival.

Overflow, ō-vėr-flō', vt. (pp. overflowed and overflown). To flow or spread over; to flood; to overwhelm.—vi. To be so full that the contents run over; to abound.—n. ō'vėr-flo. An inundation; superabundance.

Overhang, ō-vėr-hang', vt. and i. To hang, impend, jut, or project over.

Overhaul, ō-vėr-hal', vt. To examine thoroughly with a view to repairs; to re-examine; to gain upon or overtake.—n. ō'vėr-hal. Examination; inspection; repair.

Overhead, ō-vėr-hed', adv. Above; aloft.

Overhear, ō-vėr-hēr', vt. To hear by accident or stratagem.

Overjoy, ō-vėr-joi', vt. To give excessive joy to.—n. ō'vėr-joi. Joy to excess.

Overland, ō'vėr-land, a. Passing by land; made upon or across the land.

Overlap, ō-vėr-lap', vt. To lap or fold over.—n. ō'vėr-lap. The lapping of one thing over another.

Overlay, ō-vėr-lā', vt. To lay over; to coat or cover; to smother.

Overload, ō-vėr-lōd', vt. To load too much; to overburden.

Overlook, ō-vėr-luk', vt. To oversee; to superintend; to view from a higher place; to pass by indulgently.

Overnight, ō'vėr-nīt, adv. Through or during the night; in the night before.

Overpower, ō-vėr-pou'ėr, vt. To be too powerful for; to bear down by force; to overcome; to subdue; to crush.

Overrate, ō-vėr-rāt', vt. To rate at too much; to regard too highly.

Overreach, ō-vėr-rēch', vt. To reach over or beyond; to deceive by artifice; to outwit.

Override, ō-vėr-rīd', vt. To ride over; to supersede; to set at naught.

Overrule, ō-vėr-röl', vt. To control; to govern with high authority; to disallow.

Overrun, ō-vėr-run', vt. To run or spread over; to ravage; to outrun.—vi. To overflow; to run over.

Oversea, ō'vėr-sē, a. Foreign; from beyond sea.—**Overseas,** ō-vėr-sēz, adv. Abroad.

Oversee, ō-vėr-sē', vt. To see or look over; to overlook; to superintend.

Overshadow, ō-vėr-sha'dō, vt. To throw a shadow over; to shelter.

Overshoe, ō'vėr-shö, n. A shoe worn over another; an outer waterproof shoe.

Overshot, ō-vėr-shot', p.a. Shot beyond; having the water flowing on to the top, as a waterwheel.

Oversight, ō'vėr-sit, n. Superintendence; a mistake, error, omission, neglect.

Overstate, ō-vėr-stāt', vt. To state in too strong terms; to exaggerate in statement.

Overstep, ō-vėr-step', vt. To step over or beyond; to exceed.

Overt, ō-vėrt, a. Open to view; manifest; not hidden; public; apparent.

Overtake, ō-vėr-tāk', vt. To come up with; to catch, to take by surprise.

Overthrow, ō-vėr-thrō', vt. To throw or turn over; to overset; to defeat; to destroy.—n. ō'vėr-thrō. Ruin; defeat.

Overtime, ō-vėr-tim, n. Time during which one works beyond the regular hours.

Overture, ō'vėr-tūr, n. A proposal; offer; a musical introduction to oratorios, operas, etc.

Overturn, ō-vėr-tėrn', vt. To overset or overthrow; to capsize; to subvert; to ruin.

Overweening, ō-vėr-wēn'ing, a. Haughty; arrogant; proud; conceited.

Overweight, ō-vėr-wāt', vt. To overburden.—n. Excess of weight; preponderance.

Overwhelm, ō-vėr-whelm', vt. To whelm entirely; to swallow up; to submerge; to crush.

Overwork, ō-vėr-werk', vt. To work beyond strength; to tire with labor.—n. ō'vėr-werk. Work done beyond one's strength or beyond the amount required.

Overwrought, ō-vėr-rat', p.a. Wrought to excess; excited to excess; tasked beyond strength.

Ovine, ō'vin, a. Pertaining to sheep; consisting of sheep.

Oviparous, ō-vip'a-rus, a. Bringing forth eggs; producing young from eggs.

Ovoid, ō'void, a. Egg-shaped.

Ovoviviparous, ō'vō-vi-vip''a-rus, a. Producing eggs which are hatched within the body (as is the case with vipers): opposed to *oviparous*.

Ovum, ō'vum, n.; pl. **ova.** A small vesicle within the ovary of a female, when impregnated becoming the embryo.

Owe, ō, vt. (owing, owed). To be indebted in; to be obliged or bound to pay; to be obliged for.

Owl, oul, n. A nocturnal bird of prey.

Own, ōn, a. Belonging to: used, distinctively and emphatically, after a possessive pronoun, or a noun in the possessive.—vt. To hold or possess by right; to acknowledge or avow; to concede.

Owner, ōn'ėr, n. One who owns; the rightful possessor or proprietor.

Ox, oks, n.; pl. **Oxen,** oks'en. Any animal of the bovine genus; a male of the bovine genus castrated.

Oxide, oks'īd, n. A compound of oxygen with another element.

Oxidize, oks'id-īz, vt. To convert into an oxide; to cause to combine with oxygen.—vi. To change into an oxide.

Oxygen, oks'i-jen, n. A gaseous element, a component of atmospheric air and water, and essential to animal and vegetable life and combustion.

Oxygenate, oks'i-jen-āt, vt. To unite or cause to combine with oxygen.

Oyster, ois'tėr, n. A bivalve shell-fish or mollusk.

Ozone, ō'zōn, n. A kind of gas with a peculiar odor, a modification of oxygen existing in the atmosphere.

P

Pabulum, pab'ū-lum, n. Food; that which feeds either mind or body.

Pace, pās, n. A step; space between the two feet in walking; distance of 2½ feet or 5 feet; gait; rate of progress.—vi. (pacing, paced). To step; to walk slowly; to move by lifting the legs on the same side together; as a horse.—vt. To measure by steps; to accompany and set a proper rate of motion; to race.

Pacific, pa-sif'ik, a. Suited to make peace; pacifying; calm.—**The Pacific Ocean,** the ocean between America, Asia, and Australia.

Pacification, pa'si-fi-kā''shon, n. Act of making peace; appeasement.

Pacify, pa'si-fī, vt. (pacifying, pacified). To give peace to; to appease; to allay.

Pack, pak, n. A bundle; a bale; a set of playing-cards; a set of hounds or dogs; a gang.—vt. To make up into a bundle; to fill methodically with contents; to manipulate with fraudulent design; to dismiss without ceremony; to stuff.—vi. To make up bundles; to depart in haste (with *off* or *away*).

Package, pak'āj, n. A bundle or bale; a packet; charge for packing goods.

Pack-horse, pak'hors, n. A horse employed in carrying goods and baggage on its back.

Pack-saddle, pak'sad-l, n. The saddle of a pack-horse, made for bearing burdens.

Pact, pakt, n. A contract; an agreement or covenant.

Pad, pad, n. An easy-paced horse; a robber who infests the road on foot; a soft saddle; a cushion; a quantity of blotting-paper.—vi. (padding, padded). To walk or go on foot; to rob on foot.—vt. To furnish with padding.

Padding, pad'ing, n. Act of stuffing; material used in stuffing; literary matter inserted in a book, etc., merely to increase the bulk.

Paddle, pad'l, vi. (paddling, paddled). To play in water with hands or feet; to row.—vt. To propel by an oar or paddle.—n. A broad short oar; a float-board of a paddle-wheel.

Paddock, pad'ok, n. A toad or frog; an inclosure under pasture, usually adjoining a house.

Paddy, pad'i, n. Rice in the husk, whether in the field or gathered.

Padlock, pad'lok, n. A lock with a link to be fastened through a staple.—vt. To fasten or provide with a padlock.

Padre, päd'rā, n. A chaplain.

Paean, pē'an, n. A war-song; song of triumph.

Pagan, pā'gan, n. A heathen.—a. Heathenish; idolatrous.

Page, pāj, n. A young male attendant on persons of distinction; one side of a leaf of a book; a written record.—vt. (paging, paged). To number the pages of.

Pageant, pa'jent, n. Something intended for pomp; a show, as at a public rejoicing.—a. Showy; pompous.

Pagination, pa-jin-ā'shon, n. Act of paging; figures indicating the number of pages.

Pagoda, pa-gō'da, n. A Hindu or Buddhist temple.

Paideutics, pā-dū'tiks, n. The science of teaching.

Pail, pāl, n. An open vessel for carrying liquids.

Pain, pān, n. A penalty; bodily suffering; distress; anguish; pl. The throes of childbirth; labor; diligent effort.—vt. To cause pain to; to afflict; to distress.

Painstaking, pānz'tāk-ing, a. Giving close application; laborious and careful.—n. The taking of pains; careful labor.

Paint, pānt, vt. To represent by colors and figures; to cover with color; to portray; to delineate.—vi. To practice painting.—n. A substance used in painting; a pigment; rouge.

Painting, pānt'ing, n. Art or employment of laying on colors; art of representing objects by colors; a picture; colors laid on.

Pair, pār, n. Two things of like kind, suited, or used together; a couple; a man and his wife; two members on opposite sides in parliament, etc., who agree not to vote for a time.—vi. To join in pairs; to mate.—vt. To unite in pairs.

Pajamas, pā-jäm-az, n.pl. A sleeping-suit.

Palace, pa'lās, n. The house in which an emperor, king, bishop, etc., resides, a splendid residence.

Paleography, pal-ē-og'ra-fi, n. The art of deciphering ancient writing.

Paleolithic, pal'ē-ō-lith''ik, a. Belonging to the earlier stone period, when rude unpolished stone implements were used.

Paleontology, pal'ē-on-tol''o-ji, n. The science of fossil organic remains.

Paleozoic, pal'ē-ō-zō''ik, a. In *geology*, applied to the lowest division of stratified groups.

Palatable, pa'lat-a-bl, a. Agreeable to the palate or taste; savory.

Palate, pa'lāt, n. The roof of the mouth; taste; relish; intellectual taste.

Palatial, pa-lā'shal, a. Pertaining to a palace; becoming a palace; magnificent.

Palaver, pa-la'vėr, n. A long or serious conference; idle talk.—vt. To flatter or humbug.—vi. To talk idly; to engage in a palaver.

Pale, pāl, n. A pointed stake; an inclosure; sphere

or scope.—*vt.* (paling, paled). To inclose with pales; to fence in.—*vi.* To turn pale.—*a.* Whitish; wan; deficient in color; not bright; dim.

Palestra, pa-les'tra, *n.* A place of wrestling; wrestling or other athletic exercises.

Palette, pa'let, *n.* A thin oval board on which a painter lays his pigments.

Paling, pāl'ing, *n.* A fence formed with pales, or vertical stakes or posts.

Palingenesis, pal-in-jen'e-sis, *n.* A transformation; a great geological change.

Palisade, pa-li-sād', *n.* A fence or fortification of pales or posts.—*vt.* (palisading, palisaded). To surround or fortify with stakes.

Pall, pal, *n.* An outer mantle of dignity; a cloth thrown over a coffin at a funeral; a linen cloth to cover a chalice; a covering.—*vt.* To cover with a pall; to shroud; to make vapid; to cloy.—*vi.* To become vapid or cloying.

Palladium, pal-lā'di-um, *n.* A statue of the goddess Pallas; bulwark; safeguard; a grayish-white hard malleable metal.

Pallet, pal'et, *n.* A palette; a tool used by potters, etc.; a small rude bed.

Palliate, pal'i-āt, *vt.* To extenuate; to mitigate; to lessen, abate, alleviate.

Pallid, pal'id, *a.* Pale; wan.

Pallor, pal'or, *n.* Paleness.

Palm, päm, *n.* The inner part of the hand; a measure of 3 or 4 inches; a name of plants constituting an order of endogens; a branch or leaf of such a plant; victory; triumph.—*vt.* To conceal in the palm of the hand; to impose by fraud.

Palmate, pal'māt, *a.* Having the shape of a hand; entirely webbed, as feet.

Palmistry, pam'is-tri, *n.* The art of telling fortunes by the hand.

Palm-oil, päm'oil, *n.* A fatty substance resembling butter, obtained from palms.

Palm-Sunday, päm'sun-dā, *n.* The Sunday next before Easter.

Palpable, pal'pa-bl, *a.* Perceptible by the touch; plain; obvious.

Palpably, pal'pa-bli, *adv.* Plainly; obviously.

Palpitate, pal'pi-tāt, *vi.* (palpitating, palpitated). To pulsate rapidly; to throb; to tremble.

Palpitation, pal-pi-tā'shon, *n.* Act of palpitating; violent pulsation of the heart.

Palsy, pal'zi, *n.* Paralysis, especially of a minor kind.—*vt.* (palsying, palsied). To affect with palsy; to paralyze.

Paltry, pal'tri, *a.* Mean and trivial; trifling; worthless; contemptible.

Paludal, pal'ū-dal, *a.* Pertaining to marshes. Also *paludine, palustral, palustrine.*

Pampas, pam'pas, *n.pl.* The immense grassy treeless plains of South America.

Pamper, pam'pér, *vt.* To gratify to the full; to furnish with that which delights.

Pamphlet, pam'flet, *n.* A small book, stitched but not bound; a short treatise.

Pan, pan, *n.* A broad and shallow vessel, of metal or earthenware; a pond for evaporating salt water to make salt; part of a gun-lock holding the priming; the skull; the Greek and Roman god of flocks and herds.

Panacea, pan-a-sē'a, *n.* A remedy for all diseases; a universal medicine.

Pancake, pan'kāk, *n.* A thin cake fried in a pan or baked on an iron plate.

Pancreas, pan'krē-as, *n.* A fleshy gland or organ between the bottom of the stomach and the vertebrae; the sweet-bread in cattle.

Pandemonium, pan-dē-mō'ni-um, *n.* The abode of the evil spirits; any lawless, disorderly place or assemblage.

Pander, pan'dér, *n.* A pimp; a male bawd.—*vi.* To act as agent for the lusts of others; to be subservient to lust or desire. Also *Pandar.*

Pane, pān, *n.* A plate of glass inserted in a window, door, etc.; a panel.

Panegyric, pa-ne-ji'rik, *n.* A laudatory speech; eulogy; encomium; laudation.

Panel, pa'nel, *n.* A surface distinct from others adjoining in a piece of work; a sunk portion in a door, etc.; a piece of wood on which a picture is painted; list of Health Insurance doctors for a district; a doctor's list of insured persons; list of those summoned to serve on a jury; in Scotland, the accused.—*vt.* (panelling, panelled). To form with panels.

Pang, pang, *n.* A sharp and sudden pain; painful spasm, throe.

Panic, pan'ik, *n.* A sudden fright; terror inspired by a trifling cause.—*a.* Extreme, sudden, or causeless: said of fright.

Pannier, pa'ni-ér, *n.* A wicker-basket; a basket for a person's or beast's back.

Panoply, pa'nō-pli, *n.* Complete armor of defense; a full suit of armor.

Panorama, pan-ō-rā'ma, *n.* A picture presenting from a central point a view of objects in every direction.

Pansy, pan'zi, *n.* A garden variety of violet; heart's-ease.

Pant, pant, *vi.* To breathe quickly; to gasp; to desire ardently.—*n.* A gasp; a throb.

Pantaloons, pan'ta-lönz, *n.pl.* Tightly fitting trousers; trousers in general.

Pantheism, pan'thē-izm, *n.* The doctrine that the universe is God, or that all things are manifestations of God.

Pantheon, pan'thē-on, *n.* A temple dedicated to all the gods; all the divinities collectively worshipped by a people.

Panther, pan'thér, *n.* A spotted carnivorous animal, otherwise called the leopard.

Pantomime, pan'tō-mim, *n.* A representation in dumb-show; a Christmas stage entertainment of the burlesque kind.

Pantry, pan'tri, *n.* An apartment in which provisions are kept, or where plate and knives, etc., are cleaned.

Pap, pap, *n.* A kind of soft food for infants; the pulp of fruit; a teat; a round hill.

Papa, pa-pä', *n.* A childish name for father.

Papacy, pā'pa-si, *n.* The office and dignity of the pope; the popes collectively; papal authority or jurisdiction; popedom.

Paper, pā'pér, *n.* A substance formed into thin sheets used for writing, printing, etc.; a leaf, or sheet of this; a journal; an essay or article; promissory notes, bills of exchange, etc.—*a.* Made or consisting of paper; appearing merely in documents without really existing; slight.—*vt.* To cover with paper; to inclose in paper.

Paper-money, pā'pér-mun-i, *n.* Bank-notes or the like circulated instead of coin.

Papier-mâché, pap-yā-mä-shā, *n.* A material prepared by pulping different kinds of paper into a mass, which is molded into various articles, dried, and japanned.

Papillary, pap'il-la-ri, *a.* Pertaining to or resembling the nipple. Also *papillose.*

Papist, pā'pist, *n.* A Roman Catholic.

Papyrus, pa-pī'rus, *n.*; pl. -**ri.** An Egyptian sedge, the stems of which afforded an ancient writing material; a written scroll of papyrus.

Par, pär, *n.* State of equality; equality in condition or value; state of shares or stocks when they may be purchased at the original price.

Parable, pa'ra-bl, *n.* An allegorical representation of something real in life or nature, embodying a moral.

Parabola, pa-ra'bō-la, *n.* A conic section, shown when a cone is cut by a plane parallel to one of its sides; the curve described theoretically by a projectile.

Parachute, pa'ra-shöt, *n.* An apparatus like a large umbrella, enabling a safe drop to the ground from an aircraft.

Paraclete, pa'ra-klēt, *n.* One called to aid or support; the Holy Spirit.

Parade, pa-rād', *n.* Ostentation; show; military display; place where such display is held.—*vt.* (parading, paraded). To exhibit in ostentatious manner; to marshal in military order.—*vi*. To walk about for show; to go about in military procession.

Paradigm, pa'ra-dim, *n*. A pattern, model, or example.

Paradise, pa'ra-dis, *n*. The garden of Eden; a place of bliss; heaven.

Paradox, pa'ra-doks, *n*. An assertion or proposition seemingly absurd, yet true in fact; a seeming contradiction.

Paraffin, pa'ra-fin, *n*. A solid white substance obtained from the distillation of wood, bituminous coal or shale, etc.

Paragon, pa'ra-gon, *n*. A model; a perfect example of excellence.

Paragraph, pa'ra-graf, *n*. The character ¶ used as a reference, etc.; a distinct section of a writing, distinguished by a break in the lines; a brief notice.

Parallax, pa'ral-laks, *n*. The apparent change of position of an object when viewed from different points; the difference between the place of a heavenly body as seen from the earth's surface and its center at the same time.

Parallel, pa'ral-lel, *a*. Extended in the same direction, and in all parts equally distant, as lines or surfaces; running in accordance with something; equal in all essential parts.—*n*. A line which throughout its whole length is equidistant from another line; conformity in all essentials; likeness; comparison; counterpart.—*vt*. To place so as to be parallel; to correspond to; to compare.

Parallelogram, pa-ral-lel'ō-gram, *n*. A quadrilateral, whose opposite sides are parallel and equal.

Paralogism, pa-ral'o-jism, *n*. A fallacious argument; an illogical conclusion.

Paralysis, pa-ral'i-sis, *n*. A diseased state of nerves by which the power of action or sensation is lost.

Paralyze, pa'ra-līz, *vt*. (paralyzing, paralyzed). To affect with paralysis; to reduce to a helpless state.

Paramount, pa'ra-mount, *a*. Chief; superior to all others.

Paramour, pa'ra-mör, *n*. A lover; one who wrongfully holds the place of a spouse.

Parapet, pa'ra-pet, *n*. A wall or rampart breast-high; a wall on the edge of a bridge, quay, etc.

Paraphernalia, pa'ra-fér-nä''li-a, *n.pl*. That which a bride brings besides her dowry, as clothing, jewels, etc.; personal attire; trappings.

Paraphrase, pa'ra-fräz, *n*. A statement giving the meaning of another statement; a loose or free translation; a sacred song based on a portion of Scripture.—*vt*. To make a paraphrase of; to explain or translate with latitude.

Parasite, pa'ra-sīt, *n*. One who frequents the rich, and earns his welcome by flattery; a sycophant; an animal that lives upon or in another; a plant which grows on another.

Parasol, pa'ra-sol, *n*. A small umbrella used to keep off the sun's rays.

Parcel, pär'sel, *n*. A portion of anything; a small bundle or package; a collection.—*vt*. (parcelling, parcelled). To divide into portions; to make up into packages.

Parcel-post, pär'sel-pōst, *n*. Department of a post-office by which parcels are sent.

Parch, pärch, *vt*. To dry to extremity; to scorch.—*vi*. To become very dry; to be scorched.

Pardon, pär'don, *vt*. To forgive; to forbear to exact a penalty for; to overlook; to excuse.—*n*. Forgiveness; remission of a penalty.

Pare, pär, *vt*. (paring, pared). To trim by cutting; to dress; to cut away by little and little; to diminish.

Paregoric, pa-re-go'rik, *a*. Encouraging; soothing; assuaging pain.—*n*. An anodyne.

Parent, pä'rent, *n*. One who brings forth or begets; a father or mother; a progenitor; cause; origin.

Parenthesis, pa-ren'the-sis, *n*.; pl. **-theses.** A sentence or words inserted in another sentence, usually in brackets, thus, ( ).

Parhelion, pär-hē'li-on, *n*.; pl. **-lia.** A mock sun or meteor, appearing as a bright light near the sun.

Pariah, pā'ri-a, *n*. One of the lowest class of people in Hindustan; an outcast.

Parietal, pa-rī'et-al, *a*. Pertaining to a wall.

Paring, pär'ing, *n*. That which is pared off; rind; act of slicing off and burning the surface of grass-land.

Parish, pa'rish, *n*. An ecclesiastical division under the care of a priest or parson; a subdivision of a county for civil purposes.—*a*. Belonging to a parish; parochial.

Parity, pa'ri-ti, *n*. Equality; likeness; like state or degree; analogy.

Park, pärk, *n*. A piece of ground inclosed; ornamental ground adjoining a house; ground in a town for recreation; an assemblage of heavy ordnance.—*vt*. To inclose in a park; to bring together, as artillery; to draw up motorcars and leave them for a time in an inclosed space, or at the side of the road.

Parka, pär'ka, *n*. Hooded skin jacket of Eskimos.

Parlance, pär'lans, *n*. Conversation; talk; idiom.

Parley, pär'li, *vi*. To confer; to discuss orally.—*n*. Mutual discourse; conference with an enemy in war.

Parliamentary, pär'li-ment''a-ri, *a*. Pertaining to, done by, or according to the rules and usages of parliament.

Parlor, pär'lér, *n*. The sitting-room in a house which the family usually occupy.

Parochial, pa-rō'ki-al, *a*. Belonging to a parish; narrow in views; provincial.

Parody, pa'rod-i, *n*. An adaptation of the words of an author, etc., to a different purpose; a burlesque imitation.—*vt*. (parodying, parodied). To imitate in parody.

Parole, pa-rōl', *n*. Words or oral declarations; word of honor; a promise by a prisoner of war not to bear arms against his captors for a certain period, or the like; a military countersign.

Paroxysm, pa'roks-izm, *n*. A violent access of feeling (as of rage); convulsion; spasm.

Parquetry, pär'ket-ri, *n*. Inlaid wood-work, principally used for floors.

Parrakeet, pa'ra-kēt, *n*. A small parrot of the eastern hemisphere.

Parricide, pa'ri-sīd, *n*. A person who murders his father or mother; the murder of a parent.

Parrot, pa'rot, *n*. A family of birds, including parrakeets, macaws, cockatoos, etc.; a bird which can imitate the human voice.

Parry, pa'ri, *vt*. and *i*. (parrying, parried). To ward off.

Parsimonious, pär-si-mō'ni-us, *a*. Niggardly; miserly; penurious.

Parsimony, pär'si-mō-ni, *n*. The habit of being sparing in expenditure of money; excessive frugality; miserliness; closeness.

Parsley, pärs'li, *n*. A garden vegetable, used for flavoring in cooking.

Parsnip, pärs'nip, *n*. An umbelliferous plant with a fleshy esculent root.

Parson, pär'sn, *n*. The priest or incumbent of a parish; a clergyman.

Part, pärt, *n*. A portion or piece of a whole; a section; a constituent or organic portion; share; lot; party; duty; business; character assigned to an actor in a play; *pl*. faculties; superior endowments; regions; locality.—*vt*. To divide; to sever; to share; to distribute; to separate; to intervene.—*vi*. To become separated, broken, or detached; to quit each other; to depart.

Partake, pär-tāk', *vi*. (partaking, pret. partook, pp. partaken). To take or have a part with others; to share; to have something of the nature, claim, or right.—*vt*. To share.

Partial, pär'shal, *a*. Belonging to or affecting a part only; not general; biased to one party; having a fondness.

Partiality, pär'shi-al''i-ti, *n.* Unfair bias; undue favor shown; a liking or fondness.

Partially, pär'shal-li, *adv.* With undue bias; in part; to some extent.

Participate, pär-tis'i-pāt, *vi.* and *t.* To partake, share.

Participle, pär'ti-si-pl, *n.* A word having the properties of both an adjective and verb.

Particle, pär'ti-kl, *n.* An atom; a jot; a very small portion; a word not inflected.

Particular, pär-tik'ū-lėr, *a.* Pertaining to a single person or thing; private; special; exact; precise; circumstantial; notable; fastidious.—*n.* A single instance; detail; distinct circumstance.

Particularize, pär-tik'ū-lėr-iz, *vt.* To make particular mention of; to specify in detail.—*vi.* To be particular to details.

Parting, pärt'ing, *p.a.* Serving to part or divide; given at separation; departing.—*n.* Division; separation; leave-taking.

Partisan, pär'ti-zan, *n.* An adherent of a party or faction; a party man.—*a.* Adhering to a faction.

Partition, pär-ti'shon, *n.* Act of parting or dividing; division; a division-wall; part where separation is made.—*vt.* To divide by partitions; to divide into shares.

Partner, pärt'nėr, *n.* One who shares with another; an associate in business; a husband or wife.

Partnership, pärt'nėr-ship, *n.* Fellowship; the association of two or more persons in any business; joint interest or property.

Partridge, pär'trij, *n.* A game bird of the grouse family.

Parturition, pär-tū-ri'shon, *n.* The act of bringing forth young.

Party, pär'ti, *n.* A body of individuals; one of two litigants; a company made up for an occasion; a single person; a detachment of troops.—*a.* Of or pertaining to a party.

Parvenu, pär've-nū, *n.* An upstart; a person who has newly risen to eminence.

Pas, pä, *n.* A step; precedence.

Paschal, pas'kal, *a.* Pertaining to the passover or to Easter.

Pasquin, Pasquinade, pas'kwin, pas-kwin-ād', *n.* A lampoon; a satirical publication.—*vt.* To lampoon.

Pass, päs, *vi.* (pret. and pp. passed or past). To go by or past; to change; to die; to elapse; to be enacted; to be current; to thrust in fencing or fighting; to go successfully through an examination.—*vt.* To go past, beyond, or over; to cross; to live through; to undergo with success (as an examination); to circulate; to utter; to take no notice of; to enact; to thrust, to void, as feces.—*n.* A passage; a defile; a license to pass; a thrust; manipulation; condition; extremity.

Passage, pas'āj, *n.* Act of passing; transit; a journey, especially by a ship; road; channel; a gallery or corridor; access; episode; part of a book, etc., referred to; enactment; an encounter.

Passé, Passée, pas-ā, *a.* Past; faded, past the heyday of life.

Passenger, pas'en-jėr, *n.* A traveller; one who travels in a public conveyance; one who does not pull his weight in a crew or team

Passim, pas'im, *adv.* Here and there.

Passing, päs'ing, *p.a.* Current; cursory; fleeting.—*adv.* Exceedingly; very.

Passion, pa'shon, *n.* A suffering or enduring; the last suffering of Christ; a strong feeling or emotion; violent anger; ardor; vehement desire; love.

Passion-play, pa'shon-plā, *n.* A play representing scenes in the passion of Christ.

Passion-Sunday, pa'shon-sun-dā, *n.* The fifth Sunday in Lent.

Passive, pas'iv, *a.* Capable of feeling; suffering; not acting; unresisting; inert; in *grammar,* expressing that the nominative is the object of some action or feeling.

Passover, päs'ō-vėr, *n.* A feast of the Jews commemorative of the deliverance in Egypt, when the destroying angel passed over the houses of the Israelites; the sacrifice offered.

Passport, päs'pōrt, *n.* A license empowering a person to travel; that which enables one to reach some desired object.

Past, päst, *p.a.* Gone by or beyond; belonging to an earlier period; spent; ended.—*n.* Former time.—*prep.* Beyond; out of reach of; after.—*adv.* By; so as to pass.

Paste, pāst, *n.* A mass of a semi-fluid state; a mixture of flour, etc., used in cookery, or to cause substances to adhere; a mixture of clay for pottery; a brilliant glassy substance, used in making imitations of gems.—*vt.* (pasting, pasted). To unite or fasten with paste.

Pasteboard, pāst-bōrd, *n.* A thick paper formed of sheets pasted together; cardboard.

Pastel, pas'tel, *n.* A colored crayon; a drawing made with colored crayons; the art of drawing with colored crayons.

Pastern, pas'tėrn, *n.* The part of a horse's leg between the joint next the foot and the hoof.

Pasteurization, past'ur-i-zā''shun, *n.* Checking the activity of bacteria in milk, etc., by heating it to 60° or 70° C.

Pastime, pas'tim, *n.* Recreation; diversion; sport; play.

Pastor, pas'tor, *n.* A minister of a church.

Pastoral, pas'tor-al, *a.* Pertaining to shepherds; rustic; rural; relating to the care of souls, or to a pastor.—*n.* A poem dealing with shepherds; a poem of rural life; a letter addressed by a bishop to the clergy and people of his diocese.

Pastry, pās'tri, *n.* Eatables made of paste; crust of pies, tarts, etc.

Pasture, pas'tūr, *n.* Grass for the food of cattle; grazing ground; grass land.—*vt.* (pasturing, pastured). To feed on growing grass.—*vi.* To graze.

Pat, pat, *n.* A light stroke with the fingers or hand; a tap; a small lump of butter beaten into shape.—*vt.* (patting, patted). To strike gently; to tap.—*a.* Hitting the mark; apt; convenient.—*adv.* Fitly; just in the nick.

Patch, pach, *n.* A piece of cloth sewn on a garment to repair it; a small piece of silk stuck on the face for adornment; a small piece of ground.—*vt.* To mend by sewing on a patch; to repair clumsily; to make hastily without regard to forms (with *up*).

Patchwork, pach'wėrk, *n.* Work composed of varied pieces sewn together; work composed of pieces clumsily put together.

Pate, pāt, *n.* The head, or rather the top of the head.

Patella, pa-tel'la, *n.* A small pan, vase, or dish; the knee-pan.

Paten, pa'ten, *n.* A metallic flat dish; the plate on which the consecrated bread in the eucharist is placed.

Patent, pā'tent or pa'tent, *n.* A writing (called *letters patent*) granting a privilege, as a title of nobility; a similar writing, securing exclusive right to an invention or discovery.—*a.* Open; manifest; secured by patent; lacquered (leather).—*vt.* To secure, as the exclusive right of a thing to a person.

Paterfamilias, pā'tėr-fa-mil''i-as, *n.* The head or father of a family.

Paternal, pa-tėr'nal, *a.* Fatherly; derived from the father; hereditary.

Paternoster, pa'tėr-nos-tėr, *n.* The Lord's prayer; a rosary; every tenth bead in a rosary.

Path, päth, *n.* A way beaten by the feet of man or beast; a footway; course or track; way or passage; course of life.

Pathetic, pa-thet'ik, *a.* Full of pathos; affecting; exciting pity, sorrow, etc.

Pathology, pa-thol'o-ji, *n.* That part of medicine which explains the nature of diseases, their causes and symptoms.

Pathos, pā'thos, *n.* Expression of strong or deep feeling; that quality which excites tender emotions, as pity, sympathy, etc.

Patience, pā'shens, *n.* Quality of being patient; endurance; composure; forbearance; a card game for one.

Patient, pā'shent, *a.* Enduring without murmuring; not easily provoked; persevering; not hasty.—*n.* A person or thing passively affected; a person under medical treatment.

Patina, pat'i-na, *n.* The fine green rust on ancient bronzes, copper coins, etc.

Patois, pat-wä, *n.* A rustic or provincial form of speech.

Patriarch, pā'tri-ärk, *n.* The chief of a race, tribe, or family; a dignitary above an archbishop in the Greek Church.

Patrician, pa-tri'shan, *a.* Belonging to the senators of ancient Rome; of noble birth.—*n.* A person of noble birth.

Patrimony, pat'ri-mo-ni, *n.* A paternal inheritance; a church estate or revenue.

Patriot, pā'tri-ot or pat', *n.* A person who loves his country, and zealously defends its interests.—*a.* Patriotic.

Patriotism, pā'tri-ot-izm or pat', *n.* The qualities of a patriot; love of one's country.

Patrol, pa-trōl', *n.* The marching round by a guard at night to secure the safety of a camp; the guard who go such rounds; on active service, a small party sent out to harass the enemy (fighting patrol), or to get information (reconnaissance patrol).—*vi.* (patrolling, patrolled). To go the rounds as a patrol.—*vt.* To pass round, as a guard.

Patron, pā'tron, *n.* A protector; one who supports or protects a person or a work; one who has the disposition of a church-living, professorship, or other appointment; a guardian saint.

Patronize, pat'ron-īz or pā', *vt.* To act as patron of; to countenance or favor; to assume the air of a superior to.

Patter, pat'ér, *vi.* To make a sound like that of falling drops; to move with quick steps; to mumble; to talk in a glib way.—*n.* A quick succession of small sounds; chatter; prattle.

Pattern, pat'érn, *n.* A model proposed for imitation; a sample; an ornamental design.

Paucity, pa'si-ti, *n.* Fewness; scarcity; smallness of quantity.

Pauline, pal'īn, *a.* Pertaining to St. *Paul,* or to his writings.

Paunch, pansh, *n.* The belly, and its contents; the abdomen.

Paunchy, pansh'i, *a.* Big-bellied.

Pauper, pa'pér, *n.* A poor person; one dependent on the public for maintenance.

Pause, paz, *n.* A temporary cessation; cessation proceeding from doubt; suspense.—*vi.* (pausing, paused). To make a short stop; to delay; to deliberate; to hesitate.

Pave, pāv, *vt.* (paving, paved). To cover with stone, brick, etc., so as to make a level and solid surface for carriages or foot-passengers.

Pavement, pāv'ment, *n.* The solid floor of a street, courtyard, etc.; paved part of a road used by foot-passengers; material with which anything is paved.

Pavilion, pa-vil'yon, *n.* A tent; a small building having a tent-formed roof; a building of ornamental character for entertainments; the outer ear.—*vt.* To furnish with pavilions; to shelter with a tent.

Paw, pa, *n.* The foot of animals having claws.—*vi.* To draw the fore-foot along the ground.—*vt.* To scrape with the fore-foot; to handle roughly.

Pawn, pan, *n.* Something given as security for money borrowed; a pledge; state of being pledged; a pawnship; a man of the lowest rank in chess.—*vt.* To give in pledge; to pledge with a pawnbroker.

Pawnbroker, pan'brōk-ér, *n.* A person licensed to lend money at a legally fixed rate of interest on goods deposited with him.

Pay, pā, *vt.* (paying, paid). To give money, etc., for goods received or service rendered; to reward; to discharge, as a debt; to give; to cover with tar or pitch.—*vi.* To make a payment; to be profitable or remunerative.—*n.* An equivalent for money due, goods, or services; salary; wages; reward.

Pea, pē, *n.*; pl. **Peas, Pease.** A well-known flowering plant cultivated for its seeds; one of the seeds of the plant.

Peace, pēs, *n.* A state of quiet; calm; repose; public tranquillity; freedom from war; concord.

Peaceful, pēs'ful, *a.* Free from war, noise, or disturbance; quiet; mild.

Peach, pēch, *n.* A well-known tree and its fruit, allied to the almond.—*vi.* To betray one's accomplice.

Peacock, pē'kok, *n.* A large gallinaceous bird with rich plumage: properly the male bird.

Pea-jacket, pē'jak-et, *n.* A thick woollen jacket worn by seamen, fishermen, etc.

Peak, pēk, *n.* A projecting point; the top of a mountain ending in a point; the upper corner of a sail extended by a yard; also, the extremity of the yard or gaff.—*vi.* To look sickly; to be emaciated.

Peal, pēl, *n.* A series of loud sounds, as of bells, thunder, etc.; a set of bells tuned to each other; chime.—*vi.* To give out a peal.—*vt.* To cause to ring or sound.

Pear, pår, *n.* A well-known fruit-tree; one of the fruits of the tree.

Pearl, pérl, *n.* A smooth lustrous whitish gem produced by certain mollusks; something resembling a pearl; a small printing type; what is choicest and best.—*a.* Relating to or made of pearl or mother-of-pearl.—*vt.* To set or adorn with pearls.

Peasant, pe'zant, *n.* A rustic; one whose business is rural labor.—*a.* Rustic.

Peat, pēt, *n.* A kind of turf used as fuel; a small block of this cut and dried for fuel.

Pebble, peb'l, *n.* A stone rounded by the action of water; agate and rock-crystal used for glass in spectacles.

Pecan, Pecan-nut, pē-kan', pē-kan'nut, *n.* A species of hickory and its fruit.

Peccadillo, pek-a-dil'lō, *n.* A slight trespass or offense; a petty crime or fault.

Peck, pek, *n.* A dry measure of eight quarts.—*vt.* and *i.* To strike with the beak, or something pointed; to pick up, as food, with the beak.

Pectic, pek'tik, *a.* Having the property of forming a jelly.

Pectinate, pek'tin-āt, *a.* Toothed like a comb.

Pectoral, pek'to-ral, *a.* Pertaining to the breast.—*n.* A breastplate; a medicine for the chest and lungs.

Peculate, pe'kū-lāt, *vi.* To appropriate money or goods intrusted to one's care.

Peculiar, pē-kū'li-ér, *a.* One's own; characteristic; particular; unusual; odd.

Peculiarity, pē-kū'li-a'ri-ti, *n.* Quality of being peculiar; something peculiar to a person or thing.

Pecuniary, pē-kū'ni-a-ri, *a.* Relating to or connected with money; consisting of money.

Pedagogue, ped'a-gog, *n.* A teacher of children; a schoolmaster.

Pedal, pēd'al, *a.* Pertaining to a foot or to a pedal.—*n.* pe'dal. A lever to be pressed by the foot; a part of a musical instrument acted on by the feet.

Pedant, pe'dant, *n.* One who makes a vain display of his learning; a narrow-minded scholar.

Pedantry, pe'dant-ri, *n.* The qualities or character of a pedant; boastful display of learning; obstinate adherence to rules.

Peddle, ped'l, *vi.* and *t.* (peddling, peddled). To travel and sell small-wares; to trifle.

Pedestal, pe'des-tal, *n.* The base or support of a column, pillar, statue, vase, etc.

Pedestrian, pe-des'tri-an, *a.* Going on foot; performed on foot.—*n.* One who journeys on foot; a remarkable walker.

Pedigree, pe'di-grē, *n.* Lineage; line of ancestors; genealogy.

Pediment, pe'di-ment, *n.* The triangular mass resembling a gable at the end of buildings in the Greek style; a triangular decoration over a window, a door, etc.

Pedometer, pe-dom'et-ėr, *n.* An instrument which measures how far a person walks.

Peel, pēl, *vt.* To strip off, as bark or rind; to flay; to pare; to pillage.—*vi.* To lose the skin, bark or rind; to fall off, as bark or skin.—*n.* The skin or rind; a baker's wooden shovel.

Peep, pēp, *vi.* To chirp as a chicken; to begin to appear; to look through a crevice.—*n.* A chirp; a look through a small opening; first appearance.

Peer, pēr, *n.* One of the same rank; an equal; an associate; a nobleman (duke, marquis, earl, viscount, or baron).—*vi.* To appear; to peep out; to look narrowly.

Peerless, pēr'les, *a.* Matchless.

Peevish, pē'vish, *a.* Fretful; querulous; hard to please; froward.

Peg, peg, *n.* A piece of wood used in fastening things together; the pin of a musical instrument; a pin on which to hang anything.—*vt.* (pegging, pegged). To fasten with pegs.—*vi.* To work diligently.

Pekoe, pē'kō, *n.* A fine black tea.

Pelagic, pe-laj'ik, *a.* Belonging to the ocean; inhabiting the open ocean.

Pelican, pel'i-kan, *n.* A large web-footed bird with a very large bill.

Pellet, pel'et, *n.* A little ball; one of the globules of small shot.

Pell-mell, pel'mel, *adv.* With confused violence; in utter confusion.

Pellucid, pel-lū'sid, *a.* Transparent; not opaque; translucent.

Pelt, pelt, *n.* A raw hide; a blow; a heavy shower.—*vt.* To strike with something thrown.—*vi.* To throw missiles; to fall in a heavy shower.

Pelvis, pel'vis, *n.* The bony cavity forming the framework of the lower part of the abdomen.

Pen, pen, *n.* An instrument for writing with ink; style or quality of writing; a small inclosure for cows, etc.; a fold.—*vt.* (penning, penned). To write; to coop or shut up.

Penal, pē'nal, *a.* Relating to, enacting, or incurring punishment.

Penalty, pen'al-ti, *n.* Punishment for a crime or offense; forfeit for non-fulfilment of conditions; sum to be forefeited; a fine

Penance, pen'ans, *n.* An ecclesiastical punishment imposed for sin; voluntary suffering as an expression of penitence.

Penchant, päng'shäng, *n.* Strong inclination; bias.

Pencil, pen'sil, *n.* A small brush used by painters; an instrument of black-lead, etc., for writing and drawing; a converging or diverging aggregate of rays of light.—*vt.* (pencilling, pencilled). To write or mark with a pencil.

Pend, pend, *vi.* To impend; to wait for settlement.

Pendant, pen'dant, *n.* Anything hanging down by way of ornament; a hanging apparatus for giving light, etc.; an appendix or addition; a flag borne at the mast-head.

Pendent, pen'dent, *a.* Hanging; pendulous; projecting.—*n.* Something hanging.

Pendulous, pen'dū-lus, *a.* Hanging; hanging so as to swing; swinging.

Pendulum, pen'dū-lum, *n.* A body suspended and swinging; the swinging piece in a clock which regulates its motion.

Penetrable, pen'e-tra-bl, *a.* That may be entered or pierced; susceptible of moral or intellectual impression.

Penetrate, pen'e-trāt, *vt.* and *i.* To enter or pierce, as into another body; to affect, as the mind; to cause to feel; to understand.

Penguin, pen'gwin, *n.* A web-footed, flightless sea bird.

Penicillin, pen-i-sil'in, *n.* A bacteria-destroying substance derived from a mold.

Peninsula, pen-in'sū-la, *n.* A portion of land almost surrounded by water.

Penis, pē'nis, *n.* The male organ of generation.

Penitent, pe'ni-tent, *a.* Suffering sorrow on account of one's own sins; contrite.—*n.* One who repents of sin.

Penitentiary, pe-ni-ten'sha-ri, *a.* Relating to penance.—*n.* One who does penance; an office or official of the R. Catholic church connected with the granting of dispensations, etc.; a house of correction.

Penknife, pen'nif, *n.* A small pocket-knife.

Pennant, pen'ant, *n.* A small flag; a pennon; a pendant.

Penniless, pen'i-les, *a.* Without money.

Penny, pen'i, *n.*; pl. **Pennies** or **Pence,** pen'iz, pens. (*Pennies* denotes the number of coins; *pence* the value.) A bronze coin; money.

Pension, pen'shon, *n.* A stated yearly allowance in consideration of past services; a boarding-house on the Continent (pronounced päng-syong).—*vt.* To grant a pension to.

Pensive, pen'siv, *a.* Thoughtful; expressing thoughtfulness with sadness.

Pentagon, pen'ta-gon, *n.* A plane figure having five angles and five sides.

Pentateuch, pen'ta-tūk, *n.* The first five books of the Old Testament.

Pentecost, pen'tē-kost, *n.* A festival of the Jews on the fiftieth day after the Passover; Whitsuntide.

Penultimate, pen-ul'ti-māt, *a.* The last but one.—*n.* The last syllable but one; penult.

Penumbra, pen-um'bra, *n.* The partial shadow on the margin of the total shadow in an eclipse; the point of a picture where the shade blends with the light.

Penurious, pe-nū'ri-us, *a.* Pertaining to penury; parsimonious; niggardly.

Penury, pe'nū-ri, *n.* Poverty; indigence; want of the necessaries of life.

Peon, pē'on, *n.* An attendant; a native constable; a day-laborer; a kind of serf

Peony, pē'o-ni, *n.* A genus of plants of the ranunculus family, with large flowers.

People, pē'pl, *n.* The body of persons who compose a community, race, or nation; persons indefinitely.—*vt.* (peopling, peopled). To stock with inhabitants, to populate.

Pepper, pep'ėr, *n.* A plant and its aromatic pungent seed, much used in seasoning, etc.—*vt.* To sprinkle with pepper; to pelt with shot or missiles; to drub thoroughly.

Pepper-corn, pep'ėr-korn, *n.* The berry or fruit of the pepper plant.

Peppermint, pep'ėr-mint, *n.* A plant of the mint genus having a penetrating aromatic smell and a strong pungent taste.

Pepsin, Pepsine, pep'sin, *n.* The active principle of gastric juice.

Peptic, pep'tik, *a.* Promoting digestion; relating to digestion; digestive.

Per, pėr, *prep.* A Latin preposition used in the sense of *by* or *for,* chiefly in certain Latin phrases, as *per annum,* by or for the year.

Perceive, pėr-sēv', *vt.* (perceiving, perceived). To apprehend by the organs of sense or by the mind; to observe; to discern.

Percentage, pėr-sent'āj, *n.* The allowance duty, rate of interest, proportion, etc., reckoned on each hundred.

Perception, pėr-sep'shon, *n.* Act, process, or faculty of perceiving; discernment.

Perch, pėrch, *n.* A spiny fresh-water fish; a roost for fowls; an elevated place or position; 5½ yards, also called a rod or pole; 30¼ square yards, a square rod.—*vi.* To sit on a perch; to light, as a bird.—*vt.* To place on a perch.

Percipient, pér-sip'i-ent, a. Perceiving; having the faculty of perception.

Percolate, pér'kō-lāt, vt. and i. To strain through; to filter.

Percuss, pér-kus', vt. To strike against; to tap or strike in medical practice.

Percussion, pér-ku'shon, n. Collision; impact; the act of striking the surface of the body to determine by sound the condition of the organs subjacent.

Perdition, pér-di'shon, n. Entire ruin; utter destruction; eternal death.

Perdu, Perdue, pér'dū or pér-dū', a. Hid; in concealment; out of sight.

Peregrinate, pe're-grin-āt, vi. To travel from place to place; to wander.

Peremptory, pe'remp-to-ri, a. Such as to preclude debate; decisive; absolute.

Perennial, pe-ren'i-al, a. Lasting through the year; perpetual; unceasing.—n. A plant whose root remains alive more years than two.

Perfect, pér'fekt, a. Finished; complete; fully informed; completely skilled; faultless; in *grammar*, denoting a tense which expresses an act completed.—vt. To accomplish; to make perfect; to make fully skilful.

Perfection, pér-fek'shon, n. State of being perfect; an excellence perfect in its kind.

Perfidious, pér-fi'di-us, a. Guilty of or involving perfidy; treacherous; faithless.

Perfidy, pér'fi-di, n. Act of breaking faith or allegiance; the violation of a trust reposed; treachery; disloyalty.

Perforate, pér'fo-rāt, vt. To bore or penetrate through; to pierce with a pointed instrument.

Perform, pér-form', vt. To accomplish; to effect; to do; to act.—vi. To act a part; to play on a musical instrument, etc.

Performance, pér-form'ans, n. Act of performing; deed; achievement; a literary work; exhibition on the stage; entertainment at a place of amusement.

Perfume, pér'fūm or pér-fūm', n. A pleasant scent or smell; fragrance.—vt. (perfuming, perfumed). To scent with perfume; to impregnate with a grateful odor.

Perfunctory, pér-fungk'to-ri, a. Done carelessly or in a half-hearted manner; negligent.

Perhaps, pér-haps', adv. It may be; peradventure; perchance; possibly.

Pericardium, pe-ri-kär'di-um, n. The membranous sac that incloses the heart.

Peridot, pe'ri-dot, n. A variety of the precious stone, chrysolite.

Perigee, pe'ri-jē, n. That point in the moon's orbit nearest the earth.

Perihelion, pe-ri-hēl'i-on, n. That point of the orbit of a planet or comet nearest the sun.

Peril, pe'ril, n. Risk; hazard; danger.—vt. (perilling, perilled). To hazard; to expose to danger.

Perilous, pe'ril-us, a. Dangerous; hazardous; full of risk.

Perimeter, pe-rim'et-ér, n. The outer boundary of a body or figure.

Period, pē'ri-od, n. The time taken up by a heavenly body in revolving round the sun; the time at which anything ends; end; an indefinite portion of any continued state or existence; a complete sentence; the point that marks the end of a sentence, thus (.).

Periodical, pē-ri-od'ik-al, n. A magazine, newspaper, etc., published at regular periods.—a. Periodic.

Peripatetic, pe'ri-pa-tet''ik, a. Walking about; itinerant; pertaining to Aristotle's system of philosophy, taught while walking.—n. One who walks; a follower of Aristotle.

Periphery, pe-rif'ér-i, n. The boundary line of a figure.

Periscope, pe'ri-skōp, n. An apparatus or structure rising above the deck of a submarine vessel, giving by means of mirrors, etc., a view of outside surroundings, though the vessel itself remains submerged; a similar device used in trenches.

Perish, pe'rish, vi. To die; to wither and decay; to be destroyed; to come to nothing.

Peritoneum, pe'ri-tō-nē''um, n. A membrane investing the internal surface of the abdomen, and the viscera contained in it.

Peritonitis, per'i-tō-ni''tis, n. Inflammation of the peritoneum.

Perjure, pér'jūr, vt. (perjuring, perjured). To forswear; wilfully to make a false oath when administered legally.

Perjury, pér'jū-ri, n. Act or crime of forswearing; act of violating an oath or solemn promise.

Perk, pérk, a. Trim; spruce; pert.—vi. To hold up the head pertly.—vt. To make trim; to prank; to hold up (the head) pertly.

Permanent, pér'ma-nent, a. Lasting; durable; not decaying; abiding; fixed.

Permeate, pér'mē-āt, vt. (permeating, permeated). To pass through the pores or interstices of; to penetrate without rupture or displacement of parts.

Permissive, pér-mis'iv, a. That permits; granting persmision or liberty; allowing.

Permit, pér-mit', vt. and i. (permitting, permitted). To allow; to grant; to suffer; to concede.—n. per'mit. A written permission or license given by competent authority.

Permutation, pér-mū-tā'shon, n. Interchange; in *mathematics*, any of the ways in which a set of quantities can be arranged.

Pernicious, pér-ni'shus, a. Having the quality of destroying or injuring; destructive; deadly; noxious.

Perorate, pe'rō-rāt, vi. To make a peroration; to speechify; to spout.

Peroxide, pér-ok'sid, n. The oxide of a given base which contains the greatest quantity of oxygen.

Perpendicular, pér-pen-di'kū-lér, a. Perfectly upright or vertical; being at right angles to a given line or surface.—n. A line at right angles to the plane of the horizon or to another line.

Perpetrate, pér'pe-trāt, vt. To do in a bad sense; to be guilty of; to commit.

Perpetual, pér-pe'tū-al, a. Continuing without end; permanent; everlasting.

Perpetuate, pér-pe'tū-āt, vt. To make perpetual; to preserve from oblivion.

Perpetuity, pér-pe-tū'i-ti, n. State or quality of being perpetual; endless duration; something of which there will be no end.

Perplexity, pér-pleks'i-ti, n. State of being puzzled, or at a loss; bewilderment; state of being intricate or involved.

Perquisite, pér'kwi-zit, n. Something in addition to regulr wages or salary.

Persecute, pér'se-kūt, vt. (persecuting, persecuted). To harass with unjust punishment; to afflict for adherence to a particular creed.

Persevere, pér-se-vēr', vi. (persevering, persevered). To continue steadfastly in any business; to pursue steadily any design.

Persiflage, pér'sē-flāzh, n. Idle bantering talk.

Persist, pér-sist', vi. To continue steadily in any business or course; to persevere; to continue in a certain state.

Persistence, Persistency, pér-sist'ens, pér-sist'en-si, n. Act or state of persisting; perseverance; continuance; obstinacy.

Person, pér'son, n. An individual human being; each of the three beings of the Godhead; bodily form;; one of the three inflections of a verb.—In person, by oneself; not by representatives.

Personable, pér'son-a-bl, a. Having a well-formed body; of good appearance.

Personage, pér'son-āj, n. A person of importance; a man or woman of distinction.

Personal, pér'son-al, a. Pertaining to a person; peculiar or proper to him or her; belonging to face and figure; denoting the person in a grammatical sense.

Personality, pér-son-al'i-ti, n. State of being personal; that which constitutes an individual a distinct person; disparaging remark on one's conduct and character; in *law*, personal estate.

Personally, pėr'son-al-li, *adv.* In person; with respect to an individual; particularly.

Personalty, pėr'son-al-ti, *n.* Personal property, in distinction from real property.

Personification, pėr-son'i-fi-kā''shon, *n.* Act of personifying; embodiment; a metaphor which represents inanimate objects as possessing the attributes of persons.

Personify, pėr-son'i-fi, *vt.* To represent with the attributes of a person; to impersonate.

Personnel, pėr-son-el', *n.* The body of persons employed in any occupation.

Perspective, pėr-spek'tiv, *n.* The art of representing objects on a flat surface so that they appear to have their natural dimensions and relations; a representation of objects in perspective; view.—*a.* Pertaining to the art of perspective.

Perspicacious, pėr-spi-kā'shus, *a.* Quick-sighted; of acute discernment.

Perspicuous, pėr-spi'kū-us, *a.* Clear to the understanding; lucid.

Perspiration, pėr-spi-rā'shon, *n.* Act of perspiring; exudation of sweat; sweat.

Perspire, pėr-spīr', *vi.* (perspiring, perspired). To emit the moisture of the body through the skin; to sweat; to exude.—*vt.* To emit through pores.

Persuade, pėr-swād', *vt.* (persuading, persuaded). To influence by argument, advice, etc.; to induce; to prevail on.

Persuasive, pėr-swā'siv, *a.* Having the power of persuading; calculated to persuade.—*n.* That which persuades; an incitement.

Pert, pėrt, *a.* Lively; brisk; saucy; bold.

Pertain, pėr-tān', *vi.* To belong; to relate; to concern; to regard.

Pertinacious, pėr-ti-nā'shus, *a.* Obstinate; inflexible; determined; persistent.

Pertinent, pėr'ti-nent, *a.* Related to the subject or matter in hand; apposite; fit.

Perturb, pėr-tėrb', *vt.* To disturb; to agitate; to disquiet; to confuse.

Peruse, pe-rūz', *vt.* (perusing, perused). To read through; to read with attention; to examine carefully.

Pervade, pėr-vād', *vt.* (pervading, pervaded). To pass or flow through; to permeate; to be diffused through.

Perverse, pėr-vėrs', *a.* Obstinate in the wrong; stubborn; untractable; petulant.

Perversely, pėr-vėrs'li, *adv.* Stubbornly; obstinately in the wrong.

Perversion, pėr-vėr'shon, *n.* A diverting from the true intent or object; misapplication.

Pervert, pėr-vert', *vt.* To turn from truth or proper purpose; to corrupt; to misinterpret; to misapply.—*n.* pėr'vert. One who has been perverted.

Pervious, pėr'vi-us, *a.* That may be penetrated; permeable.

Pessimism, pes'im-izm, *n.* The doctrine that the present state of things tends only to evil; the tendency always to look at the dark side of things.

Pessimist, pes'im-ist, *n.* One who believes in pessimism, or takes an unfavorable view of affairs.

Pest, pest, *n.* A deadly epidemic disease; plague; pestilence; a mischievous person.

Pester, pes'tėr, *vt.* To plague; to trouble; to annoy with little vexations.

Pestilence, pes'ti-lens, *n.* Any contagious disease that is epidemic and fatal; something morally evil or destructive.

Pestle, pes'l, *n.* An instrument for pounding substances in a mortar.—*vt.* and *i.* (pestling, pestled). To pound with a pestle.

Pet, pet, *n.* A darling; any little animal fondled and indulged; fit of peevishness.—*vt.* (petting, petted). To fondle; to indulge.

Petal, pe'tal, *n.* A flower leaf.

Petite, pe-tēt', *a.* Small in figure; tiny.

Petition, pē-ti'shon, *n.* An entreaty, supplication, or prayer; a written application in legal proceedings.—*vt.* To supplicate; to solicit.

Petrifaction, pet-ri-fak'shon, *n.* the process of changing into stone; a fossil.

Petrify, pet-ri-fī, *vt.* To turn into stone or a fossil; to paralyze or stupefy.—*vi.* To become stone, or of a stony hardiness.

Petrol, pet'rol, *n.* Petroleum spirit; refined petroleum used as the source of power for the internal-combustion engines of automobiles, airplanes, etc.

Petroleum, pe-trō'lē-um, *n.* Rock-oil; an inflammable liquid found in the earth.

Petrology, pe-trol'o-ji, *n.* The study of rocks.

Petticoat, pet'i-kōt, *n.* A loose under-garment worn by women.

Petty, pet'i, *a.* Small; little; trifling; trivial.

Petulant, pe'tū-lant, *a.* Irritable; peevish; fretful; saucy; pert; capricious.

Pew, pū, *n.* An inclosed seat in a church.

Pewter, pū'tėr, *n.* An alloy mainly of tin and lead; a vessel made of pewter.—*a.* Relating to or made of pewter.

Phalange, fa-lanj', *n.* One of the small bones of the fingers and toes.

Phallus, fal'lus, *n.* The emblem of the generative power in nature, especially in certain religious usages.

Phantasm, fan'tazm, *n.* An apparition; a phantom; an idea, notion, or fancy.

Phantasmagoria, fan-tas'ma-gō''ri-a, *n.* An exhibition of figures by shadows, as by the magic lantern; illusive images.

Phantom, fan'tom, *n.* An apparition; a specter; a fancied vision; a phantasm.

Pharisaic, Pharisaical, fa-ri-sā'ik, fa-ri-sā'ik-al, *a.* Pertaining to or resembling the Pharisees; hypocritical.

Pharisee, fa'ri-sē, *n.* A Jew strict in religious observances; a hypocrite.

Pharmaceutic, Pharmaceutical, fär-ma-sū'tik, fär-ma-sū'tik-al, *a.* Pertaining to the knowledge or art of pharmacy.

Pharmacology, fär-ma-kol'o-ji, *n.* The science of drugs; the art of preparing medicines.

Pharmacopeia, fär'ma-kō-pē''a, *n.* A book describing the preparation of medicines.

Pharmacy, fär'ma-si, *n.* The art or practice of preparing medicines.

Pharynx, fä'ringks, *n.* The muscular sac between the mouth and the esophagus.

Phase, fāz, *n.* A particular stage of the moon or a planet in respect to illumination; state of a varying phenomenon; one of the various aspects of a question.

Pheasant, fe'zant, *n.* A bird commonly reared and preserved for sport and food.

Phenomenon, fē-no'me-non, *n.*; pl. **-mena.** An appearance; anything visible; an appearance whose cause is not immediately obvious; something extraordinary.

Phial, fī'al, *n.* A small glass bottle.

Philanthropist, fi-lan'throp-ist, *n.* One devoted to philanthropy; one who exerts himself in doing good to his fellowmen.

Philanthropy, fi-lan'thro-pi, *n.* The love of man or of mankind; benevolence towards the whole human family.

Philatelist, fi-lat'e-list, *n.* One who collects postage-stamps.

Philharmonic, fil-här-mon'ik, *a.* Loving harmony; musical.

Philistine, fi-lis'tin or fil'is-tin, *n.* A person deficient in culture, and wanting in taste; a person of narrow views.

Philology, fi-lol'o-ji, *n.* The study of language; linguistic science.

Philosopher, fi-los'o-fėr, *n.* A person versed in philosophy; one who studies moral or mental science.

Philosophy, fi-los'o-fi, *n.* The science which tries to account for the phenomena of the universe;

metaphysics; the general principles underlying some branch of knowledge; practical wisdom.

Philter, fil'tėr, n. A love-charm; a potion supposed to excite love.

Phlebitis, flē-bi'tis, n. Inflammation of a vein.

Phlebotomy, flē-bot'o-mi, n. The act or practice of opening a vein; blood-letting.

Phlegm, flem, n. The viscid matter of the digestive and respiratory passages; bronchial mucus; coldness; indifference.

Phoenix, fē-niks, n. A bird of ancient legend, said to live 500 years, when it burnt itself, and rose again from its ashes; an emblem of immotality; a paragon.

Phonetics, fō-net'iks, n.pl. The doctrine or science of sounds, especially of the human voice; the representation of sounds.

Phonograph, fō'nō-graf, n. An instrument for registering and reproducing sounds; a predecessor of the gramophone.

Phosgene, fos'jēn, n. A poison gas, carbon oxychloride.

Phosphate, fos'fāt, n. A salt of phosphoric acid.

Phosphoresce, fos-for-es', vi. To give out a phosphoric light.

Phosphorescent, fos-for-es'ent, a. Shining with a faint light like that of phosphorus; luminous without sensible heat.

Phosphorus, fos'for-us, n. An elementary substance which undergoes slow combustion at common temperatures.

Photograph, fō-'tō-graf, n. A picture obtained by photography.—vt. To produce a representation of by photographic means.

Photography, fō-tog'ra-fi, n. The art or practice of producing representations of scenes and objects by the action of light on chemically prepared surfaces.

Photology, fō-tol'o-ji, n. The doctrine or science of light.

Photometer, fō-tom'et-ėr, n. An instrument for measuring the intensity of lights.

Phrase, frāz, n. A short sentence or expression; an idiom; style; diction.—vt. and i. (phrasing, phrased). To style; to express.

Phraseology, frā-zē-ol'o-ji, n. Manner of expression; peculiar words used in a sentence; diction; style.

Phrenetic, fre-net'ik, a. Having the mind disordered; frantic.—n. A frenzied person.

Phrenic, fren'ik, a. Belonging to the diaphragm.

Phrenology, fre-nol'o-ji, n. The doctrine that a person's endowments may be discovered by the configuration of the skull.

Phthisis, thi'sis, n. A wasting disease of the lungs, commonly called consumption.

Phylactery, fi-lak'tėr-i, n. An amulet worn by the Jews, containing a strip of parchment inscribed with Old Testament texts.

Physical, fi'zik-al, a. Pertaining to nature or natural productions; bodily, as opposed to mental or moral; material; pertaining to physics.

Physician, fi-zi'shan, n. A person skilled in the art of healing; a doctor.

Physics, fi'ziks, n. That branch of science which deals with mechanics, dynamics, light, heat, sound, electricity, and magnetism; natural philosophy.

Physiognomy, fi-zi-og'no-mi, n. The art of perceiving a person's character by his countenance; particular cast or expression of countenance.

Physiography, fi-zi-og'ra-fi, n. The science of the earth's physical features and phenomena; physical geography.

Physiology, fi-zi-ol'o-ji, n. The science of the phenomena of life; the study of the functions of living beings.

Physique, fi-zēk', n. A person's physical or bodily structure or constitution.

Phytology, fi-tol'o-ji, n. The science of plants; botany.

Pianist, pi'an-ist, n. A performer on the piano.

Piano, pi-an'ō, n. A musical metal-stringed instrument with a key-board, sounded by hammers acting on the strings.

Piazza, pi-az'za, n. A rectangular open space surrounded by colonnades.

Pica, pī'ka, n. A printing type having six lines in an inch, used as the standard size.

Picaresque, pik-a-resk', a. Pertaining to rogues; describing the fortunes of adventurers.

Piccolo, pik'ko-lō, n. A small flute with shrill tones; an octave flute.

Pick, pik, vt. To strike at with something pointed; to peck at; to clean by the teeth, fingers, etc.; to select; to pluck; to gather.—vi. To eat slowly; to nibble; to pilfer.—n. A pointed tool; a pick-axe; choice; selection.

Pickaxe, pik'aks, n. A sharp-pointed iron tool used in digging, mining, etc.

Picket, pik'et, n. A pointed stake used in fortification; a pale; an advanced guard or outpost; a game at cards.—vt. To fortify with pickets; to post as a guard of observation.

Pickle, pik'l, n. Brine; a solution of salt and water for preserving flesh, fish, etc.; vegetables preserved in vinegar; a state of difficulty or disorder; a troublesome child.—vt. (pickling, pickled). To preserve in or treat with pickle.

Pickpocket, pik'pok-et, n. One who steals from the pocket of another.

Picnic, pik'nik, n. and a. A pleasure-party the members of which carry provisions with them.—vi. (picnicking, picnicked). To take part in a picnic party.

Pictorial, pik-tō'ri-al, a. Pertaining to or forming pictures; illustrated by pictures.

Pictorially, pik-tō'ri-al-li, adv. In a pictorial manner; with pictures or engravings.

Picture, pik'tūr, n. A painting, drawing, etc., exhibiting the resemblance of anything; any resemblance or representation; pl. the moving photographs shown in cinematography; the cinema.—vt. To represent pictorially; to present an ideal likeness of; to describe in a vivid manner.

Picturesque, pik-tūr-esk', a. Forming, or fitted to form, a pleasing picture; abounding with vivid imagery; graphic.

Pie, pi, n. A paste baked with something in or under it; a mass of types unsorted; the magpie.

Piebald, pi'bald, a. Having spots or patches of various colors; pied; mongrel.

Piece, pēs, n. A portion of anything; a distinct part; a composition or writing of no great length; a separate performance; a picture; a coin; a single firearm.—vt. (piecing, pieced). To patch; to join.—vi. To unite or join on.

Piecemeal, pēs'mēl, adv. In or by pieces; in fragments; by little and little.

Piece-work, pēs'wėrk, n. Word done by the piece or job; work paid by quantity.

Pier, pėr, n. A mass of solid stonework for supporting an arch, bridge, etc.; a projecting wharf or landing-place.

Pierce, pėrs, vt. (piercing, pierced). To stab or perforate with a pointed instrument; to penetrate; to move deeply.—vi. To enter; to penetrate.

Piety, pi'e-ti, n. Reverence or veneration towards God; godliness; devotion; religion.

Pig, pig, n. A young swine; a swine in general; an oblong mass of unforged metal.—vt. or i. (pigging, pigged). To bring forth pigs; to act like pigs.

Pigeon, pi'jon, n. A well-known bird of many varieties; a dove; a simpleton; a gull.

Pigeon-hole, pi'jon-hōl, n. A hole for pigeons to enter their dwelling; a division in a desk or case for holding papers.

Pig-iron, pig'i-ėrn, n. Iron in pigs, as it comes from the blast-furnace.

Pigment, pig'ment, n. Paint; any preparation used by painters, dyers, etc., to impart colors to bodies; coloring matter.

Pig-skin, pig'skin, n. The skin of a pig, especially

when prepared for saddlery, etc.

Pig-tail, pig´tāl, n. The tail of a pig; the hair of the head tied behind in a tail.

Pile, pīl, n. A heap; a large mass of buildings; a galvanic or voltaic battery; hair; nap on cloth; a beam driven into the ground to support some superstructure; a heraldic figure like a wedge.—vt. (piling, piled). To heap; to amass; to drive piles into; to support with piles.

Piles, pīlz, n.pl. A disease of the rectum near the anus; hemorrhoids.

Pilferer, pil´fér-ér, n. One who pilfers.

Pilgrim, pil´grim, n. A wanderer; one who travels to visit a holy place or relics.

Pilgrimage, pil´grim-āj, n. A journey to some holy place; the journey of human life.

Pill, pil, n. A medicine in the form of a little ball; anything nauseous to be accepted.—vt. To dose with pills; to form into pills; to rob; to plunder.

Pillage, pil´āj, n. Act of plundering; plunder; spoil.—vt. (pillaging, pillaged). To rob by open violence; to plunder.

Pillar, pil´ér, n. A column; a perpendicular support; a supporter.

Pillory, pil´o-ri, n. A frame of wood with movable boards and holes, through which were put the head and hands of an offender.—vt. (pillorying, pilloried). To punish with the pillory; to expose to ridicule, abuse, etc.

Pillow, pil´ō, n. A long soft cushion; something that bears or supports.—vt. To rest or lay on for support.

Pilot, pi´lot, n. One whose occupation is to steer ships; a guide; a director of one's course.—vt. To act as pilot of; to guide through dangers or difficulties.

Pimp, pimp, n. A man who provides gratifications for others' lusts; a procurer.—vi. To pander; to procure women for others.

Pimpernel, pim´pér-nel, n. A little red-flowered annual found in British cornfields.

Pimple, pim´pl, n. A small elevation of the skin, with an inflamed base.

Pin, pin, n. A longish piece of metal, wood, etc., used for a fastening, or as a support; a peg; a bolt.—vt. (pinning, pinned). To fasten with a pin or pins; to hold fast.—vt. To inclose, to pen or pound.

Pincers, pin´sérz, n.pl. An instrument for gripping anything; nippers; prehensile claws.

Pinch, pinsh, vt. To press hard or squeeze; to nip; to afflict.—vi. To press painfully; to be sparing.—n. A close compression, as with the fingers; a nip; a pang; straits; a strong iron lever, as much as is taken by the finger and thumb, a small quantity.

Pin-cushion, pin´ku-shon, n. A small cushion in which pins are kept.

Pine, pīn, n. A valuable evergreen coniferous tree, furnishing timber, turpentine, pitch, and resin; the pine-apple.—vi. (pining, pined). To languish; to grow weakly with pain, grief, etc.

Pineal, pin´ē-al, a. Resembling a pine-cone in shape.

Pineapple, pīn´ap-l, n. A fruit like the cone of a pine-tree but different in character; the plant itself.

Pinion, pin´yon, n. A bird's wing; the joint of a wing remotest from the body; a large wing-feather; a small toothed wheel; a fetter for the arms.—vt. To bind the wings of; to cut off, as the first joint of the wing; to fetter.

Pink, pingk, n. A garden flower; a light rose-color or pigment; the flower or something supremely excellent.—a. Of a fine light rose-color.—vt. To work in eyelet-holes; to scallop; to stab.—vi. To wink or blink.

Pinnacle, pin´a-kl, n. A rocky peak; the summit; a minor structure or turret above a building.

Pint, pint, n. The eighth part of a gallon.

Pioneer, pi-on-ér´, n. One whose business is to prepare the road for an army, make entrenchments, etc.; one who leads the way.—vt. To pre-

pare a way for.—vi. To act as pioneer.

Pious, pī´us, a. Devout; godly; holy; proceeding from piety.

Pip, pip, n. The kernel or seed of fruit; a spot on cards; a disease of fowls.

Pipe, pīp, n. A wind-instrument of music; a long tube; a tube with a bowl at one end for tobacco; the windpipe; a call of a bird; a wine measure containing about 105 imperial gallons.—vi. (piping, piped). To play on a pipe; to whistle.—vt. To utter in a high tone; to call by a pipe or whistle.

Pipe-clay, pīp´kla, n. The purest kind of potter's-clay.—vt. To whiten with pipe-clay.

Piping, pīp´ing, p.a. Giving out a whistling sound; accompanied by the music of the pipe; boiling.—n. Pipes, as for water, etc.; a jointed stem for propagating plants.

Piquant, pē´kant, a. Making a lively impression; sharp; lively; interesting; pungent.

Pique, pēk, n. Irritation; offense taken; slight anger.—vt. (piquing, piqued). To nettle; to touch with envy, jealousy, etc.; to pride or value (oneself).—vi. To cause irritation.

Piracy, pi´ra-si, n. The act or practice of robbing on the high seas; infringement of the law of copyright.

Pirate, pi´rāt, n. A robber on the high seas; a ship engaged in piracy; one who publishes others' writings without permission.—vi. (pirating, pirated). To rob on the high-seas.—vt. To take without right, as writings.

Pirogue, pi-rōg´, n. A canoe made from a trunk of a tree hollowed out.

Pirouette, pi´rö-et, n. A turning about on the toes in dancing.—vt. To make a pirouette; to whirl about on the toes.

Piscatorial, Piscatory, pis-ka-tō´ri-al, pis´ka-to-ri, a. Related to fishing.

Pisces, pis´sēz, n.pl. The Fishes, a sign in the zodiac; the vertebrate animals of the class fishes.

Piss, pis, vi. To discharge urine.—vt. To eject, as urine.

Pistachio, pis-tä´shi-ō, n. The nut of a small tree cultivated in S. Europe for its fruit; the tree itself, also called pistacia.

Pistil, pis´til, n. The seed-bearing organ of a flower.

Pistol, pis´tol, n. A small firearm fired with one hand.—vt. (pistolling, pistolled). To shoot with a pistol.

Piston, pis´ton, n. a cylindrical piece of metal which fits exactly into a hollow cylinder, and works alternately in two directions.

Piston-rod, pis´ton-rod, n. A rod which connects a piston to some other piece, and either moved by the piston or moving it.

Pit, pit, n. A hollow in the earth; the shaft of a mine; a vat in tanning, dyeing, etc.; a concealed hole for catching wild beasts; a small cavity or depression; part of the floor of a theater.—vt. (pitting, pitted). To lay in a pit or hole; to mark with little hollows; to set in competition.

Pitch, pich, vt. To thrust, as a pointed object; to fix; to set; to throw; to set the key-note of; to set in array; to smear or cover with pitch.—vi. To settle; to fall headlong; to fix choice; to encamp; to rise and fall, as a ship.—n. A throw; degree of elevation; highest rise; descent; elevation of a note; (cricket) prepared ground between wickets; a thick dark resinous substance obtained from tar.

Pitcher, pich´ér, n. A vessel with a spout, for holding liquors.

Pitchfork, pich´fork, n. A fork used in throwing hay, etc.; a tuning-fork. vt. To lift or throw with a pitchfork; to put suddenly into any position.

Pitch-pipe, pich´pip, n. A small pipe used in finding or regulating the pitch of a tune.

Piteous, pi´tē-us, a. That may excite pity; sorrowful; sad; miserable; pitiful.

Pith, pith, n. The spongy substance in the center of exogenous plants; the spinal cord or marrow of an animal; strength or force; energy; co-

P

gency; essence.

Pithy, pith'i, a. Consisting of pith; terse and forcible; energetic; sententious.

Pitiably, pi'ti-a-bli, adv. Woefully.

Pitiful, pi'ti-ful, a. Full of pity; compassionate; woeful; to be pitied; paltry; despicable.

Pitiless, pi'ti-les, a. Feeling no pity; hard-hearted; merciless; relentless; unmerciful.

Pittance, pit'ans, n. A very small portion allowed or assigned; a charity gift.

Pity, pi'ti, n. Sympathy or compassion; ground of pity; thing to be regretted.—vt. (pitying, pitied). To feel pain or grief for; to sympathize with.—vi. To be compassionate.

Pivot, pi'vot, n. A pin on which something turns; a turning-point; that on which important results depend.—vt. To place on or furnish with a pivot.

Placable, pla'ka-bl, a. Readily appeased or pacified; willing to forgive.

Placard, plak'ērd or pla-kärd', n. A written or printed bill posted in a public place; a poster.—vt. To post placards.

Place, plās, n. An open space in a town; a locality, spot, or site; position; room; an edifice; quarters; a passage in a book; rank; office; calling; ground or occasion; stead.—vt. (placing, placed). To put or set; to locate; to appoint or set in an office, rank, or condition; to invest; to lend.

Placenta, pla-sen'ta, n. The after-birth; an organ developed in mammals during pregnancy, connecting the mother and fetus; the part of the seed-vessel to which the seeds are attached.

Placid, pla'sid, a. Gentle; quiet; mild; unruffled; calm.

Plagiarism, plā'ji-a-rizm, n. The act of plagiarizing; literary theft.

Plagiarize, plā'ji-a-rīz, vt. To purloin the published thoughts or words of another.

Plague, plāg, n. A stroke or calamity; severe trouble; a pestilential disease; a person who annoys or troubles.—vt. (plaguing, plagued). To vex; to scourge as with disease or any evil.

Plain, plān, a. Without elevations and depressions; smooth; level; clear; undisguised; artless; sincere; simple; mere; bare; evident; obvious.— n. A piece of level land.—adv. Distinctly.

Plaintiff, plānt'if, n. In law, the person who commences a suit before a tribunal for the recovery of a claim: opposed to defendant.

Plaintive, plānt'iv, a. Expressive of sorrow or grief; repining; mournful; sad.

Plait, plāt, n. A fold; a doubling of cloth, etc.; a braid, as of hair, etc.—vt. To fold; to double in narrow strips; to braid.

Plan, plan, n. The representation of anything on a flat surface; sketch; scheme; project; method; process.—vt. (planning, planned). To form a plan or representation of; to scheme.—vi. To form a scheme.

Plane, Plane-tree, plān, plān'trē, n. A forest tree with a straight smooth stem and palmate leaves; a kind of maple.

Planet, pla'net, n. A celestial body which revolves about the sun or other center.

Plank, plangk, n. A flat broad piece of sawed timber.—vt. To cover or lay with planks.

Plant, plant, n. One of the living organisms of the vegetable kingdom; a herb; a shoot or slip; the machinery, etc., necessary to carry on a business.—vt. To set in the ground for growth; to set firmly; to establish; to furnish with plants; to set and direct, as cannon.—vi. To set plants in the ground.

Plantar, plan'tar, a. Pertaining to the sole of the foot.

Plantation, plan-tā'shon, n. The act of planting; the place planted; a wood or grove; a colony; an estate cultivated by non-European laborers.

Plantigrade, plan'ti-grād, a. Walking on the sole of the foot and not on the toes.

Plaque, plak, n. An ornamental plate; a flat plate on which enamels are painted; a brooch; t plate of a clasp.

Plasma, plas'ma or plaz'ma, n. Formless matt the simplest form of organized matter in t vegetable and animal body.

Plaster, pläs'tér, n. An adhesive substance us in medical practice; a mixture of lime, wat sand, etc., for coating walls; calcined gypsu used with water for finishing walls, for cas cement, etc.—vt. To overlay with plaster; to l on coarsely.

Plastic, plas'tik, a. Having the power to gi form to matter; capable of being molded; ε plied to sculpture, as distinguished from pai ing, etc.—**Plastics,** plas'tiks, n. The science craft of converting various resins into dural materials; the articles so made.

Plat, plat, vt. (platting, platted). To plait; to wea to make a ground-plan of.—n. A plot of grou devoted to some special purpose.

Plate, plāt, n. A flat piece of metal; gold and silv wrought into utensils; a shallow flattish di for eatables; an engraved piece of metal I printing; a page of stereotype for printing.— (plating, plated). To cover with a thin coating metal, as of silver.

Plateau, pla-tō', n.; pl. **-teaux** or **-teaus** (-tōz). ₁ elevated, broad, flat area of land; a table-lar

Plate-glass, plāt'glās, n. A superior kind of thi glass used for mirrors, windows, etc.

Plate-mark, plāt'märk, n. A mark on gold a silver articles to indicate their quality.

Platform, plat'form, n. A raised structure witl flat surface; the place where guns are mount on a battery; the raised walk at a railwε station; a structure for speakers at public me ings; a declared system of policy.

Plating, plāt'ing, n. The art of covering artic with gold or silver; the coating itself.

Platinum, pla'tin-um, n. The heaviest of metals, hard, ductile, malleable, and of a s very color.

Platitude, pla'ti-tūd, n. A trite or stupid remaε a truism.

Platoon, pla-tön', n. A quarter of a company infantry, usually 30 to 40 men, commanded by subaltern.

Platter, plat'ér, n. A large flat dish.

Plaudit, pla'dit, n. Applause; acclamation: us ally in pl.

Plausible, plaz'i-bl, a. Apparently worthy praise; apparently right; specious; fairspoke

Play, plā, vi. To do something for amusement; sport; to gamble; to perform on an instrume of music; to act with free motion; to personat character.—vt. To put in action or motion; use, as an instrument of music; to act; to cc tend against; to perform.—n. Any exercise ₹ diversion; sport; gaming; action; use; practi a drama; motion; scope; swing.

Player, plā'ér, n. An actor; musician; gameste

Playful, plā'ful, a. Full of play; sportive; given levity; indulging a sportive fancy.

Playground, plā'ground, n. A piece of ground ε apart for open-air recreation.

Playwright, plā'rīt, n. A maker of plays.

Plea, plē, n. A suit or action at law; that which alleged in support, justification, or defense; excuse; a pleading.

Plead, plēd, vi. (pleading, pleaded or pled). To ₹ gue in support of or against a claim; to prese an answer to the declaration of a plaintiff; supplicate with earnestness; to urge.—vt. discuss and defend; to argue; to offer in excus to allege in a legal defense.

Pleasant, ple'zant, a. Pleasing; agreeable; gra ful; humorous; sportive.

Please, plēz, vt. (pleasing, pleased). To exc agreeable sensations or emotions in; to delig to gratify; to seem good to.—vi. To give ple sure; to be kind enough.

Pleasurable, ple'zhūr-a-bl, a. Pleasing; givi pleasure; affording gratification.

Pleasure, ple'zhŭr, n. The gratification of the senses or of the mind; agreeable emotion; delight; joy; approbation; choice; will; purpose; command; arbitrary will or choice.

Plebeian, ple-bē'an, a. Pertaining to the common people; vulgar; common.—n. One of the lower ranks of men; one of the common people of ancient Rome.

Plebiscite, pleb'i-sit or pleb'i-sīt, n. A vote of a whole people or community.

Pledge, plej, n. Personal property given in security of a debt; a pawn; a surety; a hostage; the drinking of another's health.—vt. (pledging, pledged). To deposit as a security; to engage solemnly; to drink a health to.

Pleiad, plī'ad, n.; pl. **Pleiads, Pleiades,** plī'adz, plī'å-dēz. Any one of the cluster of seven stars situated in the neck of the constellation Taurus.

Plenary, plē'na-ri, a. Full; complete.

Plenipotent, ple-nip'o-tent, a. Possessing full power.

Plenipotentiary, ple'ni-pō-ten''shi-a-ri, n. A person with full power to act for another; an ambassador with full power.—a. Containing or invested with full power.

Plentiful, plen'ti-ful, a. Being in plenty or abundance; copious; ample; abundant.

Plenty, plen'ti, n. Abundance; copiousness; sufficiency.—a. Plentiful; abundant.

Plethora, pleth'o-ra, n. Excess of blood; repletion; superabundance; a glut.

Pleura, plū'ra, n.; pl. **-ae.** A thin membrane which covers the inside of the thorax, and invests either lung.

Pleurisy, Pleuritis, plū'ri-si, plū-rī'tis, n. An inflammation of the pleura.

Plexus, plek'sus, n. A net-work of vessels, nerves, or fibers.

Pliable, plī'a-bl, a. Easy to be bent; flexible; supple; liant; easily persuaded.

Pliant, plī'ant, a. Pliable; readily yielding to force or pressure without breaking; flexible; plastic; limber.

Pliers, plī'érz, n.pl. A small pair of pincers for bending wire, etc.

Plight, plīt, vi. To pledge, as one's word or honor; to give as a security; never applied to property or goods.—n. A pledge, a solemn promise; predicament; risky or dangerous state.

Plinth, plinth, n. A flat square slab, serving as the foundation of a column or pedestal.

Pliocene, plī'ō-sēn, a. and n. A term applied to the most modern division of the tertiary strata.

Plod, plod, vi. (plodding, plodded). To trudge or walk heavily; to toil; to drudge.—vt. To accomplish by toilsome exertion.

Plot, plot, n. A small piece of ground; a plan, as of a field, etc., on paper; a scheme; a conspiracy; the story of a play, novel, etc.—vt. (plotting, plotted). To make a plan of; to devise.—vi. To conspire; to contrive a plan.

Plow, plou, n. An instrument for turning up the soil.—vt. To turn up with the plow; to make grooves in; to run through, as in sailing.—vi. To turn up the soil with a plow; to use a plow.

Plowshare, plou'shär, n. The part of a plow which cuts the ground at the bottom of the furrow.

Pluck, pluk, vt. To pick or gaher; to pull sharply; to twitch; to strip by plucking; to reject as failing in an examination.—n. The heart, liver, and lights of a sheep, ox, etc.; courage or spirit.

Plucky, pluk'i, a. Spirited; courageous.

Plug, plug, n. A stopple or stopper; a bung; a peg; a quid of tobacco.—vt. (plugging, plugged). To stop with a plug; to make tight by stopping a hole.

Plum, plum, n. A fleshy fruit containing a kernel; the tree producing it; a raisin; a handsome sum or fortune generally.

Plumage, plöm'åj, n. The feathers of a bird.

Plumb, plum, n. A plummet; a perpendicular position.—a. Perpendicular.—adv. In a perpendicular direction.—vt. To set perpendicularly; to sound with a plummet; to ascertain the capacity of; to sound.

Plumb-line, plum'lin, n. A line with a weight attached, used to determine a perpendicular; a plummet.

Plume, plöm, n. The feather of a bird; a feather or feathers worn as an ornament; an ostrich's feather.—vt. (pluming, plumed). To pick and adjust, as feathers; to strip of feathers; to adorn with feathers; —refl. to pride.

Plummet, plum'et, n. A piece of lead, etc., attached to a line, used in sounding the depths of water; a plumb-line.

Plump, plump, a. Fat; stout; chubby.—vt. To make plump; to dilate.—vi. To plunge or fall like a heavy mass; to fall suddenly; to vote for only one candidate.—adv. Suddenly; at once; flatly.

Plunder, plun'dér, vt. To deprive of goods or valuables; to pillage; to spoil.—n. Robbery; pillage; spoil; booty.

Plunge, plunj, vt. (plunging, plunged). To thrust into water or other fluid; to immerse; to thrust or push; to cast or involve.—vi. To dive or rush into water, etc.; to pitch or throw oneself headlong; to throw the body forward and the hindlegs up, as a horse.—n. Act of plunging into water, etc.; act of throwing oneself headlong, like an unruly horse.

Plunger, plunj'ér, n. One who or that which plunges; a diver; a solid cylinder used as a piston in pumps.

Pluperfect, plö'pér-fekt, a. Applied to that tense of a verb which denotes that an action was finished at a certain period, to which the speaker refers.

Plural, plö'ral, a. Relating to, containing, or expressing more than one.—n. The number which designates more than one.

Plurality, plö-ral'i-ti, n. State of being plural; two or more; majority; more than one benefice held by the same clergyman.

Plus, plus, n. A character (+) noting addition.

Plush, plush, n. A textile fabric with a velvet nap on one side.

Plutocrat, plö'to-krat, n. A person possessing power on account of his riches.

Plutonium, plö tōn'i um, n. An element got from uranium by bombarding it with neutrons.

Pluvial, plö'vi-al, a. Relating to rain; rainy.

Ply, plī, vt. (plying, plied). To employ with diligence; to work at; to assail briskly; to beset; to press.—vi. To work steadily; to go in haste; to run regularly between any two ports, as a vessel.—n. A fold; a plait.

Pneumatic. nū-mat'ik, a. Pertaining to air; moved or played by means of air; filled with or fitted to contain air.

Pneumatics, nū mat'iks, n. That branch of physics which treats of the mechanical properties of elastic fluids and particularly of air.

Pneumonia, nū-mō'ni-a, n. An inflammation of the lungs.

Poach, pōch,vt. To cook (eggs) by breaking and pouring among boiling water; to pierce; to tread or stamp.—vt. To encroach on another's ground to steal game; to kill game contrary to law; to be or become swampy.

Pocket, pok'et, n. A small bag or pouch in a garment, a mass of rich ore.—vt. To put in the pocket; to take clandestinely.

Pocket-money, pok'et mun i, n. Money for the pocket or for occasional expenses.

Pod, pod, n. The seed-vessel of certain plants, as peas, etc.—vi. (podding, podded). To produce pods, to swell and appear like a pod.

Poem, pō'em, n. A piece of poetry; a composition in verse.

Poet, pō'et, n. The author of a poem; a peson distinguished for poetic talents.

Poetic, poetical, pō-et'ik, pō-et'ik-al, a. Pertaining or suitable to poetry; expressed in poetry or measure; possessing the peculiar beauties of poetry.

Poetry, pō'et·ri, *n.* The language of the imagination or emotions expressed rhythmically; the artistic expression of thought in emotional language; whatever appeals to the sense of ideal beauty; verse; poems.

Poignant, poin'ant, *a.* Sharp to the taste; pointed; keen; bitter; severe; piercing.

Point, point, *n.* The sharp end of anything; a small headland; sting of an epigram; telling force of expression; exact spot; verge; stage; degree; a mark of punctuation; a mark or dot; end or purpose; characteristic; argument; (cricket) fielder square with wicket on off side; *pl.* The movable guiding rails at junctions on railways.—*vt.* To make pointed; to aim; to indicate; to punctuate; to fill the joints of with mortar.—*vi.* To direct the finger to an object; to indicate the presence of game, as dogs do; to show distinctly.

Point-blank, point-blangk, *a.* and *adv.* Having a horizontal direction; direct; express.

Poise, poiz, *n.* Weight; balance; that which balances.—*vt.* (poising, poised). To balance in weight; to hold in equilibrium.—*vi.* To be balanced or suspended; to depend.

Poison, poi'zn, *n.* Any agent capable of producing a morbid effect on anything endowed with life.—*vi.* To infect with poison; to taint, impair, or corrupt.

Poke, pōk, *n.* A bag or sack; a pouch; a gentle thrust.—*vt.* (poking, poked). To thrust or push against with something pointed; to stir; to jog.—*vi.* To grope; to search.

Poker, pōk'ẽr, *n.* One who or that which pokes; an iron bar used in poking a fire; a game at cards.

Polar, pō'lẽr, *a.* Pertaining to the pole or poles; situated near or proceeding from one of the poles; pertaining to the magnetic poles.

Polarity, pō·la'ri·ti, *n.* State of being polar; property of pointing towards the poles.

Polarize, pō·lẽr·īz, *vt.* To communicate polarity or polarization to.

Pole, pōl, *n.* A long piece of wood; a measure of 5½ yards or 30¼ square yards; one of the extremities of the axis of the celestial sphere or the earth; the pole-star; one of the two points in a magnet in which the power seems concentrated; (with cap.) a native of Poland.—*vt.* (poling, poled). To furnish with poles; to impel by poles.

Pole-cat, pōl'kat, *n.* A carnivorous animal, nearly allied to the weasel, distinguished by its offensive smell.

Polemic, pō·lem'ik, *a.* Pertaining to controversy; disputative.—*n.* A disputant.

Polemics, pō'lem'iks, *n.* Disputation; controversial writings.

Pole-star, pōl'stär, *n.* A star situated close to the North Pole; a lode-star.

Police, pō·lēs', *n.* The internal government of a community; a body of civil officers for enforcing order, cleanliness, etc.—*vt.* (policing, policed). To guard or regulate by police.

Policy, po'li·si, *n.* The governing a city, state, or nation; line of conduct with respect to foreign or internal affairs; dexterity of management; pleasure-grounds around a mansion; contract of insurance.

Poliomyelitis, pol'i·ō·mī·el·it''is, *n.* Inflammation of the grey matter of the spinal cord; infantile paralysis.

Polish, po'lish, *vt.* To make smooth and glossy; to refine.—*vi.* To become smooth or glossy.—*n.* Gloss; elegance of manners.

Polite, pō·līt', *a.* Polished in manners; refined; urbane; elegant; well-bred.

Politic, po'li·tik, *a.* Showing policy; adapted to the public prosperity; sagacious; subtle; well devised.—**Body politic,** the citizens of a state.

Political, pō·lit'ik·al, *a.* Belonging or pertaining to a nation or state; public; derived from connection with government; politic; treating of politics.

Politician, po·li·ti'shan, *n.* One versed in or occupying himself with politics.

Politics, po'li·tiks, *n.* The science of government political affairs, or the contests of parties for power.

Polity, po'li·ti, *n.* The form or system of civil government; method of government.

Polka, pōl'ka, *n.* A dance of Bohemian origin; the air played to the dance.

Poll, pōl, *n.* The head or the back part of the head; register of persons; the voting of electors an election.—*vt.* To lop or clip; to enrol or register; to receive or give, as votes.

Polled, pōld, *p.a.* Lopped, cropped, or clipped having no horns or antlers.

Pollen, pol'en, *n.* The fecundating dust or male element of flowers.

Pollinate, pol'i·nāt, *vt.* To pollenize.

Pollute, pol·lūt', *vt.* (polluting, polluted). To defile to profane; to taint morally; to debauch.

Pollution, pol·ū'shon, *n.* Act of polluting; defilement; uncleanness.

Polo, pō'lō, *n.* A game at ball resembling hockey played on horseback.

Polyandry, po·li·an'dri, *n.* The practice of having more husbands than one at the same time.

Polygamy, po·lig'a·mi, *n.* The practice of having more wives or husbands than one at the same time.

Polyglot, po'li·glot, *a.* Many-tongued; containing speaking, or knowing several languages.—*n.* A book (as a Bible) printed in several languages in parallel columns.

Polygon, po'li·gon, *n.* A plane figure of many angles and sides.

Polygyny, po·lij'i·ni, *n.* The practice of having more wives than one at the same time.

Polyhedron, po·li·hē'dron, *n.* A body or solid contained by many sides or planes.

Polysyllabic, po'li·sil·lab''ik, *a.* Consisting of many syllables.

Polysyllable, po·li·sil'la·bl, *n.* A word of more syllables than three.

Polysynthesis, po·li·sin'the·sis, *n.* A compounding of several elements.

Polytechnic, po·li·tek'nik, *a.* Comprehending many arts; designating a school teaching many branches of art or science.—*n.* A school of instruction in arts.

Polytheism, po'li·thē·izm, *n.* The doctrine of a plurality of gods.

Pomade, pō·'mäd', *n.* Perfumed ointment; pomatum.

Pomander, pom'an·dẽr, *n.* A perfume ball.

Pomegranate, pŏm'gran·āt, *n.* A fruit of the size of an orange, containing numerous seeds; the tree producing the fruit.

Pommel, pum'el, *n.* A knob or ball; the knob on the hilt of a sword; the protuberant part of a saddle-bow.—*vt.* (pommelling, pommelled). To beat; to belabor.

Pomp, pomp, *n.* A showy procession; display pageantry; splendor; parade.

Pomposity, pom·pos'i·ti, *n.* Ostentation; vainglorious show.

Pompous, pomp'us, *a.* Displaying pomp; showy ostentatious; high-flown.

Pond, pond, *n.* A body of water less than a lake artificial or natural.

Ponder, pon'dẽr, *vt.* To weigh in the mind; to consider.—*vi.* To deliberate.

Ponderous, pon'dẽr·us, *a.* Heavy; weighty; massive.

Pontiff, pon'tif, *n.* A high-priest; applied particularly to the pope.

Pontifical, pon·tif'ik·al, *a.* Belonging to a high priest or to the pope.—*n.* A book containing rites performable by a bishop; *pl.* the dress of a priest or bishop.

Pontoon, pon·tön, *n.* A kind of boat for supporting temporary bridges; a water-tight structure to assist in raising submerged vessels.

Pony, pō'ni, *n.* A small horse.

Poodle, pö'dl, *n.* A small dog with long silky curling hair.

Pool, pöl, *n.* A small pond; a puddle; a hole in the course of a stream; the stakes at cards, etc.; a variety of play at billiards.

Poop, pöp, *vt.* The stern of a ship; the highest and aftmost deck of a ship.

Poor, pör, *a.* Needy; indigent; destitute of value or merit; infertile; mean; paltry; lean; weak; impotent; unhappy; wretched.

Pop, pop, *n.* A small, smart sound.—*vi.* (popping, popped). To make a small, smart sound; to enter or issue forth suddenly.—*vt.* To offer with a quick sudden motion; to thrust or push suddenly.—*adv.* Suddenly.

Pop-corn, pop'korn, *n.* Parched maize.

Pope, pöp, *n.* The head of the Roman Catholic church.

Popery, pöp'é-ri, *n.* The doctrins and practices of the Roman Catholic church (a Protestant term).

Poplin, pop'lin, *n.* A fabric made of silk and wool, of many varieties.

Poppy, pop'i, *n.* A plant with showy flowers and yielding opium.

Populace, po'pū-lās, *n.* The common people; the multitude; the mob.

Popular, po'pū-lėr, *a.* Pertaining to the common people; familiar; plain; liked by people in general; prevalent.

Popularize, po'pū-lėr-iz, *vi.* To make popular or suitable to the common mind; to spread among the people.

Populate, po'pū-lāt, *vt.* To people; to furnish with inhabitants.

Population, po-pū-lā'shon, *n.* Act or process of populating; number of people in a country, etc.; the inhabitants.

Porcelain, pör'se-lăn, *n.* The finest species of pottery ware.

Porch, pörch, *n.* A portico; covered approach at the entrance of buildings.

Porcine, pör'sin, *a.* Pertaining to swine; like a swine; hog-like.

Porcupine, por'ku-pin, *n.* A rodent animal, about 2 feet long, with erectile spines.

Pore, pör, *n.* A minute opening in the skin, through which the perspirable matter passes; a small interstice.—*vi.* (poring, pored). To look with steady attention; to read or examine with perseverance.

Pork, pörk, *n.* The flesh of swine, fresh or salted, used for food.

Pornography, por-nog'ra-fi, *n.* Literature in which prostitutes figure.

Porphyry, por'fi-ri, *n.* A reddish Egyptian stone like granite; a hard igneous rock containing crystals of felspar, etc.

Porpoise, por'pus, *n.* A small cetaceous mammal of the Northern Seas.

Porridge, po'rij, *n.* A kind of soup or broth; a dish of oatmeal boiled in water till thickened.

Port, port, *n.* A harbor or haven; a gate; an opening in the side of a ship; a port-hole; the left side of a ship; mien; demeanor.—*vt.* To carry (as a rifle) slanting upwards towards the left; to turn to the left, as the helm.

Portable, pört'a-bl, *a.* That may be carried; not bulky or heavy.

Portage, pört'āj, *n.* Act of carrying; carriage; freight.

Portal, pört'al, *n.* A door or gate; the main entrance of a cathedral, etc.—*a.* Belonging to a vein connected with the liver.

Portend, por-tend', *vt.* To foretoken; to presage; to threaten.

Portent, pör'tent, *n.* That which foretokens; an omen of ill.

Portentous, por-tent'us, *a.* Ominous; foreshowing ill; monstrous; wonderful.

Porter, pör'tér, *n.* A doorkeeper; a carrier; a dark brown malt liquor.

Portfolio, pört-fö'li-ö, *n.* A case for drawings, pa-

pers, etc.; office and functions of a minister of state.

Port-hole, pört'hōl, *n.* The embrasure of a ship of war.

Portico, pör'ti-kō, *n.* A colonnade or covered walk; a porch.

Portion, pör'shon, *n.* A part; a share or allotment; fate; final state.—*vt.* To parcel; to divide.

Portly, pört'li, *a.* Of noble carriage or bearing; stately; rather tall, and inclining to stoutness.

Portrait, pör'trāt, *n.* A picture of a person; a vivid description.

Portray, pör-trā', *vt.* To delineate; to depict; to describe in words.

Portuguese, por'tū-gēz, *a.* Pertaining to Portugal.—*n.* The language of Portugal; the people of Portugal.

Pose, pöz, *n.* Attitude or position; an artistic posture.—*vi.* (posing, posed). To attitudinize; to assume characteristic airs.—*vt.* To cause to assume a certain posture; to state or lay down; to perplex or puzzle.

Position, pö-zi'shon, *n.* State of being placed; place; posture; rank; state; principle laid down; thesis.

Positive, poz'it-iv, *a.* Definitely laid down; explicit; absolute; actual; confident, dogmatic, affirmative; noting the simple state of an adjective; applied to the philosophical system of Auguste Comte, which limits itself to human experience; applied to electricity produced by rubbing a vitreous substance.—*n.* That which is positive; the positive degree.

Possess, po-zes', *vt.* To have and hold; to own; to affect by some power or influence; to pervade; to put in possession; to furnish or fill.

Possession, po-ze'shon, *n.* Act or state of possessing; ownership; occupancy; land, estate, or goods owned.

Possessive, po-zes'iv, *a.* Pertaining to possession; expressing or denoting possession.—*n.* The possessive case; a pronoun or other word denoting possession.

Possible, pos'i-bl, *a.* That may be or exist; that may be done; practicable; not impossible, though improbable.

Post, post, *n.* A piece of timber, etc., set upright; a place assigned; a military or other station; office or employment; a carrier of letters, messages, etc.; a system for the public conveyance of letters, etc.; a post-office; a size of paper, about 18 or 19 inches by 15.—*vt.* To travel with post-horses; to hasten on.—*vt* To place; to place in the post-office; to transfer (accounts or items) to the ledger; to make master of full details; to fix up in some public place.—*a.* Used in travelling quickly.—*adv.* Travelling as a post; swiftly.

Postage, post'āj, *n.* The charge for conveying letters or other articles by post.

Post-date, pöst-dāt', *vt.* To inscribe with a later date than the real one.

Poster, pöst'ér, *n.* One who posts; a courier; a large printed bill for advertising.

Posterior, pos-tė'ri-or, *a.* Later or subsequent; hinder.—*n.* A hinder part; *pl.* the hinder parts of an animal.

Posterity, pos-te'ri-ti, *n.* Descendants; succeeding generations.

Post-haste, pöst-hāst', *n.* Haste or speed.—*adv.* With speed or expedition.

Posthumous, post'ū-mus, *a.* Born after the death of the father; published after the death of the author; existing after one's decease.

Postman, pöst'man, *n.* A post or courier; a letter-carrier.

Postmeridian, pöst-me-rid'i-an, *a.* After the meridian; being in the afternoon.

Post-mortem, pöst-mor'tem, *a.* After death.

Post-office, pöst'of-is, *n.* An office where letters are received for transmission; a government department that has the duty of conveying letters, etc.

Postpone, pöst-pön, *vt.* (postponing, postponed).

To put off to a later time; to set below something else in value.

Post-prandial, pŏst-pran'di-al, *a.* Happening after dinner.

Postscript, pŏst'skript, *n.* A paragraph added to a letter after it is signed; something added on to a book, etc., by way of supplement.

Postulate, pos'tū-lāt, *n.* Something assumed for the purpose of future reasoning; enunciation of a self-evident problem.—*vt.* To assume or take for granted.

Posture, pos'tūr, *n.* Attitude; relative position of parts; situation; condition.

Pot, pot, *n.* A metallic or earthenware vessel more deep than broad; the quantity contained in a pot; a sort of paper of small-sized sheets.—*vt.* (potting, potted). To put in a pot; to preserve in pots; to plant in a pot of earth.

Potable, pō'ta-bl, *a.* Drinkable.

Potash, pot'ash, *n.* Vegetable alkali in an impure state, procured from the ashes of plants.

Potassium, pō-tas'si-um, *n.* The metallic basis of potash, a soft, white, light metal.

Potato, pō-tā'tō, *n.*; pl. **-oes.** A well-known plant and its esculent tuber.

Pot-boiler, pot'boil-ėr, *n.* A work of art executed merely to earn money.

Poteen, po-tēn', *n.* Irish whisky, especially illicitly distilled whisky.

Potent, pō'tent, *a.* Mighty; strong; powerful; efficacious.

Potentate, pō'ten-tāt, *n.* One who possesses great power or sway; a monarch.

Potential, pō-ten'shal, *a.* Possible; latent; that may be manifested.

Potentiality, pō-ten'shi-al''i-ti, *n.* Quality of being potential; possibility; not actuality.

Potion, pō'shon, *n.* A draught; a liquid medicine; a dose to be drunk.

Pot-luck, pot'luk, *n.* What may be for a meal without special preparation.

Pot-pourri, pō-pö-rē, *n.* A mixed dish of meat and vegetables; a medley.

Potsherd, pot'shėrd, *n.* A piece or fragment of an earthenware pot.

Potter, pot'ėr, *n.* One who makes earthenware vessels or crockery.—*vi.* To busy oneself about trifles; to move slowly.

Pottery, pot'e-ri, *n.* The ware made by potters; place where earthen vessels are made.

Pouch, pouch, *n.* A pocket; a small bag.—*vt.* To put into a pouch; to pocket.

Poultice, pōl'tis, *n.* A soft composition applied to sores.—*vt.* (poulticing, poulticed). To apply a poultice to.

Poultry, pōl'tri, *n.* Domestic fowls.

Pounce, pouns, *n.* A fine powder to prevent ink from spreading on paper; the claw or talon of a bird.—*vt.* (pouncing, pounced). To sprinkle or rub with pounce.—*vi.* To fall on and seize with the pounces or talons; to fall on suddenly.

Pound, pound, *n.* A standard weight of 12 ounces troy or 16 ounces avoirdupois; a money of account; an inclosure for cattle.—*vt.* To confine in a public pound; to beat; to pulverize.

Pour, pōr, *vt.* To flow or issue forth in a stream.—*vt.* To let flow out or in; to emit; to throw in profusion.

Pout, pout, *vi.* To thrust out the lips; to look sullen; to be prominent.—*n.* Protrusion of the lips.

Poverty, po'vėr-ti, *n.* State of being poor; indigence; want; defect; insufficiency.

Powder, pou'dėr, *n.* A dry substance of minute particles; dust; gunpowder.—*vt.* To reduce to fine particles; to sprinkle with powder; to corn, as meat.—*vi.* To fall to dust; to use powder for the hair or face.

Power, pou'ėr, *n.* Ability to act or do; strength; influence; talent; command; authority; one who exercises authority; a state or government; warrant; a mechanical advantage or effect; product of the multiplication of a number by itself.

Practicable, prak'ti-ka-bl, *a.* That may be done or

effected; feasible; passable.

Practical, prak'ti-kal, *a.* Pertaining to practice, action, or use; not merely theoretical; skilled in actual work.

Practice, prak'tis, *n.* A doing or effecting; custom; habit; actual performance; exercise of any profession; medical treatment; training; drill; dexterity.

Practice, prak'tis, *vt.* (practicing, practiced). To put in practice; to do or perform frequently or habitually; to exercise, as any profession; to commit; to teach by practice.—*vi.* To perform certain acts frequently for instruction or amusement; to exercise some profession.

Practitioner, prak-ti'shon-ėr, *n.* One engaged in some profession, particularly law or medicine.

Pragmatic, Pragmatical, prag-mat'ik, prag-mat'ik-al, *a.* Meddling; impertinently busy or officious.

Prairie, prā'ri, *n.* An extensive tract of grassy land, generally destitute of trees.

Praise, prāz, *n.* Approbation or admiration expressed; eulogy; honor; gratitude or homage to God, often in song; the object, ground, or reason of praise.—*vt.* (praising, praised). To extol; to commend; to honor.

Prance, prans, *vt.* (prancing, pranced). To spring, leap, or caper, as a horse; to strut about ostentatiously.

Prank, prangk, *vt.* To adorn in a showy manner; to dress up.—*vi.* To have a showy appearance.—*n.* A merry trick; a caper.

Prate, prāt, *vi.* (prating, prated). To babble, chatter, tattle.—*vt.* To utter foolishly.—*n.* Trifling talk; unmeaning loquacity.

Prattle, prat'l, *vi.* (prattling, prattled). To talk much and idly, like a child; to prate.—*n.* Trifling or puerile talk.

Pray, prā, *vi.* and *t.* To beg, supplicate, or implore; to address God.

Prayer, prā'ėr, *n.* One who prays; the act of praying; a petition; a solemn petition to God; a formula of worship, public or private; that part of a written petition whihc specifies the thing desired to be granted.

Preach, prēch, *vi.* To deliver a sermon; to give earnest advice.—*vt.* To proclaim; to publish in religious discourses; to deliver in public, as a discourse.

Preamble, prē-am'bl or prē', *n.* An introduction; introductory part of a statute.

Precarious, prē-kā'ri-us, *a.* Depending on the will of another; uncertain; insecure.

Precaution, prē-ka'shon, *n.* Previous care; caution to prevent evil or secure good.—*vt.* To caution beforehand.

Precede, prē-sēd', *vt.* (preceding, preceded). To go before in time, rank, or importance; to preface.

Precedence, Precedency, prē-sed'ens, prē-sēd'en-si, *n.* Act or state of preceding; priority; order according to rank; superior importance.

Precedent, prē-sēd'ent, *a.* Preceding; going before in time; anterior.

Precedent, prē' or prē'sē-dent, *n.* Something done or said, serving as an example or rule.

Precept, prē'sept, *n.* Anything enjoined as an authoritative rule of action; injunction; doctrine; maxim.

Precession, prē-se'shon, *n.* Act of going before; advance.

Precinct, prē'singt, *n.* A bounding line; a part near a border; a minor territorial division.

Precious, pre'shus, *a.* Of great worth or value; costly; cherished; affected.

Precipice, pre'si-pis, *n.* A headlong declivity; a steep or overhanging cliff.

Precipitance, Precipitancy, prē-si'pi-tans, prē-si'pi-tan-si, *n.* Headlong hurry; rash or excessive haste.

Precipitant, prē-si'pi-tant, *a.* Falling or rushing headlong; precipitate.

Precipitate, prē'si'pi-tāt, *vt.* and *i.* To throw or

hurl headlong; to hasten excessively; to cause to sink or to fall to the bottom of a vessel, as a substance in solution.—*a.* Headlong; overhasty.—*n.* A substance deposited from a liquid in which it has been dissolved.

Precipitous, prē-si'pi-tus, *a.* Very steep; headlong in descent.

Précis, prā-sē', *n.* A concise or abridged statement; a summary; an abstract.

Precise, prē-sis', *a.* Sharply or exactly defined; exact; strictly accurate or correct; particular; formal; punctilious.

Preclude, prē-klōd', *vt.* (precluding, precluded). To shut out; to hinder; to render inoperative by anticipative action.

Precocious, prē-kō'shus, *a.* Ripe before the natural time; acting like an adult though not grown up.

Precognition, prē-kog-ni'shon, *n.* Previous knowledge; preliminary examination, as of a witness befor a trial (*Scots law*).

Preconceive, prē-kon-sēv', *vt.* To form a conception or opinion of beforehand.

Precursor, prē-ker'ser, *n.* A forerunner; a harbinger.

Predaceous, prē-dā'shus, *a.* Living by prey, given to prey on other animals.

Predatory, pred'a-to-ri, *a.* Plundering; pillaging; practicing rapine.

Predecessor, prē-dē-ses'er, *n.* One who has preceded another in any state, office, etc.

Predestination, prē-des'ti-nā''shon, *n.* The act of foredaining events; the doctrine that God has from eternity determined whatever comes to pass, and has preordained men to everlasting happiness or misery.

Predestine, prē-des'tin, *vt.* To decree beforehand; to foreordain.

Predetermination, prē-dē-ter'mi-nā''shon, *n.* Purpose formed beforehand.

Predicable, pre'di-ka-bl, *a.* That may be attributed to something.—*n.* Anythng that may be affirmed of another.

Predicament, prē-dik'a-ment, *n.* Class or kind; condition; dangerous or trying state.

Predicate, pre'di-kāt, *vt.* and *i.* To affirm one thing of another; to assert.—*n.* In *logic,* that which is affirmed or denied of the subject; in *grammar,* the word or words which express what is affirmed or denied of the subject.

Predict, prē-dikt', *vt.* To foretell; to prophesy.

Predictive, prē-dik'tiv, *a.* Foretelling.

Predilection, prē-di-lek'shon, *n.* A previous liking or preference; a prepossession of mind in favor of a person or thing.

Predispose, prē-dis-pōz', *vt.* To dispose before hand; to fit or adapt previously.

Predominance, Predominancy, prē-dom'i-nans, prē-dom'i-nan-si, *n.* Prevalence over others; superiority; ascendency.

Predominant, prē-dom'i-nant, *a.* Predominating; prevalent; ruling; controlling.

Predominate, prē-dom'i-nāt, *vi.* and *t.* To have surpassing power or authority; to rule.

Pre-eminent, prē-em'i-nent, *a.* Eminent above others; surpassing or distinguished.

Pre-emption, prē-em'shon, *n.* The act or right of purchasing before others.

Preen, prēn, *vt.* To trim with the beak: said of birds dressing their feathers.

Pre-exist, prē-egz-ist', *vi.* To exist beforehand, or before something else.

Prefabricate, prē-fab'ri-kāt, *vt.* To manufacture separately parts, of a building, etc., designed to be easily fitted together afterwards.

Preface, pre'fās, *n.* Introduction to a discourse or book, etc.—*vt.* (prefacing, prefaced). To introduce by preliminary remarks.

Prefect, prē'fekt, *n.* One placed over others; a governor, chief magistrate; a senior pupil entrusted with the maintenance of discipline.

Prefer, prē-fer', *vt.* (preferring, preferred). To bring or lay before; to present, as a petition,

etc.; to exalt; to set higher in estimation; to choose rather.

Preference, pre'fer-ens, *n.* Act of preferring; state of being preferred; choice.

Preferential, pre-fer-en'shal, *a.* Implying preference.

Prefiguration, prē-fig'ūr-ā''shon, *n.* Antecedent representation by similitude.

Prefigure, prē-fig'ūr, *vt.* To exhibit by antecedent representation; to foreshow.

Prefix, prē-fiks', *vt.* To put before or at the beginning of something.—*n.* prē'fiks, A letter, syllable, or word added at the beginning of a word.

Pregnant, preg'nant, *a.* Being with young; full of meaning or consequence.

Prehensible, prē-hen'si-bl, *a.* That may be seized.

Prehensile, prē-hen'sīl, *a.* Fitted for seizing or laying hold; grasping.

Prehistoric, prē-his-tor'ik, *a.* Relating to a time anterior to written records.

Prejudge, prē-juj', *vt.* To judge beforehand; to condemn unheard.

Prejudice, pre'jū-dis, *n.* An unwarranted bias; prepossession; detriment; injury.—*vt.* To bias the mind of; to do harm to.

Preliminary, prē-lim'in-a-ri, *a.* Introductory; preparatory; prefactory.—*n.* Something introductory; preface; prelude.

Prelude, prel'ūd or prē-lūd', *vt.* (preluding, preluded). To introduce; to preface.—*vi.* To form a prelude.—*n.* prel'ūd or prē'lūd. Something preparatory; a musical introduction.

Premature, pre'ma-tūr, *a.* Happening, performed, etc., too early; untimely.

Premeditate, prē-me'di-tāt, *vt.* and *i.* To meditate upon beforehand; to contrive previously; to deliberate.

Premier, pre'mi-er, *a.* First; chief.—*n.* The first minister of state; prime minister.

Premise, prē-miz', *vt.* (premising, premised). To put forward by way of preface; to lay down, as antecedent to another statement.—*vi.* To make an introductory statement.

Premium, prē'mi-um, *n.* A reward or prize; a bonus; a bounty; sum paid for insurance; increase in value.

Premonition, prē-mō-ni'shon, *n.* Previous warning, notice, or information.

Preoccupation, prē-ok'kū-pā''shon, *n.* Act of preoccupying; prior possession; state of being preoccupied.

Preoccupy, prē-ok'kū-pī, *vt.* To occupy before another; to engross before another; to engross beforehand.

Preordain, prē-or-dān', *vt.* To appoint before hand; to foreordain.

Preparation, pre-pa-rā'shon, *n.* Act or operation of preparing; that which is prepared; state of being prepared.

Prepare, prē-pār', *vt.* and *i.* (preparing, prepared). To make ready; to adjust; to provide; to procure as suitable.

Prepay, prē-pā', *vt.* To pay in advance.

Prepense, prē-pens', *a.* Premeditated.

Preponderant, prē-pon'der-ant, *a.* Superior in power, influence, or the like.

Preponderate, prē-pon'der-āt, *vi.* To outweigh; to exceed in influence or power.

Preposition, pre-pō-zi'shon, *n.* A word governing a noun, pronoun, or clause.

Prepossess, prē-po-zes', *vt.* To take possession of beforehand; to preoccupy; to prejudice.

Prepossessing, prē-po-zes'ing, *p.a.* Creating a favorable impression; attractive.

Preposterous, prē-pos'ter-us, *a.* Absurd; irrational; monstrous; utterly ridiculous.

Prerogative, prē-ro'ga-tiv, *n.* A prior claim or title; an exclusive privilege; an official and hereditary right.

Presage, prē'sāj or pres'āj, *n.* a presentiment; a prognostic, omen, or sign.—*vt.* and *i.* prē-sāj', (presaging, presaged). To betoken; to forebode;

to predict.

Presbyterian, pres-bi-tē'ri-an, *a.* Pertaining to presbyters; pertaining to ecclesiastical government by presbyteries.—*n.* A member of one of the Christian churches who vest church governments in presbyteries.

Presbytery, pres'bi-te-ri, *n.* A body of presbyters; a church court consisting of the presbyterian pastors within a district, and one elder from each church.

Prescience, prē'shi-ens, *n.* Foreknowledge.

Prescind, prē-sind', *vt.* To consider apart from other ideas or notions.

Prescribe, prē-skrīb', *vt.* (prescribing, prescribed). To lay down authoritatively for direction; to direct to be used as a remedy.—*vi.* To give directions; to give medical directions; to become of no validity through lapse of time.

Prescription, prē-skrip'shon, *n.* Act of prescribing; that which is prescribed; a claim or title based on long use; the loss of a legal right by lapse of time.

Prescriptive, prē-skrip'tiv, *a.* Consisting in or acquired by long use.

Presence, pre'zens, *n.* State of being present; existence in a certain place; company; sight; port; mien; the person of a great personage; an appearance or apparition; readiness.

Present, pre'zent, *a.* Being at hand, in view, or in a certain place; now existing; ready at hand; quick in emergency.—*n.* Present time; *pl.* term used in a legal document for the document itself.

Present, prē-zent', *vt.* To introduce to or bring before a superior; to show; to give or bestow; to nominate to an ecclesiastical benefice; to lay before a public body for consideration; to point or aim, as a weapon.—*n.* pre'zent. A donation; a gift.

Preservation, pre-zér-vā'shon, *n.* Act of preserving; state of being preserved; safety.

Preservative, prē-zérv'at-iv, *a.* Tending to preserve.—*n.* That which preserves; a preventive of injury or decay.

Preserve, prē-zérv', *vt.* (preserving, preserved). To save from injury; to keep in a sound state; to maintain; to restrict the hunting of, as game.— *n.* Something that is preserved, as fruit, vegetables, etc.; ground set apart for animals intended for sport or food.

Preside, prē-zid', *vi.* (presiding, presided). To exercise authority or superintendence; to have the post of chairman.

President, pre'zi-dent, *n.* One who presides; the head of a province or state; the highest officer of state in a republic.

Press, pres, *vt.* To bear or weigh heavily upon; to squeeze; to urge; to enforce; to emphasize; to solicit earnestly; to force into service.—*vi.* To bear heavily or with force; to crowd; to push with force.—*n.* A pressing; a crowd; an instrument for squeezing or crushing; a machine for printing; the art or business of printing; periodical literature; an upright cupboard; urgency.

Pressman, pres'man, *n.* One who attends to a printing press; a journalist.

Pressure, pre'shůr, *n.* The act of pressing; the force of one body acting on another; moral force; distress or difficulty; urgency.

Prestidigitation, pres'ti-di'ji-tā''shon, *n.* Skill in legerdemain; juggling.

Prestige, pres'tij or pres-tēzh', *n.* Influence based on high character or conduct.

Presumable, prē-zūm'a-bl, *a.* That may be presumed.

Presume, prē-zūm', *vt.* (presuming, presumed). To take for granted; to take the liberty; to make bold.—*vi.* To infer; to act in a forward way.

Presumptuous, prē-zum'tū-us, *a.* Taking undue liberties; arrogant; overweening.

Presuppose, prē-sup-pōz', *vt.* To suppose or imply as previous; to take for granted.

Pretend, prē-tend', *vt.* To feign; to simulate; to assume or profess to feel; use as a pretest.—*vi.* To assume a false character; to sham; to put in a claim.

Pretense, prē-tens', *n.* Act of pretending; simulation; feint; pretext.

Pretension, prē-ten'shon, *n.* Claim true or false; an assumed right.

Preternatural, prē-tėr-na'tūr-al, *a.* Beyond what is natural; abnormal; anomalous.

Pretext, prē'tekst or prē-tekst', *n.* An ostensible reason or motive; a pretense.

Pretty, prit'i, *a.* Having diminutive beauty; of a pleasing form without dignity; comely; neatly arranged; affectedly nice; foppish.—*adv.* Moderately.

Prevail, prē-vāl', *vi.* To gain the victory or superiority; to be in force; to succeed; to gain over by persuasion.

Prevalent, pre'va-lent, *a.* Prevailing; predominant; extensively existing.

Prevaricate, prē-va'ri-kāt, *vi.* To act or speak evasively; to shuffle; to quibble.

Prevarication, prē-va'ri-kā''shon, *n.* Act of prevaricating; a shuffling or quibbling; misrepresentation by giving evasive evidence.

Prevent, prē-vent', *vt.* To stop or intercept; to impede; to thwart.

Prevention, prē-ven'shon, *n.* The act of preventing; a hindering by previous action; measure of precaution.

Preventive, prē-vent'iv, *a.* Tending to prevent.—*n.* That which prevents; an antidote previously taken. Also *Preventitive.*

Previous, prē'vi-us, *a.* Antecedent; prior.

Prevision, prē-vi'zhon, *n.* Foresight.

Prey, prā, Property taken from an enemy; spoil; booty; a victim.—*vi.* To take prey or booty; to get food by rapine; to cause to pine away; with *on.*

Price, pris, *n.* The value which a seller sets on his goods; cost; value; worthy.—*vt.* (pricing, priced). To set a price on; to ask the price of.

Priceless, pris'les, *a.* Too valuable to admit of a price; invaluable; inestimable.

Prick, prik, *n.* A slender pointed thing that can pierce; a thorn; a puncture by a prick; a sting; tormenting thought.—*vt.* To pierce with a prick; to erect, as ears; to spur; to sting with remorse; to trace by puncturing.—*vi.* To spur on; to ride rapidly; to feel a prickly sensation.

Prickle, prik'l, *n.* A small sharp-pointed shoot; a thorn; a small spine.—*vt.* To prick; to cause a prickly feeling in.

Pride, prid, *n.* State or quality of being proud; inordinate self-esteem; a cause of pride; glory or delight; highest pitch; splendid show.—*vt.* To indulge pride; to value (oneself).

Priest, prēst, *n.* A man who officiates in sacred offices; a clergyman above a deacon and below a bishop.

Priesthood, prēt'hud, *n.* The office or character of a priest; the order of priests.

Prig, prig, *n.* A conceited, narrow-minded fellow; one who affects superiority; a thief.—*vt.* (prigging, prigged). To steal.

Prim, prim, *a.* Formal; affectedly nice; demure.— *vt.* (primming, primmed). To deck with nicety.

Primacy, pri'ma-si, *n.* Position of chief rank; the office or dignity of primate or archbishop.

Prima donna, prē'ma don'na. The first or chief female singer in the opera.

Prima facie, pri'ma fā'shi-ē. At first view or appearance.

Primal, pri'mal, *a.* Primary; primitive.

Primary, pri'ma-ri, *a.* First; chief; first in time; original; elementary; radical.—*n.* That which stands first or highest in importance; a large feather of a bird's wing.

Primate, pri'māt, *n.* A chief ecclesiastic; an archbishop.

Prime, prim, *a.* Foremost; first; original; first in rank, excellence, or importance; not divisible by any smaller number.—*n.* The earliest stage; full health; strength; or beauty; the best part.— *vt.* (priming, primed). To make ready for action; to supply with powder for communicating fire to a charge; to instruct or prepare beforehand; to lay on the first color in painting.

Primeval, prim-ē'val, *a.* Being of the earliest age or time; original; primitive.

Priming, prīm'ing, *n.* The powder used to ignite a charge; a first layer of paint; water carried over with the steam into the cylinder.

Primitive, prim'it-iv, *a.* Being the first or earliest of its kind; original; antiquated; primary; radical; not derived.—*n.* That which is original; an original word.

Primordial, prim-or'di-al, *a.* First of all; first in order; original; earliest formed.—*n.* First principle or element.

Primrose, prim'rōz, *n.* An early flowering plant.—*a.* Resembling a yellow primrose in color; abounding with primroses.

Prince, prins, *n.* A chief ruler; the son of a king or emperor; the chief of any body of men.

Princess, prin'ses, *n.* A female of the rank of a prince; the consort of a prince.

Principal, prin'si-pal, *a.* First; chief; most important or considerable.—*n.* A chief or head; the president, governor, or chief in authority; one primarily engaged; a capital sum lent on interest.

Principality, prin-si-pal'i-ti, *n.* Sovereignty; territory of a prince; a prince.

Principally, prin'si-pal-li, *adv.* Chiefly; mainly.

Principle, prin'si-pl, *n.* Cause or origin; a general truth; a fundamental law; a rule of action; uprightness; an element.

Print, print, *vt.* To mark by pressure; to stamp; to form or copy by pressure; as from types, etc.— *vi.* To use or practice typography; to publish.— *n.* A mark made by pressure; an engraving, etc.; state of being printed; a newspaper; printed calico.

Printer, print'ėr, *n.* One who prints; more especially, the printer of letterpress.

Printing, print'ing, *n.* The act, art, or practice of impressing letters or figures on paper, cloth, etc.; typography.

Printing-press, print'ing-pres, *n.* A press for the printing of books, etc.

Prior, prī'or, *a.* Preceding; earlier.—*adv.* Previously.—*n.* A monk next in dignity to an abbot.

Priority, prī-or'i-ti, *n.* State of being prior; pre-eminence; preference.

Prism, prizm, *n.* A solid whose ends are any similar, equal, and parallel plane figures, and whose sides are parallelograms.

Prison, pri'zn, *n.* A place of confinement; a jail.— *vt.* To imprison.

Pristine, pris'tin, *a.* Original; first; earliest.

Private, pri'vat, *a.* Separate from others; solitary; personal; secret; not having a public or official character.—**In private,** secretly.—*n.* A common soldier.

Privation, prī-vā'shon, *n.* Act of depriving; state of being deprived; destitution; want; hardship.

Privative, pri'va-tiv, *a.* Causing deprivation.—*n.* A prefix to a word which gives it a contrary sense.

Privet, priv'et, *n.* A shrub much used for ornamental hedges.

Privilege, pri'vi-lej, *n.* A separate and personal advantage; a prerogative, immunity, or exemption.—*vt.* To grant some right or exemption to; to authorize.

Privy, pri'vi, *a.* Private; assigned to private uses; secret; privately knowing (with *to*).—*n.* A water closet or necessary house.

Prize, priz, *n.* That which is seized; that which is deemed a valuable acquisition; a reward.—*vt.* (prizing, prized). To value highly.

Prize-fight, priz'fit, *n.* A boxing-match for a prize.

Probability, pro-ba-bil'i-ti, *n.* Likelihood; appearance of truth.

Probate, prō'bāt, *n.* The proceeding by which a person's will is established and registered; official proof of a will.

Probation, prō-bā'shon, *n.* Act of proving; proof, trial; period of trial; novitiate.

Probationary, prō-bā'shon-a-ri, *a.* Serving for probation or trial.

Probative, Probatory, prō'bat-iv, prō-ba-to-ri, *a.* Serving for trial or proof.

Probe, prōb, *n.* A surgeon's instrument for examining a wound, ulcer, or cavity.—*vt.* (probing, probed). To apply a probe to; to examine thoroughly.

Probity, prō'bi-ti, *n.* Uprightness; honesty; rectitude; integrity.

Problem, prob'lem, *n.* A question proposed for solution; a knotty point to be cleared up.

Proboscis, prō-bos'is, *n.*; pl. **Proboscides,** prō-bos'i-dēz. The snout or trunk of an elephant, etc.; the sucking-tube of insects.

Procedure, prō-sēd'ūr, *n.* Act or manner of proceeding; conduct; management.

Proceed, prō-sēd,' *vi.* To go forth or forward; to issue, arise, emanate; to prosecute any design; to carry on a legal action; to take a university degree.

Proceeds, prō'sēdz, *n.pl.* Money brought in by some piece of business.

Process, prō'ses, *n.* A proceeding or moving forward; gradual progress; course; method of manipulation; lapse; course of legal proceedings; a projecting portion.

Procession, prō-se'shon, *n.* A marching forward; a train of persons moving with ceremonious solemnity.

Proclaim, prō-klam', *vt.* To announce publicly; to promulgate; to publish.

Proclamation, pro-kla-mā'shon, *n.* Act of claiming; an official public announcement.

Proclivity, prō-kliv'i-ti, *n.* Inclination; propensity; tendency.

Procrastinate, prō-kras'ti-nāt, *vt.* and *i.* To put off from day to day; to postpone.

Procreate, prō'krē-āt, *vt.* To beget; to generate; to engender.

Procumbent, prō-kum'bent, *a.* Lying down; prone; trailing on the ground.

Procurable, prō-kūr'a-bl, *a.* Obtainable.

Procuration, pro-kūr-ā'shon, *n.* Service rendered as procurator; agency.

Procurator, pro-kūr'āt-or, *n.* The manager of another's affairs as his representative; legal agent or prosecutor.

Procure, prō-kūr', *vt.* (procuring, procured). To obtain; to cause, effect, contrive.—*vi.* To pimp.

Procurer, prō-kūr'ėr, *n.* A pimp.

Prod, prod, *n.* A pointed instrument; as a goad; a stab.—*vt.* (prodding, prodded). To prick with a pointed instrument; to goad.

Prodigal, prod'i-gal, *a.* Lavish; wasteful.—*n.* A waster; a spendthrift.

Prodigality, prod-i-gal'i-ti, *n.* Extravagance in expenditure; profusion; waste.

Prodigious, prō-dij'us, *a.* Portentous; extraordinary; huge; enormous.

Prodigy, prod'i-ji, *n.* A portent; a wonder or miracle; a monster.

Produce, prō-dūs'v, *vt.* (producing, produced). To bring forward; to exhibit; to bring forth, bear, yield; to supply; to cause; to extend, as a line.— *n.* prō'dūs, What is produced; outcome; yield; agricultural products.

Product, pro'dukt, *n.* That which is produced; result; effect; number resulting from multiplication.

Production, prō-duk'shon, *n.* Act or process of producing; product; performance; literary composition.

Productive, prō-duk'tiv, *a.* Having the power of producing; fertile; causing to exist; producing commodities of value.

Profane, prō-fān', a. Not sacred; secular; irreverent; blasphemous; impure.—vt. (profaning, profaned). To treat with irreverence; to desecrate.

Profanity, prō-fan'i-ti, n. Quality of being profane; profane language or conduct.

Profess, prō-fes', vt. To avow; to ackowledge; to declare belief in; to pretend; to declare oneself versed in.—vi. To declare openly.

Profession, prō-fe'shon, n. Act of professing; declaration; vocation; such as medicine, law; etc.; the body of persons engaged in such calling.

Professional, prō-fe'shon-al, a. Pertaining to a profession.—n. A member of any profession; one who makes a living by arts, sports, etc., in which amateurs engage.

Professor, prō-fes'or, n. One who professes; a teacher of the highest rank in a university, etc.

Proffer, prof'èr, vt. (proffering, proffered). To offer for acceptance.—n. An offer made.

Proficiency, Proficience, prō-fi'shen-si, prō-fe'shens, n. State of being proficient; skill and knowledge acquired.

Proficient, prō-fi'shent, a. Fully versed; competent.—n. An adept or expert.

Profile, prō'fil, n. An outline; an outline of the human face seen sideways; the side face.—vt. To draw in profile.

Profit, pro'fit', n. Any advantage, benefit, or gain; pecuniary gain.—vt. To benefit; to advance.—vi. To derive profit; to improve; to be made better or wiser.

Profitable, pro'fit-a-bl, a. Bringing profit or gain; lucrative; beneficial; useful.

Profligate, pro'fli-gāt, a. Abandoned to vice; utterly dissolute.—n. A depraved man.

Profound, prō-found', a. Deep; deep in skill or knowledge; far-reaching; bending low; humble.—n. The ocean, the abyss.

Profuse, prō-fūs', a. Lavish; exuberant.

Profusion, prō-fū'zhon, n. State or quality of being profuse; exuberant plenty.

Progenitor, prō-jen'i-tor, n. A forefather.

Progeny, pro'je-ni, n. Offspring; descendants.

Prognathic, Prognathous, prog-nath'ik, prog-nā'thus, a. Having projecting jaws.

Prognosis, prog-nō'sis, n. A forecast of the course of a disease.

Prognosticate, prog-nos'tik-āt, vt. To foretell; to predict; to foreshow.—vi. To judge or pronounce from prognostics.

Program, prō'gram, n. A plan of proceedings; statement of the order of proceedings in any entertainment.

Progress, pro'gres, n. A going forward; a journey of state; a circuit; advance; development.—vi. prō-gres'. To advance; to improve.

Progressive, prō-gres'iv, a. Making steady progress; advancing; advocating progress.

Prohibit, prō-hib'it, vt. To forbid; to interdict by authority; to prevent.

Prohibition, prō-hi-bi'shon, n. Act of prohibiting; an interdict; inhibition; the forbidding by law of the manufacture, importation, or sale of alcoholic liquors for ordinary use.

Project, prō-jekt', vt. To throw out or forth; to scheme; to delineate.—vi. To shoot forward; to jut.—n. pro'jekt. A scheme, plan.

Projectile, prō-jek'til, a. Throwing forward.—n. A body impelled forward; a missile from a gun.

Projection, prō-jek'shon, n. Act of projecting; a prominence; representation of something by lines, etc., drawn on a surface.

Projector, prō-jek'tor, n. One who plans; that which casts something forward.

Prolapse, Prolapsus, prō-laps', prō-lap'sus, n. A falling down of some internal organ from its proper position.

Prolegomenon, prō-le-gom'e-non, n.; pl. **-mena.** A preliminary observation; pl. an introduction.

Prolepsis, prō-lep'sis, n. Something of the nature of an anticipation; a rhetorical figure.

Proletarian, prō-le-tā'ri-an, n. and a. Applied to a member of the poorest class.

Prolific, prō-lif'ik, a. Fruitful; productive.

Prolix, prō'liks, a. Long and wordy; diffuse.

Prologue, prō'log, n. A preface or introduction; address spoken before a dramatic performance.—vt. To preface.

Prolong, prō-long,' vt. To lengthen out; to protract; to postpone.

Prolusion, prō-lū'zhon, n. A prelude; a preliminary trial.

Promenade, pro-me-näd', n. A walk for pleasure; a place set apart for walking.—vi. (promenading, promenaded). To walk for pleasure.

Prominent, pro'mi-nent, a. Jutting out; protuberant; eminent.

Promiscuous, prō-mis'kū-us, a. Confused; indiscriminate; miscellaneous.

Promise, pro'mis, n. A statement binding the person who makes it; ground or basis of expectation; pledge.—vt. (promising, promised). To make a promise of; to afford reason to expect.—vi. To make a promise; to afford expectations.

Promissory, pro'mis-o-ri, a. Containing a promise or binding declaration.

Promontory, pro'mon-to-ri, n. A headland; a cape.

Promote, prō-mōt', vt. (promoting, promoted). To forward or further; to advance; to encourage; to exalt; to form (a company).

Promotion, prō-mō'shon, n. Act of promoting; advancement; encouragement.

Prompt, promt, a. Ready; unhesitating; done without delay.—vt. To incite to action; to tell a speaker words he forgets; to suggest.

Promulgate, prō-mul'gāt, vt. (promulgating, promulgated). To publish; to proclaim.

Prone, prōn, a. Bending forward; lying with the face downward; sloping; apt.

Prong, prong, n. A spike, as of a fork.

Pronominal, prō-nom'in-al, a. Belonging to or of the nature of a pronoun.

Pronoun, prō'noun, n. A word used instead of a noun.

Pronounce, prō-nouns', vt. and i (pronouncing, pronounced). To articulate by the organs of speech; to utter formally; to declare or affirm.

Pronounced, prō-nounst', p.a. Strongly marked or defined; decided; glaring.

Proof, prōf, n. Something which tests; trial; what serves to convince; evidence; firmness; a certain standard of strength in spirit; an impression in printing for correction; early impression of an engraving.—a. Impenetrable; able to resist.

Prop, prop, n. A body that supports a weight; a support.—vt. (propping, propped). To support by a prop; to sustain generally.

Propaganda, pro-pa-gan'da, n. An institution or system for propagating any doctrine.

Propagate, prō'pa-gāt, vt. To multiply by generation or reproduction; to diffuse; to increase.—vi. To have young or issue; to be multiplied by generation, etc.

Propel, prō-pel', vt. (propelling, propeled). To drive, push, or thrust forward.

Propensity, prō-pens'i-ti, n. Bent of mind; natural tendency; disposition.

Proper, pro'pèr, a. One's own; peculiar: used as the name of a particular person or thing; adapted; correct; real.

Property, pro'pèr-ti, n. A peculiar quality or attribute; characteristic; ownership; the thing owned; estate; a stage requisite.

Prophecy, pro'fe-si, n. A foretelling; a prediction; inspired prediction or utterance.

Prophesy, pro'fe-sī, vt. To foretell; to predict.—vi. To utter prophecies.

Prophet, pro'fet, n. One who foretells future events.

Prophylactic, prō-fi-lak'tik, a. Preventive of disease.—n. A medicine which preserves against disease.

Propinquity, prō-pin'kwi-ti, n. Nearness; vicinity; kindred.

Propitiation, prō-pi'shi-ā''shon, n. Act of propitiating or what propitiates; atonement.

Propitiatory, prō-pi'shi-a-to-ri, a. Having the power to make propitious; conciliatory.—n. Among the Jews, the mercy-seat.

Propitious, prō-pi'shus, a. Favorable; disposed to be gracious or merciful.

Proportion, pro-pōr'shon, n. Comparative relation; relative size and arrangement; symmetry; just or equal share; lot; that rule which enables us to find a fourth proportional to three numbers.—vt. To adjust in due proportion; to form with symmetry.

Proportionate, pro-pōr'shon-āt, a. Proportional.—vt. To make proportional.

Propose, prō-pōz', vt. (proposing, proposed). To offer for consideration.—vi. To make a proposal; to purpose; to offer oneself in marriage.

Proposition, pro-po-zi'shon, n. That which is proposed; a proposal; offer of terms; a form of speech in which something is affirmed or denied.

Propound, prō-pound', vt. To propose; to offer for consideration; to put, as a question.

Proprietary, prō-prī'e-ta-ri, a. Belonging to a proprietor.—n. A proprietor; a body of proprietors.

Proprietor, pro-prī'e-tor, n. An owner; one who has legal right to anything.

Propriety, prō-prī'e-ti, n. State of being proper; fitness; consonance with established principles or customs; justness.

Propulsion, prō-pul'shon, n. Act of propelling or of driving forward.

Prosaic, prō-zā'ik, a. Pertaining to prose; dull; commonplace.

Proscribe, prō-skrīb', vt. To outlaw; to condemn as dangerous; to interdict.

Prose, prōz, n. Speech or language not in verse.—vi. (prosing, prosed). To write or speak in a dull, tedious, style.—a. Relating to prose; prosaic.

Prosecute, pro'se-kūt, vt. and i (prosecuting, prosecuted). To persist in; to carry on; to pursue at law.

Prosecution, pro-se-kū'shon, n. Act of prosecuting; the carrying on of a suit at law; the party by whom criminal proceedings are instituted.

Proselyte, pro'se-līt, n. A convert to the Jewish faith; a new convert.—vt. To make a convert of.

Prospect, pros'pekt, n. A distant view; sight; scene; outlook; exposure; expectation.—vt. and i. pros-pekt'. To make search for precious stones or metals.

Prospective, pros-pek'tiv, a. Looking forward; regarding the future.

Prospectus, pros-pek'tus, n. A statement of some enterprise proposed, as a literary work, a new company, etc.

Prosper, pros'pér, vi. To increase in wealth or any good; to thrive.—vt. To make to succeed.

Prosperity, pros-pe'ri-ti, n. Flourishing state; satisfactory progress; success.

Prostitute, pros'ti-tūt, vt. (prostituting, prostituted). To offer publicly for lewd purposes for hire; to devote to anything base.—a. Openly devoted to lewdness.—n. A female given to indiscrimate lewdness.

Prostitution, pros-ti-tū'shon, n. Practice of offering the body to indiscriminate intercourse with men; debasement.

Prostrate, pros'trāt, a. Lying with the body flat; lying at mercy.—vt. (prostrating, prostrated). To lay flat or prostrate; to bow in reverence; to overthrow; to ruin.

Protean, prō'tē-an, a. Assuming different shapes; variable; changeable.

Protect, prō-tekt', vt. To shield from danger, injury, etc.; to guard against foreign competition by tariff regulations.

Protection, prō-tek'shon, n. Act of protecting; shelter; defence; the system of favoring articles of home production by duties on foreign articles.

Protective, prō-tekt'iv, a. Affording protection; sheltering; defensive.

Protector, prō-tekt'or, n. One who protects; a defender; a guardian; a preserver.

Protégé, pro-tā-zhā; fem. **Protégée**, pro-tā-zhā, n. One under the care of another.

Proteid, prō'tē-id, n. A name of certain nitrogenous substances forming the soft tissues of the body, and found also in plants.

Protect, prō-test', vi. To affirm with solemnity; to make a formal declaration of opposition.—vt. To assert; to mark for non-payment, as a bill.—n. prō'test. A formal declaration of dissent; a declaration that payment of a bill has been refused.

Protestant, pro'test-ant, n. One of the party who adhered to Luther at the Reformation; a member of a reformed church.—a. Belonging to the religion of the Protestants.

Protocol, prō'tō-kol, n. A diplomatic document serving as a preliminary to diplomatic transactions.

Proton prō'ton, n. A positively charged particle, the nucleus of a hydrogen atom.

Protoplasm, prō'tō-plazm, n. A substance constituting the basis of living matter in animals and plants.

Prototype, prō'tō-tīp, n. An original type or model; a pattern.

Protract, prō-trakt', vt. To prolong; to delay; to defer; to draw to a scale.

Protractor, prō-trakt'or, n. One who or that which protracts; an instrument for surveying; a muscle which draws forward a part.

Protrude, prō-tröd', vt. and i (protruding, protruded). To thrust forward; to project.

Protuberance, prō-tū'ber-ans, n. A swelling or tumor; a prominence; a knob.

Protuberant, prō-tū'ber-ant, a. Swelling; bulging out.

Proud, proud, a. Having a high opinion of oneself; haughty; of fearless spirit; ostentatious; magnificent.—**Proud flesh**, an excessive granulation in wounds or ulcers.

Prove, pröv, vt. (proving, proved). To try by experiment: to test; to establish the truth or reaity of; to demonstrate; to obtain probate of.—vi. To be found by experience or trial; to turn out to be.

Provenance, prov'e-nans, n. Origin.

Provender, prov'en-dér, n. Dry food or fodder for beasts; provisions; food.

Proverb, pro'vérb, n. A popular saying, expressing a truth or common fact; an adage; a maxim; a by-word; a dark saying.

Provide, prō-vīd', vt. and i (providing, provided). To procure beforehand; to prepare; to supply; to stipulate previously

Provided, prō-vīd'ed, conj. On condition.

Providence, pro'vi-dens, n. Foresight; the care which God exercises over his creatures; God; a providential circumstance

Provident, pro'vi-dent, a. Foreseeing and providing for wants; prudent; frugal.

Province, pro'vins, n. A territory at some distance from the metropolis; a large political division; sphere of action; department.

Provincial, prō-vin'shal, a. Pertaining to or forming a province; characteristic of the people of a province; rustic.—n. A person belonging to a province.

Provision, prō-vi'zhon, n. Act of providing; preparaton; stores provided; victuals; stipulation; proviso.—vt. To supply with provisions.

Provisional, prō-vi'zhon-al, a. Provided for present need; temporary.

Proviso, prō-vi'zō, n. An article or clause in any statute or contract; stipulation.

Provocative, prō-vok'a-tiv, a. Serving to provoke; exciting.—n. A stimulant.

Provoke, prō-vōk', vt (provoking, provoked). To incite; to stimulate; to incense; to irritate.—vi. To produce anger.

Prow, prou, n. The forepart of a ship.

P

Prowess, prou'es, *n.* Bravery; boldness and dexterity in war; gallantry.

Prowl, proul, *vi.* and *t.* To roam or wander stealthily.—*n.* Act of one who prowls.

Proximity, proks-im'i-ti, *n.* State of being proximate; immediate nearness.

Proxy, proks'i, *n.* Agency of a substitute; a deputy; a writing by which one authorizes another to vote in his stead.

Prude, pröd, *n.* A woman affecting great reserve and excessive delicacy.

Prudent, prö'dent, *a.* Provident; careful; discreet; judicious.

Prudish, pröd'ish, *a.* Like a prude; affecting excessive modesty or virtue.

Prune, prön, *vt.* (pruning, pruned). To trim; to cut or lop off; to clear from superfluities.—*n.* A plum, particularly a dried plum.

Prurient, prö'ri-ent, *a.* Itching after something; inclined to lascivious thoughts.

Pry, prī, *vi.* (prying, pried). To peep narrowly; to look closely; to peer.—*n.* A keen glance.

Psalm, säm, *n.* A sacred song or hymn.

Psalter, sal'ter, *n.* The Book of Psalms; a book containing the Psalms separately.

Pseudo-, sū'dō. A prefix signifying false or spurious.

Pseudonym, sū'dō-nim, *n.* A false or feigned name; a name assumed by a writer.

Psychiatry, sī'ki-at-ri, *n.* Medical treatment of diseases of the mind.

Psychic, Psychical, sī'kik, sī'kik-al, *a.* Belonging to the soul; psychological; pertaining to that force by which spiritualists aver they produce "spiritual" phenomena.

Psychology, sī-kol'o-ji, *n.* That branch of knowledge which deals with the mind; mental science.

Ptomaine, tō'mān, *n.* A name of certain substances generated during putrefaction or morbid conditions prior to death.

Puberty, pū'ber-ti, *n.* The age at which persons can beget or bear children.

Pubescent, pū-bes'ent, *a.* Arriving at puberty; covered with fine soft hairs.

Public, pub'lik, *a.* Not private; pertaining to a whole community; open or free to all; common; notorious.—*n.* The people, indefinitely.—**In public,** in open view.

Publication, pub-li-kā'shon, *n.* Act of publishing; announcement; promulgation; act of offering a book, etc., to the public by sale; any book, etc., published.

Publicity, pub-lis'i-ti, *n.* State of being made public; notoriety; currency.

Publish, pub'lish, *vt.* To make public; to proclaim, promulgate; to cause to be printed and offered for sale.

Pucker, puk'er, *vt.* and *i* To gather into small folds; to wrinkle.—*n.* A fold or wrinkle, or a collection of folds.

Pudding, pud'ing, *n.* An intestine; a sausage; a dish variously compounded, of flour, milk, eggs, fruit, etc.

Puddle, pud'l, *n.* A small pool of dirty water; clay worked into a mass impervious to water.—*vt.* (puddling, puddled). To make muddy; to make water-tight with clay; to convert pig-iron into wrought-iron.

Pudgy, puj'i, *a.* Fat and short.

Puerperal, pū-er'per-al, *a.* Pertaining to child-birth.

Puff, puf, *n.* A sudden emission of breath; a whiff; a short blast of wind; a puff-ball; piece of light pastry; a consciously exaggerated commendation.—*vi.* To give a quick blast with the mouth; to breathe hard after exertion.—*vt.* To drive with a blast; to inflate; to praise extravagantly.

Puff-adder, puf'ad-er, *n.* A venomous snake which swells out the upper part of its body.

Puff-ball, puf'bal, *n.* A ball-shaped fungus which when ripe discharges a fine powder.

Pugilism, pū'jil-izm, *n.* The practice of boxing or fighting with the fist.

Pugnacious, pug-nā'shus, *a.* Disposed to fight; quarrelsome.

Pug-nose, pug'nōz, *n.* A nose turned up at the end; a snub-nose.

Puissant, pū'is-ant, *a.* Powerful; strong; mighty; forcible.

Puke, pūke, *vi.* and *t.* (puking, puked). To vomit.

Pulchritude, pul'kri-tūd, *n.* Beauty; comeliness.

Pule, pūl, *vi.* (puling, puled). To cry like a chicken; to whine; to whimper.

Pull, pul, *vt.* To draw towards one; to tug; to rend; to pluck; to gather.—*vi.* To draw; to tug.—*n.* Act of pulling; a twitch; act of rowing a boat; a drink; a struggle.

Pullet, pul'et, *n.* A young hen.

Pulley, pul'i, *n.* A small wheel in a block, used in raising weights.

Pull-over, pul'ō-ver, *n.* A knitted jersey without buttons, pulled over the head when put on.

Pulmonary, pul'mon-a-ri, *a.* Pertaining to or affecting the lungs.

Pulp, pulp, *n.* Moist, soft animal or vegetable matter.—*vt.* To make into pulp; to deprive of the pulp.

Pulpit, pul'pit, *n.* An elevated place for a preacher; preachers generally.

Pulsate, pul'sāt, *vi.* To beat or throb.

Pulsation, pul-sā'shon, *n.* The beating of the heart or an artery; a throb.

Pulse, puls, *n.* The beating of the heart or an artery; vibration; leguminous plants or their seeds, as beans, etc.—*vi.* (pulsing, pulsed). To beat or throb.

Pulverize, pul'ver-īz, *vt.* To reduce to dust or fine powder.

Puma, pū'ma, *n.* A carnivorous quadruped of the cat kind; the cougar.

Pumice, pū'mis or pum'is, *n.* A light and spongy stone, used for polishing.

Pump, pump, *n.* A machine for raising water or extracting air; a shoe used in dancing.—*vi.* To work a pump.—*vt.* To raise with a pump; to free from liquid by a pump; to put artful questions to extract information.

Pumpkin, pump'kin, *n.* A plant and its fruit; a kind of gourd or vegetable marrow.

Pun, pun, *n.* A play on words like in sound, but different in meaning; a kind of quibble.—*vi.* (punning, punned) To make a pun or puns.

Punch, punsh, *n.* An instrument for driving holes in metal, etc.; a blow or thrust; a beverage of spirits, lemon-juice, water, etc.; a buffoon; a short-legged, barrel-bodied horse; a short fat fellow.—*vt.* To stamp or perforate with a punch; to hit with the fist.

Punctual, pungk'tū-al, *a.* Exact; made or done at the exact time.

Punctuate, pungk'tū-āt, *vt.* To mark with the points necessary in writings.

Punctuation, pungk-tū-ā'shon, *n.* The act, art, or system of punctuating a writing.

Puncture, pungk'tūr, *n.* The act of pricking; a small hole thus made.—*vt.* (puncturing, punctured). To pierce with a small point.

Pundit, pun'dit, *n.* A learned Brahman; an Indian scholar; any learned man.

Pungent, pun'jent, *a.* Biting; acrid; caustic; keen; stinging.

Punish, pun'ish, *vt.* To inflict pain or any evil on, as a penalty; to chastise; to hurt.

Punitive, pū-ni-tiv, *a.* Pertaining to, awarding, or involving punishment.

Punning, pun'ing, *p.a.* Given to make puns; containing a pun or puns.

Puny, pūn'i, *a.* Small and weak; petty.

Pup, pup, *n.* A puppy.—*vi.* (pupping, pupped). To bring forth whelps.

Pupil, pū'pil, *n.* A young person under the care of a tutor; the aperture in the iris through which the rays of light pass.

Pupilary, (or -il-), pū'pil-a-ri, *a.* Pertaining to a

pupil or ward, or to the pupil of the eye.

Puppet, pup´et, *n.* A small figure in the human form mechanically worked; a person who is a mere tool.

Puppy, pup´i, *n.* A whelp; a young dog; a conceited, foppish fellow.

Purchase, pėr´chãs, *vt.* (purchasing, purchased). To buy; to obtain by labor, danger, etc.—*n.* Acquisition of anything by money; what is bought; mechanical advantage.

Pure, pūr, *a.* Clean; clear; unmixed; spotless; chaste; genuine; sincere; absolute.

Purgative, pėr´ga-tiv, *a.* Having the power of purging.—*n.* A medicine that purges.

Purgatory, pėr´ga-to-ri, *a.* Tending to purge or cleanse.—*n.* In the R. Catholic religion, a place in which souls after death are purified from sins; any place or state of temporary suffering.

Purge, pėrj, *vt.* and *i.* (purging, purged). To make pure or clean; to clear from accusation; to evacuate the bowels of.—*n.* The act of purging; a cathartic medicine.

Purify, pū´ri-fi, *vt.* (purifying, purified). To make pure or clear; to free from admixture; to free from guilt.—*vi.* To become pure or clear.

Purist, pūr´ist, *n.* One excessively nice in the use of words, etc.

Puritan, pūr´i-tan, *n.* One very strict in religious matters or in conduct; an early Protestant dissenter from the Church of England.—*a.* Pertaining to the Puritans.

Purity, pūr´i-ti, *n.* State or quality of being pure; cleanness; innocence; chastity.

Purl, pėrl, *n.* Spiced malt liquor; gentle murmur of a stream.—*vi.* To murmur, as a stream; to reverse a stitch in knitting.

Purlieu, pėr´lū, *n.* Part lying adjacent; outskirts; generally in *pl.*

Purloin, pėr-loin´, *vt.* To steal or pilfer; to filch; to take by theft or plagiarism.

Purple, pėr´pl, *n.* A color produced by mixing red and blue; a purple robe, the badge of the Roman emperors; regal power.—*a.* Of a color made of red and blue; dyed with blood.—*vt.* (purpling, purpled). To make purple.

Purport, pėr´pôrt, *n.* Meaning; import.—*vt.* To signify; to profess.

Purpose, pėr´pos, *n.* End or aim; design; intention; matter in question.—*vt.* and *i.* (purposing, purposed). To propose; to intend.

Purr, pėr, *vi.* To murmur, as a cat when pleased.—*n.* The sound of a cat when pleased.

Purse, pėrs, *n.* A small bag or receptacle for money; money collected as a prize or a present; finances.—*vt.* (pursing, pursed). To put in a purse; to pucker.

Pursuant, pėr-sū´ant, *a.* Done in prosecution of anything; conformable.

Pursue, pėr-sū´, *vt.* (pursuing, pursued). To follow with a view to overtake; to chase; to use measures to obtain; to carry on.—*vi.* To go in pursuit; to act as prosecutor.

Pursuit, pėr-sūt´, *n.* Act of pursuing; chase; quest; business occupation.

Purulent, pū´ru-lent, *a.* Consisting or of the nature of pus.

Purvey, pėr-vā´, *vt.* To provide.—*vi.* To supply provisions, especially for a number.

Purveyance, pėr-vā´ans, *n.* Act of purveying; the former royal prerogative of obtaining necessaries on easy terms.

Purview, pėr´vū, *n.* The body of a statute; the scope of a statute; limit; sphere.

Pus, pus, *n.* The soft yellowish substance formed in suppuration; matter of a sore.

Push, push, *vt.* To press against with force; to thrust or shove; to enforce; to urge; to prosecute energetically.—*vi.* To make a thrust or effort; to force one's way.—*n.* Act of pushing; vigorous effort; emergency; enterprise.

Pusillanimous, pū-sil-lan´im-us, *a.* Without strength of mind; timid; cowardly.

Pustule, pus´tūl, *n.* A small blister; small eleva-

tion of the cuticle, containing pus.

Put, put, *vt.* (putting, put). To place in any position or situation; to apply; to propose or propound; to state in words.

Put, Putt, put, *vt.* (putting, putted). To throw (a heavy stone) from the shoulder; in golf, to play the ball into the hole.—*n.* A rustic; a silly fellow.

Putrefy, pū´trē-fi, *vt.* (putrefying, putrefied). To render putrid.—*vi.* To decay; to rot.

Putrescence, pū-tres´ens, *n.* State of becoming rotten; a putrid state.

Putrid, pū´trid, *a.* In a state of decay; rotten; corrupt.

Putter, put´ėr, *n.* One who puts, sets, or places; a kind of golfing club (pron. put´ėr).

Putting-green, put´ing-grēn, *n.* A smooth piece of sward round a hole in a gold course.

Putty, put´i, *n.* A paste made of whiting and linseed-oil.—*vt.* To cement or fill with putty.

Puzzle, puz´l, *vt.* (puzzling, puzzled). To perplex; to entangle.—*vi.* To be bewildered.—*n.* Perplexity; something to try ingenuity.

Puzzling, puz´ling, *p.a.* Such as to puzzle; perplexing; embarrassing; bewildering.

Pygmy, pig´mi, *n.* A dwarf; anything little.—*a.* Dwarfish; little.

Pylorus, pi-lō´rus, *n.* The lower orifice of the stomach.

Pyramid, pi´ra-mid, *n.* A solid body having triangular sides meeting in a point at the top.

Pyre, pir, *n.* A heap of combustibles for burning a dead body; a funeral pile.

Pyrites, pi-ri´tēz, *n.* A mineral combining sulphur with iron, copper, cobalt, etc.

Pyroligneous, pi-rō-lig´nē-us, *a.* Generated by the distillation of wood.

Pyrology, pi-rol´o-ji, *n.* The science of heat.

Pyrometer, pi-rom´et-ėr, *n.* An instrument for measuring high degrees of heat.

Pyrotechnics, Pyrotechny, pi-rō-tek´niks, pi-rō-tek´ni, *n.* The art of making fireworks; the use of fireworks.

Pyrrhic, pi´rik, *n.* and *a.* An ancient Grecian warlike dance; a metrical foot of two short syllables.—**Pyrrhic victory,** a victory like those of Pyrrhus of Epirus over the Romans, costing more to the victor than to the vanquished.

Python, pi´thon, *n.* A large non venomous serpent.

Pyx, piks, *n.* A vessel used in the R. Catholic Church for holding the host; a box or chest for specimen coins at the British Mint; the metallic box containing the nautical compass-card.—**Trial of the Pyx,** the trial by weight and assay of the gold and silver coins of the United Kingdom.—*vt.* To test by weight and assay.

Q

Quack, kwak, *vi.* To cry like a duck; to boast; to practice quackery.—*n.* The cry of a duck; a pretender to skill or knowledge, especially medical.—*a.* Pertaining to quackery.

Quackery, kwak´e-ri, *n.* Practice or boastful pretenses of a quack, particularly in medicine.

Quadragesima, kwod-ra-je´si-ma, *n.* Lent.

Quadrangle, kwod-rang-gl, *n.* A plane figure, have four angles and sides; an inner square of a building.

Quadrant, kwod´rant, *n.* The fourth part of a circle or its circumference; an old instrument for taking altitudes and angles; an old form of sextant.

Quadrat, kwod´rat, *n.* A piece of type-metal for leaving a blank in printing.

Quadrate, kwod´rāt, *a.* Square.—*n.* A square surface or figure.—*vi.* To square with; to agree or suit.

Quadratic, kwod-rat´ik, *a.* In *algebra*, involving the square of an unknown quantity.

Quadrennial, kwod-ren´ni-al, *a.* Comprising four

years; occurring once in four years.

Quadrilateral, kwod-ri-lat'er-al, *a.* Having four sides and four angles.—*n.* A plane figure having four sides and angles.

Quadrillion, kwod-ril'yon, *n.* The fourth power of a million; a number represented by a unit and 24 ciphers.

Quadruped, kwod'ru-ped, *n.* An animal with four legs or feet.

Quadruple, kwod'ru-pl, *a.* Fourfold.—*n.* Four times the sum or number.—*vt.* To make fourfold.—*vi.* To become fourfold.

Quaff, kwäf, *vt.* and *i.* To drain to the bottom; to drink copiously.

Quagmire, kwag'mīr, *n.* A piece of soft, wet, boggy land; a bog; a fen.

Quail, kwäl, *vi.* To shrink; to flinch; to cower.—*n.* A small bird allied to the partridge.

Quaint, kwānt, *a.* Fanciful; curious; odd and antique; singular; whimsical.

Quake, kwāk, *vi.* (quaking, quaked). To shake; to tremble; to quiver.—*n.* A shake; tremulous agitation.

Quaker, kwāk'er, *n.* One who quakes; one of the religious sect called the *Society of Friends*.

Qualification, kwo'li-fi-kā''shon, *n.* Act of qualifying; state of being qualified; suitable quality or characteristic; legal power; ability; modification; restriction.

Qualify, kwo'li-fi, *vt.* (qualifying, qualified). To give proper or suitable qualities to; to furnish with the knowledge, skill, etc., necessary; to modify or limit; to soften or moderate; to dilute.—*vi.* To become qualified or fit.

Quality, kwo'li-ti, *n.* Sort, kind, or character; a distinguishing property or characteristic; degree of excellence; high rank.

Qualm, kwäm, *n.* A sudden fit of nausea; a twinge of conscience; compunction.

Quandary, kwon-dā'ri or kwon'da-ri, *n.* A state of perplexity; a predicament.

Quantify, kwon'ti-fi, *vt.* To determine the quantity of; to modify with regard to quantity.

Quantity, kwon'ti-ti, *n.* That property in virtue of which a thing is measurable; bulk; measure; amount; metrical value of syllables.

Quantum, kwan'tum, *n.* A quantity; an amount; a sufficient amount.

Quarantine, kwo'ran-tin, *n.* The period during which a ship suspected of being infected is obliged to forbear all intercourse with a port.—*vt.* To cause to perform quarantine.

Quarrel, kwo'rel, *n.* An angry dispute; a brawl; cause of dispute; a dart for a crossbow; a glazier's diamont.—*vi.* (quarrelling, quarelled). To dispute violently; to disagree.

Quarry, kwo'ri, *n.* A place where stones are dug from the earth; any animal pursued for prey; game killed.—*vt.* (quarrying, quarried). To dig or take from a quarry.

Quart, kwart, *n.* The fourth part of a gallon; two pints.

Quarter, kwar'ter, *n.* The fourth part of anything; 28 lbs; 8 bushels; any direction or point of the compass; a district; locality; division of a heraldic shield; proper position; mercy to a beaten foe; *pl.* shelter or lodging; encampment.—*vt.* To divide into four equal parts; to cut to pieces; to furnish with lodgings or shelter; to add to other arms on an heraldic shield.—*vi.* To lodge.

Quarterly, kwar'ter-li, *a.* Recurring each quarter of the year.—*adv.* Once in a quarter of a year.—*n.* A periodical published quarterly.

Quarter-master, kwar'ter-mäs-ter, *n.* An officer who has charge of the barracks, tents, stores, etc., of a regiment; a petty officer in the navy, who steers, signals, etc.

Quartet, kwar-tet', *n.* A musical composition in four parts; the performers of such a composition.

Quartz, kwartz, *n.* A pure variety of silica, a constituent of granite and other rocks.

Quash, kwosh, *vt.* To subdue or quell; to sup-

press; to annul or make void.

Quasi, kwä'sī. A prefix implying appearance without reality; sort of; sham.

Quatercentenary, kwa-ter-sen'te-na-ri, *n.* A four hundredth anniversary.

Quaternary, kwa-ter'na-ri, *a.* Consisting of four; arranged in fours; applied to the strata above the tertiary.

Quaternion, kwa-ter'ni-on, *n.* A set of four; a quantity employed in mathematics.

Quaver, kwä'ver, *vi.* To have a tremulous motion; to vibrate.—*vt.* To utter with a tremulous sound.—*n.* A shake or rapid vibration of the voice, or on a musical instrument; a musical note equal to half a crotchet.

Quay, kē, *n.* A built landing-place for vessels; a wharf.

Queasy, kwē'zi, *a.* Sick at the stomach; inclined to vomit; fastidious; squeamish.

Queen, kwēn, *n.* The wife of a king; a female sovereign; a pre-eminent woman; the sovereign of a swarm of bees; a playing-card; a piece at chess.

Queer, kwēr, *a.* Odd; droll; peculiar.

Quell, kwel, *vt.* To subdue; to allay.

Quench, kwensh, *vt.* To put out, as fire; to allay or slake, as thirst; to repress.

Quenchless, kwensh'les, *a.* That cannot be quenched; inextinguishable; irrepressible.

Querimonious, kwe-ri-mō'ni-us, *a.* Apt to complain; complaining; querulous.

Quern, kwern, *n.* A stone hand-mill for grinding grain.

Querulous, kwe'rū-lus, *a.* Complaining; murmuring; peevish.

Query, kwē'ri, *n.* A question; the mark of interrogation (?).—*vi.* (querying, queried). To ask a question or questions.—*vt.* To question; to mark with a query.

Quest, kwest, *n.* Act of seeking; search; pursuit; inquiry; solicitation.

Question, kwest'yon, *n.* Act of asking; an interrogation; inquiry; discussion; subject of discussion.—*vi.* To ask a question; to doubt.—*vt.* To interrogate; to doubt; to challenge.

Questionnaire, kwest'yon-ār, kest-ê-on-ār', *n.* A list or series of questions designed to elicit information on a specific subject.

Queue, kū, *n.* The tail of a wig; a pigtail; a file of persons waiting, in the order of their arrival, to be served in a shop or admitted to a theater, etc.—*vi.* To join or wait in a queue.

Quibble, kwib'l, *n.* A turn of language to evade the point in question; a pun.—*vi.* (quibbling, quibbled). To evade the question or truth by artifice; to prevaricate; to pun.

Quick, kwik, *a.* Alive; brisk; swift; keen; sensitive; irritable.—*n.* A growing plant, usually hawthorn, for hedges; the living flesh; sensitiveness.—*adv.* Quickly; soon.

Quicken, kwik'n, *vt.* To revive or resuscitate; to cheer; to increase the speed of; to sharpen; to stimulate.—*vi.* To become alive; to move quickly or more quickly.

Quicksand, kwik'sand, *n.* A movable sandbank under water; sand yielding under the feet; something treacherous.

Quicksilver, kwik'sil-ver, *n.* Mercury.

Quid, kwid, *n.* A piece of tobacco chewed and rolled about in the mouth.

Quiescence, kwi-es'ens, *n.* Rest; repose.

Quiet, kwi'et, *a.* At rest; calm; still; peaceful; patient; secluded; not glaring or showy.—*n.* Rest; repose; peace; security.—*vt.* To make quiet; to calm; to lull; to allay.

Quill, kwil, *n.* The strong feather of a goose, etc.; a feather made into a pen; the spine of a porcupine; a piece of reed used by weavers; a plait of a ruffle.—*vt.* To plait.

Quilt, kwilt, *n.* A padded bed-cover.—*vt.* To form into a quilt; to sew pieces of cloth with soft substance between.

Quince, kwins, *n.* The fruit of a tree allied to the

pear and apple; the tree itself.

Quincentenary, kwin-sen'te-na-ri, n. A five hundredth anniversary.

Quinine, kwin'ēn or kwin-ĭn', n. An alkaline substance obtained from the bark of trees of the cinchona genus.

Quintessence, kwint-es'ens, n. The fifth or highest essence of a natural body; the purest or most essential part of a thing.

Quintet, kwin-tet', n. A musical composition in five parts; the performers of such a composition.

Quintuple, kwin'tu-pl, a. Fivefold.—vt. To make fivefold.

Quip, kwip, n. A sharp sarcastic turn; a severe retort; a gibe.

Quirk, kwerk, n. An artful turn for evasion; a shift; a quibble.

Quit, kwit, a. Discharged; released; free; clear.—vt. (quitting, quitted). To discharge; to rid; to acquit; to leave; to abandon.

Quite, kwit, adv. Completely; wholly; entirely; altogether; very.

Quiver, kwi'vér, n. A case or sheath for arrows.—vi. To shake with small rapid movements; to tremble; to shiver.

Quixotic, kwiks-ot'ik, a. Chivalrous to extravagance; aiming at visionary ends.

Quiz, kwiz, n. A hoax; a jest; one who quizzes; one liable to be quizzed; a game or test in which two or more persons or teams compete in answering questions.—vt. (quizzing, quizzed). To make fun of, as by obscure questions; to look at inquisitively; to tease; to test by questioning.

Quoit, koit, n. A flattish ring of iron, thrown at a mark.—vi. To throw or play at quoits.

Quorum, kwō'rum, n. A number of the members of any body competent to transact business.

Quota, kwō'ta, n. A share or proportion assigned to each.

Quotation, kwōt-ā'shon, n. Act of quoting; passage quoted; the naming of the price of commodities, or the price specified.

Quote, kwōt, vt. (quoting, quoted). To adduce or cite, as from some author; to name as the price of an article.

Quotient, kwō'shent, n. The number obtained by dividing one number by another.

R

Rabbi, rab'bī, n. A Jewish teacher or expounder of the law.

Rabbit, rab'it, n. A burrowing rodent allied to the hare.

Rabble, rab'l, n. A crowd of vulgar, noisy people; the mob; the lower class of people.

Rabid, ra'bid, a. Raving; furious; mad.

Rabies, rā'bĭ-ēs, n. A disease affecting certain animals, especially dogs, from which hydrophobia is communicated.

Raccoon, Racoon, ra-kön', n. An American carnivorous animal.

Race, rās, n. A body of individuals sprung from a common stock; a breed or stock; a running; a contest in speed; a course or career; a rapid current or channel.—vi. (racing, raced). To run swiftly; to contend in running.—vt. To cause to contend in speed.

Racial, rā'si-al, a. Pertaining to race or lineage; pertaining to the races of man.

Rack, rak, vt. To stretch unduly; to distort; to punish on the rack; to torture; to strain.—n. Something used for stretching; an instrument of torture; torment; anguish; a frame for fodder, etc.; a bar with teeth on one of its edges; flying broken clouds; wreck.

Racket, rak'et, n. A confused din; clamor; the bat used in tennis, etc.; pl. a game like tennis.—vi. To make a racket; to frolic.

Radar, rā'där, n. A method of finding the position of an object (ship, aircraft, etc.) by reflection of radio waves.

Radiance, rā'di-ans, n. Brightness shooting in rays; luster; brilliancy; splendor.

Radiate, rā'di-āt, vi. To emit rays of light; to shine; to spread about as in rays.—vt. To emit in divergent lines; to enlighten.—a. Having rays or lines resembling radii.

Radical, ra'di-kal, a. Pertaining to the root; original; thorough-going; native; underived; relating to radicals in politics.—n. A root; a simple, underived word; one who advocates extreme political reform.

Radio, rā'di-ō, n. A combining form used in compound words as equivalent to *wireless*; also used as a noun for the wireless system of transmission.

Radish, ra'dish, n. A plant, the young root of which is eaten raw, as a salad.

Radium, rā'di-um, n. An intensely radio-active element extracted from pitchblende, and used in medicine.

Radius, rā'di-us, n.; pl. **-ii, -iuses.** A straight line from the center of a circle to the circumference; a bone of the forearm.

Radix, rā'diks, n. A root, as of a plant or a word; source; origin.

Raffle, raf'l, n. A kind of lottery.—vi. (raffling, raffled). To engage in a raffle.—vt. To dispose of by raffle.

Raft, räft, n. Logs fastened together and floated; a floating structure.

Rafter, räf'tér, n. A large sloping piece of timber supporting a roof.

Rag, rag, n. A rough separate fragment; a tattered cloth; a shred; a tatter.

Rage, rāj, n. Violent anger; fury; enthusiasm; rapture.—vi. (raging, raged). To be furious with anger; to be violently agitated.

Ragged, rag'ed, a. Rent or worn into rags; tattered; rugged; wearing tattered clothes.

Ragout, ra-gö', n. A dish of stewed and highly seasoned meat and vegetables.

Raid, rad, n. A hostile incursion; a foray.—vi. To engage in a raid.—vt. To make a raid on.

Rail, rāl, n. A horizontal bar of wood or metal; a connected series of posts; a railing; one of the parallel iron bars forming a track for locomotives, etc.; a railway; a grallatorial bird.—vt. To inclose with rails; to furnish with rails.-vi. To use abusive language; to scold; to inveigh.

Raillery, rāl'é-ri, n. Light ridicule or satire; banter; jesting language.

Railway, rāl'wā, n. A road having iron rails laid in parallel lines, on which carriages run; all the land, buildings, and machinery required for traffic on such a road.

Raiment, rā'ment, n. Clothing; vestments.

Rain, rān, n. The moisture of the atmosphere falling in drops; a shower of anything.—vi. To fall in drops from the clouds; to fall like rain.—vt. To pour or shower down.

Rainbow, rān'bō, n. An arc of a circle, consisting of all the prismatic colors, appearing in the heavens opposite the sun.

Raise, rāz, vt. (raising, raised). To cause to rise; to lift upward; to excite; to recall from death; to stir up; to construct; to levy; to breed; to originate; to give vent to; to inflate; to cause to be relinquished (a siege).

Raisin, rā'zn, n. A dried grape.

Rake, rāk, n. An implement for collecting hay or straw, smoothing earth, etc.; a dissolute, lewd man; slope.—vt. (raking, raked). To apply a rake to; to gather with a rake; to ransack; to enfilade.—vi. To use a rake; to search minutely; to incline; to slope, aft, as masts.

Rally, ral'i, vt. (rallying, rallied). To reunite, as disordered troops; to collect, as things scattered; to attack with raillery; to banter.—vi. To recover strength or vigor.—n. A stand made by retreating troops; recovery of strength.

Ram, ram, n. The male of the sheep; a battering-ram; the loose hammer of a pile-driving machine; a heavy steel beak of a war-vessel; an iron-clad ship with such a beak; one of the signs of the zodiac.—vt. (ramming, rammed). To strike with a ram; to batter; to cram.

Ramble, ram'bl, vi. (rambling, rambled). To roam carelessly about; to talk incoherently; to have parts stretching irregularly.—n. An irregular excursion.

Ramification, ra'mi-fi-kā''shon, n. The act or process of ramifying; a branch or set of branches; an offshoot.

Ramify, ra'mi-fi, vt. To divide into branches.—vi. To be divided; to branch out.

Ramp, ramp, vi. To climb, as a plant; to rear on the hind-legs; to spring.—n. A spring or leap; a slope; a swindle; an attempt to get money under false pretenses.

Rampage, ram'pāj or ram-pāj', vi. To prance about; to rage and storm.—n. Violent conduct.

Rampant, ram'pant, a. Rank in growth; exuberant; unrestrained; in heraldry, standing up on the hind-legs.

Ranch, ranch, n. In North America, a farming establishment for rearing cattle and horses.

Rancid, ran'sid, a. Having a rank or stinking smell; strong-scented; sour; musty.

Rancor, rang'kor, n. Deep-seated enmity; malice; malignity.

Random, ran'dum, n. Action without definite object; chance; caprice.—**At random,** in a haphazard manner.—a. Left to chance; done without previous calculation.

Range, rānj, vt. (ranging, ranged). To set in a row; to dispose systematically; to wander through or scour.—vt. To rank; to rove about; to fluctuate.—n. A row; a rank; compass or extent; a kitchen grate; distance to which a projectile is carried; a place for gun practice.

Rank, rangk, n. A row; a line; a social class; comparative station; titled dignity.—vt. To place in a line; to classify.—vi. To belong to a class; to put in a claim against a bankrupt.—a. Luxuriant in growth;; strong-scented; utter; coarse; disgusting.

Rankle, rang'kl, vi. (rankling, rankled). To fester painfully; to continue to irritate.—vt. To irritate; to inflame.

Ransack, ran'sak, vt. To plunder; to search thoroughly.

Ransom, ran'sum, n. Release from captivity by payment; price paid for redemption or pardon.—vt. To pay a ransom for; to buy off; to deliver.

Rant, rant, vi. To speak in extravagant language.—n. Boisterous, empty declamation; bombast.

Rap, rap, n. A quick smart blow; a knock.—vi. (rapping, rapped). To strike a quick, sharp blow.—vt. To strike with a quick blow.

Rapacious, ra-pā'shus, a. Greedy of plunder; subsisting on prey; extortionate.

Rape, rāp, n. A seizing by violence; carnal knowledge of a woman against her will; a plant of the cabbage kind, whose seeds yield an oil.—vt. (raping, raped). To carry off violently; to ravish.

Rapid, ra'pid, a. Very swift; speedy; hurried.—n. A swift current in a river.

Rapine, ra'pin, n. Act of plundering; violent seizure of goods; pillage.

Rapt, rapt, a. Transported; enraptured.

Rapture, rap'tūr, n. Extreme joy or pleasure; ecstasy; transport; enthusiasm.

Rare, rār, a. Not dense or compact; sparse; not frequent; uncommon; very valuable; underdone, as meat.

Rarefy, rā'rē-fi, vt. and i. (rarefying, rarefied). To make or become less dense.

Rarity, ra'ri-ti, n. State of being rare; a thing valued for its scarcity; tenuity.

Rascal, ras'kal, n. A scoundrel; a rogue.—a. Worthless; mean; low; base.

Rash, rash, a. Precipitate; hasty; overbold; incautious.—n. An eruption on the skin.

Rasher, rash'er, n. A thin slice of bacon.

Rasp, räsp, vt. To rub with something rough; to grate; to utter harshly.—vi. To rub or grate.—n. A coarse file; a raspberry.

Raspberry, räz'be-ri, n. The fruit of a plant allied to the bramble; the plant itself.

Raspy, räsp'i, a. Grating; harsh; rough.

Rat, rat, n. A small rodent; one who deserts his party.—vi. (ratting, ratted). To catch or kill rats; to desert one's party.

Ratchet, rach'et, n. A catch which abuts against the teeth of a wheel to prevent it running back.

Rate, rāt, n. Proportion; standard; degree; degree of speed; price; a tax; assessment.—vt. (rating, rated). To fix the value, rank, or degree of; to appraise; to reprove; to scold.—vi. To be classed in a certain order.

Rather, räᴛʜ'er, adv. More readily; preferably; more properly; somewhat.

Ratify, ra'ti-fi, vt. (ratifying, ratified). To confirm; to approve and sanction.

Ratio, rā'shi-ō, n. Relation or proportion; rate.

Ratiocination, ra-shi-os'i-nā''shon, n. The act or process of reasoning.

Ration, ra'shon, n. A daily allowance of provisions; allowance.—vt. To supply with rations.

Rational, ra'shon-al, a. Endowed with reason; agreeable to reason; judicious.

Rationale, ra-shon-ā'lē, n. Exposition of the principles of some process, action, etc.

Rationalism, ra'shon-al-izm, n. A system of opinions deduced from reason, as distinct from inspiration or opposed to it.

Rattle, rat'l, vi. and t. (rattling, rattled). To clatter; to chatter fluently.—n. A rapid succession of clattering sounds; an instrument or toy which makes a clattering sound; one who talks much and rapidly.

Rattlesnake, rat'l-snāk, n. A venomous American snake, with horny pieces at the point of the tail which rattle.

Raucous, ra'kus, a. Hoarse; harsh.

Ravage, ra'vāj, n. Devastation; havoc.—vt. (ravaging, ravaged). To lay waste; to pillage.

Rave, rāv, vi. (raving, raved). To be delirious; to speak enthusiastically; to dote.

Ravel, ra'vel, vt. (ravelling, ravelled). To disentangle; to make intricate; to involve.

Raven, rā'vn, n. A bird of prey of the crow kind, of a black color.

Ravenous, rav'en-us, a. Furiously voracious; hungry even to rage.

Ravine, ra-vēn', n. A long hollow formed by a torrent; a gorge or pass.

Raving, rāv'ing, n. Irrational, incoherent talk; delirious utterances.

Ravish, ra'vish, vt. To carry away by violence; to enrapture; to commit a rape upon.

Raw, ra, a. Not cooked or dressed; not manufactured; unfinished; not diluted; bare, as flesh; galled; sensitive; inexperienced; cold and damp.

Ray, rā, n. A line of light; a gleam of intellectual light; one of a number of diverging radii; a flatfish.—vt. and i. (raying, rayed). To shine forth; to radiate; to streak.

Rayon, rā'on, n. Artificial silk, made from cellulose.

Raze, rāz, vt. (razing, razed). To graze; to lay level with the ground; to efface.

Razor, rā'zor, n. A knife for shaving off hair.

Reach, rēch, vt. To extend; to hand; to extend or stretch from a distance; to arrive at; to gain.—vi. To extend; to stretch out the hand in order to touch; to make efforts at attainment.—n. Act or power of extending to; straight course of a river; scope.

React, rē-akt', vi. To act in return; to return an impulse; to act reciprocally upon each other.—vt. To perform anew.

Reaction, rē-ak'shon, n. A reacting; reciprocal

action; tendency to revert to a previous condition; exhaustion consequent on activity, and *vice versa.*

Read, rēd, *vt.* (reading, read). To peruse; to utter aloud, following something written or printed; to explain.—*vi.* To peruse; to study; to stand written or printed; to make sense.—*a.* red. instructed by reading; learned.

Readiness, re'di-nes, *n.* Quickness; promptitude; facility; aptitude; alacrity.

Ready, re'di, *a.* Prepared; in order; prompt; willing; inclined; at hand; opportune.

Reagent, rē-ā'jent, *n.* Anything that produces reaction; a substance employed chemically to detect the presence of other bodies.

Real, rē'al, *a.* Actual; true; genuine; in *law,* pertaining to things fixed or immovable, as lands and houses.

Realism, rē'al-izm, *n.* The endeavor in art or literature to reproduce nature or describe life as it actually appears.

Reality, rē-al'i-ti, *n.* State or quality of being real; actuality; fact; truth.

Realize, rē'al-īz, *vt.* (realizing, realized). To make real; to convert into money; to impress on the mind as a reality; to render tangible or effective; to acquire; to gain.

Realm, relm, *n.* The dominions of a sovereign; a region, sphere, or domain.

Realty, rē'al-ti, *n.* The fixed nature of property termed *real;* real property.

Ream, rēm, *n.* A package of paper, consisting generally of 20 quires, or 480 sheets.

Reanimate, rē-an'i-māt, *vt.* To animate again; to revive, to infuse new life into.

Reap, rēp, *vt.* and *i.* To cut with a scythe, etc., as grain; to gather; to clear of a grain crop; to receive as a reward of labor, etc.

Rear, rēr, *n.* The part behind; the part of an army behind the rest; the background.—*vt.* To raise; to bring up, as young; to breed, as cattle; to build up.—*vi.* To rise on the hind-legs, as horse; to become erect.

Rearmost, rēr'mōst, *a.* Farthest in the rear; last of all.

Rearrange, rē'a-rānj, *vt.* To arrange again; to put in different order.

Reason, rē'zn, *n.* A motive or cause; explanation; faculty for logical operations; justice; equity; moderate demands.—*vi.* To exercise the faculty of reason; to argue; to discuss.—*vt.* To examine or discuss by arguments; to persuade by reasoning.

Reasonable, rē'zn-a-bl, *a.* Having the faculty of reason; rational; conformable to reason; moderate; fair; tolerable.

Reasoning, rē'zn-ing, *n.* The act or process of exercising the faculty of reason; arguments employed.

Reassurance, rē-a-shōr'ans, *n.* Act of reassuring; a second assurance against loss.

Reassure, rē-a-shōr', *vt.* To assure anew; to free from fear or terror; to reinsure.

Reave, rēv, *vt.* (reaving, reaved or reft). To take away by violence; to bereave.

Rebate, rē-bāt', *vt.* (rebating, rebated). To blunt; to diminish; to make a discount from.

Rebel, re'bel, *n.* One who makes war against or opposes constituted authorities.—*a.* Rebellious; acting in revolt.—*vi.* rē-bel' (rebelling, rebelled). To oppose lawful authority; to revolt; to conceive a loathing.

Rebound, rē-bound', *vi.* To spring or bound back; to recoil.—*n.* The act of flying back on collision; resilience.

Rebuff, rē-buf', *n.* A sudden check; a repulse; refusal.—*vt.* To beat back; to check; to repel the advances of.

Rebuke, rē-būk', *vt.* (rebuking, rebuked). To reprimand; to reprove sharply.—*n.* A direct and severe reprimand; reproof.

Rebus, rē'bus, *n.* A set of words represented by pictures of objects; a kind of puzzle made up of such pictures.

Rebut, rē-but', *vt.* (rebutting, rebutted). To repel; to refute; in *law,* to oppose by argument, plea, or countervailing proof.

Recalcitrant, rē-kal'si-trant, *a.* Not submissive; refractory.

Recalcitrate, rē-kal'si-trāt, *vi.* To show resistance; to be refractory.

Recall, rē-kal', *vt.* To call or bring back; to revive in memory.—*n.* A calling back.

Recant, rē-kant', *vt.* To retract, as a declaration.—*vi.* To retract one's words.

Recapitulate, rē-ka-pit'ū-lāt, *vt.* To give a summary of.—*vi.* To repeat briefly.

Recapture, rē-kap'tūr, *n.* Act of retaking; a prize retaken.—*vt.* To retake.

Recast, rē-kast', *vt.* To throw again; to mold anew.

Recede, rē-sēd', *vi.* (receding, receded). To go back; to withdraw.—*vt.* To cede back.

Receipt, rē-sēt', *n.* Act of receiving; that which is received; a written acknowledgment of something received; a recipe.—*vt.* To give a receipt for; to discharge, as an account.

Receive, rē-sēv', *vt.* (receiving, received). To take, as a thing offered; to admit; to entertain; to contain; to be the object of; to take stolen goods.

Recension, rē-sen'shon, *n.* A revision of the text of an author; an edited version.

Recent, rē'sent, *a.* New; late; fresh.

Receptacle, rē-sep'ta-kl, *n.* A place or vessel in which anything is received; repository.

Reception, rē-sep'shon, *n.* Act or manner of receiving; welcome; a formal receiving of guests; admission or acceptance.

Receptive, rē-sep'tiv, *a.* Such as to receive readily; able to take in or contain.

Recess, rē-ses', *n.* A withdrawing; place or period of retirement; time during which business is suspended; a niche in a wall; an alcove.

Recipe, re'si-pē, *n.* A medical prescription; a statement of ingredients for a mixture.

Recipient, rē-si'pi-ent, *n.* One who or that which receives; a receiver.

Reciprocal, rē-sip'rō-kal, *a.* Reciprocating; alternate; done by each to the other; mutual; interchangeable.

Reciprocate, rē-sip'rō-kāt, *vi.* To move backward and forward; to alternate.—*vt.* To exchange; to give in requital.

Reciprocity, re-si-pros'i-ti, *n.* Reciprocation; interchange; reciprocal obligation; equal commercial rights mutually enjoyed.

Recital, rē-sīt'al, *n.* Act of reciting; narration; a musical entertainment.

Recitation, re-si-tā'shon, *n.* Recital; the delivery before an audience of the compositions of others.

Recite, rē-sīt', *vt.* and *i.* (reciting, recited). To repeat aloud, as a writing committed to memory; to relate; to recapitulate.

Reckless, rek'les, *a.* Heedless; careless; rash.

Reckon, rek'n, *vt.* and *i.* To count; to estimate; to account, consider.

Reckoning, rek'n-ing, *n.* Calculation; a statement of accounts with another; landlord's bill; calculation of a ship's position.

Reclaim, rē-klām', *vt.* To claim back; to reform; to tame; to recover; to reduce to a state fit for cultivation.

Recline, rē-klīn', *vt.* and *i* (reclining, reclined). To lean; to rest or repose.

Recluse, rē-klōs', *a.* Retired; solitary.—*n.* A person who lives in seclusion; a hermit.

Recognition, re-kog-ni'shon, *n.* Act of recognizing; avowal; acknowledgment.

Recognizance, rē-kog'niz-ans or rē-kon'i-zans, *n.* Recognition; an obligation, as to appear at the assizes, keep the peace, etc.

Recognize, re'kog-nīz, *vt.* (recognizing, recognized). To know again; to admit a knowledge of; to acknowledge formally; to indicate one's notice by a bow, etc.; to indicate appreciation of.

Recoil, rē-koil', *vi.* To move or start back; to retreat; to shrink; to rebound.—*n.* A starting or falling back; rebound, as of a gun.

Recommend, re-kom-mend', *vt.* To praise to another; to make acceptable; to commit with prayers; to advise.

Recompense, re'kom-pens, *vt.* (recompensing, recompensed). To compensate; to requite; to make amends for.—*n.* Compensation; reward; amends.

Reconcile, re'kon-sīl, *vt.* (reconciling, reconciled). To make friendly again; to adjust or settle; to harmonize.

Reconciliation, re'kon-si-li-ā''shon, *n.* Act of reconciling; renewal of friendship.

Recondite, rē-kon'dīt or re'kon-dīt, *a.* Abstruse; profound.

Reconnaissance, re-kon'nā-sans,*n.* The act or operation of reconnoitering.

Reconnoiter, re-kon-noi'tér, *vt.* and *i.* (reconnoitering, reconnoitered). To make a preliminary survey of; to survey for military purposes.

Reconsideration, rē-kon-si'dèr-ā''shon, *n.* Act of reconsidering; renewed consideration.

Record, rē-kord', *vt.* To preserve in writing; to register; to chronicle.—*n.* rek'ord. A written memorial; a register; a public document; memory; one's personal history; best results in contests.

Recount, rē-kount', *vt.* To relate in detail; to count again.—*n.* A second counting.

Recoup, rē-köp', *vt.* To recompense or compensate; to indemnify.

Recourse, rē-kōrs', *n.* A going to with a request, as for aid; resort in perplexity.

Recover, rē-kuv'ér, *vt.* To get back; to regain; to revive; to rescue; to obtain in return for injury or debt.—*vi.* To grow well; to regain a former condition.

Recovery, rē-kuv'èr-i, *n.* Act of recovering; restoration from sickness, etc.; the obtaining of something by legal procedure.

Recreant, re'krē-ant, *a.* Craven; cowardly; apostate.—*n.* One who basely yields in combat; a cowardly wretch.

Recreate, re'krē-āt, *vt.* To revive; to enliven; to amuse.—*vi.* To take recreation.

Recreation, re-krē-a'shon, *n.* Refreshment of the strength and spirits after toil; amusement; entertainment.

Recriminate, rē-krim'in-āt, *vi.* To return one accusation with another.—*vt.* To accuse in return.

Recruit, rē-kröt', *vt.* To repair; to supply with new soldiers.—*vi.* To gain new supplies of anything; to raise new soldiers.—*n.* A soldier newly enlisted.

Rectangle, rek'tang-gl, *n.* A quadrilateral having all its angles right angles.

Rectification, rek'ti-fi-kā''shon, *n.* Act or operation of rectifying; process of refining by repeated distillation.

Rectify, rek'ti-fī, *vt.* (rectifying, rectified). To correct; to refine by repeated distillation.

Rectilineal, Rectilinear, rek-ti-lin'ē-al, rek-ti-lin'ē-èr, *a.* Consisting of straight lines.

Rectitude, rek'ti-tūd, *n.* Integrity; probity; uprightness; honesty.

Rector, rek'tor, *n.* A ruler; an Episcopal clergyman who has the cure of a parish; a head of certain institutions, chiefly academical.

Rectory, rek'to-ri, *n.* A church or living held by a rector; a rector's house.

Rectum, rek'tum, *n.* The lowest part of the large intestine opening at the anus.

Recumbent, rē-kum'bent, *a.* Leaning; reclining; reposing; inactive.

Recuperate, rē-kū'pèr-āt, *vt.* and *i.* (recuperating, recuperated). To recover.

Recur, rē-kèr', *vi.* (recurring, recurred). To return; to be repeated at a stated interval.

Recurrent, rē-ku'rent, *a.* Recurring from time to time.

Recusancy, Recusance, re'kū-zan-si, re'kū-zans, *n.* Nonconformity.

Red, red, *a.* Of a color resembling that of arterial blood.—*n.* A color resembling that of arterial blood; a red pigment.

Redact, rē-dakt', *vt.* To edit; to give a presentable literary form to.

Redden, red'n, *vt.* To make red.—*vi.* To become red; to blush.

Redeem, rē-dēm', *vt.* To buy back; to ransom; to rescue; to save; to atone for; to employ to the best purpose; to perform, as what has been promised.

Redeemer, rē-dēm'èr, *n.* One who redeems; Jesus Christ.

Redemption, rē-dem'shon, *n.* The act of redeeming; state of being redeemed; ransom; release; deliverance.

Red-lead, red'led, *n.* An oxide of lead of a fine red color, used in painting, etc.; minium.

Red-letter, red'let-èr, *a.* Having red letters; fortunate or auspicious.

Redolent, re'dō-lent, *a.* Emitting an odor; having or diffusing a sweet scent.

Redouble, rē-du'bl, *vt.* To double again.—*vi.* To become twice as much.

Redoubtable, rē-dout'a-bl, *a.* Such as to cause dread; formidable; valiant.

Redound, rē-dound', *vi.* To conduce; to contribute; to have effect.

Redout, Redoubt, rē-dout', *n.* A small inclosed fortification.

Redraft, rē-dräft', *vt.* To draft anew.—*n.* A second draft; a second order for money.

Redraw, rē-dra', *vt.* To draw again.—*vi.* To draw a new bill of exchange.

Redress, rē-dres', *vt.* To set right; to adjust; to repair; to relieve.—*n.* Relief; deliverance; reparation.

Red-tape, red'tāp, *n.* Excessive official routine and formality.—*a.* Characterized by excessive routine or formality.

Reduce, rē-dūs', *vt.* (reducing, reduced). To bring down; to decrease; to degrade; to subdue; to bring under rules or within categories; to restore to its proper place.

Reduction, rē-duk'shon, *n.* Act of reducing; diminution; conversion into another state or form; subjugation.

Redundant, rē-dun'dant, *a.* Superfluous; having more words than necessary.

Reduplication, rē-dü'pli-kā''shon, *n.* Act of reduplicating; the repetition of a root or initial syllable.

Redwood, red'wud, *n.* A name of various reddish timbers.

Reed, rēd, *n.* A tall broad-leaved grass growing in marshy places, or its hollow stems; a musical instrument; a rustic pipe.

Reedy, rēd'i, *a.* Abounding with reeds; harsh and thin, as a voice.

Reef-point, rēf'point, *n.* One of the small pieces of line for tying up a sail when reefed.

Reek, rēk, *n.* Vapor; steam; exhalation; smoke.—*vi.* To smoke; to exhale.

Reel, rēl, *n.* A bobbin for thread; a revolving appliance for winding a fishing-line; a staggering motion; a lively Scottish dance.—*vt.* To wind upon a reel; to stagger.

Re-establish, rē-es-tab'lish, *vt.* To establish anew; to fix or confirm again.

Re-export, rē-eks-pōrt', *vt.* To export after having been imported.—*n.* rē-eks'pōrt. Any commodity re-exported.

Re-fashion, rē-fa'shon, *vt.* To fashion or form into shape a second time.

Refectory, rē-fek'to-ri, *n.* A room for refreshment or meals.

Refer, rē-fèr', *vt.* (referring, referred). To trace or carry back; to attribute; to appeal; to assign.—*vi.* To respect or have relation; to appeal; to apply; to allude.

Referee, ref-èr-ē', *n.* One to whom a matter in dispute is referred for decision; an umpire.

Reference, re'fèr-ens, *n.* Act of referring; allusion;

relation; one of whom inquiries may be made.

Referendum, ref-er-en'dum, *n.* The referring of a measure passed by a legislature to the people for final approval.

Refine, rē-fīn', *vt.* (refining, refined). To increase the fineness of; to purify; to make elegant; to give culture to.—*vi.* To become purer; to indulge in hair-splitting.

Refined, rē-fīnd', *p.a.* Free from what is coarse, rude, etc.; polished; polite.

Refinery, rē-fīn'er-i, *n.* A place and apparatus for refining sugar, metals, etc.

Refit, rē-fit', *vt.* and *i* (refitting, refitted). To fit anew; to repair.—*n.* Repair.

Reflect, rē-flekt', *vt.* To cast back; to throw off, as light or heat, after striking the surface; to mirror.—*vi.* To throw back light or heat; to meditate; to bring reproach.

Reflection, rē-flek'shon, *n.* Act of reflecting; that which is produced by being reflected; meditation; a censorious remark; reproach.

Reflective, rē-flekt'iv, *a.* Throwing back rays; meditating.

Reflex, rē'fleks, *a.* Bent or directed back; done involuntarily or unconsciously.—*n.* A reflection.

Reflexive, rē-flek'siv, *a.* Reflective; having respect to something past; in *grammar,* having for its object a pronoun which stands for the subject, also applied to such pronouns.

Reflux, rē'fluks, *n.* A flowing back; ebb.

Reform, rē-form', *vt.* and *i.* To change from worse to better; to amend; to form anew.—*n.* A beneficial change; amendment; a change in the regulations of parliamentary representation.

Reformation, re-for-mā'shon, *n.* Act of reforming; amendment; the Protestant revolution of the sixteenth century.

Reformatory, rē-for'ma-to-ri, *n* An institution for reclaiming young criminals.

Reformer, rē-form'er, *n.* One who reforms; one who took a part in the Reformation; one who promotes political reform.

Refract, rē-frakt', *vt.* To bend back sharply; to deflect (a ray of light) on passing from one medium into another.

Refraction, rē-frak'shon, *n.* Act of refracting; a change of direction in rays on passing from one medium into another.

Refractory, rē-frak'to-ri, *a.* Sullen in disobedience; tubborn; unmanageable; resisting ordinary treatment

Refrain, rē-frān', *vt.* To restrain; to keep (oneself) from action.—*vi.* To forbear; to abstain.—*n.* The burden of a song; part repeated at the end of every stanza.

Refresh, rē-fresh', *vt.* To revive; to reanimate; to freshen.

Refreshing, rē-fresh'ing, *a.* Invigorating; reanimating; enlivening.

Refrigerate, rē-fri'je-rāt, *vt.* To cool.

Refrigeration, rē-fri'je-rā''shon, *n.* Act of refrigerating; abatement of heat.

Refrigerator, rē-frij'e-rāt-er, *n.* That which refrigerates; an apparatus for cooling or for making ice; a refrigerant.

Refrigent, rē-frin'jent, *a.* Refractive; refracting.

Refuge, re'fūj, *n.* Protection from danger or distress; a retreat; a shelter; a device; contrivance; shift.—*vt.* and *i.* To shelter.

Refugee, re-fū-jē', *n.* One who flees for refuge; one who flees to another country or place for safety

Refulgent, rē-ful'jent, *a.* Casting a bright light; shining; splendid.

Refund, rē-fund', *vt.* To pay back; to repay; to reimburse

Refuse, rē-fūz', *vt.* (refusing, refused). To deny, as a request or demand; to decline; to reject.—*vi.* To decline a request or offer.

Refuse, re'fūz, *a.* Rejected; worthless.—*n.* Waste matter; dregs.

Refutation, re-fūt-ā'shon, *n.* Act or process of refuting; disproof.

Refute, rē-fūt', *vt.* (refuting, refuted). To disprove; to overthrow by argument.

Regain, re-gān', *vt.* To gain anew; to recover; to retrieve; to reach again.

Regal, rē'gal, *a.* Kingly; royal.

Regale, rē-gāl', *vt.* and *i.* (regaling, regaled). To refresh sumptuously; to feast.—*n.* A splendid feast; a treat.

Regality, rē-gal'i-ti, *n.* Royalty; kingship.

Regard, rē-gärd', *vt.* To notice carefully; to observe; to respect; to heed; to view in the light of; to relate to.—*n.* Look or gaze; respect; notice; heed; esteem; deference; *pl.* good wishes.

Regarding, rē-gärd'ing, *prep.* Respecting; concerning; relating to.

Regardless, rē-gärd'les, *a.* Without regard or heed; heedless; negligent; careless.

Regatta, rē-gat'a, *n.* A race in which yachts or boats contend for prizes.

Regency, rē'jen-si, *n.* Government of a regent; men intrusted with the power of a regent.

Regenerate, rē-jen'e-rāt, *vt.* To generate anew; to bring into a better state.—*n.* Born anew; changed to a spiritual state.

Regeneration, rē-jen'e-rā''shon, *n.* Act of regenerating; that change by which love to God is implanted in the heart.

Regent, rē'jent, *a.* Ruling.—*n.* A ruler; one who governs during the minority or disability of the king.

Regicide, re'ji-sīd, *n.* One who kills a king; the murder of a king.

Regime, rā-zhēm', *n.* Mode of management; administration; rule.

Regimen, re'ji-men, *n.* Orderly government; regulation of diet, exercise, etc.

Region, rē'jun, *n.* A tract of land; country; territory; portion of the body.

Register, re'jis-ter, *n.* An official record; a roll; a book for special entries of facts; device for indicating work done by machinery; musical compass; a stop in an organ.—*vt.* To record; to insure (a letter).—*vi.* To enter one's name.

Registrar, re'jis-trär, *n.* An officer who keeps a public register or record.

Registry, re'jis-tri, *n.* Registration; place where a register is kept; an entry.

Regress, rē'gres, *n.* Return; power of returning. —*vi.* rē-gres'. To go back.

Regret, rē-gret', *n.* Grief at something done or undone; remorse; penitence. —*vt.* (regretting, regretted). To be sorry for; to lament.

Regular, re'gū-ler, *a.* Conformed to a rule, law, or principle; normal; methodical; uniform; having the parts symmetrical; thorough.—*n.* A monk who has taken the vows in some order; a soldier of a permanent army.

Regulate, re'gū-lāt, *vt.* (regulating, regulated). To adjust by rule; to put or keep in good order; to direct.

Regurgitate, rē-ger'jit-tāt, *vt.* and *i.* To pour or cause to surge back.

Rehabilitate, rē-ha-bil'i-tāt, *vt.* To restore to a former capacity or position; to re-establish in esteem.

Rehearse, rē-hers', *vt.* (rehearsing, rehearsed). To repeat; to recite; to relate; to repeat in private for trial.

Reign, rān, *vi.* To be sovereign; to rule; to prevail.—*n.* Royal authority; supremacy; time of a sovereign's supreme authority.

Reimburse, rē-im-bers', *vt.* To refund; to pay back.

Reimport, rē-im-pōrt', *vt.* To carry back to the country of exportation.—*n.* rē-im'pōrt. Something reimported.

Rein, rān, *n.* The strap of a bridle, by which a horse is governed; an instrument for restraining; restraint.—*vt.* To govern by a bridle; to restrain.—*vi.* To obey the reins.

Reindeer, rān'der, *n.* A deer of northern parts, with broad branched antlers.

Reinforce, rē-in-fōrs', *vt.* To strengthen by new

assistance, as troops.—*n.* An additional thickness given to an object to strengthen it.

Reinstate, rē-in-stāt', *vt.* To instate anew; to restore to a former position.

Reiterate, rē-it'ėr-āt, *vt.* To repeat again and again; to do or say repeatedly.

Reject, rē-jekt', *vt.* To cast off; to discard; to repel; to forsake; to decline.

Rejoice, rē-jois', *vi.* (rejoicing, rejoiced). To be glad; to exult.—*vt.* To gladden; to cheer.

Rejoinder, rē-join'dėr, *n.* An answer to a reply.

Rejuvenate, rē-jū'ven-āt, *vt.* To restore to youth; to make young again.

Relapse, rē-laps', *vi.* (relapsing, relapsed). To slip back; to return to a former state.—*n.* A falling back, either in health or morals.

Relate, rē-lāt', *vt.* (relating, related). To tell; to narrate; to ally by kindred.—*vi.* To refer; to stand in some relation.

Relation, rē-lā'shon, *n.* Act of relating; account; reference; connection; kindred; a relative; proportion.

Relative, re'lat-iv, *a.* Having relation or reference; not absolute or existing by itself; relevant.—*n.* Something considered in its relation to something else; one allied by blood; a word which relates to or represents another word or sentence.

Relax, rē-laks', *vt.* To slacken; to loosen or weaken; to unbend.—*vi.* To become loose, feeble, or languid; to abate in severity.

Release, rē-lēs', *vt.* (releasing, released). To liberate; to disengage; to acquit.—*n.* Liberation; discharge; acquittance.

Relegate, re'lē-gāt, *vt.* To consign to some remote destination; to banish.

Relent, rē-lent', *vi.* To soften in temper; to yield or become less severe.

Relentless, rē-lent'les, *a.* Unmerciful; implacable; pitiless.

Relevant, re'le-vant, *a.* Applicable; pertinent; to the purpose.

Reliable, rē-li'a-bl, *a.* That may be relied on; trustworthy.

Reliant, rē-li'ant, *a.* Confident; self-reliant.

Relic, re'lik, *n.* A remaining fragment; the body of a deceased person (usually in *pl.*); a memento or keepsake.

Relief, rē-lēf', *n.* Ease or mitigation of pain; succor; remedy; redress; assistance given to a pauper; one who relieves another by taking duty; prominence of figures above a plane surface in sculpture, carving, etc.; prominence or distinctness.

Relieve, rē-lēv', *vt.* (relieving, relieved). To remove or lessen, as anything that pains; to ease; to succor; to release from duty; to give variety to; to set off by contrast; to give the appearance of projection to.

Religion, rē-li'jon, *n.* An acknowledgment of our obligation to God; practical piety; devotion; any system of faith and worship.

Religious, rē-li'jus, *a.* Pertaining to religion; teaching religion; used in worship; devout; scrupulously faithful.

Relinquish, rē-ling'kwish, *vt.* To give up; to leave; to resign; to renounce.

Relish, re'lish, *vt.* To enjoy the taste of; to have a taste for; to give an agreeable taste to.—*vi.* To have a pleasing taste.—*n.* Taste, usually pleasing; fondness; flavor; something to increase the pleasure of eating.

Reluctant, rē-luk'tant, *a.* Loath; averse; acting with slight repugnance.

Rely, rē-li', *vt.* (relying, relied). To rest with confidence; to trust; with *on* or *upon.*

Remain, rē-mān', *vi.* To continue in a place or condition; to abide; to be left; to last.—*n.* That which is left; *pl.* a dead body; literary works of one who is dead.

Remainder, rē-mān'dėr, *n.* That which remains; residue; remnant; an estate limited so as to be enjoyed after the death of the present possessor or otherwise.—*a.* Left over.

Remand, rē-mand', *vt.* To call or send back; to send back to jail.

Remark, rē-märk', *n.* Notice; an observation in words; a comment.—*vt.* To observe; to utter by way of comment.

Remarkable, rē-märk'a-bl, *a.* Worthy of remark; conspicuous; unusual; extraordinary.

Remediable, re-mē'di-a-bl, *a.* Curable.

Remedial, re-mē'di-al, *a.* Affording a remedy; healing; intended for a remedy.

Remedy, re'me-di, *n.* That which cures a disease; that which counteracts an evil; redress.—*vt.* (remedying, remedied). To cure; to repair; to redress; to counteract.

Remember, rē-mem'bėr, *vt.* To have in the memory; to think of; to observe; to give a gratuity for service done.—*vi.* To have something in remembrance.

Remembrance, rē-mem'brans, *n.* The keeping of a thing in mind; memory; what is remembered; a memorial; a keepsake.

Remind, rē-mind', *vt.* To put in mind; to cause to remember.

Reminiscence, re-mi-nis'ens, *n.* Recollection; what is recalled to mind; account of past incidents within one's knowledge.

Remiss, rē-mis', *a.* Careless; negligent; heedless; slack.

Remission, rē-mi'shon, *n.* Act of remitting; relinquishment; abatement; pardon.

Remit, rē-mit', *vt.* (remitting, remitted). To relax; to abate; to relinquish; to forgive; to transmit or send.—*vi.* To slacken; to abate in violence for a time.

Remittent, rē-mit'ent, *a.* Temporarily ceasing.—*n.* A remittent fever.

Remnant, rem'nant, *n.* That which is left; a scrap, fragment.—*a.* Remaining.

Remonstrance, rē-mon'strans, *n.* Act of remonstrating; expostulation; strong representation against something.

Remonstrate, rē-mon'strāt, *vi.* To present strong reasons against an act; to expostulate.

Remorse, rē-mors', *n.* Reproach of conscience; compunction for wrong committed.

Remorseless, rē-mors'les, *a.* Without remorse; ruthless; relentless; merciless.

Remote, rē-mōt', *a.* Distant in place or time; not immediate or direct; slight; inconsiderable.

Remove, rē-möv', *vt.* (removing, removed). To move from its place; to take away; to displace from an office; to banish or destroy.—*vi.* To be moved from its place; to change the place of residence.—*n.* A removal; departure.

Remunerate, rē-mū'nė-rāt, *vt.* To reward for service; to recompense.

Renaissance, re-nā'sans, *n.* Revival; the revival of letters and arts in the fifteenth century.

Renal, rē'nal, *a.* Pertaining to the kidneys.

Renard, re'närd, *n.* A fox.

Renascent, rē-nas'ent, *a.* Springing into being again; reappearing; rejuvenated.

Rencounter, ren-koun'tėr, *n.* An abrupt meeting of persons; a casual combat; encounter.—*vi.* To meet an enemy unexpectedly.

Rend, rend, *vt.* (rending, rent). To force asunder; to tear away; to sever.—*vi.* To be or become torn; to split.

Render, ren'dėr, *vt.* To give in return; to give back; to present; to afford; to invest with qualities; to translate; to interpret; to clarify, as tallow.

Rendezvous, ren'de-vö, *n.* A place of meeting.—*vi.* To meet at a particular place.

Rendition, ren-di'shon, *n.* A rendering; interpretation; translation; surrender.

Renegade, re'nē-gād, *n.* An apostate; a deserter.

Renew, rē-nū', *vt.* To make new again; to repair; to repeat; to grant anew; to transform.—*vi.* To grow or begin again.

Reniform, rē'ni-form, *a.* Having the shape of the kidneys.

Rennet, ren'et, n. The prepared inner membrane of the calf's stomach, which coagulates milk; a kind of apple.

Renounce, rē-nouns', vt. (renouncing, renounced). To disown; to reject; to forsake.—vi. To revoke

Renovate, re'nō-vāt, vt. To renew; to restore to freshness.

Renown, rē-noun', n. Fame; glory; reputation.—vt. To make famous.

Rent, rent, n. Money, etc., payable yearly for the use of lands or tenements; a tear; a schism.—vt. To let on lease; to hold on condition of paying rent.—vi. To be leased or let for rent.

Renunciation, rē-nun'si-ā''shon, n. Act of renouncing; disavowal; abandonment.

Repair, rē-pār', vt. To restore; to refit; to mend; to retrieve.—vi. To betake oneself; to resort.—n. Restoration; supply of loss; state as regards repairing; a resorting; abode.

Reparation, re-pa-rā'shon, n. Act of repairing; restoration; satisfaction for injury; amends.

Repartee, re-pär-tē', n. A smart, ready, and witty reply.

Repast, rē-past', n. Act of taking food; food taken; a meal.—vt. and i. To feed.

Repatriate, rē-pā'tri-āt, vt. To restore to one's own country.

Repay, re-pa', vt. To pay back or again; to refund; to requite.

Repeal, rē-pēl', vt. To recall; to revoke; to abrogate, as a law.—n. Act of repealing; abrogation.

Repeat, rē-pēt', vt. To do or utter again; to recite; to recapitulate.—n. Repetition.

Repeating, rē-pēt'ing, a. Producing a like result several times in succession.

Repel, rē-pel', vt. (repelling, repelled). To drive back; to resist successfully.—vi. To cause repugnance; to shock.

Repellent, rē-pel'ent, a. Having the effect of repelling; repulsive; deterring.

Repent, rē-pent', vi. To feel regret for something done or left undone; to be penitent.—vt. To remember with self-reproach or sorrow.

Repentance, rē-pent'ans, n. Act of repenting; sorrow for sin; penitence; contrition.

Repercussion, rē-pér-ku'shon, n. Act of driving back, reverberation.

Repertoire, rep'ér-twär, n. The aggregate of pieces that an actor or company performs.

Repetition, rē-pē-ti'shon, n. Act of repeating; recital; that which is repeated.

Replace, re-plas', vt. (replacing, replaced). To put again in the former place; to put in the place of another; to take the place of.

Replenish, rē-plen'ish, vt. To fill again; to fill completely; to stock abundantly.

Replete, rē-plēt', a. Filled up; full; abounding; thoroughly imbued.

Replevy, rē-plev'i, vt. (replevying, replevied). To reclaim (as goods wrongfully seized) upon giving security to try the cause in court.

Replica, rep'li-ka, n. A copy of a picture or a piece of sculpture made by the hand that executed the original; facsimile.

Reply, rē-pli', vi. and t. (replying, replied). To answer; to respond; to do something in return.—n. An answer; a response; a rejoinder.

Report, rē-pōrt', vt. and i. To bring back, as an answer; to relate; to give an official statement of; to take down from the lips of a speaker, etc.; to lay a charge against.—n. An account; rumor; repute; noise of explosion; official statement; account of proceedings.

Reporter, rē-pōrt'ér, n. One who reports; one of a newspaper staff who gives accounts of public meetings, events, etc.

Repose, rē-pōz', vt. (reposing, reposed). To lay at rest.—vi. To lie at rest; to rely.—n. A lying at rest; tranquillity; composure; absence of show of feeling.

Repoussé, rē-pös'sā, a. Embossed.

Reprehend, re-prē-hend', vt. To charge with a fault; to reprove; to censure.

Reprehension, re-prē-hen'shon, n. Act of reprehending; reproof; censure; blame. Containing reprehension or reproof.

Represent, re-prē-zent', vt. To exhibit by a likeness of; to typify; to act the part of; to describe; to be a substitute for; to exemplify.

Representation, re'prē-zen-tā''shon, n. The act of representing; an image or likeness; dramatic performance; a remonstrance; the representing of a constituency.

Representative, re-prē-zent'a-tiv, a. Fitted or serving to represent; conducted by the agency of delegates; typical.—n. One who or that which represents; a person elected to represent a constituency.

Repress, rē-pres', vt. To press back; to check; to quell.

Reprieve, rē-prēv', vt. (reprieving, reprieved). To grant a respite to; to relieve temporarily.—n. Suspension of the execution of a criminal's sentence; respite.

Reprimand, rep'ri-mand, n. A severe reproof for a fault.—vt. rep-ri-mand'. To administer a sharp rebuke to.

Reprint, rē-print', vt. To print again.—n. rē'print. A second or new edition.

Reprisal, rē-priz'al, n. Seizure from an enemy by way of retaliation; retaliation.

Reproach, rē-prōch', vt. To charge severely with a fault; to censure.—n. Censure; blame; source of blame; disgrace.

Reprobate, re'prō-bāt, a. Morally abandoned; profligate.—n. A wicked, depraved wretch.—vt. To disapprove strongly; to reject.

Reproduce, rē-prō-dūs', vt. To produce again; to generate, as offspring; to portray or represent.

Reproduction, rē-prō-duk'shon, n. Act or process of reproducing; that which is produced anew; an accurate copy.

Reproof, rē-pröf', n. Words intended to reprove; rebuke.

Reprove, rē-pröv', vt. (reproving, reproved). To charge with a fault orally; to chide; to rebuke.

Reptile, rep'til, a. Creeping; grovelling.—n. An animal that moves on its belly, or by means of small short legs.

Republic, rē-pub'lik, n. A commonwealth; a state in which the supreme power is vested in elected representatives.

Repudiate, rē-pū'di-āt, vt. (repudiating, repudiated). To divorce; to reject; to disavow.

Repugnance, rē-pug'nans, n. Aversion; reluctance; dislike; inconsistency.

Repulse, rē-puls', n. Act of repelling; a check or defeat; refusal; denial.—vt. (repulsing, repulsed). To repel.

Repurchase, rē-pér'chās, vt. To buy back.—n. Purchase again of what has been sold.

Reputable, re'pūt-a-bl, a. Held in esteem; estimable.

Reputation, re-pūt-ā'shon, n. Character derived from public opinion; repute; good name; honor; fame.

Repute, rē-pūt', vt. (reputing, reputed). To estimate; to deem.—n. Reputation; character; good character.

Request, rē-kwest', n. An expressed desire; a petition; thing asked for; a state of being asked for.—vt. To ask; to beg.

Requiem, rē'kwi-em, n. A mass for the dead in the R. Catholic Church; music for this mass.

Require, rē-kwir', vt. (requiring, required). To ask as of right; to demand; to have need for; to find it necessary.

Requisite, re'kwi-zit, a. Necessary; essential.—n. Something indispensable.

Requisition, re-kwi-zi'shon, n. Act of requiring; demand; a written call or invitation.—vt. To make a demand upon or for.

Requite, rē-kwit', vt. (requiting, requited). To repay; to reward; to retaliate on.

Rescind, rē-sind', vt. To abrogate; to annul; to re-

R

peal; to revoke.

Rescue, res'kū, *vt.* (rescuing, rescued). To deliver from confinement, danger, or evil.—*n.* Act of rescuing; deliverance.

Research, rē-sėrch', *n.* A diligent seeking of facts or principles; investigation.—*vt.* To search again.

Resemblance, rē-zem'blans, *n.* Likeness; similarity; something similar; similitude.

Resemble, rē-zem'bl, *vt.* (resembling, resembled). To be like; to liken; to compare.

Resent, rē-zent', *vt.* To take ill; to consider as an affront; to be angry at.—*vi.* To feel resentment.

Resentment, rē-zent'ment, *n.* Deep sense of injury; indignation; revengeful feeling.

Reservation, re-zėrv-ā'shon, *n.* Act of reserving; reserve; concealment; state of being treasured up; proviso.

Reserve, rē-zėrv', *vt.* (reserving, reserved). To keep in store; to retain.—*n.* Act of reserving; that which is retained; retention; habit of restraining the feelings; coldness towards others; shyness; troops kept for an exigency.

Reservoir, re'zėr-vwar, *n.* A place where anything is kept in store; an artificial lake to supply a town with water.

Reside, rē-zid', *vi.* (residing, resided). To have one's abode; to dwell; to inhere.

Residential, re-zi-den'shal, *a.* Pertaining to or suitable for residence.

Residual, rē-zid'ū-al, *a.* Left after a part is taken.

Residue, re'zi-dū, *n.* That which remains after a part is taken; remainder.

Resign, rē-zin', *vt.* To give up; to renounce; to submit, as to Providence.

Resignation, re-zig-nā'shon, *n.* Act of resigning; state of being resigned; habitual submission to Providence.

Resigned, rē-zind', *a.* Submissive; patient.

Resilience, Resiliency, rē-si'li-ens, rē-si'li-en-si, *n.* Act of resiling or rebounding; rebound from being elastic.

Resilient, rē-si'li-ent, *a.* Inclined to resile; rebounding.

Resin, re'zin, *n.* An inflammable vegetable substance; the hardened juice of pines.

Resist, rē-zist', *vt.* and *i.* To withstand; to oppose; to struggle against.

Resistant, Resistent, rē-zis'tent, *a.* Making resistance.—*n.* One who or that which resists.

Resolute, re-zō-lūt, *a.* Having fixedness of purpose; determined; steadfast.

Resolution, re-zō-lū'shon, *n.* Character of being resolute; determination; a formal decision; operation of separating the component parts; solution.

Resolve, rē-zolv', *vt.* (resolving, resolved). To separate the component parts of; to analyze; to solve; to determine; to decide.—*vi.* To separate into component parts; to melt; to determine; to decide.—*n.* Fixed purpose of mind; resolution.

Resonant, re'zo-nant, *a.* Resounding; full of sounds.

Resort, rē-zort', *vi.* To have recourse; to go; to repair frequently.—*n.* Recourse; concourse; a haunt.

Resound, rē-zound', *vt.* To give back the sound of; to echo; to praise.—*vi.* To sound again; to echo; to be much praised.

Resource, rē-sōrs', *n.* Any source of aid or support; expedient; *pl.* funds; means.

Respect, rē-spekt', *vt.* To regard; to relate to; to honor; to have consideration for.—*n.* Regard; attention; due deference; bias; a point or particular; reference.

Respectable, rē-spekt'a-bl, *a.* Worthy of respect; held in good repute; moderately good.

Respectful, rē-spekt'ful, *a.* Marked by respect; civil; dutiful; courteous.

Respecting, rē-spekt'ing, *prep.* In regard to; regarding; concerning.

Respire, rē-spīr', *vi.* and *t.* (respiring, respired). To breathe; to recover one's breath.

Respite, res'pit, *n.* Temporary intermission; interval; a reprieve.—*vt.* (respiting, respited). To grant a respite to; to reprieve.

Resplendent, rē-splen'dent, *a.* Very bright; shining with brilliant luster.

Respond, rē-spond', *vi.* To answer; to suit.—*n.* A short anthem; response.

Response, rē-spons', *n.* An answer; reply.

Responsibility, rē-spons'i-bil''i-ti, *n.* State of being responsible; that for which one is responsible; ability to answer in payment.

Responsible, rē-spons'i-bl, *a.* Answerable; accountable; important.

Responsive, rē-spons'iv, *a.* Making reply; answering; correspondent; suited.

Rest, rest, *n.* Cessation of action; peace; sleep; an appliance for support; a pause; remainder; the others.—*vi.* To cease from action; to lie for repose; to be supported; to be in a certain state; remain; to be left.—*vt.* To lay at rest; to place, as on a support.

Restaurant, res'tō-rong, *n.* An establishment for the sale of refreshments.

Restaurateur, res-tō'ra-tėr, *n.* The keeper of a restaurant.

Restitution, res-ti-tū'shon, *n.* Act of restoring; reparation; amends.

Restive, res'tiv, *a.* Stubborn; fidgeting; impatient under restraint or opposition.

Restless, rest'les, *a.* Without rest; disturbed; uneasy; anxious.

Restore, rē-stōr', *vt.* (restoring, restored). To make strong again; to repair; to cure; to reestablish; to give back.

Restrain, rē-strān', *vt.* To hold back; to curb; to check to repress; to restrict.

Restrict, rē-strikt', *vt.* To limit; to curb.

Restriction, rē-strik'shon, *n.* Act of restricting; limitation; a reservation.

Result, rē-zult', *vi.* To rise as a consequence; to issue; to ensue; to end.—*n.* Consequence; effect; issue; outcome.

Resume, rē-zūm', *vt.* (resuming, resumed). To take up again; to begin again.

Résumé, rā'zō-mā, *n.* A recapitulation; a summary.

Resurgent, rē-sėr'jent, *a.* Rising again.

Resurrection, re-zėr-rek'shon, *n.* A rising again; the rising of the dead at the general judgment.

Resuscitate, rē-sus'i-tāt, *vt.* and *i.* To revive.

Retail, rē-tāl', *vt.* To sell in small quantities; to tell to many.—*n.* rē'tāl. The sale of commodities in small quantities; used also as *adj.*

Retain, rē-tān', *vt.* To hold back; to keep in possession; to detain; to hire; to engage.

Retainer, rē-tān'ėr, *n.* One who retains; an adherent or dependent; a fee to engage a counsel.

Retaliate, rē-ta'li-āt, *vi.* and *t.* To return like for like; to repay; to take revenge.

Retaliation, rē-ta'li-ā''shon, *n.* The return of like for like; requital; reprisal.

Retard, rē-tärd', *vt.* To render slower; to impede; to delay; to postpone.

Retch, rech, *vi.* To make an effort to vomit; to strain, as in vomiting.

Retention, rē-ten'shon, *n.* Act or power of retaining; maintenance; memory.

Reticent, re'ti-sent, *a.* Having a disposition to be silent; reserved.

Reticular, re-tik'ū-lėr, *a.* Having the form or character of a net.

Retina, re'ti-na, *n.* One of the coats of the eye, where visual impressions are received.

Retinue, re'ti-nū, *n.* A train of attendants; a suite.

Retire, rē-tīr', *vi.* (retiring, retired). To go back; to withdraw from business or active life; to go to bed.—*vt.* To remove from service; to pay when due, as a bill of exchange.

Retiring, rē-tīr'ing, *a.* Reserved; unobtrusive; granted to one who retires from service.

Retort, rē-tort', *vt.* To retaliate; to throw back.—*vi.* To return an argument or charge.—*n.* A severe reply; a repartee; a chemical vessel for distilling.

Retouch, rē-tuch´, *vt.* To improve by new touches, as a picture, etc.

Retract, rē-trakt´, *vt.* To draw back; to recall.—*vi.* To unsay one's words.

Retractile, rē-trakt´il, *a.* Capable of being drawn back, as claws.

Retractor, rē-trakt´er, *n.* One who retracts; a muscle that draws back some part.

Retreat, rē-trēt´, *n.* Act of retiring; seclusion; a shelter; the retiring of an army from an enemy.—*vi.* To draw back; to retire from an enemy.

Retrench, rē-trensh´, *vt.* To lessen; to limit or restrict.—*vi.* To economize.

Retribution, re-tri-bū´shon, *n.* Act of rewarding; a requital for evil done.

Retributive, Retributory, rē-tri´būt-iv, rē-tri´bū-to-ri, *a.* Making retribution; entailing justly deserved punishment.

Retrieve, rē-trēv´, *vt.* (retrieving, retrieved). To recover; to regain; to repair.

Retriever, rē-trēv´er, *n.* A dog that brings in game which a sportsman has shot.

Retroact, rē-trō-akt´ or ret´rō-akt, *vi.* To act backward, in opposition, or in return.

Retrocede, rē-trō-sēd´ or ret´, *vi.* To go back; to retire.—*vt.* To cede back.

Retrograde, ret´rō-grād or rē´, *a.* Going backward; appearing to move from east to west in the sky.—*vi.* To go backward.

Retrospect, ret´rō-spekt or rē´, *n.* A view of things past; backward survey.

Retrospection, ret-rō-spek´shon or rē-, *n.* Act or faculty of looking on things past.

Return, rē-tėrn´, *vi.* To come or go back; to recur.—*vt.* To send back; to repay; to report officially; to elect; to yield.—*n.* Act of returning; repayment; election of a representative; profit; an official statement; *pl.* tabulated statistics; a light tobacco.

Retuse, rē-tūs´, *a.* Having a rounded end, with a slight hollow or indentation, as a leaf.

Reunion, rē-ūn´yon, *n.* Union after separation; a meeting for social purposes.

Reunite, rē-ū-nīt´, *vt.* and *i.* To unite again; to reconcile after variance.

Reveal, rē-vēl´, *vt.* To disclose; to divulge; to make known by divine means.

Reveille, re-vel´ye, *n.* A bugle-call sounded at sun-rise.

Revel, re´vel, *n.* A feast with noisy jollity.—*vi.* (revelling, revelled). To carouse; to delight.

Revelation, re-ve-lā´shon, *n.* Act of revealing; that which is revealed; divine communication; the Apocalypse.

Revenge, rē-venj´, *vt.* and *i.* (revenging, revenged). To take vengeance for; to avenge.—*n.* Act of revenging; retaliation; deliberate infliction of injury in return for injury; vindictive feeling.

Revenue, re´ve-nū, *n.* Income, the annual income of a state.

Reverberate, rē-vėr´be-rāt, *vt.* and *i.* To return, as sound; to echo; to reflect, as heat or light.

Revere, rē-vēr´, *vt.* (revering, revered). To regard with awe and respect; to venerate.

Reverence, rev´er-ens, *n.* Awe combined with respect; veneration; an obeisance; a reverend personage; a title of the clergy.—*vt.* To revere; to pay reverence to.

Reverent, rev´er-ent, *a.* Expressing reverence; humble; impressed with reverence.

Reverie, re´ver-i, *n.* A loose train of thoughts; a day-dream; a visionary project.

Reverse, rē-vėrs´, *vt.* (reversing, reversed). To alter to the opposite; to annul.—*n.* A reversal; a complete change or turn; a check; a defeat; the contrary; the back or under-surface.—*a.* Turned backward; opposite.

Revert, rē-vėrt´, *vt.* To reverse.—*vi.* To return to a former position, habit, statement, etc.; to return to the donor.

Revetment, rē-vet´ment, *n.* A facing to a wall or bank; a retaining wall.

Review, rē-vū´, *vt.* To view again; to reconsider; to write a critical notice of; to inspect.—*vi.* To write reviews.—*n.* A re-examination; a criticism; a periodical containing criticisms; official inspection of troops.

Revile, rē-vil´, *vt.* (reviling, reviled). To vilify; to upbraid; to abuse.

Revise, rē-viz´, *vt.* (revising, revised). To go over with care for correction.—*n.* A revision; a second proof-sheet in printing.

Revision, rē-vi´zhon, *n.* Act of revising; revisal; what is revised.

Revival, re-viv´al, *n.* Act of reviving; restoration from neglect or depression; religious awakening.

Revive, rē-vīv´, *vi.* (reviving, revived). To return to life; to recover new vigor.—*vt.* To bring again to life; to refresh; to bring again intouse or notice.

Revoke, rē-vōk´, *vt.* (revoking, revoked). To repeal; to annul.—*vi.* In *card playing*, to neglect to follow suit.

Revolt, rē-vōlt´, *vi.* To renounce allegiance; to rebel; to be disgusted: with *at*.—*vt.* To shock.—*n.* Rebellion; mutiny.

Revolution, re-vō-lū´shon, *n.* Act of revolving; rotation; a turn; circuit; a cycle of time; a radical change; overthrow of existing political institutions.

Revolutionary, re-vō-lū´shon-a-ri, *a.* Pertaining to or tending to produce a revolution.—*n.* A revolutionist.

Revolutionize, re-vō-lū´shon-iz, *vt.* To bring about a complete change in.

Revolve, rē-volv´, *vi.* (revolving, revolved). To turn round an axis or center.—*vt.* To cause to turn round; to consider attentively.

Revolver, rē-volv´er, *n.* A pistol having a revolving set of cartridge chambers, so constructed as to discharge several shots in quick succession without being reloaded.

Revue, rē-vū´, *n.* A loosely-constructed and spectacular theatrical exhibition, depending on music and scenic and staging effects.

Revulsion, rē-vul´shon, *n.* A violent drawing away; a violent change, especially of feeling.

Reward, rē-ward´, *n.* What is given in return for good done; recompense; punishment.—*vt.* To repay; to requite.

Rhapsody, rap´so-di, *n.* A short epic poem, or portion of an epic; a confused series of extravagantly enthusiastic statements.

Rhetoric, re´to-rik, *n.* The art of using language effectively; the art which teaches oratory, eloquence; flashy oratory; declamation.

Rheum, rūm, *n.* A thin serous fluid secreted by the mucous glands, etc.

Rheumatism, rū´mat-izm, *n.* A painful disease of the muscles and joints.

Rhinal, rī´nal, *a.* Pertaining to the nose.

Rhinoceros, ri-nos´e-ros, *n.* A large hoofed animal, allied to the hippopotamus, with one or two horns on the nose.

Rhododendron, rō-dō-den´dron, *n.* An evergreen shrub with large brilliant flowers.

Rhomb, Rhombus, rom, rom´bus, *n.* A quadrilateral whose sides are equal, but the angles not right angles.

Rhomboid, rom´boid, *n.* A quadrilateral whose opposite sides only are equal, and whose angles are not right angles.

Rhubarb, rö´bärb, *n.* A plant of which the leaf-stalks are used in cookery, and the roots of some species in medicine.

Rhyme, rim, *n.* A correspondence of sound in the ends of words or verses; a short poem; a word rhyming with another.—*vi.* (rhyming, rhymed). To make verses; to accord in sound.—*vt.* To put into rhyme.

Rhythm, rithm, *n.* Periodical emphasis in verse or music; metrical movement; harmony; rhyme;

meter; verse.

Rib, rib, *n.* One of the curved bones springing from the backbone; something resembling a rib; a long ridge on cloth.—*vt.* (ribbing, ribbed). To furnish with ribs; to inclose with ribs.

Ribald, ri'bald, *n.* A low, lewd fellow.—*a.* Low; obscene.

Ribbon, ri'bon, *n.* A narrow band of silk, satin, etc.

Rice, ris, *n.* A cereal plant, whose seed forms a light nutritious food.

Rich, rich, *a.* Having abundant possessions; wealthy; costly; valuable; fertile; plentiful; bright; mellow; highly flavored; highly provocative of amusement.

Rick, rik, *n.* A stack or pile of grain or hay.—*vt.* To pile up in ricks, as hay.

Rickets, rik'ets, *n.pl.* A disease of children in which there is usually some distortion of the bones.

Ricochet, rik'o-shet, *n.* A rebounding from a flat, horizontal surface.—*vt.* and *i.* rik-o-shet'. To operate upon by ricochet firing; to rebound.

Rid, rid, *vt.* (ridding, rid). To make free; to clear; to disencumber.—*a.* Free; clear.

Riddle, rid'l, *n.* A puzzling question; an enigma; a coarse sieve.—*vt.* (riddling, riddled). To solve; to sift; to make many holes in.

Ride, rid, *vi.* (riding, pret. rode, pp. ridden). To be borne on horseback, in a vehicle, etc.; to have ability as an equestrian; to be at anchor.—*vt.* To sit on, so as to be carried; to go over in riding; to domineer over.—*n.* An excursion on horseback, or in a vehicle; a road for the amusement of riding.

Ridge, rij, *n.* A long narrow prominence; strip thrown up by a plow; a long crest of hills; upper angle of a roof.—*vt.* (ridging, ridged). To form into ridges.

Ridicule, ri'di-kūl, *n.* Laughter with contempt; mockery; satire.—*vt.* To treat with ridicule; to make sport of.

Ridiculous, ri-dik'ū-lus, *a.* Worthy of or fitted to excite ridicule; droll; absurd.

Rife, rif, *a.* Abundant; prevalent; replete.

Riffraff, rif'raf, *n.* Refuse; the rabble.

Rifle, ri'fl, *n.* A gun the inside of whose barrel is grooved; *pl.* a body of troops with rifles.—*vt.* (rifling, rifled). To groove spirally the bore of; to rob; to plunder.

Rift, rift, *n.* An opening; a cleft; a fissure.—*vt.* and *i.* To cleave; to split.

Rig, rig, *vt.* (rigging, rigged). To clothe; to accoutre; to fit with tackling.—*n.* Dress; style of the sails and masts of a ship.

Rigging, rig'ing, *n.* The ropes which support the masts, extend the sails, etc., of a ship.

Right, rit, *a.* Straight; upright; just; suitable; proper; real; correct; belonging to that side of the body farther from the heart; to be worn outward; perpendicular; formed by one line perpendicular to another.—*adv.* Justly; correctly; very; directly; to the right hand.—*n.* What is right; rectitude; a just claim; authority; side opposite to the left.—*vt.* To put right; to do justice to; to restore to an upright position.—*vi.* To resume a vertical position.

Righteous, rit'yus, *a.* Upright; pious; just; honest; virtuous; equitable.

Rigid, ri'jid, *a.* Stiff; unyielding; not pliant; strict; stern; rigorous.

Rigor, ri'gor, *n.* A sudden coldness attended by shivering.

Rigor, rig'or, *n.* Stiffness; strictness; austerity; severity; intense cold.

Rim, rim, *n.* The border or edge of a thing; brim.—*vt.* (rimming, rimmed). To put a rim round.

Rime, rim, *n.* White or hoar frost; a chink; rhyme.

Rimy, rim'i, *a.* Abounding with rime; frosty.

Rind, rind, *n.* The outward coat of trees, fruits, etc.; bark; peel.

Ring, ring, *n.* Anything in the form of a circle; a circle of gold, etc., worn on the finger; an area in which games, etc., are performed; a group of persons; sound of a bell; a metallic sound.—*vt.* To encircle; to cause to sound; to repeat often or loudly.—*vi.* To sound; to resound; to tingle.

Ringlet, ring'let, *n.* A small ring; a curl.

Ringworm, ring'werm, *n.* A contagious skin disease forming discolored rings.

Rink, ringk, *n.* A portion of a sheet of ice marked off for curling; a smooth flooring for skating on with roller-skates.

Rinse, rins, *vt.* (rinsing, rinsed). To wash by laving water over; to cleanse the interior by the introduction of any liquid.

Riot, ri'ot, *n.* An uproar; a tumult; wild and loose festivity; revelry.—*vi.* To engage in a riot; to revel.

Riotous, ri'ot-us, *a.* Indulging in riot or revelry; tumultuous; seditious; excessive.

Rip, rip, *vt.* (ripping, ripped). To tear or cut open; to take out by cutting or tearing.—*n.* A rent; a scamp.

Ripe, rip, *a.* Brought to perfection in growth; mature; complete; ready for action or effect.—*vt.* and *i.* (riping, riped). To mature.

Ripple, rip'l, *vi.* (rippling, rippled). To show a ruffled surface, as water; to make a gentle sound, as running water.—*vt.* To clean the seeds from, as flax.—*n.* A ruffle of the surface of water; a comb for separating the seeds from flax.

Rise, riz, *vi.* (rising, pret. rose, pp. risen). To pass to a higher position; to stand up; to bring a session to an end; to arise; to swell by fermentation; to slope upwards; to become apparent; to come into existence; to rebel.—*n.* Act of rising; ascent; elevation; origin; beginning; appearance above the horizon; increase; advance.

Risk, risk, *n.* Hazard; peril; jeopardy.—*vt.* To hazard; to dare to undertake.

Rite, rit, *n.* A formal act of religion, etc.; form; ceremony; observance; usage.

Ritual, rit'ū-al, *a.* Pertaining to rites.—*n.* A book containing the rites of a church; a system of rights; ceremonial.

Rival, ri'val, *n.* One who pursues the same object as another; a competitor.—*a.* Having the same pretensions or claims; competing.—*vt.* (rivalling, rivalled). To strive to excel; to compete with.

Rive, riv, *vt.* and *i* (riving, rived, pp. rived and riven). To tear or rend; to split; to cleave.

River, ri'ver, *n.* A large stream of water on land; a copious flow; abundance.

Rivet, ri'vet, *n.* A metallic bolt whose end is hammered broad after insertion.—*vt.* (riveting, riveted). To fasten with rivets; to clinch; to make firm.

Rivulet, ri'vū-let, *n.* A small stream.

Road, rōd, *n.* An open way or public passage; a highway; a means of approach; a roadstead (usually in *plural*).

Roam, rōm, *vi.* To wander; to rove; to ramble.

Roan, rōn, *a.* Of a mixed color with a shade of red predominant.—*n.* A roan color, or horse of this color; a leather prepared from sheep-skin.

Roar, rōr, *vi.* To cry with a full, loud sound; to bellow; to bawl or squall.—*vt.* To cry out aloud.—*n.* A full, loud sound of some continuance; cry of a beast.

Roaring, rōr'ing, *n.* Loud, continued sound; a bronchial disease in horses.—*a.* Characterized by noise; disorderly; very brisk.

Roast, rōst, *vt.* To cook by exposure to a fire; to parch by heat; to banter severely.—*vi.* To become roasted.—*n.* Roasted meat; part selected for roasting.—*a.* Roasted.

Rob, rob, *vt.* (robbing, robbed). To strip unlawfully and by force; to deprive by stealing; to deprive.

Robe, rōb, *n.* A gown, or long, loose garment, worn over other dress; an elegant dress.—*vt.* (robing, robed). To put a robe upon; to invest.

Robin, rob'in, *n.* The European bird called also redbreast.

Robot, rŏb'ot, n. Any mechanical contrivance designed to perform work normally requiring the exercise of human intelligence.

Robust, rō-bust', a. Sturdy; vigorous; muscular.

Rock, rok, vt. To move backwards and forwards without displacing; to swing.—vi. To sway; to reel.—n. A large mass of stone; defense; source of peril or disaster; a kind of solid sweetmeat.

Rocker, rok'er, n. One who rocks; a curving piece on which a cradle, etc., rocks; a trough for washing ore by agitation.

Rocket, rok'et, n. A projectile firework; a similar device used as a lethal weapon; a garden plant.

Rock-salt, rok'salt, n. Mineral salt; common salt found in masses in the earth.

Rococo, ro-kō'kō, n. and a. A meaninglessly decorative style of ornamentation of the time of Louis XIV and XV.

Rod, rod, n. A straight slender stick; a badge of office; an enchanter's wand; a fishing-rod; a measure of 5 1/2 lineal yards.

Rodent, rō'dent, a. Gnawing; belonging to the gnawing animals (Rodentia).—n. An animal that gnaws, as the squirrel.

Rodeo, rōd-ā'o, n. A public exhibition of horse-breaking, lariat-throwing, etc.

Roe, rō, n. The spawn of fishes; female of the hart.

Rogue, rōg, n. A knave; a wag; a sly fellow.

Roil, roil, vt. To render turbid by stirring.

Roister, rois'ter, vi. To bluster; to swagger.

Rôle, rōl, n. A part represented by an actor; any conspicuous part or function.

Roll, rōl, vt. To turn on its surface; to wrap on itself by turning; to involve in a bandage or the like; to press with a roller.—vi. To turn over and over; to run on wheels; to be tossed about; to sound with a deep prolonged sound.—n. Act of rolling; something rolled up; an official document; a catalogue; a cake of bread; a roller; a prolonged deep sound.

Roller, rōl'er, n. One who or that which rolls; a cylinder for smoothing, crushing, etc.; that on which something may be rolled up; a long, heavy, swelling wave.

Rolling, rōl'ing, p.a. Revolving; making a continuous noise; undulating.

Roman, rō'man, a. Pertaining to Rome or its people and to the Roman Catholic religion; applied to the common upright letter in printing.

Romance, rō-mans', n. A tale in verse in a Romance dialect; a popular epic or tale in prose or verse of some length; a tale of extraordinary adventures; tendency to the wonderful or mysterious; a fiction.—a. (with cap.). A term applied to the languages sprung from the Latin.—vi. To tell fictitious stories.

Romantic, rō-man'tik, a. Pertaining to romance; fanciful; extravagant; wildly picturesque.

Romanticism, rō-man'ti-sizm, n. State or quality of being romantic; a reaction in literature or art from classical to mediaeval or modern qualities; romantic feeling.

Romp, romp, n. Rude play or frolic; a boisterous girl.—vi. To play boisterously; to frisk about.

Roof, rōf, n. The cover of any building; a canopy; the palate; a house.—vi. To cover with a roof; to shelter.

Rook, ruk, n. A kind of crow; a cheat; a piece in chess.—vi. and t. To cheat; to rob.

Room, rōm, n. Space; scope; opportunity; stead; apartment in a house; chamber.

Roomy, röm'i, a. Spacious; wide; large.

Roost, röst, n. The pole on which birds rest at night; a collection of fowls resting together.—vi. To occupy a roost; to settle.

Rooster, röst'er, n. The male of the domestic fowl; a cock.

Root, röt, n. That part of a plant which fixes itself in the earth; lower part of anything; origin; a form from which words are derived.—vi. To fix the root; to be firmly fixed.—vt. To plant deeply; to impress durably; to tear up or out; to eradicate.

Rooted, röt'ed, a. Fixed; deep; radical.

Rope, röp, n. A cord or line of some thickness; a row or string of things united.—vi. (roping, roped). To draw out in threads.—vt. To pull by a rope; to fasten or inclose with a rope.

Ropy, röp'i, a. Stringy; viscous; glutinous.

Rosary, röz'a-ri, n. A garland of roses; an anthology; a string of beads on which R. Catholics number their prayers.

Rose, röz, n. A plant and its flower, of many species; an ornamental knot of ribbon; a perforated nozzle of a spout, etc.—a. Of a purplish-red color.

Roseate, röz'ē-āt, a. Rosy; blooming.

Rosemary, röz'ma-ri, n. An evergreen shrub, yielding a fragrant essential oil.

Rose-water, röz'wa-ter, n. Water tinctured with roses by distillation.

Rosewood, röz'wud, n. The wood of a tree used in cabinet-work, when freshly cut having a faint smell of roses.

Rosin, ro'zin, n. The resin left after distilling off the volatile oil from turpentine; resin in a solid state.—vt. To rub with rosin.

Roster, ros'ter, n. A list showing the rotation in which individuals, regiments, etc., are called on to serve.

Rostrum, ros'trum, n.; pl. **-tra.** The beak or bill of a bird; the ram of an ancient ship; pl. a platform or pulpit.

Rot, rot, vi. (rotting, rotted). To become rotten; to decay.—vt. To make rotten.—n. Putrid decay; a fatal distemper of sheep; a disease injurious to plants; nonsense.

Rotary, rō'ta-ri, a. Turning, as a wheel on its axis.

Rotate, rō'tāt, vi. (rotating, rotated). To revolve round a center or axis, like a wheel; to act in turn.—vt. To cause to turn like a wheel.

Rote, röt, n. Repetition of words by memory; mere effort of memory.

Rotten, rot'n, a. Decomposed; decaying; putrid; unsound; corrupt; fetid.

Rotund, rō-tund', a. Round; spherical.

Rotunda, rō-tun'da, n. A round building.

Roué, rö-ā, n. A man devoted to pleasure and sensuality; a licentious man; a rake.

Rouge, rözh, n. A cosmetic to impart ruddiness to the complexion.—vt. and i (rouging, rouged). To paint with rouge.

Rough, ruf, a. Not smooth; rugged; boisterous; harsh; rude; cruel; vague; hasty.—vt. To make rough; to rough-hew.—**To rough it,** to submit to hardships. n. State of being rough or unfinished; a rowdy.

Roulette, rö-let', n. A game of chance; an engraver's tool with a toothed wheel.

Round, round, a. Circular; spherical; large; open; candid; brisk, as a trot; not minutely accurate, as a number.—n. That which is round; rung of a ladder; a circular course or series; circuit made by one on duty, a vocal composition in parts; ammunition for firing once; a turn or bout.—vt. To make round; to encircle; to make full and flowing; to pass round.—vi. To become round or full; to make a circuit.—adv. In a circle; around; not directly.—prep. About; around.

Roundabout, round'a-bout, a. Indirect; circuitous.—n. A revolving structure on which children ride.

Rouse, rouz, vt. (rousing, roused). To arouse; to awaken; to stir up.—vi To awake; to arise.—n. A carousal; a drinking frolic.

Rout, rout, n. A crowd; a rabble; a fashionable evening assembly; total defeat of troops; confusion of troops defeated.—vt. To defeat and throw into confusion; to overthrow; to rouse or drive out.

Route, röt, n. A course or way.

Routine, rö-tēn', n. A round of business or pleasure; regular course.

Rove, röv, vi. (roving, roved). To move about aimlessly; to roam; to ramble.—vt. To wander over;

to card into flakes, as wool.

Row, rō, *n.* A series in a line; a rank; a line of houses; an excursion in a boat with oars.—*vt.* To impel by oars, as a boat; to transport by rowing.—*vi.* To work with the oar.

Row, rou, *n.* A noisy disturbance; a riot.—*vt.* To scold.

Rowdy, rou'di, *n.* A turbulent fellow; a rough.—*a.* Disreputable; blackguardly.

Rowel, rou'el, *n.* The little wheel of a spur, formed with sharp points.

Royal, roi'al, *a.* Pertaining to a king; regal; kingly; august.—*n.* A large kind of paper; a shoot of a stag's antlers.

Royalty, roi'al-ti, *n.* State or character of being royal; a royal personage; share paid to a superior, inventor, or author.

Rub, rub, *vt.* (rubbing, rubbed). To move something along the surface of with pressure; to scour; to remove by friction; to chafe.—*vi.* To move along with pressure; to fret.—*n.* Act of rubbing; friction; obstruction; difficulty; a gibe.

Rubber, rub'ėr, *n.* One who rubs; thing used in polishing or cleaning; india-rubber; obstruction or difficulty; contest of three games in whist.

Rubbish, rub'ish, *n.* Refuse; debris; trash.

Rubble, rub'l, *n.* Broken stones of irregular shapes; masonry of such stones.

Rubescent, rö-bes'ent, *a.* Becoming red; blushing.

Rubicund, rö'bi-kund, *a.* Red or highly colored, as the face; ruddy.

Rubric, rö'brik, *n.* Important words in a manuscript, etc., colored red; a heading or title; direction in a prayer-book.

Ruby, rö'bi, *n.* A very valuable gem or precious stone of various shades of red; a fine red color; a blotch on the face; a small printing type.—*vt.* To make red.—*a.* Red.

Rucksack, ruk'sak, *n.* A bag made to strap on the shoulders, and used by walkers, climbers, etc.

Rudder, rud'ėr, *n.* The instrument by which a ship is steered.

Ruddy, rud'i, *a.* Of a red color; reddish; of a lively flesh color.—*vt.* (ruddying, ruddied). To make red or ruddy.

Rude, röd, *a.* Unformed by art or skill; rough; uncivilized; uncivil; impudent; violent.

Rudiment, rö'di-ment, *n.* The original of anything; a first principle; an undeveloped organ; *pl.* first elements of a science or art.

Rudimentary, rö-di-ment'a-ri, *a.* Pertaining to rudiments; consisting in first principles; initial; in an undeveloped state.

Rue, rö, *vt.* (ruing, rued). To repent of; to regret.—*vi.* To become sorrowful or repentant.—*n.* An acrid ill-smelling plant.

Ruffian, ruf'i-an, *n.* A boisterous brutal fellow.—*a.* Like a ruffian; brutal.

Ruffle, ruf'l, *vt.* (ruffling, ruffled). To rumple; to derange; to disturb.—*vi.* To bluster.—*n.* A plaited cambric, etc., attached to one's dress; frill; state of being agitated; low vibrating beat of a drum.

Rug, rug, *n.* A heavy fabric used to cover a bed, protect a carpet, etc.; a mat.

Rugby, rug'bi, *n.* One of the two principal varieties of football, played by fifteen men a side, with an oval ball, handling being permitted.

Rugged, rug'ed, *a.* Full of rough projections; rough; harsh; crabbed.

Ruin, rö'in, *n.* Destruction; fall; overthrow; anything in a state of decay; that which destroys; *pl.* remains of a city, house, etc.; state of being destroyed.—*vt.* To bring to ruin; to destroy; to impoverish.

Rule, röl, *n.* A ruler or measure; a guiding principle or formula; a precept, law, maxim; government; control; regulation; order; method.—*vt.* (ruling, ruled). To govern; to manage; to decide; to mark with lines by a ruler.—*vi.* To exercise supreme authority; to maintain a level, as the market price; to settle, as a rule of court.

Rumble, rum'bl, *vi.* (rumbling, rumbled). To make a dull, continued sound.—*n.* A low, heavy, continued sound; a seat for servants behind a carriage.

Ruminate, rö'min-āt, *vi.* To chew the cud; to meditate.—*vt.* To meditate on.

Rummage, rum'āj, *vt.* (rummaging, rummaged). To search narrowly but roughly; to ransack.—*n.* A careful search; turning about of things.

Rumor, rö'mėr, *n.* A current story; a mere report.—*vt.* To report; to spread abroad.

Rump, rump, *n.* End of an animal's backbone; buttocks; fag-end of something.

Rumpus, rum'pus, *n.* A great noise; disturbance.

Run, run, *vi.* (running, pret. ran, pp. run). To move by using the legs more quickly than in walking; to take part in a race; to flee; to spread; to ply; to move or pass; to become fluid; to continue in operation; to have a certain direction; to have a certain purport; to be current; to continue in time.—*vt.* To cause to run; to pursue, as a course; to incur; to break through (a blockage); to smuggle; to pierce; to melt; to carry on.—*n.* Act of running; course or distance run; a trip; course, tenor, etc.; general demand, as on a back; place where animals may run; generality.

Rune, rön, *n.* One of a set of alphabetic characters peculiar to the ancient northern nations of Europe.

Rung, rung, *n.* A heavy staff; the round or step of a ladder.

Runner, run'ėr, *n.* One who runs; a messenger; a bird of the order Cursores; a stem running along the ground and taking root; that on which something runs or slides.

Runt, runt, *n.* A dwarfed animal; a variety of pigeon; stalk of a cabbage.

Rupture, rup'tür, *n.* Act of breaking or bursting; fracture; breach; open hostility; hernia.—*vt.* (rupturing, ruptured). To cause a rupture in; to break.

Rural, rö'ral, *a.* Pertaining to the country; rustic.

Ruse, röz, *n.* Artifice; trick; deceit.

Rush, rush, *vi.* To move with great speed; to enter over-hastily.—*n.* A violent motion or course; an eager demand; a plant found in damp places; a reed.

Russet, rus'et, *a.* Of a reddish-brown color; coarse; homespun; rustic.—*n.* A reddish-brown color; coarse country cloth; a kind of winter apple.

Russian, ru'shi-an, *a.* Pertaining to Russia.—*n.* A native of Russia; the language of Russia.

Rust, rust, *n.* The red coating formed on iron exposed to moisture; a parasitic fungus; loss of power by inactivity.—*vi.* To contract rust; to degenerate in idleness.—*vt.* To make rusty.

Rustic, rus'tik, *a.* Pertaining to the country; rural; homely; unpolished.—*n.* A country-man, a peasant; a clown.

Rustle, rus'l, *vi.* and *t.* (rustling, rustled). To make the noise of things agitated; as straw, leaves, etc.—*n.* The noise of things that rustle; a slight sibilant sound.

Rut, rut, *n.* The track of a wheel; a line cut with a spade; line of routine; time during which certain animals are under sexual excitement.—*vt.* (rutting, rutted). To cut in ruts.—*vi.* To be in heat, as deer.

Ruthless, röth'les, *a.* Cruel; pitiless.

Rye, rī, *n.* A cereal plant and it seed.

Rye-grass, rī'gräs, *n.* A kind of grass much cultivated for cattle and horses.

S

Sabbath, sa'bath, *n.* The day of rest; Sunday.

Sabbatic, Sabbatical, sa-bat'ik, sa-bat'ik-al, *a.* Pertaining to the Sabbath; pertaining to a recurrence by sevens.

Saber, sä'ber, n. A sword with one edge; a cavalry sword.—vt. (sabering, sabered). To strike or kill with a saber.

Sable, sä'bl, n. A small animal of the weasel family; the fur of the sable; black.—a. Black; dark.

Sabotage, sä-bō-täzh, n. Malicious destruction of employers, property or national plant by employees on strike or during war-time.

Sac, sak, n. A bag; receptacle for a liquid.

Saccharin, sak'a-rin, n. A substance of great sweetness obtained from coal-tar.

Saccharine, sak'ka-rin, a. Pertaining to or of the nature of sugar; sugary.

Saccharose, sak'a-rōs, n. A chemical name for pure or crystalline sugar.

Sacerdotal, sa-ser-dōt'al, a. Pertaining to priests or the priesthood; priestly.

Sachet, sä-shä, n. A small bag for odorous substances.

Sack, sak, n. A bag for flour, wool, etc.; that which a sack holds; a sort of jacket; a dry wine; pillage of a town.—vt. To put in sacks; to pillage, as a town.

Sacrament, sa'kra-ment, n. A solemn religious ordinance observed by Christians, as baptism or the Lord's Supper.

Sacred, sa'kred, a. Set apart for a holy purpose; consecrated; religious; set apart to some one in honor; venerable.

Sacrifice, sa'kri-fis, n. The offering of anything to God; anything offered to a divinity; surrender made in order to gain something else.—vt. (sacrificing, sacrificed). To make an offering or sacrifice of.—vi. To offer up a sacrifice to some deity.

Sacrilege, sa'kri-lej, n. Violation of sacred things.

Sacristan, sa'krist-an, n. A church officer who has the care of the sacred utensils.

Sacristy, sa'krist-i, n. An apartment in a church where the sacred utensils, vestments, etc., are kept; the vestry.

Sacrosanct, sa'krō-sangt, a. Sacred and inviolable; holy and venerable.

Sacrum, sä'krum, n. The bone forming the lower extremity of the vertebral column.

Sad, sad, a. Sorrowful; affected with grief; gloomy; distressing; calamitous.

Saddle, sad'l, n. A seat for a rider on a horse's back; something like a saddle in shape or use.—vt. (saddling, saddled). To put a saddle on; to burden.

Sadducee, sad'ū-sē, n. One of a sect among the Jews who denied the resurrection and the existence of angels or spirits.

Sadism, säd'ism, n. A form of sexual perversion, in which pleasure is taken in the cruel treatment of the companion.

Safe, säf, a. Secure; free from danger; unharmed; no longer dangerous; trustworthy.—n. A strong box or chamber for securing valuables; a cool receptacle for meat.

Safeguard, säf'gärd, n. One who or that which guards; a defense; protection; a passport.—vt. To guard.

Safety-match, säf'ti-mach, n. A match which lights only on a special substance.

Safety-valve, säf'ti-valv, n. A valve on a boiler, which lets the steam escape when the pressure becomes too great.

Saffron, saf'ron, n. A bulbous plant allied to the crocus, with flowers of a rich orange color.—a. Of a deep yellow.

Sag, sag, vi. (sagging, sagged). To sink in the middle; to yield under care, difficulties, etc.

Sagacious, sa-gä'shus, a. Quick of perception; shrewd; sage.

Sagacity, sa-gas'i-ti, n. Quickness of discernment; shrewdness; high intelligence.

Sage, säj, a. Wise; sagacious; well-judged; grave.—n. A wise man; a man venerable for years, and of sound judgment; a labiate plant.

Sagittarius, sa-ji-tä'ri-us, n. The archer, a sign of the zodiac.

Sago, sä'gō, n. A starchy substance much used as food, prepared from the pith of several species of palms.

Sail, säl, n. A piece of cloth to catch the wind and so move a ship; a ship; a passage in a ship.—vi. To be carried over the water by sails or steam, etc.; to begin a voyage; to glide.—vt. To pass over by means of sails; to navigate.

Sailing, säl'ing, p.a. Moved by sails and not by steam.—n. Act of setting sail; art or rules of navigation.

Sailor, säl'or, n. A seaman; a mariner.

Saint, sänt, n. One eminent for piety and virtue; one of the blessed; a person canonized.—vt. To canonize.

Sake, säk, n. Cause; purpose; regard.

Salacity, sa-las'i-ti, n. Lust; lecherousness.

Salad, sa'lad, n. A dish of certain vegetables, as lettuce, cress, etc., dressed and eaten raw.

Salamander, sa-la-man'der, n. A small harmless amphibian; a kind of lizard formerly believed able to live in fire.

Salary, sa'la-ri, n. A stipulated recompense for services; stipend; wages.

Sale, säl, n. Act of selling; power or opportunity of selling; market; auction; state of being to be sold.

Salicylic, sal-i-sil'ik, n. An acid used as an antiseptic, etc.

Salient, sä'li-ent, a. Springing; darting; projecting, conspicuous.

Saline, sa-lin', a. Consisting of salt; salt.—n. A salt spring.

Saliva, sa-li'va, n. The fluid secreted by certain glands, which moistens the mouth and assists digestion.

Salivate, sa'li-vät, vt. To produce an unusual secretion and discharge of saliva.

Sallow, sal'ō, a. Having a pale, sickly, yellowish color.—n. A kind of willow.

Sally, sal'i, n. A leaping forth; a rush of troops from a besieged place; a dart of intellect, fancy, etc.; frolic.—vi. (sallying, sallied). To leap forth; to issue suddenly.

Salmon, sa'mun, n. A large fish highly valued as food.

Salon, sä-long, n. An apartment for the reception of company; a saloon.

Salsify, sal'si-fi, n. A plant cultivated for its edible root.

Salt, salt, n. A sbustance for seasoning and preserving food; a compound produced by the combination of a base with an acid, taste, savor, piquancy, an old sailor.—a. Impregnated with salt; pungent.—vt. To sprinkle or season with salt.

Saltant, sal'tant, a. Leaping; dancing.

Saltation, sal-tä'shon, n. A leaping; beating or palpitation.

Salt-mine, salt'min, n. A mine where rocksalt is obtained.

Saltpeter, salt'pe-ter, n. Niter.

Salts, salts, n.pl. Salt used as a medicine.

Salubrious, sa-lū'bri-us, a. Healthful.

Salutary, sa'lū-ta-ri, a. Healthful; wholesome; beneficial; profitable.

Salute, sa-lut', vt. (saluting, saluted). To greet; to greet by a bow, etc.; to kiss; to honor.—vi. To perform a salutation; to greet each other.—n. Act of saluting; greeting; a kiss; a bow; discharge of artillery, etc.

Salvage, sal'väj, n. Act of saving a ship or goods from shipwreck, fire, etc.; an allowance for the saving of property; goods thus saved.

Salvation, sal-vä'shon, n. Act of saving; redemption of man from sin; that which saves.

Salve, salv or säv, n. A healing ointment; remedy.—vt. (salving, salved). To apply salve to; to remedy.

Salver, sal'ver, n. A tray on which articles are presented.

Salvo, sal'vō, A reservation; excuse; salute of guns; a shouting or cheering.

Sambo, sam'bō, n. The offspring of a black person and a mulato.

Same, sām, a. Identical; not different or other; of like kind; just mentioned.—**All the same,** nevertheless.

Sameness, sām'nes, n. Similarity; identity; monotony.

Sample, sam'pl, n. A specimen; a part presented as typical of the whole.—vt. (sampling, sampled). To take a sample of.

Sanatorium, san-a-tō'ri-um, n. A place to which people go for the sake of health.

Sanctification, sangk'ti-fi-kā''shon, n. Act of sanctifying; consecration.

Sanctify, sangk'ti-fi, vt. (sanctifying, sanctified). To make holy; to hallow; to make pure from sin.

Sanctimonious, sangk-ti-mō'ni-us, a. Making a show of sanctity; hypocrtical.

Sanction, sangk'shon, n. Confirmation; ratification; authority.—vt. To ratify; to authorize; to countenance.

Sanctity, sangk'ti-ti, n. State of being sacred; holiness; inviolability.

Sanctuary, sangk'tū-a-ri, n. A sacred place; a place of worship; part of a church where the altar is placed; a place of protection to criminals, debtors, etc.; shelter.

Sanctum, sangk'tum, n. A sacred place; a private room.

Sand, sand, n. Fine particles of stone; pl. tracts of sand on the sea-shore, etc.—vt. To sprinkle or cover with sand.

Sandal, san'dal, n. A kind of shoe consisting of a sole fastened to the foot.

Sand-blast, sand'blast, n. Sand driven by a blast of steam or air, and used in engraving and cutting glass, etc.

Sand-paper, sand'pā-pėr, n. Paper coated with fine sand, used to smooth and polish.

Sandstone, sand'stōn, n. A stone composed of agglutinated grains of sand.

Sandwich, sand'wich, n. Slices of bread, with meat or something savory between.—vt. To insert like the meat in a sandwich; to fit between two other pieces.

Sane, sān, a. Sound in mind; discreet.

Sang-froid, sang'frwä, n. Coolness; imperturbable calmness.

Sanguine, sang'gwin, a. Consisting of blood; full of blood; of the color of blood; cheerful; confident.

Sanitary, san'i-ta-ri, a. Pertaining to or designed to secure health; hygienic.

Sanitation, san-i-tā'shon, n. The adoption of sanitary measures for the health of a community.

Sanity, san'i-ti, n. State of being sane; soundness of mind.

Sans, sanz, prep. Without; deprived of.

Sap, sap, vt. (sapping, sapped). To undermine; to destroy by some invisible process.—vi. To proceed by undermining.—n. A trench; vital juice of plants.

Sapient, sā'pi-ent, a. Wise; sage; discerning; now generally ironic.

Sapling, sap'ling, n. A young tree.

Saponify, sa-pon'i-fi, vt. To convert into soap by combination with an alkali.

Sapphic, saf'fik, a. Pertaining to Sappho, a Grecian poetess, or to a kind of verse invented by her.—n. A Sapphic verse.

Sapphire, saf'fir, n. A precious stone of very great hardness, and of various shades of blue; a rich blue color; blue.

Sarcasm, sär'kazm, n. A bitter cutting jest; a severe gibe; keen irony.

Sarcastic, sär-kas'tik, a. Containing sarcasm; scornfully severe; taunting.

Sarcode, sär'kōd, n. Structureless gelatinous matter forming the bodies of animals belonging to the protozoa.

Sarcoid, sär'koid, a. Resembling flesh.

Sarcophagus, sär-kof'a-gus, n.; pl. -gi and -guses. A coffin of stone.

Sard, Sardine, särd, sär'din, n. A variety of carnelian of a deep blood-red color.

Sardine, sär'dėn, n. Pilchars and other small fish preserved in olive oil and tinned.

Sardonic, sär-don'ik, a. Forced, as a laugh; bitterly ironical; sarcastic.

Sardonyx, sär'dō-niks, n. A precious stone, a variety of onyx, with layers of sard.

Sartorial, sär-tō'ri-al, a. Pertaining to a tailor.

Sash, sash, n. A long band or scarf worn for ornament; the frame of a window; a frame for a saw.—vt. To furnish with sashes or sash windows.

Sassafras, sas'a-fras, n. A kind of laurel, the root of which has medicinal virtues.

Satan, sā'tan, n. The devil or prince of darkness; the chief of the fallen angels.

Satchel, sa'chel, n. A little sack or bag; a bag for a school-boy's books.

Sate, sāt, vt. (sating, sated). To satiate; to satisfy the appetite of; to glut.

Satellite, sa'tel-lit, n. An attendant; an obsequious dependant; a small planet revolving round another.

Satiate, sā'shi-āt, vt. (satiating, satiated). To fully satisfy the desire of; to surfeit; to glut.—a. Filled to satiety.

Satin, sa'tin, n. A glossy close-woven silk cloth.— a. Belonging to or made of satin.

Satire, sa'tir, n. A writing ridiculing vice or folly; an invective poem; sarcastic or contemptuous ridicule.

Satirize, sa'ti-riz, vt. To expose by satire; to censure in a satiric manner.

Satisfaction, sa-tis-fak'shon, n. Act of satisfying; gratification of desire; contentment; payment; compensation.

Satisfy, sa'tis-fi, vt. and i. (satisfying, satisfied). To gratify fully; to content; to fulfil the claims of; to answer; to free from doubt.

Saturate, sa'tūr-āt, vt. To imbue till no more can be received; to soak thoroughly.

Saturday, sa'tėr-dā, n. The seventh day of the week.

Saturn, sa'tėrn, n. An ancient Roman diety; a planet.

Saturnalian, sa-tėr-na'li-an, a. Loose; dissolute.

Saturnine, sa'tėrn-in, a. Morose; gloomy; phlegmatic.

Sauce, sas, n. A liquid to be eaten with food to give it relish; pertness.—vt. To make savory with sauce; to be pert to.

Saucer, sa'sėr, n. A piece of china, etc., in which a cup is set.

Saucy, sas'i, a. Showing impertinent boldness; pert; impudent; rude.

Saunter, sän'tėr, vi. To stroll about idly; to loiter.— n. A stroll; a leisurely pace.

Saurian, sa'ri-an, a. Pertaining to the lizards.— n. A scaly reptile, as the lizard.

Sausage, sa'sāj, n. The prepared intestine of an ox, etc., stuffed with minced meat.

Savage, sa'vāj, a. wild; uncultivated; barbarous; brutal.—n. One who is uncivilized; a barbarian.

Savant, sä-väng', A man of learning; a man eminent for his scientific acquirements.

Save, sāv, vt. (saving, saved). To preserve; to protect; to rescue; to spare; to keep from doing or suffering; to reserve; to obviate.—vi. To be economical.—prep. Except.

Saving, sāv'ing, a. Thrifty; that secures from evil; containing some reservation.—n. What is saved; sums accumulated by economy: generally pl.—prep. Excepting.

Savior, sāv'yėr, n. One who saves from evil, destruction, or danger; Christ.

Savor, sā'vor, n. Taste; flavor; odor; distinctive quality.—vi. To have a particular taste; to partake of some characteristic of something else.— vt. To taste or smell with pleasure; to like.

Savory, sā'vo-ri, *a.* Having a good savor; palatable; agreeable.

Savoy, sav'oi, *n.* A variety of cabbage with crisp leaves for winter use.

Saw, sa, *n.* A instrument consisting of a thin blade of steel with a toothed edge; a saying or maxim.—*vt.* and *i.* To cut with a saw.

Sawdust, sa'dust, *n.* Small fragments of wood produced by the action of a saw.

Saw-mill, sa'mil, *n.* A mill for sawing timber, driven by water, steam, etc.

Saxophone, saks'ō-fōn, *n.* A wind-instrument similar to the sax-horn, with a clarinet mouthpiece.

Say, sā, *vt.* (saying, said). To utter in words; to speak; to declare; to assume.—*vi.* To speak; to relate.—*n.* A speech; statement.

Saying, sā'ing, *n.* Something said; speech; an adage; a maxim; a proverb.

Scab, skab, *n.* An incrusted substance over a sore in healing; a disease of sheep; the mange in horses.

Scabbard, skab'ard, *n.* The sheath of a sword.

Scabious, skā'bi-us, *a.* Consisting of scabs; rough; itchy; leprous.

Scaffold, skaf'old, *n.* A temporary platform for workmen; an elevated platform for the execution of a criminal.—*vt.* To furnish with a scaffold.

Scagliola, skal-yō-'la, *n.* A composition gypsum, splinters of marble, etc., imitative of marble, and used in decoration.

Scald, skald, *vt.* To burn or injure with hot liquor; to expose to a boiling or violent heat.—*n.* An injury caused by a hot liquid.—*a.* Covered with scurf; scabby; paltry.

Scale, skāl, *n.* A thin flake on the skin of an animal; dish of a balance; balance itself (generally *pl.*), anything graduated used as a measure, series of steps or ranks; relative dimensions; succession of notes; gamut.—*vt.* (scaling, scaled). To weigh, as in scales; to strip of scales; to clean; to climb, as by a ladder.—*vi.* To come off in thin layers.

Scalene, skā'lēn, *a.* A term applied to a triangle of which the three sides are unequal.

Scallion, skal'yun, *n.* A shallot.

Scallop, skal'op or skol'op, *n.* An edible bivalve of the oyster family; a curving on the edge of anything.—*vt.* To cut the edge of into scallops or segments of circles.

Scalloped, skal'opt, *p.a.* Cut at the edge into segments of circles.

Scalp, skalp, *n.* The skin of the top of the head, with the hair on it.—*vt.* To deprive of the scalp.

Scapel, skal'pel, *n.* A knife used in anatomical dissections.

Scamp, skamp, *n.* A knave; swindler; rogue.—*vt.* To do in a perfunctory manner.

Scamper, skam'per, *vi.* To run with speed; to scurry.—*n.* A hurried run.

Scan, skan, *vt.* (scanning, scanned). To measure by the metrical feet, as a verse; to scrutinize; to eye.

Scandal, skan'dal, *n.* Public reproach; shame; defamatory talk; slander.

Scandalize, skan'dal-īz, *vt.* To offend by some action deemed disgraceful; to shock.

Scandent, skan'dent, *a.* Climbing.

Scant, skant, *a.* Not full; scarcely sufficient; scarce.—*vt.* To limit; to stint; to grudge.—*adv.* Scarcely; hardly.

Scanty, skant'i, *a.* Scant; insufficient.

Scape, skāp, *n.* A stem rising directly from a root and bearing the fructification without leaves; the shaft of a feather or column —*vt.* and *i.* To escape.

Scape-goat, skāp'gōt, *n.* One made to bear the blame of others.

Scapula, skap'ū-la, *n.* The shoulder-blade.

Scapular, Scapulary, skap'ū-lėr, skap'ū-la-ri, *n.* A monastic garment resting on the shoulders, with a flap hanging down in front and another behind.

Scar, skär, *n.* The mark of a wound or ulcer; a cicatrix; a cliff; a bare place on the side of a hill.—*vt.* (scarring, scarred). To mark with a scar; to wound.

Scarce, skärs, *n.* Not plentiful; deficient; uncommon.

Scarcity, skärs'i-ti, *n.* State or condition of being scarce; deficiency; dearth.

Scare, skär, *vt.* (scaring, scared). To strike with sudden terror; to frighten.—*n.* A sudden fright, a causeless alarm.

Scarecrow, skär'krō, *n.* Anything set up to scare birds from crops; anything terrifying without danger; a ragged or very odd-looking person.

Scarf, skärf, *n.*; pl. **Scarfs,** skärfs, and **Scarves,** skärvz. A light article of dress worn round the neck, etc.; a joint in timber.—*vt.* To unite (timber) by means of a scarf.

Scarify, ska'ri-fī, *vt.* (scarifying, scarified). To make small superficial incisions in the skin; to remove the flesh about a tooth.

Scarlatina, skar-la-tē'na, *n.* A malady characterized by fever and a red rash.

Scarlet, skär'let, *n.* A bright-red color.—*a.* Of a bright-red color.

Scathe, skäth, *n.* Damage; injury.—*vt.* (scathing, scathed). To injure; to harm.

Scathing, skäth'ing, *p.a.* Injuring; harming; blasting.

Scatter, skat'er, *vt.* To disperse; to spread; to strew; to disunite.—*vi.* To be dispersed; to straggle apart.

Scatter-brain, skat'èr-brän, *n.* A thoughtless person.

Scattered, skat'ėrd, *p.a.* Thinly spread; loose and irregular in arrangement.

Scavenger, ska'ven-jèr, *n.* One employed to clean the streets.

Scene, sēn, *n.* A stage; a distinct part of a play; a painted device on the stage; place of action or exhibition; general appearance of any action; a view; display of emotion.

Scenery, sēn'e-ri, *n.* The painted representations on the stage; pictorial features; landscape characteristics.

Scent, sent, *n.* That which causes the sensation of smell; odor; fragrance; power of smelling; chase followed by the scent; track.—*vt.* To perceive by the sense of smell; to imbue with odor.

Sceptic, skep'tik, *n.* One who doubts or disbelieves.—*a.* Sceptical.

Scepticism, skep'ti-sizm, *n.* Doubt; incredulity.

Scepter, sep'ter, *n.* A staff or baton carried by a ruler as a symbol of authority.

Schedule, shed'ūl, sed'ūl, *n.* A paper containing a list, and annexed to a larger writing, as to a will, deed, etc.; an inventory.—*vt.* (scheduling, scheduled). To place in a schedule.

Scheme, skēm, *n.* A combination of things adjusted by design; a system; project; diagram.—*vt.* and *i.* (scheming, schemed). To plan, contrive, project.

Schemer, skēm'ėr, *n.* A contriver; plotter.

Scherzo, skert'so, *n.* A passage of a sportive character in musical pieces.

Schism, sizm, *n.* A separation; breach among people of the same religious faith.

Scholar, skol'ėr, *n.* One who attends a school; a pupil; a learned person; a junior member of an English university who is aided by college revenues.

Scholarship, skol'ėr-ship, *n.* Erudition, a foundation for the support of a student.

School, skōl, *n.* A place of instruction; a body of pupils; disciples; sect or body; a system or custom; a shoal (of fishes).—*a.* Relating to a school, scholastic.—*vt.* To instruct; to reprove.

Schooner, skön'ėr, *n.* A vessel with two or more masts, her chief sails fore-and-aft.

Sciatic, Sciatical, sī-at'ik, sī-at'ik-al, *a.* Pertaining to the hip or to sciatica.

Sciatica, sī-at'i-ka, *n.* Neuralgia or inflammation

S

of the sciatic never or great nerve of the thigh.

Science, si'ens, *n.* Knowledge reduced to a system; the facts pertaining to any department of mind or matter in their due connections; skill resulting from training.

Scientific, sī-en-tif'ik, *a.* Pertaining to science; versed in science; according to the rules or principles of science.

Scintilla, sin-til'la, *n.* A spark; glimmer; trace.

Scintillate, sin'til-lāt, *vi.* To emit sparks; to sparkle, as the fixed stars.

Sciolism, sī'ol-izm, *n.* Superficial knowledge.

Sciolist, sī'ol-ist, *n.* One who knows things superficially; a smatterer.

Sciomachy, Sciamachy, sī-om'ak-i, sī-am'ak-i, *n.* A fighting with a shadow.

Scion, sī'on, *n.* A cutting or twig; a young shoot; a descendant; an heir.

Scirrhus, Scirrhosis, ski'rus or si'rus, ski-rō'sis or si-rō'sis, *n.* A hard tumor.

Scission, si'zhon, *n.* Act of cutting; state of being cut; division.

Scissors, siz'ėrz, *n.pl.* A cutting instrument consisting of two blades.

Scleroma, Sclerosis, sklē-rō'ma, sklē-rō'sis, *n.* Induration of the cellular tissue.

Scoff, skof, *n.* An expression of derision or scorn; a gibe.—*vi.* To utter contemptuous language; to jeer; to mock.—*vt.* To mock at.

Scold, skōld, *vi.* To find fault with rude clamor; to utter harsh, rude rebuke.—*vt.* To reprimand loudly; to chide.—*n.* A clamorous, foul-mouthed woman.

Sconce, skons, *n.* A case or socket for a candle; a projecting candlestick; a detached fort; a headpiece; the skull.—*vt.* To ensconce.

Scoop, sköp, *n.* An implement for liting things; an instrument for hollowing out; the act of scooping.—*vt.* To take out with a scoop; to lade out; to hollow out.

Scope, skōp, *n.* An aim or end; intention; amplitude or range; space; sweep.

Scorbutic, skor-būt'ik, *a.* Pertaining to or diseased with scurvy.

Scorch, skorch, *vt.* To burn superficially; to singe; to parch.—*vi.* To be as hot as to burn a surface; to be dried up; to ride a cycle at excessive speed.

Score, skōr, *n.* A notch; a long scratch or mark; an account or reckoning; the number twenty; a debt; the number of points made in certain games; motive; ground; draft of a musical composition.—*vt.* (scoring, scored). To make scores or scratches on; to record; to get for oneself, as points, etc., in games.

Scoria, skō'ri-a, *n.*; pl. **-ae.** Dross; cinder; the cellular, slaggy lavas of a volcano.

Scorn, skorn, *n.* Extreme contempt; subject of contempt.—*vt.* To hold in extreme contempt; to despise.—*vi.* To feel or show scorn.

Scornful, skorn'ful, *a.* Filled with or expressing scorn; contemptuous.

Scorpion, skor'pi-on, *n.* An animal of the class Arachnida, with a jointed tail terminating with a venomous sting; a sign of the zodiac.

Scot, skot, *n.* A native of Scotland; a tax or contribution.

Scotch, skoch, *a.* Pertaining to Scotland or its inhabitants; Scottish.—*n.* The dialect of Scotland; the people of Scotland.

Scotch, skoch, *vt.* To cut with shallow incisions; to notch.—*n.* A slight cut.

Scot-free, skot'frē, *a.* Free from payment of scot; untaxed; unhurt; clear; safe.

Scotia, skō'ti-a, *n.* A hollow molding in the base of a column.

Scots, skots, *a.* Scottish.—*n.* The Scottish language.

Scotsman, skots'man, *n.* A native of Scotland.

Scottish, skot'ish, *a.* Pertaining to Scotland, its inhabitants, or language.

Scoundrel, skoun'drel, *n.* A mean, worthless fellow; a rascal.—*a.* Base; unprincipled.

Scoundrelly, skoun'drel-li, *a.* Base; mean.

Scour, skour, *vt.* and *i.* To clean by rubbing; to purge violently; to range for the purpose of finding something; to pass swiftly over.

Scourge, skėrj, *n.* A lash; a whip; an affliction sent for punishment; one who harasses.—*vt.* (scourging, scourged). To lash; to chastise; to harass.

Scout, skout, *n.* A person sent to obtain intelligence regarding an enemy; a college servant.—*vi.* To act as a scout.—*vt.* To watch closely; to treat with disdain.

Scout-master, skout-mäs'tėr, *n.* The leader of a troop of Boy Scouts.

Scow, skou, *n.* A flat-bottomed boat.

Scowl, skoul, *vi.* To wrinkle the brows, as in displeasure; to frown.—*n.* A deep angry frown; gloom.

Scrabble, skrab'l, *vi.* and *t.* To scrawl; to scribble.—*n.* A scribble.

Scrag, skrag, *n.* Something dry, or lean with roughness.

Scramble, skram'bl, *vi.* (scrambling, scrambled). To move or climb on all-fours; to push rudely in eagerness for something.—*n.* Act of scrambling; eager contest.

Scrap, skrap, *n.* A small piece; a fragment; a little picture for ornamenting screens, etc.

Scrap-book, skrap'buk, *n.* A book for preserving extracts, drawings, prints, etc.

Scrape, skrāp, *vt.* (scraping, scraped). To rub with something hard; to clean by a sharp edge; to act on with a grating noise; to erase; to collect laboriously.—*vi.* To roughen or remove a surface by rubbing; to make a grating noise.—*n.* Act of scraping; an awkward bow; an awkward predicament.

Scraper, skrāp'ėr, *n.* One who or that which scrapes; an instrument for scraping or cleaning.

Scratch, skrach, *vt.* and *i* To mark or wound with something sharp; to tear with the nails; to withdraw from the list of competitors.—*n.* A score in a surface; a slight wound; a line from which runners start, etc.; one most heavily handicapped in a contest.—*a.* Taken at random; hastily collected.

Scrawl, skral, *vt.* and *i* To write or draw carelessly or awkwardly.—*n.* Inelegant or hasty writing.

Scream, skrēm, *vi.* To shriek; to utter a shrill cry.—*n.* A sharp, shrill cry.

Screech, skrēch, *vi.* To scream; to shriek.—*n.* A sharp, shrill cry.

Screech-owl, skrēch-oul, *n.* An owl that screeches, in opposition to one that hoots.

Screed, skrēd, *n.* A strip of cloth; a lengthy statement; a harangue.

Screen, skrēn, *n.* An article to intercept heat, cold, etc.; a shelter; a kind of sieve; an ornamental partition in a church.—*vt.* To shelter; to conceal; to sift.

Screw, skrö, *n.* A cylinder with a sprial ridge which enables it when turned to enter another body; a screw-propeller; a twist or turn; a niggard.—*vt.* To fasten by a screw; to twist; to oppress.

Screw-driver, skrö'drīv-ėr, *n.* An instrument for turning screw-nails.

Screw-nail, skrö'nāl, *n.* A nail grooved like a screw.

Screw-propeller, skrö'prō-pel-ėr, *n.* An apparatus on the principle of the common screw, for propelling boats and ships.

Scribble, skrib'l, *vt.* and *i.* (scribbling, scribbled). To write with haste or without care; to tease coarsely, as cotton or wool.—*n.* Careless writing; a scrawl.

Scribe, skrīb, *n.* A writer; notary; copyist; doctor of the law among the Jews.

Scrimmage, skrim'āj, *n.* A tussle; a confused, close struggle in football.

Scrimp, skrimp, *vt.* To make too small or short; to

scant; to limit.—a. Scanty.

Scrip, skrip, n. A small bag; a wallet; a small writing; a certificate of stock.

Script, skript, n. Handwriting; printing type resembling handwriting.

Scriptural, skrip'tūr-al, a. Contained in or according to the Scriptures; biblical.

Scripture, skrip'tūr, n. The Old and New Testaments; the Bible: often pl.—a. Scriptural.

Scrivener, skri'ven-ėr, n. An old name for a notary; a money-broker; a writer; a poor author.

Scrofula, skro'fū-la, n. A disease, a variety of consumption, often showing itself by glandular tumors in the neck which suppurate.

Scroll, skrōl, n. A roll of paper or parchment; a draft or first copy; a spiral ornament; a flourish added to a person's name.

Scrotum, skro'tum, n. The bag which contains the testicles.

Scrub, skrub, vt. (scrubbing, scrubbed). To rub hard with something rough, to make clean or bright.—vi. To be diligent and penurious.—n. One who labors hard and lives sparingly; a mean fellow; a worn-out brush; low underwood.—a. Mean.

Scruple, skrö'pl, n. A weight of 20 grains; doubt; hesitation; backwardness.—vi. (scrupling, scrupled). To doubt; to hesitate.

Scrupulous, skrö'pū-lus, a. Having scruples; cautious; conscientious; exact.

Scrutinize, skrö'ti-nīz, vt. and i. To examine closely; to investigate.

Scrutiny, skrö'ti-ni, n. Close search; careful investigation; an authoritive examination of votes given at an election.

Scud, skud, vi. (scudding, scudded). To run quickly; to run before a strong wind with little or no sail.—vt. To pass over quickly.—n. Act of scudding; loose, vapory clouds.

Scuffle, skuf'l, n. A confused struggle.—vi. (scuffling, scuffled). To strive confusedly at close quarters.

Scull, skul, n. A short oar, used in pairs.—vt. To propel by sculls, or by moving an oar at the stern.

Sculptor, skulp'tor, n. One who works in sculpture; an artist who carves or models figures.

Sculpture, skulp'tūr, n. The art of carving wood or stone into images; an image in stone, etc.—vt. (sculpturing, sculptured). To carve; to form, as images on stone, etc.

Scum, skum, n. Impurities which rise to the surface of liquors; refuse.—vt. (scumming, scummed). To take the scum from.—vi. To throw up scum.

Scumble, skum'bl, vt. To cover thinly with opaque colors to modify the effect.

Scummy, skum'i, a. Covered with scum.

Scupper, skup'ėr, n. A hole for carrying off water from the deck of a ship.

Scurf, skėrf, n. Dry scales or flakes on the skin; matter adhering to a surface.

Scurrilous, sku'ril-us, a. Foul-mouthed; abusive, obscenely jocular.

Scurry, sku'ri, vi. (scurrying, scurried). To run rapidly; to hurry.—n. Hurry; haste.

Scurvy, skėr'vi, n. A disease caused by insufficiency of vegetable food. a. Vile; mean; malicious.

Scuttle, skut'l, n. A broad basket; a pail for coals; a hatchway in a ship's deck; a short run; a quick pace.—vt. (scuttling, scuttled). To sink by making holes in (a ship).—vi. To scurry.

Scythe, sīтн, n. An implement for mowing grass, etc.—vt. To cut with a scythe.

Sea, sē, n. The mass of salt water covering most of the earth; some portion of this; a name of certain lakes; a large wave; a surge; a flood.

Sea-anemone, sē'a-nem'o-nē, n. A beautiful seashore, plant-like animal.

Sea-breeze, sē'brēz, n. A wind or current of air blowing from the sea upon land.

Sea-calf, sē'käf, n. The common seal.

Sea-coast, sē'kōst, n. The land adjacent to the sea or ocean.

Seafarer, sē'fār-ėr, n. One who fares or travels by sea; a mariner; a seaman.

Sea-going, sē'gō-ing, a. Travelling by sea, as a vessel which trades with foreign ports.

Sea-horse, sē'hors, n. The walrus; a small fish with head shaped like a horse's.

Seal, sēl, n. A hard substance bearing some device, used to make impressions; the wax stamped with a seal; assurance; that which makes fast; a carnivorous marine mammal.—vt. To set a seal to; to confirm; to fasten; to shut or keep close.

Sea-legs, sē'legz, n.pl. The ability to walk on a ship's deck when pitching or rolling.

Sealer, sēl'ėr, n. One who seals; an officer in Chancery who seals writs, etc.; one engaged in the seal-fishery.

Sea-level, sē'le-vel, n. The level of the surface of the sea.

Sealing-wax, sēl'ing-waks, n. A resinous compound used for sealing letters, etc.

Sea-lion, sē'li-on, n. The name of several large seals.

Seam, sēm, n. The joining of two edges of cloth; a line of juncture; a vein of metal, coal, etc.; a scar.—vt. To unite by a seam; to scar.

Seamanship, sē'man-ship, n. The art or skill of a seaman; art of managing a ship.

Seamstress, sēm'stres, n. A woman whose occupation is sewing; a sempstress.

Seamy, sēm'i, a. Having a seam; showing seams; showing the worst side; disagreeable.

Séance, sā-angs, n. A session, as of some public body; a sitting with the view of evoking spiritual manifestations.

Sea-port, sē'port, n. A harbor on the seacoast; a town on or near the sea.

Sear, sēr, n. A catch in the mechanism of a rifle which holds back the cocking-piece.

Search, sėrch, vt. To look through to find something; to examine.—vi. To seek diligently; to inquire.—n. Act of searching; examination; inquiry.

Searching, sėrch'ing, a. Penetrating; trying; closely scrutinizing.

Sea-scape, sē'skāp, n. A picture representing a scene at sea; a sea-piece.

Sea-shore, sē'shōr, n. The shore of the sea; ground between high and low water mark.

Sea-sick, sē'sik, a. Affected with sickness caused by the motion of a vessel at sea.

Season, sē'zn, n. A division of the year; a suitable time; a time; time of the year marked by special activity; seasoning.—vt. To accustom; to acclimatize, to flavor. vi. To become suitable by time.

Seasonable, sē'zn-a-bl, a. Natural to the season; opportune; timely.

Seasoning, sē'zn-ing, n. Something added to food to give it relish; relish; condiment.

Seat, sēt, n. That on which one sits; a chair; stool, etc.; place of sitting; a right to sit; residence; station.—vt. To place on a seat; to settle; to locate; to assign seats to; to fit up with seats.

Sea-worthy, sē'wėr-тнi, a. Fit to go to sea; fit for a voyage.

Sebaceous, sē-bā'shus, a. Made of, containing, or secreting fatty matter.

Sebiferous, sē-bif'ėr-us, a. Producing fat.

Secant, sē'kant, a. Cutting.—n. A straight line that cuts a curve or figure.

Secede, sē-sēd', vi. (seceding, seceded). To withdraw from fellowship or association.

Secern, sē-sėrn', vt. To separate; to distinguish; to secrete.

Secessionist, sē-se'shon-ist, n. One who advocates or engages in a secession.

Seclude, sē-klōd', vt. (secluding, secluded). To shut up apart; to separate; refl. to withdraw into solitude.

Seclusion, sē-klö'zhon, n. Act of secluding; re-

S

tired mode of life; privacy.

Second, se'kund, a. Next after the first; repeated again; inferior; other.—n. One who or that which comes next a first; one who supports another; attendant in a duel; sixtieth part of a minute; a lower part in music; pl. a coarse kind of flour.—vt. To follow in the next place; to support; to join with in proposing some measure.

Secondary, se'kun-da-ri, a. Of second place; subordinate; not elementary.

Second-cousin, se'kund-ku-zn, n. The child of a parent's first-cousin.

Seconder, se'kund-ėr, n. One who supports what another attempts, affirms, or proposes.

Second-hand, se'kund-hand, a. Received not from the original possessor; not new.

Second-sight, se'kund-sīt, n. The power of seeing things future; prophetic vision.

Secrecy, sē'kre-si, n. State or character of being secret; seclusion; fidelity to a secret.

Secret, sē'kret, a. Hidden; concealed; private; unseen.—n. Something hidden or not to be revealed; a mystery.

Secretary, se'krē-ta-ri, n. A person employed to write orders, letters, etc.; an escritoire; one who manages the affairs of a department of government.

Secrete, sē-krēt', vt. (secreting, secreted). To hide; to separate from the blood in animals or from the sap in vegetables.

Secretive, sē-krēt'iv, a. Causing secretion; secretory; given to secrecy; reticent.

Sect, sekt, n. A body of persons united in tenets, chiefly in religion or philosphy; a school; a denomination.

Sectarian, sek-tā'ri-an, a. Pertaining to a sect or sectary.—n. One of a sect.

Sectile, sek'til, a. Capable of being cut in slices with a knife.

Section, sek'shon, n. Act of cutting; a distinct part; subdivision of a chapter, etc.; representation of an object as if cut asunder by an intersecting plane; a quarter of a platoon of infantry, the normal fire-unit.

Sector, sek'tor, n. A part of a circle between two radii; a mathematical instrument useful in making diagrams.

Secular, se'kū-lėr, a. Pertaining to things not spiritual or sacred; worldly; temporal; coming once in a century.

Secularism, sek'ū-lėr-izm, n. The elimination of the religious element from life.

Secure, sē-kūr', a. Free from care or danger; heedless; undisturbed; safe; confident.—vt. (securing, secured). To make safe or certain; to seize and confine; to guarantee; to fasten.

Security, sē-kū'ri-ti, n. Safety; confidence; protection; a guarantee; a surety; an evidence of property, as a bond, a certificate of stock, etc.

Sedate, sē-dāt', a. Composed in manner; staid; placid; sober; serious.

Sedative, se'da-tiv, a. Tending to soothe; assuaging pain.—n. A medicine which assuages pain, etc.

Sedentary, se'den-ta-ri, a. Accustomed to sit much; requiring much sitting.

Sederunt, se-dē'runt, n. A sitting of a court or the like; a formal meeting.

Sedge, sej, n. A coarse grass-like plant growing mostly in marshes and swamps.

Sediment, se'di-ment, n. That which settles at the bottom of liquor; lees.

Sedition, sē-di'shon, n. A commotion in a state; insurrection; civic discord.

Seduce, sē-dūs', vt. (seducing, seduced).To lead astray; to corrupt; to entice to a surrender of chastity.

Seduction, sē-duk'shon, n. Act of seducing; allurement; the persuading of a female to surrender her chastity.

Sedulity, se-dū'li-ti, n. Unremitting industry; diligence; assiduity.

See, sē, vt. (seeing, pret. saw, pp. seen). To per-

ceive by the eye; to notice; to discover; to understand; to receive; to experience; to attend.—vi. To have the power of sight; to understand; to consider.—interj. Lo! look!—n. A seat of episcopal power; a diocese.

Seed, sēd, n. That product of a plant which may produce a similar plant; seeds collectively; the semen; first principle; offspring.—vi. To produce seed; to shed the seed.—vt. To sow; to supply with seed.

Seedling, sēd'ling, n. A plant reared from the seed.

Seed-time, sēd'tīm, n. The season proper for sowing.

Seedy, sēd'i, a. Abounding with seeds; run to seed; shabby; feeling or appearing wretched.

Seeing, sē'ing, conj. Since; inasmuch as.

Seek, sēk, vt. and i (seeking, sought). To search for; to solicit; to have recourse to.

Seem, sēm, vi. To appear; to look as if; to imagine; to feel as if.

Seeming, sēm'ing, p.a. Appearing; specious.—n. Appearance; semblance.

Seemly, sēm'li, a. Becoming; suitable; decorous.—adv. In a suitable manner.

Seer, sēr, n. One who sees into futurity; a prophet.

See-saw, sē'sa, n. A swinging movement up and down; a game in which children swing up and down on the two ends of a balanced piece of timber.—vi. and t. To move up and down or to and fro.

Seethe, sēᴛʜ, vt. (seething, seethed). To boil; to soak.—vi. To be in a state of ebullition; to be hot.

Segment, seg'ment, n. A part cut off; a section; a natural division of a body (as an orange).

Segregate, se'grē-gāt, vt. To set apart or separate.

Seine, Sein, sēn or sān, n. A large fishing net.—vt. (seining, seined). To catch with a seine.

Seismic, Seismal, sīs'mik, sīs'mal, a. Pertaining to earthquakes.

Seismograph, sīs'mō-graf, n. An instrument to register shocks of earthquakes.

Seismology, sīs-mol'o-ji, n. The science of earthquakes.

Seize, sēz, vt. (seizing, seized). To lay hold of suddenly; to take by force or legal authority; to attack, as a disease, fear, etc.; to comprehend; to put in possession.—vi. To take hold or possession.

Seldom, sel'dom, adv. Rarely; not often.

Select, sē-lekt', vt. To choose; to pick out; to cull.—a. Chosen; choice; exclusive.

Selection, sē-lek'shon, n. Act of selecting; a collection of things selected.

Selenium, sē-lē'ni-um, n. A non-metallic element akin to sulphur and tellurium.

Selenology, sel-ē-nol'o-ji, n. That branch of astronomy which treats of the moon.

Self, self, n.; pl. **Selves,** selvz. One's individual person; personal interest; a blossom of a uniform color (with pl. **Selfs**).—a. or pron. Same. Affixed to pronouns and adjectives to express emphasis or distinction, or reflexive usage.

Self-command, self-kom-mand' a. Command of one's powers or feelings; coolness.

Self-conceit, self-kon-sēt', n. A high opinion of oneself; vanity; self-suffciency.

Self-confident, self-kon'fi-dent, a. Confident of one's own strength or abilities.

Self-conscious, self-kon'shus, a. Conscious of one's personal states or acts; apt to think of how oneself appears.

Self-contained, self-kon-tānd', a. Wrapped up in oneself; reserved.

Self-control, self-kon-trōl', n. Control exercised over oneself; self-command.

Self-denial, self-dē-nī'al, n. The forebearing to gratify one's own desires.

Self-denying, self-dē-nī'ing, a. Denying oneself; forbearing to indulge one's own desires.

Self-educated, self-ed'ū-kāt-ed, a. Educated by one's own efforts.

Self-esteem, self-es-tēm', *n*. The esteem or good opinion of oneself; vanity.

Self-evident, self-ev'i-dent, *a*. Evident in its own nature; evident without proof.

Self-government, self-gu'vern-ment, *n*. The government of oneself; government by rulers appointed by the people.

Self-important, self-im-pōrt'ant, *a*. Important in one's own esteem; pompous.

Self-imposed, self'im-pōzd, *a*. Imposed or voluntarily taken on oneself.

Selfish, self'ish, *a*. Devoted unduly to self; influenced by a view to private advantage.

Self-made, self'mād, *a*. Made by oneself; risen in the world by one's exertions.

Self-respect, self'rē-spekt, *n*. Respect for oneself; proper pride.

Self-righteous, self-rīt'yus, *a*. Righteous in one's own esteem; sanctimonious.

Self-same, self'sām, *a*. Exactly the same; the very same; identical.

Self-seeking, self'sēk-ing, *a*. Selfish.

Self-styled, self'stīld, *a*. Called by a title assumed without warrant.

Self-sufficient, self-suf-fi'shent, *a*. Having too much confidence in oneself; conceited; assuming; overbearing.

Self-willed, self'wild, *a*. Wilful; obstinate.

Sell, sel, *vt*. (selling, sold). To give in exchange for money, etc.; to betray.—*vi*. To practice selling; to be sold.

Selvedge, Selvage, sel'vej, sel'vāj, *n*. The edge of cloth; border of close work.

Semaphore, se'ma-fōr, *n*. An apparatus for signalling at a distance, usually a pole supporting a movable arm.

Semblance, sem'blans, *n*. Similarity; resemblance; image; appearance.

Semeiotics, sē-mi-ot'iks, *n*. The science of signs; the doctrine of symptoms of disease.

Semen, sē'men, *n*. The seed or fecundating fluid of male animals; sperm.

Semicircle, se'mi-sėr-kl, *n*. The half of a circle.

Semicolon, se'mi-kō-lon, *n*. The point (;), marking a greater break than a comma.

Semi-detached, se'mi-dē-tacht'', *a*. Partly separated; joined on to another house, but the two detached from other buildings.

Seminal, se'min-al, *a*. Pertaining to seed; germinal; rudimental.

Seminary, se'min-a-ri, *n*. A school or academy; a place for educating for the priesthood.

Semination, se-min-ā'shon, *n*. Act of sowing; the natural dispersion of seeds.

Semite, sem'īt, *n*. A descendant of Shem; one of the Semitic race; a Shemite.

Semi-vowel, se'mi-vou-el, *n*. A sound partaking of the nature of both a vowel and a consonant, as *l*, *m*, *r*.

Semolina, se-mō-li'na, *n*. The large hard grains of flour, separated from the fine flour.

Sempiternal, sem-pi-tėrn'al, *a*. Everlasting.

Senary, sē'na-ri, *a*. Of six; belonging to six, containing six.

Senate, se'nāt, *n*. The legislative body in ancient Rome; the upper branch of a legislature; the governing body of a university, etc.

Send, send, *vt*. (sending, sent). To cause to go or be carried; to transmit; to direct to go and act; to make befall.—*vi*. To dispatch an agent or message.

Senescence, sē-nes'ens, *n*. State of growing old.

Senile, sē'nīl, *a*. Pertaining to old age; characterized by the failings of old age.

Senior, sē'ni-or, sēn'yor, *a*. Older; older or more advanced in office.—*n*. One older in age or office.

Senna, sen'na, *n*. The dried leaves of certain plants used as a purgative; the plant itself.

Sensation, sen-sā'shon, *n*. Impression made through the senses; feeling; power of feeling; what produces excited interest.

Sensational, sen-sā'shon-al, *a*. Relating to sensa-

tion; producing excited interest.

Sense, sens, *n*. The faculty of receiving impressions; a separate faculty of perception; sight; hearing, taste, smell, or touch; consciousness; discernment; understanding; good judgment; meaning.

Senseless, sens'les, *a*. Wanting sense; unfeeling; unreasonable; foolish.

Sensibility, sens-i-bil'i-ti, *n*. State or quality of being sensible; acuteness of perception; delicacy of feeling.

Sensible, sens'i-bil, *a*. That may be perceived by the senses; perceptible; sensitive; easily affected; cognizant; reasonable.

Sensitive, sens'i-tiv, *a*. Having the capacity of receiving impressions; easily affected; having the feelings easily hurt.

Sensitize, sens'i-tīz, *vt*. To render sensitive; to make capable of being acted on by the rays of the sun.

Sensorium, sen-sō'ri-um, *n*. The common center at which all the impressions of sense are received; the brain.

Sensual, sens'ū-al, *a*. Pertaining to the senses, as distinct from the mind; carnal; voluptuous; indulging in lust.

Sensuality, sens-ū-al'i-ti, *n*. Quality of being sensual; indulgence in lust.

Sensuous, sens'ū-us, *a*. Pertaining to the senses; readily affected through the senses.

Sentence, sen'tens, *n*. Opinion; a maxim; a judgment; a number of words containing complete sense.—*vt*. (sentencing, sentenced). To pass sentence upon; to condemn.

Sententious, sen-ten'shus, *a*. Abounding in maxims; terse; gravely judicial.

Sentient, sen'shi-ent, *a*. Having the capacity of sensation; perceptive; sensible.

Sentiment, sen'ti-ment, *n*. Thought prompted by emotion; tenderness of feeling; sensibility; a thought or opinion.

Sentimental, sen-ti-men'tal, *a*. Having sentiment; apt to be swayed by emotional feelings; mawkishly tender.

Sentinel, sen'ti-nel, *n*. One who is set to keep watch; a sentry (now archaic or poetical).

Sentry, sen'tri, *n*. A soldier placed on guard; guard; watch; sentinel's duty.

Separate, se'pa-rāt, *vt*. (separating, separated). To put or set apart; to disjoin.—*vi*. To go apart; to cleave or split.—*a*. Detached; distinct; individual.

Separation, se-pa-rā'shon, *n*. Act of separating; disunion; incomplete divorce.

Sepia, sē'pi-a, *n*. The cuttle-fish; a brown pigment obtained from the cuttle-fish.

September, sep-tem'bėr, *n*. The ninth month of the year.

Septenary, sep'ten-a-ri, *a*. Consisting of or proceeding by sevens; lasting seven years.

Septic, sep'tik, *a*. Promoting or causing putrefaction.—*n*. A substance causing putrefaction.

Septicemia, sep-ti-sē'mi-a, *n*. Blood-poisoning by absorption of putrid matter.

Septuagenarian, sep'tū-a-jen-ā''ri-an, *n*. A person seventy years of age.

Septuagesima, sep'tū-a-jes''i-ma, *n*. The third Sunday before Lent.

Septuagint, sep'tū-a-jint, *n*. A Greek version of the Old Testament, finished about 200 B.C.

Septum, sep'tum, *n*.; pl. **-ta.** A wall separating cavities, as in animals or plants.

Sepulcher, se'pul-kėr, *n*. A tomb.—*vt*. To bury.

Sepulture, se'pul-tūr, *n*. Burial.

Sequacious, sē-kwā'shus, *a*. Following; logically consistent; consecutive.

Sequel, sē'kwel, *n*. That which follows; a succeeding part; result; issue.

Sequence, sē'kwens, *n*. A coming after; succession; arrangement; series.

Sequester, se-kwes'tėr, *vt*. To set apart, *refl.* to retire into seclusion; in *law*, to separate from the owner until the claims of creditors be satisfied; to appropriate.

Sequestered, se-kwes'terd, a. Secluded.

Seraglio, se-räl'yō, n. Originally the old palace of the Turkish sultan at Constantinople; so a harem.

Seraph, se'raf, n.; pl. **-phs** or **phim.** An angel of the highest rank or order.

Serenade, se-rē-nād', n. Music played at night under the windows of ladies.—vt. (serenading, serenaded). To entertain with a serenade.—vi. To perform a serenade.

Serene, sē-rēn', a. Clear; bright; calm; unruffled; formerly a form of address for princes, etc., in Germany and Austria.—n. Serenity; what is serene.

Serenity, sē-ren'i-ti, n. State of being serene; peace; calmness; coolness.

Serf, sérf, n. A villein; a forced laborer attached to an estate; a bondman.

Sergeant, sär'jant, n. A noncommissioned officer above corporal; a police officer.

Serial, sē'ri-al, a. Pertaining to a series; forming a series.—n. A written composition issued in numbers.

Seriatim, sē-ri-ā'tim, adv. In regular order; one after the other.

Sericeous, sē-ri'shus, a. Pertaining to silk; silky.

Sericulture, sē'ri-kul-tůr, n. The breeding and treatment of silk-worms.

Series, sē'ri-ēz or sē'rēz, n.; pl. the same. A succession of things; sequence; course.

Serious, sē'ri-us, a. Grave; earnest; momentous; attended with danger.

Sermon, sér'mon, n. A religious discourse by a clergyman; a homily.—vt. To tutor; to lecture.

Serous, sēr'us, a. Pertaining to serum; thin; watery; like whey; secreting serum.

Serpent, sér'pent, n. A scaly reptile without feet; a bass musical instrument of wood; a firework.—a. Pertaining to a serpent.

Serpentine, sér'pent-in, a. Resembling or pertaining to a serpent; spiral.—n. A rock resembling a serpent's skin in appearance, used for decoration.—vi. To wind like a serpent.

Serrate, Serrated, ser'rāt, ser'rāt-ed, a. Notched on the edge like a saw; toothed.

Serration, ser-rā'shon, n. Formation in the shape of a saw.

Serried, se'rid, a. Crowded; in close order.

Serum, sē'rum, n. The watery part of curdled milk; whey; the thin part of the blood, etc.

Servant, serv'ant, n. One who serves; an attendant in a household; a drudge.

Serve, sérv, vt. (serving, served). To work for and obey; to minister to; to set on a table for a meal; to conduce to; to be sufficient for; to manage or work; to deliver or transmit to; to perform the conditions of.—vi. To perform offices for another; to perform duties; to suffice; to suit.

Service, sérv'is, n. Act of one who serves; employment; kind office; military or naval duty; period of such duty; usefulness; public religious worship; liturgy; set of dishes for the table; supply of things regularly provided.

Serviette, sér-vi-et', n. A table-napkin.

Servile, sér'vil, a. Slavish; mean; dependent; fawning; meanly submissive.

Servility, sér-vil'i-ti, n. State of being servile; mean submission.

Servitude, sérv'i-tůd, n. State of a slave; slavery; compulsory labor.

Sesame, ses'a-me, n. An annual herbaceous plant, the seeds of which yield a fine oil.

Sessile, ses'il, a. Attached without any sensible projecting support; having no stalk.

Session, se'shon, n. The sitting of a court, etc., for business; time or term of sitting.—**Court of Session,** the highest civil court of Scotland.

Set, set, vt. (setting, set). To put or dispose in a certain place or position; to fix; to appoint; to estimate; to regulate or adjust; to fit to music; to adorn; to intersperse; to incite.—vi. To disap-

pear below the horizon; to solidify; to tend; to point out game; to apply oneself.—p.a. Placed, fixed, etc.; determined; established.—n. The descent of the sun, etc.; attitude, position; turn or bent; number of things combining to form a whole; a complete assortment; a clique.

Setaceous, se-tā'shus, a. Bristly.

Set-off, set'of, n. Any counterbalance; and equivalent; a counter claim.

Setose, sē'tōs, a. Bristly.

Settee, set-tē', n. A long seat with a back to it; a kind of sofa.

Setter, set'ér, n. One who or that which sets; a sporting dog.

Setting, set'ing, n. Act of sinking below the horizon; that in which something, as a jewel, is set; music set for certain words.

Settle, set'l, n. A bench with a high back and arms.—vt. (settling, settled). To place in a more or less permanent position; to establish; to quit; to determine; to reconcile; to pay; to square or adjust; to colonize.—vi. To become fixed; to fix one's abode; to subside; to become calm; to adjust differences or accounts.

Settled, set'ld, p.a. Established; steadfast; stable; methodical.

Settlement, set'l-ment, n. Act of settling; establishment in life; colonization; a colony; adjustment; liquidation; arrangement; settling of property on a wife.

Set-to, set-tö', n. A sharp contest.

Seven, se'ven, a. and n. One more than six.

Seventeen, se'ven-tēn, a. and n. Seven and ten.

Seventh, se'venth, a. Next after the sixth; containing or being one part in seven.—n. One part in seven.

Seventy, se'ven-ti, a. and n. Seven times ten.

Sever, se'vér, vt. To separate by violence; to keep distinct.—vi. To separate.

Several, se'vér-al, a. Separate; distinct; more than two, but not very many.

Severalty, se'vér-al-ti, n. A state of separation from the rest, or from all others.

Severance, se'vér-ans, n. Act of severing; separation.

Severe, sē-vér', a. Serious; grave; harsh; stern; austere; rigidly exact; keen.

Severity, sē-ve'ri-ti, n. State or quality of being severe; rigor; intensity; austerity.

Sevres, sä-vr, n. A kind of beautiful porcelain, made of Sèvres, near Paris.

Sew, sō, vt. and i. To unite or make by needle and thread.

Sewage, sū'āj, n. The filthy matter which passes through sewers.

Sewer, sū'ér, n. A subterranean drain, as in a city, to carry off water, filth, etc.

Sewer, sō'ér, n. One who sews.

Sewing, sō'ing, n. Act of using a needle; that which is sewed; stitches made.

Sex, seks, n. That character by which an animal is male or female.

Sexagenarian, seks-a-jen-ā''ri-an, n. A person sixty years of age.—a. Sixty years old.

Sexagesima, seks-a-jes'i-ma, n. The second Sunday before Lent.

Sextant, seks'tant, n. The sixth part of a circle; an instrument for measuring the angular distances of objects by reflection.

Sexton, seks'ton, n. An under officer of a church who takes care of the sacred vessels, acts as janitor, etc.

Sextuple, seks'tū-pl, a. Sixfold.

Sexual, seks'ū-al, a. Pertaining to, proceeding from, characterized by sex.

Shabby, shab'i, a. Poor in appearance; threadbare; mean; paltry; stingy.

Shackle, shak'l, n. A fetter; a manacle; that which obstructs free action.—vt. (shackling, shackled). To bind with shackles; to hamper.

Shade, shād, n. Obscurity caused by the interception of light; obscure retreat; twilight dimness; a screen; darker part of a picture;

gradation of light; a scarcely perceptible degree or amount; a ghost.—*vt.* (shading, shaded). To screen from light; to obscure; to protect; to darken; to mark with gradations of color.

Shadow, sha'dō, *n.* A figure projected by the interception of light; shade; an inseparable companion; an imperfect representation; a spirit; protection.—*vt.* To shade; to cloud; to screen; to represent faintly; to follow closely.

Shady, shād'i, *a.* Abounding in shade; affording shade; of dubious morality.

Shaft, shäft, *n.* The long part of a spear or arrow; body of a column; spire of a steeple, etc.; pole of a carriage; a kind of large axle; a narrow passage, as into a mine.

Shafting, shäft'ing, *n.* A system of shafts communicating motion in machinery.

Shag, shag, *n.* Coarse hair or nap; cloth with a coarse nap; tobacco leaves shredded for smoking.—*vt.* (shagging, shagged). To make shaggy.

Shake, shāk, *vt.* (shaking, pret. shook, pp. shaken). To cause to move with quick vibrations; to agitate; to move from firmness; to cause to waver; to trill.—*vi.* To tremble; to shiver; to quake.—*n.* A wavering or rapid motion; tremor; shock; a trill in music; a crack in timber.

Shaker, shāk'ėr, *n.* A person or thing that shakes; a member of a religious sect.

Shaky, shāk'i, *a.* Apt to shake or tremble; unsteady; feeble.

Shale, shāl, *n.* A fine-grained rock; a clay rock having a slaty structure.

Shall, shal, *verb auxiliary;* pret. *should,* shud. In the first person it forms part of the future tense; in the second and third persons it implies authority.

Shallot, sha-lot', *n.* A species of onion.

Shallow, shal'ō, *a.* Not deep; superficial; simple; silly.—*n.* A place where the water is not deep; a shoal.

Sham, sham, *n.* That which appears to be what it is not; imposture; humbug.—*a.* False; counterfeit.—*vt.* and *i.* (shamming, shammed). To feign, pretend.

Shamanism, shā'man-izm, *n.* An idolatrous religion of Northern Asia, etc., characterized by a belief in sorcery and in demons who require to be propitiated.

Shamble, sham'bl, *vi.* (shambling, shambled). To walk awkwardly, as if the knees were weak.—*n.* The gait of one who shambles.

Shambling, sham'bling, *p.a.* Walking with an irregular, clumsy pace.

Shame, shām, *n.* A painful sensation excited by guilt, disgrace, etc.; reproach; disgrace.—*vt.* (shaming, shamed). To make ashamed; to disgrace.

Shamefaced, shām'fāst, *a.* Easily put out of countenance; modest; bashful.

Shameful, shām'ful, *a.* Full of shame; disgraceful; scandalous; infamous.

Shameless, shām'les, *a.* Destitute of shame; immodest; unblushing.

Shampoo, sham-pō', *vt.* (shampooing, shampooed). To press and rub the body after a hot bath; to wash and rub thoroughly the head.

Shamrock, sham'rok, *n.* A trefoil plant, the national emblem of Ireland.

Shank, shangk, *n.* The leg; the shin-bone; the part of a tool connecting the acting part with a handle; the stem of an anchor.

Shanty, shan'ti, *n.* A hut or mean dwelling; song sung by sailors working together.

Shape, shāp, *vt.* (shaping, shaped). To form; to mold; to adjust.—*vi.* To suit.—*n.* Form or figure; make; a model; a dish of blancmange, etc.

Shapeless, shāp'les, *a.* Destitute of any regular form; deformed.

Shard, shärd, *n.* A fragment of an earthen vessel; the wing-case of a beetle.

Share, shār, *n.* A part bestowed or contributed;

lot or portion; a plow-share.—*vt.* (sharing, shared). To part among two or more; to participate in.—*vi.* To have part.

Shareholder, shār'hōld-ėr, *n.* One who holds shares in a joint property.

Shark, shärk, *n.* A voracious sea-fish; an unscrupulous person; a sharper.

Sharp, shärp, *a.* Having a very thin edge or fine point; keen; abrupt; not blurred; shrewd; acid; shrill; fierce; short and rapid; biting; barely honest; in *music,* raised a semitone.—*n.* A note raised a semitone, marked by the sign (#); the sign itself; *pl.* the hard parts of wheat.—*vt.* To sharpen.—*adv.* Sharply; exactly; rapidly.

Sharpen, shärp'n, *vt.* To make sharp or sharper; to whet.—*vi.* To become sharp.

Sharpness, shärp'nes, *n.* Keenness; pungency; acuteness.

Sharp-shooter, shärp'shöt-ėr, *n.* A soldier skilled in shooting with exactness.

Shatter, shat'ėr, *vt.* To break into many pieces; to overthrow, destroy.—*vt.* To be broken into fragments.—*n.* A fragment.

Shave, shāv, *vt.* (shaving, shaved). To cut off the hair from the skin with a razor; to cut off thin slices from; to skim along; to fleece.—*vi.* To cut off the beard with a razor.—*n.* A cutting off of the beard; a thin slice; an exceedingly narrow escape.

Shaving, shāv'ing, *n.* Act of one who shaves; a thin slice pared off.

Shawl, shal, *n.* An article of dress, used mostly as a loose covering for the shoulders.

She, shē, *pron. nominative.* The feminine pronoun of the third person.

Sheaf, shēf, *n.*; *pl.* **Sheaves,** shēvz, A bundle of the stalks of wheat, oats, etc.; any similar bundle.—*vt.* To make into sheaves.—*vi.* To make sheaves.

Shear, shēr, *vt.* and *i.* (pret. sheared or shore, pp. sheared or shorn). To cut with shears; to clip the wool from; to cut from a surface; to fleece.

Shears, shērz, *n.pl.* An instrument of two blades for cutting.

Shear-steel, shēr'stēl, *n.* Steel prepared from bars of common steel, heated, beaten together, and drawn out.

Sheath, shēth, *n.* A case for a sword, etc.; a scabbard; wing case of an insect.

Sheathe, shēᴛʜ, *vt.* (sheathing, sheathed). To put into a sheath; to protect by a casing.

Shed, shed, *vt.* (shedding, shed). To cast or throw off; to emit or diffuse; to let fall in drops; to spill.—*vi.* To let fall seed, a covering, etc.—*n.* A watershed; the opening between threads in a loom through which the shuttle passes; a penthouse; a hut; a large open structure.

Sheen, shēn, *n.* Brightness; splendor.—*a.* Bright; shining: *poetical.*

Sheep, shēp, *sing.* and *pl.* A ruminant animal valued for its wool and flesh; a silly or timid fellow.—**Sheep's eye,** a loving or wistful glance.

Sheepish, shēp'ish, *a.* Like a sheep; foolish; bashful; over-modest or diffident.

Sheep-skin, shēp'skin, *n.* The skin of a sheep prepared with the wool on; leather prepared from it.

Sheer, shēr, *a.* Mere; downright; precipitous.—*vi.* To deviate from the proper course.—*n.* The upward bend of a ship at stem or stern.

Sheet, shēt, *n.* A broad, thin piece of anything; broad expanse; piece of linen or cotton spread on a bed, piece of paper, a rope fastened to the lower corner of a sail.—*vt.* To furnish with sheets; to shroud.

Sheeting, shēt'ing, *n.* Linen or cotton cloth for making bed-sheets.

Shelf, shelf, *n.*; *pl.* **Shelves,** shelvz. A board fixed along a wall to support articles; a ledge, a ledge of rocks in the sea.

Shell, shel, *n.* A hard outside covering; an outside crust; framework; any slight hollow structure; a projectile containing a bursting charge.—*vt.* To strip off the shell of; to throw bomb-shells into or among.—*vi*. To cast the exterior covering.

Shellac, shel-lak', *n*. Lac melted and formed into thin cakes.

Shell-fish, shel'fish, *n. sing.* and *pl*. A mollusk or a crustacean whose external covering consists of a shell.

Shell-shock, shel'shok, *n*. Neurosis caused by shell-fire.

Shelter, shel'tèr, *n*. A protection; asylum; refuge; security.—*vt*. To protect; to screen.—*vi*. To take shelter.

Shelve, shelv, *vt*. (shelving, shelved). To place on a shelf; to dismiss from use or attention; to furnish with shelves.—*vi*. To slope.

Shepherd, shep'érd, *n*. One who tends sheep.

Sherbet, sher'bet, *n*. An Eastern drink of water, the juice of fruits, and sugar.

Sheriff, she'rif, *n*. An officer in each county to whom is entrusted the administration of the law; in Scotland, the chief judge of a county.

Sherry, she'ri, *n*. A wine of southern Spain.

Shibboleth, shib'bò-leth, *n*. The watchword of a party; a cry or motto.

Shield, shèld, *n*. A broad piece of armor carried on the arm; protection; an escutcheon with a coat of arms.—*vt*. To cover, as with a shield; to protect.

Shift, shift, *vi*. To change; to change place or direction; to manage; to practice indirect methods.—*vt*. To remove; to alter; to dress in fresh clothes.—*n*. A change; expedient; evasion; an under garment; a squad of workmen; the working time of a relay of men; the spell of work.

Shiftless, shift'les, *a*. Destitute of expedients; wanting in energy or effort.

Shimmer, shim'èr, *vi*. To emit a faint or tremulous light; to glisten.—*n*. A glistening.

Shin, shin, *n*. The fore-part of the leg, between the ankle and the knee.

Shine, shin, *vi*. (shining, shone). To give out a steady brilliant light; to be lively, bright, or conspicuous.—*vt*. To cause to shine.—*n*. Brightness; fair weather.

Shingle, shing'gl, *n*. A thin piece of wood used in covering roofs; loose gravel and pebbles.—*vt*. To cover with shingles; to hammer so as to expel slag or scoriae from in puddling iron.

Shingles, shing'glz, *n*. An eruptive disease which spreads around the body.

Shining, shin'ing, *a*. Bright; illustrious.

Shiny, shin'i, *a*. Bright; brilliant; clear.

Ship, ship, *n*. A vessel of some size adapted to navigation; a three-masted, square-rigged vessel.—*vt*. (shipping, shipped). To put on board of a ship; to transport in a ship; to hire for service in a ship; to fix in its place.—*vi*. To engage for service on a ship; to embark.

Shipboard, ship'bòrd, *n*. The deck or interior of a ship: used in *on shipboard*.

Ship-builder, ship'bild-èr, *n*. One who builds ships; a naval architect; a shipwright.

Shipmate, ship'māt, *n*. One who serves in the same ship; a fellow-sailor.

Shipment, ship'ment, *n*. Act of putting goods on board of a ship; goods shipped.

Shipper, ship'èr, *n*. One who sends goods on board a ship for transportation.

Ship-shape, ship'shāp, *a*. Having a seamanlike trim; well arranged.

Shipwreck, ship'rek, *n*. The wreck or loss of a ship; destruction; ruin.—*vt*. To wreck; to cast away; to ruin.

Shipwright, ship'rit, *n*. A builder of ships or other vessels; a ship-carpenter.

Shirk, shèrk, *vt*. and *i* To avoid unfairly; to seek to avoid duty.

Shirt, shèrt, *n*. A man's loose under garment of linen, etc.; a lady's blouse.—*vt*. To clothe with a shirt.

Shiver, shi'vèr, *vt*. To shatter.—*vi*. To fall into many small pieces; to tremble, as from cold; to

shudder.—*n*. A small fragment; a shaking fit; shudder.

Shoal, shòl, *n*. A multitude; a crowd; a sandbank or bar; a shallow.—*vi*. To become more shallow.—*a*. Shallow.

Shock, shok, *n*. A violent striking against; violent onset; a sudden disturbing emotion; a stook; a thick mass of hair.—*vt*. To give a shock to; to encounter violently; to disgust; to make up into shocks or stooks.

Shocking, shok'ing, *a*. Serving to shock; dreadful; disgusting; offensive.

Shod, shod, pret. and pp. of *shoe*.

Shoddy, shod'i, *n*. Fiber obtained from old woollen fabrics mixed with fresh wool and manufactured anew; inferior cloth made from this.—*a*. Made of shoddy; trashy.

Shoe, shö, *n*. A covering for the foot; a plate of iron nailed to the hoof of a horse, etc.—*vt*. (shoeing, shoed). To furnish with shoes.

Shoe-horn, Shoeing-horn, shö'horn, shö'ing-horn, *n*. A curved implement used to aid in putting on shoes.

Shone, shon, pret. and pp. of *shine*.

Shook, shuk, pret. and pp. of *shake*.—*n*. The staves for a single barrel made into a package.

Shoot, shöt, *vt*. (shooting, shot). To cause to fly forth; to discharge; to hit or kill with a missile; to empty out suddenly; to thrust forward; to pass rapidly under, over, etc.—*vi*. To charge a missile; to dart along; to sprout; to project.—*n*. A shooting; a young branch; a sloping trough; a place for shooting rubbish.

Shooting, shöt'ing, *n*. Sport of killing game with firearms; tract over which game is shot; sensation of a darting pain.—*a*. Pertaining to one who shoots.

Shop, shop, *n*. A place where goods are sold by retail; a building in which mechanics work; one's special business.—*vi*. (shopping, shopped). To visit shops for purchasing goods.

Shop-lifter, shop'lift-èr, *n*. One who steals in a shop on pretense of buying.

Shore, shòr, *n*. Land along the edge of the sea; the coast; a prop.—*vt*. To support by props: pret. of *shear*.

Shorn, shörn, pp. of *shear*.

Short, short, *a*. Not long or tall; scanty; deficient; concise; snappish; severe; brittle.—*adv*. Abruptly; insufficiently.—*n*. Something short; *pl*. garments resembling trousers, but ending above the knee.—**In short,** in few words; briefly.

Shortage, short'āj, *n*. Amount short or deficient; deficit.

Shortcoming, short'kum-ing, *n*. A failing of the usual quantity; a delinquency.

Shorthand, short'hand, *n*. A shorter mode of writing than is usually employed.

Short-handed, short'hand-ed, *a*. Not having the usual number of assistants.

Short-lived, short'livd, *a*. Not living or lasting long; of short continuance.

Short-sighted, short'sit-ed, *n*. Unable to see far; myopic; wanting foresight.

Short-winded, short'wind-ed, *a*. Affected with shortness of breath.

Shot, shot, *n*. Act of shooting; a projectile; a bullet; bullets collectively; range or reach; a marksman; the number of fish caught in one haul; a reckoning.—*vt*. (shotting, shotted). To load with shot.—*a*. Having a changeable color, as silk; interwoven.

Should, shud, the pret. of *shall*, denoting present or past duty or obligation, or expressing a hypothetical case.

Shoulder, shol'dér, *n*. The joint by which the arm or the fore-leg is connected with the body; a projection; support.—*vt*. To push with the shoulder; to put upon the shoulder.—*vi*. To push forward.

Shoulder-blade, shol'dèr-blād, *n*. The bone of the shoulder; scapula.

Shoulder-strap, shol'dèr-strap, *n*. A strap worn

on the shoulder, either to support dress, or as a badge of distinction.

Shout, shout, *vi.* To utter a loud and sudden cry.—*vt.* To utter with a shout.—*n.* A loud sudden cry.

Shove, shuv, *vt.* and *i* (shoving, shoved). To push forward; to press against; to jostle.—*n.* Act of shoving, a push.

Shovel, shu'vel, *n.* An instrument with a broad shallow blade, for lifting earth, etc.—*vt.* (shovelling, shovelled). To throw with a shovel.

Show, shō, *vt.* (pret. showed; pp. shown or showed). To display to the view of others; to let be seen; to make known; to prove; to bestow, afford.—*vi.* To appear.—*n.* Act of showing; exhibition; appearance; pretense; pageant; things exhibited for money.

Shower, shou'er, *n.* A fall of rain, etc.; a copious supply.—*vt.* To water with a shower; to bestow liberally.—*vi.* To rain in showers.

Show-room, shō'rōm, *n.* A room in which a show is exhibited; an apartment where goods are displayed.

Shrapnel, shrap'nel, *n.* A shell filled with bullets, timed to burst at any given point.

Shred, shred, *vt.* (shredding, shred or shredded). To tear into small pieces.—*n.* A long, narrow piece cut off; a tatter.

Shrew, shrō, *n.* A peevish, ill-tempered woman; a scold; a shrew-mouse.

Shrewd, shröd, *a.* Astute; sagacious; discerning; sharp.

Shrewish, shrö'ish, *a.* Having the qualities of a shrew; peevish; vixenish.

Shriek, shrēk, *vi.* To cry out shrilly; to scream.—*n.* A shrill cry; a scream.

Shrike, shrīk, *n.* An insessorial bird which feeds on insects, small birds, etc.; a butcher-bird.

Shrill, shril, *a.* Sharp or piercing in sound; uttering an acute sound.—*vi.* and *t* To utter an acute piercing sound.

Shrimp, shrimp, *n.* A small crustacean allied to the lobster; a mannikin.

Shrine, shrīn, *n.* A case, as for sacred relics; a tomb; altar; a place hallowed from its associations.—*vt.* (shrining, shrined). To enshrine.

Shrink, shringk, *vi.* (pret. shrank or shrunk, pp. shrunk or shrunken). To contact spontaneously; to shrivel; to withdraw, as from danger; to flinch.—*vt.* To cause to contract.—*n.* Contraction.

Shrive, shrīv, *vt.* (shriving, pret. shrove or shrived, pp. shriven or shrived). To hear the confession of; to confess and absolve.

Shrivel, shri'vel, *vi.* and *t* (shrivelling, shrivelled). To shrink into wrinkles; to shrink and form corrugations.

Shroud, shroud, *n.* That which clothes or covers; a winding-sheet; one of the large ropes in a ship supporting the mast.—*vt.* To cover; to dress for the grave; to screen.

Shrove-Tuesday, shrōv'tūz-dā, *n.* The Tuesday before the first day of Lent.

Shrub, shrub, *n.* A woody plant less than a tree; a plant with several woody stems from the same root; a beverage containing the juice of fruit, etc.

Shrubbery, shrub'er-i, *n.* An ornamental plantation of shrubs; shrubs collectively.

Shrug, shrug, *vt.* and *i* (shrugging, shrugged). To draw up or to contract, as the shoulders.—*n.* A drawing up of the shoulders.

Shuck, shuk, *n.* A shell or husk.

Shudder, shud'er, *vi.* To tremble with fear, horror, etc.; to quake.—*n.* A tremor.

Shuffle, shuf'l, *vt.* (shuffling; shuffled). To shove one way and the other; to confuse; to change the position of cards.—*vi.* To change position; to quibble; to move with a dragging gait; to scrape the floor in dancing.—*n.* An evasion; mixing cards; scraping movement in dancing.

Shun, shun, *vt.* (shunning, shunned). To avoid; to refrain from; to neglect.

Shunt, shunt, *vi.* and *t.* In railways; to turn from one line of rails into another; to free oneself of.

Shut, shut, *vt.* (shutting, shut). To close or stop up; to bar; to preclude; to exclude; to confine.—*vi.* To close itself; to be closed.—*a.* Made close; closed; not resonant.

Shutter, shut'er, *n.* One who shuts; a moveable covering for a window or aperture.

Shuttle, shut'l, *n.* An instrument used by weavers for shooting the thread of the woof between the threads of the warp.

Shuttle-cock, shut'l-kok, *n.* A cork stuck with feathers, and struck by a battledore.—*vt.* To throw backwards and forwards.

Shy, shī, *a.* Timid; retiring; reserved; coy; cautious; wary.—*vi.* (shying, shied). To start suddenly aside, as a horse.—*vt.* To throw.—*n.* The starting suddenly aside of a horse.

Sibilant, si'bi-lant, *a.* Hissing.—*n.* A letter uttered with a hissing, as *s* and *z*.

Sibilation, si-bi-lā'shon, *n.* The act of sibulating; a hiss.

Sic, sik, *adv.* Thus; it is so: often used within brackets in quoting, to note that a peculiarity in the quotation is literally exact.

Siccate, sik'āt, *vt.* To dry.

Sick, sik, *a.* Affected with disease of any kind; ill; inclined to vomit; disgusted or weary; pertaining to those who are sick.

Sick-bay, sik'bā, *n.* A ship's hospital.

Sicken, sik'n, *vt.* To make sick; to disgust.—*vi.* To become sick; to be disgusted; to languish.

Sickle, sik'l, *n.* An instrument for cutting grain, used with one hand; a reaping-hook.

Sickness, sik'nes, *n.* Disease; ill-health; illness; nausea.

Side, sīd, *n.* The broad or long surface of a body; edge, border; right or left half of the body; part between the top and bottom; any party or interest opposed to another.—*a.* Being on, from, or toward the side; indirect.—*vi.* (siding, sided). To embrace the opinions of one party.

Sideboard, sīd'bōrd, *n.* A piece of furniture used to hold dining utensils, etc.

Sidelong, sīd'long, *adv.* Laterally; obliquely.—*a.* Lateral; oblique.

Sidereal, sī-dē'rē-al, *a.* Pertaining to stars; measured by the motion of the stars.

Sidewalk, sīd'wak, *n.* A raised walk for footpassengers by the side of a street or road.

Sidewise, sīd'wīz, *adv.* Toward one side; laterally; on one side.

Siding, sīd'ing, *n.* A short additional line of rails laid for the purpose of shunting.

Sidle, sīd'l, *vi.* (sidling, sidled). To go or move side foremost; to move to one side.

Siege, sēj, *n.* A regular attack on a fortified place; continued endeavor to gain possession.

Sienna, sē-en'na, *n.* An earth of a fine yellow color, used as a pigment.

Siesta, sē-es'ta, *n.* A sleep or rest in the hottest part of the day.

Sieve, siv, *n.* A utensil for separating the smaller particles of a loose substance.

Sift, sift, *vt.* To separate by a sieve; to examine minutely.—*vi.* To pass as if through a sieve.

Sigh, sī, *vi.* To make a long breath audibly, as from grief; to make a melancholy sound.—*n.* A long breath made audibly, as in grief.

Sight, sīt, *n.* Act or power of seeing; view; vision; visibility; estimation; a show; an appliance for guiding the eye.—*vt.* To see; to descry; to give the proper elevation and direction to, as a piece of ordnance.

Sightless, sīt'les, *a.* Wanting sight; blind.

Sightly, sīt'li, *a.* Pleasing to the sight or eye; agreeable to look on.

Sight-seeing, sīt'sē-ing, *n.* The act of seeing sights or visiting scenes of interest.

Sign, sīn, *n.* A mark or stamp indicative of something; a token; indication; emblem; a symbol or character.—*vt.* To express by a sign; to affix a signature to.—*vi.* To make a sign or signal.

S

Signal, sig'nal, *n.* A sign to communicate intelligence, orders, etc., at a distance.—*a.* Worthy of note; remarkable.—*vt.* or *i.* (signalling, signalled). To communicate by signals.

Signalize, sig'nal-īz, *vt.* To make remarkable; to distinguish by some fact or exploit.

Signatory, Signatary, sig'na-to-ri, sig'na-ta-ri, *a.* Relating to the signing of documents.—*n.* One who signs; a state representative who signs a public document.

Signature, sig'na-tūr, *n.* A mark impressed; the name of a person written by himself; in *printing,* a distinctive letter or mark at the bottom of the first page of each sheet.

Signer, sīn'ėr, *n.* One who signs.

Signet, sig'net, *n.* A seal; seal used by the sovereign in sealing private letters.

Significant, sig-ni'fi-kant, *a.* Signifying something; indicative; important.

Signification, sig'ni-fi-kā''shon, *n.* Act of signifying; meaning; import; sense.

Signify, sig'ni-fī, *vt.* (signifying, signified). To make known either by signs or words; to betoken; to mean; to imply; to import.

Silence, sī'lens, *n.* State of being silent; quiet; secrecy; absence of mention.—*vt.* To put to silence; to quiet; to cause to cease firing.

Silent, sī'lent, *a.* Not speaking; mute; dumb; taciturn; making no noise.

Silhouette, sil'ö-et, *n.* A profile portrait filled in with a dark color.

Silicate, sīl'i-kāt, *n.* A compound of silica with certain bases.

Silicon, Silicium, sil'i-kon, si-lis'i-um, *n.* The nonmetallic element of which silica is the oxide.

Silicosis, si-li-kō'sis, *n.* A disease of the lungs caused by inhaling small particles of silica.

Silk, silk, *n.* The fine thread produced by various caterpillars, particularly the silk-worm; cloth made of silk; garment made of this cloth.—*a.* Pertaining to silk; silken.

Silk-worm, silk'wėrm, *n.* A worm which produces silk; the larva of various moths which spin a silken cocoon for the chrysalis.

Sill, sil, *n.* The timber or stone at the foot of a door or window; the threshold; the floor of a gallery in a mine.

Silly, sil'li, *a.* Weak in intellect; foolish; unwise.

Silo, sī'lō, *n.* The pit in which green fodder is preserved in the method of ensilage.

Silt, silt, *n.* A deposit of fine earth from running or standing water.—*vt.* To fill with silt.

Silurian, sī-lū'ri-an, *a.* Applied to the lowest division of the paleozoic strata.

Silver, sil'vėr, *n.* A precious metal of a white color; money; plate made of silver.—*a.* Made of silver; silvery.—*vt.* and *i.* To cover with a coat of silver; to tinge with gray.

Silversmith, sil'vėr-smith, *n.* One whose occupation is to work in silver.

Silvery, sil'vėr-i, *a.* Like silver; covered with silver; clear as the sound of a silver bell.

Simian, Simious, si'mi-an, si'mi-us, *a.* Pertaining to apes or monkeys; ape-like.

Similar, si'mi-lėr, *a.* Like; resembling; having like parts and relations but not of the same magnitude.

Simile, si'mi-lē, *n.* A figure of speech consisting in likening one thing to another.

Similitude, si-mil'i-tūd, *n.* Likeness; resemblance; comparison.

Simmer, si'mėr, *vi.* To boil gently.

Simper, sim'pėr, *vi.* To smile in a silly manner.—*n.* A silly or affected smile.

Simple, sim'pl, *a.* Not complex; single; not involved; clear; artless; mere; plain; sincere; silly.—*n.* Something not mixed; a medicinal herb.

Simpleton, sim'pl-ton, *n.* A simple or silly person; one easily deceived.

Simplicity, sim-plis'i-ti, *n.* State or quality of being simple; singleness; artlessness; sincerity; plainness; foolishness.

Simplify, sim'pli-fī, *vt.* To make simple; to make plain or easy.

Simulacrum, sim-ū-lā'krum, *n.*; pl. -**cra.** An image or likeness; a phantom.

Simulate, sim'ū-lāt, *vt.* To counterfeit; to feign.

Simultaneous, si-mul-tā'nē-us, *a.* Taking place or done at the same time.

Sin, sin, *n.* A transgression of the divine law; moral depravity; an offense in general.—*vi.* (sinning, sinned). To violate the divine law or any rule of duty.

Sinapism, sin'a-pizm, *n.* A mustard poultice.

Since, sins, *adv.* From that time; from then till now; ago.—*prep.* Ever from the time of; after.—*conj.* From the time when; because that.

Sincere, sin-sēr', *a.* Pure; unmixed; real; genuine; guileless; frank; true.

Sincerity, sin-se'ri-ti, *n.* Honesty of mind or intention; freedom from hypocrisy.

Sinciput, sin'si-put, *n.* The fore part of the skull.

Sine, sīn, *n.* A geometrical line drawn from one end of an arc perpendicular to the diameter through the other end.

Sinecure, sī'nē-kūr, *n.* An ecclesiastical benefice without cure of souls; a paid office without employment.

Sinew, si'nū, *n.* The fibrous cord which unites a muscle to a bone; a tendon; strength.—*vt.* To bind, as by sinews; to strengthen.

Sinful, sin'ful, *a.* Full of sin; wicked; iniquitous; wrong.

Sing, sing, *vi.* (pret. sang, sung, pp. sung). To utter sounds with melodious modulations of voice; to have a ringing sensation.—*vt.* To utter with musical modulations of voice, to celebrate in song; to tell.

Singe, sinj, *vt.* (singeing, singed). To burn slightly; to burn the surface of.—*n.* A burning of the surface.

Single, sing'gl, *a.* Being one or a unit; individual; unmarried; performed by one person; simple; sincere.—*vt.* (singling, singled). To select individually; with *out.*

Single-entry, sing'gl-en-tri, *n.* A system of book-keeping in which each entry appears only once on one side or other of an account.

Single-handed, sing'gl-hand-ed, *a.* Unassisted; by one's own efforts.

Single-minded, sing'gl-mīnd-ed, *a.* Free from guile; honest; straightforward.

Sing-song, sing'song, *n.* A drawling tone; repetition of similar words or tones.

Singular, sing'gū-lėr, *a.* That is single; expressing one person or thing; remarkable; rare; odd.—*n.* The singular number.

Singularity, sing-gū-la'ri-ti, *n.* Peculiarity; eccentricity.

Sinister, si'nis-tėr, *a.* Left; evil; baneful; malign; unlucky.

Sink, singk, *vi.* (pret. sank or sunk, pp. sunk). To descend in a liquid; to subside; to enter; to decline in worth, strength, etc.—*vt.* To immerse; to submerge; to make by digging; to depress; to degrade.—*n.* A receptacle for liquid filth; a sewer; place where iniquity is gathered.

Sinker, singk'ėr, *n.* One who sinks; a weight on some body to sink it.

Sinless, sin'les, *a.* Free from sin; innocent.

Sinner, sin'ėr, *n.* One who sins; a transgressor; offender; criminal.

Sinology, si-nol'o-ji, *n.* The knowledge of the Chinese language, etc.

Sinter, sin'tėr, *n.* Stony matter precipitated by springs.

Sinuate, sin'ū-āt, *a.* Winding.

Sinuous, sin'ū-us, *a.* Bending or curving in and out; crooked.

Sinus, sī'nus, *n.* A curved opening; a bay; a cavity containing pus; a fistula.

Sinusitis, sī-nū-zī'tis, *n.* Inflammation of one of the air-cavities of the skull connecting with the nose.

Sip, sip, *vt.* (sipping, sipped). To drink in small

quantities; to drink out of.—*vi*. To take a fluid with the lips.—*n*. A small quantity of liquid taken with the lips.

Siphon, si'fon, *n*. A bent tube used for drawing off liquids, as from a cask, etc.

Sir, sėr, *n*. A word of respect used to men; title distinctive of knights and baronets.

Sire, sīr, *n*. A respectful word of address to a king; a father; male parent of a horse, etc.

Siren, si'ren, *n*. A sea-nymph who enticed sea men by songs, and then slew them; a woman dangerous from her fascinations; a fog-signal; a signal used as an air-raid warning—*a*. Bewitching.

Sirius, si'ri-us, *n*. The Dog-star.

Sirloin, sėr'loin, *n*. The upper part of a loin of beef; a loin of beef.

Sister, sis'tėr, *n*. A female born of the same parents; a female of the same kind, society, etc.; a senior hospital nurse.

Sisterhood, sis'tėr-hud, *n*. State or condition of a sister; a society of females.

Sister-in-law, sis'tėr-in-la, *n*. A husband or wife's sister.

Sit, sit, *vi*. (sitting, sat). To rest on the lower extremity of the body, to incubate; to remain; to be placed; to suit; to have a seat in Parliament, etc.; to hold a session.—*vt*. To keep the seat upon (a horse, etc.).

Site, sīt, *n*. Situation; a plot of ground for building on.

Sitology, si-tol'o-ji, *n*. Dietetics.

Situate, sit'ū-āt, *a*. Placed with respect to any other object.

Situated, sit'ū-āt-ed, *a*. Having a site or position; situate; circumstanced.

Situation, sit-ū-ā'shon, *n*. Position; station; plight; post or engagement.

Six, siks, *a*. and *n*. One more than five.

Sixfold, siks'fōld, *a*. and *adv*. Six times.

Sixteen, siks'tēn, *a*. and *n*. Six and ten.

Sixteenth, siks'tēnth, *a*. The sixth after the tenth.—*n*. One of sixteen equal parts.

Sixth, siksth, *a*. Next after the fifth.—*n*. One part in six.

Sixty, siks'ti, *a*. and *n*. Six times ten.

Sizable, Sizeable, sīz'a-bl, *a*. Of considerable bulk; of reasonable size.

Size, sīz, *n*. Comparative magnitude; bigness; bulk; a glutinous substance used by painters, etc.—*vt*. (sizing, sized). To arrange according to size; to take the size of; to cover with size.

Sizing, sīz'ing, *n*. Size or weak glue; act of covering with size.

Skein, skān, *n*. A small hank of thread.

Skeleton, ske'le-ton, *n*. The bony framework of an animal; general structure or frame; outline.—*a*. Resembling a skeleton.

Skeleton-key, ske'le-ton-ke, *n*. A thin light key that opens various locks.

Sketch, skech, *n*. An outline or general delineation; a first rough draft.—*vt*. To draw a sketch of; to give the chief points of; to plan.—*vi*. To practice sketching.

Sketchy, skech'i, *a*. Having the nature of a sketch; unfinished; incomplete.

Skew, skū, *a*. Oblique. *adv*. Awry; obliquely.—*vt*. To put askew.

Skewer, skū'ėr, *n*. A pin for fastening meat.—*vt*. To fasten with skewers.

Ski, skē, *n*. A long, narrow snow-shoe for running or travelling over snow.

Skid, skid, *n*. A drag for the wheels of a vehicle.—*vt*. (skidding, skidded). To check with a skid.—*vi*. To slip sideways on mud, ice, etc., as a cycle.

Skilful, skil'ful, *a*. Skilled; dexterous; expert; clever.

Skill, skil, *n*. Ability; knowledge united with dexterity; aptitude.

Skillet, skil'et, *n*. A small vessel of metal, with a long handle, for heating water, etc.

Skim, skim, *vt*. (skimming, skimmed). To remove the scum from; to take off from a surface; to

pass lightly over; to glance over superficially.—*vi*. To glide along.

Skim-milk, skim'milk, *n*. Milk from which the cream has been taken.

Skin, skin, *n*. The natural outer coating of animals; a hide; bark; rind.—*vt*. (skinning, skinned). To strip the skin from; to cover superficially.—*vi*. To be covered with skin.

Skin-deep, skin'dēp, *a*. Superficial; slight.

Skinflint, skin'flint, *n*. A niggard.

Skinny, skin'i, *a*. Consisting of skin or nearly so; wanting flesh.

Skip, skip, *vi*. (skipping, skipped). To leap lightly; to bound; to spring.—*vt*. To pass with a bound; to omit.—*n*. A light leap; a large basket on wheels, used in mines.

Skipping-rope, skip'ing-rōp, *n*. A small rope swung by young persons under their feet and over their heads in play.

Skirmish, skėr'mish, *n*. A slight battle; a brief contest.—*vi*. To fight in short contests or in small parties.

Skirt, skėrt, *n*. The lower and loose part of a garment; border; a woman's garment like a petticoat.—*vt*. To border.—*vi*. To be on the border.

Skit, skit, *n*. A satirical or sarcastic attack; a pasquinade; a squib.

Skittish, skit'ish, *a*. Timorous; wanton; frisky; hasty; fickle.

Skulk, skulk, *vi*. To lurk; to sneak out of the way; to shun doing one's duty.

Skull, skul, *n*. The bony case which contains the brain.

Skull-cap, skul'kap, *n*. A cap fitting closely to the head.

Skunk, skungk, *n*. An animal of the weasel family, with glands that emit a fetid fluid.

Sky, skī, *n*. The apparent arch of the heavens; the region of clouds; climate.

Sky-light, skī'līt, *n*. A window in the roof of a building.

Slab, slab, *n*. A thin flat piece of anything, as marble.—*a*. Thick and slimy.

Slack, slak, *a*. Not tight or tense; loose; remiss; backward; not busy.—*adv*. In a slack manner; partially; insufficiently.—*n*. The part of a rope that hangs loose; small broken coal.—*vt*. and *i*. To slacken; to slake.

Slacken, slak'n, *vi*. To become slack; to abate; to flag.—*vt*. To lessen the tension of; to relax.

Slag, slag, *n*. The scoria from a smelting furnace or volcano; fused dross of metal.

Slake, slāk, *vt*. (slaking, slaked). To quench, as thirst or rage; to extinguish.—*vi*. To abate; to become extinct.—*n*. A muddy tract adjoining the sea.

Slam, slam, *vt*. and *i*. (slamming, slammed). To shut with violence; to bang.—*n*. A violent shutting of a door.

Slander, slan'dėr, *n*. A false report maliciously uttered; defamation. *vt*. To defame; to calumniate.

Slang, slang, *n*. and *a*. A class of expressions not generally approved of, as being inelegant or undignified.—*vt*. To address with slang; to abuse vulgarly.

Slant, slant, *a*. Sloping.—*vt*. and *i*. To turn from a direct line; to slope; to incline.—*n*. A slope.

Slap, slap, *n*. A blow with the open hand, or something broad.—*vt*. (slapping, slapped). To strike with the open hand.—*adv*. With a sudden and violent blow.

Slash, slash, *vt*. To cut by striking violently and at random.—*vi*. To strike violently and at random with a cutting instrument.—*n*. A long cut; a cut made at random.

Slat, slat, *n*. A narrow strip of wood.

Slate, slāt, *n*. Rock which splits into thin layers; a slab of smooth stone for covering buildings; a tablet for writing upon.—*vt*. (slating, slated). To cover with slates; to criticize severely.

Slattern, slat'ėrn, *n*. A female who is not tidy; a

S

slut.—*a.* Slatternly.

Slaughter, sla'tèr, *n.* A slaying; carnage; massacre; a killing of beasts for market.—*vt.* To slay; to kill for the market.

Slav, Slavonian, släv, sla-vō'ni-an, *n.* One of a race of Eastern Europe, comprising the Russians, Poles, Bohemians, Bulgarians, etc.

Slave, släv, *n.* A person wholly subject to another; a bondman; drudge.—*vi.* (slaving, slaved). To labor as a slave.

Slave-driver, släv'drīv-èr, *n.* An overseer of slaves; a severe or cruel master.

Slaver, sla'vèr, *n.* Saliva drivelling from the mouth; drivel.—*vi.* To suffer the saliva to issue from the mouth.—*vt.* To smear with saliva.

Slavish, släv'ish, *a.* Pertaining to slaves; servile; mean; oppressively laborious.

Slay, slä, *vt.* (pret. slew, pp. slain). To kill by violence; to murder; to destroy.

Sleazy, slē'zi, *a.* Thin; flimsy; wanting firmness of texture, as silk. Also *Sleezy.*

Sled, sled, *n.* A sledge.—*vt.* (sledding, sledded). To convey on a sled.

Sledge, Sledge-hammer, slej, slej'ham-èr,*n.* A large, heavy hammer, used by iron-workers.

Sleek, slēk, *a.* Smooth and glossy.—*vt.* To make smooth and glossy.

Sleep, slēp, *vi.* (sleeping, slept). To take rest by a suspension of voluntary exercise of the powers of body and mind; to be dormant or inactive.—*vt.* To pass in sleeping; to get rid of by sleeping; with *off.*—*n.* That state in which volition is suspended; slumber; death; dormant state.

Sleeper, slēp'èr, *n.* One that sleeps; a timber supporting a weight; in railways, a beam of wood supporting the rails.

Sleet, slēt, *n.* Hail or snow mingled with rain.—*vi.* To snow or hail with rain.

Sleeve, slēv, *n.* That part of a garment covering the arm.—*vt.* (sleeving, sleeved). To furnish with sleeves.

Sleigh, slä, *n.* A vehicle on runners for transporting persons on snow or ice.

Sleight, slīt, *n.* A sly artifice; an artful trick; dexterity.

Slender, slen'dèr, *a.* Thin; slim; slight; feeble; meager; scanty.

Slice, slīs, *vt.* (slicing, sliced). To cut into thin pieces; to divide.—*n.* A thin, broad piece cut off; a broad flat utensil.

Slide, slid, *vi.* (sliding, pret. slid, pp. slid, slidden). To move along a surface by slipping; to pass smoothly or gradually.—*vt.* To thrust smoothly along a surface.—*n.* A smooth and easy passage; that part of an apparatus which slides into place.

Sliding, slid'ing, *a.* Make so as to slide freely; fitted for sliding.—*n.* The act of one who slides; lapse; backsliding.

Sliding-scale, slid'ing-skäl, *n.* A sliding-rule; a varying rate of payment.

Slight, slīt, *a.* Small; trifling; not thorough; slender; frail.—*n.* Intentional disregard.—*vt.* To disregard; to treat with disrespect.

Slim, slim, *a.* Slight; slender; thin; flimsy; cunning.—*vi.* To reduce weight by means of dieting.

Slime, slīm, *n.* A soft or glutinous substance; moist earth or mud; viscous substance exuded by certain animals.—*vt.* (sliming, slimed). To cover with slime; to make slimy.

Sling, sling, *vt.* (slinging, slung). To throw; to hang so as to swing; to place in a sling.—*n.* An instrument for throwing stones; a bandage to support a wounded limb; a rope for raising heavy articles.

Slink, slingk, *vi.* (slinking, slunk). To sneak; to steal away.—*vt.* To cast prematurely.—*n.* A premature calf.

Slip, slip, *vi.* (slipping, slipped). To move smoothly along; to glide; to depart secretly; to have the feet slide; to err; to escape insensibly.—*vt.* To put or thrust secretly; to

omit; to disengage oneself from; to make a slip of for planting.—*n.* A sliding of the feet; an unintentional error; a twig cut for planting or grafting; a long narrow piece; a leash by which a dog is held; a long strip of printed matter; a loose covering; an inclined plane upon which a ship is built.

Slipper, slip'èr, *n.* One who slips or lets slip; a loose light shoe for household wear.

Slipshod, slip'shod, *a.* Shod with slippers; having shoes down at heel; slovenly.

Slit, slit, *vi.* (slitting, slit or slitted). To cut lengthwise; to cut into long strips.—*n.* A long cut or opening.

Sliver, sli'vèr, or sli'vèr, *vt.* To cleave; to cut into long thin pieces.—*n.* A long piece cut off; a splinter.

Slobber, slob'èr, *vi.* and *t.* To slaver; to slabber.—*n.* Slaver; liquor spilled.

Slogan, slō'gan, *n.* A war-cry; a watchword.

Slop, slop, *vt.* (slopping, slopped). To soil by liquid; to spill.—*n.* Water carelessly thrown about; a smock-frock; *pl.* mean liquid food; waste dirty water; wide breeches; ready-made clothing.

Slope, slōp, *n.* An oblique direction; a declivity.—*vt.* and *i.* (sloping, sloped). To form with a slope; to incline.

Sloppy, slop'i, *a.* Muddy; plashy; slovenly.

Slot, slot, *n.* A bolt or bar; an oblong hole; track of a deer.—*vt.* (slotting, slotted). To make a slot in.

Sloth, slōth or sloth, *n.* Indolence; laziness; idleness; a South American mammal.

Slouch, slouch, *n.* A stoop in walking; an ungainly gait; a droop.—*vi.* To hang down; to have a drooping gait.—*vt.* To cause to hang down.

Slouching, slouch'ing, *a.* Drooping downward; walking heavily and awkwardly.

Slough, slou, *n.* A place of deep mud; a hole full of mire.

Slovenly, slu'ven-li, *a.* Disorderly; not neat or tidy.—*adv.* In a negligent manner.

Slow, slō, *a.* Moving little in a long time; not rapid; dilatory; heavy in wit; dull; behind in time.—*vt.* and *i.* To delay; to slacken in speed.

Slubber, slub'èr, *vt.* To slobber; to soil; to do lazily or carelessly.

Sludge, sluj, *n.* Mire; soft mud.

Slue, slō, *vt.* (sluing, slued). To turn or swing round (as the yard of a ship).

Slug, slug, *n.* A sluggard; a shell-less snail injurious to plants; a piece of metal used for the charge of a gun.

Sluggish, slug'ish, *a.* Lazy; slothful; inert; not quick.

Sluice, slös, *n.* A contrivance to control the flow of water in a river, dam, etc.; a trough to separate gold from sand, etc.; flood-gate.—*vt.* (sluicing, sluiced). To wet abundantly; to cleanse by means of sluices.

Slum, slum, *n.* A low, dirty street of a city.—*vi.* (slumming, slummed). To visit slums from benevolent motives.

Slumber, slum'bèr, *vi.* To sleep; to be inert or inactive.—*n.* Light sleep; repose.

Slump, slump, *n.* The whole number taken in one lot; a sudden fall in prices or values.—*vt.* To throw into one lot.—*vi.* To sink in walking, as in snow.

Slur, slèr, *vt.* (slurring, slurred). To soil; to traduce; to pass lightly over; to pronounce in a careless indistinct manner.—*n.* A slight reproach; a stain or stigma.

Slush, slush, *n.* Sludge or soft mud; wet, half-melted snow.

Slut, slut, *n.* A woman negligent of tidiness and dress; a slattern.

Sly, slī, *a.* Cunning; crafty; wily; shrewd.

Smack, smak, *vi.* To make a sharp noise with the lips; to taste; to savor.—*vt.* To make a sharp noise with; to slap.—*n.* A loud kiss; a sharp noise; a smart blow; a slap; a slight taste; a smattering; a fishing-vessel.

Small, smal, *a.* Little; petty; short; weak; gentle;

not loud; narrow-minded; mean.—*n.* The small part of a thng; *pl.* small-clothes.

Smart, smärt, *n.* A quick, keen pain; pungent grief.—*a.* Keen; quick; sharp; brisk; witty; spruce; well dressed.—*vt.* To feel a sharp pain; to be acutely painful; to be punished

Smartly, smärt'li, *adv.* Keenly; briskly; sharply; wittily; sprucely.

Smash, smash, *vt.* To dash to pieces.—*vi.* To go to pieces.—*n.* A breaking to pieces; ruin; bankruptcy.

Smatter, smat'èr, *vi.* To have a slight knowledge; to talk superficially.—*n.* A superficial knowledge.

Smear, smèr, *vt.* To overspread with anything adhesive; to daub; to soil.

Smell, smel, *vt.* (smelling, smelled). To perceive by the nose; to perceive the scent of; to detect.—*vi.* To give out an odor.—*n.* The faculty by which odors are perceived; scent; perfume.

Smelt, smelt, *vt.* To melt, as ore, to separate the metal.—*n.* A small fish allied to the salmon.

Smile, smīl, *vi.* (smiling, smiled). To show pleasure, sarcasm, pity, etc., by a look; to appear propitious.—*vt.* To express by a smile; to affect by smiling.—*n.* A set of the features expressing pleasure, scorn, etc.; favor.

Smiling, smīl'ing, *p.a.* Wearing a smile; gay in aspect

Smirch, smèrch, *vt.* To stain; to smudge.

Smirk, smèrk, *vi.* To smile affectedly or pertly.—*n.* An affected smile.

Smite, smīt, *vt.* (smiting, pret. smote, pp. smit, smitten). To strike; to slay; to blast; to afflict; to affect with love, etc.—*vi.* To strike; to clash together.

Smith, smith, *n.* One who works in metals.

Smithy, smith'i, *n.* The shop of a smith.

Smock, smok, *n.* A chemise; a smock-frock.—*vt.* To clothe with a smock; to pucker diagonally.

Smocking, smok'ing, *n.* An ornamental diagonal puckering, in form of a honey-comb, and capable of being expanded.

Smoke, smōk, *n.* The exhalation from a burning substance; vapor; idle talk; nothingness; a drawing in and puffing out of tobacco fumes.—*vi.* (smoking, smoked). To emit smoke; to use tobacco.—*vt.* To apply smoke to; to befoul by smoke; to fumigate; to use in smoking.

Smooth, smōтн, *a.* Even on the surface; glossy; moving equably; not harsh; bland.—*n.* Smooth part of anything.—*vt.* To make smooth; to level; to make easy; to palliate; to soothe.

Smother, smuтн'èr, *n.* Stifling smoke; suffocating dust.—*vt.* To stifle; to suffocate; to suppress.—*vi.* To be suffocated or suppressed; to smoulder.

Smoulder, smōl'dèr, *vi.* To burn and smoke without flame; to exist in a suppressed state.

Smudge, smuj, *vt.* (smudging, smudged). To stain with dirt or filth; to smear.—*n.* A stain; a smear.

Smug, smug, *a.* Neat; spruce; affectedly nice.—*vt.* (smugging, smugged). To make smug.

Smuggle, smug'l, *vt.* (smuggling, smuggled). To import or export secretly and in defiance of law; to convey clandestinely.

Smut, smut, *n.* A spot or stain; a spot of soot, etc.; a disease in grain; obscene language.—*vt.* and *i.* (smutting, smutted). To stain with smut; to tarnish.

Smutty, smut'i, *a.* Soiled with smut; affected with mildew; obscene.

Snack, snak, *n.* A small portion of food; a hasty repast; a bite; a share.

Snaffle, snaf'l, *n.* A bridle consisting of a slender bitmouth without a curb.—*vt.* To bridle; to manage with a snaffle.

Snag, snag, *n.* A short projecting stump; a shoot; the tine of a deer's antler; a tree in a river dangerous to vessels.

Snail, snäl, *n.* A slimy, slow-creeping mollusk; a slug; a sluggard.

Snake, snäk, *n.* A serpent.

Snap, snap, *vt.* (snapping, snapped). To bite or

seize suddenly; to break with a sharp sound; to break short.—*vi.* To try to seize with the teeth; to break suddenly or without bending.—*n.* A quick eager bite; a sudden breaking; a sharp noise; a kind of biscuit.

Snare, snär, *n.* A line with a noose for catching animals; anything that entraps.—*vt.* (snaring, snared). To catch with a snare; to ensnare.

Snarl, snärl, *vi.* To growl, as an angry dog; to talk in rude murmuring terms.—*vt.* To entangle.—*n.* A sharp angry growl; a knot; embarrassment.

Snatch, snach, *vt.* To seize hastily or abruptly.—*vi.* To make a grasp.—*n.* A hasty catch; a short fit or turn; a small portion; a snack.

Sneak, snēk, *vi.* To creep privately; to go furtively; to crouch.—*n.* A mean fellow; one guilty of underhand work.

Sneaking, snēk'ing, *p.a.* Pertaining to a sneak; mean; servile; underhand.

Sneer, snēr, *vi.* To show contempt by a look; to jeer; to speak derisively.—*n.* A look or grin of contempt; a scoff; a jeer.

Sneeze, snēz, *vi.* (sneezing, sneezed). To emit air through the nose, etc., by a kind of involuntary convulsive effort.—*n.* A single act of sneezing.

Sniff, snif, *vi.* To draw air audibly up the nose; to snuff.—*n.* A slight smell; snuff.

Snigger, snig'èr, *vi.* To laugh in a suppressed manner.—*n.* A suppressed laugh; a giggle.

Snip, snip, *vt.* (snipping, snipped). To cut off at a stroke with shears; to clip.—*n.* A single cut with shears; a bit cut off.

Snippet, snip'et, *n.* A small part or share.

Snivel, sni'vel, *vi.* (snivelling, snivelled). To run at the nose; to whimper.—*n.* Whimpering; maudlin sentiment.

Snivelling, sni'vel-ing, *p.a.* Apt to snivel or whine; tearful; weakly sentimental.

Snob, snob, *n.* A shoemaker; one who apes gentility; a would-be aristocrat.

Snooze, snōz, *n.* A nap or short sleep.—*vi.* (snoozing, snoozed). To take a short nap.

Snore, snōr, *vi.* (snoring, snored). To breathe with a rough, hoarse noise in sleep.—*n.* A breathing with a hoarse noise in sleep.

Snort, snort, *vi.* To force air with violence through the nose.—*n.* A loud sound produced by forcing the air through the nostrils

Snout, snout, *n.* The projecting nose of a beast; muzzle; nozzle.

Snow, snō, *n.* Watery particles congealed in the air, and falling in flakes.—*vi.* To fall in snow; used impersonally.—*vt.* To scatter like snow.

Snow-plow, snō'plou, *n.* An implement for clearing away the snow from roads, etc.

Snow-shoe, snō'shō, *n.* A light frame worn on each foot to keep the wearer from sinking in snow; a snow-boot.

Snub, snub, *vt.* (snubbing, snubbed). To stop or rebuke with a tart, sarcastic remark; to slight designedly.—*n.* A check; a rebuke.

Snub-nose, snub'nōz, *n.* A flat nose.

Snuff, snuf, *vt.* To draw up through the nose; to smell; to crop, as the snuff of a candle.—*vi.* To draw up air or tobacco through the nose; to take offense.—*n.* A drawing up through the nose; resentment; burned wick of a candle; pulverized tobacco.

Snuffer, snuf'èr, *n.* One who snuffs; *pl.* instrument for removing the snuff of a candle.

Snuffle, snuf'l, *vi.* (snuffling, snuffled). To speak through the nose; to breathe hard through the nose.—*n.* A sound made by air drawn through the nostrils; nasal twang; *pl.* an ailment accompanied by snuffling with the nose.

Snug, snug, *a.* Neat, trim, cozy.

Snuggle, snug'l, *vi.* (snuggling, snuggled). To lie close for convenience or warmth; to nestle.

So, sō, *adv.* In this or that manner, to that degree, thus; extremely; very; the case being such; thereby.—*conj.* Provided that; in case that; therefore; accordingly.

Soak, sōk, *vt.* To let lie in a fluid till the substance has imbibed all that it can; to steep; to wet thoroughly.—*vi.* To steep; to enter by pores; to tipple.

Soap, sōp, *n.* A compound of oil or fat with an alkali, used in washing.—*vt.* To rub or cover with soap.

Soar, sōr, *vi.* To mount upon the wing; to rise high; to tower.—*n.* A towering flight; a lofty ascent.

Sob, sob, *vi.* (sobbing, sobbed). To sigh or weep convulsively; to make a similar sound.—*n.* A convulsive catching of the breath in weeping or sorrow.

Sober, sō'bėr, *a.* Temperate; not drunk; calm; cool; staid; grave; dull-looking.—*vt.* To make sober.—*vi.* To become sober.

Sobriety, sō-brī'e-ti, *n.* Temperance; abstemiousness; moderation; saneness; sedateness; gravity.

Sobriquet, so-brē-kā, *n.* A nickname.

Sociable, sō'shi-a-bl, *a.* Fond of companions; inclined to mix in society; social.

Social, sō'shal, *a.* Pertaining to society; sociable; consisting in union or mutual converse; living in communities.

Socialism, sō'shal-izm, *n.* A theory of social organization aiming at co-operative action and community of property.

Society, sō-si'e-ti, *n.* Fellowship; company; a body of persons united for some object; persons living in the same circle; those who take the lead in social life.

Sociology, sō-shi-ol'o-ji, *n.* The science which treats of society, its development, the progress of civilization, etc.

Sock, sok, *n.* The shoe of the ancient actors of comedy; a short woven covering for the foot.

Socket, sok'et, *n.* A cavity into which anything is fitted.

Sod, sod, *n.* That layer of earth which is covered with grass; piece of turf.

Soda, sō'da, *n.* The alkali carbonate of sodium used in washing, glass-making, etc., and extensively made from salt.

Soda-water, sō'da-wa'tėr, *n.* An effervescent drink generally consisting of water into which carbonic acid has been forced.

Sodden, sod'n, *a.* Seethed; saturated; soaked and soft; not well baked; doughy.

Sodium, sō'di-um, *n.* A soft light silvery metal.

Sodomy, sod'om-i, *n.* A carnal copulation against nature.

Sofa, sō'fa, *n.* A long seat with a stuffed bottom, back, and ends.

Soffit, sof'it, *n.* The lower surface of an arch, architrave, or overhanging cornice, etc.

Soft, soft, *a.* Easily yielding to pressure; delicate; mild; effeminate; not loud or harsh; not strong or glaring.—*adv.* Softly.—*interj.* Be soft; stop; not so fast.

Soften, sof'n, *vt.* To make soft or more soft; to mollify; to alleviate; to tone down.—*vi.* To become soft; to relent; to become milder.

Soil, soil, *vt.* To sully; to tarnish; to manure; to feed (cattle) indoors with green fodder.—*vi.* To tarnish.—*n.* Dirt; ordure; tarnish; the upper stratum of the earth; mould; loam; earth; land; country.

Soiree, swa'rā, *n.* A meeting of some body at which there are tea and other refreshments, with music, speeches, etc.

Sojourn, sō'jėrn, *vi.* To reside for a time.—*n.* A temporary residence or stay.

Solace, so'lās, *vt.* (solacing, solaced). To cheer or console; to allay.—*n.* Consolation; comfort; relief; recreation.

Solar, sō'lėr, *a.* Pertaining to the sun, or proceeding from it; sunny; measured by the progress of the sun.

Solder, sol'dėr, *vt.* To unite metals by a fused metallic substance; to patch up.—*n.* A metallic cement.

Soldier, sōl'jėr, *n.* A man in military service; a man of distinguished valor.

Sole, sōl, *n.* The under side of the foot; the bottom of a shoe; a marine fish allied to the flounder.—*vt.* (soling, soled). To furnish with a sole, as a shoe.—*a.* Single; individual; only; alone.

Solecism, so'le-sizm, *n.* A grammatical error; deviation from correct idiom.

Solely, sōl'li, *adv.* Singly; alone; only.

Solemn, so'lem, *a.* Marked with religious gravity or sanctity; impressive; earnest; affectedly grave.

Solicit, sō-lis'it, *vt.* and *i.* To ask earnestly; to beg; to invite; to disquiet; to incite.

Solicitation, sō-lis'it-ā''shon, *n.* Earnest request; supplication; entreaty.

Solicitous, sō-lis'it-us, *a.* Anxious; very desirous; concerned; apprehensive.

Solid, so'lid, *a.* Resisting pressure; not liquid or gaseous; not hollow; cubic; sound; not frivolous.—*n.* A body that naturally retains the same shape.

Solidarity, so-li-dar'i-ti, *n.* Unity or communion of interests and responsibilities.

Soliloquy, sō-lil'ō-kwi, *n.* A speaking to oneself; discourse of a person alone.

Solitaire, so'li-tār, *n.* A solitary; an article of jewelry in which a single gem is set; a game for a single person.

Solitary, so'li-ta-ri, *a.* Being alone; lonely; retired; not much frequented; shared by no companions; single; sole.—*n.* A hermit; a recluse.

Solitude, so'li-tūd, *n.* State of being alone; a lonely life; a lonely place.

Solo, sō'lō, *n.* A tune or air for a single instrument or voice.

Solstice, sol'stis, *n.* The time when the sun arrives at the point farthest north or south of the equator, namely 21st June and 22nd Dec.; either of the two points in the ecliptic where the sun then appears to be.

Soluble, so'lū-bl, *a.* Susceptible of being dissolved in a fluid; capable of being solved, as a problem.

Solution, so-lū'shon, *n.* A dissolving; preparation made by dissolving a solid in a liquid; act of solving; explanation; termination or crisis of a disease.

Solve, solv, *vt.* (solving, solved). To explain; to make clear; to unravel; to work out.

Solvent, sol'vent, *a.* Having the power of dissolving; able to pay all debts.—*n.* A fluid that dissolves any substance.

Somatic, sō-mat'ik, *a.* Corporeal; bodily.

Somatology, sō-ma-tol'o-ji, *n.* The doctrine of living bodies; the science of matter.

Somber, som'bėr, *a.* Dark; gloomy; dismal.—*vt.* (sombring, sombred). To make somber.

Sombrero, som-brär'ō, *n.* A broad-brimmed hat.

Some, sum, *a.* A certain; a; a little; indefinite and perhaps considerable; about or near.—*pron.* An indefinite part, quantity, or number; certain individuals.

Somebody, sum'bo-di, *n.* A person indeterminate; a person of consideration.

Somehow, sum'hou, *adv.* In some way not yet known; one way or another.

Somersault, Somerset, sum'ėr-salt, sum'ėr-set, *n.* A leap in which the heels turn over the head; a turn of the body in the air.

Something, sum'thing, *n.* A thing, quantity, or degree indefinitely; a person or thing of importance.—*adv.* Somewhat.

Sometime, sum'tim, *adv.* Once; formerly; by and by.—*a.* Former; whilom.

Somewhat, sum'whot, *n.* Something; more or less.—*adv.* In some degree; a little.

Somite, sō'mīt, *n.* A single segment in the body of an articulated animal.

Somnambulism, som-nam'bū-lizm, *n.* The act or practice of walking in sleep.

Somniferous, som-nif'ėr-us, *a.* Bringing or causing sleep; soporific.

Somniloquence, Somniloquism, som-nil'ō-kwens, som-nil'ō-kwizm, *n.* The act of talking in sleep.

Somnolence, som'nō-lens, *n.* Sleepiness.

Son, sun, *n.* A male child.

Sonant, sō'nant, *a.* Sounding; uttered with voice and not breath merely.—*n.* A sonant letter.

Sonata, sō-nä'tä, *n.* A musical composition of several movements for a solo instrument.

Song, song, *n.* That which is sung; vocal music or melody; a poem to be sung; a lyric; poetry; a trifle.

Son-in-law, sun'in-la, *n.* A man married to one's daughter.

Sonorous, sō-nō'rus, *a.* Giving sound when struck; resonant; high-sounding.

Soon, sōn, *adv.* In a short time; shortly; early; quickly; promptly; readily; gladly.

Soot, sōt, *n.* A black substance formed from burning matter.—*vt.* To cover or foul with soot.

Soothe, sōᴛʜ, *vt.* (soothing, soothed). To please with soft words; to flatter; to pacify; to assuage; to soften.

Soothing, sōᴛʜ'ing, *p.a.* Serving to soothe, calm, or assuage; mollifying.

Soothsayer, sōth'sā-ėr, *n.* One who foretells or predicts; a prophet.

Sop, sop, *n.* Something dipped in broth or liquid food; anything given to pacify.—*vt.* (sopping, sopped). To steep in liquor.

Sophism, sof'izm, *n.* A specious but fallacious argument; a subtlety in reasoning.

Sophistic, Sophistical, sō-fist'ik, sō-fist'ik-al, *a.* Pertaining to sophistry; fallaciously subtle; not sound in reasoning.

Sophistry, sof'ist-ri, *n.* Fallacious reasoning.

Soporiferous, sō-pō-rif'ik, *a.* Causing sleep.—*n.* A drug or anything that induces sleep.

Soprano, sō-prä'nō, *n.* The highest female voice; a singer with such a voice.

Sorcerer, sōr'sėr-ėr, *n.* A wizard; an enchanter; a magician.

Sorcery, sōr'sėr-i, *n.* Magic; enchantment; witchcraft.

Sordid, sor'did, *a.* Dirty; foul; vile; base; niggardly; covetous.

Sore, sōr, *a.* Painful; severe; distressing; tender; galled.—*n.* An ulcer, wound, etc.—*adv.* Severely; sorely.

Sorghum, sor'gum, *n.* A kind of millet.

Sorrel, so'rel, *n.* A plant allied to the docks; a reddish or yellow-brown color.—*a.* Of a reddish color.

Sorrow, so'rō, *n.* Affliction or distress of mind; grief; regret.—*vi.* To feel sorrow; to grieve.

Sorry, so'ri, *a.* Feeling sorrow; grieved; sorrowful; wretched; pitiful.

Sort, sort, *n.* Nature or character; kind; species; manner; a set.—*vt.* To assort; to arrange; to reduce to order.—*vi.* To consort; to agree.

Sortilege, sor'ti-lej, *n.* Act or practice of drawing lots; divination by lots.

Sot, sot, *n.* A dolt or blockhead; an habitual drunkard.

Soufflé, sōf-la, *n.* A light dish, partly composed of white of eggs.

Sough, suf, *vi.* To emit a rushing or roaring sound like wind; to sound like the sea.—*n.* A rushing sound; a deep sigh.

Soul, sōl, *n.* The spiritual principle in man; the moral and emotional part of man's nature; elevation of mind; fervor; essence; an inspirer or leader; a person.

Sound, sound, *a.* Not in any way defective; healthy; valid; free from error; orthodox; just; heavy.—*n.* A narrow channel of water; a strait; air-bladder of a fish; that which is heard; noise.—*vt.* To measure the depth of; to examine medically, to try to discover the opinion, etc., of; to cause to give out a sound; to pronounce.—*vi.* To give out a sound; to appear on narration; to be spread or published.

Soundings, sound'ingz, *n.pl.* The depths of water in rivers, harbors, etc.

Soundless, sound'les, *a.* That cannot be fath-

omed; noiseless.

Soundness, sound'nes, *n.* Healthiness; solidity; validity; orthodoxy.

Soup, sōp, *n.* A liquid food made generally from flesh and vegetables.

Sour, sour, *a.* Acid or sharp to the taste; tart; peevish; morose.—*vt.* To make sour; to make cross or discontented; to embitter.—*vi.* To become sour or peevish.

Source, sōrs, *n.* That from which anything rises; the spring, etc., from which a stream proceeds; first cause; origin.

Souse, sous, *n.* Pickle; the ears, feet, etc., of swine pickled; a swoop.—*vt.* (sousing, soused). To steep in pickle; to plunge into water.—*vi.* To swoop.—*adv.* With sudden descent or plunge.

South, south, *n.* The region in which the sun is at mid-day.—*a.* Being in or toward the south; pertaining to or from the south.—*adv.* Toward the south.

South-east, south'ēst, *n.* The point midway between the south and east.—*a.* Pertaining to or from the south-east.—*adv.* Toward the south-east.

South-west, south'west, *n.* The point mid-way between the south and west.—*a.* Pertaining to or from the south-west.—*adv.* Toward the south-west.

Souvenir, sö-ve-nēr', *n.* A keepsake.

Sovereign, so've-rin, *a.* Supreme in power; chief.—*n.* A monarch; the standard British gold coin.

Soviet, sov'i-et, *n.* The method of government in Russia since the Revolution, local soviets (elected councils) sending delegates to larger bodies, and these, in their turn, to the Supreme Congress, which elects the Supreme Council.

Sow, sou, *n.* The female of the swine.

Sow, sō, *vt.* (pret. sowed, pp. sowed or sown). To scatter seed over; to spread abroad.—*vi.* To scatter seed for growth.

Sower, sō'ėr, *n.* One who sows.

Soy, soi, *n.* A sauce prepared in China and Japan from a bean; the plant producing the bean.

Spa, spa, *n.* A place to which people go on account of a spring of mineral water.

Space, spās, *n.* Extension; room; interval between points or objects; quantity of time; a while.—*vt.* (spacing, spaced). To arrange at proper intervals; to arrange the spaces in.

Spacious, spā'shus, *a.* Roomy; widely extended; ample; capacious.

Spade, spād, *n.* An instrument for digging; a playing card of a black suit. *vt.* (spading, spaded). To dig with a spade; to use a spade on.

Span, span, *n.* Reach or extent in general; space between the thumb and little finger; nine inches; a short space of time; the stretch of an arch; a yoke of animals.—*vt.* (spanning, spanned). To extend across; to measure with the hand with the fingers extended.

Spangle, spang'gl, *n.* A small glittering metal ornament; a small sparkling object.—*vt.* (spangling, spangled). To adorn with spangles.

Spaniel, span'yel, *n.* A dog of several breeds; a cringing, fawning person.

Spank, spangk, *vi.* To move or run along quickly.—*vt.* To slap or smack.

Spar, spär, *n.* A long piece of timber; a pole; a crystalline mineral; boxing-match; flourish of the fists.—*vi.* (sparring, sparred). To fight in show; to box; to bandy words.

Spare, spär, *a.* Scanty; thin; sparing or chary; superfluous; held in reserve.—*vt.* (sparing, spared). To use frugally; to dispense with; to omit; to use tenderly; to withhold from.—*vi.* To be frugal; to use mercy or forbearance.

Sparing, spär'ing, *a.* Saving; economical.

Spark, spärk, *n.* A particle of ignited substance which flies off from burning bodies; a small transient light; a gay man; a lover.—*vi.* To emit particles of fire; to sparkle.

Sparkle, spär'kl, *n.* A little spark; luster.—*vi.*

S

(sparkling, sparkled). To emit sparks; to glitter; to be animated.

Sparrow, spa´rō, n. A bird of the finch family.

Sparse, spärs, a. Thinly scattered; not thick or close together.

Spartan, spär´tan, a. Pertaining to ancient Sparta; hardy; undaunted; enduring.

Spasm, spazm, n. A violent contraction of a muscle; a convulsive fit.

Spasmodic, spaz-mod´ik, a. Relating to spasm; convulsive; overstrained in expression or style.

Spatial, spā´shal, a. Pertaining to space; existing in space.

Spatter, spat´ėr, vt. To scatter a liquid substance on; to sprinkle; to asperse.—n. Act of spattering; something sprinkled.

Spatula, spat´ū-la, n. A broad thin flexible blade, used by painters, apothecaries, etc.

Spavin, spa´vin, n. A disease of horses affecting the joint of the hind-leg between the knee and the fetlock, and causing lameness.

Spawn, span, n. The eggs or ova of fish, frogs, etc., when ejected; offspring, in contempt.—vt. and i. To eject or deposit as spawn.

Spay, spā, vt. To destroy the ovaries of, as is done to female animals.

Speak, spēk, vi. (pret. spoke, spake, pp. spoken). To utter words; to talk; to deliver a speech; to argue; to plead; to be expressive.—vt. To utter with the mouth; to pronounce; to accost; to express.

Spear, spēr, n. A long, pointed weapon; a lance.—vt. To pierce or kill with a spear.

Special, spe´shal, a. Pertaining to a species; particular; distinctive; having a particular purpose or scope.

Specialist, spe´shal-ist, n. One who devotes himself to some particular subject.

Specialize, spe-shal-īz, vt. To assign a specific use to.—vi. To apply oneself to a particular subject.

Specialty, spe´shal-ti, n. Special characteristic; a special pursuit; a special product.

Specie, spē´shi, n. Metallic money; coin.

Species, spē´shēz, n. sing. and pl. Outward appearance; a kind, sort, or variety; a class.

Specific, spe-sif´ik, a. Pertaining to, designating or constituting a species; definite; precise.—n. A remedy which exerts a special action in the cure of a disease; an infallible remedy.

Specification, spe´si-fi-kā´´shon, n. The act of specifying; details of particulars; particular mention; statement.

Specify, spe´si-fi, vt. (specifying, specified). To make specific; to state in detail.

Specimen, spe´si-men, n. A sample; a part intended to typify the whole.

Specious, spē´shus, a. Superficially correct; appearing well at first view; plausible.

Speck, spek, n. A small spot; a stain; a flaw; an atom.—vt. To spot.

Speckle, spek´l, n. A speck; a small colored marking.—vt. (speckling, speckled). To mark with small specks.

Spectacle, spek´ta-kl, n. A show; a sight; an exhibition; a pageant; pl. glasses to assist or correct defective vision.

Spectacular, spek-tak´ū-lėr, a. Pertaining to or of the nature of a show.

Spectator, spek-tā´tor, n. A looker-on; a beholder; an eye-witness.

Specter, spek´tėr, n. An apparition; a ghost; a phantom.

Spectroscope, spek´trō-skōp, n. The instrument employed in spectrum analysis.

Spectrum, spek´trum, n.; pl. **-tra.** An image seen after the eyes are closed; the colored band of light, showing prismatic colors, produced when a beam of light is subjected to analysis by a spectroscope.

Specular, spek´ū-lär, a. Having a smooth reflecting surface.

Speculate, spek´ū-lāt, vi. (speculating, speculated). To meditate; to engage in risky financial transactions with a view to profit.

Speculator, spek´ū-lāt-or, n. A theorizer; one who speculates in business.

Speech, spēch, n. The faculty of speaking; language; talk; a formal discourse; oration.

Speed, spēd, n. Success; velocity; haste.—vi. (speeding, sped). To make haste; to prosper.—vt. To dispatch in haste; to help forward; to dismiss with good wishes.

Speedometer, spēd-om´et-ėr, n. A speed-indicator.

Speedway, spēd´wā, n. The track on which automobile and motor-cycle races are run.

Spell, spel, n. An incantation; a charm; fascination; a turn of work; a period.—vt. (pret. and pp. spelled or spelt). To give the letters of in order; to read; to import.—vi. To form words with the proper letters.

Spend, spend, vt. (spending, spent). To lay out, as money; to squander; to pass, as time; to exhaust of force.—vi. To spend money; to be dissipated.

Spendthrift, spend´thrift, n. and a. One who spends improvidently; a prodigal.

Spent, spent, p.a. Wearied; exhausted; having deposited spawn.

Sperm, spėrm, n. The seminal fluid of animals.

Spermaceti, spėr-ma-se´ti, n. A fatty material obtained from a species of whale.

Spermatic, spėr-mat´ik, a. Seminal.

Spermatozoon, spėr´ma-to-zō´´on, n.; pl. **-oa.** One of the microscopic bodies in the semen of animals essential to impregnation.

Spew, spū, vt. To vomit; to cast out with abhorrence.—vi. To vomit.

Sphenoid, sfē´noid, a. Resembling a wedge.—n. A wedge-shaped body.

Sphere, sfēr, n. An orb; a ball; a globe; a sun, star, or planet; circuit of motion, action, etc.; range; province; rank.—vt. (sphering, sphered). To place in a sphere or among the spheres.

Spheroid, sfēr´oid, n. A body like a sphere, but not perfectly spherical.

Sphincter, sfingk´tėr, n. A ring-like muscle closing the external orifices of organs, as the mouth or anus.

Sphygmograph, sfig´mō-graf, n. An instrument to indicate the nature of the pulse.

Spice, spīs, n. A vegetable production, aromatic to the smell and pungent to the taste; something piquant; flavor; smack.—vt. (spicing, spiced). To season with spice; to flavor.

Spicy, spīs´i, a. Producing or abounding with spice; pungent; piquant; racy.

Spider, spī´dėr, n. An animal that spins webs for taking its prey.

Spigot, spi´got, n. A peg to stop a faucet or cask.

Spike, spīk, n. A piece of pointed iron; an ear of corn, etc.—vt. (spiking, spiked). To fasten or set with spikes; to stop the vent of a cannon with a nail, etc.; to fix upon a spike.

Spikenard, spīk´närd, n. An aromatic plant of the East Indies; a fragrant essential oil; an ancient unguent.

Spill, spil, vt. (pret. and pp. spilled or split). To suffer to fall, flow over, etc.; to shed.—vi. To be shed; to be suffered to fall, be lost, or wasted.—n. A spigot; piece of wood or paper used to light a lamp, etc.; a fall.

Spin, spin, vt. (spinning, spun). To draw out and twist into threads; to protract; to whirl; to make threads, as a spider.—vi. To work at drawing and twisting threads; to rotate; to go quickly.—n. Act of spinning; a rapid run.

Spinach, Spinage, spin´āj, n. A culinary vegetable.

Spinal, spīn´al, a. Pertaining to the spine.

Spindle, spin´dl, n. A pin carrying a bobbin in a spinning machine; a small axis; a long, slender stalk; a measure of yarn.—vi. To grow in a long slender stalk.

Spine, spīn, n. A prickle; a thorn; a thin, pointed spike in animals; the backbone or spinal column.

Spinel, Spinelle, spi-nel', n. A kind of gem or hard stone.

Spinnaker, spin'a-kėr, n. A triangular sail carried by yachts on the opposite side to the mainsail in running before the wind.

Spiny, spīn'i, a. Thorny; difficult.

Spiracle, spi'ra-kl or spī'ra-kl, n. Any aperture in animals for breathing.

Spirea, spī-rē'a, n. A genus of flowering plants.

Spiral, spī'ral, a. Pertaining to a spire; winding like a screw.—n. A curve winding like a screw.

Spire, spīr, n. A winding line like a screw; a spiral; a wreath; a convolution; a steeple; a stalk or blade of grass, etc.—vi. (spiring, spired). To taper up.

Spirit, spi'rit, n. The breath of life; the soul; a spectre; vivacity; courage; mood; essence; real meaning; intent; a liquid obtained by distillation; pl. alcoholic liquor.—vt. To infuse spirit into; to encourage.

Spirited, spi'rit-ed, p.a. Showing spirit; animated; lively; bold; courageous.

Spiritual, spi'rit-ū-al, a. Pertaining to spirit; not material; mental; intellectual; divine; pure; ecclesiastical.

Spiritualism, spi'rit-ū-al-izm, n. State of being spiritual; doctrine of the existence of spirit distinct from matter; belief that communication can be held with departed spirits

Spirituality, spi'rit-ū-al'i-ti, n. Quality or state of being spiritual; spiritual nature or character.

Spirt, spėrt, vt. To force out in a jet; to squirt.—vi. To gush out in a jet.—n. A jet of fluid.

Spit, spit, n. A prong on which meat is roasted; low land running into the sea.—vt. (spitting, spitted). To put on a spit; to pierce.

Spit, spit, vt. and i. (spitting, spat). To eject from the mouth, as saliva.—n. What is ejected from the mouth; spittle.

Spite, spīt, n. A feeling of ill-will; malice; rancour.—**In spite of,** notwithstanding.—vt. (spiting, spited). To mortify or chagrin; to thwart.

Spittle, spit'l, n. Saliva; the moist matter ejected from the mouth.

Splash, splash, vt. and i. To bespatter with liquid matter.—n. A quantity of wet matter thrown on anything; a noise from water dashed about; a spot of dirt.

Splay, splā, vt. To slope or form with an angle.—n. A sloped surface.—a. Turned outward, as a person's feet.

Spleen, splēn, n. The milt, an organ in the abdomen connected with digestion; spite; ill-humor; low spirits.

Splendid, splen'did, a. Brilliant; magnificent; famous; celebrated.

Splendor, splen'dėr, n. Brilliancy; magnificence; display; pomp; grandeur.

Splice, splis, vt. (splicing, spliced). To unite, as two ropes, by interweaving the strands; to unite by overlapping, as timber.—n. Union of ropes by interweaving; piece added by splicing.

Splint, splint, n. A splinter; piece of wood to confine a broken bone when set.

Splinter, splint'ėr, n. A piece of wood, or other solid substance, split off.—vt. To split into splinters; to shiver.

Split, split, vt. (splitting, split). To divide lengthwise; to cleave; to rend; to burst.—vi. To part asunder; to burst; to crack; to differ in opinion.—n. A rent; fissure; breach or separation.—a. Divided; rent; deeply cleft.

Splutter, splut'ėr, n. A bustle; a stir.—vi. To speak confusedly; to sputter.

Spode, spōd, n. A material composed of calcined ivory, of which vases, etc., are made.

Spoil, spoil, n. Pillage; booty; plunder.—vt. To plunder; to impair; to ruin; to injure by over-indulgence.—vi. To grow useless; to decay.

Spoke, spōk, n. A bar of a wheel; the round of a ladder; a bar.—vt. (spoking, spoked). To furnish

with spokes. Pret. of *speak.*

Spoken, spōk'n, p.a. Oral; speaking (as in fair-spoken).

Sponge, spunj, n. A soft porous marine substance which readily imbibes liquids; a mean parasite.—vt. (sponging, sponged). To wipe with a sponge; to wipe out completely; to harass by extortion; to get by mean arts.—vi. To imbibe; to act as a hanger-on.

Sponsor, spon'sor, n. A surety or guarantor; a godfather or godmother.

Spontaneity, spon-ta-nē'i-ti, n. Self-originated activity; readiness.

Spontaneous, spon-tā'nē-us, a. Voluntary; self-originated; acting by its own impulse.

Spook, spök, n. A ghost, an apparition

Spool, spöl, n. A reel to wind thread or yarn on.

Spoon, spön, n. A domestic utensil for taking up liquids, etc., at table.—vt. To take up with a spoon.

Spoor, spör, n. The track or trail of an animal.

Sporadic, spō-rad'ik, a. Scattered; occurring here and there in a scattered manner.

Spore, spör, n. The reproductive germ of a cryptogamic plant; a germ of certain animal organisms.

Sport, spört, n. A game; a merry-making; out-of-door recreation, as shooting, horse-racing, etc.; jest; object of mockery; a plant or animal that differs from the normal type.—vt. To divert (oneself); to wear in public.—vi. To play; to frolic; to practise the diversions of the field.

Sportsman, spörts'man, n. One who engages in shooting, fishing, etc.

Spot, spot, n. A place discolored; a speck; a blemish; a flaw; a locality.—vt. (spotting, spotted). To make a spot on; to stain; to catch with the eye.—vi. To act as observer of enemy's position, of effect of gunfire, or of approach of hostile aircraft.

Spotless, spot'les, a. Free from spots; unblemished; pure; immaculate.

Spotted, spot'ed, a. Marked with spots; speckled.

Spouse, spouz, n. A husband or wife.

Spout, spout, n. A nozzle, or projecting mouth of a vessel; a water-spout; a jet or gush of water.—vt. and i. To discharge in a jet and with some force; to mouth or utter pompously.

Sprain, sprān, vt. To overstrain, as the muscles or ligaments of a joint.—n. A violent strain of a joint without dislocation.

Sprawl, spral, vi. To struggle or show convulsive motions; to lie or crawl with the limbs stretched.

Spray, sprā, n. A twig; collection of small branches; water or any liquid flying in small drops or particles.—vt. To cause to take the form of spray; to treat with spray.

Spread, spred, vt. (spreading, spread). To stretch or expand; to overspread; to disseminate; to emit; to diffuse.—vi. To stretch out; to be diffused.—n. Extent; diffusion; a meal or banquet.

Spree, sprē, n. A merry frolic; a carousal.

Sprig, sprig, n. A small shoot or twig; a spray; a scion; a small square brad.

Sprightly, sprīt'li, a. Full of spirit; lively; brisk; gay; vivacious.

Spring, spring, vi. (pret. sprang or sprung, pp. sprung). To leap; to start up; to dart; to warp; to become cracked; to originate.—vt. To start or rouse; to propose on a sudden; to crack; to jump over. n. A leap; resilience; an elastic body, made of various materials, especially steel; cause; an issue of water; source of supply; season of the year when plants begin to grow; a crack in timber.

Springy, spring'i, a. Elastic; light of foot; abounding with springs; wet; spongy.

Sprinkle, spring'kl, vt. and i. (sprinkling, sprinkled). To scatter in small drops; to bedew.—n. A small quantity scattered in drops.

Sprint, sprint, n. A short swift foot-race; a spurt.

Sprite, sprīt, *n.* A spirit; a kind of goblin.

Sprout, sprout, *vi.* To bud; to push out new shoots.—*n.* A shoot of a plant; *pl.* young coleworts; Brussels sprouts.

Spruce, sprös, *a.* Neat in dress; trim; smug.—*n.* A pine-tree yielding valuable timber.

Spry, sprī, *a.* Nimble; active; lively.

Spume, spūm, *n.* Froth; foam.—*vi.* To froth.

Spunk, spungk, *n.* Touchwood; tinder; mettle; pluck; courage.

Spur, spėr, *n.* An instrument with sharp points, worn on horsemen's heels; incitement; stimulus; a sharp outgrowth; a mountain mass that shoots from another.—*vt.* (spurring, spurred). To prick with a spur; to incite; to put spurs on.—*vi.* To travel with great expedition.

Spurious, spū'ri-us, *a.* Bastard; not genuine; counterfeit; false.

Spurn, spėrn, *vt.* To drive away, as with the foot; to reject with disdain; to treat with contempt.—*vi.* To kick up the heels; to manifest disdain.

Spurt, spėrt, *vt.* and *i.* To spirt.—*n.* A gush of liquid; sudden effort for an emergency; sudden increase of speed.

Sputter, sput'ėr, *vi.* To emit saliva in speaking; to throw out moisture; to speak hastily and indistinctly.

Spy, spī, *vt.* (spying, spied). To gain sight of; to gain knowledge of by artifice; to explore.—*vi.* To pry.—*n.* One who keeps watch on the actions of others; a secret emissary.

Squabble, skwob'l, *vi.* (squabbling, squabbled). To dispute noisily; to wrangle.—*n.* A scuffle; a brawl.

Squad, skwod, *n.* A small party of men assembled for drill; any small party.

Squadron, skwod'ron, *n.* The principal division of a regiment of cavalry, usually from 100 to 200 men; a division of a fleet; a group of some twelve or so military airplanes.

Squalid, skwo'lid, *a.* Foul; filthy.

Squall, skwal, *vi.* To cry out; to scream violently.—*n.* A loud scream; a violent gust of wind; a brief storm of wind.

Squalor, skwol'ėr, *n.* Foulness; filthiness.

Squander, skwon'dėr, *vt.* To spend lavishly; to fling away; to waste.

Square, skwār, *a.* Having four equal sides and four right angles; forming a right angle; just; honest; even; suitable.—*n.* A figure having four equal sides and right angles; any similar figure or area; an instrument having one edge at right angles to another; product of a number multiplied by itself; level; equality.—*vt.* (squaring, squared). To make square; to form to right angles; to adjust; to fit; to settle (accounts); to multiply a number by itself.—*vi.* To suit; to spar (colloq.).

Squash, skwosh, *vt.* To crush; to beat or press into pulp or a flat mass.—*n.* Something easily crushed; sudden fall of a heavy soft body; a kind of gourd.

Squat, skwot, *vi.* (squatting, squatted). To sit upon the hams or heels; to cower; to settle on land without any title.—*a.* Cowering; short and thick.—*n.* The posture of one who squats.

Squawk, skwak, *vi.* To cry with a harsh voice.

Squeak, skwēk, *vi.* To utter a sharp, shrill sound.—*n.* A sharp, shrill sound.

Squeal, skwēl, *vi.* To cry with a sharp, shrill voice.—*n.* A shrill, sharp cry.

Squeamish, skwēm'ish, *a.* Having a stomach easily turned; fastidious.

Squeeze, skwēz, *vt.* (squeezing, squeezed). To subject to pressure; to harass by extortion; to hug.—*vi.* To press; to crowd.—*n.* An application of pressure; compression.

Squelch, skwelch, *vt.* To crush; to destroy.—*vi.* To be crushed.—*n.* A flat heavy fall.

Squid, skwid, *n.* A cuttle-fish.

Squint, skwint, *a.* Looking obliquely or different ways.—*n.* An oblique look; an affection in which the optic axes do not coincide.—*vi.* To look obliquely.

Squirm, skwėrm, *vi.* To wriggle; to writhe.—*n.* A wriggling motion.

Squirrel, skwi'rel, *n.* A rodent with a long bushy tail, living in trees.

Squirt, skwėrt, *vt.* To eject out of an orifice in a stream.—*vi.* To spurt.—*n.* An instrument which ejects a liquid in a stream; a syringe; a small jet; a spurt.

Stab, stab, *vt.* and *i.* (stabbing, stabbed). To pierce or kill with a pointed weapon; to wound figuratively; to injure secretly.—*n.* A thrust or wound with a pointed weapon; underhand injury; poignant pain.

Stable, stā'bl, *a.* Firm; firmly established; steadfast.—*n.* A house for horses, etc.—*vt.* (stabling, stabled). To put or keep in a stable.—*vi.* To dwell in a stable.

Stack, stak, *n.* A large, regularly built pile of hay, grain, etc.; a number of chimneys standing together; a single tall chimney; a high rock detached.—*vt.* To build into a stack; to pile together.

Staff, stäf, *n.*; pl. **Staves** or **Staffs,** stävz, stäfs. A stick or rod; a prop or support; a baton; the five parallel lines on which musical characters are written; a body of officers attached to an army as a whole (pl. *staffs*); a body of persons assisting in any undertaking.

Stag, stag, *n.* A male animal, especially the male red-deer; a hart.

Stage, stāj, *n.* An elevated platform; the platform on which theatrical performances are exhibited; place of action; a halting-place; distance between two stopping-places; degree of progression; point reached.—*vt.* To put upon the theatrical stage.

Stagger, stag'ėr, *vi.* To reel; to totter; to waver.—*vt.* To cause to waver; to amaze; to arrange working hours so that employees enter and leave their place of work at intervals in batches, instead of simultaneously.—*n.* A sudden swaying of the body; *pl.* a disease of cattle, etc., attended with giddiness.

Staid, stād, *a.* Sober; grave; sedate.

Stain, stān, *vt.* To mark or spot; to discolor; to soil; to disgrace; to tinge with color.—*vi.* To take stains; to become stained.—*n.* A discoloration; a spot; disgrace; a color.

Stair, stār, *n.* One of a set of steps to go up or down by; a series of connected steps.

Stake, stāk, *n.* A sharpened piece of wood; a post; that which is pledged or wagered; hazard (preceded by *at*).—*vt.* (staking, staked). To support, defend, or mark with stakes; to pledge; to wager.

Stalactite, sta-lak'tīt, *n.* A mass of calcareous matter attached, like an icicle, to the roof of a cavern.

Stalagmite, sta-lag'mīt, *n.* A deposit of stalactitic matter on the floor of a cavern.

Stale, stāl, *a.* Vapid; tasteless; not new; musty; trite.—*vt.* (staling, staled). To make stale.—*vi.* To discharge urine, as cattle.—*n.* Urine of horses and cattle.

Stalk, stak, *n.* The stem of a plant; part that supports a flower, leaf, fruit, etc.; a stately step or walk.—*vi.* To walk in a dignified manner.—*vt.* To watch and follow warily, as game, for the purpose of killing.

Stall, stal, *n.* A place where a horse or ox is kept and fed; division of a stable; a bench or shed where anything is exposed to sale, etc.; the seat of a clerical dignitary in the choir; a seat in a theatre.—*vt.* To put into a stall; to plunge into mire.

Stallion, stal'yun, *n.* A horse not castrated.

Stalwart, Stalworth, stal'wėrt, stal'wėrth, *a.* Stout-hearted; tall and strong.

Stamina, sta'mi-na, *n.pl.* Whatever constitutes the principal strength; robustness; power of endurance.

Stammer, stam'ėr, *vt.* and *t.* To make involuntary

breaks in utterance; to stutter.—*n*. Defective utterance; a stutter.

Stamp, stamp, *vt*. To strike by thrusting the foot down; to impress; to imprint; to affix a postage-stamp to; to coin; to form.—*vi*. To strike the foot forcibly downward.—*n*. Act of stamping; an instrument for crushing or for making impressions; mark imprinted; a postage-stamp; character; sort.

Stampede, stam-pēd′, *n*. A sudden fright and flight, as of horses.—*vi*. (stampeding, stampeded). To take sudden flight.—*vt*. To cause to break off in a stampede.

Stanch, Staunch, stänsh, stansh, *vt*. To stop from running, as blood; to stop the flow of blood from.—*vi*. To cease to flow.—*a*. Strong and tight; constant and zealous; loyal.

Stanchion, stan′shon, *n*. A prop or support; a post of timber or iron.

Stand, stand, *vi*. (standing, stood). To be upon the feet in an upright position; to be on end; to have locality; to stop; to endure; to persevere; to be as regards circumstances; to be equivalent; to become a candidate; to hold a certain course; to be valid.—*vt*. To set on end; to endure.—*n*. Act of standing; a stop; a halt; a station; a small table or frame; platform for spectators at gatherings

Standard, stan′därd, *n*. A flag of war; a banner; a rule or measure; criterion; test; a certain grade in schools; an upright support.—*a*. Serving as a standard; satisfying certain legal conditions; not trained on a wall, etc., but standing by itself.

Stannary, stan′a-ri, *n*. A tin mine.—*a*. Relating to the tin mines or works.

Stanza, stan′za, *n*. A verse or connected number of lines of poetry.

Staple, stā′pl, *n*. An emporium; a principal commodity; chief constituent; thread or pile of wool, cotton, or flax; raw material; an iron loop with two points.—*a*. Chief; principal; established in commerce.—*vt*. (stapling, stapled). To adjust the staples of, as wool.

Star, stär, *n*. Any celestial body except the sun and moon; a heavenly body similar to our sun; a figure with radiating points; a badge of honor; an asterisk, thus *; a brilliant theatrical performer.—*vt*. (starring, starred). To adorn with stars; to bespangle.—*vi*. To shine as a star; to appear as an eminent actor among inferior players.

Starboard, stär′bōrd, *n*. and *a*. The right-hand side of a ship.

Starch, stärch, *n*. A vegetable substance, employed for stiffening linen, etc.; stiffness of behavior.—*vt*. To stiffen with starch.

Stare, stär, *vi*. (staring, stared). To look with fixed eyes wide open; to gaze; to stand out stiffly.—*vt*. To affect or abash by staring.—*n*. A fixed look with the eyes; a starling.

Stark, stärk, *a*. Stiff; rigid; strong; mere; downright.—*adv*. Wholly.

Start, stärt, *vi*. To move with sudden quickness; to wince; to deviate; to set out; to begin; to move from its place.—*vt*. To rouse suddenly; to startle; to originate; to dislocate.—*n*. A sudden motion; a twitch; outset; a handicap.

Startle, stärt′l, *vi*. (startling, startled). To move suddenly.—*vt*. To cause to start; to frighten.—*n*. A start, as from fear.

Starve, stärv, *vi*. (starving, starved). To perish with cold; to suffer from hunger; to be very indigent.—*vt*. To kill or distress with hunger or cold; to make inefficient through insufficient expenditure.

State, stāt, *n*. Condition; situation; rank; pomp; grandeur; an estate (of the realm); a commonwealth; a nation; civil power.—*a*. National; public; governmental.—*vt*. (stating, stated). To express the particulars of; to narrate.

Stately, stāt′li, *a*. Such as pertains to state; august; grand; lofty; dignified.

Statesman, stāts′man, *n*. A man versed in state affairs or in the arts of government.

Statical, stat′ik-al, *a*. Pertaining to bodies at rest or in equilibrium.

Station, stā′shon, *n*. Place where anything stands; post assigned; situation; social position; a regular stopping-place, as on railways, etc.—*vt*. To assign a position to; to post.

Stationary, stā′shon-a-ri, *a*. Fixed; not moving; not appearing to move.

Stationery, stā′shon-ē-ri, *n*. and *a*. Articles sold by stationers, as paper, ink, etc.

Statistics, sta-tist′iks, *n*. A collection of facts, tabulated numerically; the science of subjects as elucidated by facts.

Statue, stat′ū, *n*. An image of a human figure or animal in marble, bronze, or other solid substance.

Stature, stat′ūr, *n*. The height of anyone standing; bodily tallness.

Status, stā′tus, *n*. Social position; rank; condition; position of affairs.

Statute, stat′ūt, *n*. A law passed by the legislature of a state; an enactment; a fundamental or permanent rule or law.

Statutory, stat′ū-to-ri, *n*. Enacted by statute.

Stave, stāv, *n*. A pole; one of the pieces of timber of casks, etc.; a stanza, in *music*, the staff.—*vt*. (staving, staved). To break in a stave of; to break a hole in (pret. & pp. also *stove*).—**To stave off**, to put off; to delay.

Stay, stā, *vt*. (pret. & pp. stayed or staid). To prop; to stop; to delay; to await.—*vi*. To remain; to reside; to delay; to forbear to act; to stop.—*n*. Sojourn; stop; obstacle; a prop; a rope to support a mast; *pl*. a stiffened bodice worn by females; a corset.—**To miss stays**, to fail in the attempt to tack about.

Stead, sted, *n*. Place or room which another had or might have; assistance: preceded by *in*.—*vt*. To be of use to.

Steadfast, sted′fäst, *a*. Firm; constant; resolute; steady.

Steady, sted′i, *a*. Firm; stable; constant; regular; equable.—*vt*. (steadying, steadied). To make or keep firm.

Steak, stāk, *n*. A slice of beef, etc., broiled or cut for broiling.

Steal, stēl, *vt*. (pret. stole, pp. stolen). To take feloniously; to pilfer; to gain by address or imperceptibly; to perform secretly.—*vi*. To pass silently or privily; to practice theft.

Stealth, stelth, *n*. A secret method of procedure; a proceeding by secrecy.

Steam, stēm, *n*. The vapor of water; aeriform fluid generated by the boiling of water.—*vi*. To give out steam; to rise in vaporous form; to sail by means of steam.—*vt*. To expose to steam, to apply steam to.

Steed, stēd, *n*. A horse; a horse of high mettle, for state or war.

Steel, stēl, *n*. A very hard form or iron, produced by addition of carbon; weapons, swords, etc.; a knife-sharpener; sternness; rigor.—*a*. Made of or like steel; unfeeling; rigorous.—*vt*. To furnish with steel; to harden.

Steep, step, *a*. Sloping greatly; precipitous.—*n*. A precipitous place; a cliff; process of steeping; liquid in which something is steeped.—*vt*. To soak; to imbue.

Steeple, stē′pl, *n*. A lofty erection attached to a church, etc.; spire.

Steeple-chase, stē′pl-chās, *n*. A horse-race across country and over obstacles.

Steer, stēr, *vt*. and *i*. To direct and govern, as a ship; to guide; to pursue a course in life.—*n*. A young ox; a bullock.

Stela, Stele, stē′la, stē′lē, *n*.; pl. -lae. A small column serving as a monument.

Stellar, Stellary, stel′ör, stel′a-ri, *a*. Pertaining to stars; astral; starry.

Stellate, stel′lāt, *a*. Resembling a star; radiated.

Stem, stem, *n*. The principal body of a tree, shrub, etc.; the stalk; stock or branch of a fam-

S

ily; the prow of a vessel—*vt.* (stemming, stemmed). To make way against; to press forward through; to dam up; to check.

Stench, stensh, *n.* An ill smell; stink.

Stencil, sten'sil, *n.* A thin plate with a pattern cut through it, brushed over with color to mark a surface below.—*vt.* (stenciling, stenciled). To form by a stencil; to color with stencils.

Stenographer, Stenographist, ste-nog'ra-fẽr, sten-nog'ra-fist, *n.* One who is skilled in stenography or shorthand.

Stenography, ste-nog'ra-fi, *n.* The art of writing in shorthand; shorthand.

Stentorian, sten-tō'ri-an, *a.* Extremely loud; able to utter a loud and deep sound.

Step, step, *vi.* (stepping, stepped). To move the leg and foot in walking; to walk.—*vt.* To set (the foot); to fix the foot of, as of a mast.—*n.* A pace; a small space; a grade; a rise; footprint; gait; footfall; action adopted; something to support the feet in ascending; round of a ladder; *pl.* a step-ladder.

Stepbrother, step'brŭTH-ẽr, *n.* A father's or mother's son by another marriage.—Also *stepsister.*

Stepfather, step'fä-THẽr, *n.* A mother's second or subsequent husband.—Also *stepmother.*

Step-ladder, step'lad-ẽr, *n.* A portable self-supporting ladder.

Stepping-stone, step'ing-stōn, *n.* A stone to raise the feet above a stream or mud; a means of progress or advancement.

Stepson, step'sun, *n.* The son of a husband or wife by a former marriage.—Also *stepdaughter, stepchild.*

Stereography, ste-rō-og'ra-fi, *n.* The art of delineating solid bodies on a plane.

Stereotype, ste'rē-ō-tīp, *n.* and *a.* A metal plate presenting a facsimile of a page of type; an electrotype plate.—*vt.* To make a stereotype of; to fix unchangeably.

Sterile, ste'ril, *a.* Barren; unfruitful; incapable of reproduction; barren of ideas.

Sterling, stẽr'ling, *a.* An epithet distinctive of English money; genuine; of excellent quality.

Stern, stẽrn, *a.* Austere; harsh; rigid; stringent.— *n.* The hind part of a ship.

Sternum, stẽr'num, *n.* The breast-bone.

Stertorous, stẽr'to-rus, *a.* Characterized by deep snoring.

Stethoscope, ste'thō-skōp, *n.* An instrument for sounding the chest, lungs, etc.

Stevedore, stē've-dōr, *n.* One who loads or unloads vessels.

Stew, stū, *vt.* To boil slowly in a closed vessel.—*vi.* To be cooked slowly.—*n.* Meat stewed; a bathing house with hot baths; a brothel; a state of excitement.

Stick, stik, *vt.* (sticking, stuck). To pierce or stab; to fasten by piercing, gluing, etc.; to fix; to set.— *vi.* To adhere; to abide firmly; to be brought to a stop; to scruple.—*n.* A rod or wand; a staff; a stiff, awkward person.

Stickler, stik'lẽr, *n.* One who stickles; an obstinate contender about trifles.

Stiff, stif, *a.* Rigid; tense; not moving easily; thick; not natural and easy; formal in manner; stubborn; difficult; strong.

Stiff-necked, stif'nekt, *a.* Stubborn; inflexibly obstinate; contumacious.

Stiffness, stif'nes, *n.* Want of pliancy; rigidity; viscidness; stubbornness; formality.

Stifle, stī'fl, *vt.* and *i.* (stifling, stifled). To suffocate; to smother; to suppress.—*n.* The joint of a horse next to the buttock.

Stigma, stig'ma, *n.*; pl. **-mas** or **-mata.** A brand made with a red-hot iron; any mark of infamy; part of a flower pistil which receives the pollen; pl. *stigmata,* bodily marks like Christ's wounds impressed supernaturally.

Stigmatize, stig'mat-īz, *vt.* To characterize by some opprobrious epithet.

Stiletto, sti-let'tō, *n.* A small strong dagger; a

pointed instrument for making eyelet-holes.— *vt.* (stilettoing, stilettoed). To stab or pierce with a stiletto.

Still, stil, *a.* At rest; calm; silent; not loud; soft; not effervescing.—*vt.* To make still; to check; to appease or allay.—*adv.* To this time; always; nevertheless; yet.—*n.* A vessel or apparatus for distilling; a distillery.

Still-born, stil'born, *a.* Dead at the birth; abortive; produced unsuccessfully.

Stilt, stilt, *n.* Either of a pair of poles, with a rest for the foot, used for raising the feet in walking.

Stilted, stilt'ed, *a.* Elevated as if on stilts; stiff and bombastic; jerky.

Stimulant, stim'ū-lant, *a.* Serving to stimulate.— *n.* An agent which produces an increase of vital energy; an intoxicant.

Stimulate, stim'ū-lāt, *vt.* To rouse up; to incite; to excite greater vitality in.

Stimulus, stim'ū-lus, *n.* pl. **-li.** Something that stimulates; an incitement.

Sting, sting, *vt.* (stinging, stung). To pierce, as wasps, etc.; to prick, as a nettle; to pain acutely.—*n.* A sharp-pointed defensive organ of certain animals; the thrust of a sting into the flesh; something that gives acute pain; the biting effect of words.

Stingily, stin'ji-li, *adv.* In a stringy or niggardly manner; meanly; shabbily.

Stingy, stin'ji, *a.* Very niggardly; meanly avaricious; scanty.

Stink, stingk, *vi.* (stinking, stunk). To emit a strong offensive smell; to be in disrepute.—*n.* A strong offensive smell.

Stint, stint, *vt.* To restrict; to make scanty.—*vi.* To cease; to desist from.—*n.* Limit; restraint; restriction.

Stipend, stī'pend, *n.* Yearly allowance; salary.

Stipple, stip'l, *vt.* (stippling, stippled). To engrave by means of dots.—*n.* A process of engraving by means of dots.

Stipulate, stip'ū-lāt, *vi.* (stipulating, stipulated). To make an agreement; to contract; to settle terms.

Stir, stẽr, *vt.* (stirring, stirred). To put into motion; to agitate; to rouse; to provoke; to disturb.—*vi.* To move oneself; not to be still; to be awake or out of bed.—*n.* Commotion; bustle; disorder.

Stirrup, sti'rup, *n.* A metal loop, suspended by a strap, to support the foot in riding.

Stitch, stich, *n.* A sharp pain; one complete movement of a needle in sewing; a complete turn or link in knitting, netting, etc.—*vt.* and *i.* To sew by making stitches in; to unite by stitches.

Stoat, stōt, *n.* The ermine in its summer fur.

Stock, stok, *n.* A post; a lifeless mass; stem of a tree; wooden piece of a rifle; a stiff cravat; an original progenitor; lineage; capital invested in any business; money funded in government securities; store; animals belonging to a farm; liquor used to form a foundation for soups and gravies; a sweet-smelling garden-plant; *pl.* an instrument of punishment confining the offender's ankles or wrists; timbers on which a ship is supported while building.—*vt.* To provide with a stock; to lay up in store.—*a.* Kept in stock; standing; permanent.

Stockade, stok-ād', *n.* A defense of strong posts stuck close to each other; an enclosure made with posts.—*vt.* (stockading, stockaded). To fortify with posts fixed in the ground.

Stockbroker, stok'brō-kẽr, *n.* A broker who buys and sells stocks or shares for others.

Stock-exchange, stok'eks-chānj, *n.* The place where stocks or shares are bought and sold; an organized association of stockbrokers.

Stockholder, stok'hōld-ẽr, *n.* A shareholder or proprietor of stock.

Stocking, stok'ing, *n.* A close-fitting knitted covering for the foot and leg.

Stodgy, stoj'i, *a.* Crammed together roughly; crude and indigestible.

Stoicism, stō'i-sizm, *n.* Indifference to pleasure

or pain.

Stoke, stōk, vt. (stoking, stoked). To keep supplied with fuel, as a fire.

Stolidity, sto-lid'i-ti, n. Dullness of intellect; stupidity.

Stoma, stō'ma, n.; pl. -ata. A minute orifice or pore in plants or animals.

Stomach, stum'ak, n. A membranous sac, the principal organ of digestion; appetite; inclination.—vt To brook; to put up with.

Stone, stōn, n. A hard mass of earthy or mineral matter; a pebble; a precious stone; concretion in the kidneys or bladder; a testicle; the nut of a fruit; a measure of 14 lbs. avoirdupois.—a. Made of stone; like stone.—vt. (stoning, stoned). To pelt with stones; to free from stones; to provide with stones.

Stone-ware, stōn'wār, n. Common glazed pottery ware.

Stony-hearted, stōn'i-härt-ed, a. Hard-hearted; cruel; pitiless; unfeeling.

Stool, stöl, n. A portable seat without a back for one person; the seat used in evacuating the bowels; a discharge from the bowels.

Stoop, stöp, vi. To bend the body forward and downward; to yield; to deign; to pounce.—n. Act of stooping; bend of the back or shoulders; a condescension; swoop.

Stop, stop, vt. (stopping, stopped). To stuff up; to close; to arrest the progress of; to put an end to; to regulate the sounds of musical strings by the fingers, etc.—vi. To cease from any motion; to come to an end; to stay; to remain.—n. Obstruction; interruption; pause; a series of pipes in an organ giving distinctive sounds; a point in writing.

Stop-watch, stop'woch, n. A watch one of the hands of which can be stopped instantaneously so as to mark with accuracy any point of time.

Store, stōr, n. A large quantity for supply; abundance; a place where goods are kept; a shop; pl. necessary articles laid up for use.—a. Pertaining to a store; kept in store.—vt. (storing, stored). To amass; to supply; to reposit in a store for preservation.

Storehouse, stōr'hous, n. A place in which things are stored; a repository.

Stork, stork, n. A large grallatorial or wading bird resembling the heron.

Storm, storm, n. A violent disturbance of the atmosphere; a tempest; an outbreak; assault on a strong position.—vt. To take by assault; to attack.—vi. To be in violent agitation; to rage.

Stormy, storm'i, a. Abounding with storms; boisterous; passionate; angry.

Story, stō'ri, n. A narrative; an account; a tale; a fiction; a falsehood.

Story, Storey, stō'ri, n. A state or floor of a building.

Stout, stout, a. Bold; valiant; sturdy; bulky; corpulent.—n. A dark-brown malt liquor.

Stove, stōv, n. An apparatus for warming a room, cooking, etc.—vt. (stoving, stoved). To heat in a stove. Pret. of stave.

Stow, stō, vt. To put in a suitable place; to pack; to compactly arrange anything in.

Stowaway, stō'a-wā, n. One who hides himself on a ship to obtain a free passage.

Straddle, strad'l, vt. and t. (straddling, straddled). To spread the legs wide; to sit astride; to stride across, to drop bombs along or across a target so as to cover a large area.

Straggle, strag'l, vi. (straggling, straggled). To rove; to wander in a scattered way; to occur at intervals.

Straight, strāt, a. Stretched tight; direct; correct; upright.—n. A straight part or piece; straight direction.—adv. Immediately; directly.—vt. To straighten.

Straightforward, strāt'for-werd, a. Proceeding in a straight course; candid; honest; frank; open.—adv. Directly forward.

Strain, strān, vt. To stretch tightly; to exert to the utmost; to overtask; to sprain; to carry too far; to wrest; to filter.—vi. To exert oneself; to filter.—n. Violent effort; excessive stretching or exertion; tenor; theme; a lay; tune; race; family blood; tendency.

Strainer, strān'er, n. One who strains; an instrument for filtration.

Strait, strāt, a. Confined; narrow; close; strict.—n. A narrow passage; a narrow stretch of water (often pl.); a position of hardship or difficulty.

Straiten, strāt'n, vt. To make strait; to distress; to hamper.

Strand, strand, n. The shore of a sea or lake; one of the twists of a rope.—vt. and i. To drive or be driven ashore.

Strange, strānj, a. Foreign; wonderful; odd; not familiar.

Stranger, strān'jer, n. A foreigner; an alien; one unknown; a visitor.

Strangle, strang'gl, vt. (strangling, strangled). To choke; to throttle; to suppress or stifle.

Strangulate, strang'gū-lāt, vt. To strangle; to stop vital action in by compression.

Strap, strap, n. A long narrow slip of leather, etc.; a plate or strip of metal.—vt. (strapping, strapped). To beat with a strap; to fasten with a strap.

Strapping, strap'ing, a. Tall and well made; handsome.

Stratagem, stra'ta-jem, n. A piece of generalship; an artifice in war; a wile.

Strategic, Strategical, stra-tej'ik, stra-tej'ik-al, a. Pertaining to strategy; effected by strategy.

Strategy, stra'te-ji, n. The science of military operations; generalship.

Stratosphere, stra'tō-sfēr, n. The upper region of the earth's atomosphere.

Stratum, strā'tum, n.; pl. -ta. A layer of any substance, as sand, clay, etc., especially when one of a number.

Stratus, strā'tus, n. A low horizontal cloud.

Straw, stra, n. The dry stalk of grain, pulse, etc.—a. Made of straw.

Strawberry, stra'be-ri, n. A herbaceous plant and its succulent fruit.

Stray, strā, vi. To go astray; to err; to roam.—a. Having gone astray; straggling.—n. Any domestic animal that wanders at large, or is lost.

Streak, strēk, n. A long mark; a stripe; appearance of a mineral when scratched.—vt. To form streaks in.

Stream, strēm, n. A river or brook; a current; drift. vi. and t. To move in a stream; to stretch in a long line; to float at full length in the air

Streamline, strēm-lin', vt. To shape so as to reduce resistance to air and water.

Street, strēt, n. A road in a town or village; the roadway and houses together.

Strength, strength, n. Property of being strong; force or energy; power; support; vigor; intensity, amount or numbers of an army, fleet, or the like.—**On the strength of**, in reliance upon, on the faith of.

Strenuous, stren'ū-us, a. Energetic; vigorous; zealous; ardent; earnest.

Stress, stres, vt. To put in difficulties; to subject to emphasis.—n. Constraint; pressure; weight; violence, as of weather; emphasis.

Stretch, strech, vt. To draw out tight; to extend; to straighten; to strain; to exaggerate.—vi. To reach or extend; to spread; to have elasticity.—n. Strain; extent; scope; expanse; a turn or spell.

Stretcher, strech'er, n. One who stretches; a contrivance for stretching things; a litter for carrying persons.

Strew, strō or strō, vt (pp. strewed or strewn). To scatter or sprinkle; to cover by scattering; to besprinkle.

Stria, strī'a, n.; pl. -iae. A term for fine streaks on surfaces of minerals, plants, etc.

Strict, strikt, a. Tight; tense; exact; severe; rigor-

S

ous; not loose or vague.

Stricture, strik'tŭr, *n.* A contraction of any canal of the body; a critical remark; censure.

Stride, strīd, *vi.* (striding, pret. strode, pp. stridden). To walk with long steps; to straddle.—*vt.* To pass over at a step.—*n.* A long step; a measured tread.

Strident, stri'dent, *a.* Harsh; grating.

Strife, strīf, *n.* Act of striving; struggle; contest; discord; conflict; quarrel or war.

Strike, strīk, *vi.* (striking, pret. struck, pp. struck, stricken). To move or turn aside rapidly; to light (upon); to make a blow; to hit; to be stranded; to yield; to quit work to compel better terms.—*vt.* To smite; to mint; to thrust in; to notify by sound; to occur to; to impress strongly; to effect at once; to lower, as the flag or sails of a vessel.—*n.* Act of workmen who quit work to force their employer to give better terms; a strickle.

String, string, *n.* A small cord; a piece of twine; a line with the things on it; chord of a musical instrument; a series.—*vt.* (stringing, strung). To furnish with string; to put on a string; to make tense.

Stringent, strin'jent, *a.* Strict; rigorous; rigid.

Strip, strip, *vt.* (stripping, stripped). To deprive of a covering; to skin; to deprive; to pillage.—*vi.* To take off the covering or clothes.—*n.* A long narrow piece.

Stripe, strīp, *n.* A long narrow division or marking; a streak; a strip; a stroke with a lash; a wale or weal.—*vt.* (striping, striped). To form or variegate with stripes.

Stroke, strōk, *n.* A blow; calamity; attack; striking of a clock; touch; a masterly effort; a dash in writing or printing; a touch of the pen; a line; a gentle rub; the sweep of an oar; a stroke-oar.—*vt.* (stroking, stroked). To rub gently with the hand.

Stroll, strōl, *vi.* To ramble; to rove; to roam.—*n.* A short leisurely walk.

Strong, strong, *a.* Having power or force; robust; not easily broken; firm; effectual; earnest; containing much alcohol; glaring; forcible; tending upwards in price; effecting inflection by internal vowel change.

Strontium, stron'shi-um, *n.* A metal of a yellow color, somewhat harder than lead.

Strop, strop, *n.* A strip of leather, etc., for sharpening razors.—*vt.* (stropping, stropped). To sharpen on a strop.

Structure, struk'tŭr, *n.* A building of any kind; manner of building; make; organization.

Struggle, strug'l, *vi.* (struggling, struggled). To make great efforts; to strive; to contend.—*n.* A violent effort of the body; forcible effort; contest; strife.

Strum, strum, *vi.* and *t.* (strumming, strummed). To play unskilfully on a stringed instrument; to thrum.

Strut, strut, *vi.* (strutting, strutted). To walk with affected dignity.—*n.* A lofty, proud step or walk; a strengthening piece placed diagonally in a framework.

Strychnia, Strychinine, strik'ni-a, strik'nīn, *n.* A vegetable alkaloid poison obtained from the seeds of nux-vomica.

Stubble, stub'l, *n.* The stumps of a grain crop left in the ground after reaping.

Stubborn, stub'orn, *a.* Not to be moved or persuaded; obstinate; intractable.

Stucco, stuk'kō, *n.* A fine plaster; work made of stucco; plaster of Paris or gypsum.—*vt.* (stuccoing, stuccoed). To overlay with stucco.

Stud, stud, *n.* A post; a prop; a nail with a large head; an ornamental button; a set of breeding horses; a person's horses collectively.—*vt.* (studding, studded). To adorn with studs; to set thickly, as with studs.

Student, stū'dent, *n.* One who studies; a scholar; a bookish person.

Stud-horse, stud'hors, *n.* A breeding horse.

Studied, stu'did, *a.* Made the object of study; qualified by study; premeditated.

Studio, stū'di-ō, *n.* The work-place of a painter or sculptor.

Study, stu'di, *n.* Earnest endeavor; application to books, etc.; subject which one studies; apartment devoted to study; a reverie; a preparatory sketch.—*vt.* and *i.* (studying, studied). To apply the mind to; to investigate; to have careful regard to.

Stuff, stuf, *n.* Substance indefinitely; material; cloth; a light woollen fabric; goods; trash.—*vt.* To pack; to thrust in; to fill, as meat with seasoning; to fill, as an animal's skin to preserve the form.—*vi.* To cram; to feed gluttonously.

Stuffy, stuf'i, *a.* Difficult to breathe in; close; stifling.

Stultify, stul'ti-fī, *vi.* To prove foolish; to cause to seem absurd; to make a fool of.

Stumble, stum'bl, *vi.* (stumbling, stumbled). To trip in moving; to walk unsteadily; to fall into error; to light by chance (with *on*).—*n.* A trip in walking or running; a blunder.

Stump, stump, *n.* The part of a tree, limb, etc., left after the rest is cut off or destroyed; a worndown tooth; a wicket in cricket.—*vt.* To lop, as trees; to make a tour through, delivering speeches; to put out of play in cricket by knocking down a stump.—*vi.* To walk stiffly or noisily.

Stun, stun, *vt.* (stunning, stunned). To overpower the sense of hearing of; to stupefy; to make senseless with a blow; to surprise completely.

Stunt, stunt, *vt.* To stop the growth of; to dwarf.—*n.* A check in growth.

Stupefy, stū'pe-fī, *vt.* (stupefying, stupefied). To deprive of sensibility.

Stupendous, stū-pen'dus, *a.* Of astonishing magnitude; grand or awe-inspiring.

Stupid, stū'pid, *a.* Struck senseless; foolish; dull in intellect; nonsensical.

Stupor, stū'por, *n.* A condition in which the faculties are deadened; torpor; insensibility.

Sturdy, ster'di, *a.* Stout; strong; hardy; firm; robust; vigorous.

Stutter, stut'er, *vi.* To stammer.—*n.* A stammer; broken utterance of words.

Sty, stī, *n.* An inclosure for swine; a pig-sty; any filthy hovel or place.—*vt.* (stying, stied). To shut up in a sty.

Stye, stī, *n.* A small inflammatory tumor on the edge of the eyelid.

Style, stīl, *n.* A burin; pin of a sun-dial; manner of writing with regard to language; a characteristic mode in the fine arts; type; external manner, mode, or fashion; title; in *botany,* a slender prolongation of the ovary supporting the stigma.—*vt.* (styling, styled). To term; to designate.

Styptic, stip'tik, *a.* Able to stop bleeding.—*n.* A substance which stops a flow of blood.

Suave, swäv, *a.* Gracious in manner; blandly polite; pleasant.

Subcommittee, sub-kom-mit'tē, *n.* An under committee; a division of a committee.

Subcutaneous, sub-kū-tā'nē-us, *a.* Situated immediately under the skin.

Subdivide, sub-di-vid', *vt.* To divide part of into more parts.—*vi.* To be subdivided; to separate.

Subdue, sub-dū', *vt.* (subduing, subdued). To subjugate; to overpower; to tame; to soften; to tone down.

Subject, sub'jekt, *a.* Ruled by another; liable; prone; submissive.—*n.* One who owes allegiance to a ruler or government; matter dealt with; theme; topic; the nominative of a verb; the thinking agent or principle.—*vt.* sub-jekt'. To subdue; to make liable; to cause to undergo.

Subjective, sub-jekt'iv or sub'jekt-iv, *a.* Relating to the subject; belonging to ourselves, the conscious subject; exhibiting strongly the personality of the author.

Subjugate, sub'jū-gāt, *vt.* To subdue; to conquer and compel to submit.

Subjunctive, sub-jungk'tiv, *a.* and *n.* Applied to a

mood of verbs that expresses condition, hypothesis, or contingency.

Sublimate, sub'li-māt, *vt.* To raise by heat into vapor, as a solid, which, on cooling, returns again to the solid state; to refine; to elevate.—*n.* The product of sublimation.

Sublimation, sub-li-mā'shon, *n.* The process or operation of sublimating; exaltation; a highly refined product.

Sublime, sub-līm', *a.* High in place or excellence; affecting the mind with a sense of grandeur; noble; majestic.—**The sublime,** the grand in the works of nature or of art; grandeur of style; highest degree.—*vt.* (subliming, sublimed). To render sublime; to sublimate.—*vi.* To be susceptible of sublimation.

Submarine, sub-ma-rēn', *a.* Being under the surface of the sea.—*n.* A vessel which can be submerged at will and which can travel under the water.

Submerge, sub-mėrj', *vt.* and *i.* (submerging, submerged). To put under or cover with water; to drown; to sink.

Submersion, sub-mėr'shon, *n.* Act of submerging; state of being under fluid; a dipping or plunging.

Submission, sub-mi'shon, *n.* Act of submitting; surrender; humble behavior; obedience; resignation.

Submissive, sub-mis'iv, *a.* Yielding; obedient; compliant; humble; modest.

Submit, sub-mit', *vt.* (submitting, submitted). To yield or surrender; to refer; to state, as a claim.—*vi.* To surrender; to acquiesce; to suffer without complaint.

Subordinate, sub-or'din-āt, *a.* Inferior; occupying a lower position.—*n.* One who stands in rank, power, etc., below another.—*vt.* To place in a lower order or rank.

Suborn, sub-orn', *vt.* To bribe to commit perjury; to bribe to some wickedness.

Subpoena, sub-pē'na, *n.* A writ summoning a witness under a penalty.—*vt.* (subpoenaing, subpoenaed). To serve with a writ of subpoena.

Subscribe, sub-skrīb', *vt.* and *i.* (subscribing, subscribed). To append one's own signature to; to promise to contribute (money) by writing one's name; to assent.

Subscription, sub-skrip'shon, *n.* Act of subscribing; signature; attestation; a sum subscribed.

Subsequent, sub'sē-kwent, *a.* Following in time; succeeding; next.

Subside, sub-sīd', *vt.* (subsiding, subsided). To sink or fall to the bottom; to settle down; to abate.

Subsidiary, sub-si'di-a-ri, *a.* Pertaining to a subsidy; aiding; assistant; subordinate.—*n.* An assistant.

Subsidize, sub'si-dīz, *vt.* (subsidizing, subsidized). To furnish with a subsidy; to purchase the assistance of another by a subsidy.

Subsidy, sub'si-di, *n.* A sum of money granted for a purpose; a sum given by a government to meet expenses.

Subsist, sub-sist', *vi.* To have existence; to live; to inhere.

Subsistent, sub-sist'ent, *a.* Having being or existence; inherent.

Subsoil, sub'soil, *n.* The bed or stratum of earth below the surface soil.

Substance, sub'stans, *n.* That of which a thing consists; material; a body; essence; purport; means and resources.

Substantial, sub-stan'shal, *a.* Actually existing; real; solid; strong; moderately wealthy.

Substantiate, sub-stan'shi-āt, *vt.* To give substance to; to prove.

Substantive, sub'stan-tiv, *a.* Expressing existence; independent; real; of the nature of a noun.—*n.* A noun.

Substitute, sub'sti-tūt, *vt.* To put in the place of another; to exchange.—*n.* A person or thing in the place of

another; a deputy.

Substructure, sub'struk-tūr, *n.* An under structure; a foundation.

Subsume, sub-sūm', *vt.* (subsuming, subsumed). In *logic,* to include under a more general category.

Subtend, sub-tend', *vt.* To stretch or extend under, or be opposite to.

Subterfuge, sub'tėr-fūj, *n.* An artifice to escape or justify; evasion; a dishonest shift.

Subterranean, Subterraneous, sub-te-rā'nē-an, sub-te-rā'nē-us, *a.* Being under the surface of the earth.

Subtle, sut'l, *a.* Thin or tenuous; acute; sly; cunning; artful.

Subtlety, sut'l-ti, *n.* Quality of being subtle; delicacy; craft; cunning; acuteness; nicety of distinction; something subtle.

Subtract, sub-trakt', *vt.* To withdraw or take from; to deduct.

Subtraction, sub-trak'shon, *n.* The taking of a number or quantity from a greater.

Suburb, sub'ėrb, *n.* An outlying part of a city or town.

Subversion, sub-vėr'shon, *n.* Act of subverting; overthrow; destruction; ruin.

Subvert, sub-vėrt', *vt.* To ruin utterly; to overturn; to pervert.

Subway, sub'wā, *n.* An underground passage.

Succedaneum, suk-se-da'nē-um, *n.*; pl. **-nea.** A substitute.

Succeed, suk-sēd', *vt.* To follow in order; to take the place of; to come after.—*vi.* To follow in order; to ensue; to become heir; to obtain the end or object desired; to prosper.

Success, suk-ses', *n.* Issue; favorable result; good fortune; prosperity; something that succeeds.

Succession, suk-se'shon, *n.* A following of things in order; series of things; lineage; right of inheriting; act or right of succeeding to an office, rank, etc.

Successor, suk-ses'or, *n.* One who succeeds or follows another.

Succinct, suk-singkt', *a.* Compressed into few words; brief; concise.

Succor, suk'ėr, *vt.* To help when in difficulty; to aid; to relieve.—*n.* Aid; help; assistance given in distress; the person or thing that brings relief.

Succulent, suk'kū-lont, *a.* Full of sap or juice; sappy; juicy.

Succumb, suk-kum', *vt.* To yield; to submit; to sink unresistingly.

Such, such, *a.* Of like kind or degree; similar; like; the same as mentioned.

Suck, suk, *vt.* and *i.* To draw with the mouth; to draw milk from with the mouth; to imbibe; to absorb.—*n.* Act of sucking; milk drawn from the breast.

Sucker, suk'ėr, *n.* One who or that which sucks; an organ in animals for sucking; piston of a pump; shoot of a plant; the sucking-fish.

Suckling, suk'ling, *n.* A young child or animal nursed by the mother's milk.

Sucrose, sū'krōs, *n.* A name for the sugars identical with cane-sugar.

Suction, suk'shon, *n.* Act of sucking; the sucking up of a fluid by the pressure of the external air.

Sudden, sud'en, *a.* Happening without warning; abrupt; quick; hasty; violent.

Sudorific, sū-do-rif'ik, *a.* Causing sweat.—*n.* A medicine that produces sweat.

Suds, sudz, *n.pl.* Water impregnated with soap and forming a frothy mass.

Sue, sū, *vt.* (suing, sued). To seek justice from by legal process; to seek in marriage.—*vi.* To woo; to prosecute a suit at law; to petition.

Suet, sū'et, *n.* The harder fat of an animal about the kidneys and loins.

Suffer, suf'ėr, *vt.* To endure; to undergo; to be affected by; to permit.—*vi.* To undergo pain; to be injured.

Sufferance, suf'ėr-ans, *n.* Endurance; pain endured; passive consent; allowance.

S

Suffice, suf'fīs, *vi.* (sufficing, sufficed). To be sufficient.—*vt.* To satisfy; to content.

Sufficient, suf-fi'shent, *a.* Adequate; enough; competent; fit; able.

Suffix, suf'fiks, *n.* A letter or syllable added to the end of a word.—*vt.* To add a letter or syllable to a word.

Suffocate, suf'fō-kāt, *vi.* (suffocating, suffocated). To stifle; to choke by stopping respiration; to kill by depriving of oxygen.

Suffrage, suf'frāj, *n.* A vote; assent; right of voting for a representative.

Suffuse, suf-fūz', *vt.* (suffusing, suffused). To overspread, as with a fluid or a color.

Sugar, shu'gėr, *n.* A sweet granular substance, manufactured from sugar-cane, maple, beet, etc.; something sweet like sugar.—*a.* Belonging to or made of sugar.—*vt.* To season, mix, etc., with sugar; to sweeten.

Suggest, su-jest' or sug-jest', *vt.* To hint; to insinuate; to propose; to intimate.

Suggestion, su-jest'yon, *n.* A hint; a tentative proposal; insinuation; intimation.

Suicide, sū'i-sīd, *n.* Self-murder; one guilty of self-murder.

Suit, sūt, *n.* Act of suing; a request; courtship; a suing at law; a set of things.—*vt.* and *i.* To adapt; to fit; to be agreeable to; to agree.

Suitable, sūt'a-bl, *a.* That suits; fitting; proper; appropriate; becoming.

Suite, swēt, *n.* A company of attendants; a retinue; a connected series, as of apartments.

Suitor, sūt'or, *n.* One who sues; one who prosecutes a suit at law; a wooer.

Sulcate, Sulcated, sul'kāt, sul'kāt-ed, *a.* Furrowed; grooved; channelled.

Sulk, sulk, *vi.* To indulge in a sulky or sullen fit or mood.

Sullen, sul'en, *a.* Gloomily angry and silent; morose; sour; dismal; somber.

Sully, sul'i, *vt.* (sullying, sullied). To soil; to tarnish; to stain or pollute.—*vi.* To be soiled.—*n.* Soil; tarnish; spot.

Sulphate, sul'fāt, *n.* A salt of sulphuric acid.

Sulphide, sul'fid, *n.* A combination of sulphur with another element.

Sulphur, sul'fėr, *n.* Brimstone; a simple mineral substance of a yellow color which burns with a pale-blue flame.

Sulphurous, sul'fėr-us, *a.* Impregnated with or containing sulphur; like sulphur.

Sultry, sul'tri, *a.* Very hot; oppressive; close and heavy.

Sum, sum, *n.* The whole; aggregate; essence or substance; a quantity of money; an arithmetical problem.—*vt.* (summing, summed). To add into one whole; to reckon up; to recapitulate.

Summarize, sum'a-rīz, *vt.* To make a summary, abstract, or abridgment of.

Summary, sum'a-ri, *a.* Concise; brief; intended to facilitate dispatch.—*n.* An abridged account; an abstract.

Summer, sum'ėr, *n.* The warmest season of the year; a lintel; a girder.—*a.* Relating to summer.—*vi.* To pass the summer.—*vt.* To keep or carry through the summer.

Summit, sum'it, *n.* The top; highest point; highest degree; acme.

Summon, sum'un, *vt.* To call by authority to appear at a place, especially a court of justice; to send for; to call up.

Sumptuary, sump'tū-a-ri, *a.* Relating to expense; regulating expenditure.

Sumptuous, sump'tū-us, *a.* Very expensive or costly; splendid; magnificent.

Sun, sun, *n.* The self-luminous orb which gives light and heat to all the planets; sunshine or sunlight; sunny position; chief source of light, glory, etc.; a year.—*vt.* (sunning, sunned). To expose to the sun's rays.

Sunbeam, sun'bēm, *n.* A ray of the sun.

Sun-burn, sun'bėrn, *vt.* To discolor or scorch by the sun; to tan.

Sunday, sun'dā, *n.* The Christian Sabbath; the first day of the week.—*a.* Belonging to the Christian Sabbath.

Sunder, sun'dėr, *vt.* To part; to separate; to disunite in any manner.

Sun-dial, sun'dī-al, *n.* An instrument to show the time by a shadow cast by the sun.

Sundry, sun'dri, *a.* Several; divers; various; a few.

Sunken, sungk'en, *p.a.* Sunk; covered with water; below the general surface.

Sunny, sun'i, *a.* Like the sun; brilliant; exposed to the sun; having much sunshine; bright or cheerful.

Sunrise, Sunrising, sun'rīz, sun'rīz-ing, *n.* The first appearance of the sun in the morning; time of such appearance; the east.

Sunset, Sunsetting, sun'set, sun'set-ing, *n.* The descent of the sun below the horizon; evening; close or decline; the west.

Sunstroke, sun'strōk, *n.* A bodily affection produced by exposure to the sun.

Sup, sup, *vt.* (supping, supped). To take into the mouth with the lips, as a liquid.—*vi.* To take supper.—*n.* A sip; a small mouthful.

Superable, sū'pėr-a-bl, *a.* That may be overcome or surmounted.

Superabundance, sū'pėr-a-bun''dans, *n.* Excessive abundance; more than enough.

Superannuate, sū-pėr-an'nū-āt, *vt.* To pension off on account of old age.—*vi.* To retire on a pension.

Superb, sū-pėrb', *a.* Magnificent; sumptuous; splendid; august; grand.

Supercilious, sū-pėr-sil'i-us, *a.* Lofty with pride; haughty; overbearing.

Supererogation, sū-pėr-e'rō-gā''shon, *n.* Giving more than enough; performance of more than duty requires.

Superficial, sū-pėr-fi'shal, *a.* Being on the surface; shallow; not thorough.

Superfluous, sū-pėr'flu-us, *a.* Being more than is wanted; redundant; unnecessary.

Superhuman, sū-pėr-hū'man, *a.* Above or beyond what is human; divine.

Superimpose, sū'pėr-im-pōz'', *vt.* To lay or impose on something else.

Superinduce, sū'pėr-in-dūs'', *vt.* To bring in or on as an addition to something.

Superintend, sū'pėr-in-tend'', *vt.* To have the charge and oversight of; to direct or manage; to take care of with authority.

Superintendent, sū'pėr-in-tend''ent, *n.* One who manages and directs; an overseer.—*a.* Overlooking others with authority.

Superior, sū-pē'ri-or, *a.* Higher; higher in rank or dignity; greater in excellence.—*n.* One who is superior to another; chief of a monastery, convent, or abbey.

Superlative, sū-pėr'lat-iv, *a.* Highest in degree; supreme.—*n.* That which is superlative; the highest degree of adjectives or adverbs.

Supernal, sū-pėr'nal, *a.* Relating to things above; celestial; heavenly.

Supernatant, sū-pėr-nā'tant, *a.* Swimming above; floating on the surface.

Supernatural, sū-pėr-na'tūr-al, *a.* Being above or beyond nature; miraculous.

Supernumerary, sū-pėr-nū'me-ra-ri, *a.* Exceeding the number stated, necessary, or usual.—*n.* A person or thing beyond a number stated, but required on an emergency.

Superscription, sū-pėr-skrip'shon, *n.* Act of superscribing; that which is written or engraved above or on the outside; address on a letter, etc.

Supersede, sū-pėr-sēd', *vt.* (superseding, superseded). To set aside; to take the place of; to supplant.

Supersonic, sū-pėr-son'ik, *a.* Faster than sound; above the audible limit.

Superstition, sū-pėr-sti'shon, *n.* Groundless belief in supernatural agencies; a popular belief held without reason.

Superstructure, sū·pér·struk'tūr, *n.* Any structure raised on something else.

Supervene, sū·pér·vēn', *vi.* (supervening, supervened). To come, as something extraneous; to happen.

Supervise, sū·pér·vīz', *vt.* (supervising, supervised). To oversee and direct; to superintend; to inspect.

Supine, sū·pīn', *a.* Lying on the back; indolent; careless.—*n.* sū'pīn. A part of the Latin verb.

Supper, sup'ér, *n.* The last meal of the day; the evening meal.

Supplant, sup·plant', *vt.* To take the place of, usually by stratagem.

Supple, sup'l, *a.* Pliant; flexible; yielding.—*vt.* (suppling, suppled). To make supple.—*vi.* To become supple.

Supplement, sup'lē·ment, *n.* An addition; an appendix.—*vt.* sup·lē·ment'. To increase or complete by a supplement.

Suppliant, sup'li·ant, *a.* Supplicating; entreating earnestly; beseeching.—*n.* A supplicant; a humble petitioner.

Supplicant, sup'li·kant, *a.* Suppliant.—*n.* One who supplicates; a suppliant.

Supplicate, sup'li·kāt, *vt.* (supplicating, supplicated). To beg humbly for; to entreat; to address in prayer.—*vi.* To beg; to petition; to beseech.

Supply, sup·plī', *vt.* (supplying, supplied). To furnish; to provide; to satisfy.—*n.* Act of supplying; quantity supplied; store; *pl.* stores or articles necessary; money provided for government expenses.

Support, sup·pōrt', *vt.* To rest under and bear; to prop; to endure; to assist; to second; to maintain; to provide for.—*n.* Act of supporting; a prop; help; sustenance; maintenance.

Suppose, sup·pōz', *vt.* (supposing, supposed). To lay down or regard as matter of fact; to take for granted; to imagine; to imply.—*vi.* To think; to imagine.

Suppress, sup·pres', *vt.* To put down; to crush; to quell; to check; to conceal.

Suppression, sup·pre'shon, *n.* Act of suppressing; concealment; morbid retention of discharges; ellipsis.

Suppurate, sup'pū·rāt, *vi.* (suppurating, suppurated). To form or generate pus; to fester.

Supramundane, sū·pra·mun'dān, *a.* Being above the world; celestial.

Supreme, sū·prēm', *a.* Highest in authority; utmost; greatest possible.

Sural, sū'ral, *n.* Pertaining to the calf of the leg.

Surcease, ser·ses', *vi.* To cease; to leave off.—*n.* Cessation; stop: *poetical.*

Surcharge, sér·chärj', *vt.* To overload.—*n.* An excessive load; an overcharge.

Surcingle, sér'sing·gl, *n.* A belt, band, or girth for a horse.

Sure, shör, *a.* Certain; positive; unfailing; stable; secure.—*adv.* Certainly.

Surety, shör'ti, *n.* State of being sure; certainty; security; one who gives security; a bail.

Surf, sérf, *n.* The swell of the sea which breaks on the shore, rocks, etc.

Surface, sér'fās, *n.* The exterior part of anything that has length and breadth; outside; external appearance.—*a.* Pertaining to the surface; superficial.

Surfeit, sér'fit, *n.* An overloading of the stomach; disgust caused by excess; satiety.—*vt.* and *i.* To feed to excess; to nauseate; to cloy.

Surge, sérj, *n.* The swelling of a wave; a large wave; a rolling swell of water.—*vi.* (surging, surged). To swell; to rise high and roll, as waves.

Surgeon, sér'jon, *n.* A medical man who treats diseases or injuries of the body by manual operation.

Surgery, sér'je·ri, *n.* The operative branch of medical practice; a doctor's consulting room and dispensary.

Surly, sér'li, *a.* Gloomily sour or morose; churlish; boisterous; dismal.

Surmise, sér·mīz', *n.* A supposition; conjecture; speculation.—*vt.* (surmising, surmised). To guess; to imagine; to suspect.

Surmount, sér·mount', *vt.* To mount or rise above; to overcome.

Surname, sér'nām, *n.* The family name of an individual.—*vt.* To give a surname to.

Surpass, sér·päs', *vt.* To go beyond; to excel; to outdo.

Surplus, sér'plus, *n.* and *a.* Excess beyond what is required; balance.

Surprise, sér·prīz', *n.* Act of coming upon unawares, or of taking suddenly; emotion excited by something unexpected; astonishment.—*vt.* (surprising, surprised). To fall upon unexpectedly; to take unawares; to astonish.

Surrealism, sér·ē'al·izm, *n.* A form of art which claims to express the unconscious mind.

Surrender, sér·ren'dér, *vt.* To deliver up; to yield to another; to resign; to relinquish.—*vi.* To yield.—*n.* Act of surrendering; a yielding or giving up.

Surreptitious, sér·rep·ti'shus, *a.* Done by stealth; clandestine; underhand.

Surrogate, su'rō·gāt, *n.* The deputy of a bishop or his chancellor.

Surround, sér·round', *vt.* To be round about; to encompass; to invest.

Surtax, sér'taks, *n.* A tax heightened for a particular purpose; an extra tax.

Surveillance, sér·vāl'yans, *n.* A keeping watch over; superintendence; oversight.

Survey, sér·vā', *vt.* To oversee; to examine; to measure and value, as land, etc.; to determine the boundaries, natural features, etc., of.—*n.* sér'vā or sér·vā'. A general view; examination; determination or account of topographical particulars.

Surveying, sér·vā'ing, *n.* The art or practice of measuring and delineating portions of the earth's surface.

Survival, sér·viv'al, *n.* A living beyond the life of another person, thing, or event; old habit, belief, etc., existing merely from custom.

Survive, sér·viv', *vt.* (surviving, survived). To outlive; to live beyond the life of; to outlast.—*vi.* To live after another or after anything else.

Susceptible, sus·sep'ti·bl, *a.* Capable of admitting any change of influence; impressible; sensitive.

Suspect, sus·pekt', *vt.* To imagine as existing; to mistrust; to imagine to be guilty; to doubt.—*vi.* To have suspicion.—*n.* sus'pekt. A suspected person.

Suspend, sus·pend', *vt.* To hang; to cause to cease for a time; to debar temporarily; to stay.

Suspender, sus·pend'ér, *n.* One who suspends; *pl.* braces.

Suspense, sus·pens', *n.* State of being uncertain; indecision; cessation for a time.

Suspension, sus·pen'shon, *n.* Act of suspending; intermission; abeyance; deprivation of office or privileges for a time.

Suspicion, sus·pi'shon, *n.* Act of suspecting; fear of something wrong; mistrust.

Suspicious, sus·pi'shus, *a.* Mistrustful; inclined to suspect; apt to raise suspicion; doubtful.

Sustain, sus·tān', *vt.* To rest under and bear up; to support; to aid effectually; to undergo; to endure; to hold valid; to confirm; to continue.

Sustenance, sus'ten·ans, *n.* Act of sustaining; support; maintenance; food.

Suture, sū'tūr, *n.* A sewing together; a seam; the uniting of the parts of a wound by stitching; seam or joint of the skull.

Swab, swob, *n.* A mop for cleaning floors, decks, etc.—*vt.* (swabbing, swabbed). To clean with a swab.

Swag, swag, *vi.* (swagging, swagged). To sway, as something heavy and pendent; to sag.

Swagger, swag'ér, *vi.* To strut; to bluster.—*n.* Pretentious strut; bluster.

Swallow, swol'ō, *vt.* To receive through the gullet

into the stomach; to ingulf; to absorb; to believe readily; to put up with.—*n*. The gullet; voracity; capacity of swallowing; a small migratory bird.

Swamp, swomp, *n*. A piece of wet spongy land; a fen; a bog.—*vt*. To sink in a swamp; to overwhelm; to overset or fill, as a boat in water.

Swan, swon, *n*. A long-necked web-footed bird of the duck family.

Swap, swop, *vt*. (swapping, swapped). To barter; to exchange.—*n*. An exchange.

Swarm, swarm, *n*. A large body of small insects; a multitude.—*vi*. To depart from a hive in a body; to crowd; to abound; to climb a tree, pole, etc., by clasping it with the arms and legs.

Swarthy, swarth'i, *a*. Being of a dark hue or dusky complexion; tawny; black.

Swash-buckler, swosh-buk-lèr, *n*. A swaggering fellow; a bravo; a bully.

Swastika, swas'tik-a, *n*. An ancient Aryan symbol adopted by Nazi Germany. It consists of a cross with arms of equal length, each arm having a prolongation at right angles. It was intended to represent the sun.

Swath, swath or swäth, *n*. A line of mown grass or grain; track formed by mowing; sweep of a scythe in mowing.

Swathe, swāTH, *vt*. (swathing, swathed). To bind with a bandage; to swaddle.—*n*. A bandage.

Sway, swā, *vi*. To swing or vibrate; to incline; to govern.—*vt*. To swing; to wield; to bias; to influence; to rule.—*n*. Swing or sweep; preponderance; power; rule; ascendency.

Swear, swār, *vt*. and *t*. (swearing, pret. swore, pp. sworn). To make a solemn declaration, with an appeal to God for its truth; to make promise upon oath; to cause to take an oath; to curse.

Sweat, swet, *n*. The moisture which comes out upon the skin; labor; moisture resembling sweat.—*vi*. (pret. and pp. sweated or sweat). To emit sweat or moisture; to toil.—*vt*. To exude; to cause to perspire; to employ at starvation wages.

Sweater, swet'èr, *n*. A heavy woollen jersey.

Sweep, swēp, *vt*. (sweeping, swept). To rub over with a brush; to carry with a long swinging motion; to drive off in numbers at a stroke.—*vi*. To pass with swiftness and violence; to pass with pomp; to move with a long reach.—*n*. Reach of a stroke, etc.; range; rapid survey; a curve; one who sweeps chimneys.

Sweeping, swēp'ing, *a*. Wide and comprehensive in scope.

Sweepstake, Sweepstakes, swēp'stāk, swēp'stāks, *n*. A prize made up of several stakes.

Sweet, swēt, *a*. Agreeable to the taste or senses; having the taste of honey or sugar; fragrant; melodious; beautiful; not salt or sour; gentle.—*n*. A sweet substance; a bonbon; a word of endearment.

Sweetheart, swēt'härt, *n*. A lover, male or female.

Swell, swel, *vi*. (pp. swelled or swollen). To grow larger; to heave; to bulge out; to increase.—*vt*. To expand or increase; to puff up.—*n*. Act of swelling; gradual increase; a rise of ground; a wave or surge; an arrangement in an organ for regulating the intensity of the sound; an important person; a dandy.

Swelling, swel'ing, *a*. Tumid; turgid.—*n*. A tumor; a protuberance.

Swelter, swel'tèr, *vi*. To be overcome with heat; to perspire.—*vt*. To oppress with heat.

Swerve, swèrv, *vi*. (swerving, swerved). To deviate; to turn aside; to waver.

Swift, swift, *a*. Speedy; rapid; fleet; ready; prompt.—*n*. A bird like the swallow.

Swig, swig, *vt*. and *i*. (swigging, swigged). To drink in large gulps.—*n*. A large draft.

Swill, swil, *vi*. To swallow large drafts; to drink greedily.—*n*. Drink taken in large quantities; liquid food given to swine.

Swim, swim, *vi*. (swimming, pret. swam, swum, pp. swum). To float; to move through water by

the motion of the limbs or fins; to be flooded; to be dizzy.—*vt*. To pass by swimming.—*n*. Act of swimming; distance swum; air-bladder of fishes.

Swimming, swim'ing, *n*. The act or art of moving on the water by means of the limbs; a dizziness or giddiness in the head.

Swindle, swin'dl, *vt*. (swindling, swindled). To cheat; to defraud deliberately.—*n*. A scheme to dupe people out of money; fraud.

Swine, swin, *n. sing.* and *pl.* A hog; a pig; a sow or boar; *pl*. hogs collectively.

Swing, swing, *vi*. (swinging, swung). To move to and fro, as a body suspended; to turn round at anchor; to be hanged.—*vt*. To make to oscillate; to brandish.—*n*. Sweep of a body; swinging gait; apparatus for persons to swing in; free course.

Swingeing, swinj'ing, *a*. Great; large; excessive.

Swipe, swip, *vt*. and *i*. (swiping, swiped). To strike with a sweeping blow.—*n*. A sweeping blow.

Swirl, swèrl, *vi*. To form eddies; to whirl in eddies.—*n*. An eddy.

Swish, swish, *vt*. To swing or brandish; to lash.—*n*. A sound as of a switch in the air, a scythe in cutting grass, etc.

Switch, swich, *n*. A small flexible twig or rod; a movable rail at junctions; a device for changing the course of an electric current.—*vt*. To strike with a switch; to shunt.

Swivel, swi'vel, *n*. A link in a chain partly consisting of a pivot turning in a hole in the next link; a fastening that allows the thing fastened to turn round freely.—*vi*. (swivelling, swivelled). To turn on a swivel.

Swoon, swön, *vi*. To faint.—*n*. A fainting fit; a faint; syncope.

Swoop, swöp, *vi*. To dart upon prey suddenly; to stoop.—*vt*. To take with a swoop.—*n*. The pouncing of a bird on its prey; a falling on and seizing.

Sword, sörd, *n*. A military weapon consisting of a long steel blade and a hilt, used for thrusting or cutting; the emblem of justice, authority, war, or destruction; the military profession.

Swordsman, sördz'man, *n*. A man who carries a sword; a man skilled in the sword.

Sworn, swörn, *p.a.* Bound by oath; having taken an oath; closely bound.

Sybarite, sib'a-rit, *n*. A person devoted to luxury and pleasure.

Sycamore, si'ka-mör, *n*. A fruit-tree of the fig family; a maple naturalized in Britain; the plane-tree of America.

Sycophancy, si'kö-fan-si, *n*. Obsequious flattery; servility.

Sycophant, si'kö-fant, *n*. A servile hanger-on of great people; a parasite; mean flatterer.

Syllabary, sil'a-ba-ri, *n*. A catalogue of the primitive syllables of a language.

Syllable, sil'la-bi, *n*. A sound or combination of sounds uttered with one effort; the smallest expressive element of language.—*vt*. To articulate.

Sylph, silf, *n*. A fabulous aerial spirit; a woman of graceful and slender proportions.

Sylvan, sil'van, *a*. Pertaining to a wood; wooded; rural.

Sylviculture, sil-vi-kul'tūr, *n*. The culture of forest trees; arboriculture.

Symbol, sim'bol, *n*. A sign; an emblem; a type; a figure; an attribute; a creed or summary of articles of religion.

Symbolism, sim'bol-izm, *n*. The attributing to things a symbolic meaning; meaning expressed by symbols; use of symbols.

Symbolize, sim'bol-īz, *vt*. To represent by a symbol; to typify; to treat as symbolic.—*vi*. To express or represent in symbols.

Symmetrical, sim-met'rik-al, *a*. Having symmetry; proportional in all its parts; finely or regularly made.

Symmetry, sim'me-tri, *n*. Due proportion of parts

or elements; harmony; correspondence of arrangement.

Sympathetic, Sympathetical, sim-pa-thet'ik, sim-pa-thet'ik-al, *a.* Able to participate in the sorrows and joy of others; compassionate.

Sympathize, sim'pa-thīz, *vi.* (sympathizing, sympathized). To have sympathy; to feel in consequence of what another feels; to condole; to harmonize.

Sympathy, sim'pa-thi, *n.* Fellow-feeling; compassion; agreement of inclinations; correspondence of sensations or affections.

Symphonist, sim-fo'nist, *n.* A composer of symphonies.

Symphony, sim'fo-ni, *n.* Unison of sound; a musical composition for a full orchestra.

Symposium, sim-pō'zi-um, *n.*; pl. **-ia.** A merry feast; a convivial party; a discussion by different writers in a periodical.

Symptom, sim'tom, *n.* That which indicates the existence and character of something else; a mark, sign, or token.

Synagogue, sin'a-gog, *n.* A congregation of Jews met for worship; a Jewish place of worship.

Synchronism, sin'kron-izm, *n.* Concurrence of events in time; tabular arrangement of history according to dates.

Synchronize, sin'kron-īz, *vi.* To agree in time.—*vt.* To make to agree in time.

Synclinal, sin-klī'nal, *a.* In *geology,* dipping in opposite directions toward a common line or plane.

Syncopate, sin'ko-pāt, *vt.* To contract by omission of letters from the middle; to prolong a note in music.

Syncretism, sin'krēt-izm, *n.* The attempted blending of irreconcilable principles, as in philosophy or religion.

Syndesmology, sin-des-mol'o-ji, *n.* The department of anatomy that deals with the ligaments.

Syndic, sin'dik, *n.* A magistrate; one chosen to transact business for others.

Syndicate, sin'di-kāt, *n.* A body of syndics; office of a syndic; body of persons associated to promote some enterprise.—*vt.* To form a syndicate or body for the use of.

Synecdoche, sin-ek'do-kē, *n.* A rhetorical figure by which the whole of a thing is put for a part, or a part for the whole.

Syneresis, si-nē're-sis, *n.* The contraction of two syllables into one.

Synod, sin'od, *n.* A council or meeting of ecclesiastics; an ecclesiastical court; a meeting or council in general.

Synonym, sin'ō-nim, *n.* A word having the same signification as another.

Synopsis, sin-op'sis, *n.*; pl. **-ses.** A summary; brief statement of topics; conspectus.

Syntax, sin'taks, *n.* The construction of sentences in grammar; due arrangement of words in sentences.

Synthesis, sin'the-sis, *n.*; pl. **-ses.** The putting of things together to form a whole; composition or combination.

Syphilis, sif'i-lis, *n.* A contagious and hereditary venereal disease.

Syringe, si'rinj, *n.* A tube and piston serving to draw in and expel fluid.—*vt.* (syringing, syringed). To inject by a syringe; to cleanse by injections from a syringe.

Syrup, si'rup, *n.* A strong solution of sugar in water; any sweet thick fluid; the uncrystallizable fluid separated from crystallized sugar in refining.

System, sis'tem, *n.* An assemblage of things forming a connected whole; a complex but ordered whole; the body as a functional unity; a plan or scheme; method.

Systematic, Systematical, sis-tem-at'ik, sis-tem-at'ik-al, *a.* Pertaining to system; methodical.

Systemic, sis-tem'ik, *a.* Pertaining to a system, or to the body as a whole.

Systole, sis'to-lē, *n.* The contraction of the heart

and arteries for driving onwards the blood and carrying on the circulation.

Syzygy, siz'i-ji, *n.* The conjuction or opposition of any two heavenly bodies.

T

Tab, tab, *n.* A small flap or projecting piece.

Tabby, tab'i, *n.* A rich watered silk or other stuff; a cat of a brindled color; a female cat.—*vt.* To water or cause to look wavy.

Tabernacle, tab'ėr-na-kl, *n.* A booth; a temporary habitation; a place of worship; a repository for holy things.—*vi.* To sojourn.

Table, tā'bl, *n.* A thing with a flat surface; an article of furniture having a flat surface; fare or eatables; persons sitting at a table; a syllabus; index; list.—*vt.* (tabling, tabled). To tabulate; to lay on the table.—*a.* Appertaining to a table.

Tableau, tab-lō', *n.*; pl. **Tableaux,** tab-loz'. A picture; a striking group or dramatic scene.

Table d'hôte, tā'bl-dōt, *n.* A common table for guests at a hotel.

Tablet, tab'let, *n.* A small slab for writing on; a slab bearing an inscription; a small flattish cake, as of soap, etc.

Taboo, ta-bö', *n.* The setting of something apart from human contact; prohibition of contact or intercourse.—*vt.* (tabooing, tabooed). To interdict approach to or contact with.

Tabor, tā'bor, *n.* A small drum.—*vt.* To play on a tabor.

Taboret, tā'bor-et, *n.* A small tabor; a frame for embroidery.

Tabular, ta'bū-lėr, *a.* In form of a table; having a flat surface; set in columns.

Tabulate, ta'bū-lāt, *vt.* (tabulating, tabulated). To set down in a table of items.—*a.* Tabular.

Tacit, ta'sit, *a.* Implied, but not expressed in words; silent; unspoken.

Taciturn, ta'si-tėrn, *a.* Habitually silent; not apt to talk or speak.

Tack, tak, *n.* A small nail; a slight fastening; a rope for certain sails; course of a ship as regards the wind; in *Scots law,* a lease.—*vt.* To fasten by tacks; to attach slightly, to append. *vi.* To change the course of a ship so as to have the wind acting from the other side.

Tackle, tak'l, *n.* Gear or apparatus; pulleys and ropes for moving weights; ropes and rigging, etc., of a ship.—*vt.* (tackling, tackled). To supply with tackle; to set vigorously to work upon; to seize.

Tact, takt, *n.* Touch, nice perception or discernment; adroitness in words or actions.

Tactics, tak'tiks, *n.pl.* The science and art of disposing forces in order for battle, and performing evolutions.

Tactile, tak'til, *a.* Capable of being touched or felt; pertaining to the sense of touch.

Tactless, takt'les, *a.* Destitute of tact.

Tadpole, tad'pōl, *n.* The young of the frog in its first state from the spawn.

Tag, tag, *n.* A metallic point to the end of a string; an appendage; catch-word of an actor's speech.—*vt.* (tagging, tagged). To fit with a tag; to tack or join.

Tail, tāl, *n.* The projecting termination of an animal behind; the hinder or inferior part; the reverse of a coin; limited ownership.

Tailor, tā'lor, *n.* One who makes men's outer garments.—*vi.* To practice making men's clothes.

Taint, tānt, *vt.* To defile; to infect; to vitiate.—*vi.* To be infected or corrupted.—*n.* Infection; corruption; a stain; a blemish on reputation.

Take, tāk, *vt.* (taking, pret. took, pp. taken). To receive or accept; to capture; to captivate; to understand; to feel concerning; to employ; to need; to form or adopt; to assume; to note down; to be infected or seized with; to bear; to conduct, carry; to leap over.—*vi.* To direct one's course; to please; to have the intended effect; to admit of being made a portrait of.

Talc, talk, *n.* A magnesian mineral, unctuous to the touch.—*vt.* To rub with talc.

Tale, tāl, *n.* Number counted; reckoning; a story; a narrative.

Talent, ta'lent, *n.* An ancient weight and denomination of money; a special faculty; general mental power; people of high abilities collectively.

Talisman, ta'lis-man, *n.* A charm; a magical figure cut or engraved on stone or metal; something producing extraordinary effects.

Talk, tak, *vi.* To utter words; to converse.—*vt.* To speak; to gain over by persuasion; to discuss.— *n.* Familiar conversation; report; rumor; subject of discourse; discussion.

Tall, tal, *a.* High in stature; lofty; remarkable; extravagant.

Tallow, tal'ō, *n.* The fat of oxen, sheep, etc., melted and separated from the fibrous matter.—*vt.* To smear with tallow.

Tally, tal'i, *n.* A piece of wood on which notches are cut to keep accounts; anything made to suit another.—*vt.* (tallying, tallied). To record on a tally; to make to correspond.—*vi.* To correspond or agree exactly.

Talmud, tal'mud, *n.* The Hebrew civil and canonical laws, traditions, etc.

Talon, ta'lon, *n.* The claw of a bird of prey.

Talus, tā'lus, *n.* The ankle; slope; a sloping heap of broken rocks.

Tamarind, tam'a-rind, *n.* A tropical leguminous tree and its fruit.

Tambour, tam'bör, *n.* A drum; a cylindrical stone, as in a column; a circular frame for embroidery.—*vt.* and *i.* To embroider with a tambour; to work on a tambour frame.

Tambourine, tam-bö-rēn', *n.* A musical instrument of the drum species played on with the hand, and having jingles attached.

Tame, tām, *a.* Having lost its natural wildness; domesticated; spiritless; insipid.—*vt.* (taming, tamed). To make tame; to subdue; to depress.

Tamp, tamp, *vt.* To ram tight with clay, etc.; to stamp or make firm.

Tamper, tam'pèr, *vi.* To meddle or interfere; to influence secretly.

Tan, tan, *vt.* (tanning, tanned). To convert into leather, as skins; to make sunburnt; to flog.—*vi.* To become tanned.—*n.* Bark used for tanning; a yellowish-brown color.—*a.* Like tan in color; tawny.

Tandem, tan'dem, *adv.* With two horses harnessed singly one before the other.—*n.* A wheeled carriage so drawn; a cycle for two persons, one behind the other.

Tang, tang, *n.* A taste; characteristic flavor or property; part of a tool which fits into the handle; tongue of a buckle.

Tangent, tan'jent, *n.* A straight line which touches a circle or curve, but which, when produced, does not cut it.

Tangible, tan'ji-bl, *a.* That may be touched; real actual; evident.

Tangle, tang'gl, *vt.* (tangling, tangled). To unite confusedly; to involve; to complicate.—*n.* A confused knot of threads, etc.; an embarrassment; a species of sea-weed.

Tank, tangk, *n.* A storage vessel to contain liquids or gas; a reservoir; an armored car with caterpillar wheels, protected by guns fired from inside.

Tankard, tang'kärd, *n.* A large drinking vessel, often with a cover.

Tanner, tan'ėr, *n.* One who tans hides, or converts them into leather by the use of tan.

Tannic, tan'ik, *a.* Applied to an acid in oak, gall-nuts, etc., the efficient substance in tanning.

Tantalize, tan'ta-līz, *vt.* (tantalizing, tantalized). To torment by presenting something desirable which cannot be attained; to excite by hopes that are never realized.

Tantamount, tan'ta-mount, *a.* Equal; equivalent in value, force, or effect.

Tantrum, tan'trum, *n.* A fit of ill-humor; display of temper; chiefly in *pl.*

Tap, tap, *n.* A plug to stop a hole in a cask; a spigot; a faucet; a gentle blow; a pat.—*vt.* (tapping, tapped). To broach, as a cask; to draw liquid from; to strike gently.—*vi.* To strike a gentle blow.

Tape, tāp, *n.* A narrow strip of woven work, used for strings and the like.

Tape-line, Tape-measure, tāp'līn, tāp'me-zhür, *n.* A tape marked with feet, inches, etc., used in measuring.

Taper, tā'pėr, *n.* A long wick coated with wax; a small light; tapering form; gradual diminution of thickness.—*vi.* To become gradually smaller.—*vt.* To cause to taper.

Tapestry, ta'pes-tri, *n.* A kind of rich woven hangings of wool and silk, with pictorial representations.—*vt.* To adorn with tapestry.

Tape-worm, tāp'wėrm, *n.* A parastic worm found in the intestines of animals.

Tapioca, tap-i-ō'ka, *n.* A farinaceous substance prepared from cassava meal.

Tap-room, tap'röm, *n.* A room in which beer is served from the tap.

Tap-root, tap'röt, *n.* Main root of a plant.

Tar, tär, *n.* A thick, dark, viscid substance obtained from pine or fir, coal, shale, etc.; a sailor.—*vt.* (tarring, tarred). To smear with tar.

Tarantula, ta-ran'tū-la, *n.* A kind of spider found in S. Italy; the dance tarantella.

Tardy, tär'di, *a.* Slow; dilatory; late; backward; reluctant.

Target, tär'get, *n.* A small circular shield; a mark shot at in rifle practice, etc.

Tariff, ta'rif, *n.* A list of goods with the duties to be paid; a list of charges generally.

Tarnish, tär'nish, *vt.* To sully; to dim.—*vi.* To lose luster.—*n.* A spot; soiled state.

Tarpaulin, Tarpauling, tä4r-pa'lin, tär-pa'ling, *n.* Canvas covered with tar.

Tarry, ta'ri, *vi.* (tarrying, tarried). To stay; to delay.—*vt.* To wait for.

Tarsia, tär'si-a, *n.* A kind of Italian marquetry, representing landscapes, flowers, etc.

Tarsus, tär'sus, *n.*; pl. **-si.** The ankle or ankle-joint.

Tart, tärt, *a.* Sharp to the taste; sour; acid; severe; snappish.—*n.* A species of pastry, consisting of fruit baked in paste.

Tartan, tär'tan, *n.* Cloth woven in colors in a checkered pattern; a Mediterranean vessel somewhat resembling a sloop.—*a.* Consisting of or resembling tartan.

Tartar, tär'tar, *n.* A native of Tartary; a very irascible or rigorous person; a shrew; a reddish crust deposited by wine on casks; a concretion formed on the teeth.

Task, täsk, *n.* A piece of work imposed by another or requiring to be done; burdensome employment; toil.—*vt.* To impose a task upon.

Tassel, tas'el, *n.* An ornament consisting of a knob with hanging threads.—*vi.* (tasseling, tasseled). To put forth a tassel or flower, as maize.—*vt.* To adorn with tassels.

Taste, tāst, *vt.* (tasting, tasted). To test by the tongue and palate; to perceive the flavor of; to experience; to partake of.—*vi.* To make trial by the tongue and palate; to have a flavor; to have experience.—*n.* Act of tasting; sense of tasting; flavor; intellectual relish or discernment; manner or style.

Tasty, tāst'i, *a.* Having or showing good taste; tasteful; palatable; nice; fine.

Tatter, tat'ėr, *n.* A rag or part torn and hanging to the thing.

Tatting, tat'ing, *n.* A kind of crochet, made with a shuttle-shaped needle.

Tattle, tat'l, *vi.* (tattling, tattled). To talk idly; to gossip.—*n.* Prate; idle talk.

Tattoo, tat-tö', *n.* A beat of drum and bugle-call at

night, calling soldiers to their quarters.—*vt.* and *i.* To prick the skin and stain the punctured spot with colors.

Taunt, tant, *vt.* To reproach with severe or sarcastic words; to upbraid.—*n.* A bitter or sarcastic reproach.

Taurus, ta'rus, *n.* The Bull, one of the twelve signs of the zodiac.

Taut, tat, *a.* Tight; not slack.

Tautology, ta-tol'o-ji, *n.* Needless repetition of the same meaning in different words.

Tavern, ta'vern, *n.* A house where liquors are sold; an inn.

Taw, ta, *vt.* To make into white leather for gloves, etc., by treating skins with alum, salt, and other matters.—*n.* A marble to be played with; a game at marbles.

Tawdry, ta'dri, *a.* Tastelessly ornamental; cheap and showy.

Tawery, ta'e-ri, *n.* A place where skins are tawed or treated with alum, etc.

Tax, taks, *n.* A contribution levied by authority; a rate, duty, or impost charged on income or property; a burdensome duty; an exaction.—*vt.* To impose a tax on; to put to a certain effort; to accuse.

Taxation, taks-ā'shon, *n.* Act of levying taxes; the aggregate of taxes.

Taxicab, Taxi, tak'si-kab, tak'si, *n.* An automobile provided with a meter which shows distance run and fare due.

Taxidermy, tak'si-dėr-mi, *n.* The art of stuffing animals, or of preserving the skins.

Taxonomy, tak-son'o-mi, *n.* That department of natural history which treats of the laws and principles of classification.

Tea, tē, *n.* The dried leaves of plants cultivated in China, Assam, Ceylon, etc.; the plant itself; a decoction of tea leaves in boiling water; any decoction of vegetables.—*vi.* (teaing, teaed). To take tea.

Teach, tēch, *vt.* (teaching, taught). To instruct; to inform; to make familiar with.—*vi.* To practice giving instruction.

Teak, tēk, *n.* An E. Indian tree which furnishes hard and valuable timber.

Team, tēm, *n.* A brood; horses or other beasts harnessed together; a side in a game, match, etc.

Tea-pot, tē'pot, *n.* A vessel in which tea is infused.

Tear, tēr, *n.* A drop of the watery fluid appearing in the eyes; any transparent drop.

Tear, tār, *vt.* (pret. tore, pp. torn). To pull in pieces; to rend; to wound; to drag; to pull with violence; to make by rending.—*vi.* To be rent or torn; to rage.—*n.* A rent.

Tease, tēz, *vt.* (teasing, teased). To pull apart the fibers of; to annoy; to torment.

Tea-service, tē'sėr-vis, *n.* A complete set of dishes or utensils for the tea-table.

Teat, tēt, *n.* The projecting part of the female breast; pap; nipple.

Technical, tek'ni-kal, *a.* Pertaining to an art, science, pofession, handicraft, etc.

Technique, tek-nēk', *n.* Method of manipulation in an art; artistic execution.

Technology, tek-nol'o-ji, *n.* The science of the industrial arts.

Tectonic, tek-ton'ik, *a.* Pertaining to building or construction.

Tedious, tē'di-us, *a.* Tiresome; wearisome; irksome; fatiguing; dilatory; tardy.

Tedium, tē'di-um, *n.* Irksomeness.

Tee, tō, *n.* A point of aim or starting-point in certain games, as quoits and golf; a small cone of sand, rubber, etc., on which a golfer places his ball when driving off. *vt.* To place (ball) on tee.

Teem, tēm, *vi.* To bring forth young; to be prolific.—*vt.* To bring forth.

Teens, tēnz, *n.pl.* The years of one's age having the termination *-teen.*

Teethe, tēTH, *vi.* (teething, teethed). To have the teeth growing or cutting the gums.

Teetotaler, Teetotaller, tē'tō-tal-ėr, *n.* A total abstainer from intoxicants.

Tegular, teg'ū-lėr, *a.* Resembling a tile; consisting of tiles.

Tegument, teg'ū-ment, *n.* A cover or covering; an integument.

Telegram, tel'e-gram, *n.* A communication sent by telegraph.

Telegraph, tel'e-graf, *n.* Any apparatus for transmitting messages to a distance; an apparatus for transmitting messages along a wire by electricity, but now also wireless.—*vt.* To convey or announce by telegraph.

Telemeter, te-lem'et-er, *n.* A range-finder or similar instrument; an instrument to transmit variations marked by some physical instrument.

Teleology, tel-ē-ol'o-ji, *n.* The science or doctrine of final causes.

Telepathy, te-lep'a-thi or tel'e-path-i, *n.* Occult communication between persons at some distance.

Telephone, tel'e-fōn, *n.* An instrument transmitting sound to a distance by means of electricity and telegraph wires.—*vt.* (telephoning, telephoned). To transmit by means of the telephone.

Telescope, tel'e-skōp, *n.* An optical instrument for viewing distant objects.—*vt.* (telescoping, telescoped). To drive the parts of into each other, like the joints of a telescope.

Television, tel'e-vizh'un, *n.* Radio transmission of scenes or pictures so that they can be received at a distance (on a cathode ray tube screen).

Tell, tel, *vt.* (telling, told). To number; to relate; to disclose; to explain; to distinguish; to inform; to bid.—*vi.* To give an account; to take effect.

Teller, tel'ėr, *n.* One who tells; an officer of a bank who receives and pays money; one appointed to count votes.

Telling, tel'ing, *p.a.* Having great effect.

Tell-tale, tel'tāl, *a.* Telling tales; blabbing; serving to betray; informative.—*n.* One who discloses private concerns, or what he should suppress.

Tellurian, tel-ū'ri-an, *a.* Pertaining to the earth.— *n.* An inhabitant of the earth.

Tellurium, tel-ū'ri-um, *n.* A non-metallic element of a tin-white crystalline appearance.

Temerarious, tem-ē-rā'ri-us, *a.* Reckless.

Temerity, tē-me'ri-ti, *n.* Contempt of danger; extreme boldness; rashness.

Temper, tem'pėr, *vt.* To proportion duly; to moderate; to form to a proper hardness.—*n.* Due mixture; disposition of the mind; temperament; irritation; state of a metal as to its hardness; medium.

Temperament, tem'pėr-a-ment, *n.* Due mixture of qualities; combined mental and physical constitution; disposition.

Temperance, tem'pėr-ans, *n.* Moderation in indulgence of the natural appetites; sobriety; abstinence from intoxicants.

Temperature, tem'pėr-a-tūr, *n.* State with regard to heat or cold; climatic heat.

Tempered, tem'pėrd, *a.* Having a certain disposition or temper; disposed.

Tempest, tem'pest, *n.* A violent storm; hurricane; violent tumult or commotion.

Tempestuous, tem-pest'ū-us, *a.* Very stormy; turbulent; subject to storms of passion.

Temple, tem'pl, *n.* A place of worship; a church; part of the head between the forehead and the ear.

Templet, Template, tem'plet, tem'plāt, *n.* A board whose edge is shaped so as to serve as a guide in making an article with a corresponding contour.

Tempo, tem'pō, *n.* The time of a piece of music; musical time.

Temporal, tem'pō-ral, *a.* Pertaining to time; pertaining to this life; not spiritual or ecclesiastical, secular; pertaining to the temples of the head.—*n*. Anything temporal or secular; a temporality.

Temporarily, tem'pō-ra-ri-li, *adv*. For a time only; provisionally.

Temporary, tem'pō-ra-ri, *a*. Lasting but for a time; transient; provisional.

Temporize, tem'pō-rīz, *vi*. To comply with the time or occasion; to trim.

Tempt, temt, *vt*. To incite to an evil act; to provoke; to entice; to put to a test.

Temptation, tem-tā'shon, *n*. Act of tempting; state of being tempted; enticement to evil; an allurement.

Tempting, temt'ing, *p.a.* Adapted to tempt; attractive; seductive.

Temulence, tem'ū-lens, *n*. Drunkenness.

Ten, ten, *a*. and *n*. Twice five; nine and one.

Tenable, te'na-bl, *a*. That may be held or maintained.

Tenacious, te-nā'shus, *a*. Holding fast; retentive; adhesive; stubborn.

Tenacity, te-nas'i-ti, *n*. State or quality of being tenacious; adhesiveness; glutinousness; toughness; cohesiveness.

Tenancy, te'nan-si, *n*. A holding lands or tenements as a tenant; tenure.

Tenant, te'nant, *n*. One who occupies lands or houses for which he pays rent.—*vt*. To hold as a tenant.—*vi*. To live as a tenant; to dwell.

Tend, tend, *vi*. To move in or have a certain direction; to conduce; to attend.—*vt*. To attend; to guard; to take care of.

Tendency, ten'den-si, *n*. Inclination; leaning; bent; proneness.

Tender, ten'dėr, *n*. One who attends; a small vessel employed to attend on a larger one; a carriage with fuel, etc., attached to a locomotive; an offer of money or service; an estimate; thing offered.—*vt*. To present for acceptance.—*a*. Fragile; delicate; compassionate; kind.

Tenderly, ten'dėr-li, *adv*. In a tender manner; with tenderness; mildly; fondly.

Tendinous, ten'din-us, *a*. Pertaining to a tendon; full of tendons; sinewy.

Tendon, ten'don, *n*. A sinew; a hard, insensible cord or bundle of fibers by which a muscle is attached to a bone.

Tendril, ten'dril, *n*. A slender, twining growth, by which a plant adheres to something.

Tenebrosity, te-nē-bros'i-ti, *n*. Darkness.

Tenement, te'nē-ment, *n*. An abode; a habitation; a block of buildings divided into separate houses.

Tenet, te'net, *n*. A doctrine, opinion, principle, or dogma.

Tenfold, ten'fōld, *a*. Ten times more.

Tennis, ten'is, *n*. A game in which a ball is driven against a wall, and caused to rebound; in ordinary use, lawn-tennis.

Tenon, ten'on, *n*. The specially shaped end of a piece of wood, etc., to be inserted into the mortise to form a joint.

Tenor, ten'or, *n*. A prevailing course or direction; purport; substance, as of a discourse; the highest of the male adult chest voices; one who sings a tenor part.—*a*. Adapted for singing or playing the tenor.

Tense, tens, *n*. Inflection of a verb to express time.—*a*. Stretched; tight; strained to stiffness; rigid; not lax.

Tension, ten'shon, *n*. Act of stretching; state of being stretched; tightness; strain; intensity; elastic force.

Tensor, ten'sor, *n*. A muscle that extends or stretches the part to which it is fixed.

Tent, tent, *n*. A portable shelter consisting of some flexible covering; a roll of lint, etc., to dilate a sore.—*vi*. To lodge in a tent.—*vt*. To supply with tents; to probe; to keep open with a tent, as a sore.

Tentacle, ten'ta-kl, *n. sing*. and *pl*. A filiform organ of various animals, used for prehension or as a feeler.

Tentative, ten'ta-tiv, *a*. Experimental; empirical.—*n*. An essay; a trial.

Tenter, ten'tėr, *n*. A machine for stretching cloth; a tenter-hook; a person in a manufactory who looks after machines.—*vt*. To hang or stretch on tenters.

Tenth, tenth, *a*. Next after the ninth.—*n*. One of ten equal parts.

Tenuity, ten-ū'i-ti, *n*. State of being thin or fine; thinness; slenderness; rarity.

Tenuous, ten'ū-us, *a*. Thin; slender.

Tenure, ten'ūr, *n*. A holding or manner of holding real estate; condition of occupancy; manner of possessing in general.

Tepid, te'pid, *a*. Moderately warm; lukewarm.

Teratology, ter-a-tol'o-ji, *n*. The science of monsters or malformations.

Tercentenary, tėr-sen'ten-a-ri, *a*. Comprising three hundred years.—*n*. The three-hundredth anniversary.

Terebene, ter'ē-bēn, *n*. A liquid hydrocarbon produced by treating oil of turpentine with sulphuric acid.

Terebinth, te'rē-binth, *n*. The turpentine-tree.

Terete, te-rēt', *a*. Cylindrical and smooth; long and round.

Tergal, tėr'gal, *a*. Pertaining to the back.

Term, tėrm, *n*. A limit; boundary; time for which anything lasts; period of session, etc.; day on which rent or interest is paid; a word; a word having a technical meaning; *pl*. conditions; relative position or footing.—*vt*. To name; to call.

Termagant, tėr'ma-gant, *n*. A brawling woman; a shrew; a scold.—*a*. Quarrelsome; shrewish.

Terminal, tėr'min-al, *a*. Pertaining to or forming the end; terminating.—*n*. An extremity; the clamping screw at each end of a voltaic battery.

Terminate, tėr'min-āt, *vt*. and *i*. (terminating, terminated). To bound; to limit; to end.—*a*. Limited.

Terminology, tėr-min-ol'o-ji, *n*. The science or theory of technical or other terms; terms used in any art, science, etc.

Terminus, tėr'mi-nus, *n*.; *pl*. **-ni**. A boundary; a limit; station at the end of a railway, etc.

Termite, tėr'mīt, *n*. A neuropterous insect commonly called the white ant.

Ternary, tėr'na-ri, *a*. Proceeding by threes; consisting of three.

Terra, ter'ra, *n*. Earth; the earth.—**Terra firma,** dry land.

Terrace, te'räs, *n*. A raised level bank of earth; a raised flat area; a row of houses; flat roof of a house.—*vt*. (terracing, terraced). To form into or furnish with a terrace.

Terra-cotta, ter'ra-kot-a, *n*. A kind of pottery, commonly of a reddish color; a work of art in terra-cotta.

Terrapin, te'ra-pin, *n*. A fresh-water tortoise.

Terrene, te-rēn', *a*. Earthly; terrestrial.

Terrestrial, te-res'tri-al, *a*. Pertaining to the earth; mundane; pertaining to land.—*n*. An inhabitant of the earth.

Terrible, te'ri-bl, *a*. Adapted to arouse terror; dreadful; fearful; extraordinary.

Terrify, te'ri-fī, *vt*. (terrifying, terrified). To cause or produce terror in; to alarm.

Territory, te'ri-to-ri, *n*. A definite piece of land under any distinct administration; a dominion; region; country.

Terror, te'ror, *n*. Such fear as agitates body and mind; dread; alarm; cause of fear.

Terrorism, te'ror-izm, *n*. A system of government by terror; intimidation.

Terse, tėrs, *a*. Free from superfluities of language; concise; forcible; pithy.

Tertiary, tėr'shi-a-ri, *a*. Third; applied to the third great division of stratified rocks, resting on the chalk.—*n*. The tertiary system of rocks.

Tessera, tes'e-ra, *n*.; *pl*. **-rae**. A small cube of marble, ivory, etc., used for mosaic work.

Test, test, *n*. A vessel used in trying or refining gold, etc.; a cupel; examination; means of trial; a standard; oath taken before admission to privileges; a hard outer covering.—*vt.* To put to a trial; to refine; to examine; to prove; to attest.

Testaceous, tes-tā'shus, *a.* Having a molluskous shell; pertaining to shell-fish.

Testament, tes'ta-ment, *n.* In *law,* a person's will; (with cap.) one of the two general divisions of the Scriptures.

Testamentary, tes-ta-ment'a-ri, *a.* Pertaining to a will; bequeathed or done by will.

Testate, tes'tāt, *a.* Having left a will.

Testicle, tes'ti-kl, *n.* One of the two glands which secrete the seminal fluid in males.

Testify, tes'ti-fī, *vi.* (testifying, testified). To bear witness; to give evidence.—*vt.* To bear witness to.

Testily, tes'ti-li, *adv.* Irritably; peevishly.

Testimonial, tes-ti-m'ō'ni-al, *n.* A certificate of qualifications; a gift in token of appreciation or esteem.

Testimony, tes'ti-mo-ni, *n.* Witness; evidence; affirmation; attestation; profession; divine revelation; law of God.

Testy, tes'ti, *a.* Fretful; peevish; petulant.

Tetantus, tet'a-nus, *n.* Spasm with rigidity; lockjaw.

Tête-à-tête, tāt-ā-tāt, *adv.* Face to face; in private.—*n.* A private interview or talk.

Tether, teʀн'ėr, *n.* A rope confining a grazing animal with certain limits; scope allowed.—*vt.* To confine with a tether.

Tetrahedron, te-tra-hē'dron, *n.* A solid body having four equal triangles as its faces.

Tetter, tet'ėr, *n.* A cutaneous disease.

Teuton, tū'ton, *n.* A person of Germanic race in the widest sense of the term.

Text, tekst, *n.* An author's own work as distinct from annotations; a passage of Scripture selected as the subject of a discourse; a topic; a large kind of handwriting; particular kind of lettering.

Textile, teks'til, *a.* Woven; capable of being woven.—*n.* A fabric made by weaving.

Textual, teks'tū-al, *a.* Contained in the text; pertaining to the text.

Texture, teks'tūr, *n.* A web; that which is woven; a fabric; manner in which constituent parts are connected; the grain or peculiar character of a solid.

Thalamus, thal'a-mus, *n.*; pl. **-mi.** A large ganglion in the brain; the receptacle of a flower, or part on which the carpels are placed.

Thallus, thal'us, *n.* A solid mass of cells, forming the substance of the thallogens.

Than, тнan, *conj.* A particle used after certain adjectives and adverbs expressing comparison or diversity, as *more, other,* etc.

Thank, thangk, *n.* Expression of gratitude; an acknowledgment of favor or kindness; almost always in *pl.—vt.* To give thanks to; to express gratitude to for a favor.

Thankful, thangk'ful, *a.* Grateful; impressed with a sense of kindness received, and ready to acknowledge it.

Thanksgiving, thangks'giv-ing, *n.* Act of giving thanks; public celebration of divine goodness.

That, тнat, *a.* and *pron.*; pl. **Those,** тнōz. A pronominal adjective pointing to a person or thing mentioned or understood; a demonstrative pronoun; a relative pronoun equivalent to *who* or *which.—conj.* Introducing a reason, purpose, or result, a noun clause, or a wish.

Thatching, thach'ing, *n.* Act or art of covering buildings with thatch; material so used.

Thaumaturgy, tha'ma-tėr-ji, *n.* Miracle-working; magic; logerdemain.

Thaw, tha, *vt.* To melt, as ice or snow; to cease to freeze; to become genial.—*vt.* To melt; to make less cold or reserved.—*n.* The melting of ice or snow; warmth after frost.

The, тнē or тнi, *def. art.* Used before nouns with a specifying or limiting effect; used before adjectives and adverbs in the comparative degree it means by so much.

Theater, thē'a-tėr, *n.* A house for the exhibition of dramatic performances; a place of action; a room for anatomical demonstrations, etc.

Theft, theft, *n.* Act of stealing; unlawful taking of another's goods; thing stolen.

Their, тнāʀ, *pronominal* or *possessive adj.* Pertaining or belonging to them.—**Theirs,** possessive case of *they,* used without a noun.

Theism, thē'izm, *n.* Acknowledgment of the existence of a God; belief in gods.

Them, тнem, *pron.* The dative and objective case of *they*; those persons or things.

Theme, thēm, *n.* A subject or topic; short dissertation by a student; leading subject in a musical composition.

Then, тнen, *adv.* At that time, past or future; soon afterwards.—*conj.* In that case; therefore.

Theocracy, thē-ok'ra-si, *n.* Government by the immediate direction of God; the state thus governed.

Theocrasy, thē-ok'ra-si, *n.* Intimate union of the soul with God in contemplation.

Theodicy, thē-od'i-si, *n.* A vindication of the ways of God in creation; a doctrine as to the providential government of God.

Theology, thē-ol'o-ji, *n.* The science of God and divine things; divinity.

Theophany, thē-of'an-i, *n.* The actual appearing of God to man.

Theorem, thē'ō-rem, *n.* A proposition to be proved by reasoning; a speculative truth.

Theoretic, Theoretical, thē-ō-ret'ik, thē-ō-ret'ik-al, *a.* Pertaining to theory; speculative; not practical.

Theory, thē'ō-ri, *n.* Speculation; hypothesis to explain something; rules or knowledge of an art as distinguished from practice.

Therapeutics, the-ra-pūt'iks, *n.* That part of medicine which deals with the application and operation of remedies.

There, тнāʀ, *adv.* In or at that place; at that point; thither.

Thereabout, Thereabouts, тнāʀ-a-bout', тнāʀ-a-bouts', *adv.* About that; near that place; nearly.

Thereafter, тнāʀ-aft'ėr, *adv.* After that; accordingly; afterward.

Thereby, тнāʀ-bī', *adv.* By that; in consequence of that; near that place; nearly.

Therefore, тнāʀ'for, *adv.* or *conj.* For that or this reason; consequently.

Therein, тнāʀ-in', *adv.* In that or this place, time, thing, or respect.

Thereof, тнāʀ-ov', *adv.* Of that or this.

Thereon, тнāʀ-on', *adv.* On that or this.

Thereupon, тнāʀ-up-on', *adv.* Upon that or this; in consequence of that; immediately.

Theriotomy, thē-ri-ot'o-mi, *n.* The anatomy of animals.

Thermal, Thermic, thėr'mal, thėr'mik, *a.* Pertaining to heat; warm; hot.

Thermograph, Thermometrograph, thėr'mōgraf, thėr'mō-met-ro-graf, *n.* An instrument for recording variations of temperature.

Thermometer, thėr-mom'et-ėr, *n.* An instrument for measuring temperature.

Thermotics, thėr-mot'iks, *n.* The science of heat.

Thesaurus, the-sa'rus, *n.* A treasury; a lexicon.

These, тнēz, *pronominal adj.* Pl. of this.

Thesis, thē'sis, *n.*; pl. **-ses.** A proposition which a person advances; a theme; an essay written for a candidate for a degree.

Thespian, thes'pi-an, *a.* Relating to dramatic acting.

Theurgy, thē'ėr-ji, *n.* The working of a divine agency in human affairs.

Thews, thūz, *n.pl.* Muscles; sinews; strength.

They, тнā, *pron. pl.* The plural of *he, she,* or *it*; sometimes used indefinitely.

Thick, thik, *a.* Having extent measured through; dense; foggy; crowded; close; stupid; gross.—*n.* The thickest part.—*adv.* In close succession; fast or close together.

Thickening, thik'n-ing, *n.* Something put into a

liquid or mass to make it more thick.

Thicket, thik'et, *n.* A wood or collection of trees or shrubs closely set.

Thickness, thik'nes, *n.* Measure through and through; thick part; denseness.

Thickset, thik'set, *a.* Thickly planted; stout; stumpy.—*n.* A close hedge; dense underwood.

Thick-skinned, thik'skind, *a.* Having a thick skin or rind; callous; insensible.

Thief, thēf, *n.*; pl. **Thieves,** thēvz. A person who steals or is guilty of theft.

Thigh, thī, *n.* The thick part of the leg above the knee; the femur.

Thimble, thim'bl, *n.* A metal cover for the finger in sewing.

Thimble-rig, thim'bl-rig, *n.* A sleight-of-hand trick with three thimbles and a pea.

Thine, ᴛʜīn, *prominal, adj., poss.* of *thou.* Thy; belonging to thee.

Thing, *n.* Whatever may be thought of or spoken of; any separate entity; a creature; matter, circumstance, event; *pl.* clothes, personal belongings, etc.

Think, thingk, *vi.* (thinking, thought). To have the mind occupied on some subject; to judge; to intend; to imagine; to consider.—*vt.* To imagine; to believe; to consider.

Thinking, thingk'ing, *p.a.* Having the faculty of thought; cogitative.—*n.* Act or state of one who thinks; thought.

Thin-skinned, thin'skind, *a.* Having a thin skin; unduly sensitive; irritable.

Third, thėrd, *a.* The next after the second; being one of three equal parts.—*n.* The third part of anything.

Thirst, thėrst, *n.* The desire or distress occasioned by want of water; eager desire after anything.—*vi.* To feel thirst; to desire vehemently.

Thirteen, thėr'tēn, *a.* and *n.* Ten and three.

Thirteenth, thėr'tēnth, *a.* The third after the tenth.—One of thirteen equal parts.

Thirtieth, thėr'ti-eth, *a.* The next after the twenty-ninth.—One of thirty equal parts.

Thirty, thėr'ti, *a.* and *n.* Thrice ten.

This, ᴛʜis, *a.* and *pron.*; pl. **These,** ᴛʜēz. A demonstrative, used with or without a noun, referring to something present, near, or just ended.

Thistle, this'l, *n.* A prickly composite plant, the national emblem of Scotland.

Thong, thong, *n.* A strap of leather, used for fastening anything.

Thorax, thōraks, *n.*; pl. **-races.** That part of the human body which contains the lungs, heart, etc.; the chest.

Thorn, thorn, *n.* A tree or shrub armed with spines or prickles; a prickle; anything troublesome.

Thorough, thu'rō, *a.* Passing through or to the end; complete; perfect.

Thorough-bred, thu'rō-bred, *a.* Bred from pure and unmixed blood, as horses; completely bred or accomplished; high-spirited.—*n.* An animal of pure blood.

Thoroughfare, thu'rō-fār, *n.* A passage through; unobstructed way; power of passing.

Those, ᴛʜōz, *a.* and *pron.* Pl. of *that.*

Thou, ᴛʜou, *pron.* The second personal pronoun singular: in ordinary language supplanted by the plural form *you.*

Though, ᴛʜō, *conj.* Granting it to be the fact that; notwithstanding that; if.—*adv.* However.

Thought, that, *n.* The power or act of thinking; idea; opinion; judgment; notion; purpose; contemplation; care; concern.

Thoughtful, that'ful, *a.* Full of thought; meditative; careful; considerate; anxious.

Thousand, thou'zand, *a.* and *n.* Ten hundred; a great number indefinitely.

Thraldom, thral'dom, *n.* Bondage.

Thrash, Thresh, thrash, thresh, *vt.* To beat out the grain or seeds from; to beat soundly; to drub.

Thrashing, Threshing, thrash'ing, thresh'ing, *n.* Act of beating out grain; a sound drubbing.

Thread, thred, *n.* A fine cord; any fine filament; prominent spiral part of a screw; continued course or tenor; general purpose.—*vt.* To pass a thread through; to pass or pierce through.

Threadbare, thred'bār, *a.* Having the nap worn off; worn out; trite; hackneyed.

Threat, thret, *n.* A menace; declaration of intention to punish or hurt.

Threaten, thret'n, *vt.* To use threats towards; to menace; to show to be impending.—*vi.* To use threats.

Three, thrē, *a.* and *n.* Two and one.

Threefold, thrē'fōld, *a.* Consisting of three in one; triple.—*adv.* Trebly.

Three-ply, thrē'plī, *a.* Threefold; consisting of three strands, as cord, yarn, etc.

Threescore, thrē'skōr, *a.* Three times a score; sixty.

Threnetic, thren-et'ik, *a.* Mournful.

Threnody, thren'o-di, *n.* A song of lamentation; a dirge.

Threshold, Thresh'ōld, *n.* The stone or piece of timber which lies under a door; a doorsill; entrance; outset.

Thrift, thrift, *n.* Frugality; economy; sea-pink.

Thrifty, thrift'i, *a.* Characterized by thrift; frugal; economical.

Thrill, thril, *vt.* To send a quiver through; to affect with a keen tingling.—*vi.* To quiver; to move tremulously.—*n.* A warbling; thrilling sensation.

Thrips, thrips, *n.* A minute insect, destructive to wheat.

Thrive, thrīv, *vi.* (thriving, pret. throve, pp. thriven). To prosper; to grow vigorously; to flourish.

Throat, thrōt, *n.* The fore part of the neck of an animal; the opening downward at the back of the mouth.

Throb, throb, *vi.* (throbbing, throbbed). To beat, as the heart, with unusual force or rapidity; to palpitate.—*n.* A beat or strong pulsation.

Throe, thrō, *n.* Extreme pain; anguish of travail in childbirth.—*vi.* (throeing, throed). To struggle in extreme pain.

Thrombosis, throm'bō-sis, *n.* The obstruction of a blood-vessel by a clot of blood.

Thrombus, throm'bus, *n.* A clot of blood.

Throne, thrōn, *n.* The seat of a king or ruler; sovereign power and dignity.—*vt.* (throning, throned). To place on a royal seat; to enthrone; to exalt.

Throng, throng, *n.* A crowd; a great number.—*vi.* and *t.* To crowd or press together.

Throttle, throt'l, *n.* The windpipe or trachea; the throat; the gullet.—*vt.* (throttling, throttled). To choke; to strangle.

Through, thrō, *prep.* From end to end of; by means of; on account of; throughout.—*adv.* From end to end; to completion.—*a.* Going with little or no interruption from one place to another.

Throughout, thrō-out', *prep.* Quite through; in every part of.—*adv.* In every part.

Throw, thrō, *vt.* (pret. threw, pp. thrown). To fling or cast; to propel; to twist filaments of together; to venture at dice; to shed; to utter; to overturn.—*vi.* To cast; to case dice.—*n.* Act of one who throws; a cast; distance to which a thing is thrown; ventured.

Throw-back, thrō'bak, *n.* Reversion to an ancestral or earlier type; atavism.

Thrush, thrush, *n.* A singing bird; a disease affecting the lips and mouth; also a disease in the feet of the horse.

Thrust, thrust, *vt.* (pret. and pp. thrust). To push or drive with force; to shove; to stab; to obtrude (oneself).—*vi.* To make a push; to make a lunge with a weapon; to intrude.—*n.* A violent push; a stab; a horizontal outward pressure.

Thud, thud, *n.* The dull sound of a blow; a blow

causing a dull sound.

Thumb, thum, *n.* The short thick finger of the hand.—*vt.* To soil or handle awkwardly with the fingers.

Thump, thump, *n.* A dull, heavy blow; sound made by such a blow.—*vt.* and *i.* To strike with something thick or heavy.

Thunder, thund'dèr, *n.* The sound which follows lightning; any loud noise.—*vi.* To emit the sound of thunder; to make a loud noise.—*vt.* To emit with noise and terror; to publish, as any denunciation.

Thunderbolt, thun'dèr-bōlt, *n.* A shaft of lightning; a daring hero; a fulmination.

Thundering, thun'dèr ing, *a.* Producing or accompanied by a noise like thunder; extraordinary or excessive.

Thunder-storm, thun'dèr-storm, *n.* A storm accompanied with thunder.

Thursday, thèrz'dā, *n.* The fifth day of the week.

Thus, THUS, *adv.* In this manner; to this degree or extent; accordingly.

Thwack, thwak, *vt.* To strike, bang, beat.—*n.* A heavy blow; a bang.

Thwart, thwart, *a.* Transverse; being across.—*vt.* To cross; to frustrate or defeat.—*n.* The bench on which the rowers sit, athwart the boat.

Thyme, tim, *n.* A small aromatic shrub.

Tiara, ti-a'ra, *n.* An ornament worn on the head, the pope's triple crown.

Tibia, tib'i-a, *n.* A kind of ancient musical pipe; the shin-bone.

Tic, tik, *n.* Facial neuralgia.

Tick, tik, *vi.* To make a small noise by beating, etc.—*vt.* To mark with a tick or dot.—*n.* A small distinct noise; a small dot; a small parasitical mite; cover continaining the feathers, etc., of a bed; credit.

Ticket, tik'et, *n.* A label; a card or paper enabling one to enter a place, travel in a railway, etc.—*vt.* To put a ticket on; to label.

Ticking, tik'ing, *n.* A striped closely-woven cloth containing the feathers, etc., of beds.

Tickle, tik'l, *vt.* (tickling, tickled). To touch and cause a peculiar thrilling sensation in; to please; to flatter; to puzzle.

Ticklish, tik'lish, *a.* Easily tickled; touchy; liable to be overthrown; difficult; critical.

Tide, tid, *n.* Time; season; the rising and falling of the sea; flow; current.—*vt.* or *i.* (tiding, tided). To drive with the tide.—**To tide over,** to surmount

Tidings, ti'dingz, *n.pl.* News; intelligence.

Tidy, ti'di, *a.* Clean and orderly; neat; trim; moderately large.—*vt.* (tidying, tidied). To make tidy.—*n.* A piece of fancy work to throw over a chair, etc.

Tie, ti, *vt.* (tying, tied). To bind; to fasten; to oblige; to constrain.—*n.* That which binds or fastens together; a fastening; a neck-tie; bond; obligation; an equality in numbers.

Tier, tēr, *n.* A row; a rank.

Tiff, tif, *n.* A fit of peevishness; a slight quarrel; small draft of liquor.—*vi.* To be in a pet.—*vt.* To sip.

Tiger, ti'gèr, *n.* An Asiatic carnivorous striped mammal of the cat family as large as the lion; a boy in livery.

Tight, tit, *a.* Compact; well-knit; stanch not loose; fitting close or too close; taut; slightly intoxicated; difficult to obtain; as money.

Tights, tits, *n.pl.* A tight-fitting covering for the legs or whole body.

Tile, til, *n.* A slab of baked clay for covering roofs, floors, walls, etc.—*vt.* (tiling, tiled). To cover with tiles; to guard against the entrance of the uninitiated.

Till, til, *n.* A money box or drawer for money in a shop, etc.—*prep.* To the time of; until.—*vt* To cultivate, to plow and prepare for seed.

Tiller, til'èr, *n.* One who tills; the handle of a rudder; shoot of a plant springing from the root.—*vi.* To put forth shoots from the root.

Tilt, tilt, *vi.* To run or ride and thrust with a lance;

to joust; to lean or slope; to heel over.—*vt.* To set in a sloping position; to cover with an awning.—*n.* Inclination forward; a military contest with lances on horseback; a tilt-hammer; an awning.

Timber, tim'bèr, *n.* Wood suitable for building purposes; trees yielding such wood; one of the main beams of a fabric.—*vt.* To furnish with timber.

Timbre, tim'br or tam'br, *n.* Characteristic quality of sound.

Time, tim, *n.* The measure of duration; a particular part or point of duration; occasion; season; epoch; present life; leisure; rhythm' rate of movement.—*vt.* (timing, timed). To adapt to the time or occasion; to regulate or measure as to time.

Time-honored, tim'on-èrd, *a.* Honored for a long time.

Time-keeper, tim'kēp-èr, *n.* A clock; one appointed to keep the workmen's time.

Timeless, tim'les, *a.* Untimely; eternal.

Timely, tim'li, *a.* Being in good time; opportune.—*adv.* Early; in good season.

Timid, ti'mid, *a.* Fearful; timorous; wanting courage; faint-hearted; shy.

Timorous, ti'mor-us, *a.* Fearful of danger; timid.

Tin, tin, *n.* A malleable metal of a white color tinged with gray; a dish made of tin.—*vt.* (tinning, tinned). To cover with tin; to put in a tin.

Tincture, tingk'tūr, *n.* A tinge, tint, or shade; slight quality added to anything; flavor; extract or solution of the active principles of some substance.—*vt.* (tincturing, tinctured). To tinge; to imbue.

Tinder, tin'dèr, *n.* An inflammable substance used for obtaining fire from a spark.

Tine, tin, *n.* The tooth of a fork or harrow; a prong; point of a deer's horn.

Tinge, tinj, *vt.* (tingeing, tinged). To give a certain hue or color to; to tint; to imbue.—*n.* A slight color; tint; tincture; smack.

Tingle, ting'gl, *vi.* (tingling, tingled) To feel a kind of thrilling sensation.—*vt.* To cause to give a sharp, ringing sound.

Tinker, ting'ker, *n.* A mender of kettles, pans, etc.; a botcher.—*vt.* and *i.* To mend; to cobble; to botch.

Tinkle, ting'kl, *vi.* (tinkling, tinkled). To make small, sharp sounds; to tingle; to clink.—*vt.* To cause to clink.—*n.* A sharp, ringing noise.

Tinkling, ting'kling, *n.* A small, sharp, ringing sound.

Tinsel, tin'sel, *n.* Thin, glittering metallic sheets; cloth overlaid with foil; something superficially showy.—*a.* Consisting of tinsel; showy to excess.—*vt.* (tinselling, tinselled). To adorn with tinsel.

Tint, tint, *n.* a tinge; a slight coloring; hue.—*vt.* To tinge.

Tintinnabular, Tintinnabulary, tin-tin-nab'ū-lèr, tin-tin-nab'ū-lar-ri, *a.* Relating to bells or their sound.

Tiny, ti'ni, *a.* Very small; little; puny.

Tip, tip, *n.* A small end or point; a tap; a small present in money.—*vt.* (tipping, tipped). To form the tip of; to cant up, as a cart; to give a small money-gift to.

Tipsy, tip'si, *a.* Fuddled; affected with strong drink; intoxicated.

Tiptoe, tip'tō, *n.* The tip or end of the toe.

Tirade, ti-rād', *n.* A violent declamation; an invective; a harangue.

Tire, tir, *n.* A head-dress; a band or hoop round a wheel; attire.—*vt.* (tiring, tired). To fatigue; to weary; to adorn; to attire.—*vi.* To become weary.

Tiresome, tir'sum, *a.* Wearisome; tedious.

Tissue, ti'shū, *n.* Any woven stuff; a textile fabric; a primary layer of organic substance; a fabrication.

Tissue-paper, ti'shū-pā-pèr, *n.* A very thin paper, used for protecting or wrapping.

Titanium, ti-tā'ni-um, *n.* A metallic element

somewhat resembling tin.

Tithe, tīтн, *n.* The tenth part of anything; tenth part allotted to the clergy; any small part.—*vt.* (tithing, tithed). To levy a tithe on.—*vi.* To pay tithes.

Tithonic, ti´thon´ik, *a.* Pertaining to the chemical rays of light.

Titillate, ti´til-lāt, *vi.* To tickle.

Titillation, ti-til-lā´shon, *n.* Act of tickling; state of being tickled; any slight pleasure.

Title, tī´tl, *n.* An inscription put over anything; heading; name; appellation of dignity; a right; document which is evidence of a right.—*vt.* (titling, titled). To entitle; to name.

Title-role, tī´tl-rōl, *n.* The part in a play which gives its name to it.

Titration, ti-trā´shon, *n.* A process for ascertaining the quantity of a chemical constituent in a compound by means of a liquid of known strength.

Titter, tit´ėr, *vi.* To laugh with restraint.—*n.* A restrained laugh.

Titular, tit´ū-lėr, *a.* Holding a position by title or name only; nominal.

To, tu or tō, *prep.* Denoting motion towards; indicating a point reached, destination, addition, ratio, opposition, or contrast; marking an object; the sign of the infinitive mood.—*adv.* Forward; on.

Toad, tōd, *n.* A reptile resembling the frog, but not adapted for leaping.

Toady, tō´di, *n.* A base sycophant; a flatterer.—*vt.* (toadying, toadied). To fawn upon.

Toast, tōst, *vt.* To scorch by the heat of a fire; to warm thoroughly; to drink in honor of.—*n.* Bread scorched by the fire; anyone or anything honored in drinking; a sentiment proposed in drinking.

Tobacco, tō-bak´ō, *n.* A narcotic plant of the potato family; its leaves prepared for smoking.

Tobaggan, Tobogan, tō-bog´an, *n.* A kind of sled used for sliding down snow-covered slopes.—*vi.* To use such a sled.

Tocsin tok´sin, *n.* An alarm-bell.

Today, tu-dā´, *n.* The present day; also, on this day, adverbially.

Toddle, tod´l, *vi.* (toddling, toddled). To walk with short, tottering steps.—*n.* A little toddling walk.

Toe, tō, *n.* One of the small members forming the extremity of the foot.—*vt.* (toeing, toed). To touch or reach with the toes.

Together, tu-geтн´ėr, *adv.* In company; in concert; without intermission.

Toil, toil, *vi.* To labor; to work; to drudge. —*n.* Labor with fatigue; a string or web for taking prey.

Toilet, toi´let, *n.* A cloth over a table in a dressing room; a dressing-table; act or mode of dressing; attire.

Token, tō´kn, *n.* A mark; sign; indication; souvenir; keepsake; a piece of money current by sufferance, not coined by authority.

Tolerance, tol´ė-rans, *n.* The quality of being tolerant; toleration; endurance.

Tolerate, tol´ė-rāt, *vt.* (tolerating, tolerated). To allow or permit; to treat with forbearance; to put up with; to allow religious freedom to.

Toleration, tol´ė-rā´shon, *n.* Act of tolerating; allowance given to that which is not wholly approved; recognition of the right of private judgment in religion.

Toll, tōl, *n.* A tax on travellers or vehicles passing along public roads, etc.; stroke of a bell.—*vi.* To pay or take toll; to sound, as a bell, with slow, measured strokes.—*vt.* To take toll from; to sound (a bell); to ring on account of.

Tomahawk, to´ma-hak, *n.* A hatchet used in war by the North American Indians—*vt.* To cut or kill with a tomahawk.

Tomato, tō-mä´tō, *n.;* pl. **-toes.** A tropical plant and its fruit, now widely cultivated.

Tomb, tōm, *n.* A grave; a sepulchral structure,—*vt.* To bury; to entomb.

Tomboy, tom´boi, *n.* A wild, romping girl.

Tombstone, tōm´stōn, *n.* A stone erected over a grave; a sepulchral monument.

Tom-cat, tom´kat, *n.* A full-grown male cat.

Tome, tōm, *n.* A volume; a large book.

Tomfoolery, tom-fōl´é-ri, *n.* Foolishness; trifling; absurd knick-knacks.

Tomorrow, tō-mo´rō, *n.* The day after the present; on the day after the present, adverbially.

Ton, tun, *n.* A weight equal to 20 hundred-weight or 2,240 pounds avoirdupois (the long ton used in Great Brittain); a weight equal to 2,000 pounds avoirdupois (the short ton used in the United States, Canada and South Africa).

Tone, tōn, *n.* Any sound in relation to its pitch, quality, or strength; sound as expressive of sentiment; timbre; healthy activity of animal organs; mood; tenor; prevailing character.—*vt.* (toning, toned). To give a certain tone to.—**To tone down,** to soften.

Tongs, tongz, *n.pl.* A metal instrument for taking hold of coals, heated metals, etc.

Tongue, tung, *n.* The fleshy movable organ in the mouth, of taste, speech, etc.; speech; a language; strip of land; a tapering flame; pin of a buckle.—*vt.* To utter; to scold; to modify with the tongue in playing, as in the flute.

Tonic, ton´ik, *a.* Increasing strength; restoring healthy functions; relating to tones or sounds.—*n.* A medicine that gives tone to the system; the key-note in mucic.

Tonicity, to-nis´i-ti, *n.* The elasticity of living parts, as muscles.

Tonight, tō-nit´, *n.* The present night; in the present or coming night, adverbially.

Tonsil, ton´sil, *n.* One of the two oblong glands on each side of the throat.

Tonsile, ton´sil, *a.* That may be shorn.

Tonsure, ton´sùr, *n.* The act of clipping the hair; the round bare place on the heads of the Roman Catholic priests.

Tontine, ton´tin, *n.* An annuity shared by subscribers to a loan, and going wholly to the last survivor.

Too, tō, *adv.* Over; more than sufficiently; very; likewise; also; besides.

Tool, tōl, *n.* Any instrument to be used by the hands; a person used as an instrument by another.—*vt.* To shape or mark with a tool.

Toot, töt, *vi.* To make a noise like that of a pipe or horn.—*vt.* To sound, as a horn.—*n.* A sound blown on a horn.

Tooth, tōth, *n.;* pl. **Teeth,** tēth. A bony growth in the jaws for chewing; any projection resembling a tooth.—*vt.* To furnish with teeth; to indent.

Toothache, tōth´āk, *n.* A pain in the teeth.

Toothpick, tōth´pik, *n.* An instrument to pick out substances lodged among the teeth.

Toothsome, tōth´sum, *a.* Grateful to the taste; palatable.

Top, top, *n.* The highest part of anything; highest rank; platform in ships surrounding the head of the lower masts; a whirling toy.—*a.* Being on the top; highest.—*vi.* (topping, topped). To rise aloft; to be eminent.—*vt.* To cap; to surmount; to rise to the top of.

Topaz, tō´paz, *n.* A transparent or translucent gem of various light colors.

Top-heavy, top´he-vi, *a.* Having the top or upper part too heavy for the lower.

Topiary, tō´pi-a-ri, *a.* Shaped by clipping, pruning, or training.

Topic, to´pik, *n.* Subject of any discourse; matter treated of.

Topically, to´pik-al-li, *adv.* Locally; with application to a particular part.

Topmost, top´mōst, *a.* Highest; uppermost.

Topographic, Topographical, to-po-graf´ik, to-po-graf´ik-al, *a.* Descriptive of a place.

Topography, to-pog´ra-fi, *n.* The description of a particular place, tract of land, etc.

Topple, top´l, *vi.* (toppling, toppled). To fall, as with the top first,—*vt.* To throw forward.

Torch, torch, n. A light to be carried in the hand; a flambeau.

Toreador, tor′e-a-dor′′, n. A Spanish bull-fighter, especially one on horseback.

Torment, tor′ment, n. Extreme pain; torture; that which gives pain.—vt. tor-ment′. To torture; to distress; to tease.

Tornado, tor-nā′dō, n.; pl. -oes. A violent whirling wind; a hurricane.

Torpedo, tor-pē′do, n.; pl. -oes. A fish allied to the rays; an explosive engine propelled under water.

Torpid, tor′pid, a. Numb; stupefied; stupid; sluggish; inactive.

Torpor, tor′por, n. State of being torpid; numbness; loss of motion; sluggishness.

Torrent, to′rent, n. A violent rushing stream.

Torrid, to′rid, a. Parched; violently hot; burning or parching.

Torsion, tor′shon, n. The act of twisting; the force with which a body, such as a wire, resists a twist; the twisting of the cut end of an artery to stop the flow of blood.

Torso, tor′sō, n. The trunk of a statue deprived of its head and limbs.

Tort, tort, n. Wrong; injury.

Tortive, tor′tiv, a. Twisted.

Tortoise, tor′tois or tor′tis, n. A reptile covered with a flattened shell; a turtle.

Tortuous, tor′tū-us, a. Twisted; circuitous and underhand; roundabout.

Torture, tor′tūr, n. Extreme pain; agony; torment.—vt. (torturing, tortured). To pain to extremity; to torment; to harass.

Toss, tos, vt. To pitch; to fling; to jerk, as the head; to agitate.—vi. To roll and tumble; to be in violent commotion.—n. A throw; pitch; throw of the head.

Toss-up, tos′up, n. The throwing up of a coin to decide something; an even chance.

Tot, tot, n. Anything small or insignificant.—vt. (totting, totted). To sum (with up).

Total, tō′tal, a. Pertaining to the whole; complete.—n. The whole; an aggregate.

Totalitarian, tō-tal′it-ār′′i-an, a. Applied to states under a highly centralized government which suppresses all rival political parties.

Totality, tō′tal′i-ti, n. Total amount.

Totem, tō′tem, n. A figure, as of an animal, plant, etc., used as a badge of a tribe or family among rude races.

Totter, tot′er, vi. To threaten to fall; to vacilate; to shake; to reel.

Toucan, tö′kan, n. A scansorial bird of tropical America having an enormous beak.

Touch, tuch, vt. To perceive by the sense of feeling; to come in contact with; to taste; to reach or arrive at; to refer to; to affect.—vi. To be in contact; to take effect; to make mention; to call when on a voyage.—n. Act of touching; contact; sense of feeling; a trait; a little; a stroke; distinctive handling; in football, etc., part of the field beyond the flags.

Touching, tuch′ing, a. Affecting; moving; pathetic.—prep. Concerning; with respect to.

Touchstone, tuch′stōn, n. A compact, dark-colored, siliceous stone used in testing gold and silver; a test or criterion.

Touchy, tuch′i, a. Irritable; irascible; apt to take offense.

Tough, tuf, a. Flexible and not brittle; tenacious; durable; viscous; stiff; stubborn.

Toughen, tuf′n, vi. To grow tough.—vt. To make tough.

Toupee, Toupet, tö-pē′, tö′pē, n. A curl or artificial lock of hair; a small wig or upper part of wig.

Tour, tör, n. A journey; a lengthy jaunt or excursion.—vi. To make a tour.

Tourist, tör′ist, n. One who makes a tour.

Tourmalin, Tourmaline, tör′ma-lin, n. A mineral of various colors, possessing strong electrical properties.

Tournament, tör′na-ment, n. A martial sport performed by knights on horseback; contest in which a number take part.

Tourniquet, tör′ni-ket, n. A bandage tightened by a screw to check a flow of blood.

Tousle, tou′zl, vt. (tousling, tousled). To dishevel.

Tout, tout, vi. To ply or seek for customers.—n. One who plies for customers.

Tow, tō, vt. To drag, as a boat, by a rope.—n. Act of towing; state of being towed; coarse part of flax or hemp.

Toward, Towards, tō′ērd, tō′ērdz, prep. In the direction of; regarding; in aid of; for; about.—adv. At hand; going on.

Towel, tou′el, n. A cloth for drying the skin after washing, or for domestic purposes.

Tower, tou′ér, n. A lofty narrow building; a citadel; a fortress.—vi. To soar; to be lofty; to stand sublime.

Towering, tou′ér-ing, a. Very high; extreme; violent.

Town, toun, n. Any collection of houses larger than a village; a city; borough; inhabitants of a town; the metropolis.—a. Pertaining to a town.

Town-hall, toun′hal, n. A building belonging to a town in which the town council ordinarily hold their meetings.

Township, toun′ship, n. Territory of a town; division of certain parishes.

Townspeople, tounz′pē-pl, n.pl. The inhabitants of a town.

Toxic, Toxical, tok′sik, tok′sik-al, a. Pertaining to poisons; poisonous.

Toxicant, tok′si-kant, n. A poison of a stimulating, narcotic, or anesthetic nature.

Toxicology, toks-i-kol′o-ji, n. That branch of medicine which treats of poisons and their antidotes.

Toxin, toks′in, n. A poisonous substance generated in an animal body.

Toy, toi, n. A plaything; a bauble; a trifle.—vi. To dally; to trifle.

Trace, trās, n. A mark left by anything; footstep; vestige; track; one of the straps by which a carriage, etc., is drawn.—vt. (tracing, traced). To track out; to follow by marks left; to draw or copy with lines or marks.

Tracery, trās′ē-ri, n. A species of rich open work, seen in Gothic windows, etc.

Trachea, trā′kē-a, n. The wind-pipe.

Tracheotomy, tra-ke-ot′o-mi, n. The operation of cutting into the trachea, as in suffocation.

Tracing, trās′ing, n. Act of one who traces; copy of a design made by following its lines through a transparent medium.

Track, trak, n. A footprint; rut made by a wheel; trace; beaten path; course.—vt. To trace; to follow step by step; to tow by a line from the shore.

Tract, trakt, n. A region of indefinite extent; a short dissertation.

Tractable, trakt′a-bl, a. That may be easily managed; docile; manageable.

Tractate, trak′tāt, n. A treatise; tract.

Traction, trak′shon, n. The act of drawing a body along a surface of land or water.

Tractor, trak′tor, n. A powerful motor-driven vehicle for pulling heavy loads, particularly farm machinery; a heavy truck used primarily for pulling cargo trailers, etc.

Trade, trād, n. Employment; commerce; traffic; those engaged in any trade.—a. Pertaining to trade.—vi. (trading, traded). To traffic; to carry on commerce; to have dealings.—vt. To sell or exchange in commerce.

Trade-mark, trād′märk, n. A distinctive mark put by a manufacturer on his goods.

Trades-union, trādz-ūn′yon, n. A combination of workmen in a trade to secure conditions most favorable for labor.

Trade-wind, trād′wind, n. A periodic wind blowing for six months in one direction.

Trading, trād′ing, p.a. Carrying on commerce; engaged in trade; venal.

Tradition, tra-di'shon, *n.* The handing down of opinions, stories, etc., from father to son, by oral communication; a statement so handed down.

Traduce, tra-dūs', *vt.* (traducing, traduced). To calumniate; to vilify; to defame.

Traffic, traf'ik, *n.* An interchange of commodities; commerce; goods or persons passing along a road, railway, etc.; dealings.—*vi.* (trafficking, trafficked). To trade; to deal; to trade meanly or mercenarily.

Tragacanth, trag'a-kanth, *n.* A leguminous plant yielding a mucilaginous substance called gum-dragon.

Tragedian, tra-jē'di-an, *n.* A writer of tragedy; an actor of tragedy.

Tragedy, tra'je-di, *n.* A drama representing an important event generally having a fatal issue; a fatal and mournful event; a murderous or bloody deed.

Tragic, Tragical, tra'jik, tra'jik-al, *a.* Pertaining to tragedy; murderous; calamitous.

Trail, trāl, *n.* Something dragged behind; a train; the end of a field gun-carriage that rests on the ground in firing; a path; track followed by a hunter; the position of a rifle when carried horizontally at the full extent of the right arm.—*vt.* To draw behind or along the ground; to drag.—*vi.* To be dragged along a surface; to hang down loosely; to grow along the ground.

Trailer, trāl'ėr, *n.* One who trails; a plant which cannot grow upward without support; a carriage dragged by a motor vehicle; a series of excerpts advertising coming attractions at the cinema.

Train, trān, *vt.* To draw; to entice; to rear and instruct; to drill; to bring into proper bodily condition; to shape; to bring to bear, as a gun.—*vi.* To undergo special drill.—*n.* A trail; that part of a gown which trails; tail; a series; course; retinue; line of carriages and an engine on a railway; line to conduct fire to a charge or mine.

Trained, trānd, *p.a.* Formed by training; exercised; instructed; skilled by practice.

Traipse, trāps, *vi.* (traipsing, traipsed). To gad about in an idle way.

Trait, trāt or trā, *n.* A stroke; touch; feature; characteristic; peculiarity.

Traitor, trā'tor, *n.* One who betrays his trust or allegiance; one guilty of treason.

Trajectory, tra-jek'to-ri, *n.* The path described by a body, as a planet, projectile, etc.

Trammel, tram'el, *n.* A net for birds or fishes; shackles for regulating the motions of a horse; whatever hinders or confines; an iron hook.—*vt.* (trammelling, trammelled). To impede; to shackle.

Tramp, tramp, *vt.* and *i.* To tread under foot; to travel on foot.—*n.* A tread; scund made by the feet in walking; journey on foot; a strolling beggar; a cargo steamer which makes irregular and usually short voyages.

Trample, tram'pl, *vt.* (trampling, trampled). To tread on heavily; to tread down; to treat with pride or insult.—*vi.* To treat in contempt; to tread with force.

Trance, trans, *n.* A state of insensibility; ecstasy; catalepsy.—*vt.* (trancing, tranced). To entrance; to enchant.

Tranquil, tran'kwil, *a.* Quiet; calm; undisturbed; peaceful.

Tranquillize, tran'kwil-īz, *vt.* To render tranquil; to quiet;; to compose.

Transact, trans-akt', *vt.* and *i.* To carry through; to perform; to manage.

Transaction, trans-ak'shon, *n.* The doing of any business; affair; proceeding; *pl.* reports of proceedings of societies.

Transatlantic, trans-at-lan'tik, *a.* Being beyond or crossing the Atlantic.

Transcend, trans-send', *vt.* To rise above; to surpass; to outgo; to excel; to exceed.

Transcendent, trans-send'ent, *a.* Supreme in ex-

cellence; transcending human experience.

Transcendentalism, trans-send-ent'al-izm, *n.* A system of philosophy which claims to go deeper than experience can.

Transcribe, tran-skrīb', *vt.* (transcribing, transcribed). To write over again or in the same words; to copy.

Transcription, tran-skrip'shon, *n.* Act of transcribing; a copy; transcript.

Transept, tran'sept, *n.* The transverse portion of a church built in form of a cross.

Transfer, trans-fėr', *vt.* (transferring, transferred). To convey from one place or person to another; to make over.—*n.* trans'fėr. Act of trarnsferring; removal of a thing from one place or person to another; something transferred.

Transference, trans'fėr-ens, *n.* Act of transferring; passage of anything from one place to another.

Transfiguration, trans-fig'ūr-ā''shon, *n.* A change of form or figure; the supernatural change in the appearance of Christ on the mount; a Church feast held on the 6th of August, in commemoration of this change.

Transfigure, trans-fig'ūr, *vt.* To change in form or shape; to idealize.

Transfix, trans-fiks', *vt.* To pierce through; to cause to be immovable.

Transfluent, trans'flu-ent, *a.* Flowing or running across or through.

Transform, trans-form', *vt.* To change the form of; to change, as the natural disposition of.—*vi.* To be changed in form.

Transformation, trans-for-mā'shon, *n.* Act of transforming; an entire change in form, disposition, etc.

Transfuse, trans-fūz', *vt.* (transfusing, transfused). To transfer by pouring; to cause to pass from one to another.

Transfusion, trans-fū'zhon, *n.* Act of transfusing, as the blood of one animal into another.

Transgress, trans-gres', *vt.* To break or violate; to infringe.—*vi.* To do wrong; to sin.

Transgression, trans-gre'shon, *n.* Act of transgressing; a trespass; offense; crime.

Transient, tran'si-ent, *a.* Passing quickly; fleeting; momentary; fugitive.

Transit, tran'sit, *n.* Act of passing; passage; passage of a heavenly body over the disk of a larger one.

Transition, tran-zi'shon, *n.* Passage from one place, state, or topic to another.—*a.* Pertaining to passage from one state, etc., to another.

Transitive, tran'sit-iv, *a.* In *grammar,* taking an object after it, as a verb.

Transitory, tran'si-to-ri, *a.* Passing away; fleeting; transient.

Translate, trans-lātu', *vt.* (translating, translated). To remove from one place to another; to transfer; to render into another language.

Translation, trans-lā'shon, *n.* Act of translating; removal; act of turning into another language; interpretation; a version.

Transliterate, trans-lit'ėr-āt, *vt.* To write or spell in different characters intended to express the same sound.

Translucent, trans-lū'sent, *a.* Transmitting rays of light, but not so as to render objects distinctly visible; transparent; clear.

Transmigrate, trans'mi-grāt, *vi.* To pass from one country or body to another.

Transmigration, trans-mi-grā'shon, *n.* Act of transmigrating; the passing of a soul into another body after death.

Transmissible, Transmittable, trans-mis'i-bl, trans-mit'i-bl, *a.* That may be transmitted.

Transmission, trans-mi'shon, *n.* Act of transmitting; transference; a passing through any body, as of light through glass, the gear box of an automobile by which engine power is transmitted to the wheels.

Transmit, trans-mit', *vt.* (transmitting, transmitted). To send from one person or place to another; to hand down; to allow to pass through.

ransmogrify, trans-mog'ri-fi, *vt.* To transform; to change the appearance of.

ransmutation, trans-mū-tā'shon, *n.* Act of transmuting; conversion into something different.

ransmute, trans-mūt', *vt.* (transmuting, transmuted). To change from one nature or substance into another.

ransoceanic, trans'ō-shē-an''ik, *a.* Beyond the ocean; crossing the ocean.

ransom, tran'sum, *n.* A strengthening horizontal beam; a cross-bar.

ransparent, trans-pā'rent, *a.* That can be seen through distinctly; not sufficient to hide underlying feelings.

ranspire, trans-pīr, *vt.* (transpiring, transpired). To emit through the pores of the skin; to send off in vapor.—*vi.* To exhale; to escape from secrecy; to become public.

ransplant, trans-plant', *vt.* To remove and plant in another place.

ransport, trans-pōrt', *vt.* To carry from one place to another; to carry into banishment; to carry away by violence of passion; to ravish with pleasure.—*n.* trans'pōrt. Transportation; a ship employed to carry soldiers, warlike stores, etc.; passion; ecstasy.

ransportation, trans-pōrt-ā'shon, *n.* Act of transporting; banishment to a penal settlement; transmission; conveyance.

ranspose, trans-pōz', *vt.* (transposing, transposed). To change the order of things by putting each in the other's place; to cause to change places.

ransposition, trans-pō-zi'shon, *n.* Act of transposing; state of being transposed; change of the order of words for effect.

ransversal, trans-vèrs'al, *a.* Transverse; running or lying across.

ransverse, trans'vèrs or trans-vèrs', *a.* Lying or being across or in a cross direction.

rap, trap, *n.* A contrivance for catching unawares; an ambush; a contrivance in drains to prevent effluvia rising; a carriage of any kind, on springs; a kind of movable ladder; an igneous rock.—*vt.* (trapping, trapped). To catch in a trap; to insnare; to adorn.—*vi.* To set traps for game.

rap-door, trap'dōr, *n.* A door in a floor or roof, with which when shut it is flush.

rapeze, tra-pēz', *n.* A sort of swing, consisting of a cross-bar suspended by cords, for gymnastic exercises.

rapezium, tra'pē'zi-um, *n.*; pl. **-ia** or **-iums.** A plane figure contained by four straight lines, two of them parallel; a bone of the wrist.

rapezoid, tra'pē-zoid, *n.* A plane four-sided figure having no two sides parallel.

rappings, trap'ingz, *n.pl.* Ornaments; dress; decorations; finery.

rappist, trap'ist, *n.* A member of an ascetic order of the Roman Catholic Church.

rash, trash, *n.* Loppings of trees; broken pieces; rubbish; refuse.—*vt.* To lop.

rashy, trash'i, *a.* Worthless; useless.

aumatic, tra-mat'ik, *a.* Pertaining to wounds.—*n.* A medicine useful in the cure of wounds.

avail, tra'vāl, *vi.* To labor; to toil; to suffer the pangs of childbirth.—*n.* Labor; severe toil; childbirth.

ravel, tra'vel, *n.* Act of journeying; journey to a distant country; *pl.* account of occurrences during a journey.—*vi.* (travelling, travelled). To journey; to go to a distant country; to pass; to move.

raveller, tra'vel-èr, *n.* One who travels; one who travels from place to place to solicit orders for goods, etc.

avelling, tra'vel-ing, *p.a.* Pertaining to, used in, or incurred by travel.

averse, tra'vèrs, *a.* Transverse.—*n.* Something that is transverse; something that thwarts; a

denial.—*vt.* (traversing, traversed). To cross; to thwart; to cross in travelling; to deny.—*adv.* Athwart; crosswise.

Travertin, tra'vèr-tin, *n.* A white limestone deposited from the water of springs holding carbonate of lime in solution.

Travesty, tra'ves-ti, *vt.* (travestying, travestied). To transform so as to have a ludicrous effect; to burlesque.—*n.* A burlesque treatment; parody.

Trawl, tral, *vi.* To fish with a trawl-net; to drag, as a net.—*n.* A trawl-net.

Trawl-net, tral'net, *n.* A long purse-shaped net for deep-sea fishing, dragged behind a vessel.

Tray, trā, *n.* A sort of waiter or salver, of wood, metal, etc., on which dishes and the like are presented.

Treacherous, trech'èr-us, *a.* Guilty of treachery; faithless; traitorous; perfidious.

Treachery, trech'èr-ri, *n.* Violation of allegiance or of faith; perfidy; treason.

Treacle, trēkl, *n.* The uncrystallizable part of sugar obtained in refineries; molasses.

Tread, tred, *vi.* (pret. trod, pp. trod, trodden). To set the foot on the ground; to step; to walk with a measured step; to copulate, as fowls.—*vt.* To plant the foot on; to trample; to dance; to walk on in a formal manner; to copulate with, as a bird.—*n.* A step; gait; horizontal part of the step of a stair.

Treadmill, tred'mil, *n.* A mill worked by persons or animals treading on movable steps.

Treason, trē'zon, *n.* A betrayal; breach of allegiance; treachery; disloyalty.

Treasure, tre'zhūr, *n.* Wealth accumulated; great abundance; something very much valued.—*vt.* (treasuring, treasured). To lay up or collect; to prize.

Treasury, tre'zhū-ri, *n.* A place where treasure is laid up; department of government which controls the revenue; a book containing much valuable material.

Treat, trēt, *vt.* To handle; to act towards; to discourse on; to entertain; to manage.—*vi.* To handle; to discourse; to negotiate.—*n.* An entertainment given as a compliment; an unusual gratification.

Treatise, trē'tiz, *n.* A written composition on some particular subject; a dissertation.

Treatment, trēt'ment, *n.* Act or manner of treating; management; usage.

Treaty, trē'ti, *n.* Negotiation; agreement between two or more nations.

Treble, tre'bl, *a.* Threefold; triple; in *music,* pertaining to the highest sounds.—*n.* The highest part in a concerted piece of music; a soprano.—*vt.* and *i.* (trebling, trebled). To make or become thrice as much.

Tree, trē, *n.* A perennial plant having a woody trunk and branches; something resembling a tree; a cross; a wooden piece in machines, etc.—*vt.* (treeing, treed). To cause to take refuge in a tree.—*vi.* To take refuge in a tree.

Trefoil, trē'foil, *n.* A three-leaved plant, as clover; an architectural ornament, consisting of three cusps.

Trek, trek, *vi.* (trekking, trekked). To travel by wagon.

Trellis, trel'is, *n.* A structure of cross-barred work or lattice-work.—*vt.* To furnish with a trellis; to form like a trellis.

Tremble, trem'bl, *vi.* (trembling, trembled). To shake involuntarily; to quiver; to vibrate.—*n.* An involuntary shaking; a tremor.

Tremendous, trē-men'dus, *a.* Such as may cause trembling; terrible; extraordinary.

Tremor, tre'mor, *n.* An involuntary trembling; a shivering; vibration.

Tremulous, tre'mū-lus, *a.* Trembling; shaking; quivering; vibratory.

Trench, trensh, *vt.* To dig a ditch in; to turn over and mix, as soil.—*vi.* To cut a trench or trenches; to encroach (with *on* or *upon*).—*n.* A long narrow excavation; a deep ditch cut for de-

T

fense.

Trenchant, tren'shant, *a.* Cutting; keen; severe.

Trencher, trensh'er, *n.* A wooden plate on which meat may be carved; food; pleasures of the table.

Trend, trend, *vi.* To extend in a particular direction.—*n.* Direction; tendency.

Trepan, trē-pan', *n.* A surgical saw for removing a portion of the skull.—*vt.* (trepanning, trepanned). To perforate with a trepan; to insnare.

Trephine, tre-fēn', *n.* An improved form of the trepan.—*vt.* (trephining, trephined). To perforate with a trephine.

Trepidation, tre-pid-ā'shon, *n.* Confused alarm; perturbation; involuntary trembling.

Trespass, tres'pas, *vi.* To enter unlawfully upon the land of another; to do wrong; to offend.—*n.* An offense; a sin; wrong done by entering on the land of another.

Tress, tres, *n.* A braid, lock, or curl of hair.

Trestle, tres'l, *n.* A frame for supporting things; a frame with three or four legs attached to a horizontal piece.

Triad, trī'ad, *n.* A union of three; a trinity.

Trial, trī'al, *n.* Act of trying; examination by a test; experience; probation; temptation; judicial examination.

Triangle, trī-ang'gl, *n.* A figure having three sides and angles.

Tribalism, trī'bal-izm, *n.* The state of existence in separate tribes; tribal feeling.

Tribe, trīb, *n.* A division or class of people; a family or race; a class of animals or plants.

Tribulation, tri-bū-lā'shon, *n.* Severe trouble or affliction; distress; trial; suffering.

Tribunal, trī-bū'nal, *n.* The seat of a judge; a court of justice.

Tribune, trī'būn, *n.* Among the ancient Romans, a magistrate chosen by the people, to protect them from the patricians; a platform; tribunal; throne of a bishop.

Tributary, tri'bū-ta-ri, *a.* Paying tribute to another; subject; contributing.—*n.* One that pays tribute; a stream which falls into another.

Tribute, tri'būt, *n.* A sum paid by one prince or nation to another; personal contribution.

Tricennial, trī-sen'ni-al, *a.* Belonging to the period of thirty years, or occurring once in that period.

Tricentenary, trī-sen'ten-a-ri, *n.* A period of three hundred years; the three hundredth anniversary.

Trichina, tri-kī'na, *n.*; pl. **-nae.** A minute nematoid worm, the larva of which causes disease in the flesh of mammals.

Trichiniasis, Trichinosis, trik-i-nī'a-sis, trik-i-nō'sis, *n.* The disease produced by trichinae.

Trick, trik, *n.* An artifice; a crafty device; fraud; a knack or art; a personal practice or habit; a prank; all the cards played in one round.—*vt.* To deceive; to impose on, to cheat; to draw in outline; to dress; to adorn (often with *out*).

Trickery, trik'e-ri, *n.* Artifice; imposture.

Trickle, trik'l, *vi.* (trickling, trickled). To fall in drops; to flow gently.

Tricky, trik'i *a.* Trickish; mischievous.

Tricostate, trī-kos'tāt, *a.* Having three ribs or ridges.

Tricuspid, Tricuspidate, trī-kus'pid, trī-kus'pi-dāt, *a.* Having three cusps or points.

Tricycle, trī'si-kl, *n.* A cycle with three wheels.

Trident, trī'dent, *n.* Any instrument of the form of a fork with three prongs.

Tried, trīd, *p.a.* Tested by trial or experience; staunch; true.

Triennial, trī-en'ni-al, *a.* Continuing three years; happening every three years.

Trifle, trī'fl, *n.* Something of no moment or value; a kind of fancy confection.—*vi.* (trifling, trifled). To act with levity; to play or toy; to finger lightly.—*vt.* To waste.

Trifoliate, trī-fō'li-āt, *a.* Having three leaves.

Triform, trī'form, *a.* Having a triple form or shape.

Trifurcate, trī-fer'kāt, *a.* Having three branches or forks.

Trig, trig, *vt.* (trigging, trigged). To stop or fasten as a wheel.—*a.* Trim; spruce; neat.

Trigger, trig'er, *n.* The catch which, on being pressed, liberates the striker of a gun.

Trigonometry, tri-gon-om'et-ri, *n.* The science o determining the sides and angles of triangles; geometrical method of calculation.

Trihedron, trī-hē'dron, *n.* A solid figure havin three equal sides.

Trilateral, trī-lat'er-al, *a.* Having three sides, as triangle.

Trilith, Trilithon, trī'lith, trī'lith-on, *n.* Thre large blocks of stone placed together like doo posts and a lintel, and standing by themselves as in sundry ancient monuments.

Trill, tril, *n.* A shake of the voice in singing; a qua vering sound.—*vt.* To sing with a quaverin voice; to sing sweetly or clearly.—*vi.* To soun with tremulous vibrations; to pipe; to trickle.

Trillion, tril'yon, *n.* The product of a million mu tiplied twice by itself.

Trilobate, trī-lō'bāt, *n.* Having three lobes.

Trilogy, tril'o-ji, *n.* A series of three connecte dramas, each complete in itself.

Trim, trim, *vt.* (trimming, trimmed). To put in o der; to embellish; to clip or pare; to adjust.—*v* To hold a middle course between parties.—*c* Set in good order; properly adjusted; nea tidy.—*n.* Condition; order; mood; dress.

Trimester, trī-mes'tér, *n.* A term or period of thre months.

Trimly, trim'li, *adv.* Neatly; smartly.

Trine, trīne, *a.* Threefold.—*n.* Postion of planet distant from each other 120 degrees.

Trinity, tri'ni-ti, *n.* A union of three in one; the ur ion of one Godhead of the Father, Son, and Hol Spirit.

Trinket, tring'ket, *n.* A small ornament; a trifle.— *vi.* To intrigue; to traffic.

Trinomial, trī-nō'mi-al, *a.* Consisting of thre terms connected by the signs + or −.

Trio, trī'ō or trē'ō, *n.* Three united; musical con position for three voices or instruments; pe formers of a trio.

Trip, trip, *vi.* (tripping, tripped). To run or ste lightly; to skip; to stumble; to err.—*vt.* To caus to fall or stumble; to loose an anchor.—*n.* stumble; a light short step; an excursion o jaunt; a mistake.

Tripartite, trip'ar-tit or trī-pärt'īt, *a.* Divided int three parts; made between three parties.

Tripe, trīp, *n.* The stomach of ruminating an mals prepared for food.

Triphthong, trif'thong or trip'thong, *n.* A unio of three vowels in one syllable, as in *adieu*.

Triple, tri'pl, *a.* Threefold; treble.—*vt.* (triplin tripled). To treble.

Triplet, trip'let, *n.* Three of a kind: three lines o poetry rhyming together; one of three childre born at a birth.

Triplicate, tri'pli-kāt, *a.* Threefold.—*n.* A thir thing corresponding to two others.

Tripod, trī'pod, *n.* A three-footed pot, seat, o stand.

Triptych, trip'tik, *n.* A picture or carving in thre compartments side by side; a treatise in thre sections.

Trisect, tri-sekt', *vt.* To cut into three equal part

Trisyllable, tri-sil'la-bl, *n.* A word consisting c three syllables.

Trite, trīt, *a.* Hackneyed; threadbare; stale.

Triturate, tri'tū-rāt, *vt.* (triturating, triturated). T rub or grind to a very fine powder.

Triumph, trī'umf, *n.* A magnificent procession i honor of a victorious Roman general; victor achievement; joy for success.—*vi.* To rejoice fo victory; to obtain victory; to exult insolently.

Triumphant, trī-umf'ant, *a.* Feeling triumph; vic torious; celebrating victory; expressing joy fo success.

Triumvirate, trī-um′vėr-āt, n. A coalition of three men in office or authority.

Trivet, tri′vet, n. Anything supported by three feet; an iron frame whereon to place vessels before or over a fire.

Trivial, tri′vi-al, a. Common; commonplace; trifling; insignificant.

Troche , trōch or trosh, n. A small circular lozenge containing a drug.

Trochee, trō′kē, n. A metrical foot of two syllables, the first long and the second short.

Troglodyte, trō′glod-īt, n. A cave-dweller; one living in seclusion.

Trojan, trō′jan, a. Pertaining to ancient Troy.—n. An inhabitant of ancient Troy; a jolly fellow; a plucky determined fellow.

Troll, trōl, vt. To roll; to pass round; to sing in a full, jovial voice.—vi. To go round; to fish for pike by trolling.—n. A going round; a part-song; a reel on a fishing-rod; a dwarfish being in Scandinavian mythology, dwelling in caves and mounds.

Trolley, Trolly, trol′i, n. A kind of small truck; a small narrow cart.

Trolling, trōl′ing, n. Act of one who trolls; a method of rod-fishing for pike with a dead bait; trawling.

Trollop, trol′lop, n. A woman loosely dressed; a slattern; a drab.

Trombone, trom′bōn, n. A deep-toned instrument of the trumpet kind.

Troop, tröp, n. A collection of people; a company; a body of soldiers; pl. soldiers in general; a troupe.—vi. To collect in numbers; to march in a body.

Trope, trōp, n. A word used figuratively; a figure of speech.

Trophy, trō′fi, n. A memorial of some victory; an architectural ornament representing the stem of a tree, hung with military weapons.

Tropic, tro′pik, n. Either of two circles on the celestial sphere, limiting the sun's apparent annual path; either of two corresponding parallels of latitude including the torrid zone; pl. the regions between or near these.—a. Pertaining to the tropics.

Trot, trot, vi. (trotting, trotted). To run with small steps; to move fast.—vt. To cause to trot.—n. Pace of a horse more rapid than a walk.

Troubador, trō′ba-dör, n. one of a class of poets who flourished in S. Europe, especially in Provence, from the eleventh to the end of the thirteenth century.

Trouble, tru′bl, vt. (troubling, troubled). To disturb; to distress; to busy.—n. Distress; agitation; affliction; labor.

Trough, trof, n. A long vessel for holding water or food for animals; a depression between two waves.

Trounce, trouns, vt. (trouncing, trounced). To punish or to beat severely.

Troupe, tröp, n. A troop; a company of performers, as acrobats.

Trousers, trou′zėrz, n.pl. A garment for men; covering the lower part of the trunk and each leg separately.

Trousseau, trō-sō, n. The clothes and general outfit of a bride.

Trout, trout, n. A fresh-water fish of the salmon tribe.

Trover, trō′vėr, n. The gaining possession of goods by finding them, or otherwise than by purchase.

Trow, trou or trō, vi. To believe; to suppose.

Trowel, trou′el, n. A hand-tool for lifting and dressing mortar and plaster, etc., a gardener's tool.—vt. (trowelling, trowelled). To dress or form with a trowel.

Troy, Troy-weight, troi, troi′wāt, n. A weight used for gold and silver, divided into 12 ounces, each of 20 pennyweights, each of 24 grains, so that a pound troy = 5760 grains.

Truant, trö′ant, n. One who shirks duty; one who stays from school without leave.—a. Idle; wilfully absenting oneself.

Truce, trös, n. A temporary cessation of hostilities; armistice; short quiet.

Truck, truk, vi. and t. To barter.—n. Exchange of commodities; barter; payment of workmen's wages partly in goods; a small wheel; a barrow with two low wheels; an open railway wagon for goods; a motor driven vehicle used to carry heavy loads or general freight; the cap at the end of a flagstaff or topmast.

Truckle, truk′l, n. A small wheel or castor.—vt. (truckling, truckled). To move on rollers; to trundle.—vi. To yield obsequiously; to submit.

Truculence, Truculency, tru′kū-lens, tru′-kū-len-si, n. Ferocity; fierceness.

Truculent, tru′kū-lent, a. Terrible of aspect; fierce; wild; savage; fell.

Trudge, truj, vi. (trudging, trudged). To walk with labor or fatigue; to walk heavily.

True, trö, a. Conformable to fact; truthful; genuine; constant; faithful; loyal; honest; exact; correct; right.

Truffle, truf′l, n. An edible fungus growing beneath the surface of the ground.

Truism, trö′izm, n. A self-evident truth.

Trump, trump, n. A winning card; one of a suit for the time being superior to the others; a person upon whom one can depend; a trumpet.—vt. To take with a trump card; to concoct or forge.

Trumpery, trum′pe-ri, n. Worthless finery; trifles; trash.—a. Worthless.

Trumpet, trum′pet, n. A metal wind-instrument of music; one who praises.—vt. To publish by sound of trumpet; to noise abroad; to sound the praises of.

Truncate, trung′kāt, vt. To cut off; to lop.—a. Truncated.

Trundle, trun′dl, vi. (trundling, trundled). To roll, as on little wheels or as a bowl.—vt. To cause to roll.—n. A little wheel; a small truck.

Trunk, trungk, n. The woody stem of a tree; body of an animal without the limbs; main body; chest for containing clothes, etc.; a long wooden tube.

Truss, trus, n. A bundle, as of hay or straw; a bandage used in cases of rupture; a combination of timbers constituting an unyielding frame.—vt. To put in a bundle; to make tight or fast; to skewer.

Trust, trust, n. Reliance, confidence, hope, credit, that which is intrusted; safe-keeping; care; management.—vt. To rely on; to believe; to intrust; to sell to upon credit; to be confident.—vi. To have reliance; to confide readily.—a. Held in trust.

Trustee, trus-tē′, n. One appointed to hold property for the benefit of those entitled to it.

Trustworthy, trust′wėr-тHi, a. Worthy of trust or confidence; faithful; reliable.

Truth, tröth, n. Conformity to fact or reality; integrity; constancy; exactness; reality; verified fact.

Truthful, tröth′ful, a. Closely adhering to truth; veracious; correct; true.

Try, trī, vt. (trying, tried). To test; to make trial of; to afflict; to examine judicially; to attempt.—vi. To endeavor.—n. The act of trying; a trial; experiment; in Rugby football, the right of trying to kick a goal, obtained by carrying the ball behind the opponents' goal-line and touching it down.

Trying, trī′ing, a. Severe; afflictive.

Tryst, trist, n. An appointment to meet; a rendezvous.—vi To agree to meet at any particular time or place.

Tsetse, tset′se, n. An African fly whose bite is often fatal to horses and cattle.

T-square, tē′skwär, n. A sort of ruler shaped like a T, used in drawing straight or perpendicular lines.

Tub, tub, n. An open wooden vessel; a small cask; a clumsy boat; a vessel used as a bath.—vt.

(tubbing, tubbed). To set in a tub.—vi. To make use of a bathing-tub.

Tuba, tū'ba, n. A large musical instrument of brass, low in pitch.

Tube, tūb, n. A pipe; a hollow cylinder; the underground electric railway system in London.—vt. (tubing, tubed) To furnish with a tube.

Tuber, tū'bėr, n. An underground fleshy stem or root; a knot or swelling in any part.

Tubercle, tū'bėr-kl, n. A small tuber; a little projecting knob; a small mass of morbid matter developed in different parts of the body.

Tubercular, tū-bėr'kū-lėr, a. Pertaining to or affected with tubercles; consumptive. Also *Tuberculate, Tuberculose, Tuberculous.*

Tuberculosis, tū-bėr'kū-lō''sis, n. A disease due to the formation of tubercles; consumption.

Tubing, tūb'ing, n. Act of providing with tubes; a length of tube; series of tubes.

Tuck, tuk, vt. To gather into a narrower compass; to fold in or under.—n. A horizontal fold in a garment to shorten it.

Tuesday, tūz'dā, n. The third day of the week.

Tuft, tuft, n. A cluster; clump; head of flowers.—vt. To adorn with tufts.

Tug, tug, vt. and i. (tugging, tugged). To pull with effort; to haul along; to drag by steam-tug.—n. A drawing or pulling with force; a tug-boat.

Tug-of-war, tug'ov-war, n. A trial of strength between two parties of men tugging at opposite ends of a rope.

Tulip, tū'lip, n. A plant of the lily family with richly-colored flowers.

Tumble, tum'bl, vi. (tumbling, tumbled). To roll about; to lose footing and fall.—vt. To throw about; to rumple; to overturn.—n. A fall; a somersault.

Tumefaction, tū-me-fak'shon, n. Act of swelling; a tumor; a swelling.

Tumefy, tū'me-fī, vt. To cause to swell.—vi. To swell; to rise in a tumor.

Tumid, tū'mid, a. Swollen; distended; pompous; inflated; bombastic.

Tumor, tū'mor, n. A morbid swelling in some part of the body.

Tumult, tū'mult, n. A commotion or disturbance; uproar; high excitement.

Tumultuous, tū-mul'tū-us, a. Full of tumult; disorderly; turbulent; violent.

Tumulus, tū'mū-lus, n.; pl. -li. A mound or large heap of earth; a barrow.

Tundra, tun'dra, n. An immense stretch of flat boggy country in the arctic parts of Siberia.

Tune, tūn, n. A short air or melody; harmony; correct intonation; state of an instrument when it can give the proper sounds; frame of mind; mood.—vt. (tuning, tuned). To put into tune; to adapt.

Tungsten, tung'sten, n. A heavy metal of a grayish-white color.

Tunic, tū'nik, n. A garment of various kinds; an ecclesiastical vestment worn over the alb; a full-dress military coat; a covering membrane; an integument.

Tuning, tūn'ing, n. The art or operation of bringing musical instruments into tune.

Tuning-fork, tūn'ing-fork, n. A steel two-pronged instrument for regulating the pitch of voices or instruments.

Tunnel, tun'el, n. A tubular opening; a funnel; a subterranean passage cut through a hill, etc.—vt. (tunnelling, tunnelled). To form a tunnel through or under.

Turban, tėr'ban, n. A head-dress worn by the Orientals, consisting of a fez and a sash wound round it; a kind of head-dress worn by ladies.

Turbid, tėr'bid, a. Muddy; having the sediment disturbed; not clear.

Turbine, tėr'bin, n. A kind of water-wheel, usually horizontal, made to revolve under the influence of pressure derived from a fall of water; a similar contrivance driven by steam.

Turbulent, tėr'bū-lent, a. Being in violent commotion; refractory; disorderly.

Tureen, tu-rēn', n. A large and deep dish for holding soup at table.

Turf, tėrf, n. The grassy layer on the surface of the ground; a sod.—**The turf,** the race-course; the business of horse-racing.—vt. To cover with turf or sod.

Turgid, tėr'jid, a. Swelling; swollen; bloated; inflated; bombastic.

Turkey, tėr'ki, n. A large gallinaceous fowl.

Turkey-red, tėr'ki-red, n. A brilliant and durable red dye on cotton cloth.

Turkish, tėr'kish, a. Pertaining to Turkey, or to the Turks, or to their language.—n. The language spoken by the Turks.—**Turkish bath,** n. A hot-air or steam bath, inducing copious perspiration, followed by shampooing and massage, etc.

Turmeric, tėr'mer-ik, n. An E. Indian plant of the ginger family yielding a condiment, a yellow dye, and a test for alkalies.

Turmoil, tėr'moil, n. Disturbance; trouble; disquiet.—vt. To harass.

Turn, tėrn, vt. To cause to move round; to shape by a lathe; to direct; to alter in course; to blunt; to reverse; to change.—vi. To revolve; to depend; to change position or course; to return; to have recourse; to become; to become sour; to reel; to become nauseated; to result.—n. Act of turning; a revolution; a bend; a short walk; an alteration of course; occasion; occasional act of kindness or malice; purpose; character; short spell, as a work; nervous shock.

Turn-coat, tėrn'kōt, n. One who meanly forsakes his party or principles.

Turning-point, tėrn'ing-point, n. The point on which or where a thing turns; the point at which a deciding change takes place.

Turnip, tėr'nip, n. A plant of the cabbage genus, cultivated for its bulbous esculent root.

Turnkey, tėrn'kē, n. A person who has charge of the keys of a prison.

Turn-out, tėrn'out, n. A coming forth; persons who have come out on some particular occasion; an equipage; the net quantity of produce yielded.

Turn-over, tėrn'ō-vėr, n. The amount of money turned over or drawn in a business.

Turnstile, tėrn'stīl, n. A post at some passage surmounted by horizontal arms which move as a person pushes through.

Turpentine, tėr'pen-tīn, n. A resinous substance flowing from trees, as the pine, larch, fir, etc.; the oil distilled from this.

Turpitude, tėr-pi-tūd, n. Inherent baseness or vileness; moral depravity.

Turquoise, tėr'koiz, n. A greenish-blue or blue opaque precious stone.

Turret, tu'ret, n. A little tower on a larger building; a strong cylindrical iron structure on an iron-clad.

Turtle, tėr'tl, n. A species of small pigeon; the sea-tortoise.

Turtle-dove, tėr'tl-duv, n. The European turtle or pigeon.

Tusk, tusk, n. A long prominent tooth of certain animals, as the elephant.

Tusker, tusk'ėr, n. An elephant that has its tusks developed.

Tussle, tus'l, n. A struggle; scuffle.

Tussock, tus'ok, n. A clump, tuft, or small hillock of growing grass.

Tutelage, tū'tel-āj, n. Guardianship; protection; state of being under a guardian.

Tutor, tū'tor, n. A guardian; a private instructor; a fellow of an English college who superintends the studies of undergraduates.—vt. To instruct.

Tutorage, tū'tor-āj, n. Guardianship.

Twain, twān, a. Two.—n. A pair.

Twang, twang, vi. To make the sound of a string which is stretched and suddenly pulled.—vt. To make to sound sharply.—n. A sharp vibrating sound; a nasal sound.

Tweak, twĕk, *vt.* To twitch; to pinch and pull suddenly.—*n.* A sharp pinch or jerk.

Tweed, twēd, *n.* A twilled woollen fabric made in mixed colors.

Tweezers, twē'zėrz, *n.pl.* Small-pincers to pluck out hairs, etc.; small forceps.

Twelfth, twelfth, *a.* The second after the tenth.—*n.* One of twelve equal parts.

Twelfth-day, twelfth'dā, *n.* The twelfth day after Christmas; festival of the Epiphany.

Twelfth-night, twelfth'nīt, *n.* The evening of the festival of the Epiphany.

Twelve, twelv, *a.* and *n.* Ten and two.

Twenty, twen'ti, *a.* and *n.* Two tens, or twice ten.

Twice, twīs, *adv.* Two times; doubly.

Twig, twig, *n.* A small shoot or branch.—*vt.* and *i.* (twigging, twigged). To observe; to understand.

Twilight, twī'līt, *n.* The faint light of the sun reflected after sunset and before sunrise; dubious view or conditon.—*a.* Faint; seen or done by twilight.

Twill, twil, *vt.* To weave so as to produce a kind of diagonal ribbed appearance.—*n.* A textile fabric with a kind of diagonal ribbed surface; surface of this kind.

Twin, twin, *n.* One of two born together; one of a pair or couple.—*a.* Being one of two born at a birth; very similar; two-fold.

Twine, twīn, *n.* A strong thread composed of two or three strands; a twist.—*vt.* and *i.* (twining, twined). To twist; to weave; to coil; to wrap closely about.

Twinge, twinj, *vt.* and *i.* (twinging, twinged). To affect with or have a sharp, sudden pain.—*n.* A sudden, sharp, darting pain.

Twinkle, twingk'l, *vi.* (twinkling, twinkled). To sparkle; to shine with a quivering light.—*n.* A gleam or sparkle.

Twinkling, twingk'ling, *n.* A quick movement of the eye; a wink; an instant; the scintillation of the stars.

Twirl, twėrl, *vt.* and *i.* To turn round with rapidity; to spin.—*n.* A rapid whirl.

Twist, twist, *n.* Something twined, as a thread, etc.; roll of tobacco; a spiral; contortion; mental or moral bent.—*vt.* and *i.* To form into a cord; to twine; to contort; to insinuate; to pervert.

Twitch, twich, *vt.* To pull with a sudden jerk; to tug.—*vi.* To be suddenly contracted.—*n.* A sudden pull; short spasmodic contraction of a muscle.

Twitter, twit'ėr, *vi.* To utter small, tremulous notes, as birds; to chirp.—*n.* A chirp or continued chirping.

Two, tö, *a.* and *n.* One and one together.

Two-faced, tö'fāst, *a.* Having two faces; insincere; given to double-dealing.

Twofold, tö'föld, *a.* Double.—*adv.* Doubly; in a double degree.

Tympanum, tim'pa-num, *n.*; pl. **-na.** The drum of the ear.

Type, tīp, *n.* A distinguishing mark; emblem; symbol; ideal representative; model; letter used in printing; such letters collectively.

Typesetter, tīp'set-ėr, *n.* One who sets up type; a compositor; a type-setting machine.

Typewriter, tīp'rīt-ėr, *n.* A machine used as a substitute for the pen, producing letters by inked types.

Typhoid, tī'foid, *n.* A fever characterized by abdominal pains and diarrhea; enteric fever.

Typhoon, tī-fön', *n.* A violent hurricane on the coasts of China and Japan.

Typhus, tī'fus, *n.* A contagious or epidemic fever characterized by a deep livid eruption.

Typical, tip'ik-al, *a.* Pertaining to a type; emblematic; symbolic; representative.

Typify, tip'i-fī, *vt.* To serve as a type of, to represent; to exemplify.

Typographic, Typographical, tī-po-graf'ik, tī-po-graf'ik-al, *a.* Pertaining to typography or printing.

Typography, tī-pog'ra-fī, *n.* The art of printing; style of printing.

Typology, tī-pol'o-ji, *n.* A discourse on types; the doctrine of types in Scripture.

Tyranny, ti'ran-i, *n.* Rule of a tyrant; despotic exercise of power; oppression.

Tyrant, tī'rant, *n.* A despot; a cruel sovereign or master; an oppressor.

U

Ubiety, ū-bī'e-ti, *n.* The state of being somewhere.

Ubiquity, ū-bi'kwi-ti, *n.* Existence everywhere at the same time; omnipresence.

Udder, ud'ėr, *n.* The glandular organ of cows, etc., in which the milk is produced.

Ugly, ug'li, *a.* Repulsive; disagreeable in appearance; hateful; ill-omened.

Ukulele, ū'ku-lā''lē, *n.* A small Hawaiian guitar.

Ulcer, ul'sėr, *n.* A sore that discharges pus.

Ulcerate, ul'sėr-āt, *vt.* To affect with an ulcer.—*vi.* To become ulcerous.

Uliginous, ū-li'ji-nus, *a.* Oozy; slimy.

Ulna, ul'na, *n.* The larger of the two bones of the forearm.

Ulterior, ul-tē'ri-or, *a.* Being beyond or on the farther side; more remote; distant; not avowed; reserved.

Ultimate, ul'ti-māt, *a.* Farthest; last or final; extreme; arrived at as a final result.

Ultimatum, ul-ti-mā'tum, *n.*; pl. **-ta** or **-tums.** The last offer; a final proposition which being rejected may be followed by war.

Ultra, ul'tra, *prefix, a.* Beyond due limit; extreme.—*n.* An ultraist.

Ultramarine, ul'tra-ma-rēn'', *a.* Being beyond the sea.—*n.* A beautiful and durable sky-blue.

Ultramundane, ul-tra-mun'dān, *a.* Being beyond the world.

Ultra-violet, ul'tra-vī''ö-let, *a.* Of the part of the spectrum beyond the violet end of the visible spectrum.

Umber, um'bėr, *n.* A soft earthy pigment of an olive-brown color in its raw state, but redder when burnt.

Umbilicus, um-bi-li'kus, *n.* The navel.

Umbra, um'bra, *n.* The total shadow of the earth or moon in an eclipse.

Umbrage, um'brāj, *n.* Shade; obscurity; jealousy; offense; resentment.

Umbrella, um-brel'la, *n.* A portable shade which opens and folds, for sheltering the person from the sun or rain.

Umlaut, um'lout, *n.* The change of a vowel in one syllable through the influence of a different vowel in the syllable immediately following.

Umpire, um'pīr, *n.* A person to whose decision a dispute is referred; a judge, arbiter, or referee.

Unable, un-ā'bl, *a.* Not able; not having sufficient ability; not equal for some task.

Unacceptable, un-ak-sept'a-bl, *a.* Not acceptable or pleasing; unwelcome.

Unaccommodating, un-ak-kom'mö-dāt-ing, *a.* Not ready to oblige; uncompliant.

Unaccomplished, un-ak-kom'plisht, *a.* Not performed completely; not having accomplishments.

Unaccountable, un-ak-kount'a-bl, *a.* Not to be accounted for; not responsible.

Unaccustomed, un-ak-kus'tumd, *a.* Not accustomed; not habituated; unusual.

Unacquainted, un-ak-kwānt'ed, *a.* Not acquainted; not having familiar knowledge.

Unadorned, un-a-dornd', *a.* Not adorned; not embellished.

Unadvisable, un-ad-vīz'a-bl, *a.* Not advisable; not expedient; not prudent.

Unaffected, un-af-fekt'ed, *a.* Not affected; natural; simple; sincere; not moved.

Unalterable, un-al'tėr-a-bl, *a.* Not alterable; unchangeable; immutable.

Unanimous. ū-nan'i-mus, *a.* Being of one mind;

U

agreeing in determination; formed by unanimity.

Unappealable, un-ap-pēl'a-bl, a. Not appealable; admitting no appeal; that cannot be carried to a higher court by appeal.

Unappreciated, un-ap-prē'shi-āt-ed, a. Not duly estimated or valued.

Unapproachable, un-ap-prōch'a-bl, a. That cannot be approached; inaccessible.

Unappropriate, un-ap-prō'pri-āt, a. Not appropriate; inappropriate.

Unarmed, un-ärmd', a. Not having arms or armor; not equipped.

Unaspiring, un-as-pīr'ing, a. Not ambitious.

Unassailable, un-as-sāl'a-bl, a. Not assailable; that cannot be assaulted.

Unassuming, un-as-sūm'ing. a. Not assuming; retiring; modest.

Unassured, un-a-shörd', a. Not confident; not to be trusted; not insured.

Unattended, un-at-tend'ed, a. Having no attendants; not medically attended.

Unauthorized, un-a'thor-īzd, a. Not authorized; not warranted.

Unavailable, un-a-vāl'a-bl, a. Not available; vain; useless.

Unavailing, un-a-vāl'ing, a. Of no avail; ineffectual; useless.

Unavoidable, un-a-void'a-bl, a. Not to be shunned; inevitable.

Unbearable, un-bār'a-bl, a. Not to be endured; intolerable.

Unbecoming, un-bē-kum'ing, a. Not becoming; improper.

Unbelief, un-bē-lēf', n. Incredulity; infidelity; disbelief of the gospel.

Unbridled, un-brī'dld, a. Unrestrained.

Unbroken, un-brōk'n, a. Not broken; not tamed; not interrupted.

Uncalled, un-kald', a. Not called; not summoned; not invited.

Uncanny, un-kan'i, a. Not canny; mysterious; of evil and supernatural character.

Uncared, un-kārd', a. Not regarded; not heeded; often with *for*.

Unceasing, un-sēs'ing, a. Not ceasing; continual.

Uncertain, un-sėr'tān, a. Not certain; doubtful; inconstant.

Unchallenged, un-chal'lenjd, a. Not objected to; not called in question.

Unchanging, un-chānj'ing, a. Not changing; suffering no change.

Uncharitable, un-cha'rit-a-bl, a. Not charitable; ready to think evil; harsh.

Unchristian, un-kris'ti-an, a. Contrary to the spirit or laws of Christianity.

Uncinate, un'si-nāt, a. Hooked at the end; unciform.

Uncle, ung'kl, n. The brother of one's father or mother.

Unclean, un-klēn' a. Not clean; foul; dirty; morally impure; lewd.

Uncomfortable, un-kum'fort-a-bl, a. Not comfortable; uneasy; ill at ease.

Uncommon, un-kom'mon, a. Not common; rare; strange; remarkable.

Uncommunicative, un-kom-mū'ni-kāt-iv, a. Not apt to communicate; reserved.

Uncompromising, un-kom'prō-mīz-ing, a. Not agreeing to terms; unyielding.

Unconcern, un-kon-sėrn', n. Want of concern; apathy; indifference.

Unconditional, un-kon-di'shon-al, a. Not limited by conditions; absolute.

Unconfined, un-kon-find', a. Not confined; free from restraint or control.

Unconfirmed, un-kon-fėrmd', a. Not confirmed; not firmly established.

Unconnected, un-kon-nekt'ed, a. Not connected; separate; incoherent; loose.

Unconquerable, un-kong'kėr-a-bl, a. Not conquerable; insuperable.

Unconscious, un-kon'shus, a. Not conscious; not

perceiving; unaware.

Unconstitutional, un-kon'sti-tū''shon-al, a. Not agreeable to the constitution; against the law.

Unconverted, un-kon-vėrt'ed, a. Not converted; not regenerated.

Uncork, un-kork', vt. To draw the cork from.

Uncorrected, un-ko-rekt'ed, a. Not corrected; not revised; not reformed.

Uncouple, un-ku'pl, vt. To loose, as dogs coupled together; to disjoin.

Uncouth, un-köth', a. Strange; odd in appearance; awkward.

Uncover, un-ku'vėr, vt. To divest of a cover; to disclose.—vi. To take off the hat.

Unction, ungk'shon, n. Act of anointing; an unguent; religious fervor; sham devotional fervor; oiliness.

Unctuous, ung'tū-us, a. Oily; greasy; nauseously emotional; oily; fawning.

Uncultivated, un-kul'ti-vāt-ed, a. Not cultivated; not tilled; boorish or rude.

Undaunted, un-dant'ed, a. Intrepid; fearless.

Undecided, un-dē-sīd'ed, a. Not decided; hesitating; irresolute.

Undefined, un-dē-find', a. Not defined; lacking in clearness or definiteness.

Undeniable, un-dē-nī'a-bl, a. incapable of being denied; indisputable.

Under, un'dėr, prep. Below; beneath; undergoing; affected by; subject to; inferior; during the time of; included in; in accordance with.—adv. In a lower condition or degree.—a. Lower; subject; subordinate.

Undercharge, un-dėr-chärj', vt. To charge insufficiently.—n. un'der-chärj. Too low a charge or price.

Underclothes, Underclothing, un'dėr-klōтнz, un'dėr-klōтн-ing, n. Clothes worn under others or next to the skin.

Undercurrent, un'dėr-ku-rent, n. A current below another; some movement or influence not apparent.

Undergo, un-dėr-gō, vt. To bear; to experience; to suffer.

Undergraduate, un-dėr-grad'ū-āt, n. A student who has not taken his first degree.

Underground, un'dėr-ground, a. and adv. Below the surface of the ground; operating in secret.

Undergrowth, un'dėr-grōth, n. Shrubs or small trees growing among large ones.

Underhand, un'dėr-hand, a. Working by stealth; secret; deceitful.—adv. In a clandestine manner.

Underlie, un-dėr-lī', vt. To lie beneath; to be at the basis of.

Underline, un-dėr-līn', vt. To mark with a line below the words.

Undermine, un-dėr-mīn', vt. To sap; to injure by underhand means.

Underneath, un-dėr-nēth', adv. Beneath; below.—prep. Under; beneath.

Underrate, un-dėr-rāt', vt. To rate too low; to undervalue.

Undersized, un'dėr-sīzd, a. Being of a size or stature less than common; dwarfish.

Understand, un-dėr-stand', vt. To comprehend; to see through; to suppose to mean; to infer; to assume; to recognize as implied although not expressed.—vi. To comprehend; to learn.

Understate, un-dėr-stāt', vt. To state too low or as less than actually.

Undertake, un'dėr-tāk, vt. To take in hand; to engage in; to attempt; to guarantee.—vi. To take upon oneself; to promise; to stand bound.

Undertaker, un'dėr-tāk-ėr, n. One who undertakes; one who manages funerals.

Undertaking, un'dėr-tāk-ing, n. That which is undertaken; enterprise; promise.

Underwear, un'dėr-wār, n. Underclothes.

Underworld, un'dėr-wėrld, n. The lower world; this world; the antipodes; the place of departed souls; Hades.

Underwrite, un-dėr-rīt, vt. To write under; to subscribe one's name and become answerable for a certain amount.

Undetermined, un-dē-tér'mind, a. Not determined; not decided, fixed, or settled.

Undeterred, un-dē-térd', a. Not restrained by fear or obstacles.

Undigested, un-di-jest'ed, a. Not digested; not properly prepared or arranged; crude.

Undignified, un-dig'ni-fid, a. Not dignified; showing a want of dignity.

Undisguised, un-dis-gīzd', a. Not disguised; open; candid; artless.

Undisputed, un-dis-pūt'ed, a. Not disputed; not called in question; incontestable.

Undistinguished, un-dis-ting'gwisht, a. Not having any distinguishing mark; not famous; not possessing distinction.

Undisturbed, un-dis-térbd', a. Free from disturbance; calm; tranquil; not agitated.

Undivided, un-di-vid'ed, a. Not divided; whole; entire.

Undo, un-dö', vt. To reverse what has been done; annul; to loose; to take to pieces; to ruin.

Undoubtedly, un-dout'ed-li, adv. Without doubt; without question; indubitably.

Undress, un-dres', vt. To divest of dress or clothes; to strip.—n. un'dres. A loose negligent dress; ordinary dress.

Undue, un-dū', a. Not due; not yet demandable by right; not right; inordinate.

Undulate, un'dū-lāt, vi. To have a wavy motion; to wave.—vt. To cause to wave.

Unduly, un-dū'li, adv. In an undue manner; unlawfully; unwarrantably; excessively.

Undutiful, un-dū'ti-ful, a. Not dutiful; not obedient; rebellious; irreverent.

Undying, un-dī'ing, a. Not dying; imperishable.

Unearned, un-érnd', a. Not merited by labor or services.—**Unearned increment,** the increase in the value of property not due to any expenditure on the part of the owner.

Unearth, un-érth', vt. To drive or bring from the earth; to uncover; to discover.

Uneasy, un-ēz'i, a. Restless; disturbed; somewhat anxious; unquiet; stiff; not graceful; unpleasing; irksome.

Uneducated, un-ed'ū-kāt-ed, a. Not educated; illiterate; ignorant.

Unemotional, un-ē-mō'shon-al, a. Not emotional; impassive.

Unemployed, un-em-ploid', a. Not employed; having no work; not being in use.

Unending, un-end'ing, a. Not ending; perpetual; eternal.

Unendurable, un-en-dūr'a-bl, a. Intolerable.

Unenlightened, un-en-lit'nd, a. Not enlightened; not illuminated, mentally or morally.

Unenterprising, un-en'tér-prīz-ing, a. Wanting in enterprise; not adventurous.

Unenviable, un-en'vi-a-bl, a. Not enviable; Not to be envied.

Unequal, un-ē'kwal, a. Not equal; inadequate; insufficient; not equable.

Unequivocal, un-ē-kwiv'ō-kal, a. Not equivocal; not doubtful; clear; evident.

Unerring, un-er'ing, a. Not erring; incapable of error; certain.

Unessential, un-es-sen'shal, a. Not essential; not absolutely necessary.

Uneven, un-ē'vn, a. Not even or level; rough; crooked; not fair or just; odd.

Unexpected, un-eks-pekt'ed, a. Not expected; not looked for; sudden.

Unexpired, un-eks-pird', a. Not expired; not having come to the end of its term.

Unexplored, un-eks-plörd', a. Not explored; not visited by any traveller.

Unfading, un-fād'ing, a. Not fading; not liable to wither or decay; ever fresh.

Unfailing, un-fāl'ing, a. Not liable to fail; that does not fail; certain.

Unfair, un-fār', a. Not honest or impartial; not just; inequitable; disingenuous.

Unfamiliar, un-fa-mil'i-èr, a. Not familiar; not accustomed; strange.

Unfashionable, un-fa'shon-a-bl, a. Not fashionable or according to the fashion.

Unfasten, un-fäs'n, vt. To loose; to unfix.

Unfathomable, un-faᴛн'um-a-bl, a. That cannot be fathomed; incomprehensible.

Unfavorable, un-fā'ver-a-bl, a. Not favorable; not propitious; discouraging.

Unfeeling, un-fēl'ing, a. Devoid of feeling; hardhearted; harsh; brutal.

Unfit, un-fit', a. Not fit; unsuitable; not competent.—vt. To make unfit.

Unflinching, un-flinsh'ing, a. Not flinching; not shrinking; resolute.

Unfold, un-föld', vt. To open the folds of; to display.—vi. To open out.

Unforgiving, un-for-giv'ing, a. Not forgiving; implacable.

Unfortunate, un-for'tū-nāt, a. Not fortunate; unlucky; unhappy.—n. One who is unfortunate; a prostitute.

Unfounded, un-found'ed, a. Having no real foundation; groundless; idle.

Unfruitful, un-fröt'ful, a. Not fruitful; barren.

Unfurl, un-férl', vt. To loose from a furled state; to expand to catch the wind.

Unfurnished, un-fér'nisht, a. Not furnished; unsupplied; unprovided.

Ungainly, un-gān'li, a. Not handsome; uncouth; clumsy; awkward; ill-shaped.

Ungentlemanly, un-jen'tl-man-li, a. Not becoming a gentleman.

Ungodly, un-god'li, a. Not godly; wicked.

Ungovernable, un-gu'vern-a-bl, a. That cannot be governed; wild; refractory.

Ungracious, un-grā'shus, a. Not gracious; uncivil; rude; impolite.

Ungrateful, un-grāt'ful, a. Not grateful; not thankful; unpleasing; harsh.

Ungrounded, un-ground'ed, a. Having no foundation or support; groundless.

Ungrudging, un-gruj'ing, a. Without a grudge; freely giving; hearty; liberal.

Unguarded, un-gärd'ed, a. Not guarded; not cautious; negligent.

Unguent, un'gwent, n. An ointment.

Unhallowed, un-hal'ōd, a. Not hallowed or sanctified; profane; unholy.

Unhand, un-hand', vt. To loose from the hand or hands; to lose hold of.

Unhappy, un-hap'i, a. Not happy; sad; unfortunate; unlucky; evil; ill omened.

Unhealthy, un-helth'i, a. Not healthy; sickly; insalubrious; unwholesome.

Unheard, un-herd', a. Not heard; not admitted to audience; not known (with of).

Unhesitating, un-he'zi-tāt-ing, a. Not hesitating; not remaining in doubt; prompt.

Unhinge, un-hinj', vt. To take from the hinges; to unfix; to loosen; to derange.

Unholy, un-hō'li, a. Not holy; not sacred; unhallowed; profane; impious; wicked.

Unicorn, ū'ni-korn, n. A fabulous animal like a horse, with a long single horn on the forehead.

Unification, ū'ni-fi-kā''shon, n. The act of unifying or uniting into one.

Uniform, ū'ni-form, a. Having always one and the same form; equable; invariable; consistent.—n. A distinctive dress worn by the members of the same body.

Uniformity, ū-ni-for'mi-ti, n. State or character of being uniform; conformity to one type; agreement; consistency.

Unify, ū'ni-fi, vt. To form into one.

Unimaginable, un-im-aj'in-a-bl, a. Not imaginable; inconceivable.

Unimpaired, un-im-pärd', a. Not impaired; not diminished; uninjured.

Unimpassioned, un-im-pa'shond, a. Not impassioned; tranquil; not violent.

Unimpeachable, un-im-pēch'a-bl, a. Not impeachable; blameless; irreproachable.

U

Unimportant, un-im-pōr'tant, *a.* Not important; not of great moment.

Unimproved, un-im-prövd', *a.* Not improved; not cultivated.

Uninhabited, un-in-ha'bit-ed, *a.* Not inhabited by men; having no inhabitants.

Unintelligible, un-in-tel'i-ji-bl, *a.* Not intelligible; meaningless.

Unintentional, un-in-ten'shon-al, *a.* Not intentional; done without design.

Uninterested, un-in'tėr-est-ed, *a.* Not interested; having no interest or concern.

Uninterrupted, un-in'tėr-rupt''ed, *a.* Not interrupted; unintermitted; incessant.

Uninviting, un-in-vīt'ing, *a.* Not inviting; unattractive; rather repellent.

Union, ūn'yon, *n.* Act of joining; combination; agreement; harmony; marriage; confederacy; a trades-union; a mixed fabric of cotton, flax, jute, silk, or wool, etc.; a certain kind of flag.

Uniparous, ū-nip'a-rus, *a.* Producing one at a birth.

Unique, ū-nēk', *a.* Without a like or equal; unmatched; unequalled.

Unison, ū-ni-son, *n.* Accordance; agreement; harmony; concord.

Unit, ū'nit, *n.* A single thing or person; an individual; the number 1; a dimension or quantity assumed as a standard.

Unitarian, ū-ni-tā'ri-an, *n.* One who ascribes divinity to God only, and denies the Trinity.—*a.* Pertaining to Unitarians.

Unite, ū-nīt', *vt.* (uniting, united). To combine; to connect; to associate.—*vi.* To become one; to combine; to concur.

Unity, ū'ni-ti, *n.* State of being one; concord; agreement; harmony; artistic harmony and symmetry.

Universal, ū-ni-vėrs'al, *a.* Pertaining to all; total; whole.—*n.* A general notion or idea.

Universe, ū'ni-vėrs, *n.* The whole system of created things; the world.

University, ū-ni-vėrs'i-ti, *n.* An institution for instruction in science and literature, etc., and having the power of conferring degrees.

Unjust, un-just', *a.* Not just, upright, or equitable.

Unkempt, un-kempt', *a.* Uncombed; rough.

Unkind, un-kīnd', *a.* Not kind; cruel.

Unknown, un-nōn', *a.* Not known; not discovered, found out, or ascertained.

Unlawful, un-la'ful, *a.* Not lawful; illegal.

Unlearned, un-lėr'ned, *a.* Not learned or erudite; illiterate; (un-lėrnd') not known.

Unless, un-les', *conj.* If it be not that; if . . . not; except; excepting.

Unlicensed, un-li'senst, *a.* Not having a license; done without due license.

Unlike, un-līk', *a.* Not like; dissimilar; having no resemblance; diverse.

Unlimited, un-lim'it-ed, *a.* Not limited; boundless; indefinite.

Unload, un-lōd', *vt.* To take the load from; to discharge; to empty out.

Unlock, un-lok', *vt.* To unfasten; to open.

Unlucky, un-luk'i, *a.* Not lucky; unfortunate; not successful; ill-omened.

Unmanageable, un-man'āj-a-bl, *a.* Not manageable; beyond control.

Unmannerly, un-man'ėr-li, *a.* Not mannerly; rude; ill-bred.

Unmask, un-mask', *vt.* To strip of a mask; to expose.—*vi.* To put off a mask.

Unmatched, un-macht', *a.* Matchless.

Unmeasured, un-me'zhūrd, *a.* Not measured; immense; infinite; excessive.

Unmentionable, un-men'shon-a-bl, *a.* Not mentionable.

Unmerciful, un-mėr'si-ful, *a.* Not merciful; cruel; merciless.

Unmerited, un-mer'it-ed, *a.* Not deserved.

Unmindful, un-mīnd'ful, *a.* Not mindful; regardless.

Unmistakable, Unmistakeable, un-mis-tāk'a-bl, *a.* Not capable of being mistaken; clear; obvious.

Unmoved, un-mövd', *a.* Not moved; firm; calm; cool.

Unnamed, un-nāmd', *a.* Not having received a name; not mentioned.

Unnatural, un-na'tūr-al, *a.* Not natural; contrary to nature; affected; artificial.

Unnecessary, un-ne'ses-sa-ri, *a.* Not necessary; needless.

Unnerve, un-nėrv', *vt.* To deprive of nerve, strength, or composure; to enfeeble.

Unnoticed, un-nōt'ist, *a.* Not observed.

Unobjectionable, un-ob-jek'shon-a-bl, *a.* Not liable to objection; unexceptionable.

Unobservant, Unobserving, un-ob-zėrv'ant, un-ob-zėrv'ing, *a.* Not observant.

Unobtrusive, un-ob-trö'siv, *a.* Not obtrusive; not forward; modest; retiring.

Unoccupied, un-ok'kū-pid, *a.* Not occupied; not possessed; at leisure.

Unofficial, un-of-fi'shal, *a.* Not official.

Unopposed, un-op-pōzd', *a.* Not opposed; not meeting with any obstruction.

Unorthodox, un-ōr'tho-doks, *a.* Not orthodox; heterodox.

Unpack, un-pak', *vt.* To take from a package; to unload.

Unpaid, un-pād', *a.* Not paid; remaining due; not receiving a salary.

Unpalatable, un-pa'lat-a-bl, *a.* Not palatable; disagreeable to the taste or feelings.

Unparalleled, un-pa'ral-eld, *a.* Having no parallel; unequalled; matchless.

Unpardonable, un-pär'dn-a-bl, *a.* Not to be forgiven; incapable of being pardoned.

Unpatriotic, un-pā'tri-ot''ik, *a.* Not patriotic; wanting in patriotism.

Unpleasant, un-ple'zant, *a.* Not pleasant. **Unpolished,** un-po'lisht, *a.* Not polished; rude; plain.

Unpopular, un-po'pū-lėr, *a.* Not popular.

Unprecedented, un-pre'sē-dent-ed, *a.* Having no precedent; unexampled.

Unprejudiced, un-pre'jū-dist, *a.* Not prejudiced; free from bias; impartial.

Unpremeditated, un-prē-me'di-tāt-ed, *a.* Not previously meditated; spontaneous.

Unprepared, un-prē-pārd', *a.* Not prepared.

Unprincipled, un-prin'si-pld, *a.* Not having settled principles; immoral.

Unproductive, un-prō-duk'tiv, *a.* Not productive; infertile; not returning a profit.

Unprofessional, un-prō-fe'shon-al, *a.* Contrary to the customs of a profession; not belonging to a profession.

Unprofitable, un-pro'fit-a-bl, *a.* Not profitable; useless; profitless.

Unpromising, un-pro'mis-ing, *a.* Not giving promise of success, etc.

Unproved, un-prövd', *a.* Not proved; not established as true by proof.

Unqualified, un-kwo'li-fīd, *a.* Not qualified; not having the requisite qualifications; not modified by conditions.

Unquestionable, un-kwest'yon-a-bl, *a.* Not to be called in question; indubitable.

Unquiet, un-kwī'et, *a.* Not quiet; disturbed.

Unravel, un-ra'vel, *vt.* To disentangle; to disengage or separate; to solve.

Unreadable, un-rēd'a-bl, *a.* Incapable of being read; illegible; not worth reading.

Unready, un-re'di, *a.* Not ready; not prompt to act.

Unreal, un-rē'al, *a.* Not real; not substantial.

Unreason, un-rē'zn, *n.* Want of reason; folly; absurdity.

Unrecorded, un-rē-kord'ed, *a.* Not recorded or registered; not kept in remembrance by documents or monuments.

Unredeemed, un-rē-dēmd', *a.* Not redeemed; not fulfilled; unmitigated.

Unrefined, un-rē-fīnd', *a.* Not refined or purified;

not polished in manners, taste, etc.

Unregenerate, un-rē-jen'ē-rāt, a. Not regenerated or renewed in heart.

Unrelated, un-rē-lāt'ed, a. Not connected by blood; having no connection.

Unrelenting, un-rē-lent'ing, a. Not relenting; relentless; hard; pitiless.

Unreliable, un-rē-li'a-bl, a. Not reliable; untrustworthy.

Unrelieved, un-rē-lēvd', a. Not relieved; monotonous.

Unremitting, un-rē-mit'ing, a. Not remitting or abating; incessant; continued.

Unrequited, un-rē-kwit'ed, a. Not requited; not recompensed.

Unreserved, un-rē-zėrvd', a. Not reserved or restricted; full; free; open; frank.

Unrest, un-rēst', n. Disquiet; uneasiness.

Unrestrained, un-rē-strānd', a. Not restrained; licentious; loose.

Unrighteous, un-rit'yus, a. Not righteous; not just; wicked.

Unripe, un-rip', a. Not ripe; not mature; not fully prepared; not completed.

Unrivaled, un-ri'vald, a. Having no rival; incomparable.

Unromantic, un-rō-man'tik, a. Not romantic; not given to romantic fancies.

Unruffled, un-ruf'ld, a. Not ruffled; calm; tranquil; not agitated; not disturbed.

Unruly, un-rö'li, a. Disregarding rule; turbulent; ungovernable; disorderly.

Unsafe, un-sāf', a. Not safe; perilous.

Unsaid, un-sed', a. Not spoken.

Unsatisfactory, un-sa'tis-fak''to-ri, a. Not satisfactory; not satisfying.

Unsavory, un-sā'vo-ri, a. Not savory; insipid; unpleasing; offensive.

Unscathed, un-skāтнd', a. Not scathed; uninjured.

Unscrew, un-skrö', vt. To draw the screw from; to unfasten by screwing back.

Unscrupulous, un-skrö'pū-lus, a. Having no scruples; regardless of principle.

Unseasonable, un-sē'zn-a-bl, a. Not seasonable; ill-timed; untimely.

Unseen, un-sēn', a. Not seen; invisible.

Unselfish, un-sel'fish, a. Not selfish.

Unsettle, un-set'l, vt. To change from a settled state; to unhinge; to derange.

Unshaken, un-shā'kn, a. Not shaken; resolute; firm.

Unshrinking, un-shringk'ing, a. Not shrinking; not recoiling; fearless.

Unsightly, un-sit'li, a. Not sightly; repulsive; ugly; deformed.

Unsociable, un-sō'shi-a-bl, a. Not sociable.

Unsoiled, un-soild', a. Not soiled; pure.

Unsolicited, un-sō-lis'it-ed, a. Not asked.

Unsophisticated, un-sō-fist'ik-āt-ed, a. Pure; natural, artless; simple.

Unsound, un-sound', a. Not sound; erroneous; not orthodox.

Unsparing, un-spār'ing, a. Not sparing; profuse; severe; rigorous.

Unspeakable, un-spēk'a-bl, a. Incapable of being spoken or uttered; unutterable.

Unspoken, un-spō'kn, a. Not spoken.

Unstable, un-stā'bl, a. Not stable; inconstant; irresolute; wavering.

Unsteady, un-sted'i, a. Not steady; shaking; fickle; varying.

Unstop, un-stop', vt. To free from a stopper, as a bottle, to free from obstruction.

Unstrung, un-strung', a. Deprived of strings; having the nerves shaken.

Unsubstantial, un-sub-stan'shal, a. Not substantial; not real; not nutritive.

Unsuccessful, un-suk-ses'ful, a. Not successful; not fortunate in the result.

Unsuitable, un-sūt'a-bl, a. Not suitable; ill adapted; unfit.

Unsullied, un-sul'id, a. Not sullied; pure.

Unsung, un-sung', a. Not sung; not celebrated in song or poetry.

Unsurpassed, un-sėr-past', a. Not surpassed, excelled, or outdone.

Unsuspecting, un-sus-pekt'ing, a. Not suspecting; free from suspicion.

Unswerving, un-swėrv'ing, a. Not swerving; unwavering; firm.

Untainted, un-tānt'ed, a. Not tainted.

Untamable, Untameable, un-tām'a-bl, a. Not capable of being tamed.

Untasted, un-tāst'ed, a. Not tasted; not experienced.

Untaught, un-tat', a. Not educated; unlettered; ignorant.

Untenable, un-ten'a-bl, a. Not to be maintained by argument; not defensible.

Unthinkable, un-thingk'a-bl, a. That cannot be made an object of thought.

Unthinking, un-thingk'ing, a. Not given to think; not heedful; inconsiderate.

Unthread, un-thred', vt. To draw or take out a thread from.

Unthrifty, un-thrift'i, a. Not thrifty, prodigal; lavish; wasteful.

Untidy, un-ti'di, a. Not tidy; slovenly.

Untie, un-ti', vt. (untying, untied). To loosen, as a knot; to undo; to unfasten.

Until, un-til', prep. or conj. Till; to; till the time or point that.

Untimely, un-tim'li, a. Not timely; ill timed; inopportune.—adv. Unseasonably.

Untiring, un-tir'ing, a. Not tiring; unwearied.

Unto, un'tö, prep. To.

Untold, un-tōld', a. Not told; not revealed or counted.

Untouched, un-tucht', a. Not touched; uninjured; not affected.

Untoward, un-tō'wėrd, a. Not toward; froward; awkward; vexatious.

Untractable, un-trak'ta-bl, a. Not tractable; refractory.

Untraveled, un-tra'veld, a. Not trodden by passengers; not having traveled.

Untried, un-trid', a. Not tried; not attempted; not yet experienced; not determined in law.

Untroubled, un-tru'bld, a. Not troubled; not agitated or ruffled; not turbid.

Untrue, un-trö', a. Not true; false.

Untrustworthy, un-trust'wėr-тнi, a. Not worthy of being trusted; unreliable.

Unused, un-ūzd', a. Not used; not put to use, not accustomed.

Unusual, un-ū'zhū-al, a. Not usual; rare.

Unutterable, un-ut'ėr-a-bl, a. That cannot be uttered; inexpressible.

Unvarnished, un-vär'nisht, a. Not varnished; not artfully embellished; plain.

Unveil, un-vāl', vt. To remove a veil from; to uncover; to disclose to view.

Unwarranted, un-wo'rant-ed, a. Not warranted; unjustifiable; not certain.

Unwary, un-wā'ri, a. Not cautious.

Unwashed, un-wosht', a. Not washed; dirty.

Unwavering, un-wā'vėr-ing, a. Not wavering; steady; steadfast.

Unwearied, un-wē'rid, a. Not wearied or tired; indefatigable; assiduous.

Unwed, un-wed', a. Unmarried.

Unwelcome, un-wel'kum, a. Not welcome; not pleasing or grateful.

Unwholesome, un-hōl'sum, a. Not wholesome; insalubrious; causing sickness.

Unwieldy, un-wēl'di, n. Movable with difficulty; unmanageable.

Unwilling, un-wil'ing, a. Not willing; loath; disinclined; reluctant.

Unwise, un-wiz', a. Not wise; injudicious.

Unwitting, un-wit'ing, a. Not knowing; unconscious; unaware.

Unwomanly, un-wu'man-li, a. Not womanly; unbecoming a woman.

Unworldly, un-wėrld'li, a. Not worldly; not influ-

U

enced by worldly or sordid motives.

Unworthy, un-wẻr'THi, a. Not worthy; worthless; base; not becoming or suitable.

Unwrap, un-rap', vt. To open or undo, as what is wrapped up.

Unwritten, un-rit'n, a. Not written; blank; understood though not expressed.

Unyielding, un-yẻld'ing, a. Stiff; firm; obstinate.

Up, up, adv. Aloft; in or to a higher position; upright; above the horizon; out of bed; in a state of sedition; from the country to the metropolis; quite; to or at an end.—prep. To a higher place or point on; towards the interior of.

Upbraid, up-brād', vt. To reproach; to chide; to taunt.

Upbringing, up'bring-ing, n. Training; education; breeding.

Upheaval, up-hẻv'al, n. Act of upheaving; lifting of a portion of the earth's crust.

Uphill, up'hil, a. Leading or going up a rising ground; difficult; fatiguing.

Uphold, up-hōld', vt. To hold up; to keep erect; to support; to sustain.

Upkeep, up'kẻp, n. Maintenance.

Upland, up'land, n. Higher grounds; hillslopes.—a. Pertaining to uplands.

Uplift, up-lift', vt. To lift up.—n. up'lift. A raising; rise; exaltation.

Upmost, up'mōst, a. Highest; uppermost.

Upon, up-on', prep. Up and on; resting on; on.

Upper, up'er, a. Higher in place or rank.—n. The upper part of a shoe.

Upper-hand, up'ẻr-hand, n. Superiority.

Uppermost, up'ẻr-mōst, a. superl. Highest in place, rank, or power.

Upright, up'rit, a. Straight up; erect; honest; just.—n. A vertical piece.

Uprising, up-riz'ing, n. Rise; ascent or acclivity; a riot; a rebellion.

Uproar, up'rōr, n. A great tumult; violent disturbance; bustle and clamor.

Uproot, up-rōt', vt. To tear up by the roots.

Upset, up-set', vt. To overturn; to discompose completely.—n. up'set. Act of upsetting.—a. Fixed; determined.—**Upset price,** the price at which anything is exposed to sale by auction.

Upshot, up'shot, n. Final issue; end.

Upstairs, up'stärz, a. or adv. Ascending the stairs; in or pertaining to the upper part of a house.

Upstart, up-stärt', vi. To start up suddenly.—n. up'stärt. A parvenu.

Upward, up'wẻrd, a. Directed to a higher place; ascending.—adv. Upwards.

Uranium, ū-rā'ni-um, n. A rare metal, colored like nickel or iron.

Uranus, ū'ra-nus, n. The most distant of all the planets except Neptune and Pluto.

Urban, ẻr'ban, a. Of or belonging to a city or town.

Urbane, ẻr-bān', a. Courteous; polite.

Urchin, ẻr'chin, n. A hedgehog; a sea-urchin; a child or small boy.

Ureter, ū-rē'tẻr, n. The duct that conveys the urine from the kidney to the bladder.

Urethra, ū-rē'thra, n. The duct by which the urine is discharged from the bladder.

Urge, ẻrj, vt. (urging, urged). To press to do something; to incite; to solicit; to insist on.—vi. To press forward.

Urgency, ẻrj'en-si, n. Pressure of difficulty or necessity; importunity.

Uric, ū'rik, a. Pertaining to or obtained from urine.

Urinate, ū'ri-nāt, vi. To discharge urine.

Urine, ū'rin, n. An animal fluid secreted by the kidneys and stored in the bladder before being discharged.

Urn, ẻrn, n. A vase swelling in the middle; a vessel for water.

Us, us, pron. The objective case of we.

Usable, ūz'a-bl, a. That may be used.

Usage, ūz'āj, n. Act or manner of using; treat-

ment; practice; custom; use.

Use, ūs, n. Act of employing anything; employment; utility; need; practice; wont.—vt. ūz (using, used). To put to use; to employ; to accustom; to treat.—vi. To be accustomed.

Usher, ush'ẻr, n. A door-keeper; an officer who introduces strangers, etc.; a subordinate teacher.—vt. To give entrance to; to introduce.

Usual, ū'zhū-al, a. Customary; common; frequent; ordinary; general.

Usurp, ū-zẻrp', vt. To seize and hold without right; to appropriate wrongfully.

Usury, ū'zhū-ri, n. Extortionate interest for money; practice of taking exorbitant interest.

Utensil, ū-ten'sil, n. That which is used; an instrument; implement.

Uterus, ū'tẻr-us, n.; pl. **-ri.** The womb.

Utilitarian, ū-til'i-tā''ri-an, a. Pertaining to utility or utilitarianism.—n. One who holds the doctrine of utilitarianism.

Utility, ū-til'i-ti, n. State or quality of being useful; usefulness; a useful thing.

Utilize, ū'til-īz, vt. (utilizing, utilized). To render useful; to put to use; to make use of.

Utmost, ut'mōst, a. Being farthest out; uttermost; extreme.—n. The greatest power, degree, or effort.

Utopia, ū-tō'pi-a, n. A place or state of ideal perfection.

Utter, ut'ẻr, a. Complete; total; absolute.—vt. To give vent to; to put into circulation; to declare; to speak.

Utterly, ut'ẻr-li, adv. Totally; absolutely.

Uvula, ū'vū-la, n. The small fleshy body which hangs over the root of the tongue.

V

Vacant, vā'kant, a. Empty; void; unoccupied; leisure; thoughtless; inane.

Vacate, va-kāt', vt. (vacating, vacated). To make vacant; to leave unoccupied; to annul.

Vacation, va-kā'shon, n. Act of vacating; intermission; recess; holidays.

Vaccinate, vak'si-nāt, vt. To inoculate with the cow-pox, in order to ward off small-pox.

Vacillate, va'sil-lāt, vi. To sway; to waver; to fluctuate.

Vacuity, va-kū'i-ti, n. Emptiness; vacancy; inanity; vacant expression.

Vacuous, va'kū-us, a. Empty; void; vacant; inane; inexpressive.

Vacuum, va'kū-um, n. Empty space; a void; an enclosed space void of air.—**Vacuum cleaner,** n. An apparatus used for removing dust from carpets, etc., by means of suction.

Vagabond, va'ga-bond, a. Wandering to and fro; pertaining to a vagrant.—n. A wanderer; a vagrant; a rascal.

Vagary, va-gā'ri, n. A wild freak; a whim.

Vagina, va-ji'na, n. A sheath; the canal in females leading inwards to the uterus.

Vagrant, vā'grant, a. Wandering; unsettled.—n. A wanderer; a vagabond; a sturdy beggar; a tramp.

Vague, vāg, a. Indefinite; hazy; uncertain.

Vain, vān, a. Without real value; empty; worthless; ineffectual; light-minded; conceited.—**In vain,** to no purpose.

Valance, Valence, val'ans, val'ens, n. The drapery hanging round a bed, couch, etc.

Valedictory, va-lẻ-dik'to-ri, a. Bidding farewell; pertaining to a leave-taking.

Valence, Valency, vā'lens, vā'len-si, n. The force which determines with how many atoms of an element an atom of another element will combine chemically.

Valentine, va'len-tin, n. A sweetheart selected or got by lot on St. Valentine's Day, 14th February; a missive of an amatory or satirical kind, sent on this day.

Valet, va'let or va'lā, *n.* A man-servant.—*vt.* To attend on a gentleman's person.

Valiant, val'yant, *a.* Brave; courageous; intrepid; heroic.

Valid, va'lid, *a.* Well based or grounded; sound; just; good or sufficient in law.

Valley, val'i, *n.* A low tract of land between hills; a river-basin.

Valor, va'lor, *n.* Bravery; courage; intrepidity; prowess in war.

Valuable, va'lū-a-bl, *a.* Of great worth; precious; worthy.—*n.* A thing of value; choice article of personal property; usually in *pl.*

Value, va'lū, *n.* Worth; utility; importance; import; precise signification.—*vt.* (valuing, valued). To rate at a certain price; to estimate; to esteem; to prize; to regard.

Valve, valv, *n.* A leaf of a folding door; a lid for an orifice, opening only one way and regulating the passage of fluid or air; a separable portion of the shell of a mollusk.

Vamp, vamp, *n.* The upper leather of a boot; a piece added for appearance sake.—*vt.* To repair; to furbish up; to patch.

Vampire, vam'pir, *n.* A dead person believed to have an unnatural life so as to be able to leave the grave at night and suck the blood of living persons; an extortioner; a blood-sucker; a vampire-bat.

Van, van, *n.* The front of an army or fleet; foremost portion; a winnowing fan; a covered vehicle for goods.

Vandal, van'dal, *n.* One who willfully or ignorantly destroys any work of art or the like.

Vane, vān, *n.* A weathercock; the broad part of a feather on either side of the shaft; blade of a windmill, etc.

Vanilla, va-nil'a, *n.* A tropical orchid; a fragrant substance obtained from it, used for seasoning.

Vanish, va'nish, *vi.* To disappear; to pass away.

Vanity, va'ni-ti, *n.* Quality or state of being vain; worthlessness; vain pursuit; desire of indiscriminate admiration; conceit; a trifle.

Vanquish, vang'kwish, *vt.* To conquer; to overcome; to confute.

Vantage, van'tāj, *n.* Advantage; vantage-ground; in lawn tennis, being in a position to win the game by winning the next point.

Vapid, va'pid, *a.* Spiritless; flat; dull.

Vaporize, vā-por-iz, *vt.* To convert into vapor.—*vi.* To pass off in vapor.

Vapor, vā'por, *n.* An exhalation or fume; visible moisture or steam; hazy matter; a vain imagination; *pl.* a nervous hysterical affection; the blues.—*vi.* To boast; to bully.

Variable, vā'ri-a-bl, *a.* That may vary or alter; changeable; fickle; unsteady.

Variation, vā-ri-ā'shon, *n.* Act or process of varying; alteration; amount or rate of change; inflection; deviation.

Varicose, va'ri-kōs, *a.* Exhibiting a morbid enlargement or dilation, as the veins.

Variegate, vā'ri-e-gāt, *vt.* (variegating, variegated). To diversify in appearance; to mark with different colors.

Variety, va-rī'e-ti, *n.* State or quality of being varied or various; diversity; a varied assortment; a sort; a kind.

Various, vā'ri-us, *a.* Different; several; changeable; uncertain; diverse.

Varnish, vär'nish, *n.* A clear solution of resinous matter, for coating surfaces and giving a gloss; outside show; gloss.—*vt.* To lay varnish on; to gloss over.

Vary, vā'ri, *vt.* (varying, varied) To change; to diversify.—*vi.* To alter; to change; to differ, to swerve; to disagree.

Vascular, vas'kū-lėr, *a.* Pertaining to those vessels that have to do with conveying blood, chyle, etc.

Vase, vāz, *n.* A vessel of some size and of various materials and forms, generally ornamental rather than useful.

Vast, väst, *a.* Of great extent; immense; mighty; great in importance or degree.—*n.* A boundless space; immensity.

Vat, vat, *n.* A large vessel for holding liquors; a tun; a wooden tank or cistern.—*vt.* (vatting, vatted). To put in a vat.

Vatican, vat'i-kan, *n.* The palace of the Pope at Rome; the papal power or government.

Vaudeville, vōd'vēl, *n.* A light, gay song; a ballad; a dramatic piece with light or comic songs.

Vault, valt, *n.* An arched roof; a subterranean chamber; a cellar; a leap; a leap with the hand resting on something.—*vt.* To arch.—*vi.* To leap; to bound.

Vaunt, vant, *vi.* To brag; to exult.—*vt.* To boast of; to make a vain display of.—*n.* A boast.

Veal, vēl, *n.* The flesh of a calf.

Veer, vėr, *vi.* To change direction; to turn round.—*vt.* To direct to a different course.

Vegetable, ve'je-ta-bl, *a.* Belonging to or like plants.—*n.* A plant; a plant for culinary purposes.

Vegetarian, ve-je-tā'ri-an, *n.* One who abstains from animal food and lives on vegetables.

Vegetate, ve'je-tāt, *vi.* (vegetating, vegetated). To grow as plants; to live a monotonous, useless life; to have a mere existence.

Vehemence, vē'he-mens, *n.* Ardor; violence; force; impetuosity; fury.

Vehement, vē'he-ment, *a.* Very eager or urgent; ardent; violent; furious.

Vehicle, vē'hi-kl, *n.* Any kind of carriage moving on land; conveyance; medium.

Veil, vāl, *n.* A screen; an article of dress shading the face; a covering or disguise; the soft palate.—*vt.* To cover with a veil; to envelop; to disguise.

Vein, vān, *n.* A blood-vessel which returns impure blood to the heart and lungs; a blood-vessel; a sap tube in leaves; a crack in a rock, filled up by substances different from the rock; a streak; disposition; mood.—*vt.* To fill or variegate with veins.

Vellum, vel'um, *n.* A fine parchment made of calf's skin.

Velocity, vē-los'i-ti, *n.* Rate of motion; speed; rapidity.

Velvet, vel'vet, *n.* A rich silk stuff with a close, fine, soft pile.—*a.* Made of or like velvet.

Velveteen, vel-vet-ēn', *n.* A cloth made of cotton in imitation of velvet; cotton velvet.

Venal, vē'nal, *a.* Ready to accept a bribe; mercenary.

Vend, vend, *vt.* To sell.

Vendetta, ven-det'ta, *n.* A blood feud; the practice of the nearest of kin executing vengeance on a murderer.

Vendor, ven'dor, *n.* A vender; a seller.

Veneer, ve-nēr', *n.* A thin facing of fine wood glued on a less valuable sort; any similar coating; fair outward show.—*vt.* To overlay with veneer; to put a fine superficial show on.

Venerate, ve'nē-rāt, *vt.* (venerating, venerated). To reverence; to revere; to regard as sacred.

Veneration, ve-nē-rā'shon, *n.* The highest degree of respect and reverence; respect mingled with some degree of awe.

Venereal, ve-nē'rē-al, *a.* Pertaining to sexual intercourse.

Venetian, vē-nē'shi-an, *a.* Belonging to Venice; denoting a window blind made of thin slats of wood.

Vengeance, venj'ans, *n.* Punishment in return for an injury; penal retribution.

Venial, vē'ni-al, *a.* That may be pardoned or forgiven; excusable.

Venison, ven'zn or ven'i-zn, *n.* The flesh of deer.

Venom, ve'nom, *n.* Poison; spite; malice; malignity; virulency.

Venous, vē'nus, *a.* Pertaining to a vein; contained in veins, as blood; venose.

Vent, vent, *n.* A small opening; flue or funnel; an outlet; the anus; utterance; expression; sale;

V

market.—*vt.* To let out; to publish.

Venter, ven'tẽr, *n.* The abdomen; in *law,* the uterus.

Ventilate, ven'ti-lãt, *vt.* (ventilating, ventilated). To winnow; to expose to the air; to supply with fresh air; to let be freely discussed.

Ventilation, ven-ti-lã'shon, *n.* Act of ventilating; replacement of vitiated air by fresh air, a bringing forward for discussion.

Ventral, ven'tral, *a.* Belonging to the belly; abdominal.

Ventricle, ven'tri-kl, *n.* A small cavity in an animal body; either of two cavities of the heart which propel the blood into the arteries.

Ventriloquism, Ventriloquy, ven-tri'lo-kwizm, ven-tri'lo-kwi, *n.* The art of uttering sounds so that the voice appears to come not from the actual speaker.

Venture, ven'tūr, *n.* An undertaking which involves hazard or danger; a commercial speculation; thing put to hazard; chance.—*vi.* (venturing, ventured). To make a venture; to dare.—*vt.* To risk.

Venue, ven'ū, *n.* A thrust; the place where an action is laid or the trial of a cause takes place.

Venus, vē'nus, *n.* The Roman goddess of beauty and love; a planet.

Veracious, ve-rã'shus, *a.* Observant of truth; truthful; true.

Veracity, ve-ras'i-ti, *n.* Truthfulness; truth; that which is true.

Veranda, Verandah, ve-ran'da, *n.* An open portico or light gallery along the front of a building.

Verb, vẽrb, *n.* The part of speech which signifies to be, to do, or to suffer.

Verbal, vẽrb'al, *a.* Relating to words; spoken; literal; derived from a verb.—*n.* A noun derived from a verb.

Verbalism, vẽrb'al-izm, *n.* Something expressed orally.

Verbatim, vẽr-bã'tim, *adv.* Word for word; in the same words.

Verbose, vẽr-bõs', *a.* Wordy; prolix.

Verbosity, vẽr-bos'i-ti, *n.* Superabundance of words; wordiness; prolixity.

Verdant, vẽr'dant, *a.* Green with herbage or foliage; simple and inexperienced.

Verdict, vẽr'dikt, *n.* The answer of a jury; decision in general; opinion.

Verdigris, Verdegris, vẽr'di-gris, vẽr'de-gris, *n.* The rust of copper; a substance obtained by exposing copper to the air in contact with acetic acid.

Verdure, vẽr'dūr, *n.* Greenness; freshness of vegetation; green vegetation.

Verge, vẽrj, *n.* A rod of office; a mace; a wand; brink; margin; compass; scope.—*vi.* (verging, verged). To incline; to tend; to border.

Verification, ve'ri-fi-kã''shon, *n.* Act of verifying; confirmation.

Verify, ve'ri-fī, *vt.* (verifying, verified). To prove to be true; to confirm; to fulfil.

Verisimilitude, ve'ri-si-mil''i-tūd, *n.* The appearance of truth; probability; likelihood.

Veritable, ve'ri-ta-bl, *a.* True; real; actual.

Vermeil, vẽr'mil, *n.* Vermilion; silver or bronze gilt.

Vermicelli, vẽr-mi-chel'li, *n.* An Italian article of food made of flour, etc., in the form of long threads.

Vermicular, vẽr-mik'ū-lẽr, *a.* Pertaining to worms; like a worm; vermiculated.

Vermiculate, vẽr-mik'ū-lãt, *vt.* To ornament so as to suggest worms or a worm-eaten surface.—*a.* Worm-like in appearance.

Vermifuge, vẽr'mi-fūj, *n.* A medicine that expels intestinal worms.

Vermilion, vẽr-mil'yon, *n.* Cinnabar or red sulfide of mercury; a beautiful red color.—*vt.* To color with vermilion.

Vermin, vẽr'min, *n. sing.* and *pl.* A term for all sorts of small noxious mammals or insects.

Verminous, vẽr'min-us, *a.* Pertaining to vermin; like vermin; caused by vermin; infested by vermin.

Vernacular, vẽr-nak'ū-lẽr, *a.* Belonging to the country of one's birth or the everyday idiom of a place.—*n.* The native idiom of a place.

Vernal, vẽr'nal, *a.* Pertaining to the spring; belonging to youth.

Vernier, vẽr'ni-ẽr, *n.* A small sliding scale, parallel to the fixed scale of a barometer, or other graduated instrument, and subdividing the divisions into more minute parts.

Versatile, vẽrs'a-til, *a.* Readily turning; inconstant; having many accomplishments.

Versatility, vẽrs-a-til'i-ti, *n.* Aptness to change; facility in taking up various intellectual pursuits.

Verse, vẽrs, *n.* A line of poetry; meter; poetry; versification; a stanza; a short division of any composition.

Versed, vẽrst, *a.* Conversant; practiced; skilled; with *in.*

Versify, vẽrs'i-fī, *vi.* (versifying, versified). To make verses.—*vt.* To form or turn into verse.

Version, vẽr'shon, *n.* Act of translating; a translation; rendering; account.

Verso, vẽr'sõ, *n.* A left-hand page.

Versus, vẽr'sus, *prep.* Against.

Vertebra, vẽr'te-bra, *n.*; pl. **-rae.** One of the bones of the spine; *pl.* the spine.

Vertebrata, vẽr-te-brã'ta, *n.pl.* The highest division of animals, consisting of those which possess a backbone.

Vertebrate, vẽr'te-brãt, *a.* Having a backbone.—*n.* One of the Vertebrata.

Vertex, vẽr'teks, *n.*; pl. **-texes** or **-tices.** The highest point; top; apex; zenith.

Vertical, vẽr'ti-kal, *a.* Pertaining to the vertex; directly over the head; perpendicular to the horizon; upright.

Vertiginous, vẽr-ti'jin-us, *a.* Giddy or dizzy; affected with vertigo.

Vertigo, vẽr-tī'gõ or vẽr'ti-gõ, *n.* Dizziness or swimming of the head; giddiness.

Verve, vẽrv, *n.* Spirit; energy.

Very, ve'ri, *a.* True; real; actual.—*adv.* Truly; in a great or high degree.

Vesical, ve'si-kal, *a.* Pertaining to the bladder.

Vesicate, ve'si-kãt, *vt.* To blister.

Vesicle, ve'si-kl, *n.* A small bladder-like structure or cavity; a little sac or cyst.

Vesper, ves'pẽr, *n.* The evening; the evening-star; *pl.* evening worship or service.—*a.* Relating to the evening or to vespers.

Vessel, ves'el, *n.* A hollow utensil for holding liquids or solids; a ship; a tube or canal for blood or sap; a person.

Vest, vest, *n.* Undergarment for the upper part of the body; a waistcoat.—*vt.* To clothe; to endow; to invest.—*vi.* To descend to; to devolve; to take effect, as a title or right.

Vested, vest'ed, *a.* Clothed or habited; robed; well settled or established.

Vestibule, ves'ti-būl, *n.* A passage or hall inside the outer door of a house.

Vestige, ves'tij, *n.* Footprint; mark or trace of something; mark or remnant left.

Vestment, vest'ment, *n.* A garment; a special article of dress worn by clergymen when officiating.

Vestry, ves'tri, *n.* A room connected with a church, where the ecclesiastical vestments are kept; a body of ratepayers elected for the local government of a parish.

Veteran, ve'te-ran, *a.* Having been long exercised; long experienced in war.—*n.* An old soldier; a man of great experience.

Veterinary, ve'te-ri-na-ri, *a.* Pertaining to the art of healing the diseases of domestic animals.

Veto, vē'tõ, *n.* The power or right of forbidding; any authoritative prohibition or refusal.—*vt.* (vetoing, vetoed). To forbid; to interdict.

Vex, veks, *vt.* To irritate; to torment; to annoy; to

distress; to make sorrowful.

Vexation, veks-ā'shon, *n.* Irritation; annoyance; grief; affliction.

Vexed, vekst, *a.* Annoyed; troubled; much disputed or contested.

Via, vī'a, *prep.* By way of.

Viable, vī'a-bl, *a.* Capable of living, applied to a new-born child.

Viaduct, vī'a-dukt, *n.* A long bridge for carrying a road or railway over a valley.

Vial, vī'al, *n.* A phial; a small glass bottle.

Viand, vī'and, *n.* Meat dressed; food; victuals: used chiefly in *pl.*

Vibrate, vī'brāt, *vi.* (vibrating, vibrated). To swing; to quiver; to be unstable.—*vt.* To wave to and fro; to cause to quiver.

Vicar, vi'kėr, *n.* A substitute in office; deputy; the priest of a parish in England who receives the smaller tithes, or a salary.

Vicarage, vi'kėr-āj, *n.* The benefice of a vicar; residence of a vicar.

Vicarious, vī-kā'ri-us, *a.* Pertaining to a substitute; deputed, substituted or suffered for or in the place of another.

Vice, vīs, *n.* A blemish; fault; moral failing; profligacy; a fault or bad trick in a horse; an iron instrument which holds fast anything worked upon; a prefix denoting position second in rank.

Vice-admiral, vis-ad'mi-ral, *n.* A naval officer, the next in rank to an Admiral.

Vice-chancellor, vis-chan'sel-lor, *n.* An officer acting as deputy for a chancellor.

Vice-consul, vis-kon'sul, *n.* One who acts for a consul; a consul of subordinate rank.

Vicegerent, vīs-jē'rent, *n.* One who acts in the place of a superior; a substitute.

Vice-president, vis-pre'zi-dent, *n.* An officebearer next in rank below a president.

Viceroy, vis'roi, *n.* One who governs in place of a king or queen.

Vicinity, vi-sin'i-ti, *n.* Neighborhood; proximity.

Vicious, vi'shus, *a.* Characterized by vice; faulty; depraved; immoral; spiteful.

Vicissitude, vi-sis'i-tūd, *n.* Change or alternation; one of the ups and downs of life.

Victim, vik'tim, *n.* A living being sacrificed; a person or thing destroyed; a person who suffers; a gull.

Victor, vik'tor, *n.* One who conquers; one who proves the winner.—*a.* Victorious.

Victorious, vik-tō'ri-us, *a.* Having gained victory; conquering; indicating victory.

Victory, vik'to-ri, *n.* Conquest; a gaining of the superiority in any contest.

Victual, vit'l, *n.* Food provided; provisions: generally in *pl.*—*vt.* (victualling, victualled). To supply with victuals or stores.

Vicugna, Vicuña, vi-kön'ya, *n.* A South American animal yielding a wool used for delicate fabrics.

Vide, vī'dē, *vt.* See; refer to.

Videlicet, vi-del'i-set, *adv.* To wit; that is; namely: usually abbreviated to *viz.*

Vie, vī, *vi.* (vying, vied). To contend.

View, vū, *n.* A look; inspection; consideration; range of vision; power of perception; sight; scene; pictorial sketch; judgment; intention.—*vt.* To see; to survey; to consider.—*vi.* To look.

Vigesimal, vi-jes'i-mal, *a.* Twentieth.

Vigil, vi'jil, *n.* Act of keeping awake; a devotional watching, the eve or day preceding a church festival.

Vigilance, vi'ji-lans, *n.* Watchfulness.

Vigilant, vi'ji-lant, *a.* Watchful; circumspect; wary; on the outlook; alert.

Vignette, vin-yet' or vi-net', *n.* Flowers, head and tail pieces, etc., in books; a wood-cut without a definite border; a small photographic portrait; a small attractive picture.

Vigorous, vi'gor-us, *a.* Full of vigor; strong; lusty; powerful; energetic.

Vigor, vi'gor, *n.* Active force or strength; physical force; strength of mind.

Viking, vīk'ing, *n.* An ancient Scandinavian rover or sea-robber.

Vile, vīl, *a.* Morally worthless; despicable; depraved; bad.

Vilify, vi'li-fī, *vt.* (vilifying, vilified). To defame; to traduce; to slander.

Villa, vil'a, *n.* A country seat; a suburban house.

Village, vil'āj, *n.* A collection of houses, smaller than a town and larger than a hamlet.

Villain, vil'an or vil'ān, *n.* A feudal serf; a peasant; a knave or scoundrel.

Villainous, vil'an-us, *a.* Base; vile; wicked; depraved; mean.

Villi, vil'lī, *n.pl.* Fine small fibers; soft hairs on certain fruits, flowers, etc.

Villous, Villose, vil'lus, vil'lōs, *a.* Having a velvety, shaggy, or woolly surface.

Vim, vim, *n.* Vigor; energy.

Vinaceous, vī-nā'shus, *a.* Belonging to wine or grapes; of the color of wine.

Vinaigrette, vin-ā-gret, *n.* A small box, with perforations on the top, for holding smelling-salts.

Vincible, vin'si-bl, *a.* Conquerable.

Vindicate, vin'di-kāt, *vt.* (vindicating, vindicated). To prove to be just or valid; to maintain the rights of; to defend; to justify.

Vindictive, vin-dik'tiv, *a.* Revengeful.

Vine, vīn, *n.* A climbing plant producing grapes; the slender stem of any climbing plant.

Vinegar, vi'nē-gėr, *n.* Diluted and impure acetic acid, obtained from wine, beer, etc.; sourness of temper.

Vineyard, vin'yärd, *n.* A plantation of vines producing grapes.

Vintage, vint'āj, *n.* The gathering of the grape crop; the crop itself; the wine produced by the grapes of one season.

Vintner, vint'nėr, *n.* One who deals in wine; a wine-seller; a licensed victualler.

Viol, vī'ol, *n.* An ancient musical instrument like the violin.

Viola, vē-ō'la, *n.* The tenor violin.

Violate, vī'ō-lāt, *vt.* (violating, violated). To injure; to outrage; to desecrate; to profane; to transgress.

Violation, vī-ō-lā'shon, *n.* Infringement; transgression; desecration; rape.

Violence, vī'ō-lens, *n.* Quality of being violent; vehemence; outrage; injury.

Violent, vī'ō-lent, *a.* Impetuous; furious; outrageous; fierce; severe.

Violet, vī'ō-let, *n.* A genus of plants that includes the pansy, etc.; a plant having a bluish purple flower with a delicious smell; a rich bluishpurple.—*a.* Of a bluish-purple color.

Violin, vī-ō-lin', *n.* A musical instrument with four strings, played with a bow; a fiddle.

Violist, vī'ō-list, *n.* A player on the viola.

Violoncellist, vī'ō-lon-sel''ist, *n.* A player on the violoncello.

Violoncello, vī'ō-lon-sel''lō or vē'ō-lon-chel''lō, *n.* A large and powerful bow instrument of the violin kind.

Viper, vī'pėr, *n.* A venomous serpent.

Virago, vi-rā'gō, *n.* A man-like woman; a termagant.

Virescent, vī-res'sent, *a.* Slightly green; beginning to be green.

Virgin, vėr'jin, *n.* A woman who has had no carnal knowledge of man; a maid; a sign of the zodiac.—*a.* Chaste; maidenly; unsullied.

Virgo, vėr'gō, *n.* The Virgin in the zodiac.

Viridity, vi-rid'i-ti, *n.* Greenness; verdure.

Virile, vi'ril or vi'ril, *a.* Pertaining to a man; masculine; manly; strong.

Virility, vi-ril'i-ti, *n.* Manhood; the power of procreation; masculine action or vigor.

Virtual, vėr'tū-al, *a.* Being in essence or effect, not in name or fact.

Virtue, vėr'tū, *n.* Moral goodness; rectitude; morality; chastity; merit; efficacy.

Virtuoso, vėr-tū-ō'sō, *n.*; pl. **-osos** or **-osi.** A man

V

skilled in the fine arts, or antiquities, curiosities, etc.

Virtuous, vėr'tū-us, a. Marked by virtue; morally good; pure or chaste.

Virulence, vi'rū-lens, n. Acrimony; malignity; rancor.

Virulent, vi'rū-lent, a. Very poisonous or noxious; bitter in enmity; malignant.

Virus, vī'rus, n. Contagious poisonous matter; extreme acrimony; malignity.

Vis, vis, n. Force; power; energy.

Visage, vi'zāj, n. The face or countenance.

Vis-à-vis, vē-zä-vē, adv. Face to face.—n. One placed face to face with another; a light carriage for two persons sitting face to face.

Viscera, vis'e-ra, n.pl. The entrails.

Viscid, vis'id, a. Sticky or adhesive; glutinous; tenacious.

Viscidity, vis-id'i-ti, n. Glutinousness.

Viscous, vis'kus, a. Glutinous; viscid.

Visé, vē-zä, n. An endorsation upon a passport denoting that it has been examined and found correct.

Visible, vi'zi-bl, a. Perceivable by the eye; apparent; open; conspicuous.

Vision, vi'zhon, n. Act of seeing; sight; that which is seen; an apparition; a fanciful view.

Visionary, vi'zhon-a-ri, a. Pertaining to visions; imaginative; imaginary; not real.—n. One who is visionary; one who upholds impracticable schemes.

Visit, vi'zit, vt. To go or come to see; to view officially; to afflict.—vi. To practice going to see others; to make calls.—n. Act of visiting; a call.

Visitation, vi-zit-ä'shon, n. Act of visiting; a formal or official visit; special dispensation of divine favor or retribution.

Visitor, vi'zit-or, n. One who visits; a caller; an inspector.

Visor, Vizor, vī'zor, n. The movable faceguard of a helmet; a mask.

Vista, vis'ta, n. A view through an avenue; trees, etc., that form the avenue; an extended view.

Visual, vi'zhū-al, a. Pertaining to sight or vision; used in seeing.

Vital, vī'tal, a. Pertaining to life; necessary to life; indispensable; essential.

Vitality, vī-tal'i-ti, n. State or quality of having life; principle of life; animation.

Vitalize, vi'tal-īz, vt. To give life to; to furnish with the vital principle.

Vitals, vī'talz, n.pl. Parts essential to life.

Vitamin, vī'ta-min, n. One of several substances necessary for animal nutrition, and occurring in minute quantities in natural foods; numerous types have been distinguished, and designated by the letters of the alphabet.

Vitiate, vi'shi-āt, vt. (vitiating, vitiated). To make faulty; to impair; to corrupt; to invalidate.

Vitreous, vit're-us, a. Glassy; pertaining to glass; resembling glass.

Vitrescent, vi-tres'ent, a. Tending to become glass or glassy.

Vitrifaction, Vitrification, vit-ri-fak'shon, vit'ri-fi-kä''shon, n. The act, process, or operation of converting into glass by heat.

Vitrify, vit'ri-fī, vt. To convert into glass by heat.—vi. To become glass.

Vitriol, vit'ri-ol, n. Sulphuric acid or one of its compounds.

Vitriolic, vit'ri-ol'ik, a. Pertaining to vitriol; like vitriol; very biting or sarcastic.

Vituperate, vėr-tū'pe-rāt, vt. To abuse; to censure offensively; to rate.

Vituperative, vī-tū'pe-rāt-iv, a. Containing vituperation; abusive; railing.

Vivacious, vi-vā'shus or vi-, a. Lively; brisk; sprightly; tenacious of life.

Vivacity, vī-vas'i-ti or vi-, n. Animation; spirit; liveliness; briskness.

Viva voce, vī'va vō'sē, adv. By word of mouth; orally; sometimes used adjectively.

Vivid, vi'vid, a. Bright, clear, or lively; forcible;

striking; realistic.

Vivify, vi'vi-fī, vt. (vivifying, vivified). To make alive; to endure with life; to animate.

Viviparous, vī-vip'a-rus, a. Producing young in a living state.

Vivisection, vi-vi-sek'shon, n. Act of experimenting on a living animal.

Vixen, viks'en, n. A she-fox; a snappish, bitter woman; a termagant.

Vocable, vō'ka-bl, n. A word; a term.

Vocabulary, vō-kab'ū-la-ri, n. A list of words arranged alphabetically and explained briefly; range of expression.

Vocal, vō'kal, a. Pertaining to the voice; uttered by the voice; endowed with a voice; having a vowel character.

Vocalist, vō'kal-ist, n. A vocal musician; a public singer.

Vocally, vō'kal-li, adv. With voice; with an audible sound; in words.

Vocation, vō-kä'shon, n. A calling; employment; profession; business.

Vocative, vo'ka-tiv, a. Relating to calling by name.—n. The vocative case.

Vociferate, vō-sif'e-rāt, vi. and t. (vociferating; vociferated). To cry out with vehemence, to exclaim.

Vociferous, vō-sif'ėr-us, a. Making a loud outcry; clamorous; noisy.

Vodka, vod'ka, n. An intoxicating spirit distilled from rye, much used in Russia.

Vogue, vōg, n. Temporary mode or fashion.

Voice, vois, n. The sound uttered by the mouth; articulate human utterance; state of vocal organs; speech; sound emitted; right of expressing an opinion; vote; a form of verb inflection.—vt. (voicing, voiced). To utter or express; to declare.

Void, void, a. Empty; devoid; ineffectual; null.—n. An empty space.—vt. To make vacant; to quit; to nullify; to emit; to evacuate from the bowels.

Voidance, void'ans, n. Act of voiding; ejection from a benefice; vacancy.

Volant, vō'lant, a. Flying; nimble; rapid.

Volatile, vo-la-til, a. Readily diffusible in the atmosphere; flighty; airy; fickle; fugitive.

Volatility, vo-la-til'i-ti, n. Quality of being volatile; capability of evaporating; flightiness; fickleness; levity.

Volatilize, vo'la-til-īz, vt. To cause to exhale or evaporate.—vi. To become vaporous.

Volcanic, vol-kan'ik, a. Pertaining to volcanoes; produced by a volcano.

Volcano, vol-kä'no, n.; pl. -oes. A mountain emitting clouds of vapor, gases, showers of ashes, lava, etc.

Volition, vō-li'shon, n. Act or power of willing; will.

Volley, vol'i, n. A discharge of a number of missile weapons, as small-arms; emission of many things at once.—vt. and i. To discharge or be discharged in a volley; to sound like a volley; to strike and return a ball (in lawn-tennis, etc.) before it touches the ground.

Volt, vōlt, n. A sudden movement in fencing to avoid a thrust; the unit of electromotive force.

Voltage, vōlt'āj, n. Electromotive force as measured in volts.

Voltaism, vol'ta-izm, n. Electricity produced by chemical action; galvanism.

Volubility, vo-lū'bil'i-ti, n. Great readiness or fluency of speech.

Voluble, vo'lū-bl, a. Rolling round or revolving; glib in speech; over fluent.

Volume, vo'lūm, n. Something rolled up; a book; a coil; a convolution; mass or bulk; quantity or strength.

Volumetric, vo-lū-met'rik, a. Pertaining to the measurement of volumes of substances.

Voluminous, vō-lū'min-us, a. Bulky; being in many volumes; having written much; copious.

Voluntarily, vo'lun-ta-ri-li, adv. Spontaneously; of one's own free will.

Voluntary, vo'lun-ta-ri, *a.* Willing; free to act; spontaneous; regulated by the will.—*n.* A volunteer; a supporter of voluntaryism; an organ solo during a church service.

Volunteer, vo-lun-tēr', *n.* A person who enters into military or other service of his own free will.—*a.* Pertaining to volunteers.—*vt.* To offer or bestow voluntarily.—*vi.* To enter into any service voluntarily.

Voluptuary, vō-lup'tū-a-ri, *n.* One addicted to luxury; a sensualist.

Voluptuous, vō-lup'tū-us, *a.* Pertaining to sensual pleasure; luxurious.

Vomit, vo'mit, *vi.* To eject the contents of the stomach by the mouth.—*vt.* To eject from the stomach; to belch forth.—*n.* Matter ejected from the stomach; an emetic.

Voodoo, vō-dö, *n.* A person among the American negroes who professes to be a sorcerer; sorcery; an evil spirit.

Voracious, vō-rā'shus, *a.* Eating or swallowing greedily; ravenous; rapacious.

Vortex, vor'teks, *n.*; pl. **-tices** or **-texes.** A whirling motion in any fluid; a whirlpool or a whirlwind; an eddy.

Vortical, vor'tik-al, *a.* Pertaining to a vortex; whirling.

Votary, vō'ta-ri, *n.* One who is bound by a vow; one devoted to some particular service, state of life, etc.

Vote, vōt, *n.* Act or power of expressing opinion or choice; a suffrage; thing conferred by vote; result of voting; votes collectively.—*vi.* (voting, voted). To give a vote.—*vt.* To choose or grant by vote.

Votive, vōt'iv, *a.* Pertaining to a vow; promised or given, in consequence of a vow.

Vouch, vouch, *vt.* To attest; to affirm; to answer for.—*vi.* To bear witness; to stand surety.

Voucher, vouch'er, *n.* One who vouches; a paper which serves to vouch the truth of accounts, or to confirm facts of any kind; a written evidence of the payment of money.

Vouchsafe, vouch-sāf', *vt.* (vouchsafing, vouchsafed). To condescend to grant; to concede.—*vi.* To deign.

Vow, vou, *n.* A solemn promise; an oath; promise of fidelity.—*vt.* To promise solemnly; to dedicate, as to a divine power.—*vi.* To make vows.

Vowel, vou'el, *n.* A sound produced by opening the mouth and giving utterance to voice; the letter which represents such a sound.—*a.* Pertaining to a vowel; vocal.

Voyage, voi'āj, *n.* A journey by water to a distance.—*vi.* (voyaging, voyaged). To pass by water.

Vulcanism, vul'kan-izm, *n.* The phenomena of volcanoes, hot springs, etc.

Vulcanize, vul'kan-iz, *vt.* To harden (india-rubber) by combining with sulphur, etc.

Vulgar, vul'ger, *a.* Pertaining to the common people; vernacular; common; coarse.—**The vulgar,** the common people.

Vulgarism, vul'ger-izm, *n.* A vulgar phrase or expression; vulgarity.

Vulgarity, vul-ga'ri-ti, *n.* Coarseness; an act of low manners.

Vulgate, vul'gāt, *n.* The Latin version of the Scriptures used by the R. Catholic church.

Vulnerable, vul'ner-a-bl, *a.* That may be wounded; liable to injury.

Vulpine, vul'pin, *a.* Pertaining to the fox; cunning; crafty.

Vulture, vul'tūr, *n.* A bird of prey which lives chiefly on carrion.

W

Wad, wod, *n.* A soft mass of fibrous material, used for stuffing; material for stopping the charge in a gun.—*vt.* (wadding, wadded). To furnish with a wad or wadding.

Waddle, wod'l, *vi.* (waddling, waddled). To walk with a rolling gait; to toddle.

Wade, wād, *vi.* (wading, waded). To walk through a substance that hinders the lower limbs, as water, to move or pass with labor.—*vt.* To ford.

Wafer, wā'fer, *n.* A thin cake, as of bread; a thin disc of paste for fastening letters.—*vt.* To seal with a wafer.

Waft, wäft, *vt.* To impel through water or air.—*vi.* To sail or float.—*n.* A sweep, as with the arm; a breath of wind.

Wag, wag, *vt.* and *i.* (wagging, wagged). To swing or sway; to wave; to nod.—*n.* A wit; a joker.

Wage, wāj, *vt.* (waging, waged). To carry on; to engage in, as in a contest.—*n.* Payment for work done; hire; recompense; generally in *pl.*

Wager, wā'jer, *n.* A bet; stake laid; subject on which bets are laid.—*vt.* and *i.* To bet; to stake.

Waggish, wag'ish, *a.* Roguish in merriment; jocular; sportive.

Waggle, wag'l, *vi.* and *t.* (waggling, waggled). To sway; to wag with short movements.

Wagon, Waggon, wag'on, *n.* A four-wheeled vehicle for heavy loads.

Waif, wāf, *n.* A stray article; a neglected, homeless wretch.

Wail, wāl, *vt.* To lament; to bewail.—*vi.* To weep.—*n.* A mournful cry or sound.

Wailing, wāl'ing, *n.* Loud weeping.

Wainscot, wān'skot, *n.* The timber-work that lines the walls of a room.—*vt.* (wainscoting, wainscotted). To line with wainscot.

Waist, wāst, *n.* That part of the human body between the ribs and hips; middle part of a ship.

Waistband, wāst'band, *n.* The band of trousers, etc., which encompasses the waist.

Waistcoat, wāst'kōt, *n.* A short sleeveless garment worn under the coat; a vest.

Wait, wāt, *vi.* To stay in expectation; to continue in patience; to attend; to serve at table.—*vt.* To await.—*n.* Act of waiting; ambush; a musician who promenades in the night about Christmas time.

Waiter, wāt'er, *n.* One who waits; a male attendant; a small tray or salver.

Waitress, wāt'res, *n.* A female waiter.

Waive, wāv, *vt.* (waiving, waived). To relinquish; to forgo.

Wake, wāk, *vi.* (waking, woke or waked). To be awake; to awake; to become active.—*vt.* To rouse from sleep; to arouse.—*n.* The feast of the dedication of a parish church; a vigil; the watching of a dead body prior to burial; track left by a ship; track in general.

Wakeful, wāk'ful, *a.* Keeping awake in bed; indisposed to sleep; watchful; vigilant.

Waken, wāk'n, *vi.* To wake.—*vt.* To rouse from sleep; to rouse into action.

Walk, wak, *vi.* To advance by steps without running; to go about; to behave.—*vt.* To pass over or through on foot; to lead about.—*n.* A short excursion on foot; gait; an avenue; promenade; etc.; sphere; way of living; tract of ground for grazing.

Walking, wak'ing, *n.* The act or practice of moving on the feet without running; practice of taking walks; pedestrianism.

Walking-stick, wak'ing-stik, *n.* A staff or stick carried in the hand in walking.

Wall, wal, *n.* A structure of stone or brick, enclosing a space, forming a division, supporting a weight, etc.; side of a building or room; means of protection.—*vt.* To enclose with a wall; to defend by walls.

Wallop, wol'op, *vt.* To beat; to drub; to thrash.

Wallow, wol'ō, *vi.* To tumble and roll in water or mire; to live in filth or gross vice.

Walnut, wal'nut, *n.* A valuable tree, a native of Persia; the edible nut of the tree.

Walrus, wol'rus, *n.* A hugh marine carnivorous mammal inhabiting the arctic seas.

Waltz, walts, *n.* A kind of dance for two persons;

W

music for the dance.—*vi.* To dance a waltz.

Wan, won, *a.* Dark or gloomy; languid of look; pale.

Wand, wond, *n.* A long flexible stick; a rod; a staff of authority; a baton.

Wander, won'dèr, *vi.* To ramble here and there; to roam; to rove; to err; to be delirious.—*vt.* To traverse.

Wandering, won'dèr-ing, *a.* Given to wander; unsettled.—*n.* A traveling without a settled course; aberration.

Wane, wán, *vt.* (waning, waned). To diminish; to grow less, as the moon; to fail; to decline.—*n.* Decline; decrease.

Want, wont, *n.* State of not having; deficiency; lack; need; indigence.—*vt.* To be without; to lack; to require; to desire.—*vi.* To be deficient; to be in want.

Wanton, won'ton, *a.* Not kept in due restraint; unprovoked; lustful; frolicsome; rank.—*n.* A lewd person; a trifler.—*vi.* To revel unrestrainedly; to sport lasciviously.

War, war, *n.* A contest between nations or parties carried on by force of arms; profession of arms; art of war; hostility; enmity.—*vi.* (warring, warred). To make or carry on war; to strive.

Warble, war'bl, *vt.* and *i.* (warbling, warbled). To utter musically in a quavering manner; to carol; to sing musically.—*n.* A quavering melodious sound; a song.

War-cry, war'krī, *n.* A word, cry, motto, or phrase used in common by troops in battle.

Ward, ward, *vt.* To guard; to fend off; to turn aside.—*n.* Guard; a defensive motion or position in fencing; custody; guardianship; a minor who is under guardianship; a division of a town or county; apartment of an hospital; a piece in a lock.

Warden, war'den, *n.* A guardian; a keeper; head of a college; superior of a conventual church; member of organization for assistance of civil population in air-raids.

Wardrobe, ward'rōb, *n.* A piece of furniture in which wearing apparel is kept; a person's wearing apparel collectively.

Ware, war, *n.* Articles of merchandise; goods: generally in *pl.*; sea-weeds, employed as a manure, etc.—*a.* On one's guard; aware; *poet.*—*vt.* To beware of: *poet.*

Warehouse, war'hous, *n.* A storehouse for goods; a large shop.—*vt.* To deposit or secure in a warehouse.

Warfare, war'fār, *n.* Military service; war; contest; hostilities.

Warily, wā'ri-li, *adv.* Cautiously.

Warm, warm, *a.* Having moderate heat; flushed; zealous; excitable; brisk; rich.—*vt.* To make warm; to animate; to interest.—*vi.* To become warm or animated.

Warm-hearted, warm'härt-ed, *a.* Having warmth of heart; cordial; sincere; hearty.

Warmth, warmth, *n.* Gentle heat; cordiality; ardour; animation; enthusiasm; slight anger or irritation.

Warn, warn, *vt.* To caution against; to admonish; to advise; to inform previously.

Warning, warn'ing, *n.* Act of one who warns; caution against danger, etc.; admonition; previous notice.

Warp, warp, *vt.* and *i.* To turn or twist out of shape; to contort; to pervert; to move, as a ship, by a rope attached to something.—*n.* The threads extended lengthwise in a loom; a rope used in moving a ship; deposit of rich mud; twist of wood in drying.

Warrant, wo'rant, *vt.* To guarantee; to authorize; to justify.—*n.* An act or instrument investing one with authority; guarantee; document authorizing an officer to seize an offender; authority; a voucher; right.

Warranty, wo'ran-ti, *n.* Warrant; guarantee; authority; a legal deed of security.

Warren, wo'ren, *n.* Ground appropriated for rab-

bits; a preserve in a river for fish.

Warrior, wa'ri-or, *n.* A soldier; a brave or able soldier.

Wart, wart, *n.* A hard dry growth on the skin.

Wary, wā'ri, *a.* Cautious; prudent.

Was, woz, *v.* The first and third person singular of the past tense of *to be.*

Wash, wosh, *vt.* To apply water, etc., to, to cleanse; to flow along or dash against; to remove by ablution; to tint lightly.—*vi.* To cleanse oneself by water; to stand the operation of washing; to stand the test.—*n.* Act of washing; clothes washed on one occasion; flow or dash of water; sound made by water; a shallow; swill; lotion; thin coat of color or metal.

Washer, wosh'èr, *n.* One who or that which washed; a ring of iron, leather, etc., used under a nut that is screwed on a bolt.

Washing, wosh'ing, *n.* Act of cleansing with water; ablution; clothes washed.

Wash-out, wosh'out, *n.* A shot which misses the target, so a complete failure (used of persons and things).

Wash-tub, wosh'tub, *n.* A tub in which clothes are washed.

Washy, wosh'i, *a.* Watery; highly diluted; thin; weak; feeble; worthless.

Wasp, wosp, *n.* An active, stinging, winged insect, resembling the bee.

Waspish, wosp'ish, *a.* Like a wasp; venomous; irritable; snappish.

Wassail, wos'el, *n.* A festive occasion with drinking of healths; a drinking bout; liquor used on such occasions.—*vi.* To hold a merry drinking meeting.

Waste, wāst, *vt.* (wasting, wasted). To make desolate; to ravage; to wear away gradually; to squander.—*vi.* To decrease gradually.—*a.* Desolate; spoiled; refuse.—*n.* Act of wasting; prodigality; refuse matter; gradual decrease; a desert region.

Wasteful, wāst'ful, *a.* Causing waste; destructive; ruinous; lavish; prodigal.

Waste-pipe, wāst'pīp, *n.* A pipe for carrying off waste water, etc.

Wasting, wāst'ing, *a.* Such as to waste; desolating; enfeebling.

Watch, woch, *n.* A keeping awake to guard, etc.; vigilance; a guard; time during which a person is on guard or duty; a small pocket timepiece.—*vi.* To keep awake; to give heed; to act as a guard, etc.; to wait.—*vt.* To look with close attention at or on; to tend; to guard.

Watch-dog, woch'dog, *n.* A dog kept to guard premises and property.

Watchful, woch'ful, *a.* Keeping on the watch; vigilant; attentive; cautious.

Watch-maker, woch'māk-èr, *n.* One who makes or repairs watches.

Watchman, woch'man, *n.* A guard; a caretaker on duty at night.

Watchword, woch'wèrd, *n.* A word by which sentinels distinguish a friend from an enemy; a motto.

Water, wa'tèr, *n.* A transparent fluid; a fluid consisting of hydrogen and oxygen; the sea; rain; saliva; urine; color or luster of a diamond, etc.— *vt.* To wet or supply with water; to give a wavy appearance to, as silk.—*vi.* To shed liquid matter; to take in water; to gather saliva; to have a longing desire.

Water-bed, wa'tèr-bed, *n.* An india-rubber bed or mattress filled with water.

Water-closet, wa'tèr-kloz-et, *n.* A privy in which the discharges are carried away by water.

Water-color, wa'tèr-kul-èr, *n.* A pigment ground up with water and isinglass or other mucilage instead of oil.

Watered, wa'tèrd, *a.* Having a wavy and shiny appearance on the surface.

Waterfall, wa'tèr-fal, *n.* A fall or steep descent in a stream; a cascade.

Water-level, wa'tèr-le-vel, *n.* The level at which

water stands; a levelling instrument in which water is employed.

Water-logged, wa'tér-logd, a. Floating but full of water, as a ship.

Water-mark, wa'tér-märk, n. A mark indicating the rise and fall of water; a mark made in paper during manufacture.

Water-polo, wa'tér-pō''lō, n. A ball-game played by swimmers, who try to throw the ball into their opponents' goal.

Water-power, wa'tér-pou-ér, n. The power of water employed to drive machinery.

Waterproof, wa'tér-pröf, a. So compact as not to admit water.—n. Cloth made waterproof; a garment of such cloth.—vt. To render impervious to water.

Watershed, wa'tér-shed, n. A rise of land from which rivers, etc., naturally flow in opposite directions.

Water-spout, wa'tér-spout, n. A column of spray or water drawn up from the sea or a lake by a violent whirlwind.

Water-tight, wa'tér-tit, a. So tight as to retain or not to admit water; stanch.

Water-works, wa'tér-wérks, n.pl. The works and appliances for the distribution of water to communities; ornamental fountains.

Wattle, wot'l, n. A hurdle of interlaced rods. —vt. (wattling, wattled). To interlace (twigs or branches); to plat.

Watt, wot, n. The practical unit of power, or rate of conveying energy, used in electricity.

Wave, wāv, vi. and t. (waving, waved). To sway or play loosely; to undulate; to brandish; to beckon.—n. A swell or ridge on moving water; anything resembling a wave; an undulation; a signal made by waving the hand, a flag, etc.

Waver, wā'vér, vi. To wave gently; to fluctuate; to be undetermined.

Wavy, wāv'i, a. Rising or swelling in waves; full of waves; undulating.

Wax, waks, n. A tenacious substance excreted by bees or in the ear; any similar substance; sealing-wax.—vt. To smear or rub with wax.—vi. To increase; to grow; to become.

Wax-work, waks'wérk, n. Work in wax; figures of persons in wax as near reality as possible.

Way, wā, n. A track, path, or road of any kind; distance traversed; progress; direction; line of business; condition; device; method; course; pl. the timbers on which a ship is launched.

Wayfarer, wā'fār-ér, n. One who fares or travels; a traveller; a foot-passenger.

Waylay, wā-lā', vt. To lay oneself in the way of; to beset in ambush.

Wayward, wā'wérd, a. Full of troublesome whims; froward; peevish; perverse.

We, wē, pron. Plural of I.

Weak, wēk, a. Not strong; feeble; infirm; frail; silly; vacillating; wanting resolution; wanting moral courage; ineffective; denoting verbs inflected by adding a letter or syllable.

Weakness, wēk'nes, n. The state or quality of being weak; irresolution; want of validity; a failing.

Weal, wēl, n. Welfare; prosperity; happiness; mark of a stripe, wale.

Wealth, welth, n. Riches; affluence; opulence; abundance.

Wealthy, welth'i, a. Possessing wealth; rich; opulent; abundant; ample.

Wean, wēn, vt. To accustom to do without the mother's milk; to alienate; to disengage from any habit.

Weapon, we'pon, n. Any instrument of offense or defense.

Wear, wār, vt. (pret. wore, pp. worn). To carry as belonging to dress; to have on; to waste by rubbing; to destroy by degrees; to produce by rubbing; to exhibit.—vi. To last well or ill; to waste gradually; to make gradual progress.— n. Act of wearing; diminution by friction, use, time, etc.; fashion.

Wear, wār, vt. (pret. & pp. wore). To bring on the other tack by turning the ship round, stern towards the wind.

Wearing, wār'ing, a. Used by being worn; such as to wear; exhausting.

Wearisome, wē'ri-sum, a. Causing weariness; tiresome; fatiguing; monotonous.

Weary, wē'ri, a. Having the strength or patience exhausted; tired; disgusted; tiresome.—vt. (wearying, wearied). To make weary; to tire.—vi. To become weary.

Weasel, wē'zl, n. A small carnivorous animal akin to the ferret, etc.

Weather, weTH'ér, n. The general atmospheric conditions at any particular time. a. Turned towards the wind; windward.—vt. To affect by the weather; to sail to the windward of; to bear up against and overcome.

Weather-cock, weTH'ér-kok, n. Something in the shape of a cock, etc., for showing the direction of the wind; a vane; a fickle person.

Weather-glass, weTH'ér-gläs, n. A barometer.

Weather-wise, weTH'ér-wiz, a. Wise or skilful in forecasting the weather.

Weave, wēv, vt. (weaving, pret. wove, pp. woven). To form by interlacing thread, yarn, etc.; to form a tissue with; to work up; to contrive.—vi. To practice weaving; to be woven.

Weaving, wēv'ing, n. Act or art of producing cloth or other textile fabrics.

Web, web, n. The whole piece of cloth woven in a loom; a large roll of paper; membrane which unites the toes of water-fowl; the threads which a spider spins; a cobweb; anything carefully contrived.

Webbed, webd, a. Having the toes united by a membrance or web.

Webbing, web'ing, n. A strong fabric of hemp, two or three inches wide.

Weber, vā'ber, n. The electric unit of magnetic quantity.

Web-foot, web'fut, n. A foot whose toes are united by a membrane.

Wed, wed, vt. and i. (wedding, wedded and wed). To marry; to unite closely.

Wedding, wed'ing, n. Marriage; nuptials.

Wedge, wej, n. A body sloping to a thin edge at one end.—vt. (wedging, wedged). To drive as a wedge is driven; to crowd or compress; to fasten or split with a wedge

Wedlock, wed'lok, n. The wedded state; marriage.

Wednesday, wenz'dā, n. The fourth day of the week.

Wee, wē, a. Small; little.

Weed, wēd, n. Any plant regarded as useless or troublesome; a sorry, worthless animal; a cigar; pl. mourning dress of a widow or female.—vt. To free from weeds or anything offensive.

Week, wēk, n. The space of seven days; space from one Sunday to another.

Week-day, wēk'dā, n. Any day of the week except Sunday.

Weekly, wēk'li, a. Coming or done once a week; lasting for a week.—n. A periodical appearing once a week.—adv. Once a week.

Weep, wēp, vi. (pret. and pp. wept). To manifest grief, etc., by shedding tears; to drip; to droop.—vt. To lament; to shed or drop, as tears; to get rid of by weeping.

Weeping, wēp'ing, n. Lamenting; the shedding of tears.

Weevil, wē'vil, n. An insect of the beetle family, destructive to grain, fruit, etc.

Weft, weft, n. The woof of cloth.

Weigh, wā, vt. To raise; to find the heaviness of; to allot or take by weight; to consider; to balance; to burthen.—vi. To have weight; to amount to in weight; to bear heavily.

Weight, wāt, n. Heaviness; gravity; the amount which anything weighs; a metal standard for weighing; a heavy mass; pressure; burden; importance; moment.—vt. To add to the heaviness of.

Weighty, wāt´i, a. Heavy; important; momentous; cogent.

Weird, wērd, n. Destiny; fate.—a. Connected with fate; unearthly.

Welcome, wel´kum, a. Received with gladness; grateful; pleasing.—n. Greeting or kind reception.—vt. (welcoming, welcomed). To receive kindly and hospitably.

Weld, weld, vt. To melt together, as heated iron; to unite closely.—n. A junction by fusion of heated metals; a species of mignonette used as a yellow dye.

Welfare, wel´fār, n. Well-being; prosperity; happiness.

Well, wel, n. A spring; a pit sunk for water; perpendicular space in a building in which stairs or a hoist is place.—vi. To bubble up; to issue forth.

Well, wel, adv. In a proper manner; rightly; commendably; considerably.—a. Being in health; comfortable; fortunate; convenient; proper.

Well-being, wel´bē-ing, n. State of being well; prosperity; happiness; welfare.

Well-bred, wel´bred, a. Of good breeding; polite; refined.

Well-meaning, wel´mēn-ing, a. Having a good intention.

Well-spring, wel´spring, n. A fountain; a source of continual supply.

Welsh, welsh, a. Pertaining to Wales or to its people.—n. The language of Wales; pl. the inhabitants of Wales.

Welt, welt, n. A border or edging; a strip of leather sewed round the upper of a boot to which the sole is fastened.—vt. To furnish with a welt; to beat severely.

Welter, welt´ėr, vi. To roll; to tumble about; to wallow.—n. A turmoil.—a. Said of a horse race in which extra heavy weights are laid on some horses.

Wen, wen, n. A harmless fatty tumor.

Wench, wensh, n. A young woman; a woman of loose character.—vi. To frequent the company of women of ill-fame.

Wend, wend, vt. To go; to direct.—vi. To go; to travel.

Went, went. Used as the pret. of go.

Were, wer, v. The past tense plural indicative and the past subjunctive of be.

Werwolf, wėr´wulf, n. A man transformed into a wolf.

West, west, n. The point where the sun sets, opposite to the east.—a. Being in or towards the west; coming from the east.—adv. To the west.

Western, west´ėrn. a. Being in or moving toward the west; coming from the west.

Westernmost, west´ėrn-mōst, a. Farthest to the west.

Westward, west´wėrd, adv. Toward the west.

Wet, wet, a. Covered or soaked with water; moist; rainy.—n. Water; moisture; rain.—vt. (wetting, wetted). To make wet; to soak in liquor.

Wether, weᴛʜ´ėr, n. A ram castrated.

Wet-nurse, wet´nėrs, n. A nurse engaged to suckle an infant.

Whack, whak, vt. and i. To thwack; to give a resounding blow to.—n. A resounding blow; a thwack.

Whale, whāl, n. The largest of sea animals, a mammal.

Whalebone, whāl´bōn, n. An elastic horny substance obtained from the upper jaw of certain whales; baleen.

Wharf, wharf, n.; pl. -fs or -ves. A quay for loading or unloading ships.

What, whot, pron. An interrogative pronoun used chiefly of things; employed adjectively as equivalent to how great, remarkable, etc.; substantively as equivalent to the thing (or things) which.

Whatever, whot-ev´ėr, pron. Used as substantive, anything that; all that; used as an adj., of any kind.

What-not, whot´not, n. A piece of household furniture with shelves for books, etc.

Wheat, whēt, n. A cereal plant; its seeds, which yield a white nutritious flour.

Wheedle, whē´dl, vt. and i. (wheedling, wheedled). To flatter; to cajole; to coax.

Wheel, whēl, n. A circular frame turning on an axis; an old instrument of torture; a revolution; a cycle.—vt. To cause to turn round.—vi. to revolve; to roll forward.

Wheel-barrow, whēl´ba-rō, n. A barrow with one wheel.

Wheeze, whēz, vi. (wheezing, wheezed). To breathe hard and audibly, as persons affected with asthma.

Whelk, whelk, n. A shell-fish, a species of periwinkle or mollusk; a pustule.

Whelp, whelp, n. A puppy; a cub; a young man.—vi. To bring forth whelps.—vt. To bring forth; to originate.

When, when, adv. and conj. At what or which time; while; whereas; used substantively with since or till.

Where, whār, adv. and conj. At or in what place; at the place in which; whither.

Whereabout, whār´a-bout, adv. and conj. About what place; concerning which.

Whereabouts, whār´a-bouts, adv. and conj. Near what or which place; whereabout; often used substantively.

Whereas, whār-az´ conj. Things being so; when really or in fact.

Whereat, whār-at´, adv. and conj. At which or what.

Whereby, whār-bi´, adv. and conj. By which or what.

Wherefore, whār´for, adv. and conj. For which reason; consequently; why.

Wherein, whār-in´, adv. and conj. In which; in which thing, time, respect, etc.

Whereinto, whār-in-tö´, adv. and conj. Into which or what.

Whereof, whār-ov´, adv. and conj. Of which or what.

Whereon, whār-on´, adv. and conj. On which or on what.

Whereto, whār-tö´, adv. and conj. To which or what; to what end.

Whereupon, whār-up-on´, adv. Upon which or what; in consequence of which.

Wherewith, Wherewithal, whār-with´, whār-with-al´, adv. and conj. With which or what.—n. Means or money.

Wherry, whe´ri, n. A light river boat for passengers.

Whet, whet, vi. (whetting, whetted or whet). To rub to sharpen; to edge; to excite; to stimulate.—n. Act of sharpening; something that stimulates the appetite.

Whether, weᴛʜ´ėr, pron. Which of two.—conj. or adv. Which of two or more, introducing alternative clauses.

Whetstone, whet´stōn, n. A stone used for sharpening instruments by friction.

Whey, whā, n. The thin part of milk, from which the curd, etc., have been separated.

Which, which, pron. An interrogative pronoun, used adjectively or substantively; a relative pronoun, the neuter of who; an indefinite pronoun, any one which.

Whichever, Whichsoever, which-ev´ėr, which-sō-ev´ėr, pron. No matter which; anyone.

Whiff, whif, n. A puff of air; a puff conveying a smell.—vt. and i. To puff; to throw out whiffs; to smoke.

While, whīl, n. A time; short space of time.—conj. During the time that; though.—vt. whiling, whiled). To cause to pass pleasantly: usually with away.

Whim, n. A sudden fancy; a caprice.

Whimper, whim´pėr, vi. To express grief with a whining voice.—vt. To utter in a low, whining tone.—n. A peevish cry.

Whimsical, whim'zik-al, a. Full of whims; capricious; odd; fantastic.

Whimsy, Whimsey, whim'zi, n. A whim; a caprice; a capricious notion.

Whine, whīn, vi. (whining, whined). To express distress by a plaintive drawling cry.—n. A drawling plaintive tone; mean or affected complaint.

Whinny, whin'i, vi. (whinnying, whinnied). To neigh, especially in a low tone.—n. Neigh of a horse.—a. Abounding in whins.

Whip, whip, vt. (whipping, whipped). To put or snatch with a sudden motion; to flog; to drive with lashes; to beat into a froth.—vi. To start suddenly and run.—n. A lash; the driver of a carriage; a member of parliament who looks after the attendance of his party; the summons he sends out.

Whip-hand, whip'hand, n. The hand that holds the whip; control.

Whipping, whip'ing, n. Act of striking with a whip; flagellation.

Whir, whėr, vi. (whirring, whirred). To fly, revolve, etc., with a whizzing or buzzing sound; to whiz.—n. A buzzing sound.

Whirl, whėrl, vt. and i. To turn round rapidly; to move quickly.—n. A rapid turning.

Whirlpool, whėrl'pōl, n. An eddy or gulf where the water moves round in a circle.

Whirlwind, whėrl'wind, n. A whirling wind; a violent wind moving as if round an axis, this axis at the same time progressing.

Whisk, whisk, vt. To sweep or agitate with a light rapid motion.—vi. To move nimbly.—n. A rapid, sweeping motion; a small besom; an instrument for frothing cream, eggs, etc.

Whisker, whis'kėr, n. Long hair growing on the cheek.

Whisky, Whiskey, whis'ki, n. An ardent spirit distilled generally from barley; a light one-horse chaise.

Whisper, whis'pėr, vt. To speak with a low sibilant voice; to converse secretly.—vt. To utter in a whisper.—n. A low soft sibilant voice; a faint utterance.

Whispering, whis'pėr-ing, a. Speaking in a whisper; having or giving a soft sibilant sound.—n. Act of one who whispers; talebearing.

Whistle, whis'l, vi. (whistling, whistled). To utter a clear shrill sound by forcing the breath through the lips; to warble; to sound shrilly.—vt. To utter or signal by whistling.—n. Sound produced by one who whistles; any similar sound; a small pipe blown with the breath; instrument sounded by breath.

White, whīt, a. Being of the color of pure snow; pale; pallid; pure and unsullied.—n. The color of snow; a white pigment; white of an egg, eye, etc., —vt. (whiting, whited). To make white.

White-lead, whīt'led, n. A carbonate of lead much used in painting; ceruse.

Whiten, whīt'n, vt. To make white; to bleach; to blanch. —vi. To grow white.

Whitewash, whīt'wosh, n. A composition of lime or whiting and water, for whitening walls, etc. —vt. To cover with whitewash; to restore the reputation of

Whither, whiTH'ėr, adv. To what or which place; where.

Whithersoever, whiTH'ėr-sō-ev-ėr, adv. To whatever place.

Whitlow, whit'lō, n. A swelling about the small bones of the fingers, generally terminating in an abscess.

Whit-Monday, whit'mun-dā, n. The Monday following Whitsunday.

Whitsun, whit'sun, a. Pertaining to Whitsuntide.

Whitsunday, whit'sun-dā, n. The seventh Sunday after Easter.

Whitsuntide, whit'sun-tīd, n. The season of Pentecost.

Whittle, whit'l, n. A large knife.—vt. (whittling, whittled). To cut or pare with a knife

Whiz, whiz, vi. (whizzing, whizzed). To make a humming or hissing sound.—n. A hissing and humming sound.

Who, hö, pron.; possessive **Whose,** höz; objective **Whom,** höm. A relative and interrogative pronoun always used substantively and with reference to persons.

Whoever, hö-ev'ėr, pron. Any one without exception; any person whatever.

Whole, hōl, a. Sound; healthy; healed; intact; entire.—n. An entire thing; total assemblage of parts.

Wholesale, hōl'sāl, n. Sale of goods by the entire piece or in large quantities.—a. Pertaining to trade in large quantities; extensive and indiscriminate.

Wholesome, hōl'sum, a. Tending to promote health; salubrious; useful; salutary.

Wholly, hōl'li, adv. As a whole; entirely.

Whoop, whöp or höp, vi. To shout loudly; to hoot.—vt. To shout at; to hoot; to insult with shouts.—n. A shout; a loud clear call.

Whopper, whop'ėr, n. Anything uncommonly large; a manifest lie.

Whore, hōr, n. A prostitute; a harlot.—vi. (whoring, whored). To have to do with prostitutes.

Whose, höz, pron. The possessive case of who or which.

Whosoever, hö-sö-ev'ėr, pron. Any person whatever; any one.

Why, whi, adv. and conj. For what reason; wherefore.

Wick, wik, n. The loose spongy string or band in candles or lamps.

Wicked, wik'ed, a. Evil in principle or practice; sinful; immoral; bad; roguish.

Wickedness, wik'ed-nes, n. Immorality; depravity; sin; a wicked act.

Wicker, wik'ėr n. A small pliable twig; work made of such twigs.—a. Made of plaited twigs.

Wicket, wik'et, n. A small gate; in cricket, the three upright rods and the bails which rest on them at which the bowler aims.

Wide, wīd, a. Having a great extent each way; broad; extensive; liberal; remote from anything—adv. At or to a distance, far from; astray.

Widen, wid'n, vt. To make wide or wider.—vi. To grow wide or wider.

Widow, wi'dō, n. A woman whose husband is dead.—vt. To bereave of a husband.

Widower, wi'dō-ėr, n. A man whose wife is dead.

Widowhood, wi'dō-hud, n. The condition of being a widow or a widower.

Width width, n. Breadth; extent from side to side.

Wield, wēld, vt. To manage freely in the hands; to sway; to exercise.

Wife, wīf, n.; pl. **Wives,** wīvz. A married woman.

Wig, wig, n. An artificial covering of hair for the head.

Wight, wit, n. A human being; a person.—a. Strong and active; of warlike prowess.

Wild, wild, a. Living in a state of nature; not tame; not cultivated; desert; stormy; furious; frolicsome; rash; extravagant; excited —n An uncultivated tract.

Wilderness, wil'dėr-nes, n. A desert; waste; irregular collection of things.

Wildfire, wild'fir, n. A kind of lightning unaccompanied by thunder; erysipelas.

Wile, wil, n. An artifice; stratagem; trick.—vt. wiling, wiled. To entice; to while.

Wiliness, wi'li-nes, n. Cunning; guile.

Will, wil, vi. aux. (past. would), expresses futurity in the second and third persons, and willingness, etc., or determination in the first.—vt. and i. To determine by choice; to wish; to bequeath.—n. Wish; choice; determination; purpose; legal declaration of a person as to what is to be done after his death with his property; faculty by which we determine to do or not to do something; volition.

Willful, wil'ful, *a.* Under the influence of self-will; obstinate; wayward; intentional.

Willing, wil'ing, *a.* Ready; desirous; spontaneous; voluntary; prompt.

Willow, wil'ō, *n.* A tree or shrub, valuable for basket-making, etc.

Willowy, wil'o-i, *a.* Abounding with willows; slender and graceful.

Wilt, wilt, *vi.* To fade; to wither or droop.

Wily, wi'li, *a.* Using wiles; cunning; sly.

Wimple, wim'pl, *n.* A female head-dress still worn by nuns.—*vt.* (wimpling, wimpled). To cover with a wimple; to hoodwink.—*vi.* To ripple; to undulate.

Win, win, *vt.* (winning, won). To gain; to be victorious in; to allure; to reach; to attain.—*vi.* To gain the victory.

Wince, wins, *vi.* (wincing, winced). To shrink, as from pain; to start back.—*n.* A start, as from pain.

Winchy, winsh, *n.* The bent handle for turning a wheel, etc.; a kind of windlass turned by a crank handle.

Wind, wind, in poetry often wīnd, *n.* Air in motion; a current of air; breath; power of respiration; empty words; flatulence.—*vt.* wind (pret. & pp. wound, sometimes winded). To blow, as a horn.—*vt.* wind (pret. & pp. winded). To follow by the scent; to render scant of wind; to let rest and recover wind.

Wind, wīnd, *vt.* (pret. & pp. wound). To bend or turn; to twist; to coil.—*vi.* To twine or twist; to crook; to bend; to meander.

Winder, wīnd'ėr, *n.* One who or that which winds; an instrument for winding yarn, etc.

Windfall, wind'fal, *n.* Fruit blown down; an unexpected legacy or advantage.

Winding, wīnd'ing, *a.* Bending; twisting; spiral.—*n.* A turn or turning; a bend.

Wind-instrument, wind'in-stru-ment, *n.* An instrument of music played by wind or breath, as an organ, flute, etc.

Windlass, wind'las, *n.* A revolving cylinder on which a rope is wound, used for raising weights, etc., by hand or other power.

Windmill, wind'mil, *n.* A mill driven by the wind.

Window, win'dō, *n.* An opening in a wall for the admission of light or air; the frame (usually fitted with glass) in this opening.

Window-sash, win'dō-sash, *n.* The light frame in which glass is set in windows.

Windpipe, wind'pip, *n.* The cartilaginous pipe or passage for the breath; the trachea.

Wind-up, wind-up, *n.* The conclusion or final settlement of any matter; the close.

Windward, wind'wėrd, *n.* The point from which the wind blows.—*a.* and *adv.* Towards the wind.

Wine, win, *n.* An intoxicating liquor obtained from the fermented juice of grapes, etc.

Wine-cellar, win'sel-ėr, *n.* An apartment or cellar for storing wine.

Wine-glass, win'gläs, *n.* A small glass in which wine is drunk.

Wine-press, win'pres, *n.* An apparatus in which the juice is pressed out of grapes.

Wine-taster, win'tåst-ėr, *n.* A person employed to judge of wine for purchasers.

Wing, wing, *n.* One of the anterior limbs in birds; organ of flight; flight; a lateral extension; side; side division of an army, etc.—*vt.* To furnish with wings; to fly; to traverse by flying; to wound in the wing.

Winged, wingd, *a.* Having wings; swift.

Wink, wingk, *vi.* To shut and open the eyelids; to give a hint by the eyelids; to connive; to be willfully blind (with *at*).—*n.* Act of shutting and opening the eyelids rapidly; a twinkling; a hint given by means of the eye.

Winning, win'ing, *a.* Attractive; charming.—*n.* The sum won by success in competition; chiefly in *pl.*

Winnow, win'ō, *vt.* To separate the chaff from by

wind; to fan; to sift; to scrutinize.—*vi.* To separate chaff from corn.

Winsome, win'sum, *a.* Attractive; winning.

Winter, win'tėr, *n.* The cold season of the year; a year; any cheerless situation.—*a.* Belonging to winter—*vi.* To pass the winter.—*vt.* To keep or feed during winter.

Wintry, Wintery, win'tri, win'tėr-i, *a.* Pertaining or suitable to winter; cold; stormy.

Wipe, wīp, *vt.* (wiping, wiped). To clean by gentle rubbing; to strike gently; to efface.—*n.* A rub for the purpose of cleaning; a gibe.

Wire, wīr, *n.* A thread of metal; a telegraph wire; the telegraph.—*vt.* (wiring, wired). To bind with wire; to put a wire on; to send by telegraph.—*vi.* To communicate by telegraph.

Wireless, wir'les, *n.* Wireless telegraphy or telephony; communication between distant places by means of electromagnetic waves, without the use of wires.

Wiry, wīr'i, *a.* Made of or like wire; tough; lean and sinewy.

Wisdom, wiz'dom, *n.* Sound judgment and sagacity; prudence; learning or erudition.

Wisdom-tooth, wiz'dom-tōth, *n.* A large back double tooth, the last to come.

Wise, wīz, *a.* Having wisdom; sagacious; judicious; skilled; sage.—*n.* Manner; mode.

Wish, wish, *vi.* To have a desire; to long; with *for.*—*vt.* To desire; to long for; to invoke.—*n.* A desire; the thing desired.

Wishful, wish'ful, *a.* Desirous; eager; earnest.

Wisp, wisp, *n.* A small bundle of straw, etc.

Wistful, wist'ful, *a.* Thoughtful; attentive; earnest; pensive; longing.

Wit, wit, *vt.* and *i.* (pres. tense, wot, pret. wist, pres. part. witting and wotting). To know; to be aware.—**To wit,** namely; that is to say.—*n.* Understanding; sense; wisdom; intelligence; faculty of associating ideas cleverly and in apt language; a person possessing this faculty; cleverness.

Witch, wich, *n.* A woman who practises sorcery.—*vt.* To bewitch.

Witchcraft, wich'kraft, *n.* Sorcery; enchantment; fascination.

Witchery, wich'e-ri, *n.* Witchcraft; fascination.

With, wiTH, *prep.* Against; in the company of; among; showing; marked by; immediately after; through; by.—*n.* With or with. A withe.

Withal, wiTH-al', *adv.* Moreover; likewise; at the same time.—*prep.* With: used after relatives at the end of a clause.

Withdraw, wiTH-dra, *vt.* To draw back or away; to retract; to cause to retire.—*vi.* To retire; to secede.

Wither, wiTH'ėr, *vi.* To fade or shrivel; to become dry and wrinkled; to decline.—*vt.* To cause to fade; to prove fatal to.

Withers, wiTH'ėrz, *n.pl.* The junction of the shoulder-bones of a horse, forming the highest part of the back.

Withhold, wiTH-hōld,' *vt.* To hold back; to restrain; to retain; not to grant.

Within, wiTH-in', *prep.* In the interior of; in the compass of.—*adv.* In the inner part; inwardly; indoors; at home.

Without, wiTH-out', *prep.* On the outside of; out of; beyond; not having.—*adv.* On the outside; outwardly; out-of-doors.

Withstand, wiTH-stand', *vt.* and *i.* To oppose; to resist.

Witless, wit'les, *a.* Destitute of wit; thoughtless; indiscreet; silly.

Witness, wit'nes, *n.* Testimony; attestation of a fact or event; one who knows or sees anything; one who gives evidence in a trial.—*vt.* To attest; to see the execution of a legal instrument, and subscribe it.—*vi.* To bear testimony.

Witticism, wit'i-sizm, *n.* A witty remark.

Wittingly, wit'ing-li, *adv.* Knowingly; by design.

Witty, wit'i, *a.* Possessed of wit; full of wit; keenly or brilliantly humorous; facetious.

Wizard, wiz'ard, *n*. A wise man or sage; a sorcerer; a magician; a conjurer.

Wizen, Wizened, wiz'n, wiz'nd, *a*. Hard, dry, and shrivelled; withered; weazen.

Wobble, wob'l, *vi*. (wobbling, wobbled). To move unsteadily in rotating; to rock.

Woe, Wo, wō, *n*. Grief; misery; affliction.

Woebegone, wō'bē-gon, *a*. Overwhelmed with woe; sorrowful; melancholy.

Woeful, Woful, wō'fl, *a*. Full of woe; sorrowful; afflicted; wretched; pitiful.

Wolf, wulf, *n*.; *pl*. **Wolves**, wulvz. A carnivorous quadrüped akin to the dog, crafty and rapacious; a cruel or cunning person.

Woman, wu'man, *n*.; *pl*. **Women**, wi'men. The female of the human race; the female sex; an adult female.

Womanhood, wu'man-hud, *n*. The state, character, or qualities of a woman.

Womanly, wu'man-li, *a*. Becoming a woman; feminine in a praiseworthy sense.

Womb, wöm, *n*. The uterus; place where anything is produced; any deep cavity.

Wombat, wom'bat, *n*. A marsupial mammal about the size of a badger.

Wonder, wun'dér, *n*. Something very strange; a prodigy or marvel; feeling excited by something strange.—*vi*. To be struck with wonder; to marvel; to entertain some doubt and curiosity.

Wonderful, wun'dér-ful, *a*. Marvellous; surprising; strange; astonishing.

Wonderment, wun'dér-ment, *n*. Wonder; surprise; astonishment.

Wondrous, wun'drus, *a*. Wonderful; strange.—*adv*. Remarkably.

Won't, wönt. A contraction for *will not*.

Wont, wönt or wunt, *a*. Accustomed.—*n*. Custom; habit; use.—*vi*. (pret. & pp. wont, sometimes wonted). To be accustomed to use.

Woo, wö, *vt*. and *i*. (wooing, wooed). To make love to; to solicit in love; to court.

Wood, wud, *n*. A large collection of growing trees; the hard or solid substance of trees; timber.—*vi*. To take in or get supplies of wood.—*vt*. To supply with wood.

Wood-cut, wud'kut, *n*. An engraving on wood, or a print from such engraving.

Wooden, wud'n, *a*. Made of wood; clumsy; awkward; dull.

Wood-engraving, wud'en-grāv-ing, *n*. The art of producing designs in relief on the surface of a block of wood; an impression from such a block.

Woodland, wud'land, *n*. Land covered with wood.—*a*. Relating to woods; sylvan.

Woodpecker, wud'pek-ér, *n*. A climbing bird which feeds on insects and their larvae on trees.

Woody, wud'i, *a*. Abounding with wood; wooded; consisting of wood; like wood.

Woof, wöf, *n*. The threads that cross the warp in weaving; the weft; texture in general.

Wool, wul, *n*. That soft species of hair on sheep; any fleecy substance resembling wool.

Wool-gathering, wul'gaᴛн-ér-ing. *n*. Act of gathering wool; indulgence of idle fancies; a foolish or fruitless pursuit.

Woollen, wul'en, *a*. Made of or pertaining to wool.—*n*. Cloth made of wool.

Word, wérd, *n*. An articulate sound expressing an idea; a term; information; a saying; motto; order; assertion or promise; in *pl*., talk; wrangle.—*vi*. To express in words.

Word-book, wérd'buk, *n*. A vocabulary; a dictionary.

Wording, wérd'ing, *n*. The mode of expressing in words; form of stating.

Wordy, wérd'i, *a*. Using many words, verbose.

Work, wérk, *n*. Effort; labor; employment; a task; achievement; a literary or artistic performance; some extensive structure; establishment where labor of some kind is carried on; result of force acting.—*vi*. (pret. and pp. worked or wrought).

To put forth effort; to labor; to take effect; to tend or conduce; to seethe; to ferment.—*vt*. To bestow labor upon; to bring about; to keep at work; to influence; to achieve; to fashion; to embroider; to cause to ferment.

Workaday, wérk'a-dā, *a*. Working-day; everyday; toiling.

Worker, wérk'ér, *n*. One that works; a toiler; a laborer; a working bee.

Working, wérk'ing, *a*. Engaged in bodily toil; industrious.—*n*. Act of laboring; movement; operation; fermentation; *pl*. portions of a mine, etc., worked.

Working-class, wérk'ing-klas, *n*. Those who earn their bread by manual labor.

Working-day, wérk'ing-dā, *n*. A day on which labor is performed.—*a*. Relating to such days; laborious.

Workman, wérk'man, *n*. An artisan; mechanic; laborer; worker.

Workmanlike, wérk'man-līk, *a*. Like a proper workman; skilful; well performed.

Workmanship, wérk'man-ship, *n*. Skill or art of a workman; style or character of execution; art; dexterity; handicraft.

Workshop, wérk'shop, *n*. A shop or building where any craft or work is carried on.

World, wérld, *n*. The whole creation; the earth; any celestial orb; a large portion of our globe; sphere of existence; a domain or realm; mankind; the public; great degree or quantity.

Worldly, wérld'li, *a*. Relating to this world or this life; secular; carnal; sordid.

Worm, wérm, *n*. A small creeping animal; an intestinal parasite; *pl*. the disease caused by such parasites; something vermicular or spiral.—*vi*. To wriggle; to work gradually and secretly.—*vt*. To effect by stealthy means; *refl*. to insinuate oneself; to extract cunningly.

Worm-eaten, wérm'ēt-n, *a*. Gnawed by worms; having cavities made by worms.

Worn-out, wörn'out, *a*. Useless from being much worn; wearied; exhausted.

Worry, wu'ri, *vt*. (worrying, worried). To tear with the teeth, as dogs; to harass; to annoy.—*vi*. To trouble oneself; to fret.—*n*. Trouble; care; anxiety.

Worse, wérs, *a*. Bad or ill in a greater degree; inferior; more unwell; more ill off.—**The worse**, defeat; disadvantage.—*adv*. In a manner or degree more evil or bad.

Worsen, wér'sn, *vi* and *t*. To grow or make worse.

Worship, wér'ship, *n*. Dignity; honor; a title of honor; religious service; adoration; reverence.—*vt*. (worshiping, worshipped). To adore; to pay divine honors to; to idolize.—*vi*. To perform religious service.

Worst, wérst, *a*. Bad or evil in the highest degree.—*n*. The most evil state or action.—*adv*. Most extremely.—*vt*. To defeat.

Worsted, wust'ed, *n*. Yarn spun from wool, and used in knitting.—*a*. Made of worsted.

Worth, wérth, *a*. Equal in value or price to; deserving of; possessing.—*n*. Value; price; merit; excellence.—*vi*. To be; to betide.

Worthy, wér'ᴛнi, *a*. Possessing worth; estimable; virtuous; deserving; fitting.—*n*. A man of eminent worth; a local celebrity.

Would, wud, Pret. of *will*, mainly used in subjunctive or conditional senses.

Would-be, wud'bē, *a*. Wishing to be; vainly pretending to be.—*n*. A vain pretender.

Wound, wönd, *n*. A cut or stab, etc.; injury; hurt or pain to the feelings; damage.—*vt*. or *i*. To inflict a wound on; to pain.

Wraith, rāᴛн, *n*. An apparition of a person about to die or newly dead.

Wrangle, rang'gl, *vi*. (wrangling, wrangled). To dispute angrily; to argue.—*n*. A dispute.

Wrap, rap, *vt*. (wrapping, wrapped or wrapt). To fold or roll; to cover by something wound; to envelop.—*n*. An outer article of dress for warmth.

W

Wrath, räth or rath, *n.* Violent anger; rage; fury.

Wrathful, räth'fŭl or rath'ful, *a.* Full of wrath; furious; wroth.

Wreak, rēk, *vt.* To revenge or avenge; to inflict; to gratify by punishment.

Wreath, rēth, *n.* Something twisted or curled; a garland; a chaplet; a snow-drift.

Wreathe, rēᴛн, *vt.* (wreathing, wreathed). To twist into a wreath; to entwine; to encircle; to dress in a garland.—*vi.* To be entwined.

Wreck, rek, *n.* Ruin; overthrow; a ruin; destruction of a vessel at sea.—*vt.* To cause to become a wreck; to ruin.

Wrecker, rek'ėr, *n.* One who causes shipwrecks or plunders wrecks; one who recovers goods from wrecked vessels.

Wrench, rensh, *n.* A violent twist; injury by twisting; an instrument for screwing a bolt or nut.—*vt.* To pull with a twist; to distort.

Wrest, rest, *vt.* To twist; to take or force by violence; to distort.—*n.* Act of wresting; a wrench; an implement to tune stringed instruments with.

Wrestle, res'l, *vi.* (wrestling, wrestled). To contend by grappling and trying to throw down; to struggle.—*vt.* To contend with in wrestling.—*n.* A bout at wrestling.

Wretch, rech, *n.* A miserable person; a mean, base, or vile creature.

Wretched, rech'ed, *a.* Very miserable; distressing; worthless; despicable.

Wriggle, rig'l, *vi.* and *t.* (wriggling, wriggled). To move with writhing or twisting.—*n.* A quick twisting motion.

Wright, rit, *n.* An artisan or artificer; a worker in wood; a carpenter.

Wring, ring, *vt.* (wringing, wrung). To twist with the hands; to twist and compress; to torture; to extort.—*vi.* To writhe.

Wrinkle, ring'kl, *n.* A small ridge or furrow; a crease; a hint; a notion.—*vt.* and *i.* (wrinkling, wrinkled). To form into wrinkles; to contract into furrows; to crease.

Wrist, rist, *n.* The joint by which the hand is united to the arm.

Wristband, rist'band, *n.* The band of a sleeve covering the wrist.

Writ, rit, *n.* That which is written; the Scriptures; a legal document commanding a person to do some act.

Write, rit, *vt.* (writing, pret. wrote, pp. written). To form by a pen, etc.; to set down in letters or words; to cover with letters; to send in writing; to compose.—*vi.* To trace characters with a pen, etc.; to be engaged in literary work; to conduct correspondence.

Writhe, rīᴛн, *vt.* (writhing, writhed). To twist or distort, as the body or limbs.—*vi.* To twist and turn; to be distorted, as from agony.

Writing, rit'ing, *n.* Act of one who writes; a book, manuscript, or document; style.

Wrong, rong, *a.* Not right; not fit; not what ought to be; erroneous.—*n.* What is not right; an injustice; injury.—*adv.* In a wrong manner.—*vt.* To do wrong to; to treat with injustice.

Wrong-doer, rong'dö·ėr, *n.* One who does wrong.

Wrong-headed, rong'hed·ed, *a.* Obstinately or perversely wrong; stubborn.

Wroth, roth, *a.* Very angry; indignant.

Wrought, rat, pret. and pp. of *work.*

Wry, ri, *a.* Crooked; twisted; askew.

X

Xanthin, Xanthine, zan'thin, *n.* A yellow coloring matter.

Xanthous, zan'thus, *a.* Fair-haired.

Xerotes, zē'ro·tēz, *n.* A dry habit of the body.

Xiphoid, zif'oid, *a.* Shaped like a sword.

X-rays, eks'rāz, or **Röntgen rays,** runt'gen, *n.* Electromagnetic waves of high frequency, which penetrate most substances, except bones, metal, etc., and enable photographs to be taken of these in the living body.

Xylograph, zī'lo·graf, *n.* A wood-engraving.

Xyloid, zī'loid, *a.* Having the nature of wood; resembling wood.

Xylonite, zī'lō·nit, *n.* Celluloid.

Xylophagous, zī·lof'a·gus, *a.* Wood-eating.

Xylophone, zī·lo·fōn, *n.* A musical instrument in which the notes are given by pieces of wood struck with hammers.

Xyst, Xystus, zist, zis'tus, *n.* A covered portico or open court for athletic exercises.

Y

Yacht, yot, *n.* A light vessel used for racing, pleasure, etc.—*vi.* To sail in a yacht.

Yachtsman, yots'man, *n.* One who keeps or sails a yacht.

Yak, yak, *n.* A wild ox with long silky hair.

Yam, yam, *n.* A climbing plant, cultivated in tropical climates for its large roots.

Yankee, yang'kē, *n.* A citizen of New England; a native of the United States.

Yap, yap, *vi.* (yapping, yapped). To yelp; to bark,—*n.* Cry of a dog; yelp.

Yard, yärd, *n.* A standard measure of 3 feet; a long beam slung crosswise to a mast and supporting a sail; piece of enclosed ground.

Yard-stick, yärd'stik, *n.* A stick 3 feet in length.

Yarn, yärn, *n.* Thread prepared from wool or flax for weaving; a story.

Yaw, ya, *vi.* To swerve suddenly in sailing.—*n.* The sudden temporary deviation of a ship.

Yawn, yan, *vi.* To have the mouth open involuntarily while a deep breath is taken; to gape.—*n.* A gaping; act of yawning; a chasm.

Yea, yā, *adv.* Yes: the opposite of *nay.*

Yean, yēn, *vi.* and *i.* To bring forth young, as a goat or sheep.

Year, yėr, *n.* The period of time during which the earth makes one revolution in its orbit; twelve months; *pl.* old age; time of life.

Year-book, yėr·buk, *n.* A book published every year giving fresh information regarding matters that change.

Yearling, yėr'ling, *n.* A young beast one year old. —*a.* Being a year old.

Yearly, yėr'li, *a.* Annual; happening every year.—*adv.* Once a year.

Yearn, yėrn, *vi.* To feel uneasiness of mind from longing or pity; to long.

Yeast, yēst, *n.* A yellowish substance produced in alcoholic fermentation; barm.

Yell, yel, *vi.* To cry out with a loud piercing noise; to scream.—*n.* A loud, piercing outcry.

Yellow, yel'ō, *a.* Being of a bright golden color.—*n.* A bright golden color.

Yelp, yelp, *vi.* To utter a sharp bark or cry, as a dog.—*n.* A sharp cry of a dog.

Yes, yes, *adv.* Even so; expressing affirmation or consent; opposed to *no.*

Yesterday, yes'tėr·dā, *n.* The day before the present.—*adv.* On the day last past.

Yestereve, Yestereven, yes'tėr·v, yes'tėr·ē·vn, *n.* The evening last past.

Yestermorn, Yestermorning, yes'tėr·morn, yestėr·mor'ning, *n.* The morn or morning last past.

Yesternight, yes'tėr·nit, *n.* The night last past.

Yet, yet, *adv.* In addition; still; hitherto; nevertheless.—*conj.* Nevertheless, however.

Yew, yū, *n.* An evergreen tree, with poisonous leaves, and yielding a hard durable timber.

Yield, yēld, *vt.* To produce in return for labor, etc.; to afford; to grant; to give up.—*vi.* To submit; to comply; to produce.—*n.* Amount yielded; product; return.

Yodel, Yodle, yō'dl, *vt.* and *i.* (yodelling, yodling; yodelled, yodled). To sing like the Swiss and Tyrolese mountaineers by changing suddenly from the natural voice to the falsetto.

Yoke, yōk, *n.* Gear connecting draught animals by passing across their necks; a pair of draught animals; something resembling a yoke; shoulder-piece of a garment supporting the rest; servitude; burden; a bond; a tie.—*vt.* (yoking, yoked). To put a yoke on; to couple; to enslave.

Yokel, yō'kl, *n.* A rustic; an ignorant peasant; a country bumpkin.

Yolk, yōk, *n.* The yellow part of an egg.

Yonder, yon'dėr *a.* That or those away there.—*adv.* At or in that place there.

Yore, yōr, *adv.* Long ago; in old time: now used only in the phrase *of yore.*

You, yö, *pron.* The nominative and objective plural of *thou*: commonly used when a single person is addressed.

Young, yung, *a.* Being in the early stage of life; youthful.—*n.* The offspring of an animal.

Youngster, yung'stėr, *n.* A young person.

Your, yör, possessive corresponding to *ye, you.* Pertaining or belonging to you.

Yours, yörz, *poss. pron.* That or those which belong to you. **Yourself,** Yör-self' *pron.*; pl. **-selves.** You, used distinctively or reflexively.

Youth, yöth, *n.* State or quality of being young; period during which one is young; a young man; young persons collectively.

Youthful, yöth'ful, *a.* Young; pertaining to youth; fresh or vigorous, as in youth.

Yowl, youl, *vi.* To give a long distressful or mournful cry, as a dog.—*n.* A mournful cry.

Yule, yöl, *n.* Christmas.

Z

Zany, zā'ni, *n.* A buffoon or merry-andrew.

Zeal, zēl, *n.* Eagerness; passionate ardour; enthusiasm.

Zealot, ze'lot, *n.* One who is zealous; a fanatical partisan; a bigot.

Zealous, ze'lus, *a.* Inspired with zeal; fervent; eager; earnest.

Zebra, zē'bra, *n.* A striped South African animal allied to the horse and ass.

Zebu, zē'bū, *n.* The humped ox of India.

Zenith, zē'nith or zen'ith, *n.* The point of the heavens right above a spectator's head; highest point.

Zephyr, zet'ėr, *n.* The west wind; any soft, mild, gentle breeze.

Zero, zē'rō, *n.* Number or quantity diminished to nothing; a cipher; lowest point.

Zest, zest, *n.* Orange or lemon peel, used to flavor liquor; relish; charm; gusto.

Zigzag, zig'zag, *n.* Something in the form of straight lines with sharp turns.—*a.* Having sharp turns or bends.—*vi.* (zigzagging, zigzagged). To move in a zigzag fashion; to form zigzags.

Zinc, zingk, *n.* A metal of bluish-white color, used for roofing, to form alloys, etc.

Zincode, zingk'ōd, *n.* The positive pole of a galvanic battery.

Zincography, zing-kog'ra-fi, *n.* A mode of printing similar to lithography, a plate of zinc taking the place of the stone.

Zip-fastener, zip-fas'n-ėr, *n.* A kind of fastener, pulled open or shut by a tag, and joining two edges together, used on purses, tobacco-pouches, golf-bags, etc.

Zircon, zer'kon, *n.* A hard lustrous mineral, one of the gems called also jargon.

Zither, Zithern, zith'ėr, zith'ern, *n.* A flat musical instrument with from twenty-nine to forty-two strings, played with the fingers.

Zodiac, zō'di-ak, *n.* An imaginary belt or zone in the heavens, within which the apparent motions of the sun, moon, and principal planets are confined, divided into twelve equal parts or signs.

Zoetrope, zō'ē-trōp, *n.* An optical contrivance by which, when the instrument revolves, certain painted figures inside appear to move in a life-like manner.

Zone, zōn, *n.* A girdle or belt; one of the five great divisions of the earth, bounded by circles parallel to the equator; any well-defined belt.

Zoography, zō-og'ra-fi, *n.* The description of animals.

Zooid, zō'oid, *a.* Resembling or pertaining to an animal.—*n.* An organism, in some respects resembling a distinct animal.

Zoolite, zō'ol-līt, *n.* An animal substance petrified or fossil.

Zoology, zō-ol'o-ji, *n.* The science of the natural history of animals.

Zoon, zō'on, *n.* An animal.

Zoophagous, zō-of'a-gus, *a.* Feeding on animals; carnivorous.

Zoophyte, zō'o-fit, *n.* A name applied to many plant-like animals, as sponges.

Zoroastrianism, zor-o-as'tri-an-izm, *n.* The ancient Persian religion founded by Zoroaster, one feature of which was a belief in a good and an evil power perpetually at strife; the religion of the Parsees; fire-worship.

Zymic, zim'ik, *a.* Pertaining to fermentation.

Zymology, zi-mol'o-ji, *n.* The doctrine of ferments and fermentation.

Zymotic, zi-mot'ik, *a.* Pertaining to fermentation; applied to epidemic and contagious diseases, supposed to be produced by germs acting like a ferment.

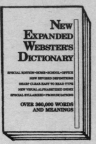